Our Sexuality

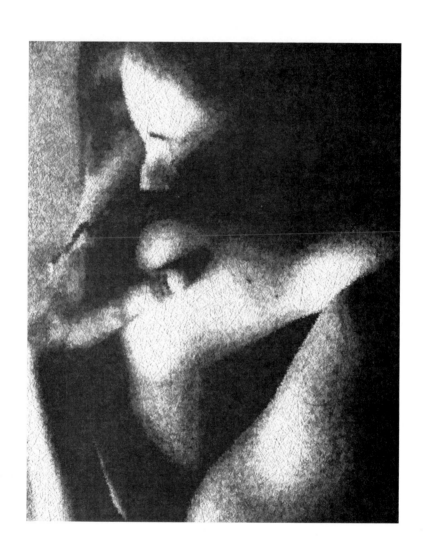

Our Sexuality

Fifth Edition

Robert Crooks
Portland Community College

Karla Baur
Oregon Health Sciences University, School of Medicine

The Benjamin/Cummings Publishing Company, Inc.
Redwood City, California • Menlo Park, California • Reading, Massachusetts • New York
Don Mills, Ontario • Wokingham, U.K. • Amsterdam • Bonn • Sydney
Singapore • Tokyo • Madrid • San Juan

Sponsoring Editor: Pat Coryell
Developmental Editor: Jamie Spencer
Marketing Manager: John Harpster
Art and Design Manager: Michele Carter
Senior Production Editor: John Walker
Copyeditor: Brian Jones
Text and Cover Designer: Jeanne Calabrese
Photo Researchers: Cecilia Mills, Kelli West
Cover, Frontispiece, Part and Chapter Opener Photographer: Robert Farber
Illustrators: Edith Algood, Barbara Hack, Heather Preston, Connie Warton, Martha Weston
Composition and Film: GTS Graphics
Printer and Binder: Arcata Graphics

Credits for photographs and excerpts appear at the end of the book, right before the index.

Library of Congress Cataloging-in-Publication Data
Crooks, Robert, 1941–
      Our sexuality / Robert Crooks, Karla Baur. — 5th ed.
            p.   cm.
      Includes bibliographical references (p.   ) and index.
      ISBN 0-8053-0212-3 30 2|2
      1. Sex.   2. Sex customs—United States.   I. Baur, Karla.
      II. Title.
      HQ21.C698   1992
      306.7—dc20
                                                                                    92-23485
                                                                                    CIP

12345678910—KP—9796959493

The Benjamin/Cummings Publishing Company, Inc.
390 Bridge Parkway
Redwood City, California 94065

For our families and friends

About the Authors

The integration of psychological, social, and biological components of human sexuality in this text is facilitated by the blending of the authors' academic and professional backgrounds. Robert Crooks has a Ph.D. in psychology. His graduate training stressed clinical and physiological psychology. In addition, he has considerable background in sociology, which served as his minor throughout his graduate training. He is currently involved in a number of research and writing projects, and teaches classes at Portland Community College.

Karla Baur has a master's degree in social work; her advanced academic work stressed clinical training. She is a licensed clinical social worker with a specialty in sex therapy and director of Baur Clinical Associates. Karla has been certified as a sex educator, therapist, and sex therapy supervisor by the American Association of Sex Educators, Counselors, and Therapists. She has instructed sexuality classes at several colleges and universities and is an adjunct Assistant Professor of Obstetrics and Gynecology at Oregon Health Sciences University, School of Medicine.

The authors have a combined total of 41 years of teaching, counseling, and research in the field of human sexuality. Together they team taught sexuality courses at Portland Community College for a number of years. They present workshops and guest lectures to a wide variety of professional and community groups, and they counsel individuals, couples, and families on sexual concerns. Their combined teaching, clinical, and research experiences, together with their graduate training, have provided them with an appreciation and sensitive understanding of the highly complex and personal nature of human sexuality.

It is the authors' belief that a truly sensitive understanding of our sexuality must be grounded in *both* the female and the male perspectives and experiences. In this sense, their courses, their students, and this text have benefited from a well-balanced perception and a deep appreciation of human sexual behavior.

Foreword

The first time I taught an undergraduate course on human sexual behavior was in 1970, at the University of Oregon. Since then I have taught the course many times, to many students, at four different universities. In developing my courses on human sexuality over the past 22 years, the search for the best textbook has been a recurring issue. In the early years of teaching this course, and to a certain degree even today, most of the available books were sex education texts. Rather than focusing on human sexuality—attitudes, emotions, and behavior patterns—these books dealt mainly with the "plumbing" aspects of sex—anatomy and physiology of the reproductive system. Furthermore, many human sexuality texts are very value-laden, initially with conservative and sexist values, and more recently with "politically correct" silliness that reduces the serious issues of sexism, racism, and human diversity to trivial word games.

After using this type of sex education–oriented texts over a few semesters, I received feedback from students that confirmed my initial misgivings. The students did not find the anatomy and physiology very interesting—they wanted to read about *sexuality,* not about reproduction. The conservative values struck many of the students as hopelessly out of touch with current reality, and many students were offended by the implicitly sexist views in these books. Today, most students find politically correct terminology amusing at best, and frequently a barrier to thinking seriously about important issues.

Not being too obtuse or a terribly slow learner, I eventually stopped using this sort of text, and instead began to use collections of articles from professional journals. However, this alternative turned out to have two problems. First, the articles were often overly detailed and uninteresting to students. Second, without the use of a text that covered anatomy and physiology, many students lacked the basic knowledge required to understand the lecture material. The sex education material is a necessary but not sufficient part of a text on human sexuality.

I eventually arrived at a combination of a basic sex education text, a collection of readings, and a collection of photocopied materials gathered from a variety of sources. What this combination did not cover was the *human* or personal side of human sexuality—the struggles we all go through as we attempt to come to terms with what it means to be a sexual being. Obviously, a course in sexuality has enormous personal relevance to students, and their reactions to both readings and lectures are often more personal than intellectual. My office hours began to assume certain aspects of a sex counseling service. I reached the point where I was actually *glad* when a student would come in merely to complain about a grade. Reflecting on their reactions to the course and readings, I realized the students needed and wanted something that would help them integrate their own life experiences—exciting, confusing, gratifying, or frustrating—with the academic material.

During this period, I often found myself wishing that my life could be much less complicated. If there were a single really good sexuality text available, it would be much easier to teach human sexuality. In thinking about what would constitute an ideal text, I came up with a shopping list:

1. The basic biology of sexuality must be covered thoroughly.

2. The psychology and sociology of human sexuality must be emphasized, covering behavior patterns, emotions, sociocultural issues, and so forth.

3. There should be some integration of both sorts of academic material with personal experiences of real people.

4. Self-help problem-solving advice in the text would be very useful.

5. The text should not be overly political or stridently polemical about sexual and sex-role values, in either conservative or liberal politically correct directions. Given that some values obviously must appear when presenting life histories and self-help material, my preference would be for a book committed to equality in male and female roles and relationships, to racial equality, and to acceptance of a wide range of sexual lifestyles as normal and healthy.

Over the next few years, I evaluated each new textbook that appeared against my shopping list. Some excellent texts appeared, including ones that met almost all my criteria. What never did appear was a solid academic text with a personal focus: that is, one that included life histories and personal problem-solving material. Thus, when I first saw a new text by Robert Crooks and Karla Baur, I was immediately intrigued. Here, at last, seemed to be two people who had obviously taught human sexuality for some time and had been willing to listen to their students and respond to *their* needs in writing a text.

The earlier editions of this text were excellent books, and were very well received. Indeed, this book has become one of the most widely used texts in college-level courses in human sexuality. Among the book's virtues is that the academic material is presented clearly yet is not oversimplified. The personal material is fascinating, and makes the text one that students read out of interest rather than to study for the exams. The self-help material is very straightforward, and is relevant and useful for most students. The values of the authors are not presented in a strident way, and are indeed egalitarian and nonjudgmental.

Not content to rest on their laurels, Crooks and Baur continually updated and revised this text, culminating in this, the fifth edition. It is not easy to improve on an already excellent text, but the authors have managed to do so. Crooks and Baur have added, over the years and editions, much new material on topics such as homosexuality, love, marriage, divorce, sexual disabilities, rape, incest, child sexual abuse, sex and the law, and sexual transmitted diseases, including the latest information about AIDS. These are all topics of great current interest, and the focus of public policy debate. This fifth edition continues their tradition, with especially noteworthy new material on hormone–behavior relationships, biological factors in gender identity formation, interviews with leading sex researchers, and new attention to ethical and legal issues in human sexuality.

In closing my foreword to the earlier editions, I concluded that at last an academically sound, personally relevant text was available for courses in human sexuality. This fifth edition only reinforces my earlier judgment. The current students—and teachers—of human sexuality are indeed fortunate to have this book available.

Joseph LoPiccolo, Ph.D.
Professor of Psychology
University of Missouri–Columbia

Preface

Our major goal for the fifth edition of *Our Sexuality* is essentially the same as for the first four editions. To provide a *comprehensive* and *academically sound* introduction to the biological, psychosocial, behavioral, and cultural aspects of sexuality, in a way that is *personally meaningful to students.* The enthusiastic response to the earlier editions of our text has been gratifying, and has encouraged us to revise the book with the dual aim of updating it and making it even more effective as a learning tool.

Like the previous four editions, the fifth edition covers a broad array of subjects in considerable detail. We have included some topics that are frequently either omitted or discussed superficially in other texts—for example, gender identity and gender roles, love and the development of relationships, communicating about sex, improving sexual satisfaction, sexuality throughout the life cycle, cross-cultural variations in sexual expression, and chronic illness, disability, and sexuality. While we have avoided being overly technical in our presentation of data, we have been scholarly and thorough in our review of the human sexuality research. The fifth edition has been updated in every area and includes approximately 600 new citations from 1991 and 1992 literature.

New in This Edition

- More than **800 new citations,** of which almost 600 are from 1991 and 1992 literature.

- **Interviews with distinguished researchers** who have made significant contributions to our understanding of human sexuality. These interviews, conducted by the authors and appearing throughout the text, provide valuable perspectives and insights regarding a number of issues relevant to human sexual behavior. A list of the interviewees and topics addressed follows:

- John Bancroft, M.D.: The relationship of reproductive hormones to sexual behavior (Chapter 6).

- Evelyn Hooker, Ph.D.: Homosexuality (Chapter 10).

- Richard Paulson, M.D.: Infertility treatments (Chapter 12).

- Wendy Maltz, M.S.W.: The impact of childhood sexual abuse on adult sexual functioning (Chapter 16).

- Paul Volberding, M.D.: The AIDS epidemic (Chapter 19).

- Charlene Muehlenhard, Ph.D.: Sexual coercion and acquaintance rape (Chapter 21).

- **Ethical/Legal Issues in Human Sexuality boxes.** These boxes, interspersed throughout the text, deal with topics that embrace important ethical and/or legal issues pertaining to human sexuality. Topics include sex research, male circumcision, homosexuality, procreative options, sex between therapist and client, prostitution, and rape.

- **Significant reduction in text length.** Without sacrificing important content areas, we have reduced the overall length of our text so that it will be more manageable within the allocated time frame of most human sexuality courses.

- **Thirty-three new Critical Thinking questions** are interspersed throughout the text.

- New information about **gender-based communication styles.**

- A new box discussing the **men's movement of the 1990s.**

- Expanded coverage of **circumcision,** including the latest medical findings regarding health issues.

- The latest information on the role of **hormones in sexual arousal.**

- A **major revision of Chapter 7,** "Love and the Development of Sexual Relationships," with new coverage of Sternberg's triangular theory of love and Lee's styles of loving.

- Discussion of **new research on sexual orientation** that strengthens the argument for biological contributions.

- A new section on **predicting marital satisfaction.**

- Expanded discussion of **social issues regarding sexual orientation.**

- New information about **contraceptive advances**—Norplant, the female condom, no-scalpel vasectomy, and RU-486.

- Current developments in **legal and social issues pertaining to abortion.**

- Updates on **hormone replacement therapy.**

- Significantly updated chapter on **STDs** (Chapter 19), with the latest information on causes, treatment, and prevention (significantly expanded prevention information).

- Updated and revised chapter on **sexual victimization** (Chapter 21), with the latest information on acquaintance rape.

- Updated and improved text **supplements.**

Continuing Features

A Personal Approach

Users of the text have responded favorably to our attempts to humanize and personalize the subject matter, and in the fifth edition we have retained and strengthened the elements that contribute to this approach.

- **Readable, Personal Style.** The book is written in a clear and interesting style that facilitates understanding. We have maintained a personal focus throughout. For example, when we present the anatomy and physiology of sexual functions, we frequently provide perspectives of people's feelings about their bodies.

- **Authors' Files.** Excerpts from our files relating experiences and observations by students, clients, and colleagues are interspersed throughout the text. In some instances, they were provided to us in the form of written personal reflections. Here, only minor changes have been made to preserve anonymity (any names that appear are fictitious). In other cases, where they were related verbally, we have recorded the accounts as accurately as our memories allow. These quotations, printed in color, help dramatize important concepts and the many dimensions of human sexuality.

- **Nonjudgmental Perspective.** Consistent with our personal focus, we have avoided a prescriptive stance on the issues introduced in the text. We have attempted to provide information in a sensitive, nonsexist, nonjudgmental manner that assumes the reader is best qualified to determine what is most valid and applicable to her or his life.

- **Psychosocial Orientation.** We focus on the roles of psychological and social factors in human sexual expression, reflecting our belief that human sexuality is governed more by psychosocial factors than by biological factors. At the same time, we provide the reader with a solid basis in the anatomy and physiology of human sexuality.

- **Practical Information.** Many chapters offer practical information and suggestions for readers to use, if they wish. Some examples: how to enhance sexual communication, options for contraception and childbirth, how to improve sexual satisfaction, how to avoid contracting sexually transmitted diseases, when and where to seek professional counseling, rape prevention strategies, guidelines for parents and other caregivers who wish to reduce a child's vulnerability to sexual abuse, and suggestions for dealing with sexual harassment in the workplace.

- **Cross-Cultural and Historical Boxes.** To help students understand that sexual values are shaped by history and culture, we have placed cross-cultural and historical information in "Other Times, Other Places" boxes throughout the text. These boxes cover such topics as the changing role of women across historic periods of human development, a view of homosexuality from a cross-cultural perspective, and sexuality and aging in other cultures.

- **Critical Thinking Questions.** These questions, integrated into the text and marked by a "thinker" icon in the margin, are designed to encourage students to apply their knowledge and experience in developing their own thoughts about the topic under discussion. Each question encourages students to stop and think about what they are reading in an attempt to facilitate higher-order processing of information and learning.

- **Superb Illustrations.** The biological and diagrammatic art is clear and instructive. Enhancing the text are sensitive drawings and photographs, many of which are new to this edition. The illustrations are not limited to portrayals of young and attractive couples but include a wide variety of individuals. In this edition we have also included full-color art in the anatomy and physiology and conception and pregnancy chapters—Chapters 4, 5, and 12—to help students visualize difficult topics more easily.

A Complete Set of Supplements

Lecture preparation and student understanding are enhanced when a complete package of learning and teaching aids is employed. The fifth edition of *Our Sexuality* is accompanied by the following new and improved supplements:

- The **Instructor's Guide** by Sanford Lopater, Ph.D., of Christopher Newport University is written specifically to accompany the fifth edition of *Our Sexuality*. This innovative guide provides different teaching methods and approaches that help the instructor broach sensitive subjects, accommodate different student learning styles, explore topics from alternative points of view, and stimulate thoughtful classroom discussions. It features both informational and attitudinal learning objectives, lecture outlines, alternative approaches to the material, student exercises, provocative issues and ways to examine them in class, and a selection of transparency masters.

- The all-new **Test Bank,** by Lauren Kuhn of Portland Community College, offers a full range of multiple choice, true/false, and short answer essay questions. These questions test both knowledge and application: how much students have learned and how well they apply what they've learned to practical, real-life situations.

- A **Computerized Test Bank** is available for IBM computers (on both 5¼″ and 3½″ disks) and the Macintosh, providing a flexible, time-saving method of creating challenging and original tests. The software is documented with a printed test bank and with system instructions.

- The student **Study Guide,** by Lauren Kuhn of Portland Community College, helps students master the ideas introduced in the text and lecture hall. Each chapter of the guide begins with a list of learning objectives. The review and reinforcement exercises include chapter overviews with fill-ins, and multiple choice, matching, and short-answer questions. Anatomical diagrams with fill-ins accompany the two anatomy and physiology chapters, and flash cards listing key terms and concepts are provided at the end of each chapter. Student learning is guided by the same objectives that appear in the Instructor's Guide and is assessed by the questions in the Test Bank.

Organization

The organization of the book has been designed to reflect a logical progression of topics. We begin, in Part One, with the social and cultural legacy of sexuality in our society. We then describe how major research studies have increased our knowledge in recent years, and discuss the difficulties of gathering information in this sensitive area of human behavior. We conclude the opening unit with a detailed exploration of a variety of gender issues.

The three chapters of Part Two present the biological foundations of sexuality, with sexual arousal and sexual response patterns integrated into one chapter, Chapter 6. In Part Three, a variety of sexual behaviors are discussed.

In Part Four, we discuss contraception, pregnancy, and issues pertaining to sexuality throughout the life cycle. Sexual problems and their treatment, and a chapter on chronic illness, disabilities, and sexuality constitute the four chapters of Part Five.

The final section, Part Six, includes discussions of atypical sexuality, sexual victimization, and pornography and prostitution.

Learning Aids Within the Text

Individuals learn in different ways. We therefore provide a variety of pedagogical aids to be used as the student chooses. At the beginning of the book is a **Health Capsules** feature that brings together key facts with page references for five health topics that are dealt with over several chapters. Each chapter opens with an **Outline** of topic headings. **Key words** are boldfaced within the text and selected key words are followed by a **Pronunciation Guide**. The chapters also contain **Critical Thinking Questions,** set off in italics with a "thinker" icon in the margin. These questions ask students to stop and think about the information they have already learned and to make decisions based on that information. Each chapter concludes with a **Summary** in outline form for student reference, followed by several **Thought Provokers**—questions designed to stimulate thought and discussion. Annotated **Suggested Readings** are included with each chapter, and a complete **Bibliography** is provided at the end of the book. A comprehensive **Glossary** facilitates quick reference to terminology.

- A collection of 47 two- and four-color **Transparency Acetates** has been assembled for the fifth edition, which include illustrations of male and female sexual anatomy and physiology, hormonal interactions, childbirth, and sexual behavior patterns.

- The **Slide Set** of 60 full-color slides taken from the text and outside sources includes photographs, line art, drawings, tables, and charts—all of which illustrate key topics in sexuality.

- **The Sexuality and Health Forum Newsletter,** published biannually, contains current information on relevant topics and trends.

- *Our Sexuality*'s **Exclusive Video Library** offers videotapes on such important topics as sexually transmitted diseases, AIDS, and pressured sex. One of these videos, *STD's and Safer Sex,* is a frank discussion of risks, symptoms, and preventive measures introduced by two student hosts and punctuated by remarks from a medical doctor.

Acknowledgments

This book represents a combination of talents and insights that extend beyond those of the authors. We are particularly indebted to the reviewers of our manuscripts, the staff of Benjamin/Cummings, and our students, whose combined contributions have added much to the quality of the text.

As we worked on this project, we came to appreciate the indispensable value of the review process. Individuals representing a variety of disciplines and perspectives have read and evaluated the manuscript for each edition at various stages of completion. For help with the first edition we owe special gratitude to Carol Ellison. Our work on the second edition was facilitated by the suggestions of Valerie Pinhas, John Petras, and Joseph LoPiccolo, who reviewed the manuscript throughout its development. Valerie Pinhas again provided invaluable guidance on the direction of the third edition as we began to revise, and Sherman Sowby provided equally valuable feedback on our revised material. In the fourth edition, Charlene Muehlenhard drew on her wealth of knowledge and research experience as she provided excellent advice for the upgrading and expansion of our coverage of rape and sexual coercion. The thorough review and excellent input of Sanford Lopater contributed much of value to the fifth edition revision process. Speciality reviews by Nancy Salisbury, Tom Britton, Joseph LoPiccolo, and Brian McNaught added state-of-the-art polish to the pregnancy, contraceptive, sex therapy, and Homosexuality chapters. We also received helpful comments and suggestions from many sexuality educators who reviewed either the entire manuscript or portions of it. We appreciate the efforts of all these reviewers, whose names are listed at the end of this preface. Special thanks are extended to Sami Tucker, consummate journal researcher, whose exhaustive search of the recent literature contributed immeasurably to the very current nature of our text.

The staff of the Benjamin/Cummings Publishing Company has consistently performed beyond our highest expectations. Our sponsoring editor on the first edition, Larry Wilson, maintained a sense of perspective, direction, and infectious enthusiasm that saw us through many difficult times. Jane Gillen, who assumed the role of sponsoring editor on the second edition, provided invaluable direction and support. Diane Bowen, sponsoring editor on the third edition, carried on the established tradition of editorial excellence and insightful guidance. The fourth edition placed us in the very capable hands of Connie Spatz, who envisioned and implemented a major upgrading of the design and visual appearance of our text. The tradition of excellence characteristic of all previous sponsoring editors was maintained by Pat Coryell, whose insights and guidance helped immeasurably to forge a plan for improving our text for the fifth edition. Margaret Moore, Pat Burner, Betsy Dilernia, and Janet Vail, production editors for the first, second, third, and fourth editions, respectively, deserve a special thanks for providing the kind of organization essential to the success of a project of this nature. John Walker performed the same critical function on the fifth edition in a superbly efficient manner.

The developmental editing on the first four editions, by Jean Stein, Beverly Azarin, Robin Fox, and Margy Kuntz, was extremely valuable and contributed much to the book's quality. Jamie Spencer provided developmental editing on the fifth edition, and her efforts were beneficial and greatly appreciated. We are also indebted to Brian Jones, who performed superlative copyediting on the fifth edition. Special thanks also go to Cecilia Mills and Kelli West, photo editor and assistant photo editor, respectively, who researched new photographs for the fifth edition.

We are deeply grateful for the support and encouragement our families and friends have so generously and patiently provided throughout the writing of this book. Karla would like to give special thanks for the active and loving support of her husband, Jim Hicks. Bob wishes to acknowledge the nurturing and loving support of his wife, Sami Tucker.

Finally, we owe our greatest gratitude to the thousands of students who have attended our classes. In many ways, *Our Sexuality* reflects the thoughts and experiences of this diverse group. Their contributions have enriched the text. We hope that readers of our book will derive at least a portion of the benefits that we have gathered from our opportunity to share in this collective fund of human experience.

Robert Crooks and Karla Baur

REVIEWERS

First, Second, and Third Editions

Daniel Adame
Emory University

Linda Anderson
University of North Carolina

Jane Blackwell
Washington State University

John Blakemore
Monterey Peninsula College

Marvin J. Branstrom
Cañada College

Charles Carroll
Ball State University

Joan Cirone
California Polytechnic
State University

Bruce Clear
The First Unitarian Church,
Portland

David R. Cleveland
Honolulu Community College

Brenda M. DeVellis
University of North Carolina

Lewis Diana
Virginia Commonwealth University

Judy Drolet
Southern Illinois University,
Carbondale

Carol Ellison
Clinical Psychologist

Andrea Parrot Eggleston
Cornell University

Catherine Fichten
Dawson College

Karen Lee Fontaine
Purdue University,
Calumet

Glen G. Gilbert
Portland State University

Steven Harmon
University of Utah

Claudette Hastie-Beahrs
Clinical Social Worker

Thomas Johns
American River College

David Johnson
Portland State University

Richard A. Kaye
Kingsborough Community College

Miriam LeGare
California State University,
Sacramento

Frank Ling
University of Tennessee

Roger W. Little
University of Illinois,
Chicago

Joseph LoPiccolo
State University of New York,
Stony Brook

Leslie McBride
Portland State University

Deborah Miller
College of Charleston

John Money
Johns Hopkins University

Denis Moore
Honolulu Metropolitan Community
Church

Teri Nicoll-Johnson
Modesto Junior College

Bruce Palmer
Washington State University

Monroe Pasternak
Diablo Valley College

Mark Perrin
University of Wisconsin,
River Falls

John W. Petras
Central Michigan University

Valerie Pinhas
Nassau Community College

Robert Pollack
University of Georgia

Deborah Richardson
University of Georgia

Barbara Safriet
Lewis and Clark Law School

Marga Sarriugarte
Portland Rape Victim Advocate Project

Dan Schrinsky
Obstetrician/Gynecologist

Cynthia Schuetz
San Francisco State University

Sherman Sowby
California State University,
Fresno

Wendy Stock
Texas A&M University

Thomas Tutko
San Jose State University

James E. Urban
Kansas State University

Peter Vennewitz
Portland Planned Parenthood

Margaret Vernallis
California State University,
Northridge

John P. Vincent
University of Houston

Donald Wagner
University of Cincinnati

Michael G. Walraven
Jackson Community College

Elaine Walster
University of Wisconsin

William Yarber
Indiana University

Marianne K. Zalar
University of California,
San Francisco

Fourth Edition

Wayne Anderson
University of Missouri, Columbia

Tom Britton, M.D.
Planned Parenthood

Joan Cirone
California Polytechnic State University

Beverly Drinnin
Des Moines Area Community College

Judy Drolet
Southern Illinois University

Karen Lee Fontaine
Purdue University

Gene Fulton
University of Toledo

Stephen Harmon
University of Utah

Sandra Leiblum
University of Medicine and Dentistry/
Robert Wood Johnson Medical School

Frank Ling
University of Tennessee

Charlene Muehlenhard
University of Kansas

James Nash
California Polytechnic State
University

J. Mark Perrin
University of Wisconsin,
River Falls

Ollie Pocs
Illinois State University

Valerie Pinhas
Nassau Community College

Robert Pollack
University of Georgia

Patty Reagan
University of Utah

Dan Schrinsky, M.D.
Portland, Oregon

Lois Shofer
Essex Community College

Sherman Sowby
California State University, Fresno

Wendy Stock
Texas A&M University

Diana Taylor
Oregon Health Sciences University

Margaret Vernallis
California State University, Northridge

Donald Wagner
University of Cincinnati

Terri Warren
Private Counseling Practice
Portland, Oregon

William Yarber
Indiana University

Fifth Edition

Veanne Anderson
Indiana State University

Betty Sue Benison
Texas Christian University

M. Betsy Bergen
Kansas State University

Tom Britton, M.D.
Planned Parenthood, Portland, Oregon

Joseph Darden
Kean College

Pat Koch
Pennsylvania State University

Virginia Kreisworth
San Diego State University

Sanford Lopater
Christopher Newport University

Joseph LoPiccolo
University of Missouri

Peter Maneno
Normandale College

Deborah McDonald
New Mexico State University

Louis Munch
Ithaca College

Ronald Murdoff
San Joaquin Delta College

Brian McNaught
Gloucester, Massachusetts *no affiliation*

Robert Pollack
University of Georgia

Patty Reagan
University of Utah

Nancy Salisbury, M.D.
Portland, Oregon

Perry Treadwell
Decatur, Georgia *no affiliation*

Larry Wise
Mount Hood Community College

Brief Contents

Detailed Contents

Health Capsules

Sexual health is an important part of sexuality. There are some practical steps you can take that will help you prevent and/or reduce your chances of having health problems. Each of the following Health Capsules summarizes the major practical points made on a health topic and includes the page numbers where the topics are discussed in detail.

Preventive Health Care and Hygiene

For Women

Most women are susceptible to infections of the vagina and/or urinary tract. There are some precautions that may help prevent these infections. (pp. 84–86, 93, 553–559)

- Eat a well-balanced diet low in sugar and refined carbohydrates.
- Maintain good health with adequate sleep, exercise, and emotional release.
- Practice good hygiene, including the following:
  1. Bathe regularly.
  2. Wipe from front to back after urinating or having bowel movements.
  3. Wear clean cotton underpants instead of nylon.
  4. Avoid use of feminine-hygiene sprays, colored toilet paper, bubble bath, and other people's washcloths.
  5. Make sure that your partner's hands and genitals are clean before sexual activity.
- Be sure you have adequate lubrication before coitus; use a sterile, water-soluble lubricant if needed.
- Use condoms if either you or your partner is nonmonogamous.
- For women who are prone to yeast infections after menstruation, douche with two tablespoons of white vinegar in a quart of warm water once the flow ceases.

To help avoid urinary tract infections:

- Wash genital and rectal areas thoroughly each day.
- Urinate as soon as you feel the urge.
- Have your health care practitioner recheck the fit of your diaphragm.

♀ Most women experience some physical or psychological changes, or both, during their menstrual cycles. Women may be able to alleviate some of the unpleasant symptoms accompanying menstruation by their own actions. Following are some suggestions. (pp. 113–115)

- Engage in moderate exercise throughout the month.
- Eat a proper diet.
    1. Increase fluids and fibers to help prevent constipation.
    2. Decrease salt intake to help reduce swelling and bloating.
    3. Use food supplements such as calcium, magnesium, and B vitamins to help relieve cramps and bloating.
    4. Avoid caffeine, nicotine, and other stimulants, and eat small, frequent meals of low-carbohydrate, low-fat, high-protein foods to help decrease anxiety and irritability.
- Engage in stress-reduction techniques.

♀ Toxic shock syndrome, a rare but potentially fatal disease, occurs most often in menstruating women. Some guidelines have been developed that may help prevent toxic shock. (p. 115)

- Use sanitary napkins instead of tampons.
- Use regular instead of superabsorbent tampons and change them 3 or 4 times during the day; and use napkins for some time during each day of menstrual flow.

♀ Menopause, or the permanent cessation of menstruation, occurs as the result of certain physiological changes, and takes place at a mean age of 51. Some women experience menopause-related problems such as hot flashes, depression, sleep disturbances, and anxiety. Taking supplemental estrogen as part of hormone-replacement therapy (HRT) may help reduce these symptoms. Estrogen also provides significant protection against osteoporosis and cardiovascular disease. (pp. 463, 465–466)

♀ Thorough prenatal care is essential for promoting the health of both the mother and the fetus. Components of optimal prenatal care include good nutrition, general good health, adequate rest, routine health care, exercise, and childbirth education. Certain medications, recreational drugs, alcohol, and tobacco, when used by the mother, can easily cross through the placenta and be damaging to the developing fetus. (pp. 372–376)

For Men

♂ Men should be aware of any changes that occur to their genitals.

- Occasionally the prostate gland becomes enlarged and inflamed as a result of various infectious agents. This condition, known as prostatitis, should be checked by a health care practitioner. (pp. 125–127, 467–468)
- Sometimes the glans or shaft of the penis may develop an eczema-like reaction, becoming weepy and sore. This may result from an allergic reaction to your partner's vaginal secretions. Wearing a condom may help alleviate the condition. (p. 130)
- Undescended testes (cryptorchidism) may result in infertility. Surgery or hormonal therapy may be necessary to allow the testes to descend. (pp. 120–121)

Some men experience retrograde ejaculation, during which the semen is expelled into the bladder rather than out the penis. A man who consistently experiences this response should seek medical attention to rule out the possibility of an underlying health problem. (p. 134)

To avoid infections or unnecessary injuries, there are some self-care guidelines that men can follow. (pp. 130–131)

- Wash the penis with soap and water at least once a day. Uncircumcised men should take care to wash the head of the penis beneath the foreskin.

- Avoid placing the penis in potentially harmful places such as vacuum-cleaner hoses, mouths with herpes blisters, and vaginas with obvious infections.

For Men and Women

Self-exams are a good way for both men and women to learn about their bodies and to notice any changes that may require medical attention.

- A vaginal self-exam can help detect infection. (p. 94)

- A monthly self-exam of the breasts should be done to check for possible cancerous lumps. (pp. 99–104)

- Men should check their genitals for any lumps or swollen, tender areas that may indicate cancer or infections. (pp. 122–123)

Cancer of the reproductive organs can impair the hormonal, vascular, and neurological functioning necessary for normal sexual activity in both women and men. There are several tests that help screen for cancer. (p. 538)

- Men should perform self-exams for early detection of testicular cancer. During the early stages of this cancer, there are usually no symptoms beyond a hard or irregular mass within the testicle. (pp. 122–123, 539)

- The older a man gets, the more likely he is to develop prostate cancer. An early diagnosis may be accomplished by a physical examination. Men over the age of 40 should have yearly prostate examinations. (pp. 125–127, 467–468)

- The Pap smear, a screening test for cervical cancer, is an essential part of a woman's routine preventive health care. Depending on a woman's individual situation and her health care provider's recommendations, she may have this test every two years, every year, twice a year, or even more frequently. Because Pap smears are not 100% accurate in detecting cervical cancer, more frequent tests increase the likelihood of discovering cancer. (pp. 94–95)

- The best method for early detection of breast cancer is a combination of monthly self-exams, routine exams by a health care practitioner, and mammography, a highly sensitive X-ray screening test for cancerous breast lumps. The American Cancer Society currently recommends a baseline mammogram between the ages of 35 and 40, a routine mammogram every one to two years between the ages 40 and 49, and yearly mammograms over the age of 50. (pp. 99–102)

Acquired Immunodeficiency Syndrome (AIDS)

AIDS results from infection with a virus called human immunodeficiency virus (HIV). HIV specifically targets and destroys the body's CD4 lymphocytes, also called helper T cells, which in healthy people stimulate the immune system to fight disease. The resulting impairment of the immune system leaves the body vulnerable to a variety of cancers and opportunistic infections. (p. 579)

Until recently, HIV infection was diagnosed as AIDS only when the immune system became so seriously impaired that the infected individual developed one or more severe, debilitating diseases, such as pneumonia or cancer. However, effective April 1992, The Centers for Disease Control (CDC) broadened its definition of AIDS to include anyone with a CD4 count of 200 cells per cubic centimeter of blood. Normal CD4 cell counts in healthy people not infected with HIV range from 800 to 900 cells per cubic millimeter of blood. (p. 580)

♂♀ HIV has been found in the semen, blood, vaginal secretions, saliva, tears, urine, and breast milk of infected individuals, and in any other bodily fluids that may contain blood. Blood and semen are the two bodily fluids that most consistently contain high concentrations of the virus in infected people. It is believed that the risk of transmitting HIV via saliva, tears, and urine is extremely low. There is no evidence that the virus can be transmitted through casual or nonsexual contact. (pp. 581–582)

♂♀ HIV is most commonly transmitted from an infected person to a noninfected person in the following ways. (p. 581)

- Exchange of bodily fluids during unprotected anal or vaginal intercourse or oral–genital contact.
- Sharing of blood-contaminated needles by intravenous (IV) drug users.
- Perinatal transmission from an infected woman to her fetus or infant before, during, or shortly after birth.
- Transfusions of infected blood or blood products.

♂♀ Sexual transmission of HIV is not dependent on sexual orientation. Rather, engaging in the following high-risk behaviors increases the risk of HIV infection. (p. 582)

- Having multiple sexual partners.
- Engaging in unprotected sex (sex without condoms and virus-killing spermicides).
- Sexual contact with people known to be at high-risk (e.g., IV drug users, prostitutes, and people with multiple sexual partners).
- Sharing injection equipment for IV drug use.

♂♀ The only certain way to avoid contracting AIDS sexually is either to remain celibate or to be involved in a monogamous relationship with one mutually faithful, uninfected partner. If neither of these conditions applies, the following safer sex practices will help reduce your risk of contracting HIV: (pp. 590–591)

- If you use IV drugs, do not share needles or syringes (boiling does not guarantee sterility). If needle sharing continues, use bleach to clean and sterilize your needles and syringes.
- Avoid oral, vaginal, or anal contact with semen.
- Avoid anal intercourse.
- Do not engage in the insertion of fingers or fists into the anus as an active or receptive partner.
- Avoid oral contact with the anus.
- Avoid oral contact with vaginal fluids.
- Do not allow a partner's urine to enter your mouth, anus, eyes, or open cuts or sores.
- Because of the remote possibility that HIV may be transmitted via saliva, it might be wise to avoid prolonged open mouth wet kissing.

- Do not share razor blades, toothbrushes, or other implements that could become contaminated with blood.
- Avoid sexual contact with prostitutes (male or female).

♂♀ The symptoms of HIV and AIDS are many and varied. Because many of the physical manifestations may only indicate common, everyday ailments, there is no need to be alarmed unless you have engaged in high-risk behavior. Some common symptoms include: (p. 588)

- Persistent or periodically repeating fevers or night sweats.
- Unexplained weight loss.
- Loss of appetite.
- Chronic fatigue or a tendency to tire quickly when performing routine tasks.
- Swollen lymph nodes in the neck, armpits, or groin.
- Persistent and unexplained diarrhea or bloody stools.
- Easy bruising or atypical bleeding from any body opening.
- Skin rashes or discoloration of the skin.
- Persistent severe headaches.
- A chronic dry cough unrelated to smoking or a cold.
- A persistent whitish coating on the tongue or throat.

♂♀ HIV infection may be detected by standard blood tests for serum antibodies to HIV. Within a few months of being infected with HIV, most people develop antibodies to the virus. A more sophisticated test such as the polymerase chain reaction test may be performed to see if a silent or latent infection is present. However, some silent infections cannot be detected even by sophisticated tests. (p. 583)

♂♀ At present, there is still no cure for AIDS. Efforts toward halting the disease include the development of drugs to treat opportunistic infections, the search for antiviral drugs that will kill or neutralize HIV, attempts to rebuild compromised immune systems, and the development of a vaccine to prevent infection by the virus. The best hope for curtailing the spread of HIV and AIDS remains with education and behavior change. (pp. 589–591)

Other Sexually Transmitted Diseases (STDs)

♂♀ In the United States there is an increasing incidence of sexually transmitted diseases (STDs). It is estimated that approximately 50% of the U.S. population will acquire one or more STDs by ages 30–35, and that 86% of these STDs will occur among 15–29-year-olds. These diseases, which range from mild to life-threatening, can be prevented and in most cases successfully treated. (p. 552)

♂♀ There are many types of STDs. The most common include (Chapter 19)
Vaginal infections in women. Caused by *Gardnerella, Candida,* or *Trichomonas,* these infections are often transmitted sexually, though they can also be transmitted by nonsexual means. (pp. 93, 553–559)

- Chlamydia. One of the most prevalent and most damaging of all STDs, chlamydia is caused by bacteria. It is often asymptomatic, and can be diagnosed by a culture analysis and treated with antibiotics other than penicillin. Untreated chlamydia frequently causes sterility, cervicitis, and pelvic inflammatory disease in women. It can also be transmitted to newborns, who develop severe eye infections or pneumonia. (pp. 559–561)

- Gonorrhea. Caused by the gonococcus bacterium, gonorrhea can be diagnosed with a blood test or a culture and is treated with ampicillin or penicillin. Left untreated, gonorrhea can lead to pelvic inflammatory disease and sterility in women and prostate and kidney problems in men. (pp. 561–564)

- Nongonococcal urethritis. Frequently caused by the organism that causes chlamydia, nongonococcal urethritis is treated with antibiotics. This disease is often seen in men. (pp. 564–565)

- Syphilis. Diagnosed by a blood test and treated with penicillin, syphilis has four stages: primary syphilis, secondary syphilis, latent syphilis, and late syphilis. During the late phase the most severe symptoms arise: blindness, paralysis, and mental illness may occur. (pp. 565–568)

- Pubic lice, or "crabs." These tiny biting insects may be transmitted through sexual contact or by using sheets or clothing contaminated by an infected individual. A variety of prescription and nonprescription medications effectively kill pubic lice. (pp. 568–570)

- Herpes. The most common varieties of herpes are types 1 and 2. Painful blisters appear during flare-ups. There is no cure for herpes, only symptom relief. A woman with genital herpes may also infect her newborn child. (pp. 570–575)

- Viral hepatitis. There are two types of sexually transmitted hepatitis (a viral infection of the liver). Hepatitis A seems to be transmitted via oral–anal contact, while Hepatitis B may be transmitted via blood or blood products, semen, vaginal secretions, and saliva. There is no specific therapy for treating hepatitis, but most infected people recover in a few weeks with adequate bed rest. (pp. 576–577)

- Genital warts. Caused by a virus similar to that which produces warts on other parts of the body, genital warts can be treated by applications of topical agents, cauterization, surgical removal, or vaporization by a carbon dioxide laser. (pp. 577–578)

♂♀

There are several preventive measures that you can take to reduce the likelihood of contracting an STD. None is 100% effective, but each acts to significantly reduce the chances of infection. (pp. 592–597)

- Take the time, ideally several months, to get to know a prospective sexual partner before engaging in genital sex.

- Obtain prior medical examinations.

- Use condoms and spermicides containing nonoxynol-9.

- Avoid sexual activity with multiple partners.

- Inspect your partner's genitals for signs of an STD.

- Wash your and your partner's genitals before and after sexual contact.

- For people who are sexually active and have multiple partners, obtain periodic medical evaluations.

♂♀

If you suspect or know that you have an STD, get prompt treatment by a physician or a local clinic. In addition, you should inform any potential partner of the problem before you engage in sexual activity. The following are some guidelines that may help you tell a partner that you have an STD. (pp. 598–599)

- Be honest—don't downplay the potential risks.

- Even if you suspect that your partner is the source of the infection, try not to blame him or her.

- Try to present the facts in as clear and calm a fashion as you can manage.

- Be sensitive to your partner's feelings.

- Do not engage in sexual activity until you are no longer contagious.

- Offer to pay for some or all of the expenses for the medical examination and treatment of the STD, to maintain goodwill in the relationship.

- In the case of herpes, where recurrences are unpredictable and the possibility of infection is an ongoing concern, tell your partner about the herpes before sexual intimacies take place.

Increasing Sexual Satisfaction

Good sex is a combination of many factors, including effective communication and physical and mental readiness.

Kegel exercises can help both men and women strengthen muscle tone in the genital area, increase sensation during intercourse, and experience stronger and more pleasurable orgasms. (pp. 88–89, 130)

Communicating about sex can contribute greatly to the satisfaction of an intimate relationship. While talking can be difficult, there are some simple guidelines that can make communication about sex more effective. (pp. 224– 237)

- Try to listen effectively and avoid being judgmental.

- Seek information about your partner's needs and share information about your own.

- Use "I" language when making requests.

- Select a time when you are both relaxed to express sexual concerns.

- Try to temper critical comments with praise.

- Try to avoid sending mixed messages.

Sensate touching, a series of touching exercises, can be used to initiate sexual intimacy, reduce anxiety, increase communication and closeness, and enhance sexual enjoyment. (pp. 512–513)

Women who wish to become orgasmic may benefit from programs that include masturbation, sensate focus, mutual genital exploration, and nondemand genital pleasuring. (pp. 514–519)

Women who have problems with insufficient vaginal lubrication can try using a water-soluble lubricant that contains no alcohol. (pp. 91–92, 488)

Women who have problems with vaginismus may be able to alleviate the spasms through a series of relaxation, self-awareness, and vaginal dilation exercises. (pp. 489–490, 519–520)

Although premature ejaculation in men is a common dissatisfaction, there are some strategies that will help delay ejaculation. (pp. 486, 520–522)

- Ejaculate more frequently.

- Find a coital position that allows you to relax during coitus.

- Communicating during coitus about the need to reduce stimulation may help you prolong the experience.

- Consider alternatives to coitus, such as manual or oral–genital stimulation.

- Consider using the stop–start technique, which gives you a chance to become acquainted with, and ultimately control, your ejaculatory reflex.

Men who have had problems with psychologically based erectile inhibition might try a behavioral approach designed to reduce anxiety. This treatment has several phases: sensate focus, followed by genital stimulation, and then penetration. (pp. 523–524)

Acquaintance Rape

♂♀

The legal definition of rape varies from state to state, but most states define rape as sexual intercourse that occurs under actual or threatened forcible compulsion that overcomes the earnest resistance of the victim. (p. 628)

♂♀

Acquaintance rape (or date rape, because many acquaintance rapes occur in dating situations) is committed by someone who is known to the rape victim. A majority of rapes are committed by acquaintances rather than strangers. (p. 628)

♂♀

There are a number of reasons, many common to both sexes, for engaging in unwanted sexual acts where physical force is not employed. (p. 641)

- Enticement (being turned on by a partner's actions or touches and later regretting it).
- Threats to end a relationship.
- Desire to be popular.
- Peer pressure.
- Intoxication.
- Time or money expended by a partner makes you feel obligated.
- For men, the societal stereotype that a "real" man should always make sexual advances if the opportunity is there.
- Misinterpretation of a partner's intentions (e.g., cuddling and kissing are interpreted as a desire for intercourse).
- Mixed messages interpreted as token resistance.

♀

There is no guarantee a woman can avoid rape even if she leads an extremely cautious and restricted life. However, there are strategies for making rape as difficult as possible for the rapist. The following suggestions may help reduce a woman's chances of being raped by an acquaintance or date. (pp. 646–647)

- When dating someone for the first time, seriously consider doing so in a group situation or meeting him at a public place.
- Watch for inclinations that your date may be a controlling or dominating person who may try to control your behavior in an intimate setting.
- Contribute to the expenses of the date so the man is less inclined to use the rationale of "getting what he paid for" to justify sexually coercive actions.
- Avoid using alcohol or other drugs when you definitely do not wish to be sexually intimate with your date.
- Avoid behavior that may be interpreted as "teasing." Clearly state to your date what you do and do not wish to do in regard to intimate contact.
- If, despite direct communication about your intentions, your date behaves in a sexually coercive manner, you may use a strategy of escalating forcefulness—direct refusal, vehement verbal refusal, and, if necessary, physical force—to stop unwanted advances.

♂♀

If you have been raped, you will have to decide whether to report the attack to the police. If you decide to report the rape, keep in mind the following suggestions.(p. 647)

- Any information you can provide to the police, even if the rape attempt was unsuccessful, may prevent another woman from being raped.
- Any information you can remember about the attack will be helpful, including the assaulter's physical characteristics, voice, clothes, car, or an unusual smell.
- If you have been raped, call the police as soon as possible; do not bathe or change clothes.

Our Sexuality

PART ONE

Introduction

The type of fig leaf which each culture employs to cover its social taboos offers a two-fold description of its morality. It reveals that certain unacknowledged behavior exists and it suggests the form that such behavior takes.

Freda Adler
Sisters in Crime (1975)

CHAPTER 1

Perspectives on Sexuality

*P*erhaps all of us have had the experience of walking into a class for the first time, wondering what the course and the teacher would be like. On that first day, the instructor's candor in freely expressing the philosophy and focus of the course is a great help in setting the stage for all that is to follow. Our primary purpose for including this opening chapter is the same as that of an instructor's opening remarks — to acquaint you, the student reader, with the focus, philosophy, and perspectives we bring to this text.

We offer this book as a tool for the development of your own personal perspectives on human sexuality. We will present a wide array of information about attitudes, ideas, and behaviors, but we wish to emphasize that the final expert on your sexuality is *you*. Therefore, we encourage you to evaluate all the information we present within the framework of your own experiences and convictions.

The Authors' Perspectives

It is safe to assume that any controversial topic will elicit a wide range of responses. As one writer has put it, "Few topics evoke so much anxiety and pleasure, pain and hope, discussion and silence as the erotic possibilities of our bodies" (Weeks, 1985, p. ix). In any beginning sexuality class — or in almost any other group, for that matter — attitudes toward sexuality will likely range from very liberal to extremely conservative. It is also reasonable to assume that students in sexuality classes represent a wide range of ages, sexual and other life experiences, and preferences. Some have had sexual encounters with one or many partners; some have had long-term partnerships in marital or other ongoing frameworks; others have not been sexually involved with another person. Many people relate sexually exclusively to members of the other sex;* some prefer sexual relations with members of the same sex; still others are comfortable relating sexually to either sex. There are virtually no universals in sexual attitudes, experiences, or preferences.

With this broad spectrum in mind, we have attempted to bring a nonlimiting philosophy to our book. We think a human sexuality text should be written for all prospective readers, not just for one or two groups that may happen to be statistically more common than others. We hope there will be something of value in the following pages for *all* our readers. At the same time, we do speak from a distinct point of view. It is appropriate to tell you about our perspective — our orientation and our biases — so you can recognize and evaluate it for yourself as you read the text.

A Psychosocial Orientation

This book has a **psychosocial** orientation, reflecting our view that human sexuality is governed more by psychological factors (motivational, emotional, attitudinal) and by social conditioning (the process by which we learn our society's expecta-

---

*We use the term "other sex" instead of "opposite sex" to emphasize that men and women are similar or alike in more ways than they are "opposite."

Sexual attitudes and experiences vary from person to person.

tions and norms) than by the effects of biological factors such as hormones and instincts. The psychological and social factors are so intertwined that it is often difficult to distinguish clearly between the two.

We may not always be aware of it, but our sexual attitudes and behaviors are strongly shaped by our society. The subtle ways in which we learn society's expectations regarding sexuality often lead us to assume that our behaviors or feelings are biologically innate, or natural. However, an examination of sexuality in other societies (or even in different cultural groups within our own society) and in other historical periods reveals a broad range of acceptable behavior. For example, lovers rubbing noses and brides engaging in coitus with many different men on their wedding day are legitimate forms of sexual expression in certain other cultures, though certainly not in North American society today. What we regard as natural is clearly relative.

It is certainly clear that the physiology of sex plays an important role in human sexuality, and we will be looking in some detail at the biological foundations of sexual behavior. But understanding the impact of culture and individual experience can make it easier to make decisions about our own sexuality. Therefore, our major emphasis in this book will be on the psychosocial aspects of human sexuality.

Our Cultural Legacy: Questioning Two Themes

Besides a psychosocial orientation, we admit to some biases. These have to do with our opposition to two themes pertaining to sexuality, themes that are of long standing in most Western cultures.

One of these themes we refer to as "sex for reproduction," the idea that reproduction is the only legitimate reason for sexual activity. This idea is a legacy rooted in our Judeo–Christian heritage (Elia, 1987). In our culture, one of the most prominent ways that the reproductive theme is expressed is in the notion that sex is synonymous with penile–vaginal intercourse (or coitus). Certainly coitus can be a very fulfilling part of sexual expression. However, we believe that excessive emphasis on penile–vaginal intercourse often has negative consequences. For one, it perpetuates the notion that sexual response and orgasm are supposed to occur during penetration. Such a narrow focus places tremendous performance pressures on both women and men, and creates enormous expectations of coitus itself.

The sex-for-reproduction view also may result in devaluing other forms of sexual behavior. Some activities — for instance, affectionate kissing, body caresses, and manual or oral stimulation of the genitals — are often relegated to the secondary status of *foreplay* (usually considered to be any activity before intercourse), implying that they are to be followed by the "real sex" of coitus. Sexual activity between members of the same sex also does not fit into the model of sex-for-reproduction. These and other noncoital sexual behaviors — such as masturbation, sexual fantasy, and anal intercourse — have been defined at various times and places in our own and other cultures as immoral, sinful, perverted, or illegal. However, we present them in this text as viable sexual options for those who choose them.

The other theme we oppose is the rigid distinction between male and female roles. This legacy is based on far more than the physiological differences between the sexes. Research does show certain sex differences in some areas. However, socialization shapes and exaggerates our biological tendencies. Human beings begin learning in early infancy to be "opposites." For example, one of our students describes seeing this behavior at a baby shower for fraternal twins:

Except for the color of their clothes, the twins sure looked the same to me. But the women handled each of them differently; they gave soft, cooing sounds and delicate touches to the girl and energetic words and bouncing to the boy. (Authors' files)

We believe that rigid gender-role conditioning limits each person's full range of human potential and produces a negative impact on our sexuality. For example, teaching "appropriate" behavior for men and women may contribute to the limiting notion that the man must always initiate sexual activity while the woman must respond. We believe that such assumptions place tremendous responsibility on the male and severely limit the woman's likelihood of discovering her own needs. Moreover, such assumptions discourage the man from expressing his receptivity — and the woman from experiencing her assertiveness.

Our psychosocial orientation and our biases — our opposition to the sex-for-reproduction theme and our belief that rigid gender roles are limiting — will appear throughout this text. In this chapter, we want to explore these ideas more thoroughly, first from an historical and then from a cross-cultural perspective.

The Sex-for-Reproduction Legacy

We have noted that a strong idea in our culture is that the purpose of sexual activity should be procreation. Where did this idea come from, and how relevant is it to us today?

The idea of sex for reproduction is associated with the Judeo–Christian tradition. Childbearing was tremendously important to the ancient Hebrews. Their history of being subjected to slavery and persecution made them determined to preserve their people—to "be fruitful, and multiply, and replenish the earth" (Genesis 1:28). Yet to "know" a partner sexually, within marriage, was also recognized as a profound physical and emotional experience (Carswell, 1969). The Song of Solomon in the Old Testament contains some of the most sensuous love poetry in Western literature. The bridegroom speaks:

> How fair is thy love, . . . my spouse!
>
> how much better is thy love than wine!
>
> and the smell of thine ointments than all spices!
>
> Thy lips, oh my spouse, drop as the honeycomb
>
> honey and milk are under thy tongue. (Solomon 4:10–11)

And the bride:

> I am my beloved's and his desire is toward me.
>
> Come, my husband, let us go forth into the field;
>
> Let us lodge in the villages . . .
>
> There will I give thee my loves. (7:10–13)

This joyful appreciation of sexuality was a part of the Judaic tradition, as was the notion that sex was for procreation. It would later be eclipsed, however, by the teachings of the medieval church. To understand why this happened, it is necessary to look at the social context in which Christianity developed.

By the first century B.C., after the Roman Empire had reached its height, social instability and sexual decadence were pervasive. Many exotic cults were imported to Rome from Greece, Persia, Palestine, and other parts of the empire to provide sexual entertainment and amusement. The cult of Bacchus (the god of wine) became one of the most notorious. In the Bacchanalia ceremony, which ultimately became so offensive that the Roman Senate banned it, young male initiates raced to the banks of the Tiber River, where they were forced to have intercourse with members of the cult or be killed.

We know very little about Jesus' views on sexuality. But in the years after his death, his followers showed their reaction against activities like the Bacchanalia by their association of sex with sin. Paul of Tarsus, whose influence upon the early church was crucial (he died in A.D. 66, and many of his writings were incorporated into the New Testament), emphasized the importance of overcoming "desires of the flesh"—including anger, selfishness, hatred, and nonmarital sex—to inherit the Kingdom of God. He associated spirituality with sexual abstinence and saw **celibacy** (SEL-a-ba-sē), the state of being unmarried and therefore abstaining from sexual intercourse, as superior to marriage. Other church fathers expanded on the theme of sex as sin in the following centuries. Augustine (354–430) declared that lust was the original sin of Adam and Eve; his writings formalized the notion that intercourse could take place only within marriage for the purpose of procreation.

The belief that sex is sinful persisted throughout the Middle Ages (the period from the fall of the Western Roman Empire in A.D. 476 to the beginning of the Renaissance, about 1400), and Thomas Aquinas (1225–1274) further refined this

Paul of Tarsus, a highly influential Christian leader, endorsed the view of sex as sinful, justifiable only in marriage for the purpose of procreation.

idea in a small section of his *Summa Theologica.* In a detailed list of rules about sexual behavior, Aquinas maintained that human sexual organs were designed for procreation and that any other use — as in homosexual acts, oral-genital sex, anal intercourse, or sex with animals — was against God's will and therefore heretical. Aquinas's teachings were so influential that from then on homosexuals were to find neither refuge nor tolerance anywhere in the Western world (Boswell, 1980).

The ideas of Augustine and Aquinas dominated Western thought until the Protestant Reformation in the sixteenth century. One of Martin Luther's (1483–1546) disagreements with official church doctrine centered around chastity and celibacy. Sex, he believed, was as necessary to humans as eating and drinking. He argued that clergy should be permitted to marry; and after he left the priesthood, he married and fathered several children. Another reformer, John Calvin (1509–1564), recognized that sex could have purposes other than procreation. Marital sex was permissible, he claimed, if it stemmed "from a desire for children, or to avoid fornication, or to lighten and ease the cares and sadnesses of household affairs, or to endear each other" (Taylor, 1971, p. 62). The Puritans, a group often maligned for having rigid views about sex, also shared an appreciation of sexual expression within marriage as a part of their emphasis on the family unit (D'Emilio and Freedman, 1988). One man was expelled from Boston when, among other offenses, "he denied . . . conjugal . . . fellowship unto his wife for the space of 2 years . . ." (Morgan, 1978, p. 364). Thus, the Reformation groups saw sexual intercourse as a human necessity, not just a requirement for procreation — but with marriage providing the proper context for it.

One other influence should be mentioned in any discussion of the sex-for-procreation legacy: the availability of modern contraception, which permits intercourse without procreation more reliably than do older methods. Contraceptive devices have been used for centuries (Pomeroy, 1975). Condoms made from goat bladders were used by men in ancient times. In Rome during the first century B.C., women used amulets, magic, and the rhythm method (which was highly ineffective at that time, because the Romans mistakenly believed that the most fertile period was at the end of menstruation). They also inserted soft wool pads to block the cervix — a precursor, perhaps, to the modern diaphragm, which was developed in Europe in the 1870s, but was not introduced to the United States until the 1920s.

With the possible exception of the diaphragm, none of these methods was as reliable as the oral contraceptive pill, introduced in the late 1950s and early 1960s, soon to be followed by the intrauterine device (IUD), "morning-after pills," and spermicides. These contraceptives have given men and women increased control over their reproductive capacities; their widespread acceptance has permitted sexuality to be separated from procreation in a way that it has never been before. The world has changed, too, so that today many people are concerned with the ecological and economic costs of bearing children, costs that were not as relevant in the preindustrial world. Despite these changes, however, the legacies of the Old and New Testaments, of Augustine and Thomas Aquinas, and of the Reformation are still very much with us. Thus, the sex-for-reproduction issue in the twentieth-century Western world represents a complex conflict among the values of personal pleasure, practicality, and tradition.

OTHER TIMES, OTHER PLACES

When God Was a Woman

Accurate knowledge of sexuality and gender roles in early human history is virtually impossible. Available information is sparse and subject to distorted interpretation by historians influenced by their own cultural biases. The following paragraphs summarize the provocative historical thesis of art historian Merlin Stone (1976).

In prehistoric and early historic periods of human development (about 7000 B.C.–A.D. 599), religions existed in which people revered great goddesses who had life-giving and important roles. In nearly all areas of the world, female deities were extolled as healers. Some were powerful, courageous warriors and leaders in battle. The Greek goddess Demeter and the Egyptian goddess Isis were both invoked as lawgivers and dispensers of wisdom and justice. In the ancient Middle East, where some of

the earliest evidence of agricultural development has been found, the goddess Ninlil was revered for having provided her people with an understanding of planting and harvesting.

As the role of the male in reproduction came to be understood and male kinship lines became important, religions headed by female deities were persecuted and suppressed by the newer religions, which held male gods supreme.

Through the imposition and eventual acceptance of the male-centered religions, women came to be regarded as inferior creatures, divinely intended for the production of children and the pleasure of men. In their new role as silent and obedient vessels, women were far removed from the status of the ancient goddesses.

The Egyptian goddess Isis.

The Gender-Role Legacy

A second issue about which we have a bias is the legacy of gender roles. Roles of women and men are changing in modern Western society, but each change, going as it does against tradition, has been difficult to achieve.

How far back do we have to look to find the roots of this legacy? Certainly by the time Hebraic culture was established, gender roles were highly specialized. The Book of Proverbs lists the duties of a good wife: She must instruct servants, care for her family, and keep household accounts. In addition, she must look on the future with optimism, be kind, and never be idle. Charm and beauty were not required, but bearing children (especially sons) was essential; so was obedience to the husband. In return for all this, the wife was granted the right to her husband's sexual favors — although she might share this right with one or more secondary wives or concubines!

In the Middle Ages, two contradictory images of women evolved: (a) women as pure and untouchable, exemplified by the Virgin Mary, and (b) women as evil, exemplified by Eve as the temptress.

(a)   (b)

Christianity reaffirmed Judaism's traditional gender roles. One of the major topics in the writings of Paul of Tarsus was the status of women. Paul used man's creation before woman's and Eve's disobedience to God to explain why women should be submissive:

> I permit no woman to teach or to have authority over men. . . . For Adam was formed first, then Eve; and Adam was not deceived, but the woman was deceived and became a transgressor. (I Timothy 2:11–15)

The view that women should be subservient to men prevailed throughout the Middle Ages. During this period, however, two contradictory images of women evolved, gaining strength so that each had its own impact on women's place in society. The first was the image of the Virgin Mary; the second, the image of Eve as an evil temptress.

The cult of the Virgin was imported to the West by crusaders returning from Constantinople. Mary had been a vague figure of secondary importance in the Western church, but now she was transformed into a gracious, compassionate protector of the poor and wretched, an exalted focus of religious devotion. The practice of *courtly love,* which evolved at about this time, reflected a compatible image of woman as pure and above reproach. Ideally, a young knight would fall in love with a married woman of higher rank. After a lengthy pursuit, he would find favor, but his love would remain unconsummated because her marriage vows ultimately proved inviolable. This paradigm caught the medieval imagination, and troubadours performed ballads of courtly love throughout the courts of Europe.

The other medieval image provides a counterpoint to the unattainable, compassionate Madonna: Eve as the evil temptress of the Garden of Eden. This image,

Antagonism toward women
reached a climax during the
witch-hunts of the fifteenth
century.

promoted by the church, reflected an increasing emphasis on Eve's sin and an antagonism toward women. This antagonism reached its climax in the witch-hunts that began in the late fifteenth century — after the Renaissance was well under way — and lasted for close to 200 years. Queen Elizabeth I (1533–1603), who ruled during the Renaissance, helped elevate women's status and brought England to new heights of power; yet during her reign, thousands of women were tortured and executed as witches in both Europe and America.

Witch-hunting had ended by the time of the eighteenth-century Enlightenment, which was partly an outgrowth of the new scientific rationalism: ideas were now based on facts that could be objectively observed and measured, rather than on subjective beliefs. Women were to enjoy a new equality, at least for a short time. Some women, like Mary Wollstonecraft, of England, were famous for their intelligence, wit, and vivacity. Wollstonecraft's book, *The Vindication of the Rights of Women* (1792), attacked the prevailing practice of giving young girls dolls rather than schoolbooks. Wollstonecraft also asserted that sexual satisfaction was as important to women as to men, and that premarital and extramarital sex were not sinful.

Unfortunately these progressive views did not prevail. The Victorian era, which took its name from the queen who ascended the British throne in 1837, brought a sharp turnaround. The sexes had highly defined roles. Upper- and middle-class Victorian women were valued for their spirituality and delicacy — and consequently constrained by such restrictive devices as corsets, hoops, and bustles, which prevented them from freely moving their bodies. Popular opinion of female sexuality was reflected by the widely quoted physician William Acton, who wrote, "The majority of women are not very much troubled with sexual feelings of any kind" (Degler, 1980, p. 250). Women's duties centered around fulfilling their families' spiritual needs, and providing a comfortable home for their husbands to retreat to after working all day. Ladylike manners and domestic skills were con-

In the Victorian era, the marriageable woman possessed morals that were as tightly laced as her corset. Ironically, prostitution flourished at this time.

sidered very important. Magazines such as *Godey's Lady's Book* instructed women on the proper forms for such virtues. The world of women was clearly separated from that of men. Intensely passionate friendships sometimes developed between women, providing the support and comfort often absent in marriage.

Victorian men were expected to conform to the strict propriety of the age, but (alas!) they were often forced to lay aside morality in the pursuit of business and political interests. They also sometimes laid aside morality in the pursuit of sexual companionship, because the separation of the worlds of husbands and wives created an emotional (and physical) distance in many Victorian marriages. Ironically, prostitution flourished at this time, right alongside propriety and sexual repression. Victorian men could smoke, drink, and joke with the women who had turned to prostitution out of economic necessity. Furthermore, social pressure encouraged men to marry only after they had accumulated money and established a comfortable home. Confronted with many years without a wife, then marriage to a sheltered bride many years younger than himself, a man paid prostitutes for companionship as well as sexual contact.

Perhaps more than any age, the nineteenth century was full of sexual contradictions. Women's sexuality was polarized between the opposing images of Madonna and whore. Men were trapped between the ideal of purity and the frank pleasures of physical expression.

The twentieth century changed this precarious dichotomy. The suffrage movement, which began in the late nineteenth century with the goal of giving women the right to vote, grew out of several related developments such as the temperance movement, the abolition of slavery, and the demand that women be permitted to attend universities and hold property. The passage in 1920 of the Eighteenth Amendment to the U.S. Constitution, which guaranteed women the right to vote,

A woman warrior in New Guinea. In many societies, bare female breasts are not generally viewed as erotic stimuli.

did not usher in a new era of equality. But World War II created an environment for increased equality and further disintegration of gender roles, as thousands of women left the traditional homemaker role and took paying jobs for the first time. Not until the 1960s, however, after the flurry of postwar marriages, the baby boom, and widespread disappointment in the resulting domesticity of women, did a new movement for gender-role equality begin. Yet we still carry the legacy of Victorianism and earlier traditions in the gender roles we all learn as children, and this legacy limits both men and women. In Chapter 3, we will discuss the impact of gender roles on contemporary American women and men.

A Cross-Cultural Perspective: Social Norms and Sexuality

What constitutes normal sexual behavior? Many of us have our own ideas about what is normal and what is not, but often the meaning of a given act (sexual or otherwise) can be fully understood only by looking at the cultural and historical context within which it occurs. There is such cultural diversity among the peoples of the world that even the idea of what is sexually arousing varies greatly. For example, exposed female breasts often trigger sexual arousal in Western males, but they induce little or no erotic interest in the males of New Guinea. Furthermore, the acceptability of sexual activity varies enormously from one culture to another. In some societies, such as the Mangaian society of Polynesia, sex is highly valued, and almost all manifestations of it are considered beautiful and natural. Other societies, such as the Manus society of New Guinea, view almost any sexual act as undesirable and shameful.

Do you think there are any rules governing sexual behavior that apply to all cultures? If so, what might these rules be? Take a moment to consider the answers to these questions before reading on.

The diversity of sexual expression throughout the world tends to mask a fundamental generalization that can be applied without exception to all social orders: Within the cultural mores of all societies, there are rules regulating the conduct of sexual behavior. For example, all cultures practice marriage in one form or another, and marriage provides sanctioned sexual privileges and obligations. Although exact regulations vary from one society to the next, no social order has seen fit to allow sexuality to remain totally unregulated. "Every society shapes, structures and constrains the development and expression of sexuality in all of its members" (Beach, 1978, p. 116). Thus, the sexual inclinations of human males and females are never allowed free rein within the context of any formally organized social group.

Data Sources: Methods and Limitations

Before we discuss cultural diversity in sexual attitudes and behavior, we would like to present some information on how the data on these cultures are obtained — and the limitations of such data. Most of our data about sexual expression in other societies have been derived from the fieldwork of **ethnographers** (eth-NOG-ra-fers), anthropologists who specialize in studying the cultures of different societies. Fieldwork consists of careful observation (the researcher may live with the population for several months or years) and in-depth interviews and discussions. It is a method of study that can produce detailed information about the beliefs and behaviors of a small, representative group.

Because sexuality is such a fascinating topic, many ethnographers must have studied it extensively. Do you think this is a true statement or not? Why? Give yourself a few moments to think about your answer before reading on.

Unfortunately, fieldwork has usually focused on religion, economics, technology, and social organization, and has rarely examined sexual mores and behaviors. The scarcity of data about sexual expression probably results in part from the cultural bias of many researchers. Most ethnographers have come from Western societies, where sex is considered a private matter, and they may therefore have been reluctant to pursue the subject. (In fact, Western social scientists and historians have been reluctant to study sexuality in their own culture [Freedman and Emilio, 1990].) Furthermore, some of these investigators made assumptions about other societies on the basis of their own culturally determined attitudes

(a)

(b)

(c)

(d)

All cultures practice marriage in one form or another. Shown here: (a) A Korean Buddist ceremony. (b) A Jewish wedding ceremony. (c) A Hindu wedding ceremony. (d) A Christian wedding ceremony.

(Bleibtreu-Ehrenberg, 1991). In addition, even when field investigators are comfortable inquiring about sexual activity, their respondents may not share their comfort. Investigations of other societies rely on reported rather than observed sexual behavior, and some degree of error in the data is probable, as we will discuss in Chapter 2. In spite of these limitations, some of the available ethnographic descriptions contain valuable data about the richness and diversity of human sexual expression.

The rest of this section is devoted to discussions of sexual attitudes and behaviors in two societies—the Polynesian island of Mangaia and the Irish island we will call Inis Beag. These two cultures represent the extremely permissive and extremely restrictive ends, respectively, of the human sexuality continuum. Additional cross-cultural and historical perspectives are presented in the "Other Times, Other Places" boxes appearing throughout the text.

Mangaia

Mangaia is the southernmost island in the Polynesian Cook Island chain. When anthropologist Donald Marshall studied the people of Mangaia in the 1950s, he observed a society in which sexual pleasure and activity is a principal concern, starting in childhood (Marshall, 1971). Children have extensive exposure to sexuality: they hear folktales that contain detailed descriptions of sex acts and sexual anatomy, and they observe provocative ritual dances. During puberty, members of both sexes receive active and detailed sexual instruction. Males undergo an operation called *superincision,* which consists of cutting the tissue on top of the penis and folding it back, exposing the glans. During this period, a boy is provided with detailed information about various sexual techniques. He is taught how to stimulate a woman's genitals and breasts with his mouth, how to bring a female partner to orgasm, and how to control his urge to ejaculate. A Mangaian girl is also instructed in sexual techniques; she is taught the importance of being responsive and active during sexual encounters.

Once their instruction is completed, boys begin to seek girls. Sex occurs in "public privacy" as young males engage in a practice called *night-crawling.* At night the boy creeps quietly into the family home of a young woman with whom he wants to have sexual intercourse. If awakened, the other 5 to 15 family members in the home politely pretend to sleep. (In the 1950s, when Marshall conducted his research, most Mangaian houses had only a single sleeping area.) Parents approve of this practice and listen for sounds of laughter as a sign that their daughter is pleased with her partner. They encourage the young woman to have several partners so that she may find a sexually compatible husband. The young men gain social prestige through their ability to please their partners. These patterns persist throughout the adolescent years for unmarried males and females.

Sexual relations continue to occur frequently after marriage. Marshall estimates that an 18-year-old male experiences three orgasms per night every day of the week — and if he is skilled, his partner experiences three orgasms for every one of his. A wide range of sexual activity is socially approved, including oral–genital sex and a considerable amount of touching before and during intercourse. The Mangaians, then, not only condone but also actively encourage a high rate of sexual activity as normal behavior. In sharp contrast is the community of the Irish island Inis Beag.

Inis Beag

The inhabitants of Inis Beag (a pseudonym, to protect the privacy of this Irish island) have a very different attitude from that of the Mangaians (Messenger, 1971). Sexual expression is discouraged from infancy; mothers avoid breast-feeding their children, and after infancy parents seldom kiss or fondle them. Children learn to abhor nudity. They learn that elimination is "dirty" and that bathing must be done only in absolute privacy. Any kind of childhood sexual expression is punished.

As they grow older, children usually receive no information about sex from their parents. Young girls are often shocked by their first menstruation, and they are never given an adequate explanation of what has happened. Priests and other religious authorities teach that masturbation, sex play, and discussion of premarital sexual activity are sinful. Religious leaders on the island have denounced even *Time* and *Life* magazines as pornographic.

The average age for marriage is older than in many societies (36 for men and 26 for women), and marriages are often arranged. One of the reasons for late marriage may be the limited land resources — a man must usually wait to own land through inheritance. Marriage partners generally know little or nothing about such precoital sex play as oral or manual stimulation of breasts and genitals. Beyond intercourse, sexual activity is usually limited to mouth kissing and rough fondling of the woman's lower body by the man. Sex usually occurs while both partners are wearing night clothes. Males invariably initiate sex, using the man-on-top, face-to-face intercourse position; and after ejaculation, they tend to fall asleep. Female orgasm is unknown or considered a deviant response.

Sexual misconceptions continue through adulthood. For example, many women believe that menopause causes insanity, and some women confine themselves to bed from menopause to their death. During menstruation and during the months following childbirth, men consider intercourse to be harmful to them. Many men also believe intercourse to be debilitating, and they avoid sex the night before a strenuous job. In general, anxiety-laden attitudes and rigid social restrictions concerning sexuality are the norm on Inis Beag.

The broad range of sexual attitudes and behaviors among the Mangaians and the people of Inis Beag helps show how society shapes sexuality. Although we may not always look at it in the same light, our own customs, practices, and attitudes reflect a parallel process of societal shaping.

Sexuality: Personal or Public Domain?

The historical and cross-cultural perspectives we have used in this chapter may help us appreciate the unique position in which we currently find ourselves. Men and women in our society today have new freedoms and responsibilities. To a far greater degree than was possible for the ancient Hebrews, the early Christians, the Europeans of the Middle Ages, or the Victorians of a century ago — and to a far greater degree than is possible for many non-Western societies, such as many Arab cultures, today — we can define our own sexuality on the basis of personal choices.

This responsibility has been hard won, and it is largely a result of psychological, scientific, and social advances that have taken place primarily in the twentieth century. Psychological advances came with the work of people like Sigmund Freud (1856–1939) and Havelock Ellis (1859–1939), who recognized sexuality in both women and men as natural and recognized that different individuals have differing sexual needs; and Theodore Van de Velde (1873–1937), who emphasized the importance of sexual pleasure and satisfaction. As these ideas became accepted by more people, the result was a growing tolerance for a wider variety of behaviors.

Findings of sex researchers like Alfred Kinsey provided scientific data that brought further acceptance of masturbation, homosexuality, and nonmarital intercourse as normal expressions of sexuality. Research such as that of William Masters and Virginia Johnson brought a greater public understanding of the sexual response cycle. We will look at the work of these and other pioneering sex researchers in Chapter 2. This new awareness of sexual interests and individual variations also contributed to a greater tolerance and respect for the individual's right to make sexual decisions.

In the early 1960s, the invention of the oral contraceptive pill and the increased availability of other reliable contraceptive devices helped bring sexual decisions even more firmly into the personal domain. By the end of that decade, contraception had become accepted as a matter of personal decision. Moreover, in 1973 the U.S. Supreme Court ruled in a landmark decision that abortion is a woman's choice, one that the government cannot prohibit. In the increasingly tolerant atmosphere of the late 1960s and 1970s, attitudes began to change about another traditional taboo, homosexuality. Homosexual men and women began to openly declare their sexual orientation — and to demand that such a personal matter should not affect their rights and responsibilities as citizens. The popular stigma surrounding homosexuality had begun to dissipate when the AIDS crisis, which arose in the 1980s, dramatically increased the visibility of homosexual individuals and amplified both positive and negative public sentiments toward their lifestyle.

These many changes have come rapidly, and our society is still in a state of flux. One result has been a sense of uncertainty about personal and social values. For example, although young women and men have had more access to information, contraception, and medical care, there has been an epidemic of sexually transmitted diseases, a rise in births to unmarried adolescent women, and widespread confusion about personal values. On the other hand, the risk of contracting a terminal disease — AIDS — has led many individuals to be more conservative and cautious in their sexual behavior. In addition, we now face controversies about ethical and legal policies in almost every area related to human sexuality, from sex education to surrogate parenthood.

While some people believe personal choice should be the foundation for decisions related to sexuality, others are dedicated to limiting personal control and bringing many choices about sexuality back into the public domain. For example, antiabortion groups are attempting to make abortion again illegal. Other groups oppose certain types of contraception, rights for homosexuals, pornography, and contraceptives for adolescents; and they are attempting to enact social policy to support their views. Such conflicts between personal autonomy and attempts at social control of various aspects of our sexuality are likely to continue throughout the 1990s.

Summary

The Authors' Perspectives

The authors' psychosocial orientation means that this book stresses the role of social conditioning in shaping human sexuality.

The book critically explores the effects of two pervasive themes related to sexuality: sex for reproduction and inflexible gender roles. The authors' biases predispose them against these legacies of Western culture.

The Sex-for-Reproduction Legacy

A prominent belief in Western culture is that sex is for reproduction only. This idea has deep historical roots.

The ancient Hebrews stressed the importance of childbearing but also had an appreciation of sexuality within marriage.

Christian writers such as Paul of Tarsus, Augustine, and Thomas Aquinas contributed to the view of sex as sinful, justifiable only in marriage for the purpose of procreation.

Leaders of the Reformation of the sixteenth century challenged the requirement that clergy remain celibate, and recognized sexual expression as an important aspect of marriage.

Technical advances in contraception in the twentieth century have permitted people to separate sexuality from procreation to a degree not previously possible.

The Gender-Role Legacy

A second prominent belief in our culture is that women and men should conform to rigid gender roles. This idea, also, goes far back in Western history.

Gender-role differences between men and women were well established in ancient Hebraic culture. Women's most important roles were to manage the household and bear children, especially sons.

The New Testament writings of Paul emphasized the subservience of women.

Two contradictory images of women developed in the Middle Ages: the pure and unattainable woman-on-a-pedestal, manifest in the cult of the Virgin Mary and in courtly love; and the evil temptress represented by Eve and by the women persecuted as witches.

Women were viewed as asexual in the Victorian era, and the lives of "proper" Victorian men and women were largely separate. Men often employed prostitutes for companionship as well as sexual relations.

A Cross-Cultural Perspective: Social Norms and Sexuality

To appreciate the importance of social conditioning, we must look at sexual attitudes and behaviors in other cultures.

A high rate of sexual activity and extensive sexual instruction of young people is the accepted pattern on the Polynesian island of Mangaia.

On the Irish island of Inis Beag, sexual expression is discouraged from infancy through old age. Sexual misinformation is common, and female orgasm is practically unknown.

Sexuality: Personal or Public Domain?

Greater knowledge, more reliable contraceptives, and legal decisions have increased the contemporary individual's ability to make personal decisions regarding sexuality. Our society is changing, and a result for some has been uncertainty about personal decisions. Social policies and laws can either restrict or expand personal options.

⤳ *Thought Provokers* ⤳

1. If you could design and implement your ideal sexual norms within a society, what would these be?

2. In what ways do restrictive sexual norms contribute beneficially to a society?

3. How do you think the two contradictory images of women — the Virgin Mary and the temptress Eve — are manifest in contemporary attitudes and media images?

4. How does someone like the pop singer Madonna affect traditional images of women, and to what extent?

Suggested Readings

Boswell, John (1980). *Christianity, Social Tolerance, and Homosexuality*. Chicago: University of Chicago Press. A comprehensive study of Western beliefs concerning homosexuality from ancient Greece to the fourteenth century.

Davenport, William (1977). "Sex in Cross-Cultural Perspective," in F. Beach (Ed.), *Human Sexuality in Four Perspectives*. Baltimore: Johns Hopkins Press. (Also available in paperback from the same publisher, 1978.) An eminent anthropologist provides a comparison of human sexuality in different societies around the world.

Degler, Carl (1980). *At Odds: Women and the Family in America from the Revolution to the Present*. Oxford: Oxford University Press. A historical survey of American women and their families.

D'Emilio, John; and Freedman, Estelle (1988). *Intimate Matters*. New York: Harper & Row. A full-length examination of the history of sexuality and how the meaning and place of sexuality in the United States have changed.

Marshall, Donald; and Suggs, Robert (Eds.) (1971). *Human Sexual Behavior: Variations in the Ethnographic Spectrum*. Englewood Cliffs, N.J.: Prentice-Hall. A superb collection of eight articles that detail the sexual attitudes, behaviors, and mores of societies around the world.

Pomeroy, Susan (1975). *Goddesses, Whores, Wives, and Slaves: Women in Classical Antiquity*. New York: Schocken Books. A scholarly and readable work on women in ancient Greece and Rome.

I know of no inquiry that the impulse of man suggests, which is forbidden to the resolution of man to pursue.

Margaret Fuller
Summer on the Lakes (1844)

CHAPTER 2

Sex Research: Methods and Problems

Research Methods

What to Believe? A Statement of Perspective

*A*rticles and books that claim to contain the latest research on human sexual behavior are plentiful. "Scientific polls" urge readers to accept their findings as Truth — even though they may contradict another survey published just a month earlier. At present there is an extensive body of scientific sex research, and it is rapidly growing. Some of this research is excellent and rather remarkable; other findings have proven to be less than noteworthy. How can a reader learn to distinguish the wheat from the chaff?

You may find it helpful to keep in mind that sex research, despite its rapid growth, is still in its infancy. The pioneering work done by Alfred Kinsey, who was the first to conduct an extensive general survey of American sexual behaviors, took place only in the late 1940s and early 1950s. Sex is as old as humankind, but it is a newcomer as a subject for serious research.

It is also important to realize that the study of sexuality shares the same problems that handicap all research into human social behavior. Human subjects cannot be placed in the same kind of experimental situations as other animals; ethical considerations limit the researcher's range of options (see the box "Human Sex Research"). Moreover, human thought and behavior are extremely complex — and this complexity poses even more serious research problems. For instance, subjects second-guess the researcher, altering their responses to coincide with their expectations of what the researcher (or society) wants to hear. The very private and sensitive nature of human sexuality further complicates the process of data collecting: Many people simply do not want to answer such personal questions.

Despite these problems, research provides a growing body of knowledge about human sexuality. In this chapter, we will acquaint you with how we have come to know certain things about sexual behavior. As we discuss particular methods, problems, and examples of sex research, you may begin to appreciate what we know and do not know, and how confident we can be in the available knowledge. You may also begin to sense the directions we can take to further expand our scientific knowledge of sexual behavior. Perhaps at some future time, you will contribute to our knowledge of this important area of human experience. We invite you to do so.

Research Methods

There are a number of methods for studying sexual behavior. They range from detailed case studies of specific individuals, often in a clinical setting where the subject is being treated for a specific behavioral or medical problem, to questionnaire or interview surveys that typically produce less depth of coverage about a much larger group of people. Two less frequently used research methods are direct observation and experimental laboratory research. Each of these strategies has advantages and disadvantages for researching various kinds of questions.

Surveys

Most of our information about human sexuality has been obtained through **surveys** that ask people about their sexual experiences or attitudes. This information

ETHICAL/LEGAL ISSUES IN HUMAN SEXUALITY

Human Sex Research

Researchers in a broad array of investigative fields share a common commitment to maintain the welfare, dignity, rights, well-being, and safety of their human subjects. In the last two decades, detailed lists of ethical guidelines have been prepared by a number of professional organizations, including the American Psychological Association (1990).

These codes, or ethical guidelines, require, among other things, that researchers avoid procedures that might cause serious physical or psychological harm to human subjects. If an experiment involves even the slightest risk of harm or discomfort, investigators are required to obtain informed consent from their subjects. Researchers must also respect a subject's right to refuse to participate at any time during the course of a study. In addition, special steps must be taken to protect the confidentiality of the data and maintain participants' anonymity unless they agree to be identified.

The issue of deception in research remains controversial. Some studies would lose their effectiveness if participating subjects knew in advance exactly what the experimenter was studying. The ethical guideline generally applied to this issue is that if deception must be used, a postexperiment debriefing must thoroughly explain to participants why it was necessary. At such time, subjects must be allowed to request that their data be removed from the study and destroyed.

Sometimes it is hard for researchers to weigh objectively the potential benefits of a study against the possibility of harming its subjects. Recognizing the difficulty of this task, virtually every institution conducting research in the United States has established ethics committees that review all proposed studies. If they perceive that the subjects' (human or otherwise) welfare is insufficiently safeguarded, the proposal must be modified or the research cannot be conducted. In addition, federal funding for research is denied to any institution that fails to conduct an adequate ethics committee review prior to the collection of data.

may be obtained in two ways: either orally through a face-to-face interview or in written form on a paper-and-pencil questionnaire. Researchers use surveys when they are interested in obtaining information from a large number of people, usually more than is practical to study in a clinical setting or in the laboratory. For instance, researchers might use a survey to find out whether publicity about AIDS (acquired immunodeficiency syndrome) has changed people's sexual practices.

Although the methods of conducting written and oral surveys are somewhat different, their intent is the same. Each tries to use a relatively small group of people, called the *survey sample,* to draw inferences or conclusions about a much larger group of people with a particular characteristic (called a *population*). For example, a population might be married adults or high school adolescents.

Choosing the Sample. Most research questions relate to a population much too large to be studied in its entirety. For example, if you wished to examine the attitudes and behavior of adolescent males regarding birth control, your population would include male teenagers from all over the globe. Obviously, you cannot question all teenage males in the world. Even if you decided to limit your observations to American male adolescents, your target group would still be prohibitively large.

Sex researchers get around this difficulty by gathering data from a relatively small sample or selected segment of the population that interests them. Our ability to draw inferences or conclusions confidently about a much larger population rests chiefly on the techniques we use for selecting subjects for the sample study.

The ideal sample is called a **representative sample,** that is, a sample in which subgroups are represented according to their incidence in the larger population

Most information about human sexual behavior has been obtained through questionnaire or interview surveys.

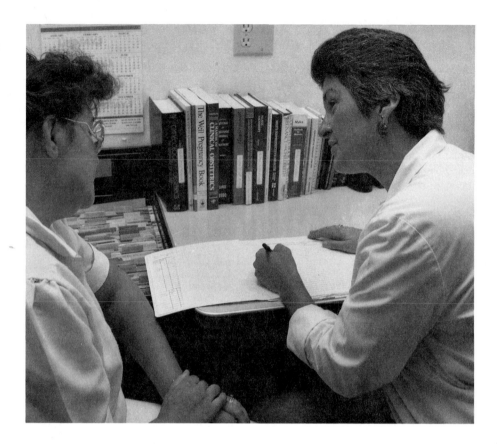

about which we wish to draw conclusions. A population could be divided into these subgroups by such criteria as sex, age, race, religious affiliation, geographic locale, and so on. In such a sample, every individual in the total population of interest has a chance to be included in the limited sample actually being studied.

How would you go about selecting a representative sample that you could use to investigate American male adolescents' attitudes and behavior regarding birth control? To draw broad conclusions about the general population (all American male teenagers), your sample would need to be representative of the group. How could you ensure this? Take a few moments to consider what procedures you might use before reading on.

You might begin by obtaining the rosters of all male high school students in a variety of geographic areas throughout the United States. You would need to select these regions very carefully to reflect the actual distribution of the population you are studying. For instance, if 30% of American male adolescents live in the Western states, 30% of your sample would be drawn from the West. Likewise, if 20% of Western male adolescents live in rural areas, 20% of the subjects selected from the West must be country dwellers.

Once the rosters were compiled in this systematic fashion, the next step would be to select the actual participants by some method that would ensure equal probability of inclusion, such as using a table of random numbers to generate random picks from the rosters. Provided that your final sample was sufficiently large, you could be reasonably confident in generalizing your findings to all American male adolescents.

Another common kind of survey sample is called a **random sample.** A random sample is selected by randomization procedures; however, the random sample may or may not be the same as a representative sample. For example, suppose that you have an opportunity to buy into a café on campus. The café has been only marginally profitable, and you think that converting to a health-food menu may help increase profitability. You decide to survey students' attitudes about patronizing a health-food restaurant on campus. Because summer provides the most free time, you decide to conduct your poll during this period. A friend who works in the registrar's office supplies you with the roster of summer session enrollees, and you randomly select your survey sample from this group.

Assuming that your question about patronizing a health-food restaurant is clearly stated and that a large percentage of the sample respond to your poll, can you be confident that your findings reflect the views of the entire student body at your school? The answer is no, for a reason you may have already guessed—students enrolled in summer classes are not necessarily representative of all students at your college or university. For example, if more graduate students enroll in the summer program, the average age will be higher than that of students in the fall and winter sessions. Differences such as this could contribute to somewhat different attitudes toward health food. For instance, there is evidence that people become more aware of the importance of a healthy diet as they grow older.

Thus, although randomization is an important tool, the sample will not be truly representative unless it includes members of specific groups (for instance, students enrolled during all seasons of the year) or proportionate numbers of individuals with certain characteristics (such as age, sex, or race).

Representative samples generally represent the total population, which they are designed to reflect, more accurately than random samples. Nevertheless, random samples are often quite adequate for many kinds of investigations. A decision whether to use a representative sample or a random sample depends both on the question(s) the researcher seeks to answer and on how precisely she or he wishes to generalize the findings to a larger population.

Questionnaires and Interviews. Once a sample is selected, survey data can be obtained in two major ways: through a questionnaire or through an interview. Both involve asking the participants a set of questions that may range in number from a few to over 1000. These questions may be multiple-choice, true–false, or discussion questions, and they may be responded to alone in the privacy of one's home or in the presence of a researcher.

Sex researchers who use surveys take into consideration the relative benefits and potential shortcomings of collecting their data via questionnaires versus interviews. Take a minute to list what you consider to be some pluses and minuses of each of these approaches before reading on.

Each of the two major survey methods has both advantages and shortcomings. Because questionnaires are more anonymous, some people may be less likely to distort information about their lives by boasting, omitting facts, and so forth. (The presence of an interviewer sometimes encourages false responses.) Questionnaires have another advantage in that they are usually cheaper and quicker than interview surveys. However, interviews have the advantage of flexibility. The interviewer may clarify confusing questions and vary the sequence of the questions in order to meet the needs of the participant. A competent interviewer can establish a rapport that may encourage more candor than that produced by an impersonal questionnaire. On the other hand, data obtained through oral interviews can be subject to bias if the researcher interprets them inaccurately.

Regardless of the particular survey strategy employed, sex researchers find that their efforts to secure a representative sample are often thwarted. This is because it is quite difficult to get people to participate in studies of this nature. For instance, assuming that you used proper sampling procedures to choose your target sample of male adolescents for the survey pertaining to birth control, how many of those included in the sample do you think would actually be willing to answer your questions? (Even if the individuals were willing, how many school officials and parents would object to such participation?) **Nonresponse,** the refusal to participate in a research study, is a common problem and one that consistently plagues sex survey research. This difficulty, together with issues related to data inaccuracy, will be explored in the following section.

Problems of Sex Survey Research: Nonresponse, Demographic Bias, and Inaccuracy. No one has ever conducted a major sex survey where 100% of the selected subjects voluntarily participated. In fact, some studies include results obtained from samples where only a small minority of those asked to respond actually did.

Nonresponse presents a major complication in sex survey research. No matter how careful the researcher has been in selecting the sample population, that sample may be distorted by the subjects' self-selection. Are the individuals who agree to participate in sex research surveys any different from those who choose not to respond? Think about this for a minute or two before reading further.

Perhaps volunteer subjects in sex research are a representative cross section of the population, but we have no theoretical or statistical basis for that conclusion. As a matter of fact, the opposite might well be true. People who volunteer to participate may be the ones who are the most eager to share their experiences, who have explored a wide range of activities, or who feel most comfortable with their sexuality. (Or it might be that the most experienced people are the ones who are least willing to respond because they feel their behaviors represent atypical or extreme levels of activity.) A preponderance of experienced, inexperienced, liberal, or conservative individuals might bias any sample.

Research on **self-selection,** or "volunteer bias," suggests that this is an important concern for sex researchers. One early study compared individuals who had volunteered for Alfred Kinsey's research with those who did not volunteer (Maslow & Sakoda, 1952). These investigators found significant differences between the two groups: The volunteers demonstrated higher levels of self-esteem and more sexual activity than those who did not volunteer. In contrast, a later study found no important differences between men and women who volunteered to fill out a

sex survey questionnaire and those who had to be persuaded to participate (Bauman, 1973). However, several more recent studies have provided strong evidence that volunteers for sex research tend to be more sexually experienced and to hold more positive attitudes toward sexuality and sex research in general than do their nonvolunteer counterparts (Morokoff, 1986; Saunders et al., 1985; Wolchik et al., 1985).

Other kinds of problems might result from subject selection. For instance, **demographic bias** has been a problem in many studies. Most of the data available from sex research in the United States have come from samples weighted heavily with white, middle-class volunteers. This was certainly true of the monumental studies of the Kinsey group in the 1940s and 1950s and of Masters and Johnson in the 1960s. Typically, college students and educated white-collar workers are disproportionately represented in these samples.

How much effect does nonresponse and demographic bias have on sex research findings? We cannot say for sure. But as long as elements of society, including the less educated and ethnic and racial minorities, are underrepresented, we must remain cautious in generalizing any findings to the population at large.

Another type of problem that hinders sex survey research has to do with the accuracy of information provided by subjects. Most of our data about human sexual behavior are obtained from respondents' self-reports of their experiences. How closely does actual behavior correspond to these subjective, after-the-fact reports?

For many reasons, there may be considerable discrepancy between actual behavior and the way people report it (Newcomer & Udry, 1988). One potential complication involves the known limitations of human memory. For instance, how many people remember accurately when they first masturbated and with what frequency? Ask yourself (if it is applicable) at what age you first experienced an orgasm. It may be quite difficult to accurately recall some information.

Some people may consciously or unconsciously conceal certain facts about their sexual histories because they view them as abnormal, silly, or perhaps too painful to remember. In areas of sexual behavior where there are strong social taboos (such as those regarding incest, homosexuality, and masturbation), people may feel pressure to deny or minimize such experiences in their own lives. Others may purposely falsify their responses to inflate their own sexual experience, perhaps out of a desire to appear sexually liberal or more experienced or proficient than they actually are.

Occasionally, false reports may result simply from misunderstandings. For example, a person with little education might answer no to the question "Did you experience penile–vaginal intercourse prior to marriage?" simply because he or she was not familiar with the terminology. That same person might respond affirmatively to the question "Did you go all the way before you got married?" Language is a problem in many types of social research; this is especially true in sex research, since there is a virtual absence of any sexual language common to all groups in our society. That is why the wording of questions becomes such a critical issue.

The studies of Alfred Kinsey are perhaps the best known and most widely cited example of survey research. Alfred Kinsey, with his associates Wardell Pomeroy, Clyde Martin, and Paul Gebhard, published two large volumes in the decade following World War II. One, on male sexuality, was published in 1948; the follow-up report on female sexuality was published in 1953. These volumes contain the results of extensive survey interviews, the aim of which was to determine patterns of sexual behavior in American males and females. These remarkably ambitious investigations remain unique in the annals of sex research as the most comprehensive of all **taxonomic surveys,** that is, investigations aimed at classifying people into behavioral categories for statistical comparisons.

Kinsey and his associates believed that attempts to secure sex histories from individuals selected by random sampling methods would result in so many refusals to participate that randomness would be destroyed. To minimize this problem of nonresponse, they sought subjects in the memberships of various social organizations, such as college classes, professional organizations, residents of rooming houses, and so forth. Initial contacts who willingly participated were urged to convince their friends to get involved. In some cases this use of peer-group assurances or pressure produced virtually 100% participation by members of the target group.

The final Kinsey subject populations consisted of 5300 white males and 5940 white females. They included people from both rural and urban areas in each state — people who represented a range of ages, marital status, occupations, educational levels, and religions.

Despite the wide subject variability in the two research samples, the failure to use random sampling procedures resulted in underrepresentation or overrepresentation of certain population subgroups. Specifically, the sample contained a disproportionately greater number of better-educated, city-dwelling Protestants,

Alfred Kinsey, a pioneer sex researcher, conducted one of the most comprehensive surveys on human sexuality.

while older people, rural dwellers, and those with less education were under-represented. Blacks and other racial minorities were completely omitted from the sample. And finally, all subjects were volunteers. Thus, in no way can Kinsey's study population be viewed as a representative sample of the American population.

Publication of the Kinsey findings generated strong reactions, both positive and negative. The most thorough review of the work was published by the American Statistical Association (Cochran et al., 1954). Despite the acknowledged problems with the sampling methods employed, this review praised Kinsey's group for their excellent use of well-planned interview techniques. While there is always the possibility of distortion whenever interviews or questionnaires are used, the Kinsey interviewers were particularly adept at establishing rapport with their subjects. They accomplished this by asking questions in a way that conveyed acceptance of any kind of response, by modifying language to fit the understanding of respondents, and by spontaneously altering the interview sequence so that particularly sensitive questions could be asked at the best time.

Kinsey's findings covered a wide range of topics, including such things as frequency and kind of sexual outlet (that is, the sources of orgasm and how often experienced), coitus outside of marriage, sexual orientation, and sexual techniques. Although published four decades ago, many of the Kinsey data are still relevant today. The passage of time has not altered the validity of certain findings — for example, that sexual behavior is influenced by educational level, or that the heterosexuality or homosexuality of a person is often not an all-or-none proposition. However, certain other areas — such as coital rates among unmarried people — are more influenced by changing societal norms. Therefore, we might expect the Kinsey data to be less predictive of contemporary practices in these areas. Nevertheless, even here the data are still relevant in that they provide one possible basis for estimating the degree of behavioral change over the years.

In summary, despite the problems inherent in the Kinsey research, it still remains a valuable source of information about patterns of human sexual behavior. If the data contained in these two volumes are interpreted cautiously, we are able to secure some important clues about the sexual behavior of white Americans, if not now, at least several decades ago.

Sample surveys via questionnaires and interviews, such as the pioneering Kinsey studies, are the most commonly used methods for studying sexual behavior and attitudes. They provide a relatively inexpensive way to obtain information about a broad range of topics from many individuals. But we cannot expect to learn all there is to know about sexuality from sample surveys. Other important sources of information include case studies, direct observation, and experimental (laboratory) research.

Case Studies

There are numerous references in the existing literature to **case studies.** These are in-depth explorations of single cases or of small groups of people who were examined individually. Unlike surveys, case studies obtain a great deal of information from one or a very few individuals.

Often people become subjects for case histories because they have some physical or emotional disorder or because they have manifested a specific atypical behavior. Thus, much of our current information about sex offenders, transsexuals, incest victims, and the like has been obtained through this approach. Also, a large portion of our information about sexual response difficulties (for instance, erectile inhibition in men and lack of orgasmic response in women) has been obtained from studies of individuals seeking treatment for these problems.

The case-study approach allows for flexible data-gathering procedures. These range from well-structured questions that offer specific response alternatives to open-ended queries that provide considerable flexibility to respondents. Some researchers criticize the case-study approach for offering little opportunity for investigative control. However, unlike survey methods, case studies often provide opportunities to acquire insight into specific behaviors. The highly personal, subjective information about how individuals actually feel about their behavior represents an important step beyond simply recording activities. So, while this method sacrifices some control, it can add considerable dimension and depth to our information. Case studies have another potential advantage. Because of their clinical nature and because they may continue for long periods of time (months or even years), the researcher may be able to explore cause-and-effect relationships in detail.

There are some important limitations to the clinical case study, however. Because proper sampling techniques are rarely observed (how could they be?), it is difficult to draw generalizations to the rest of the population. This potential source of error is illustrated in many early writings that have presented a pathologic model of homosexuality based on case studies of homosexuals who had

OUR SEXUALITY

The Elegant Prostitute: An Example of Case Study Research

In 1958, Harold Greenwald, a psychologist, published an in-depth social–psychological study of call girls, appropriately titled *The Call Girl*. An updated edition of his study, *The Elegant Prostitute* (1970), describes how call girls are the elite of the world of prostitution: They make appointments by phone, dress elegantly, and live in expensive apartments. Before Greenwald's study, little was known about the factors that contribute to call girls' choice of occupation. Greenwald became interested in the subject as a result of conducting therapy with six call girl clients. These six women shared certain experiences and attitudes, and Greenwald began to wonder if these similarities extended to other call girls. He explored this question by conducting in-depth interviews with 20 additional women who practiced the profession.

All 20 were working as call girls at the time of the interviews. They ranged in age from 19 to 43 years. Most had a high school education or better. A substantial majority had been reared in middle-income and upper-income families. Most of the information about these women was obtained through interviews that used open-ended questions such as "Tell me about yourself," or "What has your life been like up to now?"

After sifting through large quantities of interview data, Greenwald made some observations about the family backgrounds, lifestyles, feelings, and attitudes of the women in his research population. There was a marked similarity among the family atmospheres in which they were reared. "I found not one example of a permanent, well-adjusted marital relationship between the parents" (Greenwald, 1970, p. 165). Affection between parents was rarely or never displayed, and 19 of the subjects reported feeling rejected by both parents. Fifteen found themselves in broken homes before they reached adolescence, and as a result, many were passed from family to family or lived in a succession of boarding schools.

Ten of the subjects reported that at an early age they had engaged in sexual activity with an adult that resulted in some kind of reward such as affection or privileges. Greenwald suggests that these early experiences may have established a pattern of giving sexual gratification as a way of temporarily overcoming feelings of loneliness and unworthiness. Furthermore, such experiences led the women to recognize early in life that sex was a commodity with which they could barter.

Greenwald found that virtually all of his study population expressed anger and even rage over being deprived of affection and stability during their formative years. Their anger was often turned inward, resulting in very negative self-images and varying degrees of anxiety and depression. Most of them found it extremely difficult to maintain satisfactory relationships with other people.

In light of their family backgrounds and resulting negative self-images, Greenwald theorized that "becoming a call girl appeared to offer a desperate hope of halting the deterioration of self, but . . . their choice of profession made these conflicts more intense and more self-destructive" (Greenwald, 1970, p. 187).

sought treatment. As in the self-selection that can take place in survey sampling, there may be pronounced differences between homosexuals who are *not* trying to change their sexual orientation and those who *are*. In other situations, where individuals with known mental or physical disorders have been studied in depth, applying the resultant information to healthy people is questionable. For that matter, how do we know that individuals under treatment or observation are representative of the subpopulation(s) to which they belong? For example, sexually abusive fathers who have been identified by the court may not be representative of all fathers who engage in incestuous relationships with their offspring. All these general cautions can be applied to the cases we cite in our authors' files selections throughout this book. We think these cases represent especially relevant experiences and feelings, but our purpose in including them is so that readers can draw perspective from them, not conclusions. An example of case-study research is provided in the box "The Elegant Prostitute."

Direct Observation

A third method for studying human sexual behavior is **direct observation,** in which researchers observe and record several responses of participating subjects. Observational research is quite common in a variety of disciplines, particularly the social sciences of anthropology, sociology, and psychology. However, very little research of this nature occurs in the area of sexuality. Sexual expression, being a highly personal and private experience, does not readily lend itself to direct observation.

When it has been well conducted, thorough direct observation produces valuable information. There are some clear advantages to seeing and measuring sexual behavior firsthand, instead of relying on subjective reports of past experiences. Firsthand direct observation virtually eliminates the possibility of data falsification through memory deficits, boastful inflation, or guilt-induced repression. Furthermore, records of such behaviors can be retained indefinitely on videotapes or films.

But there are also some disadvantages associated with this approach. A major problem lies in the often unanswerable question of just how much a subject's behavior is influenced by the presence of even the most discreet observer. This question has been asked often since the publication of the Masters and Johnson studies (1966), which used direct observation to document male and female sexual response patterns. Researchers employing direct observation often attempt to minimize this potential complication by being as unobtrusive as possible (for example, observing from a peripheral location or behind one-way glass, or using videotapes to be viewed later). But the subject is still aware that she or he is being observed. The reliability of recorded observations can also be compromised if researchers have preexisting biases. For example, if the observer believes "swingers" experience only nonemotional sexual involvements, she or he may be less likely to interpret their interactions as expressions of affectionate intimacy.

A widely acclaimed example of direct observation research, frequently cited in our text, is the work of William Masters and Virginia Johnson. Along with the Kinsey research, Masters and Johnson's study of human sexual response is probably the most often mentioned sex research. These investigators used direct observation in a laboratory setting to learn about physiological changes during sexual arousal. (Their study remains the only major piece of research that has done this.) The product was their widely acclaimed volume *Human Sexual Response* (1966), which was based on laboratory observations of 10,000 completed sexual response cycles. Results of these observations are presented in Chapter 6.

Masters and Johnson began their research by studying a group of prostitutes (118 female and 27 male) because they assumed that "study subjects from more conservative segments of the general population would not be available (a presumption which later proved to be entirely false)" (1966, p. 10). However, they quickly determined that prostitutes were not suitable subjects, for two reasons. First, prostitutes tended to move from one city to another frequently, which discouraged study over extended periods of time. Second, female prostitutes often develop a state of chronic pelvic congestion due to repeated sexual arousal without orgasm. As a result, their physiosexual responses were somewhat different from those of other women.

William Masters and Virginia Johnson used direct observation to study the physiological sexual responses of women and men.

Masters and Johnson obtained their final research population by spreading the word in the academic community of Washington University in St. Louis that they were interested in studying normal volunteers. The response was quite enthusiastic. From 1273 who applied, they selected 382 women and 312 men. They excluded those unable to respond sexually and anyone who showed signs of emotional instability or exhibitionist tendencies. Their final sample was thus composed of sexually responsive volunteers, drawn largely from an academic community, with above-average intelligence and socioeconomic background — obviously not a representative sample of the entire U.S. population. However, the physical signs of sexual arousal, the subject of their study, appear to be rather stable across a wide range of people with diverse backgrounds.

Masters and Johnson used a number of techniques to record physiological sexual responses. These included the use of photographic equipment and instruments to measure and record muscular and vascular changes throughout the body. They also employed direct observation to record changes in sex organs. An ingenious artificial coition machine was designed to record changes that had never before been observed in internal female sex structures. This machine was equipped with an artificial penis that could be controlled voluntarily for size, as well as for depth and rapidity of thrust. It was constructed from clear plastic and contained photographic equipment for recording changes in the vagina and the lower portion of the uterus during sexual arousal. Masters and Johnson recorded responses in a variety of stimulus situations in their laboratory — masturbation, coitus with a partner, artificial coition, and stimulation of the breasts alone. Finally, as a follow-up to all recorded observations, each individual participant was extensively interviewed.

OTHER TIMES, OTHER PLACES

Foreshadowing Masters and Johnson

The Centennial Issue of the *Journal of the American Medical Association (JAMA)*, which appeared on July 8, 1983, included an article written by Denslow Lewis, M.D., titled "The Gynecologic Consideration of the Sexual Act." What is unusual about this article is that Lewis submitted it for publication in 1899, 84 years before it appeared. Unfortunately, Lewis's pioneering treatise was far ahead of his time, and publication was denied. The unwillingness of his medical colleagues to provide a forum for the issues raised in his thoughtful article is representative of the trials faced by many pioneer sex researchers in their efforts to cope with the limitations imposed by a society that is unreceptive to new and controversial information.

Lewis's article contained many sound observations that were corroborated by research conducted over half a century later. For example, he provided an illuminating description of female sexual response and suggested that it was absolutely normal for a woman to experience pleasure while actively participating in the "sexual act." Many of his observations about male–female relationships would no doubt have been considered progressive just a few years ago (perhaps even today, by some). For example, he suggested that a husband should behave more as a companion than a master, respecting and acknowledging his wife's rights as well as his own. Lewis also recommended sex education at an early age, especially for girls. This bold idea was about 60–70 years ahead of its time because sex education in the public school systems has come about only in the last 15–20 years.

In an editorial in the same issue of *JAMA,* William Masters speculated that publication of the Lewis article in 1899 might have hastened by more than 50 years investigations of the biology and psychology of sexual functioning and significantly reduced "the incredible level of sexual myth and misconception that has so handicapped medical progress well beyond the first half of this century" (p. 244).

The trials Lewis faced took place at a time when society placed much more stringent limitations on the subject matter of scientific investigations and public discussions. However, the activities of certain nationally organized groups in recent years — for example, efforts to ban sex education in schools or to restrict teenagers' access to birth control information — suggest the possibility of new limits on our access to information about our sexuality.

Employing this observational approach, Masters and Johnson obtained a wealth of information about the manner in which women and men respond physiologically to sexual stimulation. Some have suggested that their conclusions are limited because of the artificial nature of laboratory observations. Although there may be some merit to this criticism, time has nevertheless demonstrated that their research findings can be beneficially applied to such areas as sex therapy, infertility counseling, conception control, and general sex education.

Experimental Research

A fourth method, **experimental research,** is being used with increasing frequency in the investigation of human sexual behavior. In experimental (laboratory) research, subjects must be confronted with certain specific stimuli under controlled conditions so that their reactions can be reliably measured. For example, if you designed an experiment to compare the sexual responses of males and females to visual erotica, you would subject both sexes to the same stimuli under controlled conditions and then use a reliable method for measuring the results (such as physiological measures of penile erection, vaginal engorgement, and so

OUR SEXUALITY

Alcohol and Sexual Arousal: Two Examples of Experimental Research

People often believe that alcohol increases their level of sexual arousal. In one major survey of 20,000 middle-class and upper-middle-class Americans, 60% of the respondents reported that drinking increased their sexual pleasure (Athanasiou et al., 1970). However, most surveys have been limited to asking people what they *think* happens when they drink, and these subjective assessments may not match up with objective reality, as was found in two experiments on the actual effects of alcohol on human sexual arousal.

Both investigations were conducted at Rutgers University's Alcohol Behavior Research Laboratory. The first experiment involved 48 male college students between the ages of 18 and 22 (Briddell & Wilson, 1976). During an initial session, the researchers obtained baseline data on flaccid penis diameter for all subjects. The participants were then shown a 10-minute erotic film of explicit sexual interaction between male and female partners. Penile tumescence (engorgement) was measured continuously during the film by penile strain gauges (see the box "Sex Research and Technology"). In a second session, held one week later, all subjects drank measured amounts of alcohol prior to viewing a somewhat longer version of the erotic film. Subjects were assigned to four experimental groups, with 12 subjects in each group. Each subject, depending on his group assignment, consumed 0.6, 3, 6, or 9 ounces of alcohol. After a 40-minute "rest period," the subjects viewed the film, during which each person's sexual arousal was assessed by his score on three measures of penile tumescence: increase in diameter, time required to obtain an erection, and duration of the erection. The results indicated that alcohol significantly reduced sexual arousal, especially at higher intake levels. Even at low intake levels, alcohol did not enhance penile tumescence.

The second investigation was conducted with 16 college women between the ages of 18 and 22 (Wilson & Lawson, 1976). The research design was somewhat different from that employed in the Briddell and Wilson study of men. "During weekly experimental sessions, each of 16 university women received, in counterbalanced order, four doses of beverage alcohol prior to viewing a control film and an erotic film" (p. 489). Alcohol dosage levels were approximately 0.3, 1.4, 2.9, and 4.3 ounces. The control film was a boring 12-minute review of the computer facilities at Rutgers University. The erotic film portrayed explicit heterosexual interaction. Vaginal changes reflecting sexual arousal were measured continuously during film viewing by use of a vaginal photo-plethysmograph (see the box "Sex Research and Technology"). As expected, "subjects showed significantly more arousal in response to the erotic than the control film" (p. 493). More important, there was clear evidence that alcohol significantly reduced the sexual arousal of these women. The inhibitory effects were greater at higher dosages.

These two experiments suggest that "increasing intoxication in both men and women results in progressively reduced sexual arousal in response to visual erotic stimulation" (Wilson & Lawson, 1976, p. 495).

forth). Several experiments of this nature have been conducted in the last few years with rather interesting results, which will be discussed in Chapter 6.

A laboratory experiment offers the major advantage of control over variables thought to influence the behavior being studied. Often such an approach allows for direct statements about cause-and-effect that would be more speculative with other methods of data collection. However, the somewhat artificial nature of the experimental laboratory setting may influence subjects' behavior. As in direct observation research, the very fact that people know they are in an experiment can alter their responses from those that might occur outside the laboratory. Two examples of experimental research are provided in the box "Alcohol and Sexual Arousal"; while the box entitled "Sex Research and Technology" describes some applications of technology to sex research.

OUR SEXUALITY

Sex Research and Technology

Experimental research and direct observation studies of human sexual responses often employ measures of sexual arousal. Until recently, researchers had to rely largely on subjective reports of these responses. However, advances in technology have produced two devices for measuring sexual arousal: the penile strain gauge and the vaginal photoplethysmograph.

The penile strain gauge (sometimes called a penile plethysmograph) is a flexible loop that looks something like a rubber band with a wire attached. It is actually a thin rubber tube filled with a fine strand of mercury. A tiny electrical current from the attached wire flows through the mercury continuously. The gauge is placed around the base of the penis; as an erection occurs, the rubber tube stretches, and the strand of mercury becomes thinner, changing the flow of the current. These changes are registered by a recording device called a polygraph. The penile strain gauge can measure even the slightest changes in penis size and, in fact, is so sensitive that it can record every pulse of blood into the penis. In the interests of privacy, a subject can attach the gauge to his own penis.

When a woman is sexually aroused, her vaginal walls fill with blood in a manner comparable to the engorgement of a man's penis. The vaginal photoplethysmograph is a device designed to measure this increased vaginal blood volume. It consists of an acrylic cylinder about the size and shape of a tampon, which is inserted into the vagina. The cylinder contains a light that is reflected off the vaginal walls, and a photocell that is sensitive to the reflected light. When the vaginal walls fill with blood during sexual arousal, less light is reflected to the photocell. These changes in light intensity, continuously recorded by a polygraph, provide a measure of sexual arousal comparable to that provided by the penile strain gauge. Like the male device, the vaginal photoplethysmograph can be inserted in privacy by the research subject.

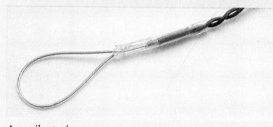

A penile strain gauge.

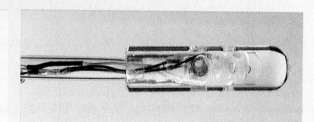

A vaginal photoplethysmograph.

What to Believe? A Statement of Perspective

The preceding discussion of the methods and problems of sex research may have left you with some unanswered questions. To what degree can we rely on the wide array of data introduced in the chapters that follow? We have learned that sex research is often hindered by difficulties in obtaining representative samples and accurate information. We have also seen that sex researchers have shown remarkable versatility in their efforts, using many different approaches to data collection. Thus, a major strength of sex research is its reliance on a wide assortment of methodological techniques.

We believe that any student of sexual behavior would do well to differentiate between nonscientific polls and opinions and the results of scientific research conducted by serious investigators. However, even in the case of carefully planned investigations, it is good to maintain a critical eye and to avoid the tendency many of us have to believe something just because it is "scientific." You may find the following checklist of questions useful in evaluating any particular piece of research.

1. Who conducted the research? Are they considered to be reputable professionals?

2. What type of methodology was employed? Were scientific principles adhered to?

3. How large was the sample group, and is there any reason to suspect bias in the selection of subjects?

4. Can the results be applied to individuals other than those in the sample group? How broad can these generalizations be and still remain legitimate?

5. Is it possible that the method used to obtain information may have biased the findings? (Did the questionnaire promote false replies? Did the cameras place limitations on the response potentials?)

6. Have there been any other published reports that confirm or contradict the particular study in question?

Keeping questions like these in mind is valuable in finding a middle ground between absolute trust and offhand dismissal of a given research study.

Summary

Research Methods

Research methods for studying sexuality include surveys, case studies, direct observation, and experimental research.

Most information about human sexual behavior has been obtained through questionnaire or interview surveys of relatively large populations of respondents. Questionnaires have the advantage of being anonymous, inexpensive, and quickly administered. Interviews are more flexible and allow for more rapport between researcher and subject.

Sex researchers who use surveys share certain problems. These include the following:

• The virtual impossibility of getting 100% participation of randomly selected subjects. (There has not yet been a true representative sample survey.) Self-selection of samples, or "volunteer bias," is a common problem.

• Biases created by nonresponse: Do volunteer participants have significantly different attitudes and behaviors from nonparticipants?

• Demographic biases: Most samples are heavily weighted toward white, middle-class, better-educated participants.

• The problem of accuracy: Respondents' self-reports may be less than accurate because of limitations of memory, boastfulness, guilt, or simple misunderstandings.

The Kinsey surveys remain the most ambitious and broad-scale studies of human sexual behavior. They were somewhat limited by sampling techniques that resulted in overrepresentation of young, educated, city-dwelling people.

Case studies typically produce a great deal of information about one or a few individuals. They have two great advantages: flexibility and the opportunity to explore specific behaviors and feelings in depth. However, poor sampling techniques often limit the possibility of making generalizations to broad populations.

There is very little direct-observation sex research due to the highly personal nature of sexual expression. When it can be done, observation significantly reduces the possibility of data falsification. However, subjects' behavior may be altered by the presence of an observer. Furthermore, the reliability of recorded observations may sometimes be compromised by preexisting researcher biases.

The laboratory observation research of William Masters and Virginia Johnson provided excellent information about the physiosexual responses of women and men. Even though their study population was biased toward high educational and socioeconomic levels, their findings have broad application to the general population.

Experimental research, although infrequently employed in investigations of human sexual behavior, offers two advantages: control over the relevant variables and direct analysis of possible causal factors. However, the artificial nature of the experimental laboratory setting may alter subject responses from those that might occur in a natural setting.

What to Believe? A Statement of Perspective

In evaluating any study of sexual behavior, it is helpful to consider who conducted the research, to examine the methods and sampling techniques carefully, and to compare the results with those of other reputable studies.

∽ *Thought Provokers* ∽

1. Of the four research techniques discussed in this chapter — surveys, clinical case studies, direct observation, and experimental laboratory studies — survey research has provided the most data about human sexuality. Why do you think this is so? Which method do you think is best for learning about our sexuality? Why?

2. A radio talk-show host informs his listening audience that women enjoy sex more in the morning than in the evening. When pressed by a questioner, he says he knows this to be true from personal experience. How would you go about determining the validity of this assertion? Which of the four methodologies discussed in this chapter could be effectively used to test this hypothesis? Why? Might you gain valuable information by applying more than one of these techniques?

Suggested Readings

Brecher, Edward (1969). *The Sex Researchers.* New York: Signet. An easy-to-read account of sex researchers and their findings. Provides a behind-the-scenes perspective and some interesting historical anecdotes.

Brecher, Ruth; and Brecher, Edward (1966). *An Analysis of Human Sexual Response.* New York: New American Library.

Besides detailing the work of Masters and Johnson, this highly readable book deals with sex research in general, particularly emphasizing its practical applications and its impact on society.

Bullough, Vern (1979). *The Frontiers of Sex Research.* Buffalo, N.Y.: Prometheus. An overview of research into various fields of sexuality. Contains several excellent articles dealing with the issues and implications of sex research.

Byrne, Donn; and Kelley, Kathryn (Eds.) (1986). *Alternative Approaches to the Study of Sexual Behavior.* Hillsdale, N.J.: Lawrence Erlbaum. This informative book provides in-depth discussions of the investigative methods employed by contemporary sex researchers.

Pomeroy, Wardell (1972). *Dr. Kinsey and the Institute for Sex Research.* New York: Harper & Row. An informed and entertaining look at Kinsey and his research, as seen through the "insider" eyes of one of his original research colleagues.

The Journal of Sex Research, February 1986, Volume 22. A special issue of this journal devoted entirely to issues related to methodology in sex research. The many excellent articles in this volume address such topics as sampling bias, the interaction of volunteer bias with different forms of sex research techniques, the relationship between objective and subjective measures of sexual responsiveness, and a critical analysis of sex research methodology.

One has noticed in a certain species the female more beautiful, stronger, more active, more intelligent, and one has noticed the opposite. One has seen the male larger, or smaller; one has seen and will see him a parasite, or provider, permanent master of the couple or the group, fugitive lover, a slave sacrificed by the female after the completion of her pleasure. All attitudes, and

the same ones, are attributed by nature to either of the sexes; there is not, apart from the specific functions, a male or female role.

Remy de Gourmont
The Natural Philosophy of Love (1904)

CHAPTER 3

Gender Issues

Male and Female, Masculine and Feminine

Gender-Identity Formation

Gender Roles

*E*xamine the following sentence and fill in the blanks: In this particular society, "the _____ is the dominant, impersonal, managing partner, the _____ the less responsible and the emotionally dependent person." Did you assume that *man* goes in the first space and *woman* in the second? In fact, the reverse is true. But how can this be? Is it not human nature for men the world over to take charge in their relationships with women? Are not women always the more dependent partners? Things may be getting a bit more equal between the sexes (at least in some societies), but a complete reversal of the traditional roles? How can that happen?

This is the first, incredulous comment people typically voice after being told about the Tchambuli society of New Guinea, where traditional masculine and feminine behavior patterns are complete opposites of those typical of American society (Mead, 1963). This cultural difference raises certain fundamental questions: What constitutes maleness and femaleness? What is the relationship between male–female and masculine–feminine? Which of the behavioral differences between women and men have a biological basis? A psychosocial basis? Both?

Male and Female, Masculine and Feminine

Through the ages people have held to the belief that we are born males or females and just naturally grow up doing what men or women do. The only explanation required has been a simple allusion to "nature taking its course." This viewpoint has a simplicity that helps make the world seem an orderly place. However, closer examination reveals a much greater complexity in the process whereby our maleness and femaleness are determined, and in the way they influence our behavior, sexual and otherwise. This fascinating complexity is our focus in the pages that follow. But first it will be helpful to clarify a few important terms.

Sex and Gender

Many writers use the terms *sex* and *gender* interchangeably. However, each word has a specific meaning. **Sex** refers to our biological femaleness or maleness. There are two aspects of biological sex: *genetic sex*, which is determined by our sex chromosomes, and *anatomical sex*, the obvious physical differences between males and females. **Gender** is a concept that encompasses the special psychosocial meanings added to biological maleness or femaleness. Thus, while our sex is linked to various physical attributes (chromosomes, penis, vulva, and so forth), our gender refers to the social accoutrements of sex — or in other words, our femininity or masculinity. In this chapter, we use the terms *masculine* and *feminine* to characterize the behaviors that are typically attributed to males and females. One undesirable aspect of these labels is that they may limit the range of behaviors that people are comfortable expressing (Sheinberg & Penn, 1991). For example, a man might hesitate to be nurturing lest he be labeled feminine, and a woman might be reticent to act assertively for fear of being considered masculine. It is not our intention to perpetuate the stereotypes often associated with these labels. However, we find it necessary to use these terms when discussing gender issues.

When we meet people for the first time, most of us quickly note their sex and make assumptions based on their maleness or femaleness about how they are likely to behave: these are **gender assumptions.** For most people, gender assumptions are an important part of routine social interaction. We identify people as being either the same sex as ourselves or the other sex. (We have avoided using the term *opposite sex* because we believe it overstates the differences between males and females.) Many of us may find it hard to interact with a person whose gender is ambiguous. When we are unsure of our identification of someone's gender, we may become confused and uncomfortable.

Gender Identity and Gender Role

Gender identity refers to our own personal, subjective sense that "I am a male" or "I am a female." Most of us realize that we are either male or female, masculine or feminine, in the first few years of life. However, there is no guarantee that a person's gender identity will be consistent with his or her biological sex, and some people experience considerable confusion in their efforts to identify their own maleness or femaleness. We will look into this area in more detail later in this chapter.

Gender role (sometimes called sex role) refers to a collection of attitudes and behaviors that are considered normal and appropriate in a specific culture for people of a particular sex. Gender roles establish sex-related behavioral expectations that people are expected to fulfill. Behavior thought to be socially appropriate for a male is called masculine, for a female, feminine. When we use the terms *masculine* and *feminine* in subsequent discussions, we are referring to these socialized notions.

Gender-role expectations are culturally defined and vary from society to society. For example, the Tchambuli society considers emotionally expressive behavior appropriate for males. Obviously, American society takes a somewhat different view. A kiss on the cheek is considered a feminine act and therefore inappropriate between men in American society. In contrast, such behavior is consistent with masculine-role expectations in many European and Middle Eastern societies.

Besides being culturally based, our notions of masculinity and femininity are also era-dependent. For example, if an American male went to a hairdresser for a permanent in the 1960s, he would probably have been ridiculed for his "effeminate" behavior. In the 1990s, an abundance of curly-headed men indicates that gender-role expectations for hairstyle have changed significantly. Such changes are becoming increasingly common; more than any other time in our history, the present era is marked by redefinition of male and female roles. Many people are no longer content to live with traditional gender roles. Many of us who have grown up subjected to strong gender-role conditioning are now exploring how these roles have shaped our lives and are seeking to break away from their limiting influences. Being part of this change can be both exciting and confusing. We will consider the impact of traditional and changing gender roles later in this chapter (and also throughout our text). But first let us turn our attention to the processes whereby we acquire our gender identity.

Gender-Identity Formation

How do we come to think of ourselves as male or female? This question has at least two answers. The first centers on biological factors: The most obvious reason we think of ourselves as female or male is our biological sex. The second answer

FIGURE 3.1

A normal male has two sex chromosomes — an X (top right) and a Y (bottom right). A normal female has two X chromosomes and no Y chromosomes.

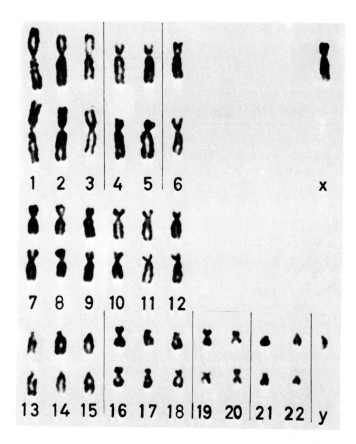

is based on social-learning theory, which says that our identification as either feminine or masculine results primarily from social and cultural influences during early development. We begin our discussion by first considering the biological influences that shape our sense of femaleness or maleness.

Gender Identity as a Biological Process: Normal Prenatal Differentiation

Research efforts to isolate the many biological factors that influence gender identity have led to the identification of six biological categories or levels of sex differentiation: chromosomal sex, gonadal sex, hormonal sex, sex of the internal reproductive structures, sex of the external genitals, and sex differentiation of the brain.

Chromosomal Sex.   At the first level of differentiation, our biological sex is determined by the sex chromosomes present in the reproductive cells (sperm and ova) at the moment of conception. With the exception of the reproductive cells, body cells of humans contain a total of 46 chromosomes, arranged as 23 pairs (see Figure 3.1). Twenty-two of these pairs are matched; that is, the two chromosomes of each pair look almost identical. These matched sets, called **autosomes,** are the same in males and females and do not significantly influence sex differentiation. One chromosome pair, however — the **sex chromosomes** — differs in females and males. Females have two similar chromosomes, labeled XX, whereas males have dissimilar chromosomes, labeled XY.

As noted above, the reproductive cells are an exception to the 23-pair rule. As a result of a biological process known as *meiosis,* mature reproductive cells contain only half the usual complement of chromosomes — one member of each pair. (This process is necessary to avoid a doubling of the chromosome total when sex cells merge at conception.) A normal female **ovum** (or egg) contains 22 autosomes plus an X chromosome. A normal male **sperm** cell contains 22 autosomes plus either an X or Y chromosome. Fertilization of the ovum by a sperm carrying a Y chromosome produces an XY combination, resulting in a male child. Fertilization by an X-bearing sperm results in an XX combination and a female child.

Although we do not yet have a complete understanding of the role of sex chromosomes in determining biological sex, certain facts seem well established. Two X chromosomes are needed for the complete development of both internal and external female sexual and reproductive structures; and the Y chromosome must be present to ensure the complete development of internal and external male sexual and reproductive organs (Harley et al., 1992; Kolata, 1986; Page et al., 1987). The presence of at least one Y chromosome (regardless of the number of X chromosomes) allows the development of male structures.

Recent research has suggested that a single gene, located on the short arm of the human Y chromosome, is responsible for initiating the sequence of events that leads to testis formation and hence to male development (Cherfas, 1991; Koopman et al., 1991). In the absence of this gene, called TDF (for testis-determining factor), female development occurs. At present it is unclear what TDF gene product (or substance produced via a genetic trigger) induces the development of testes. Furthermore, most researchers involved in unraveling the mystery of how sex is determined in mammals believe that it is unlikely that a single TDF gene and gene product are the sole determinants of male gonadal sex. Rather, it is anticipated that further research will uncover a battery of genes that interact in a cooperative manner to unleash the gene product(s) that shape(s) gonadal differentiation (Bianchi, 1991; Cherfas, 1991; Mittwoch & Burgess, 1991).

Gonadal Sex. During the first weeks of prenatal development, the **gonads** — the structures containing the cells that will develop into the reproductive organs — are alike in the two sexes (see Figure 3.2a), with the capacity to become either testes or ovaries. Without specific masculinizing signals, the gonads develop as ovaries. However, the presence of a TDF gene product (or products) triggers the transformation of the embryonic gonads into testes, a process of differentiation that begins about six weeks after conception. In the absence of the testis-determining factor, the undifferentiated gonadal tissue develops into ovaries. Thus, the presence or absence of specific genes on sex chromosomes triggers differentiation of the gonads into ovaries or testes. Once this happens, the presence or absence of the fetus's own gonadal sex hormones becomes the critical factor in determining the differentiation of the internal and external sex structures and the brain.

Hormonal Sex. As soon as the gonads differentiate into testes or ovaries, the control of biological sex determination passes to the sex hormones, and genetic influence ceases. It will be easier to understand the role of hormones if we first briefly examine the endocrine system and its function in human sexual development and behavior.

The **endocrine** (EN-do-krin) **system** consists of several ductless glands located throughout the body. The major endocrine glands include the pituitary, gonads,

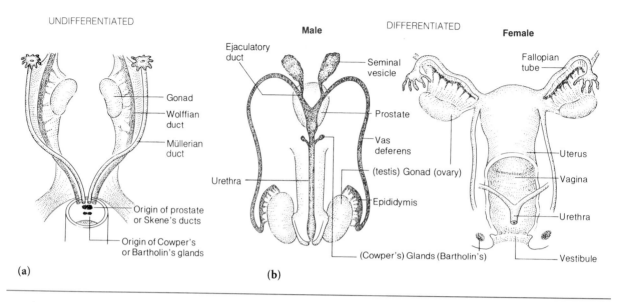

UNDIFFERENTIATED

Male   DIFFERENTIATED   Female

- Gonad
- Wolffian duct
- Müllerian duct

Origin of prostate or Skene's ducts

Origin of Cowper's or Bartholin's glands

(a)

Ejaculatory duct

- Seminal vesicle
- Prostate
- Vas deferens
- (testis) Gonad (ovary)
- Epididymis

Urethra

(Cowper's) Glands (Bartholin's)

(b)

Fallopian tube

- Uterus
- Vagina
- Urethra
- Vestibule

FIGURE 3.2

Prenatal development of male and female internal duct systems from (a) undifferentiated (before sixth week) to (b) differentiated.

thyroid, parathyroids, adrenals, and pancreas. Each produces hormones and secretes them directly into the bloodstream. Our interest here is in the gonads and in the sex hormones they secrete that influence sexual differentiation and development. All sex hormones belong to the general family known as *steroids*. Ovaries produce two classes of hormones: **estrogens** and **progestational compounds.** Estrogens, the most important of which is *estradiol,* influence the development of female physical sex characteristics and help regulate the menstrual cycle. Of the progestational compounds, only *progesterone* is known to be physiologically important. Its function is to help regulate the menstrual cycle and stimulate development of the uterine lining in preparation for pregnancy. The primary hormone products of the testes are **androgens**. The most important androgen is *testosterone,* which influences both the development of male physical sex characteristics and sexual motivation. In both sexes the adrenal glands also secrete sex hormones, including small amounts of estrogen and greater quantities of androgen.

Considerable research has shown how gonadal sex hormones contribute to differentiation of the internal and external sex structures. If fetal gonads differentiate into testes, they soon begin to secrete androgens, which in turn stimulate the development of male structures. If for some reason a male fetus does not produce enough androgen secretions, its sex organs will develop as female in form and appearance, despite the presence of the male chromosome (Money, 1968). Thus, a specific female hormone does not seem necessary to instigate development of female structures in a fetus; in the absence of male hormones, the developmental pattern is female. Maleness, however, depends on secretion of the right amount of male hormone at the crucial time.

Sex of the Internal Reproductive Structures. At about eight weeks after conception, internal reproductive structures begin to differentiate from two paired internal duct systems, the **Müllerian ducts** and the **Wolffian ducts** (see Figure 3.2a). If the embryo is chromosomally male and if the gonads have previously differentiated into testes, the newly formed testes begin secreting two substances. One of these chemicals, **Müllerian-inhibiting substance (MIS),** causes the Müllerian ducts to shrink rather than develop into internal female structures. At the same time, the testes begin to produce androgens, primarily testosterone. These hor-

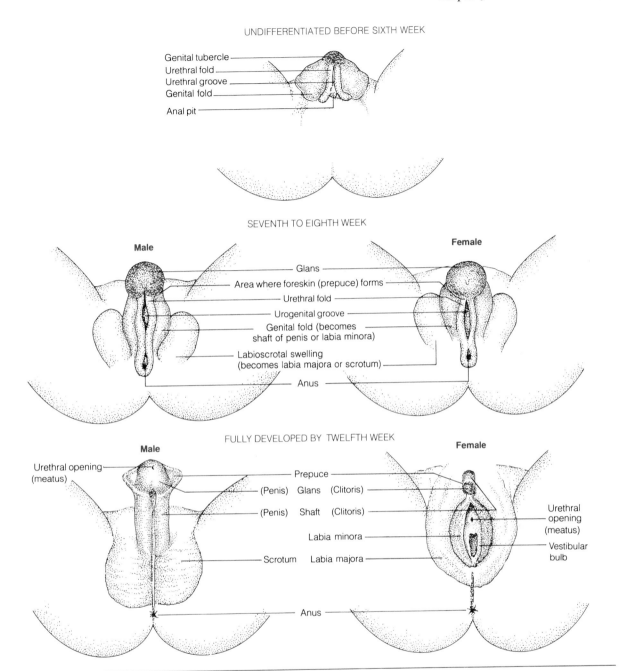

UNDIFFERENTIATED BEFORE SIXTH WEEK

Genital tubercle
Urethral fold
Urethral groove
Genital fold
Anal pit

SEVENTH TO EIGHTH WEEK

Male   **Female**

Glans
Area where foreskin (prepuce) forms
Urethral fold
Urogenital groove
Genital fold (becomes
shaft of penis or labia minora)
Labioscrotal swelling
(becomes labia majora or scrotum)
Anus

FULLY DEVELOPED BY TWELFTH WEEK

Male   **Female**

Urethral opening
(meatus)

Prepuce
(Penis)   Glans   (Clitoris)
(Penis)   Shaft   (Clitoris)
Labia minora
Scrotum   Labia majora
Anus

Urethral
opening
(meatus)
Vestibular
bulb

FIGURE 3.3

Prenatal development of male and female external genitals from undifferentiated to fully differentiated.

mones stimulate the development of the Wolffian ducts into internal male reproductive structures: the vas deferens, seminal vesicles, and ejaculatory ducts (see Figure 3.2b).

In contrast, hormones do not appear to guide the process of female sexual differentiation. When not suppressed by testis-produced MIS and testosterone, Müllerian ducts develop into internal female structures: the fallopian tubes, uterus, and inner third of the vagina (see Figure 3.2). Without testosterone to stimulate its growth, the Wolffian duct system degenerates.

Sex of the External Genitals. External genitals develop according to a similar pattern (see Figure 3.3). Prior to the completion of the sixth week of prenatal

TABLE 3.1   *Homologous Sex Organs*

Female	Male
Clitoris	Glans of penis
Hood of clitoris	Foreskin of penis
Labia minora	Shaft of penis
Labia majora	Scrotal sac
Ovaries	Testes
Skene's ducts	Prostate gland
Bartholin's glands	Cowper's glands

development, all human embryos possess undifferentiated rudimentary external genital tissue, located below the umbilical cord, which consists of the *genital tubercle, genital folds,* and *labioscrotal swelling.* These tissues develop into either male or female external genitals, depending on the presence or absence of testosterone. When testosterone begins circulating in the bloodstream of males, it is converted in some tissues into a hormone called *dihydrotestosterone* (DHT). DHT stimulates the labioscrotal swelling to become the scrotum, and the genital tubercle and genital folds to differentiate into the glans and shaft of the penis, respectively. (The genital folds fuse around the urethra to form the shaft of the penis, and the two sides of the labioscrotal swelling fuse to form the scrotum; these fusions do not occur in females.) In the absence of testosterone, female genitals evolve from the undifferentiated tissues. The genital tubercle becomes the clitoris, the genital folds become the inner vaginal lips (labia minora), and the two sides of the labioscrotal swelling differentiate into the outer vaginal lips (labia majora). By the twelfth week, the differentiation process is complete: the penis and scrotum are recognizable in males; the clitoris and labia can be identified in females.

Thus, the human form is biologically sex-neutral until critical physiological events in the early stages of prenatal development begin the complex process of sex differentiation. We have seen that without the additional input of certain key masculinizing influences, the human embryo naturally develops in the female direction. As John Money and Anke Ehrhardt succinctly summarize, "Nature's rule is, it would appear, that to masculinize, something must be added" (1972, p. 7). This extra "something" is the combined input of a TDF gene product, MIS, and testosterone.

Because the external genitals, gonads, and some of the internal structures of males and females originate from the same embryonic tissues, it is not surprising that they have corresponding, or homologous, parts. Table 3.1 summarizes these male and female counterparts. We will look at the form and function of human sex organs in more detail in Chapters 4 and 5.

Sex Differentiation of the Brain. Strong evidence indicates that some important structural and functional differences exist in the brains of males and females and

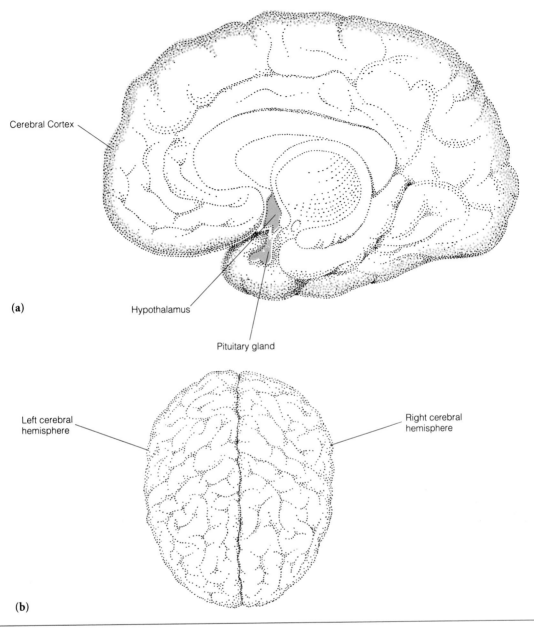

Cerebral Cortex

(a)

Hypothalamus

Pituitary gland

Left cerebral
hemisphere

Right cerebral
hemisphere

(b)

FIGURE 3.4

Parts of the brain: (a) Cross
section of the human brain
showing the hypothalamus;
(b) top view showing the left
and right cerebral
hemispheres.

that the process of sex differentiation of human brains occurs largely, if not exclusively, during prenatal development (Lish et al., 1991; MacLusky & Naftolin, 1981; Witelson, 1991). These differences appear to involve at least two major brain areas: the **hypothalamus** (hy-poh-THAL-ah-mus) and the left and right **cerebral hemispheres**.

A number of studies reveal that a marked sex differentiation occurs in the hypothalamus (see Figure 3.4a for the location of this structure), and that this process is influenced by the presence or absence of circulating testosterone, much like the differentiation of internal and external sex structures (Dorner, 1988; MacLusky & Naftolin, 1981; Reinisch et al., 1991; Swaab & Fliers, 1985; Witelson, 1991). The hypothalamus is a critical brain structure; among other functions, it plays a major role in controlling the production of sex hormones, and it mediates fertility and menstrual cycles through its interaction with the pituitary gland. It appears that the presence or absence of circulating testosterone during prenatal differentiation determines the estrogen sensitivity of certain cells in the hypothalamus. In the male, testosterone causes these specialized receptor cells to become insensitive to estrogen. In the female, the absence of testosterone allows these cells to develop extreme sensitivity to estrogen in the bloodstream.

The consequences of prenatal sex differentiation of the hypothalamus become most apparent at the onset of puberty. A hypothalamus that has undergone female differentiation directs the pituitary to release hormones in a cyclic fashion, creating the menstrual cycle. In contrast, the male-differentiated hypothalamus directs a relatively steady, or acyclic, production of sex hormones. Thus, hypothalamic sex differences are the reason why female fertility is cyclic and male fertility is not.

There is also considerable evidence for sex differences in the cerebral hemispheres of the brain (Bloom et al., 1985). If the top of a person's skull were removed and you looked straight down on the brain, you would see that it is divided into a left and a right side by a long, deep cleft running from front to back (see Figure 3.4b). The resulting two cerebral hemispheres are almost mirror images of each other. Although the hemispheres look alike, they are somewhat specialized in their functions. In most people the left hemisphere is more specialized for verbal functions (understanding and using language), whereas the right side of the brain is more specialized for spatial tasks (the ability to recognize objects and shapes and to perceive relationships among them).

A large body of evidence suggests that there are sex differences in verbal and spatial skills. Females frequently score higher than males on tests of verbal skills, while the reverse is often true when spatial abilities are tested (Burnstein et al., 1980; Deno, 1982; Halpern, 1989; Hyde, 1990; Hyde & Linn, 1986 & 1988; Sanders et al., 1982; Singleton, 1987). However, new research suggests that these sex differences in cognitive skills have declined sharply in recent years (Feingold, 1988; Hyde et al., 1990; Linn & Hyde, 1989). To the extent that sex differences in cognitive skills do exist, however small they may be, theorists continue to debate why they occur. Are they primarily a function of the way males and females are socialized in this society, or are biological factors their major cause?

Several researchers have reported sex differences in the structure of the brain that suggest a possible biological basis for differences in the cognitive skills of males and females (Witelson, 1988 & 1991). For example, in male rats the cerebral cortex is thicker in the right hemisphere than in the left, with the reverse being the case for female rats (Diamond et al., 1979). (The *cerebral cortex* — see Figure 3.4a — is the thin outer covering of the two hemispheres, the part of the brain responsible for higher mental processes like thinking, remembering, language use, and the ability to perceive spatial relationships.) Because the right hemisphere is the primary repository of spatial abilities, it is not surprising that male rats, with quantitatively superior right hemispheres, perform better than their female counterparts on maze-learning tasks that require skill with spatial relationships (Beatty, 1979). Studies of human subjects have also reported evidence indicative of sex differences in the degree of hemispheric specialization (Diamond 1991; Inglis et al., 1982; McGlone, 1978; Witelson 1991).

One investigator, Norman Geschwind (Geschwind & Behan, 1982 & 1984), believes that testosterone influences the rate of hemispheric growth in the developing fetus. He suggests that the greater quantity of circulating testosterone in the brains of prenatal males slows the growth rate of the left hemisphere and results in relatively greater development of the right hemisphere; lack of testosterone in prenatal females causes the reverse development. Some support for Geschwind's interpretation was provided by a recent study that demonstrated a relationship between testosterone levels and cognitive ability patterns in adult men and women (Gouchie & Kimura, 1991). If Geschwind's theory is ultimately supported by further research, we will have hard evidence of a biological basis for alleged sex differences in verbal and spatial skills. However, it is important to note that these reported differences are also likely to be influenced by psychosocial factors (Archer & Lloyd, 1985; Feingold, 1988; Geary, 1989; Hanna, 1988; Hyde, 1991).

Some theorists suggest that sex differences in the brain, besides contributing to differences in certain cognitive abilities, may also have a significant impact on a variety of behaviors, most notably sexual and aggressive behaviors. However, at this time we do not fully understand the manner in which sex differences in the brains of humans are related to behavioral differences between the sexes. Certainly, it is premature, and probably inaccurate, to suggest that brain differences play the most important role.

Abnormal Prenatal Differentiation

Thus far we have considered only normal prenatal differentiation. However, much of our understanding of biological sex differentiation and its impact on the ultimate development of our gender identities comes from studies of abnormal prenatal differentiation.

We have seen that the differentiation of internal and external sex structures occurs under the influence of biological cues. When these signals deviate from normal patterns, the result can be ambiguous biological sex. People with ambiguous or contradictory sex characteristics are sometimes called **hermaphrodites** (her-MAF-roh-dites), a term derived from the mythical Greek deity Hermaphroditus, who was thought to possess attributes of both sexes. This unusual situation can result from a variety of biological errors that produce markedly atypical patterns of hormonally induced prenatal sex differentiation.

We can distinguish between *true hermaphrodites* and *pseudohermaphrodites*. True hermaphrodites, who have both ovarian and testicular tissue in their bodies, are exceedingly rare (Verp et al., 1992). Their external genitals are often a mixture of female and male structures. Pseudohermaphrodites are much more common. They also possess ambiguous internal and external reproductive anatomy, but unlike true hermaphrodites, pseudohermaphrodites are born with gonads that match their chromosomal sex. Studies of pseudohermaphrodites have helped to clarify the relative roles of biology and social learning in the formation of gender identity. We consider evidence from three varieties of pseudohermaphrodites: fetally androgenized females, androgen-insensitive males, and DHT-deficient males. Table 3.2 summarizes the outstanding features of these examples.

TABLE 3.2   *Summary of Some Examples of Abnormal Prenatal Sex Differentiation*

Syndrome	Chromosomal Sex	Gonadal Sex	Reproductive Internal Structures	External Genitals	Fertility	Secondary Sex Characteristics	Gender Identity
Fetally androgenized females	46, XX	Ovaries	Normal female	Ambiguous (typically more male than female)	Fertile	Normal female (individuals with adrenal malfunction must be treated with cortisone to avoid masculinization)	Female, but significant level of dissatisfaction with female gender identity; very oriented toward traditional male activities
Androgen insensitivity syndrome	46, XY	Undescended testes	Lacks a normal set of either male or female internal structures	Normal female genitals and a shallow vagina	Sterile	At puberty breast development and other signs of normal female sexual maturation appear, but menstruation does not occur	Female
DHT-deficient males	46, XY	Undescended testes at birth; testes descend at puberty	Vas deferens, seminal vesicles, and ejaculatory ducts but no prostate; partially formed vagina	Ambiguous at birth (more female than male); at puberty genitals are masculinized	Produce viable sperm but unable to inseminate	Female before puberty; become masculinized at puberty	Prepuberty gender identity difficult to ascertain (lack of data); approximately 90% have assumed traditional male gender role at puberty

Fetally Androgenized Females. Occasionally a chromosomally normal female (XX) is exposed to an excessive amount of androgens or androgenlike substances during the critical period of prenatal sex differentiation. These androgens may have two possible sources. First, the female fetus's own adrenal glands may malfunction, producing abnormally high levels of androgens (Money, 1988). Alternately, androgens may be introduced by drugs the mother takes during pregnancy. (In the 1950s, for instance, some pregnant women were administered androgenlike synthetic hormones to reduce the risk of miscarriage.)

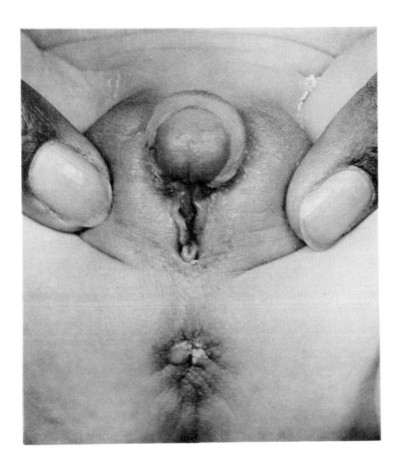

FIGURE 3.5

Masculinized external genitals of a fetally androgenized female baby.

Regardless of the source, the effect of these prenatal androgens is similar. The internal reproductive structures of these chromosomal females do not appear to be affected, but the external genitals resemble those of male infants to varying degrees (see Figure 3.5). The clitoris is often enlarged and may be mistaken for a penis, and the labia are frequently fused so that they look like a scrotum. Physicians faced with such gender ambiguities typically obtain additional information about the composition of the chromosomes and the nature of the gonads to determine the infant's sex. Thus, most of these **fetally androgenized females** are correctly identified and reared as girls. Usually only a relatively minor amount of surgery and hormone therapy is necessary to make the appearance of their external genitals consistent with their internal sex structures.

Some years ago, John Money and Anke Ehrhardt (1972) provided some fascinating data from an extensive study of 25 fetally androgenized females. Their subjects, all of whom had received appropriate medical treatment and had been reared from infancy as girls, were matched with a group of nonandrogenized girls who shared similar characteristics of age, race, and socioeconomic status.

Would you expect that Money and Ehrhardt found differences in the behavior of the fetally androgenized females as compared to those in the nonandrogenized group? Take a few moments to consider this question before reading on.

Money and Ehrhardt found marked differences in the behaviors of these two groups. Of the 25 fetally androgenized girls, 20 identified themselves as "tomboys" — a label with which their parents and friends concurred. These girls tended to be active and aggressive and to engage in traditionally male activities such as rough-and-tumble athletics and pushing trucks in dirt piles. They demonstrated little interest in bride and mother roles, disliked handling infants, and were uninterested in makeup, hairstyling, and jewelry. In contrast, only a few of the girls in the matched group of nonandrogenized girls claimed to be tomboys.

Androgen Insensitivity Syndrome.   A second pseudohermaphroditic condition is **androgen insensitivity syndrome (AIS).** A chromosomally normal (XY) male fetus develops testes that produce normal levels of prenatal androgens. However, as a result of a genetic defect, his body cells are insensitive to the action of testosterone and other androgens, with the result that prenatal development is feminized. Internal reproductive structures of either sex do not develop, the external genitals fail to differentiate into a penis and a scrotum, and the testes do not descend. (Testes normally descend from their position inside the abdomen to the scrotum during the seventh month of prenatal development.) Instead, the newborn has normal-looking female external genitals and a shallow vagina. (Remember, in the absence of male hormones — or in this case, as a consequence of insensitivity to androgen — the developmental pattern is female.) At birth, nothing unusual is suspected, and such babies are considered girls and raised accordingly.

At puberty, breast development and other signs of normal female sexual maturation appear — the result of estrogen production from the undescended testes. The flaws in the child's sex differentiation and development may not be discovered until adolescence or later, often as a result of medical consultation to determine why menstruation has not occurred.

Money and his colleagues (1968) reported an in-depth study of 10 androgen-insensitive males who had been raised as girls. Only one, a young girl with a very disturbed family background, showed any gender-identity confusion. The other nine were strongly identified as female by themselves and others, demonstrating strong preferences for the role of homemaker, fantasizing about becoming pregnant and raising a family, and engaging in typically female play with traditional girls' toys such as dolls. In short, there was nothing that could be viewed as traditionally masculine in the way these girls behaved, despite their XY chromosomes and male gonads.

The findings of this study contrast markedly with the study of fetally androgenized females mentioned earlier. Whereas the behavior of fetally androgenized females seems to reflect biological factors, it is social learning that seems to have played the decisive role in influencing the behavior of individuals with androgen insensitivity syndrome.

DHT-Deficient Males.   Still other evidence comes from a genetic disorder that prevents conversion of testosterone into dihydrotestosterone (DHT), a hormone that is necessary for normal development of male external genitals. A team of Cornell University researchers studied 18 **DHT-deficient males** raised in two rural communities in the Dominican Republic (Imperato-McGinley et al., 1979). In all of these boys, the internal sex structures had developed normally, and appropriate prenatal androgen levels were present. However, their testicles were undescended at birth, their stunted penises resembled clitorises, and they had partially formed vaginas and incompletely formed scrotums that looked like labia — features that caused them to be incorrectly identified as female and raised as girls. At puberty, however, their as-yet-undescended testes began accelerated testosterone production, causing the most amazing things to happen: Their voices deepened, their clitoris-like organs enlarged and became penises, and their testes finally descended.

In response to these marked biological changes in their bodies, all but two of the 18 adopted the culturally mandated male gender roles, including occupational inclinations and patterns of sexual activity. Of the remaining two, one acknowledged that he was male but continued to dress as a woman; the other maintained a female gender identity, married, and sought a sex-change operation.

The Dominican study challenged some widely held assumptions — most notably the notions that gender identity is primarily learned, and that once it is established during the critical early years of life, it cannot be changed without creating severe emotional problems. Certainly, this important research suggests that gender identity may be more malleable than previously thought. However, important questions remain unanswered about the psychological environments of these Dominican youths. For example, because the study was conducted after the subjects had become adults, we cannot be sure that their early gender socialization was unambiguously female. Furthermore, we must consider the possibility that these individuals converted to a male identity because of extreme social pressure (locals sometimes made the boys objects of ridicule and referred to them as *quevote*, which means "penis at 12," or *machihembra*, "first woman, then man"), or because the culture of this Caribbean country so heavily favors males. (Some of the parents were proud to discover that their daughter was actually their son.)

Support for a sociocultural explanation of why the Dominican Republic youths were able to successfully change from a female to a male gender identity is provided by a second investigation of DHT-deficient males, this one among the Sambia society of Papua, New Guinea. The authors of this study assert that sociocultural factors play a primary role in facilitating gender-identity change in DHT-deficient males. They conclude that "cultural valuation of the male role makes gender-switching from female to male pragmatically adaptive" (Herdt & Davidson, 1988, p. 33).

The three types of hormone-based differentiation errors we have just described provide seemingly contradictory evidence. In the first case, chromosomal females who were masculinized before birth by excessive androgens tended to manifest typically masculine behavior despite having been raised as girls. In contrast, the chromosomal males in the second example who were insensitive to androgens behaved in a typically feminine manner, consistent with their socialization. While in the third case, chromosomal males whose biological maleness did not become known until puberty were able to successfully alter their gender identity to male, even though they had apparently been reared as girls. Are the results of these investigations at odds with one another? Or is there a way to explain the apparent inconsistencies in these varied results? Think about these questions for a few minutes before reading on.

The apparent inconsistencies among these studies may not be contradictory at all when evaluated from a biological perspective. As we discussed earlier, mounting evidence suggests that prenatal androgens play a key role in prenatal sex differentiation of the human brain. Using this evidence as a foundation, we might theorize that prenatal androgens also masculinize the brain — just as they trigger masculinization of the sex structures. This hypothesis could explain the masculine behavior of fetally androgenized females. Furthermore, the same genetic defect that prevents masculinization of the genitals of individuals with AIS may also prevent the masculinization of their brains.

What about the Dominican and Sambia boys who seem to have converted so smoothly from a female to a male gender identity? Presumably, these individuals had normal androgen levels during critical prenatal stages of development and were able to respond normally to these hormones; the lack of DHT affected only their external genital development. Thus their brains might already have been programmed along male lines by prenatal androgens. It seems plausible that prenatal androgens, besides instigating proper differentiation of biological sex, may also masculinize the brain, thereby predisposing a person toward a male gender identity.

The results of the investigations of these varied biological accidents raise a fundamental question: Just what makes us male or female? Our chromosomes? Our hormones? The characteristics of our sexual structures? The sex we are identified as at birth? Clearly, there is no simple answer. Biological sex is determined by a complex process involving several interacting levels. Many steps, each susceptible to errors, are involved in sex differentiation prior to birth. We now turn our attention to the social-learning factors that influence gender-identity formation *after* birth.

Social-Learning Factors in Gender Identity

Thus far we have considered only the biological factors involved in the determination of gender identity. Our sense of femaleness or maleness is not based exclusively on biological conditions, however. Social-learning theory suggests that our identification with either masculine or feminine roles or a combination thereof (androgyny) results primarily from the social and cultural models and influences we are exposed to during our early development.

What do you consider to be some of the important social and cultural influences that shape our gender identities? See what you can think of before reading on.

At birth, parents label their children as male or female with the announcement "It's a boy!" or "It's a girl!" From this point on, children are exposed to people who tend to react to them in a manner dictated by their gender-role expectations (Sedney, 1987). Parents typically dress boys and girls differently, decorate their rooms differently, provide them with different toys, and even respond to them differently. Parents and others actively teach little boys and girls what gender they are by how they describe them. Expressions such as "You are a sweet little girl" or "You are a bright little boy" are common. Small children may not comprehend what makes them biologically male or female, but they definitely are not confused

cathy®   **by Cathy Guisewite**

about whether they are boys or girls — just try calling a two-year-old boy a girl, or vice versa, and observe the indignant manner in which you are set straight.

Understandably, parents and others have certain preconceived ideas about how boys and girls differ, and they communicate these views to their children from the very beginning. For example, in one study parents were asked to describe their infants within 24 hours of birth. All babies included in this sample were approximately the same height, weight, and muscle tone. Parents of girls tended to describe their daughters as soft, sweet, fine-featured, and delicate. On the other hand, parents of boys were inclined to use words like strong, well-coordinated, active, and robust to describe their sons (Rubin et al., 1974). These perceptions remain after the child is brought home from the hospital, and they may influence the nature of parent–child interactions.

A child's own actions probably strongly influence the process whereby his or her gender identity is established. Most children have developed a firm sense of being a boy or a girl by the age of 18 months. Once this takes place, they typically acquire a strong desire to adopt behaviors appropriate for their sex (Kohlberg, 1966; Sedney, 1987); that is, they try to find out how boys or girls are supposed to behave and then act accordingly.

Anthropological studies of other cultures also lend support to the social-learning interpretation of gender-identity formation. In several societies, the differences between males and females that we often assume to be innate are simply not evident. In fact, Margaret Mead's classic book *Sex and Temperament in Three Primitive Societies* (1963) reveals that other societies may have very different views about what is considered feminine or masculine. In this widely quoted report of her fieldwork in New Guinea, Mead discusses two societies that minimize differences between the sexes. She noted that among the Mundugumor, both sexes exhibit aggressive, nonnurturing behaviors that would be considered masculine by our society's norms. In contrast, among the Arapesh, both males and females exhibit gentleness, nurturing, and nonaggressive behaviors that would be judged feminine in our society. In a third society studied, the Tchambuli, Mead observed an actual reversal of our typical masculine and feminine gender roles. Recall from the opening of this chapter that Tchambuli women tend to be dominant, assertive, and very much in charge, whereas Tchambuli men are quiet, undemanding, and emotionally dependent. Because there is no evidence that people in these societies are biologically different from Americans, their often diametrically different interpretations of what is masculine and what is feminine seem to result from different processes of social learning.

Some of the most impressive evidence in support of the social-learning viewpoint has emerged from the research of John Money and his colleagues. Perhaps the most persuasive of these studies have concerned children whose external genitals represent such a mixture of male and female characteristics that biological sex identification is difficult. Money and his co-workers found that, in most of the cases they evaluated, children whose assigned sex did not match their chromosomal sex developed a gender identity consistent with the manner in which they were reared (Hampson & Hampson, 1961; Money, 1965; Money et al., 1955; Money & Ehrhardt, 1972). (As we have learned, fetally androgenized females tend to manifest some dissatisfaction with their gender identity, but they do not express a desire to actually change their sex.)

One particularly unusual study of two identical twin boys (Money, 1975; Money & Ehrhardt, 1972) has frequently been cited in support of the social-learning interpretation. At the age of seven months, a circumcision accident destroyed most of the penile tissue of one of the boys. Because no amount of plastic surgery could adequately reconstruct the severely damaged penis, it was recommended that the child be raised as a female and receive appropriate sex-change surgery. When the child was 17 months old, the parents decided to begin raising him as a girl. Shortly thereafter, initial genital surgery was performed. Follow-up studies of these unusual twins revealed that, despite possessing identical genetic materials, they responded to their separate social-learning experiences by developing opposite gender identities. Furthermore, the child reassigned to the female gender appeared to demonstrate no confusion about her identity during her early developmental years.

If the story of these twins ended here, we would have strong evidence of the dominant role of social learning in gender-identity formation. However, in 1979 the psychiatrist following this case revealed that the assigned female member of the pair was experiencing considerable difficulty in making her adjustment as a woman (Williams & Smith, 1979). Apparently, her appearance and behavior was so unfeminine during her school years that classmates heartlessly taunted her as a "cave woman" (Diamond, 1982). Thus, the efforts to alter her biological potential as a male appear not completely successful. The reasons for this circumstance are not entirely clear. Maybe her parents waited too long to make their decision — the probability of successful reassignment of sex diminishes with increasing age. Perhaps prenatal masculinization of the brain by androgens is a factor in this case. If biological and social-learning factors interact in the formation of gender identity after birth, the unfolding results of this twin study may be understandable and perhaps even predictable. In the next section, we briefly explore this interactional interpretation of the formation of gender identity.

The Interactional Model

Perhaps you have already surmised, quite correctly, that an explanation of how we acquire our gender identity must involve both biology and social learning.

Many social scientists have a propensity to emphasize learned over biological causes of behavior. Perhaps this may explain why some tend to de-emphasize the biological evidence. Others may fear that acknowledging the role of biology in gender development implies that gender roles are unchangeable or that biology denies the importance of life experiences in establishing our own subjective sense of masculinity or femininity. However, few researchers today believe in an exclusively biological basis for human gender-identity formation. The evidence supporting the role of social learning is simply too pervasive. In a later section of this chapter, we will consider the many forces at work in the socialization of gender roles.

Today virtually all researchers and theorists embrace the interactional model, wherein gender identity is considered to result from a complex interplay of biological and social-learning factors. The question of which plays the greater role in shaping gender identity undoubtedly will be debated for years to come, as new evidence is gathered.

A Special Case of Gender-Identity Difficulty: Transsexualism

The **transsexual** is a person whose gender identity is opposite to his or her biological sex (Pauly, 1990; Pauly & Edgerton, 1986). He or she feels trapped in a body of the wrong sex, a condition known as **gender dysphoria** (dis-FŌR-ē-a) (Blanchard et al., 1987). Thus, an anatomically male transsexual feels that he is a woman betrayed by some quirk of fate that provided him with male genitals. He is a woman-identified man, and this is the source of his acute discomfort. He wishes to be socially identified as the woman he sincerely believes himself to be. Rather than experiencing sexual excitement when cross-dressing, as is the case with transvestism, he experiences a sense of comfort with himself. (We will discuss transvestism in Chapter 20.)

In the 1960s and early 1970s, when medical procedures for altering sex were first being developed in this country, approximately three out of every four people requesting a sex change were men who wished to be women (Green, 1975). More recently, this ratio has narrowed to approximately one to one, and current data suggest that the incidence of transsexualism is comparable among both males and females (Pauly, 1990).

A vast accumulation of clinical literature has focused on the characteristics, causes, and treatment of transsexualism. Certain things are well established: We know that most transsexuals are biologically normal individuals with healthy sex organs, intact internal reproductive structures, and the proper complement of XX or XY chromosomes. What is less understood is why the transsexual rejects his or her anatomy. A leading scholar in this area, Leslie Lothstein (1984), published a critical review of 30 years of psychological evaluation of transsexuals, in which he concluded that no clear understanding of the nature and etiology of transsexualism has yet emerged. Considerable controversy also exists regarding the most appropriate clinical strategies for dealing with this condition. Keeping this continued debate in mind, we will summarize our current tenuous state of knowledge about this highly unusual gender-identity difficulty.

Many transsexuals develop a sense of being at odds with their genital anatomy in very early childhood; some recall identifying strongly with characteristics of the other sex as early as five, six, or seven years of age. In some cases these children's discomfort is partially relieved by imagining themselves to be a member of the other sex, but many of them eventually progress beyond mere imagining to actual cross-dressing. Less commonly, a strong identity with the other sex may not emerge until the adolescent or adult years. There is evidence that anatomically female transsexuals tend to display cross-gender behavior at an earlier age than do their male counterparts (Verschoor & Poortinga, 1988).

Male-to-female transsexuals (that is, those who are anatomically male) often exhibit much more interest as children in playing with dolls and dressing up in pretty dresses than in rough-and-tumble games and other typically boyish pursuits. In adolescence and adulthood, many engage in what has been described as hyperfeminine behavior, in which their use of perfumes, cosmetics, clothing, gestures, and styles of sitting, standing, and walking represent a somewhat exaggerated expression of stereotyped femininity (Barlow et al., 1980; Pauly, 1974). They may be aware of an emotional attachment and sexual attraction to males, but typically they do not view this (or even sexual activity with men) as an indication of homosexuality because they consider themselves female. Male-to-female transsexuals who marry women before undergoing sex-reassignment procedures may be able to engage in sex only by fantasizing that they are being penetrated by a penis.

Most female-to-male transsexuals recall thinking of themselves as boys long before the emergence of adolescence. Usually, they dressed like boys and engaged in typically masculine activities, formed close friendships with boys rather than girls, showed no interest in babies, and expressed rejection of the wife and mother roles. Adolescence is a particularly traumatic period for females who consider themselves male; they often feel intense revulsion at the onset of menstruation and may try to disguise their developing breasts. Female-to-male transsexuals who relate sexually to men prior to sex-reassignment surgery may accept clitoral stimulation but frequently refuse to allow vaginal penetration or breast stimulation. Those who have sex with women do not typically regard these encounters as homosexual because they consider themselves male.

What do you think causes transsexualism? Think about this for a moment before reading on.

There are many theories about the origins of transsexualism, but at the present time the evidence is insufficient to draw any absolute conclusions. Some writers maintain that biological factors may play a decisive role. One theory suggests that prenatal exposure to inappropriate hormones of the other sex might cause improper brain differentiation (Pauly, 1974). There is no solid evidence from research with humans that supports this speculation, so it must remain merely a theory (Ehrhardt et al., 1985). It has also been suggested that transsexualism may be induced by abnormal levels of adult sex hormones. However, this explanation also lacks support in light of numerous indications that sex hormone levels are comparable in adult transsexuals and nontranssexual individuals (Meyer et al., 1986).

A more popular theory of the causes of transsexualism, for which there is some supporting evidence, holds that social-learning experiences contribute significantly to the development of this condition. A child may be exposed to a variety of conditioning experiences that support behaving in a manner traditionally attributed to the other sex (Green, 1974; Money & Primrose, 1968). The child may develop a close, identifying relationship with the parent of the other sex, and this identification may be strongly reinforced by the adult's reaction. The little boy may play at being a girl, and the girl may be "Daddy's little man." Such cross-gender behaviors may be so exclusively rewarded that it may be difficult or impossible for the individual to develop the appropriate gender identity.

Several studies have reported unusual attachments between male-to-female transsexuals and their mothers; whereas the presence of cold, rejecting mothers and unusual identification with their fathers have been found in the early development of female-to-male transsexuals (Pauly, 1974; Stoller, 1968 & 1972). A recent study of transsexuals, who were aware of their cross-gender identification during their youth, revealed a high incidence of early traumatic experiences in a disturbed family environment (Meyer & Dupkin, 1985).

Difficult as it is to determine the causes of transsexualism, perhaps even more challenging is to find ways to resolve the problem of reversed gender identity. As previously indicated, most transsexuals follow a heterosexual script and prefer to have sexual relations with a member of the other sex. However, for them the other sex happens to have the same genitals as they. Whom then do they relate to sexually? Most want to interact with heterosexuals: A male transsexual wants to be desired as a woman by a heterosexual man, and most transsexual women would not be satisfied with a lesbian relationship.

These sexual needs are often hard to meet. Heterosexuals and homosexuals can generally find willing sex partners who match their orientations, but transsexuals' most desired partners are likely to reject them for making "unnatural" advances.

Psychotherapy, without accompanying biological alterations, has generally been reported to be unsuccessful in helping transsexuals adjust to their bodies (Benjamin, 1967; Roberto, 1983; Tollison & Adams, 1979). It would seem then that the best course of action might be for them to change their bodies to match their minds, through surgical and hormonal alteration of genital anatomy and body physiology. Beneficial as it may be, however, the process of medical alteration is not a simple solution, for it is both time-consuming and costly. Furthermore, one leading authority on the treatment of transsexualism recently suggested that all possible alternatives in the management of this challenging condition, including psychotherapy, be explored before considering irreversible sex-change surgery (Pauly, 1990).

The initial step of a sex change involves extensive screening interviews, during which the person's motivations for undergoing the change are thoroughly evaluated. Those with real conflicts and confusion about their gender identity (that is, who are not really sure which sex they are) or those seeking the operation on a whim are not considered for surgical alteration. Individuals who appear to exhibit a genuine incongruence between their gender identity and biological sex are then instructed to adopt a lifestyle consistent with their gender identity (i.e., dress style and behavior patterns). If, after a period of several months to a year or longer, it appears that the individual has successfully adjusted to the gender identity congruent with that lifestyle, the next step is hormone therapy, a process

FIGURE 3.6

The genitals following sex change surgery: (a) Male-to-female sex-change surgery is generally more effective than (b) female-to-male sex-change surgery.

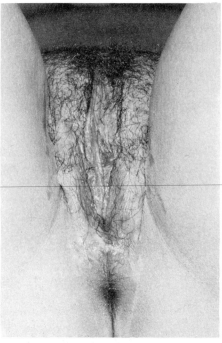

(a)

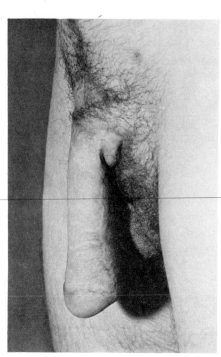

(b)

designed to accentuate some of the person's latent other-sex traits. Transsexual males wishing to be females are given drugs that inhibit testosterone production together with doses of estrogen that induce some breast growth, soften the skin, reduce growth of facial and body hair, and contribute to some feminization of the body contours (Prior et al., 1989). Muscle strength also diminishes, as does sexual interest, but there is no alteration of vocal pitch. Transsexual women who desire a male identity are treated with testosterone, which has a masculinizing effect apparent in increased growth of body and facial hair, a deepening of the voice, and a slight reduction in breast size. Testosterone also suppresses menstruation. Most health professionals providing the sex-change procedures require that a candidate live for one year or more as a member of the other sex, while undergoing hormone therapy, before taking the final, drastic step of surgery. At any time during this phase, the process can be successfully reversed, although few transsexuals choose this option.

The final step of a sex change is surgery (see Figure 3.6). Surgical procedures are most effective for men wishing to be women. The scrotum and penis are removed, and a vagina is created through reconstruction of pelvic tissue (see Figure 3.6a). During this surgical procedure, great care is taken to maintain the sensory nerves that service the skin of the penis, and this sensitive skin tissue is relocated to the inside of the newly fashioned vagina. Intercourse is possible, although use of a lubricant may be necessary, and many male-to-female transsexuals report postsurgical capacity to experience sexual arousal and orgasm (Blanchard et al., 1987; Money & Walker, 1977). Hormone treatments may produce sufficient breast development, but some individuals also receive implants. Body and facial hair, which has been reduced by hormone treatments, may be further removed by electrolysis.

Biological females who desire to be male generally have their breasts, uteri, and ovaries surgically removed and their vaginas sealed off. The process of constructing a penis is much more difficult than that of fashioning a vagina. Generally, the penis is fashioned from abdominal skin or from tissue from the labia and perineum (see Figure 3.6b). This constructed organ is not capable of natural erection in response to sexual arousal. However, several artificial devices are available for providing a rigid penis for purposes of intercourse. One involves fashioning a small, hollow skin tube on the underside of the penile shaft into which a rigid silicone rod can be inserted. Another alternative is to use an implanted inflatable device, which will be described in Chapter 17. If erotically sensitive tissue from the clitoris is left embedded at the base of the surgically constructed penis, erotic feelings and orgasm are sometimes possible.

Several reports provide some basis for optimism about the potential success of sex-reassignment surgery. One important publication summarized the conclusions that could realistically be drawn from three worldwide literature reviews on the outcome of sex-change surgery (Lundstrom et al., 1984). Among the reported findings was that approximately 9 out of 10 transsexuals undergoing hormonal and surgical sex-reassignment procedures experience a satisfactory result. This high incidence of positive outcomes appears to be equally likely for male-to-female and female-to-male transsexuals. Another study, which used a large sample of males-to-females and females-to-males, reported that 94% of this study population stated that they would have the surgery again if they had it to do over (Blanchard et al., 1985). Still another investigation revealed that transsexuals who undergo surgery demonstrate markedly better social adjustment than those who have not been surgically altered (Kockott & Fahrner, 1987). Finally, another report indicated that major determinants of healthy postoperative psychological adjustment of transsexuals include such factors as receiving social support from friends, obtaining positive reactions from family members, and securing surgical results that allow them to "pass" as the other sex (Ross & Need, 1989).

At the time of this writing, controversy continues in the scientific community over the relative benefits of sex-change surgery. Clearly, we do not have the complete picture at the present time, and there is a vital need for continued research in this area. However, there does appear to be a growing trend among health professionals to accept sex-reassignment surgery as an option for some individuals who experience great distress as a result of a strong identification with the other biological sex. Most professionals stress the importance of careful diagnostic screening to determine who is most likely to be aided by surgery, and the need to use good surgical procedures to yield an aesthetically pleasing result. Perhaps, as one writer suggests, we may eventually come to view such procedures as "sex confirmation" rather than sex reassignment (Edgerton, 1984).

Gender Roles

The issue of gender goes beyond the processes whereby we acquire our own subjective sense of maleness or femaleness. Society is not content merely to allow us to identify our gender. Rather, it ascribes to us a set of behaviors that are con-

OUR SEXUALITY

The Men's Movement of the 1990s: The New Politics of Masculinity

In the early 1990s, interest in men's issues mushroomed across America, prompted in part by Bill Moyers's 1990 PBS special, "A Gathering of Men," and by a growing realization that men are hurting, often very grievously. Three best-selling books, *Iron John* by Robert Bly (1990), *Fire in the Belly* by Sam Keen (1991), and *King Warrior Magician Lover* by Robert Moore and Douglas Gillette (1990), have given substance and impetus to the men's movement by portraying the issues, dilemmas, and emotional pain of contemporary American men.

Why are men hurting? Many contemporary writers stress that men have been devastated by a socioeconomic system that has forced them off the land, out of the family, and into the factory and office (Kimbrell, 1991). As Robert Bly (1990) points out, ever since the industrial revolution created a separate sphere of "work" for men, the father has been wrenched from the home. Even when he returns to his home, the contemporary American father is often too tired or too irritable from work to become integrally involved in family activities. Consequently, "his children receive only his temperament, and not his teaching" (p. 96). The family, and especially sons, lose an important male role model and father figure. Bly and other stalwarts of the men's movement contend that this pro-

duces for men lives blighted by "father-hunger," which manifests itself in emotional pain, unhappiness, and difficulties in intimate relationships.

Thus the historical image of men as nurturers and protectors of land and family has been replaced by the current reality: men who have lost touch with earth and family, who are forced into an impersonal system whose ultimate goal is "to turn one man against another in the competitive 'jungle' of industrialized society" (Kimbrell, 1991, p. 67). And what kind of life does the office or factory offer? In a socioeconomic system that continues to empower only a small percentage of men, most males lead subservient, stressful lives at work. Men are confused and distressed when they confront the disparity between the macho images of masculinity presented in the media and their own sense of powerlessness and subservience on the job. An abundance of data reveal that the stress of men's lives is taking a terrible toll. Suicide, alcohol and substance abuse, cancer, heart disease, and other stress-related problems and illnesses all occur with a much higher frequency among men than among women.

In countless male gatherings across the U.S., men also acknowledge that they lack friendship and close emotional ties or bonds with other men. The major reason for a shortage of genuine, caring, and com-

mitted friendships between and among men in America is that our culture discourages it (Letich, 1991). Our economic system places men in the position of competing with other men for jobs and promotions. Men often learn not to trust one another, and may even be made to feel neglectful or irresponsible for channeling any of their limited time and emotional needs in any direction other than their careers and immediate families.

Men are now awakening to a crisis of their gender and, tired of leading lives of quiet desperation, they are seeking solace and comfort through gatherings with other similarly distraught and dissatisfied men. In hundreds of meetings throughout the U.S., men are gathering to speak of the emotional, personal, and spiritual costs of being "success objects"— valued only for the money they make — and the pain they encounter in the dehumanizing, family-insensitive world of corporate America. They attend mountain retreats where they sit around a campfire or divide into small groups to discuss and share their "hidden pain, guilt, fear, and shame" (Cooney, 1991, p. 7). The Native American traditions of drumming, chanting, dancing, and sweat lodge rituals have helped men to connect with their own feelings and with one another to overcome the cultural taboo against males revealing and ex-

sidered normal and appropriate for our particular sex. These normative standards are typically labeled **gender roles** (or sex roles).

The ascribing of gender roles leads naturally to certain assumptions about how people will behave. For example, men in North American society are expected to act independently and aggressively, while women are supposed to be dependent and submissive. Once these expectations are widely accepted, they may begin to function as stereotypes. A **stereotype** is a generalized notion of what a person is

pressing emotions. As men come together during such weekends in the woods, they have an opportunity to reestablish their ties to the earth and to each other while mourning lost fathers and sons. The healing support that they get when expressing deeply felt feelings and needs, such as "father-hunger," comes from the other male participants. In addition to personal development, these gatherings of men help to promote concern and commitment for the wellness of the environment. Men can learn that rather than nature being something to be dominated, the earth's elements and creatures are to be valued and

protected as family (Keen, 1991).

Deepening vulnerability and emotional intimacy in relationships with others of their own gender is a powerful experience for many men whose only prior intimate relationships have been with women — their mothers, girlfriends, and wives. Some men are now beginning to realize that they have often mistakenly attempted to establish a sense of themselves as men solely from their intimate relationships with women instead of also from intimate friendships with other men — including their own fathers and sons.

Some observers of the men's movement, while acknowledging the deep psychological benefits of retreats and gatherings, suggest that these experiences are not enough to reverse the victimization of men. What the men's movement needs now, they argue, is a serious political or social agenda (Adler et al., 1991). Andrew Kimbrell (1991), an activist in the men's movement, suggests that as the movement gathers strength, it is essential that the increasing sense of personal liberation experienced by participants be channeled into political action. Kimbrell maintains that "a coordinated movement pressing for the liberation of men could be a key factor in ensuring that the struggle for a sustainable future for humanity and the earth succeeds" (p. 72). Key aspects of Kimbrell's recently outlined political platform or manifesto for men include supporting parental-leave legislation, increasing male involvement in raising and educating children, supporting programs that promote better health in men, taking a united stand against war and military spending, increased male involvement in organizing support for the protection of nature, and forming a united, high-profile coalition of men's groups to gain the political clout needed to implement a comprehensive platform of men's concerns at the national level.

like based only on that person's sex, race, religion, ethnic background, or similar category; stereotypes do not take individuality into account.

There are many common gender-based stereotypes that are widely accepted in our society. Some of the prevailing notions about men maintain that they are aggressive (or at least assertive), logical, unemotional, independent, dominant, competitive, objective, athletic, active, and above all, competent. Conversely, women are frequently viewed as passive, nonassertive, illogical, emotional,

OUR SEXUALITY

Gender-Based Communication Styles: Talking Across Two Different Cultures

Deborah Tannen, a professor of linguistics at Georgetown University, recently wrote a fascinating and widely praised book called *You Just Don't Understand: Women and Men in Conversation* (1990), which deals with the complexities of communication between the sexes. Drawing upon a distinguished research career, Tannen presents vivid examples of how women and men are socialized to relate and dialogue with others in such pronouncedly different ways that the two sexes often stumble in their efforts to connect. In various public lectures as well as in her book, which was a national best-seller, Tannen maintains that the sexes are, in a very real sense, communicating from the perspective of two different cultures.

Tannen contends that men use language to convey information, to achieve status in a group, to challenge others, and to keep from getting pushed around. Women, on the other hand, use language to achieve and share intimacy with others, to promote closeness and equality in a group, and to prevent others from pushing them away. Stated another way, men often grow up thinking that people will try to push them around if given a chance, and thus often enter into conversations concerned about who is one-up and who is one-down. From this perspective, communication becomes something of a contest in which a man endeavors to avoid being put in a one-down position. A man operating within this framework might be expected to be overly sensitive about asking advice or directions, being told to do something, or engaging in any other behavior or dialogue that even remotely resembled being in a one-down or pushed-around position. Tannen illustrates this point with the example of a man whose wife has requested that he do some specific task around

the house: Rather than complying with her request immediately, he might wait and let some time pass before responding, so it will not appear that he is being told what to do. In contrast, women are not typically socialized to use language as a defensive weapon to avoid being dominated or controlled. Rather, their concern is often to use dialogue as a way to get close to another — and as a way to judge how close or distant they are from a valued partner.

Tannen has some particularly enlightening things to say about women and men engaging in what she calls *troubles talk:*

Women and men are both frustrated by the other's way of responding to their expression of troubles. And they are further hurt by the other's frustration. If women resent men's tendency to offer solutions to problems, men complain about women's refusal to take action to solve the problems they complain about. Since many men see themselves as problem solvers, a complaint or a trouble is a challenge to their ability to think of a solution, just as a woman presenting a broken bicycle or stalling car poses a challenge to their ingenuity in fixing it. But whereas many women appreciate help in fixing mechanical equipment, few are inclined to appreciate help in "fixing" emotional troubles. (pp. 51–52)

A woman may talk about her problems to foster a sense of sharing and rapport and to achieve a feeling of "I am not alone." What she wants is a response that says, "I understand; I have been there too." For a woman, "troubles talk is intended to reinforce rapport by sending the message 'We're the same; you're not alone'" (p. 53). Such a response would put both communicators on an equal footing, thus allowing intimacy to be

built around equality. However, when a man responds with advice when his partner is only looking for understanding, his response frames him "as more knowledgeable, more reasonable, more in control — in a word, one-up. And this contributes to the distancing effect" (p. 53). Tannen encourages women to minimize this relationship-eroding influence by clearly telling their male partners that when dealing with emotional troubles, they do not want solutions, just someone to listen.

Other key gender differences in communication styles discussed by Tannen include women's inclinations to think a relationship is working if both partners continue to talk about it, contrasted with men's tendencies to think things are okay if they do *not* need to keep talking about their relationship; women using face-to-face eye contact during dialogue more than men; and men's propensities to clam up at home, a place where they feel free *not* to talk (no need to keep their edge in a competitive, one-up world), as opposed to women's tendencies to open up in the comfort of home, where they feel free to talk.

Tannen stresses that the first step in improving communication is understanding and accepting that there are systematic gender differences in communication styles, and that it is not a question of one style being more right or wrong than the other. Tannen reports that many people have indicated to her that once they came to understand these differences in how the sexes use language, they were better able to put their problems of communication with the other sex in a manageable context — and often to arrive at solutions to seemingly unresolvable predicaments.

dependent, subordinate, warm, and nurturing. Not all people adhere to these gender-role stereotypes, but there is strong evidence of their pervasiveness within our society (Archer & Lloyd, 1985; Doyle, 1985; Hyde, 1991; Smith & Midlarsky, 1985). However, recent research suggests that women may be less entrenched than men in rigid gender-role stereotypes and are perhaps more inclined to embrace positions of equality in relation to men (Larsen & Long, 1988). Furthermore, research has indicated that sex-based stereotyping can be reduced or eliminated when individuals are provided with information about the tendencies of people to engage in either male-typed or female-typed behaviors (Pratto & Bargh, 1991).

Finally, gender-role socialization may also influence how men and women communicate with each other. Some of the misunderstandings between the sexes may be attributed to gender-based communication styles. This issue is addressed in the box at left, "Gender-Based Communication Styles: Talking Across Two Different Cultures".

The Socialization of Gender Roles

Despite the potentially limiting impact of rigid and stereotypic gender roles on our lives, many individuals are comfortable fulfilling a traditional masculine or feminine role. We do not wish to demean or question the validity of their lifestyles. Rather, we are concerned with why these gender roles are so prevalent in our society. Are they biologically mandated, or are they learned? It seems reasonable to suspect that at least some of the behavioral differences between males and females may be related to biological factors such as differences in muscle mass, hormonal variations, and brain differences (Bloom et al., 1985; Diamond, 1977 & 1979; Diamond & Karlen, 1980). Nevertheless, most theorists, including ourselves, believe that gender roles result largely from the manner in which we are socialized as males and females. **Socialization** refers to the process whereby society conveys behavioral expectations to an individual. In the following sections, we examine the role of parents, peers, schools, textbooks, and television as agents in the socialization of gender roles.

Take a few moments to think about the respective roles of parents, peers, schools, textbooks, and television as socializers of gender roles. In what way do each of these influences shape our sense of masculinity or femininity? Are some of these agents more influential than others? Which played the strongest roles in your own life? Give these questions some thought before reading on.

Parents as Shapers of Gender Roles. Parents undoubtedly play a role in the socialization of gender roles in their children. However, there is some question about the strength of parental influence in this regard. A recent study suggested that parental impact may not be as powerful a factor in the socialization of gender roles as previously believed. This research, conducted by Hugh Lytton and David Romney (1991), employed a technique called *meta-analysis*—a complex statistical procedure whereby data from many studies are combined and collectively analyzed. The findings of 172 separate investigations of the role of parents as shapers of gender roles were included in this analysis. Lytton and Romney reported that of a possible 19 different kinds of parental influences on gender-role socialization of their children, the only area shown to exhibit "a significant effect for both par-

The establishment of stereotypic masculine or feminine roles may be influenced by traditional childrearing practices.

ents [was] encouragement of sex-typed activities" (p. 267). Other than this one area, these investigators found little evidence of parents' differential socialization of boys and girls.

These findings stand in sharp contrast to the opinions of many social scientists who view parents as influential agents of gender-role socialization (Block, 1983; Fagot et al., 1992; Huston, 1983; Sedney, 1987). Certainly the role of parents as instigators of sex-typed gender roles is open to further investigative analysis and debate.

Researchers have reported, among other findings, that parents often interact differently with girls and boys. Baby girls are frequently treated as if they were more fragile than boys (Doyle, 1985; Jacklin et al., 1984; Ross & Taylor, 1989), and they may receive more attention than baby boys (Thoman et al., 1972). Parents often encourage boys to suppress emotion and to be independent, nonnurturing, and aggressive, while girls are expected to display the opposite characteristics (Gagnon, 1977; Hyde, 1991; Mosher & Tomkins, 1988; Siegal, 1987). As reported in the Lytton and Romney investigation, parents often encourage their children to engage in sex-typed behaviors by emphasizing sex stereotypes in play activities and household chores.

Although increasing numbers of parents are becoming sensitive to the gender-role implications of a child's playthings, many others still encourage their children to play with toys and engage in activities that help prepare them for specific adult gender roles. Tea sets, dolls, and dollhouses are still common girls' toys, while boys often receive trucks, toy guns, and footballs. Such parental influences may combine to produce men who are comfortable being assertive and competitive, and women who are inclined to be domestic, nonassertive, and nurturing.

The Peer Group. The peer group is another agent of socialization, particularly during late childhood and adolescence (Adams, 1973; Doyle, 1985; Hyde, 1991). Most individuals in this age group have fairly rigid views of what is and is not gender appropriate. For girls, being popular and attractive may be very important. In contrast, boys may try to prove their worth on the athletic field. Individuals

Parents, particularly fathers, tend to interact with their sons in a more boisterous manner than they do with their daughters.

who do not conform to these traditional roles may be subjected to ridicule, teasing, questions, or other forms of pressure. One particularly negative aspect of adolescent gender typing is the notion that one cannot be both feminine and an achiever. The potential impact of this limiting assumption is revealed in the following account:

I like high school, and I am a good student. In fact, I could be an outstanding student. But I am afraid of what others might think of me if I do too well. My boyfriend is into sports and not schoolwork. We take some classes together. Many times I purposely score below my ability on tests so as not to show him up. What would he think about his girlfriend being a brain? (Authors' files)

Psychologist Eleanor Maccoby (1985) has noted a pronounced segregation between the sexes that begins very early in life. This separation of the sexes is another aspect of the peer-group structure that perpetuates traditional gender roles. Research conducted by Maccoby and Carol Jacklin (1987) suggests that even preschool children select same-sex playmates about 80% of the time. By the time they enter the first grade, children voluntarily select other-sex playmates only about 5% of the time.

Schools, Textbooks, and Gender Roles. Still another influence in the development and perpetuation of gender roles is the school. Teachers' responses to their students are often guided by their own stereotypes about males and females (Rogers, 1987). It is common for instructors to expect girls to excel in subjects like English and literature, whereas boys are often believed to be more proficient in math and science. Guided by such assumptions, teachers may differentially

Although parents are becoming more sensitive to the kinds of toys children play with, many still choose different toys and play activities for boys than for girls. Tea sets, dolls, and dollhouses are still common girls' toys; trucks, toy guns, and footballs are common boys' toys.

One aspect of peer-group structure among American children that helps to perpetuate traditional gender roles is the tendency to select same-sex playmates most of the time.

encourage and reward boys' and girls' performances in these particular subjects. Furthermore, girls often learn that acting dependent is a good way to get their teachers' attention, whereas boys learn that independent or aggressive behavior works better (Serbin, 1980). Research also shows that elementary school boys are much more likely to receive praise, criticism, and/or remedial help from their teachers than are elementary school girls (Sadker & Sadker, 1985).

Unfortunately, school textbooks have also tended to perpetuate gender-role stereotypes. Two major investigations of children's textbooks conducted in the early 1970s found that girls were typically depicted as domestic, dependent, fearful, unambitious, and not very successful or clever. In contrast, boys were brave, strong, independent, ambitious, very active (even aggressive), successful, and in charge of their fates (Saario et al., 1973; Women on Words and Images, 1972).

In recent years, textbook publishers have begun to make an effort to avoid gender stereotypes. For example, one study reported that men played the dominant roles in about two out of every three stories in American reading texts in the early 1980s, in contrast with approximately four out of every five stories in the early 1970s (Britton & Lumpkin, 1984). But textbooks — like the culture they represent — are still far from completely rid of stereotyped gender roles.

Gender-Role Stereotypes via Television. Many children regularly spend long hours in front of the TV, and it would hardly be surprising to discover that television portrayals of men and women influence their learning of gender-role behaviors. Television is often quite blatant in depicting stereotyped gender roles. In a major investigation during the 1970s, commercials were found to depict men as authoritative sources on most topics (McArthur & Reski, 1975). More recent research revealed that men continued to dominate television commercials in the 1980s (Breth & Cantor, 1988). An earlier study of prime-time shows also found that women were commonly portrayed as seductive sex objects who were incompetent, domestically inclined, passive, and unintelligent. In contrast, men were typically shown as competent, intelligent, brave, adventurous, active, and in charge (Women on Words and Images, 1975).

The prime-time TV show "Murphy Brown," with its portrayal of a woman as an assertive and independent person, illustrates a shift away from traditional gender-role stereotyping.

Recent years have witnessed a dramatic change in prime-time television, characterized by an increased propensity to portray women in lead roles as active, assertive, independent, and effective. At the time of this writing, some of television's hottest series feature women in central roles — programs such as "Murphy Brown," "L.A. Law," "Designing Women," "Murder, She Wrote," "Who's the Boss?" and "The Golden Girls." This shift toward powerful women on television reflects in large part a demographic shift in which "female viewers have seized control of the prime-time dial" (Waters & Huck, 1989, p. 48).

Market research also suggests that products advertised on television are more likely to be purchased by women than men. Hence, the increased presence of women on television may have more to do with ratings and product marketing than with efforts to reverse the negative effects of traditional gender-role stereotypes. A recent study by the Women, Men and Media Project, under the direction of Betty Friedan, revealed that men continue to dominate television news, which suggests that gender-role stereotyping is still characteristic in this segment of the media. Friedan and her associates found that women reported fewer stories in 1990 than they did in 1989, and that men accounted for 84% of the newsmakers interviewed for television news.

We see then that family and friends, schools and textbooks, television, and other media that we haven't discussed (movies, trade books, newspapers and magazines, popular music, advertising billboards, and so forth) frequently help develop and reinforce traditional gender-role assumptions and behaviors within our lives. We are all affected by gender-role conditioning to some degree, and we might discuss at great length how this process discourages development of the full range of human potential in each of us. However, this is a text dealing with our sexuality, so it is the impact of gender-role conditioning on this aspect of our lives that we examine in greater detail in the following section.

What are some ways in which gender-role expectations and stereotypes have influenced your views of sexuality and the manner in which you relate intimately to others? Pause for a moment to consider this before reading on.

The Impact of Gender Roles on Our Sexuality

Gender-role expectations exert a profound impact on our sexuality. Our beliefs about males and females, together with our assumptions about what constitutes appropriate behaviors for each, may affect many aspects of sexual experience. Our assessment of ourselves as sexual beings, the expectations we have for intimate relationships, our perception of the quality of such experiences, and the responses of others to our sexuality may all be significantly influenced by our identification as male or female.

In the following pages, we examine some of the potential effects of our gender-role assumptions on relations between the sexes. However, we do not mean to imply that only heterosexual couples are limited by these assumptions. Gender-role stereotypes may affect people regardless of their sexual orientation; however, homosexual couples may be affected somewhat differently by them. For example, problems of initiating sexual activity may be particularly pronounced for a lesbian couple, both of whom have been socialized not to initiate, whereas a male homosexual couple may have trouble establishing an emotional bond in their relationship because both partners have probably been socialized to hide their feelings.

Women as Undersexed, Men as Oversexed. A long-standing, slow-to-die assumption in many societies is the mistaken belief that women are inherently less sexually inclined than men. Such gender stereotypes may result in women being subjected to years of negative socialization during which they are taught to suppress or deny their natural sexual feelings. Legions of women have been told by parents, peers, and books that sex is something a woman engages in to please a man, preferably her husband. A related gender assumption pervasive in our society is the onerous view that "normal women" do not enjoy sex as much as men.

Although these stereotypes are beginning to fade as people strive to throw off some of the behavior constraints of generations of misguided socialization, many women are still burdened by such views. How can a woman express interest in being sexual or actively seek her own pleasure if she is laboring under the mistaken assumption that women are not supposed to have sexual needs? Some women, believing that it is not appropriate to be easily aroused sexually, may direct their energies to blocking or hiding these normal responses. Some people adhere to these stereotypes so rigidly that they believe any woman who openly expresses sexual interest or responds sexually is "easy," "sleazy," or a "slut." However, men who manifest similar behavior may be characterized as "studs," "casanovas," or "playboys," terms that are often meant to be ego enhancing rather than demeaning.

Males may be harmed by being stereotyped as supersexual. A man who is not instantly aroused by a person he perceives as attractive and/or available may feel somehow inadequate. After all, are not all men supposed to be instantly eager when confronted with a sexual opportunity? We believe that such an assumption is demeaning and reduces men to insensitive machines that respond instantly when the correct button is pushed. Male students in our classes frequently express their frustration and ambivalence over this issue. The following account is typical of these observations:

When I take a woman out for the first time, I am often confused over how the sex issue should be handled. I feel pressured to make a move, even when I am not all that inclined to hop into

the sack. Isn't this what women expect? If I don't even try, they may think there is something wrong with me. I almost feel like I would have to explain myself if I acted uninterested in having sex. Usually it's just easier to make the move and let them decide what they want to do with it. (Authors' files)

Clearly, this man believes he is expected to pursue sex, even when he doesn't want to, as part of his masculine role. This stereotypical view of men as the initiators of sex in developing relationships can be distressing for both sexes, as we see in the next section.

Men as Initiators, Women as Recipients. In our society men traditionally initiate intimate relationships, from the opening invitation for an evening out to the first overture toward sexual activity. As the following comments expressed by men during small-group discussions reveal, this can make males feel burdened and pressured:

Women should experience how anxiety-provoking it can be to provide an invitation with the ever-present potential of being turned down. (Authors' files)

I feel that every woman I date expects me to put the move on her. (Authors' files)

During lovemaking my wife usually expects me to make all the initial moves. Sometimes I wish I could just lie back and be taken over sexually instead of being the one who must orchestrate the whole thing. (Authors' files)

This last comment reflects a concern voiced by many of our male students and clients. Men who grow up being socialized to be active, assertive, and even aggressive are usually accustomed to being in control in most situations. It may be very difficult to relinquish this role in the bedroom. Thus, even though a man may fantasize about being taken over sexually, actually having such an experience can be stressful.

Even in established relationships, men are frequently expected to initiate each sexual encounter. This may result in sex becoming more of a duty than a pleasure.

My wife never initiates sex. It is always up to me. It's almost like making decisions about sex has become my job in the relationship. I wish she would hustle my body for a change. Maybe then sex would be a little more unpredictable and exciting for me. (Authors' files)

A woman who feels compelled to accept the female role of passivity may have a very difficult time initiating sex. It could be even harder for her to assume an active role during the sexual activity. Many women are frustrated, regretful, and understandably angry that such cultural expectations are so deeply ingrained within our society. The following comments, expressed by women talking together, reflect some of these thoughts:

It has been my experience that men may say they want women to be more assertive, but when we take the initiative they frequently act shocked, put off, or threatened. (Authors' files)

I like to ask men out, and have often done so. But it's frustrating when many of the men I ask out automatically assume that I want to jump in bed with them just because I take the initiative to make a date. (Authors' files)

It is hard for me to let my man know what I like during lovemaking. After all, he is supposed to know, isn't he? If I tell him, it's like I am usurping his role as the all-knowing one. (Authors' files)

The last comment relates to another common gender myth about sexual functioning—the notion that men are more knowledgeable and better able than women to direct a sexual encounter.

Men as "Sexperts." Considering that gender-role socialization conditions males to be competent leaders and females to be not-so-competent followers, is it any wonder that men are expected to act as experts in sexual matters? Men are not the only ones who see themselves as "sexperts"; women, in fact, may coerce them into playing the expert role by subscribing to this mistaken notion. In one study, roughly half the women questioned believed that a "real man" should be skilled in bed (Tavris, 1977). Some men enjoy being cast as "teacher" or "mentor." However, others may feel quite burdened by the need to play the expert and thus, by implication, to be responsible for the outcome of sexual sharing. As one man states:

Sometimes sex is more like work than fun. I have to make all the decisions—when and where we are going to have sex and what we are going to do together. It's my responsibility to make sure it works out good for both of us. This can put a lot of pressure on me and it gets real tiring always having to run the show. It would be nice to have someone else call the shots for a change. Only it has been my experience that women are real reluctant to take the lead. (Authors' files)

Fortunately, some of these destructive patterns are showing signs of eroding. Many of our male students speak with a sense of delight and relief about their sexual encounters with women who initiate sex, play an active role during lovemaking, and assume responsibility for their own pleasure. In recent years women too have seemed more inclined to view men as sexual equals rather than all-knowing experts.

Women as Controllers, Men as Movers. Many women grow up believing that men always have sex on their minds. For such a woman, it may be a logical next step to become the controller of what takes place during sexual interaction. By this we do not mean actively initiating certain activities—she sees that as the prerogative of men, the movers. Rather, a woman may see her role as controlling her male partner's rampant lust by making certain he does not coerce her into unacceptable activities. Thus, instead of enjoying how good it feels to have her breasts caressed, she may concentrate her attention on how to keep his hand off her genitals. This concern with control may be particularly pronounced during the adolescent dating years. It is not surprising that a woman who spends a great deal of time and energy regulating sexual intimacy to preserve her "honor" (something else she learns from gender-role conditioning) may have difficulty experiencing sexual feelings when she finally allows herself to relinquish her controlling role.

Conversely, men are often conditioned to see women as sexual challenges and to go as far as they can during sexual encounters. They too may have difficulty appreciating the good feelings of being close to and touching someone when all they are thinking about is what they will do next. Men who routinely experience this pattern may have a hard time relinquishing the mover role and being receptive rather than active during sexual interaction. They may be confused or even threatened by a woman who switches roles from controller to active initiator.

Men as Unemotional and Strong, Women as Nurturing and Supportive. Perhaps one of the most undesirable of all gender-role stereotypes is the notion that being emotionally expressive, tender, and nurturing is appropriate only for women. We have already seen that men are often socialized to be unemotional (Mosher & Tomkins, 1988). This conditioning can make it exceedingly difficult for a man to develop emotionally satisfying relationships. A man who is trying to appear strong may find it difficult to express vulnerability, deep feelings, and doubts. In such a situation, it can be very hard to share intimately with another person.

For example, a man who accepts the assumption of nonemotionality may approach sex as a purely physical act during which expressions of feelings have no place. This results in a limited kind of experience that can leave both parties feeling dissatisfied. Women often have a negative reaction when they encounter this characteristic in men because women tend to place great importance on openness and willingness to express feelings in a relationship. However, we need to remember that many men must struggle against a lifetime of "macho" conditioning when they try to express long-suppressed emotions. For some, even an expression of tenderness may be an exceedingly difficult break from the tough-guy image. Women, on the other hand, may grow tired of their role as nurturers, particularly when their efforts are greeted with little or no reciprocity. Tenderness and supportiveness can dwindle rapidly unless fueled by similar offerings from those for whom we care.

We have discussed how strict adherence to traditional gender roles may limit and restrict the ways we express our sexuality. These cultural legacies may often be expressed more subtly today than in the past, but rigid gender-role expectations linger on, inhibiting our growth as multidimensional people and our capacity to be fully ourselves with others. Also, while many people are breaking away from stereotyped gender roles and learning to accept and express themselves more fully, we cannot underestimate the extent of gender-role learning that occurs in our society. Images like the photos on the next two pages underscore this point; they will probably cause most readers to do at least a slight double take.

There is growing evidence, however, that many people are now striving to integrate both masculine and feminine behaviors into their lifestyles. This trend, often referred to as androgyny, is the focus of the final section in this chapter.

Transcending Gender Roles: Androgyny

The word **androgyny** (an-DRAW-jin-ē), meaning "having characteristics of both sexes," is derived from the Greek roots *andr,* meaning man, and *gynē,* meaning woman. The term is used to describe flexibility in gender role. Androgynous individuals are those who have integrated aspects of masculinity and femininity into their personalities and behavior. Androgyny offers the option of expressing whatever behavior seems appropriate in a given situation instead of limiting responses to those considered gender-appropriate. Thus, androgynous men and women might be assertive on the job but nurturing with friends, family members, and lovers. Many men and women possess characteristics consistent with traditional gender assumptions but also have interests and behavioral tendencies typically ascribed to the other sex. Actually, people may range from being very masculine or feminine to being *both* masculine and feminine — that is, androgynous.

Many individuals are now
pursuing inclinations and
expressing aspects of
themselves previously
discouraged by stereotypic
gender roles.

A social psychologist, Sandra Bem (1974), developed a paper-and-pencil inventory for measuring the degree to which individuals are identified with masculine or feminine behaviors or a combination thereof. Other devices for measuring masculine, feminine, or androgynous identifications have been developed since Bem's pioneering work (Spence & Helmreich, 1978). Armed with these devices for measuring androgyny, a number of researchers have investigated how androgynous individuals compare with strongly gender-typed people.

A number of studies indicate that androgynous people are more flexible in their behaviors, less limited by rigid gender-role assumptions, have higher levels of self-esteem, and exhibit more social competence and motivation to achieve than do people who are strongly gender-typed or those who score low in both areas (Bem, 1979 & 1980; Bem & Lenney, 1976; Flaherty & Dusek, 1980; Lott, 1987; O'Connor et al., 1978; Spence & Helmreich, 1978). Research also demonstrates that masculine and androgynous people of both sexes are more independent and less likely to have their opinions swayed than are individuals who are strongly identified with the feminine role (Bem, 1975). In fact, both androgyny and high masculinity appear to be adaptive for both sexes at all ages (Sinnott, 1986). However, feminine and androgynous people of both sexes appear to be significantly more nurturing than are those who adhere to the masculine role (Bem et al., 1976).

There are indications that we need to be cautious about concluding that androgyny is an ideal state, free of potential problems. One study found that masculine-typed males demonstrated better overall emotional adjustment than

People who integrate aspects of masculinity and femininity into their lifestyles can move beyond traditional gender roles.

androgynous males (Jones et al., 1978). A study of college professors in the early stages of their careers found that androgynous individuals exhibited greater personal satisfaction but more job-related stress than those who were strongly gender-typed (Rotheram & Weiner, 1983). In a large sample of college students, the presence of masculine personality characteristics was more closely associated with being versatile and adaptable than was the trait of androgyny (Lee & Scheurer, 1983). Clearly, more information is necessary for a complete picture of the impact of androgyny on personal adjustment and satisfaction.

What are the implications of androgyny for sexual behavior? Give this some thought before reading on.

There is evidence that androgynous individuals, both male and female, have more positive attitudes toward sexuality than those who are traditionally gender-typed (Walfish & Myerson, 1980). Androgynous people also appear to be more tolerant and less likely to judge or criticize the sexual behaviors of others (Garcia, 1982). Studies have found that androgynous women are more orgasmic and experience more sexual satisfaction than do feminine-typed women (Kimlicka et al., 1983; Radlove, 1983). However, two separate investigations revealed that masculine males were significantly more comfortable with sex than were androgynous females, indicating that biological sex may still exert a stronger effect than gender typing (Allgeier, 1981; Walfish & Myerson, 1980).

Our own guess is that androgynous people tend to be flexible and comfortable in their sexuality. We would expect such people, whether men or women, to have great capacity to enjoy both the emotional and the physical aspects of sexual intimacy. Androgynous lovers are probably comfortable both initiating and responding to invitations for sexual sharing, and they are probably not significantly limited by preconceived notions of who must do what — and how — during their lovemaking.

Research on androgyny continues, and we certainly have good reasons to be cautious about an unequivocally enthusiastic endorsement of this behavioral style. Nevertheless, most of the evidence thus far collected suggests that people who are able to transcend traditional gender roles may be able to function more comfortably and effectively in a wider range of situations. Androgynous individuals can select from a broad repertoire of feminine and masculine behaviors. They may choose to be independent, assertive, nurturing, or tender, based not on gender-role norms but rather on what provides them and others optimum personal satisfaction in a given situation.

Summary

Male and Female, Masculine and Feminine

The processes whereby our maleness and femaleness are determined and the manner in which they influence our behavior, sexual and otherwise, are highly complex.

Sex refers to our biological maleness or femaleness as reflected in various physical attributes (chromosomes, reproductive organs, genitals, and so forth).

Gender refers to the social concomitants of sex, or, in other words, our masculinity or femininity. Our ideas of masculinity and femininity involve gender assumptions — assumptions about behavior based on a person's sex.

Gender identity is a term used to describe our personal, subjective sense that we are male or female, masculine or feminine.

Gender role refers to a collection of attitudes and behaviors considered normal and appropriate in a specific culture for people of a particular sex.

Gender roles establish sex-related behavioral expectations, which are culturally defined and therefore vary from society to society and era to era.

Gender-Identity Formation

Research efforts to isolate the many biological factors that influence a person's gender identity have resulted in the identification of six biological categories, or levels: chromosomal sex, gonadal sex, hormonal sex, sex of the internal reproductive structures, sex of the external genitals, and sex differentiation of the brain.

Under normal conditions these biological variables interact harmoniously to determine our biological sex. However, errors may occur at any of the six levels. The resulting abnormalities in the development of a person's biological sex may seriously complicate acquisition of a gender identity.

The social-learning interpretation of gender-identity formation suggests that our identification with either masculine or feminine roles results primarily from the social and cultural models and influences to which we are exposed.

Most contemporary theorists embrace an interactional model in which gender identity is seen as a result of a complex interplay of biological and social-learning factors.

Transsexualism is a special case of gender-identity difficulty in which a person's gender identity is different from his or her biological sex. The scientific community has not reached a consensus about the causes and best treatment of this condition. However, some transsexuals have changed their bodies to match their identities by means of hormone treatments and surgery.

Gender Roles

Widely accepted gender-role assumptions may begin to function as stereotypes, which are notions about what people are like based not on their individuality but on their inclusion in a general category such as age or sex.

There are many common gender-based stereotypes in our society that may encourage us to prejudge others and restrict our opportunities.

Socialization refers to the process whereby society conveys its behavioral expectations to us. Parents, peers, schools, textbooks, and television all act as agents in the socialization of gender roles.

Gender-role expectations exert a profound impact on our sexuality. Our assessment of ourselves as sexual beings, the expectations we have for intimate relationships, our perception of the quality of such experiences, and the responses of others to our sexuality may all be significantly influenced by our own perceptions of our gender roles.

Androgynous individuals are people who have moved beyond traditional gender roles by integrating aspects of masculinity and femininity into their lifestyles.

⤳ *Thought Provokers* ⤳

1. We have seen that gender-identity formation is influenced by both biological and social-learning factors. Do you think the evidence more strongly supports one or the other as the major contributor to gender-identity formation? Why or why not?

2. In exploring the origins of your own gender identity, do you believe that you were socialized to be strongly gender-typed, or were you raised in a manner supporting androgynous behavior? Do you believe these socialization experiences have had any impact on how you feel about masculinity and femininity, and your sexual attitudes and behaviors?

3. Which gender-role assumptions have had the least impact on your sexuality? The greatest impact? Have you ever had a relationship in which any of these assumptions became a significant issue?

Suggested Readings

Cook, Ellen (1985). *Psychological Androgyny.* New York: Pergamon Press. An excellent review of the pertinent androgyny research literature. Also provides relevant practical information about androgynous lifestyles.

Doyle, James (1983). *The Male Experience.* Dubuque, Iowa: William C. Brown. A relatively current and comprehensive summary of what is known about men and male roles in American society.

Gilligan, Carol (1982). *In a Different Voice.* Cambridge, Mass.: Harvard University Press. An important, provocative work presenting the thesis that in this society men see the world in terms of their autonomy and are threatened by intimacy, whereas women view the world in terms of relationships and connectedness and are threatened by isolation.

Hurley, Timothy (1984). "Constitutional Implications of Sex-Change Operations." *The Journal of Legal Medicine.* Volume 5, 633–664. A comprehensive article that provides an illuminating discussion of the legal issues involved in sex-reassignment surgery.

Hyde, Janet (1991). *Half the Human Experience: The Psychology of Women* (4th ed.). Lexington, Mass.: D. C. Heath. An excellent summary of theories and research dealing with the psychology of women.

Kelly, Kathryn (Ed.) (1987). *Females, Males, and Sexuality: Theories and Research.* Albany, N.Y.: State University of New York Press. A superb collection of scholarly articles that reduces to an understandable level the complex and broad array of material dealing with male and female similarities and differences.

Mead, Margaret (1963). *Sex and Temperament in Three Primitive Societies.* New York: Morrow. An eminent anthropologist's analysis of three societies in which male and female gender roles differ from those of North American society.

Money, John (1980). *Love and Love Sickness: The Science of Sex, Gender Difference, and Pair-Bonding.* Baltimore: Johns Hopkins Press. A complex and scholarly text that covers a broad range of topics in human sexuality, including some provocative concepts related to gender identity and gender role.

Money, John; and Ehrhardt, Anke (1972). *Man and Woman, Boy and Girl.* Baltimore: Johns Hopkins Press. An in-depth analysis of the psychosocial and biological factors that influence the development of gender identity. Must reading for anyone desiring a more thorough understanding of the processes of gender identity and gender role.

Morris, Jan (1974). *Conundrum.* New York: New American Library. A widely acclaimed personal account of the transsexual experience.

Reinisch, June; and Rosenblum, Leonard (Eds.) (1987). *Masculinity-Femininity: Basic Perspectives.* New York: Oxford University Press. A collection of articles, written by internationally renowned authors, that deal with sex and gender differences from seven distinct but interrelated perspectives: psychobiological, neuroscientific, evolutionary, behavior genetics, developmental, psychosocial, and cultural.

PART TWO

Biological Basis

There's the vulva, the vagina, and the jolly perineum,
There's the hymen which is sometimes found in brides,
There's the uterus, the clitoris, the ovum and the oviducts,
The ovaries and lord knows what besides—

Algernon Swinburne
"Protest by the Medical Profession" (1863)

CHAPTER 4

Female Sexual Anatomy and Physiology

Genital Self-Exam

The Vulva

Underlying Structures

Internal Structures

The Breasts

Menstruation

I had three children and was 45 years old before I ever really looked at my genitals. I was amazed at the delicate shapes and subtle colors. I'm sorry it took me so long to do this because I now feel more sure of myself sexually after becoming more acquainted with *me*. (Authors' files)

Many women are as unacquainted with their genitals as this woman was. However, gaining knowledge and understanding of her body can be an important aspect of a woman's sexual well-being. This chapter presents a detailed description of all female genital structures, external and internal. It is intended to be easy to use for reference, and we encourage women readers to do a self-exam as part of reading it. We begin with a discussion of the genital self-exam and the external structures, then discuss the underlying structures and the internal organs. The chapter closes with information about the breasts and menstruation.

Genital Self-Exam

We are born with curiosity about our bodies. In fact, physical self-awareness and exploration are important steps in a child's development. Unfortunately, many of us receive negative conditioning about the sexual parts of our bodies from earliest childhood. We learn to think of our genitals as "privates," "down there," not to be looked at, touched, or enjoyed. It is common for people to react with discomfort to the suggestion of a genital self-exam.

The following paragraphs describe a self-exploration exercise designed to help you become more aware of your genitals. Some readers may choose to read about the exercise but not do it. Others may wish to try some or all of the steps. If you choose to do the exploration, you may experience a variety of feelings. Some people feel selfish for spending time on themselves. You may find it difficult to remain focused on the experience instead of thinking about daily concerns. The exercise may be enjoyable for some people and not for others. Primarily, it provides an opportunity to learn about yourself — your body and your feelings.

The exercise serves another purpose as well. Besides helping us feel more comfortable with our anatomy and sexuality, periodic self-examinations, particularly of the genitals, can augment routine medical care. For this reason, we have included other specific suggestions for self-exams throughout the text. For self-examinations to be most effective, do them regularly at least once a month: people who know what is normal for their own bodies can often detect small changes and seek medical attention promptly. Problems usually require less extensive treatment when they are detected early. If you discover any changes, consult a health practitioner immediately. **Gynecology** (gī'-na-KOL-ō-jē) is the medical specialty for female sexual and reproductive anatomy.

To begin the examination, look at your genitals thoroughly. Use a hand mirror, perhaps in combination with a full-length mirror, to look at them from different angles and postures — standing, sitting, lying down (see Figure 4.1). As you are looking, try to become aware of whatever feelings you have about your genital anatomy. You may find it helpful to draw a picture of your genitals and label the parts (identified in Figure 4.2). All women have the same parts, but the shades of color, shapes, and textures vary from woman to woman.

Besides examining yourself visually, use your fingers to explore the various surfaces of your genitals. Focus on the sensations produced by the different kinds of touching. Note which areas are most sensitive and how the nature of stimu-

FIGURE 4.1

Routine self-examination is an aspect of preventive health care.

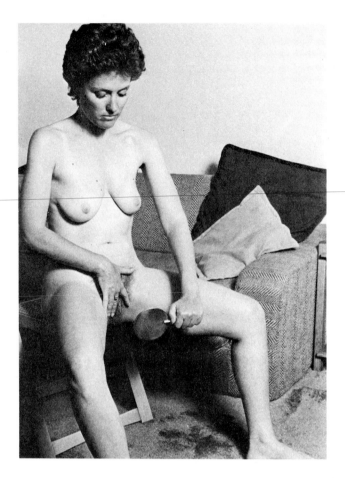

lation may vary from place to place. The primary purpose of doing this exercise is to explore, not to become sexually aroused. However, if you do become sexually excited during this self-exploration, you may be able to notice changes in the sensitivity of different skin areas that occur with arousal.

Women have different kinds of reactions to looking at their vulvas:

I don't find it to be an attractive part of my body. I wouldn't go as far as to call it ugly. I think it would be easier to accept if it was something you weren't taught to hide and think was dirty, but I've never been able to understand why men find the vulva so intriguing. (Authors' files)

I think it looks very sensuous; the tissues look soft and tender. I was told by a previous partner that my vulva was very beautiful. His comment made me feel good about my body. (Authors' files)

The Vulva

The **vulva** encompasses all female external genital structures — the hair, the folds of skin, and the urinary and vaginal openings. *Vulva* is the term we use most frequently in this text to refer to the external genitals of the female. For reference, see Figure 4.2.

F I G U R E 4.2

The structures and variations of the vulva: (a) external structures and (b)–(d) different shapes. There are many normal variations of external female genitals.

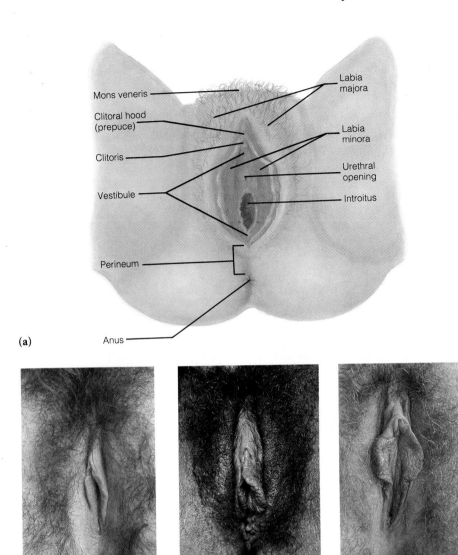

(a)

(b)   (c)   (d)

The appearance of the vulva, which varies from person to person (Gardner, 1992), has been likened to that of certain flowers, seashells, and other forms found in nature. Vulvalike shapes have been used in artwork, including "The Dinner Party" by Judy Chicago. This work consists of 39 ceramic plates, many of which have vulval shapes, representing significant women in history.

The Mons Veneris

Translated from Latin, **mons veneris** means "the mound of Venus." Venus was the Roman goddess of love and beauty. The mons veneris, or *mons*, is the area covering the pubic bone. It consists of pads of fatty tissue between the bone and

Two examples of the plates in Judy Chicago's "The Dinner Party," an exhibit symbolizing women in history. On the left is the Georgia O'Keeffe plate and on the right, the Emily Dickinson plate.

 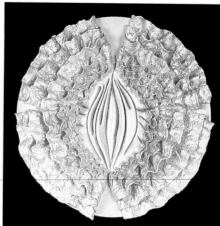

the skin. Touch and pressure on the mons can be sexually pleasurable, due to the presence of numerous nerve endings.

At puberty the mons becomes covered with hair that varies in color, texture, and thickness from woman to woman. Sometimes women are concerned about these differences:

I always felt uncomfortable in college physical education classes because I had very thick, dark pubic hair, more so than most other women. One day my best friend and I were talking and she mentioned that she felt self-conscious in the showers after P.E. class because her pubic hair was light-colored and sparse. I told her my concerns. We laughed and both decided to stop worrying about it. (Authors' files)

During sexual arousal the scent that accompanies vaginal secretions is held by the pubic hair and can add to sensory erotic pleasure.

The Labia Majora

The **labia majora** (LĀ-bē-a ma-JO-ra), or outer lips, extend downward from the mons on each side of the vulva. They begin next to the thigh and extend inward, surrounding the labia minora and the urethral and vaginal openings. Next to the thigh, the outer lips are covered with pubic hair; their inner parts, next to the labia minora, are hairless. The skin of the labia majora is usually darker than the skin of the thighs. The nerve endings and underlying fatty tissue are similar to those in the mons.

The Labia Minora

The **labia minora** (LĀ-bē-a min-OR-a), or inner lips, are located within the outer lips and often protrude between them. The inner lips are hairless folds of skin that join at the **prepuce** (PRĒ-poos), or clitoral hood, and extend downward past the urinary and vaginal openings. They contain sweat and oil glands, extensive blood vessels, and nerve endings. They also vary considerably in size, shape, and color from woman to woman, as Figure 4.2 shows. During pregnancy, the inner lips

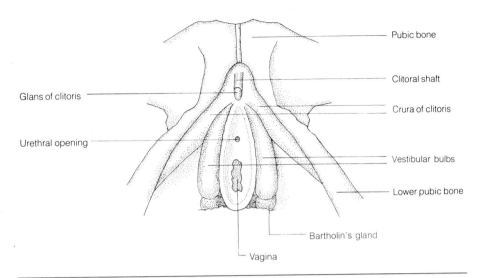

The underlying structures of the vulva.

become darker in color. In the Hottentot culture of Africa, pendulous labia are considered a sign of beauty, and women start pulling on them early in childhood in an effort to increase their size.

The Clitoris

The **clitoris** (KLIT-o-ris) comprises the external **shaft** and **glans** and the internal **crura** (KROO-ra). The shaft and glans are located just below the mons area, where the inner lips converge. They are covered by the clitoral hood, or prepuce. Genital secretions, skin cells, and bacteria combine to form **smegma,** which may accumulate under the hood and occasionally form lumps and cause pain during sexual arousal or activity. Smegma can be prevented from collecting in this area by drawing back the hood when washing the vulva. If the smegma is already formed, a health care practitioner can remove it.

If you look at Figure 4.3, which shows the clitoris with the hood removed, you can see that the glans is supported by the shaft. The shaft can be felt and its shape seen through the hood. It contains two small spongy structures called the **cavernous bodies.** These become the crura (internal leglike stalks) as they extend into the pelvic cavity. The glans is often not visible under the clitoral hood, but it can be seen if a woman gently parts the labia minora and retracts the hood. The glans looks smooth, rounded, and slightly translucent.

How important is the clitoris in sexual arousal? Take a few moments to consider what you already know about the role of the clitoris in sexual arousal. Think about what you have read, heard, and experienced personally. See how your ideas match the information that follows.

Initially, it may be easier for a woman to locate her clitoris by touch rather than sight because of its sensitive nerve endings and small size. The external part of the clitoris, although tiny, has about the same number of nerve endings as the head of the penis. The clitoral glans in particular is highly sensitive, and women usually stimulate this area with the hood covering it to avoid direct stimulation, which may be too intense. Research into female masturbation patterns has produced findings in keeping with the physiological data about the location and concentrations of nerve endings. Clitoral stimulation, not vaginal insertion, is the most common way women achieve arousal and orgasm when masturbating themselves.

Although other sexual organs have additional functions in reproduction or the elimination of wastes, the only purpose of the clitoris is sexual arousal. The size, shape, and position of the clitoris varies from woman to woman. Although women are sometimes concerned that their clitorises are too small or too large, these normal differences have no known relation to sexual arousal and functioning (Money, 1970).

A good deal of controversy has surrounded the role of the clitoris in sexual arousal and orgasm. Despite long-existing scientific knowledge about the highly concentrated nerve endings in the clitoris, the erroneous belief has persisted that vaginal rather than clitoral stimulation is — or should be — exclusively responsible for female sexual arousal and orgasm. However, there are relatively few nerve endings in the vagina as compared with the clitoris, and the clitoris is more sensitive to touch than the vagina (Schultz et al., 1989). Some nerve endings respond to light touch in the outer third of the vagina, but almost none are present in the inner two-thirds. (This is why women do not feel tampons or diaphragms when they are correctly in place in the vagina.) Nevertheless, many women experience erotic feelings in the vagina and find the internal pressure and stretching sensations during manual stimulation or intercourse highly pleasurable. Some experience more intense arousal from vaginal than from clitoral stimulation. As more and more scientific research is done, a wider range of individual variation becomes apparent (Alzate, 1985).

The Vestibule

The **vestibule** (VES-ti-byool) is the area of the vulva inside the labia minora. It is rich in blood vessels and nerve endings, and its tissues are sensitive to touch. (In architectural terminology, the word *vestibule* refers to the entryway of a house.) Both the urinary and the vaginal openings are located within the vestibule.

The Urethral Opening

Urine collected in the bladder passes out of a woman's body through the urethral opening. The **urethra** (yoo-RĒ-thra) is the short tube connecting the bladder to the urinary opening, which is located between the clitoris and the vaginal opening.

Urinary Tract Infections.   Women often develop infections of the *urinary tract,* the organ system that includes the urethra, bladder, and kidneys. If the infection progresses all the way to the kidneys, severe illness can result. About one out of every five women will have a urinary tract infection in her lifetime; many will have more than one (American College of Obstetricians and Gynecologists, 1984a).

Urinary tract infections are usually caused by bacteria from the rectum or vagina, or infectious agents from a partner's sexual organs, that enter the urethral

OTHER TIMES, OTHER PLACES

Female Genital Mutilation

Some form of female genital mutilation has been practiced at some time in almost all parts of the world (including the United States, from 1890 through the late 1930s). Today it continues in many areas of Africa, the Middle East, and Asia (Lightfoot-Klein & Shaw, 1990). Women in these parts of the world undergo several types of genital mutilation. The simplest procedure, *circumcision,* consists of cutting off the clitoral hood. Another common practice is the removal of the clitoris itself, called *clitoridectomy.* In the most extreme practice, *genital infibulation,* the clitoris is entirely removed and the labia cut off. Then both sides of the vulva are scraped raw and stitched up (sometimes with thorns) so that they grow together, leaving only a small opening for urine and menstrual flow to pass through (Davies, 1992). Serious gynecological and obstetrical complications often arise from genital infibulation. Fetal death sometimes occurs because of difficult birth due to extensive vaginal scarring. It is esti-

mated that 84 million women and girls now living have undergone one of these mutilating "surgeries" (Hosken, 1989).

The main objective of genital mutilation is to ensure virginity before marriage. A Somalian grandmother states that infibulation "takes away nothing that she needs. If she does not have this done, she will become a harlot" (Harden, 1985a). Young girls are considered unmarriageable if they do not have the prescribed excision. Because marriage is the most important duty of a woman in these cultures, her future and her family's pride depend on upholding this tradition (Harden, 1985).

Besides the numerous and severe medical problems that arise from these procedures (shock, infections, urinary retention, chronic pelvic and urinary tract infections, cyst formation, menstrual pain, childbirth complications, and infertility), African and Arab physicians and health workers report widespread sexual problems among women who have

had clitoridectomies and infibulations. One physician reported that 80% of infibulated women he had examined over the years said they had never experienced any sexual pleasure. Another physician reported similar findings on women who had undergone clitoridectomies. In recent years there has been such an outcry over female genital mutilation, particularly from women in Western nations, that the United Nations has agreed in this case to suspend its policy of nonintervention in the cultural practices of individual nations. In 1980, the World Health Organization (WHO) and the United Nations Children's Fund (UNICEF) jointly adopted a plan to encourage leaders of nations where such practices occur to use their influence to bring them to an end. In 1990, the Organization of African Unity condemned traditional practices harmful to children. Unfortunately, the strength of cultural tradition in many societies remains difficult to overcome.

opening. Coitus is the most frequent means by which *pathogenic* (disease-causing) bacteria enter the urinary tract (Leiter, 1984). Bacteria can be massaged into the urethra by the thrusting motions of intercourse. Bladder infections often occur during periods of frequent intercourse with a new partner, and are therefore sometimes referred to as "honeymoon cystitis." Poor hygiene or wiping the genitals from back to front after defecation can also introduce infection-causing bacteria into the urethra.

Other factors, including diabetes, pregnancy, a history of childhood urinary tract infections, and being postmenopausal, increase a woman's likelihood of having a urinary tract infection. An improperly fitting diaphragm that presses on the opening of the bladder and prevents a woman from voiding completely can also cause such infections (Gillespie, 1984). Delaying urination can also lead to this problem: Repeatedly stretching the bladder muscle beyond its normal capacity (which is reached with the first urge to urinate) weakens the muscle so that it cannot expel all the urine; thus some urine remains in the bladder, increasing the risk of infection.

The symptoms of urinary tract infections are usually intensely uncomfortable and include a frequent need to urinate, a severe burning sensation when urinating, blood or pus in the urine, and sometimes lower pelvic pain. A conclusive diagnosis of a urinary tract infection requires laboratory analysis of a urine sample. Such an infection generally responds to short-term antibiotic treatment. A follow-up urine test is done after treatment to ensure that the infection has been cured.

Observing a few routine precautions may help women prevent urinary tract infections. Careful wiping from front to back after both urination and bowel movements helps keep bacteria away from the urethra. Washing the genital and rectal areas thoroughly each day, urinating as soon as you feel the urge, and having your health care practitioner recheck the fit of your diaphragm during your routine exam will also help protect against a urinary tract infection. For those who have frequent problems with such infections, washing before and after intercourse may help. A woman's sexual partner can also help by washing his or her hands and genitals before sexual contact; intercourse positions that cause less friction against the urethra may also help. Urinating immediately after intercourse helps wash out bacteria. Women can also use sterile, water-soluble lubricating jelly (not petroleum jelly) when vaginal lubrication is insufficient, because irritated tissue is more susceptible to infection. It can also be helpful to drink plenty of liquids, especially juices (such as cranberry juice) high in vitamin C, and to avoid substances like coffee, tea, and alcohol, which have an irritating effect on the bladder (Greenwood, 1989a).

The Introitus and the Hymen

The opening of the vagina is referred to as the **introitus** (in-TRŌ-i-tus). It is located between the urinary opening and the anus. Partially covering the introitus is a fold of tissue called the **hymen,** which is typically present at birth and usually remains intact until initial coitus (Kuhns & Arakawa, 1987). Occasionally, this tissue may be too thick to break easily during intercourse; it may then require a minor incision by a medical practitioner. In rare cases, the hymen completely covers the vaginal opening, and when the young woman begins to menstruate, this *imperforate hymen* causes the menstrual flow to collect inside the vagina. When this condition is discovered, a medical practitioner can open the hymen with an incision. Usually, the vaginal opening is partially open and flexible enough to insert tampons before the hymen has been broken. Although such cases have been rare, it is possible for a woman to become pregnant even if her hymen is still intact and she has not experienced penile penetration. If semen is placed on the labia minora, the sperm can swim from outside to inside the vagina and fertilize an ovum.

Although the hymen may serve to protect the vaginal tissues early in life, it has no other known function. Nevertheless, many societies, including our own, have placed great significance on its presence or absence. (Attitudes and behavior regarding virginity will be discussed in Chapter 13.) The following quote from a woman who was an adolescent in the 1950s illustrates the hymen's importance in our own society:

> The hymen obsessed everyone, though it was never called by its proper name. It was referred to as your "innocence," your "purity," your "goodness," your "maidenhead," your "mark," as in "mark of Cain," and your "shield." . . . We were told that "men

can tell" and warned not to wipe ourselves too hard, which led to untold confusion about the logistics of sexual congress. (King, 1976, p. 49)

In our society and many others, people have long believed that a woman's virginity can be proved by the pain and bleeding that may occur with initial coitus. This is not always true. Although pain or bleeding sometimes occur, the hymen can be partial, flexible, or thin enough for there to be no discomfort or bleeding; it may even remain intact after intercourse. One study found that 25% of women reported no pain with first intercourse, 40% reported moderate pain, and 33% severe pain. Women who experienced pain during first intercourse were younger than women who did not, had more conservative sexual values, more often had negative feelings about their partner and about intercourse with him, and more often had expected no pain (Weis, 1985).

If a woman manually stretches her hymen before initial intercourse, she may be able to minimize the discomfort that sometimes occurs. To do this, she first inserts a lubricated finger (using saliva or a sterile lubricant such as K-Y jelly) into the vaginal opening and presses downward toward the anus until she feels some stretching. After a few seconds, she releases the pressure and relaxes. This step is repeated several times. The next step is to insert two fingers into the vagina and stretch the sides of the vagina by *opening* the fingers. The downward stretching is repeated with two fingers as well.

The Perineum

The **perineum** (per'-a-NE-am) is the area of smooth skin between the vaginal opening and the anus (the sphincter through which bowel movements pass). The perineal tissue is endowed with nerve endings and is sensitive to the touch.

During childbirth, an incision called an *episiotomy* is sometimes made in the perineum to prevent the ragged tearing of tissues that may happen as the newborn passes through the birth canal. Many medical practitioners believe this incision is essential, but other health care specialists disagree. We will consider this issue in more detail in Chapter 12.

Underlying Structures

If the hair, skin, and fatty pads were removed from the vulva, several underlying structures could be seen (see Figure 4.3). The shaft of the clitoris would be visible, no longer concealed by the hood. Also detectable would be the crura, or roots, projecting inward from each side of the clitoral shaft. These bodies extend into the pelvic cavity to the bony pelvis, and they are part of the vast network of bulbs and vessels that engorge with blood during sexual arousal. The **vestibular** (ves-TIB-yoo-lar) **bulbs** alongside the vagina also fill with blood during sexual excitement, causing the vagina to increase in length and the vulvar area to become swollen. These bulbs are similar in structure and function to the spongy tissue in the penis that engorges during arousal and causes an erection.

Bartholin's glands on each side of the vaginal opening were once believed to be the source of vaginal lubrication during sexual arousal; however, they typically produce only a drop or two of fluid just prior to orgasm. The glands are usually

FIGURE 4.4

The underlying muscles of the vulva. These muscles can be strengthened using the Kegel exercises described in the text.

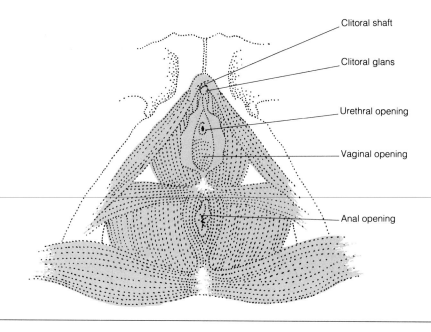

Clitoral shaft

Clitoral glans

Urethral opening

Vaginal opening

Anal opening

not noticeable, but sometimes the duct from the Bartholin's gland becomes clogged, and the fluid that is normally secreted remains inside and causes enlargement. If this occurs and the swelling does not subside within a few days, it is best to see a physician.

Besides the glands and network of vessels, a complex musculature underlies the genital area (see Figure 4.4). The *pelvic floor muscles* have a multidirectional design that allows the vaginal opening to expand greatly during childbirth and to close afterward.

The pelvic floor muscles contract involuntarily at orgasm; they also can be trained to contract voluntarily, through a series of exercises known as **Kegel** (KEG-al) **exercises.** These exercises were developed by Arnold Kegel in 1952 as a way of helping women regain control of urination after childbirth. It is common for postpartum women (women who have recently given birth) to lose urine when they cough or sneeze. This is due to the loss of muscle tone in the perineal area caused by excessive stretching and tearing of the muscles during childbirth. Not only are Kegel exercises effective in restoring muscle tone, but many women who do them regularly for about six weeks report an increase in sensation during intercourse, as well as a general increase in genital sensitivity. This seems to be the result of their increased awareness of their sex organs, as well as their improved muscle tone.

The steps for the Kegel exercises are as follows:

1. Locate the muscles surrounding the vagina. This can be done by stopping the flow of urine to feel which muscles contract. The muscles that control the flow of urine are the same muscles you contract during Kegel exercises.

2. Insert a finger into the opening of your vagina and contract the muscles you located in step 1. Feel them squeeze your finger.

3. Squeeze the same muscles for three seconds. Relax. Repeat.

4. Squeeze and release as rapidly as possible, 10 to 25 times. Repeat.

5. Imagine trying to suck something into your vagina. Hold for three seconds.

6. Push out as during a bowel movement, only with the vagina. Hold for three seconds.

7. Repeat steps 3, 5, and 6 ten times each and step 4 once. This exercise series should be done three times a day. (Adapted from Barbach, 1976, pp. 54–55.)

Internal Structures

Internal female sexual anatomy consists of the vagina, cervix, uterus, and ovaries. These are discussed in the following sections. Refer to Figure 4.5 for cross-section and front views of the female pelvis.

The Vagina

The **vagina** opens between the labia minora and extends into the body, angling upward toward the small of the back. Women who are unfamiliar with their anatomy may have a difficult time when they first try inserting tampons into the vagina:

No matter how hard I tried, I couldn't get a tampon in until I inserted a finger and realized that my vagina slanted backwards. I had been pushing straight up onto the upper wall. (Authors' files)

The nonaroused vagina is approximately 3–5 inches long. The walls form a flat tube. The analogy of a glove is often used to illustrate the vagina as a potential rather than actual space, with its walls able to expand enough to serve as a birth passage. In addition, the vagina changes in size and shape during sexual arousal, as we will discuss in Chapter 6.

The vagina contains three layers of tissue: mucous, muscle, and fibrous tissue. All these layers are richly endowed with blood vessels. The **mucosa** (myoo-KŌ-sa) is the layer of mucous membrane that a woman feels when she inserts a finger inside her vagina. The folded walls, or **rugae** (ROO-jē), feel soft, moist, and warm, resembling the inside of one's mouth. The walls normally produce secretions that help maintain the chemical balance of the vagina. During sexual arousal, a lubricating substance exudes through the mucosa.

Most of the second layer, composed of muscle tissue, is concentrated around the vaginal opening. Because of the concentration of musculature in the outer one-third and the expansive ability of the inner two-thirds of the vagina, a situation often develops that can be at best funny and at worst embarrassing. During headstands and certain yoga or coital positions with the pelvis elevated, gravity causes the inner two-thirds to expand and draws air into the vagina. The outer muscles tighten, and the trapped air is forced back out through the tightened muscles, creating a sound we usually associate with a different orifice. One student has suggested calling this phenomenon ''varting'' since the sound is similar to that of a fart (fortunately, there is no unpleasant smell). Varting occurs in gym classes and bedrooms across the nation and may be cause for great consternation. We

FIGURE 4.5

Internal female sexual anatomy: (a) cross-section side view of female internal structures; (b) front view of the internal organs. Parts of the ovaries, uterus, and vagina are shown cut away.

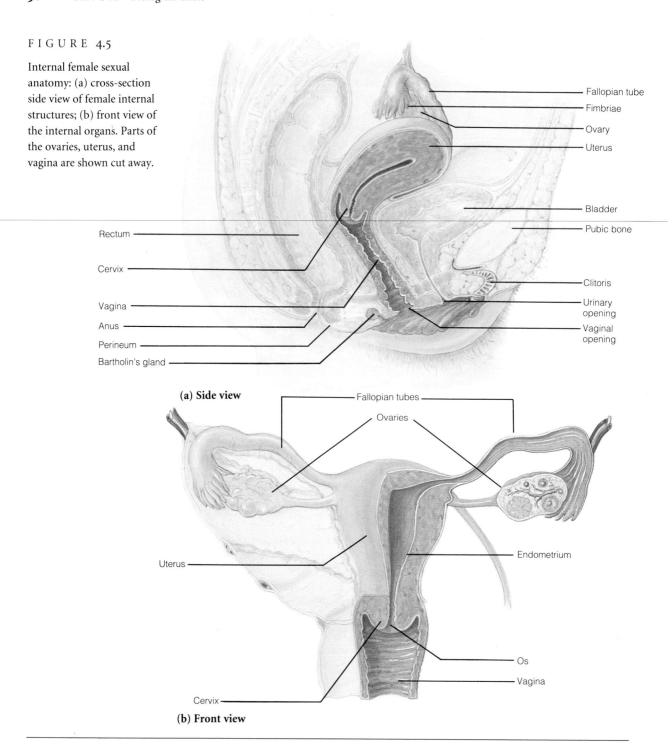

(a) **Side view**

(b) **Front view**

hope this discussion of varting will help people feel more at ease if and when it occurs.

I stopped taking gymnastics in high school because every time I did a nice tuck-roll out of a headstand, pppppppppttttt! It was just too embarrassing. (Authors' files)

When I have intercourse on my back with my legs on his shoulders, invariably my vagina fills with air. I just don't know what to do when those sounds start happening except to say, "I promise, it's not the real thing," and laugh. Only laughing just makes them louder. (Authors' files)

Surrounding the muscular layer is the innermost vaginal layer, composed of fibrous tissue. This layer aids in vaginal contraction and expansion and acts as connective tissue to other structures in the pelvic cavity.

In about 1 out of every 4000 to 5000 girls born, the vagina is absent. Congenital absence of the vagina is often not diagnosed until adolescence when menstruation does not occur. Typically, a vagina can be surgically constructed in these instances (Harnish, 1988).

Arousal and Vaginal Lubrication. So far in this chapter, we have described the parts of the female sexual anatomy, but we have said relatively little about how these structures function. Because lubrication is a unique feature of the vagina, the process is explained here. Other physiological aspects of female arousal will be discussed in Chapter 6.

During sexual arousal, a clear, slippery fluid begins to appear on the vaginal mucosa within 10–30 seconds after effective physical or psychological stimulation begins. In the past, both the cervix and Bartholin's glands were believed to be the source of this increased vaginal lubrication during sexual arousal. However, Masters and Johnson's research revealed that this lubrication is a result of **vasocongestion,** the pooling of blood in the pelvic area. During vasocongestion the extensive network of blood vessels in the tissues surrounding the vagina engorge with blood. Clear fluid seeps from the congested tissues to the inside of the vaginal walls to form the characteristic slippery coating of the sexually aroused vagina. Masters and Johnson's laboratory research firmly established vasocongestion as the source of vaginal lubrication: A clear, phallus-shaped camera was inserted into the vagina and filmed the internal changes.

Nature has designed the lubrication response of the human female to sexual arousal. What advantages does this physiological process provide? Take a moment to think about this before reading on.

Vaginal lubrication serves two functions. First, it enhances the possibility of conception by helping to alkalinize the normally acidic vaginal chemical balance. Sperm travel faster and survive longer in an alkaline environment than in an acidic one. (The seminal fluid of the male also helps alkalinize the vagina.) Second, vaginal lubrication can increase sexual enjoyment. During manual–genital stimulation, the slippery wetness can increase the sensuousness and pleasure of touching. During oral–genital sex, some women's partners enjoy the erotic scent and taste of the vaginal lubrication. During intercourse, vaginal lubrication makes the walls of the vagina slippery, which facilitates entry of the penis into the vagina. Lubrication also helps make the thrusting of intercourse pleasurable. Without adequate lubrication, entry of the penis into the vagina and subsequent thrusting can be very uncomfortable for the woman — and often for the man. Irritation and small tears of the vaginal tissue can result.

Individual females vary in the amount of vaginal lubrication that occurs during sexual arousal. Several factors can inhibit vaginal lubrication. Anxiety about oneself, one's partner, or the situation; the use of some drugs; and changes in hormone balance can all affect the vasocongestive response. Some women who take birth control pills find that vaginal lubrication is reduced. Many women experience a decrease in lubrication due to the hormonal changes after childbirth and following menopause. We will discuss each of these situations in more detail in later sections of the text.

There are several ways to remedy insufficient vaginal lubrication, depending on the source of the difficulty. Changing the anxiety-producing circumstances and engaging in effective stimulation are important. Saliva, K-Y jelly, lubricated condoms, or a nonirritating, water-soluble lotion can be used to provide additional lubrication. Occasionally, hormone treatment is necessary.

The Grafenberg Spot. The **Grafenberg spot** is an area located within the anterior (or front) wall of the vagina, about one centimeter from the surface and one-third to one-half the way in from the vaginal opening. It is reported to consist of a system of glands (Skene's glands) and ducts that surround the urethra (Heath, 1984). This area is believed to be the female counterpart to the male prostate gland, developed from the same embryonic tissue (Belzer, 1981; Heath, 1984).

The Grafenberg spot has generated considerable interest because of reports that some women experience sexual arousal, orgasm, and perhaps even an ejaculation of fluid when stimulated there (Darling et al., 1990). There is wide variation in response from woman to woman (Zaviacic et al., 1988a). We will discuss the role of the Grafenberg spot in female sexual response further in Chapter 6.

Vaginal Secretions and Chemical Balance of the Vagina. Both the vaginal walls and the cervix produce secretions that are white or yellowish in color. These secretions are normal and are a sign of vaginal health. They vary in appearance according to hormone-level changes during the menstrual cycle. (Keeping track of these variations is the basis for one method of birth control, discussed in Chapter 11.) The taste and scent of vaginal secretions may also vary with the time of a woman's cycle and her level of arousal. One study reports that men found vaginal secretion odors more pleasant during ovulation than during other times in the cycle (Doty et al., 1975).

The vagina's natural chemical and bacterial balance helps promote a healthy mucosa. The chemical balance is normally rather acid (pH 4.0 to 5.0).* A variety of factors can alter this balance and result in vaginal problems. Among these are too-frequent **douching** (rinsing out the inside of the vagina) and using feminine-hygiene sprays. Advertising has played on our cultural negativity about female sexual organs, turning misguided attempts to eradicate normal secretions and scents into an extremely profitable business. Women grow up hearing slogans such as "Unfortunately, the trickiest deodorant problem a girl has isn't under her pretty little arms," and "Our product eliminates the moist, uncomfortable feeling most women normally have just because they're women." However, douching is definitely *not* necessary for routine hygiene; and frequent douching can alter the natural chemical balance of the vagina (Aral et al., 1992; Gardner et al., 1991), thereby increasing susceptibility to infections. Feminine-hygiene sprays can cause irritation, allergic reactions, burns, infections, dermatitis of the thighs, and numerous other problems. Deodorant tampons are another example of a product women

---

*pH is a measure of acidity or alkalinity. A neutral substance (neither acid nor alkaline) has a pH of 7. A lower number means a substance is more acid; a higher number means more alkaline.

do not need: menstrual fluid has virtually no odor until it is outside the body. Regular bathing with a mild soap and washing between the folds of the vulva is all that is necessary for proper hygiene.

Vaginal Infections. When the natural balance of the vagina is disturbed or a non-native organism introduced, a vaginal infection, or **vaginitis** (vaj′-a-NI-tis), can result. Usually the woman herself first notices symptoms of vaginitis: irritation or itching of the vagina and vulva, unusual discharge, and sometimes a disagreeable odor. (An unpleasant odor can also be due to a forgotten tampon or diaphragm.) Some of the different types of vaginal infections are yeast infections, bacterial infections, and trichomoniasis. These are all discussed in detail in Chapter 19.

A number of factors increases a woman's susceptibility to vaginitis: the use of antibiotics, emotional stress, a diet high in carbohydrates, hormonal changes caused by pregnancy or birth control pills, chemical irritants, coitus without adequate lubrication, and heat and moisture retained by nylon underwear and pantyhose. One study found that women who wear pantyhose had three times more yeast infections than those who do not (Heidrich et al., 1984). Menstrual flow increases the alkalinity of the vagina, which promotes yeast growth in some women.

It is important for vaginitis to be treated and cured. Chronic irritation resulting from long-term infections may play a part in predisposing a woman to cervical cell changes that can lead to cancer. Over-the-counter treatments for yeast infections are now available. Some health care practitioners provide suggestions for nondrug treatment of vaginitis. The following suggestions may help prevent vaginitis from occurring in the first place (Solomini, 1991).

1. Eat a well-balanced diet low in sugar and refined carbohydrates.

2. Maintain general good health with adequate sleep, exercise, and emotional release.

3. Use good hygiene, including the following:

   a. Bathe regularly with mild soap.

   b. After urinating and having bowel movements, wipe from front to back, vulva to anus.

   c. Wear clean cotton underpants (nylon holds in heat and moisture that encourages bacterial growth).

   d. Avoid using feminine-hygiene sprays, colored toilet paper, bubble bath, and other people's washcloths or towels to wash or wipe your genitals.

   e. Ensure that your sexual partner's hands and genitals are clean before beginning sexual activity.

4. Be sure you have adequate lubrication before coitus: natural lubrication or a sterile, water-soluble lubricant such as K-Y jelly. Do not use petroleum-based lubricants (such as Vaseline), because they are not water-soluble and are likely to remain in the vagina and harbor bacteria (petroleum-based lubricants can also weaken and will eventually degrade latex condoms).

5. Use condoms if you or your partner are nonmonogamous.

6. Women who are prone to yeast infections after menstruation may find it helpful to douche with two tablespoons of white vinegar in a quart of warm water once the flow ceases.

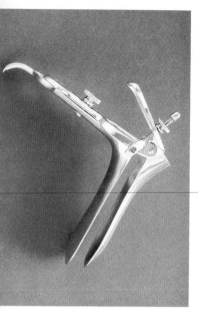

A speculum, like the one shown, is used to hold open the vaginal walls during an exam. They can also be purchased to use at home.

Self-Exams and Vaginal Health Care. A self-exam can sometimes help detect vaginal infection. The skin of the genital area may turn red instead of its usual pink, and this along with irritation is a sign that treatment may be necessary. Many health care practitioners use a mirror to show a woman the inside of her vagina during her regular exam, and some will teach her how to use the **speculum,** the instrument that holds the vaginal walls open. They may also give the woman a plastic speculum that she can use during vaginal self-exams at home.

The Cervix

The **cervix,** located at the back of the vagina, is the small end of the pear-shaped uterus (see Figure 4.5; see also Figure 12.1). The cervix contains mucus-secreting glands. Sperm pass through the vagina into the uterus through the **os,** the opening in the center of the cervix.

A woman can see her own cervix if she learns to insert a speculum into her vagina. She can also ask for a mirror when she has her pelvic exam. A woman can feel her own cervix by inserting one or two fingers into the vagina and reaching to the end of the canal. (Sometimes squatting and bearing down brings the cervix closer to the vaginal entrance.) The cervix feels somewhat like the end of a nose, firm and round in contrast to the soft vaginal walls.

The Pap Smear.   The **Pap smear,** a screening test for cervical cancer, is taken from the cervix. The vaginal walls are held open with a speculum, and a few cells are removed with a small wooden spatula; these cells are put on a slide and sent to a lab to be examined. The cells for a Pap smear are taken from the part of the cervix where long column-shaped cells called *columnar cells* meet flat-shaped cells called *squamous cells* (Jones, 1992). A Pap smear is not painful because there are so few nerve endings on the cervix.

The Pap smear is an essential part of a woman's routine preventive health care. Since its widespread use beginning in the 1950s, the death rate from cervical cancer has decreased by more than 70% (Given & Jones, 1992) yet remains the ninth most common cause of cancer death among women in the U.S. (Butterworth et al., 1992). Depending on a woman's individual situation and her health care provider's recommendation, she may have this test once every two years, every year, twice a year, or even more frequently. Pap tests are not 100% accurate in detecting cervical cancer (Ruffin & Van Noord, 1991). Therefore, more frequent tests increase the likelihood of discovering cancer.

When the results of a Pap smear indicate possible cancer cells, further tests are necessary before a conclusive diagnosis can be made. A *colposcopy* (an exam using a special microscope) and a tissue *biopsy* (surgical removal of a small piece of cervical tissue, which is then examined under a microscope) are two of the kinds of further testing that can be done (Miller et al., 1992; Pollack, 1991a).

There are several simple, highly effective, lifesaving treatments for cervical cancer. *Cryosurgery* (freezing of tissues) is one method of removing small numbers of cancerous cells from the surface of the cervix. Elimination of the malignant tissue by means of a biopsy is also often effective. In more severe cases, a woman needs to have a complete *hysterectomy* (surgical removal of the cervix and uterus), a procedure that will be discussed further in a later section.

Research indicates that women who have had genital warts (Pfenniger, 1992), have had a large number of sexual partners (Hellberg et al., 1983), had first coitus

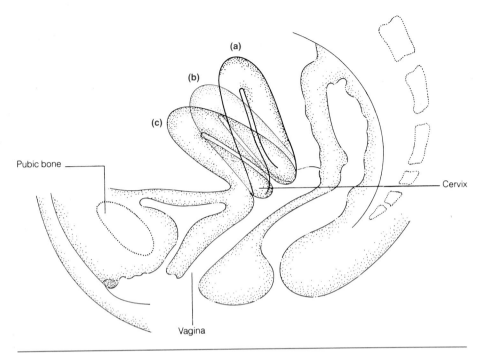

Pubic bone

Cervix

Vagina

FIGURE 4.6

Various positions of the uterus in the pelvic cavity: (a) retroflexed, (b) midline, and (c) anteflexed.

at an early age (Clarke et al., 1985), or have husbands at increased risk of cancer from occupational contact with toxic materials (Robinson, 1983) have an increased risk of developing cervical cancer. Women who smoke cigarettes or are exposed to the cigarette smoke of others also have increased rates of cervical cancer (Daling et al., 1992; Gram et al., 1992). In addition, the general incidence of cervical cancer has increased in recent years in women under the age of 35, including adolescents (Campion, 1992).

The Uterus

The **uterus** (YOO-te-rus), or womb, is a hollow, thick, pear-shaped organ, approximately 3 inches long and 2 inches wide in a *nulliparous* woman (one who has never had a child). It is somewhat larger after pregnancy. The *fundus* is the top area of the uterus, where the uterine walls are especially thick. The **myometrium** (mi′-o-MĒ-trē-um) consists of the longitudinal and circular muscle fibers that interweave like the fibers of a basket and enable the uterus to stretch during pregnancy and contract during labor and orgasm. The **perimetrium** (per-i-MĒ-trē-um) is a thin membrane that covers the myometrium and constitutes the external surface of the uterus. The uterus is suspended in the pelvic cavity by six ligaments and is capable of some movement. It is normal for the uteri of different women to be in different positions, from tipped forward toward the abdomen (anteflexed) to tipped back toward the spine (retroflexed), as shown in Figure 4.6. At one time it was believed that a retroflexed, or tipped, uterus interfered with conception. Women with retroflexed uteri may be more likely to experience menstrual discomfort or to have difficulty with diaphragm insertion, but their fertility is not impaired by the position of the uterus.

Fertilization usually occurs not in the uterus but in the fallopian tubes (which are described in the next section), as the egg travels from the ovary. Once fertilization has taken place, the *zygote* (united sperm and egg) travels down the tube and becomes implanted in the uterus, where it develops into the fetus. In preparation for this event, the **endometrium** (en′-dō-ME̅-trē-um), or uterine lining, becomes thickened. This thickening occurs in response to hormone changes during the monthly menstrual cycle, which will be discussed later in this chapter. The endometrium is also a source of hormone production (Hufnagel & Golant, 1988).

The Fallopian Tubes

Each of the two 4-inch **fallopian** (fa-LO̅-pē-an) **tubes** extends from the uterus toward the left or the right side of the pelvic cavity. The outside end of each tube is shaped like a funnel, with fringelike projections called **fimbriae** (FIM-brē-a) that almost reach the ovary. When the egg leaves the ovary, it is drawn into the tube by the fimbriae.

Once the egg is inside the tube, the movements of tiny, hairlike *cilia* and the contractions of the tube walls move it along the tube at a rate of approximately one inch every 24 hours. The egg remains viable for fertilization for about 24–48 hours. Therefore, fertilization occurs while the egg is still close to the ovary. After fertilization, the zygote begins developing as it continues traveling down the tube to the uterus.

Ectopic Pregnancy.   Sometimes the zygote becomes implanted in a location outside the uterus, a condition known as an **ectopic** (ek-TOP-ik) **pregnancy**. The most common site of an ectopic pregnancy is the fallopian tube, so the condition is often called a tubal pregnancy. Research indicates this occurs in one out of 100 pregnancies (Siller & Azziz, 1991), and that the incidence of ectopic pregnancies has increased almost fivefold since 1970 (Ory, 1992). A tubal pregnancy is often difficult to diagnose because some of the possible symptoms (abdominal pain, a missed menstrual period, a pelvic mass, or irregular bleeding) are similar to those found with other problems. Without surgical treatment, though, an ectopic pregnancy may ultimately rupture the fallopian tube and result in severe bleeding, shock, and even death. Ectopic pregnancies are more likely to occur in women with a history of pelvic inflammatory disease or tubal surgery, and in women currently using an IUD and women who smoke cigarettes (Pansky et al., 1991; Phillips et al., 1992).

The Ovaries

The two **ovaries** are structures about the size and shape of almonds. They are located at the ends of the fallopian tubes, one on each side of the uterus. They are connected to the pelvic wall and the uterus by ligaments. The ovaries are endocrine glands that produce two classes of sex hormones. The estrogens, as mentioned in Chapter 3, influence development of female physical sex characteristics and help regulate the menstrual cycle. The progestational compounds also help regulate the menstrual cycle; they also stimulate development of the uterine lining in preparation for pregnancy. Around the onset of puberty, the female sex hor-

At ovulation, the mature egg leaves the ovary and is drawn into the fallopian tube by the fringelike fimbriae.

mones play a critical role in initiating maturation of the uterus, ovaries, and vagina, and in the development of the *secondary sex characteristics,* such as pubic hair and breasts.

The ovaries contain 40,000–400,000 immature ova, which are present at birth. During the years between puberty and menopause, one ovary typically releases an egg each cycle. An average woman will release approximately 450 eggs in her lifetime. **Ovulation** (ō-vyoo-LĀ-shun), or egg maturation and release, occurs as the result of the complex chain of events we know as the menstrual cycle. We will look at the menstrual cycle more closely at the end of this chapter.

Surgical Removal of the Uterus and Ovaries

Sometimes a woman needs to have a **hysterectomy** (his′-te-REK-tō-mē), surgical removal of the uterus, or an **oophorectomy** (ō-of-ō-REK-tō-mē), surgical removal of the ovaries, or both. Various medical problems necessitate these procedures, including cervical, uterine, or ovarian cancer; the presence of benign (noncancerous) tumors (West, 1992a); or severe pelvic infections. The potential physical complications of these operations are similar to those of any major surgery.

Hysterectomy is the most frequently performed major operation in the United States with an estimated 33% of women having a hysterectomy by age 60 (Center for Disease Control, 1992d). In some situations, the reasons for performing a hysterectomy are discretionary: a woman can often be treated successfully with other medical options (Hufnagel, 1988; Roman et al., 1992). Before consenting to undergo a hysterectomy or similar surgery, it is important for a woman to obtain a second opinion; to fully inform herself of the benefits, risks, and alternatives to such surgery; and to obtain thorough preoperative and postoperative information and counseling (Easterday et al., 1983).

The effects of this type of surgery on a woman's sexuality vary. Some women find that the elimination of medical problems and painful intercourse, assured protection from unwanted pregnancy, and lack of menstruation may enhance their sexual functioning. Research indicates that women have intercourse as frequently after recovering from a hysterectomy as before the surgery (Kilkku, 1983).

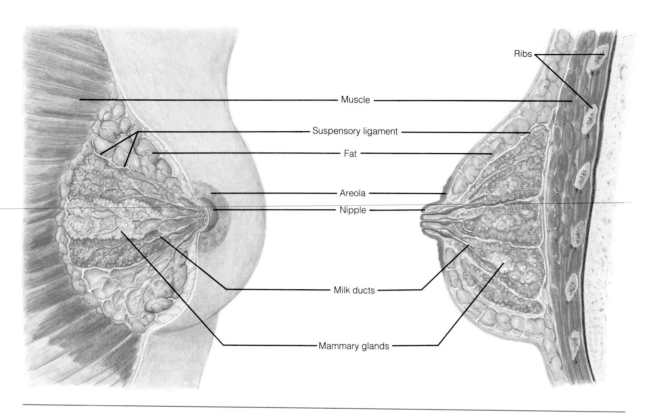

Muscle
Suspensory ligament
Fat
Areola
Nipple
Milk ducts
Mammary glands
Ribs

FIGURE 4.7

Cross-section front and side views of the female breast.

However, other women may experience an alteration or decrease in their sexual response after removal of the uterus. Sensations from uterine vasocongestion and elevation during arousal, as well as contractions during orgasm, will be absent and may change the physical experience of sexual response (Williamson, 1992; Zussman et al., 1981). Some changes may result from damage to the innervation of the vagina and cervix. Scar tissue or alterations to the vagina may also have an effect (Kilkku et al., 1983). Often the crucial variable in postsurgical sexual adjustment is how the woman and her partner perceive the surgery (Williamson, 1992). In a few instances, continued general physical or emotional problems may interfere with sexual functioning. These problems can range from diminished vaginal lubrication (due to the absence of ovarian estrogen) to depression over the loss of reproductive ability or the symbolic loss of femininity (Easterday et al., 1983).

The Breasts

Breasts are not a part of the internal or external female genitalia. The **breasts** are **secondary sex characteristics** (physical characteristics other than genitals that distinguish male from female). In a physically mature woman, they are composed internally of fatty tissue and **mammary** (MAM-ar-ē), or milk, **glands** (see Figure 4.7). There is little variation from woman to woman in the amount of glandular

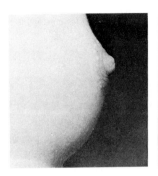 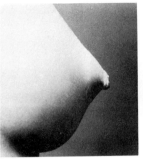 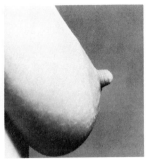 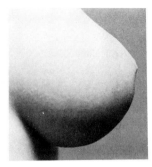

Breast size and shape vary from woman to woman.

tissue present in the breast, despite differences in size. This is why the amount of milk produced after childbirth does not correlate to the size of the breasts. Variation in breast size is due primarily to the amount of fatty tissue distributed around the glands. It is common for one breast to be slightly larger than the other.

Breast size is a source of considerable preoccupation for many women and men in our society. Large breasts are often considered to be linked with "sexiness." Surgeries to enlarge or reduce breast size reflect the dissatisfaction many women feel because their breasts do not fit the cultural ideal. (Prior to the January 1992 ban on implants, 150,000 women a year received implants [Schwartz and Kaplan, 1991]). The ideal may be difficult to define, with contradictory images of the slender, small-breasted, elegant cover girl on the one hand, and the voluptuous type on the other. Many women believe that their breasts are too small, too big, or not the right shape:

In talking with my friends about how we feel about our breasts, I discovered that not one of us feels really comfortable about how they look. I've always been envious of women with large breasts because mine are small. But my friends with large breasts talk about feeling self-conscious about their breasts too. (Authors' files)

The glandular tissue in the breast responds to sex hormones. During adolescence, both the fatty and the glandular tissue develop markedly. Breasts show some size variations at different phases of the menstrual cycle and when influenced by pregnancy, nursing, or birth control pills.

The **nipple** is in the center of the **areola** (a-RĒ-ō-la), the darker area of the external breast. The areola contains sebaceous (oil-producing) glands that help lubricate the nipples during breast-feeding. The openings of the mammary glands are in the nipples. Some nipples point outward from the breast, others are flush with the breast, and still others sink into the breast. The nipples become erect when small muscles at the base of the nipple contract in response to sexual arousal, tactile stimulation, or cold.

Breast Self-Exam

A monthly breast examination is an important part of self-health care for women. This exam can help a woman know what is normal for her own breasts. She can do the breast exam herself and can also teach her partner to do it. The steps of a breast exam are illustrated in the box "How to Examine Your Breasts." Because

FIGURE 4.8

It is helpful to use a chart
similar to this one to keep
track of lumps in the breasts.

Fill out this chart each month when you examine your breasts. Record the date you do the examination and the date your last period started. For any lump you find, mark

(a) its location
(b) its size (BB, pea, raisin, grape)
(c) its shape (rounded or elongated)

Compare each month's record with the last one, and consult your health care provider if there are any changes. A new or changing lump should be checked as soon as possible, although most such lumps will prove to be benign.

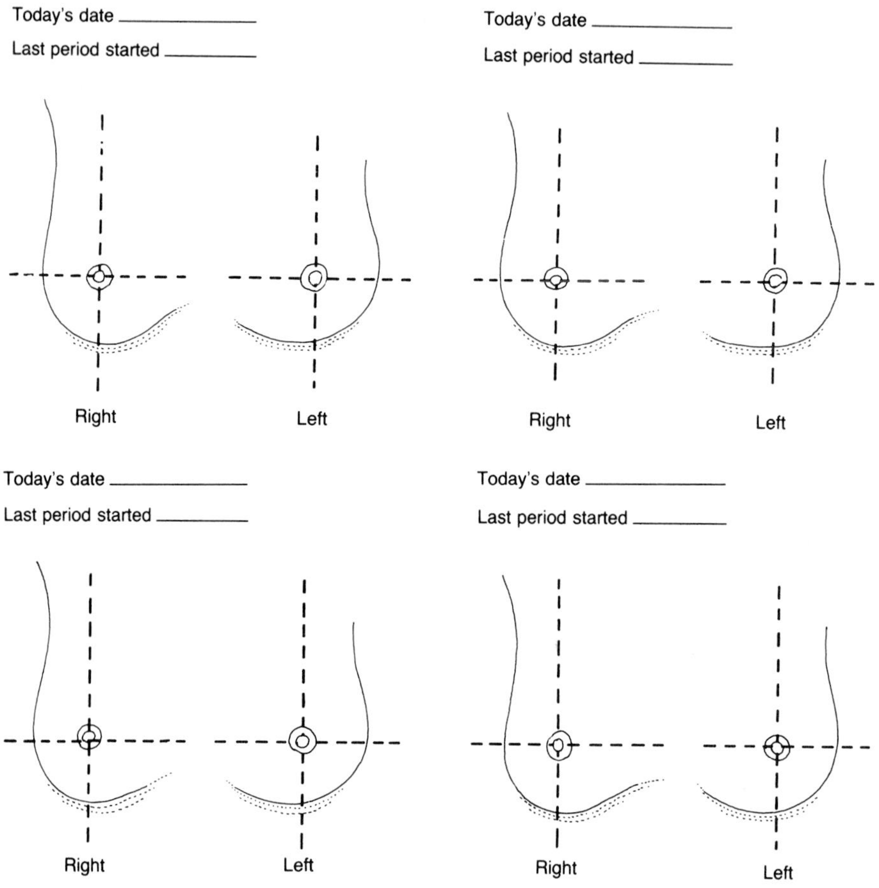

Concept from Kaiser Foundation Health Plan of Oregon.
Adapted with permission of Kaiser Permanente.

of cyclic changes in the breast tissue, the best time to do the routine exam is following menstruation. For a woman who is not menstruating (during pregnancy, or after menopause or a hysterectomy), doing the exam at the same time each month is best. Many breasts normally feel lumpy. Once a woman becomes familiar with her own breasts, she can notice any changes. If there is a change, she should consult a physician, who may recommend further diagnostic testing. It is helpful to fill out a chart, like the one shown in Figure 4.8, to keep track of lumps in the breasts. Most breast cancer is found by self-examination (Schifeling & Hamblin, 1991).

OUR SEXUALITY

How to Examine Your Breasts

1. In the shower

Examine your breasts during bath or shower; hands glide more easily over wet skin. With fingers flat, move your hands gently over every part of each breast. Use your right hand to examine your left breast, left hand for your right breast. Check for any lump, hard knot, or thickening.

2. Before a mirror

Inspect your breasts with arms at your sides. Next, raise your arms high overhead. Look for any changes in the contour of each breast: a swelling, dimpling of the skin, or changes in the nipple.

Then, rest your palms on your hips and press down firmly to flex

your chest muscles. Left and right breasts will not match exactly — few women's breasts do.

3. Lying down

To examine your right breast, put a pillow or folded towel under your right shoulder. Place your right hand behind your head — this distributes breast tissue more evenly on the chest. With your left hand, fingers flat, press gently in small circular motions around an imaginary clock face. Begin at the outermost top of your right breast for twelve o'clock, then move to one o'clock, and so on around the circle back to twelve. A ridge of firm tissue in the lower curve of each breast is normal. Then move in an inch, toward the nipple, and keep circling to examine *every part of your breast,* including the nipple. This requires at least three more circles. Now slowly repeat this procedure on your left breast.

Finally, squeeze the nipple of each breast gently between thumb and index finger. Any discharge, clear or bloody, should be reported to your doctor immediately — as should the discovery of any unusual lump, swelling, or thickening anywhere in the breast.

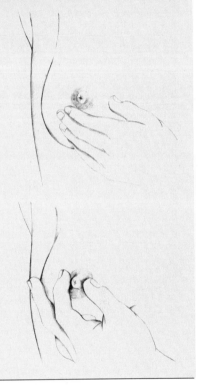

Mammography (mam-OG-ra-fē) is a highly sensitive X-ray screening test for cancerous breast lumps. It uses low levels of radiation to create an image of the breast, called a *mammogram,* on film or paper. Mammography can often detect a breast lump up to several years before it can be felt manually; it can also sometimes find cancerous cell changes that occur even before a lump develops (Bassett & Butler, 1991).

Mammography is used to detect cancerous breast lumps.

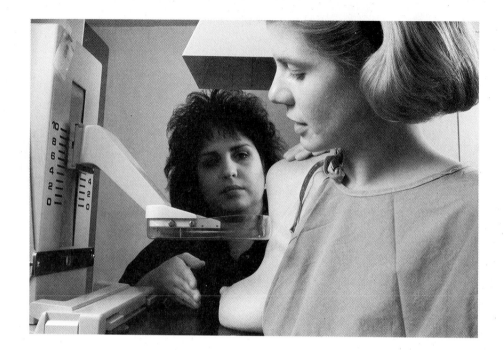

The American Cancer Society currently recommends a baseline mammogram between the ages of 35 and 40, a routine mammogram every one to two years during the 40s, and yearly mammograms after age 50. Unfortunately, many physicians do not recommend mammograms. Therefore, women may need to request this test themselves (Edell, 1989). A large survey by the American Cancer Society and the National Cancer Institute showed that regular mammograms significantly improved women's breast cancer survival rate (National Cancer Institute, 1986). Although mammography is a highly effective screening test, it is not 100% effective. In fact, one study showed that mammograms did not detect cancer previously diagnosed by biopsy in about 22% of cases (Edeiken, 1988). The best method for early detection of breast cancer is a combination of monthly manual self-exams, routine exams by a health care practitioner, and mammography as recommended.

Breast Lumps

Three types of lumps can occur in the breasts. The two most common are *cysts,* which are fluid-filled sacs, and *fibroadenomas,* which are solid, rounded tumors. Both are benign (not cancerous or harmful) tumors, and together they account for approximately 80% of breast lumps. In some women the lumps create breast tenderness ranging from mild to severe discomfort, which is called *fibrocystic disease* (Deckers & Ricci, 1992). The causes of fibrocystic disease are unknown but believed to be hormonally related (Sloane, 1985). Some researchers believe that caffeine in coffee, tea, cola drinks, and chocolate can contribute to the development of benign breast lumps. They report that breast lumps disappeared in many patients who eliminated caffeine from their diet (Minton et al., 1979). Other dietary changes that have helped some women reduce their symptoms include a diet high in fish, chicken, veal, and grains, and low in red meat, salt, and fats.

*Risk Factors for Breast Cancer**	TABLE 4.1

Higher Risk	Lower Risk
Older than age 50	Younger than age 50
Family history of breast cancer	No family history of breast cancer
No pregnancies	Both ovaries removed early in life
First child after age 30	First child before age 30
Menstruation onset before age 12	Menstruation onset after age 12
Menopause after age 50	Early menopause
Obesity	Slenderness
High-fat diet	Low-fat diet
Cancer in one breast	No cancer

* 80% of women who develop breast cancer have *no* known risk factors

Vitamin supplements of 600 units of vitamin E and vitamin-B complex in 110-mg daily doses have also helped some women (Sloane, 1985).

The third kind of breast lump is a *malignant tumor* (a tumor made up of cancer cells). Breast cancer is the most common type of cancer in women (NIH Consensus Conference, 1991), affecting approximately one in ten American women (Wertheimer, 1991). It is the leading cause of death from cancer in women age 35–54 (American College of Obstetricians and Gynecologists, 1991). Certain risk factors increase or decrease a woman's chances of developing breast cancer as shown in Table 4.1. However, about 80% of women with breast cancer do not have any of the known risk factors (Chittoor & Swain, 1991).

If a lump is found, further diagnostic testing is necessary. *Needle aspiration* involves inserting a fine needle into the lump to determine if there is fluid inside. If so, it is usually a cyst and can be drained. A biopsy of the tissue of any lump can be analyzed for cancer cells (Cowley & Rosenberg, 1992).

Once breast cancer has been diagnosed, several forms of treatment may be used. Radiation therapy, chemotherapy, hormone therapy, immunotherapy, **mastectomy** (surgical removal of all or part of the breast), or a combination of these procedures may be performed (Bernstein et al., 1992). With mastectomy, how much of the breast and surrounding tissue is removed by surgery varies from *radical mastectomy* (the entire breast, underlying muscle, and lymph nodes are removed) to *simple mastectomy* (breast tissue, the nipple and areola, and a sample of lymph nodes are removed) to *partial mastectomy* or *lumpectomy* (only the lump and small amounts of surrounding tissue are removed) (Margolis et al., 1992). If the cancer has not spread too far, a partial mastectomy provides as good a chance of a cure as a radical mastectomy (Fisher et al., 1985). Research also indicates that sexual adjustment is better following partial than radical mastectomy (Steinberg et al., 1985).

Breast cancer and its treatments may adversely affect a woman's sexuality (Dean, 1987). Beyond the physical recuperation from surgery and side effects of other treatments, the loss of one or both breasts almost certainly has special meaning to a woman and her present or future partners. In our culture, a woman's breast is often considered a symbol of femininity and is therefore a vital part of her body image. The stimulation of a woman's breasts during lovemaking—by massaging, licking, or sucking—and the stimulation her partner receives from doing these things and from simply looking at her breasts—are often important components of sexual arousal, for both the woman and her partner; consequently, surgical removal of one or both breasts may create problems in sexual adjustment for the couple (Margolis & Goodman, 1984).

A mastectomy presents unique problems to a woman who is not in a long-term relationship. She may have difficulty deciding when to tell someone she is dating about her surgery. Her own feelings of acceptance and comfort and her judgment about timing are important. Also, she needs to understand that her partner will require some time to adjust to the information about her mastectomy. Still, it may help her to keep in mind that a loving relationship is based on more than physical characteristics.

The American Cancer Society's Reach to Recovery program provides a very important service to women with breast cancer; volunteers in the program, who have all had one or both breasts removed, meet with a woman who has recently undergone a mastectomy and offer her emotional support and encouragement. They also provide positive models of women who have made a successful adjustment to the results of their surgery.

Reconstructive breast surgery may enhance a woman's general and sexual adjustment following a mastectomy. In many cases, a new breast can be made from a pouch containing silicone gel or saline water and placed under the woman's own skin and chest muscle. To improve the possibilities for breast reconstruction, it is helpful to have presurgical discussions with both the surgeon removing the tissue and the plastic surgeon doing the reconstruction (Becker & Maraist, 1987). Implants had been widely available for 30 years — and over 2 million women in the U.S. had received them (Skolnick, 1992) — before the FDA began clinical trials testing the safety of breast implants in early 1992. Implants continue to be available for mastectomy patients while the FDA studies potential problems (Selgmann & Church, 1992).

Because cancer spreads, it is especially important to remember to do regular breast exams and screenings. Early detection can lead to a higher survival rate, less drastic surgery, and easier and more successful breast reconstruction.

Menstruation

Menstruation (men'-stroo-ā-shun) is a sign of normal physical functioning, but negative attitudes about it persist in contemporary American society. One survey revealed that 66% of the adults sampled believe menstruation should not be discussed at work or socially, and 25% believed it should not be discussed within the family (Milow, 1983).

Common American folklore reveals many interesting ideas about menstruation. It has been thought that a woman should not bathe or wash her hair during her menstrual period because she would become ill or stop menstruating. In the 1920s, women commonly believed that a permanent wave given during menstru-

OTHER TIMES, OTHER PLACES

Menstruation

Many societies have viewed menstruation as unhealthy or supernatural. Both great powers and danger have been attributed to menstruation. The Roman historian Pliny wrote that bees will leave their hive, boiling linen will turn black, and razors will become blunt if touched by a menstruating woman. In some societies a menstruating woman is restricted from certain activities or from contact with men. She may also be isolated from the entire community into a menstrual hut, as with the Arapesh in New Guinea. The Bible states, "And if a woman have an issue, and her issue in her flesh be blood, she shall be put apart seven days: and whosoever toucheth her shall be unclean until the even" (Leviticus 15:19). Some writers believe that menstrual myths and taboos serve to control women and maintain their inferior social status (Weidiger, 1976).

In a few cultures, menstruation is described in lyrical words and positive images. The Japanese expression for a girl's first menstruation is "the year of the cleavage of the melon," and one Indian description of menstruation is the "flower growing in the house of the god of love" (Delaney et al., 1976).

---

ation would not curl their hair. Other myths include the belief that it is harmful for a woman to be physically active during menstruation, that a menstruating woman would wilt a corsage if she wore one, and that a filling in a tooth that was done during menstruation would fall out (Milow, 1983).

Despite these myths and negative societal attitudes toward menstruation, most women associate regular menstrual cycles with healthy functioning and femininity (Woods et al., 1986). Some women and families are redefining it more positively. For example, some may have a celebration or give a gift to a young woman when she starts her first menstrual period. One of the aspects of the menstrual cycle that people often see as positive is its cyclic pattern typical of many natural phenomena. The poet May Sarton describes the analogy of the menstrual cycle and nature in this 1937 poem:

> There were seeds
> within her
> that burst at intervals
> and for a little while
> she would come back
> to heaviness,
> and then before a surging miracle
> of blood,
> relax,
> and re-identify herself,
> each time more closely
> with the heart of life.
>
> 'I am the beginning,
> the never-ending,
> the perfect tree.'
> And she would lean
> again as one
> on the great curve of the earth,
> part of its turning,
> as distinctly part
> of the universe as a star —
> as unresistant,
> as completely rhythmical.

The menstrual cycle usually begins in the early teens, between the ages of 11 and 15, although some girls begin earlier or later. The first menstrual bleeding is called the **menarche** (me-NAR-kē). The timing of the menarche appears to be related to heredity, general health, and altitude (the average menarche is earlier in lower altitudes) (Sullivan, 1971) and occurs during a time of other changes in body size and development (Forbes, 1992). The average age of menarche in the United States is 12.8 years old (Golub, 1983). Menstrual cycles end at menopause, which in most women occurs between the ages of 45 and 55.

Differences in the age at which menarche occurs are often a concern for young women, especially those who begin earlier or later than the norm:

I felt very alone when I first started my periods late in the fifth grade because none of my friends had. In our school there were no Kotex machines in the kids' bathroom stalls, so I had to carry them in my purse and was afraid someone would see them. (Authors' files)

Almost everyone had been menstruating for years before I started. I thought something was wrong with me, but Mom said she started late, too. (Authors' files)

Although many people believe menstruation should be kept private, accurate information about this significant physiological development in young women is important to both boys and girls. Do you think most parents provide their children with sufficient information on menstruation? Why or why not? Think about your answer for a moment before reading on.

Many young women are not adequately informed about the developments and changes that accompany the onset of menstruation. One study found that 43% of women reported feeling confused, frightened, panicky, or ill when they started their first period, and one-third of the women surveyed did not know about menstruation before they began to menstruate (Research Forecasts, 1981). The information girls do receive may be scanty, confusing, or frightening.

Young men are probably even less likely to receive information about menstruation. One study found that men are most likely to learn about menstruation from friends (31%), school (21%), and mothers (20%). Ninety-one percent of both men and women thought that information about menstruation should be provided in schools (Research Forecasts, 1981).

Menstrual Physiology

During the menstrual cycle, the uterine lining is prepared for the implantation of a fertilized ovum. If conception does not occur, the lining sloughs off and is discharged as menstrual flow. The length of the menstrual cycle is usually measured from the beginning of the first day of flow to the day before the next flow begins. The menstrual period itself typically lasts two to six days (Johnson, 1991). It is normal for the volume of the menstrual flow (usually 6–8 ounces) to vary. The cycle length is often 28 days but also varies from woman to woman; it can be anywhere from 21 to 40 days. These time differences occur in the phase before ovulation. Fourteen days, plus or minus two days, is the interval between ovulation and the onset of menstruation, even when there is several weeks' difference in the total length of the cycle. Life changes and stress can affect cycle length (Harlow and Natanowski, 1991). If a woman experiences a dramatic change in her usual pattern, she should seek medical attention.

An interesting phenomenon known as **menstrual synchrony** sometimes occurs among women who live together and have considerable contact with one another: They develop similar menstrual cycles. The function of the uniform cycles is unknown, but the trigger is believed to be related to the sense of smell (Jarrett, 1984; McClintock, 1971).

How might researchers test the hypothesis that menstrual synchrony is related to the sense of smell? Think of a possible research design before reading on.

To test this hypothesis, researchers had subjects with normal menstrual cycles swab their upper lips with either perspiration extract from other women or with plain alcohol. Within three menstrual cycles, 80% of the subjects who had received the perspiration extract were menstruating in sync with their perspiration donors. The control group showed no menstrual cycle changes (Cutler et al., 1986).

Close physical contact with men may also influence ovulation. One study showed that women who had spent two or more nights with a man over a 40-day period were almost twice as likely to ovulate as women who had spent no more than one night with a man (Veith et al., 1983).

The menstrual cycle is divided into three stages, or phases: the **proliferative phase,** the **secretory phase,** and the **menstrual phase.** The menstrual cycle is regulated by intricate relationships among the hypothalamus and the pituitary gland (both located within the brain), the adrenal glands, and the ovaries and the uterus (see Figure 4.9). The cycle is a self-regulating and dynamic process in which the level of a particular hormone retards or increases the production of the same and other hormones. We will describe the action of the regulatory hormones briefly here and in more detail in the discussions of the three phases.

The hypothalamus monitors the hormone levels in the bloodstream throughout the cycle, sending chemical messages to the pituitary gland, which in turn releases hormones to stimulate the ovaries (see Figure 4.10). The hypothalamus produces chemicals known as *hypothalamic releasing factors.* The most important hypothalamic releasing factors related to menstruation are the *gonadotropic releasing factors,* which stimulate the pituitary to produce hormones that affect the ovaries. Once the pituitary gland receives the appropriate releasing factors from the hypothalamus, it produces **follicle-stimulating hormone (FSH)** or **luteinizing** (LOO-tē-n-īz-ing) **hormone (LH).** These two hormones have the general name of *gonadotropins* because they stimulate the gonads (ovaries and testes). In the female, FSH stimulates ovarian production of estrogen and the maturation of the ova and *follicles* (small sacs, each of which contains an ovum). LH induces the mature ovum to burst from the ovary, and it stimulates the development of the **corpus luteum** (the portion of the follicle that remains after the egg has matured). The corpus luteum produces the hormone progesterone.

These glands do not produce a steady stream of hormones; there is a complex interaction among the glands that signals when to increase or decrease secretions. A hormone is secreted until the organ it acts on is stimulated; at that point the organ releases a substance that circulates back through the system to reduce hormonal activity in the initiating gland. This *negative-feedback mechanism* provides an internal control that regulates fluctuations of hormonal production. Besides the hormonal and ovarian changes already mentioned, the phases of the menstrual cycle involve changes in the uterine lining. The ovarian and uterine changes, which we will now discuss, are shown in Figure 4.11. Figure 4.12 shows ovarian follicle development in more detail.

FIGURE 4.9

The interrelated parts of the menstrual cycle: (a) The fluctuating levels of gonadotropins (FSH and LH) that help regulate the events of the menstrual cycle. (b) The fluctuating levels of ovarian hormones (estrogen and progesterone) that cause endometrial changes. (c, d) The ovarian and uterine changes during the 28 days of the cycle.

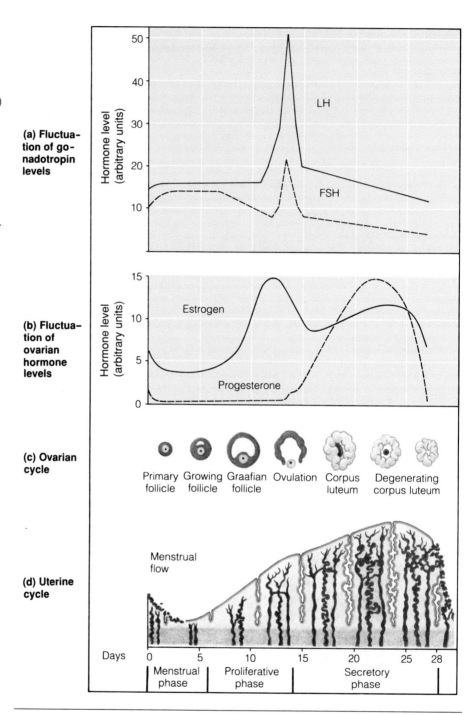

Proliferative Phase. During the proliferative phase of the menstrual cycle (see Figure 4.11a), the pituitary gland increases production of FSH, which stimulates the developing follicles to mature and to produce several types of estrogen. Estrogen in turn causes the endometrium to thicken. Although several follicles begin to mature, usually only one, the **graafian follicle** (GRAF-ē-an FOL-i-kal), reaches maturity; the other follicles degenerate. When the level of ovarian estrogen cir-

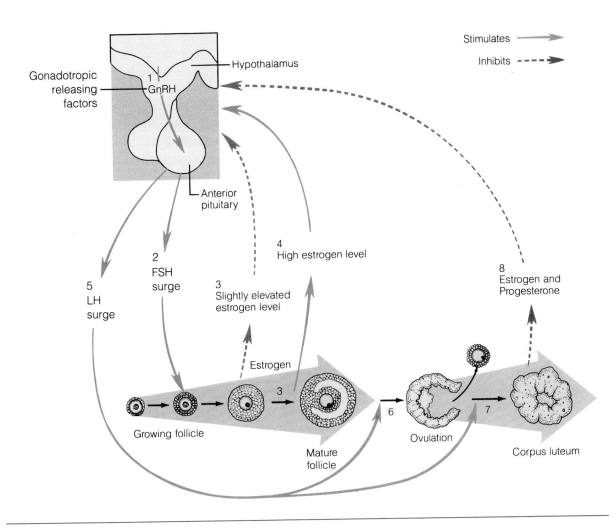

Stimulates ──────▶
Inhibits ------▶

Hypothalamus

Gonadotropic
releasing
factors

1
GnRH

Anterior
pituitary

2
FSH
surge

5
LH
surge

3
Slightly elevated
estrogen level

4
High estrogen level

8
Estrogen and
Progesterone

Estrogen

3

Growing follicle

Mature
follicle

6

Ovulation

7

Corpus luteum

FIGURE 4.10

The complex interactions among the hypothalamus, the pituitary gland, and the regulatory hormones during the menstrual cycle. The numbers indicate the order in which events occur.

culating in the bloodstream reaches a peak, the pituitary gland depresses the release of FSH and stimulates LH production.

At approximately 14 days *before* the onset of the *next* menstrual period, **ovulation** occurs (Willson, 1987). In response to the spurt of LH secreted by the pituitary gland, the mature follicle ruptures, and the ovum is released. Some women experience a twinge, cramp, or pressure in the lower abdomen, called *mittelschmerz* (German for *middle pain*), at ovulation. Mittelschmerz is caused by the swelling and bursting of the follicle or by a little fluid or blood from the ruptured follicle irritating the sensitive abdominal lining. The released ovum then travels to the fimbria of the fallopian tube. Occasionally, more than one ovum is released. If two ova are fertilized, fraternal twins will develop. When one egg is fertilized and then divides into two separate zygotes, identical twins result.

Around the time of ovulation, there is an increase and a change in cervical mucus secretions, due to increased levels of estrogen. The mucus becomes clear, slippery, and stretchy. The pH of this mucus is more alkaline; as noted earlier, a more alkaline vaginal environment contributes to sperm motility and longevity. This is the time in the cycle when a woman can most easily become pregnant.

FIGURE 4.11

The changes to the ovaries and uterus during (a) the proliferative phase, including ovulation, (b) the secretory phase, and (c) the menstrual phase of the menstrual cycle.

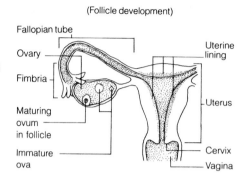

(Follicle development)

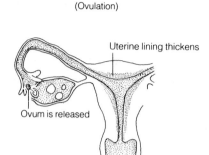

(Ovulation)

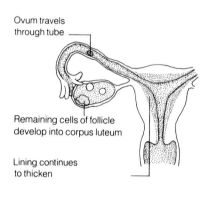

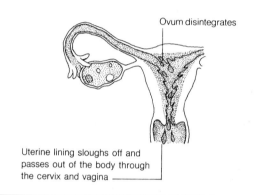

Secretory Phase. During the secretory phase (see Figure 4.11b), continued pituitary secretions of LH cause the cells of the ruptured follicle to develop into a yellowish bump called the corpus luteum. The corpus luteum secretes progesterone, which inhibits the production of the cervical mucus produced during ovulation. Progesterone, together with estrogen produced by the ovaries, causes the endometrium to thicken and engorge with blood in preparation for implantation of a fertilized egg. If implantation does not occur, the pituitary gland, in response to high estrogen and progesterone levels in the bloodstream, shuts down production of LH and FSH. This deprives the corpus luteum of the necessary chemical stimulation to produce hormones; the corpus luteum degenerates, and estrogen and progesterone production decreases. This reduction of hormone levels triggers the sloughing off of the endometrium during the menstrual phase.

Menstrual Phase. During the menstrual phase (see Figure 4.11c), the uterus sheds the thickened inner layer of the endometrium, which is discharged through the cervix and vagina as menstrual flow. Menstrual flow typically consists of blood, mucus, and endometrial tissue.

　　As we have noted, the shedding of the endometrium is the result of reduced amounts of progesterone and estrogen. As the hormone level in the bloodstream continues to fall, the hypothalamus responds to the reduction by stimulating the

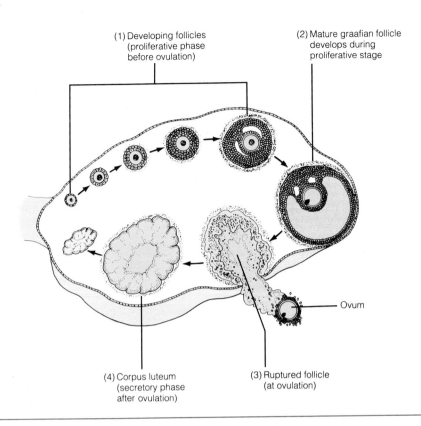

(1) Developing follicles
(proliferative phase
before ovulation)

(2) Mature graafian follicle
develops during
proliferative stage

— Ovum

(4) Corpus luteum
(secretory phase
after ovulation)

(3) Ruptured follicle
(at ovulation)

FIGURE 4.12

Ovarian follicle development.
A cross section of an ovary
showing different stages of
follicle development.

pituitary to release FSH. The release of FSH initiates the maturation process of several follicles, and the cycle begins again.

Sexual Activity and the Menstrual Cycle

A number of studies have attempted to determine whether a correlation exists between menstrual cycle changes and sexual behavior. There is some inconsistency in the findings of various researchers. Some studies show no significant variations in sexual arousal at different points in the menstrual cycle (Meuwissen & Over, 1992; Morrell et al., 1984). Others indicate a pattern of increase in sexual feelings and behavior during the ovulatory phase (Harvey, 1987) and during menstruation and the preceding few days (Friedman, 1980). In an attempt to control for external variables such as contraceptive use, fear of pregnancy, and male influence, one study examined the relationship between cycle phase and sexual response and activity in a sample of lesbians. In this sample, partner and self-initiated sexual activity increased in frequency at midcycle, as did orgasm, but sexual thoughts and fantasies peaked in the first three days following the onset of menstruation (Matteo & Rissman, 1984). There is great individual variation from woman to woman. We encourage women readers and their partners to notice their own patterns.

There is a taboo in our culture against having intercourse during menstruation. One phone interview survey found that 51% of men and 56% of women believed that women should abstain from intercourse during menstruation (Research Forecasts, 1981). Another study found that both men and women ini-

OUR SEXUALITY

Men, Lovemaking, and Menstruation

Men who make love with women have to deal in some way with menstruation. Caring about a woman's experience of her period may help avoid misunderstandings and build intimacy.

A man might ask his lover if she gets cramps and, if so, how they feel. Pain is not the only consideration. The bloated feeling caused by water retention may not *hurt*, but it can be fairly uncomfortable. In some women with pronounced menstrual water retention, it can feel like the flu.

A man can do several things to help a woman deal with dysmenorrhea. He might make her a cup of soothing herbal tea — chamomile and mint herb teas may be especially effective — or massage her lower back or abdomen.

A man could try to discuss with his lover how she feels about making love premenstrually or during her period. Some women prefer not to; discomfort can interfere with the undivided attention lovemaking deserves. On the other hand, some women say lovemaking right before or during menstruation helps alleviate cramps. During orgasm the uterus contracts, and the cervix opens. This helps speed menstrual flow and can reduce the duration of cramps. Men should bear in mind, however, that this is not an experience shared by all women. A man might also inquire about breast tenderness and keep it in mind during sensual explorations.

Different cultures and religions have different perspectives on lovemaking during a woman's period. As a result, many people — both men and women — have deep feelings about it. It is important to listen carefully to a lover's feelings about making love during menstruation and to try to respect them.

For couples who do make love during a woman's period, there are several things to remember. Menstruation may change a woman's natural vaginal lubrication. Menstrual fluid irritates some penises, but a man can use a condom if this is a problem. Intercourse with a tampon in place is not recommended, but a woman can use a diaphragm or cervical cap to catch the flow. Even if a barrier method is not your primary or preferred form of contraception, you may want to use one at this time.

If a couple would rather not have genital intercourse during the woman's period, there are other satisfying ways to make love (though some men and women may prefer to avoid cunnilingus during menstruation).

Whatever an individual or couple prefers, the important thing is to try to communicate as openly as possible about the issues menstruation raises — and to decide together what the most comfortable responses will be. (Adapted from Michael Castleman, 1981)

---

tiated substantially fewer sexual activities during menstruation than at any other time during the cycle (Harvey, 1987). Although we know today that from a medical point of view there are no health reasons to avoid intercourse during menstruation (except in the case of excessive bleeding or other menstrual problems), many couples do so.

Reasons for avoiding sex during a woman's period vary. Uncomfortable physical symptoms of menstruation can reduce sexual desire or pleasure, and the messiness or the spilling of blood on sheets can inhibit sexual playfulness. Religious beliefs can also be a factor. Some women and men avoid sexual activity because of culturally induced shame about menstruation.

If people do prefer to abstain from coitus during menstruation, the remaining repertoire of sexual activities is still available:

When I'm on my period, I leave my tampon inside and push the string in, too. My husband and I have manual and oral stimulation, and a great time! (Authors' files)

Some women use a diaphragm to hold back the menstrual flow during coitus. Orgasm by any means of stimulation can be beneficial to a menstruating woman. The uterine contractions and release of vasocongestion often reduce backache and feelings of pelvic fullness and cramping.

Menstrual Cycle Problems

Most women undergo some physical or mood changes, or both, during their menstrual cycles. In many cases the changes are minor. In some cases women experience heightened pleasant moods during ovulation or menstruation (McFarlane et al., 1988). Other times, problems with the menstrual cycle occur. Negative attitudes about menstruation appear to be related to disruptive and painful menstrual cycle symptoms; women who have problem symptoms have more negative attitudes about menstruation than do women with mild or no symptoms (Woods, 1986). Adolescent females report more acute menstrual distress than do adult females. The relatively unstable hormone shifts during adolescence may predispose them to more menstrual cycle problems (Wilson et al., 1991).

Premenstrual Syndrome. **Premenstrual syndrome (PMS)** is the term used to identify a myriad of physical and psychological symptoms that occur before each menstrual period and are severe enough to interfere with some aspects of life (Hurt, 1992; Schmidt et al., 1991). It is important to identify the cyclic manifestation of the symptoms in order to differentiate PMS from other physical or psychological problems. Random, community-based studies indicate that 10–20% of women experience severe symptoms, while 30–50% experience mild or moderate symptoms (Woods et al., 1987). PMS symptoms appear to remain stable over many years (Metcalf et al., 1992). The causes of PMS are unknown, but fluctuations in sex hormones and their effects on various organ systems are believed to be involved (Hammarback et al., 1989). Life stresses and marital distress have been shown to exacerbate PMS symptoms (Coughlin, 1990).

Reported PMS symptoms include negative emotions such as anxiety, irritability, depression, anger, insomnia, confusion, tearfulness, and social withdrawal; and uncomfortable physical symptoms such as fluid retention, breast tenderness, weight gain, headaches, dizziness, nausea, increased appetite, and craving for sweets (Backerman, 1991; Rossignol & Bonnlander, 1991; Stewart et al., 1992). These symptoms may vary from mild to severe, and most women experience several of them (Christensen et al., 1989). Many women also experience these symptoms during menstruation as well (Taylor, 1986; Woods et al., 1987).

Some of these symptoms can be disruptive to close relationships. One survey found that partners of women with PMS symptoms reported disruption from increased conflict and withdrawal (Brown & Zimmer, 1986).

Premenstrual tension is a complicated phenomenon. What difficulties do you think might be encountered in attempting to research this area? Please come up with your own ideas before reading on.

Research about the nature, cause, and treatment of PMS lacks consistency and offers contradictory results (Robinson, 1989). For example, the premenstrual period is defined as beginning anywhere from four to six days before menstruation and as ending at the onset or after four days of menstruation. Symptom severity is often not measured. There is no generally accepted way of rating a syndrome that more often consists of internally experienced symptoms than objective behavioral signs. There is also a lack of consistent data in support of any single cause, in part due to the differing methods used to obtain research results. In addition, some research results may be influenced by what subjects believe they are expected to experience during their menstrual cycle (Olasov & Jackson, 1987).

However, research is beginning to clarify uses of hormones (Graham & Sherwin, 1992), medications (Vellacott & O'Brien, 1987), vitamins (London et al., 1987; Stewart, 1987), and exercise (Prior & Vigna, 1987) in placebo-controlled, double-blind studies (studies in which neither experimenter nor subject knows whether the treatment or placebo is being given). Another study found that individually chosen combinations of diet change, nutritional supplements, physical activity, esteem-building, lifestyle management, and peer support were effective in alleviating or reducing symptoms of PMS (Freeman et al., 1992; Reid, 1991).

Dysmenorrhea. Painful menstruation is called **dysmenorrhea** (dis'-men-o-RĒ-a). *Primary dysmenorrhea* occurs during menstruation and is usually caused by the overproduction of **prostaglandins,** a class of chemicals produced by body tissue. Uterine prostaglandins cause the muscles of the uterus to contract. Most uterine contractions are not even noticed, but strong ones are painful. The uterus may begin to contract too strongly or too frequently and temporarily deprive the uterus of oxygen, causing pain (American College of Obstetricians and Gynecologists, 1985). Problems with primary dysmenorrhea usually appear with the onset of menses at adolescence. The symptoms are generally most noticeable during the first few days of a woman's period and include abdominal aching and/or cramping. Some women may also experience nausea, vomiting, diarrhea, headache, dizziness, fatigue, irritability, or nervousness.

Secondary dysmenorrhea occurs prior to or during menstruation and is characterized by constant and often spasmodic lower abdominal pain that typically extends to the back and thighs. The symptoms are often similar to those of primary dysmenorrhea and are caused by factors other than prostaglandin production; possible causes include the presence of an intrauterine device (IUD), pelvic inflammatory disease (chronic infection of the reproductive organs), benign uterine tumors, obstruction of the cervical opening, and **endometriosis** (en'-do-mē'-trē-ō-sis). Endometriosis, a condition in which endometrial cells from the uterine lining implant in the abdominal cavity, affects up to 15% of premenopausal women. The implanted endometrial tissue often adheres to other tissue in the pelvic cavity and reduces mobility of the internal structures. In addition, the endometrial implants engorge with blood during the proliferative phase. The engorged tissues and adhesions can cause painful menstruation, lower backache, and pain from pressure and movement during intercourse (Barbieri, 1988). Following a diagnosis of the cause of secondary dysmenorrhea, appropriate treatment can be implemented.

Amenorrhea. Besides discomfort or pain, another fairly common menstrual difficulty is **amenorrhea** (a-men'-o-RĒ-a), the absence of menstruation. There are two types of amenorrhea—primary and secondary. *Primary amenorrhea* is the failure to begin to menstruate at puberty. It may be caused by problems with the reproductive organs, hormonal imbalances, poor health, or an imperforate hymen. *Secondary amenorrhea* involves the disruption of an established menstrual cycle, with the absence of menstruation for three months or more. This is a normal condition during pregnancy and breast-feeding. It is also common in women who have just begun menstruating and women approaching menopause. Sometimes poor health and emotional distress are the causes.

Hormonal problems can also produce amenorrhea (Faye & Farber, 1989). Women with anorexia nervosa, an eating disorder that often results in extreme weight loss, frequently stop menstruating due to hormonal changes that accompany emaciation (Schweiger, 1991). Women who discontinue the birth control pill occasionally do not resume menstruation for several months, but this situation is usually temporary and resolves spontaneously. It is a good idea for a woman who does not have a period when expected to consult a health care practitioner.

Rigorous athletic training can interfere with ovulation (Prior & Vigna, 1991). Amenorrhea is more common among athletes than among the general population (Shangold, 1985). It is not known whether the disruption of normal menstrual cycles in athletes is caused by intensive exercise, low body fat, the physical or emotional stress of training and competing, or a combination of all of these (Loucks & Horvath, 1985). Amenorrhea may also be due to medical problems unrelated to athletics. Thus, it is important for a female athlete to seek medical evaluation for menstrual irregularities (Shangold, 1980).

Self-Help for Menstrual Problems. Women may be able to alleviate some of the unpleasant symptoms accompanying menstruation by their own actions. Moderate exercise throughout the month, as well as proper diet, can contribute to improvement of menstrual-related difficulties. For example, an increase in fluids and fiber helps with the constipation that sometimes occurs before and during menstruation. Decreasing salt intake and avoiding food high in salt (salad dressing, potato chips, bacon, pickles, to name a few) can help reduce swelling and bloating caused by water retention. Food supplements such as calcium, magnesium, and B vitamins also sometimes help relieve cramps and bloating. Avoiding caffeine, nicotine, and other stimulants and eating small, frequent meals of low-carbohydrate, low-fat, high-protein foods can help decrease anxiety and irritability (Price et al., 1986). Stress-reduction strategies that include relaxation techniques, taking time for oneself, and supportive counseling may also be helpful.

When a woman experiences menstrual-related pain, it can be useful for her to keep a diary to track symptoms, stresses, and daily habits such as exercise, diet, and sleep. She may be able to note a relationship between symptoms and habits and modify her activities accordingly. The information may also be helpful for specific diagnosis if she consults a health care practitioner.

Toxic Shock Syndrome

In May 1980, the Centers for Disease Control (CDC) published the first report of **toxic shock syndrome (TSS)** in menstruating women. Symptoms of TSS, which is caused by toxins produced by the bacterium *Staphylococcus aureus*, include fever, sore throat, nausea, vomiting, diarrhea, red skin flush, dizziness, and low blood pressure.

TSS is a rare disease and the number of TSS cases reported has fallen sharply since the peak in 1980, due likely to the removal of highly absorbent tampons from the market (Petitti & Reingold, 1988). TSS is associated with the use of tampons and is most likely to occur during menstruation in women between 15 and 24 years of age. However, up to 12% of all cases are nonmenstrual (Bryner, 1989). Some occur postpartum and others in connection with postoperative wounds or in children, men, and postmenopausal women (Johnson, 1985). Because TSS progresses rapidly and can cause death, a person with several of the symptoms of TSS should consult a physician immediately (Tanner et al., 1981; Taylor & Lockwood, 1981).

Some guidelines have been developed that may help prevent toxic shock. One suggestion has been to use sanitary napkins instead of tampons. Suggestions for women who want to continue using tampons include using regular instead of super-absorbent tampons, changing them three to four times during the day, and using napkins for some time during each 24 hours of menstrual flow. A woman should consult her health care practitioner for further up-to-date suggestions pertaining to prevention and detection of TSS.

Summary

Genital Self-Exam

Genital self-exploration is a good way for a woman to learn about her own body and to notice any changes that may require medical attention.

The Vulva

The female external genitals, also called the vulva, are composed of the mons veneris, labia majora, labia minora, clitoris, and urethral and vaginal openings. Each woman's vulva is unique in shape, color, and texture.

The mons veneris and labia majora have underlying pads of fatty tissue and are covered by pubic hair beginning at adolescence.

The labia minora are folds of sensitive skin, which begin at the hood over the clitoris and extend downward to below the vaginal opening, or introitus. The area between them is called the vestibule.

The clitoris is composed of the external glans and shaft and the internal crura. The glans contains densely concentrated nerve endings. The only function of the clitoris is sexual pleasure.

The urethral opening is located between the clitoris and vaginal introitus. About one out of every five women will experience a urinary tract infection caused by bacteria that enter the urethra.

Many cultures have placed great importance on the hymen as proof of virginity. However, there are various sizes, shapes, and thicknesses of hymens, and many women can have initial intercourse without pain or bleeding. Also, women who have decided to have coitus can learn how to stretch their hymens to help make their first experience comfortable.

Underlying Structures

Below the surface of the vulva are the vestibular bulbs and the pelvic floor muscles.

Internal Structures

The vagina, with its three layers of tissue, extends about 3–5 inches into the pelvic cavity. It is a potential rather than an actual space and increases in size during sexual arousal, coitus, and childbirth. The other internal reproductive structures are the cervix, uterus, fallopian tubes, and ovaries.

Vaginal lubrication, the secretion of alkaline fluid through the vaginal walls during arousal, is important both in enhancing the longevity and motility of sperm cells and in increasing the pleasure and comfort of intercourse.

The Grafenberg spot is located about one centimeter from the surface of the top wall of the vagina. Many women report erotic sensitivity to pressure in some area of their vaginas.

The vaginal walls and cervix produce normal secretions. Occasionally, a vaginal infection occurs that results in irritation, unusual discharge, or a disagreeable odor.

There is considerable medical controversy about the appropriate use of hysterectomy. A hysterectomy or oophorectomy may, in some cases, have an effect — either positive or negative — on a woman's sexuality.

The Breasts

The breasts are composed of fatty tissue and milk-producing glands. A monthly self-exam of the breasts is an important part of health care.

Three types of lumps can appear in the breasts: cysts, fibroadenomas, and malignant tumors. Careful diagnosis of a breast lump is important. Mammography, ultrasonography, and thermography can help detect and diagnose breast cancer. Less radical surgeries for breast cancer are often as effective as more severe procedures.

Menstruation

The menstrual cycle results from a complex interplay of hormones. The cycle is divided into the proliferative, the secretory, and the menstrual phases. Although negative social attitudes have been historically attached to menstruation, some people are currently redefining it in a more positive fashion.

There are usually no medical reasons to abstain from intercourse during menstruation. However, many people do limit their sexual activity during this time.

Some women have difficulties with premenstrual syndrome (PMS) or primary or secondary dysmenorrhea. Knowledge about the physiological factors that contribute to these problems is increasing, and some of the problems can be treated.

Amenorrhea occurs normally during pregnancy, while breast-feeding, and after menopause. It can also be due to medical problems or poor health.

Toxic shock syndrome (TSS) is a rare condition that occurs most often in menstruating women. Its symptoms include fever, sore throat, nausea, red skin flush, dizziness, and low blood pressure. If untreated, it can be fatal.

⤳ *Thought Provokers* ⤳

1. What do you think are some advantages and disadvantages of early and/or late physical maturation?

2. If a good friend of yours were told she needed a hysterectomy, what would you advise her?

3. What do you observe in the media and in others' comments and reactions that indicates positive and negative attitudes about menstruation?

4. Do you think the U.S. government should take any action toward countries that practice female genital mutilation? If so, what? If not, why not?

Suggested Readings

Boston Women's Health Book Collective (1985). *The New Our Bodies, Ourselves.* New York: Simon & Schuster. A thorough exploration of female sexuality, anatomy, and physiology. The book has a strong emphasis on health care and covers such topics as sexual relationships, rape, sexually transmitted diseases, birth control, parenthood, and menopause.

Harrison, Michelle (1985). *Self-Help for Premenstrual Syndrome.* New York: Random House. A thorough guide to understanding and to self-help treatments for PMS.

Love, Susan (1990). *Dr. Susan Love's Breast Book.* Reading, Mass.: Addison-Wesley. A comprehensive and extensively illustrated book about breast care and concerns.

Malesky, Gale; and Inlander, Charles (1991). *Take This Book to the Gynecologist with You.* Reading, Mass.: Addison-Wesley. A comprehensive guide to women's health care.

Meshorer, Marc; and Meshorer, Judith (1986). *Ultimate Pleasure: The Secrets of Easily Orgasmic Women.* New York: St. Martin's Press. Based on in-depth interviews with easily orgasmic women, this book describes how women take an active role in creating, building, and experiencing arousal.

Murcia, Andy; and Stewart, Bob (1989). *Man to Man: When the Woman You Love Has Breast Cancer.* New York: St. Martin's Press. Personal stories and practical information for men confronted with their partners' diagnosis of breast cancer.

Steinem, Gloria (1978). "If Men Could Menstruate." *Ms.,* October. A humorous yet provocative "political fantasy" about how menstruation would be treated in our society if men, instead of women, menstruated.

Weitzman, Sigmund; Kuter, Irene; and Pizer, H. F. (1986). *Confronting Breast Cancer.* New York: Vintage Books. A guide to the detection and treatments of breast cancer.

CHAPTER 5

Male Sexual Anatomy and Physiology

Sexual Anatomy

Male Sexual Functions

Some Concerns About Sexual Functioning

Who needs a lecture on male anatomy? Certainly not the men in this class. It's hanging out there all our lives. We handle it and look at it each time we pee or bathe. So what's the mystery? Now the female body—that's a different story. That's why I'm in the class. Let's learn something that isn't so obvious. (Authors' files)

The preceding quote, from a student in a sexuality class, illustrates two common assumptions. The first is that there is a simplicity about male sexual anatomy that requires little elaboration. A second, perhaps more subtle, implication is that female genital structures are, by comparison, considerably more complicated and mysterious. Neither of these assumptions is necessarily true. There is complexity as well as wide variation in the sexual anatomy of both men and women. Although increasing our understanding of complex biological sexual functions does not necessarily ensure sexual satisfaction, such knowledge may help us develop comfort with our bodies.

Since the 1960s, there has been a strong movement among women to assume responsibility for understanding and influencing their own sexual health. There has not yet been an equivalent movement for men. We are hopeful that this will change; books like Bernie Zilbergeld's *Male Sexuality* (1978) and Judith Silverstein's *Sexual Enhancement for Men* (1986) may help. These texts provide some excellent guidelines for a self-health program for men.

Perhaps male reluctance to move toward self-health care has been partly because a male's anatomy "hangs right out there." Nevertheless, easy accessibility does not necessarily imply familiarity—and in fact, many men are quite ill at ease with the idea of a detailed self-exam. As in Chapter 4, we encourage readers to use the pages that follow as a reference for their own self-knowledge.

Sexual Anatomy

We begin with discussions of the various structures of the male sexual anatomy. Descriptive accounts are organized according to parts of the genital system, for easy reference. Later in this chapter (and in Chapter 6), we will look more closely at the way the entire system functions during sexual arousal.

The Scrotum

The **scrotum,** or scrotal sac, is a loose pouch of skin that is an outpocket of the abdominal wall in the groin area (see Figure 5.1). Normally, it hangs loosely from the body wall, although influences such as cold temperatures or sexual stimulation may cause it to move closer to the body.

The scrotal sac consists of two layers. The outermost is a covering of thin skin that is darker in color than other body skin. It typically becomes sparsely covered with hair at adolescence. The second layer, known as the *tunica dartos,* is composed of smooth muscle fibers and fibrous connective tissue.

Within the scrotal sac are two separate compartments, each of which houses a single **testis,** or testicle. (For a diagram of the testis within the scrotal sac, see Figure 5.2.) Each testis is suspended within its compartment by the **spermatic** (sper-MAT-ik) **cord.** The spermatic cord contains the sperm-carrying tube, or *vas*

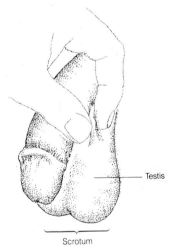

Testis

Scrotum

FIGURE 5.1

The scrotum and the testes. The spermatic cord can be located by palpating the scrotal sac above either testicle with thumb and forefinger.

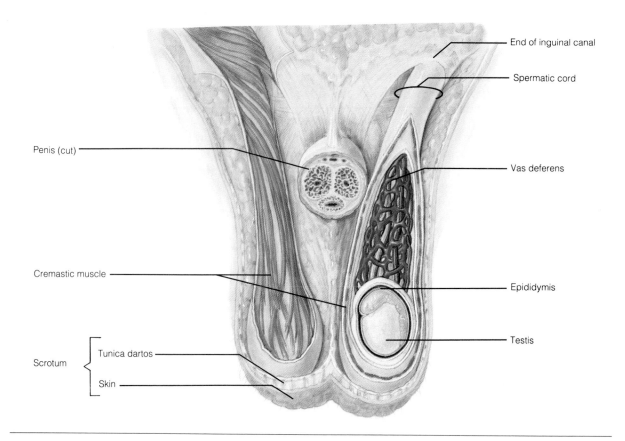

End of inguinal canal

Spermatic cord

Penis (cut)

Vas deferens

Cremastic muscle

Epididymis

Scrotum

Tunica dartos

Testis

Skin

FIGURE 5.2

Underlying structures of the scrotum. This illustration shows portions of the scrotum cut away to reveal the cremasteric muscle, spermatic cord, vas deferens, and a testis within the scrotal sac.

deferens, as well as blood vessels, nerves, and *cremasteric muscle* fibers that influence the position of the testicle in the scrotal sac. These muscles can be voluntarily contracted, causing the testicles to move upward. Most males find they can produce this effect with practice; this exercise is one way for a man to become more familiar with his body. As shown in Figure 5.1, you can locate the spermatic cord by palpating the scrotal sac above either testicle with thumb and forefinger. The cord is a firm, rubbery tube that is generally quite pronounced.

The Testes

The **testes,** or testicles, have two major functions: the secretion of male sex hormones and the production of sperm. The testes form inside the abdominal cavity, and late in fetal development they migrate from the abdomen to the scrotum (McClure, 1988). The route they take is known as the **inguinal canal.**

At birth the testes are normally in the scrotum, but in some cases one or both fail to descend. This condition is known as **cryptorchidism** (krip-TOR-ki-dizm) (meaning "hidden testis"). Evidence suggests that 3–4% of boys demonstrate cryptorchidism at birth (McClure, 1988). Undescended testicles often move into place spontaneously sometime after birth, usually in the first year or two, and no treatment is needed.

It is important to watch out for undescended testes, especially when both testicles are affected, because internal body temperature is too high to permit normal sperm production, and infertility may result (Parrott, 1989). Furthermore, cryptorchidism is frequently associated with increased risk for developing a hernia or testicular cancer (McClure, 1988; Rao et al., 1991). Surgery or hormonal treatment may be necessary to allow the testes to descend (Elder, 1989; Moul & Belman, 1988). Recent research indicates that surgical repair may not necessarily result in future fertility because cryptorchidism is often associated with anatomical abnormalities in the structure of the epididymis that interfere with sperm production and/or sperm transportation (Koff & Scaletscky, 1990).

We are not certain of the exact relationship between heat and sperm production, but we do know that average scrotal temperature is approximately 3.1 °C (5.6 °F) *lower* than body temperature (Tessler & Krahn, 1966). In fact, both early and contemporary writers have suggested that hot baths may be an effective method of male contraception. There is some supporting evidence for this notion; for example, it has been reported that a 30-minute exposure to heat within a tolerable temperature range can arrest sperm production for as long as several weeks (Dickinson, 1949). Even so, sitting in the health spa steam room or a hot tub is not a recommended method of birth control. Considering the wide range of variables involved (for instance, temperature, frequency of exposure, or time in the bath), it would be reckless to rely on such a procedure to provide sufficient protection against conception.

The scrotum is very sensitive to any temperature change, and numerous sensory receptors in its skin provide information that prevents the testicles from becoming either too warm or too cold. When the scrotum is cooled, the tunica dartos contracts, wrinkling the outer skin layer and pulling the testicles up closer to the warmth of the body. This process is involuntary, and the reaction sometimes has amusing ramifications:

When I took swimming classes in high school, the trip back to the locker room was always a bit traumatic. After peeling off my swim togs, it seemed like I had to search around for my balls. The other guys seemed to have the same problem, as evidenced by their frantic tugging and pulling as they tried to get everything back in place. (Authors' files)

Are you aware of any types of stimulation, other than cold, that influence the position of the scrotum? Think about this for a few moments before reading on.

Another kind of stimulation that causes the scrotum to draw closer to the body is sexual arousal. One of the clearest external indications of impending male orgasm is the drawing up of the testicles to a position of maximum elevation. The major scrotal muscle involved in this response is the cremasteric muscle, mentioned earlier. Sudden fear may also cause strong contractions of this muscle, and it is also possible to initiate contractions by stroking the inner thighs. This response is known as the **cremasteric reflex.**

The movements of the testes and scrotal sac are influenced by factors other than temperature change, sexual arousal, and strong emotion. These structures have the rather amazing property of virtually constant movement, a result of the continuous contraction – relaxation cycles of the cremasteric musculature.

F I G U R E 5.3

Self-examination can increase a man's familiarity with his genitals. Any irregularity, such as a lump or tender area in the scrotum, should be examined immediately by a physician.

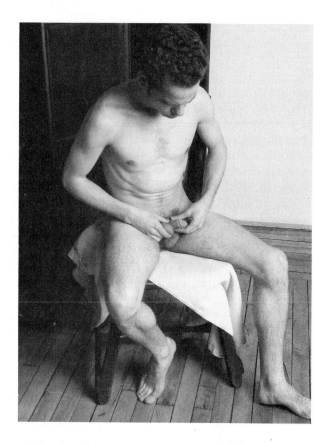

Another testicle characteristic in most men is asymmetry. Note that in Figure 5.1 the left testicle hangs lower than the right. This is the case for most men, as the left spermatic cord is generally longer than the right. This difference in positioning has often been attributed to excessive masturbation, but there is no truth to this assertion. The difference is no more unusual than a woman having one breast larger than the other. Our bodies simply are not perfectly symmetrical.

We encourage you to become familiar with the geography of your testicles and to examine them on a regular basis. Research suggests that only a very small percentage of male college students, perhaps fewer than 10%, engage in regular self-examination of the genitals (Cromer et al., 1992; Goldenring & Purtell, 1984). This is unfortunate because a variety of diseases attack these organs, including cancer, sexually transmitted diseases, and an assortment of infections. (Infections of the sex organs will be discussed in Chapter 19.) Most of these conditions produce observable symptoms, and early detection allows for rapid treatment and the prevention of more serious complications.

You can examine your testicles in a sitting position (see Figure 5.3), standing, or lying on your back. A good time for this exploration is after a hot shower or bath because the heat causes the scrotal skin to relax and the testes to descend. With the scrotum in this relaxed, accessible state, it may be easier to detect anything unusual. First, notice the cremasteric cycles of contraction and relaxation, and experiment with initiating the cremasteric reflex. Then explore the testicles one at a time. Place the thumbs of both your hands on top of a testicle and the index and middle fingers on the underside. Then apply a small amount of pressure and roll the testicle beneath your fingertips. The surface should be fairly smooth and firm in consistency. There are individual variations in the contour and texture of male testicles, and it is important to get to know your own anatomy so that you can note changes. Having two testicles allows you the opportunity for direct comparison, which is helpful in spotting abnormalities (although it is common for the two testicles to vary slightly in size).

Areas that appear swollen or are painful to the touch may indicate the presence of an infection. Along the back of each testicle lies a structure called the *epididymis,* from which the vas deferens carries sperm upward to the urethra. This structure occasionally becomes infected, sometimes causing an irregular area to become tender to the touch.

Testicular cancer is one of the most common of the malignancies that occur in young men in the 15 to 34 age group (Algood et al., 1988; Brubaker & Wickersham, 1990; Cromer et al., 1992; Vaz et al., 1989). The probability that a man will develop this form of cancer sometime during his life is only about one in 500 (Altman, 1983). During the early stages of testicular cancer, there are usually no symptoms beyond a mass within the testicle. The mass feels hard or irregular to the fingertips and is distinguishable from surrounding healthy tissue. It may be painless to touch, but some men do report tenderness in the area of the growth. Occasionally, other symptoms are reported; these may include fever, tender breasts and nipples, and painful accumulation of fluid or swelling in the scrotum. Some types of testicular cancers tend to grow more rapidly than do any other tumors that have been studied. Therefore, for successful treatment, it is important to detect the mass as soon as possible and to seek medical attention immediately (Brubaker & Wickersham, 1990). Improved therapeutic procedures have consistently yielded a very high survival rate among men treated for testicular cancer (Giguere et al., 1988; Peckam, 1988). Some men may be inclined to procrastinate in seeking medical treatment because they are afraid such procedures may create erectile problems or reduce their capacity to enjoy sexual pleasure. In fact, this occurs only rarely.

The Seminiferous Tubules. Within and adjacent to the testes are two separate areas involved in the production and storage of sperm. The first of these, the **seminiferous** (sem′-i-NI-fer-us) **tubules** (sperm-bearing tubules), are thin, highly coiled structures located in the approximately 250 cone-shaped lobes that make up the interior of each testicle (see Figures 5.4 and 5.5). **Spermatogenesis** (sper′-ma-tō-JEN-e-sis), or sperm production, takes place within these tubules. For most males this process begins sometime after the onset of puberty. Men continue to produce viable sperm cells well into their old age, often until death, although the production rate does diminish with aging. The **interstitial** (in′-ter-STISH-al) **cells,** or **Leydig's cells,** are located between the seminiferous tubules. These cells are the major source of androgen, and their close proximity to blood vessels allows for direct secretion of their hormone products into the bloodstream. (We will discuss the role of hormones in sexual behavior in Chapter 6.)

The Epididymis. The second important area for sperm processing is the **epididymis** (ep′-i-DID-i-mus) (literally, "over the testes"). The developed sperm move out of the seminiferous tubules through a maze of tiny ducts into this **C**-shaped

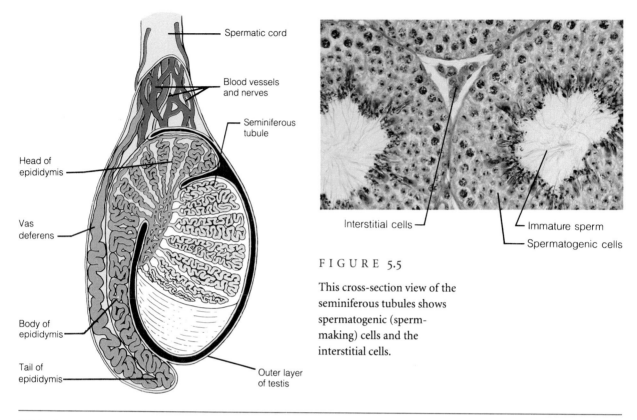

Spermatic cord

Blood vessels
and nerves

Seminiferous
tubule

Head of
epididymis

Vas
deferens

Body of
epididymis

Tail of
epididymis

Outer layer
of testis

Interstitial cells

Immature sperm

Spermatogenic cells

FIGURE 5.5

This cross-section view of the
seminiferous tubules shows
spermatogenic (sperm-
making) cells and the
interstitial cells.

FIGURE 5.4

Internal structure of a testis.
Sperm are produced in the
seminiferous tubules and
transported to the
epididymis, which serves as a
storage chamber.

structure that adheres to the back and upper surface of each testis (see Figure 5.4).
Evidence suggests that the epididymis serves primarily as a storage chamber where
the sperm cells undergo additional maturing, or ripening, for a period of several
weeks. During this time they are completely inactive. Researchers theorize that a
selection process also occurs in the epididymis, in which abnormal sperm cells are
eliminated by the body's waste removal system.

The Vas Deferens

Eventually, the sperm move through the epididymis and drain into the **vas deferens** (vas DEH-fur-renz), or ductus deferens, a long thin duct that travels up
through the scrotum inside the spermatic cord. The vas deferens is close to the
surface of the scrotum along this route, which makes the common male sterilization procedure, **vasectomy** (va-SEK-tō-mē), relatively simple. (Vasectomy will be
described in Chapter 11.)

The spermatic cord exits the scrotal sac through the inguinal canal, an opening that leads directly into the abdominal cavity. From this point the vas deferens
continues its upward journey along the top of the bladder and loops over the
ureter, as shown in Figure 5.6. (This pathway is essentially the reverse of the route
taken by the testis during its prenatal descent.) Turning downward, the vas deferens reaches the base of the bladder, where it is joined by the excretory duct of the

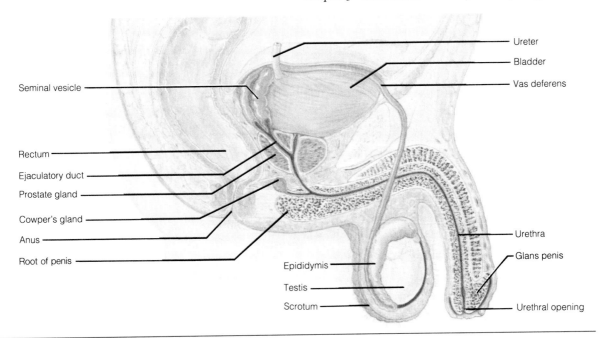

Seminal vesicle

Rectum

Ejaculatory duct

Prostate gland

Cowper's gland

Anus

Root of penis

Ureter

Bladder

Vas deferens

Urethra

Glans penis

Urethral opening

Epididymis

Testis

Scrotum

F I G U R E 5.6

Male sexual anatomy: A cross-section side view of the male reproductive organs.

seminal vesicle, forming the **ejaculatory duct.** The two ejaculatory ducts (one from each side) are very short, running their entire course within the prostate gland. At their termination, they open into the prostatic portion of the urethra.

The Seminal Vesicles

The **seminal vesicles** (SEM-i-nal VES-i-kuls) are two small glands adjacent to the terminals of the vas deferens (see Figure 5.6). Their role in sexual physiology is not completely understood at the present time. It was once assumed that they functioned primarily as storage centers for sperm. However, it is now known that they secrete an alkaline fluid that is very rich in fructose sugar. This secretion constitutes a major portion of the seminal fluid, perhaps as much as 70%, and its sugar component seems to contribute to sperm nutrition and motility (Spring-Mills & Hafez, 1980; Zaviacic et al., 1988). Up to this point in its journey from the testicle, a sperm cell is transmitted through the elaborate system of ducts by the continuous movement of **cilia** (SIL-ē-a), tiny hairlike structures that line the inner walls of these tubes. Once stimulated by the energy-giving secretions of the seminal vesicles, however, sperm propel themselves by the whiplike action of their own tails.

The Prostate Gland

The **prostate** (PROS-tāt) **gland** is a structure about the size and shape of a walnut, located at the base of the bladder (see Figure 5.6). As described earlier, both ejaculatory ducts and the **urethra** (yoo-RĒ-thra) pass through this organ. The prostate is made up of smooth muscle fibers and glandular tissue, whose secretions account for about 30% of the seminal fluid released during ejaculation.

Although the prostate is continually active in a mature male, it accelerates its output during sexual arousal. Its secretions flow into the urethra through a system of sievelike ducts, and here they combine with sperm and the seminal vesicle secretions to form the seminal fluid. The prostatic secretions are thin, milky, and alkaline in nature. This alkalinity helps counteract the unfavorable acidity of the male urethra and the female vaginal tract, making a more hospitable environment for sperm.

The prostate gland is the focal point of some of the more common physio-sexual problems in the human male. Occasionally, it becomes enlarged and inflamed as a result of various infectious agents (such as the gonococcus bacterium and *Trichomonas*). This condition, known as **prostatitis** (pros-tuh-TY-tis), may occur in a man of any age. The symptoms of prostatitis may include any or all of the following: pain in the pelvic area or base of the penis, lower abdominal ache, backache, aching testicles, feelings of urgency (needing to urinate frequently), burning sensation while urinating, a cloudy discharge from the penis, and difficulties with sexual functions such as painful erections or ejaculations and reduced sexual interest.

Some men also develop cancer of the prostate, and the potential for this becomes greater with increasing age. Prostate cancer is the most common cancer and currently the second leading cause of cancer death among men in the United States (Catalona et al., 1991; Palken et al., 1991). Approximately 30,000 men die each year from prostate cancer, the majority of whom would have been saved by early diagnosis and treatment. Consequently, it is very important for men to be aware of the early symptoms of this disease, which may include many of those listed for prostatitis (particularly pain in the pelvis and lower back and urinary complications). However, prostate cancer often lacks easily detectable symptoms in its early stages, and an early diagnosis may be accomplished by a physical examination.

A physician examines the prostate by inserting a finger into the rectum. Under normal conditions, this is only mildly uncomfortable. The discovery of a marker for prostate cancer — *prostate-specific antigen (PSA)* — detectable by a blood test, has improved the ability of physicians to diagnose early prostate cancer (Crawford et al., 1992; Jencks, 1992). In recent years transrectal ultrasound, which uses sound waves to reflect the prostate on a TV screen, has also been employed as a diagnostic tool to detect prostate cancer (Hinman, 1991; Palken et al., 1991). During these procedures the physician may also detect signs of cancer in the colon or rectum. Women too develop cancers of the rectum and colon — about 50,000 men and women die of these diseases each year. The American Cancer Society therefore recommends an annual digital rectal examination for men and women age 40 and older (Gambert, 1991).

What are some of the reasons why men are often reluctant to submit to a prostate exam, particularly the digital variety? Give this some thought before reading on.

Many men are hesitant to have rectal examinations. They may be uncomfortable about homosexual associations when the examining physician is male, or they may fear what the examination might reveal. False information abounds in the area of prostate disease, and many men incorrectly believe that prostate surgery will inevitably block sexual functioning. The reality is that surgery on the prostate only occasionally results in major impairment of the biological aspects of male sexual function. We will say more about this in Chapter 15, in which we discuss sexuality and aging.

The Cowper's Glands

The **Cowper's glands,** or **bulbourethral** (bul'-bō-yoo-RĒ-thral) **glands,** are two small structures, each about the size of a pea, located one on each side of the urethra just below where it emerges from the prostate gland (see Figure 5.6). Tiny ducts connect both glands directly to the urethra. When a man is sexually aroused, these organs often secrete a slippery, mucoid substance that appears in droplet form at the tip of the penis. Like the prostatic secretions, this fluid is alkaline in nature and helps buffer the acidity of the urethra. Furthermore, it is thought to provide lubrication for the flow of seminal fluid through the urethra. Contrary to some reports, though, it has virtually no function as a vaginal lubricant during coitus. In many men this secretion does not appear until well after the beginning of arousal, often just prior to orgasm. Other men report that it occurs immediately after they get an erection, and some individuals rarely or never produce these pre-ejaculatory droplets. All these experiences are normal variations of male sexual functioning.

The fluid from the Cowper's glands should not be confused with semen; however, it does occasionally contain active, healthy sperm. This is one reason among many why the withdrawal method of birth control is not highly effective. (Withdrawal and other methods of birth control are discussed in Chapter 11.)

Semen

As we have seen, the **semen** ejaculated through the opening of the penis comes from a variety of sources. Fluids are supplied by the seminal vesicles, prostate, and Cowper's glands, with the seminal vesicles providing the greatest portion (Eliasson & Lindholmer, 1976; Spring-Mills & Hafez, 1980). The amount of **seminal fluid** a man ejaculates—roughly one teaspoonful on the average—is influenced by a number of factors, including the length of time since the last ejaculation, the duration of arousal before ejaculation, and age (older men tend to produce less fluid). The semen of a single ejaculation typically contains between 200 and 500 million sperm, which account for only about 1% of the total volume of semen. Chemical analysis shows that semen is also made up of acids (ascorbic and citric), water, enzymes, fructose sugar, bases (phosphate and bicarbonate buffers), and a variety of other substances. None of these materials is harmful if swallowed during oral sex.

Sperm, as seen under a microscope.

The Penis

The **penis** consists of nerves, blood vessels, fibrous tissue, and three parallel cylinders of spongy tissue. It does not contain a bone, nor an abundance of muscular tissue, contrary to some people's beliefs. However, there is an extensive network

FIGURE 5.7

Interior structure of the penis: (a) side view and (b) cross section of the penis.

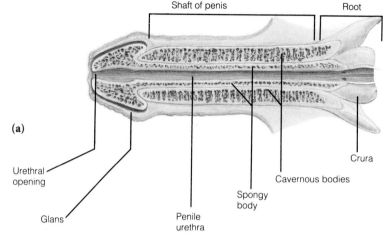

(a)

TOP OF PENIS

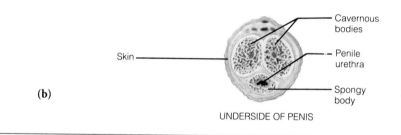

(b)

UNDERSIDE OF PENIS

of muscles around the base of the penis, and these help to eject both semen and urine through the urethra.

A portion of the penis extends internally into the pelvic cavity. This part, including its attachment to the pubic bones, is referred to as the **root.** When a man's penis is erect, he can feel this inward projection by pressing a finger up between his anus and scrotum. The external, pendulous portion of the penis, excluding the head, is known as the **shaft.** The smooth, acorn-shaped head is called the **glans.**

Running the entire length of the penis are the three chambers referred to earlier. The two larger ones, the **cavernous bodies** (corpora cavernosa), lie side by side above the smaller third cylinder, the **spongy body** (corpus spongiosum). At the root of the penis, the innermost tips of the cavernous bodies, or **crura,** are connected to the pubic bones. At the head of the penis, the spongy body expands to form the glans. These structures are shown in Figure 5.7.

All these chambers are similar in structure. As the terms *cavernous* and *spongy* imply, they are made of vast arrays of spongelike irregular spaces and cavities. Each chamber is also richly supplied with blood vessels. When a male is sexually excited, the chambers become engorged with blood, resulting in penile erection. During sexual arousal, the spongy body may stand out as a distinct ridge along the underside of the penis.

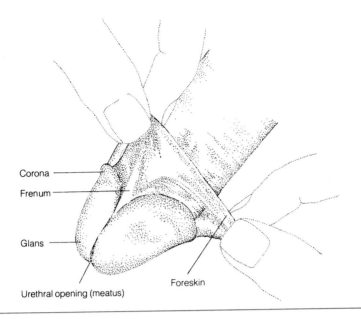

This figure shows the location of the corona and frenum — two areas on the penis that harbor a high concentration of sensitive nerve endings.

Corona

Frenum

Glans

Urethral opening (meatus)

Foreskin

The skin covering the penile shaft is usually hairless and quite loose, which allows for expansion when the penis becomes erect. Though the skin is connected to the shaft at the neck (the portion just behind the glans), some of it folds over and forms a cuff, or hood, over the glans. This loose covering is called the **foreskin**, or **prepuce**. In some males it covers the entire head, whereas in others only a portion is covered. Typically, the foreskin can be retracted (drawn back from the glans) quite easily. *Circumcision,* discussed later in the chapter, involves the surgical removal of this sleeve of skin.

While the entire penis is sensitive to tactile stimulation (touch), the greatest concentration of nerve endings is found in the glans. Although the entire glans area is extremely sensitive, there are two specific locations that many men find particularly responsive to stimulation. One is the rim, or crown, that marks the area where the glans rises abruptly from the shaft. This distinct ridge is called the **corona** (ko-RŌ-na). The other is the **frenum,** or **frenulum** (FREN-yoo-lum), a thin strip of skin connecting the glans to the shaft on the underside of the penis. The location of these two areas is shown in Figure 5.8.

While most men enjoy having the glans stimulated, particularly the two areas mentioned above, individuals vary in their preferences. Some may occasionally or routinely prefer being stimulated in genital areas other than the glans of the penis. The mode of stimulation, either manual (by self or partner) or oral, may influence the choice of preferred sites. Some of these variations and individual preferences are noted in the following accounts:

When I masturbate I frequently avoid the head of my penis, concentrating instead on stroking the shaft. What happens is that the stimulation is not so intense, which allows a longer time for buildup to orgasm. The end result is that the climax is generally more intense than if I focus only on the glans. (Authors' files)

During oral sex with my girlfriend, I sometimes have to put my hand around my penis, leaving just the head sticking out, so she will get the idea what part feels best to me. Otherwise, she spends a lot of time running her tongue up and down the shaft, which just doesn't do it for me. (Authors' files)

As previously mentioned, the internal extension of the penis is surrounded by an elaborate network of muscles. This musculature, the most important of which is the *pubococcygeus* (PC) *muscle,* is comparable to that in the female body, and strengthening these muscles by doing Kegel exercises may produce benefits for men similar to those experienced by women. In most men these muscles are quite weak because they are usually only contracted during ejaculation. The following is a brief outline of how these muscles may be located and strengthened, adapted from *Male Sexuality* (Zilbergeld, 1978, p. 109):

1. Locate the muscles by stopping the flow of urine several times while urinating. The muscles you squeeze to accomplish this are the ones on which you will concentrate. If you do a correct Kegel while not urinating, you will notice your penis move slightly. Kegels done when you have an erection will cause your penis to move up and down.

2. Begin the exercise program by squeezing and relaxing the muscles 15 times, twice daily. Do not hold the contraction at this stage. (These are called "short Kegels.")

3. Gradually increase the number of Kegels until you can comfortably do 60 at a time, twice daily.

4. Now practice "long Kegels" by holding each contraction for a count of three.

5. Combine the short and long Kegels in each daily exercise routine, doing a set of 60 of each, once or twice a day.

6. Continue with the Kegel exercises for at least several weeks. You may not notice results until a month or more has passed. By this time the exercises will probably have become automatic, requiring no particular effort.

Some of the positive changes men have reported after doing the male Kegels include stronger and more pleasurable orgasms, better ejaculatory control, and increased pelvic sensation during sexual arousal.

Caring for the penis is an important aspect of sexual self-health. Washing the penis regularly with soap and water, at least once a day, is an excellent self-health practice. (There is also evidence, discussed in Chapter 19, that washing the genitals before and after sex may reduce the chances of exchanging infectious organisms with your partner.) If you are uncircumcised, pay particular attention to drawing the foreskin back from the glans and washing all surfaces, especially the underside of the foreskin. Be aware of any unusual changes in your penis. A sore or unusual growth anywhere on its surface may be a symptom of a sexually transmitted disease. Sometimes the glans or shaft of the penis may develop an eczemalike reaction — "weepy" and sore — that may result from an allergic reaction to the vaginal secretions of your partner. Wearing a condom may help alleviate this condition, but it is important that you consult a physician to clarify its origin and treatment. (**Urology** [yoo-ROL-ō-jē] is the medical specialty that focuses on the male reproductive structures.)

It is wise to avoid abusing your penis by putting it in potentially harmful places such as partners' mouths that have herpes blisters or vaginas that manifest unusual sores, growths, odors, or discharges. There are some sexual gadgets that may also be quite hazardous to penile health. For example, never use a "cock ring" (a tight-fitting ring that encircles the base of the penis). Although this device may be successful in accomplishing its intended purpose of sustaining erections, it may also destroy penile tissue by cutting off the blood supply (Schellhammer & Donnelley, 1973). In recent years sexually oriented magazines like *Penthouse* have published testimonials attesting to the pleasure of masturbating with a vacuum cleaner. This is not a good idea! Recent research suggests that severe penile injuries (including decapitation of the glans) resulting from masturbating with vacuum cleaners and electric brooms may be much more common than reported (Benson, 1985; Grisell, 1988).

On rare occasions, the penis may be fractured (Adducci & Ross, 1991; Fitch & Hodge, 1988). This injury involves a rupture of the cavernous bodies when the penis is in an erect state. A review of the cases reported in the literature reveals that this injury most commonly occurs during coitus (Desterwitz et al., 1984). Recently, a student reported his encounter with this painful injury:

I was having intercourse with my girlfriend in a sitting position. She was straddling my legs and using the arms of the chair and her legs to move her body up and down on my penis. In the heat of passion, she raised up a little too far, and I slipped out. She sat back down hard, expecting me to repenetrate her. Unfortunately, I was off target and all of her weight came down on my penis. I heard a cracking sound and experienced excruciating pain. I bled quite a bit inside my penis, and I was real sore for quite a long time. (Authors' files)

This account suggests that it is wise to take some precautions during coitus. This injury usually happens "in the heat of passion" and often involves putting too much weight on the penis when attempting to gain or regain vaginal penetration. When the woman is on top, the risk increases. Communicating the need to go slow at these times can avert a painful injury. Treatment of penile fractures varies from measures like splinting and ice packs to surgery. Most men injured in this fashion regain normal sexual function, and surgical treatment generally provides the best results (Kalash & Young, 1984).

Male Sexual Functions

Up to this point in the chapter, we have looked at the various *parts* of the male sexual system, but we have not described their *functioning* in much detail. In the following pages, we examine two of these functions, erection and ejaculation.

Erection

An **erection** is a process coordinated by the autonomic nervous system. When a male becomes sexually excited, the nervous system transmits messages that induce expansion of the arteries leading to the three erectile chambers in the penis. This increases the rate of blood flow into these parallel cylinders. The blood flowing out of the penis through the veins cannot keep up with the dramatically increased inflow, so blood accumulates in the spongelike tissues (Bookstein & Lurie, 1988). The penis remains erect until the messages from the nervous system stop and the inflow of blood returns to normal.

The capacity for erection is present at birth. It is very common and quite natural for infant boys to experience erections during sleep or diapering, from stimulation by clothing, and later by touching themselves. Nighttime erections occur during the REM, or dreaming, stage of sleep (Chung & Choi, 1990; Fisher et al., 1965; Karacan, 1970). Erotic dreams may play a role, but the primary mechanism seems to be physiological, and erections often occur even when the dream content is clearly not sexual. Often a man awakens in the morning just after completing a REM cycle. This explains the phenomenon of "morning erections," which in the past has been erroneously attributed to a full bladder.

Although an erection is basically a physiological response, it also involves psychological components. In fact, some writers distinguish between psychogenic (from the mind) and physiogenic (from the body) erections — although in most cases of sexual arousal there are simultaneous inputs from both thoughts and physical stimulation.

How great an influence does the mind have on erections? We know that it can inhibit the response: When a man becomes troubled by erection difficulties, the problem is often of psychological origin, as we will discuss in Chapter 16. There is also extensive evidence that men are able to enhance their erection (as reflected in increased penile tumescence) by forming vivid mental images or fantasies of sexual activity (Dekker et al., 1985; Smith & Over, 1987).

 Are erections sometimes induced by nonsexual stimuli/events? If so, what kinds of nonsexual triggers are involved in erectile responses? Think about this for a couple of minutes before reading on.

Logically, one might expect erection to occur only in response to obvious sexual stimuli. That this is not always the case can be embarrassing, perplexing, amusing, or anxiety-arousing. Nearly every man can recall scenes of unwanted erections during adolescent school days — the teacher saying "Bob, come up here and do the math problem on the board," when math was the farthest thing from Bob's mind; the trips down school halls with a notebook held in a strategic location; the delayed exit from the swimming pool after playful frolicking.

Sometimes erections happen in situations that seem entirely nonsexual, such as riding a bike, lifting heavy weights, or straining during defecation (particularly in little boys). Occasionally, the occurrence of an erection produces considerable anxiety and causes a man to question his own motivations. This is evident in the following report offered by a father and former student in our sexuality class:

Sometimes when my little girl crawls up on my lap to be cuddled, I find myself getting an erection. This bothers me greatly. Does it mean I have some kind of unconscious, incestuous craving for my daughter? (Authors' files)

This kind of experience, and the anxiety associated with it, is not unusual. It is possible to experience a reflex erection from direct physical stimulation during cuddling with a child. The response may also be psychologically induced by the association of physical closeness with sex, and thus it is probably a predictable event in our culture. Consider the following account:

When I was a little boy, my father would go away on extended business trips. I missed him terribly, and when he returned I wanted to rush across the room and catapult myself into his arms. Instead, like a man, I shook his hand and said "Hi, Dad, good to see you." (Authors' files)

Like this person, many men learn very early that it is not "masculine" to cuddle and embrace those near and dear to us. Among adult males in our society, intimate physical contact occurs primarily or exclusively within a sexual context. With this kind of conditioning, the association of warm embraces and sexual excitation will be quite strong. In this sense it is not "unnatural" at all for a father to experience an erection when he holds his child closely. However, any inclination on the part of an adult to sexually fondle a child is of concern; this subject is dealt with in Chapter 21.

Ejaculation

Besides erection, the second basic male sexual function is **ejaculation** — the process whereby the semen is expelled through the penis to the outside of the body. Many writers equate orgasm and ejaculation in the male. However, these two processes do not always take place simultaneously. Prior to puberty a boy may experience hundreds of "dry orgasms" — orgasms without any ejaculation of fluid. Occasionally, a man may have more than one orgasm in a given sexual encounter, with the second or third producing little or no expelled semen. Conversely, research reveals that some men may experience a series of nonejaculatory orgasms culminating in a final orgasm accompanied by expulsion of semen (Hartman & Fithian, 1984; Robbins & Jensen, 1978). Thus, it is clear that, while male orgasm is generally associated with ejaculation, these two processes are not one and the same and do not necessarily occur together.

From a neurophysiological point of view, ejaculation — like erection — is basically a spinal reflex. Effective sexual stimulation of the penis (manual, oral, or coital) results in the buildup of neural excitation to a critical level. When a threshold is reached, this triggers several internal physical events.

The actual ejaculation occurs in two stages (see Figure 5.9). During the first stage, sometimes called the **emission phase,** the prostate, seminal vesicles, and **ampulla** (am-POOL-la) (upper portions of the vas deferens) undergo contractions. This forces their various secretions down into the ejaculatory ducts and prostatic urethra. At the same time, both internal and external **urethral sphincters** (SFINGK-ters) (two muscles, one located where the urethra exits from the bladder and the other below the prostate) are closed, trapping seminal fluid in the **urethral bulb** (the prostatic portion of the urethra, between these two muscles). The urethral bulb expands like a balloon. A man typically experiences this first stage as a subjective sense that orgasm is inevitable, the "point of no return" or "ejaculatory inevitability."

In the second stage, sometimes called the **expulsion phase,** the collected semen is expelled out of the penis by strong, rhythmic contractions of muscles that surround the urethral bulb and root of the penis. In addition, there are contractions along the entire urethral route. The external urethral sphincter relaxes, allowing fluid to pass through, while the internal sphincter remains contracted to prevent the escape of urine. The first two or three muscle contractions around the base of the penis are quite strong and occur at close intervals. Most of the seminal fluid is expelled in spurts corresponding to these contractions. Several more muscle responses typically occur, with a gradual diminishing of intensity and lengthening of time intervals between contractions. The entire expulsion stage usually occurs in three to ten seconds.

FIGURE 5.9

Male sexual anatomy during ejaculation: (a) the emission phase and (b) the expulsion phase.

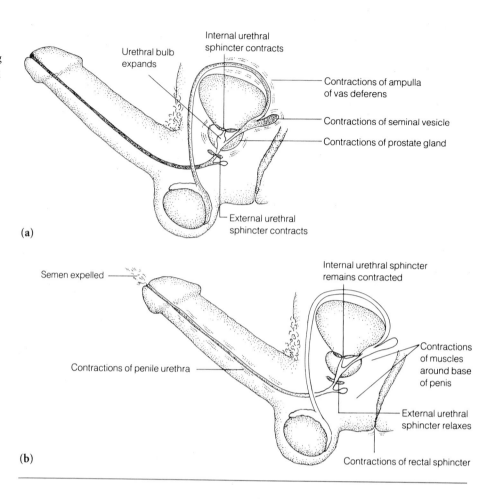

(a)

Urethral bulb expands

Internal urethral sphincter contracts

Contractions of ampulla of vas deferens

Contractions of seminal vesicle

Contractions of prostate gland

External urethral sphincter contracts

(b)

Semen expelled

Internal urethral sphincter remains contracted

Contractions of penile urethra

Contractions of muscles around base of penis

External urethral sphincter relaxes

Contractions of rectal sphincter

Some men have an experience known as **retrograde ejaculation,** in which the semen is expelled into the bladder rather than through the penis (see Figure 5.10). This results from a reversed functioning of the two urethral sphincters. The condition sometimes occurs in men who have undergone prostate surgery. In addition, illness, congenital anomaly, and certain drugs, most notably tranquilizers, can induce this reaction. Although retrograde ejaculation itself is not harmful (the seminal fluid is later eliminated with the urine), a man who consistently experiences this response would be wise to seek medical attention to rule out the possibility of an underlying health problem.

Sometimes a man experiences orgasm without direct genital stimulation. The most familiar of these occurrences are **nocturnal emissions,** commonly known as "wet dreams." The exact mechanism that produces this response is not fully understood. Women also have the capacity for experiencing orgasm during sleep. The possibility of a man using fantasy alone to reach orgasm in a waking state is exceedingly remote, and we have never heard a firsthand account of this phenomenon. Kinsey (1948) stated that only three or four of the males in his sample of over 5000 reported this experience. In contrast, significantly greater numbers of women in his sample (roughly 2%) reported orgasms from fantasy alone (Kinsey

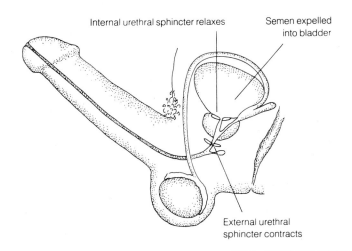

Internal urethral sphincter relaxes

Semen expelled into bladder

External urethral sphincter contracts

FIGURE 5.10

Retrograde ejaculation occurs when a reversed functioning of the urethral sphincters (internal relaxes, external contracts) results in semen being expelled *into* the bladder.

et al., 1953). Another kind of nongenitally induced ejaculation that men sometimes report is reaching orgasm during sex play (activities such as mutual kissing or manual or oral stimulation of their partner) when there is no penile stimulation.

Some Concerns About Sexual Functioning

Men frequently voice a variety of concerns about sexual functioning. Several of these will be addressed throughout our text. At this point we will discuss two areas that receive considerable attention — the significance of penis size and the necessity and impact of circumcision. Claims are frequently made that one or both of these physical characteristics may influence the sexual pleasure of a man or his partner. In the following sections, we examine the available evidence.

Penis Size

When I was a kid, my peers were unmerciful in their comments about my small size. They would say things like, "I have a penis, John has a penis, but you have a pee-pee." Needless to say, I grew up with a very poor self-image in this area. Later it was translated into anxiety-ridden sexual encounters where I would insist that the room be completely dark before I would undress. Even now, when I realize that size is an irrelevant factor in giving sexual pleasure, I am still worried that a new partner will comment unfavorably about my less than impressive natural endowment. (Authors' files)

This man is not alone in his discomfort. His feelings are echoed in more accounts than we can remember. Penis size has occupied the attention of most men and many women at one time or another. Generally, it is more than mere idle curiosity that stimulates interest in this topic. For many it is a matter of real concern, perhaps even cause for apprehension or anguish.

Preoccupation with penis size
is evident in a variety of
cultures and art forms.

It does not take much imagination to understand why penis size often takes on great importance. As a society, we tend to be overly impressed with size and quantity. Bigger cars are better than compacts, the bigger the house the better it is, and by implication, big penises provide more pleasure than smaller ones. Certainly, the various art forms, such as literature, painting, sculpture, and movies, do much to perpetuate this obsession with big penises. Consider the following excerpt from Mario Puzo's novel *The Godfather* (1969), which describes a sexual encounter between Sonny and Lucy:

> She felt something burning pass between her thighs. She let her right hand drop from his neck and reached down to guide him. Her hand closed around an *enormous*, blood-gorged pole of muscle. It pulsated in her hand like an animal and almost weeping with *grateful ecstasy* she pointed it into her own wet, turgid flesh. The thrust of its entering, the *unbelievable pleasure* made her gasp, brought her legs up around his neck, and then like a quiver, her body received the savage arrows of his lightning-like thrusts; innumerable, torturing; arching her pelvis higher and higher until for the *first time in her life* she reached a shattering climax, felt his hardness break and then the crawly flood of semen over her thighs. (p. 28, italics ours)

The modern Western world is not alone in its preoccupation with penis size, as the photograph above illustrates. Even the fascinating Indian sex manuals, the *Ananga Ranga* and the *Kama Sutra*, classify men according to three categories: the hare-man, whose erect penis measures 6 finger-widths; the bull-man (9 finger-widths long); and the horse-man (12 or more finger-widths long). In ancient Greek mythology, preoccupation with penis size found a focal point in Priapus, son of the goddess Aphrodite and the god Dionysus, who was usually portrayed as a lasciviously grinning little man with a greatly oversized penis.

The result of all this attention to penis size is that men often come to view size in and of itself as an important attribute in defining their masculinity or their worth as lovers. Such a concept of virility can contribute to a poor self-image. Furthermore, if either a man or his partner views his penis as being smaller than it should be, this can decrease sexual satisfaction for one or both of them — not because of physical limitations, but rather as a self-fulfilling prophecy.

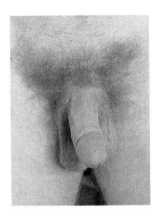

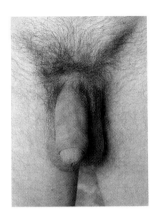

FIGURE 5.11

There are many variations in the shape and size of the male genitals. The penis in the right photo is uncircumcised.

What are your perspectives on the issue of penis size and sexual intimacy? Do you believe that a man's penis size influences his partner's pleasure during intercourse? How might you relate the information acquired in Chapter 4 to this issue? Take a few moments to consider these questions before reading on.

What are the simple physiological facts of sexual interaction and penis size? We will focus on heterosexual penile–vaginal intercourse because concerns about penis size often relate to this kind of sexual activity.

As we learned in Chapter 4, the greatest sensitivity in the vaginal canal is concentrated in its outer portion. While some women do find pressure and stretching deep within the vagina to be pleasurable, this is not usually requisite for female sexual gratification. In fact, some women may even find deep penetration painful, particularly if it is quite vigorous:

You asked if size was important to my pleasure. Yes, but not in the way you might imagine. If a man is quite large, I worry that he might hurt me. Actually, I prefer that he be average or even to the smaller side. (Authors' files)

There is a physiological explanation for the pain or discomfort some women feel during deep penetration. Because the female ovaries and male testicles originate from the same embryonic tissue source, they share some of the same sensitivity. If the penis bangs into the cervix and causes the uterus to be slightly displaced, this may in turn jar an ovary. The resulting sensation is somewhat like a male's experience of getting hit in the testicles. Fast stretching of the uterine ligaments has also been implicated in deep penetration pain. However, some women find slow stretching of these same ligaments to be pleasurable.

These observations indicate the importance of being gentle and considerate during intercourse. If one or both partners want deeper or more vigorous thrusting, they can experiment by gradually adding these components to their coital movements. It may also be helpful for the woman to be in an intercourse position other than female supine (see Figure 9.6), so she has more control over the depth and vigor of penetration.

Most textbooks on human sexuality report average dimensions of penises. We will not do this because such information seems unimportant. Figure 5.11 shows several flaccid (nonerect) penises of different sizes, all well within the normal

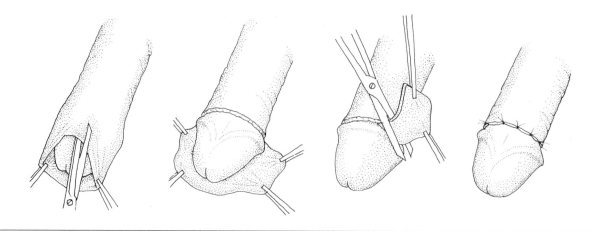

F I G U R E 5.12

Circumcision, the surgical removal of the foreskin, is practiced throughout the world.

range. It is worth noting that penis size is not related to body shape, height, length of fingers, race, or anything else (Money et al., 1984). It should also be mentioned that small flaccid penises tend to increase more in size during erection than do penises that are larger in the flaccid state (Jamison & Gebhard, 1988; Masters & Johnson, 1966). These collective facts are reflected in the comment offered by an extremely tall, husky male:

I think most people just naturally assumed, judging from my large stature, that I would have a big penis. Such is not the case. In fact, when I'm flaccid it looks like all I have is testicles and a glans. My shaft is practically invisible. However, when I get hard I know my penis is quite adequate in size. When I was a teenager the problem was how to let my buddies know this when it's not really cool to walk around with a hard-on. What I did was simply avoid taking showers with others if at all possible. Now I feel okay about my body, but for a while there I was really self-conscious. (Authors' files)

As we close this section, it is important to note that even though physiological evidence indicates that large penises are not a necessary prerequisite for female sexual pleasure during coitus, some women do have subjective preferences regarding penis size and shape, just as some men have such preferences about breasts.

Circumcision

A characteristic that many people associate with differences in male sensitivity — and also differences in hygiene — is the presence or absence of the foreskin.

Circumcision (ser′-kum-SIZH-un) is the surgical removal of the foreskin, shown in Figure 5.12. It is widely practiced throughout the world for religious, ritual, or hygienic reasons. In the United States, this operation is performed on the majority of male infants (with parental consent), generally on the second day after birth. In certain other cultures, the procedure is performed when a boy reaches adolescence, as part of the rituals of entering manhood. Some religions, including both the Jewish and Moslem faiths, mandate circumcision.

In this country, routine circumcision has reflected concern by the medical profession about hygiene. There are a number of small glands located in the foreskin *(preputial glands)* and under the corona, on either side of the frenum *(Tyson's glands).* These glands secrete an oily, lubricating substance. If these secretions are allowed to accumulate under the foreskin, they combine with sloughed-off dead skin cells to form a cheesy substance known as **smegma.** When it builds up over a period of time, smegma generally develops a strong, unpleasant odor, becomes grainy and irritating, and can serve as a breeding ground for infection-causing organisms.

There is evidence that uncircumcised males may be slightly more at risk for developing penile cancer than are their circumcised counterparts (Harahap & Siregar, 1988; McAninch, 1990; Rotolo & Lynch, 1991; Warner & Strashin, 1981). There are additional claims that smegma may harbor organisms that can cause a variety of infections in the female vaginal tract. Furthermore, some investigators have suggested that cervical cancer is more frequent in women who have sexual relations with uncircumcised partners. This assertion has generally not been supported by studies (Brinton et al., 1989; Snyder, 1991; Wallerstein, 1980). In addition, some research has indicated that there may be an increased incidence of cancer of the cervix among partners of uncircumcised men infected with the virus that causes genital warts (human papilloma virus [HPV]) (McAninch, 1989). However, other research has failed to confirm this connection between HPV, circumcision status, and cervical cancer (Brinton et al., 1989). Finally, there are some indications from data obtained in Africa that uncircumcised men may be more likely to contract AIDS via heterosexual intercourse than their circumcised counterparts (Hira et al., 1990; Jessamine et al., 1990; Marx, 1989). However, three studies in New York City failed to confirm a relationship between AIDS and circumcision (Chiasson et al., 1990). Clearly, more research is needed to clarify if AIDS and circumcision are causally related.

There are several arguments *against* routine circumcision, many of which have been raised with greater frequency in recent years. First, the foreskin may serve some important function yet to be determined. Second, some have expressed concern that sexual function may be altered by excising the foreskin; we will consider this question later in this discussion. Finally, some think performing such an unpleasant procedure on a newborn is unnecessarily traumatic and an invitation to possible surgical complications. Because the use of general anesthesia and narcotic analgesia is contraindicated for infants (Anand et al., 1992), circumcision is usually performed without anesthesia. However, "infants undergoing circumcision without anesthesia feel and respond to pain" (Schoen & Fischell, 1991, p. 429). Some of the health risks of circumcision include hemorrhage, infections, mutilation, shock, psychological trauma, and even death in rare cases (Chessare, 1992; Thompson, 1990).

In the 1960s and 1970s, the concept of circumcision as a preventative medical practice underwent serious reconsideration. This process culminated in the release of a policy statement by the American Academy of Pediatrics (AAP) in 1975, which concluded that there was no medical indication for circumcision. The AAP further recommended against the performance of routine circumcisions. Since then, several American hospitals established policies whereby circumcision was performed only at the request of parents or as elective surgery. However, parents continued to opt for this operation in most cases, no doubt due in part to the prominence of social concerns such as appearance of uncircumcised penises and perceived

ETHICAL/LEGAL ISSUES IN HUMAN SEXUALITY

Should You Have Your Son(s) Circumcised?

Consider the following scenario. A son is born to you. Neither you nor your spouse embraces a cultural or religious perspective or faith that mandates circumcision. You are aware that the American Academy of Pediatrics maintains that newborn circumcision has both potential medical benefits and advantages as well as risks and disadvantages. What do you do? Is this a decision that you or any parents should make for a newborn son? Might it be better to forgo infant circumcision, instead allowing your son to make that decision for himself later in life? Consider the following comments by a mother of a young son:

When my son was born, I agonized over the decision about whether or not he should be circumcised. My own personal preference is for circumcised penises. I also worried that by not having him circumcised, I might be setting him up for jokes or ridicule by other circumcised boys, who are certainly in the majority. But would it be right to put these values and concerns on him without his having any say in this matter? Also, the idea of subjecting my baby boy to pain was appalling to me. I knew that it must be a very painful operation. This is the major reason why my husband and I decided not to have our son circumcised. Now he is 10 years old and worries about being different. He has even asked to be circumcised now. Did we make the right decision? (Authors' files)

Clearly, when religious/cultural mandates are not present, parents could elect to leave the decision regarding circumcision up to a child when he reaches an age sufficient to make a reasoned choice. But, as pointed out by the mother above, postponing circumcision to allow individual choice opens the door to thoughtless ridicule that some uncircumcised children experience at the hands of their unenlightened peers.

A decision not to inflict pain on one's son is certainly understandable in light of clear-cut evidence that most infant circumcisions are currently performed without anesthesia and do induce vigorous pain cries and other signs of pain both during and after the procedure (Fontaine & Toffler, 1991; Myron & Maguire, 1991; Schoen & Fischell, 1991). However, physiological and behavioral indications of pain accompanying infant circumcision dim rapidly after completion of the operation and fade completely within minutes to hours following surgery (Schoen & Fischell, 1991). In contrast, an older child, adolescent, or adult undergoing circumcision can expect to experience postsurgical pain and discomfort that will persist for considerably longer, perhaps days. Thus, a decision by parents not to inflict the pain of circumcision on their son may, in fact, merely postpone the experience of

future ridicule by peers (Brown & Brown, 1987). Nevertheless, evidence suggests that in recent years the incidence of circumcision in America has declined moderately (Snyder, 1991). For example, one study of over 400,000 male infants born over a 9-year period commencing in the late 1970s revealed a decrease in the rate of circumcision from 85% to 75% (Wiswell et al., 1987). However, circumcision remains the most common surgery performed on infants in the United States, with over one million males circumcised annually (Andolsek, 1990; Schoen & Fischell, 1991).

In the late 1980s, new evidence emerged that issues a challenge to the argument that there are no significant medical reasons for circumcision. Several studies reported markedly higher rates of urinary tract infections among uncircumcised boys as compared to their circumcised counterparts (Fergusson et al., 1988; Herzog, 1989; Roberts, 1990; Wiswell et al., 1987). This new evidence played a major role in influencing the AAP to abandon its former position that there are no valid medical indications for circumcising male infants. In March 1989, the AAP announced a new neutral position, suggesting that circumcision has both medical advantages and some risks. The following recommendation was included in the AAP task force report:

pain to a time when such pain and discomfort may be felt more acutely and for much longer. In addition, circumcision after infancy includes the additional risk of general anesthesia (Larsen & Williams, 1990).

Over the last decade, an increasing number of physicians who perform infant circumcisions are injecting a local anesthetic agent directly into the penis to reduce or eliminate pain associated with circumcision. This anesthetic procedure, known as *dorsal penile nerve block,* has been shown in several recent clinical studies to have an 80–90% success rate in reducing pain and stress accompanying infant circumcision (Amir et al., 1992; Fontaine & Toffler, 1991). We anticipate that this simple, easy-to-learn technique will be used with increasing frequency as clinicians become more familiar with its effectiveness and as informed parents request it more often. Thus the issue of whether to leave the decision about circumcision

up to the individual child may become even more complex as parents learn that their infant son(s) may be circumcised with little or no pain.

What should parents make of the evidence that uncircumcised males may be slightly more at risk than their circumcised counterparts for developing urinary tract infections, penile cancer, and AIDS? Certainly such evidence merits consideration. However, parents evaluating these concerns should remember that unequivocal proof that an uncircumcised foreskin is a significant risk factor for these various diseases is currently unavailable. Furthermore, any slightly elevated risk for disease that may exist is perhaps more than offset by the risk factors associated with complications from circumcision (Chessare, 1992) . For example, one researcher recently applied both the available data on urinary tract infections in male children and the incidence of medical complications from

circumcision to a hypothetical sample of 1000 male infants subjected to circumcision. This scientist calculated that while approximately 9 baby boys would benefit by avoiding urinary tract infections, as many as 41 would be moderately or seriously adversely affected by medical complications stemming from the operation (Thompson, 1990). Considered from this perspective, the medical benefits associated with circumcision may fail to justify the risks.

Thus we see that parents who can choose whether or not to have their son(s) circumcised must confront numerous complex issues, including the possible infliction of pain and/or ridicule, their child's right of self-determination, and conflicting medical data on the potential benefits and · risks of circumcision. Clearly, it is not an easy decision.

> Newborn circumcision has potential medical benefits and advantages as well as disadvantages and risks. When circumcision is being considered, the benefits and risks should be explained to the parents and informed consent obtained. (Schoen et al., 1989, p. 390)

To put this new evidence and the altered stance of the AAP into perspective, one might ask how harmful are urinary tract infections in otherwise healthy male children. In reality, the risks associated with this kind of infection are quite low, and it is by no means clear that an increased likelihood of a urinary tract infection in uncircumcised male children is a good medical reason for routine circumcision (Andolsek, 1990; King, 1988; Lohr, 1989; Schaeffer, 1990; Snyder, 1991). Furthermore, many of the studies designed to assess the relationship between circumcision and disease are marred by methodological problems such as failure to control for variations in personal hygiene practices. For example, newborns from lower socioeconomic groups are more likely to be uncircumcised and perhaps also less likely to experience good genital hygiene. Data not corrected for these factors may be suspect (Thompson, 1990).

It seems that the widespread awareness of the medical justification for circumcision creates unnecessary potential for anxiety. In our own classes, most students assume that circumcision is important for hygiene. How do assumptions like these affect a person's self-image and sexual relations? Consider the following report provided by a surgeon:

When I was serving a stint as ship's surgeon on a large carrier, during the Vietnam conflict, I had a very interesting experience. A young sailor came to me requesting circumcision. When I queried him as to his motivation for undergoing such an operation, he stated that his wife refused to engage in oral sex because she viewed him as unclean. After performing the simple operation, an amazing thing happened. Many more men came with the same request. Apparently the word had circulated rapidly. Their reasons were essentially the same as the first seaman. They either felt unclean themselves or were viewed in this way by partners. (Authors' files)

Accounts like this one are echoed in numerous other reports. With the increasing availability of accurate information, we hope to see a time when the absence of a flap of skin will no longer be considered a sign of personal cleanliness or sexual attractiveness.

 Beyond the issue of hygiene, another question has often been raised about circumcision: Do circumcised men enjoy any erotic or functional advantages over uncircumcised men (or vice versa)? Take a minute or two to consider this question before reading on.

Some people assume that the circumcised male responds more quickly during penile–vaginal intercourse because of the fully exposed glans. However, except when there is a condition known as **phimosis** (an extremely tight prepuce), there is no difference in contact during intercourse. The foreskin of an uncircumcised man is retracted during coitus, so the glans is fully exposed. It might be assumed, in fact, that the glans of a circumcised man is less sensitive, due to the toughening effect of constant exposure to chafing surfaces. Masters and Johnson (1966) investigated both of these questions, and found no evidence of differences in responsiveness. However, the Masters and Johnson data fail to include the all-important dimension of subjective assessment by men who have experienced both conditions after achieving sexual maturity. Occasionally, we have encountered men in our classes who have been circumcised during their adult years. Some of these men have reported experiencing physiological differences in sexual arousal — such as a decrease in the sensitivity of the glans — following circumcision. But these reactions have not been consistent. Other men afforded this unique comparative opportunity have found no perceivable differences in sexual excitability. It would seem that there are still unanswered questions about the relationship between circumcision and male sexual arousal.

Summary

Sexual Anatomy

The scrotum is a loose outpocket of the lower abdominal wall, consisting of an outer skin layer and an inner muscle layer. Housed within the scrotum are the two testes, or testicles, each suspended within its respective compartment by the spermatic cord.

Human testes have two major functions: sperm production and secretion of sex hormones.

Sperm development requires a scrotal temperature slightly lower than normal body temperature.

The interior of each testicle is divided into a large number of chambers that contain the thin, highly coiled seminiferous tubules in which sperm production occurs.

Adhering to the back and upper surface of each testicle is a **C**-shaped structure, the epididymis, within which sperm maturation occurs.

Sperm travel from the epididymis of each testicle through a long, thin tube, the vas deferens, which eventually terminates at the base of the bladder, where it is joined by the ejaculatory duct of the seminal vesicle.

The seminal vesicles are two small glands, each near the terminal of a vas deferens. They secrete an alkaline fluid that constitutes about 70% of the semen and appears to nourish and stimulate sperm cells.

The prostate gland, located at the base of the bladder and traversed by the urethra, provides about 30% of the seminal fluid released during ejaculation.

Two pea-sized structures, the Cowper's glands, are connected by tiny ducts to the urethra just below the prostate gland. During sexual arousal, they often produce a few drops of slippery, alkaline fluid, which appear at the tip of the penis.

Semen consists of sperm cells and secretions from the prostate, seminal vesicles, and Cowper's glands. The sperm component is only a tiny portion of the total fluid expelled during ejaculation.

The penis consists of an internal root within the body cavity; an external, pendulous portion known as its body, or shaft; and the smooth, acorn-shaped head, called the glans. Running the length of the penis are three internal chambers filled with spongelike tissue, which become engorged with blood during sexual arousal.

Male Sexual Functions

Penile erection is an involuntary process that results from adequate sexual stimulation — physiological, psychological, or both.

Ejaculation is the process by which semen is transported out through the penis. It occurs in two stages: the emission phase, when seminal fluid is collected in the urethral bulb, and the expulsion phase, when strong muscle contractions expel the semen. In retrograde ejaculation, semen is expelled into the bladder.

Some Concerns About Sexual Functioning

Penis size does not significantly influence the ability to give or receive pleasure during penile–vaginal intercourse. Neither is it correlated with other physical variables such as body shape or height.

Circumcision, the surgical removal of the foreskin, is widely practiced in this country. Medical evidence supporting its hygienic benefits is inconclusive, as are data concerning its effect on erotic or functional elements of sexual expression.

Thought Provokers

1. If you had a newborn son, would you have him circumcised? When? Why or why not?

2. Do you believe that penis size is an important factor in a woman's coital satisfaction? What effect, if any, has the "bigger-is-better" view of penis size had on your own sexual functioning?

3. What are some of the possible negative or positive effects of nocturnal emissions in an adolescent male? What can be done to minimize any adverse consequences of this natural occurrence?

Suggested Readings

Blank, Joani (1975). *The Playbook: For Men/About Sex.* Burlingame, Calif.: Down There Press. This is an informally written self-awareness workbook for men. It includes topics such as body image, genital awareness, masturbation, sexual response, relationships, and fantasy.

Kinsey, Alfred C.; Pomeroy, Wardell B.; and Martin, Clyde E. (1948). *Sexual Behavior in the Human Male.* Philadelphia: Saunders. Besides extensive data on male sexual behaviors, this volume contains an abundance of details about a male's sexual anatomy and the manner in which he responds physiologically to sexual stimulation.

Silverstein, Judith (1986). *Sexual Enhancement for Men.* New York: Vantage Press. This book offers both a thoughtful and sensitive discussion of concerns and issues pertaining to male sexuality and some excellent suggestions for enhancing sexual functioning and for overcoming a range of sexual problems. Silverstein also puts into perspective many of the sexual myths and pressures that often erode the quality of male sexual functioning.

Simon, William (1975). "Male Sexuality: The Secret of Satisfaction." *Today's Health,* April: 32 – 34, 150 – 152. A noted sex researcher interviews four men of diverse lifestyles who candidly discuss the meaning of sexual satisfaction in their lives, with attention paid to their sexual joys, needs, uncertainties, and fears.

Zilbergeld, Bernie (1992). *The New Male Sexuality: A Guide to Sexual Fulfillment.* New York: Bantam. An exceptionally well-written and informative treatment of male sexuality, including such topics as sexual functioning, self-awareness, and overcoming difficulties.

But mark you, Venus' joys must not be hurried,

But softly coaxed in dalliance unflurried.

The spot once found wherein 'tis woman's joy

To be caressed, caress it; ne'er be coy.

Ovid
The Art of Love (English translation, 1931)

CHAPTER 6

Sexual Arousal and Response

Sexual Arousal

Sexual Response

Sexual arousal and response in humans are influenced by many factors: hormones, our brain's capacity to create images and fantasies, our emotions, various sensory processes, the level of intimacy between two people, and a host of other influences. We begin this chapter by discussing some of the things that influence sexual arousal. We then turn our attention to the ways in which our bodies respond to sexual stimulation. We concentrate primarily on biological factors and events associated with human sexual arousal and response, but this focus on physiology is not meant to minimize the importance of psychological and cultural influences. In fact, psychosocial factors probably play a greater role than do biological ones in the extremely varied patterns of human sexual response, as we will discover in later chapters.

Sexual Arousal

In this section, we single out a number of factors as we explore the complexity of human sexual arousal: the role of hormonal influences; the impact of brain functions; sensory input and the individual ways we interpret it; and, finally, the reputed effects of certain foods and drugs.

The Role of Hormones

For years sex researchers have held differing opinions about the relative importance of hormones in human sexual arousal and behavior. These differences exist for several good reasons. For one, it is extremely difficult to distinguish between the effects of physiological processes, especially hormone production, and those of psychosocial processes such as early socialization, peer-group learning, and emotional development. Furthermore, until recently much of the data relating sexuality and hormones were derived from poorly controlled studies of limited research populations. However, in recent years a number of well-designed, carefully implemented investigations have yielded data that have given us a better understanding of the complex relationship between hormones and sexual activity. As we consider this information, we will see that the evidence linking hormones to sexuality is considerably more substantial for males than for females.

 Which hormones are important in human sexuality? Have different hormones been linked with male versus female sexual functions? Take a few moments to review your knowledge relative to these questions before reading on.

Hormones in Male Sexual Behavior. We learned in Chapter 3 that the general term for male sex hormones is *androgens*. About 95% of these androgens are secreted by the testes in the form of testosterone; the remaining 5% are produced by the adrenal glands. A number of lines of research have linked androgens with sexual activity in males (Everitt & Bancroft, 1991).

One source of information has been studies of men who have undergone **castration.** This operation, called **orchidectomy** in medical language, involves removal of the testes and is sometimes performed as medical treatment for such diseases as genital tuberculosis and prostate cancer (Silver et al., 1991; Soloway et al., 1991). In one major investigation of a large group of castrated Norwegian males, most subjects reported significantly reduced sexual interest and activity within the first year after the operation (Bremer, 1959). A more recent study of 39 sex offenders in West Germany, who voluntarily agreed to surgical castration while in prison, produced similar results (Heim, 1981). However, other research suggests that castration has a highly variable effect on sexual desire and functioning. In one case, a 43-year-old man, castrated 18 years previously, reported having intercourse one to four times weekly (Hamilton, 1943). Other writers have recorded incidences of continued sexual desire and functioning for as long as 30 years following castration, without hormone treatment (Ford & Beach, 1951).

Such findings, together with numerous other investigations, suggest that while sexual interest and activity generally diminish after castration, the amount of reduction is highly variable. The fact that this reduction occurs so frequently indicates that hormones are important in instigating sexual interest. However, we cannot rule out the possible impact of psychological factors. Emotional and cognitive reactions — including embarrassment due to a sense of physical mutilation, or a self-fulfilling belief in the myth that castration abolishes erectile response — may also inhibit sexual functioning after castration.

A second line of research investigating hormones and sexual functioning involves androgen-blocking drugs. In recent years, a class of drugs known as *antiandrogens* has been used in Europe and America to treat sex offenders and certain medical conditions such as advanced prostate cancer. Antiandrogens drastically reduce the amount of testosterone circulating in the bloodstream (Pugeat et al., 1987; Rousseau et al., 1988; Silver et al., 1991). One of these drugs, *medroxyprogesterone acetate* (*MPA*, also known by its trade name, *Depo-Provera*), has received a great deal of media attention in the United States in the last few years. A number of studies have found that Depo-Provera and other antiandrogens may be effective in reducing both sexual interest and activity in human males (Cooper, 1986; Cooper & Cernovovsky, 1992; Rousseau et al., 1988 & 1990). However, altering sex hormone levels is far from a surefire treatment for sex offenders, especially in cases where sexual assaults have stemmed from nonsexual motives such as the desire to express anger or to exert control over another person.

A third source of evidence linking androgens to sexual motivation is research on **hypogonadism,** a state of androgen deprivation that results from certain diseases of the endocrine system. If this condition occurs before puberty, maturation of the primary and secondary sex characteristics is retarded, and the individual may never develop an active sexual interest. The results are far more variable if androgen deficiency occurs in adulthood. However, extensive studies of hypogonadal men conducted by a number of researchers provide strong evidence that androgens play an important role in male sexual motivation (Bancroft, 1984; Carani et al., 1990; Davidson, 1984; Zini et al., 1990). For example, it has been shown that when hypogonadal men receive hormone treatments to replace androgens in the bloodstream, they often experience a return of normal sexual interest and activity. If the treatments are temporarily suspended, sexual motivation and activity decline within two to three weeks (Carey et al., 1988; Cunningham et al., 1989; Findlay et al., 1989; Gooren, 1988).

Recent research further supports a link between male sexual functioning and androgens. In one study researchers assessed the relationship between androgen levels and sexual behavior in a group of young men with an average age of 25. The researchers found a strong positive correlation between blood androgen levels and the strength of sexual motivation as reflected by orgasm frequency (Knussmann et al., 1986). Another study provided very strong evidence of a relationship between blood androgen levels and sexual motivation and behavior in adolescent males (Udry et al., 1985). These researchers found that the higher the level of circulating androgens in the bloodstream, the more time their teenage subjects spent thinking about sex and the more likely they were to have engaged in coitus, non-coital sex play, and masturbation.

Hormones in Female Sexual Behavior. Many people assume that the female sex hormones, *estrogens,* play a major role in female sexual motivation and behavior. We do know that these hormones help maintain the elasticity of the vaginal lining and contribute to vaginal lubrication (Walling et al., 1990). However, the role of estrogens in female sexual motivation is far from clear.

A number of writers have maintained that estrogens play an insignificant role in female sexual activity. In support of this viewpoint, they quote studies of postmenopausal women (Masters & Johnson, 1966) and women who have had their ovaries removed for medical reasons (Kinsey et al., 1953). Neither change seems to have significant adverse effects on sexual arousal.

However, more recent studies of postmenopausal women or women whose ovaries have been removed suggest a more complicated picture. Some researchers have reported that when these subjects receive estrogen-replacement therapy, they experience not only heightened vaginal lubrication but also increased sexual motivation, pleasure, and orgasmic capacity (Dennerstein et al., 1980; Dow et al., 1983). At the same time, other investigators have found estrogen-replacement therapy to have no discernible impact on sexual desire and activity (Campbell, 1976; Campbell & Whitehead, 1977; Coope, 1976; Furuhjelm et al., 1984; Myers et al., 1990). In view of these contradictory findings, the role of estrogen in female sexual motivation and functioning remains unclear.

Estrogens are not the only sex hormones present in females, however. Both the ovaries and the adrenal glands produce androgens in females, and the connection between androgens and female sexual motivation seems somewhat more substantial. Some of this evidence is anecdotal. For instance, the clinical literature on gynecology cites many cases in which women undergoing androgen therapy experience increased sexual interest and activity (Bachmann, 1992; Carter et al., 1947; Dorfman & Shipley, 1956; Kupperman & Studdiford, 1953).

Better-controlled experimental evaluations of the effects of androgens on female sexuality have yielded evidence of a positive correlation between levels of circulating androgens and frequency of sexual activity (Bancroft et al., 1983 & 1991; Morris et al., 1987; Persky et al., 1978 & 1982; Sherwin, 1988; Walling et al., 1990). For instance, two investigations revealed that women who received an androgen-containing preparation after their ovaries were surgically removed reported markedly greater levels of sexual desire, sexual arousal, and sexual fantasies than subjects who received estrogen alone or a *placebo* (a pharmacologically inert substance, such as a sugar pill) (Sherwin & Gelfand, 1987; Sherwin et al., 1985). Although women who receive androgen supplements are usually pleased with their increased sexual interest, some subjects (particularly those without a sexual partner) found their heightened sex drive to be somewhat unsettling (Gallagher, 1988).

While the evidence linking androgens with female sexuality is certainly more substantial than that for estrogen, the findings are still somewhat contradictory. For instance, three systematic investigations that compared the effects of androgens on female sexuality with those of a placebo found that androgens proved no more effective than placebos (Mathews, 1981). In a more recent hormone-replacement study of postmenopausal women (mean age, 58.3 years), subjects were randomly assigned to one of four groups: estrogen alone, estrogen plus progestin, estrogen plus androgen, or a placebo. After a two-week baseline assessment period, subjects received either hormones or a placebo for two months. During this time, each subject kept a daily log in which she recorded instances of sexual desire, thoughts, and activity. The results of this investigation revealed only a relatively small effect of androgen on sexual function as reflected in reports of significantly increased pleasure from masturbation provided only by subjects in the estrogen-plus-androgen group. In addition, these researchers found a "complete lack of effect of estrogen on sexual measures" (Myers et al., 1990, p. 1130).

Future research may clarify the relationship between sex hormones and female sexual interest and behavior. At present, however, the picture is much less clear for women than for men, and the relationship between hormone levels and female sexuality is exceedingly difficult to decipher (Bancroft et al., 1991). Even in the case of male sexuality, where the role of hormones is now becoming clearer, we must continue to be aware that human sexual behavior is so tremendously individual that it is difficult to specify the precise effects of hormones on erotic arousal and expression. (See the interview with John Bancroft for additional perspectives on the relationship between hormones and sexuality.)

The Brain

From our experience, we know that the brain plays an important role in our sexuality. Our thoughts, emotions, and memories are all mediated through its complex mechanisms. Sexual arousal can occur without any sensory stimulation; it can be produced by the process of *fantasy* (in this case, thinking of erotic images or sexual interludes), and some individuals may even reach orgasm during a fantasy experience (Kinsey et al., 1948 & 1953; Whipple et al., 1992).

We know that specific events can cause us to become aroused. Less apparent is the role of individual experience and cultural influence, both of which are mediated by our brains. Clearly, we do not all respond similarly to the same stimuli. Some people may be highly aroused if their partner uses explicit sexual language; others may find such words to be threatening or a sexual turnoff. Similarly, the smell of genital secretions may be more arousing to many Europeans than to members of our own deodorant-conscious society. The brain is the storehouse of our memories and cultural values, and consequently its influence over our sexual arousability is profound.

Strictly mental events like fantasies are the product of the **cerebral cortex,** the gray matter that controls higher functions like reasoning and language abilities. But the cortex represents only one level of functioning at which the brain influences human sexual arousal and response. At a subcortical level, the **limbic system** seems to play an important part in determining sexual behavior, both in humans and in other animals.

CHAPTER 6

Interview with John Bancroft

While many sexuality researchers focus primarily on either biological or psychological topics, Dr. John Bancroft has taken on the tremendous challenge of discovering how these aspects of sexuality interact. His remarkable success at this endeavor has earned him high praise from his peers, as well as research honors in both the United States and Europe. Dr. Bancroft is a clinical consultant at the Medical Research Council Reproductive Biology Unit in Edinburgh, Scotland, and a lecturer in the Department of Psychiatry at the University of Edinburgh. He is also author of the textbook Human Sexuality and Its Problems.

A psychiatrist by training, Dr. Bancroft studies the relationship of reproductive hormones to sexual behavior, and now considers himself a behavioral endocrinologist. His wide-ranging research interests include the relationship between female reproductive hormones and sexual well-being, including the effects of oral contraceptives and the menstrual cycle on moods and sexual response; the effects of new pharmacological agents on male sexual response; and diagnostic methods of assessing male sexual dysfunction. In this interview with Robert Crooks, he describes some of

his current work and some general conclusions he's drawn from his career in this field.

How did you begin your career researching the effects of hormones on sexuality?

Early in my psychiatric training in London, I became interested in using psychophysiological techniques for assessment of sexual problems. I soon realized that sexuality is a very challenging field, because in it you have to integrate ideas and knowledge from a very broad range of disciplines. Particularly, I suppose, it appealed to the maverick in me who preferred not to be conventional and conformist in the way I approach my professional life.

I went to Oxford University for a number of years, where most of my research was on suicide and suicidal behavior, but my interest in sexuality continued. The opportunity arose in 1976 for me to go up to Scotland, to Edin-

burgh, to work in a reproductive biology unit. This provided me with an opportunity to find out more about the biological as opposed to the psychological aspects of the field. Over the years I have been involved in various aspects of sexuality, both from the clinical and the research point of view. I've done a lot of work in sex therapy, both clinical training and research; psychophysiology; pharmacology of sexual response; as well as hormonal aspects of sexuality.

You have long-standing research interests in both female and male issues. Is our understanding of how hormones affect sexuality fundamentally different for women as opposed to men?

What has struck me very forcefully over the years is that the story for the male is relatively straightforward, although by comparison there's much less research data for the male than there is for the female. There are so many more opportunities for studying hormone–behavior relationships in women: They have menstrual cycles and pregnancies and they lactate; millions of women are given contraceptives as hormonal replacements; they're much more likely to have their gonads removed than the male; they have menopause, which a man doesn't have.

There's therefore much more information for the female than there is for the male. Yet the picture of how hormones affect sexual behavior is much clearer and more consistent in the male than it is in the female. For example, it is much more difficult to predict in the case of the woman what effect a manipulation of her reproductive hormones will have on her sexuality, than it is in the case of the male.

Why do you think the data about how hormones affect women's sexual behavior are so much more complicated than the data on men?

I can give you some speculative ideas about that. One point is that this isn't just a human difference. There is a rather extraordinary consistency across the males of many animals in terms of the role that reproductive hormones have in sexuality. The role of androgens in male sexuality is strikingly similar whether you're talking about a human male, a rhesus monkey, a rat, or a deer. On the other hand, the role that hormones play in female sexual behavior varies quite a lot from one species to another. In the female of some species, estrogens play a predominant role; in some, androgens. Sometimes it's an interaction between estrogens and progesterone. There is enormous variability.

A second point is that I think women are also more variable than men in their responsiveness to reproductive hormones, so there are some women

who are quite responsive and other women who are not—although here the evidence is less strong. If that is the case, then it would go quite a long way toward explaining some of the other behavioral or psychological aspects of women's reproductive lives, such as premenstrual syndrome and postnatal depression.

You said that the effects of hormones on female sexuality vary considerably among animal species. Do the inconsistencies tend to be more pronounced as you move up the developmental scale from rodents to primates, including humans?

Sometimes people expect that as species become more developed, hormones become less and less important, but that is a gross oversimplification. For example, if you look just at the primates, you see quite striking differences in the relative importance and control of sexual behavior by hormones. You can account for a lot of that by the way that a particular species adapts to the environment. In a species like the orangutan, its environment has resulted in it leading a relatively isolated existence. The female orang and the male orang do not come into contact with one another often. Therefore it becomes particularly important that the reproductive hormones influence behavior—in this case, the female's behavior, to bring the two together to reproduce.

With chimpanzees, however, you've got a social group of animals. You can even start to think about sex play and functions of sex other than reproduction and pair bonding. You can postulate that sexuality in the chimp colony has some relevance to the integrity of the group. But you've clearly got a very different relationship between sexuality

and the reproductive factor in the chimpanzee.

In the gorilla, the female is interested in sex only around her reproductive phase. Gorillas live in groups consisting of several females and juveniles and one adult male, and much of the time the female is in lactation. It's up to her to behave appropriately when she comes into estrus—her fertile period—to ensure that mating takes place. That, again, is an entirely different reproductive strategy from the one in humans, where you have stable pairs with fairly high frequencies of sexual activity.

So hormonal effects aren't simply a matter of where the species is on the developmental scale. Rather, the species' style of adaptation to the environment, and what you might call the "constitutional level" of sexual activity in that species, are what's important.

How much of the inconsistency between hormones and sexuality in women may actually be a function of psychosocial phenomena?

This is a difficult question to answer. If you look at data on women, I think the explanation that jumps out is that women's sexuality is much more influenced by psychosocial determinants than is men's sexuality. Obviously, psychosocial factors are important in both men and women. Maybe the hormonal factors are weaker in women, so the psychosocial factors are more likely to overwhelm the hormonal ones.

In Richard Udry's fascinating study of boys and girls around puberty, there was quite striking evidence that for boys, the best predictor of whether they were sexually active and sexually interested was the level of the androgen testosterone in their blood. Whereas with the girls, although the androgens were correlated with some aspects of their sexuality, more powerful predictors—particularly of whether they were sexually active—were psychosocial factors, in particular the sort of peer-group relationships they were having. Therefore, I think we have to consider seriously that for one reason or another the emerging sexuality of the female is much more influenced by social factors.

What has your own research shown about how psychosocial factors influence how hormones affect female sexuality?

Studies we have carried out over the past 10 years have led me to think that in the presence of psychological difficulties, it is quite likely that the subtle hormone–behavior relationship will be obscured. For example, in one study we found, paradoxically, clear evidence of androgen–behavior correlations in women using oral contraceptives, but not in women who were *not* using oral contraceptives, even though the women on the pill had substantially *lower* androgen levels. The pill had obviously lowered their androgen level. Yet we saw these correlations come through in this group but not in the other group. There may be psychosocial factors involved in their decision to take oral contraceptives which also allowed this hormone–behavior relationship to exist unobscured. We're pursuing those ideas now.

Your comments illustrate how extremely complicated it can be to separate and understand the social, psychological, and hormonal factors that can influence sexual behavior. In your current studies on psychosocial factors affecting women who are taking oral contraceptives, how do you try to tease apart these components?

My previous research in that area, in collaboration with Barbara Sherwin at McGill University in Montreal, brought home two important points, both of

which we're following up in our current research program. One is that psychosocial factors can be different at different stages of women's lives. We are in the early stages of doing a study of women around menopause, looking at the relationships between androgens and sexuality. We're trying to measure as carefully as we can such factors as potentially stressful events in the woman's life at that time. We're assuming that there are important psychosocial factors, but they're probably not going to be the same psychosocial factors as in women in their early twenties.

The other lesson is more directly related to oral contraceptives. That study in Montreal brought home to me the almost total absence of any research on the psychological and psychosexual characteristics of young women *before* they started taking oral contraceptives, and relating those characteristics to how they react to the pill and whether or not they continue to use it.

So we have developed a two-stage research plan with the World Health Organization. The first stage is under way and is taking place in Edinburgh and in the Philippines. In that phase we are trying to isolate the pharmacological and hormonal effects of the pill from its psychological impact. We want to see the direct effects of these hormones on a woman's well-being and sexuality. For that purpose we are studying women who are either sterilized or who have sterilized partners.

We ask them to volunteer to take birth control pills or a placebo—a pharmacologically inert substance such as a sugar pill—over a four-month period while we monitor them with daily ratings of psychological variables.

This will hopefully lead to the second phase, which is more cross-cultural. The second study will look at women who are taking oral contraceptives for the first time. We will do a fairly thorough assessment of their personalities and their psychiatric and sexual histories, then follow them over their first year on the pill and see how they react to it and how it affects them. Although we don't really know what effect contraceptives have on women's sexuality, because we haven't got good evidence, I have no doubt that a portion of the women experience quite a marked negative effect on their sexuality.

Some of your research on men has involved assessing the causes of sexual dysfunction. Have you found that androgens have a similar effect on both sexual motivation and sexual response?

It's conceptually very difficult to distinguish between sexual desire and one's capacity for sexual arousal. The clearest evidence we have on this point comes from the studies we have done on men, which show that, first of all, sexual desire is dependent on androgens. If the androgens are low, then sexual desire goes; it returns when you replace the androgens.

Second, spontaneous erections occurring during sleep are clearly dependent on androgens. If you take a man with low androgen levels, his sleep erection will be very impaired, and if you give him androgens, it will be very much improved. We also know that sleep erections are likely to be impaired in men with low sexual desire. Looking at what these spontaneous sleep erections are doing is like having a neurophysiological window into the brain. It is a measure of the central arousability of the brain during sleep, when it is relatively free from the confounding effects of cognitive processes. So we know androgens are relevant to a man's arousability. There's probably something similar in women, but we can't be sure about that.

So it appears that a man with erection difficulties maintains his capacity to be functionally sexual, but has a decrease in the level of arousal and interest?

If the circumstances are right, yes, I think the capacity for sexual response will continue. The stimuli must be right, and must be available so the man doesn't have to look for them, which is where the motivation component comes in. And his psychological state must be right, so it is not inhibiting his response. That's a very important point, because a man who has lost his sexual desire can be in a negative psychological state, which will effectively inhibit any sort of response, regardless of what stimuli are offered.

What measurements do you use to evaluate the effects of drugs on male sexual functioning?

The sexual response of men to filmed erotic stimuli seems to be relatively independent of androgens. There's really quite striking evidence now that hypogonadal men—men who have very low

levels of androgens—will produce erections in response to certain types of stimuli. I first showed this quite a long time ago when we gave antiandrogens to sexual offenders: Although we reduced their response to fantasy, and we reduced their sexual interests and their masturbation frequency, their response to erotic films was unaffected.

So at the moment that is how we operationally define and manipulate these aspects of the man's response system. That is the basis of my experimental method for evaluating the effects of drugs on male sexual response. I compare the effects of drugs on erections during sleep with the effects of drugs on erections to visual erotic stimuli, because these are both fairly controllable situations that one can use in laboratory experiments.

There have been reports indicating that women tend to be in their thirties before they become most satisfied with their sexuality, and perhaps most sexually active, whereas men tend to experience their peak levels of sexual activity at a much younger age. To what do you attribute this difference?

There is good evidence to support that this is largely socially determined. Looking at studies done at different intervals over the last 30 or 40 years, I think that there is a clear male–female difference, particularly in unmarried young people. In earlier studies, the male was more likely to be sexually active at an early age and to be orgasmic and to masturbate and to enjoy sexuality at an earlier age than the female. Those differences have been fast disappearing. Women and men are becoming more similar in this respect. I can't see how to explain that other than on the grounds of changing social factors. In this regard, too, women might be more variable than men, but I think a majority of women have a capacity for sexual response which is just as great as in the majority of men. I don't see

any reason why they shouldn't realize that capacity just as quickly as men do.

What education and training would you suggest to a student interested in pursuing a career in the field of sex research?

I think that in the future there will be relatively few examples of what you might call specialist's training in sexology. I would recommend to them a traditional professional career. By all means, keep their interest in sex, but establish themselves in a conventional professional discipline. If their bias is toward social sciences, then perhaps do a Ph.D. in social sciences with an orientation toward sexual issues. Establish themselves in that professional group. If they are interested in physiology or psychology, they should get good credentials in those disciplines.

Would you like to see people in different areas of sexology interact even more in the future?

I think if I could work in a really good unit of sexology—sexual science which brought together good sociologists, physiologists, biochemists, animal researchers, psychologists, and so on—I would be enormously excited. My aspiration is to be able to talk intelligently with, on the one hand, a molecular biologist—and I'm struggling a little bit with that because most of my unit is into molecular biology—and then to go another day and have an equally interesting and idea-provoking discussion with a social historian, or a sociologist, or a primatologist. That's what turns me on intellectually about this field.

FIGURE 6.1

The limbic system, a region of the brain associated with emotion and motivation, is important in human sexual function. Key structures, shaded in color, include the cingulate gyrus, septal area, portions of the hypothalamus, amygdala, and the hippocampus.

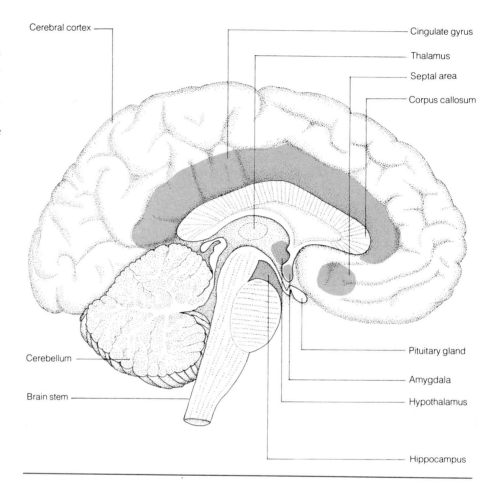

Figure 6.1 shows some key structures in the limbic system. These include the cingulate gyrus, the septal area, the amygdala, the hippocampus, and parts of the hypothalamus, which plays a regulating role. There is evidence linking various sites in this system with sexual behavior. For instance, several animal studies have implicated the hypothalamus in sexual functioning. Researchers have reported increased sexual activity in rats, including erections and ejaculations, triggered by stimulation in both anterior and posterior regions of the hypothalamus (Caggiula & Hoebel, 1966; Van Dis & Larsson, 1971; Vaughn & Fisher, 1962). When certain parts of the hypothalamus are surgically destroyed, there may be a dramatic reduction in the sexual behavior of both males and females of several species (Hitt et al., 1970; Sawyer, 1960).

In the 1950s, James Olds conducted a series of experimental investigations of brain stimulation in rats. He implanted electrodes in various regions of their limbic systems and wired the electrodes in a way that allowed the rats to stimulate their own brains by pressing a lever. When the electrodes were placed in the hypothalamus and the septal areas, the rats seemingly could not get enough stimulation. They would press the lever several thousand times per hour, often to the point of exhaustion. These animals were clearly experiencing something akin to intense pleasure, which led Olds to call these regions of the limbic system "pleasure centers" (Olds, 1956). Olds's rats were unable to tell him whether the pleasure they were experiencing was sexual in nature. Subsequent research with humans, outlined in the following paragraphs, is more enlightening.

For ethical reasons, few experiments have attempted to study the effects of brain stimulation on humans. In some cases, however, electrical and chemical brain stimulation of humans has been done for therapeutic purposes. Robert Heath, a Tulane University researcher, is one of the pioneers in this area. In the early 1970s, he experimented with limbic system stimulation of a female with epilepsy and a male troubled with emotional problems. He hypothesized that the pleasure associated with stimulation of these areas would prove to be of therapeutic value to these patients. When stimulation was delivered to the septal area, both individuals reported intense sexual pleasure. The female patient experienced multiple orgasmic response as a direct result of septal area stimulation. Provided with a self-stimulating transistorized device, the male patient stimulated himself incessantly (up to 1500 times per hour). "He protested each time the unit was taken from him, pleading to self-stimulate just a few more times" (Heath, 1972, p. 6).

It is doubtful that researchers will ever find one specific "sex center" in the brain. However, it is clear that both the cerebral cortex and the limbic system play important roles in initiating, organizing, and controlling human sexual arousal and response. In addition, the brain interprets a variety of sensory inputs that often exert a profound influence on sexual arousal. We examine this topic in the next section.

The Senses

It has been said that the brain is the most important sense organ for human sexual arousal. This observation implies that any sensory event, if properly interpreted by the psyche, can serve as an effective sexual stimulus. The resulting variety in the sources of erotic stimulation helps explain the tremendous sexual complexity of humans.

In your opinion, which of the major senses (touch, vision, smell, taste, or hearing) typically has the greatest impact on sexual interaction? Give this some thought before reading on.

Of the major senses, touch tends to predominate during sexual intimacy. However, all the senses have the potential to become involved, and sights, smells, sounds, and tastes all may be important contributors to erotic arousal. There are no blueprints for the what and how of sensory stimulation. Each of us is unique, with our own individual triggers of arousal.

Touch. Stimulation of the various skin surfaces is probably a more frequent source of human sexual arousal than any other type of sensory stimulus. The nerve endings that respond to touch are distributed unevenly throughout the body, which explains why certain areas are more sensitive than others. Those locations that are most responsive to tactile pleasuring are commonly referred to as the **erogenous zones.** A distinction is often made between primary erogenous zones — those areas that contain dense concentrations of nerve endings — and

Sensual touching is one of the most frequent sources of erotic stimulation.

secondary erogenous zones, which include other areas of the body that have become endowed with erotic significance through sexual conditioning.

A list of **primary erogenous zones** generally includes the genitals, buttocks, anus, perineum, breasts (particularly the nipples), inner surfaces of the thighs, armpits, navel, neck, ears (especially the lobes), and the mouth (lips, tongue, and the entire oral cavity). It is important to remember, however, that just because a given area qualifies as a primary erogenous zone, there is no guarantee that stimulating it will produce arousal in a sexual partner. What is intensely arousing for one person may produce no reaction in another — or it may be irritating.

The **secondary erogenous zones** include virtually all other regions of the body. For example, if your lover tenderly kissed and stroked your upper back during each sexual interlude, this area could be transformed into an erogenous zone. These secondary locations become eroticized because they are touched within the context of sexual intimacies.

Vision. In our society, visual stimuli appear to be of great importance. Prime evidence is the emphasis we often place on physical appearance, including such activities as personal grooming, wearing the right clothes, and the extensive use of cosmetics. Therefore, it is not surprising that vision is second only to touch in the hierarchy of stimuli that most people view as sexually arousing.

Do you think that there are sex differences in how males and females respond to visual erotica? Think about this before reading on.

The popularity of sexually explicit men's magazines in our society suggests that the human male is more aroused by visual stimuli than is the female. Early research seemed to support this conclusion. Kinsey found that more men than women reported being sexually excited by visual stimuli such as pinup erotica and stag shows (Kinsey et al., 1948 & 1953). However, this finding reflects several social influences, including the greater cultural inhibitions attached to such behavior in women at the time of his research and the simple fact that men had been provided far more opportunities to develop an appetite for such stimuli. This latter interpretation is supported by later research that employed physiological recording devices (see Chapter 2) to measure sexual arousal under controlled laboratory conditions. These studies have demonstrated strong similarities in the responses of males and females to visual erotica (Abramson et al., 1981; Fisher, 1983; Rubinsky et al., 1987). Recent research findings suggest that when sexual arousal is measured by self-reports rather than physiological devices, women are less inclined than men to report being sexually aroused by visual erotica (Kelley, 1985; Przybyla & Byrne, 1984). This finding may reflect the persistence of cultural influences that make women reluctant to acknowledge being aroused by filmed erotica, or it may indicate that females have greater difficulty than males identifying signs of sexual arousal in their bodies, or it may be due to a combination of these factors.

Smell. A person's sexual history and cultural conditioning often influence what smells he or she finds arousing. We typically learn through experience to view certain odors as erotic and others as offensive. From this perspective, there may be nothing intrinsic to the fragrance of genital secretions that might cause them to be perceived as either arousing or distasteful. We might also argue the contrary — that the smell of genital secretions would be universally exciting to humans were it not that some people learn to view them as offensive. This latter interpretation is supported by the fact that some societies openly recognize the value of genital smells as a sexual stimulant. For example, on the European continent, where the deodorant industry is less pervasive, some women use the natural bouquet of their genital secretions, strategically placed behind an ear or in the nape of the neck, to arouse their sexual partners.

Among other animals, smells are often more important than visual stimuli in eliciting sexual response. The females of many species secrete certain substances, called **pheromones,** during their fertile periods. Any of you who have had a female dog in heat and observed male dogs coming from miles around to scratch at your door will not doubt for a moment the importance of smell in sexual arousal. In the early 1970s, researchers isolated fatty acids called *copulins* from vaginal secretions of female rhesus monkeys; these pheromones are very strong smelling and a potent sexual attractant (Michael et al., 1971). Some years later it was discovered that sexually aroused human females secrete a vaginal substance similar to the rhesus monkey pheromone (Michael et al., 1974; Morris & Udry, 1976; Sokolov et al., 1976). Another substance that has commanded attention in the search for erotic odors in humans is a powerful pheromone called *alpha androstenal,* secreted by pigs. This substance has also been found in some human secretions, including perspiration. One investigation revealed that men and women who wore surgical masks sprayed with alpha androstenal rated women in photographs as more attractive than did subjects in a control group who wore untreated masks (Kirk-Smith et al., 1978).

Despite these suggestive results, most researchers believe that there is no convincing evidence that any smells are natural attractants for humans (Hassett, 1978; Rogel, 1978; White, 1981). The effect of pheromones on humans, if it exists at all, is probably quite weak.

The near obsession of many people in our society with masking natural body odors makes it very difficult to study the effects of these smells. Any natural odors that might trigger arousal tend to be well disguised with armpit and genital sprays. Nevertheless, each person's unique experiences may allow certain smells to acquire erotic significance, as the following anecdotes reveal:

I love the smells after making love. They trigger little flashes of erotic memories and often keep my arousal level in high gear, inducing me to go on to additional sexual activities. (Authors' files)

During oral sex the faint odor of musk from my lover's vulva drives me wild with passion. I guess it is all the memories of special pleasures associated with these smells that produces the turn-on. (Authors' files)

In a society that is often concerned about natural odors, it is nice to see that some individuals appreciate scents associated with sexual intimacy and their lovers' body.

Taste. As with smell, taste seems to play a relatively minor role in human sexual arousal. This is no doubt influenced, at least in part, by an industry that promotes breath mints and flavored vaginal douches. Besides making many individuals extremely self-conscious about how they taste or smell, such commercial products may mask any natural tastes that relate to sexual activity. Nevertheless, some people are still able to detect and appreciate certain tastes they learn to associate with sexual intimacy:

When I am sucking my man, I can taste the salty little drops that come out of his penis just before he comes. I get real excited about that time, because I know he is about to take that sweet ride home. (Authors' files)

Hearing. Whether people make sounds during sexual activity is highly variable, as is a partner's response. Some people find words, intimate/erotic conversation, moans, and orgasmic cries to be highly arousing; others prefer that their lovers keep silent during sex play. Some people, out of fear or embarrassment, may make a conscious effort to suppress spontaneous noises during sexual interaction. Because of the silent, stoical image accepted by many males, it may be exceedingly difficult for men in particular to talk, cry out, or groan during arousal. In one research study, many women reported that their male partners' silence hindered their own sexual arousal (DeMartino, 1970). Female reluctance to emit sounds during sex play may be influenced by the notion that "nice" women are not supposed to be so passionate that they make noises.

Besides being sexually arousing, talking to each other during a sexual interlude can be informative and helpful ("I like it when you touch me that way," "A little softer," and so on). If you happen to be a person who enjoys noisemaking and verbalizations during sex, your partner may respond this way if you discuss the matter beforehand. We will talk about discussing sexual preferences in Chapter 8.

Foods and Chemicals

Up to this point, we have considered the impact of hormones, brain processes, and sensory input on human sexual arousal. There are other factors, however, that may affect a person's arousability in a particular situation. Some of these directly affect the physiology of arousal; others can have a strong impact on a person's sexuality through the power of belief. In the pages that follow, we examine the effects of a number of products people use to attempt to heighten or reduce sexual arousal.

Aphrodisiacs: Do They Work? An **aphrodisiac** (ah-fro-DIZ-ē-ak) (named after Aphrodite, the Greek goddess of love and beauty) is a substance that supposedly arouses sexual desire or increases a person's capacity for sexual activities. Almost from the beginning of time, people have searched for magic potions and other agents able to revive flagging erotic interest or produce Olympic sexual performances. That many have reported finding such sexual stimulants bears testimony, once again, to the powerful role played by the mind in human sexual activity. We first consider a variety of foods that have been held to possess aphrodisiac qualities, then turn our attention to other alleged sexual stimulants, including alcohol and an assortment of chemical substances.

Do you believe that any food or chemical substances ingested by humans have genuine aphrodisiac properties? Give this some thought before reading on.

Almost any food that resembles the male external genitals has at one time or another been viewed as an aphrodisiac. Many of us have heard the jokes about oysters, although for some a belief in the special properties of this particular shellfish is no joking matter. One wonders to what extent the oyster industry profits from this pervasive myth. Other foods sometimes considered aphrodisiacs include bananas, celery, tomatoes, and potatoes. Particularly in Asian countries, there is a widespread belief that the ground-up horns of animals such as rhinoceros and reindeer are powerful sexual stimulants. (Have you ever used the term *horny* to describe a sexual state? Now you know its origin.)

A number of drugs are also commonly thought to have aphrodisiac properties. Of these drugs, perhaps more has been written about the supposed stimulant properties of alcohol than about any other presumed aphrodisiac substance. In our culture, there is widespread belief in the erotic enhancement properties of alcoholic beverages:

I am a great believer in the sexual benefits of drinking wine. After a couple glasses I become a real "hound in bed." I can always tell my wife is in the mood when she brings out a bottle of chilled rosé. (Authors' files)

Far from being a stimulant, alcohol has a depressing effect on higher brain centers, thus reducing cortical inhibitions such as fear and guilt that often block sexual expression (Cocores & Gold, 1989). Alcohol may also stimulate sexual activity by providing a convenient rationalization for behavior that might normally conflict with one's values ("I just couldn't help myself with my mind fogged by booze"). If our culture produces more sexual inhibitions in females than in males — a reasonable assumption held by many — it seems logical that alcohol is more likely to facilitate sexual activity in women than in men.

Consumption of significant amounts of alcohol, however, can have serious negative effects on sexual functioning (Cocores & Gold, 1989; Geller, 1991; Rosen, 1991). Research has demonstrated that with increasing levels of intoxication, both men and women experience reduced sexual arousal (as measured physiologically), decreased pleasurability and intensity of orgasm, and increased difficulty in attaining orgasm (Briddell & Wilson, 1976; Heaton & Varrin, 1991; Malatesta et al., 1979 & 1982; Rosen, 1991; Wilson & Lawson, 1976). Heavy alcohol use may also result in general physical deterioration, a process that commonly reduces a person's interest in and capacity for sexual activity. Recent research indicates that psychological factors may play an important role in the development of sexual problems associated with alcohol abuse (Rosen, 1991). In one study, a majority of male alcoholics demonstrated a marked improvement in sexual functioning after receiving sex therapy combined with alcoholism therapy (Fahrner, 1987).

It would appear that there may be even more serious potential consequences of alcohol use in conjunction with sexual activity. Recent research has demonstrated a strong association between the use of alcohol and an inclination to participate in sexual practices that have a high risk for contracting a life-threatening disease such as AIDS (Buffum, 1988). (Other mind-altering drugs, such as marijuana, have also been implicated in high-risk sexual behavior.) It cannot be stated with absolute confidence that this relationship is cause-and-effect (in other words, that drug use leads to high-risk sex), although the likelihood of this relationship seems quite strong.

In addition to alcohol, several other drugs have also been ascribed aphrodisiac qualities. Some of the substances included in this category are amphetamines, barbiturates, cantharides (also known as "Spanish fly"), cocaine, LSD and other psychedelic drugs, marijuana, amyl nitrite (a drug used to treat heart pain, also known as "poppers"), and L-dopa (a medication used in the treatment of Parkinson's disease). As you will see in the summary provided in Table 6.1, not one of these drugs possesses attributes that qualify it as a true sexual stimulant (Yates & Wolman, 1991). However, researchers are currently studying one drug that may eventually be shown to have genuine aphrodisiac qualities. Since the 1920s, there have been reports of the aphrodisiac properties of *yohimbine hydrochloride*, or yohimbine, a crystalline alkaloid derived from the sap of the tropical evergreen yohimbe tree that grows in West Africa. Until recently, most of these claims were dismissed by serious researchers. However, in the late 1970s, scientists at Stanford University received a grant from the National Institutes of Health to conduct research aimed at finding a drug that might be helpful in treating sexual difficulties. Experiments conducted by the Stanford team with male rats have found that injections of yohimbine induce intense sexual arousal and performance in these animals (Clark et al., 1984). The data suggest that this drug may be a true aphrodisiac, at least for rats. Several recent studies with male humans suggest that yohimbine treatment has the capacity to positively affect sexual desire or performance, at least in some people (Morales et al., 1987; Rosen, 1991; Sonda et al., 1990; Susset et al., 1989). However, these results are not conclusive at the present time in that more than half of all human subjects administered yohimbine have

Some Alleged Aphrodisiacs and Their Effects   T A B L E 6.1

Name (and Street Name)	Reputed Effect	Actual Effect
Alcohol	Enhances arousal; stimulates sexual activity	Can reduce inhibitions to make sexual behaviors less stressful. It is actually a depressant and in quantity can impair erection ability, arousal, and orgasm.
Amphetamines ("uppers"; includes Benzedrine, Dexedrine)	Elevate mood; enhance sexual experience and abilities	Central nervous system stimulants; they reduce inhibitions. Long-term use impairs sexual functioning and can reduce vaginal lubrication in women.
Amyl nitrite ("snappers," "poppers")	Intensifies orgasms and arousal	Dilates arteries to brain and also to genital area; produces time distortion, warmth in pelvic area. It can produce dizziness, headaches, and fainting.
Barbiturates ("barbs," "downers")	Enhance arousal; stimulate sexual activity	Reduce inhibitions in similar fashion to alcohol. They are physically addictive, and overdose may produce severe depression and even death due to respiratory failure.
Cantharides ("Spanish fly")	Stimulates genital area, causing person to desire coitus	Not effective as a sexual stimulant. It acts as a powerful irritant that can cause inflammation to lining of bladder and urethra; can result in permanent tissue damage and even death.
Cocaine ("coke")	Increases frequency and intensity of orgasm; heightens arousal	Central nervous system stimulant; it loosens inhibitions and enhances sense of well-being. Regular use can induce depression and anxiety. Chronic sniffing can produce lesions and perforations of nasal passage.
LSD and other psychedelic drugs (includes mescaline, psilocybin)	Enhance sexual response	No direct physiological enhancement of sexual response. May produce altered perception of sexual activity; frequently associated with unsatisfactory erotic experiences.
L-dopa	Sexually rejuvenates older males	No documented benefits to sexual ability. It occasionally produces a painful condition known as priapism (constant, unwanted erection).
Marijuana	Elevates mood and arousal; stimulates sexual activity	Enhances mood and reduces inhibitions in a way similar to alcohol. It may distort the time sense, with the resulting illusion of prolonged arousal and orgasm.
Yohimbine	Induces sexual arousal and enhances sexual performance	Appears to have genuine aphrodisiac effect on rats. Recent evidence suggests it may enhance sexual desire or performance in some humans.

Sources: Cocores & Gold, 1989: *Communicable Disease Summary,* 1985; Eisner et al., 1990; Halikas et al., 1982; Kaplan, 1974; Mendelson, 1976; Siegel, 1982; Weller & Halikas, 1984; Wesson, 1982.

experienced little or no sexual benefit from the drug (Rosen, 1991). It is hoped that further research will clarify whether yohimbine is a genuine aphrodisiac for humans.

In view of the evidence against many of the commonly held beliefs about aphrodisiacs, why do so many people around the world swear by the effects of a little powdered rhino horn, that special meal of oysters and banana salad, or the marijuana cigarette before an evening's dalliance? The answer lies in faith and suggestion — these are the ingredients frequently present when aphrodisiac claims surface. If a person believes something will improve his or her sex life, this faith is often translated into the subjective enhancement of sexual pleasure. From this perspective, literally anything has the potential of serving as a sexual stimulant.

We are not implying that all alleged aphrodisiacs owe their effects strictly to suggestion. Several substances (including alcohol, marijuana, and barbiturates) may increase sexual motivation and arousal by reducing inhibitions. However, their effects are variable and may be greatly influenced by both the particular situation and the attitudes of the person using the drug.

Anaphrodisiacs.   Several drugs are known to inhibit sexual behavior. Substances that have this effect are called **anaphrodisiacs** (an-ah-froh-DIZ-ē-aks).

A great deal of evidence indicates that regular use of *opiates,* such as heroin, morphine, and methadone, often produces a significant — and sometimes a dramatic — decrease in sexual interest and activity in both sexes (Abel, 1984). Serious impairment of sexual functioning associated with opiate use may include erectile problems and inhibited ejaculation in males and reduced capacity to experience orgasm in females.

Tranquilizers, used widely in the treatment of a variety of emotional disorders, have been shown to sometimes reduce sexual motivation, impair erection, and delay or inhibit orgasm in both sexes (Abramowicz, 1987).

Many *antihypertensives,* drugs used for treating high blood pressure, have been experimentally demonstrated to seriously inhibit erection and ejaculation, reduce the intensity of orgasm in male subjects, and reduce sexual interest in both sexes (Abramowicz, 1987; Kaplan, 1979; Rosen, 1991).

Undoubtedly, the most widely used and least recognized anaphrodisiac is *nicotine.* There is evidence that smoking can significantly retard sexual motivation and function by constricting the blood vessels (thereby retarding vasocongestive response of the body to sexual stimulation) and by reducing testosterone levels in the blood (Gilbert et al., 1986; Glina et al., 1988; Rosen, 1991). In one study, sexual arousal was physiologically monitored in 42 males while they viewed erotic films, before and after inhaling different amounts of nicotine. Subjects who smoked two low-nicotine cigarettes between viewings demonstrated no more variation in sexual responsiveness than did control subjects who ate candy. However, men who smoked two high-nicotine cigarettes experienced both delay of and decrease in sexual arousal (Hagen & D'Agostino, 1982).

Paradoxically, the most widely known substance used as an anaphrodisiac, *potassium nitrate,* or saltpeter, is completely ineffective as a sexual deterrent. Many of us have heard the joke about the newlyweds being dosed with saltpeter on their wedding night. In reality, there is no physiological basis for this kind of tale, unless the need for frequent urination can be viewed as a sexual deterrent (potassium nitrate increases urine flow through diuretic action).

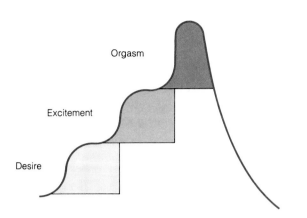

FIGURE 6.2

Kaplan's three-stage model of the sexual response cycle. This model is distinguished by its identification of desire as a prelude to sexual response. (Kaplan, 1979)

Sexual Response

Human sexual response is a highly individual physical, emotional, and mental process. Nevertheless, there are a number of common physiological changes that allow us to outline some general patterns of the sexual response cycle. Masters and Johnson (1966) and sex therapist Helen Singer Kaplan (1979) have described these patterns. We briefly outline Kaplan's ideas before turning to a detailed analysis of Masters and Johnson's work.

Kaplan's Three-Stage Model

Kaplan's model of sexual response, an outgrowth of her extensive experience as a sex therapist, contains three stages: **desire, excitement,** and **orgasm** (see Figure 6.2). She suggests that sexual difficulties tend to fall into one of these three categories, and that it is possible for a person to have difficulty in one while continuing to function normally in the other two.

One of the most distinctive features of Kaplan's model is that it includes desire as a distinct stage of the sexual response cycle. Many other writers, including Masters and Johnson, do not discuss aspects of sexual response that are separate from genital changes. Kaplan's description of desire as a prelude to physical sexual response stands as a welcome addition to the literature. However, not all sexual expression is preceded by desire. For example, a couple may agree to engage in sexual activity even though they may not be feeling sexually inclined at the time. Frequently, they may find that their bodies begin to respond sexually to the ensuing activity, despite their lack of initial desire.

Masters and Johnson's Four-Phase Model

Masters and Johnson distinguish four phases in the sexual response patterns of both men and women: **excitement, plateau, orgasm,** and **resolution.** In addition, they include a **refractory period** (a recovery stage in which there is a temporary

FIGURE 6.3

Female sexual response cycle. Masters and Johnson identified three basic patterns in female sexual response. Pattern A most closely resembles the male pattern, except that a woman can have one or more orgasms without dropping below the plateau level of sexual arousal. Variations of this response include an extended plateau with no orgasm (pattern B) and a rapid rise to orgasm with no definitive plateau and a very quick resolution (pattern C). (Masters & Johnson, 1966)

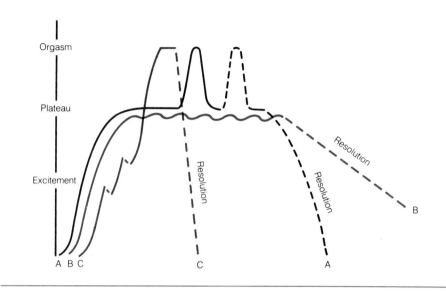

inability to reach orgasm) in the male resolution phase. Figures 6.3 and 6.4 illustrate these four phases of sexual response in women and men. These charts provide basic "maps" of common patterns, but a few cautions to the reader are in order.

First, the simplified nature of these diagrams can easily obscure the richness of individual variation that can and does occur. Masters and Johnson were charting only the physiological responses to sexual stimulation. Our biological reactions may follow a relatively predictable course, but there is tremendous variability in our individual subjective responses to sexual arousal. These personal differences are suggested in the several individual reports of arousal, orgasm, and resolution included later in this chapter.

The second caution has to do with a too literal interpretation of the so-called plateau stage of sexual response. In the behavioral sciences, the term *plateau* is typically used to describe a leveling-off period where no observable changes in behavior can be detected. For example, it might refer to a flat spot in a learning curve where no new behaviors occur for a certain period of time. It has been diagrammed in just this manner in the male chart and in pattern A of the female chart. Actually, the plateau level of sexual arousal involves a powerful surge of sexual tensions that are definitely measurable (for example, as increased heart and breathing rates), so it is far from an unchanging state.

Our third caution is a warning against a tendency to use charts like these as personal checklists. Although we encourage self-references throughout this book, this is one area where a too enthusiastic self-checking can lead to potential problems in the form of "spectatoring." The following quote illustrates this point:

After learning about the four stages of sexual response in class, I found myself "standing back" and watching my own reactions, wondering if I had passed from excitement into plateau. Also, I began to monitor the responses of my partner, looking for the telltale signs that would tell me at what point he was. Suddenly I found myself doing clinical observations rather than allowing myself to fully experience the good feelings. It was a real put-off, and I had to force myself to stop being the observer and become more of a participant. (Authors' files)

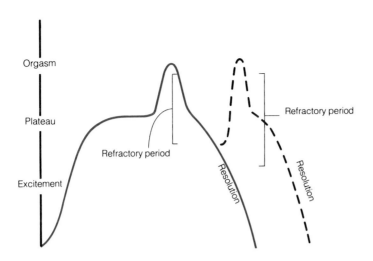

F I G U R E   6.4

Male sexual response cycle. Only one male response pattern was identified by Masters and Johnson. However, men do report considerable variation in their response pattern. Note the refractory period: Males do not have a second orgasm immediately after the first. (Masters & Johnson, 1966)

The descriptions in the following pages should not be viewed as standards for analyzing or intellectualizing your feelings or for evaluating how "normal" your reactions are. We stress that there are many natural variations from these patterns. Perhaps familiarity with these generalized descriptions may help illuminate some of the complexity of your own responses.

In much of the discussion that follows, we will be looking at the physiological reactions and subjective reports of women and men. Before we become too involved in the several specific processes of sexual response, it is important to note that the basic responses of men and women are very similar—a point that was stressed by Masters and Johnson in their research:

> Certainly there are reactions to sexual stimulation that are confined by normal anatomic variation to a single sex. There also are differences in established reactive patterns to sexual stimuli—for example, duration and intensity of response—that usually are sex-linked in character. However, parallels in reactive potential between the two sexes must be underlined. Similarities rather than differences of response have been emphasized by this investigation. (Masters & Johnson, 1966, p. 273)

Two fundamental physiological responses to effective sexual stimulation occur in both women and men. These are *vasocongestion* and *myotonia*. These two basic reactions are the primary underlying sources for almost all biological responses that take place during sexual arousal.

Vasocongestion is the engorgement with blood of body tissues that respond to sexual excitation. Usually the blood flow into organs and tissues through the arteries is balanced by an equal outflow through the veins. However, during sexual arousal the dilation of arteries increases the inflow beyond the veins' draining capacity. This results in widespread vasocongestion in both superficial and deep tissues. The congested areas that are visible may feel warm and appear swollen and red, due to their increased blood content. The most obvious manifestations of this vasocongestive response are the erection of the penis in men and lubrication of the vagina in women. In addition, other body areas may become engorged—the labia, testicles, clitoris, nipples, and even the earlobes.

The second basic physiological response is **myotonia** (mī-ō-TO-nē-a), the increased muscle tension that occurs throughout the body during sexual arousal.

Myotonia is evident in both voluntary flexing and involuntary contractions. Its most dramatic manifestations are facial grimaces, spasmodic contractions of the hands and feet, and the muscular spasms that occur during orgasm.

The phases of the response cycle follow the same general patterns regardless of the method of stimulation. Masturbation, manual stimulation by one's partner, oral pleasuring, penile – vaginal intercourse, dreaming, fantasy, and, in some women, breast stimulation can all result in completion of the response cycle. Often the intensity and rapidity of response vary according to the kind of stimulation.

In the next several pages, we outline the major physiological reactions to sexual stimulation that occur during each of the four phases of the sexual response cycle. Subjective reports of several individuals are included. For each stage we list reactions common to both sexes and those unique to just one. You will note the strong similarities in the sexual response patterns of men and women. We will discuss some important differences in greater detail at the conclusion of this chapter.

Excitement.   The first phase of the sexual response cycle, the excitement phase, is characterized by a number of responses common to men and women, including muscle tension and some increase in the heart rate and blood pressure. In both sexes, several areas of the sexual anatomy become engorged. For example, the clitoris, labia minora, vagina, nipples, penis, and testes all increase in size, and most of them deepen in color. Some responses, such as the appearance of a **sex flush** (a pink or red rash on the chest or breasts), occur in both sexes but are more common in women. Still other responses, specific to just one sex, are illustrated in Figures 6.5 – 6.8, which show changes in the sexual anatomy of women and men throughout the phases of the cycle.

The excitement phase may vary in duration from less than a minute to several hours. Both males and females may show considerable variation in the degree of their arousal during this phase. For example, a man's penis may vary from flaccid to semierect to a fully erect state. Similarly, vaginal lubrication in women may vary from minimal to copious.

Although the physiological characteristics outlined in the figures represent general patterns, different people experience these changes in differing ways. The following two reports give some indication of the subjective variations in how women describe their own feelings during sexual arousal:

Sexual arousal for me is something I look forward to when I realize my husband and I will have sex. His touching, kissing, and loving me in this way brings me to a height of excitement that is incredible. At first I felt selfish about him giving me so much satisfaction through stimulation, but he enjoys it so much, it's a wonderful time. Often we don't have intercourse because we are caught up in the "foreplay" of lovemaking. (Authors' files)

When I am aroused, I get warm all over, and I like a lot of holding and massaging of other areas of my body besides my genitals. After time passes with that particular stimulation, I prefer more direct manual stroking if orgasm is desired. (Authors' files)

Two men provide their descriptions of sexual arousal in the following accounts:

When I am sexually aroused, my whole body feels energized. Sometimes my mouth gets dry, and I may feel a little lightheaded. I want to have all of my body touched and stroked, not just my genitals. I particularly like the sensation of feeling that orgasm is just around the corner, waiting and tantalizing me to begin the final journey. Sometimes a quick rush to climax

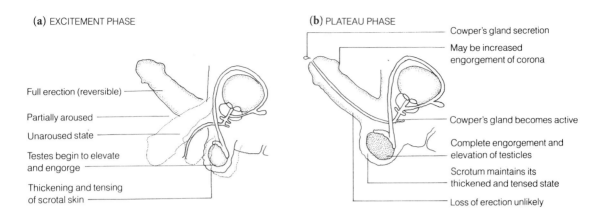

(a) EXCITEMENT PHASE

Full erection (reversible)

Partially aroused

Unaroused state

Testes begin to elevate and engorge

Thickening and tensing of scrotal skin

(b) PLATEAU PHASE

Cowper's gland secretion

May be increased engorgement of corona

Cowper's gland becomes active

Complete engorgement and elevation of testicles

Scrotum maintains its thickened and tensed state

Loss of erection unlikely

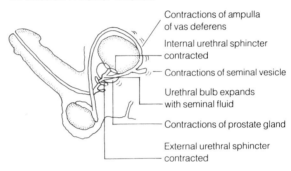

(c) EMISSION PHASE OF ORGASM

Contractions of ampulla of vas deferens

Internal urethral sphincter contracted

Contractions of seminal vesicle

Urethral bulb expands with seminal fluid

Contractions of prostate gland

External urethral sphincter contracted

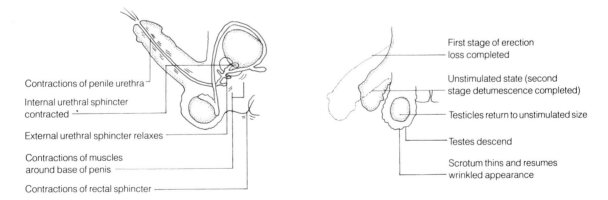

(d) EXPULSION PHASE OF ORGASM

Contractions of penile urethra

Internal urethral sphincter contracted

External urethral sphincter relaxes

Contractions of muscles around base of penis

Contractions of rectal sphincter

(e) RESOLUTION PHASE

First stage of erection loss completed

Unstimulated state (second stage detumescence completed)

Testicles return to unstimulated size

Testes descend

Scrotum thins and resumes wrinkled appearance

is nice, but usually I prefer making the arousal period last as long as I can stand it, until my penis feels like it is dying for the final strokes of ecstasy. (Authors' files)

When aroused I feel very excited, and I fantasize a lot. Then all of a sudden, a warm feeling comes over me, and it feels like a thousand pleasure pins are being stuck into my loins all at the same time. (Authors' files)

FIGURE 6.5

Major changes in external and internal male sexual anatomy during the sexual response cycle.

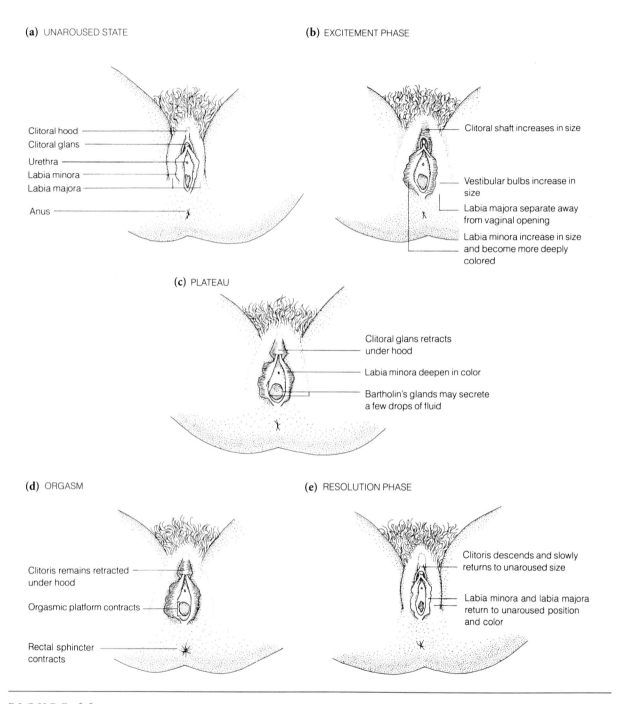

(a) UNAROUSED STATE

Clitoral hood
Clitoral glans
Urethra
Labia minora
Labia majora

Anus

(b) EXCITEMENT PHASE

Clitoral shaft increases in size

Vestibular bulbs increase in size

Labia majora separate away from vaginal opening

Labia minora increase in size and become more deeply colored

(c) PLATEAU

Clitoral glans retracts under hood

Labia minora deepen in color

Bartholin's glands may secrete a few drops of fluid

(d) ORGASM

Clitoris remains retracted under hood

Orgasmic platform contracts

Rectal sphincter contracts

(e) RESOLUTION PHASE

Clitoris descends and slowly returns to unaroused size

Labia minora and labia majora return to unaroused position and color

F I G U R E   6.6

Major changes in the external female genitals during the sexual response cycle.

Plateau. During the plateau phase, sexual tension continues to mount until it reaches the peak that leads to orgasm. It is difficult to define clearly the point at which a sexually responding individual makes the transition to this phase. Unlike the excitement phase, the plateau phase has no clear external sign such as lubrication or erection to mark its onset. Instead, several of these signs become more pronounced as they accelerate toward the peaks reached in the next phase. Both heart rate and blood pressure continue to rise; breathing grows faster; sex flushes

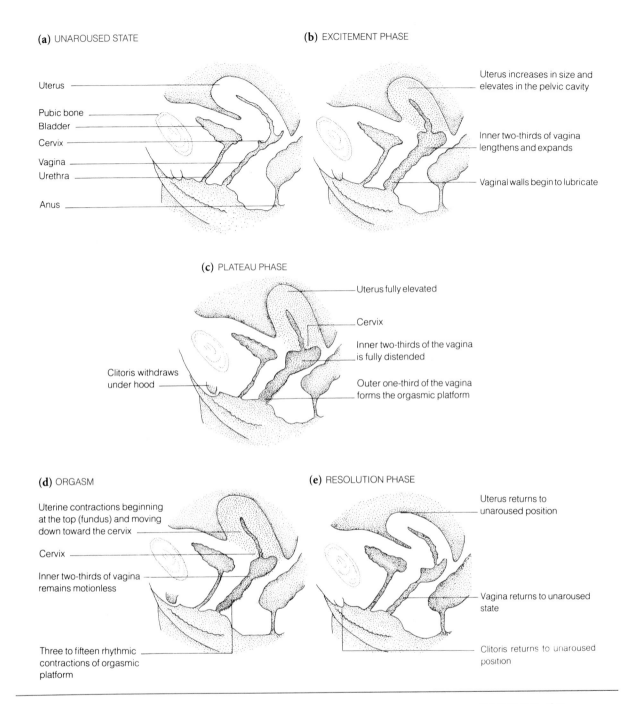

(a) UNAROUSED STATE

Uterus

Pubic bone

Bladder

Cervix

Vagina

Urethra

Anus

(b) EXCITEMENT PHASE

Uterus increases in size and elevates in the pelvic cavity

Inner two-thirds of vagina lengthens and expands

Vaginal walls begin to lubricate

(c) PLATEAU PHASE

Uterus fully elevated

Cervix

Inner two-thirds of the vagina is fully distended

Clitoris withdraws under hood

Outer one-third of the vagina forms the orgasmic platform

(d) ORGASM

Uterine contractions beginning at the top (fundus) and moving down toward the cervix

Cervix

Inner two-thirds of vagina remains motionless

Three to fifteen rhythmic contractions of orgasmic platform

(e) RESOLUTION PHASE

Uterus returns to unaroused position

Vagina returns to unaroused state

Clitoris returns to unaroused position

FIGURE 6.7

Major changes in the internal female genitals during the sexual response cycle.

and coloration of the genitals become more noticeable. Muscle tension continues to build up, and the face, neck, hands, and feet may undergo involuntary contractions and spasms in both the plateau and orgasm phases. Among women, the plateau phase is also distinguished by development of the "orgasmic platform," a term used by Masters and Johnson to describe the markedly increased engorgement of the outer third of the vagina.

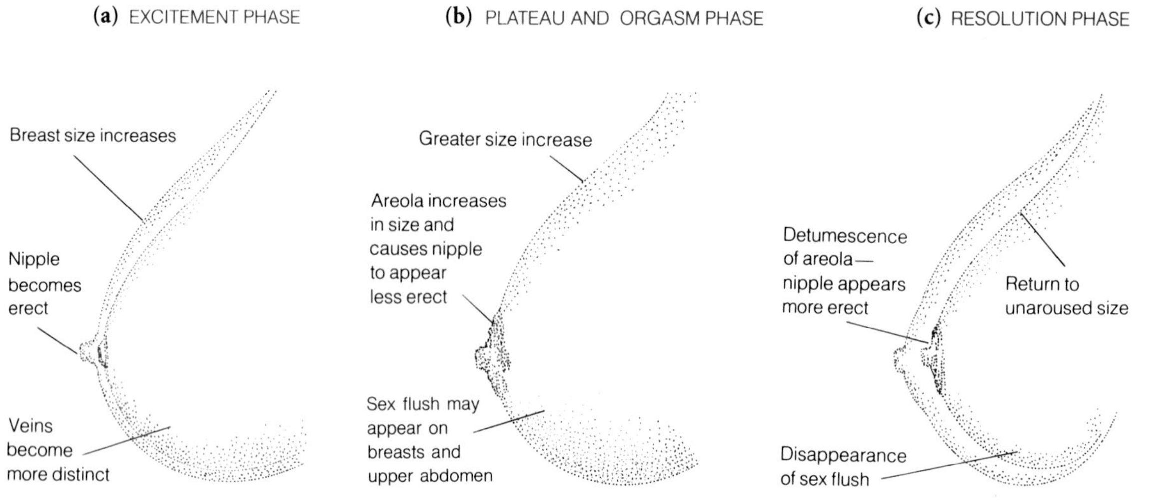

(a) EXCITEMENT PHASE   **(b)** PLATEAU AND ORGASM PHASE   **(c)** RESOLUTION PHASE

Breast size increases

Nipple becomes erect

Veins become more distinct

Greater size increase

Areola increases in size and causes nipple to appear less erect

Sex flush may appear on breasts and upper abdomen

Detumescence of areola— nipple appears more erect

Return to unaroused size

Disappearance of sex flush

FIGURE 6.8

Changes in the breasts during the sexual response cycle.

The plateau phase is often very brief, typically lasting a few seconds to several minutes. However, many people find that prolonging sexual tensions at this high level produces greater arousal and ultimately more intense orgasms. This is reported in the following subjective accounts:

When I get up there, almost on the verge of coming, I try to hang in as long as possible. If my partner cooperates, stopping or slowing when necessary, I can stay right on the edge for several minutes, sometimes even longer. I know that all it would take is one more stroke and I'm over the top. Sometimes my whole body gets to shaking and quivering, and I can feel incredible sensations shooting through me like electric charges. The longer I can make this supercharged period last, the better the orgasm. (Authors' files)

When I masturbate, I like to take myself almost to the point of climaxing and then back off. I can tell when orgasm is about to happen because my vagina tightens up around the opening, and sometimes I can feel the muscles contract. I love the sensations of balancing myself on the brink, part of me wanting to come and the other part holding out for more. The longer I maintain this delicate balance, the more shattering the climax. Sometimes the pleasure is almost beyond bearing. (Authors' files)

Orgasm. As effective stimulation continues, many people move from plateau to orgasm. This is particularly true for men, who almost always experience orgasm after reaching the plateau level. In contrast, women may obtain plateau levels of arousal without the release of sexual climax. This is often the case during penile–vaginal intercourse when the man reaches orgasm first, or when effective manual or oral stimulation is replaced with penetration as the female approaches orgasm. More will be said about this later.

Orgasm is the shortest phase of the sexual response cycle, typically lasting only a few seconds. Female orgasms often last slightly longer than do male orgasms. Figures 6.5–6.8 summarize the primary physiological responses during orgasm.

The experience of orgasm can be an intense mixture of highly pleasurable sensations. There has been considerable debate about whether women and men experience orgasm differently. This question was evaluated a few years ago in an experimental analysis of orgasm descriptions that were provided by college stu-

OUR SEXUALITY

Subjective Descriptions of Orgasm*

When I'm about to orgasm, my face feels very hot. I close my eyes and open my mouth. It centers in my clitoris, and it feels like electric wires igniting from there and radiating up my torso and down my legs to my feet. I sometimes feel like I need to urinate. My vagina contracts anywhere from 5 to 12 times. My vulva area feels heavy and swollen. There isn't another feeling like it — it's fantastic!

Orgasm for me draws all my energy in towards a core in my body. Then, all of a sudden, there is a release of this energy out through my penis. My body becomes warm and numb before orgasm; after, it gradu-ally relaxes and I feel extremely serene.

Report A. It's like an Almond Joy, "indescribably delicious." The feeling runs from the top of my head to the tips of my toes as I feel a powerful surge of pleasure. It raises me beyond my physical self into another level of consciousness, and yet the feeling seems purely physical. What a paradox! It strokes all over, inside and out. I love it simply because it's mine and mine alone.

Report B. An orgasm to me is like heaven. All my tensions and anxieties are released. You get to the point of no return, and it's like an uncontrollable desire that makes things start happening. I think that sex and orgasm are one of the greatest phenomenons that we have today. It's a great sharing experience for me.

Report C. Having an orgasm is like the ultimate time I have for myself. I am not excluding my partner, but it's like I can't hear anything, and all I feel is a spectacular release accompanied with more pleasure than I've ever felt doing anything else. (Authors' files)

*For Reports A, B, and C, try to determine if the subject was male or female. To find the answers, turn to the summary at the end of this chapter.

dents (Wiest, 1977). Using a standard psychological rating scale, this researcher found that women's and men's subjective descriptions of orgasm were indistinguishable. Similar results were obtained in an earlier study, when a group of 70 expert judges were unable to reliably distinguish between the written orgasm reports of men and women (Proctor et al., 1974).

Beyond the question of sex differences in orgasmic experiences, it is clear that there is great individual variation in how people, both men and women, describe orgasms. In the box "Subjective Descriptions of Orgasm," some subjective accounts selected from our files illustrate the diversity of these descriptions. The first one is by a woman and the second by a man. The final three — labeled Reports A, B, and C — contain no specific references that identify the sex of the describer. Perhaps you would like to try to determine whether they were reported by a man or a woman. The answers are given at the end of the chapter, following the summary.

Although the physiology of female orgasmic response can be clearly outlined, some past and present issues about its nature need to be discussed. Misinformation about female orgasm has been prevalent in our culture. Freud, writing in the early 1900s, developed a theory of the "vaginal" versus the "clitoral" orgasm that, inaccurate though it is, has had a great impact on people's thinking about female sexual response. Freud viewed the vaginal orgasm as more mature than the clitoral orgasm, and thus preferable. The physiological basis for this theory was the assumption that the clitoris is a stunted penis. This assumption led to the conclusion that erotic sensations, arousal, and orgasm resulting from direct stimulation of the clitoris were all expressions of "masculine" rather than "feminine" sexuality — and therefore undesirable (Sherfey, 1972). At adolescence a woman was supposed to transfer her erotic center from the clitoris to the vagina. If she was not able to do so at this time, psychotherapy was sometimes used to attempt to help her attain "vaginal" orgasms. Unfortunately, this theory led many women to believe incorrectly that they were sexually maladjusted.

Our modern knowledge of embryology has established the falseness of the theory that the clitoris is a masculine organ, as we have seen in our discussion of the genital differentiation process in Chapter 3. In one researcher's words, "to reduce clitoral eroticism to the level of psychopathology because the clitoris is an innately masculine organ... must now be considered a travesty of the facts" (Sherfey, 1972, p. 47). Travesty of facts or not, during Freud's time this sexual-center transfer theory was taken so seriously that surgical removal of the clitoris was recommended for little girls who masturbated, to help them later attain "vaginal" orgasms.

Surgical clitoridectomies are no longer performed in our culture. Yet social conditioning, which can be as effective as a scalpel, continues: Freud's operational definition of female sexual health is still with us in many respects. For example, a woman's reluctance to ask her partner to manually stimulate her clitoris during coitus (or to do it herself) typifies the learned belief that she "should" experience orgasm from penile stimulation alone. However, cultural conditioning can work two ways — with knowledge and support, a woman can change her attitude about her sexual feelings and behaviors.

Contrary to Freud's theory, the research of Masters and Johnson suggests that there is only one kind of orgasm in females, physiologically speaking, regardless of the method of stimulation. They state:

> From a biologic ... [and] anatomic point of view, there is absolutely no difference in the responses of the pelvic viscera to effective sexual stimulation, regardless of whether the stimulation occurs as a result of clitoral-body or mons area manipulation, natural or artificial coition, or for that matter, specific stimulation of any other erogenous area of the female body. (1966, p. 66)

Masters and Johnson's view that there is no physiological basis for defining different types of female orgasms has been contested by Josephine and Irving Singer (1972). These authors contend that, besides noting observable physiological variations, it is important to take emotional satisfaction into consideration in accounting for differences in female orgasmic response. With this in mind, the Singers have described three types of female orgasm — vulval, uterine, and blended. They suggest that a *vulval orgasm* corresponds to the type of orgasmic response described by Masters and Johnson and that it may be induced by either coital or manual stimulation. The vulval orgasm is accompanied by contractions of the orgasmic platform and typically is not followed by a refractory period. A *uterine orgasm,* in contrast, occurs only as a result of vaginal penetration and is characterized by a woman involuntarily holding her breath as orgasm approaches and explosively exhaling at climax. The Singers suggest that this type of orgasm often induces a profound sense of relaxation and sexual satiation and is typically followed by a refractory period. Finally, they describe a *blended orgasm* that is a combination of the first two types, characterized by both contractions of the orgasmic platform and breath-holding.

When the Singers' conceptualization of female orgasm was first published, many professionals in the field of sexuality assigned it little credibility. The apparent similarity of the Singers' "uterine orgasms" and Freud's "vaginal orgasms" may have caused some to fear a revival of the old theory of superior vaginal versus inferior clitoral orgasms. However, the Singers did not claim that one type of orgasm was superior to another. One of the major problems for any theory suggesting vaginal erotic response has been the widespread belief that the vagina is largely insensitive to sexual stimulation. However, this idea is being seriously called into question by the recent emergence of evidence indicating vaginal erotic sensitivity. For example, in one recent study, examiners used their fingers to apply moderate to strong rhythmic pressure to all areas of the vaginal walls of 48 subjects. Over 90% of the women stimulated in this fashion reported considerable erotic sensitivity of the vagina, most commonly on the anterior (front) wall. Some reported sensitivity in more than one area. Many of the women experienced orgasm from this manual stimulation of their vaginas (Alzate & Londono, 1984).

The Grafenberg Spot. In the last few years, a number of studies have reported that some women are capable of experiencing orgasm, and perhaps ejaculation, when an area along the anterior wall of the vagina is vigorously stimulated (Addiego et al., 1981; Davidson et al., 1989; Perry & Whipple, 1981; Whipple & Komisaruk, 1988; Zaviacic et al., 1988a). This area of erotic sensitivity, briefly mentioned in Chapter 4, has been named the *Grafenberg spot* (or *G spot*) in honor of Ernest Grafenberg (1950), a gynecologist who first noted the erotic significance of this location within the vagina 40 years ago. However, the presence of glandular structures in this area was noted in the medical literature over 100 years ago (Skene, 1880). It has been suggested that the Grafenberg spot is not a point that can be touched by the tip of one finger but, rather, a fairly large area composed of the lower anterior wall of the vagina and the underlying urethra and surrounding glands (Heath, 1984, p. 205).

Robert Mallon (1984), a pathologist and medical researcher, presented evidence of glandular material similar to prostate tissue in the Grafenberg area of 42 females examined by postmortem autopsies. Corroboration of this research was provided by another study in which complete urethras and surrounding tissue from 17 autopsied females and a portion of a urethra from one surgical specimen were examined. Over 80% of the specimens had prostatelike glandular tissue, the majority of which contained substances known to be produced by the male prostate (Heath, 1984).

The Grafenberg spot, or area, may be located by "systematic palpation of the entire anterior wall of the vagina between the posterior side of the pubic bone and the cervix. Two fingers are usually employed, and it is often necessary to press deeply into the tissue to reach the spot" (Perry & Whipple, 1981, p. 29). This exploration may be conducted by a woman's partner, as shown in Figure 6.9. Some women are able to locate their Grafenberg spots through self-exploration.

During initial searching for the sometimes elusive Grafenberg spot, a woman or her partner must rely on the sensations produced by manual stimulation. When the area is located, women report a variety of initial sensations, including a slight feeling of discomfort, a brief sensation of needing to urinate, or a pleasurable feeling. After a minute or more of stroking, the sensations usually become more pleasurable, and the area may begin to swell to a discernible size. Continued stimulation of the area may result in an orgasm that is often quite intense.

FIGURE 6.9

Locating the Grafenberg spot. Usually two fingers are used, and it is often necessary to press deeply into the anterior wall of the vagina to reach the spot.

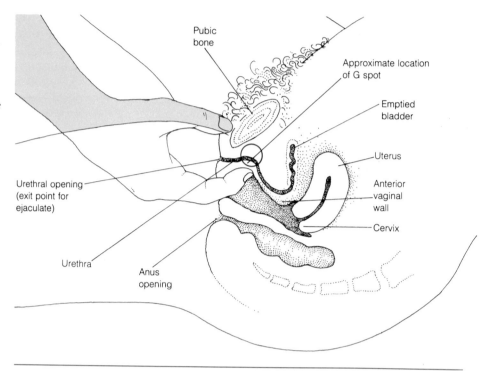

Perhaps the most amazing thing about Grafenberg spot orgasms is that they are sometimes accompanied by the ejaculation of fluid from the urethral opening. Research indicates that the source of this fluid is the "female prostate" discussed in Chapter 4. The ducts from this system empty directly into the urethra. In some women Grafenberg orgasms result in fluid being forced through these ducts and out the urethra. In view of the homologous nature of Grafenberg spot tissue and the male prostate, we might speculate that the female ejaculate is similar to the prostatic component of male seminal fluid. This notion has been supported by research in which specimens of female ejaculate were chemically analyzed and found to contain high levels of an enzyme, prostatic acid phosphatase (PAP), characteristic of the prostatic component of semen (Addiego et al., 1981; Belzer et al., 1984). Many women report that the fluid has a mild semenlike scent. A recent study found concentrations of fructose in the female ejaculate (Zaviacic et al., 1988b). (You will recall from Chapter 5 that fructose is a major component of male ejaculate.) The fructose level in the orgasmic expulsions of women is considerably higher than that found in their urine, a finding that "suggests that the female ejaculate cannot be simply regarded as urine" (Zaviacic et al., 1988b, p. 323).

Although the existence of Grafenberg spot orgasms, sometimes accompanied by ejaculation, has been reported with some degree of reliability, our understanding of this phenomenon is far from complete. For example, how common are these responses? (A recent survey of 2350 U.S. and Canadian professional women revealed that 40% of the respondents reported experiencing a fluid release ejaculation at the moment of orgasm [Darling et al., 1990].) Is there a connection between Grafenberg spot stimulation and the uterine orgasm described by the

Singers? Is the female Grafenberg area a genuine homologue of the male prostate? Clearly, considerably more research is necessary before conclusive answers can be obtained for these and other questions. In the meantime, we encourage women and their partners who want to explore this intriguing new information in relation to their own sexual response and activities to do so. However, it may be self-defeating to treat Grafenberg spot orgasm as a new sexual achievement to be relentlessly pursued. It would be unfortunate if the current reexamination of some of our beliefs about female orgasm were to lead to a reemergence of attributing emotional or physiological superiority to any one orgasmic pattern.

Resolution.   During the final phase of the sexual response cycle, the sexual systems return to their nonexcited state. If no additional stimulation occurs, the resolution begins immediately after orgasm. Some of the changes back to a nonexcited state take place rapidly, while others occur more slowly. Figures 6.5 – 6.8 summarize the major physiological changes associated with resolution.

The four self-reports that follow provide some indication of how people vary in their feelings after orgasm. The first two are by females, the second two by males.

After a satisfying experience with my husband, I want to be held, as if to finalize and complete our union. Sometimes I like to talk and sometimes I just like to be able to touch him and be touched by his whole body. (Authors' files)

After orgasm I feel very relaxed. My moods do vary — sometimes I'm ready to start all over; other times I can jump up and really get busy; and at other times I just want to sleep. (Authors' files)

After orgasm I feel relaxed and usually very content. Sometimes I feel like sleeping, and other times I feel like I want to touch my partner if she is willing. I like to hold her and just be there. (Authors' files)

After orgasm I generally experience a brief period where my sexual interest drops dramatically. While holding and being held is nice, I prefer not to continue any sexual activity, at least not for a few minutes. Usually, I feel extremely satiated, similar to the aftermath of dining on a superb meal. Talking and sharing thoughts about the experience is especially pleasant. However, sometimes I like to just roll over and quietly bask in the luxurious afterglow. (Authors' files)

These subjective reports of women and men sound very similar. But there is one significant difference in the responses of women and men during this phase — their physiological readiness for further sexual stimulation. After orgasm, the male typically enters a refractory period — a time when no amount of additional stimulation will result in orgasm. The length of this period ranges from minutes to days, depending on a variety of factors such as the age of the man, the frequency of previous sexual activity, and the degree of his emotional closeness to and sexual desire for his partner. In contrast to men, women generally experience no comparable refractory period: They are physiologically capable of returning to another orgasmic peak from anywhere in the resolution phase. However, a woman may or may not want to do so. In the next section, we take a more detailed look at male – female differences during the resolution phase, and we consider some other differences between men's and women's patterns of sexual response.

Some Differences Between the Sexes

More and more, writers are emphasizing the basic similarities of sexual response in men and women. We see this as a positive trend away from the once-popular notion that great differences exist between the sexes — an opinion that undoubtedly helped create a big market for many "love manuals" designed to inform readers about the mysteries and complexities of the "opposite sex." Now we know that much can be learned about our partners by carefully observing our own sexual patterns. Nevertheless, there are some real and important primary differences. In the following pages, we outline and discuss some of them.

What do you think are some of the significant differences between the sexes in sexual response patterns? See what you can come up with before reading on.

Greater Variability in Female Response. One major difference between the sexes is the range of variations in the sexual response cycle. Although the graphs in Figures 6.3 and 6.4 do not reflect individual differences, they do demonstrate a wider range in the female response. One pattern has been outlined for the male and three for the female.

In the female chart, the sexual response pattern represented by line A is most similar to the male pattern. It differs in an important way, however, in its potential for additional orgasms without dropping below the plateau level. Line B represents quite a different female pattern: a smooth advance through excitement to the level of plateau, where the responding woman may remain for some time without experiencing orgasm. The consequent resolution phase is more drawn out. Line C portrays a rapid rise in excitement, followed by one intense orgasm and a quick resolution.

Although it appears that women often have more variable sexual response patterns than men, this does not imply that all males experience the response cycle in exactly the same way. Men report considerable variation from the Masters and Johnson standard, including several mild orgasmic peaks followed by ejaculation, prolonged pelvic contractions after the expulsion of semen, and extended periods of intense excitement prior to ejaculation that feels like one long orgasm (Zilbergeld, 1978). In other words, there is no single pattern of sexual response, nor is there one "correct way." All patterns and variations — including one person's different reactions to sexual stimuli at different times or in different situations — are completely normal.

The Male Refractory Period. The presence of a refractory period in the male cycle is certainly one of the most significant differences in sexual responses between the sexes. Men typically find that a certain minimum time must elapse after an orgasm before they can experience another climax. Most women have no such physiologically imposed "shutdown phase."

There is considerable speculation about why only men have a refractory period. It seems plausible that some kind of short-term neurological inhibitory mechanism is triggered by ejaculation. This notion is supported by the publication of some fascinating research conducted by three British scientists (Barfield et al., 1975). These researchers speculated that certain chemical pathways between the midbrain and the hypothalamus — pathways known to be involved in regulating sleep — might have something to do with postorgasm inhibition in males. To test their hypothesis, the researchers destroyed a specific site, the *ventral medial lemniscus,* along these pathways in rats. For comparative purposes, they surgically eliminated three other areas in hypothalamic and midbrain locations in different rats. Later observations of sexual behavior revealed that the elimination of the ventral medial lemniscus had a dramatic effect on refractory periods, cutting their duration in half.

Other research with rats has provided further evidence implicating the brain in the male refractory period. In two studies, large lesions made in an area below the hypothalamus resulted in greatly increased ejaculatory behavior (Heimer & Larson, 1964; Lisk, 1966). Another investigation revealed that electrical stimulation of the posterior hypothalamus can produce dramatic declines in the intervals between a male rat's copulatory activities (Cagguila, 1970).

Some people believe that the answer to the riddle of refractory periods is somehow connected with the loss of seminal fluid during orgasm. Most researchers have been skeptical of this idea because there is no known substance in the expelled semen to account for an energy drain, marked hormone reduction, or any of the other implied biochemical explanations.

Another explanation suggests that there may be an evolutionary advantage in male refractory periods. According to this argument, because they have no sexual shutdown after orgasm, women can continue copulatory activity with other males, increasing the numbers of sperm in their reproductive tracts and thus the possibility of impregnation. From this evolutionary point of view, the presence of additional sperm might also allow for increased natural selection of the fittest (the fastest swimmers, the longest living, and so forth). Admittedly, the evidence for this theory is tenuous at best, but it is nevertheless a provocative thesis. Whatever the reason for it, the refractory period is common not just to human males but to males of virtually all other species for which data exist, including rats, dogs, and chimpanzees.

Multiple Orgasms. There is a third area of sexual response patterns where some differences between the sexes occur: the ability to experience **multiple orgasms.** Technically speaking, the term *multiple orgasms* refers to having more than one orgasmic experience within a short time interval.

Although researchers differ in their views of what constitutes a multiple orgasmic experience, for our own purposes we can say that if a man or woman has two or more sexual climaxes within a short period, that person has experienced multiple orgasms. There is, however, a distinction between males and females that is often obscured by such a definition. It is not uncommon for a woman to have several sequential orgasms, separated in time by the briefest of intervals (perhaps only seconds). In contrast, the spacing of male orgasms is typically more protracted in time.

How many women experience multiple orgasms? Kinsey (1953) reported that about 14% of his female sample regularly had multiple orgasms. In 1970 a survey of *Psychology Today* readers revealed a 16% figure (Athanasiou et al., 1970). Surveys of our own student population over the years have produced a similar percentage of women who regularly experience more than one orgasm during a single sexual encounter.

On the surface, it might seem that the capacity for multiple orgasms is limited to a minority of women. However, the research of Masters and Johnson showed this assumption to be false:

> If a female who is capable of having regular orgasms is properly stimulated within a short period after her first climax, she will in most instances be capable of having a second, third, fourth, and even a fifth and a sixth orgasm before she is fully satiated. As contrasted with the male's usual inability to have more than one orgasm in a short period, many females, especially when clitorally stimulated, can regularly have five or six full orgasms within a matter of minutes. (1961, p. 792)

Thus, we find that most women have the capacity for multiple orgasms, but apparently only a small portion of the female population experiences them. Why is there a large gap between capacity and experience? The answer may lie in the source of stimulation. The Kinsey report, the *Psychology Today* survey, and our own student surveys mentioned earlier are all based on orgasm rates during penile–vaginal intercourse. For a variety of reasons — not the least of which is the male tendency to stop after his orgasm — women are not likely to continue coitus beyond their initial orgasm. In sharp contrast, several researchers have demonstrated that women who masturbate and those who relate sexually to other women are considerably more likely both to reach initial orgasm and to continue to additional orgasms (Athanasiou et al., 1970; Masters & Johnson, 1966).

We do not mean to imply by this discussion that all women should be experiencing multiple orgasms. On the contrary, many women may prefer sexual experiences during which they have a single orgasm, or perhaps no orgasm at all. The data on multiple orgasmic capacities of women are not meant to be interpreted as the way women "should" respond. This could lead to a new kind of arbitrary sexual standard. The following quotes illustrate the tendency to set such standards:

When I was growing up, people considered any young, unmarried woman who enjoyed and sought active sexual involvements to be disturbed or promiscuous. Now I am told that I must have several orgasms each time I make love in order to be considered "normal." What a switch in our definitions of normal or healthy — from the straight-laced, noninvolved person to this incredible creature who is supposed to get it off multiply at the drop of a hat. (Authors' files)

Sometimes men ask me why I don't come more than once. It is as though they want me to perform for them. The truth is, one orgasm is all I typically need to be satisfied. Sometimes it is nice not even to worry about having a climax. All this emphasis on producing multiple orgasms is a real put-off to me. (Authors' files)

As suggested earlier, multiple orgasms are considerably less common among males. They are most often reported by very young men, their frequency declining with age. Even at college age, it is unusual to find men who routinely experience more than one orgasm during a single sexual encounter. However, we agree with Alex Comfort (1972), who asserts that most men are probably more capable of multiple orgasms than they realize. Many have been conditioned by years of masturbation to get it over as quickly as possible ("Hurry up and finish before I am discovered!"). Such a mental set hardly encourages an adolescent to continue experimenting after the initial orgasm. Through later experimentation, though, many men make discoveries similar to the one described in the following personal reflection of a middle-aged man:

Somehow it never occurred to me that I might continue making love after experiencing orgasm. For 30 years of my life, this always signaled endpoint for me. I guess I responded this way for all the reasons you stated in class and a few more you didn't cover. My wife was with me the night you discussed refractory periods. We talked about it all the way home, and the next day gave it a try. Man, am I mad at myself now for missing out on something really nice all of these years. I discovered that I could have more than one orgasm in one session, and while it may take me a long time to come again, the getting there is a very nice part. My wife likes it, too! (Authors' files)

There is evidence to suggest that some men may actually be capable of experiencing a series of orgasms in a very short time period. In one study, 13 men reported that they had the capacity to experience a series of pre-ejaculatory orgasms culminating in a final orgasm with ejaculation. Most of these men related having three to ten orgasms per sexual encounter. One man reported experiencing 30 orgasms, at intervals of one minute or less, during one intercourse session. Unfortunately, only one of these 13 individuals was studied in the laboratory, where his claim was substantiated with physiological data. Apparently, the key to these multiple responses was the men's ability to withhold ejaculation because the final orgasm in the series, accompanied by ejaculation, triggered a refractory period (Robbins & Jensen, 1978). Hartman and Fithian (1984) reported success in teaching men to experience multiple, nonejaculatory orgasms by tightening the pubococcygeus (PC) and related muscles at the point of impending orgasm. If these findings are substantiated and more men become aware of the possibility of experiencing multiple orgasms, future surveys may reveal that the percentage of men experiencing several orgasms during one sex session is closer to that of their female counterparts.

It is not necessary for lovemaking always to end with ejaculation. Many men may find it pleasurable to continue sexual activity after a climax:

One of the best parts of sex for me is having intercourse again shortly after my first orgasm. I find it is relatively easy to get another erection, even though I seldom experience another climax during the same session. The second time round I can concentrate fully on my partner's reactions without being distracted by my own building excitement. The pace is generally mellow and relaxed, and it is a real high for me psychologically. (Authors' files)

Thus multiple orgasms can be seen not as an ultimate goal to be sought above all else but rather as a possible area to explore. A relaxed approach to this possibility may give interested women and men an opportunity to experience more of the full range of their sexual potentials.

Summary

Sexual Arousal: The Role of Hormones

Although it is difficult to distinguish the effects of sex hormones and of learning experiences on sexual arousal, research does indicate that androgens appear to facilitate sexual interest in males. The relationship between female sexuality and hormones is more difficult to pinpoint.

Sexual Arousal: The Brain

The brain plays an important role in human sexual arousal by mediating our thoughts, emotions, memories, and fantasies.

There is evidence linking stimulation and surgical alteration of various brain sites with sexual arousal in humans and other animals.

The limbic system, particularly the hypothalamus and septal area, seems to play an important part in sexual function.

Sexual Arousal: The Senses

Touch tends to predominate among the senses that stimulate human sexual arousal. Locations on the body that are highly responsive to tactile pleasuring are called erogenous zones. Primary erogenous zones are areas with dense concentrations of nerve endings; secondary erogenous zones are other areas of the body that become endowed with erotic significance as the result of sexual conditioning.

Vision is second only to touch in providing stimuli that most people find sexually arousing. Recent evidence suggests that women respond as much as men to visual erotica.

It is not known whether smell and taste play a biologically determined role in human sexual arousal, but our own unique individual experiences may allow certain smells and tastes to acquire erotic significance. However, our culture's obsession with "personal hygiene" tends to mask natural smells or tastes that relate to sexual activity.

Some individuals find sounds during lovemaking to be highly arousing, whereas others prefer that their lovers be silent during love play. Besides being sexually stimulating to some, communication during a sexual interlude can be very informative.

Sexual Arousal: Foods and Chemicals

At this point there is no clear evidence that any substance that we eat, drink, or inject has genuine aphrodisiac qualities. Faith and suggestion account for the apparent successes of a variety of alleged aphrodisiacs.

Certain substances are known to have an inhibitory effect upon sexual behavior. These anaphrodisiacs include some tranquilizers, a few antihypertensives, certain antiandrogenic drugs, and nicotine.

Sexual Response: Kaplan's Three-Stage Model

Kaplan's model of sexual response contains three stages: desire, excitement, and orgasm.

This model is distinguished by its inclusion of desire as a distinct stage of the sexual response cycle separate from genital changes.

Sexual Response: Masters and Johnson's Four-Phase Model

Masters and Johnson describe four phases in the sexual response patterns of both women and men: excitement, plateau, orgasm, and resolution.

During excitement, both sexes experience increased myotonia (muscle tension), heart rate, and blood pressure. Sex flush and nipple erection often occur, especially among women. Female responses include engorgement of the clitoris, the labia, and the vagina (with vaginal lubrication), elevation and enlargement of the uterus, and breast enlargement. Males experience penile erection, enlargement and elevation of the testes, and sometimes Cowper's gland secretions.

The plateau phase is marked by dramatic accelerations of myotonia, hyperventilation, heart rate, and blood pressure. In females, the clitoris withdraws under its hood, the labia minora deepen in color, the orgasmic platform forms in the vagina, the uterus is fully elevated, and the areolas become swollen. In males, the corona becomes fully engorged, the testicles continue both elevation and enlargement, and Cowper's glands are active.

Orgasm is marked by involuntary muscle spasms throughout the body. Blood pressure, heart rate, and respiration rate peak. Orgasm is slightly longer in duration in females. Male orgasm typically occurs in two stages, emission and expulsion. It is difficult to distinguish subjective descriptions of female and male orgasms.

Masters and Johnson suggest that there is only one kind of physiological orgasm in females, regardless of the method of stimulation. Josephine and Irving Singer counter with the contention that women may experience three different kinds of orgasms.

Some women are capable of experiencing orgasm and perhaps ejaculation when the Grafenberg spot, an area along the anterior wall of the vagina, is vigorously stimulated.

During resolution, sexual systems return to their nonexcited state, a process that may take several hours, depending on a number of factors. Erection loss occurs in two stages, the first very rapid and the second more protracted.

Sexual Response: Some Differences Between the Sexes

Many writers now emphasize the fundamental similarities in the sexual responses of men and women. However, there are certain important primary differences between the sexes.

As a group, females demonstrate a wider variability in their sexual response patterns than do men.

The presence of a refractory period in the male is one of the most significant differences in the response cycles of the two sexes. No cause for this period has been clearly demonstrated, but there is some evidence that neurological inhibitory mechanisms are activated by ejaculation.

Multiple orgasms occur more often in females than in males. Women are more likely to experience multiple orgasms while masturbating than during coitus. Recent evidence suggests that some men may also be capable of experiencing a series of orgasms in a very short time period.

Answers to Quiz:

Report A = Male

Report B = Female

Report C = Female

◅ *Thought Provokers* ◅

1. Assume that research eventually reveals that yohimbine or some other substance has genuine aphrodisiac qualities. What possible benefits might be associated with its use? What possible abuses might arise? Would you consider using an aphrodisiac? If so, under what conditions?

2. It has traditionally been assumed that men have more capacity and desire for sexual expression than do women. Do you believe this is a valid assumption? Why has this viewpoint been so pervasive across most Western cultures?

3. It has been said that women enjoy hugging and touching more than genital sex, whereas men have little interest in the "preliminaries," preferring to "get down to the real thing." Do you believe this statement reflects a genuine difference between the sexes? Are there sex differences in patterns of sexual turn-ons and turn-offs? If so, are they learned or biologically determined?

4. Women collectively appear to have a greater capacity for orgasm, to experience orgasm from a wider range of stimulation, and to have more problems experiencing orgasm than men. To what factors do you attribute this greater variation in female orgasmic response patterns?

Suggested Readings

Beach, Frank (1977). "Hormonal Control of Sex-Related Behavior." In F. Beach (Ed.), *Human Sexuality in Four Perspectives*. Baltimore: Johns Hopkins Press (also available in paperback from the same publisher, 1978). A discussion of the effects of sex hormones on the behavior of humans and other animals. Although somewhat technical, this article contains a wealth of relevant facts.

Brecher, Ruth; and Brecher, Edward (1966). *An Analysis of Human Sexual Response*. New York: New American Library. A simplified, accurate reporting of the Masters and Johnson (1966) research findings.

Kaplan, Helen Singer (1979). *Disorders of Sexual Desire*. New York: Brunner/Mazel. The book deals primarily with the treatment of sexual difficulties, particularly problems of desire. It contains excellent information about the effects of a variety of drugs on sexuality.

Masters, William; and Johnson, Virginia (1966). *Human Sexual Response*. Boston: Little, Brown. This highly technical book outlines the authors' major contributions to the understanding of the physiology of human sexual response. It is a good source for those readers who would like more detailed information about physiological responses to sexual stimulation.

Rosen, Raymond; and Beck, Gayle (1988). *Patterns of Sexual Arousal: Psychophysiological Processes and Clinical Applications*. New York: Guilford. A scholarly work that provides excellent information about the psychophysiological underpinnings of sexual behavior.

PART THREE

Sexual Behavior

Life has taught us that love does not consist in gazing at each other but looking outward together in the same direction.

Antoine de Saint-Exupéry
Wind, Sand, and Stars (1939)

CHAPTER 7

Love and the Development of Sexual Relationships

*L*ove, intimacy, and sexual relationships are important and complex aspects of people's lives. In this chapter we look at these interactions from various perspectives and examine some of the research dealing with them. We consider a number of questions: What is love? What kinds of love are there? What does research on measuring love and on partner selection tell us? How does love relate to jealousy? How does sex fit into relationships? And finally, what are some factors in developing and maintaining intimacy in a relationship?

What Is Love?

> O Love is the crooked thing,
> There is nobody wise enough
> To find out all that is in it
> For he would be thinking of love
> Till the stars had run away
> And the shadows eaten the moon.
> (from Yeats, "The Brown Penney")

Love has intrigued people throughout history. Its joys and sorrows have inspired artists and poets, novelists, filmmakers, and other students of human interaction — indeed, love is one of the most pervasive themes in the art and literature of many cultures. Each of our own lives has been influenced in significant ways by love, beginning with the love we received as infants and children. Our best and worst moments in life may be tied to a love relationship. Yet, although love is of great concern to humankind, little is conclusively known about it. Researchers have explored many aspects of love, however, and in the next section we examine some of these. We begin with a look at research related to measuring love and attraction.

Measuring Love

Love is a special kind of attitude with strong emotional and behavioral components. It is also a phenomenon that eludes easy definition or explanation. The following are two contrasting definitions:

> Love is patient and kind; love is not jealous, or conceited, or proud; love is not ill-mannered, or selfish, or irritable; love does not keep a record of wrongs: love is not happy with evil, but is happy with the truth. Love never gives up: its faith, hope and patience never fail. Love is eternal. . . . There are faith, hope and love, these three; but the greatest of these is love. (New Testament, I Corinthians 13)

> Love is a temporary insanity curable by marriage or by removal of the patient from the influences under which he incurred the disorder. This disease, like caries and many other ailments, is prevalent only among civilized races living under artificial conditions; barbarous nations breathing pure air and eating simple food enjoy immunity from its ravishes. (Bierce, 1943, p. 202)

Love has been the inspiration for some of our greatest works of literature, art, and music.

Given the problematic nature of defining love, can it be meaningfully measured? Some social scientists have attempted to do so, with interesting results. Perhaps the most ambitious attempt to measure love was undertaken some years ago by psychologist Zick Rubin (1973). Based on responses to a questionnaire administered to several hundred dating couples at the University of Michigan, Rubin developed a 13-item measurement device that he called a love scale. On this scale people are asked to indicate if a particular statement accurately reflects their feelings about another person, usually someone they are interested in romantically.

Love, as measured by Rubin's scale, has three components: attachment, caring, and intimacy. *Attachment* refers to a person's desire for the physical presence and emotional support of the other person. *Caring* refers to an individual's concern for the other's well-being. *Intimacy* is the desire for close, confidential communication with the other.

Some people may argue that it is simply not possible to measure an emotion such as love, particularly with a paper-and-pencil measurement device like the love scale. Nevertheless, Rubin did obtain some evidence supporting the validity of his scale. For example, the scale was used to investigate the popular belief that lovers spend a great deal of time looking into one another's eyes (Rubin, 1970). Couples were observed through a one-way mirror while they waited to participate in a psychological experiment. The findings revealed that weak lovers (couples who scored below average on the love scale) made significantly less eye contact than did strong lovers (those with above average scores).

According to Rubin's love scale, love consists of three components: attachment, caring, and intimacy.

Types of Love

Love takes many forms. Love exists between parent and child and other family members. Love between friends, known to the Ancient Greeks as *philia,* involves concern for the other's well-being. Lovers may experience two additional types of love: passionate love and companionate love. We open this section with an analysis of these two widely discussed types of love followed by a description of two contemporary models or theories of love.

Passionate Love

Passionate love, also known as romantic love or infatuation, is a state of extreme absorption and "desire for union" with another. It is characterized by intense feelings of tenderness, elation, anxiety, sexual desire, and ecstasy. Generalized physiological arousal, including increased heart beat, perspiration, blushing, and stomach churning, along with a feeling of great excitement, often accompanies this form of love. Items on a scale measuring passionate love include statements such as "My emotions have been on a roller coaster," "Sometimes I feel I can't control my thoughts; they are obsessively on _____," "I yearn to touch and be touched," "I get extremely depressed when things don't go right in my relationship," and "No one else could love _____ like I do" (Hatfield & Rapson, 1987). Strong sexual desire is typically a major component.

Although I had never known him well, I had admired him from a distance for some time. When circumstances threw us together for that day, I felt strongly drawn to him and realized I was really in love with him. Being physically close to him was incredibly intense, and I felt as if I could never touch him enough or ever bring our bodies as close together as I yearned to do. (Authors' files)

Passionate love appears to thrive on excitement and the risks of love. One researcher states the following:

Passionate love is like any other form of excitement. By its very nature, excitement involves a continuous interplay between elation and despair, thrills and terror. . . . Sometimes men and women become entangled in love affairs where the delight is brief, and pain, uncertainty, jealousy, misery, anxiety, and despair are abundant. Often, passionate love seems to be fueled by a sprinkling of hope and a large dollop of loneliness, mourning, jealousy, and terror. (Hatfield & Rapson, 1987, pp. 262–63).

One writer speculates that emotional and physical symptoms of passionate love are related to brain chemistry changes similar to changes caused by various drugs. The initial mood lifting and energizing "high" of excitement, giddiness, and euphoria are like an amphetamine reaction; the intense experience of timelessness, beauty, and a feeling of oneness are similar to psychedelic drug experiences; and the anxiety, despair, and pain that follow loss — or even potential loss — of a romantic love relationship is like amphetamine withdrawal (Liebowitz, 1983).

Intense passionate love typically occurs early in a relationship (Hatfield & Rapson, 1987). It sometimes seems as if the less one knows the other person, the more intense the passionate love. In passionate love, people often overlook faults and avoid conflicts. Logic and reasoned consideration are swept away by the excitement the lover evokes. One may perceive the object of one's passionate love as providing complete personal fulfillment, a situation that may have unexpected consequences:

Romance is built on a foundation of quicksilver nonlogic. It consists of attributing to the other person — blindly, hopefully, but without much basis in fact — the qualities one wishes him to have, though they may not even be desirable, in actuality. Most people who select mates on the basis of imputed qualities later find themselves disappointed, if the qualities are not present in fact, or discover they are unable to tolerate the implication of the longed-for qualities in actual life. For example, the man who is attracted by his fiancee's cuteness and sexiness may spend tormented hours after they are married worrying about the effect of these very characteristics on other men. It is a dream relationship, an unrealistic relationship with a dream person imagined in terms of one's own needs. (Lederer & Jackson, 1968, p. 439)

Another characteristic of passionate love is that it often does not last very long. Love that is based on ignorance of a person's full character is bound to change with increased familiarity. Many couples choose to make some kind of commitment to each other (become engaged, move in together, get married, and so forth) while still fired by the fuel of passionate love, only to feel disillusioned later when ecstasy gives way to routine, and the everyday annoyances and conflicts typical of most ongoing relationships surface. This is the time when the previously infatuated person may begin to have some doubts about his or her partner.

The first weeks and months of my relationship with Bob were incredible. I felt like I had found the perfect partner, someone who filled all that was missing in my life. Then, suddenly, he started to get on my nerves, and we started fighting every time we saw each other. It took a while to realize that we were finally seeing each other as real people instead of dream companions. (Authors' files)

Some couples are able to work through this period to ultimately find a solid basis upon which to build a lasting relationship of mutual love. Others discover, often to their dismay, that the only thing they ever really shared was passion. Unfortunately, many people who experience diminishing passion believe that this is the end of love, rather than a possible transition into a different kind of love:

I just don't feel the same excitement and the same passion for my lover as I used to feel. I used to feel overwhelmed waiting for her to meet me. I still look forward to seeing her, but not with breathless anticipation. I guess that I must not be in love anymore. (Authors' files)

On the other hand, some people look forward to a different kind of relationship. Erich Fromm once commented, "Romantic love is a delicious art form but not a durable one. In the end, its most persistent practitioners confess that they would like to escape from its patterned illusion into the next more realistically satisfying stage of an enduring relationship" (1965, p. 252).

Companionate Love

Companionate love is a less intense emotion than is passionate love (Walster & Walster, 1978). It is characterized by friendly affection and a deep attachment that is based on extensive familiarity with the loved one. It involves a thoughtful appreciation of one's partner. Companionate love often encompasses a tolerance for another's shortcomings along with a desire to overcome difficulties and conflicts in a relationship. This kind of love is committed to ongoing nurturing of a partnership. In short, companionate love is often enduring, while passionate love is almost always transitory. The qualities of companionate love were stressed by the respondents of a *Psychology Today* readers' survey on love and romance. Respondents said that the three most important ingredients of love were friendship, devotion, and intellectual compatibility. These rated higher than the passionate love characteristics of sexual "electricity" and longing (Rubenstein, 1983).

Sex in a companionate relationship typically reflects the feelings that familiarity provides, especially the security of knowing what pleases the other. This foundation of knowledge and sexual trust can encourage experimentation and subtle communication. Sexual pleasure in a companionate relationship strengthens the overall bond of the relationship. Although sex in companionate love is usually less exciting than in passionate love, it is often experienced as richer, more meaningful, and deeply satisfying, as the following statement reveals:

Between my first and second marriages, I really enjoyed the excitement of new sexual relationships, especially after so much sexual frustration in my first marriage. Even though I sometimes miss the excitement of those times, I would never trade it for the easy comfort, pleasure, and depth of sexual intimacy I now experience in my 17-year marriage. (Authors' files)

Companionate love has also been described as a **mutative relationship** (Goethals, 1980). This notion implies that the two individuals in a love relationship, as well as the relationship itself, continually generate change. This kind of relationship has a dynamic quality that helps satisfy the often contradictory human desires for both security and excitement. The people in mutative relationships grow and change, sometimes in response to individual challenges, sometimes in response to the relationship itself. The partners share a sense of collaboration in their joint life, exhibit a great deal of empathy for each other, and demonstrate a high degree of androgyny.

Although most relationships begin with a period of passionate love and only later evolve into companionate love, some have the opposite history. Companionate love may develop first in a situation where two people know each other for an extended period as acquaintances, friends, or coworkers. Often an initial sexual attraction is not present or is de-emphasized because of circumstances. In these relationships passionate love is based on familiarity with the other person, rather than on the excitement of the unknown. One woman describes her experience:

Jim and I had been friends for several years before I even became attracted sexually to him. We would occasionally go out to dinner together, and I would always enjoy myself. We had a lot of professional interests in common, and as I came to know him more fully, I gained a deep appreciation for his personal values and integrity. But he just wasn't my "type." But one time — I'm not even sure how it happened (I guess we were both horny) — we had sex together. It was nice and comfortable, but not terrific. We continued to be sexual and as time passed we have fallen in love, and sex between us as well as our whole relationship continues to be more and more exciting. I never expected it to happen this way. (Authors' files)

Sternberg's Triangular Theory of Love

The distinction between passionate and companionate love has been further refined by psychologist Robert Sternberg (1986; 1988), who has proposed an interesting theoretical framework for conceptualizing what people experience when they report being in love. According to Sternberg, love has three faces: passion, intimacy, and decision/commitment (see Figure 7.1a). *Passion* is the component that fuels romantic feelings, physical attraction, and desire for sexual interaction. *Intimacy* encompasses the sense of being bonded with another person, including feelings of warmth, sharing, and emotional closeness. *Decision* and *commitment* refer to the conscious decision to love another and the commitment to maintain a relationship over time in spite of difficulties that may arise. Thus passion and intimacy may be viewed as the *motivational* and *emotional* components of love, respectively, while decision and commitment are the thinking or *cognitive* aspects of love.

Sternberg maintains that while both passion and intimacy tend to develop rapidly and intensely in the early stages of a love relationship, both tend to level off as the relationship progresses, passion especially. In contrast, the conscious decision to love another often comes later in the relationship, and serious commitment typically develops gradually in the early stages but more markedly as the relationship matures.

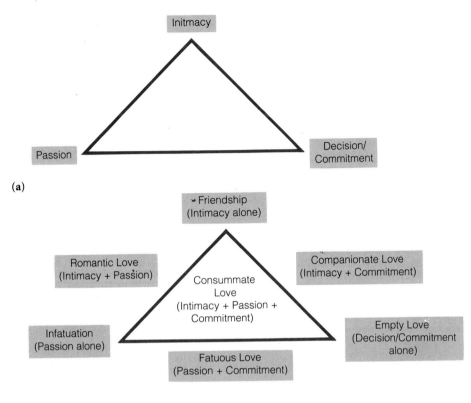

(a)

(b)

FIGURE 7.1

Sternberg's love triangle: (a) the three components of love, and (b) the various kinds of love as reflected in different combinations of the three components. Note: Nonlove is the absence of all three components.

While all three of the components just described are important dimensions of a loving relationship, they typically exist in different patterns and to varying degrees in different relationships. Moreover, they often change over time within the same relationship. Sternberg suggests that such variations yield different kinds of love, or at least differences in how people experience love. For instance, the absence of all three components yields what Sternberg calls *nonlove* (what most of us feel for casual acquaintances). When only the intimacy component is present, the experience is one of *friendship* or liking. If only passion exists, without intimacy or commitment, one experiences *infatuation*. The presence of commitment without passion and intimacy yields *empty love* (such as might be experienced in a long-term, static relationship). If intimacy and commitment exist without passion, one experiences *companionate love* (often characteristic of happy couples who have shared many years together). When passion and commitment are present but without intimacy, the experience is one of *fatuous love,* a kind of foolish involvement characteristic of whirlwind courtships or situations in which one worships and longs for another person from afar. Love characterized by passion and intimacy but no commitment is described by Sternberg as *romantic love.* Finally, when all three components are present, the experience is one of *consummate love,* the fullest kind of love that people often strive for but find difficult to achieve and/or sustain. (See Figure 7.1b for a summary of these various kinds of love.)

Empirical research on love models — including Sternberg's — is generally quite scarce. However, one study of dating couples did report that the presence of two of Sternberg's love components — intimacy and commitment — was predictive of relationship stability and longevity (Hendrick et al., 1988). However, researchers have also suggested that there may be some overlap and blurring of the boundaries between these eight patterns or types of love (Hendrick & Hendrick, 1989). We await further research to clarify the validity and utility of Sternberg's provocative theory.

Lee's Styles of Loving

Instead of attempting to describe different patterns or *types of love,* John Allan Lee (1974; 1988) has proposed a theory that describes six different *styles of loving* that characterize intimate human relationships. People with a *romantic* love style *(eros)* tend to place their emphasis on physical beauty as they search for ideal mates. A *game-playing* love style *(ludus)* is reflected in people who like to play the field and acquire many sexual "conquests" with little or no commitment. People who exhibit a *possessive* love style *(mania)* are inclined to seek obsessive love relationships, often characterized by turmoil and jealousy. *Companionate* love styles *(storage)* are expressed by people who are slow to develop affection and commitment but who tend to experience relationships that endure. An *altruistic* love style *(agape)* is characterized by selflessness and a caring, compassionate desire to give to another without expectation of reciprocity. Finally, *pragmatic* love styles *(pragma)* are most often exhibited by people who are inclined to select lovers based on rational, practical criteria (such as shared interests) that are likely to lead to mutual satisfaction.

Lee suggests that loving relationships frequently fail to thrive over time because "too often people are speaking different languages when they speak of love" (1974, p. 44). Thus a couple's efforts to create a viable foundation for a lasting involvement are often undermined by a losing struggle to integrate incompatible loving styles. In contrast, satisfaction and success in loving relationships often depend on finding a mate who "shares the same approach to loving, the same definition of love" (p. 44).

The development of a practical scale to measure Lee's six loving styles (Hendrick & Hendrick, 1986) will, we hope, generate some empirical studies of his theory. One interesting study that employed this scale did provide some support for Lee's hypothesis that relationship success is influenced by compatibility in styles of loving (Hendrick et al., 1988). However, further research is needed to clarify the value of this interesting theory.

Falling in Love: Why and with Whom?

What determines why people fall in love and with whom they fall in love? These questions are exceedingly complex. Some writers believe that people fall in love to overcome a sense of aloneness and separateness. Psychoanalyst Erich Fromm (1965) suggested that union with another person is the deepest need of humans. Another psychoanalyst and writer, Rollo May, author of *Love and Will* (1969), also believes that as people experience their own solitariness, they long for the refuge of union with another through love. Others, however, see loneliness as a by-product of our individualistic and highly mobile society rather than as an inherent part of the human condition. This view emphasizes the connectedness that people have with others through all our social relationships, language, and culture and describes love relationships as one aspect of a person's social network rather than as a cure for the "disease" of loneliness (Solomon, 1981).

What leads a person to fall in love with a particular individual? Give this some thought before reading on.

Just as we know little about why people fall in love, we have no simple explanations for why they fall in love with whom they do. There are, however, a number of factors that are often important. One of these is *proximity*. People often fall in love with individuals they see frequently — in school, at work, at church, or at social gatherings. Another factor attracting people to one another is *similarity*. Contrary to the old adage that opposites attract, people who fall in love often share common beliefs, values, attitudes, interests, and intellectual abilities (Byrne et al., 1986; Judd et al., 1983; Moreland & Zajonc, 1982; Wetzel & Insko, 1982).

Why do we feel drawn to people who are like us? For one thing, people with similar attitudes and interests are often inclined to participate in the same kinds of leisure activities. Even more important, we are more likely to communicate well with people whose ideas and opinions are similar to ours, and communication is a very important aspect of enduring relationships. It is also reassuring to be with similar people, for they confirm our view of the world, validate our own experiences, and support our opinions and beliefs (Sanders, 1982).

People tend to react positively to flattery, compliments, and other expressions of liking and affection. In the study of interpersonal attraction, this concept is reflected in the principle of **reciprocity,** which holds that when we are the recipients of expressions of liking and loving, we often tend to respond in kind (Byrne & Murnen, 1988). Furthermore, when we are provided with indications that others like us, we tend to have warm feelings about these people and to respond positively to them — a reaction that often induces them to care for us even more (Curtis & Miller, 1988).

Physical attractiveness, as you might expect, often plays a dominant role in drawing lovers together. Despite the saying that beauty is only skin-deep, it has been experimentally demonstrated that physically attractive people are more likely to be sought as friends and lovers and to be perceived as more likable, interesting, sensitive, poised, happy, sexy, competent, and socially skilled than people of average or unattractive appearance (Baron, 1986; Cash & Janda, 1984; Dion & Dion, 1987; Feingold, 1992; Hatfield & Sprechler, 1986; Solomon, 1987).

Do you think that both sexes are equally influenced by physical attractiveness in forming impressions of people they meet? Would both men and women be likely to rate good looks as a major factor in mate selection? Consider these questions before reading on.

One study indicated that male college students placed significantly more emphasis on physical appearance in selecting a partner for a sexual or long-term relationship than did females. Women placed more emphasis on interpersonal warmth and personality characteristics (Nevid, 1984). A recent cross-cultural study of sex differences in human mate preferences provided strong evidence that men worldwide place greater value than women on mates who are both young and physically attractive. In this study, conducted by psychologist David Buss (1989), subjects from 37 samples drawn from 33 countries on six continents and five islands (African, Asian, European, North and South American, and Oceanian cultures) were asked to rate the importance of a wide range of personal attributes in potential mates. These personal characteristics included such qualities as dependable character, good looks, good financial prospects, intelligence, sociability, and chastity.

In contrast to the apparent widespread male emphasis on youth and beauty, women in these cultures are more inclined to place greater value on potential mates who are somewhat older, have good financial prospects, and are dependable and industrious. This is not to say that physical attractiveness was unimportant to the women of these varied cultures. In fact, many rated physical attractiveness as important, although less so than financial responsibility and dependability.

The role of physical beauty may be most important in the early stages of a relationship: "It seems likely that the impact of physical attractiveness is greatest when we first meet someone. As a relationship progresses, physical attractiveness tends to recede in importance. And we often perceive people whom we love as being beautiful, regardless of what anyone else might think" (McNeil & Rubin, 1977, p. 581).

Love and Jealousy

Jealousy has been defined as an aversive emotional reaction evoked by a real or imagined relationship involving one's partner and a third person (Buunk & Bringle, 1987). Many people think that jealousy is a measure of devotion and, conversely, that the absence of jealous feelings implies a lack of love. However, some writers believe that jealousy is related more to injured pride, or to people's fear of losing what they want to control or possess, than to love. For example, a person who finds that a spouse enjoys someone else's company may feel inadequate and therefore jealous.

A *Psychology Today* readers' survey on jealousy defined it as the "thoughts and feelings that arise when an actual or desired relationship is threatened" (Salovey & Rodin, 1985, p. 22). This survey found that the intense emotions of jealousy are often due to our imagining and fearing the loss of the relationship. Our feelings may be further intensified by envy for the characteristics of the rival, which we may feel we lack ourselves. The survey indicated that we are likely to be jealous of those who have the qualities we desire for ourselves. In general, women were more envious of attractiveness and popularity, and men were more envious of wealth and fame. People with three specific traits were particularly prone to jealousy: having a low opinion of themselves; seeing a large discrepancy between how they are and how they would like to be; and placing a high value on traits such as wealth, fame, popularity, and physical attractiveness.

Not everyone responds to jealousy in the same way, and according to one study (Clanton & Smith, 1977), there appear to be some differences in how women and men react. In general, women are more likely to acknowledge jealous feelings and men more likely to deny them. A jealous woman more often focuses on the emotional involvement of her partner with another person, whereas a jealous man tends to be concerned with the sexual relationship between his lover and another. Women also often blame themselves, while men typically blame the third party or the woman for the jealousy. The *Psychology Today* study found few differences in men's and women's jealous feelings and behaviors, except that women in the study manifested certain kinds of jealous behavior more often than did men, such as secretly searching through a lover's belongings and extensively questioning a lover about a past romance (Salovey & Rodin, 1985). For both men and women, the feelings associated with jealousy are negative, including feeling less attractive (Bush et al., 1988).

Jealousy is an uncomfortable feeling that can stifle development and pleasure in a relationship. Jealousy has a paradoxical effect: it is a reaction aimed at maintaining one's valued relationship and self-image, yet both are likely to be damaged by the expression of jealous feelings (Buunk & Bringle, 1985). Respondents to a survey (Salovey & Rodin, 1988) described three strategies to attempt to cope with jealousy:

- "Self-reliance" involved containing any expression of jealousy.
- "Positive comparison and self-bolstering" included thinking about one's good qualities and engaging in enjoyable activities for oneself.
- "Selective ignoring" involved deciding that the desired person is not particularly important.

Walster and Walster (1978) offer the following suggestions to people who want to decrease feelings of jealousy. First, find out exactly what it is that makes you jealous. Examine your beliefs, thoughts, and feelings closely. Is it a matter of injured pride? Do you believe that the other person belongs to you like one of your possessions? Does the situation provoking jealousy lead to fears of losing this relationship? Second, it is important to put jealous feelings in perspective. One way is to ask yourself, "What is it that I want to be different? What do I really want? Why?" After understanding more fully what it is that really bothers you and leads to feelings of jealousy, the third step is for you and your partner to negotiate agreements or conditions about outside involvements. One student who did this successfully reports:

My girlfriend and I go to a lot of parties together and have a good time — except for one thing. I find myself feeling jealous when I look across the room and see her talking and laughing with another guy. And then when I'm around her, I start putting her down in subtle ways, especially to the guy she's been talking to. She pretty much ignores me when I do that, but I think it could harm our relationship. So I really gave it some thought and realized that I actually don't mind her having fun with other people; in fact, it's one of the things I like about her. What I really wanted was for her to pay a little more attention to me at parties and do things like hold my arm or give me a little kiss — little things that told others we were a couple. When I asked her to do those gestures, she was real agreeable, and parties have been a lot more fun for us since. (Authors' files)

Love and Sex

Just what is the connection between love and sex? It is certainly true that some couples, unmarried and married, engage in sexual relations without being in love with one another. Conversely, love may exist independently of any sexual attraction or expression. Nevertheless, the feelings of being in love with and sexually attracted to another person are frequently intertwined. The complex interplay between love and sex gives rise to many familiar questions. For example, does sexual intimacy typically deepen a love relationship? Are people more likely to feel that they are in love with someone *after* they have had sex? Is sex without love appropriate? We attempt to shed some light on these and other related questions in this section.

Many studies reveal a difference in men and women regarding the connection between love and sex (Leigh, 1989; Quadagno & Sprague, 1991). In response to questionnaires administered in our sexuality classes, women have consistently linked love with sex to a greater extent than have men. In a recent survey of several hundred students, roughly 36% of the women indicated that love is a necessary component of sexual relationships. In contrast, only 12% of the men indicated the same feelings. Several studies reported that men found it much easier than women to have sexual intercourse for pleasure and physical release without an emotional commitment (Carroll et al., 1985; Clark & Hatfield, 1989; Randolf & Winstead, 1988), and another study found that most women enjoy sexual intercourse only when there is a greater level of commitment within the relationship (McCabe, 1987). When other college students were asked what the most important factors were in their decision to engage in intercourse, women reported the quality and intimacy of the relationship as more important than did men (Christopher & Cate, 1984).

Other studies indicate that over the last two decades both sexes are placing increasingly greater emphasis on love and affection in sexual relationships. One study found that the first sexual intercourse for 81% of men and 91% of women occurred in a relationship in which there was affection (Kallen & Stephenson, 1982). Another found that most young men and women desire and experience sexual intercourse within a caring relationship (McCabe, 1987). A *Psychology Today* readers' survey also supported the findings that love has become more important to both men and women. In 1969, 17% of men and 29% of women believed that sex without love was either unenjoyable or unacceptable. In 1983, 29% of men and 44% of women felt this way (Rubenstein, 1983). Additionally, a *Parade* magazine nationwide survey of 1100 randomly selected men and women found that 59% of men and 85% of women reported that they found it difficult to have sex without love (Ubell, 1984). (Research note: the *Parade* survey respondents were a cross section of the U.S. population and had been contacted by the surveyors, whereas the *Psychology Today* survey respondents were mainly young, well-educated people with relatively high household incomes who had responded to the survey on their own initiative by mailing in the questionnaire. Therefore, the *Parade* study may be more representative of the general population and the *Psychology Today* survey of the college-educated population.) In addition, some individuals are waiting for more commitment in a relationship before being sexual due to concern about contracting AIDS and other health-threatening sexually transmitted diseases.

Conflict about whether to express oneself sexually, with or without love, can lead to difficulties. It is reasonable to suspect that many women (and, to a lesser extent, men) have attempted to justify their sexual behavior by deciding they are in love. It is likely that some couples even enter into premature commitments such as going steady, becoming engaged, or getting married, to convince themselves of the depth of their love and thus the legitimacy of their sexual involvement.

While many people enjoy sex without love, the activity frequently arouses strong feelings. For some, the risks of sexually transmitted diseases, especially AIDS, are not worth such involvements. Beyond this issue, others wonder, "Is it really all right for two people who are not in love to have sex?" There is no absolute answer to this question. Each of us has our own personal value system that influences the decisions we make for ourselves. Therefore, instead of attempting to answer the question about the appropriateness of sex without love, we present three differing views.

Albert Ellis, in his book *Sex Without Guilt* (1966), suggested that a sexual relationship between individuals who are not in love ought to be both socially and personally acceptable. After providing psychotherapy to individuals and couples for many years, Ellis concluded that sex without love can be quite satisfying, although sex with love is probably more so. In his book Ellis argued that many people, particularly young people, sometimes want sexual intimacy with someone with whom they are not in love. In addition, he claimed that many individuals have little or no capacity for love, and these people should not be denied the satisfaction of sexual experiences. Ellis further suggested that imposing a necessary link between sex and love may result in people feeling needlessly guilty about non-loving sexual relations.

Rollo May expressed a different view about sex without love. He observed that there have been significant changes in attitudes since earlier times in our history: "The Victorian person sought to have love without falling into sex; the modern person seeks to have sex without falling into love" (1969, p. 46). May believes that the contemporary preoccupation with technique and performance and the de-emphasis of intimacy has resulted in a lack of sexual enjoyment and passion for many people.

William Masters and Virginia Johnson describe what they believe to be the advantages of sex within a love relationship:

Sex in a warm, emotionally committed relationship may change in character and sexual response may become diffused after a while. It may not always reach the peaks of excitement that are sometimes experienced by a man and woman in their early, experimental encounters. But other dimensions of sexual pleasure may be discovered — the familiarity that is comforting, the safety that allows complete vulnerability, and the deepening sense of emotional intimacy, among other pleasures. (1975, pp. 99 – 100)

Sex and Relationships on Your Terms

The subject of sex with or without love raises the issue of decision making regarding sexual relationships. Sexual expression can have many different meanings. It can be a validation of deep intimacy within a relationship. On the other hand, people can choose to be sexual as a part of a friendship or as a way of getting to know someone. For some, reproduction may be the primary purpose. For others, reduction of sexual tension may be the motivation. Sex can be used as a way of experiencing new feelings, excitement, and risk. It can even be a kind of recreational pastime. People can use sex to try to alleviate feelings of insecurity — to prove their "manhood" or "womanhood" or to please someone or persuade that person to care. People can also use sex to experience the power to attract others or to avenge earlier rejections by enticing partners and then turning them down.

Each person has the task of deciding how she or he wants to express sexuality. This important process is complicated by the fact that many of the old rules that have governed sexual relationships are changing, as reflected in these comments of a recently divorced woman:

When I was dating 25 years ago in college, a kiss at the door on a first date was considered to mean I really liked the guy. And I was determined to be a virgin until I got married. These guidelines were held by most of my friends, and I felt a lot of security in them. Now I don't know how to behave. There really don't seem to be any standard rules. It's exciting and frightening to know I can make decisions because I want to. It is also confusing at times, and I sometimes wish the standards I used to know were still common. (Authors' files)

Some people base their decisions on sexuality on clear, preexisting rules expressed by their family, church, or peer group. Many others do not have such specific guidelines or disagree with the values they have been taught. These people need to understand their own personal values and develop their own guidelines. The following section discusses some options for establishing guidelines for decisions about sexual expression.

Know What You Want

The first step in integrating sex into your life in a meaningful way is to consider what you value in life and relationships before initiating sexual involvement with another. This is a variation on the "know thyself" theme. Consider the following:

Often when I meet a man for the first time, I end up being swept off my feet and into bed. At the time it seems like the thing to do, but afterwards I'm often left confused and a bit empty inside. It's not that I don't like sex. I'm just not sure about what role it should play in my life. (Authors' files)

This woman might be able to reduce the confusion and discomfort she experiences by evaluating her expectations and needs in the area of sexual relationships. An important question for each of us to ask ourselves is, "What role do I want relationships and sex to occupy in my life at this time?" The answer to this question often changes over time as a person faces new life situations.

As a part of this self-inventory, it might be helpful to consider the following questions:

- How comfortable am I with some of the contemporary approaches to sex and relationships?
- Which of the more traditional norms do I value?
- What are my values as they pertain to sexual relationships, and where do they come from (family, church, friends, media)?
- What will I do to protect myself and a partner from sexually transmitted diseases or unwanted pregnancy?

You can further clarify your values in relation to a specific decision about sexual activity by asking another question: "Will a decision to engage in a sexual relationship—with this person and at this time—enhance my positive feelings about myself and the other person?" The answer to this question can help you act in a way that is consistent with your value system. It can also help prevent exploitative sexual encounters in which people do not consider each other's feelings.

What if the answer to the previous question is no? Then it may be appropriate to think about what kind of relationship, if any, might enhance positive feelings. Perhaps a sexual relationship is not right, but a nonsexual friendship would be. Or perhaps you do not feel ready for a sexual relationship yet, but want to leave open that possibility. At this point communication and negotiation are important.

One of the risks of understanding and acting on your own feelings, desires, and values is that someone else may not see things the same way. Unfortunately, many people take such differences to mean that either they are wrong or the other person is wrong. However, more often than not, differences simply indicate that two people do not want the same thing at the same time. Occasionally, a relationship cannot be established without compromising one person's situation or values. When this occurs, one option is to end the relationship. Each person can then seek someone who has more similar perspectives. On other occasions clarification, negotiation, and compromise may establish a common foundation for a relationship. However, direct communication about where one stands can be difficult. One study of college students found that only 21% of those interviewed said that they asked directly about their partners' feelings for them. Others did not let themselves be so vulnerable; they used a variety of indirect means to try to find out how their partners felt about the relationship. Thirteen percent asked a third party's opinion. Other indirect tactics students used included "endurance tests" such as asking a partner to give up a ski weekend, trying to make the partner jealous, using humor or hints about the relationship's future, or making self-deprecating comments in the hope that the person would disagree (Baxter & Wilmot, 1984). The following sections illustrate some options for dealing with several specific relationship situations. Chapter 8 provides additional information on communication in sexual relationships.

Friendships Without Sex

Some people find it very difficult to communicate a desire for friendship without sex, especially when it appears that the other person wants a sexual relationship. Often they are concerned that the other person will feel bad or decide to end the relationship. However, most people would probably prefer to be told the truth directly rather than have to decipher the meaning of vague, confusing responses. The following comment is fairly typical of our students:

I hate it when I find myself in a relationship, and all I get is the runaround. I eventually get the picture when someone else doesn't reciprocate my feelings, but what a waste of time and energy. Why can't they just come out and say what they are feeling? At least I would know where I stand and could act accordingly. (Authors' files)

This person's feeling of frustration is understandable. However, one can attempt to resolve some of the uncertainty by asking the other person about his or her feelings. The following illustrates how one student did this:

Jake and I had gone out several times, and initially he acted like he was attracted to me. But then he began to treat me more like a sister. He continued to ask me out but made no sexual gestures. I finally told him I was confused about how he felt about me. He seemed very concerned about my feelings as he told me that he wanted a friendship with me instead of a romantic relationship. He wasn't sure why, but he had come to realize that's how he felt. I felt disappointed, and it was a little tough on my ego to not be desired sexually, but I decided that a friendship with him would be nice for me. And several years later, we are still friends. (Authors' files)

Saying "Not Yet" to a Sexual Relationship

One of the benefits of less rigid rules about "proper" sexual behavior is that they can make it easier for people to set their own pace in sexual relationships. It is common for a person to feel sexual attraction and to want a sexual relationship with someone — but not yet. The ability to delay sexual involvement until both people feel ready can do much to enhance the initial experience. Waiting until familiarity and trust are established and making sure that personal values are consistent with the relationship can enhance positive feelings about oneself. Also, as

Nonsexual friendships can offer companionship and enjoyment.

discussed in Chapter 19, the possibility of contracting AIDS or other serious sexually transmitted diseases may be reduced by taking some time to assess the risk status of a prospective partner before beginning sexual relations.

When sexual attraction exists within a relationship, sex is not necessarily an "either/or" situation. There are progressive stages of intimacy, from holding hands to genital contact, and some people move slowly through these stages to savor and grow comfortable with the increasingly intimate contact. Gratification may be greater with a gradual progression toward intimacy than with rushed sexual contact, as the author of the following discovered:

I felt sexually attracted to Mike the first time I met him, but somehow, almost by mutual instinct, we moved very slowly sexually. We both agreed that was how we wanted it for this relationship. We spent several extremely enjoyable months kissing, touching, holding each other, and even sleeping together before we had intercourse. The entire experience has really changed how I see "fast-food sex" and has given new light to the expression "Haste makes waste." (Authors' files)

Social expectations of "instant sex" can present a challenge to those who want to move gradually into a sexual relationship. There are several things you can do to let another person know that you are not yet ready for sex or that you want the relationship to progress slowly. It is often helpful to begin by indicating that you find the person attractive. You can acknowledge your desire for greater sexual intimacy, yet be definite about not being ready. Finally, you can let a partner know what kind of physical contact you want at a given point in the relationship; this can help avoid misunderstandings and reassure the other person.

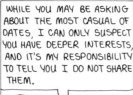

Caring Endings

Over the years our sexuality classes have included many lively discussions of the question, How do you prefer to be informed when someone does not wish to continue a relationship with you? Although students have many different opinions and experiences, the large majority want to be told in a clear, unmistakable manner that their desire for a relationship is not reciprocated. A simple statement such as "I appreciate your interest in me, but I'm not attracted to you enough to want to develop a relationship with you" is the kind of ending that most of our students have indicated they would prefer. Most students also report that it would be more difficult to make than to hear such a direct statement; there is rarely an easy way to end a relationship when one person is interested in maintaining it. This situation requires communication that is both effective and compassionate.

Managing Rejection

Fear of rejection can often inhibit people from initiating a relationship or expressing their desires within one. One man expresses his concern as follows:

I find it extremely stressful to ask a woman out for the first time. I just can't deal with the prospect of being turned down. I know it's irrational, but when someone says no, I feel lousy. (Authors' files)

To many people, a "no" affects their feelings of self-worth. A person who is rejected may feel unattractive, boring, unsexy, unintelligent, or inherently unlovable. All of us experience rejection at some time, however, because our traits cannot match every person's preferences. The very characteristics that one person finds undesirable may well appeal to another, and the right to choose not to become involved with someone is certainly a right that most people want.

Although rejection can still be a painful experience, there are some strategies for dealing with being turned down. It is important to remember that each of us has worth, regardless of whether all people approve of us. Also, defending yourself to someone who has said no is not likely to be helpful because being turned down is usually not a criticism but simply an expression of individual preferences. Finally, even though rejection may make us want to give up on continued attempts to form close relationships, we can avoid rejection completely only if we isolate ourselves from most kinds of social interaction. As one woman states:

I don't like being turned down, but I like being alone even less. Life is full of risks, and the dating game has its share. It might be safer to retreat into a social vacuum and wait for something to happen. But I like making my own choices instead of hoping the right man will ask me. If I'm turned down, someone else always comes along. It's a happy hunting ground out there, filled with all kinds of prospects, some of whom will say yes. (Authors' files)

The Development of Intimacy

A question that students and others often ask is how to acquire and maintain intimacy, satisfaction, and sexual enjoyment in a relationship. There are many opinions on this subject and no conclusive answer. This may have to do with the uniqueness of each person: what is satisfying to one person may be dissatisfying to another. Each person must, in effect, reinvent the wheel and discover for himself or herself how to develop and maintain satisfactory relationships. This section discusses some ways of thinking about developing and maintaining intimacy.

Self-Love

Satisfying intimacy within a relationship begins with self-love. How can this be? As we use the term, *self-love* does not mean conceit, selfishness, or lack of consideration of others; in fact, these qualities are usually indications of personal insecurities. By self-love we mean the kind of feeling that Leo Buscaglia (1972) described as a genuine interest, concern, and respect for ourselves — the ability to look in the mirror and appreciate the person we see and feel excited about that person's potential.

A scholar of human development, Erik Erikson (1965) believes that positive self-feelings are a prerequisite to a satisfying relationship and develop from the foundation of consistent, loving care during childhood. As people feel secure in their own worth and identity, they are able to establish intimacy with others, both in friendship and eventually in a love-based, mutually satisfying sexual relationship.

The Phases of a Relationship

One way of understanding the development of a relationship is to examine different aspects or phases of its growth; this may also give us some guidelines for maintaining a good relationship. As we discuss the various phases, it is important to remember that they are simply a convenient scheme; in reality, a relationship is fluid, dynamic, and frequently unpredictable. We mean to give our readers a framework for thinking about a relationship rather than a prescription for intimacy. Also, this discussion and the following section consider sex as only one part of the total context of a relationship.

Inclusion. Inclusion is when one person extends some kind of invitation to relate, whether by eye contact, a smile, or a friendly "Hello." It is the first step that one person takes in meeting another. Many "how-to-pick-up-dates" books specialize in tips for initial inclusion. Often, the signs can be quite subtle:

When people feel secure in their own worth and identity, they are able to establish intimacy with others.

When I go out dancing alone and want to decide who to ask to dance, I look around the room. When I see a man who returns my glance (especially if he smiles or nods), I'll go over and ask him to dance if he isn't already on his way to ask me. (Authors' files)

Inclusion continues throughout a relationship, and the nature of inclusion behaviors provides the backbone of a positive relationship. A good morning kiss, a smile and hug after a day apart, a sincere "Tell me about your day," a compliment, or an expression of appreciation are some of the kinds of inclusions that can nourish an ongoing relationship.

Response. How one responds to a gesture of inclusion may determine whether a relationship even begins. For example, quickly glancing away from someone's initial eye contact will likely deter any further initiation. However, if one responds in kind and goes a step further with a smile and a greeting, the other person will be more likely to initiate further contact. Positive inclusion and responses are dependent on each other for the interaction to progress.

As a relationship continues, certain kinds of responses typically enhance the relationship's growth. These include listening to the other person and understanding her or his point of view, following through with agreements or plans, or being enthusiastic about seeing the other person. Positive and consistent inclusions and responses are the foundation for the next important phases — care, trust, affection, and playfulness. These phases often develop simultaneously and build on each other.

Care. Care implies a genuine concern for another's welfare. Care motivates us to consider another person's desires and interests; it creates a desire to please and contribute to another's happiness.

Trust. Trust is a feeling essential to both the ongoing development of a relationship and its satisfactory continuance. It contributes to the belief that each partner will act consistently, in ways that promote the relationship's growth and stability and that affirm each partner. It means that the partners trust each other and themselves to be positive and constructive in their inclusions and responses.

I trust my partner to:
Talk to me when she's unhappy about something I've done,
Be concerned about my satisfaction when we make love,
Feel attracted to me when I am naked,
Be honorable and fair,
Take my feelings into consideration,
Use birth control. (Authors' files)

Affection. Affection is characterized by feelings of warmth and attachment. It evokes a desire to be physically close to another and is often expressed by touches, holding hands, sitting close, hugs, and caresses. Affection can be signaled nonverbally by smiles, winks, and tender looks and verbally by expressions of appreciation, liking, or loving. The following comment exemplifies a high level of affection within a friendship:

My best friend and I never get together without a hug for a greeting and a good-bye. It's also typical for us to get together at one of our houses for tea, long talks, and foot rubs. (Authors' files)

Playfulness. This is the phase in the development of an intimate relationship in which each person exhibits delight and pleasure in the other. Exhilaration, abandon, and expansive laughter often accompany playfulness, whether it is a parent playing peek-a-boo with a child or lovers having a pillow fight.

Genitality. The final phase extends the relationship to include genital contact. There may have been varying degrees of sexual feeling and expression in previous phases, but in the genitality phase a person has decided to express feelings through genital sex.

When people quickly move to genital contact before going through the other six phases, they may actually experience a reduction in feelings of emotional closeness. The following account illustrates this:

I had known Chris for some time and thought I was ready to be sexual with him. So, after an evening out together, I asked him if I could stay at his place, and he said yes. I felt really aroused as we got in bed. I really enjoyed touching the shapes and textures of his previously unknown-to-me body. As we started to touch each other's genitals, though, I felt uncomfortable. It seemed that if we were going to proceed in the direction we were headed, we would be going beyond the level of emotional intimacy I felt. It seemed that I would have to shut out the closeness I felt in order to go further. I had to choose between intimacy and genital contact. Our closeness was more important to me, and I told him that I wanted to know each other more before going further sexually. (Authors' files)

As you may have noted, the first six phases could characterize a variety of relationships, including a good friendship, a parent – child or sibling relationship, or a close mentor – student relationship. Close nonsexual friendships with members of our own and the other sex can be a very important part of our personal lives. One study found that characteristics of close friendships include enjoying one another's company; mutual trust that each will act in the other's best interest; respecting, assisting, supporting, and understanding one another; confiding experiences and feelings to each other; and being spontaneous in the relationship. This study also found that lover and spouse relationships had these general friendship qualities plus higher levels of passion, exclusiveness, self-sacrifice, and enjoyment of being together. They also had less acceptance than nonsexual friendships did and more criticism, conflict, ambivalence, and discussions about the relationship and its problems (Davis, 1985). With the foundation of the other phases, genital contact can be the culmination of deep intimacy and emotional closeness. Companionate love is an expression of all of these phases. Fromm (1965) stated that the use of the body for the purpose of seeking and expressing satisfaction with one another is what sex truly is and what gives it its most deeply felt meaning. He said further that sex is important in two ways: first, through its role in initial attraction, and second, in its cementing of a relationship through the fulfillment and pleasure it offers.

Maintaining Relationship Satisfaction

Human relationships present many challenges. To begin, there is the challenge of building a positive relationship with oneself, as described in the section on self-love. Then, there is the additional task of establishing satisfying and enjoyable relationships with family, peers, teachers, coworkers, employers, and other people within a person's social network. We also have the challenge of developing special, intimate relationships with friends and, when we want them, sexual relationships. Finally, many people confront the challenge of maintaining satisfaction and love within an ongoing, committed relationship. Commitment in a relationship is often demonstrated by the decision to marry. However, many couples have long-term committed relationships outside of marriage. This section presents some of the factors that may contribute to ongoing satisfaction in sexual relationships. We also discuss the value of sexual variety within the relationship.

An older couple's intimacy and affection develops from years of shared experiences.

There are many ingredients in a lasting love relationship. They include self-acceptance and appreciation of one another, commitment, good communication, realistic expectations, shared interests, and the ability to face conflict effectively. These characteristics are not static; they evolve and change and influence one another over time. Often they need to be deliberately cultivated. In contemporary society, the efforts of the partners are probably more important to relationship stability than in the past when marriage as an institution was sustained more strongly by culture, religion, law, and the extended family (Levinson, 1978).

A study of 300 happily married couples revealed that the most frequently named reason for an enduring and happy marriage was seeing one's partner as one's best friend. Qualities that they especially liked in one another were caring, giving, integrity, and a sense of humor. These couples were aware of flaws in their mates, but they believed that the likable qualities were more important than the deficiencies. Many said that their mates had become more interesting to them over time. They preferred shared rather than separate activities, which appeared to reflect the richness in the relationship. Another key was their belief in marriage as a long-term commitment and a sacred institution. Most of the couples were generally satisfied with their sex lives, and for some the sexual passion had become more intense over time. As one wife said, "The passion hasn't died. In fact, it has gotten more intense. The only thing that has died is the element of doubt or uncertainty that one experiences while dating or in the beginning of a marriage." However, fewer than 10% thought that good sexual relations kept their marriage together (Lauer & Lauer, 1985). The box "What Keeps a Marriage Going?" summarizes the major reasons these married people believed that their marriages were successful.

Maintaining a healthy frequency of positive interactions is crucial to the continued satisfaction of committed couples. The saying "It's the little things that count" is especially meaningful here. When one partner says to the other, "You

OUR SEXUALITY

What Keeps a Marriage Going?

Husbands and wives listed the same reasons for the success of their marriage. These were the reasons, in descending order of the frequency with which they were mentioned:

1. My spouse is my best friend.
2. I like my spouse as a person.
3. Marriage is a long-term commitment.
4. Marriage is sacred.
5. We agree on aims and goals.
6. My spouse has grown more interesting.
7. I want the relationship to succeed.

do not love me anymore," that often means, "You are not doing as many of the behaviors you used to do that I interpret as meaning you love me." The behaviors are often so small that one may not really notice them. However, when couples do fewer things that contribute to a partner's feeling of being loved, or stop doing them, the deficit is often experienced as a lack of love. On the other hand, continuing the affectionate and considerate interactions helps maintain a feeling of love. One woman writes:

The kinds of things that enhance my feeling of my partner loving me may seem quite inconsequential, but to me they aren't. When he gets up to greet me when I come home, when he takes my arm crossing the street, when he asks, "Can I help you with that," when he tells me I look great, when he holds me in the middle of the night, when he thanks me for doing a routine chore—I feel loved by him. Those little things—all added up—make a tremendous difference to me. (Authors' files)

Couples may also find that talking with one another to identify especially enjoyable actions and to explore new ideas can be useful. The golden rule ("Do unto others as you would have them do unto you") is not always applicable in relationships because people's preferences are often quite different.

Enjoyment with and appreciation of one another in nonsexual areas typically enhances sexual interest and interactions. Often couples report a lack of desire for sexual intimacy when they experience a general lack of intimacy within the relationship. People make comments like the following:

I just don't feel like having sex with him when he's been at work all day, then comes home and watches TV all night. (Authors' files)

Individual and Relationship Growth

Growth and change are important in maintaining vitality in a relationship. Each person's growth can provide an opportunity for the other partner to develop in order to appreciate and respond positively to the changes of the beloved. Partners can draw on emotional, artistic, intellectual, spiritual, and physical dimensions for growth, to enrich each other's mutual enjoyment. As a husband married for 30 years said, "I have watched her grow and have shared with her both the pain and the exhilaration of her journey. I find her more fascinating now than when we were first married" (Lauer & Lauer, 1985, p. 24).

At times this dynamic of growth and change occurs without deliberate effort; at other times it requires direct attention. Couples who maintain satisfactory levels of growth typically do not let love diminish by choosing to withdraw their energy from the relationship at the first sign of strain or boredom. Rather, they confront the difficulties and attempt to ameliorate them (Csikszentmihalyi, 1980). For example:

My husband and I found it increasingly difficult to have time together because of our busy schedules. And then when we were together, we felt a little like strangers. So we decided to structure some time together learning something new. The dancing lessons we took even rekindled some romantic feelings. (Authors' files)

Each person brings her or his strengths and weaknesses into relationships, and a relationship itself has its own combination of strengths and weaknesses. A couple is rarely fully prepared for the myriad issues that arise from this combination. It is often helpful to view problems and dissatisfactions as challenges to overcome or differences to accept, rather than as sure signs that the relationship is about to fail. Couples need to be prepared to negotiate and renegotiate what they want out of life and out of their relationship, knowing that the arrangement they work out one day may become untenable the next. At the same time, partners in a committed relationship often recognize that the love they hold for each other means accepting one another as unique human beings. These attitudes give a couple options for shaping a relationship uniquely suited to their individual and collective wants and needs (Walster & Walster, 1978).

Being in a committed relationship can itself be a source of growth. Such a relationship can make urgent demands on individuals so that they mature in directions and with a rapidity that would not otherwise occur. The "beneficial trauma" of confronting oneself intensely and learning to accept another deeply, as sometimes occurs within an intimate relationship, can facilitate individual growth. As Erich Fromm wrote, "Married lovers grow within love; they develop into better human beings" (1965, p. 288).

Sexual Variety: An Important Ingredient

There is a special little restaurant with great steaks and a cozy, intimate atmosphere that I love to visit once every few months. Good companionship, a favorite bottle of wine, a tasty cut of rare meat, and I am living. Let a friend invite me back the next day, and it is still good, but not quite so stimulating. Given an invitation for a third trip in as many days, and I might just as soon stop off for a McDonald's quarter-pounder. (Authors' files)

Many people have a strong desire to seek variety in life's experiences. They may acquire an assortment of friends, each providing a unique enrichment to their lives. Likewise, they read different kinds of books, pursue a variety of recreational activities, eat a variety of foods, and take a mixture of classes. Yet many of these same people settle for routine in their sex lives.

Unfortunately, many people enter into a committed relationship thinking that intense sexual excitement will always be a natural occurrence between two people in love. But the initial excitement must eventually be replaced by realistic and committed efforts to maintain the vitality and rewards of a working relationship. Once a person is committed to a primary partner and the variety offered by a succession of relationships is no longer available, it may be necessary to seek variety in other ways.

Not every couple feels the need for sexual variety. Many people may feel quite comfortable with established routines and have no desire to change them, as expressed in the following:

> We settled down into a variation of our own particular pattern, a seldom-deviated-from routine, a practice which *Cosmopolitan* warned was boring, stagnating, and ruinous to a marriage. . . . It has taken months, maybe years of persistent trial and error with shyly veiled hints and endless, polite "That was fine, really it was" from both of us before we each discovered what the other enjoyed, responded to, and wanted. Charlie, only slightly less shy than me, knew where I wanted to go and how to get me there, and in turn, over a period of time, I'd been able to reach through his natural reserve to the passionate man underneath. Now we had an intimate knowledge of one another and our own pace, our own rhythm, our own consistent satisfaction, and to hell with the marriage manuals. In bed, at least, we trusted one another. And shared. (Rebeta-Burditt, 1978, p. 288)

However, if you prefer to develop more variety in your sexual relationship, the following paragraphs may be helpful.

Can you think of any strategies or approaches to sexual intimacy that could add variety and zest to a couple's lovemaking in a long-term love relationship? Give this some thought before reading on.

Communication is critical. Talk to your partner about your needs and feelings. Share with him or her your desire to try something different. Perhaps some of the guidelines in Chapter 8 will facilitate making requests and exchanging information. You may want to try sharing fantasies and then acting them out.

Avoid the routine of time and place. Make love in places other than the bed (on the laundry room floor, in the shower, alongside a mountain trail) and at various times ("bird song in the morning," a "nooner," or in the middle of the night when you wake up feeling sexual).

Some of the most exciting sexual experiences may be those that take place on the spur of the moment with little or no planning. It is easy to see how these encounters might occur frequently during courtship. It is also true that they may become distant memories after couples settle into the demanding daily schedules of living together. Nevertheless, you may find that striving to maintain this spontaneity will stand you in good stead as your relationship is nurtured over the months or years of your time together.

On the other hand, planning for intimate time — sexual and nonsexual — can also help maintain closeness. Make "dates" with one another and consciously do romantic gestures that came naturally early in the relationship. Make a commitment to place your energy and time toward your sexual relationship.

Do not let questions of what is normal get in the way of an enriched and varied erotic life. Too often people refrain from experiencing something new because they feel different activities are "abnormal." In reality only you can judge what is normal for you. There is a consensus among contemporary writers in the field of human sexuality that any sexual activity is normal, as long as it gives pleasure and does not cause emotional or physical discomfort or harm to either partner. Emotional comfort is an important variable because "discomfort and conflict rather than intimacy and satisfaction can result if behaviors are tried which are too divergent from personal values and attitudes" (Barbach, 1982, p. 282).

Related to concerns about what is normal are concerns about frequency. Forget the magazine article that said that couples in your age category are having sex 2.7 times per week. The only right standard for you is to have sex as often as you and your partner desire.

Finally, partners sometimes find that books dealing with sexual techniques may benefit their erotic lives. We recommend that you read them together rather than separately. Discussing a particular written suggestion can often open up new possibilities of sexual sharing. Such books sometimes provide the necessary information and support for trying something new.

We do not mean to imply that all people must have active, varied sex lives to be truly happy; this is not the case. Some, as we have already mentioned, may find comfort and contentment in repeating familiar patterns of sexual interaction. Others may consider sex relatively unimportant compared with other aspects of their lives and may choose not to exert special efforts in pursuing its pleasures. However, if your sexuality is an important source of pleasure in your life, perhaps these suggestions and others in this text will be valuable to you.

Summary

What Is Love?

Zick Rubin's love scale is a 13-item subjective rating scale that measures what he defines as the three components of love: attachment, caring, and intimacy. Studies of eye contact and physical proximity give some support to the validity of the scale.

Types of Love

Passionate love is characterized by intense, vibrant feelings that tend to be relatively short-lived.

Companionate love is characterized by deep affection and attachment.

Sternberg's triangular theory maintains that love has three dimensions: passion and intimacy, which are the motivational and emotional components, respectively, and decision/commitment, the cognitive component. Variations in the combinations in which these three components exist yield eight different kinds of love.

Lee has proposed a theory that describes six different styles of loving: romantic, game-playing, possessive, companionate, altruistic, and pragmatic.

Falling in Love: Why and with Whom?

Falling in love has been explained as resulting from the need to overcome a sense of aloneness, from the desire to justify sexual involvement, or as a consequence of sexual attraction.

Factors known to contribute strongly to interpersonal attraction and falling in love with another include proximity, similarity, reciprocity, and physical attractiveness. We often develop loving relationships with people whom we see frequently, who share similar beliefs, who seem to like us, and whom we perceive as physically attractive.

Love and Jealousy

Some people consider jealousy a sign of love, but it may actually reflect fear of losing possession or control of another. Some research indicates that men and women react differently to jealousy.

Love and Sex

There are various perspectives on the connections between love and sex. Most students in our surveys report that love enriches sexual relations but is not necessary for enjoyment of sex.

Women consistently link love with sexual behavior more than do men, but research indicates men and women are becoming more similar on this issue.

Sex and Relationships on Your Terms

Deciding one's own values in relation to sexual experiences is especially important today, in a time of changing expectations. Asking yourself, "Will a decision to engage in a sexual relationship — with this person at this time — enhance my positive feelings about myself and the other person?" can help you act in a way that is consistent with your value system.

There are many types of intimate relationships, including friendships without sex and love relationships in which the sexual component progresses gradually.

You can develop strategies for minimizing the pain of rejection, particularly if you remember that rejection usually occurs because your traits do not match another's subjective preferences, not because you are unworthy.

The Development of Intimacy

Self-love, meaning positive and accepting feelings toward oneself, is an important foundation for intimacy with others.

The phases of an intimate relationship are inclusion, response, care, trust, affection, playfulness, and genitality. Care, trust, affection, and playfulness usually develop concurrently and reinforce one another.

Maintaining Relationship Satisfaction

Individual and relationship growth can provide challenges and stimulation to the relationship, helping maintain its vitality.

Sexual variety is often an important ingredient of enjoyable sex in a long-term relationship. For some, however, the security of routine is most satisfying.

∽ *Thought Provokers* ∽

1. The section on jealousy discussed research findings that women were more envious of attractiveness and popularity, while men were more likely to be envious of wealth and fame. What do you think accounts for this difference?

2. Assume that you are the parent of a teenager who asks, "How do I know when I should have sex?" What would you answer?

3. What do you think are the key differences between companionate and passionate love? How do these characteristics fit into the list of things that make a marriage successful?

Suggested Readings

Beck, Aaron (1988). *Love Is Never Enough*. New York: Harper & Row. This book describes specific approaches couples may use to overcome misunderstandings, resolve conflicts, and solve relationship problems.

Friday, Nancy (1985). *Jealousy*. New York: Morrow. This book is about the exploration and analysis of jealousy.

Fromm, Erich (1963). *The Art of Loving*. New York: Bantam Books. This is a classic on the topic of love. Fromm elucidates the power of love to develop human potential within oneself and within a relationship.

Lerner, Harriet (1989). *The Dance of Intimacy*. New York: Harper & Row. This book provides a framework for understanding how intimate relationships can thrive or heal.

Pogrebin, Letty (1987). *Among Friends*. New York: McGraw-Hill. This book examines the many meanings and expressions of friendship.

Human speech is like a cracked kettle on which we tap crude rhythms for bears to dance to while we long to make music that will melt the stars.

Gustave Flaubert
Madame Bovary (1857)

CHAPTER 8

Communication in Sexual Behavior

The Importance of Communication

Some Reasons Why Sexual Communication Is Difficult

Talking: Getting Started

Listening and Feedback

Discovering Your Partner's Needs

Learning to Make Requests

Giving Criticism

Receiving Criticism

Saying No

Nonverbal Sexual Communication

Impasses

213

*T*his is a chapter about sexual communication: the ways people express their feelings and convey their needs and desires to sexual partners. We consider the reasons why such attempts are sometimes unsuccessful; we also explore some ways to enhance this important aspect of our sexual lives.

The Importance of Communication

Sexual communication can contribute greatly to the satisfaction of an intimate relationship. We do not mean that extensive verbal dialogue is essential to all sexual sharing; there are times when spoken communication may be more disruptive than constructive. Nevertheless, partners who never talk about the sexual aspects of their relationship may be denying themselves an opportunity to increase their closeness and pleasure through learning about each other's needs and desires.

Central to this chapter is our belief that the basis for effective sexual communication is **mutual empathy** — the underlying knowledge that each partner in a relationship cares for the other and knows that the care is reciprocated. With this perspective in mind, we discuss various approaches to sexual communication that have proved helpful in the lives of many people. We do not claim to have the final word on the many nuances of human communication, nor do we suggest that the ideas offered here will work for everyone. Communication strategies often need to be individually modified; and sometimes the differences between two people are so profound that even the best communication cannot ensure a mutually satisfying relationship. We hope, though, that some of these shared experiences and suggestions can be helpful in your own life.

Some Reasons Why Sexual Communication Is Difficult

Why do so many people find it difficult to talk candidly with their partners about sexual needs? Before reading on, think for a minute or two about what you consider to be the major stumbling blocks in this area.

Some of the most important reasons why sexual communication is difficult lie in our socialization, the language available for talk about sex, and the fears many people have about self-expression.

The way we were reared as children often contributes to later difficulties in talking about sexual needs. Learning to cover our genitals, to think that eliminative functions are "dirty," or to hide self-pleasuring for fear of adverse reactions all may contribute to a sense of shame and discomfort with the sexual areas and functions of our bodies. The development of sexual attitudes during childhood and adolescence is discussed in Chapter 13.

Lack of communication about sexual matters in many American homes is detrimental in a number of ways. Not talking about sex at home deprives a young child of one valuable source of a vocabulary for talking about sex later in life. This lack of communication may also convey the implicit message that sex is not an acceptable topic for conversation. Furthermore, children most effectively acquire communication skills when they are provided with models of verbal interaction followed by the opportunity to express their own thoughts in an accepting atmosphere. None of these elements is typically available in a home where people simply do not talk about sex.

Lack of positive models frequently extends beyond the home. Few individuals have access to classroom or textbook sources that portray how couples talk about sex. Neither peer groups nor the popular media fill the gap by providing realistic or positive information.

Another obstacle to effective communication is the lack of a suitable language of sex. By the time we are grown up and eager to communicate sexual needs and feelings, many of us do not know how to go about doing it. The very words we have learned to describe sex may have become associated with negative rather than positive emotions. Many of us have learned to snigger over taboo sex words or to use them in an angry, aggressive, or insulting manner. Consequently, it can be very uncomfortable to use those same words to describe an activity with someone for whom we really care.

Thus, when we want to begin engaging in sexual communication, we may find ourselves struggling to find the right language for this most intimate kind of dialogue. The range of words commonly used to describe genital anatomy gives some indication of our society's mixed messages about sexuality. Two extremes tend to predominate: street language at one end and clinical terminology at the other.

One man's consternation over trying to figure out what words to use for his own genitals is revealed in the following anecdote:

I want to talk with my girlfriend about our sex life. So many times I have made up my mind to do this, but I can't seem to come up with *how* I should do this. How can I tell her about my body and its needs? What words do I use? Do I say "I like it best when you caress along the entire length of my penis" or should I say "It feels good when you touch all of my cock"? The first word sounds too clinical, but I am afraid the term "cock" might shock her and put her off. Just what words do lovers use? (Authors' files)

As this man has discovered, our language lacks a comfortable sexual vocabulary. Many of us are not at ease with the words commonly available. We may find them to be too clinical, too harsh, or too juvenile to use in a caring way. Words like *penis* and *vagina* often seem too technical or medical; but *cock, prick, cunt,* and *snatch* may sound too aggressive or insulting. And the terms available to describe sexual activity may produce similar problems. Statements like "Let's fuck" may be lovingly delivered and excitedly received by some, but they may seem too cold, graphic, or aggressive to others. But a more scientific description, such as "Let's have sexual intercourse," may seem clumsy and impersonal.*

---

*Indeed, we ourselves as authors of this textbook face the same limitations of language. What is the best word or phrase we can use to refer to the complex and varied symphony of interactions that takes place when two people interact together in explicitly sexual ways? Some of the more common street terms tend to sound crude and can objectify the participants, diminishing their interaction to the purely physical level. More formal terms such as *coitus* and *sexual intercourse* tend to put too much emphasis on heterosexual genital contact. We do not want our very language to exclude homosexual interactions, nor do we want it to exclude a whole range of nongenital interactions—including touching, talking, and communicating through facial expressions. When the context of our discussion focuses more on the physical aspects of sexual interactions, we use the terms *sexual activity* and *sexual play,* which we consider both broad and neutral. When the focus is more on the emotional and spiritual aspects of sexual interactions, we use the terms *sexual intimacy, sexual sharing,* and *lovemaking* to emphasize the larger emotional and intellectual relationship between the participants. We recognize, though, that even these terms have different connotations—both good and bad—for different people. What terms are you most comfortable with, and why?

Within the context of our culture, it is very natural — or at least common — to feel shy or embarrassed when talking about sexuality with friends and lovers. This awkwardness can often be avoided or overcome, however, and people certainly find ways of learning to live with the vocabulary. For example, the context and tone in which sexual terms are used may create totally different meanings and reactions, as this woman's comment shows:

I have very different feelings about words depending on how they are used. My lover saying "I love your sweet cunt" is very different from hearing "You stupid cunt." (Authors' files)

Also, some people give their own or their partners' genitals nicknames, such as Fuzzylove, Slurpy, Artesia, Pokey, Peter, or Moby, in an attempt to avoid negative associations with much of the existing terminology.

Later in this book (Chapter 17), we explore some of the benefits and joys associated with talking to our lovers while we touch their bodies. We will see that this is a wonderful time to develop intimacy while learning about each other's needs and preferences. It is a particularly good way to discover what words are mutually acceptable.

Beyond the handicaps imposed by socialization and language limitations, difficulties in sexual communication for some people may also be rooted in anxieties regarding self-exposure. Any sexual communication involves a certain amount of risk: By talking, people place themselves in a position vulnerable to judgment, criticism, and even rejection. The willingness to take risks may be related to the amount of trust that exists within a relationship. Some couples lack this mutual trust, and for them the risks of openly expressing sexual needs are too great to overcome. Others have a high degree of reciprocal caring and trust: for them the first hesitant steps into sexual dialogue may be considerably easier.

Even when a climate of good will prevails, however, it is sometimes still difficult to establish a satisfying pattern of sexual dialogue. In such circumstances, it may be undesirable for the couple to try to resolve their communication problems strictly on their own. Instead, they should probably seek professional counseling.*

We have outlined some reasons why many people find it difficult to engage in meaningful and effective sexual communication. Despite these difficulties, communication is an important part of sexual sharing, just as it is an important part of many other aspects of a relationship. The potential rewards are enhanced sexual experiences and enriched relationships.

Talking: Getting Started

How does one begin communicating about sex? Give this question some thought, perhaps applying your own experiences, before reading on.

There are many ways of breaking the ice, and we explore a few of them here. These suggestions may be useful not just at the beginning of a relationship but throughout its course.

Talking About Talking

When people feel uneasy about a topic, often the best place to start is by talking about talking. Discussing *why* it is hard to talk about sex can be a good place to begin. Each partner has individual reasons, and understanding those reasons can help set a relationship on a solid foundation. Perhaps you can share experiences about earlier efforts to discuss sex with parents, teachers, physicians, friends, or lovers. It may be helpful to move gradually into the arena of sexual communication by directing your initial discussions to nonthreatening, less personal topics (such as new birth control methods, pornography laws, and so forth). Later, as your mutual comfort with discussing sexual matters increases, you may be able to talk about more personal feelings and concerns.

Reading and Discussing

Because many people find it easier to read about sex than to talk about it, articles and books dealing with the subject may provide the stimulus for personal conversations. Partners can read the material separately, then discuss it together; or a couple can read it jointly and discuss their individual reactions to it. Often it is easier to make the transition from a book or article to personal feelings than to begin by talking about highly personal concerns.

---

*Chapter 17 provides some guidelines for seeking professional assistance.

Reading together facilitates
discussion of sensitive
matters.

Sharing Sexual Histories

Another way to start talking is to share sexual histories. There may be many questions that you would feel comfortable discussing with your partner. For instance: How was sex education handled in your home or at school? How did your parents relate to each other — were you aware of any sexuality in their relationship? When did you first learn about sex, and what were your reactions? Many other items could be added to this brief list; the questions depend on the feelings and needs of each individual.

Listening and Feedback

Communication, sexual or otherwise, is most successful when it is two-sided, involving both an effective communicator and an active listener. In this section we focus on the listening side of this process.

Have you ever wondered why certain people seem to draw others to themselves like metal to a magnet? With some thought you will probably conclude that, among other things, these individuals are often very good listeners. What special skills do they possess that make us feel they really care about what we have to say? Next time you are with such a person, observe closely. Make a study of his or her listening habits. Perhaps your list of good listening traits will include several of the following.

Be an Active Listener

Some people are *passive* listeners. They may stare blankly into space as their companion talks, perhaps grunting "uh-huh" now and then. Such responses may make us think that the person is indifferent, even when this is not the case, and we may soon grow tired of trying to share important thoughts with someone who does not seem to be receptive:

When I talk to my husband about anything really important, he just stares at me with a blank expression. It is like I am talking to a piece of stone. I think he hears the message, at least sometimes, but he rarely shows any response. Sometimes I feel like shaking him and screaming "Are you still alive?" Needless to say, I don't try communicating with him very much anymore. (Authors' files)

Being an *active* listener means actively communicating that you are both listening to and genuinely interested in what your partner is saying. You may communicate this through attentive body language, appropriate and sympathetic facial expressions, nodding your head, asking questions ("Could you give me an example?"), or making brief comments ("I see your point"). Sometimes it may be helpful to reciprocate in the conversation. For example, as your partner relates a feeling or incident, you may be reminded of something in your own life, related to the focus of your conversation, that you would like to share. Making these associations and candidly expressing them to your partner can encourage her or him to continue voicing important concerns.

Maintain Eye Contact

Maintaining eye contact is one of the most vital aspects of good face-to-face communication. Our eyes are wondrously expressive of feelings. When people maintain eye contact when we are sharing important thoughts or feelings with them, the message is clear: They care about what we have to say. When we fail to maintain eye contact, we deny our partners valuable feedback about how we are perceiving their messages.

Provide Feedback

The purpose of communication is to provide a message that has some impact on the listener. However, a message's impact may not always be the same as its intent, for communications can be (and often are) misunderstood. This is particularly true with a topic like sexuality, where language is often roundabout or awkward. Therefore, giving your partner some feedback, or reaction to her or his message, *in words* can be very helpful. Besides clarifying how you have perceived your partner's comments, such verbal feedback reinforces that you are actively listening.

We may also benefit by asking our partners to provide some response to a message we think is important. A comment like "What are your thoughts about what I have just said?" may encourage feedback that can help you determine the impact of your message on your partner.

Support Your Partner's Communication Efforts

Many of us can feel quite vulnerable when communicating important messages to our partners. Support for our efforts can help alleviate our fears and anxieties and can encourage us to continue building the communication skills so important for a viable relationship.

Think how good it can feel, after struggling to voice an important concern, to have a partner say, "I really appreciate your sharing your thoughts with me," or "Thanks for caring enough to tell me what was on your mind." Such supportive comments can help foster mutual empathy, while ensuring that we will continue to communicate our thoughts and feelings candidly.

Express Unconditional Positive Regard

The concept of unconditional positive regard is borrowed from the immensely popular *Client-Centered Therapy,* authored by Carl Rogers (1951). In personal relationships, it means conveying to our partners the sense that we will continue to value and care for them regardless of what they do or say. Unconditional positive regard may encourage a person to talk about even the most embarrassing or painful concerns. The following anecdote reveals one person's response to this valued attribute:

I know that my wife's love for me is unfaltering and that no matter what I say or reveal, she will continue to care for me. In an earlier marriage, I could never express any serious concerns without my wife getting defensive or just plain mean. As a consequence, I just quit talking about things that really mattered. What a relief it is to be with someone with whom I can express what is on my mind without worrying about the consequences. (Authors' files)

Use Paraphrasing

One way to increase the probability that you and your partner will listen more effectively to each other is to use a technique called **paraphrasing.** This involves a listener summarizing, in his or her own words, the speaker's message.

He: It would be nice if you could be a little gentler. Do you understand what I mean?

She: I think so — you want me to be less aggressive.

He: That's not quite what I mean. I mean that, when you touch me when we make love, I would like you to use a lighter, softer caress.

She: Oh, now I understand. I always thought you liked me to use firm pressure when I touched you. But you want light pressure — I'm sorry.

He: That's okay. You don't have to apologize. It was a misunderstanding, I guess. I'm glad you understand better now what I want.

If the paraphrase is not satisfactory, the speaker can try to express the message again in different words. Then the listener can try to paraphrase again. Several attempts may be necessary to clear away discrepancies between the speaker's intent and the listener's interpretation. As time goes by, a couple typically finds that the need to use this approach diminishes as listening skills improve.

Discovering Your Partner's Needs

Discovering what is pleasurable to your partner is an important part of sexual intimacy. Many couples want to know each other's preferences but are uncertain how to find out. In this section, we look at some effective ways of learning about our partners' wants and needs.

Asking Questions

One of the best ways to discover your partner's needs is simply to ask. However, there are several ways of asking: Some can be helpful, while others may be ineffective or even counterproductive. We review a few of the most common ways of asking questions and the effect each is likely to have.

Yes or No Questions. Imagine being asked one or more of the following questions in the context of a sexual interlude with your partner:

1. Was it good for you?
2. Do you like oral sex?
3. Was I gentle enough?
4. Did you come?
5. Do you like it when I stimulate you this way?
6. Do you like being on the bottom?
7. Is it okay if we don't make love tonight?
8. Am I a good lover?

At first glance, these questions may seem reasonably worded. However, they all share one characteristic that may reduce their effectiveness: They are **yes or no questions.** Each asks for a one-word answer, even though people's thoughts and feelings are rarely so simple.

For example, consider question 2, "Do you like oral sex?" Either answer — "Yes, I do," or "No, I don't" — gives the couple little opportunity to discuss the issue. Certainly, the potential for discussion exists. Nevertheless, in a world where sexual communication is often difficult under the best of circumstances, the asker may get no more than the specific information requested. In some situations, of course, a brief yes or no is all that is necessary. But the person responding may have mixed feelings about oral sex (for example), and the phrasing of the question leads to oversimplification. **Open-ended questions,** or questions that allow the respondent to state a preference, can make it easier for her or him to give accurate replies.

Open-Ended Questions. Some people find that asking open-ended questions is a particularly helpful way to discover their partners' desires. This approach places virtually no restrictions on possible answers; in a sense, it is like responding to a general essay question on an exam. ("What are some of the important aspects of human sexuality that you have learned thus far this term?") The following list gives some examples of open-ended questions:

1. What gives you the most pleasure when we make love?
2. What aspects of our sexual relationship would you most like to have changed or continued?
3. Where do you like to be touched?

4.   What sexual positions do you like?

5.   What is the easiest or most enjoyable way for you to reach orgasm?

6.   What are your feelings about oral sex?

A primary advantage of open-ended questions is that they allow your partner freedom to share any feelings or information she or he thinks is relevant. With no limitations or restrictions attached, you may discover much more than the bare-bones information that a simple yes or no could provide.

One possible drawback of the open-ended approach is that your partner may not know where to begin when asked such general questions. Consider being asked something like "What aspects of our lovemaking do you like best?" Some people might welcome the unstructured nature of this question, but others might find it difficult to respond to such a broad query, particularly if they are not accustomed to openly discussing sex. If this is the case, a more structured approach may have a better chance of encouraging talk. There are several ways of structuring your approach; one is the use of either/or questions.

Either/Or Questions. The following list gives some examples of **either/or questions:**

1.   Would you like the light on when we make love, or should we turn it off?

2.   Am I being gentle enough or too gentle?

3.   Is this the way you want to be touched, or should we experiment with a different kind of caress?

4.   Would you like to try something different, or should we stop and just hold each other?

5.   Would you like to talk now, or would you prefer we wait for another time?

While either/or questions offer more structure than do open-ended questions, they also encourage more participation than simple yes or no queries. People often appreciate the opportunity to consider a few alternatives. The either/or question also shows the questioner's concern about a partner's pleasure. Thus, this kind of question may encourage a response at a time when a more open-ended question might be overwhelming. However, either/or questions can still be somewhat restrictive. There is always the possibility that someone will not like either of the choices offered. In this case, the answerer can state another alternative that is preferable.

Besides asking questions, there are other ways of discovering the sexual needs of a partner. We discuss three other communication techniques here: self-disclosure, comparing notes, and giving permission.

Self-Disclosure

Direct questions often put people on the spot. Whether you have been asked "Do you enjoy oral sex?" or "How do you feel about oral sex?" it may be quite difficult to respond candidly, simply because you cannot gauge the questioner's feelings on the subject. If the topic has strong emotional overtones, it may be very difficult to reply — no matter how thoughtfully the question has been phrased. It is the content, not the communication technique, that causes the problem.

With potentially loaded topics, a way to broach the subject may be to start with a self-disclosure:

For the longest time, I was reluctant to bring up the topic of oral sex with my lover. We did about everything else, but this was one area we avoided both in action and conversation. I personally was both excited and repelled by the prospect of this kind of sex. I didn't have the slightest idea what she felt about it. I was afraid to bring it up for fear she would think I was some kind of pervert. Eventually I could no longer tolerate not knowing her feelings about what might be incredibly erotic. I brought it up by first talking about my mixed emotions, like feeling that maybe it wasn't natural but at the same time really wanting to try it out. As it turned out, she had been having similar feelings but was afraid to bring them up because of how I might react. Afterwards we laughed about how we had both been afraid to break the ice. Once we could talk freely about our feelings, it was easy to add this form of stimulation to our sex life. (Authors' files)

Personal disclosures require some give-and-take. It is much easier to share feelings about strongly emotional topics when a partner is willing to make similar disclosures. Admittedly, such an approach may have risks, and occasionally one can feel vulnerable sharing personal thoughts and feelings. Nevertheless, the increased possibility for open, honest dialogue may be worth the discomfort a person may feel about making the first disclosure.

A form of self-disclosure that some people find exciting and informative involves telling their partners about personal fantasies, as revealed in the following anecdote:

I had this sexual fantasy that kept going through my mind. I would imagine coming home after a long, hard day of classes and being met by my partner, who would proceed to take me into the bedroom and remove all my clothes. He would then pick me up and carry me into the bathroom, where a tub full of hot water and bubbles awaited. The fantasy would end with us making passionate love in the bathtub, with bubbles popping off around us. Finally, I shared my fantasy with him. Guess what happened when I came home after the next long day? It was even better than I had imagined! (Authors' files)

Understandably, many people might be concerned about the potentially negative effects of revealing such highly personal thoughts. Certain precautions can help reduce the possibility of an unpleasant outcome.

Sharing fantasies like this is usually most successful when it is mutual rather than one-way. If your partner is unwilling to engage in such a conversation, at least for the present, it would be wise to respect this wish. Sometimes starting out with very mild fantasies can help desensitize fears and embarrassment and allow you to gauge the impact of such sharing on your partner and yourself. If you sense that your companion is feeling uncomfortable, it may be best not to press. It is probably advisable to avoid altogether any fantasies that you anticipate will be shocking to your companion; fantasies that involve other lovers may be particularly threatening.

Comparing Notes

Many couples, while planning an evening out, consider it natural to discuss each other's preferences: "Do you like the symphony, the theater, movies?" "How close do you like to sit?" "Do you prefer steak or seafood?" Afterward they may candidly evaluate the evening's events: "The orchestra was great," "I think the balcony seats would be better next time," "Boy, I wouldn't order the scampi again." Yet many of the same couples never think of sharing thoughts about mutual sexual enjoyment.

Admittedly, it may be a big step from discussing an evening out to discussing sexual preferences and evaluating specific sexual encounters. Nevertheless, people do engage in this type of sexual dialogue. Some people feel comfortable discussing sexual preferences with a new lover before progressing to lovemaking. They may talk about what areas of their bodies are most responsive, how they like to be touched, what intercourse positions are particularly desirable, the easiest or most satisfying way to reach orgasm, time and location preferences, special turn-ons and turn-offs, and a variety of other likes and dislikes.

The appeal of this open, frank approach is that it allows a couple to focus on particularly pleasurable activities rather than discovering them by slow trial-and-error. However, some people may feel that preparatory dialogues are far too clinical, perhaps even robbing the sexual experience of the excitement of experimentation and mutual discovery. Furthermore, what a person finds desirable may be different with different partners, so it may be difficult to assess one's own preferences in advance.

Couples may also find it helpful to discuss their feelings after a sexual encounter. They may offer reactions about what was good and what could be better. They may use this time to reinforce the things they found particularly satisfying in their partner's lovemaking ("I loved the way you touched me with your hands"). A mutual feedback session can be extremely informative; it can also contribute to a deeper intimacy between two people.

Giving Permission

Discovering your partner's needs can be made immeasurably easier by the practice we call **giving permission.** Basically, this means providing encouragement and reassurance. One partner tells the other that it is okay to talk about certain specific feelings or needs — in fact, that he or she wants very much to know how the other feels about the subject.

He: I'm not sure how you like me to touch you when we make love.

She: Any way you want to is good.

He: Well, it would be good to know what you like best, and you can help me by saying what feels good while I touch you.

Many of us have had experiences where we have felt rebuffed in our efforts to communicate our needs to others. It is no wonder people often remain silent even when they want to share personal feelings. Giving and receiving permission to express needs freely can contribute to the exchange of valuable information.

Learning to Make Requests

People are not mind readers. Nevertheless, many lovers seem to assume that their partners know (perhaps by intuition?) just what they need. People who approach sex with this attitude are not taking full responsibility for their own pleasure. If sexual encounters are not satisfactory, it may be convenient to blame the other — "You don't care about my needs" — when it may be one's own reluctance to express one's needs that is the root of the problem. Expecting our partners to somehow know what we want without our telling them places a heavy burden on them. Many people think that they "shouldn't have to ask," but in fact, asking a partner to do something can be an affirmative, responsible action that is helpful to both people.

Taking Responsibility for Our Own Pleasure

When two people are really in harmony with each other, you don't have to talk about your sexual wants. Each will sense and respond to the other's desires. Talking just tends to spoil these magical moments. (Authors' files)

The situation this person describes seems to exist more in the fantasyland of idealized sex than in the real world. As we noted earlier, people are not mind readers, and intuition leaves much to be desired as a substitute for genuine communication. A person who expects another to know his or her needs by intuition is saying, "It's not my business to let you know my needs, but yours to know what they are"; and by inference, "If my needs are not fulfilled, it is your fault, not mine." Needless to say, this is a potentially destructive approach that may lead to blaming, misunderstandings, and unsatisfying sex.

In a similar vein, some individuals may take too much responsibility for their partners' sexual pleasure. The person says, in effect, "It is my job to satisfy you sexually. I will make all the decisions and assume responsibility for your pleasure." A person so intent on figuring out and fulfilling the needs of a partner may find that his or her own needs are largely overlooked. Furthermore, such a take-charge attitude encourages passivity and undermines a partner's inclination to assume responsibility for her or his own satisfaction.

In summary, the best way for us to get our needs met is to speak up with our requests. Two individuals willing to communicate their desires and take responsibility for their own pleasure create an excellent framework for effective, fulfilling sexual intimacy.

One woman stated her experience with assuming responsibility for her own pleasure:

For much of my life, sex has been a hit-or-miss proposition, with the miss part predominating. Only recently have I discovered how to change this pattern. I know what I need sexually to be satisfied. I am very good at giving myself pleasure. Finally it occurred to me how futile it was to hope that my partners would somehow automatically possess this knowledge that took me years to discover for myself. I decided that the better I could express myself about my sexual needs, the greater the likelihood they would be fulfilled. Assuming this responsibility for my own pleasure was a big step that I took with a great deal of hesitancy and anxiety. But I have been pleasantly surprised by most of my subsequent lovers' reactions. They are usually quite relieved to have the guesswork taken out of our sexual experiences. One man praised me for my openness and confided that my willingness to tell him what I wanted relieved him of one of his greatest concerns, namely, not knowing what his partner desired from him during sex. (Authors' files)

Deciding to assume responsibility for one's own satisfaction is an important step. Just as important are the methods a person selects for expressing his or her

needs. The way a request is made has a decided effect on the reaction it draws. Some suggestions are listed in the next two sections.

Making Requests Specific

The more specific a request, the more likely it is to be understood and heeded. This is a fact frequently noted by social psychologists and communication specialists. Nevertheless, many of us neglect to apply this sound principle to our sexual dialogues. Lovers often ask for changes in the sexual aspects of their relationships in the vaguest language. It can be quite uncomfortable, even anxiety-provoking, to be on the receiving end of an ill-defined request. Just what do we do in response? Probably very little, if anything.

The key to preventing unnecessary stress for both partners lies in delivering requests in as clear and concise a manner as possible. Thus, an alternative to the vague request "I'd like you to try touching me differently" might be something like "I would like you to touch me gently around my clitoris but not directly on it." Other examples of specific requests include the following:

1. I would like you to spend more time touching and caressing me all over before we have intercourse.

2. I want to be on top this time. It feels real good to me, and I love being able to watch you respond.

3. I like it when you lick the underside of the head of my penis during oral sex. Not too hard, though — I'll tell you if I want it harder or softer.

4. I really enjoy it when you continue kissing and caressing me after you're in-side me.
5. I would really like you to stroke my penis with your hand.

Using "I" Language

Many counselors encourage their clients to use "I" language when stating their needs to others. This forthright approach brings the desired response more often than does a general statement. For example, saying "I would like to be on top" is considerably more likely to produce that result than "What would you think about changing positions?"

Many people find it difficult to ask for what they want in such clear, unequiv-ocal language. Saying "I want ..." may seem selfish to some. However, there is a difference between being self-centered and recognizing that "I am as important as others in my life, and my needs are worthy of being met." Individuals who experience gratification of their own needs are often able to give much of them-selves to others. Conversely, the philosophy of "never put myself first" may ulti-mately produce so much frustration and resentment that a person is left with few positive feelings to share.

Expressing requests directly may not always be effective. Some people may want to make all the decisions during sex, and they may not take kindly to requests from their partners during lovemaking. To them a partner's assertiveness may be offensive. You may want to determine if this is your partner's attitude before an encounter, thereby avoiding an awkward situation later on. One way to do this is to ask the open-ended question "How do you feel about asking for things during lovemaking?" Or, you may choose to wait and find out during sex play. At any rate, if a person appears closed to direct requests, you may wish to reevaluate your strategy. Perhaps making your needs known at some time other than during sexual interaction may give your partner a more relaxed opportunity to consider your desires.

Giving Criticism

Contrary to the popular romantic image, no two people can fill all of each other's needs all of the time. It seems inevitable in an intimate relationship that people will sometimes need to register complaints and request changes. This is not an easy process for caring individuals whose involvement is characterized by mutual empathy. When the criticism pertains to the emotionally intense area of sexual intimacy, it may be doubly difficult. Partners will want to think carefully about appropriate strategies and potential obstacles to accomplishing this delicate task. Perhaps the best way to begin, before verbalizing a complaint to your partner, is to examine the motivations underlying your need to criticize.

Be Aware of Your Motivation

The way criticism is offered may depend largely on the motive of the critic. Con-sider the following two anecdotes:

My husband is a lousy lover. He doesn't know the first thing about how to turn me on, and when I tell him I don't get any pleasure out of our sex life he just clams up. I don't know what's the matter with him, but it sure burns me up. (Authors' files)

A couple of years ago I found out that my wife was involved in an affair with a man she works with. She claimed he was kind and gentle and that she couldn't help being attracted to him. Faced with my ultimatum, she changed jobs and stopped seeing him (I think). Since that time our sex life has been a real bust. She seems to lack enthusiasm, and we engage in sex much less frequently. Sometimes I think her having sex with the other guy has ruined our sex life. Maybe she thinks he was better than me. When I confront her with my dissatisfaction with her lack of enthusiasm she gets upset, and we usually end up having a fight. (Authors' files)

It seems clear that these people's motivations for criticizing are not based on a caring desire to make their relationships better. In the first example, the aim of the woman appears to be to hurt or humiliate her husband. The man in the second anecdote seems to be motivated by a desire for revenge. If the aim is to hurt, humiliate, blame, ridicule, or get even, it is likely that criticizing a partner will prove to be far more destructive than constructive. Being aware of your motives for criticizing your partner can help avoid this pitfall.

In this book we are concerned with constructive criticism that is prompted by a genuine desire for necessary change. It is not always easy to criticize effectively while maintaining mutual empathy and a sense of togetherness. There are, however, certain strategies that can help maintain empathy in a confrontational situation. One important consideration is picking the right time and place.

Choose the Right Time and Place

Whenever my lover brings up something that is bothering her about our sex life, it inevitably is just after we have made love. Here I am, relaxed, holding her in my arms, thinking good thoughts, and she destroys the mood with some criticism. It's not that I don't want her to express her concerns, but her timing is terrible. The last thing I want to hear after lovemaking is that it could have been better. (Authors' files)

This man's dismay is obvious. His partner's decision to voice her concerns during the afterglow of lovemaking worked against her purpose. He may have felt vulnerable, and he clearly resented having his good mood broken by the prospect of potentially difficult conversation. Of course, other couples may find this to be a time when they are exceedingly close to each other and, thus, a good atmosphere in which to air concerns.

Many people, like the woman in the previous example, never choose the best time to confront their lovers. Rather, the time chooses them: They jump right in when the problem is uppermost in their minds. There are some benefits to dealing with an issue immediately. However, a person who does this may be feeling disappointed, resentful, or angry, and these negative emotions, when running full tide, can easily get in the way of constructive interaction. Avoid registering complaints when anger is at its peak. Though you may have every intention of making your criticism constructive, anger has a way of disrupting a search for solutions. Sometimes, however, it may be necessary to express anger; we consider how to do so appropriately at the end of this section.

Choosing the right time and place to express sexual concerns can facilitate communication.

In most cases it is unwise to tackle a problem when either you or your partner has limited time or is tired, stressed, preoccupied, or under the influence of drugs or alcohol. Rather, try to select an interval when you have plenty of time and are both relaxed and feeling close to each other.

A pragmatic approach to the problem of timing is to simply ask your lover: "I really value our sexual relationship, but there are some concerns I would like to talk over with you. Is this a good time, or would you rather we talk later?" Be prepared for some anxiety-induced stalling. If your partner is hesitant to talk now, support his or her right to pick another time or place. However, it is important to agree on a time, particularly if you sense your partner might prefer to let the matter go.

Choosing the right place for expressing sexual concerns can be as important as timing. Some people may find that sitting around the kitchen table while sharing a pot of coffee is a more comfortable setting than the place where they make love, whereas others might prefer the familiarity of their bed. A walk through a park or a quiet drive in the country, far removed from the potential interferences of a busy lifestyle, may prove best for you. Try to sense your partner's needs. When and where is she or he most likely to be receptive to your requests for change?

Picking the right time and place to deliver criticism does not ensure a harmonious outcome, but it certainly improves the prospects of your partner responding favorably to your message. Using some other constructive strategies can also increase the likelihood of beneficial interaction. One of these is to combine criticism with praise.

Temper Criticism with Praise

The strategy of tempering criticism with praise is based largely on common sense. All of us tend to respond well to compliments, whereas harsh criticism untempered by praise is difficult to accept. The gentler approach of combining criticism with praise is a good way to reduce the negative impact of a complaint. It also gives the person who has been criticized a broader perspective from which to evaluate the criticism, and reduces the likelihood that he or she will respond in a defensive or angry manner. Consider how you might react differently to the following criticisms depending on whether or not they are accompanied by praise:

Criticism Alone	Criticism with Praise
1. When we make love you seem so inhibited.	I appreciate the way you respond to me when we make love, and I think it could be even better if you would take the initiative sometimes. Does this seem like a reasonable request?
2. I am really getting tired of your turning off the lights every time we make love.	I enjoy hearing and feeling you react when we make love. I would also like to see you respond. How would you feel about leaving the lights on sometimes?
3. I think our lovemaking is much too infrequent. It almost seems like sex is not as important to you as it is to me.	Having sex gives me a great deal of pleasure, and I value sharing it with you. My concern is that it doesn't happen as frequently as I would like. What are your thoughts about this?

Sadly, just about all of us have been on the receiving end of criticisms like those in the left column. Common reactions are anger, feeling humiliated, anxiety about our competency as lovers, and resentment. Although some people may respond to such harsh complaints with a resolve to make things better, it is more likely that this will not occur. On the other hand, affirmative criticism, like the examples in the right column, is more likely to encourage efforts to change.

There is a good deal of wisdom in the saying "People are usually more motivated to make a good thing better than to make a bad thing good." This applies as much to sexual activity as to any other area of human interaction. One of us was once approached by a woman who complained that her husband was often too rough with her during love play. She was reluctant to discuss her concern with him, however, for fear that he would feel put down or angered. She also had mixed feelings about her husband's roughness — it was part of the unbridled enthusiasm with which he related to her sexually, a zestiness she very much enjoyed. On those rare occasions when he did take the time to be gentle with her, she was very pleased. Now, the problem: How could she tell him she didn't like his roughness, while at the same time assuring that he would maintain his enthusiasm and not feel angry or inept?

What she finally told him was essentially what she had expressed in seeking advice. Sometimes it was terrific when he was gentle. She loved being pursued with enthusiasm and vigor. It could be even better if he would include more gentleness in their lovemaking. Although he was somewhat surprised and dismayed over his inability to detect her needs, her husband's response was quite positive. What do you suppose his reaction might have been had she coldly complained, "Do you have to be so rough when we make love?"

It is also a good idea to ask for feedback when delivering criticisms. Regardless of how much warmth and good will we put into this difficult process, there is always the possibility that our partners may become silent or change the subject. Asking them to talk about their reaction to our request for change helps to reduce these prospects. (Note that in the previous list, all "Criticism with Praise" examples ended with requests for feedback.)

Nurture Small Steps Toward Change

Complete behavioral changes rarely occur immediately following criticism — no matter how positively the criticism is stated. Rather, they must be patiently nurtured, with each small step along the way properly acknowledged with words of appreciation. In the example of the woman wanting more gentleness from her husband, it would have been unreasonable for her to assume that once she expressed her criticism, her partner would completely change his ways. In fact, what occurred was a noticeable but minimal effort to be less vigorous in the next sexual encounter. Soon the old patterns ingrained over many years took over again.

Backsliding is natural and predictable and, as with other unwanted behaviors, responding to it requires tact. Have you ever heard the words "I see you didn't pay a bit of attention to what I said"? Such a negative reaction could easily cool your desire to follow through with change. It is far more encouraging and reassuring to be on the receiving end of a message like the one delivered by the wife to her "trying to be more gentle" husband: "I really appreciate the time you took to be gentle when we made love. It means a great deal that you care about my needs." With such a caring and supportive reaction, few people are likely to stick to the same old behavior.

Avoid "Why" Questions

People frequently use "why" questions as thinly veiled efforts to criticize or attack their partners while avoiding full responsibility for what is said. Have you ever been asked any of the following?

1. Why don't you make love to me more frequently?
2. Why don't you show more interest in me?
3. Why don't you get turned on by me anymore?
4. Why can't you be more loving toward me?
5. Why are you so lazy?

Such queries have no place in a loving relationship. They are hurtful and destructive. Rather than representing simple requests for information, they are typically used to convey hidden messages of anger that people are unwilling to communicate honestly. These are hit-and-run tactics that give pain and seldom induce positive changes. Get rid of them. They cannot help register constructive criticism.

Express Anger Appropriately

Earlier in this chapter, we noted that it is wise to avoid confronting our partners when anger is riding high. However, there will probably be times when you feel compelled to express angry feelings. If so, certain guiding principles may help you defuse a potentially explosive situation.

Avoid focusing your anger on the character of your partner ("You are an insensitive person"). Instead, try directing your anger toward his or her behaviors ("When you don't listen to my concerns, I think they are unimportant to you and I feel angry"). At the same time, express appreciation for your partner as a person ("You are very important to me, and I don't like feeling this way"). This acknowledges that we can be angered by our partners' behaviors yet still feel loving toward them — an often overlooked but important truth.

Anger is probably best expressed with clear, honest "I" statements rather than with accusatory and potentially inflammatory "you" statements. Consider the following:

"I" Statements	"You" Statements
1. I feel ignored.	You don't give a damn about me.
2. I don't like being blamed.	You always blame me for our problems.
3. I am upset.	You make me upset.
4. I am angry.	You make me angry.
5. I feel unloved.	You don't love me.

"I" statements are self-revelations that express how we feel without placing blame or attacking our partners' character. In contrast, "you" statements frequently are interpreted as attacks on the other person's character or attempts to fix blame.

Limit Criticism to One Complaint per Discussion

Many of us are inclined to avoid confrontations with our partners. This understandable reluctance to deal with negative issues can result in an accumulation of unspoken complaints. Consequently, when we finally reach the point where we need to "say something or bust," it may be difficult to avoid unleashing a barrage of criticisms that includes everything on our current list of grievances. Such a response, though understandable, may only serve to magnify rather than resolve conflicts between lovers, as reflected in the following account:

My wife lets things eat on her without letting me know when I do something that she disapproves of. She remembers every imagined shortcoming and blows it way out of proportion. But I never learn about it until she has accumulated a lengthy list of beefs. Then she hits me with all of them at once, dredging them up like weapons in her arsenal, all designed to make me feel like an insensitive creep. I sometimes hear about things that happened years ago. She wonders why I don't have anything to say when she is done haranguing me. But what do you say when somebody has just given you 10 or 20 reasons why your relationship with her sucks? Which one do you respond to? And how can you avoid being pissed off when somebody rubs your face in all your shortcomings, real or imagined? (Authors' files)

We can reduce the likelihood of creating such a counterproductive situation in our own relationships by limiting our criticisms to one complaint per discussion. Even if you have a half-dozen complaints you want to talk about, it will probably serve your relationship better to pick one and delegate the remaining concerns to later conversations.

Receiving Criticism

Delivering complaints to our partners is difficult for caring people; likewise, receiving criticisms from a loved one can also be an emotionally rending experience. However, as we have already said, people involved in an intimate, loving relationship inevitably experience the need to register complaints on occasion. How we respond to such criticism may have a significant impact not only on our partners' inclination to openly share concerns in the future but also on the probability that the complaint will be resolved in a manner that strengthens rather than erodes the relationship.

See if you can think of some helpful strategies for responding to criticism before reading on.

When your partner delivers a criticism, take a few moments to gather your thoughts. A few deep breaths is probably a much better initial response than blurting out "Yeah, well what about the time that you . . . !" Ask yourself, "Is this person trying to give me some information that may be helpful?" In a loving relationship where mutual empathy prevails, perhaps you will be able to see some potential for positive consequences, even though you have just received a painful message. There are several ways you can respond to such a communication. We hope one or more of the following suggestions provides helpful guidelines in these circumstances.

Empathize with Your Partner and Paraphrase the Criticism

Many of us have had the experience of expressing concerns to people we care about, only to have them come back with a criticism of their own. Such a response will likely result in increased defensiveness, which may precipitate withdrawal or antagonistic confrontation. Furthermore, when people match a criticism with a countercomplaint, it appears that they are not trying to understand and empathize with the concern. In contrast, providing a paraphrase of your partner's criticism suggests you are making an effort to understand and appreciate what he or she is experiencing. For example, saying to your partner "It sounds like you have been frustrated with our lovemaking" will probably have a much more beneficial effect than a comment like "Well, you're not such a hot lover either!"

Paraphrasing a partner's criticism does not mean that you agree with it. Rather, you are simply saying "This is what I am hearing — do I understand correctly?" We can empathize with our lovers' concerns even if we have different thoughts and feelings about them. This type of positive response increases the likelihood that your partner will voice important concerns in the future.

Responding to criticism in an open manner can help strengthen a relationship.

Acknowledge a Criticism and Find Something to Agree With

Perhaps if you open yourself to listen to a criticism, you will see that there is some basis for it. For example, suppose your partner feels angry about your busy schedule and criticizes you for not devoting more time to the relationship. Maybe you think he or she is overreacting or forgetting all the time you have spent together. However, you also know that there is some basis for this expressed concern. It can be helpful to acknowledge this by saying something like, "I can understand how you might feel neglected because I have been preoccupied lately with my new job." Such constructive acknowledgment can occur even if you think the criticism is largely unjustified. By reacting in an accepting and supportive manner, you are conveying the message that you hear, understand, and appreciate the basis for your partner's concern.

Ask Clarifying Questions

In some cases your partner may deliver a criticism in such a vague manner that further clarification is needed. If this happens, ask questions. For example, suppose your partner complains that you do not take enough time in your lovemaking. You might respond by asking, "Do you mean that we should spend more time touching before intercourse, or that I should last longer before coming, or that you want to be held for a longer time after sex?"

Express Your Feelings

It can be helpful to talk about your feelings in regard to the criticism rather than letting these emotions dictate your response. For instance, your partner's criticism may cause you to feel angry, hurt, or dejected. It is probably better to verbalize these emotional reactions by expressing feeling statements rather than reacting by yelling, stomping out of the room, crying, or retreating into a shell of despair. It may help to tell your partner, "That was really hard to hear, and I am hurt," or "Right now I feel like flipping my lid, so I need to stop and take a few breaths and figure out what I am thinking and feeling."

Focus on Future Changes You Can Make

An excellent closure to receiving criticism is to focus on what the two of you can do to make things better. Perhaps this is the time to say, "My new job is really important to me, but our relationship is much more important. Maybe we can set aside some specific times each week where we both agree not to let outside concerns intrude upon our time together." Sometimes people agree to make things better but neglect to discuss concrete changes that will resolve the issue that triggered the complaint. Taking the time to identify and agree on specific future changes is a crucial step in resolving the basis for the complaint.

Saying No

Many of us have difficulty saying no to others. Our discomfort in communicating this direct message is perhaps most pronounced when it applies to intimate areas of relationships. This is reflected in the following anecdotes:

Sometimes my partner wants to be sexual when I only want to be close. The trouble is, I can't say no. I am afraid she would be hurt or angry. Unfortunately, I am the one who ends up angry at myself for not being able to express my true feelings. Sex sure isn't very good under such circumstances. (Authors' files)

It is so hard to say no to a man who suggests having sex at the end of a date. This is especially true if we have had a good time together. You never know if they are going to get that hangdog hurt look or become belligerent and angry. (Authors' files)

These accounts reveal some of the common concerns that may inhibit our inclinations to say no. We may believe that saying no will hurt the other person or perhaps cause him or her to become angry or even combative. Laboring under such fears, it may seem less stressful to simply comply with the requests of others. Unfortunately, this reluctant acquiescence can create such negative feelings that the resulting shared activity may be less than pleasurable for both ourselves and our partners.

Many of us have not learned that it is okay to say no, and perhaps more important, we have not learned strategies for doing so. In the following section, we consider some potentially useful ways to say no.

A Three-Step Approach to Saying No

Many people have found it helpful to have a definite plan or strategy in mind for saying no to invitations for intimate involvements. This can help prevent being caught off guard and not knowing how to handle a potentially unpleasant task with tact. One approach you may find helpful involves three distinct steps, or phases, outlined as follows:

Step 1. Express appreciation for the invitation ("Thanks for thinking of me," "I appreciate your attraction to me, your interest in _____ with me," and so forth). Perhaps you may also wish to validate the other person ("You are a good person").

Step 2. Say no in a clear, unequivocal fashion ("I would prefer not to make love, go dancing, get involved in a dating relationship," and so forth).

Step 3. Offer an alternative, if applicable ("I would like to have lunch sometime, give you a backrub," and so forth).

The positive aspects of this approach are readily apparent. We first indicate our appreciation for the expressed interest in us. At the same time, we clearly state our wish not to comply with the request. Finally, we end the exchange on an upbeat note by offering an alternative. Of course, this last step will not always be an option (for example, when turning down a request from someone with whom we wish to have no further social contact). Between lovers, however, there is often a mutually acceptable alternative.

Avoid Sending Mixed Messages

Saying no in clear, unmistakable language is essential to the success of the previously outlined strategy. Nevertheless, many of us are probably guilty, at least sometimes, of sending mixed messages about our sexual and other intimate needs. Consider, for example, someone who responds positively to an expressed desire for sexual intimacy but then spends an inordinate amount of time soaking in the bathtub while a patiently waiting partner falls asleep. Another version of this story involves the person who expresses a desire or willingness to have sex but instead gets engrossed in a late-night talk show. Both of these people are sending mixed messages to their partners that may reflect some of their own ambivalence about engaging in sexual relations.

The effect of such mixed messages is usually less than desirable. The recipient is often confused about the other person's intent. He or she may feel uncertain or even inadequate ("Why can't I figure out what you really want?"), and these feelings may evolve into anger ("Why do I have to guess?") or withdrawal. These reactions are understandable in such circumstances. A person faced with contradictory messages may be unsure what to do — act on the first message or on the second one? Consider the following:

It really bothers me when my partner says we will make love when I get home from night school and then she is too busy studying to take a break. Sometimes I wonder if she had any intention in the first place to follow through on her suggestion. (Authors' files)

All of us may benefit from taking stock from time to time to see if we send mixed messages. Try looking for inconsistencies between your verbal messages and your subsequent actions. Does your partner seem confused or uncertain when interacting with you? If you do spot yourself sending a double message, decide which one you really mean, then state it in unmistakable language. It may also be helpful to consider why you sent contradictory messages.

If you are the recipient of such contradictory messages, it may help to discuss your confusion and ask your partner which one of the two messages she or he would like you to act on. Perhaps your partner will recognize your dilemma and act to resolve it. If she or he seems unwilling to acknowledge the inconsistency, it may help to express your feelings of discomfort and confusion as the recipient of the two conflicting messages.

Nonverbal Sexual Communication

Sexual communication is not confined exclusively to words. Sometimes a touch or smile may convey a great deal of information. Tone of voice, gestures, facial expression, and changes in breathing may also be important elements of the communication process:

I can usually tell when my sweetheart is in the mood for some loving. There is a certain softness about her face and a huskiness that comes into her voice. She touches me more with her hands, and it almost seems like she presents her body as more open and vulnerable. Believe me, there is some truth to all this stuff about body language. She rarely needs to verbalize her desire for sex because I usually get the message. (Authors' files)

Sometimes when I want my lover to touch me in a certain place, I move that portion of my body closer to his hands or just shift my position to make the area more accessible. Occasionally, I will guide his hand with mine to show him just what kind of stimulation I want. (Authors' files)

These examples reveal some of the varieties of nonverbal communication that may have particular significance for our sexuality. In this section, we direct our attention to four important components of nonverbal sexual communication: facial expression, interpersonal distance, touching, and sounds.

Facial Expression

Facial expressions often communicate the feelings a person is experiencing. While there is certainly variation in people's expressions, most of us have learned to identify particular emotions from facial expressions with a high degree of accuracy. The rapport and intimacy between lovers may further increase the reliability of this yardstick.

A look into the faces of our lovers during sexual activity often gives us a quick reading of their level of pleasure. If we see a look of complete rapture, we are likely to continue providing the same type of stimulation. However, if the look conveys something less than ecstasy, we may decide to try something different or perhaps encourage our partners to provide some verbal direction.

Facial expressions can also provide helpful cues when talking over sexual concerns with a partner. If our lover's face reflects anger, anxiety, or some other disruptive emotion, it might be wise to deal with this emotion immediately ("I sense that you are angry with me. Would you like to talk about your feelings?"). Conversely, a face that shows interest, enthusiasm, or appreciation can encourage us to continue expressing a particular feeling or concern. It is also a good idea to be aware of the nonverbal messages you are giving your partner when she or he is sharing thoughts or feelings with you. Sometimes we may inadvertently shut down potentially helpful dialogue by setting our jaw or frowning at an inappropriate time.

Interpersonal Distance

Social psychologists and communication specialists have much to say about personal space. In essence, this idea suggests that each of us tends to maintain differing degrees of interpersonal distance between ourselves and the people we have contact with, depending on the nature of our relationship with them (actual or desired). The intimate space to which we admit close friends and lovers restricts contact much less than the distance we maintain between ourselves and the general public.

It is instructive to watch what takes place between people meeting each other at places like singles bars and parties. Consider the following:

When I meet people I am attracted to, I pay close attention to body language. If they seem uneasy or retreat when I move closer, it is a pretty good indication my interest is not reciprocated. (Authors' files)

When someone attempts to decrease interpersonal distance, it is generally interpreted as a nonverbal sign that she or he is attracted to or desirous of more intimate contact with the other person. A person's withdrawal from another's efforts to establish greater physical closeness is usually interpreted as lack of interest or a gentle kind of rejection.

Lovers, whose interpersonal distance is generally at a minimum, can use these cues to signal desire for intimacy. When your lover moves in close, making his or her body available for your touches or caresses, the message of wanting physical intimacy (not necessarily sex) is quite apparent. Similarly, when he or she curls up on the other side of the bed, it may be a way of saying, "Please don't come too close tonight."

Touching

Touch is a powerful vehicle for nonverbal sexual communication between lovers. Hands can convey special messages. For example, increasing or decreasing the tempo with which a lover's back is kneaded may signal a desire for more or less intense reciprocated stimulation. Reaching out and pulling someone closer can indicate desire and readiness for more intimate contact.

Touch can also defuse anger, heal rifts, and close the gap between temporarily alienated lovers. As one man states:

I have found that a gentle touch, lovingly administered to my partner, does wonders in bringing us back together after we have exchanged angry words. Touching her is my way of reestablishing connection. (Authors' files)

In the early stages of a developing relationship, touch can also be used to express a desire for more intimate involvement.

When I meet a man and find myself attracted to him, I use touch to convey my feelings. Touching him on the arm to emphasize a point or letting my fingers lightly graze across his hand on the table generally lets my feelings be known. (Authors' files)

Touch is a powerful vehicle for nonverbal sexual communication.

Sounds

Many people, though by no means all, like making and hearing sounds during sexual activity. Some individuals find increased breathing, moans, groans, and orgasmic cries to be extremely arousing. Also, such sounds can be helpful indicators of how a partner is responding to lovemaking. Some people find the absence of sounds to be quite frustrating:

My man rarely makes any sounds when we make love. I find this to be very disturbing. In fact, it is a real turn-off. Sometimes I can't even tell if he has come or not. If he wasn't moving, I'd think I was making love to a corpse. (Authors' files)

Some people make a conscious effort to suppress spontaneous noises during sex play. In doing so, they deprive themselves of a potentially powerful and enjoyable form of nonverbal sexual communication. Not uncommonly, their imposed silence also hinders their partners' sexual arousal, as the foregoing example illustrates.

In this section we have acknowledged that not everything has to be spoken between lovers. However, facial expression, interpersonal distance, touching, and sounds cannot convey all of our complex needs and emotions in a close relationship: Words are needed too. One writer observes, "As a supplement to verbal communication, acts and gestures are fine. As a substitute, they don't quite make it" (Zilbergeld, 1978, p. 158).

Impasses

Candid communication between caring, supportive partners often leads to changes that are mutually gratifying. However, even an ample supply of openness, candor, support, and understanding cannot assure a meeting of the minds on all issues: You may reach impasses. Your partner may simply not want to try a new coital position. Or, your suggestion to incorporate a vibrator into shared sex play may be just a bit too threatening. Perhaps the two of you cannot agree on the question of other relationships.

What does one do when communication results in a standoff? Continued discussion may be helpful. However, it is self-deceiving to assume that talk, even the most open and compassionate, will always lead to desired changes.

Sometimes it is useful to try to put yourself in your partner's shoes. Try to see things from the other person's perspective. If you have some difficulty with this, ask your partner for help ("I am having some trouble seeing this from your point of view — can you help me out?"). If you can understand his or her concern, by all means say so. Acknowledging the reasonableness of the other's viewpoint is a process called **validating** (Gottman et al., 1976). Validating does not mean that you give up your own position. You are not saying, "I am wrong and you are right." You are simply admitting that another point of view may make sense, given some assumptions that you may not share with your partner. Sometimes this process of trying to see the validity of another viewpoint may lead to new perspectives that can help end the deadlock. However, if you continue to disagree after this effort, it may be easier to accept the idea that you can both be right.

At a time of impasse, it may also be beneficial for a couple to take a break from each other for a while. Sometimes forced continuation of a discussion, particularly when emotions are strong, is counterproductive. Scheduling another time to talk can be a good tactic. Perhaps in the future, after each has had the opportunity to privately consider the other's feelings, it may be possible to readdress the issue with more tangible results.

Sometimes people cannot or will not change, often for justifiable reasons. Certainly, all of us cherish our right to refuse to do something we consider undesirable. Granting the same right to someone close to us is an important ingredient in a relationship characterized by mutual respect.

Failure to reach a solution to an impasse is not necessarily cause for despair. At least a problem has been brought out into the open, and the couple has discussed a sensitive issue. Possibly, they have also increased their understanding of each other and the level of intimacy between them. In the event that unresolved impasses threaten to erode a relationship, professional counseling may be desirable. (Chapter 17 includes guidelines for selecting a counselor.)

Summary

The Importance of Communication

Sexual communication often contributes positively to the contentment and enjoyment of a sexual relationship; infrequent or ineffective sexual communication is a common reason for people feeling dissatisfied with their sex lives.

An excellent basis for effective sexual communication is mutual empathy — the underlying knowledge that each partner in a relationship cares for the other and knows that care is reciprocated.

Some Reasons Why Sexual Communication Is Difficult

Childhood training, which often creates a sense of discomfort with sexual matters, may contribute to later difficulties in engaging in sexual communication.

Our language is characterized by a conspicuous absence of an effective, comfortable sexual vocabulary.

Some people object to sexual communication on the grounds that it disrupts spontaneity or that it may place one in a position of increased vulnerability to judgment, criticism, or rejection.

Talking: Getting Started

It is often difficult to start talking about sex. Some suggestions for doing this include talking about talking; reading about sex, then discussing the material; and sharing sexual histories.

Listening and Feedback

Communication is most successful with an active listener and an effective communicator.

The listener may facilitate communication by maintaining eye contact with the speaker; providing some feedback, or reaction, to the message; expressing appreciation for communication efforts; maintaining an attitude of unconditional positive regard; and using paraphrasing effectively.

Discovering Your Partner's Needs

Efforts to seek information from sexual partners are often hindered by the use of yes/no questions, which encourage limited replies. Effective alternatives include open-ended queries and either/or questions.

Self-disclosure may make it easier for a partner to communicate her or his own needs. Sharing fantasies, beginning with mild fantasies, may be a particularly valuable kind of exchange.

Comparing notes about sexual needs, preferences, and reactions, either before or after a sexual encounter, may be beneficial.

Giving permission encourages partners to share feelings freely.

Learning to Make Requests

Making requests is facilitated by (a) taking responsibility for one's own pleasure, (b) making sure requests are specific, and (c) using "I" language.

Giving Criticism

Be aware of your motives for criticizing. Criticism that aims to hurt or blame a partner is likely to be destructive.

It is important to select the right time and place for expressing sexual concerns. Avoid registering complaints when anger is at its peak.

Criticism is generally most effective when tempered with praise. People are usually more motivated to make a good thing better than a bad thing good.

It is beneficial to reward each small step in the process of changing undesirable behavior.

"Why" questions have no place in the process of registering constructive criticisms.

It is wise to direct anger toward behavior rather than toward a person's character. Anger is probably best expressed with clear, honest "I" statements, not with accusatory "you" statements.

Relationships are better served when criticisms are limited to one complaint per discussion.

Receiving Criticism

Paraphrasing a partner's criticisms and acknowledging an understanding of the basis for his or her concerns can help establish a sense of empathy and lead to constructive dialogue.

It can be helpful to ask clarifying questions when criticisms are vague and to calmly verbalize the feelings that are aroused when one is criticized.

An excellent closure to receiving criticism is to focus on what can be done to make things better in a relationship.

Saying No

One three-step strategy for saying no to invitations for intimate involvements includes expressing appreciation for the invitation; saying no in a clear, unequivocal fashion; and offering an alternative, if applicable.

To avoid sending mixed messages, occasionally check for inconsistencies between verbal messages and subsequent actions. Recipients of mixed messages might find it helpful to express their confusion and to ask which of the two messages they are expected to act on.

Nonverbal Sexual Communication

Sexual communication is not confined to words alone. Facial expressions, interpersonal distance, touching, and sounds also convey a great deal of information.

The value of nonverbal communication lies primarily in its ability to supplement — not to replace — verbal exchanges.

Impasses

Sexual communication, no matter how candid and compassionate, does not always lead to solutions. Trying to see things from a partner's perspective may be beneficial when deadlocks occur, and it may also be helpful to temporarily suspend the discussion so that each person can privately consider the other's point of view. An unresolved impasse does not necessarily threaten a relationship; if it does, counseling may be desirable.

⤳ *Thought Provokers* ⤳

1. Assume that you are in the early stages of a developing relationship and anticipate making love the next time you are with your new companion. In your opinion, which technique(s) described in this chapter might be most helpful in contributing to satisfying sexual relations? Which suggestion(s) would be the most difficult for you to implement? Explain.

2. Some people think that combining praise with criticism is a manipulative technique, designed to coerce behavior changes by tempering requests with insincere praise. Do you agree with this view? Why or why not?

3. What do you think about sharing sexual fantasies as a way for intimate partners to discover each other's needs?

Suggested Readings

Brenton, Myron (1973). *Sex Talk.* Greenwich, Conn.: Fawcett Publications. This book provides some good ideas for improving sexual communication between partners and between parents and children.

Gottman, John; Notarius, Cliff; Gonso, Jonni; and Markman, Howard (1976). *A Couple's Guide to Communication.* Champaign, Ill.: Research Press. This book, although not focused on sexual communication per se, provides some excellent suggestions for enhancing a couple's communication. Includes such topics as hidden agendas, negotiating agreements, listening, and getting through a crisis.

Langer, Ellen; and Dweck, Carol (1973). *Personal Politics: The Psychology of Making It.* Englewood Cliffs, N.J.: Prentice-Hall. This well-written book contains some valuable strategies for improving interpersonal communication, several of which may be applied directly to the sexual aspects of human relationships.

McKay, Matthew; Davis, Martha; and Fanning, Patrick (1983). *Messages: The Communication Book.* Oakland, Calif.: New Harbinger Publications. This practical, skills-oriented book addresses such topics as sexual communication, conflict resolution, and family communication.

Tannen, Deborah (1990). *You Just Don't Understand: Women and Men in Conversation.* New York: Morrow. (Also available in paperback from Ballantine, 1991.) This highly readable, best-selling book uses vivid examples to outline the distinctly different conversational styles of males and females, the origins of these differing linguistic styles, and how such divergent communication modes lead to difficulties in relationships between the sexes. Throughout this gem of a book, the reader will discover much that will help to improve his or her communication with the other sex.

.. alone I enjoy, with another I enjoy

... (in essence) ... twofold.

William Carlos Williams
The Embodiment of Knowledge (1977)

CHAPTER 9

Sexual Behavior Patterns

Celibacy

Erotic Dreams and Fantasy

Masturbation

Shared Touching

Oral – Genital Stimulation

Anal Stimulation

Coitus and Coital Positions

$\mathcal{P}$eople express their sexuality in many ways. The emotions they attach to sexual behavior also vary widely. In this chapter we define and explain some of the varieties of sexual expression, looking first at individuals and then at couples. We also consider some of the feelings and attitudes people have about these specific behaviors. Celibacy, the first topic we consider, may not commonly be thought of as a form of sexual expression. However, when it represents a conscious decision not to engage in sexual behavior, this decision in itself is an expression of one's sexuality.

Celibacy

A physically mature person who does not engage in sexual behavior is said to be **celibate.** There are two degrees of celibacy. In **complete celibacy** a person neither masturbates nor has sexual contact with another person. In **partial celibacy** he or she engages in masturbation but does not have interpersonal sexual contact.

Celibacy is most commonly thought of in connection with religious devotion: Joining a religious order or becoming a priest or nun often includes a vow of celibacy.

Individuals choose celibacy for a variety of reasons other than religious devotion. What do you think some of these reasons might be? Give some thought to this before reading on.

Many factors may lead a person to be celibate. Health considerations such as concerns about recurring vaginal infections or sexually transmitted diseases may prompt a decision to stop having sexual intercourse. Some people choose to be celibate until marriage because of religious or moral beliefs. Others maintain celibacy until their personal criteria for a good sexual relationship have been met. Some may choose celibacy because they have experienced confusion or disappointment in past sexual relationships, and they want to spend some time establishing new relationships without the complicating factor of sexual interaction. At times a person can be so caught up in other aspects of life that sex is simply not a priority (Laws & Schwartz, 1977).

Celibacy can also be an important aspect of treatment for individuals who are newly recovering from alcohol or drug dependency. Drug and alcohol abusers often use the substance to attempt to decrease their feelings of anxiety, and the anxiety created by involvement in sexual relationships can precipitate a return to drug or alcohol abuse. A period of celibacy affords individuals an opportunity to learn about their sexual feelings and desires without acting on them. Celibacy during recovery also lets people develop the skills to handle the anxiety involved in sexual relationships without turning to alcohol or drugs (Pinhas, 1989).

Some people find that a period of celibacy can be quite rewarding. There is often a refocusing on oneself during such a period: exploring self-pleasuring; learning to value one's aloneness, autonomy, and privacy; or giving priority to work and nonsexual relationship commitments. Friendships may gain new dimensions and fulfillment.

Some people find that celibacy lets them develop closer friendships.

Many people do not choose to be celibate, however, for despite its rewards for some individuals, celibacy also has a number of disadvantages. These can include lack of physical affection and loneliness for sexual intimacy. Coming out of a period of celibacy may be difficult, too, for reestablishing sexual relationships can be awkward and frightening. It is interesting that of the many options for sexual expression, celibacy is one choice that people sometimes have considerable trouble understanding. However, celibacy can be a personally valuable choice.

Erotic Dreams and Fantasy

Some forms of sexual experience occur within a person's mind, with or without accompanying sexual behavior. These are erotic dreams and fantasies — mental experiences that may arise from our imagination or life experience or may be stimulated by books, drawings, or photographs.

Erotic Dreams

Erotic dreams and occasionally orgasm may occur during sleep without a person's conscious direction. Like other dreams, the content of erotic dreams can be logical or quite nonsensical. Explicit sexual expression in dreams varies widely, from common sexual activities to behaviors considered to be taboo. Both erotic dreams and waking fantasy can be ways to express and explore dimensions of experiences, feelings, and desires.

Sexual fantasies can take many forms. This block print shows a young woman fantasizing about her lover while she masturbates.

Almost all the males and two-thirds of the females in Kinsey's research populations reported experiencing erotic dreams. A person may waken during such a dream and notice signs of sexual arousal: erection, vaginal lubrication, or pelvic movements. Orgasm can also occur during sleep and is called **nocturnal orgasm.** When orgasm occurs, males usually notice the ejaculate — hence the term "wet dream." Women also experience orgasm during sleep (Renshaw, 1991), but female orgasm may be more difficult to determine, due to the absence of such a visible sign. In one study of college women, 30% reported having experienced nocturnal orgasm. Another 30% had never heard of nocturnal orgasm. Women who had a higher frequency of intercourse and of orgasm with masturbation were more likely to experience and be aware of orgasms during sleep (Wells, 1983).

Erotic Fantasy

Erotic waking fantasies commonly occur during daydreams, masturbation, or sexual encounters with a partner. In the Kinsey studies, 84% of men and 67% of women reported having had sexual fantasies. A more recent study of college students found that 60% of both men and women reported fantasizing specifically during intercourse (Sue, 1979). Greater sexual experience may contribute to increased sexual fantasizing because college students with more sexual experience report more frequent use of sexual fantasies than do those with less experience, and students with liberal sexual attitudes had longer, more explicit fantasies (Gold & Chick, 1988; Pelletier & Herold, 1988).

The content of sexual fantasies varies greatly and can range from vague, romantic images to graphic representations of imagined or actual past experiences.

Fantasy Content	% Men	% Women
Intercourse with loved one	75	70
Intercourse with strangers	47	21
Sex with more than one person of the other sex	33	18
Sexual activities that would not be done in reality	19	28
Forcing someone to have sex	13	3
Being forced to have sex	10	19
Homosexual activity	7	11

Male and Female Sexual Fantasies During Masturbation   T A B L E 9.1

Source: Hunt, 1974.

Research on fantasy content reveals this diversity, as shown in Tables 9.1 and 9.2. The tables provide an idea of the range of content and suggest some male and female differences, which we discuss later in this section.

Functions of Fantasy. Erotic fantasies serve many functions, some of which are listed in Table 9.3. First, they can be a source of pleasure and arousal. Erotic thoughts typically serve to enhance sexual arousal during masturbation or partner sexual activities. Both male and female college students reported that the most common purpose of their fantasies during intercourse was to facilitate sexual arousal (Sue, 1979). The following two accounts, the first by a woman and the second by a man, show how fantasy can amplify pleasurable physical and emotional feelings:

When my partner and I make love, I let my mind leave all other thoughts behind and totally experience and feel what is happening. All aromas become much more noticeable and pleasurable. The warmth increases, and I imagine my lover and me suspended in mist upon a bed of clouds. Our bodies come close together in my mind as arousal increases, and at the moment of orgasm it is as if we were mentally and physically one. I caress my lover's body, but it is as if it were part of my own. (Authors' files)

The fantasy that recurs most when I am making love is a visualization of being on an isolated tropical beach. The warm sun is baking our bodies golden brown. The rhythmic pounding of the waves eliminates all tension and worries. My partner and I are one. (Authors' files)

Sexual fantasies may also help overcome anxiety and facilitate sexual functioning (Coen, 1978) or compensate for a somewhat negative sexual situation (Knafo & Jaffe, 1984). Fantasies can also be a way to mentally rehearse and anticipate new sexual experiences. Imagining seductive glances, that first kiss, or a novel intercourse position may help a person more comfortably implement these activities.

Some sexual fantasies allow for tolerable expression of "forbidden wishes." The fact that a sexual activity in a fantasy is "forbidden" may make it more excit-

TABLE 9.2   *Male and Female Sexual Fantasies During Intercourse*

Fantasy Content	% Men	% Women
Sex with a former lover	43	41
Sex with an imaginary lover	44	24
Oral–genital sex	61	51
Group sex	19	14
Being forced into a sexual relationship	21	36
Being observed engaging in sexual intercourse	15	20
Being found sexually irresistible by others	55	53
Being rejected or sexually abused	11	13
Forcing others to have sexual relations with you	24	16
Having others give in to you after resisting	37	24
Observing others engaging in sex	18	13
Sex with a member of the same sex	3	9
Sex with animals	1	4

Source: Sue, 1979.

ing. People in sexually exclusive relationships can fantasize about past lovers or others to whom they feel attracted, even though they are committed to a single sexual partner. In a fantasy a person can experience lustful group sex, cross-orientation sexual liaisons, brief sexual encounters with strangers, erotic relations with friends and acquaintances, incestuous experiences, sex with animals, or any other sexual activity they can imagine, without actually engaging in them. The following are examples of the variety of "forbidden wishes" fantasies. A woman's masturbation fantasy:

I fantasize about being seduced by another woman. Although I've never had an affair with another woman, it really makes me sexually excited to think of oral sex being performed on me or vice versa. (Authors' files)

A man's masturbation fantasy reflects one study's findings that one in three men have same-sex fantasies (Ellis et al., 1987):

I usually think of some woman (no one that I know), blond, beautiful, lowering herself onto me, letting me eat her out in a "69." Often times a strong and bearded man is involved and gives me oral stimulation at the same time the woman is kissing me or letting me eat her. (Authors' files)

Another function of erotic fantasy can be to provide relief from gender-role expectations (Pinhas, 1985). In fact, a degree of gender-role deviation in women may contribute to increased fantasizing. One study found that college women with more traditional feminine attitudes report fewer sexual fantasies than women who are more independent and hold more liberal views of women's roles (Brown & Hart, 1977). Women's fantasies of being the sexual aggressor and men's fantasies

Stated Purpose of Fantasies During Intercourse		T A B L E 9.3

Purpose	% Males	% Females
To facilitate sexual arousal	38	46
To imagine activities my partner and I do not engage in	18	13
To increase my partner's attractiveness	30	22
To relieve boredom	3	5
Uncertain	10	15

Source: Sue, 1979.

of being forced to have sex can offer alternatives to stereotypical roles. Three percent of women in Morton Hunt's (1974) study and 16% in David Sue's (1979) study reported fantasizing about forcing others to have sex. For example, a woman college student fantasizes an aggressive and powerful role:

I walk into a male locker room and tell them to drop their shorts. I proceed to suck them off one by one. All the others are watching and panting in anticipation. When I am done with all of them, I take off my clothes, and they all begin to kiss me and touch me very slowly. I get hotter and hotter, and we all end up in a sweaty orgy. (Authors' files)

Ten percent of men in Hunt's study and 21% in Sue's study reported fantasizing about being forced to have sex. In her first book about male sexual fantasy, Nancy Friday reported that one of the major themes is men's abdication of activity in favor of passivity:

> It may seem lusty and dashing always to be the one who chooses the women, who decides when, where, and how the bedroom scene will be played. But isn't her role safer? The man is like someone who has suggested a new restaurant to friends. What if it doesn't live up to expectations he has aroused? The macho stance makes the male the star performer. The hidden cost is that it puts the woman in the role of critic. (1980, p. 274)

Although fantasies of being forced to have sex provide an alternative to gender-role expectations for men, the same type of fantasy typically means something different to women. For women, who often learn to have mixed feelings about being sexual, this type of fantasy offers sexual adventures free from the responsibility and guilt of personal choice.

Male – Female Similarities and Differences

The similarities between men's and women's fantasy lives include the following areas: First, the frequency of fantasy is similar for both sexes during daydreams, masturbation, and sexual activity with a partner (Knafo & Jaffe, 1984). Second, both men and women indicate a wide range of fantasy content, as seen in Tables 9.1 and 9.2. Third, similar percentages of research subjects fantasize while masturbating about having intercourse with a loved one.

What are the differences between male and female fantasies? Take a moment before reading on to speculate on how men's and women's fantasies differ.

One survey of over 300 college students found substantial differences between men's and women's sexual fantasies. Compared to women's, men's fantasies contained more explicit genital images and moved more quickly to sexual acts. Women's fantasies unfolded more slowly with emphasis on emotional feelings and ambience and included more nongenital caressing. Women's fantasy partners were more likely to be someone with whom they had been involved, whereas men's fantasies featured a greater variety of lesser-known women (Ellis & Symons, 1990).

The frequency of fantasies of being forced or forcing someone to have sex differs significantly between males and females. These types of fantasies probably reflect an exaggeration of stereotypical gender roles of the male as active and the female as receptive. Research indicates that almost twice as many women as men fantasize about being forced to have sex. One study found that submission fantasies among women were more common during intercourse than during masturbation or daydreaming (Knafo & Jaffe, 1984). It is important to note, however, that enjoyment of forced sex fantasies does not mean women really want to be raped (Bond & Mosher, 1986; Gold et al., 1991). A woman is in charge of her fantasies, but as a victim of sexual aggression, she is not in control. Other studies have shown that more men than women fantasize about forcing someone to have sex (Hunt, 1974; Sue, 1979).

One study of college undergraduates found that men fantasize more about past experiences and current behavior, while women fantasize more about imaginary experiences. These researchers hypothesize that due to the female script of passivity and acquiescence, women are less able than men to initiate and act out their impulses except in their fantasy lives (McCauley & Swann, 1978).

Fantasies: Help or Hindrance?

Erotic fantasies are generally considered a healthy and helpful aspect of sexuality. Many sex therapists encourage their clients to use sexual fantasy as a source of stimulation to help them increase interest and arousal (Meuwissen & Over, 1991). Sexual fantasies help many women experience arousal and orgasm during intercourse (Davidson & Hoffman, 1986), and a deficit of erotic fantasy is often present with problems of low sexual desire and arousal (Nutter & Condron, 1983). Research has also indicated that people who experience more guilt about sex feel less arousal to sexual fantasies than subjects who do not experience as much guilt about sex (Follingstad & Kimbrell, 1986). Another study found that people who feel less guilt about sexual fantasy during intercourse reported more sexual fantasies and higher levels of sexual satisfaction and functioning than did those who felt more guilt (Cado & Leitenberg, 1990).

Although most of the available research supports erotic imagining as helpful, sexual fantasy has also been considered symptomatic of poor heterosexual relations or other problems (Hollender, 1970; Horney, 1967; Shainess & Greenwald, 1971). Private fantasies during sex with a partner may erode the trust and intimacy in a relationship (Apfelbaum, 1980). Individuals who have experienced sexual abuse as children may use particular sexual fantasies to attempt to master their past trauma, but find that these fantasies actually re-create and reinforce the orig-

MOMMA by Mell Lazarus. Courtesy of Mell Lazarus and News America.

inal abuse. Developing new fantasies based on self-acceptance and loving relationships can be a part of the healing process for these abused individuals (Maltz, 1991). Like most other aspects of sexuality, what determines whether fantasizing is helpful or disturbing to a relationship is its meaning and purpose for the individuals concerned.

Some people may decide to incorporate a particular fantasy into their actual sexual behavior. Acting out a fantasy can be pleasurable; on the other hand, if a fantasy is counter to one's value system or has possible negative consequences, one should consider the advantages and disadvantages of doing so. For some people, fantasies are more exciting when they remain imaginary and are a disappointment in actual practice.

Most people draw a distinct boundary between their fantasy world and the real world. For example, a woman who enjoys fantasizing about having intercourse with her partner's best friend might never really consider doing so. However, some people feel guilty about fantasizing; almost 20% of college men and women felt uneasy or ashamed about their fantasies during intercourse (Sue, 1979). For people who experience guilt over their fantasies, it is important to remember that thoughts and feelings are not the same as actions. As long as people feel able not to act on a fantasy that would hurt themselves or others, they probably do not need to be concerned.

In some cases, fantasy may contribute to a person acting in a way that is harmful to others. This is of particular concern with people who may sexually molest children or sexually assault adults. A person who thinks that he or she is in danger of committing such an act should seek professional psychological assistance. Chapter 21 provides further information about fantasy and sexual offenders.

Masturbation

In this text the word **masturbation** is used to describe self-stimulation of one's genitals for sexual pleasure. *Autoeroticism* is another term used for masturbation. We discuss some perspectives on and purposes of masturbation, patterns of self-stimulation through the life cycle, and specific techniques used in masturbation.

OTHER TIMES, OTHER PLACES

Masturbation: An Historical Opinion

There are various names given to the unnatural and degrading vice of producing venereal excitement by the hand, or other means, generally resulting in a discharge of semen in the male and a corresponding emission in the female.

Symptoms — The following are some of the symptoms of those who are addicted to the habit: . . . becoming timid and bashful, and shunning the society of the opposite sex; the face is apt to be pale and often a bluish or purplish streak under the eyes,

while the eyes themselves look dull and languid and the edges of the eyelids often become red and sore; the person can not look anyone steadily in the face, but will drop the eyes or turn away from your gaze as if guilty of something mean.

The health soon becomes noticeably impaired; there will be general debility, a slowness of growth, weakness in the lower limbs, nervousness and unsteadiness of the hands, loss of memory, and inability to study or learn, restless disposition, weak eyes

and loss of sight, headache and inability to sleep or wakefulness. Next come sore eyes, blindness, stupidity, consumption, spinal affection, emaciation, involuntary seminal emissions, loss of all energy or spirit, insanity and idiocy — the hopeless ruin of both body and mind.

Source: *Vitalogy,* described as an "encyclopedia of health and home" (Wood & Ruddock, 1918, p. 812).

Perspectives on Masturbation

Masturbation has been a source of social concern and censure throughout Judeo – Christian history. This state of affairs has resulted in both misinformation and considerable personal shame and fear. Many of the negative attitudes toward masturbation are rooted in the early Judeo – Christian view that procreation was the only legitimate purpose of sexual behavior. Because masturbation obviously could not result in conception, it was condemned. The "evils" of masturbation received a great deal of publicity in the name of science during the mid-eighteenth century, due largely to the writings of a European physician named Tissot. He wrote vividly about the mind- and body-damaging effects of "self-abuse." Tissot believed that semen was made from blood and that the loss of semen was debilitating to health. This view of masturbation influenced social and medical attitudes in Europe and the United States (Money et al., 1991).

In the 1800s sexual abstinence, simple foods, and fitness were lauded as crucial to health. The Reverend Sylvester Graham, who promoted the use of whole-grain flours and whose name is still attached to Graham crackers, wrote *A Lecture to Young Men.* He proclaimed that ejaculation reduced precious, health-preserving "vital fluids" and beseeched men to abstain from masturbation and even marital intercourse to avoid moral and physical degeneracy. John Harvey Kellogg, M.D., carried Graham's work further and developed the corn flake to help prevent masturbation and sexual desire (Money, 1983). False beliefs about masturbation, fostered by medical authorities and popular writings well into this century, may be one reason earlier generations of men in Kinsey's study reported less masturbation and more concern about it than did later generations (Downey, 1980).

Freud and most other early psychoanalysts recognized that masturbation does not harm physical health, and they saw it as normal during childhood. However, they believed that masturbation in adulthood could result in "immature" sexual development and in the inability to form good sexual relationships. Current

"Now they tell us masturbation is harmless!"

research indicates that masturbation does not prevent people from developing positive social and sexual relationships. In a national sample of male and female college students, a greater frequency of dating, kissing, breast and genital touching, and intercourse was found to correlate with a higher likelihood and increased frequency of masturbation (Atwood, 1981).

Contemporary views reflect conflicting beliefs about masturbation, and much of the traditional condemnation still exists. In 1976 the Vatican issued a "Declaration on Certain Questions Concerning Sexual Ethics," which described masturbation as an "intrinsically and seriously disordered act." On the other hand, many writers today view masturbation as a healthy and positive aspect of sexuality. For example, Betty Dodson, author of *Liberating Masturbation*, writes:

> Masturbation, of course, is our first natural sexual activity. It's the way we discover our eroticism, the way we learn to respond sexually, the way we learn to love ourselves and build self-esteem. Sexual skill and the ability to respond are not "natural" in our society. Doing what "comes naturally" for us is to be sexually inhibited. Sex is like any other skill — it has to be learned and practiced. (1974, p. 13)

Purposes of Masturbation

People masturbate for a variety of reasons, not the least of which is the pleasure of arousal and orgasm. In one study (Clifford, 1978), college women reported that

This Victorian device was one of several such devices used to "protect" boys from the temptation of masturbation.

experiencing pleasurable sensations and physical release of sexual tension were their primary motives for masturbation. At certain times the satisfaction from an autoerotic session may be more rewarding than an interpersonal sexual encounter, as the following quote illustrates:

I had always assumed that masturbation was a second-best sexual expression. One time, after reflecting back on the previous day's activities of a really enjoyable morning masturbatory experience and an unsatisfying experience that evening with a partner, I realized that first- and second-rate was very relative. (Authors' files)

Furthermore, some people find that the independent sexual release available through masturbation can help them make better decisions about relating sexually with other people. Within a relationship, too, masturbation can help even out the effects of dissimilar sexual interest. Masturbation can be a shared experience:

When I am feeling sexual and my partner is not, he holds me and kisses me while I masturbate. Also, sometimes after making love I like to touch myself while he embraces me. It is so much better than sneaking off to the bathroom alone. (Authors' files)

In addition, some people find masturbation to be valuable as a means of self-exploration. Sex educator Eleanor Hamilton recommends masturbation to adolescents as a way to release tension and to become "pleasantly at home with your own sexual organs" (1978, p. 33). Indeed, people can learn a great deal about their sexual responses from masturbation. Self-stimulation is often helpful for women learning to experience orgasms and for men experimenting with their response patterns to increase ejaculatory control. (Masturbation as a tool for increasing sexual satisfaction is discussed in Chapter 17.) Finally, some people find that masturbation helps them get to sleep at night, for the same generalized feelings of relaxation that often follow a sexual encounter can also accompany self-pleasuring.

Although masturbation is a widely existing practice that is being recognized more and more as a normal activity, guilt about it is still common:

Every time before I would masturbate, I would pray and say "I promise, God, this will be the last time." (Authors' files)

Most people have masturbated, but many people feel uncomfortable about it. It is also possible to feel uneasy about *not* having masturbated:

I was with a group of friends who started talking and joking about masturbation. I knew what they were talking about, but I had never done it. I didn't want to say so, though. (Authors' files)

Most people who masturbate probably view the behavior with a mix of pleasure and a socialized sense of uneasiness or guilt.

A common concern about masturbation is "doing it too much." Even in writings where masturbation is said to be "normal," masturbating "to excess" is often presented as unhealthy. A definition of excess rarely follows. If a person were masturbating so much that it significantly interfered with any aspect of his or her life, there might be cause for concern. However, in that case masturbation would be a symptom or manifestation of some underlying problem rather than the problem itself. For example, someone who is experiencing intense emotional anxiety may use masturbation as an attempt to relieve anxiety or as a form of self-comforting. The problem here is the intense emotional anxiety — not the masturbation.

Masturbation Through the Life Cycle

Masturbation often continues as part of a person's sexual expression throughout her or his life. It is normal for infants to touch their genitals and respond pleasurably to self-stimulation. Parents may express direct disapproval by a look, a slap, or moving the child's hands away. Some clinicians speculate that severe interruption of an infant's self-pleasuring activities can have serious consequences in adult sexual expression and can be the basis for compulsive and other atypical sexual behaviors, which are described further in Chapter 20 (McDougall, 1986).

In some cases parents who discover their young children masturbating punish or chastise them severely. One woman reports:

When I was about eight years old, my mother caught me masturbating in bed. She told me that I was a very bad girl and made me sleep in the hallway that night. The next weekend we had our aunt and uncle over for supper, and she told everyone at the dinner table what I had done. (Authors' files)

Even children who experience no direct disapproval from their parents or others will usually learn quickly that masturbation must be done in secret and kept private, as reflected by the following comment:

I didn't even know there was a word to describe what I was doing when I touched myself. I don't even remember being told not to, but somehow I knew I had to be very careful not to be caught. (Authors' files)

Few children receive permission for or information about self-stimulation from their parents. The perception that masturbation must be kept secret can produce feelings of guilt and shame and make it difficult for a child to ask clarifying and potentially useful questions about masturbation. Moreover, even if children do ask questions, many parents may not be supportive resources because of their own confusion and negative feelings about masturbation.

What differences in masturbation patterns between boys and girls do you think emerge beginning in adolescence? Come up with your own ideas before reading on to see what the research in this area indicates.

During adolescence, the number of boys who masturbate increases dramatically. Kinsey's figures estimated that only 21% of 12-year-old boys masturbated, compared with 82% of 15-year-old boys (1948). Corresponding statistics for girls were much lower: an initial 12% at 12 years of age, increasing to only 20% by the age of 15 (1953). More recent statistics have higher percentages for both boys and girls, but there is still a wide discrepancy between the sexes; more than twice as many high school and college men than women masturbate (Atwood & Gagnon, 1987; Hunt, 1974).

The reasons masturbation is more common among males are unknown. One factor may be that young boys are taught to hold their penises during toilet training, thus receiving some degree of encouragement to touch themselves. Adolescent males also typically begin masturbation at an earlier age and masturbate more frequently. Girls, however, learn to use toilet tissue to wipe their genitals, which may make it less likely for them to discover the pleasurable sensations that can come from self-touching.

During adolescence, the social expectations for gender-role stereotyped behavior often become stronger and more rigid, and these stereotypes may also contribute to lower masturbation rates among females. Masturbation is a direct statement of desire for one's own sexual pleasure and orgasm; it does not conform to gender-role stereotypes in which males obtain sexual satisfaction and females provide it. The lower percentage of adolescent girls who masturbate may also reflect the idea that "good girls" are not sexual. In other words, masturbation does not fit into the expectations that females often learn to have about sex. In contrast, the value of sex for pleasure and release of sexual tension meshes better with stereotypical male attitudes about sexuality. Adolescent males are probably more likely to experience peer support for masturbation, and it is not uncommon for boys to show each other how to masturbate. For females, however, the situation is often quite different; some women in Kinsey's study masturbated for the first time only after their male partners manually stimulated them. Another study also found that approximately 20% of women learned to masturbate by copying their partners' petting techniques (Clifford, 1978). These sex differences in masturbation behavior extend into young adulthood: college-age men are more likely to masturbate and do so more often than college-age women (Atwood, 1981).

How do you think masturbation patterns change in adulthood, especially following marriage? Is masturbation a form of childhood sexual expression that stops once people are grown? Consider these questions before reading on.

In adulthood, the majority of men and women, both married and unmarried, masturbate on occasion. Women tend to masturbate more after they reach their twenties than they did in their teens. Kinsey hypothesized that this was due to increased erotic responsiveness, opportunities for learning about the possibility of self-stimulation through sex play with a partner, and a reduction in sexual inhibitions.

It is common for people to continue masturbation when married. Hunt's 1974 survey reported that 72% of young husbands and 68% of young wives (in their twenties and early thirties) masturbated, on the average, twice and once a month, respectively. However, masturbation is often considered inappropriate when a person has a sexual partner. Some people believe that they should not engage in a sexual activity that excludes their partners or that experiencing sexual pleasure by masturbation deprives their partners of pleasure. Others mistakenly interpret their partners' desire to masturbate as a sign that there is something wrong with their relationship. But unless it interferes with mutually enjoyable sexual intimacy in the relationship, masturbation can be considered a normal part of each partner's sexual repertoire. Moreover, one study found that married women who masturbated to orgasm had greater marital and sexual satisfaction than women who did not masturbate (Hurlbert & Whittaker, 1991).

During the adult years, people who are not in a sexual relationship may use masturbation as a primary sexual outlet. Masturbation may be particularly valuable to older people as a way of continuing sexual expression when illness, absence, death, or divorce deprive them of a partner.

Self-Pleasuring Techniques

This section offers descriptions of self-pleasuring techniques. Self-exploration exercises can help a person become more aware of genital and whole-body sensations: readers who would like to experiment with some or all of the steps are invited to do so. It is not unusual for someone first trying self-pleasuring to feel anxious. If this happens to you, two suggestions may be helpful. First, focus for a minute on physical relaxation: take a few slow breaths, extending your belly outward as you inhale. Another way to relax yourself is to tense a body part, like an arm and hand, for a few seconds, then release the tension. Second, try to clear your mind of thoughts related to the "rightness" or "wrongness" of self-pleasuring and allow yourself to concentrate instead on the positive physical sensations that can come from self-stimulation. Because the genitals are only one part of the body, we suggest involving your entire anatomy in the self-exam, to explore your sensuality as well as specific structures. Both men and women often report that their sexual feelings are enhanced by learning to be less genitally focused and more in touch with the sensual potentials that exist throughout their bodies.

Set aside a block of time (at least one hour for the entire exercise) when you will have privacy. Allow several minutes for your mind to quiet down from the noisy clatter of the day. A good way to begin is with a relaxing bath or shower. You can start the self-exploration while bathing, washing with soapy hands in an unhurried manner. Towel off leisurely and then explore all areas of your body with your fingertips, gently touching and stroking the skin of your face, arms, legs, stomach, and feet.

As you are touching yourself, focus on the various textures and shapes. Compare the sensations when you have your eyes open and closed. You may wish to experiment with using a body lotion, oil, or powder. After gentle stroking, try firmer, massaging pressures, paying extra attention to areas that are tense. You might like to allow yourself some pleasurable fantasies during this time. Notice whether your breathing is relaxed; let it be deep and slow. When you have completed this part, notice how you feel.

For the next step, we recommend that you return to the genital self-examination exercises in Chapters 4 and 5. Once you have completed the exploration, continue experimenting with various kinds of pressure and stroking. Pay attention to what feels good. The following paragraphs offer descriptions of ways of touching that some people use during masturbation.

Specific techniques for masturbation vary. Males commonly grasp the penile shaft with one hand, as shown in Figure 9.1. Up-and-down motions of differing pressures and tempos provide stimulation. A man may also stroke the glans and frenum or caress or tug the scrotum. Or, rather than using his hands, he may rub his penis against a mattress or pillow.

Women enjoy a variety of stimulation techniques. Typically, the hand provides circular, back-and-forth, or up-and-down movements against the mons and clitoral area (see Figure 9.2). The glans of the clitoris is rarely stimulated directly, though it may be stimulated indirectly when covered by the hood. Some women thrust the clitoral area against an object such as bedding or a pillow. Others masturbate by pressing the thighs together and tensing the pelvic floor muscles that

FIGURE 9.1

Male masturbation.

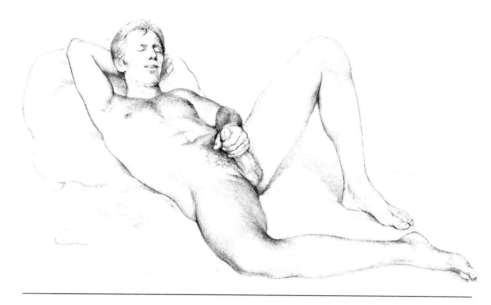

FIGURE 9.2

Female masturbation.

underlie the vulva. Contrary to what is often portrayed in pornography, few women use vaginal insertion to reach orgasm during masturbation. Only 1.5% of women in Shere Hite's survey (1976) used vaginal insertion of a finger or penis-

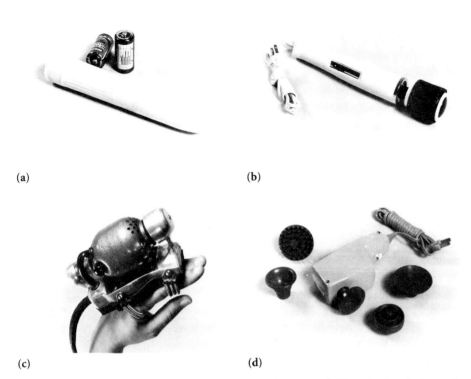

(a)

(b)

(c)

(d)

F I G U R E 9.3

Four types of vibrators: (a) phallic-shaped with batteries, (b) wand-shaped, (c) hand-strapped, and (d) hand-held with attachments.

shaped object; over half of this small group had also used clitoral stimulation prior to insertion.

Individuals and couples also use vibrators for added enjoyment or variation. Although some men enjoy using a vibrator on their genitals, women tend to be greater enthusiasts of such devices. If you want to use a vibrator for sexual plea-sure, experimentation is in order—both with the type of vibrator and with how it is used. By placing the vibrator on different areas of your body or genitals, you can find what is particularly arousing for you. Moving the pelvis or the vibrator may enhance your enjoyment.

Several different types of vibrators are available (see Figure 9.3), and people's preferences vary.* The penis-shaped, battery-operated ones usually provide less intense vibrations than do the others. These vibrators do not require an electrical outlet and are also the least expensive. Electric vibrators should never be used in or around water, as lethal electrical shock may result. Two basic kinds of *hand-held* vibrators are the wand-shaped and the multiple-attachment types. *Hand-strapped* vibrators—another option—attach to the back of the hand, causing the fingers to vibrate. The vibrations transmitted in this way are generally less intense than with hand-held vibrators, and some people prefer this. However, the hand with the vibrator attached to it may become numb or uncomfortable. Detachable, hand-held pulsating shower heads are another alternative. Some women have long known that a stream of water coursing over their genitals can be very arousing.

Although masturbating is valuable for many people in varied situations, not everyone wants to do it. Sometimes, in our attempts to help people who would

*An excellent book on vibrators is *Good Vibrations* by Joani Blank (Burlingame, Calif.: Down There Press, 1976).

like to eradicate their negative feelings about self-stimulation, it may sound as if the message is that people *should* masturbate. This is not the case. Masturbation is an option for sexual expression — not a mandate.

Up to this point in the chapter, we have been looking at ways that people express themselves sexually as individuals. However, many of the sexual behaviors with which we are concerned take place as interactions between people. In the sections that follow, we discuss some of the more common forms of shared sexual behavior. The sequence in which they are presented does not mean that such a progression is "best" in a particular sexual relationship or encounter; for example, a heterosexual couple may desire oral–genital stimulation *after* coitus rather than before. Nor is any one of these activities necessary in a given relationship or encounter: complete sexual experience may consist of any or all of them. The discussions of shared sexual activities, with the exception of coitus, are directed toward all individuals, regardless of their sexual orientation.

Although the following sections include discussions of sexual techniques, a specific technique cannot stand on its own; it must exist or be used in the context of the relationship as a whole. Feelings, desires, and attitudes strongly influence choices about sexual activity. Sensitivity to your and your partner's sexual needs will help develop shared pleasure and arousal more effectively than any specific technique. Mutual consent is an important aspect of a sexual relationship, and sexual activities that both partners are willing to engage in are more likely to provide a couple with enjoyable sexual experiences.

There may be some male–female differences to consider in regard to feelings about various sexual activities. A research study asked college students about their preferences regarding "foreplay," coitus, and "afterplay" and found that males were more likely to say they preferred coitus and females that they preferred foreplay and afterplay (none of the males said afterplay). Furthermore, females wanted to spend more time in foreplay and afterplay than did males (Denny et al., 1984). There is, of course, great individual variation in such preferences. Open communication can greatly help couples establish their unique and changing attitudes and desires.

Shared Touching

i like my body when it is with your
body. It is so quite new a thing.
Muscles better and nerves more.
i like your body. i like what it does,
i like its hows. i like to feel the spine
of your body and its bones, and the trembling
-firm-smooth ness and which i will
again and again and again

kiss, i like kissing this and that of you,
i like, slowly stroking the, shocking fuzz
of your electric fur, and what-is-it comes
over parting flesh. . . . And eyes big love-crumbs,

and possibly i like the thrill

of under me you so quite new*

---

*Reprinted from *Tulips & Chimneys* by e. e. cummings, by permission of Liveright Publishing Corporation and HarperCollins Publisher. Copyright 1923, 1925 and renewed 1951, 1953 by e. e. cummings. Copyright © 1973, 1976 by the Trustees for e. e. cummings Trust. Copyright © 1973, 1976 by George James Firmage.

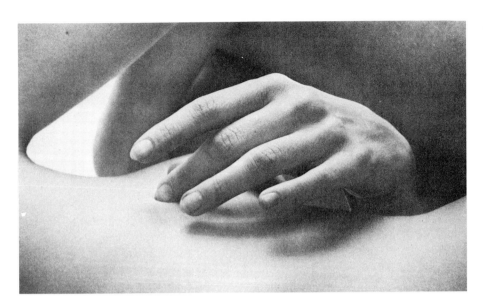

Sensual touching can be pleasurable to both the giver and the receiver.

Touch is one of the first and most important senses that we experience when we emerge into this world. Infants who have been fed but deprived of this basic stimulation have died for lack of it. A classic animal study showed that when baby monkeys' and other primates' physical needs were met but they were denied their mothers' touch, they grew up to be extremely maladjusted (Harlow, 1959). Touch forms the cornerstone of human sexuality shared with another. In Masters and Johnson's evaluation:

> Touch is an end in itself. It is a primary form of communication, a silent voice that avoids the pitfall of words while expressing the feelings of the moment. It bridges the physical separateness from which no human being is spared, literally establishing a sense of solidarity between two individuals. Touching is sensual pleasure, exploring the textures of skin, the suppleness of muscle, the contours of the body, with no further goal than enjoyment of tactile perceptions. (1976, p. 253)

Touch does not need to be directed to an erogenous area of the body to be sexual. The entire body surface is a sensory organ, and touching—almost anywhere—can enhance intimacy and sexual arousal. It is important to remember that different people may like different kinds of touching: it is therefore helpful for couples to openly discuss their preferences.

The entire body responds to touching, but some specific areas are, of course, more receptive to sexual feelings than others. Preferences vary from one person to another. Many men and women report breast stimulation (especially of the nipple) to be arousing. Others find it unenjoyable or unpleasant. A few women reach orgasm from breast stimulation alone (Masters & Johnson, 1966). The size of the breasts is not related to how erotically sensitive they are. Some women's breasts become more sensitive, even tender, during certain times of their menstrual cycles. A woman may find that a firm touch that is highly arousing one week feels uncomfortable and harsh the next. Once again, ongoing communication between partners is important.

Genital stimulation is often highly pleasurable to women and men. Many people's first experience with manual–genital stimulation comes from masturbation, and this self-knowledge can form the basis of further learning with a partner. People who have not previously masturbated can explore and learn what is enjoyable with each other. One partner can touch the other, or they can explore each other's sensations simultaneously. Manual stimulation can provide pleasure or orgasm by itself, or it can be a prelude to other activities.

Manual Stimulation of the Female Genitals

The vulval tissues are delicate and sensitive. If there is not enough lubrication to make the vulva slippery, it can become easily irritated. A lubricant such as K-Y jelly, a lotion without alcohol or perfume, or saliva can be used to moisten the fingers and vulva.

There is great variation from one woman to another in the kind of genital touches that induce arousal. Even the same woman may vary in her preference from one moment to the next. Women may prefer gentle or firm movements on different areas of the vulva. Direct stimulation of the clitoris is uncomfortable for some women; touches above or along the sides may be preferable. Insertion of a finger into the vagina may enhance arousal. Anal stimulation is erotic to some women but not to others. It is important not to touch the vulva or vagina with the same finger used for anal stimulation because bacteria that are normal in the rectum can cause infections if introduced into the vagina.

Manual Stimulation of the Male Genitals

Men also have individual preferences for manual stimulation and, as with women, may desire a firmer or softer touch — and faster or slower strokes — as their arousal increases. Gentle or firm stroking of the penile shaft and glans and light touches or tugging on the scrotum may be desired. Some men experience uncomfortable sensitivity of the penile glans when it is touched immediately following orgasm. Some men find that lubrication with a lotion or saliva increases pleasure. (With heterosexual couples, if intercourse might follow, the lotion should be non-irritating to the woman's genital tissues.) Some men also enjoy manual stimulation or penetration of the anus.

Oral – Genital Stimulation[*]

Both the mouth and genitals are primary biological erogenous zones, areas of the body generously endowed with sensory nerve endings. Therefore, couples who are psychologically comfortable with oral – genital stimulation often find both giving and receiving it to be highly pleasurable. Oral – genital contact can produce pleasure, arousal, or orgasm. As one woman states:

At first, I was very uncomfortable with the idea of oral sex. After some explanations and some showing by my partner, I realized that maybe this wasn't so bad after all. In fact, for the first time in my life, I reached orgasm. (Authors' files)

---

[*] Because oral – genital contact often involves an exchange of bodily fluids, there is a risk of transmitting or contracting the virus that causes AIDS. This virus can enter the bloodstream through small breaks in the skin of the mouth or genitals. Although the risk of transmitting the AIDS virus through oral – genital contact is thought to be relatively low, only monogamous partners who are both free from the AIDS virus are completely free from risk when engaging in such activities. (See Chapter 19 for a further discussion of precautions against transmitting the AIDS virus.)

Simultaneous oral – genital stimulation in the "69" position.

Oral – genital stimulation can be done individually (by one partner to the other) or simultaneously. Some people prefer oral sex individually because they can focus on either giving or receiving. Others especially enjoy the mutuality of simultaneous oral – genital sex. Simultaneous stimulation is sometimes referred to as "69" because of the body positions suggested by that number (Figure 9.4). Besides the one illustrated, a variety of positions can be used; lying side by side and using a thigh for a pillow is another option. As arousal becomes intense during mutual oral – genital stimulation, partners need to be careful not to suck or bite too hard.

Different terminology is used to describe oral – genital stimulation of women and oral – genital stimulation of men. **Cunnilingus** (kun-i-LIN-gus) is oral stimulation of the vulva — the clitoris, labia minora, vestibule, and vaginal opening. Many women find the warmth, softness, and moistness of the partner's lips and tongue to be highly pleasurable and effective in producing sexual arousal or orgasm. Variations of stimulation include rapid or slow circular or back-and-forth tongue movement on the clitoral area, sucking the clitoris or labia minora, and thrusting the tongue into the vaginal opening. Some women are especially aroused by simultaneous manual stimulation of the vagina and oral stimulation of the clitoral area.

Fellatio (fel-Ā-shē-ō) is oral stimulation of the penis and scrotum. Both of Kinsey's studies found that, among heterosexual couples, women were less likely to stimulate their partners orally than the reverse. Options for oral stimulation of the male genitals include gently or vigorously licking and sucking the glans, the frenum, and the penile shaft; and licking or enclosing a testicle in the mouth. Some men enjoy combined oral stimulation of the glans and manual stroking of the penile shaft, testicles, or anus.

It is usually best for the partner performing fellatio to control the other's movements by grasping the penis manually below her or his lips to prevent it from going further into the mouth than is comfortable. This helps avoid a gagging reflex. Also, too vigorous thrusting could result in lacerations of the partner's lips as he or she attempts to protect the penis from his or her teeth.

Couples differ in their preference for including ejaculation into the mouth as a part of male oral – genital stimulation. Many find it acceptable, and some find it exciting; others do not. An occasional couple avoids fellatio entirely because they want to avoid ejaculation into the partner's mouth. However, a couple can agree beforehand that the one who is being stimulated will indicate when he is close to orgasm and withdraw from his partner's mouth. For couples who are comfortable with ejaculating into the mouth, the ejaculate can be swallowed or not according to one's preference.

Some people have psychological and/or moral qualms about oral–genital stimulation. As we have seen, sexual behaviors that do not have the potential of resulting in a pregnancy within marriage have historically been labeled immoral, and many people therefore believe that oral sex is wrong. Moreover, this belief has often been institutionalized into law, and sexual behaviors other than coitus are still illegal in many states, as described in the box "The Law and Sexual Behaviors."

Other qualms arise from the belief that oral–genital stimulation is unsanitary or that the genitals are unattractive. It may be difficult for someone who has a negative image of his penis or her vulva to feel comfortable receiving oral stimulation. Many people also think that the genitals are "dirty" because they are close to the urinary opening and the anus. However, routine thorough washing of the genitals with soap and water is adequate for cleanliness.

Other reasons some people object to oral sex stem from the belief that it is a homosexual act — even when experienced by heterosexual couples. Although many homosexual people do engage in oral sex, the activity is not homosexual by nature. Rather, its homosexuality or heterosexuality depends on the sexes of the partners involved.

Given some of the concerns people may have about oral sex, how common a practice do you think it is?

Despite these negative attitudes, oral–genital contact is quite common and has become even more so in recent years (Gagnon & Simon, 1987). Moreover, it seems to have gained acceptance through a larger cross section of educational levels. Kinsey's research in the late 1940s and early 1950s revealed that 60% of college-educated couples, 20% of high school–educated couples, and 10% of grade school–educated couples had experienced oral–genital stimulation as part of their marital sex. Hunt's 1974 investigations indicated that by the 1970s, 90% of married couples under 25 years of age — regardless of educational level — had experienced oral–genital sex. Although it is likely that these different figures reflect a degree of sample bias (see Chapter 2), it also seems probable that oral–genital contact is gaining more widespread acceptance and practice. A study of 203 Canadian college women found that 61% had experienced fellatio and 68% had experienced cunnilingus. Of those who had experienced fellatio, 97% had also experienced cunnilingus (Herold & Way, 1983). Surveys from our most recent classes reveal that approximately 86% of women and 80% of men have experienced both fellatio and cunnilingus.

Anal Stimulation

Like oral–genital stimulation, anal stimulation may be thought by some to be a homosexual act. However, penile penetration of the anus is practiced regularly by about 10% of heterosexual couples* (Voeller, 1991). The anus has dense supplies

---

*There are some important health risks to consider in connection with anal intercourse (Agnew, 1986). Anal intercourse is one of the riskiest of all sexual behaviors associated with transmission of the AIDS virus, particularly for the receptive partner. (For women, the risk of contracting the AIDS virus through unprotected anal intercourse is greater than the risk of contraction through unprotected vaginal intercourse [Voeller, 1991].) Both heterosexual and homosexual people who wish to reduce their risk of transmitting or contracting this deadly virus should refrain from anal intercourse or use a condom and practice withdrawal prior to ejaculation. (Precautions against transmission of the AIDS virus are discussed more fully in Chapter 19.)

ETHICAL/LEGAL ISSUES IN HUMAN SEXUALITY

The Law and Sexual Behaviors

Many of the laws concerning specific sexual behaviors of consenting adults in private are derived from the Judeo–Christian ethic that viewed procreation as the only justification for sex. In this view, any sexual act that did not provide the possibility of conception was sinful. In the past, immorality was codified into laws that defined many nonprocreative behaviors as criminal, and many of these laws are still in effect. Although definitions are often vague and vary from state to state, oral–genital intercourse and anal intercourse are categorized as sodomy. In the 24 states where such laws still exist, it is important to note that they usually pertain to all adults — married, non-married, heterosexual, and homosexual. Often the penalties for these "crimes" (described in many statutes as "crimes against nature") are very severe. The maximum jail sentence for sodomy is 20 years in Georgia and Rhode Island and 10 years in several other states (Press et al., 1986).

In 1986, a heavily disputed U.S. Supreme Court decision upheld states' rights to have sodomy laws and to impose penalties, stating that "the proposition that any kind of private sexual conduct between consenting adults is constitutionally insulated from state proscription is insupportable" (*Hardwick* v. *Bowers*, 106 S.Ct. 2841). In his dissenting opinion, Justice Harry Blackmun emphasized the right to privacy and stated, "What the court really has refused to recognize is the fundamental interest all individuals have in controlling the nature of their intimate associations" (Hardwick v. Bowers, 106 S.Ct. 2841). Blackmun's views appear to be supported by the majority of the population. A Gallup Poll found that 57% of those surveyed thought that states should not prohibit private sexual practices between consenting adult homosexual individuals, and 74% took the same position regarding heterosexual activity (Alpern, 1986). As of 1992, 27 states allow sodomy between consenting adults — but the 23 others still have sodomy laws on the books (see the tables).

Samples of States' Penalties for Sodomy

States with Sodomy Laws	Maximum Jail Sentences for Sodomy	States with Sodomy Laws	Maximum Jail Sentences for Sodomy
Alabama	1 year	Missouri	1 year
Arizona	30 days	Montana	10 years*
Arkansas	1 year*	Nevada	6 years*
Florida	60 days	North Carolina	10 years
Georgia	20 years	Oklahoma	10 years
Idaho	5-year minimum	Rhode Island	20 years
Kansas	6 months*	South Carolina	5 years
Louisiana	5 years	Utah	6 months
Maryland	10 years	Virginia	5 years
Minnesota	1 year	Washington, D.C.	10 years
Mississippi	10 years		

*For homosexual sodomy only.
Source: National Gay and Lesbian Task Force.

States with Consenting Adult Laws

Alaska	New Mexico
California	New York
Colorado	North Dakota
Connecticut	Ohio
Delaware	Oregon
Hawaii	Pennsylvania
Illinois	South Dakota
Indiana	Texas
Iowa	Vermont
Maine	Washington
Massachusetts	West Virginia
Nebraska	Wisconsin
New Hampshire	Wyoming
New Jersey	

Source: National Gay and Lesbian Task Force.

of nerve endings that can respond erotically. Some women report orgasmic response from anal intercourse (Masters & Johnson, 1970), and heterosexual and homosexual men often experience orgasm from stimulation during penetration.

Individuals or couples may also use anal stimulation for arousal and variety during other sexual activities. Manually stroking the outside of the anal opening or inserting one or more fingers into the anus can be very pleasurable for some people during masturbation or partner sex. Hunt's (1974) survey reported that various forms of anal stimulation had been used, at least experimentally, by many of his respondents. Approximately 25% of married couples under age 35 reported that they used anal intercourse occasionally. A more recent study found that one in 10 heterosexual couples engaged in anal intercourse regularly (Voeller, 1991).

Besides the sphincter muscle, the anus is composed of delicate tissues, and some special care needs to be taken in anal stimulation. A nonirritating lubricant and gentle penetration are necessary to avoid discomfort or injury. It is helpful to use lubrication on both the anus and the penis or object being inserted. The partner receiving anal insertion can bear down (as for a bowel movement) to relax the sphincter. The partner inserting needs to go slowly and gently, keeping the penis or object tilted to follow the direction of the colon (Morin, 1981).

Heterosexual couples should never have vaginal intercourse directly following anal intercourse because bacteria that are normal in the anus often cause vaginal infections. To prevent vaginal infections from this source, a couple should have vaginal intercourse before anal intercourse, or they should use a condom during anal intercourse and wash the man's genitals thoroughly with soap and water before moving on to penile–vaginal or penile–oral contact. Oral stimulation of the anus is very risky; various intestinal infections, hepatitis, and sexually transmitted diseases can be contracted or spread through oral–anal contact.

Coitus and Coital Positions

There is a wide range of positions a couple may choose for penile–vaginal intercourse, or coitus.* Many people may have a favored position, yet enjoy others as shown in Figures 9.5–9.8. A 30-year-old man states:

Different intercourse positions usually express and evoke particular emotions for me. Being on top, I enjoy feeling aggressive; when on the bottom, I experience a special kind of receptive sensuality. In the side-by-side position, I easily feel gentle and intimate. I like sharing all these dimensions of myself with my lover. (Authors' files)

Each position provides varying opportunities for physical and emotional expression. The desirability of a particular position may change with one's mood at the moment. Alterations in health, age, weight, pregnancy, or partners may create different preferences. In some positions, one person will have greater freedom to initiate and control the tempo, angle, and style of movement to create

*Of course, a likely result of coitus is pregnancy: the subject of contraception is addressed in Chapter 11. Another possible result of genital–genital contact is the transmission of a wide range of sexually transmitted diseases, including AIDS; these are discussed fully in Chapter 19.

FIGURE 9.5

Man-above, face-to-face intercourse position.

FIGURE 9.6

Two variations of the woman-above intercourse position.

FIGURE 9.7

Face-to-face, side-lying
intercourse position.

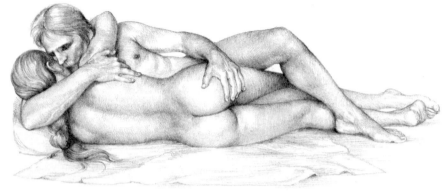

FIGURE 9.8

Rear-entry intercourse
position, with pregnant
woman simultaneously
stimulating herself manually.

arousing stimulation. In others, mutual control of the rhythm of thrusting works well. Some positions lend themselves to manual stimulation of the clitoris during intercourse, such as the woman above, sitting upright. Many couples like a position where they can have eye contact and look at each other's bodies. The face-to-face, side-lying intercourse position can provide a particularly relaxed connection, with each partner having one hand free to caress the other's body. Rear entry can be a good position during pregnancy when pressure against the woman's abdomen is uncomfortable.

Beyond options for position, cooperation and consideration are important, particularly at **intromission** (entry of the penis into the vagina). Often the woman can best guide her partner's penis into her vagina by moving her body or using her hand. If the penis slips out of the vagina, which can occur fairly easily in some positions, a helping hand will most likely be welcome. Furthermore, both non-verbal and verbal communication about preferences of position, tempo, and movement can enhance the pleasure and arousal of both partners. Intercourse can occur with or without orgasm for one or both partners.

Summary

Celibacy

Celibacy means not engaging in sexual activities. Celibacy can be complete (no masturbation or interpersonal sexual contact) or partial (the person masturbates). There are many circumstances in which celibacy is a positive way of expressing one's sexuality.

Erotic Dreams and Fantasy

Erotic dreams often accompany sexual arousal and orgasm during sleep. Erotic fantasies serve many functions: They can enhance sexual arousal, help overcome anxiety or compensate for a negative situation, allow rehearsal of new sexual experiences, permit tolerable expression of "forbidden wishes," and provide relief from gender-role expectations.

Masturbation

Masturbation is self-stimulation of the genitals, intended to produce sexual pleasure.

Past attitudes toward masturbation have been highly condemnatory. However, the meaning and purposes of masturbation are currently being more positively reevaluated.

Masturbation is an activity that is continuous throughout the life cycle, although its frequency varies with age and sex.

Shared Touching

The entire body's surface is a sensory organ, and touch is a basic form of communication and shared intimacy.

Breast stimulation is arousing to most men and women, but some people find it unenjoyable.

Preferences as to the tempo, pressure, and location of manual genital stimulation vary from person to person. A lubricant, a nonirritating lotion, or saliva on the genitals may enhance pleasure.

Oral – Genital Stimulation

Oral – genital contact has become more common in recent years. Qualms about oral – genital stimulation usually stem from ideas that it is immoral, unsanitary, or a homosexual act.

Cunnilingus is oral stimulation of the vulva; fellatio is oral stimulation of the male genitals.

Anal Stimulation

Couples may engage in anal stimulation for arousal, orgasm, and variety. Careful hygiene is necessary to avoid introducing anal bacteria into the vagina. To reduce the chances of transmitting the AIDS virus, couples should avoid anal intercourse or use a condom and practice withdrawal before ejaculation.

Coitus and Coital Positions

The diversity of coital positions offers potential variety during intercourse. The man-above, woman-above, side-by-side, and rear-entry positions are common.

Thought Provokers

1. If your 10-year-old son asked you what you think about masturbation, what would you say? If your 10-year-old daughter asked?

2. What helpful functions, if any, do you think sexual fantasies serve? When do you think a person's fantasies indicate a problem?

3. Research indicates that men prefer coitus whereas women prefer "foreplay" and "afterplay." Why do you think this is so?

Suggested Readings

Barbach, Lonnie (1986). *Erotic Interludes.* New York: Harper & Row. An edited collection of fantasy erotic experiences written by women.

Dodson, Betty (1987). *Sex for One.* New York: Harmony Books. An energetic, sometimes outrageous, book about masturbation.

Friday, Nancy (1980). *Men in Love.* New York: Delacorte Press. A collection of men's sexual fantasies and interpretations of their meaning.

Friday, Nancy (1991). *Women on Top: How Real Life Has Changed Women's Sexual Fantasies.* New York: Simon & Schuster. Research and theory about sexual fantasy as it reflects the impact of social change.

Wegscheider-Cruse, Sharon (1988). *Coupleship: How to Have a Relationship.* Deerfield Beach, Fla.: Health Communications. A book designed to help couples establish and maintain a relationship.

The lover takes courage in her certainty
of caressing a body whose secrets she
knows, whose preferences her own
body has taught her.

Colette
Ces Plaisirs (1932)

Homosexuality

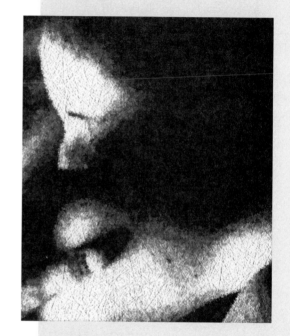

A Continuum of Sexual Orientations
Societal Attitudes
Development of Sexual Orientation
Lifestyles
The Gay Rights Movement

Over 7½ million people in the United States are homosexual.

$\mathcal{M}$any people think of homosexuality as sexual contact between individuals of the same sex. However, this definition is not quite complete. It does not take into account two important dimensions — the context within which the sexual activity is experienced and the feelings and perceptions of the people involved. Nor does it encompass all the meanings of the word **homosexual,** which can refer to erotic attraction, sexual behavior, emotional attachment, and a definition of self. The following definition incorporates a broader spectrum of elements: A homosexual person is an individual "whose primary erotic, psychological, emotional, and social interest is in a member of the same sex, even though those interests may not be overtly expressed" (Martin & Lyon, 1972, p. 1).

A homosexual person's gender identity typically agrees with his or her biological sex. That is, a homosexual person perceives himself or herself as male or female, respectively, and feels attraction toward a same-sex person.

A common synonym for homosexual is **gay.** *Gay* was initially used as a code word between homosexuals, and it has moved into popular usage to describe homosexual men and women, as well as social and political concerns related to homosexual orientation. Homosexual women are often referred to as **lesbians.** Pejorative words such as *faggot, fairy, homo, queer, lezzie,* and *dyke* have traditionally been used to demean homosexuality. However, within certain gay subcultures, some gay people use these terms with each other in positive or humorous ways.

A Continuum of Sexual Orientations

Homosexuality, bisexuality, and *heterosexuality* are words that identify one's **sexual orientation** — that is, to which of the sexes one is attracted. Attraction to same-sex partners is a homosexual orientation, and attraction to other-sex partners is

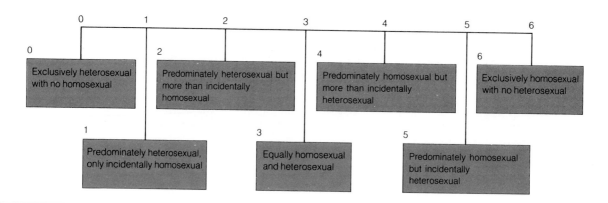

| 0 | 1 | 2 | 3 | 4 | 5 | 6 |

| 0 | | 2 | | 4 | | 6 |
| Exclusively heterosexual with no homosexual | | Predominately heterosexual but more than incidentally homosexual | | Predominately homosexual but more than incidentally heterosexual | | Exclusively homosexual with no heterosexual |

| | 1 | | 3 | | 5 | |
| | Predominately heterosexual, only incidentally homosexual | | Equally homosexual and heterosexual | | Predominately homosexual but incidentally heterosexual | |

FIGURE 10.1

Kinsey's continuum of sexual orientation. (Adapted from Kinsey et al., 1948, p. 638.)

a heterosexual orientation. **Bisexuality** refers to attraction to both same- and other-sex partners. Because sexual orientation is only one aspect of a person's life, this text uses these three terms as descriptive adjectives rather than as nouns that label one's total identity.

In our society we tend to make clear-cut distinctions between homosexuality and heterosexuality. Actually, the delineation is not so precise. A relatively small percentage of people consider themselves to be exclusively homosexual; a greater number think of themselves as exclusively heterosexual. These groups represent the opposite ends of a broad spectrum. Individuals between the ends of the spectrum exhibit varying mixtures of preference and/or experience, which may also change over time. Sexual orientation is best evaluated by observing patterns over a lifespan rather than at any given time (Fox, 1991).

Figure 10.1 shows a seven-point continuum that Alfred Kinsey devised in his analysis of sexual orientations in American society (Kinsey et al., 1948). The scale ranges from 0 (exclusive contact with and erotic attraction to the other sex) to 6 (exclusive contact with and attraction to the same sex). In between are varying degrees of homosexual and heterosexual orientation; category 3 represents equal homosexual and heterosexual attraction and experience.

 How many people in our society fall into the exclusively homosexual category on the continuum? Consider this question and make an estimate before you read on.

According to the Kinsey data, the exclusively homosexual category comprised 2% of women and 4% of men. Although this percentage of people who identified themselves as having had exclusively homosexual experiences appears small, 3% of the 250 million people in the United States is over 7½ million people. The number of predominantly homosexual people may be 10% of the population. Accurate statistics are hard to obtain because social pressures cause many homosexual people to conceal their orientation (a behavior known as being "in the closet"). Social pressure for heterosexual conformity often results in homosexual people dating, having sexual experiences with, and marrying partners of the other sex.

Between the extreme points on the continuum are many individuals who have experienced sexual contact with or been attracted to people of the same sex. Kinsey's estimate of this group's number was quite high: 37% of males and 13% of females in his research population reported having had overt homosexual experiences at some time in their lives, and even more had experienced erotic psychological responses to the same sex.

Kinsey's estimates were made some time ago, and they have been criticized. It has been suggested that the study's sample techniques (for example, making many interview contacts in gay bars) produced an inflated estimate of the number of homosexual people in our society. Morton Hunt's 1974 report revealed a somewhat lower incidence of homosexuality among his respondents, who were contacted by telephone. However, Hunt has criticized his own study for being somewhat underweighted with homosexual people. He has suggested adjusting his data upward and Kinsey's downward to arrive at what may be more accurate figures. The revised estimates after this adjustment are that approximately 2% of men and 1% of women are exclusively homosexual; about 75% of men and 85% of women are exclusively heterosexual; and roughly 23% of men and 14% of women have had both types of experiences.

Defining Bisexuality

In interpreting the continuum shown in Figure 10.1, we want to caution against too broad a use of the word *bisexual.* There is a tendency to use behavior as the only criterion for sexual orientation and to use *bisexual* as a catchall to describe the considerable number of people who fall between exclusive heterosexuality and exclusive homosexuality. This grouping fails to take into account the context within which the sexual experiences occur and the feelings and thoughts of the individuals involved. It is the context, not the contact, that may be most significant. According to one definition, a bisexual person is one who can "enjoy and engage in sexual activity with members of both sexes, or recognizes a desire to do so" (MacDonald, 1981). Bisexuality can be considered as a behavior or as an identity, and the two are not always the same. As one bisexual woman states:

> My dreams and fantasies could remain bisexual; I could continue to be sometimes equally attracted to the male and female star at the movies; still, the world would define me, not by my own sexuality, but by my lover's gender. (Orlando, 1978, p. 60)

Kinsey's continuum of sexual orientation has been questioned, especially in regard to bisexuality. On Kinsey's scale, individuals lose degrees of one orientation as they move toward the opposite end of the scale; thus, bisexual individuals are seen as a compromise between the two extremes. In another model, a bisexual orientation is viewed as showing high rather than moderate degrees of both homosexuality and heterosexuality (Storms, 1980). This view is supported by the type and frequency of sexual fantasies reported by study subjects in the various groups. As might be expected, homosexual subjects reported more fantasy about the same sex than about the other sex, while heterosexual subjects reported the reverse. But contrary to what one might predict from the Kinsey scale, bisexual subjects reported as much same-sex fantasy as homosexual individuals and as much other-sex fantasy as heterosexual individuals. In other words, bisexual people seem to have a high degree of general erotic interest.

There are several different types of bisexuality: bisexuality as a real orientation, as a transitory orientation, as a transitional orientation, or as homosexual denial (Fox, 1991; MacDonald, 1981). Bisexuality as a real orientation means that some people are born with a natural attraction to both sexes, and this attraction continues into adulthood. An individual with this orientation might or might not be sexually active with more than one partner at a time but would continue to have feelings of attraction to both sexes.

Bisexual behavior can also be transitory — a temporary involvement by people who are actually heterosexual or homosexual. These individuals will return fully to their original orientation after a period of bisexual experimentation or experiences. Transitory homosexual behavior may occur in single-sex boarding schools and prisons, yet the people involved resume heterosexual relationships when the opportunities for such are again available. Some prostitutes or male hustlers may do business with either sex and yet be involved in only heterosexual or homosexual relationships in their personal lives.

Bisexuality can also be a transitional state in which a person is changing from one exclusive orientation to another. This person will remain in the new orientation, as illustrated in the following account:

I had led a traditional life with a husband, two kids, and community activities. My best friend and I were very active in the PTA together. Much to our surprise, we fell in love. We were initially secretive about our sexual relationship and continued our marital lives, but then we both divorced our husbands and moved away to start a life together. The best way I can describe being with her is that life is now like a color TV, instead of a black-and-white. (Authors' files)

Finally, bisexuality may sometimes be an attempt to deny exclusive homosexual interests and to avoid the full stigma of homosexual identity (MacDonald, 1981). Gay men and lesbians sometimes view the bisexual person as someone who really is homosexual but lacks the courage to identify himself or herself as such. For example, there are a number of people who marry to maintain a facade of heterosexuality but continue to have strong homosexual desires or secretive homosexual contacts.

Sexual orientation is often viewed as an either/or situation — one is either heterosexual or homosexual. Researchers have had a tendency to categorize people who engage in sexual activity with both sexes as homosexual, when they would be more accurately understood as bisexual (Dixon, 1985). Consequently, self-identified bisexual individuals may be met with ambivalence and suspicion and are often pressured by heterosexual or homosexual people to adhere to one orientation (Fox, 1991). Even without pressure, they may experience self-doubt and distress due to the cultural message that one must choose between orientations (Schuster, 1988). Bisexual individuals "who associate with the gay/lesbian community as well as with the heterosexual mainstream may find themselves shifting social identities: the attempt to bridge both worlds with a single identity can be a source of stress and discomfort in both social arenas" (Paul, 1984, p. 54).

Societal Attitudes

In the Judeo–Christian tradition, homosexuality has been viewed negatively. Many religious scholars believe that the condemnation of homosexuality increased during a reformation movement beginning in the seventh century B.C., through which Jewish religious leaders wanted to develop a distinct, closed community that was different from others of the time. Homosexual activities were a part of the religious services of many groups of people in that era. Rejecting religious rituals involving homosexual activities was one way of enhancing the uniqueness of a

OTHER TIMES, OTHER PLACES

Homosexuality in Cross-Cultural Perspective

Attitudes toward homosexuality have varied considerably. A number of research studies of other cultures have revealed widespread acceptance of homosexual activities. One survey of 190 societies found that two-thirds of them considered homosexuality socially acceptable for certain individuals or on specific occasions (Ford & Beach, 1951). Homosexuality has been widely accepted in many earlier cultures. For example, over 50% of 225 Native American tribes accepted male homosexuality, and 17% accepted female homosexuality (Pomeroy, 1965). With the exception of ceremonial heterosexual contacts, homosexuality was the primary form of sexual expression among a group of eastern Peruvian native males (Schneebaum, 1975). In ancient Greece, homosexual relationships between men were considered a superior intellectual and spiritual expression of love, whereas heterosexuality provided the more pragmatic benefits of children and a family unit.

Certain general findings emerge from cross-cultural comparisons of homosexual behavior. First, male homosexuality is more common than is lesbianism in most societies. Second, the percentage of males in a given society who participate in homosexual activity at some time during their lives varies from nearly 100%, as in the Melanesian island society of East Bay (Davenport, 1965), to virtually none, as in Mangaia. Third, it appears that the societies with the lowest proportions of people who are exclusively or nearly exclusively homosexual are nonindustrialized societies like those of Africa and the South Pacific. Finally, homosexual activity has never been the predominant form of adult sexual behavior in any society for which we have data.

Some societies *require* their members to engage in homosexual activities. For example, all male members of the Sambia society of about 2300 people in the mountains of New Guinea engage in exclusively homosexual activities from approximately seven years of age until they get married, in their late teens or early twenties. The Sambia men believe that a prepubertal boy becomes a strong warrior and hunter by drinking as much semen as possible from postpubertal boys' penises. Once a boy reaches puberty, he must no longer fellate other boys but experiences erotic pleasure from fellatio by boys who can not yet ejaculate. From the start of their erotic lives and during the years of peak orgasmic capacity, young men engage in frequent, obligatory, and gratifying homoeroticism. During the same period, looking at or touching females is taboo. Yet as they approach marriage, these youths create powerful erotic daydreams about women. During the first weeks of marriage, they experience only fellatio with their wives, but they then change to include intercourse as a part of their heterosexual activity. Following marriage they stop homosexual activity, experience great sexual desire for women, and engage exclusively in heterosexual activity for the rest of their lives (Stoller & Herdt, 1985).

religion. Homosexual behaviors were then condemned as a form of pagan worship (Kosnik et al., 1977). Strong prohibitive biblical scriptures were written: "You shall not lie with a man as one lies with a female, it is an abomination" (Leviticus 18:22).

In the Judeo–Christian tradition, the primary purpose of sexual interaction is procreation, not pleasure. The pursuit of sexual pleasure outside of that purpose, whether practiced by homosexual or heterosexual individuals, was viewed as immoral.

Do all current organized religions view homosexuality negatively? Consider what you have experienced, heard, and read in the media before reading on.

Current theological positions toward homosexuality demonstrate a great range of convictions. Theologian James Nelson (1980) described four stances represented in contemporary Christianity. The first is a *rejecting–punitive* orientation, which unconditionally rejects homosexuality and bears a punitive attitude toward gay people. This position is the predominate one in Christian history. For many centuries the church ostracized homosexual people from church and community life and gave its blessings to civil persecutions, including killing discovered homosexuals. The theology of this position rests on selective biblical literalism. The Greek Orthodox church's statement from the Biennial Clergy–Laity Congress of 1976 exemplifies this theological position:

> Thus the function of the sexual organs of a man and a woman . . . are ordained by nature to serve one particular purpose, the procreation of human kind. Therefore, any and all uses of the human sex organs for purposes other than those ordained by creation, runs contrary to the nature of things as decreed by God. . . . The Orthodox Church believes that homosexuality should be treated by society as an immoral and dangerous perversion and by religion as a sinful failure. In both cases correction is called for. Homosexuals should be accorded the confidential medical and psychiatric facilities by which they can be helped to restore themselves to a self-respecting sexual identity that belongs to them by God's ordinance. (Batchelor, 1980, p. 237)

The *rejecting–nonpunitive* position maintains that homosexuality is inherently unnatural and must be condemned, but because of Christ's grace, the homosexual person must not be condemned. This position supports the civil liberties of gay people, recognizing the injustice and hypocrisy in their persecution.

The third position, *qualified acceptance,* maintains that homosexuality is a sin but acknowledges that homosexuality is largely unsusceptible to change by contemporary medical and psychological science. Therefore, homosexual people who cannot refrain from sexual interaction should maintain fully committed relationships.

The fourth major theological position is *full acceptance.* This perspective views sexuality as intrinsically important to the capacity for human love. It maintains that ethical sexual relationships include commitment, trust, tenderness, and respect for the other regardless of the sex of the partners. Full acceptance includes providing a church blessing of the union of those who vow a lifelong commitment. As another aspect of complete acceptance, gay Christians are welcomed into every aspect of the life of the congregation, including ordination as ministers. (The first major American denomination to ordain an openly gay candidate was the United Church of Christ in 1972; it was followed four years later by an Episcopalian church.) Full acceptance also includes support for the civil rights of gays and lesbians. The advocates of full acceptance are still a minority (Mitchell, 1992a).

In the early- to mid-1900s, there was a shift in attitudes toward homosexuality. The belief that homosexual people were sinners was replaced to some degree by the belief that they were "sick" (Esterberg, 1990). The medical and psychological professions have used drastic treatments in attempting to cure the "illness" of homosexuality. Surgical procedures such as castration were performed in the 1800s. Lobotomy (brain surgery that severs nerve fibers in the frontal lobe of the brain) was performed as a "cure" for homosexuality as late as 1951. Psychotherapy, drugs, hormones, hypnosis, shock treatments, and aversion therapy (pairing nausea-inducing drugs or electrical shock with homosexual stimuli) have all been used to the same end (Katz, 1976).

Actually, most current research contradicts the notion that homosexual people are "sick." The first major research to compare the adjustment of nonpatient heterosexual and homosexual individuals (described more fully in the interview with Evelyn Hooker) found no significant differences between the two groups (Hooker,

1967). Further research has supported these findings (Isay, 1989; Mannion, 1981; Wilson, 1984). Alan Bell and Martin Weinberg summarized that "homosexual adults who have come to terms with their homosexuality, who do not regret their sexual orientation, and who can function effectively sexually and socially, are no more distressed psychologically than are heterosexual men and women" (1978, p. 216). In 1973 the American Psychiatric Association, after great internal conflict, removed homosexuality per se from its diagnostic categories of mental disorders. In 1975 the American Psychological Association urged "all mental health professionals to take the lead in removing the stigma of mental illness that has long been associated with a homosexual orientation" (American Psychological Association press release, 24 January 1975). As an eminent psychiatrist stated: "I consider a person healthy if he or she gets along well with others — without a lot of anxiety, lying, crippling psychologic symptoms, inhibitions, or hatred, open or disguised — takes responsibility for his or her actions, uses his or her talents effectively, and is dependable. . . . A description such as this one includes, perhaps, several heterosexual and homosexual people" (Stoller, 1985, p. 102).

Homophobia

Some of society's antihomosexual attitudes stem from what Martin Weinberg (1973) labeled **homophobia.** Homophobia is defined as irrational fears of homosexuality in others, the fear of homosexual feelings within oneself, or self-loathing because of one's homosexuality. It stems from ignorance and popular myths that give rise to homosexual prejudice. Negative, hostile attitudes toward homosexuality have also been labeled *anti-homosexual prejudice* (Haage, 1991). The box "Assessment of Personal Homophobia" presents one scale that has been used to measure homophobic tendencies; you may want to use it to examine your own attitudes.

The recent recognition and discussion of homophobia represent a significant shift in views toward homosexuality: now homophobic attitudes are the problem rather than homosexuality itself. However, some reactions to the AIDS crisis have

CHAPTER 10

Interview with Evelyn Hooker

Seldom does a single scientific publication so dramatically and personally affect people's lives as did the landmark study reported by Dr. Evelyn Hooker in 1957. At a time when homosexuality was equated with being mentally ill, and lesbians and gay men were frequently forced out of government jobs and arrested in police raids, Dr. Hooker's study provided the first clear experimental evidence that homosexuality is not a mental illness. Her data and conclusions, published in the Journal of Projective Techniques *as "The Adjustment of the Male Overt Homosexual," were important in causing the American Psychiatric Association and the American Psychological Association to remove homosexuality from their diagnostic categories of mental illness in 1973 and 1975, respectively.*

Now a retired psychology professor from the University of California, Los Angeles (UCLA), Dr. Hooker has received high praise from scientists, mental health professionals, and gay men and lesbians. She has been the subject of a documentary film, grand marshal of the Los Angeles Gay Pride Parade, and the recipient of numerous scientific and public service awards. In August 1992, she received the Distinguished Contribution Award in the Public Interest from the

American Psychological Association. The award reads, in part: "Hooker has had a career of ground-breaking research, personal courage, and direct and significant impact on the lives of lesbians and gay men. . . . [B]y publishing and continuing to investigate controversial data, Hooker set an example of intellectual courage for all who seek to advance psychology as a science and a means of promoting human welfare."

In this interview in her home in Los Angeles, Dr. Hooker describes her research career to Karla Baur.

What events led you to begin studying whether homosexuality was a mental illness?

During World War II I was teaching a class at UCLA, and in the first or second row was a very bright student who

I got to know well. He would often talk to me at breaks and after class. Shortly after he finished my class, he visited me and my husband. When he left, my husband said, "Why didn't you tell me he was queer?" (I suppose he said "queer" in those days, although we wouldn't use that word today.) I said, "You're crazy. You couldn't know that." I was surprised.

At any rate, my husband and I got to know this gay student, Sam From, and his gay friends. His friends were very eager that we meet, and I found them fascinating. His group of friends—men, and maybe one or two women—were in the film industry; they were college professors; they were ordinary sailors; they covered the whole gamut. After about a year, my husband and I went on a trip to San Francisco with Sam and his friend. One night, Sam turned to me and said, "Now, we have let you see us as we are. It is your scientific duty to make a study of people like us."

To that, I said, "No." First of all, I was doing 10 million other things, teaching and doing animal research. But he simply wouldn't let up. He persisted and persisted. Finally I went to a colleague and told him about this. He practically leaped out of his chair and said, "You know, he's absolutely right. We scientists don't know anything about the ordinary, walking-around-outside gay. We know about patients, and we know about prisoners."

However, at this time my life changed. I was divorced, I decided to go east, and I took a position at Bryn Mawr College and dropped the whole idea. A few years later, I decided to come back to California, where I later remarried. When I returned, among the first people I saw were my gay friends. Again, they set up this plea: "You must do a study like this."

That was in 1953, and the National Institute of Mental Health (NIMH) had just been organized, and they were giving grants. It was, of course, also the peak of the McCarthy era. It was a strange time to be asking the National Institute of Mental Health for money, but I did that. I said, "If they agree with me that this is an important thing to do, I'll do it. If they don't agree with me, I'll forget it."

The next thing I knew, the director of the grants division flew out and spent a day with me. It was clear what he wanted: He wanted to see my home; he wanted to see what kind of a lady I was; obviously, he wanted to know whether I was a lesbian. He didn't ask me that. It should have become apparent to him very soon that I wasn't. If he had thought that I was a lesbian, I do not think I would have gotten the grant, courageous as they were. He said, "We are prepared to make you this grant, but everybody is being investigated, especially on the topic of homosexuality."

I had asked for research support for six months, but NIMH came back and said, "You can't do it in that amount of time. How much more time do you want—another year?" That went on and on until NIMH supported my work for 17 years. Without NIMH and their courage and foresight, I couldn't have done this work. The money for the research was the least of it; they gave me an enormous amount of support with research design and every aspect of the work. I also couldn't have done it without Sam's entree for me into the gay world.

Once you had funding, how did you carry out the study?

I knew that the scientific issue I wanted to address was that of psychopathology versus normality. To do that I would have to secure a group of gay men and a comparable group of straight men. I knew that I wanted 30 men in each group, because statistically that was the minimum number that would be meaningful. Getting the gay men was not a problem, because by that time I had so many contacts in the gay world, and they were eager to be subjects. Of course, I couldn't take anybody who was in that original group of my friends as a subject.

The gay men wanted the study very much, and you can imagine why. Since they apparently trusted me, they saw this as a way of understanding scientifically what differences existed between gay men and straight men, if any. I did not present the issue to potential subjects that way, of course. What I said was that I wanted to study personality and administer some psychological tests for that purpose in a comparable group of gays.

The biggest problem I had was getting the straight men. The gay men were eager to participate, but mention the word "sex" in that year—again, this is 1953 or '54—and the straight

men would run like the devil! I had a study in the garden of our home, without which I could never have done the research. We had an acre of ground which was surrounded by a fence. So when someone came, nobody could see them once they got inside the gate. If I had tried to do that research at UCLA, no one would have come. By that time the research I was doing was sufficiently well-known that men didn't want to be seen walking into my office and have people wonder whether they were gay.

I recruited straight men wherever I could. I recruited a fireman who came to check on whether our control of household fire hazards was adequate. One of my best friends was earning his way to a master's degree by working in the maintenance department at UCLA, and I tested three men who worked there. My husband would joke, "No man is safe on Saltair Avenue."

The excitement came, of course, in the analysis of the material. I had to submit the tests to expert judges who would not be contaminated by any prejudgment about which subjects might be homosexual. I used three nationally known psychology experts to review psychological tests of types that could not be faked. They analyzed one phase of the psychological profiles after the other and gave each subject an adjustment rating based on the Thematic Apperception Test. That rating essentially answered the question of pathology. We did the same thing with the Rorschach test, and the Make a Picture Story Test.

There are various ways of describing the lack of difference between these two groups of men. We found that if you draw a curve averaging the scores that the judges gave them, there is so little difference in psychological adjustment between the gay men and the straight men as to really be microscopic. That was very exciting. It was also not surprising because, after all, I had seen all these men and had no reason to think that there was anything maladjusted about them.

Since your original publication in 1957, what other research do you feel has been particularly important in the field of homosexuality?

I think some of the most important research has been ongoing work by Greg Herek, who is in the psychology department at the University of California, Davis. He's working on that all-important issue: the origin and nature of prejudice, particularly homophobia.

I think that some of the most important research that is going on now is being done by anthropologists. I have the book, *Culture in America,* which describes several studies done by anthropologists at the University of Chicago. There are chapters that deal with particular aspects of homosexual life—for example, the issue of adolescence and what kind of treatment adolescents should be given. Dr. Gilbert Herdt, a distinguished anthropologist at the University of Chicago, is very much concerned about youth and development, and about the social structures the gay

community builds for itself. I think one of the most interesting chapters in that book is the one about the gay parade in Chicago and its symbolic character.

What research on sexual orientation would you like to see done in the future?

homosexuality in developing adolescents. Others may disagree with me on this, but I feel there are multiple pathways which lead to an adult pattern of homosexuality. These pathways are not at all clear. I do not remember any gay person who has talked with me who would really point to a specific causative factor for his or her sexuality. I think a great many gay people believe, and would say, that the only reason they can think of that they are gay is because it must have some biological basis. It feels that strong to them.

I would like to see more of the kind of research that Dr. Joe Carrier of Pacific Palisades is doing in Guadalajara. He has been looking at the social milieu in which children develop, and the way in which highly feminine boys are pushed into a homosexual role by everybody in the environment. That

doesn't say what causes it, but it does ask, "How does it develop, and what are the factors?"

Why do you think that many fewer studies have looked at lesbians than at gay men?

After I published a few articles on gay men, whenever I would be asked to make a presentation, lesbians would say to me, "Why don't you do for us what you did for gay men?" My answer to that was, and is, "You didn't ask me." And that's true: they didn't.

However, a number of studies of lesbians were comparable to my study, although they were not as extensive. I think the studies absolutely paralleled each other. There's no need to fight that battle all over again. Ann Peplau, a professor of psychology at UCLA, studies lesbians. I once asked her how she got into this study, and she said, "They asked me." And she said she responded, "But I don't know anything." And they said, "Yes, but you can learn." And now she has written excellent articles on lesbians.

Do you think it is easier to be gay or lesbian in the 1990s than it was in the 1950s, when you began this work?

I would have thought that it was much easier today, but I've also listened to the anguish and the labels that some young people must deal with even now. There are organizations which have been founded recently which certainly make it much easier for a lot of people, such as the Gay and Lesbian Services Center in Los Angeles. Of course, gays and lesbians also have many more good role models now than before. They have baseball heroes and a lot of very believable kinds of models.

On the other hand, there's AIDS. There are hate crimes. Although gay

rights have made some progress in some places, it also sometimes brings a backlash effect.

But it seems to me that things are better now. For example, every judge who was gay had to be secretive about it in 1954, whereas today there are any number of openly gay judges on the bench. We also have two openly gay members of Congress. Congressman Barney Frank does something which I would hope might be developed further among people: I recently saw him in one of the town hall meetings, and somebody addressed him and made a joke about his being gay, and Barney laughed. It would seem to me that the resilience among these men must be absolutely incredible to allow them such an openness and sense of humor.

Do you think there are characteristics that make it easier or more difficult for lesbians or gay men to "come out"?

I have seen some people who wanted to come out and didn't have the courage to do it. What makes it easier? I don't know, but I would hazard a guess that it is easier if the person is strongly developed in his own personal identity. That's really asking a lot. When I look at somebody like Congressman Barney Frank, it seems to me that when he came out a few years ago, he was able to stand on his feet and to really say, "I mean it." But that kind of ego strength is not something we find very easily. I wish somebody would do a study examining whether there is a relationship between ego strength and the ability to come out without fear of what is going to be said.

I think that Gilbert Herdt and his colleagues are going to make a considerable dent in that question. Among their studies is one on a group of adolescents who have come out or who are coming out. They have an ongoing study which is, in part, supportive of their efforts to come out, and which is studying the process as they go along.

In retrospect, do you think your years of research on sexual orientation made any impact on your personal opinions?

No. Sometimes even gay people say to me, "Surely you must have been prejudiced at one time." And I say, "Well, if I was, I didn't know it." And that's true. But you have to look at who my teachers were—that is, my very bright student and his very bright friends. I don't think I'm a person who has prejudice in any area as far as I can tell. I came from a very poor family. My father was a tenant farmer in Nebraska and later in Colorado. I worked my way through college, and I think I made a vow that I would always be able to see beyond whatever stereotypes or prejudices people held.

Do you think that the stigma associated with homosexuality affected your career?

I'm often asked whether it damaged my career in some way. I have to answer, "No." For example, if I had wanted to be in the tenure track at UCLA, I could have been. I chose not to be. I simply have to tell you that if there were any negative effects of doing this research, I don't know what they were. Rather, I feel my career has been greatly enhanced by being involved in this important research.

From the time I officially began in 1954, I continued to have pressure and funding from the NIMH to go on and on. In 1965, for example, I said, "I've had it, I think. I really think it would be wise to not go on." But at that time the NIMH was establishing career research awards, and I was in the first group that they offered to fund, and I was the first woman. They talked me into continuing.

I can't imagine anything else I could have done with my life that I would have enjoyed more, and that I think has brought more light to more people. I feel that very strongly.

reflected strong homophobic bias. Jerry Falwell, founder of the now defunct fundamentalist political group the Moral Majority, called the outbreak of AIDS a "form of judgment of God upon a society." An executive in this same group criticized federal spending for medical research on AIDS: "What I see is a commitment to spend our tax dollars on research to allow these diseased homosexuals to go back to their perverted practices without any standards of accountability" (*U.S. News and World Report,* 2 September 1985). This view assumes that homosexuality, rather than a virus, is the cause of AIDS (Brandt, 1985), and reflects research findings that show that negative attitudes toward homosexual persons correlate with negative attitudes toward persons with AIDS (Ambrosio & Sheehan, 1991).

Homophobia can be exhibited in many ways, both subtle (even unconscious) and blatant. Telling "queer" jokes and belittling homosexuality expresses hostility that is part of the homophobic attitude. This hostility can be overt, and people who are suspected of being homosexual are sometimes subjected to verbal or physical assault:

The group I ran around with in high school used to drive downtown to where the gay bars were, pick up a swishy-looking one, beat him up, and dump him back on the street. (Authors' files)

Many psychologists believe that such aggression toward homosexuality is an attempt to deny or suppress homosexual feelings in oneself. Heterosexual men tend to express more hostile attitudes toward those who are homosexual than do women (Ambrosio & Sheehan, 1991; Herek, 1988).

Another expression of homophobia may be the careful avoidance of any behavior that might be interpreted as homosexual. In this sense, homophobia can restrict the lives of heterosexual people. For example, during lovemaking, heterosexual men may be unable to enjoy having their nipples stimulated, or may be reluctant to allow their female partners to take the lead, if they believe these behaviors demonstrate homosexual tendencies (Wells, 1991). Same-sex friends or family members may refrain from spontaneous embraces, people may shun "unfeminine" or "unmasculine" clothing, or a woman may decide not to identify herself as a feminist because she fears being called a lesbian. Homophobia may have an especially significant impact on the depth of intimacy in male friendships. Men's fear of same-sex attraction often prevents them from allowing the emotional vulnerability required for deep friendship and limits their relationships largely to competition and "buddyship" (Nelson, 1985).

Any gender-role reversal can be perceived as threatening. Male homosexuals have been seen as "defective" because they are believed to share characteristics with women — the inferior sex (Lewes, 1988). According to some research, homophobia may be related to traditional gender-role stereotypes (Whitley, 1987). This study found a correlation between attitudes about gender roles and attitudes toward homosexuality, with respondents who supported rigid gender-role stereotypes having more negative feelings about homosexuality than did others. Bell and his colleagues discussed the idea that homosexuality confronts people with their ability to tolerate diversity in gender roles:

> In a society such as ours a special loathing is reserved for any male who appears to have forfeited the privileges and responsibilities associated with upholding the conventional imagery of males. The spectre of a group of males living outside the strict confines of "masculinity" can appear as a threat to men who are not entirely certain about their own maleness and thus heighten whatever antagonisms are expressed toward those who do not follow male "rules." Similarly, to the degree that lesbianism is associated with the rejection of traditionally "feminine" roles and responsibilities, heterosexual women may feel threatened by those who do not join their ranks. (1981, p. 221)

Homophobic attitudes can change over time, with experience or deliberate thought. Education can also play a role: most students who take courses in human sexuality become more tolerant (Stevenson, 1990). One of our students described how this process occurred in his life:

My own reaction to learning that one of my fraternity brothers was gay was discomfort. I increasingly avoided him. I am sorry now that I didn't confront myself as to why I felt that way. I was homophobic. And because I didn't deal with that then, it kept me from developing a closeness with my other men friends. I lost something in those relationships because I was afraid that being physically and emotionally close to another man meant that I, too, was homosexual. I finally began to explore why I felt so uncomfortable touching or being touched by another man. Today I am no longer threatened or frightened by physical closeness from another man, even if I know his preference is other men. I am secure enough to deal with that honestly. (Authors' files)

Development of Sexual Orientation

What determines sexual orientation? Do you think sexual orientation is caused by "nature" or "nurture"? Give this some thought before reading on.

A variety of theories have attempted to explain the origins of sexual orientation, particularly homosexuality. Considerable research has been done over the years, but there are still no definitive scientific answers. In the next few pages, we consider some common notions about the causes of homosexuality and evaluate some of the research that has attempted to substantiate these ideas.

Bell and his colleagues (1981) have done the most comprehensive study to date about the development of sexual orientation. They used a sample of 979 homosexual people matched to a control group of 477 heterosexual people. All research subjects were asked questions about their childhood, adolescence, and sexual practices during four-hour, face-to-face interviews. The researchers then used sophisticated statistical techniques to analyze possible causal factors in the development of homosexuality or heterosexuality. This research is cited frequently throughout this section because of its excellent methodology.

Psychosocial Theories

Some of the theories about the development of a homosexual orientation relate to life incidents, parenting patterns, or psychological attributes of the individual. Unhappy heterosexual experiences or the inability to attract partners of the other sex are sometimes believed to cause a person to become or choose to be homosexual. Stereotypes that homosexuals are less attractive than others are common. For example, in one study college students of both sexes were shown photographs of 22 women and asked to identify the half who were reputed to be homosexuals. The students tended to identify people they perceived as less attractive as the homosexuals (Dew, 1985). Statements like "All a lesbian needs is a good lay" or "He just needs to meet the right woman" reflect the notion that homosexuality is a poor second choice for people who lack satisfactory heterosexual experiences. It is often assumed that lesbianism is due to resentment, dislike, fear, or distrust of men rather than attraction toward women. The illogic of this argument is clear if we turn it around and say that female heterosexuality is caused by a dislike and fear of women. Actually, research indicates that up to 70% of lesbians have had sexual experiences with men, and many report having enjoyed them. However, they prefer to be sexual with women (Klaich, 1974; Martin & Lyon, 1972). Bell and his colleagues' analysis of their data indicated that "homosexual orientation among females reflects neither a lack of heterosexual experience nor a history of particularly unpleasant heterosexual experiences" (1981, p. 176).

Bell and his colleagues also found that the homosexual and heterosexual groups did not differ in the frequency of dating during high school. This refutes the belief that lack of heterosexual opportunity causes homosexuality. The male and female homosexual subjects did tend, however, to feel differently about dating than did their heterosexual counterparts; fewer homosexual subjects reported that they enjoyed dating. Their feelings likely indicated less interest in heterosexual activity. For example, although the homosexual males dated as much as the heterosexual males in the study, they tended to have fewer sexual encounters with females and to have engaged in fewer types of heterosexual activities such as manual stimulation of genitals, oral–genital sex, or intercourse. The researchers suggested "that unless heterosexual encounters appeal to one's deepest sexual feeling, there is likely to be little about them that one would experience as positive reinforcement for sexual relationships with members of the opposite sex" (1981, p. 108). On the other hand, other researchers conclude that learning from intense and pleasurable sexual experiences is the strongest antecedent to later sexual orientation. Their research found that those who learned to masturbate by being manually stimulated by a person of the same sex and those whose first orgasm is in homosexual contact are more likely to have a homosexual orientation as adults (VanWyk, 1984). This is the classic "Which came first, the chicken or the egg?" question. Do the feelings guide the behavior (and if so, what causes the feelings?), or does the behavior shape the feelings? How do the feelings and the behavior interact, and how significant is each in developing sexual orientation? These are questions for continued research.

Do you think homosexuality is learned through seduction by an older homosexual person? Consider your thoughts before reading on.

Another myth that the Bell and coworkers' study showed to be false is that young men and women become homosexual because they have been seduced by older homosexuals. Their data indicated that most homosexual males and females had their first homosexual encounter with someone, usually a friend or acquaintance, about the same age as themselves. In fact, homosexual people were less likely than heterosexual people to have had initial sexual encounters with a stranger or an older person.

Some people may believe that homosexuality can be "caught" from someone else. People seem especially concerned about the influence of homosexual teachers; they are afraid that exposure to a homosexual teacher, especially a well-liked and respected one, will cause students to model after him or her and become homosexual. However, a homosexual orientation appears to be established even before school age, and modeling is not a relevant factor (Marmor, 1980).

Another prevalent theory concerning the development of homosexuality has to do with certain patterns in a person's family background. Speculation about environmental causes of homosexuality can be found in the literature of psychoanalysis. Psychoanalytic theory implicated both childhood experiences and relationships with parents. Sigmund Freud (1905) maintained that the relationship with one's father and mother was a crucial factor in the development of homosexuality. He believed that men and women were innately bisexual but, with "normal" developmental experiences, passed through a "homoerotic" phase in the process of establishing a heterosexual orientation. However, he thought that people could become "fixated" at the homosexual phase if certain kinds of life experiences occurred, especially if a male had a poor relationship with his father and an overly close relationship with his mother. Later clinical research attempted to confirm these hypotheses. A study by Irving Bieber (1962), for instance, compared homosexual and heterosexual men who were undergoing psychoanalysis. Bieber's data indicated that certain patterns were frequently found in the family backgrounds of homosexual clients—most typically, a dominant and overprotective mother and a passive and detached father. Another study gave some support to Bieber's finding. It compared homosexual and heterosexual men who had lost one or both parents before the age of 15. More of the homosexual group reported that their mothers had been overcontrolling or that their fathers had been emotionally distant toward them (Saghir & Robins, 1973).

However, it has not been clearly established that certain childhood factors are the critical determinants in the development of a homosexual orientation. Many homosexual people did not have a dominant mother and an emotionally detached father, just as many heterosexual people *were* reared in families where this pattern prevailed. Bell and his colleagues (1981) reported some interesting findings on the role of family patterns in the development of sexual orientation. Although there was some evidence that male homosexuality was related to poor father–son relationships, they stated that the traditional psychoanalytic model of the impact of parents was exaggerated. On the basis of their findings, no particular phenomenon of family life could be singled out as "especially consequential for either homosexual or heterosexual development" (p. 190). Moreover, their findings were supported by another study of homosexual and heterosexual men who had never been in therapy. Data using standardized measures of perceptions of parental rearing style failed to reveal any differences between the two groups (Ross & Arrindell, 1988).

Implicit in many psychosocial explanations of homosexuality is the assumption that homosexuality is a less permanent condition than heterosexuality. Most therapists agree that exclusive homosexuality is extremely difficult, if not impossible, to change to functional and satisfactory heterosexuality. Also, no long-term data show that short-term behavior changes affect long-term sexual orientation.

In light of contemporary research on homosexuality — and taking into account that the American Psychiatric and Psychological Associations no longer categorize homosexuality as a mental illness — most therapists and counselors have changed the focus of therapy. Rather than assuming that they must "cure" their homosexual clients by changing their sexual orientation, therapists are trying instead to help them to love, live, and work in a society that harbors considerable hostility toward them (Garnets et al., 1991; Moran, 1992). This change in therapeutic practice is significant in that it defines the problem as society's negativity toward homosexuality rather than homosexuality itself.

Biological Theories

Researchers have looked into a number of areas in an effort to establish biological causes for sexual orientation. Some researchers have speculated that hormone levels in adults may contribute to homosexuality. They have compared hormone levels in adult homosexual men and women with those in heterosexual adults. The data have been contradictory (Meyer-Bahlburg, 1977; Tourney, 1980). A leading researcher stated that studies that have controlled for the many variables operating in this experimental area — criteria for selection of subjects; use of control subjects matched for age, sex, education, and other factors; and attention to possible significance of intervening variables — indicate no difference in the circulating levels of sex hormones of adult heterosexual and homosexual males (Money, 1988).

Even if consistent differences were found in the hormonal patterns of homosexual and heterosexual adults, it would remain unknown whether the differences were a cause or a result of sexual orientation. Testosterone levels are sensitive to a number of variables, including general health, diet, drug use, marijuana use, cigarette smoking, sexual activity, and physical and emotional stress (Marmor, 1980). Many of these variables can be controlled for in careful research. However, it is important to note that the stress and anxiety many homosexual people experience as a result of societal oppression may itself have an impact on hormone levels. Others believe that adult hormone levels will prove to be irrelevant because sexual orientation is established prenatally and/or early in life (Money, 1988).

Some researchers have speculated that prenatal hormone levels can alter the masculine and feminine development of the fetal brain and that this may contribute to a homosexual orientation (Ellis & Ames, 1987; Zuger, 1989). Laboratory research with animals has demonstrated that hormones given prenatally can masculinize fetal females and demasculinize fetal males. This results in other-sex social and mating behavior when the animals mature, as this example illustrates:

> The brains and behavior of ewe lambs ... can be masculinized in utero by injecting the pregnant mother with testosterone at the critical period of gestation.... Its brain is so effectively masculinized that its mating behavior, and its urinating behavior also, are completely masculinized. It engages in mating rivalry with other rams in head-on, butting contests. Its proceptive courtship ritual is never like that of a ewe, but exactly like that of a ram, even though while it is courting a ewe in heat, its own ovaries are secreting estrogen, not androgen. Moreover, the normal rams and ewes of the flock respond to the ... ewe's masculinized mating behavior as if it were that of a normal ram. (Money, 1988, p. 26)

There is a critical period during human gestation in which the fetus is particularly sensitive to levels of sex hormones. Prenatal hormonal imbalances during this period could contribute to homosexuality. It is also possible for both prenatal masculinization and feminization to coexist to some degree, with a consequent bisexual orientation. Nutritional changes, medicine and drugs, and maternal stress alter maternal hormones in animals (Money, 1988). However, a 1991 study found no correlation between maternal stress during pregnancy and sexual orientation of the human offspring (Bailey et al., 1991). Any conclusions about humans from animal studies are uncertain, and it is scientifically unethical to experiment on human fetuses.

Research published in 1991 reported structural differences in the brains of homosexual and heterosexual men, lending weight to a biological basis for sexual orientation. Salk Institute scientist Simon LeVay (1991) studied the brains of 41 cadavers — 19 homosexual men, 16 presumed heterosexual men, and 6 presumed heterosexual women. He found that the anterior hypothalamus, an area of the brain that influences sexual behavior, was half as large in homosexual men as in heterosexual men. LeVay cautioned that the difference he observed provides no direct evidence that it causes sexual orientation. However, his findings encourage further research in this direction.

Other recent research has suggested the possibility that genetic factors may contribute to the development of male homosexuality. Researchers studied three groups: identical twins, fraternal twins, and adoptive brothers. They found that when one brother was homosexual, so were 52% of the identical twins, 22% of the fraternal twins, and 11% of the adoptive brothers. These results may also be due to some extent to environmental factors, but the large differences between identical twins and the other two groups strongly indicate a genetic component to male sexuality (Bailey & Pillard, 1991). Some researchers have hypothesized that genes affect the part of the brain that LeVay studied (Holden, 1992).

Although Bell and his coworkers did not do any hormonal studies, they maintained that their research also suggested biological causes, especially for Kinsey's category of exclusive homosexuality. They stated that, in general, homosexuality "is a pattern of feelings and reactions within the child that cannot be traced back to a single social or psychological root" (1981, p. 192) and that "a boy or girl is predisposed to be homosexual or heterosexual, and during childhood and adolescence this basic sexual orientation begins to become evident" (p. 187).

These and other researchers believe that evidence for a biological predisposition for homosexuality is the strong link between adult homosexuality and **gender nonconformity** as a child. Gender nonconformity is a variable the researchers used that measured the extent to which the research subjects conformed to stereotypic characteristics of masculinity or femininity during childhood. Respondents were asked their own perceptions of how masculine or feminine they were as children and how much they enjoyed conventional boys' or girls' activities. Both male and female homosexuals were more likely to have experienced far-ranging and deep-seated gender nonconformity than were heterosexuals. One-half of homosexual males but only one-quarter of heterosexual males did not conform to a typical "masculine" identity pattern; while about four-fifths of homosexual females but only two-thirds of heterosexual females were not highly "feminine" during childhood. Childhood gender nonconformity in homosexual people also occurs in societies other than the United States. A comparative study of males in the United States, Guatemala, and Brazil indicated that gender nonconformity related to childhood toy and activity interests, as well as sexual interest in other boys, were behavioral indicators of adult homosexual orientation (Whitam, 1980). Bell and his colleagues speculated that "if there is a biological basis for homosexuality, it probably accounts for gender nonconformity as well as for sexual orientation" (1981, p. 217). A 15-year longitudinal study that compared gender-role behavior in boys and later sexual orientation found similar results (Green, 1987). Boys who preferred dolls to other toys, disliked rough-and-tumble play, and preferred role-playing as a female rather than a male (such as playing mommy rather than daddy when playing house) were highly likely to have homosexual orientations later in life, although some of these boys were heterosexual as adults. In addition, research on cognitive abilities in adults has found that cognitive patterns of homosexual men fall between the cognitive patterns of heterosexual men and heterosexual women in regard to spatial ability and verbal fluency, again indicating brain differences (McCormick et al., 1990).

What do you think the impact would be if sexual orientation were absolutely proven to be biologically caused? Give yourself a minute to come up with your own ideas before reading on.

The possible proof of biological causation of homosexuality raises some important issues. On the one hand, if homosexuality were found to be biologically based, the assumption that homosexuality is unnatural would be challenged because something biologically innate is natural for that person. Society might thus become more accepting of homosexuality. One survey found that people who believed homosexuals were "born that way" had more positive, accepting attitudes about homosexuality than those who believed that homosexuals chose or learned to be homosexual (Gelman et al., 1992). Parents who have blamed themselves or have been blamed by others for causing what they view as an aberration could be relieved of their guilt. Society's expectations for gender-role behaviors might become more flexible given the acceptance of biologically based gender nonconformity. On the other hand, if homosexuality were shown to be biologically caused and homosexuals were labeled as biologically "defective," attempts to use abortion to eliminate homosexuality or biologic engineering to prevent or change homosexuality in utero might be implemented (Gelman et al., 1992). During the 1930s and 1940s, hormone therapy (consisting of androgen supplements) was used to try to "cure" male homosexuality, although the data were inconsistent regarding homosexuality and hormone imbalance. Such hormone therapy, while it sometimes increased sexual interest, did not result in significant changes in sexual orientation (Money & Ehrhardt, 1972).

In conclusion, research is suggesting that there is a biological predisposition to exclusive homosexuality. However, the causes of sexual orientation in general, and homosexuality specifically, remain speculative at this point (Gooren et al., 1990). It seems more appropriate to think of the continuum of sexual orientation as influenced by an interaction of various psychosocial and biological factors, which may be unique for each person, than to think in terms of a single cause for sexual orientation. More importantly, as Evelyn Hooker has stated in Gelman et al., 1992, "Why do we want to know the cause? ... If we accept it as a given, then we come much closer to the kinds of attitudes which will make it possible for homosexuals to lead a decent life in society" (p. 53).

Lifestyles

As we have discussed in the preceding section, people whose sexual orientation is homosexual cannot be clearly distinguished from heterosexual people on the basis of hormonal balance or mental health. This leads to another observation: Homosexual lifestyles are as varied as heterosexual lifestyles. All social classes, occupations, races, religions, and political persuasions are represented among homosexual people. The only characteristics homosexual people necessarily have in common are their desire for emotional and sexual fulfillment with someone of the same sex and their shared experience of oppression from a hostile social environment.

Despite their many similarities to heterosexual people and the wide variety of their lifestyles, stereotypes about homosexual people exist (Hersch, 1991a). Many of these concern their physical appearance (Terry, 1990). It is true that there are some homosexual individuals who dress and act according to commonly held stereotypes. Characteristics often associated with an identifiable homosexual man include exaggerated "feminine" gestures and tight and flashy clothing; in contrast, the image of a stereotypically recognizable lesbian includes such attributes as short hair and highly "masculine" clothing and gestures.

> Many people are astonished when a national hero, sports champion, film star, coworker, or neighbor is discovered to be a homosexual ..., because it is a common and popular misconception that all homosexual men are swishy, unmanly, and easily recognized in public because of their effeminate ways and exaggerated stereotyping of femininity. Correspondingly, a lesbian is misconstrued as always being mannish in bearing, speech, and dress, and publicly recognizable because of masculine accouterments, crudity, and exaggerated toughness. (Money, 1988, p. 122)

Although the incidence of people who fit the stereotypes is small, the stereotypes persist (Herek et al., 1991). This is in part because people who believe that homosexual individuals look a certain way notice and categorize (sometimes erro-

Contrary to popular stereotypes, homosexual individuals exhibit a wide variety of lifestyles and relationships.

neously) those who seem to fit the image. The fact that most homosexual people may not fit the stereotype at all often goes unnoticed. One study measured general gender-role attributes and found no significant differences in characteristics of masculinity and femininity among homosexual, bisexual, and heterosexual male and female college students (Storms, 1980). Another study found that neither heterosexual nor homosexual subjects could exceed chance levels of discriminating between videotaped interviews of homosexual and heterosexual men and women (Berger, 1990).

There are far more basic elements of a homosexual lifestyle than how a person dresses. We look briefly at some of these in the following sections.

Homosexual Relationships

Some people mistakenly think that homosexual partners always enact the stereotypically active "male" or passive "female" roles. This notion stems in part from the pervasive heterosexual model of relationships. Because this model of male–female role-playing has historically been the predominant one in our culture, both heterosexual and homosexual intimate relationships have typically been patterned after it. However, options for more egalitarian relationships have increased in recent years, and these are being followed by both heterosexual and homosexual couples. In this regard, a homosexual relationship may well be the more flexible in our society.

One research study that compared characteristics of homosexual and heterosexual relationships found major differences in gender roles. The study reported that heterosexual couples were likely to adhere more closely to traditional gender-role expectations than were homosexual couples. Most of the homosexual relationships studied resembled "best friendships" combined with romantic and erotic attraction. The researcher suggested that studies of homosexual couples can provide insights and models for heterosexual couples who are trying to establish more egalitarian relationships (Peplau, 1981).

There are some differences between homosexual men and women in the number of their sexual partners (Rothblum, 1989). Lesbians are likely to have had fewer than 10 sexual partners, and lesbian couples are more likely than male couples to have monogamous relationships (Thoresen, 1984). Prior to the AIDS epidemic, some homosexual men had frequent casual sexual encounters — sometimes hundreds or more (Bell & Weinberg, 1978; Kinsey et al., 1948). These encounters were sometimes exceedingly brief, occurring in bathhouses, public restrooms, or in film booths in pornography shops. This difference between homosexual men and women may reflect traditional gender-role definitions. Males learn initially to be interested in sex, while females learn initially to be interested in building relationships.

Several studies have found that homosexual women differ from homosexual men in the extent to which they associate emotional closeness with sex (Leigh, 1989; Markowitz, 1991). In one study, most of the lesbians waited to have sex with a partner until they had developed emotional intimacy. Although 46% of gay men had become friends with their partner before having sex, as a group they were more likely than lesbians to have had sexual experiences with casual acquaintances or people they had just met. In addition, gay men with primary partners were much more likely to have sexual experiences with others than were lesbians or heterosexual women and men. What explains the tendency toward less sexual exclusiveness among gay men? The researcher suggested that gender-role socialization places more emphasis on and gives more permission for casual sex for males than for females. Men's and women's motivations for sexual involvement are different, regardless of the sex of their partners (Leigh, 1989). Heterosexual relationships are to some extent a compromise between male and female gender-role expectations and thus may include exclusiveness for both partners. However, with gay male relationships this particular compromise is not typically as necessary, and casual sex outside an intimate relationship can occur more easily (Peplau, 1981).

However, sexual involvement with many partners is not universal among homosexual men (Isay, 1989). Many men feel no desire for multiple relationships, and others have decided that multiple relationships do not adequately meet their needs. Some men want to have a strong emotional relationship before becoming sexually involved. And for some men, being involved in an ongoing relationship eliminates sexual interest in other men (Tripp, 1975). In some cases the growing desire of homosexual men to modify the definition of masculinity has encouraged them to develop committed, multidimensional relationships rather than pursuing casual sexual encounters. Also, many gay men are reducing the numbers of their sexual partners or establishing monogamous relationships because of concerns about contracting AIDS (McNaught, 1991; Schecter et al., 1984; Stulberg & Smith, 1988). In addition, it is important to remember that homosexual relationships are multidimensional and not based solely on sex (Adler et al., 1986).

Peplau (1981) examined characteristics of homosexual love relationships. This study found many similarities between homosexual and heterosexual relationships, and reported that most differences in relationships have more to do with whether the partners are men or women than with whether they are homosexual or heterosexual. Matched samples (overrepresented by young, well-educated, middle-class whites) of homosexual females and males and heterosexual females and males all indicated that "being able to talk about my most intimate feelings" with a

A gay couple following their holy union ceremony.

partner was most important in a love relationship. The research also found that partners in a love relationship, regardless of sexual orientation, must deal with and attempt to reconcile desires for togetherness and independence. For many individuals these desires were not mutually exclusive; some people wanted both a secure love relationship and meaningful activities and friendships separate from the relationship. Responses from homosexual and heterosexual women were distinct in some ways from those of homosexual and heterosexual men. Women placed greater importance on emotional expressiveness within a relationship than did men. Women also gave higher ratings to the importance of having an egalitarian relationship and having similar attitudes and political beliefs.

Although marriage between two people of the same sex is not legally recognized by any state, many homosexual couples share significant one-to-one relationships. One-half of the lesbians and one-quarter of the homosexual men in Bell and Weinberg's study were in primary relationships. The Metropolitan Community Church, which primarily serves gay people, performs holy unions (this term is used because marriage is a legal contract) that provide the spiritual significance of marriage for homosexual couples. The Unitarian church and Reform Judaism also bless gay unions. In Denmark, gay people can legally marry (McNaught, 1991).

Family Life

Traditionally, a family has been considered to consist of a heterosexual couple and their offspring, but many forms of family life exist in contemporary society. Single-parent families have become more prevalent as the divorce rate has increased and as more women have decided to have children outside of marriage. Homosexual individuals also form family units, either as single parents or as couples, with children brought into the family or born through a variety of circumstances. Some homosexual individuals or couples become parents with adopted or foster children, and many homosexual people have children who were born in previous heterosexual marriages (Wyers, 1987). About one-third of lesbians are mothers from heterosexual relationships or by artificial insemination (Baker, 1990). For our purposes, therefore, "family" means any group of two or more people who are committed to caring about each other (Dahlheimer and Feigal, 1991). Supportive, involved friends often take the role of extended family (Ainslie & Feltey, 1991).

The custody of children in divorce proceedings is commonly biased toward the mother. However, if the mother is an acknowledged lesbian, this may jeopardize her claim to custody (Pollack, 1990). A homosexual father attempting to gain custody has the double disadvantage in court of being a man and a homosexual (Schwartz, 1991). Some people have challenged the ability of homosexual parents to provide a positive family environment for children. However, research has found that children of lesbian mothers are essentially no different from other children in terms of self-esteem, gender-related problems, gender roles, sexual orientation, and general development (Gibbs, 1989; Green et al., 1986; Hoeffer, 1981; Huggins, 1989; Kirkpatrick et al., 1981). Lesbian mothers have been found to be similar to heterosexual mothers in lifestyle, maternal interests, and parenting behavior (Gibbs, 1989; Kirkpatrick, 1982; Lewin, 1981).

Families headed by homosexual parents are one of several kinds of nontraditional families.

Children may also be adopted or conceived by lesbians through artificial insemination or with a partner chosen for just this purpose (Crawford, 1988; Rohrbaugh, 1989). Semen can be obtained from a sperm bank or by individual arrangements with a selected donor. One woman who became pregnant through a selected donor shared her experience:

My partner and I wanted to have a child, and we decided to ask a close male friend to be the donor. We charted my ovulation cycle for several months and then got together with him monthly for the artificial insemination. He ejaculated in privacy and brought his semen to our bedroom. We put the sperm in a cervical cap and inserted it to insure contact between the semen and the cervix. It took me about five months to become pregnant, and now we have a beautiful baby boy. (Authors' files)

A homosexual man who wants to be a father may make a personal agreement with a woman who agrees to carry his child. When a man or woman selects a surrogate or donor known to him or her, it is important for the future biological and legal parents to discuss their respective rights and responsibilities; a legal document supporting the agreement is advisable. Many new concepts of family are emerging, and the desire for legal and social recognition of gay and lesbian families increases (Ainslie & Feltey, 1991).

Sexual Expression

Homosexual individuals who are in sexual relationships engage in sexual behaviors similar to those of heterosexual persons, with the exception of penile–vaginal intercourse. Touching, kissing, body contact, manual–genital stimulation, oral–genital contact, and anal stimulation are techniques that are used during sexual interactions. Younger homosexual people are typically more likely to have experienced a greater variety of sexual behaviors than have older people (Bell & Weinberg, 1978), as is the case with the heterosexual population.

Some lesbian couples may have a more relaxed and less goal-oriented approach to sexual intimacy than do some heterosexual couples.

Sexual Behaviors Among Homosexual Women. Several misconceptions exist regarding lesbian sexual expression. One is the notion that sex between women is unsatisfactory because a penis is lacking. Kinsey's 1953 study indicated that lesbian women had orgasms in a greater percentage of sexual encounters than did heterosexual married women. After five years of marriage, 55% of heterosexual women had orgasms in 60–100% of sexual contacts. Whereas after five years of homosexual experience, 78% of homosexual women had orgasms in 60–100% of their sexual encounters. Kinsey has suggested that these results may be due to a better understanding of sexual and psychological response between members of the same sex than between those of different sexes. Shere Hite stated that greater sexual satisfaction between women may occur because "lesbian sexual relations tend to be longer and involve more all-over body sensuality" (1976, p. 413).

Another mistaken belief is that dildos (penis-shaped devices) are used extensively among lesbians. In fact, only 2% of the homosexual women in Hunt's 1974 survey had ever used a dildo. Manual stimulation, oral contact, and rubbing genitals together or against the partner's body are included in lesbian sexual behaviors (Hite, 1976; Hunt, 1974; Kinsey, 1953). Rubbing genitals against someone's body or genital area is called *tribadism*. Many lesbians like this form of sexual play because it involves all-over body contact and a generalized sensuality. Some women find the thrusting very exciting; others straddle a partner's leg and rub gently. Some rub the clitoris on the partner's pubic bone (Loulan, 1984).

It may be more difficult for lesbians to initiate a sexual relationship than for either heterosexual or male homosexual persons. One explanation for this is that society conditions women to respond to sexual initiation rather than to take the lead. Without the familiar cues of "being pursued," women may not even be aware of a mutual attraction; each is waiting for the other person to take a first step to demonstrate interest. Consequently, the sexual relationship may not even begin (Schwartz & Blumstein, 1973). A woman explains:

Like heterosexuals, homosexuals have relationships that vary from casual encounters to close, caring involvements.

> Initiating dates is difficult for lesbians because most of us never learned how to ask someone out. We were supposed to wait for the boys to ask us! Two women attempting to get together face this process with little experience and a lot of awkwardness. (Loulan, 1984, p. 20)

A survey comparing heterosexual and homosexual patterns concluded that lesbian couples have sex less frequently than do heterosexual couples. The gap between the lovemaking frequency of lesbian and heterosexual couples widens dramatically as the relationships continue over time. In the first two years of the relationship, 76% of lesbians and 83% of heterosexual couples reported making love one or more times per week. After two years, 37% of lesbians and 73% of heterosexual couples reported that same frequency (Blumstein & Schwartz, 1983). One explanation for this may be that just as women are not socialized to initiate sexual relationships, they are not socialized to initiate individual sexual encounters within such a relationship. Both partners in a long-term lesbian relationship may want to make love more frequently than they do, but neither feels comfortable initiating such activities.

Sexual Behaviors Among Homosexual Men.   Contrary to the stereotype that sexual experiences between men are completely genitally focused, extragenital eroticism and affection are important aspects of sexual contact for many homosexual men:

> No doubt most people will always conceive of male sexuality in general, and male homosexuality in particular, in terms of phallic actions.... These and similar ideas have led to a widely held impression that homosexual practices lack precisely those kinds of affection which, in fact, are usually the main motives behind them. (Tripp, 1975, p. 102)

Hugging, kissing, and total-body caressing are important, as one homosexual man clearly states:

One of the best parts of making love is the time we spend holding each other, touching each other's faces, and looking into the other's eyes. (Authors' files)

Although anal intercourse is often thought to be the most prevalent sexual behavior between homosexual men, research has shown that fellatio is in fact the most common mode of expression (Bell & Weinberg, 1978; Weinrich, 1991). Mutual masturbation is the next most common, and anal intercourse is least common. Because AIDS is spread through the exchange of bodily fluids, some gay men are changing their patterns of sexual activity by using condoms and avoiding any exchange of semen (Gochros, 1992). (Chapter 19 includes a detailed discussion of AIDS prevention strategies.)

Coming Out

The extent to which a homosexual person decides to be secretive or open about his or her sexual orientation has a significant effect on his or her lifestyle. There are various degrees of being "in the closet," and there are several steps in the process of **coming out** — acknowledging, accepting, and openly expressing one's homosexuality (Rothblum, 1989). Although these decisions are unique to each individual and situation, there are often some common elements.

Self-Acknowledgment. Very "closeted" homosexual men and women may attempt to suppress their sexual orientation even from their own awareness. These people may actively seek sexual encounters with members of the other sex, and it is not uncommon for them to marry in an attempt to convince themselves of their "normalcy." Some of the homosexual people who have previously been married (one-third of the women and one-fifth of the men in the Bell and Weinberg study) may have done so to avoid openly confronting their sexual orientation. As one man, now openly homosexual, stated:

As I look back now, I can see that my playboy lifestyle was really an attempt to convince myself that the nagging attraction I felt for John was just a good friendship. It was as if I thought I could change my feelings by having sex with enough women. (Authors' files)

The initial step in coming out is usually a person's realization that she or he feels different from the heterosexual model (Herdt, 1992). Some people report knowing they were homosexual when they were small children. Many realize during adolescence that something is missing in their heterosexual involvements and that they find same-sex peers sexually attractive (Hersch, 1991). Once individuals recognize homosexual feelings, they must confront their own internalized homophobia as they deal with the reality that they are members of a stigmatized minority group (Padesky, 1989).

Self-Acceptance. Accepting one's homosexuality is the next important step after realizing it. Self-acceptance is often difficult, for it involves overcoming the internalized negative and homophobic societal view of homosexuality:

> Initially a homosexual person often has difficulty from the pervasive condemnatory attitudes toward homosexuality. Like the prejudiced heterosexual, his early impressions about homosexuality came from the culture around him. As a child he heard the same nasty references to homosexuals. He has heard them called "queers," seen them portrayed as dissolute and sad, on stage and screen, in novels, in newspaper articles. His own attitude toward homosexuality has evolved out of a context almost wholly derogatory. His prejudice against himself is an almost exact parallel to the prejudice against homosexuals held in the larger culture. (Weinberg, 1973, p. 74)

When individuals realize that they belong to a socially stigmatized group, self-acceptance becomes a difficult but essential challenge (Margolies et al., 1988).

Gay and lesbian adolescents may experience particularly profound confusion about their feelings. They typically endorse the erroneous, negative stereotypes about homosexuality and may fail to recognize their homosexual feelings or feel particularly bad about themselves for their feelings and for the intense unhappiness, persecution, and rejection that seems inevitable (Herdt & Boxer, 1992). They are also likely to believe that they are the only young persons to feel this way — and thus to feel acutely alone and separate from their peer group, which is so important at this stage of life (Schneider & Tremble, 1986). Families that are very rigid, moralistic, and gender-role stereotyped contribute added stress to gay and lesbian adolescents (Hackenbruck, 1987). Due to these difficulties, gay and lesbian youth are two to three times more likely than other adolescents to attempt suicide (Hersch, 1991b). Isolation, low self-esteem, and physical and verbal abuse are frequently cited as the reasons for suicide attempts (Cwayna et al., 1991). It can be helpful for gay and lesbian adolescents to find at least one supportive, nonjudgmental adult with whom to talk.

Disclosure. Following acknowledgment and self-acceptance is the decision to be secretive or open. Deciding to remain in the closet may erode a person's pride and self-respect, yet concerns about consequences from disclosure often encourage secrecy (Wells & Kline, 1987). As a result, interpersonal relationships may remain distant:

> To avoid awkwardness or dishonesty, many of us just refrain from talking openly about our personal lives. Our co-workers and co-students see us as shy, withdrawn, reserved, snobbish — when actually we are trying to protect ourselves from *their homophobia!* (Loulan, 1984, p. 17)

Concealment can intensify social isolation and personal loneliness (Gartrell, 1987). It also inhibits participation in any gay rights activities. Whatever security is gained by concealment can also be jeopardized by discovery at any time. **Passing** is a term sometimes used for maintaining the false image of heterosexuality (Lynch, 1992). Passing as heterosexual is usually quite easy because most people assume that everyone is heterosexual.

Being homosexual usually requires ongoing decisions about whether to be in or out of the closet, as new relationships and situations unfold. Heterosexuals sometimes do not understand this, as exemplified by the following comment:

I don't see any reason why they have to tell anyone. They can just lead their lives without making such a big deal out of it. (Authors' files)

Openly expressing one's homosexuality can be an important part of coming out.

In most daily interactions, sexual orientation is irrelevant. However, imagine being a closeted homosexual person and hearing a friend make a derogatory reference to "fags" or "dykes," being asked "When are you going to settle down and get married?" or being invited to an office party for couples. In one writer's words, "Because of its devalued status, affirmation of homosexuality (or disclaiming it) becomes a more significant act than the same would be for a heterosexual, with significant consequences for a lifestyle" (Gagnon, 1977, p. 248). Passing can negatively affect the quality of gay and lesbian relationships (Berger, 1990). A lesbian author explains:

> The daily act of having to live a double life — one that you show in public, one that you act in private — negatively influences our sexual expression. It is difficult to be sexual with someone you have denied all week at work. Switching gears from being "friends" outside your home to passionate lovers inside has a devastating effect on our ability to be sexually free. (Loulan, 1984, p. 23)

With some exceptions, the more within "the system" a person is or desires to be, the more risk there is in being open about one's sexual orientation (Lynch, 1992). Jobs, social position, and friends may all be placed in jeopardy (Padesky, 1989). Bell and Weinberg (1978) confirmed this notion with their findings that relatively "out" homosexual men and women are more likely to have lower social status (less education and income) than do those who remain covert. The conservativeness of the surrounding community may further affect one's decisions about whether or not to come out and to whom.

OUR SEXUALITY

"Dear Abby"

Dear Abby: Some time ago you made the statement in your column that lesbians are born, not made.

Abby, I have a beautiful, talented 30-year-old daughter who is a lesbian, and I have always blamed myself for that. When she was little, she hated dresses, so I let her wear blue jeans and T-shirts just like her brothers wore. I didn't think a thing of it at the time, but now I realize I helped to make a tomboy out of her. I blame myself for not insisting that she dress and act like a girl instead of putting her in boys' clothes and encouraging her to play boys' games with her brothers and their friends.

So, my question is, if I didn't contribute to the way she turned out, how in the world did it happen? — Puzzled in Hope, Ark.

Dear Puzzled: Don't blame yourself. Millions of little girls are tomboys and prefer jeans to dresses, yet the vast majority of them do not become lesbians. The causes of lesbianism, like those of male homosexuality, are complex and not fully understood, but there is growing evidence that many lesbians are born with a predisposition in that direction.

The important thing to remember is that sexual preference is not a matter of choice; it is determined at a very early age. Children who grow up to be homosexuals need their parents' love and understanding no less than other children do. In fact, they need it more.

Coming out may be a particularly difficult issue for homosexual adults who are parents. Some stay in marriages because of being parents (Green & Clunis, 1989). Approximately 60% of homosexual men and women who have been married have at least one child (Bell & Weinberg, 1978). The difficulties a gay parent faces in attempting to attain custody or visitation rights may be severe (Erlichman, 1989). It is not unusual for gay parents to lose these rights strictly on the basis of their sexual orientation, regardless of their fitness as parents (Schwartz, 1991). Yet some courts hold that homosexuality itself is not proof of unfitness. The pattern of court decisions at this time is arbitrary and uncertain.

Telling the Family. Disclosing one's homosexuality to family can be more difficult than disclosing it to others (Cain, 1991). Coming out to one's family is a particularly significant step, as the following account by a 35-year-old man illustrates:

Most of my vacation at home went well, but the ending was indeed difficult. Gay people kept cropping up in conversation. My mother was very down on them (us), and I of course was disagreeing with her. Finally she asked me if I was "one of them." I said "yes." It was very difficult for her to deal with. She asked a lot of questions, which I answered as calmly, honestly, and rationally as I could. We spent a rather strained day together. It was so painful for me to see her suffering so much heartache over this, and not even having a clue that the issue is the oppression of gay people. I just wish my mother didn't have to suffer so much from all this. (Authors' files)

Parents often do experience difficult feelings from the revelation that a child is homosexual. They may react with anger or with guilt about what they "did wrong" (Strommen, 1989) (see the box "Dear Abby"). Because telling the family is so difficult, many homosexual people do not do so. Approximately half of the

OUR SEXUALITY

Letter from a Gay Man to His Parents

Dear Mom and Dad,

Hi! I hope that all is well with you.

Well, I was waiting to tell you about my sexuality — waiting for a time when it would be best for you to deal with it. But now that it is out in the open, I'm happy that I can share that part of my life with you. My relationship with Bob is a big part of what is positive in my life, so not being able to share that has really been difficult for me.

I would hope that my sharing this with you will bring us closer together. I would like to do anything I can to help you understand me and to understand what it's like to be gay. Please realize that you are in no way responsible for my sexual preference. What you did or didn't do as parents is not what determined my sexuality. I want to be absolutely clear — you are not to "blame," it is not your "fault" — it's just part of who I am, and it is a beautiful part of me. So do

not feel guilty. Besides, accepting my feelings has made me truly happy for the first time in my life. My being gay is not a tragedy — it's just part of who I am.

I know that my preference to be in a relationship with a man is going to be difficult for you to understand and difficult to accept. There is a lot of social pressure and programming against it. For that reason I had a hard time accepting it myself. I tried to deny it, in fact, for 29 years. I didn't want to disappoint you as parents, and I wanted to be "normal" and accepted by those around me. As I said, it was not easy to accept the social context, but I firmly believe, deep in my heart and soul, that being with another man is going to make me happy and fulfilled (it has already).

My feelings for a man are deeper, more beautiful, and more intense than anything I have felt with a woman. How can it be wrong if it fills

me full of joy and happiness? How can it be wrong when being with a man is just so comfortable and easy?

I hope you can accept my relationship because it is the most important aspect of my life — that love and caring form a base for everything else that I do. I would very much like you to share my life, and I hope that you can see that I'm still the same person that you have always loved and cared about. I definitely do not want to be in the position of having to choose between your approval and my happiness — because from my perspective, the choice would be an obvious but unfortunate one.

Also, please try to react out of love, not fear, guilt, or sadness. I tried to write this letter from my heart, and I hope that you will receive it in the same spirit in which it was written.

I love you very much,

Don

(Authors' files)

respondents in the Bell and Weinberg survey believed that their parents did not know about their homosexuality. Fathers were somewhat less likely to know than were mothers. The box "Letter from a Gay Man to His Parents" sensitively addresses many of the issues involved in coming out to parents.

In the past, each person usually decided if, when, and how to come out (except when his or her homosexuality was discovered by accident). Now, however, many homosexual men are compelled to come out when they test positive for the AIDS virus or begin exhibiting symptoms of that deadly disease. Other homosexual men and women — often celebrities or prominent business or political leaders — may find others abruptly opening the closet door for them. "Outing" is the term used when an individual or group publicizes the homosexual orientation of someone who would otherwise not be open about it. "Outing" others is something that some gay rights activists have done in recent years to try to combat homophobic attitudes and policies; it remains a highly controversial tactic (Turque et al., 1991).

Involvement in the Gay Community. The need to belong is a deeply felt human need. For homosexual individuals, a sense of community helps provide a sense of belonging and the affirmation and acceptance that is missing in the larger culture

This gay men's chorus is one of many community activities developed by homosexual people.

(Pearlman, 1988). Social and political involvement with other homosexual people is another step in the coming-out process. Some aspects of homosexual lifestyles center around various gay subcultures. In larger cities, gay and lesbian bars and cafés cater to different groups or clientele. Like heterosexual bars, these gathering places range from low-key socializing spots to establishments with reputations for casual pickups. Lesbians are far less likely to "cruise" in search of casual sexual encounters than are gay men. But many gay men do not cruise either. Particularly in years past, gay bars — as well as certain designated recreational areas, restaurants, and bathhouses — served an important function: often they were the only places where homosexual patrons could drop the facade of heterosexuality. In recent years this need has diminished to some extent. Gay people have helped found service organizations, educational centers, and professional organizations (Lukes & Land, 1990). Religious organizations for gay people have been established, including the Metropolitan Community Church and denominational groups such as Dignity for Roman Catholics and Integrity for Episcopalians. And the AIDS crisis has precipitated increased community involvement and coherence. The gay and lesbian communities have mobilized educational efforts, developed innovative programs for caring for AIDS patients, created an impressive network of volunteers to provide needed help and support for persons with AIDS, and lobbied — often quite visibly — for increased AIDS awareness and funding.

Since its beginning in the 1960s, the growing gay rights movement has provided support for many homosexual men and women to be more open about their sexual orientation. The following section describes some of the movement's activities.

The Gay Rights Movement

In the 1950s some organizations for gay people were established despite the very conservative atmosphere of the times. The Mattachine Society had chapters in many cities, providing a national network for support and communication among

Gay rights supporters want homosexual individuals to have the same rights, liberties, freedom from harassment, and legal protections that other citizens enjoy.

homosexuals. The Daughters of Bilitis, an organization of lesbians, published a journal called *The Ladder,* which contained fiction, poetry, and political articles. The goals of both organizations were to educate homosexual and heterosexual people about homosexuality, increase understanding of homosexuality, and eliminate discriminatory laws toward homosexual individuals (Katz, 1976).

During the 1960s many people began to question traditional aspects of American life in all areas, including the sexual. In this atmosphere more gay people began to respond to social and political changes and to question and challenge the social problems they faced. The symbolic birth of gay activism occurred in 1969 in New York City when police raided a gay bar, the Stonewall. Police raids on gay bars were common occurrences, but this time people in the bar resisted and fought back. A riot ensued and did not end until the following day. The Stonewall incident served as a catalyst for the formation of gay rights groups, and activities such as Gay Pride Week and parades are held in yearly commemoration of the Stonewall riot (Herrell, 1992).

Since the early 1970s, groups have worked to end various kinds of discrimination against homosexual people. The National Gay Task Force was founded in 1973 to work with homosexual men and women around the country to help achieve legal rights. The gay rights movement has been primarily concerned with legislation related to consensual sex and civil rights. Both of these legal areas are seen as essential to providing homosexual people the same legal protection that heterosexual people enjoy. The movement's central philosophy is that private consensual sexual expression is not a matter of legal concern, nor is it adequate reason to deny or rescind housing or employment. By the 1990s several states had established gay rights guarantees (McNaught, 1991). Most Americans — 71% — believe that gays should have equal job opportunities (Salholz et al., 1990a).

A major legislative goal of gay rights advocates is an amendment to the 1964 Civil Rights Act that would broaden it to include "affectional or sexual orientation" along with race, creed, color, and sex. This would make it illegal to discrim-

ETHICAL/LEGAL ISSUES IN HUMAN SEXUALITY

The Law and Homosexuality

Laws against homosexual behaviors, which stem from biblical injunctions against same-sex contact, have historically been exceedingly punitive. People with homosexual orientations have been tortured and put to death throughout Western history. In the American colonies, homosexual people were condemned to death by drowning and burning. In the late 1770s, Thomas Jefferson was among the political leaders who suggested reducing the punishment from death to castration for men who committed homosexual acts (Katz, 1976).

Today official views and actions on homosexuality reflect changed attitudes. The British Wolfenden Report of 1957 was based on a 10-year study by the Committee on Homosexual Offenses and Prostitution. The report maintained that there was no evidence that homosexual behavior contributed to "social decay," that the personal beliefs of those who consider homosexual behavior unnatural or sinful were not valid reasons to override personal privacy or to make an act criminal, that the removal of criminal sanctions against homosexual behaviors in private between consenting adults would not result in an increase in homosexuality, and that private morality was not the law's concern. The report recommended that sexual behavior in private between consenting adults should not be a criminal offense, and the British Parliament eventually supported that position.

As for our own country, although many states have passed legislation legalizing private sexual behavior between consenting adults, in many other states sexual behaviors such as oral–genital contact, manual–genital stimulation, and anal intercourse are still illegal, whether performed by same- or other-sex partners. By 1990, 47% of American adults surveyed believed that homosexual relations between consenting adults should be legal; nevertheless, 23 states still have sodomy laws. Although most of these laws prohibit certain actions without regard to who is performing them, they are usually enforced against homosexual men. Moreover, in 1986 the U.S. Supreme Court upheld states' rights to prosecute consenting adults who engage in oral and anal sex (*Hardwick* v. *Bowers,* 106 S. Ct. 2841). For a further discussion of U.S. sodomy laws, see the box in Chapter 9 titled "The Law and Sexual Behaviors."

inate in housing, employment, insurance, and public accommodations on the grounds of sexual orientation. Several large private corporations and the Federal Civil Service Commission have established equal-opportunity employment in regard to homosexuality. This means that it is illegal for these employers to discriminate against anyone in hiring or firing on the basis of sexual orientation. Some local governments have adopted laws prohibiting discrimination on the basis of sexual orientation. For example, some U.S. cities have "domestic partnership" laws that grant gays a variety of spousal rights, such as insurance benefits and bereavement leave (Salholz et al., 1990). Expansion of family rights such as the formal recognition of gay and lesbian marriages or the legal right of a coparent to raise a child upon the death of the birth mother are further goals (Pollack, 1991).

Many gay men and lesbians have become involved in gay rights advocacy for the first time as a result of their concerns about AIDS (Clarke, 1985). Much recent gay activism has focused on funding for AIDS research, providing support for victims and their friends and families, public education about AIDS, and volunteer work. As traumatic and painful as the AIDS epidemic has been, it has also strengthened the gay community (Stulberg & Smith, 1988).

Despite some gains in gay civil rights, problems continue. Antigay sentiment can escalate to drastic proportions. Many cities are reporting an increase in physical assaults on gays and others suspected of being gay (Berrill & Kane, 1992).

Many homosexuals have become involved in gay rights as a result of their concerns about AIDS. The AIDS quilt has been exhibited in cities throughout the United States. Each square of this immense quilt was made by loved ones or friends of someone who died from AIDS.

These events indicate a pathological fear and hatred of homosexuality; they deepen the commitment of gays and others sympathetic to their concerns to eradicate the attitudes that contribute to such violence. The National Gay Task Force has started a major project to monitor and document violence against homosexuals. The data will be used as a tool for civil rights advocacy and to help reduce gay victimization. In 1990 President Bush signed into law the Hate Crimes Statistics Act, which provides resources to document hate crimes in the United States. Gay rights advocates are attempting to pass antidiscriminatory legislation in various places throughout the country. It is our hope that the gay civil rights movement will prevail and that homosexual Americans will be freer to live, work, and contribute to society.

Summary

The word *homosexual* can be an objective or subjective appraisal of sexual behavior, emotional affiliation, and/or self-definition.

A Continuum of Sexual Orientations

Kinsey's seven-point continuum ranges from exclusive heterosexuality to exclusive homosexuality. Kinsey based his ratings on a combination of overt sexual behaviors and erotic attractions.

According to estimates based on methodological adjustments between the Kinsey and Hunt survey data, approximately 2% of men and 1% of women are exclusively homosexual, about 23% of men and 14% of women have had both homosexual and heterosexual experiences, and roughly 75% of men and 85% of women are exclusively heterosexual.

Bisexuality can be characterized by overt behaviors and/or erotic responses to both males and females. As with heterosexuality and homosexuality, a clear-cut definition of bisexuality is difficult to establish.

Four types of bisexuality include bisexuality as a real orientation, a transitory orientation, a transitional orientation, or homosexual denial.

Societal Attitudes

Cross-cultural attitudes toward homosexuality vary from condemnation to acceptance. Negative attitudes toward homosexuality still predominate in our society.

Current theological positions toward homosexuality include the rejecting–punitive, rejecting–nonpunitive, qualified-acceptance, and full-acceptance stances.

Homophobia is the irrational fear of homosexuality, the fear of homosexual feelings within oneself, or self-loathing because of one's own homosexuality.

Development of Sexual Orientation

There are a number of psychosocial and biological theories that attempt to explain the development of homosexuality. Some of the psychosocial theories relate to parenting patterns, life experiences, or the psychological attributes of the person. Theories of biological causation look to prenatal or adult hormone differences.

Various "treatments" have been used to attempt to change homosexual orientation to heterosexual. Such attempts in the past have not been successful, and much controversy surrounds current therapy designed to develop heterosexual functioning in homosexually oriented individuals.

Sexual orientation, regardless of where it falls on the continuum of heterosexuality and homosexuality, seems to be formed from a composite of inconsistent and undetermined elements.

Lifestyles

Contrary to popular stereotypes, homosexual individuals exhibit a wide variety of lifestyles.

As gender-role stereotyping has decreased, many homosexual and heterosexual couples have developed more egalitarian relationships. Some of the differences reported between homosexual men and homosexual women may be attributed to general gender-role differences between men and women.

The choice of coming out or being "in the closet" often has a significant impact on a homosexual person's lifestyle. The steps of coming out involve recognizing one's homosexual orientation, deciding how to view oneself, and being open about one's homosexuality.

The Gay Rights Movement

Gay rights activists have been promoting consenting adult and civil rights legislation and, more recently, campaigning for greater AIDS awareness and funding. These activities have met with opposition from various individuals and groups.

∽ *Thought Provokers* ∽

1. What do you think are the advantages and disadvantages of being bisexual, homosexual, heterosexual, or asexual?

2. How have you observed homophobia being expressed?

3. How do you think the emergence of AIDS has affected attitudes toward homosexuality? What do you think the longer-term changes will be?

Suggested Readings

Borhek, Mary (1983). *Coming Out to Parents.* New York: Pilgrim Press. This book explores the fears and misgivings of homosexual individuals coming out to their parents and their parents' disappointment, confusion, and guilt. It also provides suggestions for dealing with this process.

Boston Lesbian Psychologies Collective (1988). *Lesbian Psychologies.* Urbana: University of Illinois Press. This edited book contains a wide-ranging exploration of life issues confronting lesbians today, including sections on identity, relationships, family, therapy, and community.

Clark, Don (1987). *The New Loving Someone Gay.* Millbrae, Calif.: Celestial Arts. This book is designed to increase understanding and communication between homosexual people and their friends and families.

Gochros, Jean (1989). *When Husbands Come Out of the Closet.* New York: Haworth Press. This book explores the issues that wives confront when they learn that their husbands are sexually attracted to other men.

Griffin, Carolyn; Wirth, Marian; and Wirth, Arthur (1986). *Beyond Acceptance.* Englewood Cliffs, N.J.: Prentice-Hall. Written by and for parents of gays and lesbians, this book discusses the conflicts, problems, and solutions parents confront when they learn of their children's homosexuality.

Hanckel, Frances; and Cunningham, John (1979). *A Way of Love, A Way of Life.* New York: Lothrop, Lee & Shepard. This book is written to inform people, especially young people, about what it means to be gay. It discusses how young people who are gay can know that they are, how to develop positive attitudes about themselves, how to tell family and friends, where to go for help, the history of gay rights, and variations in lifestyles.

Isay, Richard (1989). *Being Homosexual: Gay Men and Their Development.* New York: Avon. This book explores the normal path of psychological and social development for gay men.

Loulan, JoAnn (1984). *Lesbian Sex.* San Francisco: Spinsters/Aunt Lute. This is an excellent book about lesbian sexual activities, relationships, and lifestyles, with exercises designed to enhance self-awareness and sexual expression.

McNaught, Brian (1988). *On Being Gay.* New York: St. Martin's. This book discusses the coming-out process, family relationships, lasting love relationships, and dealing with AIDS.

Schulenberg, Joy (1985). *Gay Parenting.* New York: Anchor Books. This book is a practical and comprehensive guide to dealing with becoming a parent, coming out to children, and custody issues.

Zinik, Gary (1985). "Identity Conflict or Adaptive Flexibility? Bisexuality Reconsidered." *Journal of Homosexuality* 11, 7–19. This article is about two opposing models of bisexual functioning, the "conflict model" and the "flexibility" model.

Resources

The National Gay Task Force, 1734 14th Street NW, Washington, D.C. 20009-4309; (202) 332-6483. This group provides information about social, political, and educational organizations in particular locales.

Parents and Friends of Lesbians and Gays (PFLAG), P.O. Box 27605, Washington, D.C. 20038; (202) 638-4200. This group provides support and counseling for parents and public education on gay rights.

PART FOUR

Sexuality and the Life Cycle

No woman can call herself free who
does not own and control her body.
No woman can call herself free until
she can choose consciously whether
she will not be a mother.

Margaret Sanger
Parade (1 December 1963)

CHAPTER 11
Contraception

Historical and Social Perspectives

Shared Responsibility

Currently Available Methods

New Directions in Contraception

Historical and Social Perspectives

Humankind's concern with controlling conception goes back at least to the beginning of recorded history (McLaren, 1990). In ancient Egypt women placed dried crocodile dung next to the cervix to prevent conception (Zatuchni, 1984). In sixth-century Greece, eating the uterus, testicle, or hoof paring of a mule was recommended. In more recent historical times, the eighteenth-century Italian adventurer Giovanni Casanova was noted for his animal-membrane condoms tied with a ribbon at the base of the penis. In seventeenth-century western Europe, condoms, withdrawal of the penis from the vagina before ejaculation, and vaginal sponges soaked in a variety of solutions were used for contraception.

Contraception in the United States

Although we may take for granted the variety of contraceptive, or birth control, methods available in the United States today, this state of affairs is quite recent. Throughout American history, both the methods available for contraception and the laws concerning their use have been restrictive. In the 1870s Anthony Comstock, then secretary of the New York Society for the Suppression of Vice, succeeded in having national laws enacted that prohibited disseminating contraceptive information through the U.S. mail on the grounds that such information was obscene (these were known as the Comstock Laws). At that time the only legitimate form of birth control was abstinence, and reproduction was viewed as the only acceptable reason for sexual intercourse.

Margaret Sanger was the person most instrumental in promoting the changes in birth control legislation and availability in the United States. In 1915 she opened an illegal clinic where women could obtain and learn to use the diaphragms she had shipped from Europe. She also published birth control information in her newspaper *The Woman Rebel.* As a result, Sanger was arraigned for violating the Comstock Laws. She fled to Europe to avoid certain prosecution but later returned to promote birth control – hormone research, a project financed by her wealthy friend Katherine Dexter McCormack. These women wanted to develop a reliable method by which women could control their own fertility. However, it was not until 1960 that the first birth control pills came on the U.S. market, after limited testing and research in Puerto Rico.

In 1965 the Supreme Court ruled in *Griswold* v. *Connecticut* that states could not prohibit the use of contraceptives by married people, basing the decision on the right to privacy of married couples (381 U.S. 479). In 1972 the Supreme Court case *Eisenstadt* v. *Baird* extended the right to privacy to unmarried individuals by decriminalizing the use of contraception by single people (405 U.S. 438).

Laws governing contraceptive availability continue to change. Recently, many states have liberalized their laws to allow the dispensing of contraceptives to adolescents without parental consent and the displaying of condoms and spermicidal foam on open pharmacy shelves rather than behind the counter. But many people still oppose television ads for condoms, and controversy continues on the national level about whether to require parental notification when minors receive contraceptive services from government-funded organizations. Even today, the availability and acceptability of contraception is still a contested issue.

Margaret Sanger was dedicated to helping women and families to have every child be a wanted child.

Contraception as a Contemporary Issue

In recent years the availability and use of reliable birth control has been seen as increasingly desirable for a variety of reasons. There has been a growing emphasis on having planned and wanted children. Many couples who want children wait for some years to establish their relationship and financial stability before starting a family. Birth control also enables couples and individuals to limit the size of their families. In particular, women who want to combine a career and parenthood depend on birth control. Finally, men and women who choose *not* to be parents can avoid unwanted pregnancies more successfully with effective birth control methods.

The use of birth control can also contribute to the physical health of the mother. Pregnancy itself has health risks, and spacing pregnancies usually results in better health for both mother and children, particularly when nutrition and health care are inadequate (DaVanzo et al., 1991). In some cases birth control is used to avoid the possibility of bearing children with hereditary diseases or birth defects.

Population growth is another concern that plays a part in some people's decision to limit their family size. The world's natural resources are limited, and a continually increasing population has precipitated a crisis (Alper, 1991). The current world population of 5.25 billion people is likely to double in the next century. Ninety percent of that growth is expected to occur in poorer, developing countries, where the population already exceeds the availability of bare necessities — hous-

OTHER TIMES, OTHER PLACES

The Burden of Fertility

Millions of women around the world lack the cultural support and money necessary to limit the number and timing of their children. The story of Dora Ayonga, a 23-year-old woman who lives in a village in Kenya, typifies the lives of women in many countries of the world. Her ability to have babies is her key to acceptance in the community. Dora has been pregnant five times in the last five years. One child has died, and the living children have the bloated bellies and skinny legs characteristic of malnourishment. Dora earns about 48 cents a day hoeing cornfields. A trip to the nearest family planning clinic would cost her five days' salary, equal to one week's supply of food for her family. In addition, her husband, who is out of work, wants her to have another baby. The more children he has, the higher his status in the village, where the average family has 12 children (Harden, 1985b).

ing, food, and fuel. For example, 37% of people in India cannot buy enough food to nourish themselves. Furthermore, overpopulation is a dire threat to the earth's environment. Some environmentalists urge the world to cut the growth rate in half over the next decade, which translates to limiting family size to two children across the world, with limits of one child per family in some areas (Toufexis, 1989). For these reasons, many people see population control through the use of birth control as a social necessity (Diczfalusy, 1992; Potts, 1991).

Objections to contraception often stem from religious mandate. The official doctrine of the Roman Catholic Church (as well as some other religions, such as the Fundamental Muslim faith) holds that the use of contraceptive means other than abstinence and methods based on the menstrual cycle is immoral. However, many contemporary religions approve of and even favor the use of birth control. Moreover, there is a wide diversity of views even among leaders of the Catholic Church. For example, a study commissioned by the Catholic Theological Society of America stated that "the mere fact that a couple is using artificial means of birth control cannot provide a sufficient basis to make a judgment about the morality or immorality of their married life and sexual expression" (Kosnik et al., 1977, p. 127).

Given that the official doctrine of the Roman Catholic Church prohibits the use of contraceptives, do you think Catholic women are less likely to use birth control? Come up with your own answer before reading further.

The discrepancy between doctrine and practice is wide: the majority of practicing Catholics in the United States use some kind of artificial contraception. In fact, the difference between Catholic and non-Catholic use of contraceptive devices is minimal. An investigation of birth control practices among a large sample of women of childbearing age found that 88.7% of Protestant women and 88.3% of Catholic women used some contraceptive method (Bachrach, 1984).

Shared Responsibility

In promoting contraception, Margaret Sanger's idea was to give women control over their own fertility. However, control does not necessarily mean total respon-

The fact that women bear children does not mean that men are not responsible for birth control.

Would you be more careful if it were you that got pregnant?

sibility by the woman. It may not be wise for a man to assume that a woman has "taken care of herself." Many women do not regularly practice birth control, especially if they are not in a long-term relationship, and some use various methods incorrectly. Dealing with an unwanted pregnancy is not easy, and fear of unwanted pregnancy can negatively affect both partners' sexual experience.

Sharing the responsibility of contraception can enhance a relationship. Talking about birth control can be a good way to practice discussing personal and sexual topics. Not talking about birth control can lead to the resentment women often feel when men put the entire responsibility for it on them. As one writer has stated, "Taking care of business before you get down to pleasure often enhances lovemaking by reducing stress and building trust" (Castleman, 1980). For these reasons, we recommend that women and men share the responsibility for birth control.

What are some ways of sharing the responsibility for birth control? Please come up with several ideas before reading on.

The first step in sharing contraceptive responsibility may simply be for either partner to ask the other about birth control before the first time they have intercourse. In our experience talking with students and clients, this initial question is rarely asked. Openness on the part of the male partner to using condoms or engaging in noncoital sexual activities, whether as the contraceptive method of choice or as a backup or temporary method, is another way to share responsibility for birth control. Reading about and discussing the various alternatives and their side effects and choosing the one that seems best is an important way for both partners to be involved. Most birth control clinics offer classes that are open to partners. The man can also participate by accompanying his partner when a medical exam is needed. Many physicians or nurse practitioners are comfortable with the woman's partner being present during such exams. The partner can be supportive about the cramping and discomfort some women experience from an IUD insertion and can learn to check the string. Expenses for both the exam and the birth control method can also be shared. Male partners can learn to insert the diaphragm or cervical cap and foam, and to put on condoms. We strongly believe that sharing the responsibility for birth control can help provide both better sexual relationships and improved contraceptive effectiveness.

Currently Available Methods

There are many forms of birth control. However, an ideal method — one that is 100% effective, does not rely on the user's memory, is completely safe with no side effects, reversible, separate from sexual activity, inexpensive, easy to obtain, and usable by either sex — is not available now or in the foreseeable future (Britton, 1988). Each of the methods currently available has advantages and disadvantages with regard to effectiveness, safety, and convenience. It is a good idea to be familiar with the various methods available because most people will use several of them during their active sex lives.

Effectiveness

Several variables influence the effectiveness of birth control. The theoretical effectiveness of a method does not take into account human error. Health care – practitioner error (such as improper IUD insertion or poor fitting of a diaphragm, discussed later in this chapter), poor or improper knowledge of the correct use of the method, negative beliefs about using the method, an uninvolved partner, forgetfulness, or deciding that "this time it won't matter" all greatly increase the chances of pregnancy (Jones & Forrest, 1992).

Do you think that people who feel guilty about sex are more or less likely to use contraception effectively than people who have positive attitudes about sexuality? Why or why not? Take a moment to consider these questions before reading on.

Research indicates that men and women who do not use contraception or use it ineffectively or inconsistently have several characteristics in common. Individuals who feel guilty about sex are likely to use contraception ineffectively (Strassberg & Mahoney, 1988). They have negative attitudes toward sexuality that interfere with their ability to process information about sexuality and birth control. They

TABLE 11.1   *Birth Control – Method Effectiveness*

Number of pregnancies during the first year of use per 100 nonsterile women initiating the method.

Method	Theoretical Number If Method Is Used Correctly and Consistently	Typical Number Who Become Accidentally Pregnant
"Outercourse"	0	0
Tubal sterilization	0.2	0.4
Vasectomy	0.1	0.15
Estrogen – progestin pills	0.1	3
Progestin-only pills	0.5	3
Progestasert T IUD	2	3
Copper-T IUD	0.8	3
Condom	2	12
Diaphragm and spermicide	6	18
Cervical cap	6	18
Spermicides	3	21
Sponge with spermicide	6 – 9	18 – 28
Withdrawal	4	18
Fertility awareness: "rhythm," calendar, basal body temperature, cervical mucus	1 – 9	20
No method	85	85

Source: Adapted from Hatcher et al., 1990, p. 134.

tend to choose less effective methods and to use them inconsistently. In addition, women who are uncomfortable with their sexuality are likely to take a passive role in contraceptive decision making and leave themselves vulnerable to their partners' ability to implement effective contraceptive behavior (Gerrard, 1987).

Contraceptive effectiveness is best compared by seeing how many women out of 100 get pregnant by the end of the first year of using a particular method. Table 11.1 shows the failure rates (pregnancies per 100 women per year) for a large number of women using the most common methods. As the box "Using Backup Methods to Increase Contraceptive Effectiveness" suggests, many couples may want to use backup methods to provide greater protection under certain circumstances.

Many additional factors besides effectiveness influence people's decisions about whether to use a particular birth control method. As we discuss a number of commonly used methods in the paragraphs that follow, we present more specific information on how to use each method, how it works, and its potential advantages and disadvantages.

OUR SEXUALITY

Using Backup Methods to Increase Contraceptive Effectiveness

There are a number of circumstances in which a couple may need or want to use more than one method of contraception. Backup methods can help reduce the human element in failure rates. Some examples of these circumstances include the following:

- During the first cycle of the pill.
- For the remainder of the cycle after forgetting to take one or more birth control pills or after several days of diarrhea or vomiting while on the pill.
- The first month after changing to a new brand of pills.
- During the initial one to three months after IUD insertion.
- When first learning to use a new method of birth control.
- When the couple wants to increase the effectiveness of contraception. For instance, using foam and condoms together offers very effective protection.

Abstinence from intercourse and the use of condoms, foam, or a diaphragm are possible backup methods that can be combined in many ways with other birth control methods for extra contraceptive protection.

"Outercourse"

Noncoital forms of sexual intimacy, called **outercourse**, can be a viable form of birth control (Hatcher et al., 1986). Outercourse includes all avenues of sexual intimacy other than penile–vaginal intercourse, including kissing, touching, petting, mutual masturbation, and oral and anal sex. The voluntary avoidance of coitus offers effective protection from pregnancy, providing the male does not ejaculate near the vaginal opening. This method has no undesirable side effects, and — with the notable exception of anal intercourse — reduces the chances of spreading sexually transmitted diseases. Outercourse can be used as a primary or temporary means of preventing pregnancy, and it can also be used when it is inadvisable to have intercourse for other reasons — for example, following childbirth or abortion, or during a herpes outbreak.

Oral Contraceptives

Oral contraceptives are the most commonly used reversible method of birth control in the United States today (Dawson, 1990), and the percentage of women who use the pill increases steadily each year (Winslow, 1991). Over 60 million women around the world are using the pill (Wharton & Blackburn, 1988). There are three basic types of oral contraceptives currently on the market: the constant-dose combination pill, the multiphasic pill, and the progestin-only pill (currently called the minipill) (see Figure 11.1). The **constant-dose combination pill,** which has been on the market since the early 1960s and is the most commonly used oral contraceptive in the United States today, contains two hormones, synthetic estrogen and progestin (a progesteronelike substance). There are more than 32 different varieties, containing varying amounts and ratios of the two hormones.

The **multiphasic pill,** which has been on the market since 1984, is another type of oral contraceptive. Unlike the constant-dose combination pill, which releases the two hormones at constant levels throughout the menstrual cycle, the

There are currently three basic types of pill: the combination pill, the multiphasic pill, and the progestin-only pill. Although most birth control pills come in packages of 28 pills, some types come in 21-day supplies.

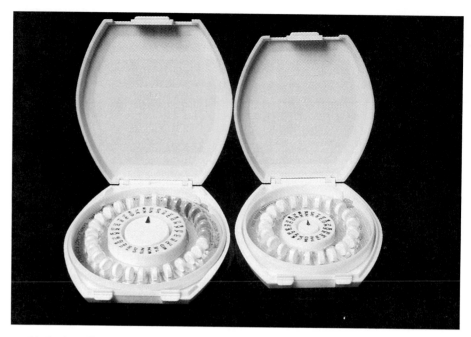

multiphasic pill provides fluctuations of estrogen and progesterone levels during the menstrual cycle. The multiphasic pill is designed to reduce the total hormone dosage and side effects while maintaining contraceptive effectiveness (Pasquale, 1984).

The **progestin-only pill,** which has been on the market since 1973, contains only 0.35 mg of progestin — about one-third the amount in an average-strength combination pill. There is no estrogen in the progestin-only pill. Like the combination pill, the progestin-only pill has a constant-dose formula.

How Oral Contraceptives Work. Both the combination pill and the multiphasic pill prevent conception primarily by inhibiting ovulation. The estrogen in these pills affects the hypothalamus, inhibiting the release of the pituitary hormones LH and FSH, which would otherwise begin the chain of events culminating in ovulation (see Chapter 4). The progestin in these pills provides secondary contraceptive protection by thickening and chemically altering the cervical mucus so that it hampers the passage of sperm into the uterus. Progestin also causes changes in the lining of the uterus, making it less receptive to implantation by a fertilized egg. In addition, progestin may inhibit ovulation by mildly disturbing hypothalamic – pituitary – ovarian function (Hatcher et al., 1990).

The progestin-only pill works somewhat differently. Most women who take the progestin-only pill probably continue to ovulate at least occasionally. The primary effect of this pill is to alter the cervical mucus to a thick and tacky consistency that effectively blocks sperm. As with the combination pill, secondary contraceptive effects may be provided by alterations in the uterine lining that make it unreceptive to implantation.

How to Use Oral Contraceptives. There are several acceptable ways to begin taking oral contraceptives; a woman who does so should carefully follow the instructions of her health care practitioner.

Forgetting to take one or more pills reduces the effectiveness of this method; taking the pill at approximately the same time each day maximizes it. Because oral contraceptives maintain particular hormone levels in the body, missing one or more pills can alter the hormone levels and allow ovulation to occur. A woman must take a missed pill as soon as she remembers to do so; she then takes the next pill at the regular time. If she forgets more than one pill, it is best for her to consult her health care practitioner. She should also use a backup method such as foam or condoms for the remainder of her cycle.

Advantages of Oral Contraceptives. Birth control pills have several advantages. They can be taken at a time separate from sexual activity, which many people believe helps maintain sexual spontaneity. If the combination pill is used correctly, it is a highly effective method, as Table 11.1 shows. The pill also often eliminates *mittelschmerz* (pain at ovulation) and reduces menstrual cramps and the amount and duration of the flow. In addition some women notice that taking oral contraceptives diminishes premenstrual tension symptoms. Oral contraceptives can also be effective in treating medical problems such as iron-deficiency anemia, endometriosis, and cysts of the ovary, and may decrease the incidence of benign breast disease (Duchin et al., 1989; Hatcher et al., 1990). The incidence of rheumatoid arthritis is lower in users than in nonusers of the pill (Hazes et al., 1990; Schlesselman et al., 1988). Use of oral contraceptives reduces the risk of endometrial cancer by 50% and ovarian cancer by 40% (Andrews and Mishell, 1988). Other potential advantages include breast enlargement and a decrease in acne. A woman who was pleased with this method explained:

I really like the pill I'm taking. My periods are light, and the bad cramps I used to have are gone. I hadn't been using anything before taking the pill. It's a tremendous relief to make love and not be afraid of getting pregnant. (Authors' files)

These advantages explain, in part, why the pill is more commonly used than any other temporary method of birth control. One study reported that over 12% of women who used the pill did so exclusively for the various noncontraceptive benefits (The Walnut Creek Contraceptive Drug Study, 1981).

The progestin-only pill has the advantage that it eliminates any estrogen-related side effects and reduces the likelihood of progestin-related problems because of the low progestin dosage. Adverse reactions to the combination pill may be reduced by switching to the progestin-only pill (Hatcher et al., 1990).

Disadvantages of Oral Contraceptives. One of the biggest disadvantages of the pill is that it does not protect against AIDS and other STDs. Condoms should be used in conjunction with the pill when protection from these diseases is desired.

Because the hormones in birth control pills circulate in the bloodstream through the entire body, there are a variety of potential side effects. However, it is important to note that most modern contraceptive pills contain less than 50 milligrams of estrogen, compared to 150 milligrams in the early birth control pills. The reduced amount of hormone reduces the risk of side effects (Gerstman et al., 1991). For most healthy women, the benefits of oral contraceptives outweigh the risks (Ory et al., 1980).

T A B L E 11.2   *Remember "ACHES" for the Pill*

Symptoms of possible serious problems with the birth control pill, represented by their initials.

Initial	Symptom	Possible Problem
A	Abdominal pain (severe)	Gallbladder disease, liver tumor, or blood clot
C	Chest pain (severe) or shortness of breath	Blood clot in lungs or heart attack
H	Headaches (severe)	Stroke, high blood pressure, or migraine headache
E	Eye problems: blurred vision, flashing lights, or blindness	Stroke, high blood pressure, or temporary vascular problems of many possible sites
S	Severe leg pain (calf or thigh)	Blood clot in legs

Source: Adapted from Hatcher et al., 1990.

Serious problems associated with the pill can be summarized by the acronym ACHES (see Table 11.2). We look first at some of the problems that have been associated with the estrogen–progestin pills, then examine possible side effects of the progestin-only pill.

The combination pill has been associated with an increased risk of blood clots in users. If a clot forms and travels to the lung or the brain, it can cause crippling or death. The symptoms of a blood clot may include severe leg or chest pains, coughing up blood, difficulty breathing, severe headache or vomiting, dizziness, fainting, disturbances of vision or speech, and weakness or numbness of an arm or leg. If a woman using an oral contraceptive experiences one or more of these symptoms, she should obtain immediate medical attention. Women who are immobilized or confined to a wheelchair are often advised against using the pill because poor circulation (sometimes related to lack of physical activity) can increase the potential for developing blood clots.

Another risk associated with the combination pill (especially those varieties with high estrogen dosages) is increased likelihood of heart attacks in women who smoke or who have underlying risk factors for heart disease (Rabe et al., 1992). High blood pressure (hypertension) is also associated with taking the pill. Pill-related high blood pressure can be reversed by discontinuing use. Periodic blood pressure measurements are important in oral contraceptive users, and women who already have high blood pressure are usually advised to use another form of contraception.

Noncancerous liver tumors can be a potential side effect of oral contraceptives. These tumors are very rare but can be fatal. Women who have used high-dose oral contraceptives for eight or more years run the greatest risk of developing liver tumors. Some liver tumors associated with oral contraceptives have been found to be cancerous, but these are even less likely to occur than noncancerous tumors (Hatcher et al., 1990).

OUR SEXUALITY

Oral Contraceptive Use for Women Over Age 40

Many health care practitioners now believe that the low-dose combination birth control pill can be prescribed safely to most women over age 40 (Upton, 1987), and many more women in this age group are currently using the pill (Rosenthal, 1991). In a 1988 study, almost 43% of physicians, nurse practitioners, and physicians' assistants believed that the birth control pill could be prescribed safely to women over age 40, with some guidelines (Contraceptive Updates, 1988a). A good candidate should be a nonsmoker in generally good health, with normal blood pressure, no risk factors for coronary heart disease or diabetes, and no contraindications for oral contraceptive use. Close monitoring of cholesterol levels, blood pressure, and blood sugar is recommended.

Use of the pill may also be related to emotional changes, although it is difficult to establish a definitive cause for any emotional state. Many women, however, see a correlation between their moods and use of oral contraceptives. Some studies have shown an increase in depression in women on the pill (Hatcher et al., 1990); because depression can affect all aspects of a woman's life, it is not to be taken lightly. A woman who suspects her depression may be pill-related can use another contraceptive method for a time and observe any changes in her mood.

Many women take the pill to increase the spontaneity and enjoyment of their sexual expression. Some women on the pill experience improvement in their sexual lives (Hatcher et al., 1990). However, a decrease in sexual motivation may also occur (Graham & Sherwin, 1992). A decline in sexual interest may be influenced by a variety of side effects including frequent yeast infections, a reduction of vaginal lubrication, and depression. Hormonal and other psychological factors may also contribute.

Oral contraceptives interact with other medications and can diminish the therapeutic effect of the medication, or the medication can diminish the contraceptive effectiveness of the pill. Some medications that can interfere with oral contraceptive effectiveness include antibiotics (tetracycline), analgesics, antihistamines, and drugs used to treat tuberculosis, epilepsy, and depression (Szoka & Edgren, 1988).

While the reduced amount of hormones in the progestin-only pill causes it to have fewer potential side effects, this pill too has some disadvantages associated with it. Irregular and "breakthrough" bleeding (a light flow between menstrual periods) happens more frequently with the progestin-only pill than with the combination pill. However, the bleeding irregularities usually diminish in two or three months, as they do with the combination pill.

Additional Comments on Oral Contraceptives. The long list of potential side effects of oral contraceptives may seem alarming. However, many informed women continue to choose the pill as their best contraceptive alternative. The physical risks associated with the pill are far lower than those of pregnancy (Kost et al., 1991)—although a Gallup Poll found that 84% of women incorrectly believed that the risks of the pill were greater than the risks of pregnancy and childbirth (American College of Obstetricians and Gynecologists, 1985).

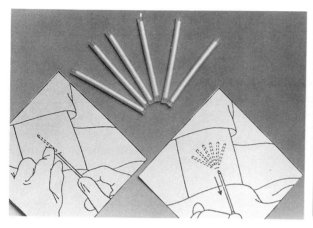 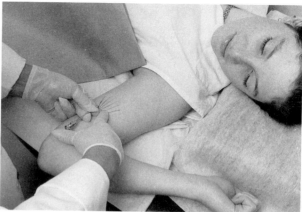

F I G U R E 11.2

How Norplant works:
Norplant capsules implanted
in a woman's arm release
progestin over a five-year
period.

Women vary in their responses to the varying hormone combinations of different oral contraceptives. Some side effects—such as nausea, fluid retention, increased appetite, acne, depression, spotting, or lack of "menstruation" (withdrawal bleeding)—can be eliminated by changing the type of pill. Generally, a woman will be given a type of pill that works well for her and that has the lowest practical hormonal potency, to reduce the possibility of side effects. Women with a history of certain conditions should use a different method of contraception; these conditions include blood clots, strokes, circulation problems, heart problems, jaundice, cancer of the breast or uterus, and undiagnosed genital bleeding. In addition, a woman who currently has a liver disease or who suspects or knows she is pregnant should not take the pill. Women who have problems with migraine headaches, depression, high blood pressure, epilepsy, diabetes or prediabetes symptoms, asthma, or varicose veins should weigh the potential risks most carefully and use the pill only under close medical supervision.

Norplant

Norplant consists of six thin, flexible capsules made of a soft, rubberlike material (called Silastic) filled with synthetic progestin. The capsules are implanted under the skin of a woman's upper arm (see Figure 11.2). Norplant has been tested for 20 years in 46 countries and became available in the United States in 1991 (Pollack, 1991b). A year after its approval, 100,000 women in the United States had received it (Lewin, 1991).

How Norplant Works. The implanted capsules release the synthetic progestin gradually into the bloodstream over a five-year period to prevent conception in the same manner as the minipill (Flattum-Riemers, 1991; Faundes et al., 1991). Norplant provides effective contraception within 24 hours of insertion (Monaghan, 1992).

How to Use Norplant. Norplant is inserted and removed by a health care practitioner. A local anesthetic is used to numb a small area; the capsules are then placed under the skin in a fan pattern through an incision about ⅛-inch long. Insertion usually takes 10 to 15 minutes. Once inserted, the capsules are not easily seen.

Advantages of Norplant. Once inserted, Norplant provides highly effective contraception for five years without the woman needing to remember to take a pill daily or use a barrier method when having sexual intercourse. Fertility is not compromised by Norplant (Sivinct et al., 1992); a woman's ability to become pregnant returns within 24 hours following removal (Filips, 1991). Norplant releases about 30 micrograms of hormone a day, compared to about 150 micrograms a day in oral contraceptives, yet it is more effective because the release is constant and there is no risk of forgetting to take a pill. One study found that most women who have used the Norplant system would recommend it to others (Pollack, 1991b).

Disadvantages of Norplant. The initial cost of using Norplant is high, approximately $500. (This is, however, less expensive than five years' worth of birth control pills.) Side effects and contraindications are the same as for oral contraceptives. The most common side effect is the same as for the minipill: menstrual irregularity (Pollack, 1991b). Menstrual irregularity decreases after the first year of use (Shoupe et al., 1991).

Diaphragms

The **diaphragm,** shown in Figure 11.3(a), is a round, soft latex dome with a thin, flexible spring around the rim. It is inserted into the vagina along with a spermicidal contraceptive cream or jelly, which comes in a tube. The diaphragm rim fits around the back of the cervix and underneath and behind the pubic bone, as shown in Figure 11.3(b). Some women's cervixes are located farther back in the vagina, and others are closer to the opening. Therefore, diaphragms vary in size from two to four inches in diameter to fit each individual correctly. Diaphragms are also made with different kinds of springs: the coil spring, the flat spring, or the arcing spring. Some women find one style easier to insert and better fitting than another. For example, the arcing spring may stay in place better than a coil spring for a woman with reduced vaginal muscle tone.

How the Diaphragm Works. When fitted and inserted properly, the diaphragm covers the cervix, thus providing a mechanical barrier to prevent sperm from entering the cervix and uterus. The spermicidal cream or jelly serves as a chemical barrier, effectively killing any sperm that might migrate around the rim of the diaphragm and toward the cervix.

How to Use the Diaphragm. The diaphragm must be fitted by a skilled practitioner. A size estimate is made during the pelvic exam; then different sizes and types are inserted until the best fit is found. It is very important for the examiner to thoroughly instruct the woman on how to insert and care for her diaphragm. Then the woman practices inserting it herself in the examination room, until she is able to do so correctly. The examiner makes a final check to confirm that the woman has learned the proper insertion technique.

Figure 11.3(b) shows how the diaphragm is used. First, a tablespoon of the spermicidal cream or jelly (available at pharmacies without a prescription) is put into the cup of the diaphragm. Some of the spermicide should also be spread around the inside of the rim. The sides of the rim are then squeezed together with one hand, while the other hand opens the inner lips of the vulva. Some women

FIGURE 11.3

(a) The diaphragm is made of a soft latex dome on a coil and is used with contraceptive cream or jelly. (b) These figures illustrate the insertion and checking of a diaphragm.

(a)

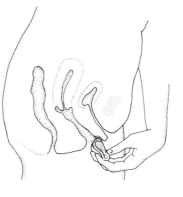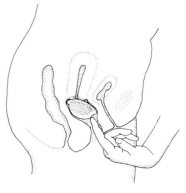

Cream or jelly

Diaphragm

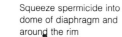

(b)   Squeeze spermicide into dome of diaphragm and around the rim

Squeeze rim together; insert jelly-side up

Check placement to make certain cervix is covered

prefer to use a plastic diaphragm introducer, whereas others prefer manual insertion. The diaphragm is then pushed into the vagina, with the cream side facing up. The woman may be standing, lying, or squatting while she or her partner inserts the diaphragm.

After the diaphragm is inserted, it is important for the woman or her partner to feel it with the fingers to determine whether the dome covers the cervix. Occasionally, the back rim lodges in front of the cervix, so that the diaphragm offers no contraceptive protection. When the diaphragm is placed correctly, it rarely can be felt by the woman or her partner during intercourse.

Some sources state that the diaphragm can be inserted up to six hours prior to intercourse; others recommend that the diaphragm be inserted no more than two hours prior to intercourse without an additional application of spermicide. The shorter time span may afford better protection. The diaphragm can also be inserted just before intercourse. Some women prefer to insert the diaphragm ahead of time, in privacy, whereas others share the insertion with their partners. As one man explained:

I have had a traditional repulsion of "just-before" birth control devices such as condoms and diaphragms. However, with my present partner the use of the diaphragm is part of sexual excitement for us. We usually become quite stimulated before reaching for the good old jelly and diaphragm, and then I continue with manual clitoral stimulation while she inserts the device. I have also learned to put it in while she continues to stimulate herself and me at the same time. Also, any leftover jelly works nicely as a lubricant. The pause between being ready for intercourse and actually doing it seems to heighten the whole thing. (Authors' files)

The diaphragm should remain in the vagina for at least eight hours following intercourse to assure that the spermicide has killed all sperm in the vaginal folds. It is important not to douche during this time. If intercourse occurs again before eight hours elapse, the diaphragm can be left in place, but additional spermicidal cream or jelly needs to be inserted with an applicator tube. Reusable plastic applicators can be purchased with the spermicide.

Several cases of toxic shock syndrome (TSS) have been reported in association with diaphragm use. Therefore, a diaphragm should not be left in the vagina for more than 24 hours (Hatcher et al., 1990). To remove it, a finger is inserted into the vagina under the front rim of the diaphragm. Squatting or bearing down may make it easier to find the rim. After a gentle pull with one finger to break the air seal, it is easier to grasp the rim with two fingers and pull the diaphragm out. After removal, the diaphragm should be washed with a mild soap and warm water. Then it should be carefully and thoroughly dried, dusted with cornstarch, and returned to its plastic case.

A well-cared-for diaphragm can last for several years. It should remain soft, flexible, and free of defects. To make certain of this, the woman should check it periodically. She can detect tiny leaks by placing water in the dome or by holding it up to the light, stretching it slightly and checking for any defects. She should bring along her diaphragm when she has her yearly Pap smear so that its fit and condition can be evaluated. A woman may need a different diaphragm after a pregnancy (including an aborted pregnancy) or a weight loss or gain of 10 pounds or more.

A most important point in using the diaphragm is to have it available. It simply will not do a woman any good at home in a drawer when she is at the beach for the weekend. Depending on a woman's lifestyle, the best place for it may be in her purse, bedroom, bathroom — wherever is most convenient for her situation. Some women prefer to own two diaphragms to assure availability.

Advantages of the Diaphragm. The recent resurgence in the popularity of the diaphragm is most likely due to concerns about the side effects of oral contraceptives and IUDs, coupled with reports of high rates of contraceptive effectiveness with diaphragm use. In studies where women were thoroughly instructed in the use and care of the diaphragm, its effectiveness was almost comparable to that of the pill and the IUD. Most important, there are no potentially dangerous side effects comparable to those encountered when using oral contraceptives and IUDs.

Through learning to use the diaphragm, a woman may become more knowledgeable and comfortable with her body. She may also find diaphragm use helpful in making decisions about relating sexually with others.

Since I've been using the diaphragm, I've moved more slowly into sexual relations. I want to discuss my method with a new partner before we have intercourse. When I'm feeling like I'm not comfortable enough to talk about birth control, I'm not ready to have intercourse. (Authors' files)

Some people think that there may be some additional positive side effects to proper use of the diaphragm. They speculate that some spermicidal jellies and creams may promote vaginal health and decrease the incidence of vaginal infections. Spermicides help prevent gonorrhea, pelvic inflammatory disease, and AIDS (Hatcher et al., 1990). In addition, the use of any barrier method may help reduce the risk of cervical cell changes that can lead to cancer (Coker et al., 1992).

Disadvantages of the Diaphragm.   The diaphragm is not without disadvantages, however. Some people may find that it is inconvenient, that using it interrupts spontaneity, or that the spermicidal cream or jelly is messy. The spermicidal cream or jelly can also interfere with the couple's enjoyment of oral – genital sex. However, a couple can engage in oral – genital contact before inserting the diaphragm, or the woman's partner can focus stimulation on the clitoral rather than the vaginal area. Occasionally, women or their partners experience irritation from a particular spermicide. Sometimes switching to a different brand takes care of any difficulty. In rare instances a woman is allergic to the latex of the diaphragm. Using a plastic diaphragm can eliminate this problem.

Poor diaphragm fit may occasionally cause problems. Because diaphragms are fitted when a woman is not sexually aroused, they may not fit as well during arousal due to the vaginal expansion that occurs. The penis may then be placed between the diaphragm and cervix. This is most likely to happen during position changes, with reinsertion of the penis, and in the woman-above position. The spermicidal cream or jelly still provides some contraceptive protection if this occurs. If either partner feels the diaphragm during intercourse, she or he should check to see if it is correctly in place. Some women report bladder discomfort, urethral irritation, or recurrent cystitis from diaphragm use (Hooten et al., 1991). Using another diaphragm size or rim type may eliminate these difficulties. A few women with certain pelvic-structure problems, such as marked loss of vaginal muscle tone and support, cannot use the diaphragm effectively.

Cervical Caps

The **cervical cap** is a thimble-shaped cup made of rubber or plastic (see Figure 11.4). The cap is like a miniature diaphragm, but it fits only over the cervix and can be left in place longer. Like the diaphragm, the cap comes in different sizes. Although it can be used alone, health care practitioners usually recommend that it be used with a spermicide (Hatcher et al., 1990).

Different versions of the cervical cap have been used for centuries. European women melted beeswax into cervical disks. In eighteenth-century Europe, Casanova promoted the idea of using a squeezed-out lemon half to cover the cervix. The modern cervical cap was developed in 1838 by a German gynecologist, who took a wax impression of each patient's cervix and made custom cervical caps out of rubber (Seaman & Seaman, 1978). Cervical caps have been widely available in Europe for many years and were finally approved for sale in the United States in 1988.

FIGURE 11.4

Cervical caps come in various sizes.

How to Use the Cervical Cap. The cervical cap comes in different sizes and must be individually fitted by a skilled practitioner. When a woman uses the cap, she or her partner fills it one- to two-thirds full with spermicide. The cap is inserted by folding its edges together and sliding it into the vagina along the vaginal floor. The cup is then pressed onto the cervix. The woman or her partner then sweeps a finger around the cap to confirm that the cervix is covered, and depresses the dome of the cap to feel the cervix through the rubber. A woman can usually reach her cervix most easily if she is in a squatting or upright sitting position. The cap can be inserted up to six hours before intercourse. It should not be removed for at least six hours following intercourse, and douching should be avoided during this period. It can be left in place up to 48 hours but should be removed by that time to avoid risk of TSS (Weiss et al., 1991). Pulling on one side of the rim breaks the suction to permit easy removal of the cap from the vagina. After removal, the cap should be washed with warm water and soap and dried.

Advantages of the Cervical Cap. A major advantage of the cervical cap is the lack of side effects. Women who cannot use the diaphragm because of pelvic-structure problems or loss of vaginal muscle tone or support can often use this method. The cap is less expensive to use than the diaphragm because it requires less spermicide, but the cap itself is two to three times more expensive than the diaphragm. Unlike the diaphragm, the cervical cap does not require repeated applications of spermicide with additional intercourse (Weiss et al., 1991).

Disadvantages of the Cervical Cap. A woman who has distortions of her cervix from cysts or lacerations or postpartum enlargement of the cervix is usually an unsuitable candidate for cervical cap use. Caps do not successfully fit about 6% of women (Klitsch, 1988a). Some women and their partners may have allergic reactions to the spermicide or rubber. The cap is usually more difficult to learn to

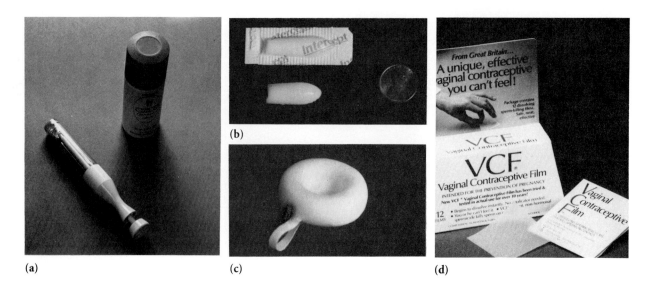

(a)   (c)   (d)

FIGURE 11.5

Vaginal spermicides are available in pharmacies without a prescription: (a) foam and applicator, (b) suppositories, (c) sponge, and (d) vaginal contraceptive film.

use than the diaphragm, and for some women it is uncomfortable to wear. There is some concern that wearing the cap for prolonged periods may cause problems by damaging the cervix or interrupting the normal discharge of secretions from the cervix. Although there are no clear data on this matter, the Food and Drug Administration (FDA) recommends a Pap smear after three months of using the cervical cap (Klitsch, 1988a). The cap may also become dislodged during intercourse, greatly reducing its contraceptive effectiveness (Hatcher et al., 1990).

Vaginal Spermicides

There are several types of **vaginal spermicides:** foam, suppositories, the contraceptive sponge, creams and jellies, and contraceptive film (see Figure 11.5). The *contraceptive sponge,* the most commonly used, is made of polyurethane and is impregnated with spermicide. It is shaped like a mushroom cap and fits in the upper vagina. *Foam* is a white substance resembling shaving cream. It comes in pressurized cans and has a plastic applicator. Foam is available in pharmacies without a prescription. (Feminine-hygiene products, although often displayed along with various brands of foam, are *not* contraceptives.) *Vaginal suppositories* have an oval shape and contain the same spermicidal chemical found in foam. Some *contraceptive creams and jellies* are made to be used without a diaphragm. However, they are not as effective as foam, and many health care practitioners recommend that they not be used without a diaphragm. Therefore, we do not discuss them in detail. *VCF,* a vaginal contraceptive film, is a paper-thin, two-inch by two-inch sheet that is laced with spermicide. It is packaged in a matchbooklike container with 10 to 12 sheets.

How Spermicidal Methods Work. Foam, suppositories, creams and jellies, and the contraceptive sponge all contain a *spermicide,* or chemical that kills sperm. When foam is inserted with the applicator, it rapidly covers the vaginal walls and the cervical os (see Figure 11.6). Contraceptive vaginal suppositories take about 20 minutes to dissolve and cover the walls. One brand of suppositories, Encare, effer-

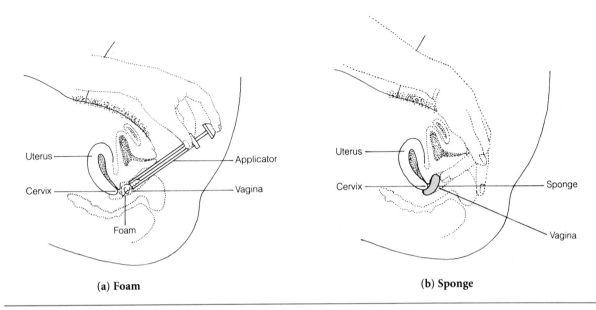

(a) Foam   **(b) Sponge**

vesces and creates a foam inside the vagina; other brands melt. The sponge works by releasing spermicide, absorbing semen, and blocking the cervical opening. Once VCF is inserted into the vagina, it dissolves into a stay-in-place gel.

How to Use Vaginal Spermicides. Complete instructions for use come with each package of vaginal spermicide. It is important to use them as directed for maximum protection. Like spermicides used with the diaphragm, another application of spermicide is necessary before each additional act of intercourse. If a woman douches, she needs to wait eight hours after intercourse before douching to assure that the spermicide has killed the sperm. It is probably better to shower than to take a bath, to prevent the spermicide from being rinsed out of the vagina.

Advantages of Vaginal Spermicides. Because spermicides, VCF, and contraceptive sponges are sold over-the-counter in pharmacies, using them does not require a visit to a physician's office. They have no known dangerous side effects to the woman, and some couples welcome the additional lubrication spermicides provide. Like the diaphragm, vaginal spermicides may give some protection against vaginal infections, sexually transmitted diseases (including AIDS), and pelvic inflammatory disease (PID) (Hatcher et al., 1990). The suppository has the advantage of being small and convenient to use. VCF can be used by people who are allergic to foams and jellies; also, unlike foams and jellies, VCF dissolves gradually and almost unnoticeably.

Disadvantages of Vaginal Spermicides. Occasionally, a woman or her partner may report irritation of genital tissues from the foam, suppositories, or sponge. Changing brands will often alleviate this difficulty, but in some cases any brand causes discomfort. Some of the suppositories may not dissolve completely and therefore feel gritty. Some women or couples dislike the additional lubrication during intercourse or the postcoital discharge following intercourse. Because of the unpleasant taste, using vaginal spermicides may limit couples who like to

FIGURE 11.6

Insertion of vaginal spermicides. (a) Insertion of foams: The filled applicator is inserted into the vagina, and the foam is deposited at the back of the vaginal canal. (b) Insertion of sponge: The sponge is moistened with tap water and then inserted deep into the vagina.

Since the advent of AIDS, condoms have become an even more popular means of birth control for both men and women.

engage in cunnilingus after intercourse (although they can still do so before inserting the foam or suppositories). These products may also have a soaplike scent that is disagreeable to some users. In addition, some people feel that insertion of spermicides, even though the procedure takes only about 30 seconds, interrupts spontaneity. Some women and their partners report difficulty in removing the sponge.

Condoms

Condoms, also called prophylactics and rubbers, are currently the only temporary method of birth control available for men. A condom is a sheath that fits over the erect penis and is made of thin surgical latex or sheep membrane. This approach to contraception has a long history. A penile sheath was used in Japan during the early 1500s, and in 1564 an Italian anatomist, Fallopius, described a penile sheath made of linen. Mass production of inexpensive modern condoms began after the development of vulcanized rubber in the 1840s (Vinson & Epperly, 1991). Condom use more than doubled in the last decade, from 21% in 1979 to 58% in 1988 (Hatcher et al., 1990).

Condoms are available without prescription at pharmacies, from family planning clinics, by mail order, and in some areas, in vending machines. Most condoms are packaged — rolled up and wrapped in foil or plastic — and come lubricated or nonlubricated. There is less chance of the condom breaking if it is lubricated, and some men report less reduction of penile sensation during intercourse with lubricated condoms. Sheep membrane, natural-skin condoms are more expensive but often interfere less with sensation than do the latex ones. *However, some sexually transmitted diseases, including the AIDS virus, can pass through*

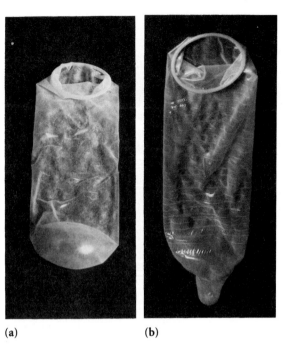

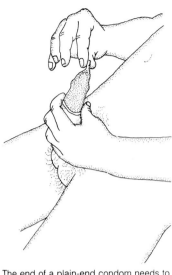

The end of a plain-end condom needs to be twisted as it is rolled onto the penis in order to leave space at the tip.

(a)   (b)   (c)

FIGURE 11.7

(a) Unrolled condom with plain end. (b) Unrolled condom with reservoir tip. (c) The correct method of using a plain-end condom.

natural-membrane condoms but not through latex condoms. The pores in natural membrane condoms are 10 times larger than the HIV virus (Robinson, 1991). Some condoms have a small nipple on the end, called a reservoir tip, and others have a contoured shape or textured surface (Figure 11.7). Some are also made with spermicide on their inner and outer surfaces. Condoms have an average shelf life of about five years, although not all packages are dated. They should not be stored in hot places like the glove compartment of a car or a back pocket because the heat can deteriorate the latex.

How the Condom Works. When a man uses a condom properly, both the ejaculate and the fluid from Cowper's glands secretions are contained within the tip. The condom thus serves as a mechanical barrier, effectively preventing any sperm from entering the vagina.

How to Use the Condom. Most condoms are packaged rolled up. Correct use includes unrolling the condom over the erect penis before any contact between the penis and the vulva occurs. Sperm in the Cowper's gland secretions or in the ejaculate can travel from outside the labia to inside the vagina. For maximum comfort and sensation, an uncircumcised man can retract the foreskin before rolling the condom over the penis. With plain-ended condoms (without the reservoir tip), the end needs to be twisted before rolling the condom down over the penis, as shown in Figure 11.7(c). This leaves some room at the end for the ejaculate and reduces the chances of the condom breaking. If a condom breaks or slips off during intercourse, contraceptive foam, cream, or jelly should be inserted into the vagina *immediately.*

A condom breaks more easily without vaginal lubrication, so if the condom is nonlubricated, some vaginal secretion, saliva, or K-Y jelly needs to be put on

OUR SEXUALITY

The Role of Women in Condom Use

The percentage of unmarried women in the United States using condoms almost doubled between 1982 and 1987. Women's opinions of condoms have become more favorable, and women purchase 50% of condoms sold today. Eighty-eight percent of women polled said that they were likely to "insist" on using a condom with their next sexual partner.

These changes represent good "condom sense," because women have much more to lose than men when a couple does not use a condom.

- If an unplanned pregnancy occurs, the woman's body will undergo the abortion or pregnancy and birth.
- A woman is three times more likely to get a sexually transmitted disease (including AIDS) from one act of intercourse than is a man.

- Bacterial STDs do much more damage to a woman's reproductive tract than to a man's and can ruin her subsequent ability to have a baby.

"It is a woman's right to say no to intercourse if her partner says no to condoms" (Hatcher et al., 1991, p. 166).

---

the vulva and outside of the condom before insertion of the penis into the vagina. Because the penis begins to detumesce, or lose its size and hardness, soon after ejaculation, it is important to hold the condom at the base of the penis before withdrawing it from the vagina. Otherwise the condom may slip off and spill semen inside the vagina:

> The first time I used a rubber, I relaxed inside her after I came, holding her for a while. Then I withdrew, leaving the rubber behind. My first thought was "Oh, no, it's dissolved." I reached inside her vagina and found the rubber. We used some foam right away but were nervous until her next period started. (Authors' files)

Condoms are best disposed of in the garbage rather than in the toilet because they have been known to clog plumbing.

Advantages of Condoms. Latex condoms provide the best protection from contracting and spreading sexually transmitted diseases (including AIDS) and vaginal infections (Grimes, 1991). Condoms containing the spermicide nonoxynol-9 provide additional protection (Rietmeijer et al., 1988). For this reason, individuals who are not in a disease-free, monogamous relationship should use spermicidal condoms.

Condoms are available without prescription. There are no harmful side effects associated with their use. If condoms are not the primary method of birth control, they are useful as a backup. Some men prefer the slightly dampened sensation they experience with condoms because they find that the duration of intercourse before ejaculation is prolonged. Because the semen is contained inside the condom, some women appreciate the tidiness:

> I really like the juiciness of sex when I can bathe afterwards, but when we go camping and don't have a stream or shower handy, my husband uses condoms so it's not as messy. (Authors' files)

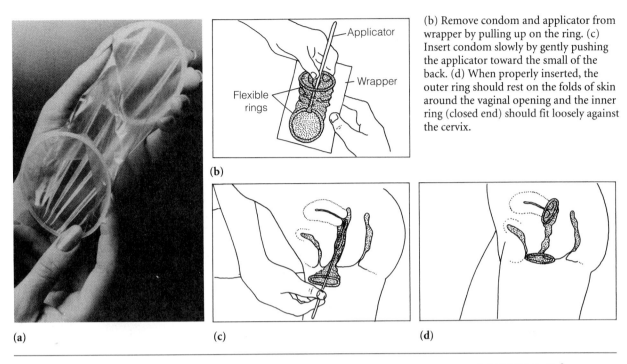

(b) Remove condom and applicator from wrapper by pulling up on the ring. (c) Insert condom slowly by gently pushing the applicator toward the small of the back. (d) When properly inserted, the outer ring should rest on the folds of skin around the vaginal opening and the inner ring (closed end) should fit loosely against the cervix.

(a)   **(c)**   **(d)**

FIGURE 11.8

A female condom consists of two diaphragmlike flexible polyurethane rings and a soft, loose-fitting polyurethane sheath.

Disadvantages of Condoms. Unless putting on the condom is incorporated as part of sexual interaction, it can interrupt spontaneity. Some men see reduced penile sensitivity as a disadvantage (Valdiserri et al., 1989). Condoms can have pinhole-sized leaks or break or slip off (Trussell et al., 1992). Also, a few people are allergic to rubber condoms.

The Female Condom. In 1988 couples in several countries began testing a "woman's condom" (*Contraceptive Technology Update*, 1988c), which was approved for sale in the United States (Segilmann, 1992). It resembles a regular condom (see Figure 11.8), but it is worn internally by the woman. A flexible plastic ring at the closed end of the sheath fits loosely against the cervix, rather like a diaphragm. Another ring encircles the labial area. The female condom covers some of the vulva and may provide more protection from sexually transmitted diseases than would traditional condoms (Soper, 1992). Although the female condom fits the contours of the vagina, the penis moves freely inside the sheath. The female condom is made of polyurethane or latex (Cates & Stone, 1992).

Intrauterine Devices

Intrauterine devices, commonly referred to as **IUDs,** are small plastic objects that are inserted into the uterus through the vaginal canal and cervical os. Several types of IUDs were available in this country during the 1960s and 1970s, but many companies removed their IUDs from the market because of litigation costs from numerous lawsuits charging that the devices caused infections, infertility, or death

SYLVIA ON SUNDAY   **by Nicole Hollander**

WHAT HAVE you SAid ReCENtLY tHAt you NeveR IMAGiNeD you'd HeAR youRSeLf SAy?

◻1. Do you CARRY ANY ULtRA-tHIN LAtex CoNdoMS witH ReSeRVoiR tips, NoN oxyNoL 9 SpeRMi cidAL LubRiCANt, ANd DecoRAted witH StARS ANd cReSCeNt MooNS oN A DARK bLue BACKGRouNd?

from infection when pregnancy occurred with an IUD in place (Pollock & Girvin, 1992). Although the companies successfully defended most suits, the legal costs were prohibitively high (Klitsch, 1988b).

Two types of IUDs currently are available: the Copper-T (ParaGard), a plastic T with copper wire wrapped around its stem and copper sleeves on the side arms, and the Progestasert T (see Figure 11.9), a plastic T with slow-releasing progesterone in the plastic. Both have fine plastic threads attached, cut to hang slightly out of the cervix into the vagina.

How the IUD Works. Recent studies have indicated that the copper and the progesterone in IUDs prevent fertilization (Connell & Grimes, 1990). Another theory is that the uterine lining is slightly irritated and inflamed due to the presence of this foreign object, and that as a result the fertilized ovum does not implant (Wilcox, 1987). The IUD also alters the delicate timing of ovum transport through the fallopian tubes.

How to Use the IUD. The IUD is inserted by a trained health care professional using sterile instruments. Most IUDs come with an inserter. The inserter and IUD are introduced through the cervical os into the uterus; the inserter is then withdrawn, leaving the IUD in place. (A woman should be screened for gonorrhea and chlamydia before she has an IUD inserted because the procedure may cause the bacteria associated with these STDs to be pushed farther into the uterus.) The Progestasert T needs to be replaced every six years because the progesterone gradually loses its effectiveness. IUDs should be removed when a woman reaches menopause and stops menstruating (Hatcher et al., 1990).

Guidelines for IUD use state that they should be used only by women in stable, monogamous relationships, with no history of sexually transmitted diseases or pelvic inflammatory disease, who have at least one child or have completed childbearing, are 25 years or older, and have ready access to medical facilities (*Contraceptive Technology Update*, 1987; Lee et al., 1988).

While a woman is using an IUD, she or her partner needs to check each month after her menstrual period to see that the string is the same length as when the device was inserted. To do this, one of them reaches into the vagina with a finger and finds the cervix. If the cervix is far back in the vagina and difficult to reach, the woman can squat or bear down to make it more accessible. The string should be felt in the middle of the cervix, protruding out of the small indentation in the center. Occasionally, it curls up in the os and cannot be felt, but any time

FIGURE 11.9

The Progestasert T intrauterine device.

a woman or her partner cannot find it, she needs to check with her health care specialist. She should also seek attention if the string seems longer or the plastic protrudes out of the os; this probably means that her body is expelling the IUD.

Advantages of the IUD. The primary advantage of the IUD is that it provides a woman with highly effective contraceptive protection with little inconvenience beyond the monthly checking of the string. The IUD allows uninterrupted sexual interaction. Beyond the initial cost of $300 – $400 for the IUD and insertion, there are no further supplies to be purchased. Although an IUD is usually not inserted until two to three months after childbirth, it does not interfere with breast-feeding (as the pill does) once it is in place. Some women who experience initial discomfort after the insertion find that this diminishes in a month or two.

Disadvantages of the IUD. The most serious complication related to IUD use is that it increases a woman's chances of pelvic inflammatory disease (Hatcher et al., 1990). PID can occur if bacteria are introduced into the sterile environment of the uterus during insertion, and the risk of infection from an IUD is largely limited to the first 20 days following insertion (Farley et al., 1992). The string of the IUD has also been suspected of providing an entryway for bacteria. An IUD is likely to aggravate a gonorrhea infection and make treatment more difficult. Most physicians recommend removal of an IUD when a woman is being treated for a uterine infection. Fallopian tube problems resulting from IUD use can also be a contributing factor in infertility (Hatcher et al., 1990). Increased risk of PID has been found almost exclusively in women involved in high-risk behaviors such as having multiple partners (Connell, 1991; Kronmal et al., 1991).

Discomfort, cramping, bleeding, or pain may occur during insertion. The discomfort or bleeding sometimes continues for a few days and occasionally much longer. The IUDs that have been withdrawn from the market typically caused increased menstrual bleeding, but the Progestasert T usually reduces bleeding to half of the regular menstrual flow (Hatcher et al., 1990).

From 2 – 20% of users expel their IUDs within the first year following insertion (Hatcher et al., 1990). The uterus reacts to the IUD as a foreign body, contracting and sometimes pushing it out. This is most likely to occur during menstruation, so a woman needs to check her tampons or sanitary napkins before disposing of them. Also, her partner might feel the IUD protruding out of the cervix during intercourse. It is wise to check the string several times a month at first because, if the IUD is incorrectly positioned in the uterus or is expelled, the woman is not protected against an undesired pregnancy.

As discussed in Chapter 4, the multidirectional muscles of the uterus are interwoven. In rare cases the IUD breaks through the uterine wall. This perforation can partially extend through the wall, or the IUD can slip completely through the uterus into the abdominal cavity. When this occurs, surgery may be necessary to remove the IUD. Occasionally (although rarely), a woman may require a hysterectomy as a result of this type of complication. In a small number of cases, the IUD perforated both the uterus and the bladder (Zakin, 1984). If an IUD string seems to become shorter, this may be an indication that the IUD is perforating, and the woman should seek immediate medical attention.

Other problems may occur if a woman becomes pregnant with an IUD in place. She has a 50% chance of a miscarriage (Hatcher et al., 1990). Because of

TABLE 11.3   ***Remember "PAINS" for the IUD***

Symptoms of possible serious problems with the IUD, represented by their initials.

Initial	Symptoms
P	Period late, no period
A	Abdominal pain
I	Increased temperature, fever, chills
N	Nasty discharge, foul discharge
S	Spotting, bleeding, heavy periods, clots

Source: Adapted from Hatcher et al., 1990.

some reports of deaths of pregnant IUD users in 1974 (primarily from the Dalkon Shield), removal of the IUD when a woman becomes pregnant is now recommended (Stubblefield et al., 1988). It is thought that as the uterus enlarges during pregnancy, the string in the vagina is drawn into the uterus and carries bacteria and viruses with it. The string may also act as a wick for bacteria, facilitating the spread of any infectious organisms. Due to the increased blood flow in the tissues of the uterus during pregnancy, such an infection travels rapidly through the woman's bloodstream and may cause death within 24–48 hours. If an IUD is removed during the first three months of pregnancy, the risk of a subsequent miscarriage is only slightly higher than for nonusers of IUDs and less than if the woman kept the IUD in place (Britton, 1988).

Finally, a number of previous or current conditions seem to be related to heightened risks in using an IUD. A woman should consult a health care practitioner if any of these conditions apply to her: a history of ectopic pregnancy; active PID, chlamydia, or gonorrhea; current or suspected pregnancy; or current conditions such as endometriosis, anemia, heavy menstrual flow or cramping, a very small or malformed uterus, uterine fibroids, heart disease, or the use of anticoagulants.

Serious problems associated with the IUD can be summarized by the acronym PAINS (see Table 11.3).

Besides the IUD and hormonal and barrier methods, a number of other contraceptive options are available. We look at these in the paragraphs that follow.

Methods Based on the Menstrual Cycle

The birth control methods we have already discussed require the use of pills or devices. Some of these methods have side effects in some users, and there may be serious health risks in the use of oral contraceptives and the IUD. Other methods we have looked at — condoms, vaginal spermicides, and the diaphragm — have fewer side effects, but they require that the couple use them each time they have intercourse.

Many couples are interested in a birth control method that has no side effects, is inexpensive, and does not interrupt spontaneity during sexual interaction. In the next paragraphs, we look at some methods of birth control based on the menstrual cycle, which may answer some of these couples' needs. These methods are sometimes referred to as *natural family planning,* or *fertility awareness* methods. A fertile woman's body reveals subtle and overt signs of cyclic fertility that can be used both to help prevent and to plan conception. The three fertility awareness methods—mucus, calendar, and basal body temperature—are most effective when used together.

Mucus Method. The **mucus method,** also called the *ovulation method,* is based on the cyclic changes of cervical mucus. (See Figure 12.1.) These natural changes, if carefully observed, reveal periods of fertility in a woman's cycle. To use this method, a woman learns to "read" the amounts and textures of vaginal secretions and to maintain a daily chart of the changes. A woman reads her mucus by wiping herself every time she goes to the toilet and observing the secretions on the tissue. After menstruation there are usually some "dry days" when there is no vaginal discharge on the vulva. When a yellow or white sticky discharge begins, unprotected coitus should be avoided. Several days later the ovulatory mucus appears. It is clear, stringy, and stretchy in consistency, similar to egg white. A drop of this mucus will stretch between an open thumb and forefinger. A vaginal feeling of wetness and lubrication accompanies this discharge, which has a chemical balance and texture that facilitate the entry of sperm into the uterus. Approximately four days after the ovulatory mucus begins and 24 hours after a cloudy discharge resumes, it is considered safe to resume unprotected intercourse. The fertile period usually totals 9 to 15 days out of each cycle. The temperature method, discussed later in this section, is often combined with the mucus method to better estimate the time of ovulation.

In many cities, classes in this method are offered at a hospital or clinic. Each woman's mucus patterns may vary, and a class is the best way to learn to interpret the changes.

The Calendar Method. With the **calendar method,** also called the *rhythm method,* a woman estimates the calendar time during her cycle when she is ovulating and fertile. To do this she keeps a chart, preferably for one year, of the length of her cycles. (She cannot be using oral contraceptives during this time because they impose a cycle that may not be the same as her own.) The first day of menstruation is counted as day one. The woman counts the number of days of her cycle, the last day being the one before the onset of menstruation. To determine the high-risk days on which she should avoid unprotected coitus, she subtracts 18 from the number of days of her shortest cycle. For example, if her shortest cycle was 26 days, day 8 would be the first high-risk day. To estimate when unprotected coitus could resume, she subtracts 10 from the number of days in her longest cycle. For example, if her longest cycle is 32 days, she would be able to resume intercourse on day 22. Thus she avoids coitus without birth control during her midcycle ovulation, either by abstaining from coitus or by using another method of contraception from days 8 through 22. Forms of lovemaking other than intercourse can continue during the high-risk days.

F I G U R E 11.10

Charting basal body temperature during a model menstrual cycle.

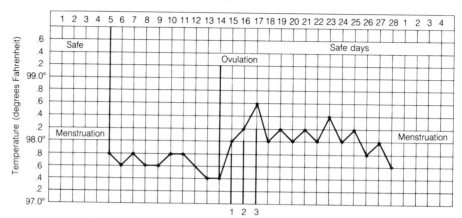

The Basal Body – Temperature Method. Another way of estimating high-fertility days is through temperature. Immediately prior to ovulation, the **basal body temperature** (BBT, the body temperature in the resting state upon waking in the morning) drops slightly. After ovulation the corpus luteum releases more progesterone, which causes the body temperature to rise slightly (0.2°F). Because these temperature changes (shown in Figure 11.10) are slight, a thermometer with easy-to-read gradations must be used. Electronic thermometers have also been developed for measuring BBT and are effective in indicating infertile and fertile times in the cycle (Royston et al., 1984).

Advantages of Menstrual Cycle – Based Methods. Major advantages of methods based on the menstrual cycle are that there are no side effects and that they are free or very inexpensive. Some women and their partners report increased comfort and appreciation of their bodies' cycles and processes when they use these methods. If they choose abstinence from penile – vaginal intercourse during the fertile days, this interval can provide time and motivation for noncoital sexual relating. Knowledge of cyclic changes can also help a couple plan a pregnancy. Also, these methods are acceptable to some religious groups that oppose other contraceptive methods.

Disadvantages of Menstrual Cycle – Based Methods. Methods based on the menstrual cycle restrict spontaneity of intercourse and ejaculation during fertile times. Furthermore, learning to accurately detect the mucus and temperature changes involves practice, and with all of these methods, a couple must keep accurate records for several cycles before beginning to rely on them for contraception. Considerable commitment is essential to maintain daily observation and charting. These methods are more difficult for women who have irregular cycles, and some women are unable to see mucus and temperature patterns clearly. Also, vaginal infections, semen, and contraceptive foams, jellies, and creams make it more difficult to accurately interpret mucus.

Although temperature changes are often good indicators of ovulation, this method is fallible. Slight temperature variations can result from many conditions — a low-grade infection or cold, unrestful sleep, and so forth. Also, because sperm can remain alive in the fallopian tubes for up to 72 hours, the preovulation temperature drop does not occur far enough ahead of time to safely avoid coitus. Although the temperature method is more effective in preventing an undesired pregnancy than no method, it is quite unreliable.

Even after careful arithmetic, the calendar method is very unreliable. Ovulation usually occurs about 14 days before the onset of menstruation; however, even with a woman who ordinarily has regular cycles, the timing of ovulation and menstruation may vary due to factors such as illness, fatigue, or excitement. For a woman who routinely or periodically has irregular cycles, the calendar method is even less safe and requires longer abstention from coitus.

Present research indicates that methods based on the menstrual cycle are considerably less effective than most others (Hatcher et al., 1990).

Postcoital Contraception

Women or couples may seek some kind of postcoital contraception following unprotected intercourse. The risk of pregnancy from unprotected midcycle intercourse is 15 – 26% (Hatcher et al., 1990). For contraception after intercourse, administration of high levels of hormones and insertion of an IUD are the methods most commonly used.

Morning-After Pills. Recent studies have shown that taking Ovral, a brand of birth control pills, within 72 hours following unprotected midcycle intercourse effectively prevented pregnancy. High doses of estrogens or progestins are also given as morning-after contraceptives. These hormone treatments are presumed to work by affecting the uterine lining so that the developing embryo cannot implant on it. Nausea or vomiting are potential side effects of morning-after pills. Long-term health effects on the woman or the fetus are unknown; the possibility of cancer in children of women who take morning-after pills but continue the pregnancy has not been ruled out. If a woman uses any kind of morning-after pill, she should be aware of and watch for pill-related side effects (Hatcher et al., 1990).

Morning-After IUD Insertion. Inserting an IUD within five to seven days following unprotected midcycle intercourse can prevent pregnancy. IUDs are believed to work by preventing implantation of the fertilized ovum, and they can be kept as an ongoing method of contraception. An IUD should not be used as a morning-after contraceptive if there has been a high risk of exposure to a sexually transmitted disease (Hatcher et al., 1990).

Sterilization

One other method of contraception has become common in recent years due to improved surgical techniques and increasing societal acceptance. *Sterilization* is the most effective method of birth control except abstinence from coitus, and its safety and permanence appeal to many who want no more children or prefer to remain childless. Sterilization is the leading method of birth control in the United States

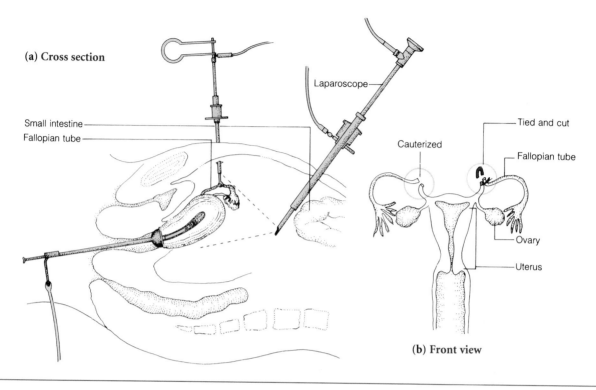

(a) Cross section

Laparoscope

Small intestine
Fallopian tube

Tied and cut
Cauterized
Fallopian tube
Ovary
Uterus

(b) Front view

FIGURE 11.11

Female sterilization by
laparoscopic ligation. (a)
Cross section: The tubes are
located using a laparoscope
and cut, tied, or cauterized
through a second incision.
(b) Front view: The tubes
after ligation.

and around the world. Although some research is being conducted on ways of reversing sterilization, at present the reversal procedures involve complicated surgery, and their effectiveness is not guaranteed. Therefore, sterilization is recommended only to those who desire a permanent method of birth control.

Because sterilization is best considered permanent, a person should carefully explore his or her situation and feelings before deciding on the procedure (Chi, 1992; Marcil-Gratton et al., 1988). Questions to consider include: Are there any circumstances under which I would want (more) children (for example, if my child died, or if I began a new relationship)? Is my sense of masculinity or femininity tied to my fertility? What are my alternatives to sterilization? How does my partner feel about the decision? In the following paragraphs, we look at the procedures for sterilization of females and males.

Female Sterilization. In recent years female sterilization has become a relatively safe, simple, and inexpensive procedure. Sterilization can be accomplished by a variety of techniques that use small incisions and either local or general anesthesia.

Tubal sterilization can be done in several ways. A *minilaparotomy* involves a small abdominal incision. Each fallopian tube is gently pulled to this incision; then they are cut and tied, or clips or rings are applied. The tubes are then allowed to slip back into place within the abdomen (Liskin et al., 1985). Another procedure, *laparoscopy,* is shown in Figure 11.11. One or two small incisions are made in the abdomen, usually at the navel and slightly below the pubic hairline. A narrow, lighted viewing instrument called a laparoscope is inserted into the abdomen to locate the fallopian tubes. The tubes are then tied off, cut, or cauterized to block passage of sperm and eggs. Other methods have also been developed to block the tubes. A band or a clip is sometimes applied to a tube instead of removing a segment. The ligated (tied) or cut tubes prevent the sperm and egg from meeting in the tube, thus preventing pregnancy. The incisions are generally so small that adhesive tape rather than stitches is used after surgery. Sometimes the incision is made through the back of the vaginal wall, and the procedure is called a *culpotomy*.

Sterilization acts only as a roadblock in the tubes. It does not further affect a woman's reproductive and sexual system. Until menopause her ovaries continue to release their eggs. The released egg simply degenerates, as do millions of other cells daily, and is carried away by the circulatory system. The woman's hormone levels and the timing of menopause are not altered. Her sexuality is not physiologically changed, but she may find that her interest and arousal increase because she no longer is concerned with pregnancy or birth control methods. Research indicates that sterilization does not have a detrimental effect on a woman's sexual satisfaction (Shain et al., 1991).

Some discomfort or complications can occur from female sterilization. A woman may experience some pain at the site of the incision, and if the tubes are sealed by burning, other tissue in the pelvic cavity may be accidentally burned. Postsurgical bleeding is also a possible complication. To minimize the possibility of complications, it is important for a woman to choose a physician who is experienced in sterilization procedures.

Surgical reversal of female sterilization is sometimes successful. Rates of postsurgical pregnancy vary from about 40–75% (Hatcher et al., 1988). One researcher found that women were most likely to have successful reversal if the previous sterilization procedure had removed or blocked only a small portion of the tube on the end close to the uterus (Silber & Cohen, 1984).

Male Sterilization. In general, male sterilization is safer, has fewer complications following surgery, is considerably less expensive, and is as effective as female sterilization. **Vasectomy** is a minor surgical procedure that involves cutting and tying the vas deferens, the two sperm-carrying ducts (Figure 11.12). The operation is typically performed in a physician's office. Under a local anesthetic, a small incision is made in the scrotal sac, well above the testicle. The vas is lifted out and a small segment removed. The free ends are tied off, clipped, or cauterized to prevent rejoining. After the procedure is repeated on the opposite side, the incisions are closed and the operation is completed, usually in less than 20 minutes. A man can expect some short-term postoperative problems such as swelling, inflammation, or bruising in the region of the surgery that last from one day to two weeks.

An improved vasectomy procedure, known as no-scalpel vasectomy, substitutes small punctures for the conventional incision. The vas deferens is lifted out of the puncture opening and ligated. Side effects are reduced with no-scalpel vasectomy (Liskin et al., 1992).

Vasectomy prevents sperm produced in the testes from entering the semen produced by the internal reproductive organs (see Chapter 5). However, because a significant number of sperm are stored beyond the site of the incision, a man remains fertile for some time after the operation. Sperm may be present in the first 10 to 20 postoperative ejaculations, or for up to several months. Therefore, effective alternative methods of birth control should be used until semen analysis reveals no sperm present in the seminal fluid. Many physicians recommend that a vasectomized man have two consecutive negative evaluations before engaging in unprotected intercourse. Generally, these checks occur six to eight weeks after the

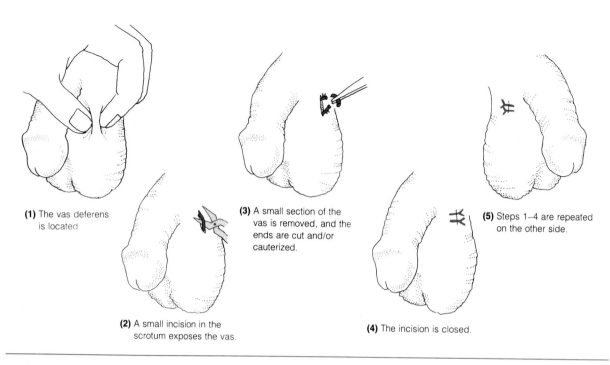

(1) The vas deferens is located

(2) A small incision in the scrotum exposes the vas.

(3) A small section of the vas is removed, and the ends are cut and/or cauterized.

(4) The incision is closed.

(5) Steps 1–4 are repeated on the other side.

F I G U R E 11.12

Male sterilization by vasectomy.

operation. In rare cases the two free ends of the severed vas grow back together (this is called *recanalization*), or the surgeon misses one of the vas deferens (Alderman, 1988).

Unlike castration, vasectomy does not alter testicular production of male sex hormones or absorption of the hormones into the bloodstream. A vasectomized man also continues to produce sperm that are absorbed and eliminated by his body. His ejaculations contain almost as much semen after the operation as before because sperm constitute less than 5% of the total ejaculate. The characteristic odor and consistency of the semen also remain the same.

Most men report that vasectomy does not affect their sexual functioning. Some report improvements, often due to greater spontaneity of sexual expression and less fear of impregnating their partners. A few report a reduction in sexual desire, which may be related to concerns about their continued masculinity.

Some preliminary research has found an association between vasectomy and an increase in prostate and testicular cancer. However, the results are inconclusive as to whether or not vasectomy contributes to the development of a later cancer; further research is needed to clarify this question (Cale et al., 1990; Perlman et al., 1991; West, 1992b).

Some men request a **vasovasostomy,** a reversal of a vasectomy. Approximately 80% of vasovasostomies are done for men in a second marriage following divorce (Fallon et al., 1981). With selected patients and experienced microsurgeons, the chances of reconnecting the vas have increased (Engleman et al, 1990). The shorter the interval between vasectomy and vasovasostomy, the better the outcome (Cos et al., 1983). However, the major problem complicating vasovasostomy is reduced fertility following reconnection of the vas. After vasovasostomy many men have low sperm counts, reduced sperm motility, or both. Another factor in reduced postvasovasostomy fertility may be the antisperm antibodies that develop in some vasectomized men. The best measure of vasovasostomy success is subsequent pregnancy; various studies report a pregnancy rate of 16 – 79% using current vaso- vasostomy techniques (Hatcher et al., 1990).

Other Methods

There are other contraceptive methods that are less commonly used than the ones we have been discussing. We mention some of them here, partly because they are used both as primary birth control methods and as backups for other methods and partly because people may have misconceptions about their effectiveness. We discuss nursing, withdrawal, and douching as methods of birth control.

Nursing. Nursing a baby delays the return to fertility after childbirth; however, it is not a reliable method of birth control because there is no way of knowing when ovulation will resume. *Amenorrhea* (lack of menstruation) usually occurs during nursing, but it is not a reliable indication of inability to conceive. Nearly 80% of breast-feeding women ovulate before their first menstrual period. The longer a woman breast-feeds, the more likely it is that ovulation will occur (Hatcher et al., 1986).

Withdrawal. The practice of the man removing his penis from the vagina just before he ejaculates is known as *withdrawal.* The oft-unfulfilled hope is that there will be no sperm present to fertilize an ovum. However, withdrawal is not very effective. It may be difficult for the man to judge exactly when he must withdraw. His likely tendency is to remain inside the vagina as long as possible, and this may be too long. Both partners may experience pleasure-destroying anxiety about whether he will withdraw in time. Furthermore, even withdrawing before ejacu- lation does not protect against pregnancy. The preejaculatory Cowper's gland secretions may contain sperm that can fertilize the egg; and if sperm are deposited on the labia after withdrawal, they can swim into the vagina.

Douching. *Douching* after intercourse is very ineffective as a method of birth con- trol. After ejaculation some sperm are inside the uterus in a matter of one or two minutes. The movement of the water from douching may actually help sperm reach the opening of the cervix. Furthermore, frequent douching can irritate vag- inal tissues.

New Directions in Contraception

The spectrum of choices available for contraception widened markedly with the advent of the pill and the IUD. Currently with hormonal contraceptives "less is better"; we now have lower-dose oral contraceptives and subcutaneous capsules. As we have seen in this chapter, however, there are still potential health hazards and inconveniences associated with available methods. The National Research Council has stated that three million unwanted pregnancies occur each year because of contraceptive and user failure. Further research is needed to improve the safety, reliability, and convenience of birth control. However, little research is being done because of fear of lawsuits involving new contraceptives (Salholtz, 1990b). Given these limitations, we look at some projected improvements for both both men and women.

New Directions for Men

Presently, male contraception is limited to condoms, vasectomy, and the highly unreliable withdrawal method. However, there are some research efforts currently underway that suggest other methods may be available in the future. These efforts have concentrated on inhibiting sperm production, motility, or maturation.

A study began in 1988 to test reversible vasectomies for men. A silicone plug is inserted into the vas deferens. In primate studies the device was 100% successful in blocking sperm passage over a 7–12-month period and was completely reversible (*Contraceptive Technology Update,* 1988b).

Some years ago it was shown that the conventional estrogen–progesterone female birth control pill induces temporary sterility in men by curtailing sperm production. This effect was presumed to result from suppression of pituitary gonadotropins, the same mechanism by which the pill induces temporary sterility in women. Unfortunately, men often reported markedly reduced interest in sex while taking the pill, a fact that seriously limited its practicality. The idea of giving men a contraceptive pill that modifies hormone levels still holds some promise, and research with various substances is ongoing (World Health Organization Task Force on Methods for the Regulation of Male Fertility, 1990; Hatcher et al., 1988).

A gonadotropin-releasing hormone inhibitor (LH–RH agonist) is currently under study as a male contraceptive. LH–RH agonist has been shown to reduce the number and motility of sperm in men who received daily injections of the substance. Testosterone levels also dropped, and inability to achieve an erection occurred in more than half of the men in the study. This side effect disappeared after treatment stopped. However, testosterone combined with LH–RH agonist is effective in maintaining sexual functioning while producing temporary infertility (Salameh et al., 1991).

Another substance under research as a male contraceptive is *gossypol,* a compound derived from the seeds, stems, or roots of cotton plants. Gossypol was first identified as an antifertility agent in China. Investigators found that there was an extremely low birthrate in an area where the local people used cottonseed oil for cooking. Clinical trials in China began in 1972, and more than 10,000 men have been studied. Among the first 400 men who received the drug for 6 months to 4 years, gossypol was reported to be 99.89% effective. Gossypol apparently inhibits enzyme activity necessary for sperm production and reduces sperm count dramatically, without affecting sex hormone levels. Some of the side effects reported included transient weakness, an increase or decrease in appetite, gastrointestinal disturbances, and a small incidence of decreased sexual interest and functioning (Nieschlag et al., 1981). Although there have been several births of healthy babies from wives of men who stopped taking gossypol (Maugh, 1981), recovery of complete sperm counts did not occur in 25% of the 2000 men who were followed up after stopping (Nieschlag et al., 1981). A great deal of further research is needed to determine the safety of gossypol as a contraceptive agent.

Several researchers are considering the possibility of developing a vaccine to immunize a man against his own sperm. The idea is to introduce a substance into a man's system that would induce his body to develop antibodies against his own sperm cells. There has even been some effort to develop an antisperm vaccine for women. However, there are still some unresolved problems with this approach, including possible genetic damage and unhealthy reactions of body tissue to the vaccine.

New Directions for Women

An array of contraceptive methods for women is currently under experimentation. All the hormonal methods have potential side effects similar to those of the pill, but these vary with the manner of administration. Injections of progesterone, given every one to three months, have been used by 200 million women in more than 90 countries, but are not currently available in the United States (Connell, 1991).

Another recently developed female contraceptive device is the "vaginal ring," which is something like a diaphragm. Each ring slowly releases low doses of estrogen and progestin, or progestin alone, for three months before needing replacement. The hormone is absorbed into the blood through the vaginal mucosa (Liskin & Blackburn, 1987). This device should be available in the mid-1990s (Monier & Laird, 1989).

As mentioned earlier, another possibility is a vaccination to develop a woman's immunity to her partner's sperm. This method is still in the experimental stages, and maintaining effectiveness of the immunity has not yet been firmly established. The use of a luteinizing hormone-releasing factor inhibitor (LH–RF agonist) as a method of contraception is also under study. Injections of LH–RF agonist for three successive days, beginning with the first day of menstruation, have been shown to induce a chain of hormonal events that results in inadequate maturation of the ovarian follicle and the uterine lining. Either of these effects would act to prevent conception. It may also be possible to use LH–RF agonist in a birth control pill taken monthly at the beginning of menstruation (Sheehan et al., 1982).

Female sterilization by injection of liquid silicone into the fallopian tubes, where it hardens and blocks passage of the sperm and egg, is also under study (Loffer, 1984).

An antiprogesterone substance, *RU-486,* has been approved for use in Great Britain, France, and China, but is not currently available in the United States. When given late in the menstrual cycle, RU-486 leads to menstruation by preventing implantation or causing the fertilized zygote to slough off of the uterine wall. When administered within 10 days of the expected onset of the missed menstrual period, 90% of women experienced menstruation (Hatcher et al., 1988). The National Right to Life Committee opposes the use of RU-486 because it can induce abortion and is campaigning to prevent it from being marketed in the United States (Lader, 1991). Although it is controversial as a method of preventing implantation, RU-486 also shows promise in slowing or stopping the growth of some types of breast tumors, treating endometriosis, assisting in cervical dilation during labor, and treating Cushing Syndrome, a serious endocrine disorder (Hodgen, 1991).

Summary

Historical and Social Perspectives

From the beginning of recorded history, humankind has been concerned with birth control.

Margaret Sanger opened the first birth control clinics in the United States at a time when it was illegal to provide birth control information and devices.

Objections to contraception stem from religious doctrine. However, most church members in the United States use some kind of artificial contraception.

Shared Responsibility

The male partner can share contraceptive responsibility by being informed, asking a new partner about birth control, accompanying his partner to her exam, using condoms and/or coital abstinence if the couple chooses, and sharing the expense of the exam and method.

Currently Available Methods

Comparison of relative convenience, safety, cost, and effectiveness may influence the choice of contraception.

People who feel guilty and have negative attitudes about sexuality are less likely to use contraception effectively than people who have positive attitudes about sexuality.

Three types of oral contraceptives are currently available. The constant-dose combination pill contains steady doses of estrogen and progestin. The multiphasic pill provides fluctuations of estrogen and progesterone levels throughout the cycle. The progestin-only pill consists of low-dose progestin.

Advantages of oral contraceptives are high effectiveness and lack of interference with sexual activity. The birth control pills are also associated with lower incidences of cancer of the uterus and ovary, ovarian cysts, benign breast disease, and pelvic inflammatory disease. An additional advantage of the combination and multiphasic pills is reduction of menstrual flow and cramps. The advantage of the progestin-only pill is the reduced chance of harmful side effects.

Some of the disadvantages of the constant-dose combination and multiphasic pills are possible side effects such as blood clots, increased probability of heart attack, high blood pressure, more rapid growth of cancer of the breast and uterus, depression, and reduced sexual interest. Disadvantages of the progestin-only pill include irregular bleeding and the possibility of additional side effects. In general, the health risks of oral contraceptives are far lower than those from pregnancy and birth.

Norplant, made of silastic rods filled with synthetic progestin, is an additional form of birth control, which became available in 1991. Its main advantages are ease of use and high effectiveness. Its main disadvantages are irregular bleeding and the potential of hormone-related side effects.

Diaphragm use is currently increasing. Advantages include lack of side effects, high effectiveness with knowledgeable and consistent use, and possible promotion of vaginal health. Some disadvantages are interruption of sexual activity, potential irritation from the spermicidal cream or jelly, and possible misplacement during insertion or intercourse.

The cervical cap has similar advantages and disadvantages to the diaphragm. Some women who have problems fitting the diaphragm can use the cervical cap, but cervical caps will not fit all women.

Vaginal spermicides (including foam, vaginal suppositories, the sponge, creams and jellies, and contraceptive film) are available without a prescription. Spermicides with nonoxynol-9 help protect against sexually transmitted diseases, including AIDS. Advantages of vaginal spermicides are lack of serious side effects, added lubrication, and possible promotion of vaginal health. Disadvantages include possible irritation of genital tissues and interruption of sexual activity.

Condoms are available in a variety of styles, including some lubricated with nonoxynol-9. Advantages include protection from sexually transmitted diseases, improved ejaculatory control, and ready availability as a backup method. Disadvantages include interruption of sexual activity and reduced penile sensation. A female condom has also been developed.

The Copper-T and the Progestasert T are currently the only intrauterine devices (IUDs) on the U.S. market. Advantages of the IUD include uninterrupted sexual interaction and simplicity of use. Disadvantages include the possibility of increased cramping, spontaneous expulsion, uterine perforation, pelvic inflammatory disease, and pregnancy complications.

Methods based on the menstrual cycle, including the mucus, calendar, and basal body–temperature methods, help in planning coital activity to avoid a woman's fertile period.

Postcoital ("morning-after") contraception may be used following unprotected intercourse. Available methods include various types of hormone administration and IUD insertion.

At this time, sterilization should be considered permanent. A decision to be sterilized should be carefully evaluated.

Tubal ligation is the sterilization procedure most commonly done for women. It does not alter a woman's hormone levels, menstrual cycle, or the timing of menopause.

Vasectomy, the sterilization procedure for men, is not effective for birth control immediately after surgery because sperm remain in the vas deferens above the incision. Most men report that vasectomy does not affect their sexual functioning.

Nursing, douching, and the withdrawal method are not reliable methods for contraception.

New Directions in Contraception

Possible contraceptive methods for men in the future include a reversible vasectomy, male pill, or a sperm-immunization vaccine.

Possible contraceptive methods for women in the future include several long-lasting hormonal alternatives injected into the bloodstream or absorbed through a vaginal ring. A reversible sterilization procedure is also under study. RU-486, an antiprogesterone substance that induces menstruation when administered within 10 days of a missed menstrual cycle, is used in Great Britain, France, and China. But political controversy exists concerning its approval for sale in the United States.

☙ *Thought Provokers* ☙

1. What do you think are the positive and negative effects of modern contraception on relationships and sexuality?

2. If you could design an ideal contraceptive, what would it be like?

3. What criteria should a married couple who do not want more children use to decide which one of them should be sterilized?

Suggested Readings

Hatcher, Robert et al. (1990). *Contraceptive Technology: 1990–1992.* New York: Irvington. A comprehensive, up-to-date book about birth control—a must for anyone who wants the latest information about the technology and effects of contraception.

Kass-Annesse, Barbara; and Danzer, Hal (1986). *The Fertility Awareness Workbook.* Atlanta: Printed Matter. This book contains fertility awareness charts, step-by-step instructions on how to record fertility signs, and specific advice on how to prevent pregnancy using fertility awareness.

Lader, Lawrence (1991). *RU-486: The Pill That Could End the Abortion Wars and Why American Women Don't Have It.* Reading, Mass.: Addison-Wesley. A pro-choice activist details the controversial suppression of RU-486 in America.

McLaren, Angus (1990). *A History of Contraception.* Oxford, England: Basil Blackwell. A scholarly and readable history of the uses and meaning of fertility control through the ages.

Resources

Mail-order condoms from The Rubber Tree, 4426 Burke Avenue N., Seattle, WA 98103; (205) 633-4750. Send a self-addressed, stamped envelope for a brochure.

A baby is an inestimable blessing and bother.

Mark Twain
Letters (1876)

CHAPTER 12

Conceiving Children: Process and Choice

*O*ne of the most important decisions you will probably make in your lifetime is whether or not to become a parent. In this chapter we address the pros and cons of parenthood. We also discuss the processes of conception, pregnancy, and birth and some of the emotions that accompany them, from the viewpoints of the mother and father. We encourage people who desire further information to seek more extensive references or to consult a health care practitioner. As a starting point, we look at the option of parenthood and some of the alternatives that are available for people who want to become mothers and fathers.

Parenthood as an Option

Parenthood is changing in contemporary American society, both in the degree of choice we have about becoming parents and with regard to the definition of parenthood itself. Until recently in human history, highly effective birth control methods were not available, and parenthood was an expected consequence of marriage. Today, however, adults have more choice about becoming parents. Couples can make conscious decisions about when or whether they would like to have children. One result of this freedom of choice is that an increasing number of people are deciding not to have children at all (Landa, 1990).

However, people who choose child-free marriage are often criticized and pressured about that decision. **Pronatalism** is the word used to describe policies and attitudes that encourage parenthood for all couples. Childless married couples are routinely asked questions like "When are you going to start your family?" or "You're *not* going to have children? Why aren't you?" (When people say they *are* planning to have children, rarely does anyone ask "Why?") Other manifestations of pronatalism are commonly held stereotypes about people, especially women, who choose not to be parents. Many women have learned to believe that motherhood is essential to their personal fulfillment and that they are selfish or "unnatural" if they choose not to be mothers. However, many women are not mothers; one in five U.S. women in their 40s is childless (Mitchell, 1992b).

What do you think are the thoughts and feelings of women who decide not to have children ? Come up with your own ideas before reading further.

One study reported that voluntarily childless women tended to be both very involved in their marriages and to feel a great deal of ambivalence about the conflict between work and motherhood. These women believed that their own parents had made financial sacrifices and had limited their travels, careers, and mobility for the sake of their children. Many of their mothers had longed for careers that they had never had or had cut short when they became parents. Most of the women in the study said that they had not had babies because of their careers. Voluntarily childless women viewed careers and childrearing as full-time commitments, and many feared that choosing one would close off the other. As one subject stated:

I wish I could decide once and for all to have a baby, or even figure out whether I want one. Then I could plan the rest of my life.... One day I'm so absorbed by my career that I think I can't possibly have a child. Then the next day, I'm staring somewhat jealously at pregnant women. I see mothers and babies everywhere. It looks good to me. But I always scare myself away before I actually do anything about it. (Faux, 1984, p. 167)

There are many potential advantages to remaining childless. Individuals and couples without children have much more time for themselves and do not have worries about providing for the physical and psychological needs of children. Nonparents can continue more spontaneous recreational, social, and work patterns. They can more fully pursue careers and may experience a great deal of challenge and fulfillment in their professional lives. Nonparents also have more financial resources available to them. There is usually more time and energy for companionship and intimacy in an adult relationship when there are no children. There is often less stress on marriages; in fact, some studies show that marriages without children are happier and more satisfying than are marriages with children (Stiglitz, 1990). However, this discrepancy may be due, in part, to the proportion of unhappily married couples who remain married because they have young children, rather than completely to the presence or absence of children in the family.

There are also many potential advantages to having children. Children themselves give and receive love, and their presence may enhance the love between couples as they share in the experiences of raising their offspring. Successfully managing the challenges of parenthood can also build self-esteem and provide a sense of accomplishment. Parenthood is often an opportunity for discovering new and untapped dimensions of oneself that can give one's life greater meaning and satisfaction. As one new father explained:

I almost didn't choose to become a father. How awful that would have been. What is worse, I never would have known what it was I was missing.... I feel somehow that I have finally joined the human race.... There is no way to describe this feeling that is neither corny nor trite. There is also no way to express the notion that we have somehow stumbled into manufacturing a perfect miniature human being ... without resorting to that hackneyed and overused word "miracle." (Greenburg, 1986, p. 92)

Many parents say that they have experienced tremendous personal growth and have become better people through parenthood. Children offer ongoing stimulation and change as they develop through childhood, as another father experienced:

His presence helped me to break out of my adult world in which everything was ordered and set, and allowed me to experience the world of childhood, where everything is free and spontaneous. Past memories, long since forgotten, of earlier years and relationships with my own family would surface, effortlessly, to my awareness. It was as if Jonathan was the door, the entryway, to my experiencing a new and different aspect of myself. At the same time, I felt even more intimately connected to him. (Greenburg, 1985, p. 7)

Adults may also want to raise children who are not biologically their own. Their desire to adopt a child or children may be partly motivated by a concern with overpopulation and a desire to give parentless children love and security. Another common reason for seeking to adopt is that the couple is unable to have children due to infertility. Currently in the United States, potential adoptive parents outnumber the healthy newborn infants available for adoption, and there is

OUR SEXUALITY

Are We Parent Material? (Or, Am I? in the Case of Single Parenthood)

1. Are my partner and I willing to devote at least 18 years of our lives to being responsible for a child?

2. How would a child affect our growth and development as individuals and as a couple? How would a child affect our careers, education, social life, recreational interests, and privacy?

3. Do my partner and I understand each other's feelings about religion, careers, family, child rearing, and future goals? Will children fit into these feelings, hopes, and plans?

4. Could we give a child a good home? Is our relationship basically happy and strong?

5. Do we like children? Do we enjoy activities that children can do?

6. How would we feel if our child's ideas and values turn out to be different from our own?

7. Do I expect a child to compensate for unhappiness in other areas of my life?

8. What do I/we really want?

Source: Adapted from a pamphlet by the National Alliance for Optional Parenthood.

a long waiting period. However, worldwide adoption has become more common, and children or adolescents who are older or disabled are being placed more and more frequently in adoptive homes.

The potential rewards of either becoming parents or remaining childless may be romanticized or unrealistic for a given person or couple. There are no guarantees that the benefits of either children or child-free living will meet one's expectations. Still, it is important to consciously consider the options beforehand because parenthood is a permanent and major life decision. The box "Are We Parent Material?" presents some important considerations for people trying to decide whether or not to have children. There are no right or wrong answers; rather, the purpose of these questions is to help you explore your feelings about parenthood. And because we all change, your feelings about parenthood may very well change during your life. As one writer put it, having children changes your life but so does not having them (Cole, 1987).

Becoming Pregnant

There are, of course, several options for becoming parents without actually experiencing pregnancy and childbirth. Most people who have children, however, are biological parents. In the remainder of this chapter, we look at some of the developments, experiences, and feelings that are involved in the physiological process of becoming parents, starting with becoming pregnant. This first step may be difficult for some couples.

Enhancing the Possibility of Conception

Picking the right time for intercourse is important in increasing the probability of conception. It is difficult to predict the exact time of ovulation, but several methods permit a reasonable approximation. One is the mucus method discussed

F I G U R E 12.1

Determining ovulation using
mucus secretions. (a) Cervix
at day 6 of the menstrual
cycle. Secretions are minimal.
(b) Cervix at ovulation on
day 14. Fertile mucus is
secreted from the os.

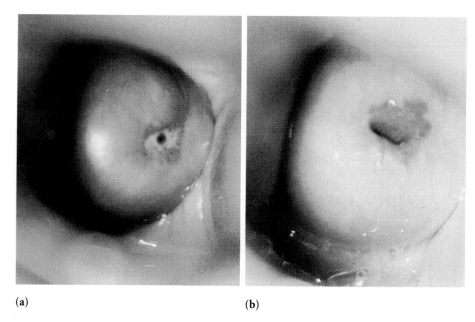

(a)   (b)

in Chapter 11, where the couple times coital activity according to the fertile period
in the woman's menstrual cycle (see Figure 12.1). Body temperature and the principles of the calendar method may also be used in estimating ovulation time. Ovu-
lation-predictor tests that measure the rise in LH in urine prior to ovulation can
accurately identify the best time for conception. However, if a couple continues
to have difficulty conceiving a child, both partners should be medically evaluated.

Infertility

It has been estimated that as many as one in six couples in the United States
experience fertility problems and seek treatment for infertility each year (Pearson,
1992). If attempts at impregnation are unsuccessful after a reasonable period of
time (usually one year), a couple should consult a physician (Waterstone, 1992).
Approximately 20–35% of couples take more than one year to conceive (Page,
1989). Because approximately 40–50% of infertility cases result from male factors,
it is important that both partners be evaluated (Grunfeld, 1989). In about 15% of
couples, factors from both partners are involved (Hudson et al., 1987). We usually
think of infertility as the inability to conceive any children, but secondary infertility — the inability to conceive a second child — is also common (Beck 1989).

Given recent medical and scientific advances, do you think the majority of infertility cases can be treated successfully? Take a moment to consider this question
and come up with an answer before reading on.

Infertility is a complex and distressing problem. The causes of infertility are sometimes difficult to determine; a cause is not found in as many as 15% of couples
(Weiss et al., 1992). In addition, as many as half the couples seeking treatment for

infertility will ultimately be unsuccessful in their efforts to conceive, despite trying various avenues of treatment (Office of Technology Assessment, 1988). In this section we look briefly at some common causes of female and male infertility and at the impact infertility can have on individuals and their sexuality.

Female Infertility. A woman may have difficulty conceiving or be unable to conceive for a number of reasons. Failure to ovulate at regular intervals is quite common. Such failure may be caused by a variety of factors, including hormone imbalances, severe vitamin deficiencies, metabolic disturbances, poor nutrition, genetic factors, emotional stress, or medical conditions. Ovulation and thus pregnancy can also be inhibited by a below normal percentage of body fat from excessive dieting or exercise. Even 10–15% below normal weight is sufficient to inhibit ovulation (Frish, 1988). Women who smoke cigarettes are less fertile and take longer to become pregnant than nonsmokers (Phipps et al., 1987). Smokers are also more likely to experience ectopic pregnancy (Laurent et al., 1992). Alcohol and drug abuse reduces fertility in women, and environmental toxins can also impair female fertility (Office of Technology Assessment, 1988). A variety of medications are sometimes used to stimulate ovulation. These medications are often successful in accomplishing their purpose. Though generally safe, they may produce certain complications, including multiple births.

If tests indicate that the woman is ovulating and that her partner's semen quality is satisfactory, the next step often is a postcoital test to see whether the sperm remain viable and motile in the cervical mucus. A woman's cervical mucus may contain antibodies against her partner's sperm, and it may form a plug that blocks their passage (Cunningham et al., 1991). In some cases several months of using condoms or abstaining from intercourse may reduce the level of sperm antibodies in the mucus sufficiently to allow fertilization to occur (Speroff et al., 1989).

Infections, as well as other abnormalities of the cervix, vagina, uterus, fallopian tubes, or ovaries, can destroy sperm or prevent them from reaching the egg. Problems with the fallopian tubes account for as many as 40% of cases of female infertility (Paterson & Petrucco, 1987). Scar tissue from old infections — in the fallopian tubes or in or around the ovaries — can block the passage of sperm and eggs (Moore et al., 1991; Safrin et al., 1992). Other major causes of female infertility are reproductive tract infections and tubal scarring from sexually transmitted diseases (STDs) (Morgan, 1991). STDs cause approximately 20% of female infertility problems (Office of Technology Assessment, 1988). IUD use also increases the risk of tubal infection and scarring. Defects in the uterine cavity can prevent implantation of the fertilized egg, and endometriosis (growths of the uterine lining that develop in the pelvic cavity) can also result in infertility (Murphy et al., 1991). Tubal problems can sometimes be resolved by surgery to remove scar tissue around the fallopian tubes and ovaries. A new treatment that is demonstrating success uses a balloon-type device that is inserted into the fallopian tube and then inflated to open the tube (Cofino, 1990).

Male Infertility. Most causes of male infertility are related to abnormalities in sperm number and/or motility (i.e., sperm cells that do not propel themselves with sufficient vigor). Infectious diseases of the male reproductive tract can alter sperm production, viability, and transport. For example, infectious diseases of the testes, particularly mumps during adulthood, can reduce sperm output; or an infection of the vas deferens can block the passage of sperm. Fertility may be decreased when a genital tract infection produces an immune response that affects sperm (Alexander & Anderson, 1987; Grunfeld, 1989). STD-caused infections are another major cause of male infertility. Environmental toxins such as toxic chemicals, pollutants, radiation, and drugs may also produce low sperm counts and abnormal sperm cells (Yazigi et al., 1991). Sperm absorb and metabolize environmental toxins more easily than other body cells because of their rapid cell division. Smoking, alcohol, and drug abuse also reduce fertility (Hurd et al., 1992).

Another major cause of infertility in men is a damaged or enlarged vein in the testes or vas deferens, called a varicocele (Schlegel, 1991). The varicocele causes blood to pool in the scrotum, which elevates temperature in the area, impairing sperm production. Varicoceles can usually be corrected surgically, and the postsurgical pregnancy rate is about 50% (Crocket, 1984).

An unlikely cause of male sterility may be undescended testes (McClure, 1988). If this condition is not corrected before puberty, sperm will be less likely to mature because of the higher temperatures within the abdomen. Hormone deficiencies may also result in an inadequate number of sperm cells in the semen. This situation can sometimes be remedied by hormone therapy.

In cases where the sperm count is low, the optimal frequency of ejaculation during intercourse is usually every other day during the week the woman is ovulating, to increase the concentration of sperm (Speroff et al., 1989). In such circumstances it is especially important for a couple to chart the woman's cycle so that they can reasonably predict her most fertile time. A man with a borderline sperm count might also want to avoid taking hot baths and wearing tight clothing and undershorts because these and similar environments subject the testicles to higher than normal temperatures.

Infertility and Sexuality. Most people grow up believing that they can conceive children when they decide to begin a family. Confronting infertility is an unanticipated shock and crisis (Forrest & Gilbert, 1992). Women tend to express more emotional distress about infertility than their partners, but both men and women experience increased anxiety, depression, and stress (Wright et al., 1991). The man is more likely to experience emotional distress when he is the cause of the infertility (Nachtigall et al., 1992). Problems with infertility can have profoundly negative effects on a couple's relationship and sexual functioning (Berg & Wilson, 1991). When a couple is first informed of their infertility, they may deny it or downplay their desire to have children. As their infertility becomes more evident and undeniable, they may feel a great sense of isolation from others during social discussions of pregnancy, childbirth, and child rearing. As one woman who has been unable to conceive stated:

Coffee breaks at work are the worst times; everyone brings out their pictures of their kids and discusses their latest trials and tribulations. I can't help feeling like there's something wrong with me for not being able to get pregnant. When one of the women complains about having problems with something like child care, I just want to shout at her and tell her how lucky she is to be able to have such a "problem." (Authors' files)

Partners may also become isolated from each other and believe that the other does not really understand. Each may feel inadequate about his or her masculinity or femininity due to problems with conceiving. Each may feel anger and guilt and wonder, "Why me?" Finally, the couple may feel grief over life experiences they can never have: namely, pregnancy, birth, and conceiving and rearing their own biological children. Intercourse itself may evoke these uncomfortable feelings and become an emotionally painful rather than pleasurable experience. One study found that 55% of infertile couples reported a decline in frequency of sexual intercourse, and 59% of the women and 42% of the men found sex less satisfactory (Sabatelli et al., 1988).

In addition, the medical procedures used in fertility diagnosis and treatment are often disruptive to the couple's sexual spontaneity. Sex can become very stressful and mechanical. Taking basal body temperature daily and timing intercourse according to ovulation can create tremendous sexual performance anxiety that can interfere with sexual arousal and emotional closeness. Because of these psychological and sexual stresses, health care practitioners who work with infertility problems need to be sensitive to and skilled in helping affected couples (Pepe & Byrne, 1991).

Alternatives to Couple Intercourse for Conception

In recent years various alternatives have been developed to help couples overcome the problem of infertility. *Artificial insemination* is one option to be considered in certain instances. In this procedure semen from a woman's partner is mechanically introduced by a health care practitioner into the woman's vagina or cervix — or in some cases, after being specially prepared, directly into her uterus. If the man is not producing adequate viable sperm or if a woman does not have a partner, artificial insemination with a donor's semen is another option. Many donor artificial insemination programs now require a 6–12 month follow-up blood sample to assure that the semen specimen does not carry the AIDS virus (Hudson et al., 1987). In addition, most programs now use frozen semen to eliminate the AIDS virus (Salisbury, 1991).

Various procedures are being developed to allow a woman or couple who cannot conceive through intercourse or artificial insemination to become pregnant. Advances in reproductive technology have developed methods that can be used when infertility is due to blocked fallopian tubes, severe endometriosis, very low sperm count, inability of sperm to survive in the woman's cervix, and unexplained infertility of two or more years' duration. The world's first "test-tube baby," born in England in 1978, provided impetus to research in this area. By the late 1980s, more than 3000 children had been born by similar methods. In *in vitro fertilization (IVF)*, the ovaries are stimulated by fertility drugs (see Figure 12.2). Then mature eggs are removed from the woman's ovary and are fertilized in a laboratory dish by her partner's sperm. After two to three days, several fertilized eggs of two to eight cells each are then introduced into the woman's uterus. If the fertilized egg is placed in the fallopian tube, the procedure is known as *zygote intrafallopian transfer (ZIFT)*. Excess embryos are often frozen if the first implantation does not take, so another implantation can be done without repeating the ova-retrieval procedures. A more recently developed procedure, *gamete intrafallopian transfer (GIFT)*, differs from IVF in that the sperm and ova are placed directly into the fallopian tube, the normal site of fertilization. If these procedures are successful, at least one egg will implant and develop. Because more than one

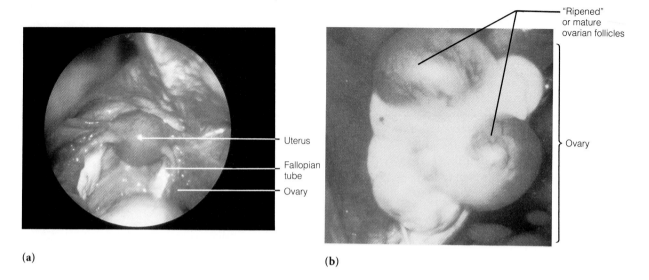

(a)   (b)

F I G U R E 12.2

The in vitro fertilization process: (a) an unstimulated ovary and (b) an ovary that has been stimulated with hormones to develop multiple mature follicles. These follicles can be seen protruding from the ovary surface.

fertilized ovum is placed in the uterus, there is about a 16–30% chance of twins or triplets (Bollen et al, 1991). Studies indicate that babies born from IVF–GIFT are as normal and healthy as others (Shoham et al., 1991).

Donated ova may be used for IVF–GIFT in cases where the woman does not have ovaries, does not produce her own ova, or has an inheritable genetic disease (Ames et al., 1991). Donation of ova is analogous to donor artificial insemination. Donors are usually patients undergoing IVF or a sister or friend of the infertile woman. When extra ova are retrieved, the women can anonymously donate them to another woman wanting the IVF–GIFT procedure. More recently, advances in ova-retrieval techniques have made the procedures safe and easy enough for women who are not undergoing IVF–GIFT ova retrieval themselves to donate ova. In certain cases where both partners are infertile, IVF–GIFT may be done with both donated sperm and ova (Seibel, 1988).

IVF–GIFT has been attempted by fewer than 1% of the estimated number of couples in the United States who have sought treatment for infertility (Office of Technology Assessment, 1988). The high cost and low success rates of these techniques are important factors. From the start of the menstrual cycle to the pregnancy test two or three weeks after transfer of the embryo, one attempt at IVF–GIFT costs around $6000; subsequent attempts are at additional cost. Because of variations in methods used to report results and select patients, it is difficult to obtain accurate rates of successful pregnancies from IVF–GIFT. The success rate at most centers is approximately 15–20% per IVF–GIFT procedure (Medical Research International, 1991).

Surrogate mothers are women who are willing to be artificially inseminated by the male partner of a childless couple, carry the pregnancy to term, deliver the child, and give it to the couple for adoption. This is done anonymously through an attorney or privately by arrangement between the woman and the couple. Surrogate mothers typically receive a fee of $10,000. About 600 surrogate mother arrangements had been concluded in the United States by the late 1980s (Office of Technology Assessment, 1988), but the personal and legal issues of such arrangements remain complex and unresolved (Schwartz, 1989). See the box "In Vitro Fertilization and Surrogate Motherhood."

ETHICAL/LEGAL ISSUES IN HUMAN SEXUALITY

In Vitro Fertilization and Surrogate Motherhood

Nontraditional methods of conception and birth raise complex legal and social issues (Halman et al., 1992). IVF – GIFT and surrogate motherhood have complicated traditional concepts of parenthood and genetic lineage, and have raised questions about the status of the resultant embryos and children (Strickler, 1992).

If a surrogate mother has a baby with birth defects, and neither she nor the adoptive couple wants the child, who is ultimately responsible for the child? When the surrogate mother decides she wants to keep the child, is the surrogate contract enforceable? Is a sperm bank liable if the inseminated mother contracts AIDS from the semen? When more ova for IVF – GIFT are fertilized in the laboratory medium than are implanted and the extra ones are discarded — is this immoral destruction of human life? (The Ethics Committee of the American Fertility Society has determined that embryos do not have the rights of persons [Seibel, 1988]). Who is legally entitled to

make decisions about how surplus in vitro embryos are used or discarded? Are the embryos the property of the genetic parents or the hospital or physician, or should they be protected by law from parental actions deemed harmful? When donor sperm or ova are used in IVF – GIFT, can the legal status of the mother or father come into question? Should children conceived by donor sperm or ova be told about their origins? What will be the long-term emotional effects on children, parents, and donors involved in once unimagined options such as surrogate motherhood, IVF – GIFT, and artificial insemination (Hunter, 1991)?

The conflict and confusion about these alternative methods of procreation are reflected by the fact that hundreds of bills to regulate or prohibit surrogacy contracts have been introduced to state legislators (Sollom, 1991): half of the states have passed laws limiting surrogacy while the other half have passed laws that facilitate surrogacy (Office of Tech-

nology Assessment, 1988). Most religions in the United States accept many necessary medical treatments for infertility. There is general acceptance of the morality of artificial insemination by the husband, considerable hesitation about donor artificial insemination, and little support for artificial insemination of single women. Most religions support IVF – GIFT using the married couple's own sperm and eggs as long as no embryos are discarded. Surrogate motherhood is largely opposed (Office of Technology Assessment, 1988).

These and other controversies and considerations will be an increasing focus of concern as reproductive technology continues to expand and more courts struggle with the resultant legal issues. In 1991 the American College of Obstetricians and Gynecologists and the American Fertility Society established a national advisory board on reproductive ethics to develop policies on such issues (McBride, 1991).

Pregnancy Detection

The initial signs of pregnancy may provoke feelings ranging from joy to dread, depending on the woman's desire to be pregnant and a variety of surrounding circumstances. Although some women may have either a light blood flow or "spotting" (irregular bleeding) after conception at the time of implantation, usually the first indication of pregnancy is the absence of the menstrual period at the expected time. Breast tenderness, nausea, vomiting, or other nonspecific symptoms (such as extreme fatigue or change in appetite) may also accompany pregnancy in the first weeks or months.

Any or all of these clues may cause a woman to suspect she is pregnant. Blood or urine tests and pelvic exams are medical techniques used to make the determination with a greater degree of certainty. The blood, and hence urine, of a pregnant woman contains the hormone **human chorionic gonadotropin,** (kō-rē-ON-ik gon'-a-dō-TRŌ-pin) **(HCG),** secreted by the **trophoblast** (TROF-ō-blast) **cells** of the placenta. Sensitive blood tests for HCG have become available that can detect

CHAPTER 12

Interview with Richard Paulson

Having children is one of the most important aspects of many people's lives, and in recent years, a variety of fertility-enhancing medical options have become available to women and men who have had difficulty conceiving. Dr. Richard Paulson is a physician who conducts research on infertility issues and specializes in treating and counseling infertile women and couples.

An associate professor of obstetrics and gynecology at the University of Southern California (USC) School of Medicine, Dr. Paulson directs USC's In Vitro Fertilization Program. In addition to his clinical practice, Dr. Paulson writes and lectures frequently, and trains other physicians and medical students in this field. His award-winning research investigates a variety of clinical and laboratory questions relating to infertility treatments such as in vitro fertilization. In this interview with Karla Baur, Dr. Paulson describes the current state of this remarkable field of medicine, and discusses some of the complex personal decisions it involves for patients.

Would you describe the various assisted reproductive techniques that are currently available to fertility specialists such as yourself?

"Assisted reproductive technique" is a generic term for various procedures that are being offered now for the treatment of infertility. The procedures are all derived from the prototype procedure of in vitro fertilization, or IVF, which was developed in the late 1970s. Basically, IVF combines the egg and the sperm outside of the body and transfers the resulting embryo back into the uterus.

We have to remember how reproduction normally takes place. The egg is ovulated, and then the fallopian tube performs three functions: it picks up the egg, it provides a place for the egg to fertilize, and it transfers the fertilized egg to the uterus. So the fertilized egg lives in the fallopian tube for two to four days before arriving in the uterus.

The assisted reproductive techniques replace some of the body's

functions in that process. For example, for a woman without fallopian tubes, IVF can perform the role of the fallopian tubes: pick up the eggs from the ovary, fertilize them outside of the body, nurture them for a couple of days, and transport them to the uterus.

Other reproductive techniques are used by patients who have functional fallopian tubes, but who are experiencing other problems such as unexplained infertility or endometriosis. In those cases, we do most of the work done in the IVF procedure, but not all of it. For example, GIFT, or gamete intrafallopian transfer, was the next assisted reproductive technique developed. In GIFT, the eggs and the sperm are collected, but instead of letting them fertilize in the laboratory, the egg and the sperm are combined and then placed in the fallopian tube. The rest is left up to the cells and the body.

Several other permutations and combinations of procedures based on IVF have also been developed. They have different names depending on

356

whether you inject the embryo into the fallopian tube or through the cervix, and depending on how long after fertilization it is transferred. They all have in common the concept of collecting the gametes, mixing them together outside of the body, and putting them back. They can be grouped into two basic categories based on whether fertilization take place in the laboratory or in the body.

There is a variety of techniques, and they have never been carefully compared by any kind of prospective study. They all yield about equal rates of success—about a 20 percent pregnancy rate per attempt. All of the procedures can of course be repeated to increase the overall likelihood of success.

After people struggle with infertility for years, how do you evaluate them and decide which treatment to try from among this array of options?

A principle in medicine says to always do the simplest treatments first. So we start off with the simple, easy, least-expensive treatments first. Once you decide that assisted reproductive techniques are going to be used, you do the procedure which, in your experience, provides the best success. For us, that happens to be IVF. I also prefer it because I think it is the least invasive technique. All the other procedures now require general anesthesia, but we can do IVF without any general anesthesia. We collect the eggs under local anesthetic, and the embryos are simply placed in the uterus, in a manner analogous to that used for artificial insemination, without requiring any anesthetic.

In these procedures, how do you cause women's ovaries to release multiple eggs for collection?

Normally there are internal mechanisms which limit humans to a single ovulation per cycle. But researchers found that in other animal species, with an appropriate hormone treatment program, they could get the ovary to produce multiple eggs, resulting in multiple gestations. In the early days of in vitro fertilization, people found that super-ovulatory medication also allows a woman to produce more than one egg at a time. As a result, their IVF success rate rose because they could obtain multiple eggs of very good quality. The super-ovulatory regimes and techniques have been perfected over the last 10 or 12 years so we are very comfortable with them.

Will it become more common in the future to have open donor relationships where the couple receiving donated eggs or sperm knows or meets the donor?

I think it will become more common in the future. As people become emotionally comfortable with the concept that the donor can contribute without threatening the subsequent relationship between the child and the parent that rears it or carries it, I think they will appreciate the advantage of having more knowledge about the donor.

For example, with an open donor relationship, you know more about the donor's personality than if somebody else picked out the donor for you. If you believe that the environment determines the child's personality, then of course the source of the gamete is immaterial. But if you believe that personality is mostly determined by genetics, then, of course, it becomes extremely important.

Artificial insemination has been going on for decades, and typically has been anonymous. The first egg donation, in 1983, was non-anonymous—the donor and the recipient knew each other. When we started doing egg donation at USC in 1987, all of our donation was also non-anonymous. We have a fair number of patients who come in with their sisters. But now it has become more common for couples to come in and say, "We are ready for an egg donation, but we would rather not know where it is coming from."

What are the typical costs for assisted reproductive techniques?

The costs for these procedures are fairly high. In Los Angeles, which happens to be an expensive area, a stimulated IVF cycle may cost as much as $10,000. Other places around the country, it is closer to $5,000. You have to compare that to other kinds of medical costs; a typical outpatient procedure for a hernia would be on the same order of cost.

There are several ways that the procedure could become less expensive. First, I hope that insurance will cover it in the future. But the best way to make the procedure cheaper is to make it more successful. If the procedure worked 99 percent of the time, more people could live with the cost. In addition, as we become more clever, perhaps we will not have to do as much monitoring as we do now, nor use super-ovulated cycles. About $2,000 of the $10,000 for the whole procedure is for the super-ovulatory drugs.

When cost is not the primary consideration, how do you counsel infertile couples about when to stop trying to conceive with assisted reproductive techniques?

IVF does not appear to stop working after any particular number of treatments. Most research implies that you can achieve pregnancies even after 12 or 13 cycles of IVF. Consequently, people who decide that they are going to stop do so for reasons that are arbitrary from the medical perspective.

In a paper I wrote recently, I contrasted this situation with cancer treatment, where there is usually a well-defined point at which treatment is stopped. If you have cancer, the doctors look at you after you receive a certain number of cycles of chemotherapy. If your tumor is still progressing, you stop and try a different chemotherapy. If that does not work, there is usually no point in doing any more chemotherapy, and you stop. With infertility, there is never that end point. There is nothing that says it is not going to work the next time.

Couples invest a lot of time and money in infertility treatments, and it's easy for them to say, "We've come this far, let's try just one more time." The best way to guard against developing a perpetual patient is to set arbitrary, but relatively firm, limits. It may be best to start by saying, "We are going to do this for a year, and if it does not work, we'll stop, or at the very least, we'll reevaluate your status. You will have time off from the clinic and have permission to go elsewhere and seek second and third opinions." That way, if people continue, they are doing it for a good reason, and are not just caught up in the emotionality of the situation.

When IVF is successful, what do you think children should be told about how they were conceived?

There are those who advocate very strongly that children should be told about it right away. My own feeling is that there is no reason to hide it, but I would probably wait until the time that gametes came up in the child's natural questioning, and then mention how the conception occurred.

In the case of gamete donation, the child's knowledge of his genetic origins becomes relevant from the perspective of family history of disease. There's also the issue of how the child might find out if the parents don't explain it. The risk may come when the child reaches high school and determines his blood type in a biology lab and finds out he is not a genetic child of his parents. What a shock to find out in that way.

What do you think are some of the key research questions in fertility research right now?

I think there are several frontiers in assisted reproductive techniques that are still quite dark. The darkest is the question of the male factor. The vast majority of infertile men produce some sperm, yet in some cases you can't get that sperm to work at all. The assisted reproductive techniques help a little because they allow high concentrations of sperm to be confined with eggs for a prolonged period of time. We have also done some work trying to "jazz up" the sperm. All kinds of substances have been tested for their ability to improve sperm function.

We have started using a substance called TEST-yolk buffer, which, when combined with the sperm, induces a re-

action on the sperm's surface that enables it to penetrate the egg. This reaction is normally induced when the sperm first binds to the outside of the egg. By inducing it with this additional chemical agent, we have been able to show an increase in fertilization rates from 45 percent to 55 percent. It's not too dramatic, but we are encouraged.

Microinjection techniques are other interesting things on the frontier. In those, a single sperm is physically injected into the egg. Another frontier, of course, is to enhance the likelihood that all of these procedures succeed. The implantation rates that we have now are on the order of 10 or 20 percent, but we should be able to increase that to 50 or 60 percent, I think.

How does the United States compare with other countries in terms of assisted reproductive techniques and their availability?

Medicine in the United States is usually a few years ahead of the rest of the world and decades ahead of some places. However, in assisted reproductive techniques, I would say we are only on a par with the rest of the world. There are two reasons for that. First, most other countries have at least partial insurance coverage, but in the United States there is none. Second, the United States has a very peculiar feeling about research in this area. This country thinks that science is fantastic as long as it is engineering or physics. But as soon as you start talking about reproductive issues, the Puritan ethic that built this country comes bubbling up and blocks research.

For example, in California there is an insurance law that mandates that infertility coverage be made available to individuals seeking medical treatment, but there is an exclusion in that law for in vitro fertilization. That exclusion is there because when we first tried to pass the law about three years ago, the antiabortion people said that in vitro fertilization creates embryos in the laboratory, and this represents an interference with the natural process. So the law died. Subsequent passage of the law was only permitted when IVF was excluded. So this is where the United States stands on issues of assisted reproduction.

How could some of the proposed antiabortion laws affect infertility treatments and research?

The antiabortion peoples' stance is that we are playing with life in the laboratory. Since we know that in IVF implantation rates are low per embryo—on the order of 10%—they conclude that we are destroying 90% of this life. That argument ignores the fact that we don't know how often a fertilized embryo would implant in vivo. But I think these are religious and emotional arguments, not scientific ones.

In many of the proposed antiabortion laws, they are trying to define human life as existing at the time of conception. That says we are working with "human life in a dish." Now, while we are extremely careful with the dishes, we are not as careful with them as one would be with an infant. You wouldn't dream of carrying an infant in the palm of your hand. You wouldn't have the infant connected to a single emergency power source. I think it is best to treat embryos on a level just a little bit higher than gametes: it belongs to you and it is essentially property; it is your tissue. I think you can go too far on this concept of the embryos being potential life.

How can college students interested in fertility get into this field?

There are a lot of different levels where a person can participate. One could get a laboratory technician degree and link up with an IVF laboratory to become specially trained in this area. People who have a Ph.D. in one of the biological sciences might do embryology research and run an embryology lab. The nurses do a tremendous amount of work in this area in terms of counseling. They essentially run the office; they are the ones who coordinate all the cycles. Currently, all the physicians who do assisted reproductive techniques are subspecialty trained in reproductive endocrinology within the specialty of obstetrics and gynecology. To do that, college students need to complete college, medical school, four years of residency, and then two years of subspecialization.

What led you to specialize in this area?

When I came upon this field, I found it absolutely fascinating that you could combine an egg and a sperm in the laboratory to create an embryo. In addition, this field attracted me because it provides the opportunity to get involved with a couple on an intense basis. Dur-

ing my training, I couldn't decide between psychiatry and surgery. Here, I've found that I have both: I get to do delicate microsurgery, and I get to sit and talk for a long time with a couple. Everybody is very emotionally involved—everybody gets very depressed when it doesn't work, and when it works, the ecstasy is unbelievable.

We had a reunion last year for all the couples that had a baby. It was so happy. It gives you a perspective on what is important in life. For some of us, fertility came without too much of a struggle. But if it were a struggle, imagine how far you would go to try to have a baby—how many thousands of dollars, and how much time and effort you would be willing to give. There is no doubt in my mind I would be one of these couples coming in for treatment.

The very first stage of pregnancy — only one of the sperm surrounding this ovum will fertilize it.

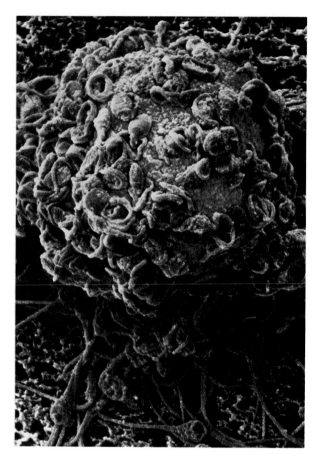

pregnancy as early as 10 days after conception. Commercially available at-home pregnancy urine tests can detect pregnancy very shortly after a missed menstrual period. However, despite manufacturers' claims of 89% accuracy, a university study found a much higher rate of these tests falsely indicating that women were not pregnant (Doshi, 1987). Elective home pregnancy tests can result in both false positive and false negative results. Their results should be taken with some reservation and should always be confirmed by a health care practitioner (Salisbury, 1991). Also, around the sixth week after conception, an experienced practitioner can feel a subtle softening of the uterus during a pelvic exam.

Spontaneous and Elective Abortion

Even when pregnancy has been confirmed, complications may prevent full-term development of the fetus. Various genetic, medical, or hormonal problems may cause **spontaneous abortion,** or **miscarriage,** to occur, terminating the pregnancy. A miscarriage is a spontaneous abortion that occurs in the first 20 weeks of pregnancy.

About 20% of pregnancies end in known miscarriage (Salisbury, 1991). The majority of miscarriages occur within the first trimester of pregnancy; many occur

OUR SEXUALITY

Preconception Sex Selection

The desire to select the sex of a child has existed since ancient times. Superstitions about this are part of our folk tradition — for example, the belief that if a man wears a hat during intercourse he will father a male child or that hanging his trousers on the left bedpost will produce a girl. Laboratory techniques to separate X- from Y-bearing sperm are now in widespread clinical use (Jancin, 1989). Once the laboratory separation process is complete, the desired X or Y fraction is introduced into the vagina by artificial insemination. Success rates of about 80% have been reported (Carson, 1988). However, the rather "unromantic" nature of semen collection and artificial insemination will probably limit the use of such sperm-separation techniques unless parents have compelling reasons to conceive a child of a particular sex (Office of Technology Assessment, 1988). Sex preselection offers benefits to couples at risk for passing on X-linked diseases to their children (Handyside et al., 1989). Additional new technology for sex preselection is on the horizon (Fox & Joyce, 1991).

How will effective and easy preconception sex selection affect society? An imbalance in sex ratios, probably in favor of males, might result. The overall birth rate could also be reduced because, once parents had a child of the sex they wanted, they would no longer continue having more children in the hope of conceiving a child of the desired sex.

before the woman knows she is pregnant. In many cases doctors are unable to determine the specific cause of the miscarriage (McBride, 1991).

Early miscarriages may appear as a heavier than usual menstrual flow; later ones may involve uncomfortable cramping and heavy bleeding. Fortunately for women who desire a child, one miscarriage rarely means that a later pregnancy will be unsuccessful.

However, miscarriage can be a significant loss for the woman or couple. If the expectant parents strongly desired the pregnancy, have been trying to conceive for some time, or have miscarried before, the emotional impact may be particularly painful. Parents may experience grief, helplessness, guilt, and anger. As one woman explained:

> I had a miscarriage. I experienced it as the death of our child ... and I am terrified of it happening again. ... People minimize our loss when they say things like, "You're young, you can have lots of babies," "It's God's will," or "It's for the best — there was probably something wrong with the baby." The truth is — as with any death — there is nothing one can say or do to fix it. ... What helps me is to know that others view my child as real — for like the Velveteen Rabbit, he was real to me. (Beck et al., 1988, p. 46)

Miscarriage can be a very lonely experience. Family and friends can be helpful by acknowledging the loss and asking what the experience has been like for the person. Listening and allowing the parents to express their emotions and unique reactions to the miscarriage, without giving advice, can also be helpful (Cole, 1987). Couples may need to grieve the loss of this hoped-for pregnancy and baby for several months before pursuing another pregnancy (Salisbury, 1991). Some parents who lose an unborn child through miscarriage find it meaningful to name the baby or have a memorial service (Beck et al., 1988).

In contrast to a spontaneous abortion, an **elective abortion** involves a decision to terminate a pregnancy by medical procedures. One point six million Amer-

A first-trimester abortion procedure.

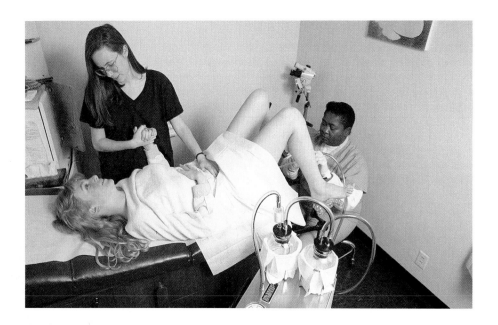

ican women terminate a pregnancy by abortion each year (Franz & Reardon, 1992). The majority of women obtaining abortions are young: 26% are between age 11–19, 33% between age 20–25; only 19% are over 30 (Alan Guttmacher Institute, 1991). Young, white, unmarried women are the largest group obtaining abortions (Henshaw, 1986), but approximately 20% of abortions are for married women (Kochanek, 1991). Catholic women are as likely to obtain an abortion as other women, and about one in 6 of all abortions are obtained by born-again and evangelical Christians (Alan Guttmacher Institute, 1991).

Medical Procedures for Abortion

There are several different abortion procedures used at different stages of pregnancy. The most common are *suction curettage, D and E,* and *prostaglandin induction.* An orally administered drug, RU-486 (discussed in Chapter 11), may be available in the United States for very early abortions (Grimes et al., 1988).

Suction curettage is usually done from 7–13 weeks after the last menstrual period. About 90% of abortions are done at or before 12 weeks (Henshaw et al., 1985). With suction curettage, the cervical os is usually dilated by graduated metal dilators or by a *laminaria,* a small cylinder of seaweed stem or artificial substance, inserted hours earlier. The laminaria slowly expands as it absorbs cervical moisture, and it gently opens the os. This gradual expansion reduces the chance of cervical trauma. During the abortion, a small plastic tube is inserted into the uterus. The tube is attached to a vacuum aspirator, which draws the fetal tissue, placenta, and built-up uterine lining out of the uterus. The suction curettage is done by physicians at clinics or hospitals; the procedure takes about 10 minutes. However, admission, preparation, counseling, and recovery take longer. A local anesthetic may be used, and in some settings general anesthesia is available. There are minor risks of uterine infection or perforation, hemorrhage, or incomplete removal of the uterine contents. If a pregnancy progresses past approximately 12 weeks, the suction curettage procedure can no longer be performed as safely. The uterine walls have become thinner, and perforation and bleeding are more likely.

D and E, or dilation and evacuation, is currently the safest and most widely used technique for pregnancy termination between 13 and 21 weeks (Schrinsky, 1988). A combination of suction equipment, special forceps, and a curette (a metal instrument used to scrape the walls of the uterus) is used. General anesthesia is usually required, and the cervix is dilated wider than with suction curettage (Hatcher et al., 1990).

Prostaglandins (a type of hormone) are one of the compounds used to induce termination of second-trimester pregnancies. (They are also sometimes used to induce labor.) The prostaglandin can be introduced into the vagina as a suppository or into the amniotic sac by inserting a needle through the abdominal wall. These hormones cause uterine contractions, and the fetus and placenta are usually expelled from the vagina within 24 hours. Complications from abortion procedures that induce labor contractions can include nausea, vomiting, and diarrhea; tearing of the cervix; excessive bleeding; and the possibility of shock and death.

Research data have indicated that a first-trimester abortion has little effect on subsequent fertility or pregnancy (Hatcher et al., 1990); but research has also indicated that having two or more abortions may lead to a higher incidence of miscarriages in subsequent pregnancies (Madore et al., 1981).

Approximately one-third of abortions are performed for women who have had at least one previous abortion (Henshaw et al., 1985). Although there are limited data about women who have had more than one abortion, the available research findings are interesting. First, the data indicated that contraceptive method failure is a major contributor to repeat abortions (Henshaw & Silverman, 1988). Another study found that repeat abortions were not the consequence of women's psychological maladjustment or negative attitudes toward using contraceptives; rather, they occurred due to frequency of sexual activity during relationships of long duration and imperfect birth control methods (Berger et al., 1984).

Shared Responsibility. After a woman confirms that she is pregnant (assuming she was not trying to conceive), she must then decide whether to carry the pregnancy and keep the child, to give it up for adoption, or to have an abortion. There are several ways in which a couple can share responsibility for this decision and for the abortion itself. First, the man can help his partner clarify her feelings and can express his own regarding the unwanted pregnancy and how best to deal with it. One study of 1000 men interviewed in abortion clinics stressed the importance of men talking about their own feelings (Shostak et al., 1984). Important topics for a couple to discuss include each person's life situation at the time; their feelings about the pregnancy, possible choices, and each other; and their future plans as individuals and as a couple. If the couple disagree on what to do, the final decision rests with the woman: male partners do not have a legal right to demand or deny abortion for the woman, although legislation may be passed requiring a husband's permission for an abortion.

Once the woman has decided to have an abortion, the man can help pay medical expenses and accompany her to the clinic or hospital. According to several studies, about three-quarters of male partners of pregnant women agreed to the abortion decision and helped pay for the procedure (Pfuhl, 1978; Shostak, 1979). The man can also be understanding about not having intercourse for at least a week following the abortion and can help in planning and implementing effective postabortion contraception. Because the abortion process is likely to evoke some difficult emotions, the couple may find it useful to continue to talk with each other about their reactions.

Choosing abortion is usually a difficult decision for a woman and her partner to make. It means weighing and examining highly personal values and priorities. When made, the decision is usually fraught with ambivalence. Even if the pregnancy was unwanted, both the woman and the man may feel loss and sadness. They may also feel regret, depression, anxiety, guilt, or anger about the abortion or what led to needing to have the abortion.

Research indicates that legal abortion does not cause lasting emotional trauma. Women who have abortions usually experience some anxiety or depression, but these feelings resolve and the women feel relief once the abortion is done (Rodman et al., 1987). Studies show that months or years following the abortion, the majority of women express positive feelings about their choice (Dagg, 1991). However, women who have repeat abortions experience higher emotional distress in interpersonal relationships than do women having a first abortion (Freeman et al., 1980). Men often find themselves experiencing feelings of hurt, guilt, and anger following their partners' abortions (Shostak et al., 1984).

A great many factors can affect the woman's and the man's emotional response to the abortion. The reactions of close friends and family, the attitude of the medical staff and physician performing the abortion, the individuals' values about abortion, the voluntariness or pressure from others about the decision, and the nature and strength of the couple's relationship all can contribute to positive or negative reactions. One study found that support from partners, friends, and families was the most important variable in the degree of anxiety and depression women felt before and after abortion (Moseley et al., 1981). Another study found that women who became pregnant while using contraception tended to be more depressed after an abortion than were women who did not use contraception. The women who had used contraception believed that they would be unable to avoid future pregnancies, whereas those who blamed themselves for not using contraception said they planned to avoid future unwanted pregnancies by using birth control (Janoff-Bulman & Golden, 1984).

The timing of the abortion may also be important: Early abortions are medically, and usually emotionally, much easier than are later abortions. A woman having a legal abortion is also less likely to be as emotionally affected as she would be having an illegal, clandestine abortion.

Pregnancy Risk Taking and Abortion

In many cases an unwanted pregnancy is clearly a matter of contraceptive failure. A woman and her partner can face a situation in which they have used an effective method of birth control correctly and consistently and the woman still became pregnant. For other women or couples seeking abortions, contraceptive risk taking can be common.

Why do you think some women risk an unwanted pregnancy by not using contraceptives reliably? Take a moment to consider this question before reading further.

To better understand the issues surrounding unwanted pregnancies not related to contraceptive failure, one researcher studied 500 women who had had abortions. This research suggested that there could be various kinds of "costs" associated with contraceptive use. Some women stopped using a method because they feared side effects. For others, obtaining birth control from a pharmacy or health care practitioner could mean acknowledging one's intent to engage in or continue nonmarital intercourse, which may conflict with one's value system, cause guilt, and result in risk taking (Luker, 1975). Another study found that young women and men with low degrees of guilt about sex were more likely to use contraception more effectively than were women with high degrees of guilt (Strassberg & Mahoney, 1988). Actively seeking and using contraception is also contrary to the traditional role of female passivity. Pregnancy prevention may interfere with romantic passion, and in some cases a woman may fear alienating her partner by asking for cooperation in contraceptive planning and implementation. Using drugs and alcohol also increases the chances of contraceptive risk taking, unless the woman is using the pill or IUD. One study found that about 9% of abortions were done for women who had never used contraception and that most of this group were teenagers (Henshaw & Silverman, 1988).

"Getting away with" contraceptive risk taking often increases carelessness. For example, a couple who does not use the diaphragm on a few occasions during one month without a pregnancy resulting is likely to increase nonuse the following month. In some cases lack of information about contraceptive methods results in risk taking. Although the majority of women in a sample of 500 had previously demonstrated contraceptive knowledge and skills, they began to take contraceptive risks, either believing that they were unlikely to become pregnant or because they placed a high social value on pregnancy. Two-thirds of the women interviewed reported that a gynecologist had told them that they would have difficulty becoming pregnant, and many were consequently not careful about birth control (Luker, 1975).

Some women may take contraceptive risks because of the high social value placed on pregnancy. Pregnancy connotes fertility, womanhood, and adulthood in our society and is accordingly often considered a measure of a woman's worth. Pregnancy can also be a bargaining chip for marriage or can be used to test or coerce a man's commitment to a relationship or parenthood, or to prevent an impending breakup. Pregnancy can be a plea for help or an attempt to punish someone — usually the woman's parents. Life transitions may also affect risk taking: the mother who has just sent her last child off to school or the woman past 30 who has never been pregnant may become more careless in contraceptive use (Luker, 1975).

The Abortion Controversy

Elective abortion continues to be a highly controversial social and political issue in the United States and other countries. Beliefs regarding the beginning of life,

Two opposing groups in the controversy over the moral and legal status of abortion in the United States.

the reproductive choices of women, the quality of life, and the role of law influence the stand one takes regarding elective termination of pregnancy.

Laws regulating abortion continue to change. Abortion early in pregnancy was legal in ancient China and Europe. In the thirteenth century, St. Thomas Aquinas delineated the Catholic Church's view that the fetus developed a soul 40 days after conception for males and 90 days for females (Rodman, 1987). In the late 1860s, Pope Pius IX declared fetal life at any stage equally important to the mother's, which has remained the position of the Roman Catholic Church (Rodman et al., 1987).

Early American law, based on English common law, allowed abortion until the pregnant woman felt fetal movement, or quickening. Quickening usually occurs during the fourth or fifth month after conception. During the 1860s abortion became illegal in the United States, except when it was necessary to save the woman's life. Some of the reasons given for making abortion illegal included the high mortality rate from abortion due to the scarcity of antiseptics and crude abortion procedures. Also, population growth was seen by some decision makers as important to the country's developing economy. Antiabortion legislation may have also been a response of the prevailing male-dominated society and political system to the emerging middle-class white women who were seeking independence and equality (Sheeran, 1987).

In the mid-twentieth century, before abortion became legal again, women desperate to terminate their unwanted pregnancies sought illegal abortions or attempted to abort themselves. Women with money could fly to Europe or Japan or persuade an American physician to perform an illegal abortion. Low-income women often resorted to unskilled, unsanitary, medically unsafe procedures. By 1967, due to the advocacy of women and men who organized to lobby for change, a few states began altering their abortion laws. In 1973, based on the right to privacy, the U.S. Supreme Court in *Roe* v. *Wade* legalized a woman's right to decide to terminate her pregnancy before the fetus has reached the age of viability. *Viability* is defined as the fetus's ability to survive independently of the woman's body. This usually occurs by the sixth or seventh month of pregnancy, but most abortions are done before the third month. The *Roe* v. *Wade* ruling returned the abortion decision to the individual conscience.

However, the legalization of abortion in 1973 did not end the controversy. Legislation in the late 1970s greatly curtailed the availability of medically safe abortions to low-income women. In July 1977 the Hyde Amendment was passed, prohibiting federal Medicaid funds for abortions; it was later upheld by the Supreme Court. (Medicaid is a state and federal joint program to provide payment of medical services for low-income citizens.) The Court also established that states are not required to provide Medicaid funds for the purpose of elective pregnancy termination. (States can use their own funds to provide abortions for low-income women; as of the early 1990s thirteen states continue to fund abortions for low-income women (Alan Guttmacher Institute, 1991).) Before this legislation, one-third of the approximately 1.5 million annual abortions had been paid for by Medicaid. Many of the low-income women who carry their unwanted pregnancies to term and do not give the child up for adoption will have larger families, making it more difficult for them and their children to break out of the cycle of poverty. While low-income women may not have the financial resources to choose a medical abortion, middle- and upper-income women could continue to obtain legal, medically safe abortions.

In 1988 the state of Missouri asked the U.S. Supreme Court to overturn *Roe* v. *Wade* and to uphold 1986 state restrictions on abortion that had been unconstitutional under *Roe* v. *Wade*. In July 1989 the Court ruled in favor of three state restrictions. These restrictions bar public employees from performing or assisting in abortions not necessary to save a pregnant woman's life; bar the use of public buildings for performing abortions, even if no public funds are involved; and require that doctors perform tests to determine whether the fetus can live outside the womb if they believe the woman requesting an abortion may be at least 20 weeks pregnant. Although this ruling did not overturn the right to abortion, it does give other state legislatures the right to impose these limitations.

In June 1991 the Supreme Court, in its *Rust* v. *Sullivan* decision, upheld the legislation barring federally funded clinics from *discussing* abortion with patients. This "gag rule" decision affects about 4000 clinics serving four and a half million mostly low-income women. Critics of the "gag rule" view the prohibition on discussing abortion as a violation of the constitutional right of free speech (McBride, 1992). Seventy-two percent of a representative sample of U.S. citizens oppose the "gag rule," and Congress has begun debating whether or not to rescind the regulation, but until that happens many clinics will forfeit federal funding in order to discuss all options for unplanned and unwanted pregnancies (Kaplan, 1991).

Further restrictions on abortion occurred in June 1992 when the Supreme Court ruled on *Planned Parenthood v. Casey*. States can now require a 24-hour waiting period before a woman can obtain an abortion, parental notification for women younger than 18 and detailed medical reports on each abortion performed. Although abortion remains legal, the cumulative restrictions limit availability of abortion, particularly to young, rural, or low-income women (Lacayo, 1992)

Abortion will continue to be a major social and political issue in the United States, characterized by highly polarized opinions for and against (Ryan, 1992) (See Figure 12.3). In 1990, 465 abortion-related bills were introduced by state legislators, three times as many as in 1989 (Sollom, 1991). As this text goes to press in 1992, the stability of *Roe* v. *Wade* is uncertain with the addition of Clarence Thomas to the Supreme Court (Kaplan, 1992). At the same time, if RU-486 is approved for sale in the United States, abortion could become more accessible to women (Lader, 1991).

A 1992 survey, representative by sex, age and income, found that 71% believe that abortion should remain legal (Clements, 1992). The central issue in the abortion controversy is the moral debate between those arguing for the fetus's right to live and those arguing for the woman's right to choose to terminate her pregnancy (Rodman, 1987). The antiabortion, or "prolife," advocates argue that life begins at conception and abortion is therefore immoral. One of their pamphlets states the following:

> At the moment of conception, all the elements that create a new human life are present. When the life-giving forces of the father and the mother unite, they form a unique human person. Life begins and from that moment, your formation has been purely a matter of development, growth and maturation. [Source not available]

Antiabortion groups want to reestablish national legislation, by constitutional amendment if necessary, to make abortion illegal and to establish the constitutional rights of the unborn fetus. Members of the antiabortion minority are waging an active battle against legal and available abortion. One of their primary tactics has been to target prochoice incumbents in Congress to attempt to prevent their reelection. Antiabortion protesters also block clinic entrances and harass patients and staff (Suh & Denworth, 1989). In 1985, 47% of abortion providers experienced some type of harassment (Forrest & Henshaw, 1987). Some extreme antiabortion activists have burned or bombed abortion clinics: there were 110 such incidents of arson or bombing between 1977 and 1988 (Grimes et al., 1991). Abortion activists also picket at the homes of doctors who perform abortions (Adler et al., 1992).

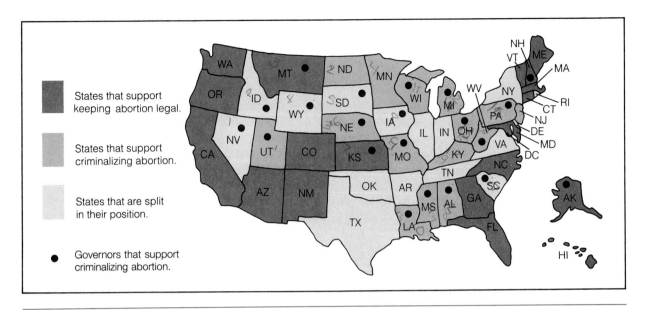

FIGURE 12.3

If *Roe* v. *Wade* were overturned by the Supreme Court, individual states would mandate the legal status of abortion. The map indicates the legislation that would likely occur in each state.

Prochoice advocates see abortion as a social necessity, due to imperfect and sometimes unavailable birth control methods and lack of education. They want abortion to be an option for women who are faced with the dilemma of an unwanted pregnancy and who decide that terminating it is their best alternative. Prochoice advocates support a woman's choice *not* to have an abortion, but they are strongly opposed to antiabortion legislation restricting others' choices. Many prestigious organizations have made public statements opposing antiabortion bills, including the National Academy of Sciences, the American Public Health Association, the American Medical Association, the American College of Obstetricians and Gynecologists, and many religious organizations. One rabbi stated the following:

> My religious tradition is one which has revered and sanctified human life for nearly four thousand years. . . . It is that regard for the sanctity of human life which prompts us to support legislation enabling women to be free from the whims of biological roulette and free mostly from the oppressive, crushing weight of ideologies and theologies which . . . continue to insist that in a world already groaning to death with overpopulation, with hate and with poverty, there is still some noble merit or purpose to indiscriminate reproduction. (Hamilton, 1983, pp. 30–31)

Individuals who hold strong prochoice beliefs also have other beliefs that differ from those of people who are antiabortion. Take a few moments before reading on to consider what some other differences between the two groups might be.

One study of recent trends in abortion attitudes found that people who approve of legally available abortions are more likely to support civil liberties and women's rights than are those who disapprove. People who disapprove of legal abortion are more likely than others to have strongly committed Catholic or fundamentalist Protestant affiliations (Granberg & Granberg, 1980); to have disapproving attitudes toward premarital sex, homosexuality, and government spending; to be politically conservative; and to have traditional attitudes about the female role (Deitch, 1983). Women who are prochoice activists tend to be college-educated, to have well-paid careers and few children, to have few ties to formal religion, and to have a strong vested interest in their work roles. Antiabortion activist women are more likely to be practicing Roman Catholics with large families, to have low-paying or no employment outside the home, and to base their self-esteem on their maternal roles. In addition, prochoice activists believe that intimacy is the most important purpose of sexuality, whereas antiabortion activists believe that procreation is the primary purpose of sexuality.

Research examining U.S. senators' and representatives' voting records demonstrates that those who are opposed to legal abortion supported the Vietnam War, support capital punishment, oppose handgun control, and oppose legislation that promotes the health and well-being of families and their children—such as school lunch and milk programs. Voting records of prochoice legislative supporters have shown the opposite trends (Prescott, 1986). One writer has elaborated on this inconsistency:

> The right to life, if it truly begins at conception, should not end at the moment of birth. . . . Although the rights of the unborn have been defended, social and health programs needed to enhance the lives of infants and children have been decimated. If we really care about children how can we allow one in five to live in poverty? . . . If we believe in the fetus's right to life, why have funds been cut for prenatal care? . . . One is left asking if the concern is really with life or with the changing roles and status of women and the liberation of women from compulsory motherhood. (Hartman, 1991, p. 468)

It is likely that the abortion debate will remain passionate and bitter because of fundamental differences in life circumstances and values of people with strong commitments to each side. However, most people experience considerable ambivalence about abortion (Connell, 1992). Many people who believe abortion is morally wrong also believe that any woman who wants an abortion should be able to obtain one legally (Stone & Waszak, 1992). As one woman stated:

> Part of my problem is that what I think and how I feel about this issue are two entirely different matters. . . . I cannot bring myself to say I am in favor of abortion. I don't want anyone to have one. I want people to use contraceptives and for those contraceptives to be foolproof. I want people to be responsible for their actions; mature in their decisions. I want children to be loved, wanted, well cared for. [At the same time,] I cannot bring myself to say I am against choice. I want women who are young, poor, single or all three to be able to direct the course of their lives. I want women who have had all the children they want or can afford or their bodies can withstand to be able to decide their future. I want women who are in bad marriages or destructive relationships to avoid being trapped by pregnancy. . . . Even as I refuse to pass judgment on other women's lives, I weep for the children who might have been. (Smith, 1985, p. 16)

A Healthy Pregnancy

Once a woman becomes pregnant, her own health care plays an important part in the development of a healthy fetus. Countless books have been written about

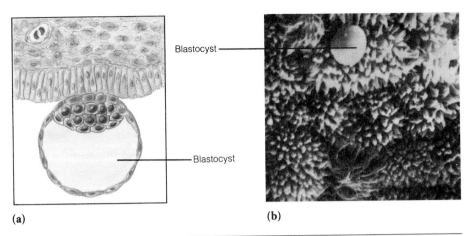

Blastocyst

Blastocyst

(a)

(b)

FIGURE 12.4

(a) As a fertilized egg travels toward the uterus, it divides to form the blastocyst. (b) The blastocyst then implants on the uterine wall. A scanning electron micrograph of a blastocyst as it begins to implant in the endometrium.

pregnancy and prenatal care (a few are listed in "Suggested Readings"); we mention only a few important points here.

Fetal Development

The nine-month (40-week) span of pregnancy is customarily divided into three 13-week segments called *trimesters.* Characteristic changes occur in each trimester.

As with all mammals, a human begins as a **zygote** (ZĪ-gōt), a united sperm cell and ovum, which develops into the multicelled **blastocyst** (BLAS-tō-sist) that implants on the wall of the uterus about one week after fertilization (see Figure 12.4). Growth progresses steadily. By 9–10 weeks after a woman's last menstrual period, the fetal heartbeat can be heard with a special ultrasound stethoscope known as the *Doppler* (MacMillan et al., 1992). By the beginning of the second month from the time of conception, the fetus is one-half to one inch long, grayish, and crescent-shaped. During this same month, the spinal canal and rudimentary arms and legs form, as do the beginnings of recognizable eyes, fingers, and toes. During the third month, internal organs such as the liver, kidneys, intestines, and lungs begin limited functioning in the 3-inch fetus.

The second trimester begins with the fourth month of pregnancy. By now the sex of the fetus can often be distinguished. External body parts including fingernails, eyebrows, and eyelashes are clearly formed. The fetus's skin is covered by fine, downlike hair. Future development primarily consists of growth in size and refinement of the features that already exist. Fetal movements can be felt by the end of the fourth month. The fetus's weight has increased to one pound by the end of the fifth month. Head hair may appear at this time, and subcutaneous fat develops. By the end of the second trimester, the fetus has opened its eyes.

In the third trimester, the fetus continues to grow and to develop the size and strength it will need to live on its own, apart from the mother's warmth and sustenance. It increases in weight from 4 pounds in the seventh month to an average of over 7 pounds at birth. The downlike hair covering its body disappears, and head hair continues growing. The skin becomes smooth rather than wrinkled. It is covered with skin that is exfoliated, which forms a protective creamy, waxy substance called the **vernix caseosa** (VER-niks kas′-ēō-sa).

Fetal development at 9 weeks.
The fetus (right) is connected
to the placenta (left) by the
umbilical cord.

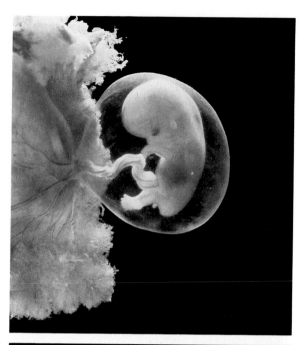

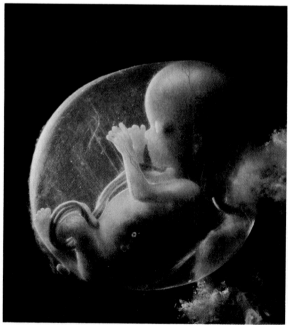

Fetal development at 14 weeks.

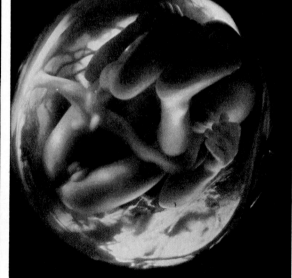

Fetal development at 20 weeks.

Prenatal Care

The developments just described take place in most pregnancies. Occasionally, however, something may go wrong. The fetus may not develop normally, or the pregnancy may terminate early, as we discussed previously. The causes of these

Close-up of fetal
development at 22 weeks.

problems may be genetic and unpreventable, but the mother's own health and
nutrition are also crucial in providing the best environment for fetal development.
This is one reason why it is important for a woman to have a complete physical
examination and health assessment before becoming pregnant (Chez, 1991). She
should also have a test to determine her immunity to rubella (German measles),
a disease that may cause severe fetal defects if the mother contracts it while she
is pregnant. A prepregnancy AIDS test should also be considered because the AIDS
virus can be transmitted to the developing fetus during pregnancy.

Thorough prenatal care is essential for promoting the health of both the
mother and the fetus (Wall et al., 1989). Components of optimal prenatal care
include good nutrition, general good health, adequate rest, routine health care,
exercise, and childbirth education. Early in the pregnancy the woman, her partner,
and her health care practitioner should discuss the health needs of both the
mother and the developing fetus; they can also begin to make plans for the birth.

As women have increasingly taken up athletic activities, many have had questions about the effects of exercise on pregnancy. Moderate exercise is commonly
recommended as important to a healthy pregnancy. See the box "Pregnancy: Latest Fitness Thinking" for current guidelines.

Risks to Fetal Development. The rapidly developing fetus is dependent on the
mother for nutrients, oxygen, and waste elimination as substances pass through
the **placenta** (a disk-shaped organ attached to the wall of the uterus, shown in
Figure 12.5). The fetus is joined to the placenta by the umbilical cord. The fetal
blood circulates independently within the closed system of the fetus and the inner
part of the placenta. Maternal blood flows in the uterine walls and outer part of

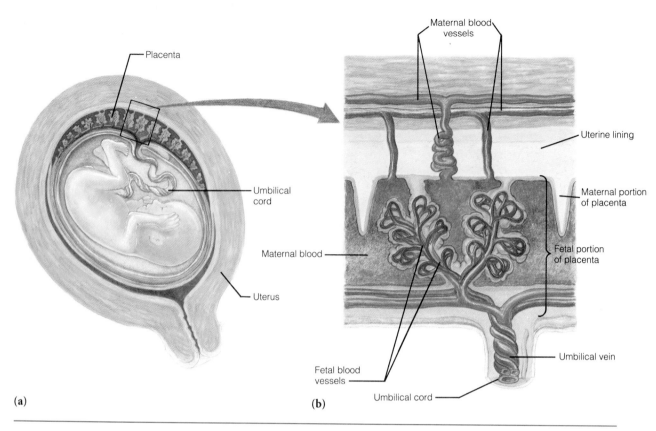

(a)

(b)

F I G U R E 12.5

The placenta exchanges nutrients, oxygen, and waste products between the maternal and fetal circulatory systems. (a) The placenta attached to the uterine wall. (b) Close-up detail of placenta.

the placenta. Fetal and maternal blood do not normally intermingle. All exchanges between the fetal and maternal blood systems occur by passage of substances through the walls of the blood vessels. Nutrients and oxygen from the maternal blood pass into the fetal circulatory system; carbon dioxide and waste products from the fetus pass into the maternal blood vessels, to be removed by the maternal circulation.

Although the placenta prevents some kinds of bacteria and viruses from passing into the fetal blood system, many do cross through the placenta, including the AIDS virus. Furthermore, many substances ingested by the mother easily cross through the placenta and can be damaging to the developing fetus. Certain medications, as well as recreational drugs, alcohol, and tobacco, are all dangerous, and there have been a number of tragic situations where children have been damaged by medications taken by their mothers during pregnancy. For example, the drug *thalidomide,* prescribed as a sedative to pregnant women in the early 1960s, was absorbed into the circulatory systems of fetuses, causing severe deformities to the extremities. A drug used to treat severe acne, Accutane, creates a risk of having a baby with a major malformation almost as high as did thalidomide (Lammer et al., 1985). Some grown children of women who took diethylstilbestrol (DES) while pregnant have developed genital tract abnormalities, including cancer. Tetracycline, a frequently used antibiotic, can damage an infant's teeth and cause stunted bone growth if it is taken after the fourteenth week of pregnancy. Antibiotics need to be prescribed selectively during pregnancy (Lynch et al., 1991). In animal studies

OUR SEXUALITY

Pregnancy: Latest Fitness Thinking

The American College of Obstetricians and Gynecologists has issued safety guidelines for women who wish to continue exercising during pregnancy. Consult your physician first. (Certain factors may be reasons to avoid exercise during pregnancy.)

Limit aerobic exercise to 15-minute sessions, and monitor your heart rate regularly. Keep it below 140 beats per minute. (Animal studies have indicated that increased body temperatures induced by too vigorous exercise could have adverse effects on the fetus.) Walking is usually excellent exercise during pregnancy.

Avoid jerky stretches and exercises. (The hormonal changes caused by pregnancy loosen the soft tissue that links bones within the joints,

making a woman more susceptible to joint injury.)

Drink fluids before and after exercise; stop immediately to drink if you become thirsty. (Dehydration occurs much more rapidly than usual during pregnancy.)

After the fourth month of pregnancy, don't do any exercises that are performed lying down on your back. (The increased size of the uterus can interfere with the blood flow to a woman's heart and to the fetus.) Have reasonable expectations from exercise. (Exercise can boost a pregnant woman's energy level; help her maintain muscle tone, strength, and endurance; and decrease the likelihood of back pain.)

even nonprescription drugs such as aspirin have been implicated in fetal abnormalities. Toxic substances found in the polluted environment can also harm fetal development (Office of Technology Assessment, 1988).

Some substances known to cause harm to the mother also pose serious hazards to a developing fetus (Sloan et al., 1992). Approximately 15% of American women of reproductive age are substance abusers and place their babies at risk for many problems (Silverman, 1989). The babies of mothers who regularly use addictive drugs such as amphetamines, heroin, cocaine, codeine, morphine, or opium during pregnancy are often born premature and with low birth weight and size. In addition, following birth these babies experience withdrawal from the drug: they have tremors, disturbed feeding and sleep patterns, and abnormal muscle tension (Dombrowski et al., 1991; Little & Snell, 1991). Approximately 100,000 cocaine-exposed infants are born each year (Segal, 1991). Children born to women who abuse cocaine may experience permanent birth defects and damage to sensory, motor, and cognitive abilities (Christmas, 1992). Mental and physical impairments in development can continue past infancy (Chasnoff et al., 1992).

Another serious health hazard for the fetus is cigarette smoking (Ventura, 1992). Approximately 25% of pregnant women smoke during their pregnancies (Jack & Culpepper, 1991). Maternal smoking increases the chances of spontaneous abortion and of pregnancy complications that can result in fetal or infant death (Samet, 1991). Smoking reduces the amount of oxygen in the bloodstream, which can adversely affect the fetus by slowing its growth. Infants of mothers who smoked during pregnancy often weigh less and are in poorer general condition

 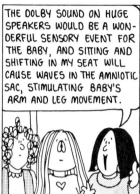 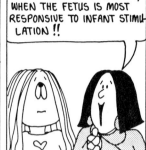 

than are infants of nonsmoking mothers. In addition, children of mothers who smoked during their pregnancies have significantly lower IQ scores and increased incidence of reading disorders compared with matched offspring of nonsmokers. Smoking also increases the incidence of serious and potentially lethal pregnancy and birth complications for the mother (McLaren & Nieburg, 1988). Additionally, evidence suggests that maternal smoking increases the risk of childhood cancer (John et al., 1991). Children in nonsmoking families are less likely to get bronchitis and pneumonia (Walters, 1991).

Fetal alcohol syndrome (FAS) is the leading cause of developmental disabilities and birth defects in the United States (Jack & Culpepper, 1991). Heavy alcohol use can cause intrauterine death and spontaneous abortion, premature birth, congenital heart defects, damage to the brain and nervous system, and numerous physical malformations of the fetus. Most babies with FAS have below-normal IQs (Roeleveld et al., 1992). Infants may be born addicted to alcohol and, consequently, experience alcohol withdrawal for several days following birth. The fetus is at risk of developing FAS if the mother drinks six or more drinks per day during her pregnancy. However, lesser amounts of alcohol can also impair the fetus (Abel, 1980). In 1981 the Food and Drug Administration advised women to abstain *completely* from alcohol use during pregnancy to avoid the risk of damage to their babies (Serdula et al., 1991). The effects of FAS continue into childhood; children with FAS continue to be small in size and mentally retarded and to have behavior problems (Day et al., 1991). Research also indicates that heavy marijuana use may cause problems similar to FAS (Hingson et al., 1982).

The extent of our knowledge about the effect of most of the drugs and other substances consumed by pregnant women is very limited; little is known of the exact risk of a given drug taken during pregnancy. Even drinking three or more cups of coffee a day during pregnancy increases the risk of having a low birth weight (Narod et al., 1991; Fenster et al., 1992). What we do know now is that we are learning of more and more potential hazards. For this reason, no medications should be used during pregnancy unless they are absolutely necessary and are taken under close medical supervision.

OUR SEXUALITY

Poverty and Prenatal Care

For those who can afford it, thorough prenatal care helps a mother have a healthy baby. Prenatal care can prevent about 50% of problems that babies can develop during pregnancy. However, about 88 out of every 1000 babies are born following inadequate prenatal care. This increases the chances of low birth weight babies with problems including lung disorders, brain damage, and abnormal growth patterns. The life stresses of a woman with few financial resources are part of the problem. A woman who is preoccupied with the necessities of day-to-day survival has little time or energy to care for the baby growing inside her. She often has other children for whom to provide and is working at a minimum-wage job without medical benefits. In addition, most states in the United States lack a comprehensive system to assure that pregnant women receive adequate prenatal care, despite the fact that funds spent on maternal care actually save money for the government over the long run by reducing the costs of long-term pediatric care for problems resulting from inadequate prenatal care (O'Neill, 1988).

Detection of Birth Defects

If a woman and her physician have some reason to suspect that there may be fetal abnormalities, a reliable and accurate test known as **amniocentesis** (am'-nē-o-sen-TĒ-sis) can help establish whether certain problems exist. The test is done during the fourteenth to sixteenth week of pregnancy. The procedure consists of inserting a needle with the assistance of ultrasound guidance through the woman's abdominal wall and into the uterine cavity to draw out a sample of the **amniotic fluid** (fluid surrounding the fetus). Fetal cells from the fluid are cultured for chromosome analysis, and the fluid is tested in procedures that take two to three weeks to produce results (Elias & Simpson, 1991). A variety of birth defects can be detected by this means. Although amniocentesis cannot detect all fetal abnormalities, the number is increasing as techniques become more sophisticated.

Another technique for detection of birth defects is called **chorionic villus** (kō-rē-ON-ik VIL-us) **sampling,** or **CVS** (Brambati, 1991). Chorionic villi are threadlike protrusions on a membrane surrounding the placenta. This test involves inserting a thin catheter with the assistance of ultrasound through the abdomen or vagina and cervix into the uterus, where a small sample of the chorionic villi is removed for analysis. This procedure has an advantage over amniocentesis: it can be done as early as the ninth week instead of the fourteenth (Lehnhoff, 1991).

Circumstances in which amniocentesis or CVS may be of benefit include maternal age over 35 years, a parent with a chromosomal defect, a previous child with defects such as *Down syndrome* (a chromosomal abnormality that results in impaired intellectual functioning and physical defects) or defects of the spine or spinal cord, or a familial background that suggests a significant risk of other disorders related to chromosomal abnormalities. If the test results reveal a serious untreatable birth defect, the mother can have the pregnancy terminated. Amniocentesis and CVS involve some risks, including damage to the fetus, induced miscarriage, and infection (Seligmann, 1992). Couples who have these procedures

Ultrasound image of a fetus. Ultrasound monitoring is used in amniocentesis and chorionic villus sampling procedures.

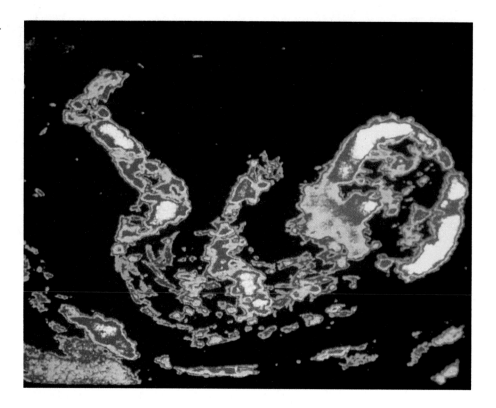

may also feel worried about harming the fetus, the possible diagnosis of abnormality, or having an abortion. For these reasons, the procedures are not recommended unless the potential risks are outweighed by the expected benefits.

Pregnancy After Age 35

Increasing numbers of women are deciding to have children after 35 years of age (Harker & Thorpe, 1992). One out of every five women in the United States has her first baby after age 35 (Nachtigall, 1991). Some couples are delaying childbearing for career, financial, or other reasons.

There are some increased risks to the fetus and mother with pregnancy at a later age. The rate of fetal defects due to chromosomal abnormalities (such as Down syndrome) rises with maternal age: the estimated rate of such fetal defects per 1000 women is 2.6 up to age 30, 5.6 at age 35, 15.8 at age 40, and 53.7 at age 45 (Hook, 1981). However, healthy older women have no higher risk than younger women of having a child with birth defects *not* related to abnormal chromosomes (Baird et al., 1991).

Until recently it was thought that women age 35 and older were far more likely to experience complications of pregnancy and birth. Recent information, however, leads physicians to believe that pregnancy over age 35 is both safe and not difficult to manage medically (Schrinsky, 1988). In fact, some research indicates that compared with first-time mothers in their mid-twenties, women age 35 and older showed less anxiety, depression, and adverse symptoms during pregnancy (Robinson, 1987). For women between ages 35 and 44, amniocentesis and elective abortion reduce the risk of bearing an infant with a severe birth defect to a level comparable with that for younger women (Goldberg et al., 1979). Furthermore, with careful monitoring and management, risks to the newborn and mother from complications of labor and birth can also be reduced almost to the level for the younger population (Kujansuu et al., 1981).

Another concern that women and their partners have when they consider postponing having a child until the woman is past her twenties is that her ability to become pregnant may be diminished. Current research indicates that as women become older, their fecundity decreases. However, "for the majority of women who want to postpone childbearing until they have completed their education and established themselves in a career, the risks they are running may be quite small compared with the benefits" (Bongaarts, 1982, p. 78).

The Experience of Pregnancy

Pregnancy is a unique and significant experience for both the woman and her partner, especially if he is involved throughout the pregnancy. In the following pages, we look at the experience and the impact it may have on the woman and the man.

The Woman's Experience

Each woman has different emotional and physical reactions to pregnancy, and the same woman may react differently to different pregnancies. Factors influencing a woman's emotional reactions can include how the decision for pregnancy was made, current and impending lifestyle changes, her relationship with others, her financial resources, her self-image, and hormonal changes. The woman's acquired attitudes and knowledge about childbearing and her hopes and fears about parenthood also contribute to her experience.

Women sometimes feel that they should experience only positive emotions when they are pregnant. However, the physical, emotional, and situational aspects of a pregnancy often elicit an array of contradictory emotions including joy, depression, excitement, impatience, and fear. Some women may feel less attractive (Sadler, 1992). One study of 1000 women found a wide range of feelings about pregnancy. Thirty-five percent loved being pregnant, 8% hated it, 40% had mixed feelings about the pregnancy experience and the remainder had varying experiences with different pregnancies. The researcher concluded that the emotional and physical experience of pregnancy were very intertwined. The degree of physical discomfort, and her feelings about the pregnancy and her life impact one another (Genevie & Margolies, 1987).

The marked changes that occur also have a significant effect on the experience of pregnancy. Several changes take place during the early stages of the first trimester. Menstruation ceases. As the milk glands in the breasts develop, the breasts increase in size. The nipples and areola usually become darker in color. Nausea, sometimes called "morning sickness," may occur. Many women experience a marked increase in fatigue:

I'm ordinarily a very energetic woman, but during the first two months of my pregnancy, I couldn't get enough sleep. This meant a drastic change in my daily routine. (Authors' files)

Vaginal secretions may change or increase. Urination may be more frequent, and bowel movements more irregular. However, there is little increase in the size of the woman's abdomen during these first three months.

In the second trimester, there are more outward signs of pregnancy. The waistline thickens, and the abdomen begins to protrude. Fetal movements may be felt in the fourth or fifth month, which is usually very exciting and reassuring to the parents-to-be. First-trimester nausea and tiredness usually disappear by now, and a woman may experience heightened feelings of well-being. The breasts may begin to secrete a thin yellowish fluid called **colostrum** (ka-LOS-tram).

During the last trimester, the uterus and abdomen increase in size (see Figure 12.6). The muscles of the uterus occasionally contract painlessly. The enlarged uterus produces pressure on the woman's stomach, intestines, and bladder. This may cause discomfort, indigestion, and frequent urination. Fetal movements can be seen and felt from the outside of the abdomen.

Being an expectant father obviously does not involve the same physical experiences that a pregnant woman has (although occasionally a "pregnant father" may report psychosympathetic symptoms such as the nausea or tiredness his partner is experiencing). However, the experiences of pregnancy and birth are often profound for the father as well.

The Man's Experience

Significant changes have occurred in the last several decades in the role of the woman's partner during pregnancy, childbirth, and child rearing. Pregnancy, once seen as predominantly the woman's domain, is now commonly viewed as a shared experience:

> For many couples the proposition is now our pregnancy and birth. With the advent of the Lamaze method and the prepared natural-childbirth movement, the man became more intimately involved in the pregnancy and childbirth experience. He attended pregnancy and childbirth classes, and even watched childbirth films. He became an aide in the process, helping with breathing exercises, listening to little heartbeats, learning to comfort and cope with the experience of the woman. There is no question that this movement brought the male closer to the pregnancy and birth experience in some cases. For that special group there is a very real sense of "our pregnancy and birth" which represents a substantial departure from the traditional involvement of the male. (Dailey, 1978, p. 43)

The author of the preceding quote is describing some of the unique experiences of the male in what he terms the "male pregnancy." Like the woman, her partner often reacts with a great deal of ambivalence. He may feel ecstatic, but he may also be fearful about the woman's and baby's well-being. Like many men, he may feel frightened about the impending birth and whether he will be able to "keep it together." He may feel especially tender toward his partner and become more solicitous. At the same time, he may feel a sense of separateness from the woman because of the physical changes only she is experiencing. He may be proud at the prospect of becoming a father, but he may question his parenting ability. He may fear losing his wife's affection and attention to the pregnancy and baby. Most men feel concern over the impending increase in financial responsibility. In all, the expectant father has special needs, as does his partner, and it is important that the woman be aware of these needs and be willing to respond to them.

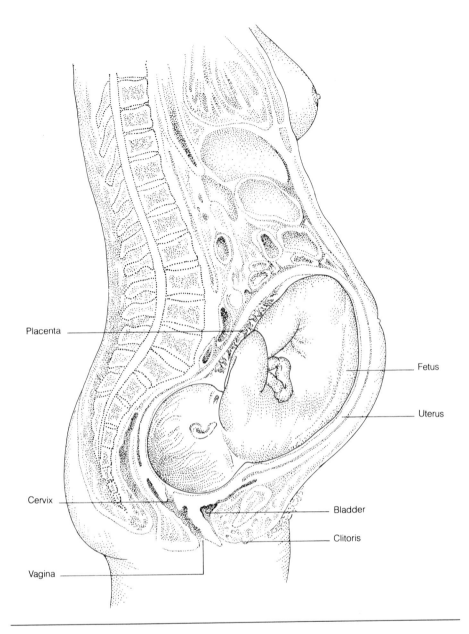

FIGURE 12.6

Pregnancy at the ninth month. The uterus and abdomen have increased in size to accommodate the fetus.

Placenta

Fetus

Uterus

Cervix

Bladder

Clitoris

Vagina

Although men are encouraged to be active participants in the pregnancy and birth experience, they sometimes feel that their feelings of anxiety, anger, sadness, or fear might upset their partners and therefore are taboo (Chapman, 1992). It is important for the father-to-be to participate fully in the process of fatherhood by recognizing his own feelings and receiving understanding from his partner, family, and health care providers. One study of expectant fathers found that when men did share their feelings with their partners, the relationships deepened (Shapiro, 1987). This mutual support can enhance the couple's level of sharing and closeness.

A man's active involvement throughout childbearing seems to initiate a positive interaction between the father and the newborn. Research supports the notion that fathers can be as nurturant of children as can mothers. Father–newborn interaction helps develop the paternal role, and programs in the hospital to increase father–newborn contact and to teach the father caregiving skills seem to facilitate this process (Sherwen, 1987).

Sexual Interaction During Pregnancy

A woman's sexual interest and responsiveness may change through the course of her pregnancy. Nausea, breast tenderness, and fatigue may inhibit sexual interest during the first trimester. A resurgence of sexual desire and arousal may occur for some women in the second trimester (Masters & Johnson, 1966), but most research shows a progressive decline in sexual interest and activity over the nine months of pregnancy, with diminished sexual desire most common in the third trimester (Bogren, 1991; Hart et al; 1991). Some of the most common reasons women give for decreasing sexual activity during pregnancy include physical discomfort, feelings of physical unattractiveness, and fear of injuring the unborn child (Colino, 1991). Women who have positive attitudes about sexuality maintain more sexual interest, activity, and satisfaction during pregnancy than do women with negative attitudes about sexuality (Fisher & Gray, 1988). Research also indicates that a planned pregnancy results in fewer sexual problems than does an unplanned one, and that women who experience more sexual arousal prior to pregnancy do not lose interest in sex as much as those who experience less sexual arousal. Many women also have increased desire for nonsexual affection as pregnancy progresses (Walbroehl, 1984). The key to sexuality and pregnancy is that feelings are highly individual:

> Some feel sexier, more attractive and more easily aroused than ever before in their life. Others are completely turned off by the mere thought of sex; they don't feel the least bit sexy, and they couldn't be less interested. (Stern, 1987, p. 71)

For some women pregnancy can result in a heightened awareness of one's body and an increased sensuality. Others feel intensely "womanly" and are less inhibited sexually. The increased vasocongestion of the genitals during pregnancy can heighten sexual desire and response for some.

The partner's feelings also affect the sexual relationship during pregnancy. Reactions to the woman's changing body and to the need for adjustment in the couple's sexual repertoire may vary from increased excitement to inhibition for the partner. Especially late in pregnancy, awareness of the baby can make lovemaking seem like a crowded event:

> Sex during the third trimester requires a sense of humor. It doesn't seem to matter where you touch her anymore; the baby pops up everywhere. You can't escape the little kicks and jabs, and the thought of tiny feet and fists inches away (or closer) can be disconcerting. (Stern, 1987, p. 78)

For most couples, pregnancy is a time of significant emotional and physical changes. Open communication, accurate information, mutual support, and flexibility in sexual frequency and activities can help maintain and strengthen the bond between the couple (Stern, 1987).

It is now generally accepted that in pregnancies where there are no risk factors, sexual activity and orgasm may be continued as desired until the onset of

Total body touching and holding can be a valuable part of sexual interaction during pregnancy.

labor. Women who are at risk for bleeding or premature labor will likely be advised differently (Schrinsky, 1988). Coitus should not occur if spotting or vaginal or abdominal pain occur or if the amniotic sac ("water bag") breaks. As with many other areas of sexual health care, a woman, her partner, and her health care practitioner can make an informed decision.

During pregnancy it may be necessary for a couple to modify intercourse positions. The side-by-side, woman-above, and rear-entry positions are generally more comfortable than the man-above position as pregnancy progresses. Oral – and manual – genital stimulation as well as total body touching and holding can continue as usual. In fact, pregnancy is a time when a couple may explore and develop these dimensions of lovemaking more fully; even if intercourse is not desired, intimacy, eroticism, and sexual satisfaction can continue.

Childbirth

The full term of pregnancy usually lasts about nine months, although there is some variation in length. Some women may have longer pregnancies; others may give birth to fully developed infants up to a few weeks before the nine-month term is over. There is a good deal of variation in the experience of childbirth also, depending on many factors: the woman's physiology, her emotional state, the baby's size and position, the kind of childbirth practices she employs, and the kind of support she receives. Despite the variations, there are three generally recognizable stages in the process of childbirth (see Figure 12.7).

Stages of Childbirth

A woman can often tell that labor has begun when regular contractions of the uterus begin. Another indication of beginning **first-stage labor,** the gradual dilation of the cervix to 10 centimeters, may be the "bloody show" (discharge of the mucus plug from the cervix). The amniotic sac may rupture in the first stage of labor, an occurrence sometimes called "breaking the bag of waters." The first stage is shown in Figure 12.7(a).

Before the first stage begins, the cervix usually has already **effaced** (flattened and thinned) and dilated slightly. It continues to dilate throughout the first stage, and it is the extent of dilation that defines the early, late, and "transition" phases of first-stage labor. The cervix is dilated up to 4 cm during the early phase, 4–8 cm in the active phase, and 8–10 cm during the final, or transition, phase of the first stage. Each phase becomes shorter, and the contractions become stronger; transition is usually the most intense. The first stage is the longest of the three stages, usually lasting 10–16 hours for the first childbirth and 4–8 hours in subsequent births.

Second-stage labor begins when the cervix is fully dilated and the infant descends farther into the vaginal birth canal. Usually the descent is head first, as shown in Figure 12.7(b). The second stage often lasts from a half-hour to two hours — although it may be shorter or longer. During this time the woman can actively push to help the baby out, and many women report their active pushing to be the best part of labor:

I knew what "labor" meant when I was finally ready to push. I have never worked so hard, so willingly. (Authors' files)

The second stage ends when the infant is born.

Third-stage labor lasts from the time of birth until the delivery of the placenta, shown in Figure 12.7(c). With one or two more uterine contractions, the placenta usually separates from the uterine wall and comes out of the vagina, generally within a half-hour after the baby is born. The placenta is also called the **afterbirth.**

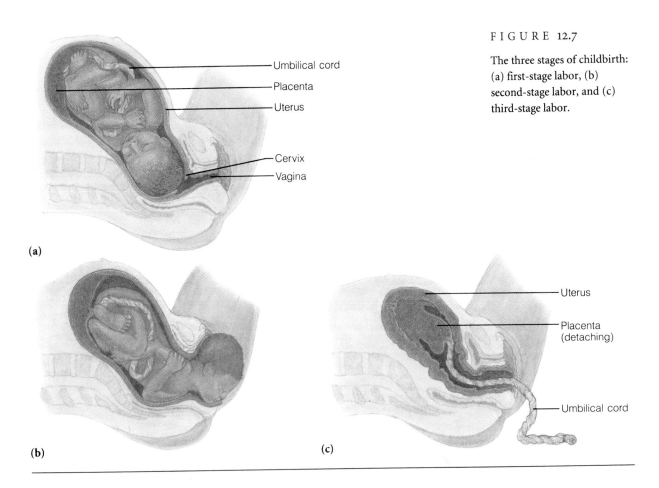

Umbilical cord
Placenta
Uterus
Cervix
Vagina

(a)

(b)

(c)

Uterus
Placenta (detaching)
Umbilical cord

FIGURE 12.7

The three stages of childbirth: (a) first-stage labor, (b) second-stage labor, and (c) third-stage labor.

Contemporary Childbirth

Today's parents-to-be can expect to work as part of a team with their health care provider in preparing and planning for their childbirth experience (Midmer, 1992). Most hospitals and health care providers are eager to help provide a safe and positive birth experience for the entire family. A cooperative effort involving all members of the team is most important. Parents-to-be often participate in childbirth classes that provide thorough information about medical interventions and the process of labor and birth. The classes also provide training for the pregnant woman and her labor coach in breathing and relaxation exercises designed to ease the pain of childbirth.

Approaches to contemporary childbirth began to develop when Grantly Dick-Read and Bernard Lamaze began presenting their ideas about childbirth in the late 1930s and early 1940s. They believed that certain attitudes and practices could help make childbirth a better experience. Dick-Read believed that most of the pain during childbirth stemmed from the muscle tension caused by fear. In an effort to reduce anxiety, he advocated education about the birth process and relaxation with calm, consistent support during a woman's labor. The Lamaze philosophy is similar. The method consists of learning to voluntarily relax abdominal and perineal muscles and to use breathing exercises to dissociate the involuntary labor

OTHER TIMES, OTHER PLACES

Childbirth in Our Recent Past

To fully appreciate today's options for childbirth, it is important to know what childbirth practices were in our recent past. From the beginning of the twentieth century through the early 1970s, few birthing alternatives were available to the pregnant family. Decision making had become the domain of hospitals and obstetrical health care providers. At the time of labor, a woman and her spouse would go to a hospital where they could expect to have the labor and birth directed by her physician and hospital rules. General anesthesia and medication to reduce a woman's recall of labor were routinely given. Medical interventions such as the use of forceps were common, even in routine births. The risks and benefits of medications and procedures were usually not discussed.

The woman went through labor and birth without the support and involvement of her partner because hospital rules did not allow husbands or labor coaches to go beyond the waiting room (thus the classic scenario of the helpless father anxiously pacing in the waiting room). After birth the newborn was promptly removed to a nursery where masked attendants cared for the new baby. Hospital personnel assumed all responsibility for infant care, and babies were only permitted to be with their mothers for feeding.

Opposition to the mechanization of childbirth gained momentum in the United States in the late 1960s. The greatest influence came from the women's movement. As feminists pursued women's rights in many areas, they stressed involvement in decision making about pregnancy and birth. They strongly argued that pregnancy was for most women a normal event rather than an illness requiring extensive medical intervention. They criticized standard hospital deliveries because of the rigid policies; the routine use of medications and medical procedures in normal births; the lack of parental involvement in decision making; and prohibitions against participation of husbands, labor coaches, and others in the birth. Extensive media coverage of these issues changed the public's concept of childbirth and led women and families to seek individuals and settings that would offer flexible, family-centered birth experiences. Many physicians and health care providers supported these changes, and economic concerns and sensitivity to consumer demands motivated most hospitals to create policy and program changes from which pregnant families benefit today (Toussie-Weingarten & Jacobwitz, 1987).

contractions from pain sensations. Although both of these methods are now incorporated into childbirth education classes throughout the United States, women in the 1950s and 1960s who wanted to use these methods frequently had difficulty finding physicians willing to support them in the hospital. By questioning established obstetrical practice, these women were often seen as compromising the health of their infants (Toussie-Weingarten & Jacobwitz, 1987).

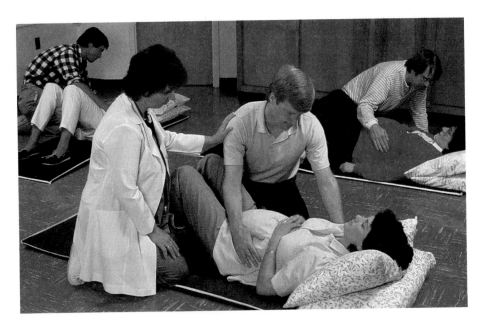

Prepared childbirth classes, such as this one, help prepare expectant mothers and fathers for childbirth.

Although they are sometimes referred to as "natural" childbirth methods, **prepared childbirth** is a more appropriate label for the Dick-Read, Lamaze, and other childbirth approaches. A woman and her partner are indeed preparing themselves when they participate in prepared-childbirth classes and rehearse these techniques during pregnancy. An additional benefit of prepared childbirth is the company and support of the labor coach, often the woman's partner (Gjerdingen et al., 1991). Hospitals now permit labor coaches in the birthing or delivery room for uncomplicated vaginal — and in many cases, cesarean — births. Recent research found that women assisted by a trained birth attendant during labor had fewer cesarean sections, less pain medications, shorter length of labor and greater satisfaction with the birth experience (Kennell et al., McNiven et al., 1992).

Birthplace Alternatives

Along with more options for childbirth practices have come new options for places where childbirth occurs. Not many years ago, a husband, partner, family member, or labor coach could not be with the woman during labor and childbirth. The hospital setting was cold and impersonal, and the woman had little control over the medical procedures used during the birth process. But in recent years, choices about labor and birth have increased greatly, and setting options now include birthing clinics and private homes as well as hospitals. Each birthplace is unique in terms of what it offers the parents and the infant.

Hospital Births. Hospitals have grown more receptive to individualized birth in recent years, and many hospitals now have birthing rooms with a homelike atmosphere. A birthing room offers families the opportunity for an emotionally supportive, homelike birth and yet has the medical backup services of the hospital. Participation of a partner, labor coach, and others; unmedicated childbirth; and

A birth of a baby in a
traditional hospital setting.

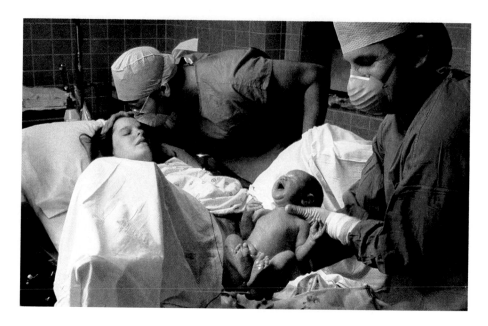

immediate postbirth parent – infant contact are increasingly available. The following account describes a hospital birth experience:

**My husband and I had a great deal of privacy during labor. We had consulted with our doctor
prior to delivery. She agreed to use no medications unless I agreed, and to let me try the
sitting-up and holding-my-knees position during second-stage pushing. Our baby stayed with
us awhile and our parents could see the baby minutes after he was born. It really felt like
our delivery rather than "being delivered." (Authors' files)**

Regulations vary among physicians and hospitals, but most hospitals provide for
experiences like this one. It is important to discuss and agree on childbirth plans
with the practitioner before the time of birth.

Sometimes medical problems arise that interfere with maternal – child contact
immediately following birth. Some child specialists have suggested that a critical
period exists for humans in the first hours after a baby is born, and that if contact
is prevented during this time, mother – infant bonding will not develop adequately
(Klaus & Kennell, 1982). This notion has received little support from research,
however (Goldberg, 1983; Lamb, 1982; Myers, 1984). Instead, the parent – child
attachment can be established throughout development.

An important aspect of the hospital setting is that it provides emergency medical care should birth complications arise. The hospital is the appropriate place
for childbirth in any high-risk pregnancy. Conditions that raise the risk of complication include premature labor, the infant in other than the head-first presentation, blood incompatibility between mother and fetus, **toxemia** (toks-Ē-mē-a)
(water retention and high blood pressure are early symptoms — the condition may
result in convulsions if untreated), **placenta previa** (pla-SEN-ta PRĒ-vē-a) (the placenta positioned over the cervical opening), multiple births, five or more previous
births, too small a pelvis, or maternal illness (Lieberman, 1987). Competent and
thorough prenatal screening can detect most of these complications. However,
even a birth that is expected to be low-risk can develop complications that require
medical intervention.

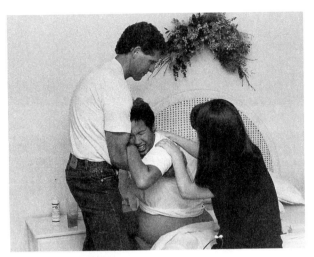
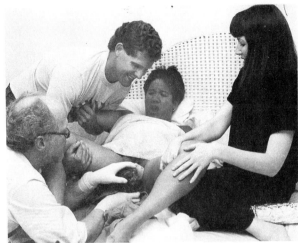
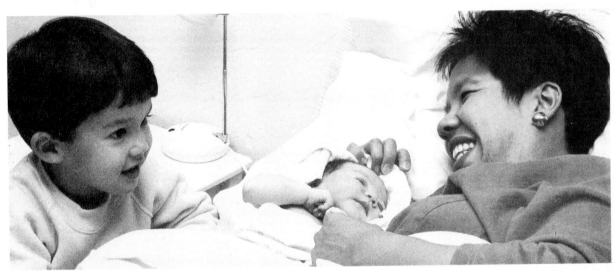

A birth in a birthing room.

Birthing Centers. Birthing centers, available in some areas, offer the homelike atmosphere of the birthing rooms in hospitals. Some are adjacent to hospitals, and others are separate, freestanding organizations. Limited emergency equipment is available at a birth center. In the event of a serious complication, however, the woman would have to be transported to a hospital — for example, if an emergency cesarean birth were required. Only women with no foreseeable likelihood of birth complications should be accepted for care in a birth center (Toussie-Weingarten & Jacobwitz, 1987).

Home Birth. Home birth became more common when families began seeking the family-centered birth experience that, in the past, hospitals did not provide. Proponents of home birth believe that with precautions — careful prenatal screening for complications, thorough preparations, a skilled attendant, and available emergency transportation — home birth can be relatively safe. However, few physicians or certified nurse–midwives will assist with home births when hospitals are available because of both the medical risks and the possibility of malpractice suits from unfavorable birth outcomes (Toussie-Weingarten & Jacobwitz, 1987). The primary advantages of home birth are the familiar surroundings, the involvement of other family members or friends, and the reduced cost.

The greatest risks associated with home births are that lifesaving emergency equipment is not readily available and that emergencies are not always predictable. Opponents to home birth believe that having a baby at home presents an unnecessary risk to mother and infant. Controversy about home birth will continue due to the lack of research studies on its safety.

Medical Interventions: Pros and Cons

Women and their partners should be aware of the possible benefits and side effects of medical procedures used during childbirth. Administering or using medications, fetal heart monitors, and forceps, and performing an episiotomy or cesarean section are common medical interventions whose advantages and disadvantages need to be evaluated carefully and discussed with the health care provider before labor begins.

The potential disadvantage of medications given to the woman during childbirth is that they can affect not only the mother but also the fetus. Research has indicated that drugs can slow, lengthen, or stop labor; decrease maternal blood pressure; eliminate the ability to push during second-stage labor; and affect fetal heart rate and oxygen supply (Willson et al., 1987). Newborn sucking behavior and alertness can be reduced by the use of certain amounts of obstetrical medications (Scanlon, 1974). Generally speaking, however, medications can have a place in the management of labor and birth. It is the responsibility of the health care provider to choose the medications and dosages properly so that the benefits they provide outweigh the potential risks. If medications are chosen and administered properly, the risks are small, and the woman can have a positive childbirth experience while being more comfortable physically during labor and childbirth (Schrinsky, 1988).

Often men and women feel pressured to have a nonmedicated "natural" birth regardless of the situation (Nadelson & Notman, 1985). But unmedicated childbirth may not be suitable for every woman. Although some women do experience "easy" labors and births, labor can be a painful and difficult experience for others, and requesting and requiring pain medication is not a sign of failure (Toussie-Weingarten & Jacobwitz, 1987).

Performing an **episiotomy** (e-pis′-ē-OT-ō-mē), or making an incision in the perineum from the vagina toward the anus, is another common intervention in hospital births (see Figure 12.8). The rationale for episiotomies is that they reduce the pressure on the infant's head and also help prevent vaginal tearing, which is more difficult to suture than a straight incision and often heals less well. Episiotomies also are thought to help preserve pelvic muscle tone and support (Borgatta et al., 1989). Although the procedure is common in the United States, it is not considered necessary in most other countries (only 8% of birthing women in Holland, for example, have episiotomies). Relaxation, proper breathing and pushing, physician patience, manual stretching of the perineum, and freedom of leg movement can eliminate the need for many routine incisions.

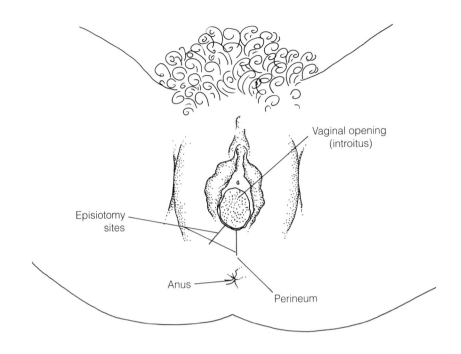

Episiotomy sites

Vaginal opening (introitus)

Anus

Perineum

F I G U R E 12.8

In an episiotomy, an incision is made in the perineum from the vagina toward the anus. Two possible incision sites are shown here.

Forceps, a medical instrument shaped like salad tongs and designed to clasp the baby's head, are sometimes used to assist the infant out of the birth canal. Forceps are often used after analgesics and anesthetics have reduced the strength of uterine contractions. Careful use of forceps is justified in appropriate circumstances but not with routine, normal births, for the use of forceps poses some risks of injury to the woman and baby. A vacuum cup placed on the emerging baby's head can also be used to help pull the infant through the birth canal.

A **cesarean** (sē-SĀR-ē-an) **section,** in which the baby is removed through an incision made in the abdominal wall and uterus, can be lifesaving surgery for the mother and child. Cesarean birth may be recommended in a variety of situations, including when the fetal head is too large for the mother's pelvic structure, during maternal illness, or when there are indications of fetal distress during labor, or birth complications such as a breech presentation (feet or bottom coming out of the uterus first) (Hage et al., 1988). Mothers who experience cesarean birth often have a spinal or epidural anesthetic and are awake to greet their infants when the baby is born. In many hospitals fathers remain with the woman during cesarean births.

A woman may have more than one baby by cesarean section. Also, most women can have subsequent vaginal births, depending on the circumstances of the earlier cesarean birth(s) and of the subsequent birth (Novas et al., 1989; Phelan et al., 1989). A vaginal birth following a cesarean one is called a VBAC (vee-bak) for *v*aginal *b*irth *a*fter *c*esarean. Although many women who have cesarean births are less satisfied with their birth experiences than are women who have vaginal births, adjustment following childbirth is similar in the two groups (Padawer et al., 1988).

The percentage of cesarean sections performed in the United States has increased dramatically since the mid-1960s. It is the most common hospital surgical procedure in the United States today (Stafford, 1991). Cesarean sections account for approximately 24 out of 100 births in the United States (Taffel et al., 1992). This increase has evoked controversy. Some maintain that the increase reflects better use of medical technology in the management of childbirth, but others believe that cesarean sections are aggressive medical interventions that are being too readily used (O'Driscoll et al., 1988).

Postpartum

The first several weeks following birth are referred to as the **postpartum period.** This is a time of both physical and psychological adjustment for each family member and is likely to be a time of intensified emotional highs and lows. Understanding that these feelings are a common response to adjustments to the new baby may help new parents cope with the stresses involved. One woman described her feelings during this time as follows:

> That calm, sure, unambivalent woman who moved through the pages of the manuals I read seemed as unlike me as an astronaut. Nothing, to be sure, had prepared me for the intensity of relationship already existing between me and a creature I had carried in my body and now held in my arms and fed from my breasts. Throughout pregnancy and nursing, women are urged to relax, to mime the serenity of madonnas. No one mentions the psychic crisis of bearing a first child, the excitation of long-buried feelings about one's own mother, the sense of confused power and powerlessness, of being taken over on the one hand and of touching new physical and psychic potentialities on the other, a heightened sensibility which can be exhilarating, bewildering, and exhausting. No one mentions the strangeness of attraction — which can be as single-minded and overwhelming as the early days of a love affair — to a being so tiny, so dependent, so folded-into itself — who is, and yet is not, part of oneself. (Rich, 1976, p. 36)

Combined with heightened excitement and happiness are often other feelings. The mother may experience what is described as "postpartum blues," during which she may cry easily and feel fearful or sad. Postpartum depression has been reported for 26–85% of mothers (O'Hara, 1991). Such reactions may be partly due to the sudden emotional, physical, and hormonal changes following birth (Gruen, 1990).

The new baby also affects the roles and interactions of all members of the family. The mother and father may experience an increased closeness to each other as well as some troublesome feelings. New fathers sometimes feel jealous of the close relationship between the mother and child. Both the man and the woman may want extra emotional support from the other, but each may have less than usual to give. A good support system for the new mother and father can be immensely helpful. The time and energy demands of caring for an infant can contribute to weariness and stress — feelings that may be compounded by the responsibility of having to care for this young being for the next 20 years. Sleep deprivation from waking many times in the night to care for the newborn is very stressful and diminishes emotional and physical reserves (Gjerdingen et al., 1991). Both new mothers and fathers may experience anxiety and concern in the postpartum period. Brothers and sisters may also be affected, as they often have some negative feelings about the attention given their new sibling. Some hospitals offer classes for expectant brothers and sisters to help them anticipate and cope with changes the new baby will bring.

Each of these feelings and concerns tends to diminish gradually as the family makes adjustments to new roles and expectations. Often, too, the adjustment is easier when family members have realistic expectations (or previous experience) to prepare them for the demands as well as the pleasure of the new arrival.

Breast-Feeding

Production of breast milk does not take place as soon as the infant is born. Right after birth the breasts produce a yellowish liquid called colostrum, which contains antibodies and protein. Lactation, or milk production, begins about one to three days after birth. Pituitary hormones stimulate milk production in the breasts in response to the stimulation of the infant suckling the nipples. If a new mother does not begin or continue to nurse, milk production subsides within a matter of days.

Nursing may temporarily inhibit ovulation, particularly for women who feed their babies only breast milk and nurse during the night and day (Kennedy & Visness, 1992; Perez et al., 1992). However, nursing is not a completely reliable method of birth control (see Chapter 11). Estrogen-containing birth control pills should not be used during nursing because the hormones reduce the amount of milk and affect milk quality as well. However, progesterone-only pills can be used because progesterone does not reduce the milk supply or affect milk quality (Salisbury, 1991).

There are many advantages to breast-feeding. Breast milk provides the infant with a digestible food filled with antibodies and other immunity-producing substances. Nursing also induces uterine contractions that help speed the return of the uterus to its prepregnancy size. Breast-feeding can be an emotional and sensual experience for the mother. For women who decide to nurse, breast-feeding is another opportunity for close physical contact with the baby. Women with more positive attitudes toward sexuality in general are more likely to breast-feed and experience sexual interest and an earlier resumption of intercourse than are women with negative attitudes about sex (Fisher & Gray, 1988). William Masters and Virginia Johnson (1966) found that sexual interest returned more rapidly in women who breast-fed than in those who bottle-fed their infants. However, most women in another study reported that breast-feeding had no effect on their sexual relationships (Ellis & Hewat, 1985). When a negative effect was reported, it was usually because of decreased sexual enjoyment because of breast tenderness, decreased vaginal lubrication, or milk leaking during sexual contact (Ellis & Hewat, 1985).

Nursing also has some disadvantages. The nursing mother's genitals may be oversensitive and become sore from intercourse because of the reduction of estrogen that nursing induces (estrogen conditions and maintains vulvar tissue). The vaginal tissue becomes thinner, and vaginal lubrication significantly decreases. The woman's breasts may also be tender and sore. Milk may be ejected involuntarily from her nipples during sexual stimulation — a source of potential embarrassment (Ellis & Hewat, 1985). Also, the tasks of caring for a baby and the physical demands of producing milk may leave the woman with little energy for sexual activities.

For women who decide to nurse, breast-feeding is another opportunity for close physical contact with the baby.

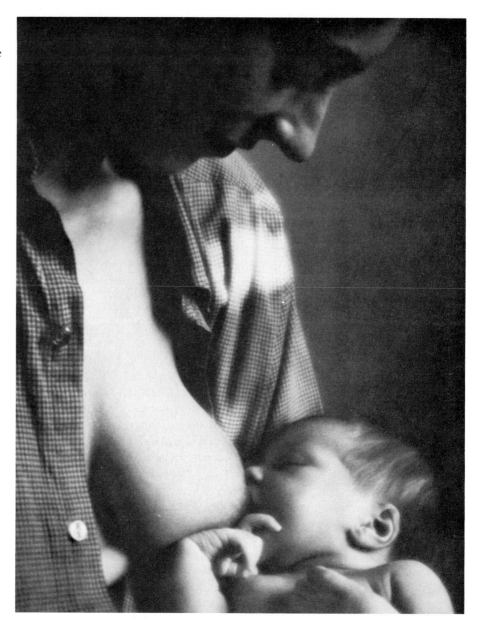

Some women may have negative feelings about breast-feeding. Many women feel ambivalent about this activity, perhaps partly because of our society's emphasis on breasts as sex symbols. Furthermore, some mothers' lives may be too disrupted by the sole feeding responsibility of nursing, particularly if they return to work shortly after childbearing (Ruben, 1992). It is often easier to share child-care responsibilities by bottle-feeding rather than nursing: the father can then play a greater role in holding and feeding the infant. However, a nursing mother can use a breast pump to extract her milk so that it is available to her partner or another caregiver for bottle-feeding the baby. Like other aspects of child care, breast-feeding is a matter of exploration and personal preference.

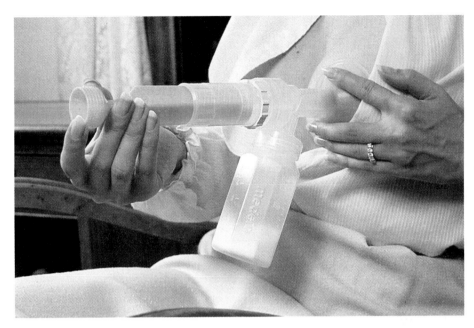

A breast pump extracts breast milk to be fed to the baby by bottle.

Sexual Interaction After Childbirth

In the past, many physicians prohibited intercourse until six weeks after childbirth. Currently, couples are commonly advised that intercourse can resume after the flow of the reddish uterine discharge, called **lochia** (LŌ-kē-a), has stopped and after episiotomy incisions or vaginal tears have healed (Masters & Johnson, 1966). An important factor to consider is when intercourse is physically comfortable for the woman. This depends on the type of birth, the size and presentation of the baby, the extent of episiotomy or lacerations, and the individual woman's rate of healing. The postpartum decrease in hormones, especially pronounced with breast-feeding, can cause discomfort during intercourse (Reamy, 1991). After a cesarean birth, the couple needs to wait until the incision has healed enough for intercourse to occur without discomfort. Other sexual and affectionate relations can be shared while waiting.

Psychological readiness for sexual activity is another important factor. The significant changes in daily life that a new baby brings can affect sexual intimacy. Desire for and frequency and satisfaction of sexual activity may decline during the first year following birth. Fatigue is a major factor. The demands on both the woman and her partner of caring for a new baby may mean that there is not much time or energy left for sexual expression. Fitting lovemaking into the baby's and parents' schedules can be quite a challenge. Concern about the baby can also interfere:

It seems that every time we start to make love, the baby cries. Even though I know he's been fed and is dry, I can't focus on my sexual feelings. And when he gets quiet, I worry that he's dead! My husband has the same reactions, so lots of times we don't get much going together. (Authors' files)

In addition, until the hormonal changes of pregnancy, birth, and breast-feeding have returned to the prepregnancy state, many women experience a decrease in sexual interest and response. It is important to note that men, as well as women, may not be particularly interested in sex in the first weeks or months following the birth of a baby (Gurian, 1988). Typically, women and men with more positive attitudes about sex in general show more sexual interest and earlier resumption of intercourse than do others with more negative attitudes about sexuality (Fisher & Gray, 1988).

Couples whose sexual activity has been disrupted by pregnancy and birth may feel "out of practice" in their sexual relationship. It is often helpful for couples to resume sexual activity in an unhurried, exploratory manner, as if they were first initiating a sexual relationship. Once intercourse is resumed, contraception is nec-traception is necessary for as long as the couple wants to avoid another pregnancy.

Summary

Parenthood as an Option

Increasing numbers of couples are choosing not to be parents. More women today choose careers over motherhood.

The realities of parenthood or child-free living are difficult to predict.

Becoming Pregnant

Timing intercourse to correspond to ovulation enhances the likelihood of conception.

Approximately one in six couples in the United States have problems with infertility, and a cause is not found in as many as 15% of infertile couples.

Failure to ovulate and blockage of the fallopian tubes are typical causes of female infertility. Low sperm count is the most common cause of male infertility.

Alcohol, drug use, cigarette smoking, and infections from sexually transmitted diseases reduce fertility in both women and men.

The emotional stress and the disruption of a couple's sexual relationship caused by infertility can result in sexual difficulties.

The legal and social issues related to artificial insemination, in vitro fertilization, and surrogate motherhood are complex and will continue to create controversy.

Artificial insemination is done with donor semen when the husband is infertile. IVF – GIFT offers a 10 – 15% chance of success with each procedure.

The first sign of a pregnancy is usually a missed menstrual period. Urine and blood tests and pelvic exams are used to determine pregnancy.

Spontaneous and Elective Abortion

Spontaneous abortion, or miscarriage, occurs in approximately 20% of pregnancies. The majority of miscarriages occur within the first three months of pregnancy.

Elective abortion is a highly controversial social and political issue in the United States today. Suction curettage, D and E, intraamniotic injections, and intravaginal suppositories of prostaglandins are the medical techniques used to induce abortion.

Contraceptive method failure is a major contributor to women having repeat abortions.

Contraceptive risk taking sometimes precedes an unplanned pregnancy and consequent abortion. There are different kinds of "costs" and "benefits" to contraceptive use for each woman and in each relationship.

In 1973 the U.S. Supreme Court legalized a woman's right to decide to terminate her pregnancy before the fetus reaches the age of viability. In 1977 the Hyde Amendment prohibited the use of federal Medicaid funds for abortion and limited low-income women's access to abortion. In the 1990s many state legislatures are imposing further limitations on the availability of abortion.

Prochoice and antiabortion advocates have fundamental differences in their beliefs about many aspects of life.

A Healthy Pregnancy

Pregnancy is divided into three trimesters, each of which is marked by fetal changes.

Nutrient, oxygen, and waste exchange between the woman and fetus occurs through the placenta. Substances harmful to the fetus can pass through the placenta from the mother's blood.

Smoking, alcohol and drug use, and certain medications can severely damage the developing fetus.

Amniocentesis and chorionic villus sampling are two tests that can be done during pregnancy to screen for certain birth defects.

More women are deciding to have children after age 35. These women have slightly decreased fecundity and a somewhat higher risk of conceiving a fetus with chromosomal abnormalities. However, with careful monitoring of pregnancy and childbirth, their risks can be reduced to the level of those of younger women.

The Experience of Pregnancy

Some first-trimester physical changes include cessation of menstruation, fatigue, and breast tenderness. In the second trimester, the woman's abdomen begins to protrude, and she can feel fetal movements. By the third trimester, the abdomen is enlarged, and fetal movements are pronounced. Emotional reactions to pregnancy vary greatly.

Men have become increasingly involved in the prenatal, childbirth, and child rearing processes.

Although changes of position may be necessary, sensual and sexual interaction may continue as desired during pregnancy, except in occasional cases of medical complications.

Childbirth

Indications of first-stage labor are regular contractions of the uterus, discharge of the mucus plug, rupture of the amniotic sac, and cervical effacement and dilation of up to 10 cm.

Second-stage labor is the descent of the infant into the birth canal, ending with birth. The placenta is delivered in the third stage.

Prepared childbirth, popularized by Bernard Lamaze and Grantly Dick-Read, has changed childbirth practices. Most hospitals now support participation of the woman's partner and a team approach to decision making about the birth process.

Birthing clinics and home birth are additional alternatives to hospital birth, but neither has the advantage of the complete emergency medical backup sometimes necessary during birth.

Medical interventions during birth (administering medications, using forceps, and performing episiotomies and cesarean sections) can be helpful in the birth process, but some people believe that these interventions and procedures are overused.

Postpartum

There are many physical, emotional, and family adjustments to be made following the birth of a baby.

Breast-feeding has regained popularity in the United States. There are advantages and disadvantages to both breast- and bottle-feeding.

Intercourse after childbirth can usually resume once the flow of lochia has stopped and any vaginal tears or the episiotomy incision has healed. However, it may take longer for sexual interest and arousal to return to normal.

⤶ *Thought Provokers* ⤶

1. If you were in a position of deciding whether a large research grant would go toward developing a perfect contraceptive or a cure for infertility, what would you decide? Why?

2. If preconception sex selection became 100% accurate and inexpensive, what do you think the consequences would be?

3. What laws, if any, should be established regarding surrogate motherhood, in vitro fertilization, artificial insemination, and embryo transfer?

4. When you were born, what was your mother's birth experience like? Your father's?

5. What are your expectations regarding pregnancy and birth? Where do these expectations come from?

Suggested Readings

Genevie, Louis; and Margolies, Eva (1987). *The Motherhood Report*. New York: Macmillan. An in-depth study of 1000 women addressing how they really feel about being mothers. It includes discussions of pregnancy, childbirth, and stages of childhood.

Gerson, Kathleen (1986). *Hard Choices*. Berkeley: University of California Press. An in-depth analysis of the individual and social forces that influence how women decide about work, career, and motherhood.

Lieberman, Adrienne (1987). *Giving Birth*. New York: St. Martin's. This comprehensive childbirth text covers the events of labor and birth, including personal stories of a variety of births and suggestions for birth plans for expectant couples.

Nilsson, Lennart (1977). *A Child is Born*. New York: Dell. A classic book of wonderful photographs of fetal development.

Reukauf, Diane; and Trause, Mary (1988). *Commonsense Breastfeeding: A Practical Guide to the Pleasures, Problems and Solutions*. New York: Atheneum. This practical approach to the realities of bringing a new baby home uses examples of real-life experiences and information to enhance the experience of breast-feeding.

Samuels, Mike and Samuels, Nancy. (1986). *The Well Pregnancy Book*. New York: Summit. A comprehensive guide for expectant parents.

Stephenson, Lynda (1987). *Give Us a Child: Coping with the Personal Crisis of Infertility*. San Francisco: Harper & Row. This comprehensive guide examines the emotional and practical concerns of coping with infertility.

Tribe, Laurence (1990). *Abortion: The Clash of Absolutes*. New York: Norton. This book explores legal, political, religious, and emotional issues from both sides of the abortion debate.

Worth, Cecelia (1988). *Birth of a Father: New Fathers Talk About Pregnancy, Childbirth and the First Three Months*. New York: McGraw-Hill. This book, written by a childbirth educator, describes fathers' reactions and insights into the uncertainties and joys of pregnancy, the surprises of labor and birth, and the realities of parenting a newborn.

Resources

International Childbirth Education Association, P.O. Box 20048, Minneapolis, MN 55420. Provides information and resources for childbirth education.

Resolve, Inc., 5 Water Street, Arlington, MA 02174-4814; (617) 643-2724. A national nonprofit organization that provides support groups, education, and publications for couples struggling with infertility.

If men and women are to understand each other, to enter into each other's nature with mutual sympathy, and to become capable of genuine comradeship, the foundation must be laid in youth.

Havelock Ellis
The Task of Social Hygiene (1912)

Sexuality During Childhood and Adolescence

*I*n many Western societies, including the United States, it has been traditional to view the period between birth and puberty as a time when sexuality remains unexpressed. However, with the widespread circulation of the findings of Alfred Kinsey and other distinguished investigators, the false assumption that childhood is a period of sexual dormancy has changed. In fact, it is now widely recognized that infants of both sexes are born with the capacity for sexual pleasure and response.

Signs of sexual arousal in infants and children, such as penile erection, vaginal lubrication, and pelvic thrusting, are often misinterpreted or unacknowledged. However, careful observers may note these indications of sexuality in the very young (Calderone, 1983; Langfeldt, 1981; Montauk & Clasen, 1989). In some cases infants, both male and female, have been observed experiencing what appears to be an orgasm. The infant, of course, cannot offer spoken confirmation of the sexual nature of such reactions. However, the behavior is so remarkably similar to that exhibited by sexually responding adults that little doubt exists about its nature.

It is impossible to determine what such early sexual experiences mean to infants, but it is reasonably certain that these activities are gratifying. Many infants of both sexes engage quite naturally in self-pleasuring unless such behavior produces strong negative responses from parents or other caretakers.

As this information demonstrates, we cannot accurately view sexuality as something that remains dormant during the early years of life. A variety of behaviors and body functions, including sexual eroticism, develop during infancy and childhood. In some ways sexuality may be especially important during this period because many experiences during these formative years may have great impact on the later expression of adult sexuality. In the opening section of this chapter, we briefly outline some typical sexual behaviors during childhood.

Sexual Behavior During Childhood

People show considerable variation in their sexual development during childhood, and many diverse influences are involved. Despite these differences, however, certain common features in the developmental sequence tend to emerge. In the next few pages, we briefly outline some of these typical behaviors, keeping in mind that each person's unique sexual history may differ from one or more of the following points. As you consider this information, it is also important to realize that most of the data about childhood sexual behavior is based on recollections of adults who are asked to recall their childhood experiences. As we noted in Chapter 2, it may be quite difficult to remember accurately experiences that occurred many years earlier.

In the first few years of life, many girls and boys discover the pleasures of genital stimulation. This often involves rubbing the genital area against an object such as a doll or pillow. With the development of coordinated hand movements, manual stimulation may become a preferred method for producing sexual pleasure. In all probability such activity is more likely to be observed in children reared in home environments where adults hold permissive attitudes toward genital touching.

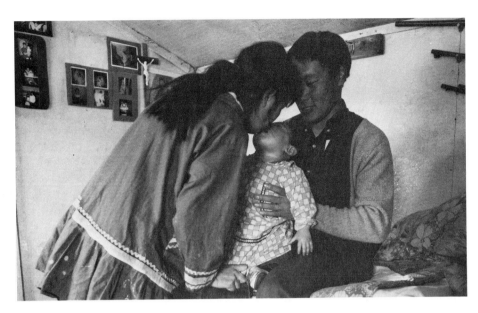

Enjoying sexual intimacies as an adult may be related to childhood experiences of warm, pleasurable contact, particularly with parents.

A child may learn to express his or her affectionate and sensual feelings through activities like kissing and hugging. The responses the child receives to these expressions of intimacy may have a strong influence on the manner in which he or she expresses sexuality in later years. The inclinations we have as adults toward giving and receiving affection seem to be related to our early opportunities for warm, pleasurable contact with significant others, particularly parents (Montauk & Clasen, 1989; Prescott, 1989). A number of researchers believe that children who are deprived of "contact comfort" (being touched and held) during the first months and years of life may have difficulty establishing intimate relationships later in their lives (Harlow & Harlow, 1962; Money, 1980; Montagu & Matson, 1979; Trause et al., 1977).

Besides self-stimulation, prepubertal children often engage in play that may be viewed as sexual in nature (Golden, 1989; Reiss, 1986). Such play takes place with friends or siblings of the same or the other sex. It may occur as early as the age of two or three, but it is more likely to take place between the ages of four and seven. Alfred Kinsey (1948 & 1953) noted that 45% of the females and 57% of the males in his sample reported having these experiences by age 12. In a more recent survey, parents of six- and seven-year-old children reported that 76% of their daughters and 83% of their sons had participated in some sex play with friends or siblings (Kolodny, 1980). The activities may range from exhibition and inspection of the genitals, often under the guise of "playing doctor," to simulating intercourse by rubbing genital regions together. While most adults, particularly parents, tend to react to the apparent sexual nature of this play, for many children the play aspects of the interaction may be far more significant than any sexual overtones:

> The sexual nature of these games is not always understood by the child and even when the small boy lies on the top of the small girl and makes what may resemble copulatory movement, there is often no realization that genital contact might be made, or that there might be an erotic reward in such activity. (Kinsey et al., 1953, p. 108)

Many children find the play aspects of interactions like this one more important than any sexual overtones.

> When we think of preadolescent activities that look sexual — we, as adults, looking back on it, or as parents looking at it in our children — we respond to the sexual aspect; the sex is very important; the play is unimportant. To the child, however, the balance is exactly the opposite. The play is the major part; whatever sex might be in it, is mainly interesting because it is forbidden, like mommy's jewel box or daddy's tool chest. (Gagnon, 1977, p. 85)

As this last quote suggests, curiosity about what is forbidden probably plays an important role in encouraging early sexual exploration. Curiosity about the sexual equipment of others, particularly the other sex, is quite normal. Many day-care centers and nursery schools now have bathrooms open to both sexes so that children can learn about sexual differences in a natural, everyday way.

Besides showing interest in sexual behaviors, many children in the five-to-seven age range begin to act in ways that mirror the predominant heterosexual marriage script in our society. This is apparent in the practice of "playing house,"

Childhood curiosity about sexuality takes many forms.

which is typical of children of this age. Some of the sex play described earlier occurs within the context of this activity.

By the time children reach the age of eight or nine, there is a pronounced tendency for boys and girls to begin to play separately, although romantic interest in the other sex may exist at the same time. Furthermore, despite an apparent decline in sex play with others, curiosity about sexual matters remains high. This is an age when many questions about reproduction and sexuality may be asked (Parsons, 1983).

Most 10- and 11-year-olds are keenly interested in body changes, particularly those involving the genitals and secondary sex characteristics such as underarm hair and breast development. They often wait in eager anticipation for these signs of approaching adolescence. Many prepubescent children may become extremely self-conscious about their bodies and may be quite reticent about exposing them to the view of others. Separation from the other sex is still the general rule, and children of this age often strongly protest any suggestions of romantic interest in the other sex (Goldman & Goldman, 1982).

Sex play with friends of the same sex is common during the late childhood years. In fact, during this time when the separation of the sexes is particularly strong, homosexual activity is probably more common than heterosexual encounters. In a survey of 432 white children, 52% of males and 35% of females reported homosexual experiences prior to puberty (Elias & Gebhard, 1969). These childhood homosexual encounters are a normal part of growing up, and in most instances they are transitory, soon replaced by the heterosexual courting of adolescence (Thornburg & Aras, 1986; Van Wyk & Geist, 1984). We encourage parents who become aware of these behaviors to avoid responding in an overly negative fashion or labeling such activity as homosexual in the adult sense (Carrera, 1981; Gadpaille, 1975).

Masturbation is one of the most common sexual expressions during the childhood years. In a study of several hundred children, 30% of the females and 56% of the males reported masturbating prior to adolescence (Elias & Gebhard, 1969). In a more recent survey, one-third of the female respondents and two-thirds of the males reported having masturbated by the age of 13 (Hunt, 1974). For both sexes masturbation is the most frequent source of preadolescent orgasm (Kinsey et al., 1948 & 1953). Most boys learn about it from friends, and some may even receive instruction in the particulars of self-stimulation, as the following account indicates:

My introduction to the fine art of masturbation was provided by an older buddy. One day in his basement, while changing from wet swim suits, he asked me if I had ever "jerked off." Well, I hadn't, and he proceeded to soap up his penis and demonstrate his technique. When I tried it, the sensations were very good but, unlike my friend, nothing came out of my penis. He told me to keep practicing, and I did. Several months later I had my first ejaculation. (Authors' files)

In contrast to boys, most young girls do not discuss masturbation with friends. For them, discovery of this activity is usually a solitary and often an accidental event:

I discovered the delights of masturbation when I was about eight years old. My mother always encouraged me to thoroughly wash my "privates." One day in the tub, I decided to make them "squeaky clean." I slid my bottom under the faucet and directed a stream of warm water over my vulva. Wow! That was one kind of washing I really liked. In short order I experienced my first orgasm. I didn't even know what you called it, but the sensations were great. I soon improvised all kinds of ways to squirt water over my clitoris. I never told anyone about my "discovery" but continued masturbating regularly with this water-spray technique. Today I have no problem understanding the popularity of hand-held water massagers. (Authors' files)

As these accounts and the preceding discussion have indicated, self-discovery and peer interactions are very important during childhood development of sexuality. These factors continue to be influential during the adolescent years, as we will discover in later portions of this chapter. But first we turn our attention to the physical changes that accompany the onset of adolescence.

The Physical Changes of Adolescence

Adolescence is a time of dramatic physiological changes and social-role development. In Western societies it is the transition between childhood and adulthood that typically spans the period from 12 to 20 years of age. Most of the major physical changes of adolescence take place during the first few years of this period (Thornburg & Aras, 1986; Wheeler, 1991). However, important and often profound changes in behavior and role expectations occur throughout this phase of life. By cross-cultural standards, adolescence in our society is rather extended. In many cultures (and in Western society in preindustrial times), adult roles are assumed at a much earlier age. Rather than undergoing a protracted period of child – adult status, the child is often initiated into adulthood upon reaching puberty.

Puberty (Latin *pubescere,* to be covered with hair) is a term frequently used to describe the period of rapid physical changes in early adolescence. The onset of puberty is approximately two years earlier for girls than for boys. Before puberty both boys and girls have been growing taller and stronger. The mechanisms that trigger the chain of developments that follow are not fully understood. However, we do know that the hypothalamus plays a key role (Foster, 1992; Stanhope & Brook, 1988; Thornburg & Aras, 1986). In general, when a child is between 8 and 14 years old, the hypothalamus increases secretions that cause the pituitary to release larger amounts of **gonadotropins** into the bloodstream. The gonadotropins, hormones that stimulate activity in the gonads, are chemically identical in men and women. However, in males they cause the testes to increase testosterone production, whereas in females they act on the ovaries to produce elevated estrogen levels.

At this point, external signs of characteristic male and female sexual maturation begin to appear in response to higher levels of the male and female hormones. The resulting developments — breasts; deepened voice; and facial, body, and pubic hair — are called **secondary sex characteristics.** Growth of pubic hair in both sexes and breast budding (slight protuberance under the nipple) in girls are usually the earliest signs of puberty. A growth spurt also follows. This spurt eventually terminates, again under the influence of sex hormones, which send signals to close the ends of the long bones. The growth spurt usually occurs approximately two years earlier in females than in males and often results in girls being taller than boys during early adolescence (Thornburg & Aras, 1986). External genitals also undergo enlargement; the penis and testes increase in size in the male, and the labia become enlarged in the female.

Under the influence of hormone stimulation, the internal organs of the male and female undergo further development during puberty. In girls the vaginal walls become thicker, and the uterus becomes larger and more muscular. The vaginal pH changes from alkaline to acidic as vaginal and cervical secretions increase in response to the changing hormone status. Eventually menstruation begins; the first menstrual period is called **menarche.** Initial menstrual periods may be irregular and occur without ovulation. Some adolescent girls may experience irregular menstrual cycles for several years before their periods become regular and predictable. Consequently, methods of birth control based on the menstrual cycle can be particularly unreliable for females in this age group. Most girls begin menstruating around the age of 12 or 13, but there is widespread variation in the age of menarche (Wheeler, 1991). Research has suggested that menarche may be triggered when a certain minimum percentage of body fat is present (Frisch & McArthur, 1974). At the onset of puberty, the average ratio of lean to fatty tissue in females is five to one (that is, approximately one-sixth of the total body weight is fat); while at menarche, it is about three to one (about one-fourth of body weight is fat). In support of the suggested connection between body fat and menarche, research has revealed that female athletes and ballet dancers who engage in prolonged and strenuous training frequently experience delayed menarche or interrupted menstruation (Frisch et al., 1980; Warren, 1982). Presumably, this results from having a low proportion of body fat.

In boys the prostate gland and seminal vesicles increase noticeably in size during this time. Although boys may experience orgasms throughout childhood, ejaculation is not possible until the prostate and seminal vesicles begin functioning under the influence of increasing testosterone levels. Typically, the first ejaculation occurs a year after the growth spurt has begun, usually around age 13 or 14, but as with menstruation, the timing is highly variable. The initial appearance of sperm in the ejaculate typically occurs at about age 14 (Kulin et al., 1989; Wheeler, 1991). Kinsey (1948) reported that in two out of three boys, initial ejaculation occurred during masturbation. There appears to be a period of early adolescent infertility in many girls and boys following initial menstruation or ejaculation. However, this should not be depended on for birth control. In some males sperm production occurs in the early stages of puberty, and even the first ejaculation may contain viable sperm (Abrahams, 1982).

Voice changes caused by growth of the voice box (larynx) occur in both sexes, but they are more dramatic in boys, who often experience an awkward time when their speech alternates between low and high pitch. Facial hair in boys and axillary (underarm) hair in both sexes usually appears approximately two years after pubic hair does. Increased activity of oil-secreting glands in the skin can cause facial blemishes, or acne.

Many of these physical developments may be sources of concern or pride to the adolescent and his or her family and friends. Feeling self-conscious is a common reaction, and individuals who mature early or late often feel particularly self-conscious:

I was the first one to get hair on my chest. At first I would cut it off so I wasn't different from everyone else in the shower room. (Authors' files)

All my friends had started menstruating a long time before, and I still had not. I started wearing pads and a belt once a month so I wouldn't feel so out of it. (Authors' files)

The physical changes we have been describing are quite dramatic and rapid. Suddenly the body one has been living in for years undergoes mysterious changes that are often disconcerting:

If given the chance, I would never repeat my early teen years. My body was so unpredictable. At the most inopportune moments, my voice was cracking, my penis was erect, or a pimple was popping out on my face. Sometimes, all these things would happen at the same time! (Authors' files)

These physical changes do not go unnoticed by adolescent peers. Boy–girl friendships often change, and adolescents are likely to become — at least temporarily — more homosocial, relating socially primarily with members of the same sex. A young woman explains:

When I was growing up, a neighbor boy and I were best buddies. We spent our summers exploring nearby fields, wrestling, and building a great tree house. When I started developing breasts, it all changed, and we didn't seem to know how to talk to each other any more. (Authors' files)

Adolescent relationships often do not remain homosocial for very long. The period of adolescence is marked not only by physical changes but also by important behavioral changes. In the following pages, we look at some important areas of adolescent sexual behavior.

Many adolescents form caring relationships with each other.

Sexual Behavior During Adolescence

Adolescence is a period of exploration, when sexual behavior — both self-stimu-lation and partner-shared — generally increases. Although much of teenage sex-uality represents a progression from childhood behaviors, a new significance is attached to sexual expression. We will look at some areas in which important developments take place during adolescence, including masturbation, petting, development of ongoing relationships, intercourse, pregnancy, the use of birth control, and homosexuality. In most areas of adolescent sexuality, the male–female double standard prevails: feelings and behaviors that are considered ac-ceptable for adolescent males are considered unacceptable or inappropriate for adolescent females. Recent research suggests that the sexual double standard among American adolescents may be on the decline (Bolton & MacEachron, 1988; Sonenstein, 1986; Sprecher, 1989). We consider the sexual double standard before turning to specific behaviors.

The Double Standard

Although children have been learning gender-role stereotypes since infancy, the emphasis on gender-role differentiation often increases during adolescence. One way that gender-role expectations for males and females are revealed is through the double standard. As we will see in Chapter 16, the double standard has profound effects on both male and female sexuality throughout our lives. The sexually emerging adolescent receives the full brunt of this polarizing societal belief.

For males the focus of sexuality may be sexual conquest. Young men who are nonexploitative or inexperienced are often labeled with highly negative terms like "sissy." On the other hand, peers often provide social reinforcement for stereotypically "masculine" attitudes and behaviors; for example, approval is given to aggressive and independent behaviors. For some young men, telling their peers about their sexual encounters is more important than the sexual act itself. As one young man stated:

My own self-image was at stake. There I was — good-looking, humorous, athletic, liked to party — but still a virgin. Everybody just assumed that I was an expert at making love. I played this role and, without a doubt, always implied, "Yes, we did and boy, was it fun." (Authors' files)

For females the message and the expectations are often very different. The following account illustrates one woman's view of both sides of the double standard:

It always seemed so strange, how society encouraged virginity in girls but it was okay for boys to lose theirs. I came from a large family, my brother being the oldest, and we girls followed him. I can remember when word got around how much of a playboy my brother was (he was about 18). My parents were not upset, but rather seemed kind of tickled. When we girls were ready to go out, our parents became suspicious. I can always remember how I felt and how if I ever became a parent I wouldn't allow such an inequality and emphasis on female virginity to take place. (Authors' files)

Many girls face a dilemma. They may learn to appear "sexy" to attract males, yet they often experience ambivalence about overt sexual behavior. A young woman expressed this feeling:

Going out with boys is hard for me when it comes to making a decision about sex. I'm afraid if I don't hold out long enough they'll think I'm easy and if I wait too long they'll lose interest. (Authors' files)

The double-standard dilemma often encompasses far more than sexual behavior. Girls may begin to define their worth by their boyfriends' accomplishments rather than their own. Wearing her boyfriend's letter jacket may bring a girl infinitely more status than earning one herself. Her abilities may even be seen as liabilities rather than assets. She may be concerned, for example, about getting better grades than her boyfriend.

Masturbation

Although a significant number of adolescents do not experience sexual intercourse by the age of 19, many masturbate. As we saw earlier in this chapter, masturbation is a common sexual expression during childhood. During adolescence the behavior tends to increase in frequency. A survey of teenage males revealed an average masturbation frequency of five times per week (Lopresto et al., 1985). Masturbation-frequency rates among females are notably lower for all age groups, including adolescents. Studies have indicated that by the time they have reached the end of adolescence, almost all males and approximately three out of four females have masturbated (Hunt, 1974; Kolodny, 1980; Sorenson, 1973).

Masturbation can serve as an important avenue for sexual expression during the adolescent years. Besides providing an always available outlet for sexual tension, self-stimulation is an excellent way to learn about one's body and its sexual potential (Weinstein & Rosen, 1991). Teenagers can experiment with different ways of pleasuring themselves, thereby increasing their self-knowledge. This information may later prove helpful during sexual interaction with another. In fact, many sex therapists believe that people who do not masturbate during adolescence may be missing an important element in their sexual development.

Petting

Another form of noncoital sexual expression provides an important way for many couples to relate to one another, often as an alternative to intercourse. A man describes this alternative:

My fiancée and I agreed that it was important for both of us to remain virgins before marriage. Neither of us felt it was a particular hardship to wait until we were married to experience coitus. Instead, we engaged in lots of necking and heavy petting, often to orgasm. (Authors' files)

Petting refers to erotic physical contact that may include kissing, holding, touching, manual stimulation, or oral–genital stimulation — but not coitus. "Necking," "making out," and "messing around" are other expressions for petting. Even very "heavy" petting is a common activity among teenagers. According to the 1974 Hunt survey, approximately one-half of the girls and two-thirds of the boys had experienced some type of petting to the point of orgasm during adolescence.

Perhaps one of the most noteworthy recent changes in the pattern of adolescent petting behaviors involves oral sex. A number of surveys have shown that the incidence of oral–genital stimulation among teenagers has risen dramatically, to a level two or three times higher than the rates reported in the Kinsey studies (Gagnon & Simon, 1987; Newcomer & Udry, 1985). Cunnilingus is more frequently reported than is fellatio by adolescents of both sexes.

"How far to go" in petting is often an issue. It can become a contest between the young man and woman, he trying to proceed as far as possible and she attempting to go only as far as is "respectable." Because "love" often motivates or justifies sexual behavior for girls, he may say "I love you" as a ploy to engage in further sexual behaviors.

However, petting is often not so narrowly goal-oriented, and it may constitute a form of sexual expression that offers both members of a couple the highly valued combination of safety and enjoyment. Petting can be an opportunity for young people to experience sexual intimacy while technically remaining virgins. The steps from holding hands to genital stimulation can progress with increasing emotional intimacy. Through petting adolescents begin to learn, within the context of an interpersonal relationship, about their own and their partners' sexual responses. They can develop a repertoire of pleasurable sexual behaviors without the risk of pregnancy, as the following account shows:

During adolescence sexual exploration and behavior generally increase.

One boy I went out with in high school and I had a great understanding. We both knew we were not ready for intercourse. Because of this mutual decision — and our mutual affection — we felt very free to experiment together and spent most of our dates making out for hours. (Authors' files)

This account illustrates not just the function petting serves as a sexual outlet but also the importance of a partner relationship in adolescent sexual behavior.

Ongoing Sexual Relationships

Despite the lingering double standard, data indicate that early petting and intercourse experiences are now more likely to be shared within the context of an ongoing relationship than they were in Kinsey's time. It appears that contemporary adolescents are most likely to be sexually intimate with someone they love or to whom they feel emotionally attached (Christopher & Cate, 1984 & 1988). Furthermore, there are noteworthy changes in both sexes that are narrowing the gender gap. There are indications that adolescent females are becoming more comfortable with having sex with someone they feel affection for rather than feeling they need to "save themselves" for a love relationship. At the same time, adolescent males are becoming increasingly inclined to have sex with someone they feel emotional connections with (affection or love) rather than engaging in sex with a casual acquaintance or stranger, which was once a typical pattern for adolescent males (Delamater & MacCorquodale, 1979; Farber, 1992; Sorenson, 1973; Zabin et al., 1984a).

Sexual Intercourse

Before beginning to discuss adolescent coital behavior, it is worthwhile to note a basic point of semantics that places some limitations on our interpretations of data.

A frequently quoted statistic in sex research is the number of people in a given category who have engaged in "premarital sex." As a statistic in sex surveys, premarital sex is defined as penile – vaginal intercourse that takes place between a couple before they are married. Do you believe this term may be misleading, and, if so, why? Think about this for a minute or two before reading on.

There are two reasons why the term *premarital sex* may be misleading. First, as a measure that is frequently used to indicate the changing sexual or moral values of American youth, it excludes a broad array of noncoital heterosexual and homosexual activities. We saw in the previous discussion that petting can include extensive noncoital types of sexual contact and that it often produces orgasm. For some people maintaining virginity prior to marriage may not reflect a lack of sexual activity. Second, the term *premarital* has connotations that may seem highly inappropriate to some people:

I really hate those survey questions that ask, "Have you engaged in premarital coitus?" What about those of us who plan to remain single? Does this mean we will be engaging in pre-

marital sex all of our lives? I object to the connotation that marriage is the ultimate state that all are supposed to evolve into. (Authors' files)

Despite these limitations of the term *premarital sex,* most of the statistics we have are based on this measure. We now turn to some of the available data on sexual intercourse during adolescence; then we look at two related areas, adolescent pregnancy and the use of contraceptives.

Incidence of Premarital Sex.   Even though many contemporary adolescents have not experienced sexual intercourse, the results of five major nationwide surveys reveal a strong upward trend in adolescent coitus over the last four decades (see Table 13.1). The most recent of these surveys, conducted by Mott and Haurin (1988), suggests that this trend leveled off in the 1980s. Further evidence of a curtailment of the upward trend is provided by a number of other studies (Gerrard, 1987; Hofferth et al., 1987; O'Connell & Rogers, 1984; Ostrov et al., 1986; Pratt et al., 1984; Sonenstein et al., 1991). There is, however, some indication that this leveling effect is not occurring among very young females, 15 and younger, who are engaging in intercourse in increasing proportions (Centers for Disease Control, 1991a; Hofferth et al., 1987; Orr et al., 1991).

In broad terms we can briefly summarize the major changes in adolescent coital activities in the last four decades. First, there has been an increase in the percentages of both young men and young women who have experienced premarital intercourse. Second, these increases have been considerably larger for females than for males. Finally, there are still fewer women than men who experience premarital intercourse. However, this difference between the sexes has been diminishing at a rapid rate.

The Effect of AIDS on Premarital Coital Rates and Teenage Sexual Behavior.
Many health professionals are concerned that American teens are particularly at risk for becoming infected with the AIDS virus (HIV) (Cates, 1991; Cora-Bramble et al., 1992; Kotloff et al., 1991; Metzler et al., 1992; Roscoe & Kruger, 1990; Wendell et al., 1992). Various surveys have shown that most adolescents in the United States are familiar with the basic facts about AIDS and are aware that high-risk activities

Percentage of Adolescents Who Reported Having Premarital Intercourse by Age 19			TABLE 13.1
	Females	**Males**	
Kinsey (1948, 1953)	20%	45%	
Sorenson (1973)	45%	59%	
Zelnick & Kantner (1977)	55%	No males in survey	
Zelnick & Kantner (1980)	69%	77%	
Mott & Haurin (1988)	68%	78%	

OTHER TIMES, OTHER PLACES

Cultural Variations in Childhood and Adolescent Sexuality

Humans are capable of experiencing sexual arousal and pleasure in the very earliest stages of their lives. However, adult acceptance of youthful sexuality, as well as the actual expression of such activity, shows enormous variation from one society to another. A few examples provide some indication of cultural diversity in this area of sexual behavior.

Many of the island societies of the South Pacific are very permissive about youthful sexual activity. Children of both sexes may engage in solo masturbation, group masturbation, and sex play with others, including manual manipulation, oral–genital contacts, and coitus. Children may receive extensive verbal instructions about sexual matters. In some areas they may be allowed to observe adult sexual activity.

Among the Mangaians of the South Pacific, children acquire a great deal of information about sexuality during their early years, as evidenced by their use of detailed vocabulary for describing sexual anatomy and function. (For example, they learn several

different terms for the clitoris.) In the 1950s Donald Marshall (1971) noted that it was quite common for an entire Mangaian family of 5 to 15 members to sleep in one room. Because a good deal of sexual activity occurred at night in this room, Mangaian children had innumerable opportunities to see and hear sexual activities. One of us, Bob Crooks, visited Mangaia in 1982 and noted that in recent years many of the island inhabitants have moved into larger homes with multiple sleeping areas, a change that may reduce the exposure of young people to sexual activity.

Like the Mangaians, the children of the Marquesas Islands in French Polynesia develop remarkable sophistication about sex early in life. They also sleep with their parents and siblings in one room, with ample opportunity to observe sexual activity. Marquesan boys begin masturbating around the age of two or three and may engage in same-sex group activities involving genital fondling by the age of five or six. Boys may also engage in casual homosexual contacts

during their youth. Marquesan girls also experience self-stimulation and homosexual contacts from an early age (Suggs, 1962).

Early childhood masturbation is common in other areas besides the South Pacific. Among the African Bala, children of both sexes are given free reign to masturbate from an early age. As in the Marquesas, Bala boys commonly engage in group masturbation.

Some of these permissive societies provide a rationale for prepubertal sexual activity. For example, the Chewa of Central Africa believe that sexual activity in children is essential to ensure adult fertility. The Lepcha of the southeastern Himalayas maintain that girls must be sexually active if they are to undergo normal growth as they develop into adulthood.

A few non-Western societies have strong prohibitions against self-stimulation similar to those of North American societies. For example, the African Ashanti forbid their children to masturbate. Little boys growing up in the Kwoma society of New Guinea

may lead to transmission of HIV (Roscoe & Kruger, 1990; Stevenson & Stevenson, 1991; Tucker & Cho, 1991). However, knowledge of these risks does not induce behavior changes in many teenagers at risk. The results of several recent studies of high school and college-age youths suggest that since most teenagers do not believe that they are at risk for contracting the virus that causes AIDS, most do not significantly alter their sexual behavior to avoid infection (Gray & Saracino, 1991; Maticka-Tyndale, 1991; Roscoe & Kruger, 1990; Sugarman, 1991). Thus knowledge of AIDS represents a necessary but apparently not sufficient condition for reduction of risky teenage sexual behavior (Andre & Bormann, 1991).

"Many adolescents believe AIDS is a concern only for 'other' people. These teenagers believe that AIDS affects only homosexual men and intravenous drug abusers or that they are not at risk because their sexual activity is infrequent. They do not see the threat of AIDS; therefore they will not take precautions" (Tucker & Cho, 1991, pp. 51–52). It is hoped that the recent announcement by the charismatic pro basketball star Earvin "Magic" Johnson, that he is HIV-infected, may help to alter the mistaken impression that AIDS happens only to "other" people.

live in fear of being caught with an erection. If they are, they may have their penises struck with a stick! Some Kwoma boys become so concerned about this possibility that they learn to urinate without touching their penises.

As with childhood sexual activity, an enormous cultural diversity exists in both attitudes toward and expression of adolescent premarital coital activity. Some societies, more restrictive than our own, apply strong punishments to individuals caught indulging in such behavior. At the other extreme, some societies encourage coital expression in unmarried young people.

The inhabitants of Romonum Island in the Truk group of the South Pacific are representative of some of the more permissive societies in this regard. The Romonum consider premarital coital activity to be both natural and desirable for both sexes starting in early adolescence. Teenage males are often introduced to coitus by older women. Initiation into coitus by older adults is also common among the Lepcha of the Himalayas. However, in the Lepcha society, it is typically the young female who, by age 11 or 12, may be engaging in intercourse with adult males.

First coital experiences occur at an even younger age in the Trobriand Islanders society, located in a group of islands off the coast of New Guinea. Here, girls as young as 6 and boys of 10 or 11 years have their first coital experiences with other children under adult tutelage.

The Marquesans also openly encourage coitus before marriage. Throughout adolescence it is considered normal for girls and boys to have frequent sexual relations. This is generally accomplished through the practice known as night-crawling, where boys enter their chosen lover's house at night and have sexual relations while other family members are sleeping nearby. The practice of night-crawling also occurs on the island of Mangaia. However, it appears that night-crawling has lost some of its appeal in the years since Marshall studied Mangaian society. Several of Crooks's adult informants in 1982 stated that it is now an uncommon practice. Some flatly denied it occurs. However, numerous youthful informants confirmed its continued existence, although in significantly altered form. It seems that parents have become less accepting of such behavior. An adolescent male caught in his lover's bedroom stands a good chance of being punished. Apparently, some Mangaian adolescents also disapprove of night-crawling. One 17-year-old woman adamantly stated to Crooks: "I'm a good girl— I'm not one of those."

What happens in permissive societies like those of Mangaia and the Marquesas when an "illegitimate" birth occurs? William Davenport provides a general answer. "Societies that permit or encourage premarital sex freedom are organized so that all children born outside marriage are fully provided for and in no way suffer social disabilities or stigma" (1978, p. 146).

The notion of the "personal fable" (Elkind, 1967) is relevant to a consideration of adolescent risk taking and sexual behavior. Adolescents are particularly susceptible to a kind of cognitive egocentrism, an illusionary belief pattern in which they view themselves as somehow invulnerable and immune to the consequences of dangerous and risky behavior (Brown et al., 1992; Gruber & Chambers, 1987; Tucker & Cho, 1991). Thus, large numbers of adolescents continue to engage in high-risk sexual behaviors, not because they are ignorant about AIDS and other sexually transmitted diseases (STDs), but rather because they falsely view themselves as being at very low (or no) risk of suffering negative consequences (Moore & Rosenthal, 1991).

Behaviors that put young people at risk for becoming infected with HIV include engaging in intercourse without condoms and spermicides; using alcohol, cocaine, and other drugs that impair judgment and reduce impulse control, thereby increasing one's inclination to engage in hazardous sexual activity; needle sharing among IV drug users; and exposing themselves to multiple sexual partners (Andre & Borman, 1991; Cates, 1991; Chitwood & Comerford, 1990; DiClemente et al., 1992; Orr et al., 1991; Smith et al., 1992; Wendell et al., 1992). The continuing trend toward a younger age of first intercourse is disturbing in that people who begin sexual activity by age 15 or younger tend to have significantly more lifetime sexual partners than those who begin having sexual intercourse at an older age (Cates, 1991). (Exposure to multiple sex partners is very high-risk sexual behavior — see Chapter 19.)

While there is some evidence of increased condom use among teenagers, those who use condoms as protection against unwanted pregnancies and STDs often do so inconsistently. "In every survey where the question was asked, less than half of teenagers who recently used condoms did so all the time" (Cates, 1991, p. 90). Family planning clinics have traditionally promoted condoms as a backup birth control method to those clients provided prescriptions for oral contraceptives. However, with growing awareness that female teenagers are at risk for HIV infection (and other STDs), most clinic counselors now encourage clients, even those on the pill, to regularly use condoms and spermicides to protect against STDs. Unfortunately, evidence suggests that women who use oral contraceptives seem reluctant to follow this advice. A recent study reported that of 308 teenage women who had received a prescription for oral contraceptives at a family planning clinic, only 16% used condoms consistently over a six-month period, in spite of the fact that 30% were judged to be at high risk for contracting HIV because of multiple sex partners. This finding suggests that "young women generally use condoms to prevent pregnancy, not STDs. The risk of disease transmission did not usually enter into their decision" (Weisman et al., 1991, p. 71).

It is hoped that national AIDS education efforts currently being implemented in America's schools will succeed in influencing adolescents both to understand and to accept their personal level of risk and to modify it, if necessary. Clearly, a reduction in coital activity among teenagers together with a move to safer sexual practices would serve to lower adolescents' risk for contracting HIV.

Homosexuality

A national survey of adolescent sexual behavior in the early 1970s (Sorenson, 1973) indicated that about 6% of adolescent females and 11% of adolescent males had experienced same-sex contact during their adolescent years. The great majority of these contacts took place not with older adults but between peers. These data, or the behaviors they describe, do not entirely reflect later orientation. Same-sex contact with the intent of sexual arousal can be either experimental and transitory or an expression of a lifelong sexual orientation. As we saw in Chapter 10, many homosexual individuals do not act on their sexual feelings until adulthood, and many people with heterosexual orientations have one or more early homosexual experiences.

Some people, however, do define themselves as homosexual during adolescence. This identification may create severe problems for the young person (Hersch, 1991; Remafed, 1987a & 1987b). It may begin with an awareness of having different feelings about sexual attractions than those commonly verbalized by peers; often a person will have a homosexual experience before she or he either applies a label of homosexuality to the behavior or understands its significance. Not being "part of the crowd" can be emotionally painful. It may be very difficult for young people to find confidants with whom they can share their concern or find guidance. Parents, ministers, physicians, and teachers often are unable to offer constructive help or support.

Most teenagers in America have little or no accurate information about homosexuality, and they may even be "activity denied objective information about the nature of sexual orientation and what it means to be gay or lesbian" (Bidwell & Deisher, 1991, p. 297). Furthermore, homosexual adolescents are often emotionally (if not physically) forsaken by their families and scorned by their peers (Hersch, 1991). The adolescent's dilemma is further complicated by the fact that homosexual organizations, although designed to provide assistance and support, are often reluctant to offer help to underage people because of possible legal action for "contributing to the delinquency of a minor." We hope that in the future there will be an increased societal acceptance of homosexuality that will help make this time of life easier for adolescents with homosexual orientations.

Adolescent Pregnancy

Although in recent years we have seen an improvement in the availability of both fertility education and reproductive health care services to American adolescents, the alarmingly high rate of teenage pregnancies in the United States continues to be a matter of urgent social concern. Our best estimate suggests that of the approximately 11 million unmarried adolescent females who are sexually active, about 1 million become pregnant each year (McGrew & Shore, 1991). Of these pregnancies, approximately 40% are aborted, 10% end in spontaneous abortions or stillbirths, and 50% result in live births (roughly one-fifth of all births annually in the United States) (Coll et al., 1987; Glasser et al., 1989; McGrew & Shore, 1991; Trussell, 1988). While the rate of births among adolescents had been declining through most of the 1970s and 1980s, recently released data from a national survey revealed a sharp increase in births among teenagers, commencing in 1987. This reversal was particularly pronounced among adolescent females in the 15 to 17 age group (National Center for Health Statistics, 1991).

These statistics represent a great deal of human suffering. A pregnant adolescent is more likely to have pregnancy complications than a woman in her 20s. These include toxemia, hemorrhage, miscarriages, and even maternal death (McGrew & Shore, 1991; Stevens-Simon & White, 1991). Adolescent pregnancy is also associated with a prenatal and infant mortality rate that is 200% higher than that exhibited among older pregnant women (Bright, 1987). However, recent research has shown that many of the adverse consequences of adolescent pregnancy have been overstated (Stevens-Simon & White, 1991; Trussell, 1988). Available data now indicate that many of these negative health consequences are primarily due to inadequate prenatal care among pregnant teenagers rather than to biological immaturity; "pregnancy outcomes among adolescents who receive good prenatal care are no different from, or are better than, those of older women" (Trussell, 1988, p. 268).

Unintended pregnancy and the decision to keep her child often have a serious negative impact on the adolescent mother's educational progress and financial

At least 1 out of every 11 unmarried American teenage women who are sexually active becomes pregnant each year, many of whom experience considerable hardship as a result of their pregnancies.

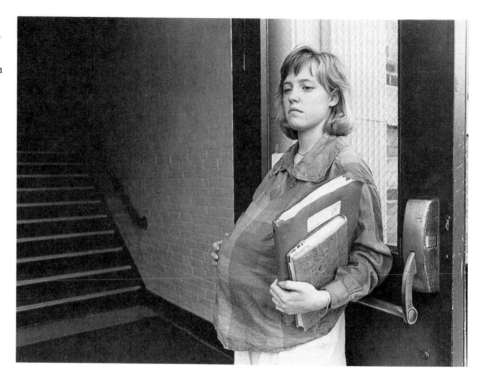

resources (McGrew & Shore, 1991; Teti & Lamb, 1989). Approximately 95% of unmarried adolescent mothers who give birth choose to keep their babies (Stevens-Simon & White, 1991). It is now illegal to bar teenagers who are pregnant or already mothers from public school. Nevertheless, a large number of these young women, perhaps as many as 80%, drop out of school and do not return (Felsman et al., 1987; Furstenberg et al., 1987; McGee, 1982; White & DeBlassie, 1992). Faced with the burden of child-care duties and an inadequate education, teenage mothers are highly likely to be underemployed or unemployed and dependent on welfare services (Felsman et al., 1987; Furstenberg et al., 1987; McGrew & Shore, 1991; Stevens-Simon & White, 1991). Furthermore, low education levels and limited employment skills severely limit the efforts of these young mothers to obtain economic independence as they move beyond their teenage years (Adams et al., 1989).

The negative impact of adolescent pregnancy is further exhibited in the lives of the resulting children. Teenage mothers often provide parenting of a lower quality than that of adult mothers (Lamb et al., 1987). Adolescent mothers, in comparison with older mothers, have also been shown to exhibit more abuse and/or neglect of their children (Felsman et al., 1987).

It has been widely reported that the offspring of teenage mothers are at a greater risk of having physical, cognitive, and emotional problems than are children of adult mothers (Dubow & Luster, 1990; Furstenberg et al., 1987; Huston et al., 1990; Stevens-Simon & White, 1991). These children of young mothers are also more likely to demonstrate deficits in intellectual ability and school performance than children of older mothers (Kinard & Reinherz, 1987; Trussell, 1988).

Use of Contraceptives

Despite the economic, lifestyle, and emotional stress pregnancy and parenthood often bring, and the availability of birth control today, consistent and effective contraceptive use is not widespread among sexually active American adolescents (DeClemente et al., 1992; Orr et al., 1992; Soskolne et al., 1991; Strassberg & Mahoney, 1988; Woods, 1991). A number of studies have revealed that many teenagers do not use any contraception at all the first few times they have sexual intercourse, and only a minority of teenagers consistently use a reliable method of birth control even after they have been sexually active for some time (Darling et al., 1992; Forrest & Singh, 1990; Furstenberg, 1984; Kisker, 1985; Zabin et al., 1984b). However, a recent study that compared data obtained from two national surveys found that the percentage of women aged 15 – 19 who used a contraceptive method in their first sexual intercourse rose from 48% in 1982 to 65% in 1988 (Forrest & Singh, 1990). Furthermore, additional data from two national surveys of adolescent males revealed that among 17 – 19-year-olds, condom use at last intercourse more than doubled from 1979 to 1988 — from 21% to 58% (Sonenstein et al., 1989). Another national survey revealed that among sexually active students in grades 9 – 12 in the 50 states, 77.7% of females and 77.8% of males used some form of contraception during their last intercourse (Centers for Disease Control, 1992a). It is, however, important to note that using contraceptives the first time and the last time is not the same as using them *every* time. Present data suggest that teenagers who use contraceptives often do so sporadically rather than consistently in each and every sexual encounter (Cates, 1991). In a more positive vein, data do indicate that as adolescent women increase their frequency of sexual intercourse, contraceptive risk taking sometimes decreases (De La Mater, 1983; Du Rant & Sanders, 1989). Studies have indicated that contraception is most likely to be employed by adolescents who are in established relationships (Baker et al., 1988). However, even adolescent couples involved in monogamous relationships in which contraception is discussed often use ineffective methods or are inconsistent in their use of more reliable techniques (Polit-O'Hara & Kahn, 1985).

Many professionals knowledgeable about teenage pregnancy believe that American culture contributes greatly to the high rate of adolescent pregnancies. The following quote provides a summary of this point of view:

> American teenagers seem to have inherited the worst of all possible worlds regarding their exposure to messages about sex: Movies, music, radio and TV tell them that sex is romantic, exciting, titillating; premarital sex and cohabitation are visible ways of life among the adults they see and hear about; their own parents or their parents' friends are likely to be divorced or separated but involved in sexual relationships. Yet, at the same time, young people get the message good girls should say no. Almost nothing that they see or hear about sex informs them about contraception or the importance of avoiding pregnancy. For example, they are more likely to hear about abortions than about contraception on the daily TV soap opera. Such messages lead to an ambivalence about sex that stifles communication and exposes young people to increased risk of pregnancy, out-of-wedlock births and abortions. (Jones et al., 1985, p. 61)

The preceding quote is from an article describing the results of an extensive, comparative study of adolescent pregnancy in a number of developed countries

(Jones et al., 1985). Besides the United States, five nations were studied in depth: Canada, England, France, Sweden, and the Netherlands. All five of these countries were found to have lower adolescent pregnancy rates than the United States. The incidence of teenage pregnancy in England, the nation with the second highest rate among the six, is less than half that of the United States. The two countries with the lowest incidence, Sweden and the Netherlands, have adolescent pregnancy rates less than one-fifth the American rate. Yet the available evidence indicates that the proportions of adolescent females who have experienced sexual intercourse are similar in all of these countries with the exception of Sweden, which has higher proportions of sexually experienced teenagers at all ages (Trussell, 1988). What then accounts for the pronounced differences in pregnancy rates? The authors of this landmark study suggested several possible contributing factors, three of which we discuss here.

First, "teenagers are much less likely to get free or very low-cost contraception services in the United States than in the other five countries studied in detail" (p. 54). One of the major problems with the American family planning clinic system is that it was originally developed primarily as a service to the poor. Consequently, teenagers often avoid birth control clinics, regarding them as places that serve only people on welfare. In contrast, adolescents in countries like Sweden and the Netherlands have access to a dense network of clinics, many of which are directed largely toward meeting the special needs of youth. Sweden is exemplary in having established a link between schools and contraceptive clinic services for adolescents. This link was initiated in 1975, just after Sweden liberalized its abortion laws. Many were concerned that increasing the availability of abortion might result in a marked rise in the number of abortions performed on teenagers. In fact, the adolescent abortion rate in Sweden has declined dramatically since school–clinic networking was established in 1975.

Second, the research team determined that the use of birth control pills is much less common among American teenagers than among the youth of the other five countries. This difference suggests that American adolescents use less effective birth control methods when they use anything at all.

Third, with the exception of Canada, school and community sex-education programs in the other five nations are much more extensive than in the United States. Sweden has established a compulsory sex-education curriculum in every school and for all grade levels. Sex education is enthusiastically supported by the vast majority of Swedish parents, most of whom had sex education while they were in school. In the Netherlands there is a national comprehensive sex education program from primary school onwards and the government encourages teaching of contraception by subsidizing mobile educational teams (Macfarlane & Mcpherson, 1992). In addition, the Dutch media present extensive information about contraception and other aspects of sexuality. Surveys of Dutch adolescents have revealed that knowledge of how to avoid pregnancy is virtually universal among them. In England and France, there is a national policy supporting the inclusion of sex education in the school curriculum. There is no such national policy in the United States or Canada.

This comparative study of adolescent pregnancy demonstrates that we need more readily available contraception and improved sex education if we are to reduce the increasing numbers of unwanted pregnancies. A number of surveys have revealed that many American adolescents, perhaps the majority, have little

Doonesbury

accurate knowledge about effective birth control. In addition, certain myths abound, such as the belief that a woman cannot get pregnant the first time she has intercourse or that infrequent coitus will not result in a pregnancy (Kisker, 1985; Ostrov et al., 1985; Trussell, 1988).

Inadequate knowledge is by no means the only reason for not using contraception. Another reason teenagers avoid birth control is that its use is an acknowledgment that one is planning to have intercourse. Some young people's attitudes reflect the value that the teenage woman who "does it" without contraceptive evidence of premeditation is more moral than the young woman who assumes responsibility for her sexual activity and uses birth control. This theme emerges in the responses we received from high school students when we asked them, "Why would a high school–age woman who didn't want to become pregnant *not* use birth control?"

She may feel guilty about planning ahead about sex.

She feels guilty. If she uses birth control, then she is admitting she is having sex.

Maybe people would think of her as a big sleaze if the word got out that she was on the pill or something.

Because she wants to consider it making love. (Authors' files)

Strategies for Reducing the Teenage Pregnancy Rate

What can be done to reverse the trend of escalating teenage pregnancies in America? In your opinion, what strategies might prove helpful in accomplishing this aim? Give this some thought before reading on.

Many authorities on adolescent sexuality agree that educational programs designed to increase adolescents' awareness of contraception and other aspects of sexuality will be much more effective if they treat sexuality as a positive aspect of our humanity rather than something that is wrong or shameful. An adolescent who has a positive and accepting attitude toward her or his sexuality is more likely to use contraceptives in an effective manner (Baker et al., 1988; Oettinger, 1979). In the European countries included in the previously discussed research, sex is viewed as natural and healthy, and there is widespread acceptance of teenage sexual activity. This stands in sharp contrast to the United States, where sex is romanticized and flaunted but also portrayed as something sinful or dirty that should be hidden (Jones et al., 1985).

We offer a list of suggestions for reducing teenage pregnancy, gleaned from the writings and research of several eminent investigators of adolescent sexuality.

1. The American family planning clinic system needs to be upgraded to provide free or low-cost contraceptive services to all adolescents who want them. Schools and the media should become more involved in publicizing the fact that these services are not limited to the poor. Of equal importance is the need to publicize the fact that clinics maintain the confidentiality of their clients. Many adolescents are reticent about visiting a family planning clinic because they think the clinic staff might contact their parents (Zabin & Clark, 1981).

2. The United States should follow the lead of several European nations, most notably Sweden, in establishing a compulsory national sex-education curriculum that is extended to all grade levels. Research data clearly reveal that teenagers who have been exposed to sex education are considerably less likely to become pregnant than those who have had no such education (Allen et al., 1990; Jones et al., 1985; Zelnick & Kim, 1982).

3. Ideally, sex-education programs provided by local school districts would be linked to family planning clinic services in a manner similar to the Swedish approach. A number of these programs, incorporating in-school sex education and counseling with clinic services, have been established in recent years (Barth et al., 1992; Kent, 1992; Kirby et al., 1991; Turque, 1987; Zabin et al., 1984b). By the early 1990s, about 300 of these school-based clinics were operating in junior and senior high schools across the United States (Kent, 1992). One good reason for anticipating positive results from these innovative programs is evidence linking ease of access and short travel time to clinics with effective contraceptive use among teenagers (Kent, 1992; Smith et al., 1987).

4. Efforts to educate adolescents in ways to prevent unwanted pregnancies must recognize that male attitudes are important for the practice and effectiveness of birth control (Glasser et al., 1989; Meyer, 1991). Adolescent boys often consider birth control to be their partners' responsibility (Cohen & Rose, 1984; Pleck et al., 1988). When we asked teenage men "Why would a high school–age man who did not want to be a father have sexual intercourse and *not* use a condom?" their responses included the following:

He may have thought that it was the girl's problem, not his.

He probably didn't want it to seem planned.

Because he didn't like the feeling of the rubber.

Embarrassed about putting them on. (Authors' files)

Educational posters aimed at teenagers attempt to combat adolescent pregnancies.

Sex-education programs should stress that responsibility for contraception is best shared by both parties. A survey of several thousand American teenagers revealed that respondents who believed responsibility for pregnancy prevention should be shared were more likely to have used effective contraception than those who felt the responsibility belonged to one or the other partner (Zabin et al., 1984a).

5. Government agencies should continue a trend toward relaxing the restrictions on the distribution and advertising of nonprescription contraceptives, particularly the condom.

In summary, we hope that in the years to come we will see widespread efforts to increase the legitimacy and availability of contraception, as well as broadly focused sex-education programs that will help reduce teenage pregnancy rates in America.

Sex Education

Many parents today want to provide some input into the sexual education of their children. Societal values about sex are rapidly changing, and we are all exposed to an abundance of contrasting opinions. How much should children see, or how much should they be told? Many parents — even some of those who are comfortable with their own sexuality — have difficulty judging the "best" way to act and react toward their children's sexuality.

Perhaps the information that we offer in the following paragraphs will help modify some of this uncertainty. We do not profess to have the last word on raising sexually healthy children, so we advise you to read this material with a critical eye. Along the way, however, you may acquire some new insights that will aid in your efforts to provide meaningful sex education for your children, either now or in the future.

We are often asked, "When should we start telling our children about sex?" One answer is, "When the child begins to ask the questions." It seems typical for children to inquire about sex along with the myriad of other questions they ask about the world around them. Research has indicated that by about age four, most children begin asking questions about how babies are made (Martinson, 1980). What is more natural than a query about where you came from? Yet this curiosity is often stopped short by parental response. A flushed face and a few stammering words, a cursory "Wait till your mother (or father) comes home to ask that question," or "You're not old enough to learn about such things" are a few of the common ways communication in this vital area is blocked before it has a chance to begin. Putting questions off at this early age means that you may be confronted with the potentially awkward task of starting a dialogue on sexual matters at a later point in your children's development.

It can be helpful for parents to include information about sex (when appropriate) in everyday conversations that their children either observe or in which they participate. Accomplishing this with a sense of ease and naturalness may increase the comfort with which the children introduce their own questions or observations about sex.

If a child's questions either do not arise spontaneously or get sidetracked at an early age, there may be a point when you as a parent will feel it is important to begin to talk about sexuality. Perhaps a good starting point is to share your true feelings with your child — that possibly you are a bit uneasy about discussing sex or that maybe you are confused about some of your own feelings or beliefs. There is something very human about a parent who can express his or her own indecision or vulnerability to a child. This may be all you will say during this initial effort, simply indicating your feelings and leaving the door open to future discussions. An incubation period is often valuable, allowing a child to reassess her or his interpretation of your willingness to talk about sexuality. If no questions follow this first effort, it might be wise to select a specific area for discussion. Some suggested open-ended questions for a not too stressful beginning might be (a) How do you feel about the changes in your body? (b) What are some of the things that the kids at school say about sex? and (c) What are your feelings about birth control? Is it "proper"? Who should be responsible, male or female or both?

Understandably, parents sometimes have a tendency to overload a child who asks a question expecting a relatively brief, straightforward answer. For example, when a five-year-old inquires "Where did I come from?" he or she is probably not asking for a detailed treatise on the physiology of sexual intercourse and conception. In such cases it may be more helpful to just briefly discuss the basics of sexual intercourse, perhaps including the idea of potential pleasure in such sharing. It is also a good idea to check to see if your child has understood your answer to his or her question. In addition, you might wish to ask if you have provided the information that was desired and also to indicate that you are open to any other questions. When young children want more information, they will probably ask for it, provided an adult has been responsive to their initial questions.

Some parents may feel that it is inappropriate to tell their children that sexual interaction is pleasurable. Others may conclude that there is value in discussing the joy of sex with their offspring, as revealed in the following account:

One evening, while sitting on my daughter's bed and discussing the day's events, she expressed some concern over her next-door playmate's announcement that her father was going to purchase a stud horse. Apparently, she had been told to have me build a higher fence to protect her mare. She asked why this was necessary. Actually, she knew all about horses mating, as evidenced by her quick acknowledgment of my brief explanation. However, such commentary on my part did produce the following inquiry, "Do you and Mom do that?" to which I replied, "Yes." "Do my uncle and aunt do that?" Again the affirmative response, which produced the final pronouncement, "I don't think I'll get married." Clearly, she was experiencing some strong ambivalence about what this sexual behavior meant to her. It seemed of critical importance to make one more statement, namely that not only did we do this but that it is a beautiful and pleasurable kind of sharing and lots of fun! (Authors' files)

Reluctance to express the message that sex can be enjoyable may stem from parents' concern that their children will rush right out to find out what kind of good times they have been missing. Yet there is little evidence to support such apprehension. There are, however, many unhappy lovers striving to overcome early messages about the dirtiness and immorality of sex.

There are some topics that may never get discussed, at least not at the proper time, unless parents are willing to take the initiative. We are referring to certain aspects of sexual maturing that the child may not consider until he or she experiences them. These include menstruation, first ejaculation, and nocturnal (nighttime) orgasms. The desirability of preparing girls for their first period well in advance of the event has been well documented. Nevertheless, a majority of women students in our classes have said that they knew little or nothing about menstruation until they were given sketchy accounts by peers or actually had their first period. It is also typical for males to be unaware of their potential for ejaculating when masturbating. Experience with first menstruation or ejaculation can come as quite a shock to the unprepared, as revealed in the following two anecdotes:

I hadn't even heard of menstruation when I first started bleeding. No one was home. I was so frightened I called an ambulance. (Authors' files)

I remember well the first time I ejaculated during masturbation. At first I couldn't believe it when something shot out of my penis. The only thing I could figure is that I had whipped up my urine. However, considering earlier lectures from my mother about the evils of "playing with yourself," I was afraid that God was punishing me for my sinful behavior. (Authors' files)

It is important that youngsters be aware of these impending physiological changes before they actually happen. A child's natural curiosity about sex may cause him or her to discuss these topics with friends, who are usually not the most reliable sources of information. It is certainly better for parents to provide a more accurate description of natural events like menstruation and ejaculation.

Some parents may find it relatively easy to discuss menstruation but quite difficult to discuss nocturnal orgasms or first ejaculations because of their associations with sexual activity. However, discussion of these events can also provide an opportunity to talk about self-pleasuring. Females as well as males may experience nocturnal orgasms. The fact that girls have no ejaculate to deal with does not eliminate possible confusion or guilt over the meaning of these occurrences.

When I was a little girl, I began to have these incredibly erotic dreams that sometimes produced indescribably good sensations. Looking back on it now, I realize these were my first experiences with nighttime orgasms. At the time I thought it was awful to have such good feelings connected with such wicked thoughts. I wish someone had told me then that my experiences were normal. It certainly would have eliminated a lot of unnecessary anxiety. (Authors' files)

Most young people prefer that their parents be the primary source of sex information and that their mothers and fathers share equally in this responsibility (Bennett, 1984; Sanders & Mullis, 1988). To the extent that parents do take an active role in the sex education of their children, mothers are far more likely than are fathers to fulfill this function (Coreil & Parcel, 1983; Thornburg, 1981). Unfortunately, most American parents do not provide sex education to their children (Fox, 1981; Sanders & Mullis, 1988). Recent research has revealed that even in families characterized by close and open communication between parents and children, sex is often not discussed (Fisher, 1987). Several studies have shown that friends are the principal source of information about sex for young people in the United States (Gebhard, 1977; Papin et al., 1988; Sorenson, 1973; Thornburg, 1981; Thornburg & Aras, 1986). Thus, the gap created by lack of information in the home is likely to be filled with incorrect information from peers and other sources. Such information can have serious consequences; for example, an adolescent may hear from friends that a girl will not get pregnant if she only has intercourse "now and then." Peers may also encourage traditional gender-role behavior, and they often put pressure on each other to become sexually active. Thus the challenge for parents is whether they want to become actively involved in their children's sex education, thereby minimizing some of the pitfalls faced by children and adolescents who turn to their peers for sex (mis)information.

Parents may hesitate to discuss sex with their children because they are concerned that such communication may encourage early sexual experimentation. However, there is no evidence that sex education leads to sexual activity. In fact, a number of studies have indicated that young people whose parents play a major role in their sex education are not as likely to engage in early sexual activity as are their less-informed counterparts (Brody et al., 1976; Goldfarb et al., 1977; Lewis, 1973; Spanier, 1977). More recently, several studies have raised doubts about whether open parent–child communication about sex actually reduces an adolescent's likelihood to engage in premarital sex (Darling & Hicks, 1982; Fisher, 1987 & 1988; Newcomer & Udry, 1985). However, none of this research supports the fear that such communication actually encourages children to experiment sexually. Furthermore, there is ample evidence that adolescent children who talk openly with their parents about sexual matters, including contraception, are far more

Although opposition to sex education in the schools continues, a majority of parents support the idea.

likely to use effective and consistent birth control than those teenagers who do not talk to their parents about sex (Baker et al., 1988; Fox, 1981; Milan & Kilmann, 1987; Shah & Zelnick, 1981).

Parents may also be reticent to become involved in educating their children about sexuality because they are unsure of how and what to communicate about this important topic. In response to this concern, sexuality educators have implemented educational programs for parents in a number of U.S. cities. The impact of one of these programs, based in San Antonio, Texas, was recently analyzed (Huston et al., 1990). In this study, 47 parents participated in four 2-hour classroom sessions that included both factual information and exercises designed to "enhance the participants' communication skills and knowledge about sexual issues" (p. 627). Discussions covered such topics as sexual anatomy, puberty, peer pressure, teenage sexual activity, contraception and pregnancy, and sexually transmitted diseases. Information obtained from participating parents via questionnaires administered before the program commenced and after it was completed revealed a significant increase in parent–child communication about sex. This finding prompted the investigators to conclude that "parent–child communication about sex can be facilitated by an educational program for parents" (p. 626).

In response to the frequent lack (or insufficiency) of information from the home and the inaccuracy of much of the information from peers, other social institutions are attempting to provide sex education. Some schools have included sex education as part of the curriculum, although the quality and extent of these programs varies considerably.

Various surveys have revealed that a majority of parents support the idea of having sex education in schools but that only a minority of American schools offer sex education courses, many of which are woefully incomplete (Alexander, 1984; Fisher, 1991; Kenney et al., 1989; Orr, 1982; Whatley, 1987). Public school sex-education programs are often hampered by pressures from well-organized and highly vocal minorities opposed to such education. In response to these pressures, many school systems completely omit sex education from their curricula, and others attempt to avert controversy by allowing only discussions of "safe" topics such as reproduction and anatomy (Whatley, 1987). As a consequence, some important areas for discussion, such as interpersonal aspects of sexuality and preventing pregnancy, are entirely overlooked. In a survey of several hundred adolescents, only about 1 out of 10 indicated that their school was teaching them what they wanted to know about sex. The top five topics they wanted to learn about, in order of importance, included feelings about the other sex, birth control, pregnancy and parenthood, abortion, and how to decide about sex (Ostrov et al., 1985). School sex education is further limited by the fact that it is typically provided during the late stages of high school, a time when most adolescents have already begun sexual experimentation.

An argument sometimes expressed by those opposed to sex education in the schools is that such programs promote sexual experimentation. There are no data to support these claims. Quite the contrary, research has strongly suggested that while formal sex-education programs promote neither experimentation nor restraint, they do tend to improve knowledge, reduce high-risk sexual behavior, enhance communication with parents and partners, and contribute to more effective use of contraception (Cora-Bramble et al., 1992; Eisen & Zellman, 1987; Green & Sollie, 1989; Weis et al., 1992).

Androgynous Child Rearing and Sexuality

The idea of rearing children in an androgynous fashion has much to offer to parents anxious to minimize the limiting influence of gender-role expectations in the lives of their children. As discussed in Chapter 3, the term *androgyny* is used to describe flexibility in gender roles. In this sense, androgynous child rearing means raising a child in a way that encourages selection of whatever feminine or masculine behaviors feel good to him or her.

On numerous occasions in this text, we have expressed our belief that strict adherence to stereotypic gender roles may have a detrimental effect on sexual functioning. The examples are many, ranging from the man who is unable to express emotion and tenderness because it is not "masculine" to do so, to the woman who has great difficulty communicating her sexual needs because she has been conditioned to be passive. Many parents may wish to counteract these limiting influences through the manner in which they rear their children. Perhaps such things as reassuring little boys that it is okay to cry and reinforcing girls for appropriate expressions of assertiveness will help offset the impact of rigid gender roles.

Encouraging a child to develop as a human being first and a male or female second is a developmental goal that is receiving increasing support in our society.

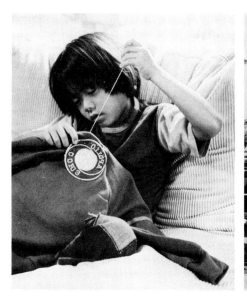 

People who do not conform to traditional gender-role stereotypes have more alternatives available to them.

Those inclined to agree with the philosophy and intent of this evolving concept of androgyny may find the most fertile ground for its implementation in the home environment.

One of the truly striking aspects of a gender-role dominated society is that boys and girls grow up playing primarily with same-sex peers. Little girls get together to see who has the latest Barbie doll fashions and boys shoot each other with mock guns. Other than dating in adolescence, this same-sex pairing generally holds up throughout the developmental years. There may be many effects of this separation of the sexes, not the least of which is the awkwardness and lack of spontaneity that characterizes many man–woman relationships. The separation of the sexes may often seem to be self-imposed — girls frequently do not want to play with boys and vice versa. However, a contributing factor may sometimes be adult approval of sex-specific play activities. Many now believe that it is acceptable for boys to play with dolls and girls to push trucks through dirt piles. Would children play so consistently in same-sex groups if gender-neutral activities were encouraged more?

Besides encouraging or discouraging types of play, parental modeling is also an important influence in rearing children in an androgynous fashion (Sedney, 1987). Parents who feel comfortable sharing child care and housework can provide models of androgynous behavior for their developing children. It may be particularly valuable to engage in behaviors that are markedly different from traditional gender-role stereotypes. For example, Dad may cook dinner or change diapers, while Mom works late at the office, changes the oil in the car, and so on.

We believe that people raised in an androgynous fashion may enjoy freedom to behave sensitively and sensibly, and that by lifting restrictive notions about "acting like a lady" or "being a man," adults can encourage their children to have a broader outlook. This potential is one of the possible benefits of this alternative approach to parenting.

Parents can provide models of nonstereotypical behavior for their developing children.

Summary

The traditional view of infancy and childhood as a time when sexuality remains unexpressed is not supported by research findings.

Infants of both sexes are born with the capacity for sexual pleasure and response, and some experience observable orgasm.

Sexual Behavior During Childhood

Self-administered genital stimulation is common among boys and girls during the first two years of life.

Sex play with other children, which may occur as early as the age of two or three, increases in frequency during the five-to-seven age range.

Separation of the sexes becomes pronounced by the age of eight or nine. However, romantic interest in the other sex and curiosity about sexual matters are typically quite high during this stage of development.

The ages of 10 and 11 are marked by keen interest in body changes, continued separation of the sexes, and a substantial incidence of homosexual encounters.

Masturbation is one of the most common sexual expressions during the childhood years. It is the most frequent source of preadolescent orgasm for both sexes.

The Physical Changes of Adolescence

Puberty refers to the physical changes that occur in response to increased hormone levels. These physical developments include maturation of the reproductive organs and consequent menstruation in girls and ejaculation in boys.

Sexual Behavior During Adolescence

The sexual double standard often pressures males to view sex as a conquest and places females in a double bind about saying yes or no.

The number of adolescents who masturbate increases between the ages of 13 and 19.

Petting is a common sexual behavior among adolescents. One-half of adolescent girls and two-thirds of adolescent boys have engaged in petting to the point of orgasm.

Adolescent sexual expression is now more likely to take place within the context of an ongoing monogamous relationship than it was during Kinsey's time.

A significant increase in the number of both young men and young women who experience intercourse by age 19 has occurred over the last four decades. These increases have been considerably more pronounced among females.

Homosexual experiences during adolescence can be experimental or an expression of permanent sexual orientation.

Adolescent Pregnancy

One in 11 sexually active adolescent females becomes pregnant each year. Adolescent pregnancy is often associated with social, medical, educational, and financial difficulties.

The majority of adolescents who have intercourse do not regularly use contraceptives.

The low rate of contraceptive use among American adolescents seems to be related to a number of factors including inadequate availability of free or low-cost contraceptive services, minimal use of the most effective birth control methods, inadequate school sex-education programs, and an attitude among teenagers that assuming responsibility for birth control implies an immoral character.

Strategies for reducing the teenage pregnancy rate in America include upgrading the family planning clinic system, establishing a compulsory national sex-education curriculum, linking school programs to contraceptive clinics, educating males about their contraceptive responsibility, and relaxing government restrictions on the distribution and advertising of nonprescription contraceptives, especially condoms.

Sex Education

One answer to the question of when to start discussing sex with our children is, "When they start asking questions." If communication does not spontaneously occur, it may be helpful for parents to initiate dialogue, perhaps by simply sharing their feelings or asking nonstressful, open-ended questions.

Some important topics — particularly menstruation, first ejaculation, and nocturnal orgasms — are rarely discussed unless parents take the initiative.

Although the majority of adolescents prefer their parents to be the primary source of sex information, evidence indicates that peers are considerably more likely than parents to provide this information, often in a biased and inaccurate manner.

Research indicates that formal sex-education programs promote neither experimentation nor restraint, but they do tend to improve knowledge, enhance communication about sexual concerns, and contribute to more effective use of contraception.

Androgynous Child Rearing and Sexuality

Besides encouraging a child to develop her or his potential, androgynous child rearing practices help break down the stereotypical gender roles that often have a negative effect on sexual functioning.

⤳ *Thought Provokers* ⤳

1. Assume that you are a parent of a seven-year-old and that one day you find your child "playing doctor" with a playmate of the same age of the other sex. Both have lowered their pants, and they seem to be involved in visually exploring each other's body. How would you respond? Would you react differently according to the sex of your child?

2. Should parents provide birth control devices to their teenage children who are actively dating or going steady?

3. It has been suggested that rearing children in an androgynous fashion may foster uncertainty and lead to confusion over their proper roles in society. Do you agree with this assertion? Why or why not?

4. There is evidence that women who have had a history of masturbating to orgasm during their childhood or adolescence have an increased probability of experiencing satisfactory sexual relations as adults. In view of this finding, do you think it is appropriate for parents to encourage their female children to engage in self-pleasuring?

Suggested Readings

Anthony, James; Green, Richard; and Kolodny, Robert (1982). *Childhood Sexuality*. Boston: Little, Brown. This book provides comprehensive information about childhood and adolescent sexuality.

Byrne, Dann; and Fisher, William (Eds.) (1983). *Adolescents, Sex, and Contraception*. Hillsdale, N.J.: Erlbaum. A thoughtful, accurate discussion of many aspects of adolescent sexuality.

Calderone, Mary; and Johnson, Eric (1981). *The Family Book About Sexuality*. New York: Harper & Row. This excellent book, helpful for both parents and children, offers practical advice and valuable insights into childhood sexuality.

Calderone, Mary; and Ramey, James (1982). *Talking with Your Child About Sex*. New York: Random House. This excellent book provides practical and wise advice for parents who wish to raise sexually healthy children.

Furstenberg, Frank (1987). *Adolescent Mothers in Later Life*. New York: Cambridge University Press. This excellent book, based on a long-term study of adolescent mothers, provides an informative discussion of the problems of adapting to teenage motherhood.

Hanckel, Frances; and Cunningham, John (1979). *A Way of Love, A Way of Life*. New York: Lothrop, Lee and Shepard. This sensitive, thoughtful book gives young people information about what it means to be homosexual.

Leight, Lynn (1990). *Raising Sexually Healthy Children*. New York: Avon. This well-written, insightful book provides a wealth of information to parents who wish to provide an atmosphere conducive to the development of positive sexual attitudes and healthy sexual behavior in their children.

Pogrebin, Letty (1980). *Growing Up Free: Raising Your Child in the '80s*. New York: McGraw-Hill. An important source for parents who wish to rear their children in an androgynous fashion.

Love seems the swiftest, but it is the slowest of all growths. No man or woman knows what perfect love is until they have been married a quarter of a century.

Mark Twain
Notebook (1894)

CHAPTER 14

Sexuality and the Adult Years

Single Living

Cohabitation

Marriage

Extramarital Relationships

Divorce

Widowhood

*I*ntimate relationships occupy a position of considerable significance in many adults' lives. An adult's relationship status — as single, married, or living with someone — becomes an important social concern, as well as an important element in that person's self-identity. A person's relationship status may also have considerable influence on the kinds of sexual interactions he or she experiences during the adult years. This chapter examines several alternatives for lifestyles and intimate relationships, which have been undergoing transition in recent years.

Single Living

Increasing numbers of people in our society are opting to remain single and postpone marriage. This increase is most pronounced among people in their 20s and early 30s. For example, a comparison of 1970 and 1990 census figures reveals that the percentage of men in the 20 – 24 age range who had not yet married increased from 55% in 1970 to 79% in 1990. Comparable figures for women demonstrated an increase from 36% to 63%. The proportion of never married for 25- to 29-year-olds more than doubled for men (from 19% to 45%) and tripled for women (from 11% to 31%) (U.S. Bureau of the Census, 1991a). The number of American households composed of only one person increased approximately 40% in the period between 1970 and 1990 (Hoffman, 1992). Persons living alone represented 25% of the total number of households in the United States in 1990 (U.S. Bureau of the Census, 1990).

These figures seem to represent a shift in adult living patterns. In the past, a far smaller percentage of adults either divorced or remained unmarried. Various factors contribute to the increasing numbers of single adults; these include people marrying at a later age, an increase in the numbers of those who never marry, more women placing career objectives ahead of marriage, an increase in the number of couples living together outside of marriage, rising divorce rates, a greater emphasis on advanced education, and an increase in the number of women who no longer must depend on marriage to ensure their economic stability (Current Population Reports, 1985; Glick & Norton, 1979; Riche, 1988). The figures also reflect what may be a change in societal attitudes. Until recently in the United States, a stigma was often attached to remaining single. This stigma applied particularly to women, as terms such as *old maid* and *spinster* indicate. (Single men would most likely be referred to by the less negative term *bachelor*.) Today these terms are heard less frequently, and it is quite possible that remaining single, either as an option to first marriage or following termination of a marriage, will play an increasingly prominent role in American culture. If this happens, we may also witness a reduction in the number of people who marry primarily for convention's sake or to avoid the negative perception of the single state. Nevertheless, single life is still often seen as the period before, in between, or after marriage.

A survey of 482 single Canadian adults in several major population centers provided both indications of what motivates people to remain single and a sense of how satisfied they are with single life (Austrom & Hanel, 1985). Almost half of the respondents considered themselves single by deliberate choice and not as a result of chance or circumstances beyond their control. The vast majority of the

482 did not believe that they were single because they were reluctant to be committed to an exclusive relationship, because they lacked desire for sexual relations with the other sex, or because high divorce rates made them apprehensive about marriage. Rather, most indicated that they were unmarried "simply because they had not met the right person and also because their expectations of a marriage partner were very high" (p. 17). There were some sex differences in the reasons expressed for being single. Women had a greater tendency to attribute their singleness to caution due to bad experiences with previous relationships. On the other hand, men were more inclined to say that there were too many interesting people to choose among. There were no sex differences in reported satisfaction with single life. Forty-seven percent indicated dissatisfaction with their present status, and the rest were either neutral (28%) or satisfied (25%). Levels of satisfaction did not seem to be a function of whether the respondents were never-married, divorced, or widowed. Being satisfied with the number and types of friends they had was positively correlated with feeling good about being single. "These results suggest that satisfaction with single life is, to some degree, a function of expressive social support, especially in the interpersonal areas of friendship and community life" (p. 19).

Single living encompasses a range of sexual lifestyles and differing levels of personal satisfaction. Levels of sexual activity among single people vary widely, just as they do among marrieds. However, evidence has suggested that singles are likely to be as sexually active as married people (Petersen et al., 1983). Some people who live alone remain celibate by choice or because of lack of available partners. Others may be involved in a long-term, sexually exclusive relationship with one partner. Some practice *serial monogamy,* moving through a succession of sexually exclusive relationships. Still others prefer concurrent sexual and emotional involvements with a number of different partners. Some single people develop a primary relationship with one partner and have occasional sex with others.

Single living is becoming more acceptable in our society. However, the majority of people still choose to enter into a long-term relationship with a partner, even though it may not be a lifelong bond. There are several kinds of long-term sexual relationships, and we examine these various options in most of the remainder of this chapter.

Cohabitation

When I was a college student in the early 1960s, the possibility of living with someone dear to me, without the sanctity of marriage, simply never entered my mind. When I met a very special person and found myself wishing for the intimacy of sharing a home together, marriage was my only option. Although we were sexual prior to marriage, there were no occasions when we even took a weekend trip together. The topic of unmarrieds living together was never discussed, although I did occasionally hear a hushed reference to someone "living in sin." (Authors' files)

This account reflects a prevalent societal attitude toward **cohabitation** (living together in a sexual relationship without being married), and this attitude has only recently begun to undergo change. In the past few decades, there has been a significant increase in both the number of people choosing this living arrangement and societal acceptance of what was once an unconventional practice. Census Bureau figures revealed that by 1990 unmarried couples living together in the United States numbered 2.9 million, an 80% increase during the past decade and more than quadruple the 523,000 cohabiting couples in 1970 (U.S. Bureau of the Census, 1991). It appears that cohabitation is now well established as a social phenomenon. In 1980 the Census Bureau formally acknowledged cohabitation by announcing a new category: POSSLQ (Persons of Opposite Sex Sharing Living Quarters).

This dramatic increase in cohabitation has been attributed to American youth's growing inclination to question traditional mores, particularly those pertaining to the value of marriage. These questioning attitudes are supported by an expanding societal awareness that sexuality is an important part of a person's life and that marriage is not the only lifestyle that legitimizes sexual relations. In addition, some social theorists have pointed to the increased availability and variety of birth control methods as influencing people's decision to live together outside of matrimony. Furthermore, living together may provide some people with a sense of being protected from the risks associated with AIDS and other sexually transmitted diseases. In the last few years, there are also indications that an increasing number of couples view their cohabitation not as a precursor to marriage but rather as an end in itself (Riche, 1988).

Many couples prefer the relative informality of cohabitation arrangements to the more official aspects of a marriage. They appreciate the sense of living together because they want to, not as a result of the binding power of a legal contract, as the following account demonstrates:

I object to people constantly asking us when we are going to get married. We live together because it feels good and because it seems like a reasonable thing to do. Neither one of us has any intention of ever getting married, to each other or to anyone else. We have been together for over two years and plan to continue for a long time. One thing is certain. We are together because we want to be, not because we are in some kind of "training for marriage." (Authors' files)

The informality of living together may have other advantages. A couple may not feel as pressured to take on the new and demanding roles of wife and husband. As a result the relationship is less likely to produce the sort of "identity crisis" that may follow when people try to live up to the social expectations attached to these roles. Another perceived advantage may be that if the relationship is not satisfactory, the stigma of failure is less than with a divorce. This does not necessarily mean that it is easy to break up after living together; terminating such a relationship can be very traumatic.

While living together offers some advantages to many couples, it also poses certain unique problems. Many of these problems stem from lack of social acceptance for this arrangement. Disapproval on the part of parents and other family members can sometimes be severe — a situation that can place considerable emotional strain on one or both partners. Some couples may also have difficulty renting or buying property together, although this problem is becoming less common. Owning property jointly does present other potential difficulties, however. Who owns the property and financial assets a former couple have shared? Without a clear written contract, legal rights upon dissolution of the relationship are less

Many college students who cohabit value sharing the day-to-day activities of living together.

clear than with a divorce. Death of one or both partners can result in legal confusion in addition to the emotional trauma. Again, unless the couple has had the foresight to write a contract or to maintain up-to-date wills, there is no clearly established legal definition of partnership rights.

The Social Impact of Living Together

The popular point of view among college students is that living together will result in happier and more stable marriages. In this view, cohabiting allows two people to explore their compatibility before making a long-term commitment. Trial experiences with the struggles and joys of an everyday relationship help individuals to identify their own needs and expectations.

The opposing view is that living together will have an overall negative impact on a possible future marriage, particularly its long-term stability. Faced with conflict, individuals who are living together may find it easier to end the relationship than to work together to resolve their problems. Once the pattern of breaking up when significant difficulties arise has been established, people may be more likely to respond to marital conflict in the same way.

What is your opinion regarding the possible impact of cohabitation on a subsequent marriage? Think about this question before reading on.

Perhaps neither of these standard views is correct, and cohabitation has no demonstrable effect on a subsequent marriage. Some evidence supports this contention. In one study, couples who had lived together before marriage were just

DOONESBURY   **by Garry Trudeau**

as likely to divorce as those who did not (Newcomb & Bentler, 1980). Another study of university students examined whether cohabitation (with either the future spouse or someone else) had any influence on subsequent marital happiness. It found no differences between cohabiters and noncohabitors on several measures, including relationship stability, sexual satisfaction, physical intimacy, and openness of communication (Jacques & Chason, 1979). A third study, in which couples were evaluated in the fourth year of their marriages, suggested that the premarital relationships of these pairs, whether traditional courtship or cohabitation, did not have a long-term effect on their marital adjustment (Watson & DeMeo, 1987).

Other research has produced results that do not support the findings of these three investigations. One study, which used interview data from a national sample of married persons, reported a moderate link between cohabitation and low marital satisfaction (Booth & Johnson, 1988). Another study of more than 300 couples found that cohabitation with one's future spouse was associated with significantly lower perceived quality of communication for wives and significantly lower marital satisfaction for both partners (DeMaris & Leslie, 1984). In still another study, data from the National Survey of Families and Households revealed that 53% of first marriages preceded by cohabitation failed within 10 years in contrast to 28% of those marriages where the couple did not live together before marriage (Riche, 1988). Finally, a recent analysis of data obtained from a national long-term study of Americans representative of high school graduates in 1972 "found that cohabiting prior to marriage, regardless of the nature of the cohabitation, is associated with an enhanced risk of later marital disruption" (DeMaris & Rao, 1992, p. 189).

Further research is necessary to clarify the nature of the relationship between cohabitation and marriage and to explain why cohabiters seem to have a higher risk of marital discord than their noncohabiting counterparts. One thing we can say with some confidence: People do not appear to be permanently substituting living-together arrangements for marriage. Despite the rapidly changing societal mores pertaining to human relationships and sexual expression, Census Bureau statistics reveal that about 9 out of every 10 adults in the United States marry, some more than once. Recent statistics show that the number of new marriages each year per 1000 U.S. residents has declined only slightly from 1970 to 1991 (see Table 14.2 later in the chapter). A closer look at the institution of marriage may provide some insight into its continuing appeal.

Marriage

Marriage is an institution that is found in virtually every society. It has traditionally served several functions, both personal and social. It provides societies with stable family units that help perpetuate social norms because children are typically taught society's rules and expectations by parents or kinship groups. In many cultures marriage defines inheritance rights to family property. Marriage performs an important function by structuring an economic partnership that ties child support and subsistence tasks into one family unit. Marriage regulates sexual behavior to maintain the family line. It also provides a framework for fulfilling people's needs for social and emotional support.

Although marriage is integral to most cultures, it assumes many different forms (Gaylin, 1991). Western society has defined its own marriage ideal. Within this ideal we can isolate a number of elements that many people take for granted—for instance, legality, permanence, heterosexuality, sexual exclusivity, emotional exclusivity, and monogamy (one man and one woman). But the elements that are traditional to marriage in most Western cultures are not necessarily the same in other societies. For example, some societies have marriages between one man and several women (polygyny); others (far less common) have recognized unions between one woman and several men (polyandry).

Changing Expectations and Marital Patterns

The institution of marriage has been both condemned and venerated in contemporary America. Currently, a large discrepancy exists between the American marriage ideal and actual marriage practices. Cohabitation, high divorce rates, and widespread extramarital sexual involvements are all antithetical to the traditional ideal of marriage.

Some of the reasons for contradictions between ideal and actual marriage practices have to do with changes that have been taking place, both in expectations for marriage and in the social framework of marriage. Historically, the function of marriage has been to provide a stable economic unit in which to raise children. People who did not want to have children were often admonished not to marry (Ritter, 1919). In many societies, and in some groups within our own society in the past, marriages were arranged through contracts between parents; "romance" was not expected to play a part. Today, however, most people expect more from marriage as they seek fulfillment for their social, emotional, financial, and sexual needs—all within the marriage relationship. Happiness itself is sometimes thought to be an automatic outcome of marriage. These are high expectations, and they are difficult to meet. As one observer stated, "Marriage was not designed

Marriage is a traditional and deeply ingrained institution in American society.

as a mechanism for providing friendship, erotic experience, romantic love, personal fulfillment, continuous lay psychotherapy or recreation" (Cadwallader, 1975, p. 134). However, many modern couples expect a satisfactory degree of all these benefits from a marital relationship.

While people's expectations for marriage have increased, our society's supportive network for marriage has decreased. Extended families and small communities have become less prevalent, and many married couples are isolated from their families and neighbors. This places further demands on the marriage to meet a variety of human needs, for there is often no place else to turn for such things as child-care assistance, emotional support, and financial or housework help. Another development that is influencing marital patterns is increased longevity. "Till death do us part" now means many more years than it did in the past. This raises the question of how long even the best marriage can be expected to fulfill all these functions.

At a personal level, courtship experiences before marriage also contribute to the discrepancy between expectations and reality. Dating rarely offers a couple the kinds of experiences that would enable them to draw a realistic picture of the marriage relationship or learn the skills that may help resolve later difficulties. Both partners frequently present their more likable, sociable side. The focus of their time together is usually on pleasurable activities, with day-to-day problems kept separate from their interactions. The fairy-tale ending to their courtship — "they married and lived happily ever after" — is often difficult to achieve. While the challenges of sharing everyday life after marriage can enrich and fulfill some couples, the lack of preparedness for meeting such challenges may disillusion others.

There are many things a couple can do that may help prepare them for the experience of marriage. Some not yet married couples make an effort to discuss such topics as finances, child rearing, and daily household responsibilities, which are often sources of disagreement within marriages. They may plan the handling of finances for shared activities or a vacation. They may also decide to divide their premarital living expenses equally or in proportion to their respective incomes.

A couple contemplating marriage needs to discuss their desires and decisions about children — whether each person wants them, how many, and when. If neither partner has children at the time, they may want to make arrangements to share volunteer child-care work or baby-sitting for friends, to help assess and discuss their child-rearing attitudes. They may also need to plan the logistics of caring for their own children. The importance of becoming clear about aspirations and expectations concerning children is made evident by the fact that married couples tend to disagree frequently about child-rearing practices (Klagsbrun, 1985; Waite & Lillard, 1991).

Some couples may work on a cooperative household project or share home-making activities. Building something together, organizing a party, trading work-days at each other's houses, or cooking meals for each other are activities that may help couples learn more about how well they can work together.

Situations in which the pair discovers problems can make the couple aware of what differences they bring into the marriage. A "good marriage" is not necessarily a problem-free marriage but rather a relationship in which two people are committed to dealing with the problems that invariably arise. Francine Klagsbrun (1985) conducted in-depth interviews with 90 couples, married 15 years or more, who rated their marriages as happy and successful. Some of the traits she found to be associated with good marriages included spending focused time together (such as might occur during the courtship days), sharing values (more important than sharing interests), and flexibility — the ability to accept change both in one's partner and in the nature of the relationship. Other research studies have provided strong evidence that positive communication, high levels of physical intimacy, shared leisure time, and perceptions of emotional closeness and mutual empathy are highly correlated with marital happiness (Hill, 1988; Tolstedt & Stokes, 1983; Zimmer, 1983).

Predicting Marital Satisfaction

Researchers have long been fascinated with the prospect of developing techniques for predicting the probability that a couple contemplating marriage will experience marital satisfaction. Until recently, these efforts have been quite unsuccessful (Gottman, 1991). However, several recent studies have revealed surprisingly effective tools for predicting marital success.

In one study psychologists John Gottman and Robert Levenson (1986 & 1988) videotaped married couples as they discussed how to resolve a major conflict in their relationship. While the couples talked, the researchers simultaneously collected physiological data (such as heart rate, blood pressure, etc.) that indicated the couples' levels of arousal. They discovered that couples who exhibited high levels of arousal during their discussions had marriages that declined in satisfaction in subsequent years. Gottman noted, "Using only physiological data we could predict, with over 95% accuracy, which couples' marriages would improve and which would deteriorate in the next three years" (1991, p. 4).

In another study Gottman and his colleagues endeavored to discover what kinds of interaction patterns were related to a decline in a couple's marital satisfaction over time. Using videotapes of couple interaction, questionnaires, and physiological data, these researchers identified a number of interactive behavior patterns that were predictive of marital discord, unhappiness, and separation. Briefly summarized, these patterns included (1) facial expressions of disgust (wife), fear (husband), and misery (both spouses); (2) defensiveness on the part of both (making excuses, denying responsibility for disagreements); (3) wife's verbal expressions of contempt; and (4) husband's "stonewalling" (presenting a stonewall of nonresponsiveness while listening to wife's concerns) (Gottman, 1991; Gottman & Krokoff, 1992). Commenting on the predictive nature of these observed patterns of interaction, Gottman noted that "if we wanted to predict marital separation four years later using our ... data we would correctly classify about 90% of the couples separated or not separated" (1991, p. 5).

Another intriguing area of research has involved assessing the effectiveness of a premarital inventory called PREPARE in predicting marital satisfaction. PREPARE is a questionnaire containing 125 items designed to identify areas of strengths and weaknesses in 11 relationship areas: (1) realistic expectations, (2) personality issues, (3) communication, (4) conflict resolution, (5) financial management, (6) leisure activities, (7) sexual relationship, (8) children and marriage, (9) family and friends, (10) egalitarian roles, and (11) religious orientation (Olson et al., 1987).

Blaine Flowers and David Olson (1986) conducted a three-year follow-up of 164 couples who had taken PREPARE prior to getting married to determine the extent to which they could predict marital success based on scores obtained on this questionnaire. Those couples who exhibited difficulties or incompatibility in several areas assessed by PREPARE were much more likely to experience marital discord and/or dissatisfaction (including separation or divorce) than were couples who were more compatible as revealed by their scores on this premarital inventory. More recently, researchers Andrea Larsen and David Olson (1989) conducted another study using PREPARE scores as a basis for predicting marital satisfaction. This investigation replicated the previous longitudinal study of Flowers and Olson (1986), and like the earlier research, 179 couples who took PREPARE before marriage were followed over a three-year period. These researchers observed, "As in the initial longitudinal study, PREPARE predicted, with about 80% accuracy, couples who got divorced from those who were happily married" (p. 311).

What are the implications of these findings regarding effective methods for predicting marital happiness? How might such discoveries be applied to our own lives? Give this some thought before reading on.

Married couples are engaging in a wider variety of sexual behaviors and enjoying sexual interaction more often.

Given that current estimates suggest that 50% or more of all first marriages in the United States will end in separation or divorce (Bumpass et al., 1991; Larsen & Olson, 1989), these research findings strongly underscore the value of obtaining premarital counseling from professionals well versed in the use of predictive devices such as PREPARE. A couple contemplating marriage might wisely choose to secure such information as they seek to make reasoned decisions about the future course of their relationship. In the event that premarital assessment methods pinpoint areas of present or potential conflict, a couple might then seek to resolve these difficulties through in-depth therapy prior to taking their vows. In situations where conflict resolution efforts are unsuccessful, a couple might reconsider entering into a marriage.

Sexual Behavior Within Marriage

Contemporary developments and changes in sexual mores and behavior are often discussed in the context of nonmarital or extramarital activities. However, the greatest impact of increased sexual liberalization may be on the marital relationship itself. As compared with the people in Kinsey's research groups, contemporary American married women and men appear to be engaging in sexual intercourse more often, experiencing a wider repertoire of sexual behaviors, and enjoying sexual interaction more. Several surveys have revealed significant changes in sexual activity among married couples in the years since Kinsey collected his data. The frequency and duration of precoital activity has increased, with more people focusing on enjoyment of the activities themselves rather than viewing them as preparation for coitus. Oral stimulation of the breasts and manual stimulation of the genitals have increased; so has oral–genital contact, both fellatio and cunnilingus (Blumstein & Schwartz, 1983; Frank & Enos, 1983; Hunt, 1974; Petersen et al., 1983; Rubin, 1976).

Married couples' experiences with coitus also seem to have changed over the years. Today's couples report using a wider variety of intercourse positions and

OTHER TIMES, OTHER PLACES

Adult Sexuality in Other Cultures

Marital coitus is the most common form of adult sexual activity in virtually all societies for which we have information. However, there is widespread variation in both the types of coital positions used and the frequency of sexual contact. Although data are limited, there is evidence that each society tends to favor a particular coital position. Whether it is man-above, woman-above, or some other variation is greatly influenced by the relative social status of the sexes in the society. In places like the Trobriand Islands off the coast of New Guinea, where women are valued, the female-above position is quite common. In societies where women are assigned low social status (for example, in the society we call Inis Beag, off the coast of Ireland), the male-above position seems to be preferred. It is interesting to note that improved social status of American women has been paralleled by an increase in the

use of coital positions other than the man-above.

It has been estimated that most married couples around the world engage in coitus between two and five times per week (Gebhard, 1971). However, in some societies the frequency may range as high as ten times a night or as low as once or twice a month. Married couples on the Polynesian island of Mangaia, although somewhat less active than during their premarital days, maintain a coital frequency far greater than that of most Western couples. In Mangaia, coital emphasis after marriage tends to shift from the number of times a man can bring his partner to orgasm during a single session to whether he can copulate with her every night of the week (Marshall, 1971). Somewhat higher frequencies are reported among the Australian Aranda, who report as many as three to five coital contacts per night. Even

higher rates (up to ten times per night) are reported by the Chagga farmers of Tanzania. The Lepcha of the southeastern Himalayas report having intercourse five to nine times a night during the early years of marriage. At the other extreme, there are societies that report an exceedingly low rate of marital coitus. Couples in the Dani culture of New Guinea seem rarely to have sexual interactions. Newlyweds wait an average of two years for their first coital experiences, and both men and women abstain from intercourse for a period of four to six years after the birth of a child. Married couples in another New Guinean society, the Kerakis, report relatively low coital frequencies of once a week.

Most societies have more restrictive norms pertaining to extramarital than to premarital sex. Nevertheless, many societies impose fewer restrictions on extramarital activity than

prolonging coitus to several times longer than the two-minute average reported in Kinsey's 1948 study (Hunt, 1974; Petersen et al., 1983). The average frequency of marital coitus also appears to have increased to approximately two or three times per week for couples in their 20s and 30s, a frequency that gradually declines with increasing age (Doddridge et al., 1987; Frank & Enos, 1983; Petersen et al., 1983; Pietropinto & Simenauer, 1979; Trussel & Westoff, 1980).

Philip Blumstein and Pepper Schwartz (1983), in their landmark national survey of American couples, found that the frequency of marital sexual interactions was strongly associated with how the over 7000 married respondents in their sample group rated their sexual satisfaction. Nine out of 10 of the married couples who were having sex three or more times a week reported satisfaction with the quality of their sex lives. In contrast only half of those who were having sex one to four times a month were satisfied. Furthermore, only a third of those with frequency rates of once a month or less reported satisfaction. As we might expect, Blumstein and Schwartz also found that sex is more exciting at the outset of marriage and that in long-term relationships sex tends to be more "bread-and-butter" rather than "champagne-and-caviar."

does our own. Some societies even have formal rules allowing such behavior under special circumstances — during celebrations, as part of the marriage ceremony, or as a form of sexual hospitality. With very few exceptions, men around the world are allowed greater access to extramarital coitus than are women. However, it appears that as many as 60% of non-Western societies studied allow some form of extramarital coitus for wives (Gebhard, 1971). A few examples illustrate the diversity of this activity in other societies.

The aborigines of western Australia's Arnhem Land openly accept extramarital sexual relationships for both wives and husbands. They welcome the variety in experience and the break in monotony offered by extramarital involvements. Many also report increased appreciation of and attachment to the spouse as a result of such experiences. The Polynesian Marquesans, although not open advocates of extramarital affairs, nevertheless exhibit covert acceptance of such activity. A Marquesan wife often takes young boys or her husband's friends or relatives as lovers. Conversely, her husband may have relations with young unmarried girls or with his sisters-in-law. Marquesan culture openly endorses the practices of partner swapping and sexual hospitality, where unaccompanied visitors are offered sexual access to the host of the other sex. Sexual hospitality is also practiced by some Eskimo groups, where a married female host has intercourse with a male visitor. The Turu of central Tanzania regard marriage primarily as a cooperative, economic, and social bond. Affection between husband and wife is generally thought to be out of place; most members of this society believe that the marital relationship is endangered by the instability of love and affection. The Turu have evolved a system of romantic love, called Mbuya, that allows them to seek affection outside the home without threatening the stability of the primary marriage. Both husband and wife actively pursue these outside relationships.

There has been a general tendency in Western societies to consider female sexual gratification unimportant. Although this is changing, particularly in the United States, there are still significant numbers of Western women who seldom experience orgasm, particularly in repressive cultures. In Inis Beag, where women are ascribed the status of second-class citizens, female orgasm is virtually unknown. In marked contrast, most island societies of the South Pacific value female sexual pleasure: here female orgasm during sexual activity is routine. An example is the Mangaian culture, where "the Mangaian male lover aims to have his partner achieve orgasm two or three times to his once" (Marshall, 1971, p. 122).

A number of factors other than frequency of sexual interaction have also been linked to satisfaction with marital sex. Mutuality in initiating sex may be an important contributor to sexual satisfaction of both wives and husbands (Blumstein & Schwartz, 1983; Tavris & Sadd, 1977). It also appears that women who take an active role during lovemaking are more likely to be pleased with their sex lives than those who assume a more passive role (Tavris & Sadd, 1977). Research also suggests a positive correlation between marital happiness and female orgasm. In one survey of over 1000 women, orgasm frequency was considerably higher among those women reporting marital happiness than in those who indicated they were unhappily married (Gebhard, 1966). There is evidence that orgasm frequency is increasing among married women (Hunt, 1974; Petersen et al., 1983; Pietropinto & Simenauer, 1979; Tavris & Sadd, 1977).

It also appears that good communication contributes greatly to sexual satisfaction within marriage. In one survey of 100,000 women, 88% of the respondents who reported always discussing their sexual feelings with their partners described their sex lives as good or very good. In contrast, only 30% of those who reported never discussing sex with their partners described their sex lives as good or very good (Tavris & Sadd, 1977). A study of married couples found that those participants who enjoyed a high-quality marital relationship also reported good sexual communication (Banmen & Vogel, 1985).

After reviewing the information just presented, one might be tempted to conclude that all is well with marital sex. However, we caution against such a generalization. One of the shortcomings of much of the available data is that they are generally collected from people involved in intact marriages, as opposed to those whose marriages have ended. This is an important biasing influence that quite possibly leads to a more positive image of marital sexual satisfaction than is justified. Furthermore, most studies focus on the frequencies of certain behaviors and attitudes rather than on people's feelings about various aspects of their marriages, including sex. One notable exception is the work of sociologist Lillian Rubin (1976). She interviewed 50 working-class and 25 professional, middle-class couples living in the San Francisco Bay area. Her interviews explored not only how her respondents behaved sexually but, perhaps more important, also how they felt about sex in their marriages. Each of the 75 couples in her study population reported some problems in sexual adjustment. Masters and Johnson (1970) also stated that marital sexual problems are quite common; they estimated that approximately half of all American married couples experience difficulties with sexual adjustment.

A number of factors may interfere with marital sexual enjoyment. When people marry, their relationship often changes. They suddenly find themselves confronted with a new set of role expectations. They are no longer just friends and lovers but also husband and wife, and the romance of the former condition may be replaced by the stress of adjusting to the latter. They no longer have the independence of living separately, and day-to-day togetherness may erode their sense of individuality and autonomy. Unfortunately, many people are less motivated to maintain personal attractiveness once they have secured a marriage partner; being overweight, out of shape, and poorly groomed may reduce one's sexual attractiveness and pleasure during sexual activity. People often get caught up in a "rat race" lifestyle that can seriously erode the quality of marital sex. Holding down a job, doing laundry, fixing the lawn mower, socializing with two sets of relatives and friends, and countless other tasks can reduce the time a couple has for intimate sharing. Couples who become parents may discover that children can place unexpected strains on their relationship, in addition to interfering with their privacy and spontaneity (Jouriles et al., 1991; Kohn, 1987; Lewis, 1988; Sander & Cairns, 1987; Waite & Lillard, 1991). Finally, boredom can be a devitalizing factor. Sex may become routine and predictable. The discussion in Chapter 7 on maintaining relationship satisfaction may be helpful in enhancing sexual enjoyment in marriages and other long-term relationships.

Extramarital Relationships

The term **extramarital relationship** is used to describe sexual interaction experienced by a married person with someone other than her or his spouse. The term is a general one that makes no distinction among the many ways in which extramarital sexual activity occurs. Such activity can be clandestine; it can also be based on an open agreement between the married partners. The extramarital relationship may be a casual encounter, or it may involve deep emotional commitment; it may last for a brief or extended time period. Sometimes this form of sexual activity occurs within the context of an alternative lifestyle such as swinging. The following discussions examine extramarital relationships, both nonconsensual and consensual.

Nonconsensual Extramarital Relationships

In **nonconsensual extramarital sex,** the married person engages in an outside sexual relationship without the consent (or presumably the knowledge) of his or her spouse. This form of behavior has been given many labels, including "cheating," adultery, infidelity, having an affair, and "fooling around."

Why do people enter into nonconsensual extramarital relationships? List as many possible reasons that you can think of before reading on.

The reasons for nonconsensual extramarital sex are varied and complex. Sometimes such relationships are motivated by a desire for excitement and variety. The person may have no particular complaints about the marital relationship but may want to enrich or broaden her or his emotional or sexual life with extramarital encounters. Some may be motivated to engage in extramarital relationships to confirm that they are still desirable to members of the other sex. In other cases people may be highly dissatisfied with their marriages. If emotional needs are not being met within the marriage, having an "illicit lover" may seem particularly inviting. In some situations affairs may also provide the impetus a person needs to end a marriage of which he or she no longer wishes to be part (Brown, 1988). Occasionally, the reason for outside involvements may be the unavailability of sex within the marriage. A lengthy separation, a debilitating illness, or a partner's inability or unwillingness to relate sexually may all contribute to a person deciding to look elsewhere for sexual fulfillment. An affair may also be motivated by a desire for revenge (Meyering & Epling-McWherter, 1986). In such instances the offending party may be quite indiscreet to ensure that the "wronged" spouse will discover the infidelity.

It is difficult to estimate the incidence of extramarital sexual involvements. Kinsey's surveys reported that approximately half of the men and a quarter of the women in his samples admitted to experiencing extramarital sexual intercourse at least once by age 40. The term *admitted* is a significant qualifier. Many writers and researchers believe that a considerable number of people are reluctant to acknowledge this kind of behavior, which may contribute to low estimates of its prevalence. This speculation has received some support from a survey of 750 individuals undergoing psychotherapy (Greene et al., 1974). Thirty percent of the sample initially admitted to having experienced extramarital involvements. After a period of extensive psychotherapy, however, an additional 30% revealed previous affairs. Furthermore, many sex surveys fail to distinguish between consensual and nonconsensual extramarital relationships—although it is reasonable to assume that the substantial majority of extramarital sexual contacts are nonconsensual. In Hunt's 1974 study, only one in five spouses whose partners had had such contacts had been told of the occurrence by their partner.

A number of surveys conducted in more recent years have yielded varying estimates of the frequency of extramarital involvements among American couples. None of these investigations was conducted with true representative samples of the U.S. population. Furthermore, each is biased by certain characteristics of its sample. However, despite drawing on widely divergent sample populations, all these surveys yield consistent evidence of an increased incidence of extramarital sexual involvements since the time of Kinsey's research, particularly among women. The following list gives the pertinent statistics from several of these investigations:

1. Of 106,000 female respondents to a *Cosmopolitan* sex survey, 50% under age 35 indicated that they had experienced one or more extramarital affairs. The figure for women over age 35 jumped to 69% (Wolfe, 1981).

2. Of 100,000 respondents to a *Playboy* sex survey, all age groups combined, 45% of the men and 34% of the women reported one or more extramarital involvements. When only the older respondents were evaluated, the number of those experiencing extramarital sex by age 50 rose to 70% of the men and 65% of the women (Petersen et al., 1983).

3. A *Redbook* survey of 100,000 women reported that approximately 30% of the overall study population had engaged in one or more extramarital involvements. However, approximately half of those respondents who worked outside the home had experienced affairs. Furthermore, women in their late teens and 20s were almost three times as likely to have experienced extramarital sex as women of the same age in Kinsey's study population (Tavris & Sadd, 1977). This latter finding of a dramatic escalation of extramarital activity among young women was duplicated by Morton Hunt's 1974 research and a *Psychology Today* survey (Athanasiou et al., 1970).

When all of these statistics are considered collectively, it seems reasonable to conclude that a substantial percentage of married American men and women will experience one or more extramarital involvements during their lifetime. Furthermore, there is clear evidence that the double standard for female and male marital infidelity, which was clearly evident in Kinsey's time, has been quite notably eroded over the last few decades. Evidence now suggests that middle-aged women are almost as likely as their husbands to have extramarital sexual relationships (Segraves, 1989; Wyatt et al., 1988).

Interestingly, two recent studies have suggested that the upward trend in the incidence of extramarital sex over the last few decades may be leveling off or perhaps even declining. Both investigations utilized a large group of adult participants from the annual General Social Survey (interviews with a national sample of American adults). In addition to being interviewed as part of the regular survey, these subjects were asked to complete another questionnaire containing items pertaining to the number and gender of sexual partners during the previous 12 months. Of those married individuals who completed the questionnaire in 1988, 96% reported that they had been monogamous over the previous year (Greeley et al., 1989). A 1989 sample surveyed in the same manner yielded a 98.5% monogamy rate for the previous year among married respondents (Smith, 1990). The authors of these two investigations have suggested that the unexpectedly high rates of monogamy reported by their married subjects were due, in large part, to fear of contracting AIDS through extramarital sexual involvements. We await further research to determine if a reversal in the trend toward increasing extramarital sex is indeed under way in America.

The effects of extramarital sex on a marriage vary. When secret involvements are discovered, the "betrayed" spouse may feel devastated. He or she may experience a variety of emotions, including feelings of inadequacy and rejection, extreme anger, resentment, shame, and jealousy. This last emotion can be very difficult to deal with, particularly when one partner has remained faithful while the other has not. Jealousy may emerge from a sense of betrayal — the belief that the spouse is giving away something that belongs exclusively to the other partner. The fear that another person will usurp one's position of preeminence in the life of one's spouse may also be involved. Particularly for men, part of sexual jealousy may stem from a sense of ownership. However, the discovery of infidelity does not inevitably erode the quality of a marriage. In some cases it may motivate a couple to search for and attempt to resolve sources of discord in their relationship — a process that may ultimately lead to an improved marriage.

Available research data provide a hazy picture regarding the impact of extramarital sex on both the individual participant and the primary couple. Blumstein and Schwartz's national survey of American couples revealed that the monogamous pairs in their sample had a lower rate of divorce than couples in which one or both had participated in extramarital relationships. This finding is consistent with other evidence indicating that extramarital relationships are often mentioned by divorced people as a cause of their marital breakup (Kelly, 1982). However, we cannot conclude that this apparent association between outside involvements and divorce necessarily reflects a cause-and-effect relationship. A plausible alternative explanation is that in at least some cases extramarital sex may be a *symptom* of a disintegrating marriage rather than its cause.

Consensual Extramarital Relationships

Consensual extramarital relationships occur in marriages where both partners are informed about and supportive of sexual involvements outside the marriage. These mutually sanctioned experiences may be primarily emotional, primarily sexual, or they may involve the couple's whole lifestyle. A variety of arrangements fall under the category of consensual extramarital involvements. We briefly examine two: open marriage and swinging.

Open Marriage. The concept of **open marriage** received widespread public attention with the 1972 publication of George and Nena O'Neill's book *Open Marriage*. For many people who are not aware of the broad scope of this concept, open marriage has become synonymous with consensual sexual involvements. However, this is an incomplete view of the open-marriage idea. The essence of the O'Neills' thesis is that one relationship is unlikely to fulfill a person's total intimacy needs throughout the adult years. In an open marriage people allow each other the freedom to have intimate emotional relationships with members of either sex without compromising their primary relationship. These intimacies do not necessarily include sexual sharing; that would be a matter for an individual couple to determine.

Those who support open marriage believe that it is confining to limit emotional or sexual intimacy to only one person. Some have even argued that it is "essentially absurd to expect that all physical sexual expression for a fifty-year period will be confined to the marriage partner" (Roy & Roy, 1973, p. 144). Other advocates of open marriage are committed to sexual exclusivity, but they find it stressful to avoid nonsexual intimacies with individuals other than their spouses. As the following anecdotes reveal, a marriage relationship that is too "closed" can have confining and potentially negative effects:

When I married my husband, it was with the intention of being totally faithful to him. I couldn't imagine myself wanting sex with another man. However, I was unprepared for the jealous way he reacts to anybody I show an interest in. If I talk too long to another man at a party, he comes unglued. He doesn't even like me to spend time with my girlfriends, and I lie to him on those rare occasions I go out to lunch or shopping with a friend. I long for the companionship of others. I still love my husband, but sometimes I just need to be close to someone else. Sometimes I think his extreme possessiveness will be the end of us. (Authors' files)

In my job I form close working relationships with both men and women. A couple of the women have become very dear friends. I wish I could feel comfortable taking them out to lunch on occasion or having them call me at home like good friends do. But my wife raises hell even when their names come up in conversation. I guess she thinks being friends and crawling into bed go hand-in-hand. (Authors' files)

Open Marriage maintains that people who are allowed the freedom to form close, meaningful relationships with others are often able to bring more contentment and satisfaction to the primary relationship with a spouse. As an alternative to the resentment and frustration evident in the preceding accounts, open marriages attempt to foster mutual trust, support, and appreciation.

We have very limited information on the incidence of sexually open relationships in American society. Blumstein and Schwartz (1983) found that in 15% of 3574 married couples, both partners indicated having "an understanding that allows nonmonogamy under some circumstances." Nearly twice as many cohabitors (28%) had a similar understanding, while 29% of lesbian couples and 65% of male homosexual couples reported sexually open relationships.

Swinging. **Swinging,** or comarital sex, refers to a form of consensual extramarital sex that a married couple share (Duckworth & Levitt, 1985; Jenks, 1985). Husband and wife participate simultaneously and in the same location, which distinguishes swinging from the extramarital sexual contact that might occur in an open marriage, where mutual participation is not usual. This activity has been labeled "wife-swapping" in the past, but this term came into disrepute among swingers because of its implications of male property rights. Most participants also object to labeling this activity as "extramarital" sex. Because they do it together, they do not consider it extraneous to but rather part of their marriage. Furthermore, many believe it to be far more acceptable morally than a secretive affair.

Swinging experienced its heyday in the 1970s and early 1980s, when most of the research on this social phenomenon was conducted. More recently, this form of consensual extramarital sex appears to be in decline. Available data suggest that fewer than 5% of American men and women have experienced swinging (Athanasiou et al., 1970; Duckworth & Levitt, 1985; Hunt, 1974; Tavris & Sadd, 1977). A review of the literature on swinging provides a composite picture of the people who engaged in this activity. They were shown to be predominantly middle-class and upper-middle-class whites with above average educations and incomes and mostly conservative or moderate in their political and social views (Bartell, 1970; Gilmartin, 1977; Karlen, 1988; Palson & Palson, 1972; Smith & Smith, 1970). The reasons respondents most commonly gave for becoming involved in swinging were boredom with their partners and a desire to introduce excitement into their sex lives.

Swinging seems to affect individuals and couples in a variety of ways. Some participants have suggested that it improved the sexual aspects of their marriage, increased togetherness, and broadened their social horizons. Gilmartin (1977) reported that the swingers in his research population, compared with a matched control group of nonswingers, had sex more often with their spouses, were slightly more happily married, and generally seemed to be less bored. However, swinging is not without potential hazards. Some of its participants have reported extreme sexual performance pressures (this is particularly true of men), guilt, jealousy, and feeling threatened. Evidence has suggested that swinging does not maintain its appeal for long; most couples stopped swinging after a brief period of experimentation (Murstein, 1978; Murstein et al., 1985).

Divorce

We have seen that people today define marriage in a variety of ways, according to their particular needs. Despite this increased flexibility, however, a significant number of marriages are ending in divorce. Current estimates suggest that half or more of all first marriages will end in divorce (Gottman, 1991; Larsen & Olson, 1989; White & Booth, 1991). These estimates are a common topic in the popular media, where the prevalence of divorce is often presented as a sign of societal rejection of the institution of marriage. This interpretation is not necessarily accurate. Available divorce statistics are not an entirely reliable indicator of the current state of American marriage.

Interpreting Divorce Statistics

Several factors have some bearing on how we interpret divorce statistics. A rise in divorce rates may reflect the increased ease of obtaining a legal marital dissolution more than a rise in dissatisfaction with marriage. Obtaining a legal divorce has become a simpler, less expensive process in recent years. Furthermore, a significant percentage of divorces involve people who have had more than one marriage and divorce. Therefore, a higher percentage of first marriages remain intact than a quick glance at the statistics indicates.

Research does confirm that the proportion of marriages ending in divorce has increased dramatically since the 1950s, as shown in Table 14.1. The ratio of divorce to marriage was one to four in 1950; by 1977 the ratio was one divorce to every two marriages. More recent statistics reveal that there were approximately 1.2 million divorces and 2.4 million marriages in 1991, still a ratio of one to two. In the

© Engleman/Rothco.

"Playing house is old-fashioned . . .
let's play divorce!"

last few years, the divorce rate itself (number of divorces per 1000 residents) has begun to level off and even decline somewhat. As you can see in Table 14.2, there were 3.5 divorces per 1000 U.S. residents in 1970, and this figure increased steadily until 1981, at which time it was 5.3 per 1000 (an increase of 51%). However, in the next 10 years, the rate dropped down to 4.7 per 1000 (a decrease of 11.3%). It has been suggested that this leveling off of the divorce rate may reflect, in part, an increase in the number of cohabiting couples in America. "This is because couples who break up before they marry don't show up in the divorce statistics" (Riche, 1988, p. 25).

Suggested Causes for High Divorce Rates

Several large-scale investigations have reported the demographic characteristics of divorced people, such as age, length of marriage, number of children, education level, profession, income, and so on. These demographic studies have provided worthwhile data that can be used to predict probabilities of divorce for individuals sharing particular characteristics. However, they generally relied on data provided by county, state, and federal bureaus, which almost never included reasons for divorce except for occasional reporting of legal grounds. In the absence of hard data, a number of writers have speculated on the factors responsible for the high divorce rates in America.

 What do you consider to be some primary causes of divorce in America? Think about what you have observed and make some reasoned guesses before reading on.

Number and Ratio of Divorces to Marriages, 1950, 1977, and 1991 TABLE 14.1

	1950	Ratio	1977	Ratio	1991	Ratio
Number of divorces	385,000		1,097,000		1,179,000	
		1:4		1:2		1:2
Number of marriages	1,667,000		2,176,000		2,446,000	

Sources: U.S. Bureau of the Census, 1978 & 1985; and National Center for Health Statistics, 1982, 1985, 1989, & 1992.

Number of Marriages and Divorces per 1000 U.S. Residents, 1970–1991 TABLE 14.2

	'70	'71	'72	'73	'74	'75	'76	'77	'78	'79	'80	'81	'82	'83	'84	'85	'86	'87	'88	'89	'90	'91
Marriages	10.6	10.6	10.9	10.8	10.5	10.0	9.9	9.9	10.3	10.4	10.6	10.6	10.6	10.5	10.5	10.2	10.0	9.9	9.7	9.7	9.8	9.7
Divorces	3.5	3.7	4.0	4.3	4.6	4.8	5.0	5.0	5.1	5.3	5.2	5.3	5.0	5.0	4.9	5.0	4.8	4.8	4.8	4.7	4.7	4.7

Source: U.S. Bureau of the Census, 1985 & 1988. National Center for Health Statistics, 1989, 1992.

Some of the causes of divorce frequently mentioned include the comparative ease of obtaining no-fault divorces since the liberalization of divorce laws during the 1970s (Day & Hook, 1987); a reduction in the social stigma attached to divorce; increasing expectations for marital and sexual fulfillment, which have caused people to become more disillusioned with and less willing to persist in unsatisfying marriages; the increased economic independence of women; a greater abundance of wealth, which makes it easier for some people to maintain multiple families; and an attitude of "me first," which places personal fulfillment ahead of the compromises and hard work that relationships often require.

A study conducted by Margaret Cleek and Allan Pearson (1985) provided some much needed empirical evidence of what divorced people perceived to be the cause(s) of their breakup. These researchers surveyed over 600 divorced men and women. The most frequently cited cause for divorce — by both sexes — was communication difficulties, followed by basic unhappiness and incompatibility.

Adjusting to Divorce

Although the chain of events leading to marriage is unique for each individual, most people marry with the hope that the relationship will last. Divorce often represents loss of this hope and other losses as well: one's spouse, lifestyle, the security of familiarity, sometimes one's children, and often part of one's identity. Many people who terminate nonmarital intimate relationships experience these losses as well.

The loss a person feels in divorce is often comparable to the loss felt when a loved one dies (Gove & Shin, 1989; Gray et al., 1991; Kitson et al., 1989). In both cases the person undergoes a grieving process (Crosby et al., 1986). There are important differences, however. When the grief is caused by death, there are rituals and social support available, which may be helpful to the survivor. In contrast, there are no recognized grief rituals to help the divorced person. Initially, a person may experience shock: "This cannot be happening to me." Disorganization may follow, a sense that one's entire world has turned upside down. Volatile emotions may unexpectedly surface. Feelings of guilt may become strong. Loneliness is common. Finally (usually not for several months or a year), a sense of relief and acceptance may come (Krantzler, 1975). If after several months of separation a person is not developing a sense of acceptance, she or he may need professional help. Although many of the feelings triggered by divorce are uncomfortable, even painful, they can be steps toward resolving the loss so that a person can reestablish intimate relationships. Grieving can lead to healing.

There is a potential for personal growth in the adjustment process that accompanies divorce. Many people experience a sense of autonomy for the first time in their lives. Others find that being single presents opportunities to experience more fully dimensions of themselves that had been submerged in their identity within a couple. Learning to reach out to others for emotional support can help diminish feelings of aloneness. Divorce can offer an opportunity to reassess oneself and one's past, a process that may lead to the evolution of a new life.

Making the transition from marital to postmarital sexual relationships often presents a challenge to divorced individuals. The newly divorced person may experience considerable ambivalence about intimacy. Feelings of anger, rejection, or fear remaining from the trauma of the divorce may inhibit openness to intimate relationships. To protect themselves from emotional vulnerability, some people may withdraw from potential sexual relationships. Others may react by seeking many superficial sexual encounters.

Despite the problems newly single people often encounter in establishing nonmarital sexual expression, Hunt's (1974) research revealed considerable sexual satisfaction and activity among the divorced people in his volunteer subject group. Specific data on the sexual activity of divorced men indicated a slightly higher frequency of coitus than for married men of the same age, while the rate for divorced women was approximately the same as for married women of the same age. In this same study, divorced respondents reported greater participation in noncoital sexual activities and more variety in intercourse positions than did married respondents. There is also evidence that divorced women may be more orgasmic in their postmarital relationships than in their previous marriages (Gebhard, 1970). In one national survey, it was reported that a majority of divorced individuals became sexually active within the first year following the breakup of their marriages (Hunt & Hunt, 1977). Another survey of several hundred divorced individuals revealed an overall increase in sexual activity following their divorces (Simenauer & Carroll, 1982). Even in recent years, with concern about AIDS widespread, people continue to be sexually active after the breakup of their marriages. In one national survey, 74% of divorced and 80% of separated respondents reported being sexually active in the previous 12 months (Smith, 1990).

The period after a divorce often involves many lifestyle changes and adjustments. However, the adjustment process can offer an opportunity for personal growth.

Approximately three out of four divorced persons remarry, most within three years of the divorce (Lown & Dolan, 1988). Many remarried people have reported that their second marriage was better than the first, but hard evidence indicates that second marriages are more likely to end in divorce than first marriages (Blumstein & Schwartz, 1983; Brooks, 1985; Cox, 1983; Ganong & Coleman, 1989; Glick & Lin, 1986; Lown et al., 1989; Lown & Dolan, 1988). Remarried people may be inclined to rate second marriages higher because they strive harder to achieve good communication, have fewer romantic illusions, and are more committed to effectively resolving conflicts. However, such people are also inclined to monitor second marriages more closely than initial marriages and are less willing to stick around when things turn sour (Cox, 1983; Spanier & Furstenberg, 1982). Some researchers also believe that second marriages are more prone to fail because the trauma of divorce has been lessened somewhat by having gone through it once already (Blumstein & Schwartz, 1983). Furthermore, the financial problems associated with remarriage (alimony and child-support payments, high costs involved with establishing a new residence, and so forth) represent a major impetus for discord and divorce in remarried families (Lown & Dolan, 1988; Morgan, 1989).

Widowhood.

Widowhood

Although a spouse can die during early or middle adult years, widowhood usually occurs later in life. In most cases it is the man who dies first, a tendency that has become more pronounced during this century. The ratio of widows to widowers has increased from less than two to one in the early 1900s to almost six to one by the 1990s (U.S. Bureau of the Census, 1991b).

The postmarital adjustment of widowhood is different in some ways from that of divorce. Widowed people typically do not have the sense of having failed at marriage. However, the anger and resentment that often help ease the emotional separation after a divorce are frequently lacking when a partner dies. The grief may be more intense, and the quality of the emotional bond to the deceased mate is often quite high. For some people this emotional tie remains so strong that other potential relationships appear dim by comparison. Nevertheless, about half of widowed men and a quarter of widowed women do eventually remarry (Lown & Dolan, 1988).

Many widowers and widows experience the same lifestyle adjustments and grieving processes described in our discussion of divorce, often to a greater degree. Further information on widowhood is included in the next chapter's discussion of aging and sexuality.

Summary

Single Living

Although single living is often seen as a transition period before, in between, or after marriage, many people choose it as a permanent lifestyle.

The proportion of individuals who have never married has almost tripled since 1970 for men and women in their late 20s and early 30s.

Cohabitation

The number of couples who cohabit (live together without marriage) more than quadrupled in the period from 1970–1990.

While cohabitors seem to have a higher risk of marital discord than noncohabitors, the exact nature of the relationship between cohabitation and marriage remains to be explained.

Marriage

The primary elements in the marriage ideal of our society are a permanent, sexually exclusive, and legal relationship between two heterosexual adults.

There are a variety of techniques for predicting, with a high degree of success, the probability that a couple will experience marital happiness. These assessment devices include questionnaires, videotapes of couple interaction, and physiological data reflective of arousal level.

Recent changes in sexual behaviors can be observed within the marital relationship. Married couples are engaging in a wider variety of sexual behaviors and experiencing coitus more often and with greater duration than in the past.

Extramarital Relationships

Nonconsensual extramarital relationships occur without the partner's consent.

Kinsey found that approximately 50% of married males and 25% of married females had experienced sexual intercourse outside marriage by age 40.

The results of several contemporary surveys suggest that a substantial majority of married American men and women will experience one or more extramarital involvements during their lifetimes.

The most notable increase in extramarital sexual intercourse in current studies is among young women.

Consensual extramarital relationships occur with the spouse's knowledge and agreement. Examples of these involvements include open marriage and swinging.

The open-marriage concept can include emotional, social, and sexual components in the extramarital relationship.

Swinging is structured to facilitate sexual expression and inhibit emotional involvement between the participants.

Divorce

The ratio of divorces to marriages has increased from one to four (1950) to one to two (1991).

In the last few years, the divorce rate (divorces per 1000 residents) has begun to level off and even decline somewhat.

Some of the causes of high divorce rates may include the liberalization of divorce laws, a reduction in the social stigma attached to divorce, unrealistic expectations for marital and sexual fulfillment, increased economic independence of women, and a "me-first" attitude.

One important study found that the most common reason given by men and women for their divorces was communication difficulty, followed by basic unhappiness and incompatibility.

Divorce typically involves many emotional, sexual, interpersonal, and lifestyle changes and adjustments.

Widowhood

The ratio of widows to widowers is now close to six to one.

⮌ *Thought Provokers* ⮌

1. Which of the following lifestyles do you consider to be viable options for your adult years: single living, cohabitation, "traditional" monogamous marriage, open marriage limited to emotional intimacy with others, open marriage that allows both emotional and sexual intimacy with someone other than your spouse, and swinging? What are some of the benefits and potential problems associated with each?

2. You and an intimate companion have decided to live together. What aspects of your cohabitation relationship would you want to discuss and reach agreement on

first? What problems would you expect to face as a result of your changed relationship? Do you think that cohabitation might affect any future marriage you enter into?

3. Among the aborigines of western Australia's Arnhem Land, extramarital relationships contribute to increased appreciation of and attachment to one's spouse. Do you think that if such involvements received more support within American society, married couples in this country would experience similar benefits?

4. Consider your married friends and relatives. Of those that have happy marriages, what seem to be the major

factors that contribute to their satisfaction? What about those that are experiencing poor adjustment within their marriages? What appear to be the primary causes for their lack of happiness?

Suggested Readings

Atwater, Lynn (1982). *The Extramarital Connection: Sex, Intimacy, and Identity.* New York: Irvington. This book provides enlightening insights into the motivations underlying women's decisions to become involved in extramarital relationships and the effect of such involvements on their marriages and their self-concepts.

Blumstein, Philip; and Schwartz, Pepper (1983). *American Couples.* New York: Morrow. This highly acclaimed book provides a wealth of information about current trends in relationships among couples — married and cohabiting, heterosexual and homosexual.

Colgrove, Melba; Bloomfield, Harold; and McWilliams, Peter (1977). *How to Survive the Loss of a Love.* New York: Bantam Books. A sensitive, warm, and practical book that can assist people in emotional healing after loss.

Krantzler, Mel (1975). *Creative Divorce.* New York: Signet Books. This book views divorce as an opportunity for personal growth and learning. It also gives readers support during the difficulties usually accompanying divorce.

Olds, Sally Wendkos (1985). *The Eternal Garden: Seasons of Our Sexuality.* Westminster, Md.: Time Books. A sensitive, informative discussion of sexuality and sexual development from young adulthood through old age.

Sarnoff, Irving; and Sarnoff, Suzanne (1989). *Love-Centered Marriage in a Self-Centered World.* New York: Hemisphere. This engaging and thoughtful book provides important insights into how couples may successfully cultivate loving relationships with their spouses that both enrich their lives and contribute to lasting marriages.

Sarrel, Lorna; and Sarrel, Philip (1984). *Sexual Turning Points: The Seven Stages of Adult Sexuality.* New York: Macmillan. An enlightening, sensitive book by respected sex therapists that provides thought-provoking discussions of many important aspects of adult sexuality, including initial pairing with an intimate companion, the experience of being a parent, divorce, and sex in the middle years and beyond.

Shahan, Lynn (1981). *Living Alone and Liking It.* New York: Stratford Press. This book examines some of the potential advantages of living alone and provides excellent advice on how to combat loneliness.

Singer, Laura (1980). *Stages: The Crises That Shape Your Marriage.* New York: Grosset & Dunlap. This book discusses the evolving pattern of predictable crisis points in marriage and provides positive suggestions to help resolve problems.

Old age has its pleasures, which, though different, are not less than the pleasures of youth.

W. Somerset Maugham
The Summing Up (1938)

CHAPTER 15

Sexuality and Aging

*D*uring the young adult years, the prospect of altered sexual expression with aging may seem remote and unimportant. However, in the later years of life most people begin to note certain changes taking place in their sexual response patterns. Some women and men who understand the nature of these variations may accept them with equanimity. Others may observe them with concern.

An important source of the confusion and frustration many aging people feel is the prevailing notion that old age is a sexless time (Lieblum & Segraves, 1989). However, as one author stated:

> The needs for an intimate relationship, for touch, caress, companionship, caring, love, dignity, identity, self-esteem, intellectual growth, and overall human interaction begin very early in human development and continue until death in old age. These needs and their realization may be even more critical in the later years, as other roles and relationships slip away. (Weg, 1983, p. 46)

In this chapter we examine some myths and facts about aging and sexuality.

Sexuality in the Later Years: Examining the Myths

Why is aging in our society often associated with sexlessness? There are a number of reasons. Part of the answer is that American culture is still influenced by the philosophy that equates sexuality with procreation. For older people, whose prospects for having babies are either nonexistent or unrealistic, this viewpoint offers little beyond self-denial.

Moreover, American society focuses on youth. The media usually link love, sex, and romance with the young. There is also an often unspoken assumption in American society that it is not quite acceptable for older people to have sexual needs. With such widespread denial of the validity of sexual expression in the "golden years," it is not surprising that many individuals are confused about aging and sexuality (Pratt & Schmall, 1989).

In examining the myth of sexless old age, two notable societal phenomena merit some special attention. These are, first, the double standard as it relates to the aging process and, second, the way nursing homes deal with the sexual needs of their residents.

The Double Standard and Aging

We have discussed the double standard as it relates to male and female sexual expression during adolescence and adulthood: feelings and behaviors that are considered acceptable for males are often considered unacceptable or inappropriate for females. The assumptions and prejudices implicit in the sexual double standard continue into old age, imposing a particular burden on women.

Although a woman's sexual capabilities continue after menopause, it is not uncommon for her to be considered past her sexual prime relatively early in life (Kite et al., 1991). The cultural image of an erotically appealing woman is commonly one of youth. As a woman grows further away from this nubile image, she is usually considered less and less attractive. In our society even young girls are

Contrary to the stereotype that older women are past their sexual prime, women such as Linda Evans prove that women over 50 can still be sexually attractive.

sometimes told not to frown ("You'll get wrinkles"); cosmetics, specially designed clothing, and even surgery are often used to maintain a youthful appearance for as long as possible.

In contrast, the physical and sexual attractiveness of men is often considered to be enhanced by the aging process. Gray hair and facial wrinkles may be thought to look "distinguished" on men — signs of accumulated life experience and wisdom. Likewise, while the professional achievements of women may be perceived as threatening to a potential male partner, it is relatively common for a man's sexual attractiveness to be closely associated with his achievements and social status, both of which may increase with age.

The pairings of powerful, older men and young, beautiful women reflect the double standard of aging. The marriage of a 55-year-old man and a 25-year-old woman would probably generate a much smaller reaction than that of a 55-year-old woman and a 25-year-old man. And as you might expect, pairings of older men and younger women occur much more commonly than the reverse. However, the percentage of marriages of women older than their husbands has increased in recent years, and about 35% of women age 45 and older marry younger men (Gavzer, 1987).

What aspects of sexuality are most important to older men's and women's sense of well-being? Do you think these aspects are the same or different for older women and men? Take a moment to consider this before reading further.

One research study (Stimson et al., 1981) suggested that the aspects of sexuality that contribute to a general feeling of well-being among the aged are different for men and women. For the older man, pride in his sexual performance and attractiveness to the other sex appeared to be crucial to his general feelings of well-being. In contrast, sexual performance did not seem related to general feelings of well-being for the older woman. However, feeling sexually attractive to the other sex was important; when the older woman no longer felt attractive, her general feelings of well-being decreased. Given that attractiveness in women is often equated with youthfulness, aging may affect a woman's sense of well-being more than a man's.

In response to the double standard of aging, Susan Sontag has presented an alternative view:

> Women have another option. They can aspire to be wise, not merely nice; to be competent, not merely helpful; to be strong, not merely graceful; to be ambitious for themselves, not merely themselves in relation to men and children. They can let themselves age naturally and without embarrassment, actively protesting and disobeying the conventions that stem from this society's double standard about aging. Instead of being girls, girls as long as possible, who then age humiliatingly into middle-aged women and then obscenely into old women, they can become women much earlier—and remain active adults, enjoying the long, erotic career of which women are capable, for longer. Women should allow their faces to show the lives they have lived. (1972, p. 38)

Sexuality and Aging in Nursing Homes

Up to this point, we have discussed sexual double standards that differentiate between females and males. But there is another sexual double standard that can restrict the sexuality of older adults of both sexes—the belief that feelings and behaviors appropriate to young or middle-aged adults are inappropriate or unacceptable for older adults, especially those in the care of others. This double standard is so ingrained in our social traditions that until recently it has rarely been questioned. However, the treatment that older people have received in some nursing homes has come under increasing public scrutiny. Nursing homes have been criticized for their insensitivity to the human rights of aged individuals. Our concern here is specifically with antisexual prejudice and practices, which are clearly demonstrated in many nursing home facilities (Pratt & Schmall, 1989). For example, researchers have often found that administrators and personnel in seniors facilities resist programs having to do with sexuality (Starr & Weiner, 1981). Sometimes staff in nursing homes separate married couples who engage in sexual activities (Falk & Falk, 1980). Of the 5% of the population over age 65 who live in nursing homes at a given time, many are denied the adult rights of sexual opportunity and privacy.

These problems can be especially acute for older homosexual partners. Antihomosexual prejudice may make it extremely difficult for a gay person to express

The need for affection and sexual intimacy extends into the older years, which can be a time of sharing and closeness.

affection much less have sexual contact with his or her lover or friend in hospital or nursing home settings (Kassel, 1983; Kelly & Rice, 1986). Even nursing homes that allow conjugal visits for their heterosexual residents are unlikely to do so for a homosexual couple.

Because older people are often assumed not to be sexual, medications are sometimes prescribed without consideration of their effects on sexuality. Some tranquilizers, antidepressants, and high blood pressure and arthritis medications can have an inhibiting effect on sexual interest and arousal. In cases where drug therapy is indicated, these side effects should be discussed with each person, and adjustments made as necessary. It is also desirable for older people to be thoroughly educated about the potential effects on sexuality of suggested surgeries, particularly those that involve the reproductive organs (Rosenthal, 1987).

Some relatives of nursing home residents and the staffs of such facilities help perpetuate difficulties like those just outlined, perhaps in part because of their own lack of knowledge or discomfort about sexuality and aging. However, concerned individuals, progressive nursing home personnel, and organizations such as the Gray Panthers and Services to Ongoing Mature Aging are beginning to have some effect on restrictive practices in nursing homes. Staff education, programs on sexuality for the residents, private lounges, and acceptance of the affectional and sexual needs and rights of elderly residents are important elements of care in these facilities. It is our hope that such progressive policies and attitudes will gain wider acceptance, so that older adults who must reside in hospitals or nursing homes can still have opportunities for sexual expression — and all the physical and emotional intimacy and joy that sexual activity can provide.

We have been looking at some of the myths about sexuality and aging that have had a particularly oppressive impact on some older people. One of the foundations of these myths is widespread ignorance about sexual functioning in elderly adults. The rest of this chapter examines some of the physiosexual changes and altered sexual responses that accompany the aging process.

Physiosexual Changes and Sexual Response: The Older Female

The term **climacteric** (klī-MAK-ter-ik) refers to the physiological changes that occur during the transition period from fertility to infertility. In women around 40 years of age, the ovaries begin to slow the production of estrogen. Menstruation continues, but cycles may become irregular as menopause approaches (Speroff, 1991). **Menopause,** one of the events of the female climacteric, refers to the permanent cessation of menstruation (Reamy & Reamy, 1991). Menopause occurs as a result of certain physiological changes and takes place at a mean age of 51 (Sherwin, 1991).

The general public and the medical community have begun to focus more on menopause because of the great increase in the number of women who live many years after menopause. In the fourteenth century, a woman's average life expectancy was 33 years (Budoff, 1987). Today the average life expectancy for women is almost 80 years. There are currently 40 million women in the United States who are postmenopausal. By the year 2020, there will be 60 million postmenopausal women, who can expect to live to be an average of 82 years old. In practical terms this means that most women experience the second half of their adult life following menopause (Beck, 1992).

During menopause the pituitary continues to secrete follicle-stimulating hormone (FSH); however, the ovaries cease production of mature ova. Ovarian estrogen output also slows, although the adrenals, liver, and adipose (fat) tissue continue to produce some estrogen after menopause. The postmenopausal ovary continues to produce androgens (Huges et al., 1991).

Menopause is often surrounded by myths and confusion (Mansfield et al., 1992). The experience will vary greatly from woman to woman (Mendham and Rees, 1992). Some women may experience few physical symptoms other than cessation of menstruation. For these women menopause is surprisingly uneventful:

After hearing comments for years about how menopause was so traumatic, I was ready for the worst. I was sure surprised when I realized I had hardly noticed it happening. (Authors' files)

In addition, most women feel relieved that they no longer need to be concerned about pregnancy, contraception, and menstruation (McKinlay et al., 1985). They may experience an increased sense of freedom in sexual intimacy as a result.

However, for many women menopause brings a range of symptoms that can vary from mild to severe. These symptoms are caused by the decline in estrogen. The most acute menopausal symptoms occur in the two years prior and two years following the last menstrual period. A woman in her 40s may first notice changes in her menstrual flow and sleep patterns. "Hot flashes" and night sweats are also common difficulties. Hot flashes can range from a mild feeling of warmth to a feeling of intense heat and profuse perspiration, especially around the chest, neck, and face. A severe hot flash can soak clothing or sheets in perspiration. The flashes usually last for three to six minutes, though they may last up to an hour. Hot flashes occur because hormones influence the nerves that control the blood vessels. As hormone levels fluctuate, the diameter of the blood vessels changes. Rapid dilation of the vessels causes a woman to experience a momentary rush of heat. The sensation can be quite disconcerting. Hot flashes can occur several times a day and during sleep; they usually cease within two years. About 80% of women will experience some degree of hot flashes (Sarrel, 1988), and about 20% have hot flashes for more than five years (Brenner, 1988). Some women report a decrease in frequency of intercourse during the period in which they are experiencing hot flashes (McCoy et al., 1985). Daily doses of 400 units of vitamin E twice a day can sometimes help alleviate the discomfort of hot flashes (Nachtigall & Heilman, 1987).

Other symptoms arising from the decrease in estrogen can significantly affect a woman's daily life. Sleep disturbance may increase during menopause. A typical example is a woman who can readily fall asleep but wakes one or more times during the night feeling agitated and has difficulty falling back to sleep. This pattern can easily result in fatigue and irritability during the day. Menopausal symptoms can also include dizziness, difficulty with balance, diminished pleasure from touch, itchy or burning skin, sensitivity to clothing or touch, and numbness or tingling in hands and feet. In addition, estrogen deficiency can cause severe headaches, short-term memory loss, difficulty concentrating, depression, and increased anxiety (Sarrel, 1988).

The Sexual Response Cycle of the Older Female

Hormonal changes of menopause also affect the sexual response of most women. In general, all phases of the response cycle continue to occur but with somewhat decreased intensity (Masters & Johnson, 1966).

The estrogen level of a particular woman appears to be a significant factor in the amount of change experienced. One study of women around age 50 found that most did not experience problems with desire, arousal, or satisfaction in their sexual lives. However, a small group of women with especially low estrogen levels tended to have reduced coital activity (Cutler et al., 1987).

Excitement Phase. The first physiological response to sexual arousal, vaginal lubrication, typically begins more slowly in an older woman. Instead of 10–30 seconds, it may take several minutes or longer before vaginal lubrication is observed. In most cases the amount of lubrication is reduced. Studies using the vaginal photoplethysmograph found that postmenopausal women's vaginal blood-volume increase during sexual arousal is smaller than in premenopausal women.

However, women in both groups reported similar levels of sexual activity and enjoyment, indicating that the somewhat lowered vasocongestion response is within the range necessary for normal function (Morrell et al., 1984; Purifoy et al., 1983).

The decrease in circulating estrogen also changes urethral and vaginal tissues. Urethral tissue can lose tone and become dry, often leading to urinary tract infections and urinary incontinence when sneezing, coughing, exercising, or engaging in sexual activity (Capewell et al., 1992; Frazer, 1987; Sarrel, 1990). Vaginal mucosa become thinner and change to a lighter pinkish color. Both the length and the width of the vagina decrease, and these changes contribute to the diminished expansive ability of the inner vagina during sexual arousal (Bachmann, 1990).

When there is considerably diminished lubrication and vaginal expansion during sexual response, uncomfortable or painful intercourse can result. In addition, some women reported decreased sexual desire and sensitivity of the clitoris, both of which interfere with sexual excitement (Sarrel, 1988).

Plateau Phase. During the plateau phase, the vaginal orgasmic platform develops, and the uterus elevates. In a postmenopausal woman, these changes occur to a somewhat lesser degree than before menopause (Masters & Johnson, 1966).

Orgasm Phase. Contractions of the orgasmic platform and the uterus continue to occur at orgasm, although the number of these contractions is typically reduced in an older woman. In some postmenopausal women, uterine contractions that take place at orgasm can be painful. Several of the women in Masters and Johnson's study continued to experience multiple orgasmic response. However, one-third of the women in another study reported significantly reduced capacity or inability to experience orgasm (Sarrel, 1988).

Orgasm appears to be an important aspect of sexual activity to older women. One survey (Starr & Weiner, 1981) found that 69% of women aged 60–91 listed "orgasm" first in response to the question, "What do you consider a good sexual experience?" Only 17% of the women answered "intercourse" to this same question. Additionally, "orgasm" was the most frequent response to the question, "What in the sex act is most important to you?" Compared with when they were younger, 65% of the women reported that their frequency of orgasm was the same, and 20% said it was increased. About 14% reported that they now experienced orgasms less often, but only 1.5% of the sample said that they never experienced orgasm.

Resolution Phase. The resolution phase typically occurs more rapidly in postmenopausal women. Labia color change, vaginal expansion, orgasmic platform formation, and clitoral retraction all disappear soon after orgasm. This is most likely due to the overall reduced amount of pelvic vasocongestion during arousal.

In summary, there is considerable variation in the effects of menopause and aging on female sexuality. Most women experience minor changes, and some others find their sexual interest, excitement, and orgasm seriously affected. An active sex life helps maintain vaginal health, and a functional and interested partner and good couple communication contribute to gratifying sexual relations for the older woman (Lieblum & Bachmann, 1988). Hormone replacement therapy, discussed in the next section, can also resolve many of the problems that interfere with enjoyable sexual response (Sarrel, 1988).

Hormone Replacement Therapy

Hormone-replacement therapy (HRT) involves taking supplemental estrogen and progesterone to compensate for the decrease in natural hormone production that occurs during the female climacteric. HRT may alleviate some of the problems resulting from the significant reduction in estrogen after menopause.

Given what you have learned about menopause, what difficulties do you think HRT could ameliorate or resolve? Take a minute to come up with your own ideas before reading on.

The estrogen in HRT can help maintain the urethral and vaginal tissues, vaginal lubrication, clitoral sensitivity, orgasmic response, and sexual interest (Walling et al., 1990). HRT can also contribute to general health by reducing hot flashes as well as the depression, sleep disturbances, and anxiety caused by estrogen deficiency (Matthews, 1992; Myers et al., 1990). In addition, estrogen provides significant protection against life-threatening *osteoporosis* (abnormal bone loss) and resultant fractures, particularly of the hip (Creasman, 1991). Estrogen also provides strong protection from cardiovascular disease (Barrett-Conner & Bush, 1991; Stampfer et al., 1991).

A significant increase in the incidence of endometrial cancer has been associated with the exclusive and continuous use of estrogen. Now, however, it is common practice to combine progestin with estrogen for about 10 days out of a 30-day cycle. The addition of progestin has almost eliminated the risk of endometrial cancer with HRT (Utian, 1990). The progestin causes the uterine lining to shed each month, and a monthly flow results. When this occurs, it is highly unlikely that the lining will develop cancer from estrogen stimulation. Women who have had a hysterectomy do not need to take progestin because they have no risk of uterine cancer.

Progestins may reduce the beneficial effect of estrogen in protecting against heart disease by unfavorably altering the type of fats in the bloodstream (Lobo & Whitehead, 1989; Luciano et al., 1988). The risks of heart disease are significantly increased in smokers, diabetics, the very obese, women who do not exercise, and women with high blood pressure and high cholesterol levels.

Women who have endometrial cancer or estrogen-dependent breast cancer cannot receive HRT because it can accelerate the rate of growth of these cancers. HRT does not cause these cancers; in fact, taking low-dose estrogen combined with progesterone reduces the chances of developing breast cancer. Women who need to be most cautious about HRT are those who have benign breast tumors or a strong family history of mothers or sisters with estrogen-dependent breast cancer (Nachtigall & Heilman, 1987). (Breast cancer that occurs after menopause is usually non–estrogen-dependent). In the past, HRT was contraindicated for women with liver impairment and gallbladder disease because it could worsen these conditions. However, vaginal creams or an estrogen patch on the skin can deliver the hormone directly into the bloodstream without passing through the digestive system.

Current research suggests that a menopausal woman should weigh the potential benefits and risks of hormone-replacement therapy against the symptoms of hormone deficiency. For many women the benefits far outweigh the potential risks

(Garnett, 1991). We recommend thorough discussion of the matter with a physician specializing in menopause and HRT.

There are also some alternatives to HRT. Continued frequent sexual activity helps maintain vaginal lubrication during sexual arousal. Research has found that vaginal changes due to aging are less pronounced in women who are sexually active through intercourse or masturbation than in sexually inactive women (Lieblum & Bachmann, 1988). Vaginal lubricants and moisturizers can also be used to help with vaginal lubrication (Notelowitz, 1990). Physical exercise, good nutrition, and food supplements can also sometimes alleviate some menopausal symptoms (Ritz, 1981).

Physiosexual Changes and Sexual Response: The Older Male

As a man grows older, certain physiosexual changes occur that are in large part related to decreased production of testosterone (Schiavi, 1990). In most men the male hormones reach their peak levels sometime between the ages of 17 and 20. Hormone output then steadily but slowly declines until around age 60, after which it remains fairly constant.

With aging, a man may note several changes in his sexual anatomy and functioning. The size and firmness of his testicles diminish somewhat. This is a normal anatomical change that is unlikely to impair his ability to function sexually. There is also a thickening and gradual degeneration of the seminiferous tubules, which generally results in reduced sperm production. However, many men retain their fertility well into their older years. There are numerous recorded cases of men older than 80 who have fathered children. Besides reduced sperm production, changes in orgasmic and erectile function also accompany the male aging process, and specific alterations occur in the prostate gland. We look at some of these changes in the following two sections.

The Sexual Response Cycle of the Older Male

Most changes in the sexual response cycle involve alterations in the intensity and duration of response (Masters & Johnson, 1966).

Excitement Phase. During youth many males are capable of achieving an erection in a few seconds. This ability is typically altered with the aging process. Instead of 8–10 seconds, a man may now require several minutes of effective stimulation to develop an erect penis (Segraves & Segraves, 1992). More direct physical stimulation, such as hand caressing or oral stimulation, may also be desirable or necessary. This slowed rate of erectile response may cause alarm, stimulating a fear of impotence in some men:

I guess it was the little things adding up that finally made me realize it was taking me longer to get a hard-on — the fact that I could go to bed with an extremely desirable woman and still be flaccid; that kissing and hugging often wasn't enough to get me started. At first I was real shaken-up at this discovery, thinking that maybe I would lose my potency. However, I

received some good advice from my physician, who assured me that while things may slow down a bit, they continue to remain functional. (Authors' files)

Fortunately, this man received good advice. Others, fearful that they will ultimately lose their erectile function, may develop such anxiety that their fears become reality. However, most men retain their erectile capacities throughout their lifetimes. The slowed rate of obtaining an erection is a natural part of the aging process. When a man and his partner understand this, the altered pattern has little or no effect on his enjoyment of sexual expression (LoPiccolo, 1991).

Plateau Phase. Older men do not typically experience as much *myotonia* (muscle tension) during the plateau phase as when they were younger. Testes may not elevate as close to the perineum. Complete penile erection is frequently not obtained until late in the plateau phase, just prior to orgasm. One result of these changes is that the older man is often able to prolong the plateau phase much longer than he did when he was younger, which may significantly enhance his pleasure. Many men appreciate this prolonged opportunity to enjoy other sensations of sexual response besides ejaculation. When a man engages in intercourse, his partner also may appreciate his greater ejaculatory control.

Orgasm Phase. Most aging males continue to experience considerable pleasure from their orgasmic responses. In fact, about 73% of older men in one study reported that orgasm was "very important" in their sexual experiences (Starr & Weiner, 1981). However, they may note a decline in intensity. Frequently absent are the sensations of ejaculatory inevitability that correspond with the emission phase of ejaculation. The number of muscular contractions occurring during the expulsion phase are typically reduced, and so is the force of ejaculation. The seminal fluid is usually less copious and somewhat thinner in consistency.

Resolution Phase. Resolution typically occurs more rapidly in older men. Loss of erection is usually quite rapid, perhaps bypassing altogether the two stages of penile detumescence characteristic of younger men. Testicles generally descend immediately after ejaculation.

While resolution becomes faster with aging, the refractory period between orgasm and the next excitement phase gradually lengthens. Men may begin to notice this as early as their 30s or 40s. Often by age 60, the refractory period may last for several hours, even days in some cases.

Another important factor is the man's partner's response to aging. A woman's sexual difficulties from menopause — pain or discomfort during intercourse or diminishing desire and enjoyment of sexual activity — can have a negative effect on the man's sexuality and may result in the man developing sexual problems.

The Prostate Gland

One of the most common physiosexual changes encountered by men during the aging process involves the prostate gland. This structure produces a large portion of the fluids contained in the ejaculate. Inflammation of the prostate, a condition known as **prostatitis** (pros-ta-TI-tis), is a difficulty that may occur in young and old alike, but it is considerably more common in older men. In most cases it results from a bacterial or viral infection, although occasionally it may be attributed to a disruption in the usual pattern of sexual behavior (either an increase or decrease in frequency). Some common symptoms of prostatitis include pain in the pelvic area, backache, urinary complications, and, occasionally, a cloudy discharge from the penis. In the case of a bacterial infection, medical treatment generally involves the administration of antibiotics. Nonbacterial prostatitis often responds to prostatic massage (the physician inserts a finger into the rectum and presses rhythmically against the prostate).

As men grow older, the prostate gland tends to increase in size, a condition called *benign prostatic hypertrophy.* The enlarged prostate tends to put pressure on the urethra, thus decreasing urine flow. If this problem is severe, surgery can correct it (Fowler et al., 1988).

It is not uncommon for aging men to develop benign or malignant tumors of the prostate (Lepor, 1992). Early detection of prostatic cancer is important to its successful treatment. Therefore, it is good preventive practice for all men past the age of 40 to have yearly prostate evaluations. The usual treatment for prostate cancer is surgical removal of the entire gland, *prostatectomy,* or treatment with female sex hormones. These treatments may contribute to a variety of problems in sexual functioning (Schmidt, 1992). Hormone treatments sometimes result in difficulty achieving an erection. Surgically removing portions of the prostate via the urethral tract damages the urethral sphincter valves, which can result in retrograde ejaculation. This produces sterility, although in some cases artificial insemination can be successfully performed with sperm removed from the man's urine. Although some prostate surgery may cause erection problems, surgical techniques that avoid cutting a small group of nerves involved in erection can maintain erectile functioning for many men following prostate surgery (Vikram & Vikram, 1988).

Sexual Development in the Later Years

As the preceding discussion of sexual responses indicates, most people retain the capacity and desire for sexual expression throughout their lives (Bachmann, 1990). As we grow older, all of us will experience some physical changes that will affect our sexual functioning. However, it is unlikely that these natural alterations will eliminate our capacity to maintain a rewarding and satisfying sex life. In the following sections, we examine some of the many factors that influence sexual development during the later years.

Sexual Expression in the Later Years

As you know from your previous reading, sexual expression can take many forms — including coitus, masturbation, kissing, and stroking. Which forms of sexual expression do you think are common among older adults? What might limit the options older adults have for expressing themselves sexually? Take a moment to list some of your ideas before reading on.

OTHER TIMES, OTHER PLACES

Sexuality and Aging in Other Cultures

We have only limited cross-cultural data about sexual expression among older men and women. However, some evidence suggests that frequency of activity is related to the status assigned older members of the community. It seems that cultures that value older people tend to be characterized by more frequent sexual expression among aging individuals. For example, the mountain people of Abkhasia, in the Caucasus region of the former Soviet Union, enjoy tremendous longevity as well as prolonged sexual activity. Sex among married couples is considered a primary pleasure in life, to be pursued for as long as possible. Most Abkhasian couples remain quite active sexually beyond the age of 70, and some even after the age of 100. Aging individuals are ascribed valued social status. They are expected to continue making productive contributions to the family and community — there is no retirement in this society. Moderation is the key cultural ethic: Older folks "continue to do what they have always done, but in gradually diminishing amounts" (Beach, 1978, p. 118).

The African Bala also seem to maintain a high degree of sexual vigor in the older years. Ethnographer Alan Merriam (1971) reported asking a small sample of men how many times they had experienced intercourse in the preceding 24 hours. The data, collected each morning for a period of 10 days, revealed that the average frequency of intercourse for several men over the age of 45 (the oldest was 66) was about 1.5 times per day. Some caution in interpreting this finding seems necessary. It is possible that being asked daily to report the frequency of coital encounters may have induced Merriam's respondents to temporarily increase or to misreport their activity levels.

The options for sexual expression may change in the later years. Men die an average of eight years earlier than women, and by age 65, more than half of married women are widows (Greene & Feld, 1989); women accustomed to expressing their sexuality exclusively within a marriage find themselves suddenly alone. Furthermore, older males without partners often seek younger female companions, whereas older women are less likely to be involved with younger men — both of which trends tend to limit the pool of potential new partners for older women.

Many older adults remain interested in sexuality (Mulligan, 1989; Mulligan & Palguta, 1991). One survey of 200 healthy people ages 80 – 102 found that 88% of the men and 72% of the women fantasized about sex (Bretschneider & McCoy, 1988). For some older women and men, widowed or divorced, masturbation can become or continue to be a form of sexual release and expression (Weizman & Hart, 1987). A study of 800 people between 60 and 91 years of age reported that women are becoming more accepting of masturbation as a means of sexual expression (Starr & Weiner, 1981). As a woman of 60 stated:

I thought my life was over when my husband of 35 years died two years ago. I have learned so much in that time. I learned to masturbate. I had my first orgasm. I had an "affair." I have established intimate relationships with women for the first time in my life. (Authors' files)

One survey found that more older people approved of masturbation (62%) than engaged in it (Brecher, 1984). This study also found that the incidence of masturbation among both male and female respondents declined with age and that a greater proportion of men than women — at all ages — reported masturbating (see Table 15.1).

Being married is no guarantee of a satisfying sexual relationship, particularly as aging occurs. One partner's sexual interest may lag behind the other's. A

TABLE 15.1   *Percentage of Older People Who Report That They Masturbate*

	Men	Women
Age 50 – 59	66	47
Age 60 – 69	50	37
Age 70 and above	43	33
Married	52	36
Unmarried	63	54

Source: Brecher, 1984.

woman who finds that her sexual needs are now greater than those of her husband or lover may find it quite difficult to seek more frequent sexual activity with him, particularly if a pattern of male initiation has been long established. Misunderstandings about altered patterns of sexual response may give rise to difficulties. A woman may misinterpret the slower erectile and ejaculation response of her husband or lover as signs of waning interest or rejection. Similarly, a man may believe that reduced vaginal lubrication is an indication that his wife or lover is less aroused by him than formerly. However, many couples find ways to successfully cope with lubrication and erection problems, as discussed later in this section (Brecher, 1984).

On the other hand, both well-established and new relationships may blossom during the later years. The opportunities for sexual expression in a relationship often increase, as pressures from work, children, and fulfilling life's goals may wane, thus allowing more time for sharing with a partner. Although it was not a representative study, one survey found that 66% of women and 80% of men age 70 and older experienced intercourse, and that 50% did so at least once a week (Brecher, 1984). Couples may increasingly emphasize quality rather than quantity of sexual experience. For example, one study of heterosexual men found that for younger men the amount of sexual activity they engaged in was an important aspect of their social confidence. However, for older men the quality of their sexual activity was the crucial factor (Stimpson et al., 1981). A small study of older gay men found something similar. Most of the homosexual respondents indicated that sex was less frequent than when they were younger, but half felt that it was more satisfying than before. As one 63-year-old man said, "Less accent on the genitals, more on the total person now" (Kimmel, 1978, p. 199).

Masters and Johnson (1966) reported that regularity of sexual expression throughout the adult years (whether by masturbation or activity with a partner) was a crucial factor in maintaining satisfactory sexual functioning beyond one's youth and middle age. This conclusion has been supported by data from Kinsey's studies (1948 & 1953), which revealed a close correlation between sexual activity levels in the earlier and later years. Other research has corroborated Kinsey's findings and has found that the differences among men and women in levels of sexual activity before middle age tended to be maintained as the men and women grew older (Bretschneider & McCoy, 1988; Lieblum & Bachmann, 1988). These findings do not necessarily demonstrate a direct cause-and-effect relationship between sex-

Sexual relationships may improve in later years when individuals redefine their sexual and affectional relationships.

ual activity in young adulthood and old age; it may simply be that those people with the strongest interest in sex in their youth maintain that interest into old age.

The stereotypical view that homosexual people as a group face a lonely and unhappy old age is not supported by the limited research available. Gay men and lesbians may be better prepared for coping with the adjustments of aging than are heterosexual men and women. Many homosexual individuals have planned for their own financial support and have consciously created a network of supportive friends (Kelly & Rice, 1986). Having successfully faced the adversities of belonging to a stigmatized group may also help them deal with the losses that come with aging (Dawson, 1982). One study found that older homosexual males match or exceed comparable groups in the general population on a measure of life satisfaction. The majority of these men reported that they socialized primarily with age peers. There was a change over time toward fewer sexual partners, but frequency of sexual activity remained quite stable, and 75% were satisfied with their current sex life (Berger, 1982). Another study of over 4000 gay men found no age-related differences in their levels of sexual activity and social interaction with other gay men. Research has also revealed that most older lesbians prefer women of similar ages as partners (Raphael & Robinson, 1980). Furthermore, lesbians do not face the same limitations as heterosexual women on the number of same-age eligible partners because their potential partners do not die younger than they do.

Intimacy, a lifelong need, may find new and deeper dimensions in later years. Some people find their sex lives markedly improved by the greater opportunities to explore relaxed and prolonged lovemaking. A few may even have more frequent sexual encounters, as revealed in one survey of people more than 65 years old (Pfeiffer, 1975). For others, genital contact may become less frequent, but interest, pleasure, and frequency of nonintercourse activities such as caressing, embracing, and kissing may remain stable or increase. As a 73-year-old man expressed it:

> I don't know if I'm oversexed, but I'm a lover. I like to pet, kiss, hug. I have more fun out of loving somebody I love than the ultimate end. You know, some people want sex and forget the rest of it — the hugging and the petting — and I think that's wrong. People say, "What will happen to me when I get older?" Well, I'm still alive! (Vinick, 1978, p. 362)

Nonsexual relationships often provide affection and closeness.

One survey found that, while sexual frequency declines, enjoyment of sex sometimes increases with age. Many respondents found techniques for maintaining or enhancing their enjoyment of sex despite the progressive physiological changes. For example, 43% of women and 56% of men provided oral stimulation to their partners. Some used fantasy or sexually explicit materials; others engaged in manual and oral stimulation of the breasts and genitals, anal stimulation, use of a vibrator, various coital positions, sex in the morning, or exclusive fondling and cuddling (Brecher, 1984). Middle-class and upper-middle-class elderly adults are more likely to include options beyond intercourse than are those in lower socioeconomic groups. In one study most of the men in the lower socioeconomic group stopped all sexual activity when they were unable to have intercourse (Cogen & Steinman, 1990). This data supports Kinsey's findings that the poor and working class were strongly oriented toward intercourse and considered other sexual alternatives unacceptable. Openness to experimenting and developing new sexual strategies together with a supportive partner are instrumental in continuing sexual satisfaction (Bachmann, 1991; Schiavi, 1990). Some older individuals and couples will participate in sex therapy to enhance their sexual lives (LoPiccolo, 1991; Schiavi, 1990).

Older people may redefine their sexual and affectional relationships. Nonsexual friendships with either sex can offer affectionate physical contact, emotional closeness, intellectual stimulation, and opportunities for socializing. One survey found that a supportive network of close friends helped minimize loneliness and maintain life enjoyment, especially for the unmarried (Brecher, 1984).

Most people who regularly hike, fish, play golf, or till a garden during their youth will continue to do so in their later years. In fact, regular physical activity (walking, jogging, swimming, and so forth) enhances sexual desire and erotic abilities, besides contributing to one's general and sexual health. Exercise and physical activity permit most individuals to be at least 10 – 20 years younger physiologically than their chronological age (Harris, 1988b). Poor health and illness have a greater impact on sexual functioning than age itself (Mulligen et al., 1988).

Far from developing a total incapacity for recreational activities, older people may simply pursue them less often and at a more leisurely pace. The same can be true of one's sex life, particularly if misconceptions and anxieties are avoided or resolved.

As one grows older, an active physical life can contribute to health and self-satisfaction.

Sex isn't as powerful a need as when you're young, but the whole feeling is there; it's as nice as it ever was. He puts his arms around you, kisses you, and it comes to you — satisfaction and orgasm — just like it always did . . . don't let anybody tell you different. Maybe it only happens once every 2 weeks, but as you get older, it's such a release from tensions. I'm an old dog who's even tried a few new tricks. Like oral sex, for instance. . . . We weren't too crazy about it though. . . . We take baths together, and he washes my body, and I wash his. I know I'm getting old and my skin could use an ironing, but we love each other — so sex is beautiful. (Wax, 1975, p. 43)

A review of the literature on sexuality and aging notes the following trends:

1. Maintenance of sexual capacity depends on regular sexual expression.

2. In the presence of reasonably good health and available partners, sexual activity among older people continues into the 70s, 80s, and 90s (Mooradian & Greiff, 1990). Even many who are no longer sexually active continue to be sexually interested.

3. Within the older age group, the range of sexual drives varies from very great to very little. Sexual capacity varies from individual to individual, and from time to time in a particular individual.

4. There is an overall pattern of decline in sexual interest and activity with advancing age. However, sexuality continues to hold a place of importance in the lives of most older people.

5. Among older women and men, sexual interest and activity are directly related to individual sexual histories. Those who described their sexual urges as strongest in youth tended to describe them as moderate in old age. Those who described their sexual feelings in youth as weak to moderate tended to describe themselves as being without sexual feelings in old age (Dressel & Avant, 1983, pp. 199–200).

Toward Androgyny in Later Life

Development toward androgyny in personal, interpersonal, and sexual styles occurs for many people in later life (Hyde et al., 1991). On a biological level, the hormonal differences between women and men tend to diminish. Estrogen levels in women decline rapidly following menopause, and androgen levels in men decline gradually from about age 30 on. The extent to which these hormonal changes contribute to increased androgyny is unknown.

On psychological and social levels, the gender-role differences between men and women also tend to diminish in later years. Expectations for gender-specific roles and responsibilities are more pronounced in younger adulthood, when the demands of supporting and rearing a family pressure men to focus on their jobs or careers and women to focus on taking care of the children. But with retirement approaching and children leaving home, such pressures tend to decline — thus freeing both women and men to develop more androgynous patterns. One study found that older men and women developed other-sex characteristics by age 50 without relinquishing same-sex characteristics:

> Individuals who were psychologically healthiest at age 50 showed increased androgyny over time. Women became more assertive and analytic while remaining nurturant and open to feelings. Men became more giving and expressive while they continued to be assertive and ambitious. (Livson, 1983, p. 112)

Another study found that men who were more emotionally expressive also experienced more sexual interest (Thomas, 1991). There is also often a shift in power within the marital relationship, with women being more likely to have increased power in later rather than in earlier life stages (Chiriboga & Thrunher, 1980).

These developments can help set the stage for a merging of sexual styles that may occur in later years. A more androgynous orientation allows individuals to expand their concepts of a sensuous man or woman (Rice & Kelly, 1987). Older males often become more like women in their sexual behavior, in that fantasy and ambience become more important and orgasm less so. Older adults may move away from the stereotypical focus of women on the relationship and men on genital sex. Over the lives of many of the subjects of one study, women developed a greater interest in genital sex and men in nongenital sexuality, thus realizing a more harmonious relationship (Bangs, 1985).

Summary

Sexuality in the Later Years: Examining the Myths

American culture continues to be influenced by the philosophy that equates sexual expression with procreation and youth.

The sexual double standard continues into old age. It often affects both sexes adversely but may impose a particular burden on women. However, marriages of older women to younger men have increased in recent years.

For the 5% of older Americans who live in nursing homes, antisexual prejudice against older people is pronounced in some of the facilities, particularly for homosexual residents.

Physiosexual Changes and Sexual Response: The Older Female

Menopause is the cessation of menstruation and signals the end of female fertility. Fifty-one is the average age of menopause. Due to increases in life expectancy, women can expect to live half of their adult lives following menopause.

Most women experience few uncomfortable symptoms during the aging process and maintain sexual interest and response. Others experience symptoms such as hot flashes, sleep disturbance, depression or anxiety, headaches, and sensitivity to touch due to declining estrogen levels.

A postmenopausal woman typically requires more time to achieve vaginal lubrication. The sexual response cycle of the older woman is also characterized by less vaginal expansion, diminished orgasmic intensity, and a more rapid resolution.

Less commonly, women may experience a decrease in sexual desire, clitoral sensitivity, and/or the capacity for orgasm.

Hormone-replacement therapy (HRT) is a medical treatment for menopausal symptoms and helps protect against osteoporosis and heart disease. Potential side effects necessitate careful use of such therapy. Continued sexual activity also helps maintain sexual functioning.

Physiosexual Changes and Sexual Response: The Older Male

After early adulthood, testosterone production declines steadily, until approximately age 60. Many physiosexual changes in the aging male result from this decreased hormone output.

Common physiosexual changes in the older male include reduction in the size and firmness of the testicles, lowered sperm production, and difficulties with the prostate gland.

The older male typically requires longer periods of time to achieve erection and reach orgasm. Greater ejaculatory control may be beneficial to sexual pleasure for both his partner and himself.

The sexual response cycle of the aging male is also characterized by less myotonia, reduced orgasmic intensity, more rapid resolution, and longer refractory periods.

Sexual Development in the Later Years

The options for sexual expression may change in the older years, as many individuals find themselves without a sexual partner. Masturbation may serve as one alternative.

Sexual relationships may improve during later years when individuals focus on intimacy and redefine their sexual and affectional relationships. Physical health and exercise can help maintain sexual functioning and satisfaction.

A blurring of stereotypic gender roles, an increase in androgyny, and a consequent merging of sexual styles often occur in later life.

It is unlikely that the physiosexual changes of aging alone will eliminate one's capacity to maintain a satisfying sex life.

∽ *Thought Provokers* ∽

1. Television programs featuring older adults, such as "Murder, She Wrote," with Angela Lansbury, and "The Golden Girls" (about four female housemates over age 50), have become more common. How do you account for the popularity of these shows, and what impact might they have on attitudes toward sexuality and older adults?

2. What policies and practices do you think nursing homes should follow regarding their residents' sexual behavior?

3. Are there any advantages to old age that you are looking forward to? Can you imagine yourself as a "sexy senior citizen"? What do you think the potential advantages and disadvantages of the development in later years toward androgyny might be?

Suggested Readings

Adelman, M. (1986). *Long Time Passing*. Boston: Alyson Publications. These are stories of the lives of older lesbians reflecting the cultural changes during their lifetimes.

Berger, Raymond (1982). *Gay and Gray*. Urbana: University of Illinois Press. An informative, research-based book that examines the lifestyles, sexuality, relationships, and life satisfaction of older homosexual men.

Butler, Robert; and Lewis, Myrna (1986). *Love and Sex After Forty*. New York: Harper & Row. This book provides extensive, down-to-earth health and living-adjustment information related to sexuality. Many useful suggestions are offered within a context of individual differences, with encouragement for personal and relationship growth.

Nachtigall, Lila; and Heilman, Joan (1987). *Estrogen: The Facts Can Change Your Life*. New York: Harper & Row. This book offers comprehensive information on menopause, hormone-replacement therapy, and alternative treatments.

Weg, Ruth (Ed.) (1983). *Sexuality in the Later Years: Roles and Behavior*. New York: Academic Press. This book provides a multifaceted approach to the understanding of sexual roles and behavior in the later years, including perspectives from anthropology, psychology, sociology, and physiology.

PART FIVE

Sexual Problems

For some years she had been thinking she was not much inclined toward sex. . . . It is not merely a lack of pleasure in sex, it is dislike of the excitement. And it is not merely dislike, it is worse, it is boredom.

Muriel Spark
Collected Stories: I (1968)

CHAPTER 16

The Nature and Origin of Sexual Difficulties

Desire Phase Difficulties

Excitement Phase Difficulties

Orgasm Phase Difficulties

Coital Pain

Origins of Sexual Difficulties

*T*he next four chapters are concerned with some of the difficulties that can hinder sexual functioning and some ways of preventing or resolving these difficulties. This chapter looks at a number of relatively common sexual problems and the factors that frequently contribute to them. First, we look at a number of specific problems related to sexual desire, arousal, and orgasm, and at problems that cause painful intercourse. We then discuss some common origins of these problems — organic, cultural, individual, and interpersonal. Chapter 17 outlines sex therapy approaches and ways of enhancing sexuality, Chapter 18 elaborates on the impact of chronic illness and disability on sexuality, and in Chapter 19 we turn our attention to understanding and preventing sexually transmitted diseases.

In reading this chapter, it is important to remember that sexual satisfaction is a subjective perception. A person or couple could experience some of the problems described in this chapter and yet be satisfied with their sex lives. In fact, some research has indicated that many of the happily married couples studied experienced problems with arousal and orgasm but felt very positive about their sexual relations and marriages (Frank et al., 1978).

How common do you think sexual problems are? Take a moment to estimate what percentage of people have sexual problems such as lack of desire, inability to experience an erection or orgasm, or rapid ejaculation.

Research indicates that sexual problems are quite common. A study of a nonclinical population of university students who responded to a mailed questionnaire found that 13% reported sexual dysfunctions (Spencer & Zeiss, 1987). A random, nationwide survey done by *Parade Magazine* found that one in seven men and women reported problems in their sex lives (Ende et al., 1984). Table 16.1 shows percentages taken from 23 different studies of people with specific sexual problems.

In the first half of this chapter, we consider some of the specific problems people encounter with the desire, excitement, and orgasm phases of sexual response. In reality there is considerable overlap: Problems with desire and arousal

---

Prevalence of Sexual Problems in Nonclinical Sample   T A B L E   16.1

Percentage of adults who reported specific sexual problems.

	Men	Women
Lack of sexual desire	16	34
Erection difficulties	4 – 9	—
Anorgasmia	0	5 – 10
Inhibited male orgasm	4 – 10	—
Premature ejaculation	36 – 38	—
Pain during intercourse	0	8 – 23

Source: Spector & Carey, 1990.

also affect orgasm, and orgasm difficulties can easily affect a person's interest and ability to become aroused.

The sexual problems we will discuss can vary in duration and focus from person to person. A specific difficulty can be of lifelong duration or appear at a certain time. A person may experience the problem in all situations with all partners (global) or only in specific situations or with specific partners (situational) (Kaplan, 1977; LoPiccolo, 1989).

The categories and labels for the problems we discuss come from a number of sources: the American Psychiatric Association's *Diagnostic and Statistical Manual (DSM III – R)*, the Stony Brook Sex Therapy Center in New York State (Schover et al., 1982), and a few additions of our own.

Desire Phase Difficulties

Problems with sexual desire have received increased attention in recent years. This section discusses inhibited sexual desire, dissatisfaction with frequency of sexual activity, and sexual aversion.

Inhibited Sexual Desire

Inhibited sexual desire (ISD) is a common sexual difficulty experienced by both men and women. It is the most frequent problem that brings people to seek sex therapy. ISD is characterized by a lack of interest in sexual activity (O'Carroll, 1991). Helen Singer Kaplan (1979) described it as a lack of "sexual appetite." ISD can be distinct from excitement and orgasm difficulties. In fact, some people who are uninterested in sex become aroused and experience orgasm when they engage in a sexual encounter. Others may experience pleasure from touching and physical closeness but have no desire for erotic excitement. Still others with ISD feel tension and anxiety with physical and sexual contact and do not experience arousal and orgasm.

Global, lifelong ISD is rare. People with this condition did not masturbate or exhibit sexual curiosity in childhood, and as adults they do not develop interest in sexual fantasy, sexual activity, or the sexual aspects of a relationship. More commonly, people develop ISD at a specific point in their lives. Some people may experience ISD in a particular situation, such as with a spouse but not with a lover or when masturbating. In general, ISD is most commonly presented as a problem when it causes distress in a relationship.

Dissatisfaction with Frequency of Sexual Activity

Sexual partners usually have normal discrepancies in their preferences for amount, type, and timing of sexual activities. Sometimes the relationship can accommodate these individual differences. However, when sexual differences are a source of significant conflict or dissatisfaction, a couple can experience considerable discomfort.

Inhibited sexual desire frequently reflects relationship problems.

Instead of moving toward some compromise, the couple may polarize in opposite directions. Feelings of resentment and power struggles may then develop. A common pattern that often emerges in these situations is that one partner feels constantly deprived and the other constantly pressured. Usually both feel unloved and guilty — one for asking too much and the other for not giving enough (Zilbergeld & Kilmann, 1984).

Sexual Aversion

When low desire for sexual activity includes a fear of sex and a compelling desire to avoid sexual situations, this is considered **sexual aversion** (Kaplan, 1987). Sexual aversion can range from feelings of discomfort, repulsion, and disgust to extreme, irrational fear of sexual activity. Even the thought of sexual contact can result in intense anxiety and panic. A person who experiences sexual aversion may exhibit physiological symptoms such as sweating, increased heart rate, nausea, dizziness, trembling, or diarrhea as a consequence of fear.

Excitement Phase Difficulties

Both men and women can experience difficulties in sexual arousal. Of course, most of us are not responsive sexually all of the time. Sometimes we may be too preoccupied with another aspect of our lives, too fatigued, or feeling somewhat distant from our partners. However, when physiological arousal, erotic sensations, or the subjective feeling of being "turned on" are chronically diminished or absent, inhibited sexual excitement exists (Schover et al., 1982). We focus here on lack of vaginal lubrication in women and the inability to achieve or maintain erections in men.

Lubrication Inhibition

As we saw in Chapters 4 and 6, vaginal lubrication is a woman's first physiological response to sexual arousal. For some women inhibited lubrication is only an occasional problem. They become sufficiently aroused to experience lubrication in certain situations but not in others. Other women have never experienced vaginal lubrication during a sexual encounter. Biological factors, including low estrogen levels, can be a factor in lack of lubrication. Nonphysiological factors such as years of learning not to experience sexual arousal frequently contribute to this difficulty. Feelings of apathy, anger, or fear may also inhibit arousal and lubrication.

Lack of lubrication in a particular situation does not necessarily mean something is wrong. Vaginal lubrication frequently decreases during prolonged coitus. This may be due to a long plateau phase (during the plateau phase, lubrication typically decreases). Or, it may be the result of exclusive coital stimulation that may not be stimulating enough to induce continued lubrication. In the latter case, if continued sexual contact is desired, simultaneous manual stimulation of the clitoris or other parts of the body or changing to noncoital activities may increase lubrication. In addition, diminished lubrication is normal while breast-feeding and following menopause.

Erectile Inhibition

The term often applied to male erection difficulty is *impotence.* The origin of this word suggests the primary reason for our opposition to its use: It comes from Latin and literally means "without power." The implication is that a man is powerless as a lover without an erection. It is likely that a man who cannot achieve or maintain an erection is deeply concerned; the implication that he is without value as a lover only contributes to this distress. As the following account indicates, however, this interpretation can be far from reality:

I met a man once whose erectile capacity was completely destroyed by a spinal-cord injury in the precise region of the lower spine where erectile function is controlled. While he couldn't get it up, he certainly had no trouble getting it on! I've often wondered if his acquired status of highly desired lover had something to do with his discovery that erections are not essential to meaningful sexual interaction. (Authors' files)

Instead of the term *impotence,* we use the more neutral term **erectile inhibition,** which adequately describes this major male difficulty without the negative connotations just mentioned. *Erectile dysfunction* is another term commonly substituted for impotence in professional literature (Levine & Althof, 1991).

OUR SEXUALITY

A Case Study in Psychologically Based Erectile Inhibition

The following case is a composite of several actual situations described to the authors by students and clients. At the end are some questions that may prove helpful as you analyze both the source(s) and potential remedies for the difficulties encountered by this hypothetical couple.

Bill and Karen attended a party, during the course of which she became quite angry over his lack of attention. As the evening wore on, her anger mounted, ultimately resulting in an argument with Bill. On the drive home, neither talked. Both felt somewhat responsible, but neither was willing to apologize. Bill was actually feeling some guilt over his actions and was determined to make up in bed. At the same time, he was still angry at Karen. He brought these conflicting feelings to bed with him and was unable to get an erection. Now Karen became openly angry and suggested that Bill's present ineptness, together with his earlier indifference at the party, clearly indicated a lack of caring on his part. He feebly

assured her that this was not the case, that he was just tired, and that everything would be back to normal next time. But would it really be fine the next time? This question bothered him as he lay awake, long after Karen had fallen asleep by his side.

The next day he could think of little else. "I have got to make it right tonight — must show her that I still care." However, as the evening approached, his anxiety mounted. By the time he was driving home, the pressure was really intense. He stopped at a bar for a drink or two to soothe his growing fears. Finally, after an evening spent trying to appear casual and collected, it was time for bed — time for him to function as a lover.

Instead of being spontaneously swept away by the passions of lovemaking, he remained focused on his penis, willing it to respond and to become erect. He had now become a spectator to his own performance, cursing his flaccid penis, sick with frustration and concern over Karen's

response to his repeated failure. Unexpectedly, but perhaps more damaging, her reaction was not overtly accusatory. Rather she simply withdrew in brooding silence, leaving him alone with his misery. At this point, he was on the merry-go-round of the failure-fear-failure syndrome.

The following are some questions for analysis:

1. What does this case illustrate about the relationship between emotional conflicts and sexual intimacy?

2. In what ways do you think Bill's and Karen's expectations of love and intimacy may have contributed to the development of their shared problem?

3. How might this situation have been averted?

4. What do you think Bill and Karen could do to resolve their sexual problem?

Erectile inhibition is a common problem among men who seek sex therapy (Spector & Carey, 1990). Erectile inhibition problems may be broadly classified into two types. Men with *lifelong erectile inhibition* have attempted but never experienced maintained penetration (either vaginally or anally) throughout their entire lives, although they may routinely experience nocturnal erections and have erections when masturbating.

The label *nonlifelong erectile inhibition* is applied to the man who has previously had erections with his partner(s) but finds himself presently unable to experience consistently a functional erection. This condition is far more prevalent than lifelong erectile difficulty. It is common for men to occasionally be unable to achieve or maintain an erection due to minor factors like fatigue or stress. Masters and Johnson stated that if a man was unable to have an erection in 25% or more of his sexual experiences, this label was appropriate for him. We believe that the percentage is not as important as whether the individual or couple sees the erectile failure as a problem.

Orgasm Phase Difficulties

The problems we have been discussing have primarily been ones of desire and excitement. Some other sexual difficulties specifically affect orgasmic response, and a variety of problems are reported by both women and men. Some of these problems are infrequency of orgasms or their total absence. Others involve reaching orgasm too rapidly or delayed climaxes. Sometimes a partner may fake orgasm to conceal its absence.

Inhibited Female Orgasm

The term *frigidity* has been used as a general, descriptive label for female sexual problems including lack of interest, arousal, or orgasm. It is both imprecise and pejorative, mistakenly implying that women with these difficulties are totally sexually unresponsive and emotionally cold or unloving. Many sexuality educators and therapists now use the word **anorgasmia** (AN-or-GAZ-mē-uh), meaning the absence of orgasm, instead.

Some women who do not achieve orgasm experience arousal, lubrication, and enjoyment from sexual contact. However, their sexual response does not increase to the point of orgasm. Some may feel satisfied with their sexual experience without orgasm; others are highly disappointed and distressed. The lack of peak arousal and physical release from orgasm can result in experiences that are less and less enjoyable.

Anorgasmia can be lifelong or nonlifelong, global or specific. A woman who has *global, lifelong anorgasmia* has never experienced orgasm by masturbation or with a partner. *Nonlifelong anorgasmia* refers to a woman who has previously experienced orgasm but no longer does so. A woman who has *specific anorgasmia* experiences orgasm rarely, or in some situations but not in others; for example, she may be orgasmic when masturbating but not with a partner, or orgasmic with manual or oral stimulation from her partner but not during intercourse.

Global, lifelong anorgasmia is quite common; surveys have indicated that approximately 5–10% of adult women in the United States have never experienced orgasm by any means of self- or partner stimulation (Spector & Carey, 1990). This figure is especially noteworthy when compared to the number of men who have never experienced orgasm in their lifetimes. We do not know exactly how many this is; because it is assumed that all males have orgasms, the question is rarely even asked. Nevertheless, some men are totally anorgasmic, although the incidence is extremely low.

There are some indications that the number of global, lifelong anorgasmic women is decreasing, and some sex therapy clinics are seeing a smaller percentage of women with this problem (LoPiccolo, 1980). This apparent decrease may be due to the accessibility of excellent self-help books for women who want to learn to experience orgasm.

The absence of routine orgasm during coitus without additional manual–clitoral stimulation is a common and normal pattern for women. *The Hite Report* (1976) asked women if they routinely experienced orgasm during coitus without simultaneous manual stimulation of the clitoral area; only 30% responded that they did. Another study found that fewer than half (44%) of 141 women attending human sexuality workshops usually or always experienced orgasm during intercourse without simultaneous manual clitoral stimulation (Ellison, 1980). Kaplan stated, "There are millions of women who are sexually responsive, and often multiply orgasmic, but who cannot have an orgasm during intercourse unless they receive simultaneous clitoral stimulation" (1974, p. 397). For many women the indirect clitoral stimulation that occurs during coitus is simply less effective than direct manual or oral stimulation of the clitoral area.

During coitus the clitoris may be stimulated indirectly in two ways. First, coital thrusting can create tension in the labia minora, which extend to the clitoral hood. Clitoral stimulation thereby occurs from pressure and movement of the hood (Masters & Johnson, 1966). Second, pressure on the mons and clitoral area from the partner's pubic bone may provide stimulation (Hite, 1976; Masters & Johnson, 1966). Although this indirect clitoral stimulation is often not sufficiently intense to result in orgasm, most women, as indicated in *The Hite Report*, report intercourse to be highly enjoyable and desirable.

Freud maintained that women who required direct clitoral stimulation to experience orgasm demonstrated immature, masculine, or neurotic development. This belief has lingered in popular mythology, contributing to misunderstanding among men and women. Unfortunately, many women believe there is something wrong with them for not experiencing orgasms during coitus — even though coitus may not fully address their physiological needs. The painfully asked question "I come when he touches me but not when he's inside me; what's wrong with me?" is very common. Women who require direct clitoral stimulation to reach orgasm may be reluctant to ask for or engage in manual stimulation or to request noncoital stimulation after their partners ejaculate. In fact, anorgasmic women report greater discomfort in communicating to a partner about their desires for direct clitoral stimulation than do women who experience orgasm during coitus (Kelly et al., 1990). Most sex therapists believe that women who enjoy intercourse and experience orgasm in some way other than during coitus do not have a sexual problem (LoPiccolo, 1985). However, some women may wish to increase their arousal and experiment with experiencing orgasm during intercourse to enhance sexual enjoyment.

Inhibited Male Orgasm

Ejaculatory inhibition generally refers to the inability of a man to ejaculate during coitus. Four to nine percent of men experience this difficulty (Spector & Carey, 1990). Most men who are troubled by inhibited ejaculation are able to reach orgasm through masturbation or manual or oral stimulation from their partners. In some cases, however, a man may not ejaculate at all during a sexual encounter, as revealed in the following account:

I began a sexual relationship several months ago with a man who has a problem I've never before encountered. He has no difficulty getting an erection. In fact, he usually seems real excited when we make love. But he never comes. The first time I thought it was great — he seemed to be able to go on forever. But after a while it started getting to me. I've tried everything — going down on him, using my hand, stroking his scrotum when he is inside me — nothing works. He doesn't want to talk about it, but I sense he is as frustrated as I am, maybe more. Once I got him to admit he climaxes when he masturbates. Why can't he come with me? (Authors' files)

Many researchers and therapists distinguish between global, lifelong and situational, nonlifelong ejaculatory inhibition. *Global, lifelong ejaculatory inhibition* applies to men who have never been able to experience intravaginal ejaculation. Most of these men are capable of ejaculating outside the vagina, through stimulation by a partner or through masturbation. However, there are extremely rare cases of men who have never experienced ejaculation in their entire lives (Kaplan, 1974). When inhibited ejaculation develops in a man who has a past history of normal ejaculatory functioning, his problem is classified as *situational, nonlifelong ejaculatory inhibition.*

Premature Ejaculation

A common male orgasm difficulty is **premature ejaculation.** We define premature ejaculation as consistently reaching orgasm so quickly that it significantly diminishes a man's own enjoyment of the experience, impairs a partner's gratification, or both. This definition eliminates arbitrary time goals, takes into account the partner's pleasure, and views the person's own subjective needs as an important determinant of what constitutes reaching orgasm too fast.

The average duration of intercourse for American couples is between five and ten minutes. Taking this norm into account, the Stony Brook group considers premature ejaculation on a continuum. First, the premature ejaculation label is not applied if neither the man nor his partner considers the rapidity of ejaculation a problem. Otherwise, ejaculation before penetration or after only a minute or two of intercourse, or needing to use intrusive and unpleasant techniques to delay ejaculation throughout the length of intercourse, is considered a problem (Schover et al., 1982).

Approximately 35–38% of men experience premature ejaculation. Masters and Johnson stated that it was the most prevalent male sexual problem and estimated that millions were troubled by it. In anonymous surveys of students enrolled in our human sexuality classes over the last several years, consistently over 75% of the men have reported that premature ejaculation was at least sometimes a problem. Twenty-five percent of our male students have reported premature ejaculation to be an ongoing difficulty.

Faking Orgasms

A final orgasmic difficulty we discuss is **faking orgasms** — pretending to experience orgasm without actually doing so. This kind of sexual deception is typically discussed in reference to women, and it happens quite often. According to a recent survey of female students in our sexuality classes, 62% have faked an orgasm at some time. Other research has indicated that nearly 66% of women and 33% of men have pretended to experience orgasm from time to time (Darling & Davidson, 1986).

What are your thoughts about why men and women fake orgasm? Develop your own ideas before reading further.

Unlike some of the other difficulties discussed in this chapter, faking orgasm reflects a conscious decision. The most common reason given by women for pretending orgasm was to avoid disappointing or hurting their partners (Darling & Davidson, 1986). A person is often motivated to engage in such deception by real or imagined performance pressures. Some additional factors related to faking orgasms may include poor communication or limited knowledge of sexual techniques, a need for partner approval, little hope of changing the partner's behavior, and an attempt to hide a deteriorating relationship or to protect a partner's ego (Lauersen & Graves, 1984). The following comments, all by women, reveal some of these motivations:

He feels badly if I don't have an orgasm during intercourse, so I fake it, even though I have real ones from oral sex. (Authors' files)

I get tired of intercourse after a certain period, and there he is, still pumping away, determined not to stop until I come, so I pretend to climax. (Authors' files)

I don't know my partner well enough to tell her what I like, but I don't want her to think it's her fault that I don't come. (Authors' files)

I started our sexual relationship faking, and I don't know how to stop. (Authors' files)

Although some women may find faking orgasm to be an acceptable solution in their individual situations, others find that faking itself becomes troublesome, as revealed in the last of the preceding comments. The effects of faking orgasm can include increased resentment, guilt, anger, and fear of being discovered (Lauersen & Graves, 1984). At the least, faking orgasms creates emotional distance at a time of potential closeness and satisfaction (Masters & Johnson, 1976).

Do you think there are any other disadvantages associated with faking orgasm? Take a few moments to think about this question before reading on.

There is often a vicious cycle involved in faking orgasms. The person's partner is likely not to know that his or her partner has pretended to climax. Consequently, the deceived partner continues to do what he or she has been led to believe is effective, and the other partner continues to fake to prevent discovery of the deception. This makes it more difficult for the couple to talk about and discover what is gratifying to both of them. Once established, a pattern of deception may be quite difficult to break.

How to best change this pattern of interaction is a matter of personal decision. Some people may not want to change because faking orgasms serves a purpose in a relationship. A person who does want to change might decide to discontinue faking orgasms without discussing the decision with her or his partner. Under such circumstances some of the procedures for enhancing sexual pleasure outlined in Chapter 17 might prove helpful. Another alternative would be to inform one's partner of one's past deception and to discuss the reasons why pretending to climax seemed necessary. Some of the communication strategies outlined in Chapter 8 may help in this process. Maybe some specific difficulties will surface as the motivation for deception, such as female orgasmic problems, or retarded ejaculation. It may be helpful, or perhaps necessary, to engage a counselor to help communicate with a partner. Seeing a counselor may also facilitate efforts to establish more rewarding sexual behaviors.

Coital Pain

Both men and women can experience coital pain, although it is more common for women to have this problem. The medical term for painful intercourse is **dyspareunia** (DIS-puh-ROO-nē-uh).

Painful Intercourse in Men

Painful intercourse in men is unusual but does occur. If the foreskin of an uncircumcised male is too tight, he may experience pain during sexual arousal and have difficulty reaching orgasm. In such circumstances minor surgery may be indicated. Inadequate hygiene of an uncircumcised penis can result in the accumulation of smegma or infections beneath the foreskin, causing irritation of the glans during sexual stimulation. This problem can be prevented by routinely pulling back the foreskin and washing the glans area with soap and water.

Another possible source of pain or discomfort for men is **Peyronie's disease** in which fibrous tissue and calcium deposits develop in the space above and between the cavernous bodies of the penis (Miller, 1989). This fibrosis results in pain and curvature of the penis with erection that, in severe cases, interferes with intercourse and can interfere with erection (Ansell, 1991; Eigner et al., 1991). Medical treatments can sometimes be effective in treating this condition (Gelbard, 1988). Finally, problems and infections of the urethra, bladder, prostate gland, or seminal vesicles may induce burning, itching, or pain during or after ejaculation (Davis & Noble, 1991). Proper medical attention can generally alleviate this source of discomfort during coitus.

Painful Intercourse in Women

Experiencing pain with intercourse is very likely to affect a woman's sexual arousal. Coital discomfort stems from a variety of causes, and for this reason it is important for the woman to determine specifically where the pain is.

Discomfort at the vaginal entrance or inside the vaginal walls is commonly due to inadequate arousal and lubrication. Physiological conditions such as insufficient hormones may also reduce lubrication. Using a lubricating jelly can provide a temporary solution so that intercourse can take place comfortably, but this may bring only short-term relief. For a more permanent solution, it would be better if the woman could discover the cause of her discomfort and then take steps to remedy the situation.

There are also a variety of other causes for vaginal discomfort during intercourse. Yeast, bacterial, and trichomoniasis infections cause inflammations of the vaginal walls and may result in painful intercourse when the infection is present. Such inflammations are often related to the problem just described: Intercourse with insufficient lubrication irritates the vaginal walls and increases the possibility of vaginal infections. Foam, contraceptive cream or jelly, condoms, and diaphragms may irritate the vaginas of some women. Pain at the opening of the vagina may also be attributed to an intact or inadequately ruptured hymen, a Bartholin's gland infection, or scar tissue at the opening (Brashear & Munsick, 1991).

Inflammation of the bladder wall can cause moderate to severe pain during intercourse.

Vulvar vestibulitis syndrome results in severe pain at the entrance of the vagina. There is typically a small reddened area that is very painful even with light pressure, but the area may be so small that it is difficult for the health care practitioner to see (Goetsch, 1991). Another area where there may be discomfort is the clitoral glans. Occasionally, smegma collects under the clitoral hood and may cause distress when the hood is moved during sexual stimulation. Gentle washing of the clitoris and hood may help prevent this.

Pain deep in the pelvis during coital thrusting may be due to jarring of the ovaries or stretching of the uterine ligaments. A woman may experience this type of discomfort only in certain positions or at certain times in her menstrual cycle. Some women report that such pain only occurs around the time they are ovulating. Avoiding positions or movements that aggravate the pain is the first solution; and if a woman has more control of the pelvic movements during coitus, she may feel more secure about being able to avoid pain.

Another source of deep pelvic pain is *endometriosis,* a condition in which tissue that normally grows on the walls of the uterus implants on various parts of the abdominal cavity. Endometrial tissue can prevent internal organs from moving freely, resulting in pain during coitus. Birth control pills are sometimes prescribed to control the buildup of tissue during the monthly cycle. Gynecological surgeries for uterine and ovarian cancer can also cause dyspareunia (Anderson et al., 1989).

Infections in the uterus, such as gonorrhea, may also result in painful intercourse. In fact, pelvic pain may often be the first physical symptom noticed by a woman who has gonorrhea. If the infection has caused considerable scar tissue to develop, surgery may be necessary. Childbirth and rape may tear the ligaments that hold the uterus in the pelvic cavity, which can result in pain during coitus. Surgery can relieve this difficulty partially or completely.

Vaginismus

Vaginismus (vaj-in-IZ-mus) is characterized by strong involuntary contractions of the muscles in the outer third of the vagina (see Figure 16.1). The contraction can be so strong that attempts at inserting a penis into the vagina are very painful to the woman. A woman with vaginismus usually but not always experiences this same contracting spasm during a pelvic exam. Even the insertion of a finger into her vagina can cause great discomfort.

An estimated 2% of women have vaginismus (Renshaw, 1990). Some women who experience vaginismus are sexually responsive and orgasmic with manual and oral stimulation, but others are unable to experience desire and arousal (LoPiccolo, 1989). However, because most couples regard coitus as a highly important component of their sexual relationship, vaginismus typically causes great concern, even if the couple is sexually involved in other ways.

Milder forms of vaginismus can produce minor unpleasant sensations that are chronically irritating—enough to have an inhibiting effect on a woman's sexual interest and arousal. It is important for women and their partners to know that intercourse, tampon use, and pelvic exams should not be uncomfortable. If they are, investigating the cause of the discomfort is essential.

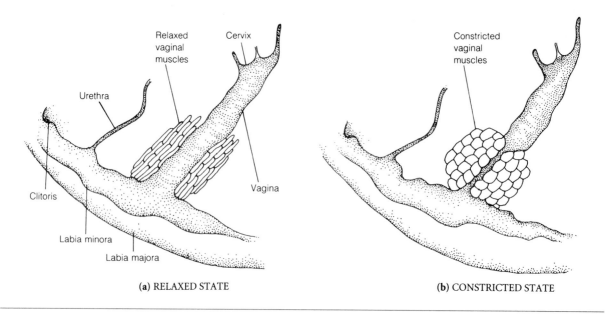

(a) RELAXED STATE   (b) CONSTRICTED STATE

Vaginismus, characterized by strong involuntary contractions of the muscles in the outer third of the vagina, is a relatively uncommon sexual difficulty. Shown here: the vaginal muscles (a) in a relaxed state and (b) during an episode of vaginismus.

Vaginismus often follows chronic painful intercourse, repeated erectile difficulties of a woman's partner, strong orthodox religious taboos about sex, a homosexual orientation, past physical or sexual assault, or feelings of hostility or fear toward a partner (Masters & Johnson, 1970; van de Weil et al., 1990). It is important to note that although a woman who experiences vaginismus can learn to prevent the contractions, she does not consciously will them to occur. Rather, they are a conditioned, involuntary response to fearful, painful, or conflicted situations or feelings. When a woman experiences physical pain from vaginismus, she will probably be anxious about pain occurring the next time she attempts intercourse. Her apprehensions will increase the likelihood of involuntary muscle contractions, and when her expectations are once again met, she will be even more anxious on subsequent occasions.

Origins of Sexual Difficulties

Determining the origins of sexual problems is often difficult and complex. There are several reasons for this. First, even when a sexual difficulty has been clearly identified, it is often hard to isolate the specific causes because many varied influences and experiences contribute to sexual feelings and behavior. Second, it is usually difficult to identify a clear and consistent cause-and-effect relationship because the experiences that contribute to a specific sexual difficulty in one person may produce no such effects in another individual (LoPiccolo, 1989).

The following paragraphs examine several factors that can interfere with or enhance sexuality. We hope that a clearer understanding of the events that shape sexuality will lead to increased satisfaction, communication, and pleasure. Organic, cultural, individual, and relationship factors can all contribute to sexual difficulties. Significant interaction among these factors also occurs. Therefore, the separate categories that we describe in the following pages are somewhat arbitrary.

Organic Factors

Physiological factors often play a role in sexual problems, so it is often desirable to have a general physical and a gynecological or urological exam to help rule out organic factors as causes. Sexual problems are frequently caused by a combination of physical and psychological factors rather than just one or the other (Bancroft, 1992; Buvat et al., 1990). Any degree of physiological impairment can make a person's sexual response and functioning more vulnerable to disruption by negative emotions or situations. For example, a man with moderate diabetes may have no difficulty achieving an erection when he is rested and feeling comfortable with his partner but may be unable to do so after a stressful day at work or when there is an unresolved conflict with his partner.

Any disturbances in the vascular, endocrine, and neurological systems can contribute to sexual problems. Medications, surgeries, illnesses, and "recreational" drugs can affect each of these systems, interfering with sexual interest and response. (The impact of some specific illnesses on sexuality will be discussed in Chapter 18.)

Medications used to treat high blood pressure are most frequently reported to interfere with sexual function (Segraves & Segraves, 1992). Antihistamines and medications used to treat gastrointestinal problems can cause lack of desire and erectile difficulty. Some medications used for psychiatric disorders and depression may impair vasocongestion and orgasmic response (Segraves, 1989; Yates & Wolman, 1991). Anticancer drugs can cause gonadal damage and reduce hormones, resulting in loss of sexual desire both during and following treatment. Insufficient hormones can impair sexual interest and response.

Alcohol and drug abuse can also result in sexual dysfunctions (Cocores & Gold, 1989). Barbiturates and narcotics (heroin, morphine, codeine, and methadone) depress the central nervous system and can seriously inhibit sexual interest and response. Chronic alcohol abuse results in physiological disturbances that can cause a variety of sexual difficulties. Alcoholism also often presents personal and interpersonal disruptions in addition to physical problems. For example, alcoholism can diminish female sexual satisfaction when either the woman or her partner is alcoholic (Peterson et al., 1984). Marijuana can decrease sexual desire and testosterone levels in addition to interfering with fertility by reducing sperm production (Nelson, 1988). Chronic cocaine use can lead to decreased sexual desire and other sexual dysfunctions (Segraves, 1988).

Recent evidence has linked tobacco smoking with erectile dysfunction. Cigarette smoking appears to adversely affect small blood vessels in the penis and to decrease frequency and duration of erections (Mohr & Beutler, 1990; Rosen et al., 1991).

More is known about how organic factors contribute to erectile problems than to other sexual difficulties. Between 33 and 66% of erectile failure cases have some degree of organic impairment (LoPiccolo, 1991). Special procedures have been developed to evaluate physical factors in erection problems (Schiavi, 1992; Zorgniotti & Lizza, 1991). A *nocturnal penile tumescence* (NPT) test can also be performed in a hospital sleep laboratory to help assess physiological erectile capability. Erections occur normally during sleep. In an NPT test, strain gauges are placed on the penis overnight to determine if erections have occurred. Some home techniques for testing erection patterns during sleep have also been developed. Unfortunately, the results of sleep laboratory and home testing procedures are not completely reliable (Morales et al., 1990).

Instruments designed to measure penile blood pressure and flow can help evaluate possible vascular problems (Melman, 1992). In addition, injections of special medications that produce an erection can be used to detect possible vascular difficulties; the injection causes an erection unless there is vascular impairment (Witherington, 1991). The injected medication works by relaxing the smooth muscles in the penis, which causes blood to fill the spaces in the corpus cavernosum, resulting in an erection.

In 1992 research was published on the role of a chemical in the body, nitric oxide, in erection. Researchers believe a lack of this substance plays an important role in many cases of erectile failure (Rajfer et al., 1992). Nitric oxide causes smooth muscles in the penis to relax and engorge with blood; researchers speculate that injected medications work by enhancing the effect or production of nitric oxide.

The problem of premature ejaculation usually does not have a physiological cause. However, some men have a particularly low threshold to physical stimulation and therefore have a physical predisposition to rapid ejaculation (Strassberg, 1990). Men who ejaculate prematurely often have fewer orgasms in a given time period and may ejaculate at a lower level of arousal than men who do not experience rapid ejaculation (Geer & O'Donohue, 1984; LoPiccolo, 1980b). Anxiety can also play a role in premature ejaculation by increasing muscle tension (myotonia), which tends to hasten orgasm.

It is rare for anorgasmia (in women) to be due to physiological causes. However, conditions or medications that impair the vascular system or nerve supply of the female genital area can inhibit orgasmic response.

Health care practitioners do not always remember to discuss potential sexual side effects of medications, so you may need to inquire about the possible effects on sexuality of any prescribed medicines. Often, another medication can be substituted that will have fewer or lesser negative effects on sexual interest, arousal, and orgasm. Much of the information on the effects of medications on sexuality is based on clinical experience rather than placebo-controlled, double-blind research (Segraves, 1988). Therefore, individual consultation with a physician is critical.

Cultural Influences

Culture strongly influences both the way we feel about our sexuality and the way we express it. This section examines some influences in Western society — and particularly in the United States — that affect our sexuality and may contribute to sexual problems.

Negative Childhood Learning. We learn many of our basic, important attitudes about sexuality during childhood. Some people's views are strongly influenced by

The way others react to childhood genital exploration may affect how children learn to feel about their sexual anatomy and sexual expression.

our cultural legacy that sex is sinful. It has been widely reported by a variety of therapist researchers that severe religious orthodoxy equating sex with sin is common to the backgrounds of many sexually troubled people. One researcher found that the more rigidly orthodox married members of Jewish, Protestant, and Catholic churches were, the less sexual interest, response, frequency, and pleasure they reported in marital sex and the more sexual inhibitions, anxiety, guilt, shame, and disgust they experienced (Purcell, 1985).

A child may or may not be directly told that sex is shameful or sinful, but this belief can be communicated in other ways. Kaplan described some aspects of childhood sexuality and the response they often evoke in our society:

> Infants seem to crave erotic pleasure. Babies of both genders tend to touch their genitals and express joy when their genitals are stimulated in the course of diapering and bathing, and both little boys and girls stimulate their penis or clitoris as soon as they acquire the necessary motor coordination. At the same time, sexual expression is, in our society, systematically followed by disapproval and punishment and denial. (1974, p. 147)

The results are often guilt feelings about sexual pleasure from touching one's genitals. Conflict about erotic pleasure may thus be initiated early in a person's life. Kaplan summarized: "The interaction between the child's developing sexual urges and the experiences of growing up in our sexually alienating society probably produces some measure of sexual conflict in all of us" (p. 145).

Do you think most contemporary American parents accept their children masturbating? Arrive at your own hypothesis before reading further.

Negative attitudes about childhood masturbation still appear to be quite common among American parents. One study found that almost 35% of parents of preteens said that their children's masturbation was wrong. Fewer than half of the parents wanted their adolescent children to have positive attitudes about masturbation. When parents were confronted with their children's masturbation, common responses were "don't touch" and "that's not nice" (Gagnon, 1985).

While growing up we learn important lessons about human relationships from our families. We observe and integrate the models we see around us. We notice how our parents use touch and how they feel about one another. One researcher found that women with inhibited sexual desire (ISD) perceived their parents' attitudes toward sex and their affectionate interaction with each other to be significantly more negative than did those without ISD (Stuart et al., 1988).

The Sexual Double Standard. Although the rigidity of the sexual double standard appears to be diminishing somewhat, opposite sexual expectations for women and men are still quite prevalent in our society. Masters and Johnson noted that "sociocultural influence more often than not places a woman in a position in which she must adapt, sublimate, inhibit or even distort her natural capacity to function sexually. . . . Herein lies a major source of woman's sexual dysfunction" (1970, p. 218). On the positive side, research has indicated that women with nontraditional gender-role attitudes are more likely to be comfortable engaging in sexual activities such as oral sex, petting, and intercourse in different positions; initiating sexual encounters; and being the more assertive partner (Koblinsky & Palmeter, 1984).

The male side of the sexual double standard is also a function of cultural expectations. Men frequently learn that sexual conquest is a measure of "manliness."

> Erotic materials portray men as always wanting and always ready to have sex, the only problem being how to get enough of it. We have accepted this rule for ourselves and most of us believe that we should always be capable of responding sexually, regardless of the time and place, our feelings about ourselves and our partners, or any other factors. We have thus accepted the status of machines, performing whenever the right button is pushed. (Zilbergeld, 1978, p. 41)

As a result of these expectations, men have often assumed that intercourse was primarily for their own pleasure and sexual release. This was true especially in the past. Today, however, men often feel overly responsible for the woman's sexual pleasure as well, and thus see sexual interaction as a "performance" (Zilbergeld, 1992).

These cultural expectations can produce discomfort, frustration, and resentment for men as well as for women. An author writing about the men's movement stated:

> Men and women end up misunderstanding and making each other crazy. We are taught to be strangers in the night, talking different languages. We expect impossible things from one another, resent and blame each other for lack of fulfillment. (Keen, 1991, p. 79)

A Narrow Definition of Sexuality. Besides early socialization experiences and continuing exposure to the sexual double standard, popular opinions about the appropriateness of sexual behaviors also influence our expressions of sexuality. Although attitudes about what is normal appear to have changed in recent years, certain assumptions still strongly affect sexual expression.

The notion that sex equals penile – vaginal intercourse is pervasive in our society, and this assumption can significantly affect erotic behavior (McCarthy, 1992a). Coitus is certainly a viable option. However, it is just one alternative — not the only, most important, or best avenue for experiencing sexual pleasure. A strong inclination to view coitus as synonymous with sex can contribute to inadequate stimulation for women and place burdensome and anxiety-provoking expectations on intercourse. This view can also lead people to overlook other sensual enjoyments in relating sexually. In Bernie Zilbergeld's words, "Many men, when asked how it felt to touch their partners or be touched by them, have said that they didn't know because they were so busy thinking about getting to intercourse. In this way we [men] rob ourselves of pleasure and of fully experiencing the stimulation necessary for an enjoyable sexual response" (1978, p. 45).

Goal Orientation. There have been a wide variety of goals prescribed for sexuality throughout history. A common one has been procreation. Another is the man's physiological release, with the woman providing it as her duty. Once the woman's pleasure began to be considered a legitimate aspect of sexual contact, the woman's orgasm and the ideal of the simultaneous orgasm became new goals to achieve. Now, as women's sexuality receives more attention, vaginal orgasms, multiple orgasms, and female ejaculation may be seen as essential to the sexual experience. The contemporary message about sexuality often appears to be "Sex is OK for both males and females, and you better be good at it" (LoPiccolo & Heiman, 1978, p. 56). What could and should be playful and pleasurable becomes work. "Performance anxiety" can block natural sexual arousal and release by diminishing the pleasurable sensations that would produce them.

Arbitrary definitions of sexuality that impose external standards of success and failure reduce the opportunities for individuals and couples to determine what is satisfactory based on their own feelings. In addition, a transitory sexual problem such as an inability to achieve an orgasm or erection due to fatigue or just "not being in the mood" can produce such concern and anxiety that the problem develops into a pattern (Dormont, 1989). One's own performance anxiety, a partner's response, or the combination of the two can turn a transitory difficulty into a serious problem (Marshall, 1989). If a partner withdraws emotionally and physically, blames him- or herself, or feels insecure about the relationship as a result of the other's reduced response, the problem may be worse the next time due to anxiety about it recurring (Aradi, 1988). Individuals or couples may also avoid sexual activity to protect themselves from experiencing embarrassment or a sense of failure from sexual experiences that do not meet an arbitrary predetermined goal.

Individual Factors

Beyond the cultural setting and the influences it has on sexual feelings and expression, sexual difficulties may also stem from other physical, emotional, or psychological factors. Each of us is a unique, complex blend of biological, cultural, and emotional elements. Our sexuality is an expression of all these aspects of ourselves, which begin forming in childhood and continue to develop throughout our lives. Personal factors are important, for human reactions to life experiences are highly variable. Two individuals may respond in totally different ways to the same situation. It is in this light that we present a discussion of some of the personal influences that help mold an individual's sexual expression and satisfaction.

Sexual Knowledge and Attitudes. The knowledge and attitudes we acquire about sex have a direct influence on our sexual options. For example, if a woman knows about the function of her clitoris in sexual arousal and believes her own sexual gratification is important, she will most likely have experiences different from a woman who has neither this knowledge nor this belief. Even education and social class have an impact on sexual attitudes and behaviors. For example, Alfred Kinsey's study found that the higher the educational and occupational level of a couple, the greater their tendency to use a variety of noncoital stimulation methods and intercourse positions (Kinsey et al., 1948 & 1953). In certain cases where difficulties are based on ignorance or misunderstanding, accurate information can sometimes alleviate sexual dissatisfaction.

Negative attitudes about sex also contribute to poor sexual responsiveness (Kelly et al., 1990). Some people may unconsciously be so fearful of sexual pleasure that they prevent themselves from feeling sexual desire. These individuals may have developed a "turn-off" mechanism, described by Kaplan:

> Most of the patients I have studied tend to suppress their desire by evoking negative thoughts or by allowing spontaneously emerging negative thoughts to intrude when they have a sexual opportunity. They have learned to put themselves into negative emotional states. . . . In this manner they make themselves angry, fearful, or distracted, and so tap into the natural physiologic inhibitory mechanisms which suppress sexual desire. (1979, p. 83)

Kaplan further explained that people were usually not aware of the active role they played in creating their inhibitions. Their lack of desire appeared to emerge automatically and involuntarily; they did not realize that they had control over the focus of their thoughts.

Self-Concept. Self-concept refers to the feelings and beliefs we have about ourselves. For example, a woman who feels comfortable with her body, believes she is entitled to sexual pleasure, and takes an active role in attaining sexual fulfillment is likely to have a more satisfying sexual relationship than a woman who lacks those feelings about herself (Koppelman, 1988). Some studies have found that men and women with sexual problems are likely to have more feelings of depression and anxiety and to have less self-confidence than men and women without sexual problems (Clement & Pfafflin, 1980; Derogatis et al., 1977). In addition, women who report disliking themselves indicate that they experience less sexual satisfaction than do women who have more positive feelings about themselves (Frank et al., 1979).

Emotional Difficulties. Often related to poor self-concept are personal emotional difficulties such as anxiety or depression. These difficulties can be a response to a current situation, or they may stem from unresolved past events. Whatever the source, emotional states have a strong impact on sexuality. Lack of sexual interest and response is a common symptom of depression (Dubovsky, 1991). Moreover, severe life problems such as a death in the family, divorce, or extreme family or work difficulties can create stress that results in lack of sexual interest.

Discomfort with certain emotions can also affect sexuality. Particularly important are one's feelings about intimacy (Levine, 1992). The desire for intimacy and apprehension about it can significantly influence sexual encounters. An individual who experiences intimacy in a sexual relationship as threatening may have considerable sexual difficulty (Kaplan, 1979). One study of individuals whose inhibited sexual desire did not improve with therapy found that they had negative feelings about closeness and intimacy in general (Chapman, 1984). On the other hand, being sexual with someone does not automatically result in emotional or psychological intimacy. In fact, sexual encounters can be used to increase or decrease interpersonal closeness. For example, people can use their sexuality to increase warmth and involvement with another person or to express hostility and rejection.

Sexual Abuse and Assault. Both childhood sexual abuse and adult sexual assault can greatly interfere with sexuality (Vanderbilt, 1992; Wyatt, 1991). Of any childhood experience, childhood sexual abuse has the greatest negative impact on adult sexual functioning as discussed more fully in the interview with Wendy Maltz. Many of the personal and relationship issues discussed in this chapter are a direct result of sexual abuse experiences.

Male and female sexual abuse survivors share common concerns. Sexual abuse lacks the essential conditions for positive sexual interaction of consent, equality, respect, trust, and safety. Children who are sexually abused experience sexual behavior and stimulation that are overwhelming for their level of physical and social development. They are robbed of the opportunity to explore and develop their sexuality at their own age-appropriate pace (Maltz, 1991). Due to the sexual abuse experiences, sexual activity becomes associated with emotional and, often, physical pain. As one woman stated:

> In retrospect, I can see how the incest experiences of over thirty years ago still govern and pattern my sexuality. I have a very diminished sexual appetite, with little curiosity or interest. It is difficult for me to anticipate, enjoy, express, and receive love in a sexual, physical form. A wall of avoidance, fear, and dread has replaced any thrill or urge or anticipation. (Maltz & Holman, 1987, p. 75)

Research has shown that women with a history of childhood sexual abuse are more likely than other women to have chronic pelvic pain (Walker et al., 1992) and to experience depression, anxiety, and low self-esteem (Bachmann et al., 1988; Feinauer, 1989). Incest survivors commonly report never having experienced orgasm (Becker et al., 1984).

In addition, sexual abuse survivors often experience specific aversion reactions to exactly what was done to them during the sexual assault (LoPiccolo & Friedman, 1988). They will have "flashbacks," sudden images of the smells, sounds, sights, feelings, or other reminders of the sexual abuse (Maltz, 1991). These reminders may dramatically interrupt any positive feelings and pleasure the sexual abuse survivor is experiencing at the time (McCarthy, 1992b). In many cases a sexual abuse survivor may have symptoms of fear or aversion to sexual contact yet have no memory of sexual abuse. As an unconscious self-protection mechanism, victims often repress memories and have no conscious recollection of the trauma. They then have symptoms they cannot explain or understand (Golden, 1988).

CHAPTER 16

Interview with Wendy Maltz

Wendy Maltz, M.S.W., is a licensed clinical social worker, a licensed marriage and family counselor, and a certified sex therapist, who has counseled survivors of sexual abuse for more than 15 years. Maltz is the author of The Sexual Healing Journey, *a book for survivors of sexual abuse, and* Partners in Healing, *a video production for couples, and coauthor of the book* Incest and Sexuality. *In private practice in Eugene, Oregon, Maltz provides training seminars nationally for other counselors and sex therapists to work with sexual abuse survivors. In addition, she markets a product called HealthySex Nightshirt, which she recently designed to help survivors and others develop positive attitudes about sex and communicating with a partner. In this interview with Karla Baur, Maltz describes how childhood sexual abuse affects adult sexual functioning, and discusses cultural attitudes toward sexual abuse.*

What aspects of sexual abuse have you been most involved in treating and researching, and how did you come to focus on these areas?

In working with survivors of sexual abuse, I have focused specifically on treating the sexual effects of the abuse. A lot of recovery work has treated general effects of sexual abuse, such as depression, low self-esteem, personality disturbances, substance abuse, and eating disorders. The sexual functioning problems and roadblocks to intimacy that can result from abuse have often gone overlooked and untreated. I help people see the word "sex" in sexual abuse, and teach them to reclaim sexuality as a birthright.

In the early 1980s I discovered that some of the people coming to me for counseling about sexual problems had sexual abuse in their background. I saw a pattern in the symptoms they displayed: withdrawal from sex, compulsive sexual activity, feeling emotionally distant during sex, having strange feelings such as fear, anger, disgust, or shame surface during sex, in addition to sexual functioning problems such as difficulty with arousal, orgasm, or specific sexual activities. I realized that there were specific ways that sexual problems manifested in survivors of sexual abuse. Very little research had been done on this topic, and virtually no therapeutic techniques had been developed for this population.

Traditional sex therapy methods didn't work. Survivors were often frightened of the exercises and didn't do them. Or they would do the exercises like robots, not benefiting from them. I realized that a whole area of study and sex therapy techniques was missing. I became curious about how to help these people. As a survivor myself, I probably also have a personal interest at stake.

I reviewed research on the interrelationship of sexuality and sexual abuse, but I just couldn't find much written. I was shocked to read books on sex therapy and not find anything listed in the index under sexual abuse, incest, or rape. Books on sexual abuse rarely mentioned sexuality. For *Incest and Sexuality*, my research began with 35 women who filled out a questionnaire on how they thought incest had affected them sexually. The research for *The Sexual Healing Journey* was a lot more extensive, including 150 twenty-page questionnaires from both men and women.

Now that you have studied and treated clients in this field for many years, how do you define sexual abuse?

Sexual abuse occurs when someone dominates or exploits you by means of sexual activity or suggestion. I use a very broad definition because I'm looking at abuse from the perspective of a sex therapist. Legal definitions are too narrow in this context. They fail to reflect emotional pain and long-term effects. Survivors seeking a therapist's help aren't in court; they are suffering from sexual problems.

When patients question whether they were sexually abused, I ask whether they had a sense of betrayal of human trust in the experience. Did lack of consent or coercion and manipulation occur? Was the episode violent or physically hurtful or emotionally hurtful? And, finally: Did it just plain feel abusive? For purposes of sexual healing, survivors and their therapists need to trust those funny feelings that maybe they were exploited, or maybe whatever happened was inappropriate.

Sexual abuse is not limited to overt attacks, such as when a stranger jumps out from behind some bushes, tackles a victim, and rapes her. It can also be very subtle and can even have pleasurable aspects—for example, a grandmother holding her grandson on her lap and stroking his genital area. But touch doesn't even have to occur for abuse to happen. A child manipulated to pose for a pornographic picture has been sexually abused. There are a lot of different types of abuse, and all of them can cause serious harm to sexual attitudes, behaviors, and experiences.

Sexual abuse attacks a victim's sexuality. It is harm directed at a person's gender, sexual body parts, and sexual functioning. It's an attempt to use sex to control and dominate.

Have you found that female and male survivors tend to differ in the types of sexual difficulties they experience?

In general, females react to sexual abuse by becoming afraid or withdrawn from sex, while males tend to engage more in sexually compulsive or addictive behavior. But I suspect that this pattern reflects cultural influences. There may be more similarity between the sexes than we realize. Due to sex-role injunctions, women who have compulsive sexual behaviors may be afraid to talk about them. Likewise, men may not reveal how they fear sex or feel withdrawn from it because of their sex-role messages. And, withdrawal and compulsive behaviors can often exist in the same person. For example, a man who compulsively masturbates might also have erectile difficulty when it comes to being sexually intimate with his partner. Compulsiveness and avoidance are two sides of the same coin—both are ways of avoiding emotional pain related to past sexual abuse.

Can you be more specific about how abuse-related emotional pain can make it difficult for survivors to experience the feelings of arousal and enjoyment?

Sexual abuse creates certain associations between sexual sensation and the feelings that were present at the time of the trauma. For example, if a woman was molested by her father and she felt disgust, fear, pain, and betrayal, she may have associated those feelings with her genital sensations and experience them now in different stages of her sexual response. She can avoid this unpleasantness by avoiding sex or by mentally "checking out" and not feeling present during sex. Either way, her sexuality suffers.

Unless survivors can identify the associations they have and work to re-solve them, their sexual lives may remain harmed for years. They may feel like their sexuality isn't their own. I help survivors identify these effects of abuse and learn skills to overcome them. There are ways out of the problems caused by abuse. A survivor who feels fear during arousal can stop and realize what's happening, learn to calm herself, physically affirm her present reality, talk about her feelings, and move on, pacing herself in a sexual experience to feel more pleasure associated with sex.

Can sexual abuse influence sexual orientation?

While sexual abuse does not cause a particular sexual orientation, it can create a lot of confusion and influence a person's choices and behaviors. Some survivors assume that their orientation is whatever it was in the abuse. If a little girl who might naturally have been drawn toward lesbian relationships is abused by her father, and feels some arousal in the abuse, she might falsely think she is heterosexual for a long time in her life because the abuse involved heterosexual activities. Likewise, a boy abused by a man might think he's gay. On the other hand, some survivors may recoil from sexual partners who are the same sex as the offender. A heterosexual woman who was abused by her father might not want to pursue heterosexual relationships because she is repulsed by male genitals and thinks all men are potentially sexually abusive. The abuse made it difficult for her to feel comfortable with her natural, innate orientation. Due to these influences, many survivors find themselves with the additional problem of trying to figure out their sexual orientation, and to learn how to separate it from the abuse.

Can the sexual repercussions of sexual abuse ever be life-threatening?

Yes. Due to the realities of AIDS and other sexually transmitted diseases, survivors who act out sexually with many partners are at great risk. To stop patterns of self-destructive sex, survivors need extra help from twelve-step recovery programs in addition to sexual healing work. These survivors need to look at how their behavior relates to the abuse. Negative sexual behaviors may be based on something the offender said, such as, "You're only good for sex," or it may be a way to self-punish or express anger or pain due to the abuse. Some promiscuous sex can be a misguided search for love in which the survivors think, "Sex equals love." Seeing the connection to the abuse is empowering. You can overcome feelings of shame and get on with making healthy changes.

What are the effects of sexual abuse for the partner of a survivor?

Partners of survivors are secondary victims of the abuse. Their lives are also affected by the harm done by the offender. Sexual abuse affects human trust. Partners who can't create an intimate connection may think they are sexually inadequate or unattractive. In fact, it's the history of abuse that is interfering with intimacy. Partners need to be involved in the sexual recovery process. Though sexual healing can feel like an extra burden on a relationship at times, in the long run it can help couples grow emotionally closer and stronger. Their sexual life together can become richer and more meaningful.

Although individuals vary widely, will you outline a typical course of therapy for a survivor of sexual abuse?

Survivors need to identify sexual effects, acknowledge abuse, and develop new, positive associations with their bodies and their sexual functioning. I begin with sexual history and assessment work to rule out medical conditions and other influences. The course of treatment varies and is woven in with general recovery from sexual abuse. We explore how the survivor views sex. Often sex is so strongly associated with abuse that the survivor is at a loss to understand how it could be something positive. Recovery involves creating a new meaning for sex, in which sex is based on caring and respect.

We explore how abuse affects the way the survivor sees himself or herself as a sexual person. There are often a lot of false assumptions that result from abuse, such as, "I'm bad," or "I'm just an object for someone else," or "I'm permanently damaged." Therapy involves being able to look at assumptions, see how they relate to abuse, undo them, and create the beginnings for a healthy sexual self-concept. Therapy also focuses on stopping negative sexual behaviors and learning new, healthy ones. Survivors often need to learn how to build friendships first, before having sex. They also need to learn to say no to sex at any time. I tell my clients, "You can't say yes to sex until you can say no, even in the midst of a hot-and-heavy interaction."

An important part of therapy is work on overcoming automatic reactions to specific touches or behaviors that have to do with sex and physical intimacy. These include dealing with flashbacks and panic reactions. In *The Sexual Healing Journey* I present exercises to relearn touch. These exercises teach skills that many survivors did not get a chance to develop because of the abuse—things like having fun with touch, learning how to be present in the moment and aware of sensations, learning how to control and initiate playful touch, and learning to stop and relax when needed.

In the later stages of recovery work on sexuality, once they have relearned touch and developed new skills, survivors can move on in therapy to address specific sexual problems that resulted from abuse—lack of orgasm, erection difficulty, painful orgasm, inability to experience penetration. At that stage of healing, patients will have more comfort in talking about sex, and they will have acquired a vocabulary for expressing their feelings and needs. They

have new skills to stop behaviors, relax, and change an experience so that it can continue comfortably. At that point, more standard sex therapy techniques can be adapted to help them. Throughout the process, the survivor needs to be able to control the pace. When particular types of touch re-trigger feelings of the abuse, survivors have new ways to deal with their response.

Do you think our culture contributes to sexual abuse?

Sexual abuse permeates our culture. We are bombarded with movies, television, magazines, and books in which sex is used to dominate or hurt someone else. If a boss molests his secretary in a soap opera, people usually don't scream, "That's sexual abuse!" The behavior is woven into the theme of a story. It is not viewed as sexual harassment and inappropriate behavior. The fact that we accept it and see it as normal means our sexuality has been corrupted by it. It damages our sexuality to experience feelings of sexual arousal to scenes of violence and humiliation.

When I present a public lecture or a training, sometimes I'll say, "Let's imag-ine a scavenger hunt. If I give you 20 minutes to run out of the auditorium and get some image or information that represents abusive sexuality, how many of you feel you could do it?" And the hands go up. Then I'll say, "In another 20 minutes I want you to run out and find an image or item that represents healthy sexuality. How many of you think you could do it?" The hands don't go up, and people look around in surprise. We are being saturated with images of abusive sexuality. There is little to compensate in terms of educating people about sex in a positive way.

What training do you suggest to college students who are interested in doing clinical or research work on sexual abuse issues?

Volunteer at crisis centers and sexual abuse treatment centers. Start working with survivors by doing support work or emergency room counseling to get a feel of what abuse is like for someone who just experienced it. Then, if you want to combine sex therapy with sexual abuse treatment, get as much training as possible in classes and outside training through professional groups. Read whatever you can find on the topic.

There is a tremendous need for people skilled in the interface between sex therapy and sexual abuse. A lot of therapists feel embarrassed by the whole subject of sexuality. They don't address those issues with clients. They want to refer to someone who has developed skill and comfort addressing sexual concerns.

How would you like to see this field change in the future?

I want to help educate the public, survivors and non-survivors, about the conditions for and elements of healthy sexuality. This merges with educational efforts triggered by the risks of AIDS and other sexually transmitted diseases. People need to learn how to be responsible in a physical sense as well as emotionally and interpersonally. We need to stop sexual disease and sexual abuse both, while remaining sex-positive.

I don't want our culture to develop a negative sexual ideology in which sex is to be feared, avoided, or engaged in with shame. Under conditions of caring, respect, and health, sex is a wonderful type of communication and pleasure. Everyone deserves to experience and enjoy it. That is why it's worth recovering from the sexual effects of sexual abuse.

Research has also indicated serious sexual consequences for survivors of adult sexual assault. One study of 372 female sexual assault survivors found that almost 59% were experiencing sexual problems following the assault. About 70% reported that these sexual problems were related to their sexual assault. Fear of sex and lack of desire or arousal were the most frequently mentioned problems (Becker et al., 1986). And the effects of sexual assault can be long-lasting; 60% of rape victims had sexual problems for more than three years after the assault (Becker & Kaplan, 1991).

Relationship Factors

Besides personal feelings and attitudes, a variety of interpersonal factors can strongly influence the satisfaction or dissatisfaction two people experience in a sexual relationship. These factors often vary according to the couple and their particular circumstances. For example, one couple may find that an argument typically ends with passionate lovemaking, whereas another couple moves to separate bedrooms for a week after a disagreement.

Judging from the popular media, it would almost seem that our sexuality is separate from the context in which we express it. Movies, magazines, and novels perpetuate the belief that if we are "sexually liberated," we can turn ourselves on and off regardless of our feelings of the moment. It is sometimes jarring to realize that as real people we cannot always relate this way.

Unresolved Relationship Problems. Unresolved resentment, a lack of trust, inability to combine love and sexual desire, dislike of a partner, lack of attraction, poor sexual skills, boredom, or fear can easily lead to sexual dissatisfaction or disinterest. The dynamics of a whole relationship are highly significant in determining sexual satisfaction or dissatisfaction—which is reflected in the strong emphasis in sex therapy on working with the couple rather than the individual. In many cases a sexual difficulty is a symptom of a more general relationship problem (Levine, 1992).

For some couples hostility or lack of trust or respect in a relationship may inhibit sexual desire and response. It is usually difficult to feel desire for someone who arouses strong negative feelings. The following anecdote describes this common situation:

Over the years of our marriage my sexual desire for my wife has diminished gradually to the point that it is presently almost nonexistent. There have been too many disputes over how we raise the children, too many insensitive comments, too many demands, not enough freedom to be my own person. When I look at her I have to acknowledge that she is a remarkably beautiful woman, just as lovely as the day I was first attracted to her. I certainly feel no physical repulsion to her body. I guess it would be more accurate to say that I simply no longer have sexual feelings for her. One feeling I do have plenty of is hostility. I suspect it is this largely suppressed anger that has been the killer of my sexual interest. (Authors' files)

Inhibited sexual desire (ISD) frequently reflects relationship problems (Beck et al., 1991; Lieblum & Rosen, 1988). One study found that women with ISD reported more dissatisfaction with relationship issues than women with other sexual problems (such as anorgasmia, vaginismus, and dyspareunia). The subjects

Without effective verbal communication, couples must base their sexual encounters on assumptions, past experiences, and wishful thinking.

reported diminished desire for their partners when affection was not freely given without expectations of intercourse, when communication and resolution of conflicts was unsatisfactory, and when the couples did not maintain love, romance, and emotional closeness. In addition, the study found that women with ISD often view intercourse as an obligation; they are more likely to engage in intercourse to fulfill a sense of marital obligation and avoid hurting their spouses' feelings than were women without ISD (Stuart et al., 1988).

Often a person who experiences a lack of power and control in a relationship unintentionally loses sexual desire or response, thereby gaining some control in the sexual aspect of the relationship (LoPiccolo, 1992). Partners need a balance of togetherness and separateness; sexual difficulties may occur when there is insufficient independence and an overabundance of dependency and closeness within the relationship (Fish et al., 1984; Lieblum & Rosen, 1992).

One partner may even use his or her lack of sexual interest, consciously or unconsciously, to hurt or punish the other. A person who is frequently pressured to engage in sex or who feels guilty about saying no may become less and less interested and feel increasingly diminished desire (Kolodny et al., 1979).

Ineffective Communication. Ineffective communication can contribute to and perpetuate sexual dissatisfaction. As we discussed in Chapter 8, verbal communication between partners is a basic tool for learning about needs and sharing desires. Without effective verbal communication, couples must base their sexual encounters on assumptions, past experiences, and wishful thinking—all of which may be inappropriate in the immediate situation.

A frequent source of communication problems is stereotyped gender roles—in particular, the myth that "sex is exclusively the man's responsibility and that sexual assertiveness in a woman is 'unfeminine'" (Kaplan, 1974, p. 350). A woman who believes that it is not her place to tell her partner that she is or is not in the mood to make love, or that she would like another kind of stimulation (or any other sex-related desire), may find that the relationship becomes increasingly frustrating simply because her partner does not know what she wants. How could he? This is compounded by the popular myth that "If she/he really loved me, she/he could read my mind!" Difficulty communicating with a partner about the desire for direct clitoral stimulation is common in women who do not experience orgasm (Kelly, 1990).

For many reasons—limited communication skills, stereotyped gender roles, stereotyped images of romance, misplaced assumptions about the other person—couples sometimes operate under the belief that communication is unnecessary in a good sexual relationship. However, communicating sexual needs is often the first step in having them met. Communication is also the basis for the negotiation often necessary to reach compromises over individual differences.

Fears About Pregnancy or Sexually Transmitted Diseases. The fear of an unwanted pregnancy may interfere with coital enjoyment in a heterosexual relationship (LoPiccolo & Friedman, 1988). Sometimes one member of the couple is ambivalent about having a child but does not feel free to be direct about his or her reluctance. If a couple uses no birth control, this may result in a pairing of intercourse with thoughts such as "I sure hope I don't get pregnant." It is not easy to enjoy sex with that concern in the back of one's mind. Furthermore, a 100% effective temporary method of birth control is simply not available at this time. The reality is that unless one of the partners is surgically sterilized, there is a risk of impregnation, however small, in all instances of heterosexual intercourse.

The relationship between pregnancy anxiety and arousal can sometimes be seen in women who are completely freed from the possibility of pregnancy through sterilization or menopause. It is not at all uncommon for sexual activity and desire to increase at this point.

On the other hand, emotional reactions to infertility can also create sexual difficulties. Many couples who want to conceive and have difficulties doing so often find that their sexual relationship becomes anxiety-ridden, especially if they have to modify and regulate the timing and pattern of sexual interaction to enhance the possibility of conception.

Anxiety about contracting a sexually transmitted disease, particularly AIDS, also can interfere with sexual arousal. For people who are not in a monogamous, disease-free relationship, some risk exists. Safer-sex guidelines are outlined in Chapter 19.

Sexual Orientation. Another reason a woman or man may not experience sexual satisfaction in a heterosexual relationship can be a preference to be involved with individuals of the same sex (LoPiccolo & Friedman, 1988). It is understandable that a person with a homosexual orientation experiences sexual difficulty or a lack of satisfaction in heterosexual relations. Sexual difficulties with heterosexual partners are most likely to be considered problems by homosexual people who are attempting to conceal their orientation by relating sexually to partners of the other sex, or by bisexual or homosexual individuals who want to change their orientation to heterosexual. Although some progress has been made by gay rights groups, a homosexual orientation is still not generally accepted in our society. Following one's homosexual inclinations therefore involves facing significant societal disapproval if not outright discrimination. To avoid these repercussions, many homosexual people attempt to relate heterosexually despite their lack of desire for such a relationship. Others have a commitment and a desire for the heterosexual relationship (often marriage) to continue and to be sexually fulfilling. Sex therapists are increasingly attempting to provide services for individuals and couples to resolve these complex difficulties (Gochros, 1978; Masters & Johnson, 1979).

This chapter has outlined some of the reasons people encounter dissatisfactions, problems, or discomfort in what can be an experience of great pleasure and joy. It remains for us to explore ways of preventing or overcoming these difficulties. This will be our focus in the next chapter.

Summary

Sexual problems in the general population appear to be common. A nationwide random survey found that one in seven people reported problems in their sex lives.

Desire Phase Difficulties

Inhibited sexual desire (ISD) is characterized by a lack of interest in sexual activity and fantasy. ISD most commonly reflects relationship problems but may also be caused by other physical or personal difficulties.

Dissatisfaction with frequency of sexual activity occurs when individual differences in sexual interest are significant and a couple is not able to compromise about their individual preferences.

Sexual aversion is an extreme, irrational fear or dislike of sexual activity. Many individuals with sexual aversion will experience physical symptoms of anxiety when they attempt to engage in sexual activity.

Excitement Phase Difficulties

A lack of vaginal lubrication indicates an inhibition of the vasocongestive response. This inhibition may be caused by physiological or psychological factors. Reduced lubrication is normal during breast-feeding and following menopause.

Erectile inhibition can be global and lifelong (never having attained vaginal or anal penetration) or situational and nonlifelong (having previously been able to maintain erections during intercourse).

Orgasm Phase Difficulties

Inhibited orgasm, or anorgasmia, occurs mostly in women.

Anorgasmia can be lifelong or nonlifelong and global or situational.

Global, lifelong anorgasmia means that a woman has never experienced orgasm by any means of self- or partner stimulation.

Nonlifelong anorgasmia means a woman has experienced orgasm but no longer does so.

Situational anorgasmia describes a woman who can experience orgasm in one situation but not another; for example, during masturbation but not with a partner.

Coitus provides mostly indirect clitoral stimulation and for many women is not sufficient to result in orgasm.

Ejaculatory inhibition is the inability of a man to ejaculate (usually during coitus).

This text defines premature ejaculation as reaching orgasm so quickly as to significantly reduce enjoyment of the experience or to interfere with the partner's gratification. Premature ejaculation is a common problem.

Some men may ejaculate quickly due to a low threshold to sexual stimulation.

Both men and women fake orgasm. Pretending usually perpetuates ineffective patterns of relating and reduces the intimacy of the sexual experience.

Coital Pain

Pain during coitus, or dyspareunia, is very disruptive to sexual interest and arousal in both women and men. Numerous physical problems can cause painful intercourse.

Peyronie's disease, in which fibrous tissue and calcium deposits develop in the penis, can cause pain and curvature of the penis during erection.

Vaginismus is an involuntary contraction of the outer vaginal muscles that makes penetration of the vagina difficult and painful. Many women who have vaginismus are interested in and enjoy sexual activity.

Origins of Sexual Difficulties

Physiological conditions can be the primary causes of sexual problems or can combine with psychological factors to result in sexual dysfunction. It is important to rule out organic causes of sexual problems through medical examinations.

Medications that can impair sexual functioning include drugs used for high blood pressure, psychiatric disorders, and depression, and anticancer drugs. Recreational drugs (including barbiturates, narcotics, and marijuana), alcohol abuse, and even tobacco smoking can interfere with sexual interest, arousal, and orgasm.

Between 33 and 66% of erectile failure cases have some degree of organic impairment. A variety of procedures can help evaluate physical factors in erection problems.

Negative attitudes about sexuality and shameful feelings about one's genitals learned during childhood can be detrimental to adult acceptance of one's body and sexual feelings.

The sexual double standard prescribes opposite expectations of sexual behavior for males and females. Both sets of expectations can have negative effects on sexuality.

The cultural notion that sex equals coitus often limits the erotic potential of sexual interactions.

Goal orientation in sexual expression is a culturally acquired attitude that can increase performance anxiety and reduce pleasurable options in lovemaking.

Sexual difficulties can be related to personal factors such as limited or inaccurate sexual knowledge, problems of self-concept, or emotional difficulties.

Experiencing sexual abuse as a child and sexual assault as an adult often leads to sexual problems. Due to the abuse experiences, sexual activity is associated with negative, traumatic feelings.

Relationship problems, ineffective communication, and fear of pregnancy or sexually transmitted diseases can often inhibit sexual satisfaction.

A woman or man whose sexual orientation is homosexual will often have difficulty with sexual interest, arousal, and orgasm in a heterosexual sexual relationship.

∽ *Thought Provokers* ∽

1. What positive and negative effects do you think traditional gender roles can have on sexual functioning?

2. Describe a hypothetical example of an individual with a sexual problem stemming from a combination of cultural, personal, interpersonal, and organic factors.

3. Do you think men or women are more prone to sexual problems? Why?

Suggested Readings

Bass, Ellen; and Davis, Laura (1988). *The Courage to Heal: A Guide for Women Survivors of Child Sexual Abuse.* New York: Harper & Row. A comprehensive guide to help women who were sexually abused as children in their recovery; includes a section specific to sexuality.

Kaplan, Helen (1983). *The Evaluation of Sexual Disorders.* New York: Brunner/Mazel. This book offers a thorough and scholarly presentation on the psychosexual and medical evaluation of sexual problems.

Lieblum, Sandra; and Rosen, Raymond (1988). *Sexual Desire Disorders.* New York: Guilford Press. A comprehensive text by leading experts about the theories, research, and treatments for sexual desire problems.

Maltz, Wendy (1991). *The Sexual Healing Journey.* New York: HarperCollins. An excellent and sensitive book for adult survivors of sexual abuse and their partners. It explores the impact of sexual abuse on sexuality and explains the steps survivors and their partners can take to reclaim their sexuality.

Zilbergeld, Bernie (1992). *The New Male Sexuality: A Guide to Sexual Fulfillment.* New York: Bantam. An exceptionally well-written and informative treatment of male sexuality, including such topics as sexual functioning, self-awareness, and overcoming difficulties.

Suggested Videotape

Maltz, Wendy (1990). *Partners in Healing.* An excellent videotape of three couples discussing the effects of childhood sexual abuse on their intimate relationships and the steps they took to recover from their traumas. Available from Independent Video Services, 401 East 10th Ave., Suite 160, Eugene, OR 97401.

We have been led astray by our economic and biological models to think that the aim of the love act is the orgasm. The French have a saying which, referring to eros, carries more truth: "The aim of desire is not its satisfaction but its prolongation."

Rollo May
Love and Will (1969)

CHAPTER 17

Sex Therapy and Enhancement

The PLISSIT Model of Sex Therapy

Basics of Sex Therapy

Specific Suggestions for Women

Specific Suggestions for Men

Treatment for Inhibited Sexual Desire

Guidelines for Seeking Professional Assistance

*T*his chapter focuses on approaches in sex therapy and methods for increasing sexual satisfaction. The activities we discuss may be pursued individually or by a couple; they range from expanding self-knowledge to sharing more effectively with a partner. Much of what follows embraces our belief that all of us have the potential for self-help. The various suggestions offered here have proved helpful in the lives of many people. However, the same techniques do not work for everyone, and exercises often need to be individually modified. Furthermore, professional help may be called for in those cases where individual efforts, couple efforts, or both do not produce the desired results. Recognizing that therapy is sometimes necessary to promote change, we have included guidelines for seeking sex therapy in the last section of this chapter. In addition, it is important to consult a physician to rule out any physical causes for the sexual difficulty.

The PLISSIT Model of Sex Therapy

There are many approaches to sex therapy. Nevertheless, most sex therapies have several elements in common. The PLISSIT model of sex therapy (Annon, 1974) specifies four levels of treatment; each successive level provides increasingly in-depth therapy. PLISSIT is an acronym for permission, limited information, specific suggestions, and intensive therapy.

Permission

A therapist can play an important role in reassuring clients that thoughts, feelings, fantasies, desires, and behaviors that enhance their satisfaction and do not have potentially negative consequences are normal. Helping individuals and couples to appreciate their unique patterns and desires instead of comparing themselves with friends or national averages of frequency is sometimes all the help they need. Another aspect of this level of therapy is giving people permission *not* to engage in certain behaviors unless they choose to do so. For example, a therapist can support a person's desire to set limits about sexual relationships, not have orgasms with every sexual encounter, or not engage in an undesired sexual activity.

Limited Information

In the limited information level of treatment, a therapist provides the client with information that is specific to his or her sexual concern. A person can use information, as well as permission, to change thoughts and feelings that impede his or her sexual satisfaction. Information that helps a person to view sexuality as positive and to think, talk, and fantasize about sex is a major component in the treatment of many sexual problems. Factual information about concerns with penis size, clitoral sensitivity, or the effects of aging or medications on sexual response can alleviate anxiety and problems related to lack of knowledge.

Specific Suggestions

Specific suggestions are the activities and "homework" exercises that therapists recommend to clients to help them reach a goal. These behavioral approaches, which form the foundation of contemporary sex therapy, were initially popularized by William Masters and Virginia Johnson (1970). Other therapists have modified and developed further techniques discussed in this chapter. Most are designed to reduce anxiety, enhance communication, and to teach new, arousal-enhancing behaviors. Masturbation techniques, sensate focus, and the stop – start technique described later in this chapter are examples of specific suggestions common in sex therapy.

A therapist may also suggest that a client read books that give permission, information, and specific suggestions. In some cases an appropriate book can help resolve problems so that therapy is no longer needed. In others it can enhance the therapy process (McGovern, 1982).

Intensive Therapy

If a client's problem has not been resolved by the first three therapy levels, intensive therapy may be required. These are likely to be cases in which personal emotional difficulties or significant relationship problems interfere with sexual expression such that behavioral techniques alone are not adequate to help the person resolve her or his difficulties.

Treatment that combines behavioral techniques with the development of insight into the origins of unconscious conflicts is an important development in the sex therapy field. In *insight-oriented therapy,* the therapist provides interpretations and reflection to help clients gain awareness and understanding of the unconscious feelings and thoughts that have been contributing to their sexual difficulties. Helen Singer Kaplan (1974) has called this **psychosexual therapy.** Kaplan has observed that many people's sexual behavior is influenced by unconscious guilt and anxiety. These people often unconsciously avoid sexually exciting positive relationships or effective forms of stimulation. For example, a woman who becomes aroused from light touching, but unconsciously experiences conflict about feeling "turned on," may interfere with her partner touching her in such a manner. When he begins to stroke her lightly, she may immediately think, "Oh, he's bored," and request intercourse, denying herself an opportunity to respond to his touches. The integration of sex therapy exercises with insight-oriented therapy can be especially useful: Discussions about clients' reactions to the behavioral touching experiences often help them realize the extent to which they avoid receiving and giving pleasure.

Insights gained in this type of intensive therapy often pertain to patterns developed in childhood that are the root of current problems. In psychosexual therapy the therapist helps the client examine how present feelings relate to childhood influences. Because intimate adult relationships can be greatly affected by the first significant relationships with parents, awareness and insight into these primary family relationships are sometimes necessary to resolve a sexual difficulty.

Another addition to the sex therapy methods is **systems therapy** (LoPiccolo, 1992). In contrast to Kaplan's psychosexual therapy, which emphasizes insight into the historical causes of a sexual problem, systems theory is based on the concept that the identified problems serve important current functions in the relationship. For example, in one case a woman's inhibited sexual desire helped maintain some separateness in an otherwise overly close relationship:

Joseph LoPiccolo is a prominent sex therapist, researcher, and educator.

> Brad and Lisa had an almost nonexistent boundary between them as individuals. When not working, they were always together, and when at home, they would stay in the same room. There was rarely a division of labor; instead, they did everything together. They shared the same soda in the therapist's office, smoked the same cigarette, talked for each other, and knew everything about their mate. They had stopped seeing old friends and had only a few acquaintances. They both . . . admitted to an almost phobic response to strangers. . . . Thus Lisa's inhibited sexual desire was an attempt to correct too much intimacy in the relationship. (Fish et al., 1984, pp. 9 –10)

An important part of systems therapy is to gain understanding about the adaptive value and function(s) that the sexual problems serve (LoPiccolo, 1991). The therapist helps the clients understand the positive value that the sexual problem provides for them as individuals and as a couple — which can then enable them to make changes so that they no longer need the sexual difficulty. For example, in the case of Brad and Lisa, the therapist would help them to be more separate in their daily lives so that they could be intimate and close sexually.

Psychosexual therapy and systems therapy are two methods of helping individuals and couples who need more intensive approaches to resolving their sexual difficulties. But let us now back up and examine some of the specific behavioral methods used in sex therapy. These techniques need not be limited to the setting of formal sex therapy; they can also be used on one's own to enhance sexual awareness and satisfaction and to add variety to a sexual relationship. Moreover, many of these suggestions are equally applicable to heterosexual and homosexual couples. Some specific approaches for homosexual people, similar to those developed for heterosexual couples, are outlined in Masters and Johnson's publication *Homosexuality in Perspective* (1979).

Basics of Sex Therapy

Many people's childhood sexual development is influenced by negative conditioning, limiting attitudes, and a lack of self-exploration. All these factors can hinder later sexual enjoyment or functioning; however, increased self-knowledge may help modify negative preconceptions and feelings. With this in mind, we briefly outline procedures for improving awareness of your body and of activities that provide the most pleasurable stimulation.

Self-Awareness

People who know themselves — their sexual feelings, their needs, and how their bodies respond — are often better able to share this valuable information with a partner than are people who are unaware of their sexual needs and potentials. A good way to increase self-awareness, as well as comfort with our sexuality, is to become well acquainted with our sexual anatomy. It is not unusual for women to report never having looked at their own vulvas. Men may not feel quite so alienated from their bodies, but many are not comfortable with their genital structure. We strongly recommend becoming familiar with your genitals by looking and touching, so as to become more comfortable with your own body. It can be helpful to examine all areas of your anatomy, not just the genital region. Examine yourself visually and experiment with different touches, perhaps using a massage lotion to make the movements more pleasant.

Some people find that knowledge obtained during self-exploration exercises may later be shared with a partner. Moreover, explorations of one's own body may provide the motivation to take the same approach in exploring and examining the body of a partner. Exchanging information can be immensely valuable in increasing both comfort with and knowledge about each other. A later section, "Sensate Focus," elaborates on mutual exploration.

Masturbation Exercises

Masturbation exercises are an effective way for a person, male or female, to learn about and experience sexual response. They can be enjoyed for themselves, and the knowledge they provide can be shared with a partner. Masturbation also can help elderly people who do not have a current partner to maintain sexual functioning (Lieblum & Segraves, 1989). Many people have some negative feelings about masturbation that intrude on sensations of pleasure. Changing these negative attitudes and increasing self-knowledge may take some time, but the rewards can be worth the effort.

If you choose to experiment with masturbation exercises, it is important to remember that the major purpose of the experience is to become more aware of your body's sensations. You may find it helpful to experiment with several positions. Some people find that lying on their backs is best; others prefer to stand or sit. Many people use sexual fantasy to enhance the sensual experience. Further information on masturbation can be found in Chapter 9 and later in this chapter in the section "Specific Suggestions for Women, Becoming Orgasmic."

Communication

Before discussing specific ways of dealing with sexual difficulties, we want to stress again the importance of good communication between partners, and encourage you to review Chapter 8. Many people find it difficult to talk about the sexual aspects of their relationships, but failure to communicate needs and expectations can hinder the resolution of sexual problems and may even contribute to some difficulties (McCabe & Delaney, 1992).

One of the primary benefits of sex therapy, whether it is learning to have orgasms with partners, how to overcome premature ejaculation, or almost any other shared problem, is that couples participating together in the treatment process often develop more effective communication skills. The following account, from one of our students, reflects this potential benefit:

When you first discussed the stop–start technique [discussed later in this chapter] in class, I was excited to try it out with my partner. However, I didn't know how to talk about it. It wasn't like he had never mentioned his problem before. He would say he was sorry he was so fast, and that maybe it would get better with time. Finally, I asked him to come to class with me the day you showed the film demonstrating the technique. Man, did we do a lot of talking after it was over. He was anxious to give it a try, and we felt that with your lectures

and the movie we could do it on our own. At first we made some mistakes, like not doing enough sensate focus and him waiting too long to tell me to stop. In fact, it was only when we were really talking openly that things began to work well. He showed me how he liked to be stimulated, things he had never told me before. During sensate focus we shared a lot of feelings. He became much more aware of my needs and what I needed to be satisfied. We really started getting into a lot of variety in our lovemaking, whereas before it had usually consisted of just kissing and intercourse. By the way, the technique did work in slowing him down, but I think the biggest benefit has been breaking down the communication barriers. Now the talking is almost as fun as the doing, and it sure makes sex a whole lot better! (Authors' files)

Communication itself may not solve a sexual difficulty. It is, however, a very important element — not only in working out a specific problem but also in establishing and maintaining mutual understanding, which can make a relationship stronger. Couples who have better communication than other couples prior to sex therapy are more likely to be successful in treatment (Hawton et al., 1992). In a study of college students, general assertiveness was a significant predictor of sexual satisfaction (Laflin, 1985).

Sensate Focus

One of the most useful couple-oriented activities for enhancing mutual sexual enjoyment is a series of touching exercises called **sensate focus** (see Figure 17.1). Masters and Johnson labeled this technique and have used it as a basic step in the treatment of many sexual problems. It can be extremely helpful in reducing anxiety caused by goal orientation and in increasing communication, pleasure, and closeness. It is by no means a technique only appropriate for sex therapy but is rather an activity all couples can use to enhance their sexual relationships. In the sensate focus touching exercises, partners take turns touching each other while following some essential guidelines. In the following descriptions, we assume that the one doing the touching is a woman and the one being touched is a man. Of course, homosexual as well as heterosexual couples can do these exercises, and in either case the partners periodically change roles.

To start, the person who will be doing the touching takes some time to "set the scene" such that it is comfortable and pleasant for herself; for example, by unplugging the phone and arranging a warm, cozy place with relaxing music and lighting. The two people then undress, and the toucher begins to explore her partner's body, following this important guideline: She is *not* to touch to please or arouse her partner, but for her *own* interest and pleasure. The goal is for the toucher to focus on her perception of textures, shapes, and temperatures. The nondemand quality of this kind of touching helps reduce or eliminate performance anxiety, which can inhibit arousal for both partners. The person being touched remains quiet except when any touch is uncomfortable. In that case he describes the uncomfortable feeling and what the toucher could do to make it more comfortable; for example, "That feels ticklish — please touch the other side of my arm." This guideline helps the toucher attend fully to her own sensations and perceptions without worrying whether something she is doing is unpleasant to her partner.

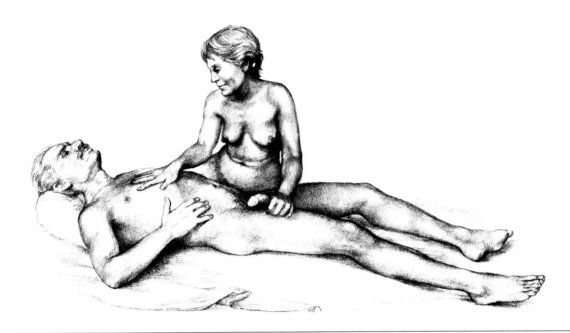

F I G U R E 17.1

The process of sensate focus, whereby partners sensually explore each other's body, can contribute to the mutual enhancement of a couple's sexual enjoyment.

In the next sensate focus exercise, the two people switch roles, following the same guidelines as before. In these first sensate focus experiences, intercourse and touching breasts and genitals are prohibited. Only after the partners have focused on touch perceptions and on communicating uncomfortable feelings do they include breasts and genitals as part of the exercise. Again, the toucher explores for her own interest and pleasure, not her partner's. After the inclusion of breasts and genitals, the partners progress to a simultaneous sensate focus experience. Now they touch one another at the same time and experience feelings from both touching and being touched.

Sensate focus is an excellent way to learn to respond erotically with all areas of the body. It is also a good exercise for learning the sensitive areas on one's partner's body. In sex therapy sensate focus exercises usually precede and form the foundation for specific techniques for resolving arousal and orgasm difficulties. These techniques are discussed later in this chapter.

Masturbation with a Partner Present

It can be particularly valuable for couples to let each other know what kind of touching they find arousing. Masturbating in the presence of a partner may be a way to share this kind of information (see Figure 17.2). A woman described how she accomplished this:

When I wanted to share with my partner what I had learned about myself through masturbation, I felt super uptight about how to do it. Finally, we decided that to begin with, I would be in the bedroom, and he would be in the living room, knowing I was masturbating. Then he would sit on the bed, not looking at me. The next step was for him to hold and kiss me while I was touching myself. Then I could be comfortable showing him how I touch myself. (Authors' files)

FIGURE 17.2

Masturbating in the presence of a partner can be an effective way for an individual to indicate what kind of touching she or he finds arousing.

Couples who feel comfortable incorporating self-stimulation into their sexual relationship open many options for themselves. When only one of them feels sexual, that person can masturbate with the other present, perhaps touching, perhaps kissing.

The experiences suggested in the preceding pages may all be helpful in increasing sexual satisfaction, whether an individual or couple have a specific difficulty or their goal is simply to find out more about themselves. Beyond these general exercises, though, specific exercises or techniques can sometimes aid in reducing or overcoming particular sexual difficulties that can be highly troublesome. We described some of these difficulties in Chapter 16, and in the remainder of this chapter we look at some strategies that have been used to deal with them. For purposes of clarity and easy reference, these strategies are organized according to whether they deal with primarily female or primarily male sexual problems, except treatment of ISD (inhibited sexual desire). We should stress, however, that these discussions are not applicable only to one sex. Men can gain some understanding of both their female partners and themselves from reading the section on specific female strategies; women can gain similarly from reading the discussions of techniques for men.

Specific Suggestions for Women

The following paragraphs suggest procedures that may be helpful to women in learning to increase sexual arousal and to reach orgasm by themselves or with a partner. They also include suggestions for dealing with vaginismus.

Becoming Orgasmic

Learning effective self-stimulation is often recommended for women who have never experienced orgasm. One advantage to self-stimulation is that a woman without a partner can learn to become orgasmic. For a woman with a sexual partner, becoming orgasmic first by masturbation may help develop a sense of sexual autonomy that can increase the likelihood of satisfaction with a partner.

Therapy programs for anorgasmia are based on progressive self-awareness activities that a woman does at home between therapy sessions. The step-by-step activities are often presented by a therapist in a small group of women who want to learn to experience orgasm. Women in the group also provide each other with support and encouragement. These same steps are also used in individual sex counseling. Both individual and group counseling for anorgasmic women can provide information, give "permission," and help solve individual problems. Other sources for learning to experience orgasms are books such as *For Yourself: The Fulfillment of Female Sexuality,* by Lonnie Barbach (1976), and *Becoming Orgasmic: A Sexual and Personal Growth Program for Women,* by Julia Heiman and Joseph LoPiccolo (1988). The following is a brief outline of the therapy program presented in Barbach's book:

1. *Time commitment.* Set aside an hour every day to do the following "home-play" exercises.

2. *Mirror exercise.* Using a full-length mirror, look at your nude body from all angles. Examine uncritically the shapes, colorations, and textures of the different areas.

3. *Body exploration.* Using your hands, and body lotion or powder if desired, explore your entire body, from your face to your toes. Take plenty of time and focus on the feelings in your fingertips and in your body. Notice differences in sensation. Compare doing this with your eyes open and closed.

4. *Vulva self-exam.* Locate and explore the different structures of the vulva. Learn and practice Kegel exercises (outlined in Chapter 4).

5. *Self-stimulation.* Find a lotion or oil that contains no alcohol and is water-soluble, and use it on your vulva to enhance the touch sensations. For the first several sessions, experiment and discover genital touches that are pleasurable, but do not attempt to reach orgasm. It is very important not to have the goal of orgasm in mind at this point. If you feel yourself becoming aroused, reduce the stimulation. Then begin again, allowing yourself to become slightly more aroused than previously. Focus on the pleasurable sensations. Allow yourself to have erotic fantasies if you desire. Experiment with Kegel squeezes during stimulation.

6. *Orgasm.* Once you are becoming aroused from self-stimulation and believe you want to proceed to orgasm, continue the touching that is most arousing. If interfering thoughts or feelings arise, allow yourself to be aware of them and then refocus on the sensations. If you experience difficulty "letting go," it may be helpful to try acting out an orgasm — exaggerate the movements and sounds you associate with orgasm.

7. *Use a vibrator.* Vibrators are a potentially pleasurable option for self-stimulation. They are sometimes used to help an anorgasmic woman experience sexual climax for the first time so she knows that she can have this response. A vibrator is often less tiring to use and supplies more intense stimulation

than the fingers, and it is sometimes recommended for a woman who has not experienced orgasm after a couple of weeks of daily self-stimulation exercises. After she has had a couple of orgasms with the vibrator, it is helpful for her to stop using it and return to manual stimulation, so she can learn to respond in this manner too. This step is important because it is easier for a partner to replicate a woman's own touch than the stimulation of a vibrator.

If following these exercises does not result in orgasm, this does not necessarily mean that something is wrong. It may be that you could benefit by reading more. The books listed earlier should be helpful, and your sexuality course teacher may have other suggestions. Counselors are also available, as mentioned earlier, to answer questions and provide more personal assistance. Sharing discoveries with a partner may be another option to explore.

Experiencing Orgasm with a Partner

As we saw in Chapter 16, the origins of difficulties in reaching orgasm may be highly complex, involving conditioning and experiences of which a person may not even be consciously aware. This is one reason why any step-by-step guidelines for learning to reach orgasm should be thought of as aids, not solutions. The steps that follow are intended to help a woman experience orgasm with a partner. They are based on techniques used in therapy.

After the couple is comfortable with the sensate focus exercises described earlier, they proceed to genital exploration. The exercise is called a *sexological exam.* Each partner takes turns visually exploring the other's genitals, locating all the parts discussed in Chapters 4 and 5. After looking thoroughly, they experiment with touch, noticing and sharing what different areas feel like (Barbach, 1976).

The next step is for the woman to stimulate herself in her partner's presence. The woman can use self-stimulation methods that she has learned are effective and share her arousal with her partner, who can be holding and kissing her or lying beside her, as is shown in Figure 17.2. This step is often a difficult one, and some women begin by asking their partners to be in another room while they are masturbating. Slowly, as the woman determines she is ready for such sharing, her partner can be progressively closer and more involved (Barbach, 1976).

Next the partner begins nondemanding manual – genital pleasuring. The couple can do this in any position that suits them. Masters and Johnson (1970) recommended the position illustrated in Figure 17.3. (We are supposing in this discussion that the partner is a man.) The partner reclines against cushions or pillows; the woman sits between his legs with her back supported by his chest. The woman places her hand over her partner's hand on her genitals to guide the stimulation. They can use lotion or oil to increase sensation. The partner is to make no assumptions about how to touch but rather be guided by the woman's words and hand. The purpose of initial sessions is for the partner to discover what is arousing to the woman, rather than to produce orgasm. If the woman thinks she is ready to experience orgasm, she indicates to her partner to continue the stimulation until she experiences climax. Orgasm will probably not occur until after several sessions.

There are several specific techniques that couples can use to increase a woman's arousal and the possibility of orgasm during intercourse. The first has to do

FIGURE 17.3

The back-to-chest position for genital sensate focus.

with when to begin intercourse. Rather than beginning intercourse after a certain number of minutes of foreplay or when there is sufficient lubrication, a woman can be guided by her feeling of what might be called "readiness." Not all women experience this feeling of readiness, but for those who do, beginning intercourse at this time (and not before) may enhance the ensuing erotic sensations. Of course, her partner will have to cooperate by waiting for the woman to indicate when she is ready and by not attempting to begin intercourse before then.

A woman who wants increased stimulation during coitus may benefit from direct manual stimulation of her clitoris — by herself or her partner (see Chapter 9, the figures on pages 267 and 268). Such direct clitoral stimulation during intercourse often results in greater arousal and sometimes orgasm. The woman-above intercourse position is commonly used when additional manual stimulation is desired. After both partners are aroused — the man with an erection and the woman with adequate lubrication — and feel ready for intercourse, she sits astride him and guides his penis into her vagina. She remains motionless for several moments, allowing both of them to be aware of sensations. Then she begins slow, exploring pelvic movements with the intention of discovering what is pleasurable to her. Her partner is to be receptive to her movements rather than actively initiating his own (Masters & Johnson, 1970). *The Hite Report* emphasized the importance of female-initiated movements:

> Orgasms during intercourse in this study usually seemed to result from a conscious attempt by the woman to center some kind of clitoral area contact for herself during

FIGURE 17.4

The use of an electric vibrator for clitoral stimulation during coitus.

intercourse, usually involving contact with the man's pubic area. This clitoral stimulation during intercourse can be thought of then as basically stimulating yourself while intercourse is in progress. Of course, the other person must cooperate. This is essentially the way men get stimulation during intercourse. They rub their penises against our vaginal walls so that the same area they stimulate during masturbation is being stimulated during intercourse. In other words, you have to get the stimulation centered where it feels good. (Hite, 1976, p. 276)

The next step is for the woman to stimulate her clitoris manually during intercourse. She can also use a vibrator, as shown in Figure 17.4. Some men report the vibrations transmitted to their penises as pleasurable. The woman can then guide her partner in touching her clitoris (Barbach, 1976). One comfortable way for him to be able to touch her clitoris is to turn his hand slightly and use his thumb. (Side-lying and rear-entry coital positions also allow either of them to touch her clitoris easily.) The woman may also find it helpful to experiment with Kegel exercises during penetration.

After several sessions of the woman controlling the pelvic movements and incorporating manual stimulation, the man initiates nondemanding thrusting. The couple can also experiment with other coital positions. For women who wish to try experiencing orgasm without direct clitoral stimulation, Kaplan (1974) has suggested the *bridge maneuver.* In this, manual stimulation during intercourse is employed until the woman is very close to climaxing. Then manual stimulation is stopped, and she actively moves her pelvis to provide sufficient stimulation to induce orgasm.

FIGURE 17.5

These plastic dilators are sometimes used to treat vaginismus — they help accustom the vaginal muscles to stretching.

The techniques just described are useful in exploring ways of relating sexually and may allow a woman to experience orgasm in some cases. A number of books are available for couples who want more information than we have had space to present here; some of these are listed in the "Suggested Readings" at the end of this chapter.

Dealing with Vaginismus

Treatment for vaginismus usually begins during a pelvic exam, with the physician demonstrating the vaginal spasm reaction to the couple. The woman is given relaxation and self-awareness exercises to do in the privacy of her own home. These include a soothing bath, general body exploration, and manual external genital pleasuring. The next steps pertain specifically to resolving the vaginismus. She puts some lubricant, such as K-Y Jelly, at the vaginal opening and practices inserting a fingertip gently into her vagina without having an involuntary spasm reaction. This may take several sessions. Once she can do this comfortably, she inserts her entire finger into the vaginal canal. After relaxing her vagina with her finger inside, she is to consciously contract and relax the vaginal muscles as with Kegel exercises. The next step is for her to insert two, then three fingers and continue to practice vaginal muscle contractions and relaxation. Dilators, cylindrical rods of graduated sizes that the woman inserts into her vagina, are also sometimes used to accustom the vaginal muscles to stretching (see Figure 17.5). Once the woman can comfortably insert one size, she allows it to remain in her vagina for several hours. Concurrently with these "homeplay" exercises, she will meet with her therapist to discuss her reactions.

When the woman has completed the preceding steps, her partner joins her in homeplay assignments. He visually examines her vulva and proceeds to insert his fingers or dilators, following the same steps she did. Open communication between the partners is essential during these steps. After the man can insert three fingers without inducing a vaginal muscle spasm, the couple continues to the next step, penile – vaginal penetration. When the penis and the vaginal opening are well lubricated, the woman slowly guides the erect penis into her vagina. Once it is inside, the couple remain motionless while the woman experiences vaginal containment of the penis. After a few moments, the man withdraws his penis. The couple will then repeat this procedure, and as they continue to be comfortable with penetration, they will add pelvic movements and pleasure focusing. Masters and Johnson (1970) reported 100% success in alleviating vaginismus using this method. However, more current research has indicated that vaginismus can sometimes be difficult to treat successfully, especially in relationships in which couples have never had penile – vaginal intercourse (LoPiccolo, 1982).

Specific Suggestions for Men

In the following paragraphs, we outline methods for dealing with the common difficulties of premature ejaculation and erectile inhibition. We also discuss a way of treating the less common condition of ejaculatory inhibition. As in the preceding discussion of women's sexual difficulties, we caution that the origins of such problems are complex and that solutions are frequently not simple. Again, we refer readers who are interested in pursuing these topics to the "Suggested Readings" and also to the discussion of "Guidelines for Seeking Professional Assistance."

Lasting Longer

Although premature ejaculation is a common dissatisfaction, the prospects for positive change are good. Most professional sex therapists use a multiphased program that focuses on the stop – start technique. The successful approaches to learning ejaculatory control are quite easy to implement, even, in some cases, without professional guidance. There are also simpler strategies for helping to delay ejaculation, and we discuss these first. Men for whom premature ejaculation is not a problem as well as women readers may find the following discussion valuable simply because they would sometimes like sexual intercourse to last longer.

Ejaculate More Frequently. Men with premature ejaculation problems sometimes find that they can delay ejaculation when they are having more frequent orgasms (Geer & O'Donohue, 1984). If partner sex is not a viable option, frequent masturbation to orgasm can be helpful.

"Come Again!" Because of the limiting assumption that male orgasm is the end point of sexual interaction, few men or their partners consider or explore the potential for slowed responsiveness after a first climax. In view of our earlier discussion of the male refractory period, however, it is clear that sexual activity that follows an initial male orgasm will not typically be characterized by rapid ejaculation. Many men might be pleased with the results of exploring the potential for continued interaction. A couple can experiment with continuing sexual interaction following the man's ejaculation and resume intercourse when his erection returns.

Change Positions. Excessive muscle tension is detrimental to a man who ejaculates rapidly. All things being equal, increased muscle tension is typically associated with a rapid sexual response cycle. Aside from certain exotic acrobatic positions, the man-above position is about the worst way to have intercourse for a man who wants to delay ejaculation. The muscle tension from supporting his own weight as he thrusts results in a more rapid ejaculation.

Many men gain a desirable amount of control by lying on their backs (see page 267 for variations of the woman-above position). An important point to note is that this position by itself is not sufficient; another requirement is relaxation. One couple who reported a lack of success with this position told us that the man's orgasm was occurring even more rapidly than before. Closer questioning revealed that he was maintaining his old custom of energetic pelvic movements. Thus, he was moving not only his own weight but that of his partner as well, increasing muscle tension to even higher levels than before. Encouraged to relax during coitus, he found that he was able to prolong intercourse. Both partners were then able to fully enjoy what had once been a fleeting and anxiety-ridden experience.

Immediate results do not always follow this position modification. Sometimes a man will experience increased arousal, stemming from the novelty of the position, that will temporarily counteract its tendency to delay ejaculation. Also, his partner may be more responsive, and he may be further excited by the increased opportunity to observe her reactions. However, after some experience with this change in position, he often experiences the advantages of increased relaxation.

Talk with Each Other. Communicating during coitus may help the couple prolong the experience. It is often essential to slow down or completely cease movements if climax is to be delayed. A partner may find it difficult to anticipate the precise moment to reduce or stop stimulation unless she or he is clearly informed by the other. The man needs to become comfortable asking his partner for help (McCarthy, 1988).

Some men find that intercourse can be maintained for very long periods of time if they allow sexual tension to rise and fall between the plateau and excitement phase levels of arousal. Not uncommonly, men report an added sense of control that comes with repeated episodes of going to the brink of orgasmic release, reducing stimulation to allow tensions to subside somewhat, and then moving once again to the edge. Often, time and practice facilitate this modulated form of activity, particularly if the partners continue to communicate.

Consider Alternatives. In minimizing performance anxiety about rapid ejaculation (and most of the other problems discussed here), it is often useful to think of intercourse as just one of the several options for sexual sharing. Many people have discovered that reaching orgasm during intercourse is not necessary for pleasure, particularly if other successful methods of orgasm-producing stimulation are used. Occasionally, a man will find that manual stimulation, oral–genital contact, or using a vibrator will reduce his performance anxiety enough to considerably help prolong his arousal. It can be comforting to know that there are many options for obtaining and giving sexual pleasure. It is also important to realize that an activity may be very enjoyable even when it does not produce orgasm.

The Stop–Start Technique. James Semans, a urologist, hypothesized that premature ejaculation stemmed from a man's lack of awareness of the neuromuscular sensations that precede orgasm and ejaculation. The man who ejaculates rapidly, for whatever reasons, has not noticed this sensory feedback, yet such awareness is essential to bringing any reflex function under control.

Working from this assumption, Semans developed a **stop–start technique.** This technique is designed to prolong the sensations prior to orgasm, thereby affording the man a chance to become acquainted with, and ultimately to control, his ejaculatory reflex. The partner is instructed to stimulate the man's penis, either manually or orally, to the point of impending orgasm — at which time stroking is stopped until the preejaculatory sensations subside (Semans, 1956).

With a less commonly used technique, the *squeeze technique,* the partner applies strong pressure with her thumb on the frenum and her second and third fingers on the top side of the penis, one above and one below the corona, until the man loses the urge to ejaculate. Initially, the man with rapid ejaculation places his hand over his partner's to demonstrate how hard to squeeze.

It is generally suggested that training sessions such as those just described last around 15–30 minutes and occur as often as once a day for several days or weeks. During each session the couple repeats the stimulation and stop–start procedure several times and then allows ejaculation to occur on the last cycle. The couple should reach an agreement about sexual stimulation and orgasm for the man's partner. If this is desired, they can engage in noncoital activity.

A man working with the stop–start technique will usually experience immediately observable benefits. As his ejaculatory control improves appreciably, the couple progresses to coital interaction, using the woman-above position shown on page 267, with the woman sitting astride. This position is especially well suited for this next stage because the man can relax his body. The first step is for the man to put his penis in the woman's vagina and lie quietly for several moments before beginning slow movements. When he begins to feel close to orgasm, they lie quietly again. This stop–start intercourse technique is continued as the man experiences progressively better ejaculatory control. In most cases the man is able to prevent a too-hasty orgasm (Masters and Johnson reported a 98% success rate). A major advantage of the stop–start technique is the almost inevitable improvement of communication that results when two people treat the problem of premature ejaculation together.

A man can benefit from using this technique on himself during solo masturbation sessions. However, to gain the full returns of improved communication, we encourage couples to practice this technique together whenever practical.

Dealing with Erectile Difficulties

With the exception of organically caused erection difficulties, anxiety is the major stumbling block to erectile response. Therefore, all behaviorally focused approaches to this problem concentrate on reducing or eliminating anxiety. A major goal is to create an atmosphere in which the man is able to achieve some success in obtaining an erection, thus restoring his confidence and diminishing performance fear.

Initially, a couple will use the sensate focus exercises discussed earlier. The emphasis is placed on sensual pleasure as each person lightly touches, strokes, and explores his or her partner's body. It is also important that both partners understand that these exercises are not designed to produce an erect penis. Neither person should enter into the experience expecting this. The main point is that the time spent touching is *not* goal-oriented. For this reason, therapists restrict coitus and ejaculation during these exercises. The following account shows how one man reacted to the regimen imposed by his therapist:

When I was told that intercourse was off-limits, at least for the time being, I couldn't believe how relieved I felt. After years of trying to make my body get up for a performance, suddenly the doctor's advice eliminated this pressure. It was like being given permission to feel again. If I couldn't get hard, so what? After all, I was told not to use it even if it happened. Looking back, I think those first few times touching and getting touched by my wife were the first really worry-free pleasurable times I had experienced in years. Soon I was getting erections all over the place. (Authors' files)

Avoiding intercourse and ejaculation does not necessarily mean that a man's partner may not have an orgasm. If a couple wants to, they can agree in advance for the partner to have an orgasm at the close of a session by whatever mode of stimulation seems comfortable to both (self-stimulation, being touched by the partner, oral stimulation, or whatever). One key restriction is that such activity is noncoital and does not result in ejaculation by the man who has the erectile difficulty. When anxiety is reduced and the couple has progressed to a point where both feel comfortable with the newly discovered pleasures of body exploration, it is time to move to the next phase. Note that, although the man who has experienced arousal difficulties will probably have begun to have spontaneous erections by this time, their occurrence is not essential to deciding to move forward. The critical condition is that both partners feel relaxed and positive about their mutually experienced sensuality. In the next phase, the two people direct their attention toward whatever kinds of genital stimulation are particularly arousing to the man. This may consist of manual or oral pleasuring, or both. The intercourse ban is still in effect. If the man achieves a complete erection, his partner should stop whatever actions have aroused him.

Why do you think stopping stimulation after the man with erection problems has an erection is helpful? Give this some thought before reading on.

Sometimes people are perplexed at this suggestion, thinking that the logical next step would be to progress to penetration. However, in view of the past history of the vast majority of men troubled by erectile inhibition, it is critical that the erection be allowed to subside at this point. Why? To alter the man's belief that once an erection is lost it will not return. When his partner stops providing optimal stimulation, the man allows his erection to subside. This may take several minutes of nonstimulation if the level of arousal is very high. This time can be spent holding each other close or exchanging nongenital caresses. When his erection has completely gone down, the man's partner again resumes the genital pleasuring that produced the original reaction. Once he experiences that erections can be lost and regained, the fear that he has "had it" if he loses the first one is diminished.

The final phase of treatment, for heterosexual couples who desire intercourse, involves penetration and coitus. A good procedure for this is to begin with sensate focus, with the man on his back and his partner astride. The couple can then move to genital stimulation; then, when he has an erection, she lowers herself onto his penis, maintaining stimulation by gentle movements of her pelvis. If his penis remains erect, vaginal stimulation should be continued until he reaches orgasm. Allowing the man to be "selfish" is quite helpful at this point (Kaplan, 1974). By this we mean that the man should be permitted to concentrate exclusively on his own erotic pleasures. If worries such as "Is she going to come?" or "Am I doing well?" intrude on his own sensual feelings, he should shift his attention back to his own sensations. Sometimes this concern for self is easier to put into practice if the partners have agreed to consider her orgasm only after he has experienced his.

Occasionally, a man will lose his erection after penetration. If this happens, it is good procedure for his partner to again provide the kind of oral or manual stimulation that originally produced his erection. If his response continues to be blocked, it is wise to stop genital contact, returning once again to the original nondemand pleasuring of sensate focus rather than forcing the issue. Erection loss after penetration is not uncommon, and couples should not be overly anxious if it happens. A few successful coital encounters will generally alleviate erectile inhibition. Should the problem recur, the couple is now experienced in techniques they can use to avoid establishing a pattern of difficulty.

Medical Treatments.   Some men who have impaired erectile functioning as the result of medical problems make a very satisfactory sexual adjustment to the absence of erection by emphasizing and enjoying other ways of sexual sharing. For other men whose illness or injury has left them unable to have erections, several types of medical treatments are available. A variety of innovative microsurgical procedures to repair vascular problems in the penis can be helpful (Melman & Tiefer, 1992). For appropriate patients, revascularization surgery can restore sexual functioning in 80% of cases (Mohr & Beutler, 1990).

Injections into the penis of medications that dilate blood vessels and cause erection are another option, developed in the early 1980s (Althof & Turner, 1992). Vasoactive medications relax smooth muscle in the spongy body of the penis; this increases blood flow into the penis, resulting in engorgement of the erectile tissue and an erection. The most commonly used medication for this purpose is papaverine, but additional medications are being tested and used (Jeremy & Mikhailidis, 1990). According to one study, 80% of the men who used such medications were able to experience erections firm enough for intercourse (Zorgniotti, 1991). These injections are particularly useful with diabetic erectile failure (Turner et al., 1990). The physician injects the medication into the corpora cavernosa and teaches the man to inject it himself. Erection typically occurs within four to ten minutes after the almost painless injection and lasts from one to four hours. Some complications reported from these injections include transitory numbness of the penile glans, infection, damage to the tissue at the injection site, prolonged erection, and poten-

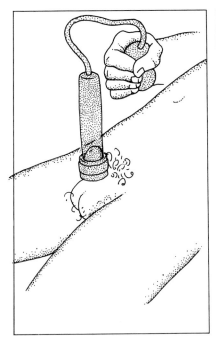 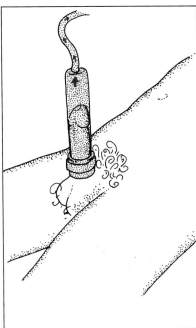 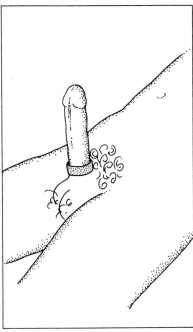

(a) Vacuum chamber is placed over flacid penis.

(b) Vacuum is applied, drawing blood into the penis to produce an erection-like state.

(c) A constriction band is guided from the vacuum chamber onto the base of the penis to maintain the errection.

FIGURE 17.6

Devices that suction blood into the penis, such as the vacuum system shown here, are used to treat erectile difficulties.

tial disruption of liver function (Renshaw, 1987a; Turner et al., 1989). In addition, long-term effects of these injections are not yet known (Malloy & Wein, 1988). At some point in the future, pills or a skin patch may be available instead of these injections.

Yohimbine, a substance found in the bark of the yohimbine plant, is occasionally prescribed for hypertension and helps induce erection in some cases. This drug is believed to work by stimulating the nerves that affect the penile blood vessels, increasing blood flow into and decreasing blood flow out of the penis (Sonda et al., 1990).

Devices that suction blood into the penis and hold it there during intercourse have also been available since the mid-1980s (Korenman & Viosca, 1992; Marmar, 1989). Available by prescription, external vacuum constriction devices consist of a vacuum chamber, pump, and penile constriction bands (see Figure 17.6). The vacuum chamber is placed over the flaccid penis. The pump creates a negative pressure within the chamber and draws blood into the penis. The elastic band is then placed onto the base of the penis to trap the blood, and the chamber is removed (Witherington, 1991).

Surgical Treatments. A surgically implanted penile prosthesis is another available option. Because the surgery is expensive and involves some risks, it is wise to evaluate this option carefully in comparison to others, and to include one's partner in pre- and postsurgical counseling (LoPiccolo, 1991). There are two basic types of penile implants. One consists of a pair of semirigid rods placed inside the cav-

FIGURE 17.7

An inflatable penile
prosthesis.

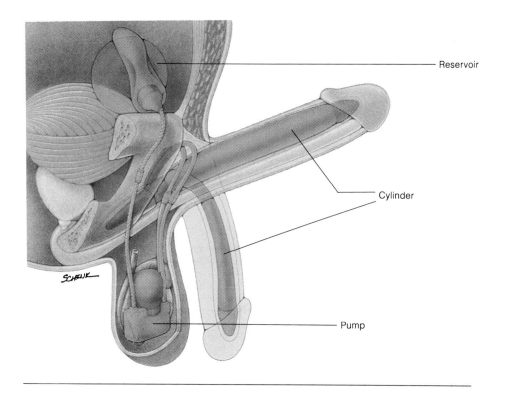

ernous bodies of the penis. They are easier to implant than the second type, but
a potential disadvantage to this method is that the penis is always semierect. The
second type of prosthesis is an inflatable device that enables the penis to be either
flaccid or erect (see Figure 17.7). Two inflatable cylinders are implanted into the
cavernous bodies of the penile shaft. They are connected to a fluid-filled reservoir
located near the bladder and to a pump in the scrotal sac. When a man wants an
erection, he squeezes the pump several times, and the fluid fills the collapsed cylinders, producing an erection. When an erection is no longer desired, a release
valve causes the fluid to go back into the reservoir. Neither of these devices can
restore sensation or the ability to ejaculate if these have been lost due to medical
problems. They do, however, provide an alternative for men who want to mechanically restore their ability to have erections (Gregoire, 1992).

 How satisfied do you think men and their partners are with penile implants? Take
a moment to think about this before reading further.

A review of research on postsurgical adjustment and satisfaction following
implantation of penile prostheses found that 80–90% of implant patients and
their partners were satisfied with the results (Witherington, 1991). Other studies
found that most implant recipients said that they would have the surgery again
(Tiefer et al., 1988) and would recommend penile implant surgery to others
(McCarthy & McMillan, 1990). A majority of the respondents also reported pos-

itive changes in the nonsexual aspects of their relationships. Men with inflatable prostheses were more satisfied than men with semirigid rods (Mohr & Beutler, 1990). Dissatisfaction with the surgery could be due to altered sensations during erection; decreased penile length, width, and firmness; and decreased sensation during ejaculation (Hrebinko et al., 1990; Steege et al., 1986). Implant recipients who were inclined to be dissatisfied with penile prostheses included men who had a low level of sexual interest prior to experiencing erectile difficulties and couples whose relationships were troubled before surgery (Meisler et al., 1988). In addition, some studies have shown that almost 10% of the men who received implants never had intercourse following the surgery (Nelson, 1988). It is important for men who are considering implants to be aware that any ability they have to experience natural erection prior to surgery will be impaired postoperatively. In rare cases the implant needs to be repaired or replaced, or infection occurs.

Impotence Anonymous is a self-help group for men and their partners. For more information about the over 100 chapters in the United States, send a stamped, self-addressed envelope to 119 S. Ruth Street, Maryville, Tennessee 37801.

Reducing Ejaculatory Inhibition

As with erectile difficulties, a behavioral approach is generally used in the treatment of ejaculatory inhibition. In addition, psychotherapy aimed at reducing resentment in the relationship may be helpful when dislike or anger toward a partner contributes to a man's ejaculatory inhibition. The program outlined in the following paragraphs is suitable for either a heterosexual or a homosexual couple; however, for purposes of descriptive simplicity, we will assume a male–female pair.

Therapy usually begins with a few days of sensate focus, during which time the man should not attempt to have an ejaculation, either intravaginally or by some other form of stimulation. If his partner desires orgasm, this may be accomplished in whatever fashion is comfortable to both, excluding coitus. It is desirable for a man to maintain this consideration for his partner's needs throughout the program.

When they have become comfortable with the nondemand pleasuring of sensate focus, the couple may move on to the next phase of treatment. Now the man should experience ejaculation by whatever method is most likely to be successful. Ideally, this will involve his partner so that he may begin to associate his orgasmic pleasure with her. Frequently the man begins by masturbating himself to orgasm after first being stimulated to a highly aroused state by his partner. If he is uncomfortable masturbating in her presence, he can leave the room after being aroused by her touch and immediately stimulate himself to orgasm. Perhaps after some experience with this activity, he will feel comfortable remaining in her presence while he masturbates, preferably with her kissing, fondling, or holding him. The essential idea is for him to begin connecting his partner's presence and activity with his own pleasure. Many couples may find that they can move successfully from sensate focus to partner stimulation without the intervening step of solo masturbation.

Once both partners feel comfortable with the man's self-stimulation in the woman's presence, the couple may move on to the next phase, where she attempts to bring him to orgasm with manual or oral stimulation. Communication is especially important at this time. The man can greatly heighten his pleasure and arousal by demonstrating or verbalizing what feels best to him. It may take several days or longer before his partner's stimulation produces an ejaculation — there is no need to rush or feel panicked if it does not happen immediately. Most therapists agree that once he can reach orgasm by her touch, an important step has been accomplished.

When the man is ejaculating consistently in response to partner stimulation, the couple may move on to the final phase of treatment, in which ejaculation takes place during vaginal penetration. The female partner assumes the woman-above position, sitting astride the man, who is lying on his back. She then stimulates him to the point where he signals that he is about to reach orgasm, at which time she inserts his penis and begins active pelvic thrusting. If he starts to ejaculate before insertion is completed, this should not be viewed as a cause for concern. If he does not ejaculate shortly after penetration, she should withdraw his penis and resume manual stimulation. When he is again about to ejaculate, she reinserts his penis, and they continue stimulation by pelvic thrusting.

Once the man experiences a few intravaginal ejaculations, the mental block that is usually associated with ejaculatory inhibition often disappears. After a few experiences with penetration followed immediately by ejaculation, he may acquire confidence in his capacity to ejaculate intravaginally. Based on limited clinical data, it appears that the probability of overcoming the problem in a therapy program is high. Masters and Johnson (1970) reported success with 10 of the 17 men they treated for this difficulty. Generally, the prognosis is better when the condition occurs independently of severe relationship problems.

Treatment for Inhibited Sexual Desire

Many therapists consider sexual desire problems the most complicated sexual difficulty to treat, requiring multifaceted interventions to help couples resolve their problems (Hawton et al., 1991; LoPiccolo, 1989). Many aspects of the treatment for inhibited sexual desire (ISD) are similar to specific suggestions for resolving other sexual problems. These include encouraging erotic responses through self-stimulation and arousing fantasies; reducing anxiety with appropriate information and sensate focus exercises; enhancing sexual experiences through improved communication and increased skills both in initiating desired and in refusing undesired sexual activity; and expanding one's repertoire of affectionate and sexual activities (LoPiccolo & Freidman, 1988). Therapeutic support to set aside more time for enjoyable couple activities and to prioritize a busy lifestyle in order not to leave sex until last when everyone is tired can also often be helpful.

ISD is likely to require more intensive therapy than problems such as rapid ejaculation, anorgasmia, or vaginismus (Lieblum & Rosen, 1988). The goal for treatment of ISD is to modify the person's pattern of inhibiting his or her erotic impulses. To achieve this, the therapist helps the client understand the underlying motivation to suppress sexual feelings and the reasons he or she refuses sexual intimacy. Most therapists combine suggestions for specific activities with insight therapy that may help the person understand and resolve unconscious conflicts about sexual pleasure and intimacy.

In addition, ISD is often a symptom of unresolved relationship problems. In these situations therapy focuses on the interactions between the couple that contribute to the lack of sexual desire. A skilled therapist helps the couple resolve such issues as a power imbalance (where one person has most of the power and control in the relationship), fears about vulnerability and closeness, or poor sexual skills (LoPiccolo & Friedman, 1988). In situations where one or both partners are overly dependent on the other and feel highly responsible for the other's happiness and well-being, low sexual desire and the distance it creates compensate for the lack of healthy separateness. Here the therapist's task is to help the individuals and couple develop a better balance between independence and interdependence within the relationship (Schwartz & Masters, 1988).

Guidelines for Seeking Professional Assistance

After exploring the information and suggestions in this text and other readings, you may continue to experience considerable sexual dissatisfaction. Perhaps you may find it difficult to progress beyond a particular stage in an exercise program. Although some people with sexual problems improve over time without therapy (De Amicis et al., 1984), you may decide to seek professional help. A skilled therapist can offer useful information, emotional support, a perspective other than your own, and specific problem-solving techniques, all of which may help you make the desired changes in your sex life.

Many people are apprehensive about going to see a sex therapist, and it can be helpful to have some idea about what to expect. Each therapist works differently, but most follow certain steps. At the first interview, the therapist will help the person or couple to clarify the problem and their feelings about it, and to identify their goals for the therapy. The therapist will usually ask questions about when the difficulty first began, how it has developed over time, what the person thinks has caused it, and how she or he has already tried to resolve the problem. The therapist will likely gather some information about medical history and current physical functioning and then make referrals, if necessary, for further physical screenings. Increasingly sophisticated and refined techniques for diagnosing vascular, neurological, and endocrine causes of sexual problems have been and continue to be developed (Fedoroff, 1991).

Over the next few sessions, the therapist may gather more extensive sexual, personal, and relationship histories. During these sessions the therapist will screen for severe depression and other major psychological problems that could interfere with therapy, explore whether the clients have a lifestyle conducive to a good emotional and sexual relationship, and determine whether they have problems with substance abuse or domestic violence (LoPiccolo, 1985). Some therapists use written questionnaires to help gather information and clarify problems.

Once the therapist and the individual or couple more fully realize the nature of the difficulty and have defined the therapy goals, the therapist helps the client(s) understand and overcome obstacles to meeting the goals as the sessions continue.

ETHICAL/LEGAL ISSUES IN HUMAN SEXUALITY

Sex Between Therapist and Client

Despite such examples as the relationship between Barbra Streisand and Nick Nolte's characters in *The Prince of Tides,* it is highly unethical for professional therapists to engage in sexual relationships with clients they have in treatment. Psychiatry, psychology, social work, and counseling professional associations have codes of ethics against sexual relations between psychotherapists and their clients. The American Association for Marriage and Family Therapy prohibits sexual contact for two years after therapy has ended, and many professionals believe that sex with a former client is unethical at any time. In addition, some states have criminalized sexual behavior with patients (Laury, 1992).

If a sexual relationship develops in the context of therapy, attention would likely be diverted from the client's original concerns, and the preexisting problems would not be resolved. In addition, the sexual involvement can have other negative effects on the client. Research has indicated that women who experienced sexual contact with their therapists (including psychotherapists in general, not just sex therapists) felt greater mistrust of and anger toward men and therapists than did a control group of women. They also experienced a greater number of psychological and psychosomatic symptoms, including anger, shame, anxiety, and depression (Feldman-Summers & Jones, 1984). If at any time your therapist makes verbal or physical sexual advances toward you, you have every right to leave immediately and terminate therapy. It would be helpful to others who may be victims of this abuse of professional power if you reported this incident to local professional organizations.

Most therapy occurs in one-hour weekly sessions, although the Masters and Johnson Institute has daily appointments for a two-week period. The therapist will often give homework assignments such as masturbation or sensate focus exercises for the client(s) to do between therapy sessions. Successes and difficulties with the assignments are discussed at subsequent meetings. Therapy is terminated when the clients reach their goals. It is often helpful for client(s) to leave with a plan for continuing and maintaining progress. The therapist and client(s) may also plan one or more follow-up sessions.

Selecting a Therapist

Depending on your situation, you may wish to see a therapist alone or with your partner. You may have a preference for a male or female therapist, or one with a particular therapeutic approach. Many women who want to learn to experience orgasm may not have an available partner or may decide they prefer to attain orgasm initially by self-stimulation; the same may be true for men with ejaculation or erection problems. Others may not have a partner or their partner may not be willing to be involved in treatment. Individual therapy can be effective (Stravynski, 1986), but most therapists believe that a couple's sexual functioning, including difficulties one or the other may experience, is based on the interaction between the two people. Therefore, most counseling is done with both partners. Masters and Johnson have also promoted the use of female and male co-therapists to work with heterosexual couples, but research has not indicated that co-therapy is more effective than an individual therapist (Arentewicz & Schmidt, 1983; Marks, 1981).

Another option in some areas is small-group therapy. Small groups in sex therapy were first extensively used with women who had not yet experienced orgasm. These women's groups combine in-group sharing and support with self-discovery exercises (Barbach, 1975). This model is also being used for groups of men (Zilbergeld, 1975) and couples (Baker & Nagata, 1978; McGovern et al., 1976). One advantage of group therapy is that it is usually less expensive than individual therapy. Also, group members often gain knowledge and support from sharing their experiences with each other.

Once a person has determined she or he wants help from a sex therapist, how is a therapist selected? To locate a therapist, you might ask your sexuality course instructor or health care practitioner for referrals. Also, the American Association of Sex Educators, Counselors and Therapists (AASECT) can send you the names of therapists in your area who have applied and qualified for AASECT certification.* Homosexual individuals or couples may find it helpful to contact a gay rights organization for names of therapists who are supportive of and knowledgeable about their clients' sexual orientations. Your doctor or friends may know therapists whom they might recommend.

After consulting some of these sources, you should have several potential therapists to choose among. There are many factors to consider in making your selection. A basic criterion is training; professionals from a variety of backgrounds do sex therapy. The title sex therapist does not assure competence: There are few regulations on the use of that title. At this time there are few advanced degree programs in sex therapy. Rather, a professional who has specialized in this area should have a minimum of a master's degree and credentials as a psychiatrist, psychologist, social worker, or counselor. To do sex therapy, he or she should also have participated in sex therapy training, supervision, and workshops. It is highly appropriate for you to inquire about the specific training and certification of a prospective therapist.

To help determine if a specific therapist will meet your needs, you may wish to cover the following topics at your first meeting:

1. What do you want from therapy? You and your therapist should reach an agreement on your and the therapist's goals. This agreement is sometimes referred to as the *therapy contract*.

2. What is the therapist's approach? You can ask about the general process in the therapy sessions (what the therapist will do) and what kind of participation is expected of you.

3. How do you feel about talking with the therapist? Therapy is not intended to be a light social interaction. It can be difficult. At times it may be quite uncomfortable for a client to discuss personal sexual concerns. However, for therapy to be useful, you will want to have the sense that the therapist is open and willing to understand you.

4. What is the therapist's fee for services, and how many sessions does she or he estimate will be needed?

After the initial interview, you can decide to continue with this therapist or ask for a referral to another therapist more appropriate to your personality or needs. If you become dissatisfied once you begin therapy, discuss your concerns with your therapist. Decide jointly, if possible, whether to continue therapy or to

*The address is AASECT, 435 N. Michigan Ave., Suite 1717, Chicago, IL 60611-4067; (312) 644-0828.

seek another therapist. It is usually best to continue for several sessions before making a decision to change. Occasionally, clients expect magic cures rather than the difficult but rewarding work that therapy often demands.

Another consideration may be the cost of therapy. Fees vary considerably. Psychiatrists (who are medical doctors) are usually at the upper end of the fee scale, psychologists (who have Ph.D.s) are in the middle, and social workers and counselors (who have master's degrees) are usually at the lower end. A higher fee does not necessarily indicate better sex therapy skills. Some mental health agencies and private practitioners offer sliding fee schedules based on the client's income.

Sex therapy can be a useful tool for individuals and couples who want to resolve their sexual difficulties. The process of sex therapy may also have additional benefits. Clients often experience reduced anxiety as well as improved communication, marital adjustment, and satisfaction following sex therapy (Zilbergeld & Kilmann, 1984). Couples may be more assertive and emotionally expressive with each other (Tullman et al., 1981). Individuals and couples who have met their goals may experience increased self-confidence and emotional satisfaction (Clement & Pfafflin, 1980). The combined efforts of the therapist and client(s) can replace doubt and anxiety with the joy of satisfying sexual intimacy.

Summary

The PLISSIT Model of Sex Therapy

The PLISSIT model outlines four progressive levels of sex therapy: permission, limited information, specific suggestions, and intensive therapy.

Intensive therapy often combines specific behavioral techniques with insight-oriented psychosocial therapy or with a systems theory approach that focuses on the function of the problem within the relationship.

Basics of Sex Therapy

Self-awareness is a good beginning for therapy. Exploring one's own body increases one's knowledge and comfort and may prepare one for exploring a partner's body.

Masturbation exercises are an effective way for an individual to learn about and experience sexual response. They can be enjoyed for themselves, and the acquired knowledge can be shared with a partner.

Good communication between partners is an important element of therapy. It can help work out specific problems and foster stronger relationships.

The experience of sensate focus, nondemand pleasuring shared by sexual partners, is an excellent vehicle for mutually enhancing sexual potentials.

Masturbating in each other's presence may be an excellent way for a couple to indicate to each other what kind of touching they find arousing.

Specific Suggestions for Women

Therapy programs for anorgasmic women are based on progressive self-awareness activities.

Women who wish to become orgasmic during lovemaking with a partner may benefit from programs that commence with sensate focus, mutual genital exploration, masturbation, and nondemand genital pleasuring by the partner.

A couple may increase the probability of female orgasm during intercourse by incorporating knowledge acquired during sensate focus and nondemand pleasuring, and by combining intercourse with manual stimulation of the woman's clitoris (by herself or her partner).

Treatment for vaginismus generally involves promoting increased self-awareness and relaxation. Insertion of a lubricated finger (first one's own and later the partner's) into the vagina is an important next step in overcoming this condition. Penile insertion is the final phase of treatment for vaginismus.

Specific Suggestions for Men

A variety of approaches may help a man learn to delay his ejaculation. Potentially helpful suggestions include ejaculating more frequently, having a second orgasm, using a more relaxed intercourse position, and openly communicating a need to modulate movements and/or engage in noncoital activities to reduce stimulation.

If a couple has the time and inclination to work together in resolving premature ejaculation difficulties, application of the stop – start or squeeze technique is often effective.

A behavioral approach designed to reduce anxiety has proven quite successful in treating psychologically based erectile inhibition. This treatment method has several phases: sensate focus, followed by genital stimulation, then penetration.

Vascular surgery, vasoactive injections, external vacuum constriction devices, and surgically implanted penile prostheses are options for men who have a permanent, physiologically caused inability to experience erections.

A behavioral approach for the treatment of ejaculatory inhibition combines sensate focus with self- and partner manual stimulation, ultimately leading to intravaginal ejaculation.

Treatment for Inhibited Sexual Desire

Problems with ISD often require more intensive therapy to help people understand and change their suppression and avoidance of sexual feelings.

Guidelines for Seeking Professional Assistance

Professional counseling is often helpful and sometimes necessary in overcoming sexual difficulties.

A skilled therapist can offer useful information, emotional support, a perspective other than your own, problem-solving strategies, and specific sex therapy techniques.

A lack of regulations governing sex therapy suggests that one should be careful in selecting a therapist. Referrals may be given by sex educators, health care practitioners, or AASECT.

➣ *Thought Provokers* ➣

1. Why might someone be reluctant to seek professional assistance for a sexual difficulty?

2. How do you think the sensate focus experience challenges gender-role stereotyped behavior of men and women?

3. If you were a man and were not able to experience erection due to irreversible physical causes, would you get a penile prosthesis? Why or why not?

Suggested Readings

Castleman, Michael (1980). *Sexual Solutions*. New York: Simon & Schuster. This excellent book encourages men to clarify their personal conditions for positive sexual experiences.

Heiman, Julia; and LoPiccolo, Joseph (1988). *Becoming Orgasmic: A Sexual and Personal Growth Program for Women*. New York: Prentice-Hall. An excellent guide for women who want to learn to experience orgasm and enhance their sexual pleasure by themselves or with a partner.

Kaplan, Helen (1987). *The Illustrated Manual of Sex Therapy*. New York: Brunner/Mazel. A readable and beautifully illustrated book with clearly explained steps in the behavioral treatment of sexual difficulties.

Lieblum, Sandra; and Rosen, Raymond (Eds.) (1989). *Principles and Practice of Sex Therapy: Update for the 1990s*. New York: Guilford Press. A comprehensive text about contemporary theory, research, and treatment of sexual disorders, edited by leaders in the sex therapy field.

McCarthy, Barry; and McCarthy, Emily (1984). *Sexual Awareness*. New York: Carroll & Graf. A straightforward and sensitive guide to improving self-awareness and pleasure in sexuality. This book offers suggestions for enhancement programs for men, women, and couples.

Yaffe, Maurice; and Fenwick, Elizabeth (1988). *Sexual Happiness: A Practical Approach*. New York: Holt, Rinehart & Winston. Developed for readers who want to enhance their sexuality or resolve specific difficulties, this book offers step-by-step self-help guidelines.

The psychology of the seriously ill put barriers between us and those who had the skill and the grace to minister to us. . . . There was an utter void created by the longing — ineradicable, unremitting, pervasive — for warmth of human contact. A warm smile and an outstretched hand were valued even above the offerings of modern science. . . .

Norman Cousins
Anatomy of an Illness (1979)

CHAPTER 18

Chronic Illness, Disability, and Sexual Adjustment

Stereotypes About Sexuality, Chronic Illness, and Disability

Chronic Illnesses

Disabilities

Coping and Enhancement Strategies

𝒫eople with chronic illnesses and disabilities often have special needs regarding their sexual behavior. Most of us will confront chronic illness or disability in our own lives to some degree; 86% of individuals over the age of 65 have one chronic disease and 50% have two or more (Rodin & Salovey, 1989). In addition, illness or disability can occur at any age: studies have estimated that 5 – 40% of children and adolescents have potentially limiting disabilities (Meeropol, 1991). In this chapter we discuss some of the special needs of people with chronic illnesses and disabilities and methods of coping with those needs, as well as some of the sexual concerns that people with chronic illnesses and disabilities have in common.

Stereotypes About Sexuality, Chronic Illness, and Disability

Most people with chronic (long-term) illnesses and disabilities must confront prevalent myths about their sexual nature and abilities. These myths often have their basis in the notion, common in our society, that the only people who are sexual are those who are young and beautiful. "Barbie and Ken" images of sexually active people are constantly reinforced by the popular media; people who are obese, old, or do not conform to current standards of sexual attractiveness are usually presented as asexual or undesirable. This narrow stereotype has been particularly damaging to physically or mentally disabled people.

In addition, people whose illnesses and disabilities make them dependent on others for care are often seen as childlike rather than as individuals interested in age-appropriate sexuality (Asch & Rousso, 1985). This "Peter Pan" myth of perpetual childhood is a stigma that many people with disabilities experience (Cornelius et al., 1982). As a woman who was paralyzed following a car accident explained, "I was still a woman, but I was helpless and people began treating me like a little girl. I was sure no one would ever want to have sex with me" (Hasslebrign, 1990, p. 25). Furthermore, the cessation of involvement in one's usual roles and activities — parent, employee, skier, and so on — can diminish self-esteem and sexual functioning (Schover, 1989).

The stereotype of the asexual ill and disabled may also be based on incorrect assumptions about the sexual limitations that certain medical problems present. Some of these assumptions are that the chronically ill or disabled person lacks genital sensation, is unable to have an erection or orgasm, or is unable to engage in penile – vaginal intercourse (in particular, that a man is unable to be on top during intercourse). It is also commonly (but wrongly) believed that the presence of a bowel or bladder apparatus, prosthetic device(s), or mechanical supports such as braces or a wheelchair, or infertility as a result of disability, all constitute or result in a loss of sexuality. However, as we stress throughout this text, sexuality is integral to all of us — regardless of whether erection, intercourse, orgasm, or pregnancy can occur and despite crutches, braces, or wheelchairs. People are sexual beings no matter what their physical appearance or level of functioning. As one writer stated:

> Hopefully, we will begin to discover that each human being has an unlimited potential for sexual well-being that is not related to neurology, the cardiovascular system, or the skeletal – muscular system. We will find out that we all have an unlimited capacity

to give and receive, to belong in the world to each other, to respect ourselves as sexual persons, and to enjoy the pleasure that life gives us, be that with ourselves or with other people. We will begin to see the effects of disability not as how they impinge on certain neurological conditions or how certain muscles respond, but how they might limit or change the way we respond to other people. If we begin to understand those issues, we might begin to see sexuality as part of the total person as opposed to limiting it to the genital area. (Daniels, 1981, p. 7)

The next sections briefly describe several chronic illnesses and disabilities and their possible impact on sexuality.

Chronic Illnesses

The diagnosis of a chronic illness is a crisis that requires adjustment and coping. Immediately following such a diagnosis, sexual concerns may have a low priority compared to survival. Reduced sexual desire and arousal can be related to loss of self-esteem and fears about the illness (Schover 1989). People often pass through several emotional phases following the diagnosis of a chronic illness, including anxiety, anger, and depression. One researcher summarized the typical reactions of a woman after learning she must have a mastectomy:

> At first there is the outcry: "Why me? Will my husband still want me? Will I die of my cancer?" Next comes denial, for example, shopping for a revealing bathing suit the week before surgery or telling friends she is just having a biopsy. After the operation come the intrusive thoughts. Every billboard and TV commercial seems to picture a large-breasted model wearing low-cut clothes. A woman friend is being cruel by ostentatiously wearing a tight sweater. A hug from the husband is a reminder of the breast prosthesis. If the woman has adequate social support and inner resources, she will work through her preoccupation with her lost breast and complete the crisis period with a return to normal life activities, including a joyful sex life. (Schover & Jensen, 1988, pp. 62–63)

The impact of a chronic illness is complex. Role changes that occur when one of the partners assumes the role of caregiver and nurse can interfere with the adult-to-adult relationship. Continued medical care following initial treatment may disrupt daily life routines.

Diseases of the neurological, endocrine, and vascular systems can directly interfere with sexual functioning. Medications can interfere with sexual interest and enjoyment (Bullard, 1988). Pain and fatigue can distract from erotic thoughts and sensations or limit specific sexual activities (Anderson et al., 1989). Surgical or medical treatments can also physically or emotionally impair sexual functioning. For example, people with kidney failure who undergo renal dialysis may have significant difficulty with sexual response (Solomon, 1986).

However, even for some people who are terminally ill, sexuality remains an important aspect of life. "Many people remain fully sexual beings from 'womb to tomb.' To the end of their lives, they continue to harbor sexual thoughts, desires, and capabilities" (Laury, 1987, p. 102). The sexuality of a person who is dying is largely determined by the physical limitations of his or her illness, his or her prior sexual adjustment, and his or her partner's feelings.

The following paragraphs describe the impact of some specific illnesses on sexuality.

Multiple Sclerosis

Multiple sclerosis (MS) is a neurological disease of the brain and spinal cord in which damage occurs to the myelin sheath that covers nerve fibers; vision, sensation, and voluntary movement are affected. It is the most common disabling neurological condition for young adults in the United States (Schover et al., 1988). Studies have found that most MS patients experienced changes in their sexual functioning and that at least half had sexual problems (Stenager et al., 1990). The person with MS may experience either a reduction or loss of sexual interest, genital sensation, arousal, or orgasm; as well as uncomfortable hypersensitivity to genital stimulation. Sexual arousal may not be possible by genital stimulation because of sensory losses (Hill & Kassam, 1984). These symptoms may vary and become worse over time.

Diabetes

Diabetes is an inherited disease that occurs when the pancreas fails to secrete insulin. It is a disease of the endocrine system and a leading organic cause of erectile problems in men. Nerve damage or circulatory problems from diabetes can cause sexual problems (Rowland et al., 1989). Many diabetic men experience a reduction or loss of their capacity for erection, and a few diabetic men ejaculate into the bladder. Heavy alcohol use and poor blood sugar control increase the chances of erectile problems in men with diabetes (McCulloch et al., 1984). Much less research has been done with women than with men on the role of diabetes in sexual problems. Research has indicated that women who developed diabetes in adolescence reported few sexual difficulties. However, women whose diabetes began in adulthood were likely to have problems with sexual desire, lubrication, and orgasm (Schreiner-Engel et al., 1987).

Diabetes is a good example to show how the interplay of physiological and psychological factors affects sexuality (Jefferson et al., 1989). Research has indicated that sexual functioning was better for diabetics who had accepted their disease and had formed new relationships or had decreased marital conflict (Jensen, 1986).

Heart Disease

Some 68 million individuals in the United States have some form of cardiovascular disease (Papadopoulos, 1991). Sexual problems following a heart attack are common and are usually due to anxiety, misinformation, and feeling stigmatized by the illness rather than organic causes (Schover & Jensen, 1988). A person or his or her partner may be worried that sexual excitement will bring on another heart attack and consequently be fearful of and avoid sexual activity (Gould, 1989). Research measuring cardiac effects in men during masturbation, noncoital stimulation, and intercourse in both the male- and the female-above intercourse positions found that cardiac expenditure during these activities was equivalent to light to moderate exercise. Some couples can benefit from using a portable heart-monitoring machine during a typical day, including sexual activity, to reassure the couple of the safety of sexual activity (Bohlen et al., 1984). It is essential for someone who has had a heart attack to consult a physician about sexual activity and to secure individualized, accurate information. One study found that individuals who received information about when it was safe for them to resume sexual activity showed less apprehension following their heart attacks than did those who received no information (Dhabuwala et al., 1986).

Cerebrovascular Accidents

Cerebrovascular accidents (CVA), commonly called strokes, often result in residual impairments of motor, sensory, emotional, and cognitive functioning that can have a negative effect on sexuality. Stroke survivors frequently report a decline in their frequency of interest, arousal, and sexual activity. Some factors that commonly influence the sexual behavior of people who have experienced a stroke include limited mobility, altered or lost sensation, impairment in verbal communication, and depression (Schover & Jensen, 1988).

Arthritis

Arthritis is a progressive, systemic disease that results in inflammation of the joints. Chronic inflammation can cause pain, destruction of the joint, or reduced joint mobility. Nerves and muscle tissue surrounding the affected joints are also often damaged. Arthritis does not directly impair sexual response, but body image problems, depression, and chronic pain and fatigue may diminish a person's interest in sex (Roth, 1989). Pain or deformities in the hands may also make masturbation difficult or impossible without assistance. Arthritic impairment of hips, knees, arms, and hands may interfere with certain intercourse positions (Ehrlich, 1988). Planning for sex when one is least tired, and using medications and moist heat prior to sex, can help those suffering from arthritis diminish pain, relax muscles, and increase range of motion (Bullard, 1988).

Cancer

Cancer and its treatment can be particularly devastating to sexuality. The disease and its therapies can impair hormonal, vascular, and neurological functions necessary for normal sexual interest and response. Pain can also greatly interfere with sexual interest and arousal (Schover, 1988). Chemotherapy and radiation therapy can cause hair loss, skin changes, nausea, and fatigue, all of which can negatively affect sexual feelings. Some cancer surgeries result in permanent scars, loss of body parts, or an ostomy (a body opening created after removal of the colon or bladder), all of which can result in a negative body image.

Although all forms of cancer can affect sexual functioning, cancers of the reproductive organs can be especially devastating and therefore are of particular concern to many people (Anderson et al., 1989). We briefly discuss these forms of cancer and examine their impact on sexuality in the following sections. Methods for early detection of cancer can be found in Chapter 4 (for cervical, uterine, and ovarian cancer) and Chapter 5 (for prostate and testicular cancer). Breast cancer is also discussed in detail in Chapter 4.

Cancer of the Cervix and Uterus. In 1991 an estimated 13,000 cases of cervical cancer and 33,000 cases of uterine cancer occurred in the United States (American Cancer Society, 1991). Treatment of cervical cancer depends on whether the cancer

ETHICAL/LEGAL ISSUES IN HUMAN SEXUALITY

Medical and Institutional Care and Sexuality

Most individuals with a chronic illness or disability will have contact with medical or institutional care. The ethical responsibility of institutional policy and practice to facilitate the sexual rights of patients is often overlooked. Health care professionals may pay attention to reproductive concerns but often ignore the emotional and social effects of a disability or illness on sexuality (Bullard, 1988; Cole, 1991; Schover & Jensen, 1988). They sometimes mistakenly assume that they should not talk about sexuality with patients to avoid adding to patients' problems and anxieties. Although those responsible for health care have become more sensitive to their patients' needs in this area, there is still a great need for sexuality education for the staff and clients of hospitals and institutions. Studies have shown that although most health care providers believed that their patients should have sexual counseling, they lacked the knowledge and training to provide it (Malloy & Herold, 1988). Health care providers need to know what potential for positive sexual experiences exists despite serious medical conditions (Bullard, 1988). Equally important for hospitalized or institutionalized people are opportunities to explore options for sexual expression — solitary and interpersonal — within their capabilities.

cells have spread beyond the cervix. If they have, surgery is required. If not, radiation therapy can be used. One report suggested that surgery is less disruptive to sexual functioning than is radiation treatment (Seibel et al., 1980). Treatment of uterine cancer ranges from hysterectomy (removal of the uterus) to radiation therapy, drug therapy, or hormonal therapy. As we discussed in Chapter 4, the effects of a hysterectomy on a woman's sexuality can vary. Some possible changes are altered physical response, diminished lubrication, painful intercourse, and depression.

Cancer of the Ovaries. An estimated 20,700 cases of ovarian cancer occurred in the United States in 1991 (American Cancer Society, 1991). Although ovarian cancer ranks second in incidence among gynecological cancers, it causes more deaths than any other cancer of the female reproductive organs. Common treatment involves an oophorectomy (removal of the ovaries), radiation therapy, and drug therapy. Removal of the ovaries reduces the levels of estrogen and androgen in females, causing reduced lubrication, altered or decreased sexual response, and/or painful intercourse.

Cancer of the Prostate. About 1 out of every 11 men will develop prostate cancer during his lifetime, usually after age 65 (American Cancer Society, 1991). This type of cancer accounted for an estimated 122,000 new cases in 1991. Surgery (prostatectomy) alone or in combination with radiation and/or hormones and anticancer drugs are all options in the treatment of prostate cancer. Nerve-sparing surgical techniques have been developed, but prostatectomy and hormone treatment can cause erectile dysfunction (Litwin & Richie, 1989). Retrograde ejaculation can also occur.

Cancer of the Testis. While the incidence of testicular cancer is fairly low — only 6100 cases occurred in 1991 (American Cancer Society, 1991) — it is one of the most common forms of cancer in men age 20 – 40. Treatment generally involves the removal of the affected testis. Sexual functioning and fertility usually remain unimpaired.

Disabilities

Major disabilities such as spinal cord injury, cerebral palsy, blindness and deafness, and mental disabilities have widely varying effects on sexual responsiveness. Some people with these disabilities are able to maintain or restore satisfying sex lives; others find their sexual expression reduced or impaired by their difficulties. In the following sections, we look at some of these disabilities and discuss some of the sexual adjustments that people with these problems can make.

Spinal-Cord Injury

People with *spinal-cord injuries (SCI)* have reduced motor control and sensation because the damage to the spinal cord obstructs the pathway between body and brain. The parts of the body that are paralyzed vary according to the location of the injury. A person can be *paraplegic* (a condition characterized by loss of feeling and voluntary muscle function of the trunk and legs) or *quadriplegic* (a condition characterized by loss of feeling and voluntary muscle function of the arms or hands, as well as of the trunk and legs). Injuries lower on the spine result in paraplegia, while higher spinal injuries cause quadriplegia.

Although the spinal-cord injury does not necessarily impair sexual desire and psychological arousal, a person with SCI may have impaired ability for arousal and orgasm; this varies according to the specific injury (Kennedy and Over, 1990). Some women and men with SCI are able to experience arousal or orgasm from psychological or physical stimulation; others are not (Kettl et al., 1991). Furthermore, a person with SCI may or may not be able to feel the arousal that he or she experiences. Some people with SCI report that the sensations they experience change or increase slightly over time. There is great individual variation in sexuality among those with spinal-cord injuries. Therefore, an individual's sexual capacity cannot be predicted solely on the basis of the nature of the injury (Narum & Rodolfa, 1984). Overall, research studies have shown that 54 – 87% of spinal-cord – injured men are able to experience erections. However, most men are unable to ejaculate or experience an orgasm, and very few are able to produce children (Cornelius et al., 1982). However, the use of a vibrator has facilitated ejaculation and impregnation (Beretta, 1989).

Much of the professional and personal sex education for individuals and couples faced with SCI consists of redefining and expanding sexual expression. For example, genital sensations may be very slight or nonexistent, but other areas of the body may increase in sexual responsiveness and may cause intense pleasure. The book *Sexual Options for Paraplegics and Quadriplegics* has described techniques to increase feelings of pleasure:

> Sensory amplification, the method used by some disabled men and women to achieve the most pleasure and satisfaction from a sensory input, is the act of thinking about a physical stimulus, concentrating on it, and amplifying the sensation in your mind to an intense degree. Thus, it is possible to achieve a higher level of satisfaction and possibly a mental orgasm. Some who have lost physical sensation in the genital area substitute or transfer a sensation to an area of the body that has retained some feeling, such as the inside of an arm, the neck, breasts, buttocks, or around the anal area. By transposing these sensations mentally, or by using your imagination to create a fantasy, you may find intense satisfaction. (Mooney et al., 1975, p. 5)

Many people with SCI have able-bodied partners who can enhance the sexual relationship by taking an active role in sex play.

Men with SCI who are unable to have erections must make some sexual adjustments; it is important for a couple in this situation to experiment with different intercourse positions to find what works best for them. Surgically inserted implants are sometimes used to make the penis erect. However, men with SCI and their partners often reevaluate the importance of penile – vaginal intercourse and develop other viable options for pleasure, such as manual and oral stimulation or the use of vibrators.

Women with spinal-cord injuries usually lose sensations in the vulva (Berard, 1989), but other body areas above the level of the injury can become increasingly sensitive to erotic stimulation. Most women with SCI do not experience orgasm, but orgasmic-type sensations have been described from erotic stimulation, fantasy, or dreams. One woman described her experience:

> My head gets to a point where I don't think about what I am doing and it slides into the sensations . . . it feels good for a while and then subsides and I feel sort of satisfied. There is no peak at the end. (Becker, 1978, p. 194)

Most women with SCI are able to conceive, carry a pregnancy, and give birth to a healthy infant. They are no more likely to require a cesarean section than other women (Cornelius et al., 1982).

Observing their partners' responses to sexual pleasure can heighten the satisfaction and enjoyment of people with SCI. Some disabled people have developed the ability to "feel" what their partners are feeling and share intensely in their partners' excitement (Mooney et al., 1975). Many people with SCI have able-bodied partners who can enhance the sexual relationship by taking an active role in sex play.

Cerebral Palsy

Cerebral palsy (CP) is caused by damage to the brain that may occur before or during birth or during early childhood; it is characterized by mild to severe lack of muscular control. Involuntary muscle movements may disrupt speech, facial expressions, balance, and body movement. Involuntary, severe muscle contractions may cause limbs to jerk or assume awkward positions. A person's intelligence may or may not be affected. Unfortunately, it is often mistakenly assumed that people with CP are mentally disabled because of their physical difficulty in communicating.

Genital sensation is unaffected by CP. Spasticity and deformity of arms and hands may make masturbation difficult or impossible without assistance, and the same problems in the hips and knees may make certain intercourse positions painful or difficult (Joseph, 1991). Chronic contraction of the muscles surrounding the vaginal opening may create pain during intercourse (Renshaw, 1987b).

The sexual adjustment of a person with CP is contingent on what is physically possible and the extent of environmental support for social contacts and privacy. People with CP and SCI may require the help of someone who can assist in preparation and positioning for sexual relations:

> Society has traditionally taught us that sexual expression is a private matter and that it should involve only the individual(s) participating in the activity. Many severely disabled cerebral palsied individuals, however, need assistance to perform daily activities of living. These same people may also require the assistance of another individual to make sexual activity possible. For example, a woman may need help in positioning herself for masturbation. A disabled couple may require an assistant to undress them and position them for sexual activity. . . . Sexuality must be treated as a normal and necessary activity for all people. (Cornelius et al., 1982)

Blindness and Deafness

The sensory losses of blindness and deafness can affect a person's sexuality in several ways. A woman with visual impairment commented:

> When I am trying to meet a person for the first time, I do not have access to eye contact. For example, I can't flirt with my eyes. . . . A new experience I had last year was being in a hot tub for the first time with three friends. I was really looking forward to this experience. I would have liked being able to see the other bodies, but I could not. I mentioned this to my boyfriend afterward. So the next time we did this, he described these people to me in graphic detail: "Her nipples point up; he's got a roll around his middle; he's got a large penis . . . it makes mine look like. . . ." His descriptions really made the experience fun for me. (Straw, 1981, pp. 37–38)

A great deal of information and many attitudes and social interaction skills are acquired by seeing or hearing others, and visual or hearing deficits impair this learning process. In addition, only 2% of parents of hearing-impaired children know sign language. Therefore, communication about sexuality between parents and deaf children is impaired (Cornelius et al., 1982). Deafness or blindness that occurs in adolescence or adulthood may cause depression, lowered self-esteem, and social withdrawal during the adjustment period. If the sensory losses are a result of disease, the disease itself may have deleterious effects on sexual functioning. In themselves, blindness and deafness do not appear to physically impair sexual interest or response.

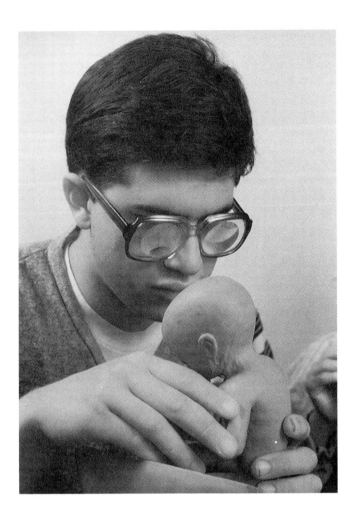

Blind students can learn a great deal about sexuality through the use of anatomical models.

Specially adapted sex-education programs are essential for people with hearing and visual impairments. What unique educational approaches might be used?

Educational resources for visually impaired individuals include written guides for parents and teachers and tapes designed to be used privately by the visually impaired child. The tape instructs the child to explore her or his own body while it describes the various body parts for both sexes and the changes that occur during adolescence. Another program uses lifelike male and female dolls, including a male with an erection and a couple having intercourse, for exploration guided by a tape (Cornelius et al., 1982).

Mental Disabilities

Mentally disabled people have below-average intellectual functioning. A person with an IQ around 70 is usually classified as mentally disabled. However, learning capabilities of such people vary greatly from one person to the next. The ability to meet age-appropriate standards of independence and responsibilities depends somewhat on intelligence, but with repetition and guidance, many people with intellectual deficits can learn adaptive behaviors related to daily living and sexuality.

Unfortunately, there are strong stereotypes that all mentally disabled people are unable to learn and are either asexual or unable to control their sexual impulses. More often than not, people with mental disabilities have not had adequate opportunities to learn about their sexuality because parents and/or health care providers have attempted to deny or repress any sexual expression rather than aid them in appropriate expression of sexual feelings (Frank, 1991; Muccigrosso, 1991). The result is usually poorly developed social and sexual skills.

Given their special needs, what do you think mentally disabled people should be taught about sexuality? Please come up with your own ideas before reading on.

Sex education is particularly important for both individuals with mental disabilities and their families. Sexual development of mentally disabled children follows typical patterns (initial involvement with masturbation followed by heterosexual and/or homosexual exploration) but with a time lag compared with nondisabled children. A crucial point in sex education is that mentally disabled people have a basic right to sexual expression. Thorough teaching of important areas of responsibility, including self-care, menstrual hygiene, use of contraceptives, and appropriateness of time and place, is essential (Ragg & Rowe, 1991). In addition, people with mental disabilities need to learn how to set limits with and report others who may attempt to exploit them sexually (Sobsey & Doe, 1991).

People with mental disabilities, their parents, and health care professionals need to be taught that masturbation in private is normal. Judgment in social situations is also a part of sex education (Monat, 1982). In institutional settings where privacy is at a minimum, "appropriateness" in terms of privacy for sexual activities should be liberally defined. The bathroom, bedroom, or secluded outdoor places can be considered appropriate for masturbation or intimacy with others. The mentally disabled share the usual human interest in and desire for closeness, affection, and physical contact, and institutions need to be sensitive to this aspect of their residents' lives (Ames, 1991).

Coping and Enhancement Strategies

Individuals and couples can best cope with the sexual limitations their illness or disability presents by accepting the limitations and developing the possible options remaining for them. For example, couples can minimize the effects of pain by planning sexual activity at optimal times of the day, using methods of pain control such as moist heat or pain medication; finding comfortable positions; and focusing on genital pleasure or arousing erotic images to distract from pain (Schover & Jensen, 1988). Expanding the definition of sexuality beyond genital arousal and intercourse to include dimensions such as erotic thoughts and sensual touch is

The mentally disabled share the usual human interest in and desire for closeness, affection, and physical contact.

also essential. Table 18.1 gives some specific suggestions for coping with the illnesses and disabilities discussed in this chapter.

Illnesses and disabilities often affect a person's body image. Accepting and positive feelings about one's physical self are an important part of sexuality; a good body image contributes to a person's perception of himself or herself as a sexual and sexually attractive individual. Chronic illnesses and physical disabilities can be devastating to this self-confidence (Schover & Jensen, 1988). People who believe that they are unattractive may avoid social situations or feel inadequate in a sexual relationship. Body image also influences how much attention a person pays to grooming and other aspects of personal physical care. A positive body image can contribute to how lovable and worthwhile one feels and what kinds of relationships a person chooses.

For individuals with physical illnesses and limitations, developing a positive body image may be particularly difficult. It can be emotionally painful to compare oneself to other people or to oneself prior to becoming ill or injured. Impaired mobility and limitations in recreation, self-care, and work performance can generate resentment and anger toward one's body. These feelings can be exacerbated by juxtaposing media images of attractiveness and one's own attributes: scars from injuries or surgery, lack of muscle tone from paralysis, or involuntary muscle spasms from neurological damage. Yet these characteristics are very much a part of a person and need to be accepted along with her or his other attributes. As one person who had polio noted:

T A B L E 18.1   *Coping Strategies*

Illness or Disability	Effects on Sexuality	Coping Strategies
Multiple sclerosis (MS)	Symptoms will vary and may come and go. Some will experience difficulty having an orgasm, decreased genital sensitivity, dryness of the vagina, muscle weakness, pain, and bowel and bladder incontinence.	Medication for spasms and pain may be helpful. For those who tire easily, try lovemaking positions that require little exertion. Lubricants may help with dryness.
Diabetes	Many diabetic men experience a reduction or loss of erection. Retrograde ejaculation can also be a problem. Women with diabetes may have problems with sexual desire, lubrication, and orgasm.	Acceptance of the disease may help improve sexual functioning. Noncoital lovemaking can be a viable option for men with loss of erection. Lubricants can help with vaginal dryness.
Heart disease	Chest pain, palpitations, and shortness of breath may limit sexual activities. Fear of stress may cause anxiety.	It is essential for someone who has had a heart attack to consult a physician before resuming sexual activity. Once sexual activity is resumed, try lovemaking positions that require little or no exertion. Go slowly to start to minimize stress and the fear of stress.
Cerebrovascular accident (CVA) (stroke)	Impaired motor coordination or paralysis may create difficulties with sexual positioning and sensitivity.	Nongenital lovemaking and/or different sexual positions may help those with paralysis or limited motor coordination.
Cancer	Pain can greatly interfere with sexual arousal and interest. Radiation therapy may cause hair loss, skin changes, nausea, and fatigue. Surgery may result in loss of body parts and/or permanent scars.	Couples can minimize the effects of pain by using pain medication, finding comfortable positions, and focusing on genital pleasure or arousing erotic fantasies.
Arthritis	Swollen, painful joints, muscular atrophy, and joint contractures may make it difficult to masturbate or make love in some positions.	To avoid pain and pressure on the affected joints, be creative in sexual positioning. Try moist heat to help alleviate pain, and choose a time when you have the least pain and stiffness to make love.
Spinal-cord injury (SCI)	Sexual functioning will depend on the location and severity of the injury. SCI may result in paralysis, spasticity, loss of sensation, incontinence, pain, lack of erection in men, and a dry vagina in women.	It may help to make love in ways other than coitus, which may be difficult, painful, or impossible. The woman-on-top position, and/or a penile prosthesis may be used if there are erectile difficulties. Spasm medication and a water-soluble vaginal lubricant may be of some assistance. If genital sensations are slight, focusing on other areas of the body may increase sexual responsiveness and may cause intense pleasure.
Cerebral palsy (CP)	Muscle spasticity, rigidity, and/or weakness may make certain sexual activities difficult or impossible. Pain and spasms may also occur during arousal.	Nongenital lovemaking, trying different positions, and propping legs up on pillows may help ease spasms. Partners can help with positions, and focusing on genital pleasure may help distract from pain.

Developing a positive body image can help chronically ill and disabled people cope with their limitations.

Before my disability I was very active. I skated, danced, and played the piano. After I was disabled, it changed my body so much. Well, it happened at 17 and was quite a shock. . . . At the present time I'm working on trying to accept my body and to be more aware of it. It is really part of my self-image. Sometimes I'd like to put it [my body] out there somewhere and act as if it's not part of me, but I'm working to admit that it's there and trying to include it as part of me. (Shaul et al., 1978, pp. 6–7)

Body image often can be improved for both disabled and nondisabled people. Many people have negative feelings about their bodies, and all of us will eventually confront body-image changes caused by wrinkles, gray hair, and reduced speed and agility. The following suggestions for helping disabled individuals improve their body image (adapted from Shaul et al., 1978) can be helpful for others as well:

1. Using a mirror, note your positive features and think about how they can be enhanced.

2. Explore and become acquainted with the features or body parts you consider least attractive.

3. Put up photographs of yourself that you like.
4. Say out loud to the mirror, the next time you go to extra effort to look good, "I look great today."
5. Pamper your body with relaxing baths, fragrances, back rubs, a new haircut, and new clothes.
6. Ask people what they find physically attractive about you.
7. Develop your physical potential with exercise and diet.
8. Talk with other people with disabilities to help overcome a sense of isolation.
9. Shop for prostheses or braces where the sales people are concerned with appearance as well as function.
10. Pay attention to the ways you've grown and improved.

Sometimes a person will face body-image changes with previously unknown reserves of emotional strength. Meeting such a challenge can promote a reevaluation of personal values and priorities. A young woman who broke her neck in a car accident reported:

I went through enormous personal changes after my accident. I had been working as a model prior to my accident and was very sought after socially, mainly because of my physical attractiveness. I didn't really reach out to others to get to know them; I always got enough attention by being pretty. But after my accident, with my hair shaved for the halo-type metal band that screwed into my skull and attached to a shoulder – neck brace, I wasn't very pretty. I had to learn to reach out to others to help them feel comfortable with me, so that I wouldn't be so alone and lonely. It has been the most valuable, and most difficult, experience in my life. (Authors' files)

Certainly, the limitations and special circumstances that illnesses and disabilities present are often a challenge for sexual adjustment. Good communication within relationships is especially important because the able-bodied partner is unlikely to know what the ill or disabled person can or cannot do or finds pleasing. Chronically ill and disabled people can greatly benefit from flexibility in sexual roles and innovation in sexual technique. As a woman with CP explained:

My disability kind of makes things more interesting. We have to try harder and I think we get more out of it because we do. We both have to be very conscious of each other — we have to take time. That makes us less selfish and more considerate of each other which helps the relationship in other areas beside sexuality. (Shaul et al., 1978, p. 5)

This kind of exploration, experimentation, communication, and learning together are ways of relating that can contribute to pleasure and intimacy in the relationships of nondisabled couples too.

Summary

Stereotypes About Sexuality, Chronic Illness, and Disability

Stereotypes about the chronically ill and disabled are often based on incorrect assumptions about the sexual limitations that certain medical problems present.

Chronic illness or disability may influence the ways in which a person expresses her or his sexuality but does not alter the inherent sexual nature of the person.

Chronic Illnesses

Chronic illnesses and their treatments can have great impact on sexuality. Diseases of the neurological, vascular, and endocrine systems can impair sexual functioning. Medications, pain, and fatigue can also interfere.

Multiple sclerosis (MS) is a neurological disease of the brain and spinal cord that can affect sexual interest, genital sensation, arousal, or capacity for orgasm. Nerve damage or circulatory problems from diabetes can cause erectile problems in men and problems with sexual desire, lubrication, and orgasm in women.

Sexual problems following heart attacks are usually due to anxiety, misinformation, and feeling stigmatized rather than organic causes.

Cerebrovascular accidents, or strokes, can reduce a person's frequency of interest, arousal, and sexual activity.

Cancer and its therapies can impair the hormonal, vascular, and neurological functions necessary for normal sexual activity. Pain can also greatly interfere with sexual interest and arousal. Cancer of the reproductive organs — cervix, uterus, ovary, prostate, and testis — can greatly influence sexual response.

Arthritis does not directly impair sexual response, but chronic pain and fatigue may lessen a person's sexual interest.

Disabilities

Individuals with disabilities have special needs for education about sexuality and sexual enhancement.

Although a spinal-cord injury does not necessarily impair sexual desire, a person with SCI may have impaired ability for arousal and orgasm; this varies according to the specific injury.

People with cerebral palsy, which is characterized by mild to severe lack of muscular control, may need help with preparation and positioning for sexual relations.

Blindness and deafness may cause depression, lowered self-esteem, and social withdrawal; however, in themselves, these conditions do not appear to physically impair sexual interest or response.

Stereotypes about the mentally disabled imply that affected people are unable to learn and are either asexual or unable to control their sexual impulses; but more often than not, mentally disabled people have not had adequate opportunities to learn about their sexuality.

Coping and Enhancement Strategies

Individuals and couples can best cope with the sexual limitations of their illness or disability by accepting the limitations and developing the possible options remaining to them.

Development of a positive body image can contribute to a person's perception of himself or herself as a sexual and sexually attractive individual.

Good communication within a relationship is a particularly important component of sexuality for ill or physically disabled people.

✑ *Thought Provokers* ✑

1. A number of myths exist about the sexuality of the chronically ill and disabled. What myths of this sort have you encountered?

2. Do you believe that institutions such as hospitals and nursing homes should provide for the sexual needs of their residents? Why or why not?

3. How would your sexuality change if you incurred a spinal-cord injury in an accident?

Suggested Readings

Boston Women's Health Book Collective (1985). *The New Our Bodies, Ourselves.* New York: Simon & Schuster. Contains detailed discussions on the detection, treatment, and aftereffects of breast and cervical cancers.

Bullard, David; and Knight, Susan (1981). *Sexuality and Physical Disability: Personal Perspectives.* St. Louis, Mo.: Mosby. Accounts of personal experiences with physical disability.

Marat, Rosalyn (1982). *Sexuality and the Mentally Retarded.* San Diego: College-Hill Press. A thoughtful overview of a much neglected topic.

Rabin, Barry (1980). *The Sensuous Wheeler: Sexual Adjustment for the Spinal-Cord Injured.* San Francisco: Multi Media Resource Center. A clearly written book for the spinal-cord injured and their partners.

Sandowski, Carol (1989). *Sexual Concerns When Illness or Disability Strikes.* Springfield, Ill.: Charles Thomas Publisher. A comprehensive book clarifying the impact of illnesses and disabilities on sexuality.

Schover, Leslie; and Jensen, Soren (1988). *Sexuality and Chronic Illness.* New York: Guilford Press. Analyzes the impact of chronic illness on sexuality and the treatment and adjustment possibilities.

I enjoy sex, but I am not willing to die
for it.

Ansell Corporation
Condom Advertisement (1986)

CHAPTER 19

Sexually Transmitted Diseases

𝐼n this chapter we discuss a variety of diseases that can be transmitted through sexual interaction. These are commonly called **sexually transmitted diseases (STDs).** Some of these conditions can be spread nonsexually as well as through sexual contact (for example, pubic lice, herpes, and genital warts). The term *venereal disease* (VD) is sometimes used interchangeably with STD. However, the term VD is traditionally applied only to those conditions whose mode of transmission is almost always sexual contact (for example, gonorrhea and syphilis). Thus, the title of this chapter, "Sexually Transmitted Diseases," is a much broader topic that includes the more limited category of VD.

Our purpose in including a chapter on STDs is to present a realistic picture of what a sexually transmitted disease is, how it can be recognized, what should be done to treat it, and what preventive measures can be taken to avoid contracting or transmitting it. Furthermore, we trust that increased knowledge about STDs will lead to thoughtful consideration of other people who might be involved. Such knowledge is particularly important considering that the incidence of many STDs is on the increase, that many people do not take appropriate action to avoid being infected, and that most of these diseases can be successfully treated. Acquisition of knowledge about STDs may be particularly relevant to adolescents and young adults in light of evidence that 86% of all STDs in the United States occur among 15 – 29-year-olds and that approximately 50% of the U.S. population will acquire one or more STDs by age 30 – 35 (Centers for Disease Control, 1992a; Handsfield, 1992).

 What are some of the factors that contribute to the rise in the incidence of STDs? Give this some thought before reading on.

It is not entirely clear why the incidence of STDs is so high. Undoubtedly, a number of factors are operating in what many writers and health authorities have labeled an epidemic. Increasing sexual activity among young people has commonly been advanced as a prime reason for the accelerating rate of STDs. A related contributory effect of "sexual liberation" has been an increasing tendency to have multiple sexual partners, particularly during one's youth, when the incidence of STDs is the highest. It is also believed that increased use of birth control pills has contributed to the rising incidence rates by reducing the use of vaginal spermicides and the condom, contraceptive methods known to offer some protection against STDs.

The spread of STDs is facilitated by the unfortunate fact that many of these diseases do not produce obvious symptoms. In some cases, particularly among women, there may be no outward signs at all. Under these circumstances people may unknowingly infect others. In addition, feelings of guilt and embarrassment that often accompany having an STD may prevent people from seeking adequate treatment or informing their sexual partners.

It is possible that the effects of these factors could be counterbalanced through general public understanding of STDs and their prevention. Unfortunately, this has not happened. We hope the present widespread ignorance will eventually be overcome by the development of more effective sex education at all levels of society.

The following sections focus on the most common STDs. There is also a large unit on AIDS, a disease that has received more attention than any other STD in the last few years. Table 19.1 summarizes the STDs discussed in this chapter. If you want more information, we recommend contacting your county health service or VD clinic or calling the National STD Hotline.* These services will answer questions, send free literature, and most important, give you the name and phone number of a local physician or public clinic that will treat STDs free or at minimal cost.

Common Vaginal Infections

Several kinds of vaginal infections can be transmitted through sexual interaction. Because they are also frequently contracted through nonsexual means, they are not generally referred to as venereal diseases. *Vaginitis* and *leukorrhea* are general terms applied to a variety of vaginal infections characterized by a whitish discharge. The secretion may also be yellow or green because of the presence of pus cells, and it often has a disagreeable odor. Additional symptoms of vaginitis may include irritation and itching of the genital tissue, burning during urination, and pain around the vaginal opening during intercourse.

Vaginal infections are far more common than some of the more serious STDs like gonorrhea and syphilis (Lefèvre et al., 1988). Practically every woman experiences one or more of these infections during her life. In fact, vaginitis is one of the most common reasons women consult physicians. Under typical circumstances, many of the organisms that cause vaginal infections are relatively harmless. In fact, some routinely live in the vagina and cause no trouble unless something alters the normal vaginal environment and allows them to overgrow. The vagina normally houses bacteria (lactobacilli) that help maintain a healthy vaginal environment (Domingue et al., 1991). The pH of the vagina is usually sufficiently acidic to ward off most infections. However, certain conditions may alter the pH toward the alkaline side, which may leave a woman vulnerable to infection. Some factors that increase the likelihood of vaginal infection include antibiotic therapy, use of contraceptive pills, menstruation, pregnancy, wearing pantyhose and nylon underwear, douching, and lowered resistance from stress or lack of sleep. A few women appear to have such a delicately balanced vaginal ecosystem that even a brief change in vaginal pH is sufficient to allow pathogenic (infection-causing) organisms to overwhelm the protective lactobacilli. These women may develop symptoms of vaginitis after each coital encounter because the alkalinity of semen may reduce vaginal acidity enough to allow the pathogenic organisms to gain control. The use of condoms or a postcoital vinegar douche will usually overcome this problem (Friedrich, 1985).

---

*The National Sexually Transmitted Disease Hotline can be dialed toll free from 8:00 AM to 8:00 PM weekdays and from 10:00 AM to 6:00 PM weekends, Pacific time. The number is (800) 227–8922 (in California, [800] 982–5883).

T A B L E 19.1   ***Common Sexually Transmitted Diseases (STDs):***
Mode of Transmission, Symptoms, and Treatment

STD	Transmission	Symptoms	Treatment
Bacterial vaginosis	The most common causative agent, the *Gardnerella vaginalis* bacterium, is sometimes transmitted through coitus.	In women, a fishy or musty smelling, thin discharge, like flour paste in consistency and usually gray. Most men are asymptomatic.	Metronidazole (Flagyl) or clinamycin
Candidiasis (yeast infection)	The *Candida albicans* fungus may accelerate growth when the chemical balance of the vagina is disturbed; it may also be transmitted through sexual interaction.	White, "cheesy" discharge; irritation of vaginal and vulval tissues.	Vaginal suppositories or cream, such as clotrimazole, nystatin, and miconazole, or oral fluconazole
Trichomoniasis	The protozoan parasite *Trichomonas vaginalis* is passed through genital sexual contact or, less frequently, by towels, toilet seats, or bathtubs used by an infected person.	White or yellow vaginal discharge with an unpleasant odor; vulva is sore and irritated.	Metronidazole (Flagyl) for both women and men
Chlamydial infection	The *Chlamydia trachomatis* bacterium is transmitted primarily through sexual contact. It may also be spread by fingers from one body site to another.	In women, PID (pelvic inflammatory disease) caused by *Chlamydia* may include disrupted menstrual periods, abdominal pain, elevated temperature, nausea, vomiting, and headache. In men, chlamydial infection of the urethra may cause a discharge and burning during urination. *Chlamydia*-caused epididymitis may produce a sense of heaviness in the affected testicle(s), inflammation of the scrotal skin, and painful swelling at the bottom of the testicle.	Tetracycline, doxycycline, erythromycin, or trimethoprim-sulfamethoxazole
Gonorrhea ("clap")	The *Neisseria gonorrhoeae* bacterium ("gonococcus") is spread through genital, oral–genital, or genital–anal contact.	The most common symptoms in men are a cloudy discharge from the penis and burning sensations during urination. If disease is untreated, complications may include inflammation of scrotal skin and swelling at base of the testicle.	Cefixime, ceftriaxone, or spectinomycin are usually effective.

T A B L E **19.1**   *(continued)*

STD	Transmission	Symptoms	Treatment
Gonorrhea ("clap") (continued)		In women, some green or yellowish discharge is produced but commonly remains undetected. At a later stage, PID (pelvic inflammatory disease) may develop.	
Nongonococcal urethritis (NGU)	Primary causes are believed to be the bacteria *Chlamydia trachomatis* and *Ureaplasma urealyticum,* most commonly transmitted through coitus. Some NGU may result from allergic reactions or from *Trichomonas* infection.	Inflammation of the urethral tube. A man has a discharge from the penis and irritation during urination. A woman may have a mild discharge of pus from the vagina but often shows no symptoms.	Doxycycline or erythromycin
Syphilis	The *Treponema pallidum* bacterium ("spirochete") is transmitted from open lesions during genital, oral–genital, or genital–anal contact.	*Primary stage:* A painless chancre appears at the site where the spirochetes entered the body. *Secondary stage:* The chancre disappears and a generalized skin rash develops. *Latent stage:* There may be no observable symptoms. *Tertiary stage:* Heart failure, blindness, mental disturbance, and many other symptoms may occur. Death may result.	Benzathine penicillin, doxycycline, tetracycline, or erythromycin
Pubic lice ("crabs")	*Phthirus pubis,* the pubic louse, is spread easily through body contact or through shared clothing or bedding.	Persistent itching. Lice are visible and may often be located in pubic hair or other body hair.	Preparations such as A-200 pyrinate or Kwell (gamma benzene hexachloride)
Herpes	The genital herpes virus (HSV–2) appears to be transmitted primarily by vaginal, anal, or oral–genital intercourse. The oral herpes virus (HSV–1) is transmitted primarily by kissing.	Small, painful red bumps (papules) appear in the region of the genitals (genital herpes) or mouth (oral herpes). The papules become painful blisters that eventually rupture to form wet, open sores.	No known cure; a variety of treatments may reduce symptoms; oral or intravenous acyclovir (Zovirax) promotes healing and suppresses recurrent outbreaks.

Continued

T A B L E **19.1**   (*continued*)

STD	Transmission	Symptoms	Treatment
Viral hepatitis	The hepatitis B virus may be transmitted by blood, semen, vaginal secretions, and saliva. Manual, oral, or penile stimulation of the anus are strongly associated with the spread of this virus. Hepatitis A seems to be primarily spread via the fecal–oral route. Oral–anal sexual contact is a common mode for sexual transmission of hepatitis A.	Vary from nonexistent to mild, flulike symptoms to an incapacitating illness characterized by high fever, vomiting, and severe abdominal pain.	No specific therapy; treatment generally consists of bed rest and adequate fluid intake.
Genital warts (*condylomata acuminata*)	The virus is spread primarily through vaginal, anal, or oral–genital sexual interaction.	Warts are hard and yellow–gray on dry skin areas; soft pinkish red, and cauliflower-like on moist areas.	Topical agents like trichloroacetic acid or podophyllin, cauterization, freezing, surgical removal, or vaporization by carbon dioxide laser
Acquired immunodeficiency syndrome (AIDS)	Blood and semen are the major vehicles for transmitting HIV, which attacks the immune system. It appears to be passed primarily through sexual contact, or needle sharing among IV drug users.	Vary with the type of cancer or opportunistic infections that afflict an infected person. Common symptoms include fevers, night sweats, weight loss, loss of appetite, fatigue, swollen lymph nodes, diarrhea and/or bloody stools, atypical bruising or bleeding, skin rashes, headache, chronic cough, and a whitish coating on the tongue or throat.	At present, therapy focuses on specific treatment(s) of opportunistic infections and tumors. Some antiviral drugs, such as zidovudine, slow the progression of AIDS and extend patients' lives.

Approximately 90% of women with vaginitis have an infection caused by *Gardnerella, Candida,* or *Trichomonas,* either alone or in combination (Friedrich, 1985). Of the infections caused by these organisms, *Gardnerella vaginalis* is the most common, followed in order of frequency by candidiasis and trichomoniasis.

Bacterial Vaginosis

Bacterial vaginosis (BV) is a vaginal infection typically caused by a bacterium known as *Gardnerella vaginalis* (Mengel et al., 1989; Platz-Christensen et al., 1989; Watts et al., 1989).

Incidence and Transmission. Not long ago the *Gardnerella vaginalis* bacterium was dismissed as a harmless organism in the normal vaginal flora. However, it is now recognized that although the presence of some *Gardnerella vaginalis* bacteria in the vaginal flora is normal, an increased growth of the organism together with a decrease in lactobacilli results in the development of bacterial vaginosis. There is evidence that overgrowth of *Gardnerella vaginalis* bacteria is perhaps the most common cause of vaginitis in American women (Easmon et al., 1992). Many male partners of women with diagnosed bacterial vaginosis also harbor the *Gardnerella vaginalis* organism, usually without any clinical symptoms. While the role of sexual transmission in BV is not fully understood, it is believed that coitus often provides a mode for transmission of the infection.

Symptoms and Complications. The most prominent symptom of bacterial vaginosis in women is a foul-smelling, thin discharge that resembles flour paste in consistency. The discharge is usually gray, but it may also be white, yellow, or green. The disagreeable odor, often noticed first by an infected woman's sexual partner, is typically described as fishy or musty (Easmon et al., 1992; Handsfield, 1992). This smell may be particularly noticeable after coitus because the alkaline seminal fluid reacts with the bacteria, causing the release of the chemicals that produce the smell. A small number of infected women experience irritation of the genital tissues and mild burning during urination. As mentioned earlier, most men are asymptomatic. However, some males infected with *Gardnerella vaginalis* develop inflammation of the foreskin and glans of the penis, **urethritis** (inflammation of the urethral tube), and **cystitis** (bladder infection) (Watson, 1985).

Treatment. The treatment of choice for bacterial vaginosis is metronidazole (Flagyl) by mouth for seven days. When this drug is contraindicated (inadvisable) because of pregnancy or other factors, the antibiotic clindamycin may be used (Handsfield & Schwebke, 1991). In cases of recurrent BV, the regular male sexual partner of the infected woman is often treated simultaneously with his partner's retreatment to avoid the possibility of "ping-ponging" the disease back and forth (Handsfield & Schwebke, 1991; Mengel et al., 1989).

Candidiasis

Candidiasis (kan-de-DĪ-a-sis), also commonly referred to as *moniliasis* or a *yeast infection,* is caused by a yeastlike fungus called *Candida albicans.*

Incidence and Transmission. The microscopic *Candida albicans* organism is normally present in the vagina of many women; it also inhabits the mouth and large intestine of large numbers of women and men. A disease state results only when certain conditions allow the yeast to overgrow other microorganisms in the vagina. This accelerated growth may result from pregnancy, use of birth control pills, or diabetes — conditions that increase the amount of sugar stored in vaginal cells (*Candida albicans* thrives in the presence of sugar). If a nonpregnant woman has repeated yeast infections, it may be advisable for her to be tested for diabetes or other blood sugar disorders. Another factor is the use of oral antibiotics, which reduce the number of lactobacilli (mentioned earlier as important for a healthy vaginal environment). This reduction permits *Candida albicans* to multiply rapidly.

It has become clear that diet can play an important role in the incidence of candidiasis. The ingestion of large amounts of dairy products, sugar, and artificial sweeteners leads to the excessive excretion of urine sugars that may promote *Candida albicans* overgrowth. Reducing the intake of these substances can lead to a dramatic reduction in the frequency of recurrences of yeast infections (Friedrich, 1985).

If the yeast organism is not already present in the woman's vagina, it may be transmitted to this area in a variety of ways. It can be conveyed from the anus by wiping back-to-front or on the surface of a menstrual pad, or it can be transmitted through sexual interaction because the organism may be harbored under the foreskin of an uncircumcised man. It may also be passed from a partner's mouth to a woman's vagina during oral sex (Markos et al., 1992).

Symptoms. A woman with a yeast infection may notice that she has a white, clumpy discharge that looks something like cottage cheese. In addition, candidiasis is often associated with intense itching and soreness of the vaginal and vulval tissues, which typically become red and dry. A woman who has a yeast infection may find coitus quite painful, and irritation from intercourse may worsen the infection.

Treatment. A variety of treatments may prove effective in combating yeast infections. Traditional treatment strategies consist of vaginal suppositories or cream such as clotrimazole, miconazole, or nystatin (Handsfield & Schwebke, 1991). A drug taken by mouth, fluconazole, has also proven to be effective in treating candidiasis (Boag et al., 1991). Because *Candida albicans* is a hardy organism, treatment should be continued for the prescribed length of time (usually several days to two weeks), even though the symptoms may disappear in two days.

Trichomoniasis

Trichomoniasis (trick-ō-mon-ī-ah-sis) is caused by a one-celled protozoan parasite called *Trichomonas vaginalis.*

Incidence and Transmission. In females trichomoniasis accounts for about one-fourth of all cases of vaginitis. Approximately eight million American women develop this condition each year (Martens & Faro, 1989). Not all infected women have noticeable symptoms. Men may carry the infection too, but it is quite difficult to spot this condition in men because they generally have no observable symptoms (Saultz & Toffler, 1989). Nevertheless, some authorities believe that most male sex partners of infected women carry the *Trichomonas vaginalis* organism in their urethras and under the foreskin if they are uncircumcised. The primary mode of transmission of this infection is through sexual contact.

Symptoms and Complications. The most common symptom of trichomoniasis infection in women is an abundant, frothy, white or yellow vaginal discharge with an unpleasant odor. The discharge frequently irritates the tissues of the vagina and vulva, causing them to become inflamed, itchy, and sore. The infection is usually limited to the vagina and sometimes the cervix, but occasionally the organism may invade the urethra, bladder, or Bartholin's glands. Some health specialists believe that long-term trichomonal infection may damage the cells of the cervix and increase susceptibility to cervical cancer. However, prompt, effective treatment prevents permanent cervical damage.

Treatment. To avoid passing the disease back and forth, it is important that the male partner(s) of the infected woman be treated even if asymptomatic (Abramowicz, 1990; Handsfield, 1992). If a male partner is not treated, the couple should use condoms to prevent reinfection. The recommended drug regimen for both sexes is a single 2-gram dose of metronidazole (Flagyl) taken by mouth (Abramowicz, 1990; Handsfield & Schwebke, 1991). Metronidazole is strongly contraindicated in the first trimester of pregnancy. Topical creams, such as clotrimazole, may provide symptomatic improvement and some cures in women unable to take metronidazole.

Chlamydial Infection

Chlamydial (clah-MID-ē-al) **infection** is caused by *Chlamydia trachomatis*, a bacterial microorganism. Although classified as a bacterium, *Chlamydia trachomatis* is like a virus in that it only grows intracellularly. This organism is now recognized as the cause of a diverse group of genital infections. *Chlamydia trachomatis* is also involved in a number of infections of newborns and is a common cause of preventable blindness.

Incidence and Transmission. It is now widely recognized that *Chlamydia trachomatis* infections are among the most prevalent and most damaging of all STDs (Aral & Holmes, 1991; Humphreys et al., 1992; Potts, 1992; Weinstock, 1992). Chlamydial infection is the most common bacterial STD in the United States (Handsfield, 1991). An estimated three to five million American men, women, and infants develop a chlamydial infection each year (Handsfield, 1991; Handsfield & Hammerschlag, 1992; Potts, 1992; Stein, 1991). Sexually active teenagers have higher infection rates than any other age group (Stein, 1991). Young women who use oral contraceptives seem to be at particularly high risk for developing a chlamydial infection if they are exposed (Aral & Holmes, 1991).

Chlamydial disease is transmitted primarily through sexual contact (Aral & Holmes, 1991; Potts, 1992). It may also be spread by fingers from one body site to another, such as from the genitals to the eyes. In areas of the world where people live in conditions of poor sanitation and overcrowding (such as the Middle East, Africa, and India), the disease is commonly spread through sexual activity and by nonsexual modes of transmission such as via hands, flies, and contact with human waste. In the United States the major mode of transmission is sexual relations.

Symptoms and Complications. There are two general types of genital chlamydial infections in females — infections of the mucosa of the lower reproductive tract, commonly manifested as *urethritis* or *cervicitis* (infection of the cervix), and invasive infections of the upper reproductive tract, which are expressed as **pelvic inflammatory disease (PID)** (Apuzzio & Hoegsberg, 1992; Expert Committee on Pelvic Inflammatory Disease, 1991; Golden et al., 1989). PID typically occurs when chlamydial or other infectious organisms spread from the cervix upward, infecting the lining of the uterus (*endometritis*), the fallopian tubes (*salpingitis*), and possibly the ovaries and other adjacent abdominal structures. *Chlamydia trachomatis* may account for as many as half of the approximately one million recognized cases of PID that occur annually in the United States (Centers for Disease Control, 1991b; Expert Committee on Pelvic Inflammatory Disease, 1991; Handsfield, 1992; Potts, 1992).

Most women with lower reproductive tract chlamydial infections have few or no symptoms (Handsfield & Hammerschlag, 1992). Symptoms, when they do occur, may include mild irritation or itching of the genital tissues, burning during urination, and a slight discharge (Stein, 1991; Handsfield & Hammerschlag, 1992). PID resulting from invasion of the upper reproductive tract by *Chlamydia trachomatis* often produces a variety of symptoms, which may include disrupted menstrual periods, pain in the lower abdomen, elevated temperature, nausea, vomiting, and headache. Chlamydial salpingitis is the primary preventable cause of female infertility and ectopic pregnancy (Aral & Holmes, 1991; Handsfield & Hammerschlag, 1992). Even after PID has been effectively treated, residual scar tissue in the fallopian tubes leaves some women sterile (Handsfield, 1992).

Are there any limitations on the kind of birth control that is appropriate for a woman who has had PID? Can you think of any post-PID complications that might be associated with a specific birth control method? If you are knowledgeable about how various birth control methods work, you may be able to answer these questions before reading on.

A woman who has had PID should be cautioned about the use of the IUD as a method of birth control. An IUD does not prevent fertilization (see Chapter 11 for an explanation of how the IUD prevents pregnancy); thus, a tiny sperm cell may negotiate a partially blocked area of a scarred fallopian tube and fertilize an ovum that, because of its larger size, subsequently becomes lodged in the scarred tube. The result is an ectopic pregnancy, a serious hazard to the woman.

In men the *chlamydia trachomatis* organism is estimated to be the cause of approximately half the cases of *epididymitis* (infection of the epididymis) and *nongonococcal urethritis* (NGU) (infection of the urethral tube not caused by gonorrhea) (Kojima et al., 1988; Potts, 1992). The symptoms of epididymitis may include a sensation of heaviness in the affected testicle(s), inflammation of the scrotal skin, and the formation of a small area of hard, painful swelling at the bottom of the testicle. Symptoms of NGU include a discharge from the penis and burning during urination (more details are provided in a later section on NGU).

One of the most disheartening aspects of this disease is the absence of symptoms in the majority of females with lower reproductive tract chlamydial infections (Freund, 1992; Stein, 1991; Weinstock et al., 1992). Most women and men with rectal chlamydial infections and as many as 30% of men with chlamydial NGU also manifest few or no symptoms (Centers for Disease Control, 1985b; Stein, 1991). Laboratory diagnostic tests are necessary to confirm the presence of

Chlamydia trachomatis. Medical specialists have access to relatively uncomplicated and inexpensive nonculture methods for diagnosing chlamydial infections (Freund, 1992; Taylor-Robinson & Thomas, 1991).

Chlamydia trachomatis also causes **trachoma** (tra-KO-ma), a chronic, contagious form of **conjunctivitis** (kon-junk′-ti-vī-tis) (inflammation of the mucous membrane that lines the inner surface of the eyelid and the exposed surface of the eyeball). Trachoma is the world's leading cause of preventable blindness (Schachter et al., 1988); it is particularly prevalent in Asia and Africa. *Chlamydia trachomatis* is also the most common cause of eye infections in newborns, who can become infected as they pass through the birth canal (Hammerschlag, 1989). Studies have variously estimated that 20 – 50% of infants born to infected mothers will develop conjunctivitis (Hammerschlag, 1989; Rivlin, 1992). In addition, many babies of infected mothers will develop chlamydial pneumonia during the first few months of their lives (Aral & Holmes, 1991; Rivlin, 1992).

Treatment. Drugs effective against *Chlamydia trachomatis* include tetracycline, doxycycline, erythromycin, and trimethoprim-sulfamethoxazole (Handsfield & Schwebke, 1991; Stein, 1991). Penicillin is not effective. Because chlamydial infection often coexists with gonorrhea, it is advisable to employ a drug regimen that is effective against both infectious organisms. Tetracycline or doxycycline is the treatment of choice for men and for nonpregnant women with uncomplicated infections of the lower reproductive tract. For pregnant women and others for whom tetracycline and doxycycline are contraindicated, an effective alternative drug is erythromycin. All sexual partners exposed to *Chlamydia trachomatis* should be examined for STDs and treated if necessary.

To reduce the risk of an infant developing chlamydial conjunctivitis after passing through the birth canal of an infected mother, either erythromycin or tetracycline ointment is put into the eyes of exposed newborns as soon as possible after birth.

Gonorrhea

Gonorrhea (gon-ō-RĒ-a), known in street language as "clap," is an STD caused by the bacterium *Neisseria gonorrhoeae* (also called "gonococcus").

Incidence and Transmission. Gonorrhea is a very common communicable disease. In 1991 approximately 600,000 cases of gonorrhea were reported in the United States, a figure that is no doubt much smaller than the number of actual cases. Public health experts believe that the majority of new cases of gonorrhea go unreported each year. (The Centers for Disease Control estimates the true incidence of gonorrhea to be three to five million cases annually.) The late 1970s witnessed the beginning of an intensified public health effort to curtail gonorrhea infections in the United States. These efforts resulted in a downward trend in the overall incidence of gonorrhea in the U.S. population, a decline that continued through the 1980s (Aral & Holmes, 1991; Schwebke, 1991a). Unfortunately, this reduction has not been consistent throughout the population, and gonorrhea rates "have escalated among heterosexual inner-city ethnic minorities of low socio-economic status" (Schwebke, 1991a, p. 42). Recent data indicate a strong link between increasing rates of gonorrhea and the exchange of sex for money or drugs, especially crack cocaine (Marx et al., 1991; Schwarcz et al., 1992).

Survival of the gonococcus bacterium is facilitated by the warm mucous membranes found in the tissues of the genitals, anus, and throat. Its mode of transmission is by sexual contact — penile – vaginal, oral – genital, or genital – anal.

Symptoms and Complications. Early symptoms of gonorrheal infection are more likely to be evident in men than women. The majority of men who experience gonococcal urethritis will have some symptoms, ranging from mild to quite pronounced. However, it is not uncommon for men with this type of infection to be asymptomatic and yet potentially infectious (Schwebke, 1991a; Starcher et al., 1983). The incidence of asymptomatic gonorrhea is considerably greater in women; as many as 80% will not detect the disease until it has progressed considerably.

Early Symptoms in the Male. In men early symptoms typically appear within one to five days after sexual contact with an infected person. However, symptoms may show up as late as two weeks after contact or, in a small number of cases, may not appear at all. The two most common signs of infection are a bad-smelling, cloudy discharge from the penis (see Figure 19.1) and burning sensations during urination. About 30 – 40% of infected men also have swollen and tender lymph glands in the groin. These early symptoms sometimes clear up on their own without treatment. However, this is no guarantee that the disease has been eradicated by the body's immune system. The bacteria may still be present, and a man may still be able to infect a partner.

Complications in the Male. If the infection continues without treatment for two to three weeks, it may spread up the genitourinary tract. Here it may involve the prostate, bladder, kidneys, and testicles. Most men who continue to harbor the gonococcus have only periodic flareups of the minor symptoms of discharge and burning during urination. In a small number of men, however, the bacteria cause abscesses to form in the prostate. These may result in fever, painful bowel movement, difficulty urinating, and general discomfort. In approximately one out of five men who remain untreated for longer than a month, the bacteria move down the vas deferens to infect one or both of the epididymal structures that lie along the back of each testicle. Generally, only one side is infected initially, usually the left. The symptoms of epididymitis were described in the discussion of chlamydial infection. Even after successful treatment, gonococcal epididymitis leaves scar tissue, which can block the flow of sperm from the affected testicle. Sterility does not usually result because this complication is typically restricted to only one testicle. However, if treatment is still not carried out after epididymitis has occurred on one side, the infection may spread to the other testicle, rendering the man permanently sterile.

Early Symptoms in the Female. As mentioned earlier, women are often unaware of the early signs of gonorrheal infection. The primary site of infection, the cervix, may become inflamed without producing any observable symptoms. A green or yellowish discharge usually results, but because this is rarely heavy, it commonly

FIGURE 19.1

A cloudy discharge symptomatic of gonorrheal infection.

remains undetected. A woman who is very aware of her vaginal secretions (perhaps from using the mucus method of birth control) is more likely to note the infection during these early stages. Sometimes the discharge may be irritating to the vulval tissues. However, when a woman seeks medical attention for an irritating discharge, her physician may fail to consider gonorrhea because many other infectious organisms produce this symptom. Also, many women who have gonorrhea also have trichomoniasis, and this condition may mask the presence of gonorrhea. Consequently, it is essential for any woman who thinks she may have gonorrhea to make certain that she is tested for gonorrhea when she is examined. (A Pap smear is *not* a test for gonorrhea.)

Complications in the Female. It is not uncommon for the Bartholin's glands to be invaded by the gonococcus organism. When this happens there are usually no symptoms. Far more serious complications result from the spread of this disease to the upper reproductive tract, where it often causes PID (pelvic inflammatory disease). The symptoms of PID, discussed in the previous section on chlamydial infection, are often more severe when the infecting organism is gonococcus rather than *Chlamydia trachomatis.* Sterility and ectopic pregnancy are very serious consequences occasionally associated with gonococcal PID. Another serious complication that may result from PID is the development of tough bands of scar-tissue adhesions that may link several pelvic cavity structures (fallopian tubes, ovaries, uterus, and so forth) to each other, to the abdominal walls, or to both. These adhesions can cause severe pain during coitus or when a woman is standing or walking.

Other Complications in Both Sexes. In about 1% of adult men and women with gonorrhea, the gonococci enter the bloodstream (a condition called *disseminated gonococcal infection*) and spread throughout the body to produce a variety of symptoms including chills, fever, loss of appetite, skin lesions, and arthritic pain in the joints (Fitzgerald, 1984; Soper, 1991). If arthritic symptoms develop, quick treatment is essential to avoid permanent joint damage. In very rare cases, the gonococcus organism may invade the heart, liver, spinal cord, and brain.

An infant may develop a gonococcal eye infection after passing through the birth canal of an infected woman (Schwebke, 1991a). The use of silver nitrate or penicillin eye drops immediately after birth averts this potential complication. There are a few rare cases recorded where adults have transmitted the bacteria to their eyes by touching this region immediately after handling their genitals. That is one reason it is important to wash with soap and water immediately after self-examination.

Oral contact with infected genitals may result in transmission of the gonococcal bacteria to the throat, causing pharyngeal gonorrhea. Most people who have pharyngeal gonorrhea are asymptomatic, but a few may have a sore throat. Rectal gonorrhea may be caused by anal intercourse or, in a woman, by transmission of the bacteria from the vagina to the anal opening via menstrual bleeding or vaginal discharge. This form of gonorrhea is often asymptomatic, particularly in females, but it may be accompanied by itching, rectal discharge, and bowel disorders.

Because infections of the throat or anus often do not produce observable symptoms, it is very important to examine laboratory cultures taken from the throats or anuses of people who have engaged in oral–genital or anal intercourse with those suspected of having gonorrhea. Health practitioners often overlook these important tests unless a person requests them.

Treatment. Because gonorrhea is often confused with other ailments, it is important to make the correct diagnosis. A coexisting chlamydial infection has been shown to be present in up to 45% of gonorrhea cases (Centers for Disease Control, 1985a). Consequently, many health practitioners use a treatment strategy that is effective against both gonorrheal and chlamydial infections. Up to 1976, all cases of gonorrhea could be effectively treated by penicillin (Aral & Holmes, 1991). Another widely used antibiotic, tetracycline, was also an effective treatment agent. However, in recent years we have seen the emergence of antibiotic-resistant strains of gonococcal bacteria (Aral & Holmes, 1991; Schwebke, 1991a; Smith et al., 1991). Consequently, current treatment guidelines suggest the use of drugs effective against both resistant and nonresistant strains of *Neisseria gonorrhoeae*. Recommended drugs include single doses of cefixime, ceftriaxone, or spectinomycin. Treatment for possible coexisting chlamydial infection consists of seven days of doxycycline or erythromycin.

A reduction in the symptoms of a gonorrheal infection does not necessarily imply total cure, and it is essential that a follow-up negative culture be obtained three to seven days after completion of treatment before a person may conclude that he or she is free of the infection. All sexual partners exposed to a person with diagnosed gonorrhea should be examined, cultured, and treated prophylactically with a drug regimen that covers both gonococcal and chlamydial infections.

Nongonococcal Urethritis

Any inflammation of the urethra that is not caused by gonorrhea is called **nongonococcal urethritis (NGU)**. Until 1974 it was not known what organisms were the cause of this very common condition. Prior to that time it was also common to call it *nonspecific urethritis* (NSU). Now it is believed that two separate microscopic organisms, *Chlamydia trachomatis* and *Ureaplasma urealyticum* (a member of a group of bacteria called mycoplasmas) are the primary causes of NGU (Handsfield, 1992; Hernández-Aguado et al., 1988). Occasionally, NGU may result from invasion by other infectious agents (such as trichomonas, fungi, or bacteria); allergic reactions to vaginal secretions; or irritation by soaps, vaginal contraceptives, or deodorant sprays.

Incidence and Transmission. NGU is quite common among men: In the United States, it now occurs much more frequently than gonococcal urethritis (Handsfield, 1992; Rosenfeld, 1991). Although NGU generally produces urinary tract symptoms only in men, there is evidence that women harbor the chlamydial or mycoplasma organisms. The most common forms of NGU, caused by these two organisms, are no doubt transmitted through coitus. That NGU rarely occurs in men who are not involved in sexual interaction supports this contention.

Symptoms and Complications. Men who contract NGU often manifest symptoms similar to those of gonorrheal infection, including discharge from the penis and mild burning during urination. Often the discharge is less pronounced than that which occurs with gonorrhea; it may be evident only in the morning before urinating.

Women infected with *Chlamydia trachomatis* or *Ureaplasma urealyticum* are generally unaware of the disease until they are informed that NGU has been diagnosed in a male partner. They frequently show no symptoms, although there may be some itching, burning during urination, and a mild discharge of pus from the vagina. (Cultures may reveal the presence of the causative organism.) An infected woman may have the infection for a long time, during which she may pass it to sexual partners.

The symptoms of NGU generally disappear after two to three months without treatment. However, the disease may still be present. If left untreated in women, it may result in cervical inflammation or PID; in men it may spread to the prostate, epididymis, or both. In rare cases NGU produces a form of arthritis.

Treatment. Many physicians assume that any penile discharge is caused by gonorrhea, and thus they may fail to diagnose NGU. Some even begin treatment for gonorrhea before confirming its existence with laboratory tests. Because penicillin, which is still sometimes used to treat gonorrhea, is not effective against NGU, it is important that an infected person make certain there has been a laboratory diagnosis before receiving treatment (Handsfield & Schwebke, 1991). Doxycycline or erythromycin usually clears up the condition. All sexual partners of individuals diagnosed as having NGU should be examined for the presence of an STD and treated if necessary.

Syphilis

Syphilis (SIF-uh-lis) is an STD caused by a thin, corkscrewlike bacterium called *Treponema pallidum* (also commonly called a "spirochete").

Incidence and Transmission. The incidence of syphilis reported in the United States rose steadily throughout the 1970s and early 1980s. This trend reversed itself from 1982 through 1986, "with much of the decrease seen in male homosexuals, probably stemming from changes in sexual behavior in response to the AIDS epidemic" (Schwebke, 1991b, p. 44). However, since the last quarter of 1986, the incidence of syphilis in both sexes has risen steadily and sharply. In 1990, 50,223 cases of syphilis were reported in the United States, a 9% increase from 1989. This number, which equals 20 cases per 100,000 persons, represents a 75% increase from 1985 (Centers for Disease Control, 1991c). This overall increase is primarily attributable to a disturbing increase in syphilis among inner-city ethnic minority groups of low socioeconomic status (Schwebke, 1991b). The following quotation provides an illuminating and disheartening perspective on the recent rapid rise in both syphilis and gonorrhea infections among inner-city populations:

> The epidemiology of both syphilis and gonorrhea appears to be closely linked to illicit drug use and prostitution. Syphilis rates began to skyrocket among inner-city populations at the same time as use of crack-cocaine reached epidemic proportions. The trading of sex for drugs at crack houses encouraged frequent sexual encounters with anonymous partners. This phenomenon ... increases a person's risk for infection. (Schwebke, 1991, p. 44)

A recent review of 16 studies, all of which examined drug use, sexual behavior, and incidence of STDs, provided evidence consistent with the perspective offered in the previous quote. Data provided by these investigations have demonstrated a clear link between increasing rates of syphilis, gonorrhea, AIDS, and other STDs and the use of crack cocaine and the exchange of sex for drugs or money (Marx et al., 1991).

Moreover, the actual incidence of syphilis is undoubtedly much higher than reported; some STD specialists speculate that as many as nine cases go unreported for each one that is recorded (Fitzgerald, 1984). Regardless of its frequency, syphilis should not be taken lightly: Unlike most STDs, syphilis can result in death.

Treponema pallidum requires a warm, moist environment for survival. It is transmitted almost exclusively from open lesions of infected individuals to the mucous membranes or skin abrasions of sexual partners through penile–vaginal, oral–genital, or genital–anal contacts. Syphilitic organisms may also be transmitted from an infected pregnant woman to her unborn child through the placental blood system. The resulting congenital syphilis can cause death or extreme damage to infected newborns (Gilstrap & Hendel, 1992; Lind, 1992). If the disease is successfully treated before the fourth month of pregnancy, the fetus will not be affected. Therefore, pregnant women should be tested for syphilis sometime during their first three months of pregnancy.

Symptoms and Complications. If untreated, syphilis can progress through four phases of development. These are known as the primary, secondary, latent, and tertiary stages. A brief description of each follows.

Primary Syphilis. In its initial or primary phase, syphilis is generally manifested in the form of a painless sore called a **chancre** (SHAN-ker), which appears at the site where the spirochete organism entered the body (see Figure 19.2). In women who have coitus with infected men, this sore most commonly appears on the inner

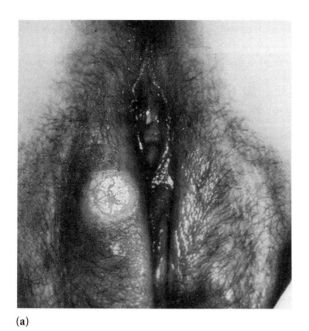

(a)

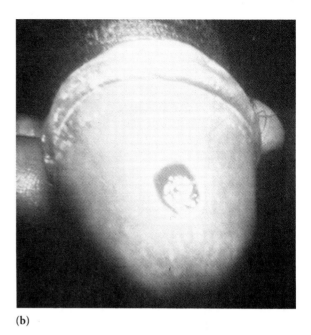

(b)

FIGURE 19.2

The first stage of syphilis. A syphilitic chancre as it appears on (a) the labia and (b) the penis.

vaginal walls or cervix. It may also appear on the external genitals, particularly the labia. In men the chancre most often occurs on the glans of the penis, but it may also show up on the penile shaft or on the scrotum (Kirchner, 1991; Mindel et al., 1989). Although 95% of chancres are genital, they may occur in the mouth or rectum or on the anus or breast. People who have had oral sex with an infected individual may develop a sore on the lips or tongue. Anal intercourse may result in chancres appearing in the rectum or around the anus. The following is an excellent description of the chancre sore:

> When the chancre first develops, it is a dull red bump about the size of a pea. The surface of the bump soon breaks down and the chancre becomes a rounded, dull red, open sore which may be covered by a yellow or grey crusty scab. The chancre is painless and does not bleed easily. In about 50% of cases, the chancre is surrounded by a thin pink border. The edges of the chancre are often raised and hard, like the edges of a button. The hardness may spread to the base of the chancre and eventually to the surrounding tissue, making the whole area feel hard and rubbery. (Cherniak & Feingold, 1973, p. 30)

In view of the typically painless nature of the chancre, it often goes undiscovered when it occurs on internal structures like the rectum, vagina, or cervix. (Occasionally, chancres may be painful, and they may occur in multiple sites.) Even when it is noticed, some people do not seek treatment. Unfortunately (from the long-term perspective), the chancre generally heals without treatment in one to five weeks after its initial appearance. For the next few weeks, the person usually has no symptoms but may infect an unsuspecting partner. After about six weeks (although sometimes after as little as two weeks or as long as six months), the disease progresses to the secondary stage.

Secondary Syphilis. This phase is characterized by the appearance of a skin rash on the body — generally on the palms of the hands and soles of the feet — that may range from barely noticeable to severe, with raised bumps that have a rubbery, hard consistency. While the rash may look terrible, it typically does not hurt or itch. If it is at all noticeable, it generally prompts a visit to a physician, if the earlier appearance of a chancre did not. Besides a generalized rash, a person may have flulike symptoms such as fever, swollen lymph glands, fatigue, and weight loss. Even if treatment is not provided, these symptoms eventually subside, usually within a few weeks. Rather than being eliminated, however, the disease may enter the potentially more dangerous latent phase.

Latent Syphilis. This stage can last for several years, during which time there may be no observable symptoms of the disease. Nevertheless, the infecting organisms may continue to multiply, preparing for the final stage of syphilitic infection. After one year of the latent stage has elapsed, the infected individual is no longer contagious to sexual partners. However, a pregnant woman with syphilis in any stage can pass the infection to her fetus. This type of syphilis, called *congenital syphilis,* causes fetal or infant death in 50% of affected pregnancies (Kirchner, 1991). Congenital syphilis can be averted by appropriate treatment of the mother during pregnancy.

Tertiary Syphilis. A small percentage of those individuals who do not obtain effective treatment during the first three stages of syphilis are affected by the tertiary stage later in life (Musher, 1991). The final manifestations of syphilis can be severe, often resulting in death. They occur anywhere from 3 to 40 years after the initial infection and may include such conditions as heart failure, blindness, ruptured blood vessels, paralysis, skin ulcers, liver damage, and severe mental disturbance. Depending on the extent of the damage, treatment even at this late stage may be beneficial.

Treatment. Primary, secondary, or latent syphilis of less than one year's duration may be effectively treated with a single intramuscular injection of benzathine penicillin (Kirchner, 1991; Schwebke, 1991b). People allergic to penicillin may be treated with doxycycline, tetracycline, or erythromycin. Syphilis of more than one year's duration is treated with intramuscular injections of benzathine penicillin once a week for three successive weeks.

All sex partners exposed to a person with infectious syphilis should be treated. All individuals who have been treated for this disease should have several diagnostic blood tests after the completion of treatment to make certain that they are completely free of the *Treponema pallidum* organism.

Pubic Lice

Pubic lice, more commonly called "crabs," belong to a group of parasitic insects called biting lice. They are known technically as *Phthirus pubis.* Although very tiny, adult lice are visible to the eye. They are yellowish gray in appearance, and under

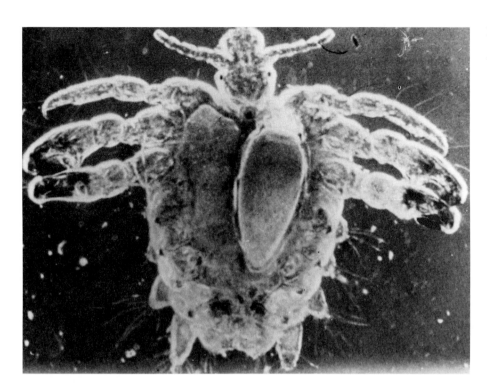

FIGURE 19.3

A pubic louse, or "crab."

magnification resemble a crab, as Figure 19.3 shows. A pubic louse generally grips a pubic hair with its claws and sticks its head into the skin, where it feeds on blood from tiny blood vessels.

Incidence and Transmission. Pubic lice are quite common and are seen frequently in public health clinics and by private physicians. They are frequently transmitted during sexual contact when two people bring their pubic areas together. Crabs may live away from the body for as long as one day, particularly if their stomachs are full of blood. They may drop off onto underclothes, bedsheets, sleeping bags, and so forth. Eggs deposited by the female louse on clothing or bedsheets may survive for several days. Thus, it is possible to get pubic lice by sleeping in someone else's bed or by wearing his or her clothes. Furthermore, a successfully treated person may be reinfected by being exposed to her or his own unwashed sheets or underclothes. Pubic lice do not necessarily limit themselves to the genital areas. They may be transmitted, usually by fingers, to the armpits or scalp.

Symptoms. Most people begin to suspect something is amiss when they start itching. Suspicions become stronger when scratching brings no relief. However, a few people seem to have great tolerance for the bite of a louse, experiencing very little if any discomfort. Self-diagnosis is possible simply by locating a louse on a pubic hair.

Treatment. Self-treatment for pubic lice can be done with an over-the-counter preparation known as A-200 pyrinate. Another commonly employed treatment is Kwell (gamma benzene hexachloride), available by prescription. Be sure to follow the accompanying instructions carefully. It is advisable to apply the solution to all areas where there are concentrations of body hair — the genitals, armpits, scalp, and even eyebrows. This should be followed by a reapplication seven days later (eggs take seven days to hatch). Be sure to wash all clothes and sheets that were used prior to treatment.

Herpes

Herpes is caused by the *Herpes simplex* virus (HSV). A virus is an organism that invades, reproduces, and lives within a cell, thereby disrupting normal cellular activities. There are five different herpes viruses that infect humans, the most common being type 1 (HSV–1) and type 2 (HSV–2). Type 1 typically manifests itself as lesions, or sores, of the type called "cold sores," or "fever blisters," in the mouth or on the lips (oral herpes). Type 2 generally causes lesions on and around the genital areas (genital herpes). Type 1 may affect the genital area, and conversely, type 2 may produce a sore in the mouth area. Genital infection with HSV–1 has been increasingly recognized. Studies have revealed that 20 – 50% of genital herpes infections are due to HSV–1 (Landry & Zibello, 1988). Cases of mixed infections of HSV–1 and HSV–2 have also been documented (Landry & Zibello, 1988).

Incidence and Transmission. Current estimates indicate that over 100 million Americans are afflicted with oral herpes and that 10 – 20 million people in the United States have genital herpes. Current estimates also suggest that there are approximately 500,000 new cases of genital herpes annually in the United States.

Genital herpes appears to be transmitted primarily by penile – vaginal, oral – genital, or genital – anal contact. Oral herpes may be transmitted by kissing, sharing towels, drinking out of the same cup, and so on. A person who has oral sex performed on her or him by a partner who has a cold sore or fever blister in the mouth region may develop genital herpes of either the type-1 or type-2 variety (McKenna et al., 1991).

When any herpes sores are present, the infected person is highly contagious, and it is extremely important that he or she avoid bringing the lesions into contact with someone else's body through touching, sexual interaction, or kissing. It was once believed that a person could transmit herpes only when symptoms were present. However, it has been demonstrated that HSV may be transmitted during asymptomatic periods (Centers for Disease Control, 1985a; Handsfield, 1992). Studies in which the sexual partners of persons with first-episode genital herpes were evaluated revealed that the frequency of HSV transmission from asymptomatic individuals may be quite high (Mertz et al., 1992; Rooney et al., 1986).

Research has shown that HSV–2 will not pass through latex condoms (Peterman et al., 1988a). The use of condoms may be effective in preventing transmission from a male whose only lesions occur on the glans or shaft of the penis. However, due to the risk of condoms breaking or coming off, many health officials recommend that men abstain from intercourse during active outbreaks. Condoms

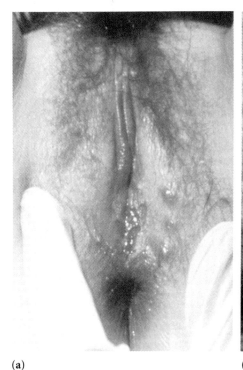
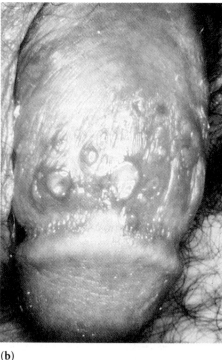

(a)   (b)

FIGURE 19.4

Genital herpes blisters as they
appear on (a) the labia and
(b) the penis.

are helpful but less effective in preventing transmission from a female to a male because vaginal secretions containing the virus may wash over the male's scrotal area.

People may also spread the virus from one part of their bodies to another by touching a sore and then scratching or rubbing somewhere else, a process referred to as *autoinoculation.* It is very important for people with herpes to wash their hands thoroughly with soap and water after touching a sore. It is better to avoid touching the sores if possible.

Symptoms and Complications. The symptoms associated with HSV–1 and HSV–2 infections are quite similar.

Genital Herpes Symptoms. Many individuals with genital herpes infections do not experience recognizable symptoms (Aral & Holmes, 1991; Handsfield & Schwebke, 1991). When symptoms are present, they consist of one or more small, painful red bumps, called *papules,* that usually appear in the genital region. In women the areas most commonly infected are the labia. The inner vaginal walls and cervix may also be affected. In men the infected site is typically the glans or shaft of the penis. Homosexual men and heterosexual women who have engaged in anal intercourse may develop eruptions in and around the anus.

Soon after their initial appearance, papules rapidly develop into tiny painful blisters filled with a clear fluid containing highly infectious virus particles (see Figure 19.4). The body then attacks the virus with white blood cells, causing the blisters to become filled with pus. Soon the blisters rupture to form wet, painful, open sores surrounded by a red ring (health practitioners refer to this as the period of "viral shedding"). A person is highly contagious during this time. About 10 days after the first appearance of the papule, the open sore forms a crust and begins to heal, a process that may take as long as 10 more days. Sores on the cervix may continue to produce infectious material for as long as 10 days after labial sores have completely healed. Consequently, it is wise during an initial episode to avoid coitus for a 10-day period after all external sores have healed.

There may be other symptoms accompanying genital herpes, including swollen lymph nodes in the groin, fever, muscle aches, and headaches. In addition, urination may be accompanied by a burning sensation, and women may experience increased vaginal discharge.

Oral Herpes Symptoms. Oral herpes is characterized by the formation of papules on the lips and sometimes on the inside of the mouth, the tongue, and the throat. (HSV–1 only infrequently occurs within the mouth, and it should not be confused with canker sores.) These blisters tend to crust over and heal within 10 – 16 days. Other symptoms include fever, general muscle aches, swollen lymph nodes in the neck, flulike symptoms, increased salivation, and sometimes bleeding in the mouth.

Recurrence. After complete healing one cannot assume that one will not experience a recurrence of the infection. Unfortunately, the herpes virus does not typically go away; instead, it retreats up the nerve fibers leading from the infected site. Ultimately, the genital herpes virus finds a resting place in nerve cells adjacent to the lower spinal column, whereas the oral herpes virus becomes lodged in nerve cells in the back of the neck (Willey et al., 1988). The virus may remain dormant in these cells, without causing any apparent damage, perhaps for the person's entire lifetime. However, in many cases there will be periodic flareups as the virus retraces its path back down the nerve fibers leading to the genitals or lips.

Although some people never experience a recurrence of herpes following the initial or primary infection, research has suggested that 10 – 40% of people who have undergone a primary episode of oral herpes experience at least one recurrence. The comparable figures for genital herpes are 30 – 70% (Gunn & Stenzel-Poore, 1981; Straus et al., 1984a). Recurrent genital lesions are less frequent with HSV–1 than with HSV–2 (Landry & Zibello, 1988). Individuals who experience recurrences may do so frequently or only occasionally. Studies have shown that the more extensive the primary attack, the greater the chance of recurrence. Symptoms associated with recurrent attacks tend to be milder than primary episodes, and the disease tends to run its course more quickly, averaging 7 – 10 days.

The majority of people prone to recurrent herpes outbreaks, perhaps as many as 75%, experience some type of **prodromal symptoms** that give advance warning of an impending eruption. These indications include itching, burning, throbbing, or "pins-and-needles" tingling at the sites commonly infected by herpes blisters and sometimes pain in the legs, thighs, groin, or buttocks. Many health authorities believe that a person's degree of infectiousness increases during this stage and that it further escalates when the lesions appear. Consequently, a person should be particularly careful to avoid direct contact from the time he or she first experiences prodromal symptoms until the sores have completely healed. Even during an outbreak, it is possible to continue sexual intimacies with a partner, as long as infected skin does not come in contact with healthy skin. During this time partners may wish to experiment with other kinds of sensual pleasuring, such as sensate focus (see Chapter 17), hugging, and oral or manual stimulation.

A variety of factors may trigger reactivation of the herpes virus, including emotional stress, acidic food, sunburn, cold, poor nutrition, being overtired or run-down, and trauma to the skin region affected. One person noted:

For several years I have been having a herpes outbreak on my lips. It usually happens just once a year and coincides with the start of fishing season when I sit in a boat too long without protection from the sun. Now that I am aware of the pattern, I plan to take proper precautions in the future. (Authors' files)

Recurrences may also be more frequent in cases where the genitals are kept tightly enclosed and warm, such as by wearing pantyhose, nylon underwear, or tight jeans (Gunn & Stenzel-Poore, 1981). There is wide individual variation in triggering factors, and it is often difficult to associate a specific event with the onset of a recurrent herpes infection.

Some people may not experience a relapse of genital herpes until several years after the initial infection. Therefore, if you have been in what you believe is a sexually exclusive relationship and your partner shows symptoms or transmits the virus to you, it does not necessarily mean that she or he contracted the disease from someone else during the course of your relationship. Furthermore, as stated earlier, most people with HSV–2 infections are asymptomatic or have such mild symptoms that they are often unrecognizable as such. Clearly then, a first episode of symptomatic genital herpes may not be due to recent sexual contact with an infected person.

Other Complications. Although the sores are painful and bothersome, it is very unlikely that men will experience any major physical complications of herpes. Women, however, may be faced with two very serious, although quite uncommon, complications: cancer of the cervix and infection of the newborn. There is evidence that the risk of developing cervical cancer is higher among women who have had genital herpes (Rapp, 1982; Trimble et al., 1986). However, it remains unclear if there is a direct causal link between genital herpes and cervical cancer. "Some medical authorities have argued that genital herpes might only be a marker for high-risk sexual behaviors that could also transmit other STDs — perhaps even an unrecognized STD that was the true cause of cervical cancer" (Aral & Holmes, 1991, p. 66). Fortunately, the great majority of women infected with herpes will never develop cancer of the cervix. Nonetheless, it is advisable for all women, particularly those who have had genital herpes, to obtain an annual cervical Pap smear for the rest of their lives. Some authorities recommend that women with genital herpes should have this test every six months.

A newborn may be infected with genital herpes while passing through the birth canal. Many newborns infected with herpes will be severely damaged or die (Apuzzio & Leo, 1991; Handsfield, 1992; Kulhanjian et al., 1992; Whitley et al., 1991). It is believed that viral shedding from the cervix, vagina, or vulva plays the primary role in transmitting the disease from mother to infant. When sufficient risk exists for transmission of HSV from a mother to her baby during birth, some health practitioners recommend "obtaining cultures from these women at delivery to allow early identification of infants who have been exposed to the virus" (Gibbs & Mead, 1992, p. 946). These specialists further suggest that exposed infants might then be followed with frequent examinations and might even be given acyclovir, a drug shown to be somewhat effective in suppressing herpes outbreaks.

There is one additional serious physical complication of herpes of which both women and men should be aware. Occasionally a person will transfer the virus to an eye after touching a virus-shedding sore. This may lead to a severe eye infection known as ocular herpes, or *herpes keratitis* (usually caused by HSV–1). This complication may best be prevented by not touching the herpes sores. If you cannot avoid contact, thoroughly wash your hands with hot water and soap immediately after touching the lesions. There are effective treatments for ocular herpes, but they must be started quickly to avoid damaging the eye.

Many people who have recurrent herpes outbreaks are troubled with mild to severe psychological distress (Aral et al., 1988; Hoon et al., 1991; Schmader et al., 1990). In view of the physical discomfort associated with the disease, the unpredictability of recurrent outbreaks, and the lack of an effective cure (see next section), it is no small wonder that people who have herpes undergo considerable stress. We believe that becoming better informed about herpes may help to alleviate some of these emotional difficulties. In addition, talking with supportive partners may facilitate a person's psychological adjustment to recurrent genital herpes infections (Aral et al., 1988). Certainly, herpes is not the dread disease that some people believe it to be. In fact, countless numbers of individuals have learned to cope quite effectively with it, as did the person in the following account:

When I first discovered I had herpes several years ago, my first reaction was "Oh no, my sex life is destroyed!" I was really depressed and angry with the person who gave me the disease. However, with time I learned I could live with it, and I even began to gain some control over it. Now, on those infrequent occasions when I have an outbreak, I know what to do to hurry up the healing process. Most of the time things are just the same as before I got it, and my sex life is only occasionally disrupted. (Authors' files)

Treatment. The most common method of diagnosing herpes is direct observation by a physician. In many cases the clinical symptoms accompanying a herpes outbreak, together with a thorough patient history, will yield an accurate diagnosis. There are also a number of laboratory tests designed to detect herpes virus infections, and one or more of these may be used in cases where the diagnosis is in question. The most accurate of these tests involves culturing a small sample taken from the base of an active lesion (Baker et al., 1989). If the virus grows in the culture medium, a definitive diagnosis of HSV can be made.

At the time of this writing, there is no medical treatment proven to be effective in curing either oral or genital herpes. However, there is mounting optimism among medical researchers who are pursuing an effective treatment on many fronts. Current treatment strategies are designed to reduce discomfort and to speed healing during an outbreak.

An antiviral drug, acyclovir, sold under the trade name Zovirax, is often highly effective in the management of herpes. There are three forms of the drug: topical (ointment), oral, and injectable. The ointment has not proven to be particularly helpful in the management of herpes outbreaks (Abramowicz, 1990). In contrast, a number of studies have shown that acyclovir administered orally or intravenously dramatically reduces the length and severity of initial herpes outbreaks

(Abramowicz, 1990; Gold et al., 1988; Sacks et al., 1988). In addition, continuously administered oral acyclovir has been shown to both suppress and reduce the duration of recurrent episodes of herpes outbreaks in individuals prone to frequent recurrences (Baker et al., 1989; Handsfield, 1992; Kaplowitz et al., 1991). Unfortunately, the resistance of HSV infections to acyclovir appears to be increasing (Arbesfeld & Thomas, 1991).

There are also a number of other ways to obtain relief from the discomfort associated with herpes. The following list of suggestions may be helpful. The effectiveness of these measures varies from person to person, and we encourage people to experiment with the various options available to find an approach to symptom relief that best meets their needs.

1. Keeping herpes blisters clean and dry will lessen the possibility of secondary infections, significantly shorten the period of viral shedding, and reduce the total time of lesion healing. Washing the area with warm water and soap two to three times daily is adequate for cleaning. After bathing, dry the area thoroughly by patting it gently with a soft cotton towel or by blowing it with a hair dryer set on cool. Because the moisture that occurs naturally in the genital area may slow the healing process, sprinkling the dried area liberally with cornstarch or baby powder can help. It is desirable to wear loose cotton clothing that does not trap the moisture (cotton underwear absorbs moisture, but nylon traps it).

2. Two aspirin every three to four hours may help to reduce the pain and itching. Ice packs applied directly to the lesions may also provide temporary relief (but avoid wetting them as the ice melts). Keeping the area liberally powdered may also alleviate itching.

3. Some people have an intense burning sensation when they urinate if the urine comes into contact with herpes lesions. This discomfort may be reduced by pouring water over the genitals while you void or by urinating in a bathtub filled with water. It may help to dilute the acid in the urine by drinking lots of fluids (but avoid liquids that make the urine more acidic, like cranberry juice).

4. Because stress has been implicated as a triggering event in recurrent herpes, it is a good idea to try to reduce this negative influence. There are a variety of approaches to stress reduction, including learning relaxation techniques, practicing yoga or meditation, and obtaining counseling about ways to cope with daily pressures.

5. If you are prone to repeated relapses of herpes, you may obtain some benefit from recording events that occur immediately before an eruption (either after the fact or as part of an ongoing journal). You may be able to recognize common precipitating events like fatigue, acidic food, or excessive sunlight, which you can then avoid in the future.

Researchers are currently working on vaccines to protect people from herpes infections. Recent research has shown that some experimental vaccines, tested on laboratory animals, show considerable promise in their capacity to protect animals from becoming infected with HSV. It is our hope that future clinical trials with human subjects will yield an effective vaccine.

Viral Hepatitis

Viral hepatitis (hep-a-TĪ-tis) is a disease in which liver function is impaired by a viral infection. There are three major types of viral hepatitis: hepatitis A (formerly called infectious hepatitis), hepatitis B (formerly called serum hepatitis), and non-A/non-B hepatitis (which is caused by at least three different viruses: types C, D, and E [Gilson, 1992; Scheig, 1991]). Each of these forms of viral hepatitis is caused by a different virus.

Incidence and Transmission.   Hepatitis B is the most common form of viral hepatitis in the United States, followed in order of frequency by hepatitis A and non-A/non-B hepatitis. Health authorities have estimated that approximately 300,000 new cases of hepatitis B occur annually in the United States (Aral & Holmes, 1991). Both the A and B types can be sexually transmitted, but sexual transmission of the non-A/non-B type is believed to be uncommon (Barrett et al., 1992; Centers for Disease Control, 1990). It is believed that hepatitis B is more often transmitted through sexual activity than is hepatitis A (Gilson, 1992).

Hepatitis B may be transmitted via blood or blood products, semen, vaginal secretions, and saliva. Manual, oral, or penile stimulation of the anus are practices strongly associated with the spread of this viral agent. Hepatitis A seems to be primarily spread via the fecal–oral route (Kools, 1992). Consequently, epidemics often occur when infected food handlers do not wash their hands properly after using the bathroom. Oral–anal sexual contact seems to be the primary mode for sexual transmission of hepatitis A.

Symptoms and Complications.   Symptoms of viral hepatitis may vary from nonexistent to mild flulike symptoms (poor appetite, upset stomach, diarrhea, sore muscles, fatigue, headache) to an incapacitating illness characterized by high fever, vomiting, and severe abdominal pain. One of the most notable signs of viral hepatitis is a yellowing of the whites of the eyes; the skin of light-complexioned people may also take on a yellow, or jaundiced, look. Hospitalization is required only in severe cases. There is some evidence that people who have had hepatitis B are at increased risk for developing cancer of the liver. On rare occasions, severe medical complications associated with viral hepatitis infections result in death (Scheig, 1991).

Treatment.   At the present time, there is no specific therapy known to be effective against the various types of viral hepatitis. However, recent research has suggested that the drug alpha interferon can prevent destruction of liver cells in some hepatitis patients (Davis et al., 1989; Scheig, 1991; Wang et al., 1991). Treatment generally consists of bed rest and adequate fluid intake to prevent dehydration. The disease generally runs its course in a matter of a few weeks, although complete recovery may take several months in cases of severe infections. An effective and safe vaccine to prevent hepatitis B infections has been available since 1982. However, "it is discouraging to note that the overall measured incidence of hepatitis B has not declined much since 1982, despite a steep decline in high-risk homosexual contacts among men and the availability of an effective vaccine" (Aral & Holmes, 1991, p. 66). Persons at high risk for contracting hepatitis B should seriously consider getting immunized with the vaccine. These high-risk people include

health care workers who are exposed to blood, IV drug users and their sex partners, homosexual and bisexual men, heterosexually active persons with multiple
sexual partners, and sexual partners or housemates of people infected with the
hepatitis B virus (Handsfield, 1992).

Genital Warts

Genital warts, sometimes referred to as *condylomata acuminata,* are caused by a
virus called the *human papilloma virus* (HPV). Application of recently developed
technology has led to the identification of more than 70 types of HPV, several of
which cause genital infections (Aral & Holmes, 1991; Beckman et al., 1991; Wik-
ström et al., 1992).

Incidence and Transmission. The incidence of genital and anal warts has been
increasing so rapidly in both sexes that the disease has reached epidemic proportions in recent years (Handsfield, 1992). At the present time, genital and anal HPV
is the most common viral STD in the United States and probably the most common of all STDs (Aral & Holmes, 1991; Beckman et al., 1991; Zazove et al., 1991).
Most genital warts are found in young, sexually active adults (Fletcher, 1991).
Research findings have suggested that 20 million or more women in the United
States are infected with HPV and that roughly three out of four male sexual partners of infected women are also infected (Zazove et al., 1991). A recent survey of
467 female undergraduates undergoing a routine gynecological examination at the
campus health service of a major California university found that 46% were
infected with HPV (Bauer et al., 1991). Present data indicate that HPV is primarily
transmitted through vaginal, anal, or oral – genital sexual interaction.

Symptoms and Complications. The incubation period for genital warts (elapsed
time from contact with an infected person to appearance of symptoms) may range
from 3 weeks to 18 months, with an average period of about 3 months. In women
genital warts most commonly appear on the bottom part of the vaginal opening.
They may also occur on the perineum, the labia, the inner walls of the vagina,
and the cervix. In men genital warts commonly occur on the glans, foreskin, or
shaft of the penis (see Figure 19.5). In moist areas (such as the vaginal opening
and under the foreskin), genital warts are pink or red and soft, with a cauliflow-
erlike appearance. On dry skin areas, they are generally hard and yellow – gray. In
many cases people may carry the virus without developing any symptoms (Handsfield, 1992; Zazove et al., 1991).

Genital warts are sometimes associated with serious complications. Sometimes
they invade the urethra, where they may cause urinary obstruction and bleeding.
Research has also revealed a strong association between HPV infections and cancers of the cervix, vagina, vulva, penis, and anus (Bauer et al., 1991; Cusick et al.,
1992; Fletcher, 1991; Handsfield, 1992; Lorincz et al., 1992; Zazove et al., 1991). At
the present time it is not known if HPV acting alone directly causes these cancers
or if it acts in conjunction with other cofactors (such as other infections, smoking,
or possibly the use of oral contraceptives) to cause genital and anal tract cancers
(Zazove et al., 1991).

F I G U R E 19.5

Genital warts on the penis.

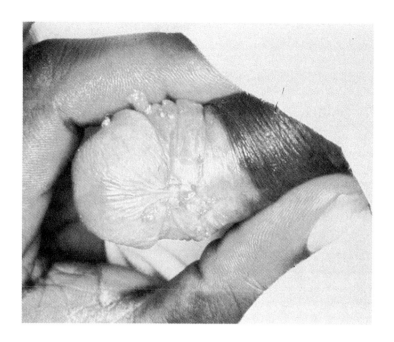

Another serious complication of HPV is that pregnant women infected with the virus may transmit it to their babies during the later stage of pregnancy or during birth (Fletcher, 1991). Infected infants may develop a condition known as *respiratory papillomatosis* that results from HPV infections of their upper respiratory tracts. Respiratory papillomatosis may have serious health consequences that produce lifelong distress and require multiple operations.

Treatment. Genital warts may spontaneously disappear, but this is a relatively rare event. Therefore, it is a good idea to obtain treatment so that they will not enlarge and spread to healthy tissue. While no standard treatment for HPV-infected lesions exists, several methods have been used for removing warts. These include vaporization by carbon dioxide laser and topical applications of trichloroacetic acid (Tri-Chlor), podophyllin, and 5-fluorouracil cream (Efudex) (Bergman & Nalick, 1991; Greenberg et al., 1991; Zazove et al., 1991). Often a second or extended period of treatment with the topical medications is necessary. Podophyllin should not be used during pregnancy and is not recommended for treatment of vaginal or cervical warts. Cauterization by electric needle, freezing with liquid nitrogen, or surgical removal may be necessary with large or persistent warts.

There is increasing evidence that many people treated for visible genital warts also have asymptomatic or subclinical HPV infections that are "extremely difficult or even impossible to eradicate" (Zazove et al., 1991, p. 1286). Follow-up medical evaluations of these individuals, every four to six months, is recommended.

Acquired Immunodeficiency Syndrome (AIDS)

The **acquired immunodeficiency syndrome (AIDS)** epidemic, which constitutes a worldwide public health threat of rapidly increasing magnitude, is now recog-

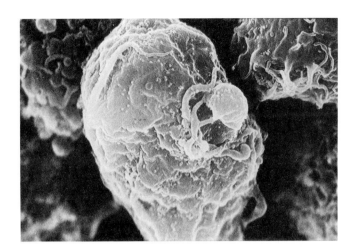

FIGURE 19.6

This scanning electron micrograph shows HIV viruses (the tiny spheres) attacking a helper T lymphocyte.

nized as the most serious disease epidemic of our time. In the United States AIDS is the second leading cause of death among men 25–44 years of age and one of the five leading causes of death among women ages 15–44 (Centers for Disease Control, 1991c). An all-out research assault on this deadly disease, unprecedented in scope and extent, is being conducted throughout the world, and new findings are surfacing with startling rapidity. Consequently, it is very likely that at least some of the information that follows will be obsolete by the time you read it.

AIDS results from infection with a virus called *human immunodeficiency virus* (HIV). (A virus is a protein-coated package of genes that invades a healthy body cell and alters the normal genetic apparatus of the cell, causing the cell to reproduce the virus. In the process, the invaded cell is often killed.) HIV falls within a special category of viruses called *retroviruses,* so named because they reverse the usual order of reproduction within the cells they infect.

In recent years it has become clear that more than one virus is linked with the development of AIDS. The first virus to be identified, and the one that causes the greatest number of AIDS cases, has been designated as human immunodeficiency virus type 1 (HIV–1). This virus appears to be the most virulent member of a growing family of AIDS and AIDS-related viruses. HIV is a formidable enemy in that it is constantly mutating and is present in multiple strains. To simplify our discussion of AIDS in the following pages, we refer to the infectious agent simply as HIV.

In spite of a great deal of speculation and theorizing, the origin of AIDS remains undetermined. It has been variously proposed that HIV came from residents of Africa or Haiti, mosquitoes, monkeys, and pigs. However, "precisely where, when, and why HIV began to spread in human populations cannot be determined. Although the first AIDS cases to be recognized and reported were in the United States in 1981, it is clear from retrospective studies that this syndrome has been occurring in several other areas of the world since the mid-1970s" (Chin & Mann, 1990, p. 128).

HIV specifically targets and destroys the body's CD4 lymphocytes, also called helper T cells (see Figure 19.6), which in healthy people stimulate the immune system to fight disease. The resulting impairment of the immune system leaves the body vulnerable to a variety of cancers and opportunistic infections (infections that take hold because an impaired immune system gives them the opportunity to thrive). Until recently, HIV infection was diagnosed as AIDS only when the immune system became so seriously impaired that the infected individual developed one or more severe, debilitating diseases, such as pneumonia or cancer. However, effective April 1, 1992, the Centers for Disease Control (CDC) broadened its definition of AIDS: Now anyone who is infected with HIV and has a CD4 count of 200 cells per cubic millimeter of blood or less is considered to have full-blown AIDS, regardless of what other symptoms that person may or may not have. (Normal CD4 cell counts in healthy people not infected with HIV range from 800 to 900 per cubic millimeter of blood.)

The serious diseases that afflict AIDS patients include Kaposi's sarcoma (an otherwise rare form of cancer that accounts for many AIDS deaths), pneumocystic carinii pneumonia (a lung disease that is also a major cause of AIDS deaths), and a variety of other generalized opportunistic infections, such as shingles (herpes zoster), encephalitis, severe fungal infections that cause a type of meningitis, yeast infections of the throat and esophagus, and infections of the lungs, intestines, and central nervous system. The incidence of tuberculosis, a disease almost eradicated in the United States by the mid-1980s, has escalated rapidly since 1986 due largely to the epidemic of HIV infection and AIDS (Onorato et al., 1992).

Many people infected with HIV will exhibit less severe manifestations of immune system impairment before the onset of life-threatening diseases characteristic of full-blown AIDS. These early signs of impaired immune response have generally been referred to as AIDS-related complex (ARC) or HIV disease. However, we can expect these terms to be used less commonly in the future in light of the newly broadened definition of AIDS. While evidence suggests that the vast majority of HIV-infected individuals eventually develop AIDS, it is not possible to say at this time whether all infected people ultimately manifest this life-threatening syndrome (Lifson et al., 1991).

Incidence and Transmission. By July 1992, over 220,000 cases of AIDS had been reported in the United States, and 141,000 persons had died of the disease since it was first diagnosed in 1981. Moreover, it is estimated that between 1 and 2 million people in the United States who do not yet show symptoms of HIV disease are infected with the virus (Centers for Disease Control, 1991c; Greene, 1991). The World Health Organization (WHO) has estimated that 8–10 million adults and 1 million children worldwide are infected with HIV. WHO has also predicted that by the year 2000, as many as 40 million men, women, and children will be HIV-infected, and nearly 10 million adults and 5 million children will have developed full-blown AIDS. The vast majority of infections will occur in people who reside in developing countries in Africa, Asia, Latin America, and the Caribbean (Chin & Mann, 1990; Mann, 1992; Palca, 1991).

The number of new AIDS cases reported annually in the United States grew rapidly through the early 1980s, reaching a peak in the middle of the decade. Thankfully, there was a marked moderation in the late 1980s in the rate at which new AIDS cases were diagnosed, probably due both to a decline in the underlying infection rate and to better treatments at early stages of HIV disease, which delayed the onset of full-blown AIDS (Brookmeyer, 1991; Centers for Disease Control, 1991d). While some experts have predicted that the AIDS incidence in Amer-

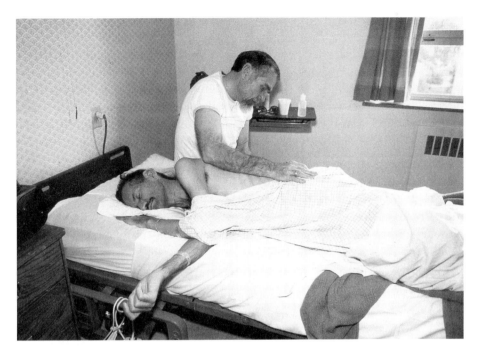

Many of the 1 – 2 million AIDS patients in the U.S. benefit from supportive interaction with caring people.

ica may plateau during the 1990s, "the demands on the U.S. health care system for treatment and care of HIV-infected individuals remain enormous" (Brook-meyer, 1991, p. 37).

HIV has been found in the semen, blood, vaginal secretions, saliva, tears, urine, and breast milk of infected individuals, and in any other bodily fluids that may contain blood (cerebrospinal fluid, amniotic fluid, etc.) (Klein, 1991; Wofsy et al., 1986). Blood and semen are the two bodily fluids that most consistently contain high concentrations of the virus in infected people. Most commonly, HIV enters the body through the exchange of bodily fluids during unprotected anal or vaginal intercourse or oral – genital contact with an infected person and via blood-contaminated needles shared by intravenous (IV) drug users. The virus can also be transmitted from an infected woman to her fetus or infant before, during, or shortly after birth (perinatal transmission) and via transfusions of infected blood or blood products (Greene, 1991; Gwinn et al., 1991; Klein, 1991; Lederman, 1992; Mann, 1992; Mano & Chermann, 1991; Sacco et al., 1991; Samuels et al., 1992).

In the early 1980s, before the federal government required screening of donated blood for HIV, contaminated blood and blood products wreaked havoc on the U.S. blood supply. An estimated 25,000 transfusion recipients and people with blood-clotting disorders (such as hemophilia) became infected with HIV (Gilbert, 1991). However, since early 1985 donated blood and blood products have been screened for the presence of HIV antibodies, and HIV-infected units have been discarded. As an added precaution, donated blood is heat treated to inacti-vate HIV (Centers for Disease Control, 1991c). Therefore, the possibility of now being infected with HIV via transfusion of contaminated blood is quite remote (Carson et al., 1992). However, precautions designed to safeguard the nation's blood supply are not foolproof. One problem is that the blood test looks for *antibodies* to HIV rather than the virus itself. And because, as we shall see, HIV antibodies take months or even years to show up in the blood, contaminated units of blood have on rare occasions slipped by. There is, however, no danger of being infected as a result of *donating* blood. Blood banks, the Red Cross, and other blood-collection centers use sterile equipment and disposable needles.

It is believed that the risk of transmitting HIV via saliva, tears, and urine is extremely low. Furthermore, there is no evidence that the virus can be transmitted by casual contact such as hugging, shaking hands, cooking or eating together, living in the same household, or other forms of nonsexual contact with an infected person (Hearst & Hulley, 1988; Lifson et al., 1988; Peterman et al., 1988).

In the developed, industrialized countries of North America, Western Europe, Australia, and New Zealand, HIV infections to date have predominantly occurred in homosexual and bisexual men and in IV drug users and their sexual partners and infants. Of the sexually transmitted HIV infections in these nations, most have been transmitted homosexually to men who practiced receptive anal intercourse. In terms of relative incidences of infection, the overall male to female ratio in these countries is about 10 to 1. In sharp contrast, in developing countries, especially in Africa, the Caribbean, and Latin America, heterosexual transmission of HIV has predominated, and the male to female ratio of HIV infection in these areas is almost 1 to 1 (Aral & Holmes, 1991; Chin & Mann, 1990; Greene, 1991). In Africa, where the majority of worldwide HIV infections exist, heterosexual transmission accounts for by far the greatest number of infections (Mann, 1992; Plummer et al., 1991; Sanders et al., 1991). WHO has estimated that to date 80% of HIV transmission worldwide is heterosexual, and that by the year 2000 up to 90% of all HIV infections in the world will be transmitted heterosexually (Aral & Holmes, 1991; Forrest, 1991; Mann, 1992).

The incidence of AIDS in the homosexual male population of America has received a great deal of public attention. Nevertheless, it is clear that the sexual transmission of HIV is not dependent on sexual orientation. Furthermore, while the heterosexual AIDS epidemic in the United States began several years later than the one affecting homosexual and bisexual men, reported cases of heterosexual transmission of HIV have been increasing steadily in recent years (Centers for Disease Control, 1992b). In fact, "in 1990, the incidence of AIDS increased most rapidly among persons exposed to HIV through heterosexual contact" (Centers for Disease Control, 1991d, p. 359).

The data just presented confirm without a doubt that it is sexual contact with an infected person, or sharing contaminated needles, rather than one's sexual orientation, that places an individual at risk of becoming HIV-infected and developing AIDS. Furthermore, engaging in certain high-risk behaviors increases one's chances of becoming infected. Behaviors that place one at increased risk of HIV infection include having multiple sexual partners, engaging in unprotected sex (sex without condoms and virus-killing spermicides), sexual contact with people known to be at high risk (e.g., IV drug users, prostitutes, and people with multiple sexual partners), and sharing injection equipment for IV drug use (Brookmeyer, 1991; Brunham, 1991; Chin & Mann, 1990; Klein, 1991; Morse et al., 1991).

Over the last few years the number of women with AIDS has increased (Allen & Marte, 1992; IcKovics & Rodin, 1992; Sweeney et al., 1992). By 1990 the number of reported female AIDS cases in the United States exceeded 15,000, an increase of 34% over the previous year (Centers for Disease Control, 1991e). While the majority of female AIDS cases are IV drug users, the proportion of American women infected with HIV through heterosexual contact has increased over time (Ellerbrock et al., 1991; Sperling et al., 1991). Research has indicated that HIV is not as easily transmitted from women to men as it is from men to women, and that the risk of becoming infected via heterosexual intercourse appears to be much greater for a female with an HIV-infected male partner than for a male who has intercourse with an infected female (Al-Nozha et al., 1990; Forrest, 1991; Padian, 1990; Padian et al., 1991).

Can you think of a plausible reason why HIV is more easily transmitted from male to female than from female to male during intercourse?

One explanation advanced to account for the greater female risk during hetero-sexual intercourse is that semen contains a much higher concentration of HIV than occurs in vaginal fluids (Forrest, 1991). Another suggested explanation is that "male-to-female transmission may be more efficient than female-to-male transmission, due in part to a greater exposed area of mucosal surface in the female genital tract" (IcKovics & Rodin, 1992, p. 3).

Within a few months of being infected with HIV, most people develop antibodies to the virus (Lifson et al., 1988). HIV infection may be detected by standard blood tests for serum antibodies to HIV (tests like ELISA and Western blot). Recent studies have revealed that "silent" HIV infections can be present in some individuals for three years or more before being detected by standard serum antibody tests (Clerici et al., 1991). A more costly and more labor-intensive test for the virus itself, such as the polymerase chain reaction (PCR), may be performed to see if one has a silent or latent infection. However, some silent infections elude detection even by such sophisticated tests (Clerici et al., 1991). Once infected with HIV, a person should be considered contagious and capable of infecting others indefinitely, regardless of whether or not clinical signs of HIV disease or AIDS are present (Centers for Disease Control, 1988b).

In the first few years after HIV antibody tests became available in 1985, many public-health officials and gay activist groups counseled people to avoid being tested lest they test positive and thus become a target of discrimination. However, with the advent of better treatment techniques, and in spite of the persistence of HIV-based discrimination, many public-health experts and leaders of gay communities began to change their minds about routine testing. Many now believe that, in light of the demonstrated ability of certain drugs to slow the HIV-induced deterioration of the immune system, there is now a moral obligation to find infected people and care for them (Findlay, 1991). Efforts to encourage testing have focused most directly on people at higher than normal risk for HIV infection, including clients at STD clinics, IV drug users, and health care workers exposed to patients' blood. Some health experts have also suggested that HIV screening should be performed on all hospital patients as well as all pregnant women (to assess the risk of perinatal transmission). Health officials, medical ethicists, and even politicians are currently embroiled in a heated controversy over whether health care workers who have direct contact with patients should be required to submit to HIV testing. (See the interview with Paul Volberding for a physician's perspective on this issue.) However, the risk of a patient contracting HIV from a

CHAPTER 19

Interview with
Paul Volberding

In the course of just a few years, the specter of AIDS has revolutionized the way people approach sexual encounters. Dr. Paul Volberding has helped lead the effort to fully understand HIV—the virus that causes AIDS—and to fully explore how best to treat the disease. Trained as a cancer specialist, Dr. Volberding is a professor of medicine in residence at the University of California, San Francisco, where he directs the Center for AIDS Research. He also heads the AIDS Program at San Francisco General Hospital. Dr. Volberding has received many humanitarian and scientific awards for his compassionate patient care, prolific research, and community and educational outreach efforts. For the next two years he will chair the AIDS Committee of the National Academy of Sciences' Institute of Medicine. In this interview with Robert Crooks, Dr. Volberding describes some of the work he has been involved with in the years since AIDS was identified, and explains how he believes society should cope with the dilemmas of the disease as it continues its course.

Since the beginning of this epidemic, what treatment and research issues have you and your colleagues focused on at the Center for AIDS Research?

We've been working with the epidemic here since 1981, when we came upon the first case of Kaposi's sarcoma in San Francisco. Since then, our experience has obviously increased enormously, and we currently care for about 30 percent of all the patients with AIDS in San Francisco. From the early days of the epidemic, we've been very interested in doing more than just taking care of patients—we're trying to learn more about the disease, trying to develop new treatments, and trying to teach other professionals about the care of patients so that care can be widely distributed. The epidemic is too big for any single institution to be the sole provider of patient care.

The approaches to treatment that we've been exploring most actively include the treatment of HIV infection itself using drugs to slow the reproduc-

tion of the virus. We hope that slowing viral reproduction will enable people to live longer, and ideally enable them to have some immune system restoration, even though they are still infected. Our research also involves the treatment and prevention of some of the complicating problems—such as pneumocystis carinii pneumonia and Kaposi's sarcoma—that we see in people with HIV disease because of their weakened immune system. We've made enormous strides there in terms of being able to diagnose using less invasive tests, and being able to treat with more oral drug therapies so that people can stay at home instead of having to come into the hospital. Probably most significantly, we've made strides in the use of antibiotics to prevent some of those infections. As a result, what we have been able to achieve, I think, is prolongation of survival in people with HIV disease and a shift away from acute hospital care to more home-based care.

What promising new drugs are being investigated for the treatment of AIDS?

At this point we're really limited in having AZT and DDI as our only two approved drugs. Perhaps we'll also have DDC soon, but that's very similar to DDI, so I'm not sure it's going to expand our palette very much. There are two classes of drugs that show promising profiles right now. One is a class of drugs which inhibit an important component of HIV, an enzyme called protease. Protease inhibitors for HIV are now being tested clinically. Several companies have prototype drugs.

Another class of drugs includes those that interfere with the genes that regulate the reproduction rate of the virus. HIV has "regulatory genes," some of which accelerate its reproduction, some of which slow it down. So we're looking at drugs which may inhibit the accelerators of the virus growth. One of the first of those is a drug to inhibit a gene called *tat*. The clinical trials for that drug are also beginning already, and we have our fingers crossed.

Do you think that in the near future we will consider people with HIV to have a chronic, but not necessarily fatal, disease?

It's obviously hard to give time lines, but I think it is a realistic goal. It is encouraging to me that we understand the life cycle of the virus quite well, and we have drugs that are being tested now that are showing encouraging activity. We know more about this than we do about any other infectious disease. Unlike the common cold, which is caused by several hundred different strains of different viruses, this involves one virus. We know what it does; we know its life cycle; it's fairly small. The tools we have give us a lot of options.

How long have HIV-infected people been known to live without developing disease symptoms?

The longest study we have is ongoing at the San Francisco STD Clinic, where a group of homosexual men has been followed as part of a hepatitis study. As part of the study, their serum was taken and frozen in the late seventies. By going back and testing that serum for HIV, we've found men who have been infected with HIV for more than 14 years. And we've found that 10 percent of those men are still free of symptoms and, in fact, have absolutely normal helper cell levels, even after more than 14 years of infection. We don't know why some people progress and die quickly and others progress much more slowly. But it does suggest that there will be people who live a long time, and probably lead a normal life, even when they are HIV-positive.

What is the state of research aimed at developing a vaccine to prevent AIDS?

There are lots of interesting vaccines being investigated. The body's immune reaction to HIV is better understood now, and that gives us something to shoot for as we develop vaccines. Clinical trials clearly show that humans can respond to vaccines by forming antibodies against the material that was injected. That is the first step.

The second step is finding out whether the people who got the vaccine have any protection against HIV if they become exposed. The problem is that most people who volunteer for a vaccination in a clinical trial are more motivated than others, more aware of the disease, and less likely to put themselves at risk for infection. If you vaccinate somebody and he always uses condoms after that, you'll never know whether the vaccine helped him or not.

So a vaccine test will require that it be done in a population where there is still some element of unsafe behavior going on, probably in the developing world. Hopefully, we won't see vaccine trials done that don't try to get people to follow safe behavior, but it's more likely that in some places, despite educational efforts in the context of a vaccine trial, people will engage in unsafe behavior.

Another question of interest is whether or not vaccines given to HIV-infected people might help them form a more effective response against their infection. So we're now trying vaccines as therapy for HIV disease.

When do you think effective vaccines will be available to the public?

People who I respect have said vaccines will be available within 10 years. I might double that estimate. It does seem to me that we will have an effective vaccine at some point. Part of my optimism is just because there are so many highly qualified scientists working on this epidemic.

I think it's quite likely that we'll have a very effective drug treatment before we have a very effective vaccine. For our own patients, I certainly hope that's the case, because my patients won't benefit from a vaccine. They need drug therapy. On the other hand, for the sake of the world's population, we should hope that a vaccine is available very soon because most of our drug therapies are absolutely irrelevant to the developing world. Some places affected by this epidemic have per capita health expenditures of three to five dollars per year. Drugs such as AZT, which costs $2,000 a year, or drugs like foscarnet, which we use for treatment of one of the complicated infections, and which costs $25,000 to $50,000 per year, will never be used in these countries. Vaccines are the hope for developing countries.

We know that HIV, like all organisms, undergoes spontaneous genetic changes, or mutations, from time to time. Has the particularly high mutation rate of HIV created difficulties in developing drugs and vaccines?

The mutability of this virus is a real problem. Although, as we discussed, there is a single species of HIV, there are probably thousands of genetic variants of HIV. If we look carefully, we can identify 15 to 20 or more different types of HIV simultaneously in each person with advanced HIV disease. Even though the person was infected with only one type to begin with, the virus mutates, and we eventually find these genetically different strains of HIV.

Although some drugs, such as AZT and DDI, seem to work quite well for long periods of time, there are other drugs to which the virus can become resistant almost immediately. That resistance is due to a mutation that can occur within the virus. For example, a few years ago we were very excited about a drug known as soluble CD4, which was designed to block the attachment of the virus to the cell. But the virus almost immediately found ways to evade that drug. With AZT and DDI, resistance does develop, but it takes quite a bit longer to happen, so it's not an absolute limitation of those drugs.

In the future, we might be able to use several drugs simultaneously, even early in the disease. Hopefully, that would slow down the growth of the virus even more than a single drug like AZT can, but we also hope it would prevent the emergence of drug resistance. That's the result when multiple

drugs are used in the treatment of tuberculosis or cancer.

HIV mutations also present problems with vaccines. The vaccines that have been prepared as prototypes for use in our clinic populations are made from strains of this virus that are so different than the strains in Africa that it's probably not going to be feasible to test them in Africa. It's likely that vaccines will have to be developed on a regional basis so that they more or less match the HIV strain found in that population. If the virus is very mutable, an additional complexity is that even though you use a vaccine against the appropriate strain of virus, the virus in that person or in that community might shift slightly, leaving the vaccine ineffective.

How do you predict the AIDS epidemic will progress in the coming years in the United States and in the world?

The pictures are going to be very different in the U.S. compared to the rest of the world. In the U.S., the disease is rapidly going to become a disease of the underclass, driven by drug use and sharing equipment, and then by sexual transmission from those infected people. So the population affected by the

disease will become increasingly heterosexual, with a heavier and heavier representation of the underclass and of ethnic and racial minorities. The progression in the broader heterosexual community will happen quite slowly in the United States, although it will spread.

Gay men have benefited most from information, education, and prevention in the past. However, there are some alarming indications recently that young gay men may be relapsing into unsafe behavior. Hopefully, we will become concerned enough about it to mount more effective prevention programs in the gay community.

In the developing world, it's very easy to predict that this is going to remain a massive epidemic. We're watching situations in India, Thailand, and the Philippines that would suggest that within the next five years or so, Asia will overtake Africa in terms of the number of infected cases. India apparently has the highest rates of untreated syphilis in the world, and any STD is a good surrogate marker for your risk of HIV infection because, after all, this is just another sexually transmitted disease.

What ethical dilemmas currently affect AIDS treatment?

I think the central problem we face is that AIDS is, has been, and probably will continue to be, a very stigmatizing disease. This stigmatization is unfair, because we have certainly learned that it is not easily transmitted. It seems to me and others that much of this is homophobia. It's fear of gays, and sexually transmitted diseases, and maybe even a fear of sexuality.

We've been very interested in why physicians and other health professionals choose to or choose not to participate in HIV care. It's a critical question, because there will be an ongoing need for more physicians to be involved in HIV care. We have found from studies so far that women have much less of a problem taking care of HIV-infected gay men than men do. I think there's less homophobia among women. I think that for many male physicians, taking care of HIV-infected people exposes them to questions about their own sexuality, so they often overtly avoid it. Other studies have looked at the role of homophobia in different medical specialties.

Do you feel that medical practitioners should be required to submit to compulsory HIV testing, and should they be protected by required testing of patients?

These are very important issues. I think the bottom line is that HIV is a difficult disease to transmit. It's difficult for patients to give to physicians, and it's difficult for physicians to give to patients.

There's a lot of anxiety, and there is some risk on the part of health care workers. There clearly have been cases where nurses and others have become infected by needle sticks in the course of taking care of patients.

To my mind, there have been no adequately documented cases of infected physicians transmitting this disease to their patients. The case of the HIV-infected dentist in Florida has so many unanswered questions that it almost needs to be set aside as a case by itself. There have been a number of surgeons who have become HIV-infected by means other than their work. When their infections were made known, thousands of their patients were called in and tested, and none had acquired HIV infection from the surgeon. So I think that the magnitude of that risk is extremely small—so small that it should be discounted in terms of policy guidelines. I don't think physicians or patients should be forced to be tested.

Knowing what we now know about AIDS, what practical advice would you give to a sexually active person in terms of preventing HIV infection?

We're dealing with a sexually transmitted disease—a disease that doesn't know who you are or who your partner is. It's a virus that can be spread by unprotected sex. It really behooves you in this day and age to insert a barrier between you and your sexual partner.

To be effective, I think we have to be quite honest. I don't think it's going to be a good strategy in the long run to exaggerate the degree of risk. I think we have to say, "Look, even if you don't do what I say, your risk is very small. You're probably going to do fine, but I don't want to live with the fear that you might get infected. I don't want to see you get this devastating disease."

We should try to work with a realistic assessment of risk, to increase the time and dialogue between partners so that decisions to engage in sexual activity can be carefully considered ones instead of ones that have to be made instantaneously with people that you don't really know. I think that the advice of knowing your partner is a good one, but can't be taken to the extreme, because you may think you know your partner very well when you really don't. Sexual experiences for many people are very private things, and people aren't always willing to say what they've done with whom. People might not know what their partners have experienced. So everything argues for taking more time, knowing your partner, and still using a condom or other barrier.

health care worker is quite minuscule (Daniels, 1992; Lo & Steinbrook, 1992). The probability of transmission of HIV from an HIV-infected surgeon to a patient has been estimated to fall in the range of one in 40,000 to one in 400,000 (the estimated risk from dentists is about 10 times lower) (Daniels, 1992).

Studies aimed at estimating the incubation time for AIDS in adults (defined as the time between infection with HIV and the onset of one or more severe, debilitating diseases associated with extreme impairment of the immune system), have suggested that incubation periods typically range from 8 to 11 years or more, with the median duration pegged at approximately 10 years (Bacchetti & Moss, 1989; Grohmann & MacDonell, 1992; Gwinn et al., 1991). Individuals infected later in this unfolding epidemic "will tend to have longer incubation periods because they have an increasingly greater opportunity to have access to treatment at an earlier point in their incubation period" (Brookmeyer, 1991, p. 38). Once an AIDS patient develops life-threatening illnesses, such as pneumonia or cancer, the disease tends to run a fairly rapid course culminating in death (Centers for Disease Control, 1989). However, a few AIDS patients continue to defy the death prognosis, years after having been diagnosed with the disease, and we cannot say for certain that AIDS is inevitably fatal to all those afflicted.

Symptoms and Complications. The symptoms of HIV disease and AIDS are many and varied, depending on the degree to which the immune system is compromised and on the particular type of cancer or opportunistic infection(s) that afflict an infected person. The following symptoms are commonly associated with HIV disease and AIDS. However, it must be emphasized that many of these physical manifestations may only indicate common, everyday ailments that are by no means life-threatening. Observing that you have one or more of these symptoms can alert you to seek a medical diagnosis of your ailment. However, do not be needlessly alarmed because, unless you have engaged in high-risk behaviors, the probability of being infected with HIV at the present time is extremely low. Some common symptoms include:

1. Persistent or periodically repeating fevers or night sweats.
2. Unexplained weight loss.
3. Loss of appetite.
4. Chronic fatigue or a tendency to tire quickly when performing routine tasks.
5. Swollen lymph nodes in the neck, armpits, or groin.
6. Persistent and unexplained diarrhea or bloody stools.
7. Easy bruising or atypical bleeding from any body opening.
8. Skin rashes or discoloration of the skin.
9. Persistent severe headaches.
10. A chronic dry cough unrelated to smoking or a cold.
11. A persistent whitish coating on the tongue or throat.

People who develop AIDS experience a multitude of serious, life-threatening complications. Over 60% of the people afflicted with AIDS in the United States have already died, which means that the mortality rate for AIDS is *at least* 60%. Many AIDS researchers believe that the true mortality rate is closer to 100%.

Treatment. As we write this updated review of current treatment strategies for AIDS, there is still no cure, and the general consensus among researchers is that the growing AIDS epidemic will not be halted any time in the near future (Findlay, 1991). However, thousands of scientists are involved in an unprecedented, world-wide effort to ultimately cure and/or prevent AIDS. These efforts are being waged on several fronts, including the development of drugs to treat opportunistic infections, the search for effective antiviral drugs that will kill or at least neutralize HIV, efforts to rebuild compromised immune systems, and attempts to develop a vaccine that will prevent infection by the virus (see the box "The Search for an AIDS Vaccine").

A variety of drugs, most of which are still experimental, have been found to slow the progressive deterioration of the immune system as the illness progresses from HIV disease to AIDS. However, none of the drugs currently being tested seems likely to provide a "cure" for AIDS. At best, we can expect these medications to improve the quality and length of lives of people infected with HIV.

Thus far the most effective of these drugs is zidovudine (formerly called azidothymidine, or AZT). This drug was approved for treatment of HIV infections by the Food and Drug Administration (FDA) in 1987. Zidovudine, like most of the drugs used against HIV, interrupts *reverse transcription* (Goodpasture, 1991), which is the process whereby the virus's genetic information, encoded on its RNA, is copied into its DNA. The DNA is then integrated into the genetic apparatus of the infected cell, resulting in mass reproduction of the virus and death of the invaded cell (Epstein, 1988). Zidovudine does not cure HIV disease and AIDS, but it has been shown to reduce the incidence of opportunistic infections, relieve the physical symptoms of HIV disease, significantly improve patients' sense of well-being, delay progression to full-blown AIDS, and increase the duration of survival for AIDS patients (Brookmeyer, 1991; Goodpasture, 1991; Hamilton et al., 1992; Moore et al., 1991; Vella et al., 1992). It is important to note that zidovudine therapy does not eliminate the potential for sexual transmission of HIV (Krieger et al., 1991). Despite the benefits of zidovudine, the search for other drugs effective against HIV has continued because of toxic side effects in some patients, the development of zidovudine-resistant HIV strains, and the possible potential for drug-induced cancer with prolonged zidovudine therapy (Boucher et al., 1992; Goodpasture, 1991; Koup et al., 1991).

Many other antiviral drugs have shown some promise in the laboratory or clinical trials. Among those most promising are dideoxyinosine (DDI) (approved by the FDA in 1991) and benzodiazapine.

Prevention. The only certain way to avoid contracting AIDS sexually is either to remain celibate or to be involved in a monogamous relationship with one mutually faithful, uninfected partner. If neither of these conditions is applicable, a wise person will act in a way that significantly reduces his or her risk of becoming infected with HIV. Safer sex practices that reduce one's risk of contracting AIDS and other STDs are described in some detail in the last section of this chapter. Most of the preventive methods discussed are directly applicable to AIDS. However, it is important to note that any strategies that reduce your risk of developing any of the other STDs discussed in this chapter will also reduce your risk of HIV infection because of the known association between AIDS and other STDs. Research throughout the world has shown that the risk of contracting HIV is

OUR SEXUALITY

The Search for an AIDS Vaccine

Researchers are hopeful that someday a vaccine will be developed that will block infection by HIV. A recent article reviewing progress in the search for an AIDS vaccine reported that despite extensive worldwide efforts, employing state-of-the-art methods, an effective vaccine has yet to be developed. Nevertheless, the authors of this report concluded that the outlook for an eventual AIDS vaccine was optimistic, even though "it is still impossible to predict with certainty that the development of an HIV/AIDS vaccine for humans will eventually be successful" (Kurth et al., 1991, p. 432). One of the major problem areas confronting vaccine researchers is that HIV is extremely complicated, is present in multiple strains, and can change rapidly due to genetic mutations (Greenberg, 1992).

An antiviral vaccine consists of either portions of the infectious virus or entire units of killed viruses that are injected into healthy people. Once injected, they induce production of certain antibodies that ward off future invasions by the live virus. Most scientists are reticent to test vaccines consisting of entire units of killed HIVs out of fear that some viruses might survive and subsequently cause rather than prevent AIDS. Consequently, efforts are focused on trying to locate subunits of the virus that, when injected into the body of healthy recipients, will stimulate the production of effective antiviral antibodies. Most vaccine researchers are focusing on one or another protein found on the outer covering of HIV that remains unchanged during its rapid mutation. The theory is that it is the outer shell of HIV that the immune system recognizes and attempts to fight with antibodies. It is thus hoped that one or more of these protein sections can serve as the basis for a vaccine that will remain effective for numerous mutations of HIV (Goldsmith, 1991).

The first experimental AIDS vaccine used in human testing in the United States caused no ill effects in 33 healthy human volunteers. Potentially protective immune responses were triggered in the majority of these subjects, but the antibody response was somewhat weak and transitory in nature (Dolin et al., 1991). At the time of this writing, 11 possible vaccines are being tested on people in limited trials designed to evaluate the safety of doses (Bolognesi, 1991). We can only hope that one or more of these candidates (or others yet to be developed) will eventually prove to be an effective AIDS vaccine and will thus prevent HIV infection.

---

elevated in people who have other STDs such as herpes, gonorrhea, syphilis, chlamydial infection, and trichomoniasis (Aral & Holmes, 1991; Goeman & Piot, 1992; Musher, 1991). STDs that cause genital ulcers, such as herpes and syphilis, have shown the highest association with HIV infection in America and Africa (Aral & Holmes, 1991; Goeman & Piot, 1992; Hook et al., 1992; Plummer et al., 1991). (Genital ulcers allow HIV easy access to the bloodstream.)

Beyond the obvious safer-sex strategies of using condoms and virus-killing spermicides and avoiding sex with multiple partners, some suggestions particularly relevant to avoiding HIV infection follow.

1. If you use IV drugs, do not share needles or syringes (boiling does not guarantee sterility). If needle sharing continues, use bleach to clean and sterilize your needles and syringes (Clayton & O'Connell, 1990). You may also wish to check with local health departments to see if a needle-exchange program exists. These programs provide clean syringes and needles on an exchange basis. A number of needle-exchange programs are currently operating in U.S. and European cities.

2. Avoid oral, vaginal, or anal contact with semen.

3. Avoid anal intercourse because this is one of the riskiest of all sexual behaviors associated with the transmission of HIV (DE Bruyn, 1992; European Study

Group, 1989; Franceschi et al., 1989; Voeller, 1991). Anal intercourse has a greater HIV infection risk for women than does vaginal intercourse, just as receptive anal intercourse carries a very high risk for males (Keet et al., 1992; Voeller, 1991). The high risk associated with anal intercourse is thought to be related to the fact that anal penetration causes small abrasions in the rectal tissues, through which HIV has easy access to the recipient's blood.

4. Do not engage in the insertion of fingers or fists ("fisting") into the anus as an active or receptive partner. Fingernails can easily cause tears in the rectal tissues, allowing direct access to the blood system.

5. Avoid oral contact with the anus (a practice commonly referred to as "rimming") (Baral et al., 1992).

6. Avoid oral contact with vaginal fluids.

7. Do not allow a partner's urine to enter your mouth, anus, eyes, or open cuts or sores.

8. In view of the remote possibility that HIV may be transmitted via saliva, it might be wise to avoid prolonged open mouth wet kissing (deep kissing or tongue kissing) (Piazza et al., 1989).

9. Do not share razor blades, toothbrushes, or other implements that could become contaminated with blood.

10. Avoid sexual contact with prostitutes (male or female). Research has found that individuals who work as prostitutes have unusually high rates of HIV infection (DE Bruyn, 1992; De Zalduondo, 1991; Dorfman et al., 1992; Morse et al., 1991; Sanders et al., 1991).

At the present time, the best hope for curtailing the epidemic spread of HIV and AIDS is through education and behavior changes (Centers for Disease Control, 1991c). Because HIV is transmitted almost exclusively through behaviors that individuals can modify, health and education officials are hopeful that educational programs aimed at encouraging people to engage in safer sexual practices will be effective in curtailing the spread of AIDS. Two experts on the global AIDS epidemic, James Chin and Jonathan Mann (1990), recently stated, "The single most important component of national AIDS programs is information, education, and communication. This is because even in the absence of an HIV vaccine or curative therapy, the first objective of the Global AIDS Strategy — to prevent HIV infection — can still be achieved, through the adoption by individuals of informed and responsible behavior and practices" (p. 134).

A number of studies of populations of gay males have shown that fear of contracting AIDS has resulted in significant changes in sexual behavior (Centers for Disease Control, 1987; Ekstrand & Coates, 1990; Lawrence et al., 1989; Lourea et al., 1986; Ruefli et al., 1992). Many of these men have reduced the number of their sexual partners or entered into monogamous relationships. We can only hope that educational efforts aimed at the broader population will accomplish similar shifts away from high-risk behaviors.

When former U.S. Surgeon General C. Everett Koop took a strong stance in 1986 supporting sex education in the schools, many health officials were hopeful that a national educational effort would make significant inroads into the HIV epidemic. At least 30 states and the District of Columbia now require HIV/AIDS education in public schools. However, the growing tolerance and willingness to talk about sex have not necessarily led to significant changes in sexual behavior in the broader population during the past decade (Blendon et al., 1992; Findlay, 1991). Recent surveys of high school- and college-age populations have indicated that few people in these groups had modified their sexual practices out of fear of getting AIDS (see Chapter 13). Unfortunately, available data indicate that "the vast majority of the public perceive their personal risk of becoming infected as low or nonexistent, which probably blunts the nation's sense of urgency about addressing the epidemic" (Blendon et al., 1992, p. 981). It is our hope that we will soon see the emergence in the United States of a more effective national AIDS program with an integrated approach to inducing behavioral change, promoting condom use, and controlling other STDs that increase susceptibility to HIV infection. Such a national program was introduced in the Netherlands in 1987 and led to a considerable decline in the ensuing years in the number of "risky" sexual contacts in the broader Netherlands population (van Haastrecht et al., 1991).

Prevention of Sexually Transmitted Diseases

Many approaches to curtailing the spread of STDs have been advocated. These range from attempting to discourage sexual activity among young people to providing easy public access to information about the symptoms of STDs, along with free medical treatment. Unfortunately, the efforts of public health agencies have not been successful in curbing the rapid spread of STDs. For this reason it is doubly important to stress a variety of specific preventive measures that may be taken by an individual or couple.

Clearly, abstinence is one virtually surefire way to avoid an STD infection. However, this alternative is not especially popular. Being disease-free and monogamous yourself and having a partner who is also disease-free and monogamous is another way to prevent contracting an STD. However, it is often very difficult for people to assess the disease risk status of prospective partners and, for that matter, how committed their prospective partners are to being monogamous. Having a frank and open discussion with someone prior to initial sexual interaction may seem difficult and embarrassing. However, in this era of epidemic health-damaging and life-threatening STDs, such discussions are essential to making sound judgments that may have profound ramifications for your physical and psychological well-being. Consequently, we address this issue early in our outline of prevention guidelines.

Prevention Guidelines

We discuss several methods of prevention — steps that can be taken before, during, or shortly after sexual contact to reduce the likelihood of contracting an STD. Many of these methods are effective against the transmission of a variety of diseases. Several are applicable to oral – genital and anal – genital contacts in addition to genital – genital interaction. None is 100% effective, but each acts to significantly reduce the chances of infection. Furthermore — and this cannot be overemphasized — the use of preventive measures may help curtail the booming spread of STDs. Because many infected people have sexual contact with one or more partners before realizing they have a disease and seeking treatment, improved prevention rather than better treatment seems to hold the key to reducing these unpleasant effects of sexual expression.

Assess Your and Your Partner's Risk Status for Transmitting STDs. As a result of informed concern about acquiring an STD, you may understandably focus on assessing the risk status of a prospective sexual partner. However, in doing so you may overlook the equally important need to evaluate your own risk status. If you have had previous sexual activity with others, is there any possibility you may harbor an STD that could be transmitted to your new partner? Have you been tested for STDs in general, not one specific infectious agent? Remember, many of the STDs discussed in this chapter may produce little or no noticeable symptoms in an infected person. If you care enough to be sexually intimate with a new partner, is it not reasonable that you should also be open and willing to share information about your own physical sexual health?

Some experts maintain that one of the single most important STD-preventive messages to convey to people is to spend time, ideally several months or more, getting to know prospective sexual partners before engaging in genital sex (Hearst & Hulley, 1988; Peterman et al., 1988). Take time to develop a warm, caring relationship in which mutual empathy and trust are key ingredients. Use this time to convey to the other person any relevant information from your sexual history regarding your risk status — and to inquire about his or her present or past behavior in the areas of sex and IV drug use. As discussed in Chapter 8, self-disclosure can be a marvelous strategy for getting a partner to open up. Thus you might begin your dialogue about these matters by discussing why you think that such an information exchange is vitally important in the AIDS era, followed by information about your own sexual history.

Getting to know someone well enough to trust his or her answers to these important questions means taking the time to assess a person's honesty and integrity in a variety of situations. If you observe your prospective partner lying to friends, family members, or you about other matters, you may rightfully question the truthfulness of her or his responses to your risk-assessment queries.

Research by Susan Cochran (1988) suggested that we cannot always assume that potential sexual partners will accurately disclose their risk for STDs. Cochran found that a sizable percentage of both men and women said that they would not be fully honest when questioned about their past sexual and drug-use histories. Of over 400 sexually experienced southern California college students surveyed by Cochran, 35% of the men and 10% of the women said that they had lied about such things as pregnancy risk and other sexual involvements in order to have sex. In addition, 47% of the men and 42% of the women said that they would report fewer previous sexual partners than they really had. Finally, 20% of the men and 4% of the women indicated that they would falsely claim that they had tested negative for HIV.

Obtain Prior Medical Examinations. It is often difficult to accurately assess risk status from conversations alone. As we just learned, people may choose to lie about STD risk factors in order to have sex. Furthermore, while people may be entirely candid about their own sexual histories, there is no way to assure that

Health departments often provide screening and treatment for STDs.

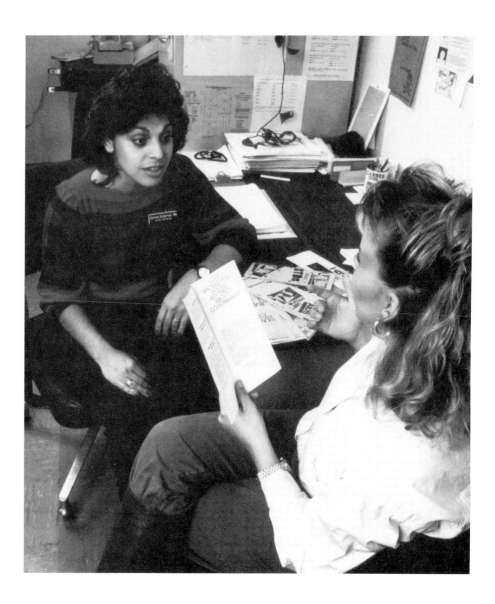

people they have previously related to sexually have been equally honest with them or, for that matter, that they even asked previous partners about STD risk status.

In view of these concerns, we strongly encourage couples who wish to commence an intimate relationship to abstain from any sexual activity that puts them at risk for STDs until they both undergo medical examinations and laboratory testing designed to rule out STDs. Undergoing such a process prior to beginning sexual relations, while greatly reducing one's chance of contracting a disease, can contribute immeasurably to a sense of mutual trust and comfort with developing intimacy. If cost is an issue, contact your campus health service or public health clinics in your area, both of which may provide examinations and laboratory testing free of charge or on a sliding-fee scale commensurate with your financial status.

Use Condoms and Spermicides. It has been known for decades that condoms, when correctly used, prevent the transmission of many STDs. The condom may be one of the great underrated aids to sexual interaction. Used in combination with vaginal spermicides, condoms are effective in preventing both undesired conception and the transmission of many STDs, including AIDS (Centers for Disease Control, 1991c; Plummer et al., 1991). The membranes of condoms made of latex do not have pores and thus offer greater protection against STDs than do natural-membrane ("skin") condoms (Peterman et al., 1988). The use of condoms plus a spermicide (foams, creams, jellies) containing nonoxynol-9 (which kills HIV and some other infectious agents as well as sperm cells) offers more protection than condoms used alone. Nonoxynol-9 is incorporated in the lubricant of some condoms. Condoms plus spermicides should be used as a protection against STDs even if contraception is not needed.

Condoms are most valuable in the prevention of sexual transmission of bacterial vaginosis, candidiasis, trichomoniasis, *Chlamydia trachomatis,* gonorrhea, NGU, syphilis, and AIDS. They are less effective against the spread of herpes and genital warts and have no value in combating pubic lice. Chapter 11 contains a description of the proper way to put on a condom. Additional recommendations for the proper use of condoms follow.

- Store condoms in a cool, dry place out of direct sunlight.
- Throw away condoms in damaged packages and any that are brittle, sticky, discolored, or show any other signs of age.
- Handle condoms with care so that they are not punctured.
- Put on a condom before any genital contact to prevent exposure to fluids that may contain infectious agents.
- Be sure the condom is adequately lubricated. If you need to add a lubricant, be sure to use only water-based products such as spermicides or K-Y jelly. Latex is weakened by petroleum- or oil-based lubricants (such as Vaseline, baby oil, cooking oils, shortening, and many body lotions).
- Do not blow up a condom like a balloon or fill it with water before using it to test for leaks. Such stretching weakens the latex and makes it more likely that the condom will break during use.
- Do not unroll the condom first and then pull it on like a sock; this also tends to weaken the latex, making it more likely that the condom will break during use. The proper way to put on a condom is to unroll it directly onto the erect penis (either while pinching the reservoir tip or while holding a twisted end to create a reservoir area).
- If a condom does break, replace it immediately.
- After ejaculation, take care that the condom does not slip off. Withdraw the condom-clad penis while the penis is still erect, holding the base of the condom firmly to prevent slippage.
- Never reuse a condom.

A final word on condoms as a preventive device: Using condoms **DOES NOT** guarantee protection against STD infections. Some critics of condom campaigns assert that people too often are lulled into a sense of false complacency — that as long as they use condoms, they are safe. However, an examination of Table 11.1 (Birth Control – Method Effectiveness) reveals that more than 1 out of 10 women who use condoms as their only method of birth control becomes pregnant in one year's time. We can safely assume that the actual failure rate of condoms (inconsistent or improper use, breakage, slippage, etc.) must be considerably higher than indicated by pregnancy statistics. (Conception can occur on only a few days each month, but an STD can be contracted any time sexual interaction with an infected person coincides with a failure of preventive methods.) One recent study reported that 14.6% of the 405 condoms used during penile – vaginal intercourse by 70 couples either broke or slipped off the penis during intercourse or withdrawal (Trussel et al., 1992). Another study revealed that even among couples proficient with condom usage, some occasionally reported intravaginal spillage of seminal fluid (Drew et al., 1990).

To be effective as STD prophylactics, condoms must be used correctly EVERY TIME a person has sex. That may be hard to do, particularly since logic has a tendency to shut down in the heat of passion. Thus, we strongly encourage you to incorporate into your sex life knowledge about both the non-foolproof nature of condoms and how they may be used most effectively to prevent both disease transmission and conception.

Avoid Sexual Activity with Multiple Partners. You may wish to reevaluate the importance of sex with multiple partners in light of the clear and extensive evidence that having many sexual partners is one of the strongest predictors of becoming infected with HIV, HSV–2, *Chlamydia trachomatis*, HPV, and numerous other sexually transmitted infections (Brookmeyer, 1991; Chin & Mann, 1990; Hearst & Hulley, 1988; Peterman et al., 1988). You may also elect not to have sex with individuals you know or suspect have had multiple partners. People with multiple partners will probably know each partner less well and thus may be less successful in avoiding people who engage in high-risk behaviors.

Inspect Your Partner's Genitals. Examining your partner's genitals prior to coital, oral, or anal contact may reveal the symptoms of an STD. Herpes blisters, vaginal and urethral discharges, chancres and rashes associated with syphilis, genital warts, and pubic lice may be seen. In most cases symptoms will be more evident in a man. (If he is uncircumcised, be sure to retract the foreskin.) The presence of a discharge, unpleasant odor, sores, blisters, rash, warts, or anything else out of the ordinary should be viewed with some concern. "Milking" the penis is a particularly effective way to detect a suspicious discharge. This technique, sometimes called the "short-arm inspection," involves grasping the penis firmly and pulling the loose skin up and down the shaft several times, applying pressure on the base-to-head stroke. Then part the urinary opening to see if any cloudy discharge is present.

People frequently find it difficult to conduct such an inspection before sexual involvement. Sometimes the simple request "let me undress you" will provide some opportunity to examine your partner's genitals. Sensate focus pleasuring, discussed in Chapter 17, could provide the opportunity for more detailed visual exploration. Some people suggest a shower before sex, with an eye toward examining a partner. This may be quite helpful for noting visible sores, blisters, and so forth, but soap and water may also remove the visual and olfactory cues associated with a discharge.

If you note signs of infection, you may justifiably and wisely elect not to have sexual relations. Your intended partner may or may not be aware of his or her symptoms. Therefore, it is important that you explain your concerns. Some people may decide to continue their sexual interaction after discovering possible symptoms of an STD; they would be wise, though, to restrict their activities to kissing, hugging, touching, and manual–genital stimulation.

Wash Your — and Your Partner's — Genitals Before and After Sexual Contact. There is some difference of opinion about the extent of benefits associated with soap-and-water washing of the genitals before sexual interaction. However, there can be little doubt that washing has some benefits. Washing the man's penis is generally more effective as a prophylactic measure, although washing the woman's vulva can also be helpful.

You may find it difficult to suggest that your partner wash (or allow you to wash) his or her genitals before having sex. However, you may accomplish this unobtrusively by including washing of the genitals in the sex play that occurs in the shower or bathtub. Or you may frankly announce that you are cleansing your partner's and your own genitals for your mutual protection.

After sexual contact, thorough washing of the genitals and surrounding areas with soap and water is highly recommended as a preventive procedure when the transmission of an infection is a possibility. We are not, however, suggesting that this procedure should always follow sexual activity. Many lovers with long-term, monogamous relationships would find this unnecessary and possibly even offensive, implying that a person is somehow unclean after sex.

Promptness is very important in postsex washing, probably as important as thoroughness. However, some people might object to jumping out of bed immediately to wash, as this may break the relaxed and intimate mood. For those uncomfortable letting their partners know that they are taking this precaution, perhaps simply announcing that you need to go to the bathroom (a not uncommon need after sex) will suffice. Women and men can wash their genitals while sitting over the sink. First fill the sink with warm, soapy water, then turn your back to it and boost yourself up to straddle it. In this position it is relatively easy to thoroughly wash your exposed genitals with a soapy washcloth.

Urinating after coitus may have some limited prophylactic benefits, particularly for men. Many infectious organisms do not survive in the urethra in the acidic environment created by urine. Urinating may also flush out disease-causing organisms.

Obtain Routine Medical Evaluations.   Many authorities recommend that sexually active people with multiple partners routinely visit their health practitioner or local STD clinic for periodic checkups, even when no symptoms of disease are evident. In view of the number of people, both women and men, who are symptomless carriers of STDs, this seems like very good advice. How often to have such examinations is a matter of opinion. Our advice to people who are sexually active with multiple partners is that they should have checkups preferably every three months and certainly no less often than twice a year.

OUR SEXUALITY

Telling a Partner

Most of us would find it difficult to discuss with our lover(s) the possibility that we have transmitted a disease to her or him during sexual activity. Due to the stigma often associated with STDs, it can be bad enough admitting to having one of these diseases. The need to tell others that they may have "caught" something from you may seem a formidable task. You might fear that such a revelation will jeopardize a valued relationship or worry that you will be considered "dirty." In relationships presumed to be monogamous, a person might fear that telling his or her partner about an STD will threaten mutual trust. "However, lovers who attempt to conceal a sex-related illness risk a good deal more in the long run than those who have the courage to discuss the situation right away" (Castleman, 1980, p. 230).

Not disclosing the existence of an STD risks the health of one's partner(s). Many people may not have symptoms and thus may not become aware that they have contracted a disease until they discover it for themselves, perhaps only after they have developed serious complications. Furthermore, if a lover remains untreated, she or he may reinfect you even after you have been cured. Unlike some diseases (like measles and chicken pox), STDs do not provide immunity against future infections. You can get one, give it to your lover, be cured, and then get it back again if he or she remains untreated (a proc-

ess some health authorities call "ping-pong VD").

The following suggestions may provide some guidelines for telling a partner about your STD. Remember, these are only suggestions that have worked for some people; they may need to be modified to fit your particular circumstances. This is a sensitive issue that requires thoughtful consideration and planning.

1. Be honest. There is nothing to be gained by downplaying the potential risks associated with STDs. If you tell a partner, "I have this little drip, but it probably means nothing," you may regret it. Stick with the facts and be sure your partner understands the importance of obtaining a medical evaluation.

2. Even if you suspect that your partner may have been the source of your infection, there is little to be gained by blaming him or her. Instead, you may wish to simply acknowledge that you have the disease and are concerned that your partner gets proper medical attention.

3. Your attitude may have considerable impact on how your partner receives the news. If you display high levels of anxiety, guilt, fear, or disgust, your partner may reflect these feelings in her or his response. Try to simply present the facts in as clear and calm a fashion as you can manage.

4. Be sensitive to your partner's feelings. Be prepared for reactions of anger or resentment. These are understandable initial responses. Being supportive and demonstrating a willingness to listen without becoming defensive may be the best tactics for diffusing negative responses.

5. Engaging in sexual intimacies after you become aware of your condition and before you obtain medical assurances that you are no longer contagious is clearly inappropriate.

6. Medical examinations and treatments for STDs, when necessary, can be a financial burden. Offering to pay for some or all of these expenses may help to maintain (or re-establish) goodwill in your relationship.

7. In the case of herpes, where recurrences are unpredictable and the possibility of infecting a new partner is an ongoing concern, it is probably a good idea to tell him or her about your herpes before sexual intimacies take place. You may wish to preface your first sexual interaction by saying "There is something we should talk over first." Be sure to emphasize that herpes is usually preventable when proper precautions are taken.

Inform Your Partner(s) If You Have an STD. The high frequency of infections without symptoms makes it imperative for infected individuals to tell their sexual partner(s) once they are diagnosed as having an STD. However, we cannot assume that a previous sexual partner will be forthcoming about a newly diagnosed STD. For example, two recent studies revealed that very few past sexual partners of individuals diagnosed as HIV-infected were informed of their risk by the infected person (Landis et al., 1992; Marks et al., 1992). In one of these studies, 111 male subjects reported a total of 926 sexual partners during the 12 months prior to testing HIV-positive. Of the total, only 51 partners (5.5%) were informed of their infection risk by the subjects (Marks et al., 1992). Furthermore, one cannot assume that a partner who has been infected with a disease during sexual interaction will have symptoms or that she or he will understand the meaning of any symptoms that might occur and seek proper medical treatment. The box "Telling a Partner" offers some suggestions that may be helpful when telling a partner about an STD infection.

Summary

In the United States, there is an increasing incidence of sexually transmitted diseases (STDs). However, public understanding of STDs, particularly of preventive measures, has not shown a comparable increase.

Common Vaginal Infections

Bacterial vaginosis, typically caused by a bacterium known as *Gardnerella vaginalis,* is the most common cause of vaginitis (vaginal infection) in American women. Many male partners of infected women also harbor the *Gardnerella vaginalis* organism, usually without clinical symptoms. Coitus often provides a mode of transmission of this infection.

The most prominent symptom of bacterial vaginosis in women is a fishy or musty smelling, thin discharge that is like flour paste in consistency. Women may also experience irritation of the genital tissues. A small number of men may develop inflammation of the foreskin and glans, urethritis, or cystitis.

The treatment for bacterial vaginosis is Flagyl. To avoid "ping-ponging" the disease back and forth, partners of infected individuals are often treated simultaneously.

Candidiasis is a yeast infection that affects many women. The *Candida albicans* organism is commonly present in the vagina but causes problems only when overgrowth occurs. Pregnancy, diabetes, the use of birth control pills or oral antibiotics, and the ingestion of large amounts of dairy products, sugar, and artificial sweeteners are conditions often associated with yeast infections. The organism can be transmitted via sexual or nonsexual means.

Symptoms of yeast infections include a white, clumpy discharge and intense itching of the vaginal and vulval tissues.

Traditional treatment for candidiasis infection consists of vaginal suppositories or creams such as clotrimazole, miconazole, or nystatin.

Trichomoniasis accounts for about one-fourth of all cases of vaginitis. Male partners of infected women are thought to carry the *Trichomonas vaginalis* organism in the urethra and under the foreskin if they are uncircumcised. The primary mode of transmission of this infection is through sexual contact.

The primary symptom of trichomoniasis in women is an abundant, unpleasant-smelling vaginal discharge, often accompanied by inflamed, itchy, and painful genital tissues. Men are rarely symptomatic.

Infected women and their male sexual partners may be successfully treated with the drug Flagyl.

Chlamydial Infection

Chlamydial infections are among the most prevalent and among the most damaging of all STDs.

Chlamydial disease is transmitted primarily through sexual contact. It may also be spread by fingers from one body site to another, as from the genitals to the eyes.

There are two general types of genital chlamydial infections in females — infections of the lower reproductive tract, commonly manifested as urethritis or cervicitis, and invasive infections of the upper reproductive tract, expressed as PID (pelvic inflammatory disease).

Most women with lower reproductive tract chlamydial infections have few or no symptoms. Symptoms of *Chlamydia*-caused PID include disrupted menstrual periods, abdominal pain, elevated temperature, nausea, vomiting, and headache.

Chlamydial salpingitis (infection of the fallopian tubes) is a major cause of infertility and ectopic pregnancy.

In men chlamydial infections are a common cause of epididymitis and NGU. Possible symptoms of chlamydial infections in men are a discharge from the penis and burning during urination.

Chlamydia trachomatis also causes trachoma, the world's leading cause of preventable blindness.

Gonorrhea

Gonorrhea, a very common communicable disease in the United States, is a bacterial infection transmitted through sexual contact. The infecting organism is commonly called a gonococcus bacterium.

Early symptoms of gonorrheal infection are more likely to be manifested by men, who will probably have a discharge from the penis and burning during urination. The early sign in women, often not detectable, is a mild vaginal discharge that may be irritating to vulval tissues.

Complications of gonorrheal infection in men include prostate, bladder, and kidney involvement and, infrequently, gonococcal epididymitis, which may lead to sterility. In women gonorrhea may lead to PID, sterility, and abdominal adhesions.

Recommended drugs for treating gonorrhea include cefixime, ceftriaxone, and spectinomycin. Because chlamydial infection often coexists with gonorrhea, many health practitioners use a treatment strategy that is effective against both infectious organisms.

Nongonococcal Urethritis

Nongonococcal urethritis (NGU) is a very common infection of the urethral passage typically seen in men. It is primarily caused by two infectious organisms transmitted during coitus.

Symptoms, most apparent in men, include penile discharge and slight burning during urination. Women may have a minor vaginal discharge and are thought to harbor the infecting organisms.

Penicillin is not effective against NGU, making definitive diagnosis essential. Doxycycline or erythromycin therapy usually clears up the condition.

Syphilis

Syphilis is less common but potentially more damaging than gonorrhea. It is almost always transmitted through sexual contact.

If untreated, syphilis may progress through four phases: primary, characterized by the appearance of chancre sores; secondary, distinguished by the occurrence of a generalized skin rash; latent, a several-year period of no overt symptoms; and tertiary, during which the disease may produce cardiovascular disease, blindness, paralysis, skin ulcers, liver damage, and severe mental pathology.

Syphilis may be treated with penicillin at any stage of its development. People allergic to penicillin may be treated with doxycycline, tetracycline, or erythromycin.

Pubic Lice

Pubic lice ("crabs") are tiny biting insects that feed on blood from small vessels in the pubic region. They may be transmitted through sexual contact or by using sheets or clothing contaminated by an infested individual.

The primary symptom is severe itching that is not relieved by scratching. Sometimes pubic lice can be seen.

A variety of prescription and nonprescription medications effectively kill pubic lice.

Herpes

There are five different herpes viruses, the most common being type 1, which generally produces cold sores on or in the mouth, and type 2, which generally infects the genital area. Type 1 may sometimes be found in the genital area and type 2 in the mouth area. Type 2 is transmitted primarily through sexual contact; type 1 may be passed by kissing or by using the toilet articles or utensils of an infected person.

It has been estimated that over 100 million Americans are afflicted with oral herpes and that 10–20 million people in the United States have genital herpes.

The presence of painful sores is the primary symptom of herpes. A person is highly contagious during a herpes eruption.

There is evidence that herpes may also be transmitted during asymptomatic periods, but the relative risk is undefined.

Genital herpes may predispose a woman to cervical cancer. It may also infect her newborn child, producing severe damage or death of the infant.

There is no known cure for herpes. Treatment is symptomatic, aimed at reducing pain and speeding the healing process. Oral acyclovir is effective in promoting healing during first episodes and, if taken continuously, in suppressing recurrent herpes outbreaks.

Viral Hepatitis

Hepatitis A, hepatitis B, and non-A/non-B hepatitis are three major types of viral infections of the liver. Both the A and B types can be sexually transmitted.

Hepatitis B may be transmitted via blood or blood products, semen, vaginal secretions, and saliva. Manual, oral, or penile stimulation of the anus are practices strongly associated with the spread of this viral agent.

Oral – anal contact seems to be the primary mode of sexual transmission of hepatitis A.

The symptoms of viral hepatitis may vary from mild to incapacitating illness. There is no specific therapy available to treat this disease. Most infected people recover in a few weeks with adequate bed rest.

Genital Warts

Genital and anal warts are the most common viral STD in the United States and probably the most common of all STDs.

Genital warts are primarily transmitted through vaginal, anal, or oral – genital sexual interaction.

Research has revealed a strong association between genital warts and cancers of the cervix, vagina, vulva, penis, and anus.

Genital warts are treated by applications of topical agents, cauterization, freezing, surgical removal, or vaporization by a carbon dioxide laser.

Acquired Immunodeficiency Syndrome (AIDS)

AIDS is caused by infection with a virus (HIV) that destroys the immune system, leaving the body vulnerable to a variety of cancers and opportunistic infections.

In spite of a great deal of speculation and theorizing, the origin of HIV remains undetermined.

Some individuals infected with HIV manifest less severe immune system impairments, referred to as AIDS-related complex (ARC) or HIV disease.

It is estimated that 1 – 2 million persons in the United States and 8 – 10 million adults and 1 million children worldwide are infected with HIV.

HIV has been found in semen, blood, vaginal secretions, saliva, tears, urine, breast milk, and any other bodily fluids that may contain blood.

Blood and semen are the major vehicles for transmitting the virus, which appears to be passed primarily through sexual contact and through needle sharing among IV drug users.

The present possibility of being infected with HIV via transfusion of contaminated blood is quite remote. Furthermore, there is no danger of being infected as a result of donating blood.

The risk of transmitting HIV via saliva, tears, and urine appears to be very low. There is no evidence that HIV can be transmitted by casual contact.

It is estimated that 80% of HIV transmission worldwide is heterosexual.

It is sexual contact with an infected person, or sharing contaminated injection equipment, rather than one's sexual orientation, that places one at risk for becoming infected with HIV.

High-risk behaviors that increase one's chances of becoming infected with HIV include having multiple sexual partners, engaging in unprotected sex, sexual contact with people known to be at high risk, and sharing injection equipment for IV drug use.

HIV is not as easily transmitted from women to men as it is from men to women.

While most people develop antibodies to HIV within months of being infected, some "silent" infections may go undetected for three years or more.

The incubation time for AIDS — defined as the time between infection with HIV and the onset of one or more severe, debilitating diseases — is estimated to range between 8 and 11 years.

The symptoms of HIV disease and AIDS are many and varied, depending on the degree to which the immune system is compromised and the particular type of cancer or opportunistic infection(s) that afflict an infected person.

Over 60% of people afflicted with AIDS in the United States have already died. Many researchers believe that the true mortality rate for AIDS is closer to 100%.

A major focus of therapy for HIV-infected people is to provide treatment for the various infections and tumors that occur as immune systems are compromised.

None of the antiviral drugs currently available seems likely to provide a "cure" for AIDS, although some do relieve symptoms, improve the quality of patients' lives, and significantly prolong their lives.

At the present time, while all efforts to develop an AIDS vaccine have failed, the outlook for an eventual effective vaccine is optimistic.

The best hope for curtailing the AIDS epidemic is through education and behavioral changes.

A person may significantly reduce her or his risk of becoming infected with HIV by following safer-sex strategies, which include, among others, using condoms and virus-killing spermicides and avoiding sex with multiple partners.

Prevention of Sexually Transmitted Diseases

Taking the time to carefully assess your and your partner's risk status for transmitting STDs is perhaps the single most important preventive strategy.

Since it is often difficult to accurately assess risk status from conversations alone, couples are encouraged to undergo medical examinations and laboratory testing to rule out STDs prior to engaging in any sexual activity that puts them at risk for STDs.

Condoms, when used correctly in conjunction with spermicides containing nonoxynol-9, offer good, but not foolproof, protection against the transmission of many STDs.

Avoid sex with multiple partners or with individuals who likely have had multiple partners.

Inspecting a partner's genitals prior to sexual contact may be a way to detect symptoms of an STD.

Washing the genitals with soap and water both before and after sexual interaction offers additional protection against being infected with an STD.

Sexually active people with multiple partners should routinely visit their health practitioner or local STD clinic for periodic checkups, even when no symptoms of disease are present.

It is imperative for infected individuals to tell their sexual partner(s) once they are diagnosed as having an STD.

✐ *Thought Provokers* ✐

1. Do you think that the threat of contracting STDs such as AIDS, herpes, or *Chlamydia trachomatis* will alter or has already altered patterns of sexual interaction among college students and other young adults? Explain your answer.

2. Many individuals with herpes have very rare outbreaks of the disease. It is also true that some people afflicted with this disease have experienced rejection by prospective sexual partners when they explain their condition. In view of these facts, do you believe that people who carefully monitor their health and take proper precautions can justifiably enter into sexual relationships without revealing that they have herpes?

3. It has been suggested that all adolescents and adults should be required to undergo screening for the presence of the AIDS virus. Do you agree with this recommendation? How might the results of such testing be effectively employed to reduce the transmission of HIV? What problems might occur as a result of compulsory screening? Do you believe that such mandatory testing would be an unjustifiable violation of privacy rights?

4. Assume that you are in the preliminary stages of a sexual encounter when you notice one or more symptoms of an STD in your partner. What would you do? Would you make up an excuse for not continuing the sexual activity, or would you tell your companion the true reason for your concerns? Would your response be different with a first-time versus a repeat lover?

Suggested Readings

AIDS Education and Prevention. This interdisciplinary journal, which is the official journal of the International Society for AIDS Education, is available in many major library systems and contains excellent information regarding the prevention of AIDS. One of the best available sources of material on AIDS education.

Centers for Disease Control. *The MMWR (Morbidity and Mortality Weekly Report)* of the national Centers for Disease Control is available in most major library systems (particularly medical libraries) and frequently contains valuable information about the nature, transmission, prevention, and treatment of STDs. It is perhaps the single best source for keeping abreast of the latest developments regarding AIDS and other STDs.

Lumiere, Richard; and Cook, Stephani (1983). *Healthy Sex and Keeping It That Way.* New York: Simon & Schuster. A valuable resource guide to genital health and disease for the layperson; contains an excellent chapter on informing sexual partners about an STD.

Shilts, Randy (1987). *And the Band Played On: Politics, People, and the AIDS Epidemic.* New York: St. Martin's Press. This compelling book, written by an investigative reporter, provides shocking information about how government incompetence and infighting among research groups in the scientific and medical communities hindered efforts to mobilize an effective campaign against the AIDS epidemic. This book also humanizes the AIDS crisis by telling personal stories of people who have lived and died with AIDS.

Resources

AIDS National Hotline, (800) 342–AIDS. An informative recording with current information. Those who have specific questions not answered by the recording can call (800) 447–AIDS. Many cities have a local AIDS information hotline; check your local white pages for listings.

The Herpes Resource Center (formerly HELP), P.O. Box 100, Palo Alto, CA 94302. For an annual membership fee, this excellent service provides a quarterly journal complete with up-to-date information about herpes, access to local chapters (support groups), and a private telephone information, counseling, and referral service.

Herpes Anonymous, P.O. Box 278, Westbury, NY 11590; (516) 334–5718. A nonprofit social organization comprised of people with herpes who wish to help others overcome the difficulties associated with this disease. Herpes Anonymous assists in developing companionable associations between people who have herpes. The organization also distributes a free newsletter containing up-to-date information about this disease.

Social Issues

CHAPTER 20
Atypical Sexual Behavior

*I*n this chapter we focus on a number of sexual behaviors that have been variously labeled as deviant, perverted, aberrant, or abnormal. More recently, the terms *variant* and *paraphilia* (PAIR-uh-FIL-ē-uh) (meaning "beyond usual or typical love") have been used to describe these somewhat uncommon types of sexual expression. These labels are less emotionally laden and judgmental and therefore preferable to the others. However, in our experience of dealing with and discussing variant sexual behaviors, only one common characteristic seems to stand out. Simply stated, each behavior in its fully developed form is not typically expressed by most people in our society. Therefore, we have elected to use the term **atypical** to describe these behaviors.

There are several points we should raise about atypical sexual expression in general before we discuss specific behaviors. First, like many other sexual expressions discussed in this book, the behaviors singled out in this chapter represent extreme points on a continuum. In reality atypical sexual behaviors exist in many gradations, ranging from mild, infrequently expressed tendencies to full-blown, regularly manifested behaviors. Although these are *atypical* behaviors, many of us may recognize some degree of such behaviors or feelings within ourselves—perhaps manifest at some point in our lives, or mostly repressed, or emerging only in very private fantasies.

A second point has to do with the state of our knowledge about these behaviors. In most of the discussions that follow, the person who shows the atypical behavior is assumed to be male. For some of the activities discussed in this chapter, this is an accurate portrayal. In other instances, however, the tendency to assume that males are predominantly involved may be influenced by the somewhat biased nature of differential reporting and prosecution. Female exhibitionism, for example, is far less likely to be reported than is a similar kind of behavior in a male. John Money (1981) has suggested that atypical sexual behavior may be decidedly more prevalent among males than females because male *erotosexual differentiation* (the development of sexual arousal in response to various kinds of images or stimuli) is more complex than that of the female and subject to more errors. In support of this contention, Money has noted that nature seems to have more difficulty producing males than females. For example, males have higher prenatal and postnatal mortality rates, and masculine development will not even occur unless triggered by sufficient levels of male hormones because the basic developmental pattern is female (see Chapter 3). Money has theorized that these facts may demonstrate that males are more susceptible to a variety of errors affecting survival, sexual differentiation, and erotosexual differentiation.

A third consideration is the impact of atypical behaviors both on the person who exhibits them and on others to whom they may be directed. People who manifest unusual sexual behaviors often depend on these acts for sexual satisfaction. The behavior is an end in itself. It is also likely that their unconventional behavior will alienate others. Consequently, these people often find it very difficult to establish satisfying relationships with partners. Instead, their sexual expression may assume a solitary, driven, even compulsive quality. Research also has suggested that such acts may have harmful effects on others (Altrocchi, 1980). People who are unwilling recipients of variant sexual expressions, such as peeping or exposing, may be psychologically traumatized. They may feel they have been violated or that they are vulnerable to physical abuse, and they may develop fears that such unpleasant episodes will recur. This is one reason many of these behaviors are illegal. On the other hand, many people who encounter such acts are not adversely affected. Because of this and because many of these behaviors do not generally involve physical or sexual contact with another, many authorities view them as minor sex offenses (sometimes called "nuisance" offenses). However, recent evidence suggests that some people progress from nuisance offenses to more serious forms of sexual abuse, a finding that may lead to a reconsideration of their classification as minor. We examine this issue in more detail later in this chapter and the next.

In the following pages, we discuss in some detail six of the most frequently expressed atypical behaviors in our society. We examine how each of these behaviors is expressed, some of the common characteristics of those exhibiting it, and the various factors thought to contribute to its development. More severe forms of sexual victimization, such as rape, incest, and child abuse, are discussed in Chapter 21.

Exhibitionism

Exhibitionism, often called "indecent exposure," refers to behavior where an individual (usually a male) exposes his genitals to an involuntary observer (usually an adult woman or female child) (Freund, 1990; Marshall et al., 1991). Typically, a man who has exposed himself obtains sexual gratification by masturbating shortly thereafter, using mental images of the observer's reaction to increase his arousal (Blair & Lanyon, 1981). Some men may fantasize about exposing themselves or replay mental images from previous episodes while having sex with a willing partner (Money, 1981). Still others may have orgasm triggered by the very act of exposure, and a few may masturbate while exhibiting themselves (American Psychiatric Association, 1987). The reinforcement of associating sexual arousal and orgasm with the actual act of exhibitionism, or with mental fantasies of exposing oneself, contribute significantly to the maintenance of exhibitionistic behavior (Blair & Lanyon, 1981). Exposure may occur in a variety of locations, most of which allow for easy escape. Subways, relatively deserted streets, parks, and cars with a door left open are common places for exhibitionism to occur. However, sometimes a private dwelling may be the scene of an exposure, as revealed in the following account:

One evening I was shocked to open the door of my apartment to a naked man. I looked long enough to see that he was underdressed for the occasion and then slammed the door in his face. He didn't come back. I'm sure my look of total horror was what he was after. But it is difficult to keep your composure when you open your door to a naked man. (Authors' files)

Certainly, many of us have exhibitionistic tendencies — we may go to nude beaches, parade before admiring lovers, or wear provocative clothes or scanty swim wear. However, such behavior is considered appropriate by a society that in many ways exploits and celebrates the erotically portrayed human body. The fact that legally defined exhibitionistic behavior involves generally unwilling observers sets it apart from the more acceptable variations of exhibitionism just described.

Our knowledge of who displays this behavior is based almost exclusively on studies of the arrested offender, a fact that may make the sample unrepresentative.

Exhibitionists often want to elicit reactions of shock, disgust, fear, or terror. The best response is to calmly ignore the person and casually go about your business.

This sampling problem is common to many forms of atypical behavior that are defined as criminal. From the available data, however limited, it would appear that most people who exhibit themselves are adult males in their 20s or 30s, and over one-half are or have been married. They are often very shy, nonassertive people who feel inadequate and insecure and suffer from problems with intimacy (Blair & Lanyon, 1981; Maletzky & Price, 1984; Marshall, 1989; Marshall et al., 1991). They may function quite efficiently in their daily lives and be commonly characterized by others as "nice, but kind of shy." Their sexual relationships with others are likely to have been quite unsatisfactory. Many were reared in atmospheres characterized by puritanical and shame-inducing attitudes toward sexuality.

What influences a person to engage in exhibitionism? What do you think might motivate such behavior? Give this some thought before reading on.

There are a number of hypotheses about the factors that influence the development of exhibitionistic behavior. Many of the individuals manifesting such behavior may have such powerful feelings of personal inadequacy that they are afraid to reach out to another person out of fear of rejection (Goldstein et al., 1986). Their exhibitionism may thus be a limited attempt to somehow involve others, however fleetingly, in their sexual expression. Limiting contact to briefly opening a raincoat before dashing off minimizes the possibility of overt rejection. Some men who expose themselves may be looking for affirmation of their masculinity. Others, feeling isolated and unappreciated, may simply be seeking attention they desperately crave. A few may feel anger and hostility toward people, particularly women, who have failed to notice them or who they believe have caused them emotional pain. In these circumstances exposure may be a form of reprisal, designed to shock or frighten the people they see as the source of their discomfort. It is not uncommon to observe exhibitionism in emotionally disturbed, intellectually disabled, or mentally disoriented individuals. In these cases the behavior may reflect a limited awareness of what society defines as appropriate actions, a breakdown in personal ethical controls, or both.

In contrast to the public image of an exhibitionist as one who lurks about in the shadows, ready to grab hapless victims and drag them off to ravish them, the majority of men who engage in exhibitionism limit their illegal behaviors to exposing themselves (American Psychiatric Association, 1987; Davison & Neale, 1986; Langevin et al., 1979; Radar, 1977). Yet the word *victim* is not entirely inappropriate, in that observers of such exhibitionistic episodes may be emotionally traumatized by the experience (Cox, 1988; Marshall et al., 1991). Some may feel that they are in danger of being raped or otherwise harmed. A few, particularly young children, may develop negative feelings about genital anatomy from such an experience.

Investigators have noted that some people who expose themselves, probably a small minority, may actually physically assault their victims. Furthermore, it also seems probable that some men who engage in exhibitionism progress from exposing themselves to more serious offenses such as rape and child molesting. In a one-of-a-kind study, Gene Abel (1981), a Columbia University researcher, conducted an in-depth investigation of the motives and behavior of 207 men who were admitted perpetrators of a variety of sexual offenses, including child molesting and rape. This research is unique in that all participants were men outside the legal system who voluntarily sought treatment after being guaranteed confidentiality. Abel found that 49% of the rapists in his sample had histories of other types of variant sexual behavior, generally preceding the onset of rape behavior. The most common of these were child molestation, exhibitionism, voyeurism, incest, and sadism. A more recent study of 274 Canadian sex offenders, all adult males, revealed that most had engaged in multiple types of variant sexual behavior, including paraphilias and more serious forms of sexual victimization, such as child molestation and rape. Overall, the 274 subjects admitted to 7,677 total incidents of sexual offenses, an average of 28 incidents per offender. These findings suggest that "paraphiliacs tend to have multiple types of sexual aberrations as well as a high frequency of deviant acts per individual" (Bradford et al., 1992, p. 104). These findings do not imply that people who engage in activities like exhibitionism and voyeurism will inevitably develop into child molesters and rapists. However, it seems clear that some people may progress beyond these relatively minor acts to far more severe patterns of sexual aggression.

While perhaps all of us would like protection against being sexually used without our consent, it seems unnecessarily harsh and punitive to imprison people manifesting exhibitionistic behavior, particularly first-time offenders. In recent years, at least in some locales, there has been some movement toward therapy as an alternative to incarceration. Often therapy is directed toward fostering feelings of personal worth and adequacy, together with supporting the development of more acceptable modes of sexual expression (Marshall et al., 1991). Various behavioral therapy methods are also sometimes used to help the offender gain control over his urge to expose (Maletzsky, 1987; Rooth & Marks, 1974). In addition, antiandrogen drugs (see Chapter 6) have been used effectively to block the inappropriate sexual arousal patterns underlying exhibitionistic behavior (Emmanuel et al., 1991; Rousseau et al., 1990). An extensive review of the literature revealed that men undergoing treatment for exhibitionism can sometimes successfully modify their behavior and overcome their inclinations to exhibit their genitals to involuntary observers (Kilman et al., 1982). However, in some individuals the urge to exhibit themselves is very powerful and thus difficult, if not impossible, to overcome (Money, 1986; Money & Lamacz, 1990).

What do you think would be an appropriate way to respond to exhibitionism? How do you think you would react personally to such an encounter? Give this some thought before reading on.

Most people who express exhibitionistic behavior want to elicit reactions of shock, disgust, fear, or terror. Although it may be difficult not to react in any of these ways, a better response to exhibitionism is to calmly ignore it and casually go about your business. Of course, it is also important to report such acts to the police as soon as possible.

Obscene Phone Calls

The characteristics of people who make obscene phone calls seem to be similar to those of people who engage in exhibitionism. They typically experience sexual arousal when their victims react in a horrified or shocked manner, and many masturbate during or immediately after a "successful" phone exchange. As one extensive study has indicated, people who manifest this behavior are typically male, and they often suffer from pervasive feelings of inadequacy and insecurity (Nadler, 1968). Obscene phone calls are frequently the only way they can find to have sexual exchanges. However, when relating to the other sex they frequently show greater anxiety and hostility than do people inclined toward exhibitionism, as revealed in the following account:

One night I received a phone call from a man who sounded quite normal until he started his barrage of filth. Just as I was about to slam the phone down, he announced, "Don't hang up. I know where you live (address followed) and that you have two little girls. If you don't want to find them all mangled up, you will hear what I have to say. Furthermore, I expect you to be available for calls every night at this time." It was a nightmare. He called night after night. Sometimes he made me listen while he masturbated. Finally, I couldn't take it any longer, and I contacted the police. They were unable to catch him, but they sure scared him off in short order, thank heaven. I was about to go crazy. (Authors' files)

Fortunately, a caller rarely follows up his verbal assault with a physical attack on his victim.

What might be the best way to handle obscene phone calls? What kinds of strategies might help end this form of harassment? Take a few moments to think about your answers to these questions before reading on.

Information about how to deal with obscene phone calls is available from most local phone company offices. Because they are commonly besieged by such queries, you may need to be persistent in your request. A few tips are worth knowing; they may even make it unnecessary to seek outside help.

First, quite often the caller has picked your name at random from a phone book or perhaps knows you from some other source and is just trying you out to see what kind of reaction he can get. Your initial response is critical in determining his subsequent actions. He wants you to be horrified, shocked, or disgusted; thus, the best response is usually not to react overtly. Slamming down the phone may reveal your emotional state and provide reinforcement to the caller. Simply set it down gently and go about your business. If the phone rings again immediately, ignore it. Chances are he will seek out other, more responsive victims.

Other tactics may also be helpful. One, used successfully by a former student, is to feign deafness. "What is that you said? You must speak up. I'm hard of hearing, you know!" Setting down the phone with the explanation that you are going to another extension (which you never arrive at) may be another practical solution. Finally, screening calls via an answering machine may also prove helpful. The caller is likely to hang up in the absence of an emotionally responding person.

If you are persistently bothered by repeated obscene phone calls, you may need to take additional steps. There are several possible ways of dealing with the situation. Your telephone company should cooperate in changing your number to an unlisted one at no charge. Some people report success with tapping a ring or some other metallic object against the mouthpiece to simulate connecting a recording device. Others cover the mouthpiece partially, announcing, "He is on the line again, Officer." It is probably not a good idea to heed the commonly given advice to blow in the mouthpiece with a police whistle (which may be quite painful and even harmful to the caller's ear) because you may end up receiving the same treatment from your caller.

Voyeurism

Voyeurism (voi-YUR-iz-um) refers to deriving sexual pleasure from looking at the naked bodies or sexual activities of others, usually strangers, without their consent (American Psychiatric Association, 1987). A degree of voyeurism is socially acceptable (witness the popularity of R- and X-rated movies and magazines like *Playboy* and *Playgirl*), and it is sometimes difficult to determine when voyeuristic behavior becomes a problem. To qualify as atypical sexual behavior, voyeurism must be preferred to sexual relations with another or indulged in with some risk (or both). People who engage in this behavior are often most sexually aroused when the risk of discovery is high, and this may explain why most are not attracted to places like nudist camps and nude beaches, where looking is acceptable (Tollison & Adams, 1979).

The common term *Peeping Tom* correctly implies that this behavior is typically, although not exclusively, expressed by males (Davison & Neale, 1990). Voyeurism includes peering in bedroom windows, stationing oneself by the entrance to women's bathrooms, and boring holes in the walls of public dressing rooms. Some men have elaborate routes that they travel several nights a week, being occasionally rewarded by a glimpse through a window of bare anatomy or, rarely, a scene of sexual interaction.

Most people inclined toward voyeurism tend to have some of the same characteristics as people who expose themselves (Gebhard et al., 1965; Langevin et al., 1979). They often have poorly developed sociosexual skills, with strong feelings of inferiority and inadequacy, particularly as directed toward potential sexual partners. They tend to be very young men, usually in their early 20s (Davison & Neale, 1990). They rarely "peep" at someone they know, preferring strangers instead. Voyeurism is not typically associated with other antisocial behavior. Most individuals who engage in such activity are content merely to look, preferring to keep their distance. However, in some instances people who engage in voyeurism go on to more serious offenses such as burglary, arson, assault, and even rape (Abel, 1981; Gebhard et al., 1965; Langevin et al., 1985; MacNamara & Sagarin, 1977).

It is difficult to isolate specific influences that trigger voyeuristic behavior, particularly because so many of us demonstrate these tendencies in a somewhat more controlled fashion. The adolescent or young adult male who displays this behavior is often an individual who feels great curiosity about sexual activity (as many of us do) but at the same time feels very inadequate or insecure. Peeping becomes a vicarious fulfillment because he may be unable to consummate sexual relationships with others without experiencing a great deal of anxiety. Some people may also have their voyeuristic behavior reinforced by feelings of power and superiority over those they secretly observe.

Sadomasochism

We have chosen to discuss sadism and masochism under the common category **sadomasochistic** (SĀ-dō-MAS-ō-kiz-tic) **behavior** (also known as SM) because they are two variations of the same phenomenon, the association of sexual expression with pain. Furthermore, the dynamics of the two behaviors are similar and overlapping. Technically, sadomasochism can be defined as obtaining sexual arousal through giving or receiving physical or mental pain (Gebhard et al., 1965).

Labeling behavior as sadistic or masochistic is complicated because many people enjoy some form of aggressive interaction during sex play (such as "love bites") for which the label SM seems inappropriate. Alfred Kinsey and his colleagues (1953) found that 22% of the males and 12% of the females in his sample responded erotically to stories with SM themes. Furthermore, over 25% of both sexes reported erotic response to receiving love bites during sexual interaction. Morton Hunt's survey (1974) found that 10% of the males and 8% of the females in his sample (under age 35) reported obtaining sexual pleasure from SM activities during interaction with a partner. Although sadomasochistic practices have the potential for being physically dangerous, most people who indulge in these behaviors generally stay within mutually agreed-on limits, often confining their activities to mild or even symbolic SM acts with a trusted partner. In mild forms of sadism, the pain inflicted may often be more symbolic than real. For example, a willing partner may be "beaten" with a feather or a soft object designed to resemble a club. Under these conditions, the receiving partner's mere feigning of suffering is sufficient to induce sexual arousal in the individual inflicting the symbolic pain.

People with masochistic inclinations may be aroused by such things as being whipped, cut, pierced with needles, bound, or spanked. The degree of pain one must experience to achieve sexual arousal varies from symbolic or very mild to, on rare occasions, severe beatings or mutilations. Masochism is also reflected in individuals who achieve sexual arousal as a result of "being held in contempt, humiliated, and forced to do menial, filthy, or degrading service" (Money, 1981, p. 83). There is a common misconception that any kind of pain, physical or mental, will sexually arouse a person with masochistic inclinations. This is not true. The pain must be associated with a staged encounter whose express purpose is sexual gratification.

Many individuals who engage in SM activities do not confine their participation to exclusive sadistic or masochistic behaviors. Some are able to alternate between the two roles, often out of necessity, because it may be difficult to find a partner who prefers only to inflict or to receive pain. A majority of these people seem to prefer one or the other role, but some may be equally comfortable in either role (Moser & Levitt, 1987; Spengler, 1977; Weinberg et al., 1984).

There are some indications that individuals with sadistic tendencies are less common than their masochistic counterparts (Gebhard et al., 1965). This imbalance may reflect a general social script — certainly, it is more virtuous to be punished than to be the perpetrator of either physical or mental aggression toward another. A person who needs severe pain as a prerequisite to sexual response may have difficulty finding a cooperative partner. Consequently, such individuals may resort to causing their own pain by burning, mutilating, or hanging themselves (which sometimes causes death). A person who needs to inflict intense pain in order to achieve sexual arousal may find it very difficult to find a willing partner, even for a price. We occasionally read of sadistic assaults against unwilling victims: the classic sex murder is often of this nature. In these instances orgasmic release may be produced by the homicidal violence itself.

Many people in contemporary Western societies view SM in a very negative light. This is certainly understandable, particularly when those who see it this way regard sexual sharing as a loving, tender interaction between partners who wish to exchange pleasure, not pain. However, much of this negativity stems from a generalized societal perception of SM activities as perverse forms of sexual expression involving severe pain, suffering, and degradation. There is a further assumption that many individuals caught up in such activities are victims rather than willing participants.

Martin Weinberg, Colin Williams, and Charles Moser maintained that these conceptions of SM were misleading "because they are not based on close examination of what the majority of SM participants actually do and how they interpret their own behavior" (1984, p. 379). These researchers suggested that the traditional medical model of SM as a pathological condition is based on a limited sample of individuals who practice SM activities and who also have personality disorders or severe emotional problems that cause them to come to the attention of clinicians. In contrast to this clinically biased sample, Weinberg and his colleagues conducted extensive fieldwork in nonclinical environments, in which they interviewed a variety of SM participants and observed their behaviors in many different settings. They did find that some of these individuals engaged in "heavy SM" that was consistent with traditional conceptions. However, for the majority of these participants, SM was an activity that involved elements of dominance and submission, role playing, and consensuality and "was simply a form of sexual enhancement which they voluntarily and mutually choose to explore" (p. 388).

What factors might motivate a person to engage in SM activity? See what ideas you can come up with before reading on.

A review of recent sociological literature has confirmed that many people who engage in SM activities are motivated by a desire to experience dominance and/or submission rather than pain (Weinberg, 1987). Studies of sexual behavior in other species reveal that many nonhuman animals engage in what might be labeled combative or pain-inflicting behavior before coitus. Some theorists have suggested that such activity has definite neurophysiological value in that it heightens many of the biological accompaniments of sexual arousal, including blood pressure, muscle tension, and hyperventilation (Gebhard et al., 1965). It may be that a number of people engage in this behavior because, for a variety of reasons (such as guilt, anxiety, or apathy), they need additional nonsexual stimuli to achieve sufficient arousal. It has also been suggested that resistance or tension between partners enhances sex and that SM is just a more extreme version of this ordinary principle (Tripp, 1975).

It has also been suggested that SM may provide participants with an escape valve and an opportunity to temporarily assume a role that may be the exact opposite of the rigidly controlled, restrictive one they manifest in their everyday, public lives. Thus, there are "men who may be brokers of immense political, business or industrial power by day, and submissive masochists begging for erotic punishment and humiliation by night" (Money, 1984, p. 169). Conversely, individuals who are normally meek may welcome the temporary opportunity to assume a powerful, dominant role within the carefully structured role-playing of SM.

Ray Baumeister (1988) has theorized that sexual masochism may represent an attempt to escape from high levels of self-awareness. According to this perspective, when a person is engaging in masochistic activity, his or her awareness of thoughts and feelings is "replaced by focus on the immediate present and on bodily sensations" (p. 28). Such escape from self-awareness may enhance sexual pleasure by blocking out unwanted thoughts and feelings, particularly those that may induce anxiety, guilt, or feelings of inadequacy or insecurity. We hope that future research will clarify the applicability of this theoretical interpretation of why some people associate masochistic acts with enhanced sexual pleasure.

Clinical case studies of individuals who engage in SM sometimes reveal early experiences that may have established a connection between sex and pain. For example, being punished for engaging in sexual activities (such as masturbation) might result in a child or adolescent associating sex with pain. A child might even experience sexual arousal while being punished — for example, getting an erection or lubricating when one's pants are pulled down and a spanking is administered (spanking is a common SM activity). Paul Gebhard and his colleagues (1965) reported one unusual case in which a man developed a desire to engage in SM activities following an episode during his adolescence in which he experienced a great deal of pain while a fractured arm was set without the benefit of anesthesia. During the ordeal he was comforted by an attractive nurse, who caressed him and held his head against her breast in a way that created a strong conditioned association between sexual arousal and pain.

Many people, perhaps the majority, who participate in SM are not dependent on these activities to achieve sexual arousal and orgasm. Those for whom it is only an occasional pursuit may find that at least some of its excitement and erotic allure stems from the fact that it represents a marked departure from more conventional sexual practices. Other people who indulge in SM acts may have acquired strong negative feelings toward sex, often believing it is sinful and immoral. For such people masochistic behavior provides a guilt-relieving mechanism: Either they get their pleasure simultaneously with punishment, or they first endure the punishment to entitle them to the pleasure. Similarly, people who indulge in sadism may be punishing partners for engaging in anything so evil. Furthermore, people who have strong feelings of personal or sexual inadequacy may resort to sadistic acts of domination over their partners to temporarily alleviate these feelings of inferiority.

Fetishism

Fetishism (FET-ish-iz-um) refers to sexual behavior in which an individual becomes sexually aroused by focusing on an inanimate object or a part of the human body. As has been the case with the behaviors we have considered so far, it is often difficult to draw the line between normal activities that may have fetishistic overtones and those that are genuinely atypical. Many people are erotically aroused by the sight of undergarments and certain specific body parts, such as legs, buttocks, thighs, and breasts. Many men and some women may use articles of clothing and other paraphernalia as an accompaniment to masturbation or sexual activity with a partner. It is only when a person becomes focused on these objects or body parts to the exclusion of everything else that the term *fetishism* is truly applicable. In some instances a person may be unable to experience sexual arousal and orgasm in the absence of the fetish object. In other situations where the attachment is not so strong, sexual response may occur in the absence of the object but often with diminished intensity. For some people fetish objects serve as substitutes for human contact and are dispensed with if a partner becomes available. Some common fetish objects include women's lingerie, shoes (particularly high-heeled), boots (often affiliated with SM themes of domination), hair, stockings (especially black mesh hose), and a variety of leather, silk, and rubber goods (American Psychiatric Association, 1987; Davison & Neale, 1990).

How does fetishism develop? Perhaps the most common way is through incorporating the object or body part, often through fantasy, in a masturbation sequence where the reinforcement of orgasm strengthens the fetishistic association. This is a kind of classical conditioning in which some object or body part becomes associated with sexual arousal. This pattern of conditioning was demonstrated some years ago by Rachman (1966), who created a mild fetish among male subjects under laboratory conditions by repeatedly pairing a photograph of women's boots with erotic slides of nude females. The subjects soon began to show sexual response to the boots alone. This reaction also generalized to other types of women's shoes.

Only rarely does fetishism develop into an offense that might harm someone. Occasionally, an individual may commit burglary to supply an object fetish, as in the following account:

Some years ago we had a bra stealer loose in the neighborhood. You couldn't hang your brassiere outside on the clothesline without fear of losing it. He also took panties, but bras seemed to be his major thing. I talked to other women in the neighborhood who were having the same problem. This guy must have had a roomful. I never heard anything about him being caught. He must have decided to move on because the thefts stopped all of a sudden. (Authors' files)

Burglary is the most frequent serious offense to be associated with a fetishistic inclination. Uncommonly, a person may do something bizarre such as cut hair from an unwilling person. In extremely rare cases, a man may murder and mutilate his victim, preserving certain body parts for fantasy – masturbation activities.

Transvestism

The term **transvestism** is applied to behaviors whereby an individual obtains sexual excitement from putting on the clothes of the other sex. In defining transvestism it is important to emphasize the differences among people who cross-dress to experience sexual arousal, female impersonators (who cross-dress to entertain), male homosexuals who occasionally "go in drag" (cross-dress), and transsexuals who, as we discussed in Chapter 3, cross-dress to obtain a partial sense of physical and emotional completeness rather than for sexual titillation.

A range of behaviors comprises the category of transvestism. Some people prefer to don the entire garb of the other sex. This is often a solitary activity, occurring privately in their homes. Occasionally, a person may go out on the town while so attired, but this is unusual. Generally, the cross-dressing is a momentary activity, producing sexual excitement that often culminates in gratification through masturbation or sex with a partner. In many cases of transvestism, a person becomes aroused by wearing only one garment, perhaps a pair of panties or a brassiere. There is a strong element of fetishism in this behavior, which has led many writers to link the two conditions. A distinguishing feature of transvestism is that the article is actually worn instead of just being viewed or fondled.

It would appear that in the majority of instances it is men who are attracted to transvestism. This seems to be true of all contemporary societies for which we have data. However, there have been a few isolated cases of female transvestism in the clinical literature (Stoller, 1982). Some writers contend that transvestism is more common among females than we are aware of because the opportunities for cross-dressing without detection are obviously much greater for women. While this may be true, we know that males who cross-dress are not aroused by wearing ambiguous or unisex attire. Rather, they prefer feminine apparel that only women wear, such as panties, bras, or nylons. Consequently, we might expect women engaging in transvestism to become sexually aroused while wearing something

Transvestism is usually a solitary activity expressed by a heterosexual male in the privacy of his own home.

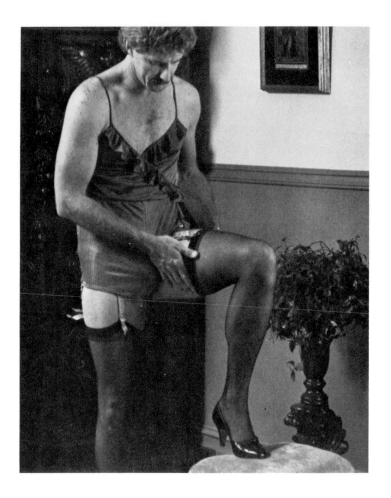

strictly identified with males, such as a pair of jocky undershorts or a jock strap rather than jeans or a flannel work shirt. These behaviors among women are extremely rare in the clinical literature.

Several studies of both clinical and nonclinical populations have indicated that cross-dressing occurs primarily among married men with predominantly heterosexual orientations (Buhrich, 1976; Prince & Bentler, 1972; Stoller, 1971; Talamini, 1982; Wise & Meyer, 1980). A survey of 504 subscribers to the magazine *Transvesti* provided some of the best evidence we have about the characteristics of individuals who practice transvestism. Ninety percent of the respondents described themselves as heterosexual, and 64% were married at the time of the survey. Only 22% had never been married. Roughly 25% had experienced sexual contact with the same sex at some time in their lives, a percentage comparable to that reported for the general male population. Approximately 75% said their fathers modeled a typically masculine role. Seventy-five percent of these men had not sought treatment for their atypical pattern of sexual arousal (Prince & Bentler, 1972). Another survey of over 200 members of an Australian male transvestite club also revealed that the majority of the respondents were married and heterosexual in orientation (Buhrich, 1976). The majority of these individuals had begun cross-dressing before they were nine years old. As adults, most practiced their atypical behavior once or twice a month.

The majority of men in both studies just described had not told their wives about their interest in cross-dressing prior to marriage, primarily because they thought their urge to engage in such behavior would disappear once they settled into married life. This did not happen, and most of the wives eventually found out. Of the 80% of the wives of the *Transvesti* respondents who made this unsettling discovery about their husbands, 23% were accepting, 20% antagonistic, and the rest somewhere between these two extremes. More recent data have suggested that most wives only tolerate rather than support the cross-dressing of their husbands (Weinberg & Bullough, 1986 & 1988). Even when the initial reaction of the partner is not particularly negative, resentment and disgust may sometimes develop, as revealed in the following account:

The first time my husband asked if he could wear my panties I thought he was joking. When he put them on, I could see that he wasn't kidding around. Actually, we had a real good session that night, and I guess this kind of blunted my concern. After a while it just started really bugging me. It seems like we can never just make love without his first putting on my underthings. Now I'm sick and tired of it. The whole thing seems real weird. (Authors' files)

What do you think might be some of the factors associated with the development of transvestism? Could there be some similarity in how this condition and fetishism evolve? Think about these questions for a couple of minutes before reading on.

Like fetishism and some other atypical behaviors, the development of transvestism often reveals a pattern of conditioning. Reinforcement, in the form of arousal and orgasm, may accompany cross-dressing activities at an early point in the development of sexual interest, as illustrated in the following anecdote:

When I was a kid, about 11 or 12, I was fascinated and excited by magazine pictures of women modeling undergarments. Masturbating while looking at these pictures was great. Later, I began to incorporate my mother's underthings in my little masturbation rituals, at first just touching them with my free hand, and later putting them on and parading before the mirror while I did my hand-job. Now, as an adult, I have numerous sexual encounters with women that are quite satisfying without the dress-up part. But, I still occasionally do the dress-up when I'm alone, and I still find it quite exciting. (Authors' files)

Some males who engage in transvestism reported having dressed up as girls during their childhood for a variety of reasons (Bullough et al., 1983). Occasionally, parents initiated this behavior by dressing their young son in dainty girl's clothes because they thought it was "cute" or because they wanted a little girl rather than a boy. Often the case histories of men who engage in transvestism have revealed that as boys they were punished by being forced to dress in girl's clothes (Stoller, 1977). This attempt to punish by humiliation is sometimes the first step toward transvestism.

Occasionally, transvestism is a behavior of the heterosexual male who is striving to explore the feminine side of his personality, an often difficult effort in a society that extols the "Marlboro Man" image. In essence, such men create two separate worlds — the one dominated by the masculine image they exhibit on the job and in most relationships and the private world of dress-up at home, where they can express their gentle, sensuous "feminine" selves.

Anthropologist Robert Munroe (1980) has noted that transvestism tends to appear most frequently in cultures where males shoulder a greater portion of the economic burden than their female counterparts. Munroe has speculated that in some instances transvestism may allow men in these cultures to temporarily unburden themselves from perceived pressures of responsibility by escaping into the female role, complete with feminine attire and behaviors.

Most people who engage in transvestism are not inclined to seek professional help. Even when therapy is undertaken, it is unlikely that the behavior will be appreciably altered (Wise & Meyer, 1980).

Other Atypical Behaviors

The six paraphilias discussed in the preceding pages, while among the most common of the atypical sexual behaviors, by no means exhaust the list of variant ways in which humans express their sexuality. Money (1984), who has written extensively about the nature and origins of the paraphilias, has categorized over 30 of these conditions. In this final section, we briefly describe six paraphilias not previously discussed. In addition, Table 20.1 lists several less common forms of variant sexual expression not discussed below.

Zoophilia

Zoophilia (zoo-FIL-ē-uh), sometimes called *bestiality*, involves sexual contact between humans and animals. Eight percent of the males and almost 4% of the females in Kinsey's sample populations reported having had sexual experience with animals at some point in their lives. The frequency of such behavior among males was highest for those raised on farms (17% of these men reported experiencing orgasm as a result of animal contact). The animals most frequently involved in sex with humans are calves, sheep, donkeys, large fowl (ducks and geese), dogs, and cats. Males are most likely to have contact with farm animals and to engage in penile–vaginal intercourse or to have their genitals orally stimulated by the animals (Hunt, 1974; Kinsey et al., 1948). Women are more likely to have contact with household pets involving the animals licking their genitals or the woman masturbating a male dog. Less commonly, some adult women have trained a dog to mount them and engage in coitus (Gendel & Bonner, 1988; Kinsey et al., 1953).

Sexual contact with animals is commonly only a transitory experience of young people to whom a sexual partner is inaccessible or forbidden (Money, 1981). Most adolescent males and females who experiment with zoophilia make a transition to normal adult sexual relations with human partners. Occasionally, an adult may engage in such behavior as a "sexual adventure" or because a human partner is unavailable (Tollison & Adams, 1979). True zoophilia exists only when sexual contact with animals is preferred regardless of what other forms of sexual expression are available. Such behavior, which is quite rare, is generally only expressed by people with deep-rooted psychological problems or distorted images of the other sex. For example, a man who has a pathological hatred of women

Miscellaneous Paraphilias	T A B L E 20.1

Apotemnophilia: Being sexually excited by the fantasy or reality of being an amputee. This behavior is often accompanied by obsessional scheming to convince a surgeon to perform a medically unnecessary amputation.

Acrotomophilia: Being sexually aroused by a partner who is an amputee.

Asphyxiophilia: A condition in which a person, most commonly an adolescent male, employs partial asphyxiation, as by hanging or strangulation, in order to achieve and maintain sexual arousal or as a way to facilitate or enhance orgasm.

Gerontophilia: The condition in which a young adult may become sexually aroused primarily or exclusively via sexual conduct with a much older person.

Mysophilia: Being sexually turned on by something soiled or filthy, such as smelly underwear or used menstrual pads.

Narratophilia: The need to listen to erotic narratives (stories) in order to achieve sexual arousal.

Pictophilia: Being dependent on sexy pictures for sexual response.

Somnophilia: Being dependent on the fantasy or actuality of intruding on and fondling a sleeping stranger in order to achieve sexual arousal.

may be attempting to express his contempt for them by choosing animals in preference to women.

Necrophilia

Necrophilia (nek-rō-FIL-ē-uh) is a rather bizarre and extremely rare sexual variation in which a person obtains sexual gratification by viewing or having intercourse with a corpse. This paraphilia appears to occur exclusively among males, who may be driven to remove freshly buried bodies from cemeteries or to seek employment in morgues or funeral homes (Tollison & Adams, 1979). However, the vast majority of people who work in these settings do not have tendencies toward necrophilia.

Due to the obvious difficulties associated with gaining access to dead bodies, some men with necrophilic preferences limit their atypical behavior to contact with simulated corpses. Some prostitutes cater to this desire by powdering themselves to produce the pallor of death, dressing in a shroud, and lying very still during intercourse. Any movement on their part may inhibit their customers' sexual arousal.

People who engage in necrophilia almost always manifest severe emotional disorders. Such men may see themselves as sexually and socially inept and may both hate and fear women. Consequently, the only "safe" woman may be one whose lifelessness represents the epitome of a nonthreatening, totally subjugated sexual partner (Mathis, 1972; Stoller, 1977).

Klismaphilia

Klismaphilia (klis-ma-FIL-ē-uh) is a very unusual variant in sexual expression in which an individual obtains sexual pleasure from receiving enemas. Less commonly, the erotic arousal may be associated with giving enemas. The case histories of many individuals who express klismaphilia reveal that as infants or young children they were frequently administered enemas by concerned and affectionate mothers. This association of loving attention with the erotic pleasure of anal stimulation may eroticize the experience for some people so that as adults they may manifest a need to receive an enema as a substitute for or necessary prerequisite to genital intercourse.

Coprophilia and Urophilia

Coprophilia (cop-rō-FIL-ē-uh) and **urophilia** (yoo'-rō-FIL-ē-uh) refer to activities in which people obtain sexual arousal from contact with feces and urine, respectively. Individuals who exhibit coprophilia achieve high levels of sexual excitement from watching someone defecate or by defecating on someone. In rare instances they may achieve arousal when they are defecated on. Urophilia is expressed by urinating on someone or being urinated on. This activity has been referred to as "water sports" and "golden showers." There is no consensus opinion as to the origins of these highly unusual paraphilias.

Frotteurism

Frotteurism (fro-TUR-izm) may be a fairly common paraphilia that goes largely unnoticed. It involves an individual, usually a male, who obtains sexual pleasure by pressing or rubbing against a fully clothed female in a crowded public place, such as an elevator, bus, or subway. The most common form of contact is between the man's clothed penis and a woman's buttocks or legs. Often the contact seems to be inadvertent, and the woman who is touched may not notice or pay little heed to the seemingly casual contact. On the other hand, she may feel victimized and angry. In rare cases she may reciprocate (Money, 1984).

The man who engages in frotteurism may achieve arousal and orgasm during the act. More commonly, he incorporates the mental images of his actions into masturbation fantasies at a later time. Men who engage in this activity have many of the characteristics manifested by those who practice exhibitionism. They are frequently plagued with feelings of social and sexual inadequacy. Their brief, furtive contacts with strangers in crowded places allow them to include others in their sexual expression in a safe, nonthreatening manner.

Sexual Addiction: Fact, Fiction, or Misnomer?

In recent years both the professional literature and the popular media have directed considerable attention to a condition commonly referred to as sexual addiction. The idea that people may become dominated by insatiable sexual needs has been around for a long time, exemplified by the terms *nymphomania*, applied to women, and *satyriasis* or *Don Juanism*, applied to men. Many professionals have traditionally reacted negatively to these labels, suggesting they are disparaging terms likely to induce unnecessary guilt in individuals who enjoy an active sex life. Furthermore, it has been argued that one cannot assign a label implying excessive sexual activity when there are no clear criteria for establishing what constitutes "normal" levels of sexual involvement. Nevertheless, the concept of compulsive sexuality achieved a heightened legitimacy with the publication of Patrick Carnes's book, *The Sexual Addiction* (1983), recently retitled *Out of the Shadows: Understanding Sexual Addiction*. A more recent Carnes book, *Don't Call It Love* (1991), based on a survey of nearly 1000 so-called sex addicts, provides additional insights into his conceptualization of sexual addiction.

According to Carnes many of the people who engage in some of the atypical or paraphilic behaviors described in this chapter (as well as victimization behaviors, such as child molesting, described in Chapter 21) are manifesting the outward symptoms of a process of psychological addiction in which feelings of depression, anxiety, loneliness, and worthlessness are temporarily relieved through a sexual high not unlike the high achieved by mood-altering chemicals such as alcohol or marijuana. Carnes suggested that a typical addiction cycle progresses through four phases: Initially, the sex addict enters a trancelike state of *preoccupation* in which obsessive thoughts about a particular sex behavior, such as exposing oneself, creates a consuming need to achieve expression of the behavior. This intense preoccupation induces certain *ritualistic* behaviors, such as running a regular route through a particular neighborhood where previous incidents of exposing have occurred. Their ritualistic behaviors tend to further intensify the sexual excitement that was initially aroused during the preoccupation phase. The next phase is the actual expression of the *sexual act,* in this case exposing oneself. This is followed by the final phase, one of *despair,* in which sex addicts are overwhelmed by feelings of worthlessness, depression, and anxiety. One way to minimize or anesthetize this despair is to start the preoccupation again. With each repetitive cycle, the addiction behavior becomes more intense and unmanageable, "thus confirming the basic feelings of unworthiness that are the core of the addict's belief system" (Carnes, 1986, p. 5).

Carnes's conception of the sexual addict has generated considerable attention within the professional community, but those who support his interpretation are in the minority. Many sexologists do not believe that sexual addiction should be a distinct diagnostic category because it is both rare and lacking in distinction from other compulsive disorders, such as gambling and eating disorders (Levine & Troiden, 1988; Money, 1988). This position is reflected in a decision not to include a category encompassing hyperactive sexuality in the most recent version of the *Diagnostic and Statistical Manual* (DSM III – R) of the American Psychiatric Association (the most widely accepted system for classifying psychological disorders).

A number of professionals acknowledge the validity of the arguments against the addiction concept but nevertheless recognize that some people may become involved in patterns of excessive sexual activity that reflect a lack of sexual control. Noteworthy in this group is sexologist Eli Coleman (1986), who prefers to describe these behaviors as symptomatic of sexual compulsion rather than addiction. Coleman has had extensive clinical experience with clients who view their sexual behavior as having elements of preoccupation, lack of control, and self-destructiveness. He has integrated information gleaned from these experiences with existing theoretical notions about compulsive behaviors to derive his own interpretation of how sexual compulsivity develops.

According to Coleman a person manifesting excessive sexual behaviors typically has grown up in a home characterized by severe "intimacy dysfunction," such as child abuse or neglect. An individual who suffers this trauma develops feelings of shame, unworthiness, inadequacy, loneliness, and low self-esteem. Such negative feelings, which continue into adolescence and adulthood, cause great psychological pain. This pain then causes the person to search for a "fix," or an agent that has pain-numbing qualities, such as alcohol, certain foods, gambling, or, in this instance, sex. Indulging oneself in this fix produces only a brief respite from the psychological pain that returns in full force, thus triggering a greater need to engage in these behaviors to obtain temporary relief. Unfortunately, these repetitive, compulsive acts soon tend to be self-defeating in that they compound feelings of shame and lead to intimacy dysfunction by interrupting the development of normal, healthy interpersonal functioning. "Thus the sexual compulsivity results from and becomes a symptom of intimacy dysfunction" (Coleman, 1986, p. 9).

We can expect that professionals within the field of sexuality will continue to debate for some time how to diagnose, describe, and explain problems of excessive or uncontrolled sexuality. Even as this discussion continues, professional treatment programs for compulsive or addictive sexual behaviors have emerged throughout the nation. For example, Carnes has established in a suburban Minneapolis hospital a treatment program that integrates principles of family therapy with the methods of Alcoholics Anonymous. Data pertaining to treatment outcomes for this and similar programs are still too limited to judge the therapeutic effectiveness of these approaches. Besides formal treatment programs, a number of community-based, self-help organizations have surfaced throughout the United States. Some of these groups are Sex Addicts Anonymous, Sexaholics Anonymous, Sexual Compulsives Anonymous, and Sex and Love Addicts Anonymous.

Summary

Atypical sexual behavior refers to a variety of sexual activities that in their fully developed form are statistically uncommon in the general population.

Such behaviors exist in many gradations, ranging from mild, infrequently expressed tendencies to full-blown, regularly manifested behaviors.

Exhibitionism

Exhibitionism refers to behavior where an individual, almost always a male, exposes his genitals to an involuntary observer.

People who exhibit themselves are usually young, adult males who have strong feelings of inadequacy and insecurity.

Sexual relationships with others, either past or present, are likely to be unsatisfactory.

Gratification is usually obtained when the reaction to exhibitionism is shock, disgust, or fear. Physical assault is generally not associated with such behavior.

Obscene Phone Calls

The characteristics of individuals who make obscene phone calls are similar to those who engage in exhibitionism.

While there may be an element of vicious verbal hostility in obscene phone calls, the caller rarely follows up his verbal assault with a physical attack on his victim.

Voyeurism

Voyeurism refers to obtaining sexual pleasure from looking at the exposed bodies or sexual activities of others, usually strangers.

People inclined toward voyeurism, typically males, are often sociosexually underdeveloped, with strong feelings of inferiority and inadequacy.

Sadomasochism

Sadomasochism (SM) may be defined as obtaining sexual arousal through receiving or giving physical and/or mental pain.

The majority of participants in SM view it as a form of sexual enhancement that they voluntarily and mutually choose to explore.

Individuals who engage in SM behavior may be seeking additional nonsexual stimuli to achieve sufficient arousal. They may also be acting out of deeply rooted beliefs that sexual activity is sinful and immoral.

For some participants SM may act as an escape valve whereby they are able to temporarily step out of the rigid, restrictive roles they play in their everyday lives.

Individuals who engage in SM sometimes describe early experiences that may have established a connection between sex and pain.

Fetishism

Fetishism is a form of atypical sexual behavior wherein an individual obtains arousal by focusing on an inanimate object or a part of the human body.

Fetishism often is a product of conditioning, where the fetish object becomes associated with sexual arousal through the reinforcement of masturbation-produced orgasm.

Transvestism

Transvestism involves obtaining sexual excitement by cross-dressing. It is usually a solitary activity, expressed by a heterosexual male in the privacy of his own home.

Like fetishism, transvestism often evolves through an early pattern of conditioning. In this case reinforcement in the form of arousal and orgasm accompanies cross-dressing activities.

Some males who engage in transvestism were dressed up as girls by parents who thought it was cute or who wanted a girl, or perhaps as a form of punishment.

Transvestism may allow some men to unburden themselves from the pressures of responsibility by temporarily escaping into the female role.

Other Atypical Behaviors

Zoophilia involves sexual contact between humans and animals; it occurs most commonly as a transitory experience of young people to whom a sexual partner is inaccessible or forbidden. Necrophilia involves obtaining sexual gratification by viewing or having intercourse with a corpse. Klismaphilia involves achieving sexual pleasure from receiving enemas. Coprophilia and urophilia refer, respectively, to obtaining sexual arousal from contact with feces or urine. Frotteurism involves obtaining sexual pleasure by pressing or rubbing against a person in a crowded public place.

Sexual Addiction: Fact, Fiction, or Misnomer?

The concept of sexual addiction suggests that some people who engage in excessive sexual activity are manifesting the outward symptoms of a process of psychological addiction in which feelings of depression, anxiety, loneliness, and worthlessness are temporarily relieved through a sexual high.

Many sexologists do not believe that sexual addiction should be a distinct diagnostic category because it is both rare and lacking in distinction from other compulsive disorders, such as gambling and eating disorders.

⤚ *Thought Provokers* ⤙

1. Which of the atypical sexual behaviors discussed in this chapter do you find to be the most unacceptable? Why?

2. Do you think that social and cultural conditioning contributes to the much higher incidence of atypical sexual behavior among men than among women? Explain.

3. People typically are much less concerned about female exhibitionism than they are about male exhibitionism. For example, if a woman were seen observing a man undressing in front of a window, the man might be accused of being an exhibitionist. However, if the roles were reversed and the woman was undressing, the man would probably be labeled a voyeur. What do you think of this sex-based inconsistency in labeling these behaviors?

Suggested Readings

Carnes, Patrick (1983). *Out of the Shadows: Understanding Sexual Addiction.* Minneapolis: Compcare Publications. A detailed description of Carnes's conception of the sexual addict diagnostic criteria, causes, and treatment. A thought-provoking and controversial book.

Docter, Richard F. (1988). *Transvestites and Transsexuals: Toward a Theory of Cross-Gender Behavior.* New York: Plenum. An excellent source of information about transvestism and transsexualism. Docter, a psychologist, details a thoughtful, theoretical conception of the development of transvestism.

Earle, Ralph; and Crow, Gregory (1989). *Lonely All the Time.* New York: Pocket Books. This book, written by two respected clinicians, explores the causes and symptoms of sexual addiction and the needs and concerns of an addict's family members.

Gebhard, Paul H.; Pomeroy, Wardell B.; Gagnon, John H.; and Christenson, Cornelia V. (1965). *Sex Offenders: An Analysis of Types.* New York: Harper & Row (also available in paperback from Bantam Books, 1967). Offers a thorough analysis of many types of atypical sexual behaviors that come under the criminal code. Contains excellent information about a variety of psychosocial factors implicated in the development of these behaviors.

Stoller, Robert (1977). "Sexual Deviations." In F. Beach (Ed.), *Human Sexuality in Four Perspectives.* Baltimore: Johns Hopkins Press (also available in paperback from the same publisher, 1978). Provides a review of several common atypical sexual behaviors with accompanying case examples.

Weinberg, Thomas; and Kamel, G. W. Levi (Eds.) (1983). *Studies in Sadomasochism.* Buffalo, N.Y.: Prometheus Books. A collection of 18 articles that provides a considerable amount of thought-provoking information about sadomasochism.

Wilson, Glenn (Ed.) (1986). *Variant Sexuality: Research and Theory.* Baltimore: Johns Hopkins University Press. An excellent sourcebook that contains a wealth of information about the varied theoretical explanations for why people engage in atypical sexual behavior.

The maiden I wronged in Peninsular
days . . .
You may prate of your prowess in lusty
times,
But as years gnaw onward you blink
your bays
And see too well your crimes!
Afeared she fled, and with heated head
I pursued to the chambers she called
her own;
When might is right no qualms deter,

And having her helpless and alone
I wreaked my will on her.
So, to-day I stand with a God-set
brand
Like Cain's, when he wandered from
kindred's ken . . .
I served through the war what made
Europe free,
I wived me in peace-year. But, hid
from men,
I bear that mark on me.

Thomas Hardy San Sebastian (1813)

A person becomes a sexual victim when she or he is deprived of free choice and coerced or forced to comply with sexual acts under duress. Sexual victimization takes many forms; for example, a teenager may threaten to break up with his girlfriend if she doesn't "put out," or an adult may feel compelled to perform a personally repugnant sexual act because his or her partner has threatened to "find it somewhere else." In this chapter we focus on three particularly abusive and exploitive forms of sexual victimization: rape, the sexual abuse of children, and sexual harassment. All these behaviors involve strong elements of coercion, sometimes even violence.

Rape

Rape, which is commonly thought of as sexual relations forced by a man upon an unconsenting woman, has occurred throughout history. The legal definition of rape varies from state to state; however, most laws define rape as sexual intercourse that occurs under actual or threatened forcible compulsion that overcomes the earnest resistance of the victim. Within this broad category are several specific kinds of rape. **Statutory rape** refers to intercourse with a person who is under the age of consent. (The age of consent varies in different states but is generally 18.) Statutory rape is considered to have occurred regardless of the apparent willingness of the underage partner. **Stranger rape** is the rape of a person by an unknown assailant. **Acquaintance rape,** or **date rape,** is committed by someone who is known to the rape victim.

Unfortunately, it is exceedingly difficult to obtain accurate statistics on the number of rapes and rape survivors in America due to the reluctance of many people to report being assaulted. Estimates of how many rapes of women are reported to the police or other public agencies range from 10% (Seligmann, 1984) to as high as 50% (Feldman-Summers & Norris, 1984). However, a number of contemporary surveys have provided some indication of the numbers of American women who have experienced attempted or completed rape. The sample size and victim percentages from five of these studies are as follows: 19% of 3700 women (Crooks, 1991); 30% of 518 women (Ward et al., 1991); 24% of 500 women (DeVisto et al., 1984); 15% of 3187 women (Koss et al., 1987); and 25% of 404 women (Mims & Chang, 1984). If we add other forms of sexual abuse to the rape statistics, it becomes clear that an alarming number of American men sexually victimize women. A survey of 190 male college students found that a significant number had engaged in a variety of sexually coercive behaviors ranging from grabs and feels (61%) to forced intercourse (15%). Men who were inclined to engage in these coercive acts tended to view relations between the sexes as adversarial, considered the use of force to be legitimate in certain sexual situations, and viewed women as manipulative and untrustworthy (Rapaport & Burkhart, 1984). Another survey of several hundred male college students revealed that 25% of the respondents reported attempting or completing forced intercourse (Kanin, 1967).

In still another study, 175 male college students were administered two questionnaires, one designed to assess callous sexual attitudes and the other to reveal how frequently the men had engaged in sexually coercive acts ranging from verbal pressure to physical force. The results indicated that a strong majority admitted to using one or more of the following coercive tactics to have sex with a date: drugs or alcohol (69%), verbal coercion (40%), anger (13%), and actual or threatened physical force (33%). The results further indicated a strong positive relationship between callous attitudes and sexually coercive behavior. The authors of this study concluded that "the socialization of the macho man, if it does not directly produce a rapist, appears to produce calloused sex attitudes toward women and rape and proclivities toward forceful and exploitive tactics to gain sexual access to reluctant women" (Mosher & Anderson, 1986, p. 91).

In the following sections, we look at some of the attitudes and beliefs people hold about rape, the psychosocial bases of rape, and the aftermath of rape.

Attitudes and Beliefs About Rape

Many contemporary attitudes, issues, and laws regarding rape stem from the historical status of women. Until very recently, rape was institutionalized by law as a violation of male property rights. For example, in ancient Babylonian law, a woman was considered to be her father's possession until sold to her husband for a bride price. The amount of payment for the bride was contingent on her virginity. Therefore, rape of an unmarried woman was considered theft of the father's market price for his daughter. In England at the close of the thirteenth century, punishment that had previously been reserved only for the forcible rape of a virgin was extended to include the rape of a married woman by a man other than her husband. The law still maintained that a husband could not legally rape his own wife because she was his possession and sexual relations were his right (Brownmiller, 1975).

Both rape and the threat of rape have served to control female sexuality and behavior for centuries. Throughout history, if a woman was to expect even a modicum of protection or recourse against rape, her sexual behavior had to remain within narrowly defined limits; that is, she must have been a virgin or a monogamous wife. The "protection" of women from rape has often been a way of preserving exclusive male sexual rights to chaste women. In the following discussions of contemporary attitudes and beliefs regarding rape, we will see that, although significant changes have occurred in how people perceive and interpret the act of rape, some of these earlier archaic and dehumanizing conceptualizations are still apparent in present-day viewpoints.

Attitudes Toward Rape in American Society. Males in our society often learn that power, aggressiveness, and getting what one wants are all part of the proper male role (Mosher & Tomkins, 1988). Furthermore, they frequently learn that they should seek sex and expect to be successful in this endeavor. It is widely recognized that many males receive a great deal of pressure from their peers to acquire sexual experiences. When this pressure is combined with callous attitudes toward women and a belief that "might makes right," we have a cultural foundation for rape and other acts of sexual coercion.

Research has revealed that some rapists have distorted perceptions of their interactions with the women they rape, both before and during the assault. They may believe that women want to be coerced into sexual activity, even to the extent of being physically abused (Abel, 1981; Beal & Muehlenhard, 1987). These distorted beliefs may help the rapist justify his reprehensible behavior; his acts are not rape but rather "normal" courtship behavior. Such a man might meet a woman in a bar, take her for a drive, park, and attempt intercourse, which he would force if she resisted. Even if he has to "slap her around" to convince her to have sex, he believes he is only acting in accordance with her wishes and expectations. Afterward, he may have little or no guilt about his behavior because in his own mind it was not rape. Of 114 imprisoned rapists who were interviewed, over 80% did not see themselves as rapists. Those who did not deny having sexual contact with their accusers used a variety of explanations to make them appear guilty, including such distorted perceptions as women say no when they mean yes, women are seducers who "lead you on," and most women eventually relax and enjoy it (Scully & Morolla, 1984). Unfortunately, there seems to be considerable support for such attitudes in the general population. Many people believe that roughing up a woman is acceptable, that many women get turned on by such activity, and that it is impossible to rape a healthy woman against her will (Burt, 1980; Gilbert et al., 1991; Malamuth et al., 1980). Thus, a rapist may find both the impetus for and support of his behavior within the fabric of society.

False Beliefs About Rape. As attitudes have begun to change and research has correspondingly improved, many past beliefs about the crime of rape, the person who rapes, and the person who is raped have been shown to be inaccurate. However, many false beliefs about rape still persist (Fonow et al., 1992; Reilly et al., 1992). In the following paragraphs, we consider some of the more common of these misconceptions.

False Belief: "You Can't Thread a Moving Needle." The belief that women can always successfully ("if they *really* want to") resist a rape attempt is false, for several important reasons. First, men are usually physically larger and stronger than women. They have been encouraged to develop their physical strength and agility throughout their lives. Boys' rough-and-tumble play and athletics encourage them to be physically forceful and confident. On the other hand, stereotypical female gender-role conditioning trains a woman to be passive — the recipient rather than the initiator of action. Smaller stature is a physical reality, but the way women feel about and use their bodies is learned. Muscles may be admired on men, but they are typically considered unattractive on women. Soft skin and physical weakness are feminine. Furthermore, a woman's clothing and shoes typically inhibit her efforts to fight or to run. Yet these are all exterior symbols of passivity, compliance, and submission that "good girls" are encouraged to incorporate in their behavior. (Paradoxically, "good girls" are also supposed to actively defend their "honor"!) These elements of gender-role conditioning limit the options a woman believes she has in resisting a rape attack. It simply may not be in her repertoire of behavior to be offensive or aggressive or to resort to socially unacceptable behaviors to defend herself against the person attacking her.

Second, the man who rapes chooses the time and place. He has the element of surprise on his side. The fear and intimidation a woman usually experiences when attacked works to the assailant's advantage. His use of weapons, threats, or physical force further encourages her compliance. Furthermore, many rapes are perpetrated by two or more attackers.

Courses on rape prevention sometimes advise women to be passive when attacked, on the assumption that resistance or fighting might increase the potential

ETHICAL/LEGAL ISSUES IN HUMAN SEXUALITY

Rape and the Legal System

Significant changes in rape laws and services to those who are raped have occurred in the past several years. Legal reform is taking place in the areas of redefinition of the crime and revision of the rules of evidence during rape trials. A few important changes have been made in many states. One is the provision that the *threat* of force is sufficient coercion — that is, that personal injury does not have to occur for an act to be considered rape. Second, the accuser's prior sexual conduct is *not* admitted as evidence in the trial. Third, the accused man's past sexual offenses may be discussed in court. A fourth reform recognizes the woman's right not to have her name printed in the newspaper.

A number of professionals who deal with sexual victimization have expressed concern about a legal system that generally requires evidence of clearly demonstrable force before labeling a sexually coercive act rape. The degree of force applied by the rapist is often judged in the context of the amount of resistance exerted by the victim. Thus under the laws of many states a rape is not construed as having occurred unless a person physically resists, even if that person does not consent to sexual intercourse. Cindy Turk and Charlene Muehlenhard (1991) recently argued that rape laws should be changed to move away from the force requirement. "One way would be for the law to demand that defendants interpret

a person's no to mean no, rather than to demand that victims use reasonable resistance. Under such a law, verbally expressing objections to sexual intercourse would be sufficient to make it clear that one does not consent to sexual intercourse, and anyone who ignored these objections would be guilty of rape" (p. 1). This suggested change in rape laws to an *expressing objections* rather than a *force* criterion seems particularly desirable in view of evidence that one of the most common ways for men to engage in sex with an unwilling partner is to simply ignore her refusals and proceed without force (Muehlenhard & Linton, 1987; Rapaport & Burkhart, 1984).

Recently, women who have been raped have begun to fight back not just in criminal court but also in civil court. Several have successfully sued their assailants. Property owners and institutions may also be found liable and forced to pay damages through civil court procedures. In one landmark case in California, a woman who had been raped in her own apartment won the right in appeals court to bring charges against her landlord for negligence in failing to provide adequate safety measures. College and university officials have also been defendants in civil litigation proceedings that contended that they had failed to provide adequate protection for women students who had been raped on campus (Keen, 1991). These developments in rape litigation

may prompt insurance companies to demand stricter enforcement of security measures before providing coverage for property owners and institutions.

In addition, the viewpoint that a husband should be allowed unrestricted sexual access to his wife has come under sharp attack in recent years in this country. By 1992 a substantial majority of states and the District of Columbia had established statutes permitting the prosecution of husbands who rape their wives. However, in a majority of the states that have established these statutes, a husband can be prosecuted for raping his wife only under certain circumstances, such as an extraordinarily violent assault. Only a minority of states (17 at last count) provide wives full legal protection against being raped by their husbands (Muehlenhard et al., 1991). A major study by Diana Russell, published in her book *Rape in Marriage* (1982), provided strong evidence that one out of every seven American women who have ever been married has been raped by a husband or ex-husband. Lenore Walker, author of *The Battered Woman* (1979), found that 60% of 430 battered women she interviewed had been raped by their husbands. These grim statistics reveal the need for legislation to make spousal rape a crime in all states of the union and to provide wives full legal protection against such sexual violence.

for violence. Yet such compliance often results in difficulties for a rape survivor if she prosecutes. Without clear signs of resistance on her part, chances of a conviction are often reduced.

Statistically, rape murders are rare. However, serious physical injury does occur in a small minority of cases. Two studies demonstrated no relationship between a rape survivor's resistance tactics and subsequent injury (Cohen, 1984;

Quinsey & Upfold, 1985). There was no evidence that physical resistance increased or decreased the likelihood of injury. However, women who physically resist their attackers may experience less postassault depression than those women who did not use physical force in an effort to escape their attackers (Amick & Calhoun, 1987; Bart & O'Brien, 1984 & 1985).

False Belief: Many Women "Cry Rape." Historically, women may have chosen to "cry rape" because they were severely condemned when they overstepped the boundaries of virgin or wife. Today false accusations rarely occur, and they are even less frequently carried as far as prosecution. Given the difficulties that exist in reporting and prosecuting a rape, few women or men could successfully proceed with an unfounded rape case.

False Belief: "All Women Want to Be Raped." Novels and films perpetuate the notion that women want to be raped. Typically, fictionalized rape scenes begin with a woman resisting her attacker, only to melt into passionate acceptance. In the rare cases where male-to-male rape is shown, as in the film *Deliverance,* the violation and humiliation of rape is more likely to be truthfully portrayed.

The fact that some women do occasionally have rape fantasies is sometimes used to support the idea that women want to be sexually assaulted. However, there are several factors that clearly discredit this belief. It is important to understand the distinction between an erotic fantasy and a conscious desire to lose one's free will to someone whose intent is to inflict harm. In a fantasy a person still retains ultimate control. But a basic element in an actual rape is the terrifying powerlessness of the woman. A fantasy carries no threat of physical harm or death; a rape does. Furthermore, many women have internalized ambivalent "good girl versus bad girl" messages about expressing their sexuality. Fantasizing about intense seduction can be a way for a woman to feel accepting of her sexual feelings without having to assume active responsibility for them.

An extremely negative consequence of the belief that women want to be raped is that many rape survivors may believe that the rape was basically their fault. Even when they may have simply been in the wrong place at the wrong time, a pervasive sense of personal guilt may remain. Unfortunately, when a woman continues to feel self-blame following a rape, the man who raped her is still indirectly maintaining some control over her life. Rape self-help groups or personal counseling may help a woman resolve these feelings.

False Belief: "It Could Never Happen to Me." Many women may think that, because they are too young, too old, too fat, married, "not that kind of girl," exceedingly cautious, or possess any of a variety of unique characteristics, they will not be raped. This belief may promote a false sense of security. It also tends, once again, to place blame for the rape on some characteristic or behavior of the woman herself. The truth is that any female is a potential victim.

Even women who are never raped live daily with the threat of a sexual attack. The possibility of rape makes it more difficult for women to lead independent lives. Although rape can happen to virtually any woman, there are some things that can be done to reduce (but not eliminate) the likelihood of its occurrence. Some suggestions for prevention, and for coping with a rape if it cannot be prevented, appear in the box "Dealing With Rape" on pages 646–647.

Boston women protest against night assaults. These women, and others like them, have helped challenge societal assumptions about rape.

The Psychosocial Bases of Rape

Why do men rape women? This is a question that researchers have attempted to answer for many years. Until very recently many of these investigative efforts were hindered by both a narrow conceptualization of rape and inadequate research methods. Our awareness of the characteristics and motivations of men who rape has been based, until recently, largely on studies of men convicted of the crime, a sample group that probably represents fewer than 1% of all males who rape. We cannot say with certainty that men who rape without being prosecuted and convicted demonstrate traits similar to those of convicted rapists. In fact, there is good reason to believe that convicted rapists are less educated, are more inclined to commit other antisocial or criminal acts, and tend to be more alienated from society than are rapists who do not pass through the criminal justice system at all (Smithyman, 1979).

Many of the men incarcerated for rape offenses appear to have a strong proclivity toward violence that is often reflected in their act of rape. This fact, along with certain assumptions about male – female relationships, resulted in a number of feminist writers taking the position that rape is not sexually motivated but rather an act of power and domination (Brownmiller, 1975). This viewpoint prevailed for a number of years, during which time the sexual component of rape and other assaultive offenses was de-emphasized. However, recent research has made it clear that while power and domination are often involved in sexual coercion, such acts are also frequently motivated by a desire for sexual gratification. Our awareness of this fact has been enhanced by several excellent recent studies of the incidence and nature of sexual coercion among populations of nonincarcerated males. Particularly noteworthy in this regard is the growing body of data pertaining to acquaintance or date rape, which we discuss shortly.

It is becoming increasingly apparent that rape is more often a product of socialization processes that occur within the fabric of "normal" society than of severe pathology of the individual rapist (Akers, 1985; Boeringer et al., 1991; Fonow et al., 1992; Gilbert et al., 1991). Strong support for the view that rape is in many ways a cultural phenomenon was provided by the research of Peggy Reeves Sanday (1981), an anthropologist who compared the incidence of rape in 95 societies. Sanday's important research revealed that women in America are several hundred times more likely to be raped than are women in certain other societies. Her research indicated that the incidence of rape in a given society is influenced by several important cultural factors: the nature of relations between the sexes, the status of women, and the attitudes boys acquire during their developmental years. Sanday found that societies with a high incidence of rape, which she labeled "rape-prone," tolerate and even glorify masculine violence. These societies encourage men and boys to be aggressive and competitive and to view physical force as a natural and exemplary expression of their nature. Men in such societies generally have special gathering spots, like a men's club or corner tavern, and women generally have less power in the economic and political aspects of life. Men in these societies also frequently demean the judgments of women as well as remaining aloof from child rearing and household duties, which they may consider to be "women's work."

In contrast, Sanday reported on 44 "rape-free" societies, where there is virtually no rape. Women and men in rape-free societies share power and authority, and both contribute equally to the community welfare. In addition, children of both sexes in these societies are raised to value nurturance and to avoid aggression and violence. With this cultural framework in mind, let us take a closer look at some of the aspects of male socialization within our own culture that contribute to the occurrence of rape and other forms of sexual coercion.

To obtain a better sense of the socialization processes that shape rapists, let us examine some comparative analyses of populations of rapists and nonrapists. Eugene Kanin (1985) reported the results of an in-depth comparison study of 71 self-disclosed date rapists (male college students who forced their female dates to engage in coitus) with a control sample of 227 nonrapists (also male college students). This important study provided several noteworthy findings.

1. The rapists were not sexually deprived — in fact, their average levels of current sexual activity and previous experiences were much greater than those of the control subjects. However, the rapists were over twice as likely to report dissatisfaction with their sex lives than were the nonrapists (79% versus 32%).

2. The rapists were much more exploitive of women in their attempts to achieve sexual contact. For example, almost 80% reported attempting to get a female drunk to gain sexual access, whereas only 23% of the nonrapists reported similar behavior. In addition, 86% of the rapists had falsely expressed love for this purpose, compared to 25% of the nonrapists.

3. There was strong evidence that the rapists were much more likely to have a peer group that legitimized "rough sex" and labeled certain types of females as legitimate targets for rape. Over half the rapists (54%) indicated that they believed their peer-group reputations would be enhanced if they tried to rape a "bar pickup," whereas only 16% of the nonrapists embraced this repugnant attitude. Eighty-one percent of the rapists thought that they would enhance

their reputations by raping a known "teaser," whereas 40% of the nonrapists expressed this belief; and 73% versus 39% thought that their reputations would be enhanced by raping a woman who economically exploited men.

4. The rapists also reported considerably more peer-group pressure to acquire sexual experience than did the nonrapists. Almost half the rapists had been involved with their peers in a sequential sex episode with one female (frequently called a "gang bang"). In addition, significantly more rapists than nonrapists had experienced sex with a woman recommended for such purposes by a friend.

5. Finally, 86% of the rapists indicated believing that rape is justified under some circumstances, whereas only 19% of the nonrapists embraced this reprehensible viewpoint.

Another study found similar correlates of male sexual aggression in a sample of 237 subjects. In this investigation sexual aggression was defined as physically forced sexual activity carried to the point where the woman was crying, fighting, or screaming. Three variables were shown to distinguish men who reported sexually aggressive behavior from those who did not. Having male friends who were sexually aggressive was the most predictive factor, followed by having served in the armed forces in Vietnam and by seeing women as legitimate targets for sexual assault. Seventy-five percent of the men in the sample who were characterized by all three of these factors had engaged in sexually aggressive behavior (Alder, 1985). Moreover, these studies of samples of nonincarcerated male rapists supported the findings of UCLA researcher Neil Malamuth (1981, 1982, & 1986), who found that a man's perception of peer-group acceptance of rape was the best predictor of his inclination to engage in rape, followed by the presence of callous attitudes toward women.

As the evidence about cultural influences accumulates, we are beginning to understand why the United States is among the societies identified by Sanday as rape-prone. Sadly, many American men seem to be socialized to view aggression as a legitimate means to achieve sexual access to women, and to treat with callous disregard women's rights to maintain the integrity and privacy of their bodies. "Sexual assault is a logical extension of a system in which men are taught to fight for what they want, whereas women are taught to be passive and yielding and to put men's needs above their own" (Muehlenhard et al., 1991, p. 161). Men who are products of a peer subculture that openly legitimizes and supports these attitudes and behaviors are particularly prone to sexually victimize women.

The Impact of Sexually Violent Media. A number of researchers have provided compelling evidence that sexually violent media (films, books, magazines, and videotapes) may contribute to some rapists' assaultive behaviors. Neil Malamuth and James Check (1981) recruited 271 college men and divided them into two groups. Subjects in one group were shown movies with nonviolent erotic themes. Participants in the other group were shown R-rated movies in which men committed sexual violence against women who eventually experienced a transformation from victim to willing erotic partner — a theme reinforcing the culturally perpetuated myth that women welcome violence. Several days after the film-viewing sessions all subjects completed a questionnaire, the results of which demonstrated that the men who viewed the violent erotica were much more inclined to have an accepting attitude toward sexual violence than those subjects exposed to consensual, nonviolent erotic themes. The results of this study, considered collectively with a number of other investigations, led Malamuth to conclude that "certain types of violent porn do encourage attitudes of violence against women" (quoted in Japenga, 1984, p. 1).

Research has demonstrated that exposure to violent erotica can decrease one's sensitivity to the tragedy of rape and the damaging impact on the victim, increase the viewer's likelihood of condoning aggressive acts against females and accepting a variety of rape myths (for instance, that women want to be coerced into sexual activity), and perhaps most alarming, increase the willingness of a man to admit that he would commit a rape if he thought he could get away with it (Donnerstein & Linz, 1984; Linz, 1989; Linz et al., 1992; Scott & Schwalm, 1988). Furthermore, a number of investigators have demonstrated that repeated exposure to sexually explicit materials and other films where violence and sex are associated may result in males becoming desensitized to violence (particularly against women), more callous in their attitudes toward women, and less inclined to see rape as a crime (Donnerstein & Linz, 1984; Gray, 1984).

Much of the research in this area has indicated that mere exposure to erotic materials may not be the key ingredient in increasing men's aggressiveness toward women. Rather, the violent nature of some of this material may be the causative ingredient (Scott & Schwalm, 1988). Several researchers have provided evidence that men who rape have "sexualized" violence. Two separate studies compared the erectile responses of matched groups of rapists and nonrapists to taped descriptions of rape and of mutually consenting sexual activity (Abel et al., 1977; Barbaree et al., 1979). Both experiments found that rapists obtained erections while listening to violent scenes of rape while their nonrapist counterparts did not. Descriptions of consenting sexual activity produced similar levels of arousal in both groups of men. Another study compared the responses of convicted rapists and non – sex offenders to audio descriptions of a variety of sexual activities, ranging from consenting heterosexual contact to rape. As in the two previously mentioned experiments, the description of rape produced greater arousal in the rapists than in the nonrapists. However, unlike those in the earlier studies, the rapists in this experiment manifested significantly less arousal than did the nonrapists to descriptions of consenting sex (Quinsey et al., 1984).

A recent study involving 222 male, nonoffender, college students provided further evidence of the association between sex and violence. Each subject was administered an attitude survey that assessed his use of pornography and self-reported likelihood of committing rape or using sexual force. Nonviolent pornography was used by 81% of these men during the previous year, whereas 35% used sexually violent pornography during the same time span. Those subjects who reported experience with sexually violent pornography were considerably more likely to indicate a likelihood of raping or using sexual force against a woman than were subjects who had limited their exposure to nonviolent pornography. The authors of this study concluded that "the specific fusion of sex and violence in some pornographic stimuli and in certain belief systems may produce a propensity to engage in sexually aggressive behavior" (Demaré et al., 1988, p. 140).

Another study demonstrated that sex offenders (rapists and child molesters) were more likely than nonoffenders to report having used sexually explicit materials during their adolescent and adult years (Marshall, 1988). This same research also revealed that rapists and child molesters often reported "frequent use of these materials while preparing themselves to commit an offense" (p. 267).

Of related interest are two studies that compared the circulation rates of adult sex magazines such as *Playboy, Penthouse,* and *Hustler* and rape rates by state. Both investigations reported a strong positive relationship between rape rates and circulation rates by state; that is, those states with high rape rates tended to have high sex magazine circulation rates (Scott & Schwalm, 1988; Straus & Baron, 1983).

Do you believe that these studies provide clear evidence that reading adult sex magazines increases one's inclination to commit rape? Is there another interpretation of the demonstrated positive relationship between these two events? Think about these questions before reading on.

We must be cautious in concluding from these results that an increase in the circulation of sex magazines necessarily causes an increase in rape rates. Another plausible explanation is that "in those areas with high rape rates the culture is such that people subscribe or purchase adult magazines more often than in areas with low rape rates" (Scott & Schwalm, 1988, p. 248).

Characteristics of Men Who Rape. Besides the different socialization processes that often distinguish rapists from nonrapists, a number of other characteristics have been linked to men who rape. Several studies have noted that rapists, particularly those who committed stranger rapes, are frequently socially inept, have difficulty establishing meaningful interpersonal relationships, have low self-esteem, are guilt-ridden, and feel inadequate (Baxter et al., 1984; Groth & Burgess, 1977; Levin & Stava, 1987; Marshall & Barbaree, 1984; Pepitone-Rockwell, 1980). To the extent that rapists lack social competence, they may be unable to establish satisfying heterosexual relationships, which may increase their negative attitudes toward women and their inclination to perpetrate acts of sexual violence (Marshall & Barbaree, 1984). However, this interpretation may be inaccurate. Several recent studies have found no support for the hypothesis that rapists have poorer social skills than nonrapists. Two studies of incarcerated rapists found that these men did not differ significantly in levels of social competence from imprisoned non–sex offenders (Segal & Marshall, 1985; Stermac & Quinsey, 1986). Another study of nonincarcerated university men also found that social competence was unrelated to rape behavior (Muehlenhard & Falcon, 1990).

Other research suggests rapists may also be characterized by a tendency to hold rather conservative attitudes toward a variety of sexual topics, such as masturbation and the appropriateness of family nudity (Allford & Brown, 1985). Men who embrace traditional gender roles, particularly the element of male dominance, are more likely than men who do not accept these attitudes to commit rape (Harney & Muehlenhard, 1991; Muehlenhard & Falcon, 1990). Many rapists were subjected to sexual abuse during childhood (Delin, 1978; Groth, 1979; Petrovich & Templer, 1984; Seghorn et al., 1987). Alcohol use may also contribute to rapists' behavior; rapists have often been drinking just prior to assaulting their victims (Ladouceur & Temple, 1985; Muehlenhard & Linton, 1987).

Some particularly illuminating evidence pertaining to the characteristics of men who rape was provided by Gene Abel (1981), a Columbia University researcher who developed an elaborate system of confidentiality that allowed over

200 New York men who had engaged in a variety of sexual victimization behaviors to participate in his research without being identified by the criminal justice system. Abel found that some of the rapists in his sample had extensive histories of fantasizing about rape and violence long before becoming rapists. Such a man might have begun masturbating frequently to the accompaniment of rape fantasies as early as his mid-teens. As he continues this pattern, his deviant urges to rape become progressively stronger. Ultimately, his attempts to resist acting on his impulses fail, and he becomes a rapist in fact. Earlier we suggested that some men sexualize the violence of rape. These observations by Abel suggest at least one mechanism whereby this effect may occur. Approximately half the rapists in Abel's sample had histories of committing other types of sexual offenses, most notably sexual abuse of children, exhibitionism, voyeurism, and sadism. This suggests that the behavior of at least some rapists may escalate through a series of progressively more violent sexual offenses.

Rapists may also be motivated by displaced anger toward women (Abel, 1981; Marshall, 1981; Yates et al., 1984). For example, a man who is unable to express his anger directly to his wife or girlfriend may inappropriately and violently direct that anger at another woman by raping her.

Types of Rapes and Rapists. One fact that has become clear in our evolving understanding of the psychosocial bases of rape is that there is no singular pattern that characterizes the violent act of rape or the men who perpetrate this crime. Rather, there is a wide range of individual differences among rapists, both in the motivations underlying the sexual assault and in how that assault is committed. From this perspective we can differentiate among four types of rape: anger rape, power rape, sadistic rape, and sexual gratification rape. The typology for the first three types of rape in this categorization was developed by Nicholas Groth and William Hobson (1983), based on over 16 years of extensive clinical experience with more than 1000 rapists in a variety of institutional and community settings.

Anger Rape. According to Groth and Hobson, "The anger rape is an unpremeditated, savage, physical attack prompted by feelings of hatred and resentment" (1983, p. 163). The assailant is motivated to vent his rage and contempt, and sexual gratification has little or nothing to do with his assaultive behavior. Anger rape is often characterized by the use of physical violence far in excess of the amount necessary to force sexual submission. Many anger rapists exhibit a pattern of long-term hostility toward women. They perceive the rape as an act of revenge in which they attempt to get even for the "put-downs," humiliation, and rejection they believe they have suffered at the hands of women.

The victim of anger rape is usually a total stranger to the perpetrator. She is often subjected to physical injury and extreme degradation. She may be forced to engage in acts such as fellatio and anal intercourse, and sometimes foreign objects are used to penetrate her vagina or anus. The anger rapist often has difficulty obtaining sufficient sexual arousal to achieve and sustain an erection, and he usually does not find the rape to be sexually gratifying.

As mentioned previously, an anger rape is not premeditated but rather occurs impulsively when some triggering event, like a conflict with a lover or spouse, causes a man to reach a breaking point under an accumulated load of anger and resentment. An anger rapist's assaults tend to be episodic in nature, which is to say they occur on an irregular schedule, often separated by months or even years.

Power Rape. A power rape is an act motivated primarily by a desire to exert control over another human being. Sexual gratification may be an aspect of this type of rape, but it is secondary to the power rapist's desire to demonstrate that he has more power than his victim and that he is able to dominate and control her. Such an offender may rape women in an "effort to resolve disturbing doubts about his masculine identity and worth," or in an attempt "to combat deep-seated feelings of insecurity and vulnerability" (Groth & Hobson, 1983, p. 165). The power rapist is often overwhelmed by an increasing sense of failure. His psychological makeup, socioeconomic background, or both ill equip him to cope with the economic and social stresses in his life. He may feel powerless, hopeless, and unable to effectively deal with escalating stress. Rape may represent his attempt to regain some of the power absent from his life.

The power rapist usually employs only enough force to cause the woman to cooperate in a submissive fashion. His intention is not to physically injure her but rather to achieve control over her. Power rapes are typically premeditated and often highly repetitive, and they may exhibit a pattern of increasing frequency over time.

Sadistic Rape. "The sadistic rape is a preplanned, ritualistic assault, frequently involving bondage, torture, and sexual abuse, in which aggression and sexuality become inseparable" (Groth & Hobson, 1983, pp. 167–68). In this type of rape, aggression is an erotic experience. Power and anger or both may be eroticized. If power is the primary source of sexual arousal, the victim may be subjected to certain ritualistic acts such as bondage, being shaved, or being assaulted with an instrument. If the anger components of rape are sexualized, the victim is likely to be subjected to torture, such as having her breasts or genitals bitten, burned, or otherwise mutilated.

The motivational forces underlying sadistic rape are complex and more difficult to delineate than in anger and power rapes. Groth and Hobson have suggested that, for this type of assailant, rape may represent a perverse attempt to regain some sense of control and psychological equilibrium, while discharging pent-up frustration over unresolved conflicts. This type of rapist is likely to exhibit a particularly strong preoccupation with violent pornography. Explicit erotica without a component of violence is unlikely to hold the interest of a sadistic rapist.

Sexual Gratification Rape. The motivation propelling this type of rape is primarily sexual in nature. A man who perpetrates this act of sexual coercion is interested in obtaining sexual gratification and willing to use varying degrees of force to obtain it. Because sexual gratification is the primary goal, this type of rapist is likely to use no more force than necessary to accomplish this end. If it becomes clear that an excessive amount of force or violence is necessary to overcome the woman's resistance, the sexual gratification rapist may terminate his assaultive act.

It is likely that a majority of acquaintance rapes fit into this category. Many men who force an acquaintance or date to submit to unwanted sexual intercourse may be acting out some of the male themes common in our culture that were discussed earlier. These include glorifying the virtues of being a strong, virile, aggressive male who gets what he wants by taking it. The "caveman" mentality of dragging a woman off by her hair for sexual conquest is, unfortunately, all too prevalent in our rape-prone society.

The sexual gratification rape is likely to be impulsive rather than planned. For example, a man may take a woman to dinner, spend some money, perceive her interactions with him as seductive, assume that he will "score" when he takes her home, and end up deciding impulsively when aroused that his desire for sexual gratification will not be thwarted by her saying no. He perceives that "she really means yes" or that she deserves what she gets because "she led me on all evening." Less commonly, sexual gratification rape may occur when a man happens on an unexpected opportunity for sexual activity and uses force to obtain it. In one example, a woman in a rural community in the state of Washington was raped by three men who met her in a bar when she was in an intoxicated state. Testimony of the assailants indicated that they believed she was a "loose woman" who was asking for it by being in a bar alone and behaving in a flirtatious manner. It is also likely that these assailants presumed that the intoxicated state of their victim would reduce her resistance and preclude her identifying and pressing charges against them.

In light of statistics suggesting a high incidence of acquaintance rape and rape by family members and friends, it is possible, even probable, that sexual gratification rape is the most common kind of rape committed in American society.

It is important to note that these four types of rape are not necessarily mutually exclusive. Any act of rape may involve components from one or more of these four types of sexual assault. However, the characteristics and motivational dynamics of one type are frequently predominant in a given assault.

Acquaintance Rape and Sexual Coercion. A majority of rapes are committed by someone who is known to the raped woman, not (as in the popular stereotype) by a stranger lurking in the bushes (Harney & Muehlenhard, 1990; Koss, 1992; Parrot & Bechhofer, 1991). A significant number of these acquaintance rapes occur in dating situations—hence, the term *date rape* (Muehlenhard & Linton, 1987; Muehlenhard et al., 1985). Acquaintance rapes are much less likely to be reported than stranger rapes (Koss et al., 1988; Lizotte, 1985; Muehlenhard & Linton, 1987; Muehlenhard et al., 1985 & 1991).

In recent years researchers have provided extensive and disheartening evidence regarding the prevalence of sexual coercion in dating situations (Grauerholz & Koralewski, 1990). These studies have revealed that although both sexes experience sexual coercion, women are more likely than men to be physically forced into unwanted sexual activity. A survey of several hundred Cornell University women revealed that 16% had been forced to have intercourse against their wills (Parrot & Allen, 1984). Thirty-five percent of 930 San Francisco women reported having been victims of either attempted or completed acquaintance rape, usually in dating situations (Russell, 1984). Fully 95.3% of 275 Arizona State University women reported having been coerced into one or more sexual behaviors (Christopher, 1988).

Charlene Muehlenhard and her colleagues have conducted a number of assessments among college women and men of the frequency of being on the receiving end of sexual coercion. The results of three of these studies, indicated by sample size and number of women and men reporting having been the victims of sexual coercion, are listed as follows: 79.7% of 375 women and 62.1% of 328 men (Muehlenhard et al., 1985); 97.5% of 486 women and 93.5% of 507 men (Muehlenhard & Cook, 1987); 84.1% of 370 women and 73.7% of 426 men (Muehlenhard & Long, 1988). Although these results indicate that almost as many men as women have experienced sexual coercion, it is important to note that although many women respondents in these studies were physically forced to engage in unwanted sex acts, physical force was rarely employed in the sexual coercion of male respondents. (See the Charlene Muehlenhard interview for additional information about her research on sexual coercion.)

What reasons or motivating factors might cause people to engage in unwanted sexual activity? Are these reasons common to both sexes, or can you think of some that might apply only to one sex? Give these questions some thought before reading on.

There are a number of reasons, many common to both sexes, for engaging in unwanted sexual acts where physical force is not employed. These include such inducements as enticement (being turned on by a partner's actions or touches and later regretting it), threats to end a relationship, a desire to be popular, peer pressure, a partner questioning one's sexuality, being intoxicated, feeling obligated because of the time or money expended by a partner, and, for men, responding to the societal stereotype that a real man should always make sexual advances if the opportunity is there, regardless of whether he wants to (Muehlenhard, 1989; Muehlenhard & Cook, 1987; Muehlenhard & Schrag, 1991; Muehlenhard et al., 1991).

In addition, men often misinterpret the actions of women (cuddling, kissing, and so on) as indicating a desire to engage in intercourse (Goodchilds & Zellman, 1984; Muehlenhard, 1988; Muehlenhard & Linton, 1987). Misinterpreting a woman's intentions may provide the basis or rationale for a subsequent rape. If the woman, who just wishes to cuddle, resists the man's advances, he may conclude that she really wants to have intercourse but that she feels the need to offer at least some token resistance so as not to appear too "easy" (Check & Malamuth, 1983; Muehlenhard & Hollabaugh, 1988; Muehlenhard & Linton, 1987). Unfortunately, a study of 610 female undergraduates revealed that 39.3% had engaged in token resistance to sex at least once. Common reasons for saying no when they really meant yes included not wanting to appear promiscuous, uncertainty about a partner's feelings, undesirable surroundings, game-playing (wanting a partner to be more physically aggressive, to beg or talk them into sex, etc.), and wanting to be in control. The authors of this study, Charlene Muehlenhard and Lisa Hollabaugh (1989), maintain that such a double message promotes rape by providing men with a rationale for ignoring sincere refusals. "If a man encounters a woman who says no and he ignores her protests and finds that she is indeed willing to engage in sex, his belief that women's refusals are not to be taken seriously will be strengthened" (p. 878).

A man who embraces this "token-no" idea may thus proceed with his sexual advances despite further protests from a companion whose resistance is genuine rather than token. Such a man may not even define his actions as rape. However, even men who believe their partners when they say no may think it is defensible to use force to obtain sex if they feel that they have been "led on." A number of studies have found that many men regard rape as justifiable if a woman leads a man on by such actions as dressing "suggestively" or going to his apartment (Goodchilds & Zellman, 1984; Kanin, 1967 & 1969; Muehlenhard & Linton, 1987; Muehlenhard et al., 1991). The implications of these findings for acquaintance rape prevention are discussed in the box "Dealing with Rape."

CHAPTER 21

Interview with Charlene Muehlenhard

Charlene Muehlenhard is a leading researcher of sexual coercion, including the phenomenon of "date rape," a widespread problem now gaining increasing attention, particularly on college campuses. Trained in clinical psychology and mathematics, Dr. Muehlenhard is a professor of psychology and women's studies at the University of Kansas. Her research has demonstrated the prevalence and causes of date rape, and has examined other sexually coercive acts experienced by both men and women. A frequent author and speaker, she and her students have also studied the characteristics of people who are the perpetrators and victims of sexual coercion. In this interview with Robert Crooks, Dr. Muehlenhard describes how her interest in studying sexual coercion evolved, and how her studies are helping elucidate the factors responsible for date rape.

How did you get interested in psychology, and what led you to do research in the area of sexuality and sexual coercion?

When I was in high school, I was ambivalent about going to college. I applied very late to the University of Cincinnati, and where the application asked, "What are some of your interests?" I wrote psychology, among other things. By psychology I meant things like discussing problems with my friends. But when I got to the university

to register, they had me listed as a psychology major. I tried it, and the first week I was hooked. I also started taking some math courses just for fun, and my calculus teacher convinced me to do a double major in math.

I decided to go to graduate school in clinical psychology at the University of Wisconsin. There I worked with Dick McFall, studying "heterosocial skills," which, in the mid-seventies, basically involved teaching men how to ask women for dates. I had for many years been asking men out, so I thought, "What are women supposed to do if they want to date men?"

My master's thesis was on men's reaction to women's dating initiation. I decided that instead of starting by actually teaching women to ask men out, first I should find out if men would react positively to that. Our conclusion was basically that, as long as women were willing to face the possibility of rejection, they had nothing to lose by asking men out. If he was interested in her he

would say yes, and if he was not then he would say no, but he would not have asked her out anyway.

I subsequently saw an article in *Ms.* magazine that made me stop and think. First, it reported that high school boys would interpret almost any initiative taken by a high school girl as a sign that she was interested in sex—even a casual phone call. Second, they found that over half the boys said that rape, or forcing a girl to have sex, would be at least somewhat justified if the girl "led the boy on."

I started to wonder, if a woman asked a man out for a date, and he interpreted that to indicate that she wanted to have sexual intercourse, and if she did not, would he still feel he was "being led on"? And would he then feel that rape was justifiable under that circumstance?

What rape studies did that lead you to?

My first study on rape looked at how men's ratings of the justifiability of rape

642

would be influenced by who initiated the date, who paid for the date, and where they went on the date. We found that men rated rape as more justifiable if the woman asked the man out than if the man asked the woman out, and more justifiable if the couple went to the man's apartment than to a movie. And they rated rape as more justifiable if the man paid for the woman's concert ticket than if they each paid for their own.

But subsequently, looking at the actual risk factors related to rape, we found that sexual aggression in dating situations was more common on dates in which the man asked the woman out, the man paid, and the man drove.

Why do you think that rapes occur more often on dates where the man asks the woman out, drives, and pays?

There are several possibilities. One is that they've started the date with the man in control, and his domination extends into the sexual arena. Possibly because he has put out effort and provided the car and the money, he feels entitled to sex in exchange. Another possible reason is a practical one: if the man asks the woman out, he is likely to be the one to decide where they go. He can pick an isolated location if he's the one driving, and she might be unable to leave.

Another possibility, for which there is very strong evidence from our studies and others, is that it is people who have traditional gender-role attitudes who view rape as justifiable. Traditional men are more likely than nontraditional men to say that they would engage in rape if they could be sure that they would not be caught. In the case of dates for which the man asks, drives, and pays, he's likely to be more traditional in general. In fact, a study we did

later found that men who have traditional gender-role attitudes were actually more likely to engage in forcible rape than nontraditional men.

Your studies have all been based on college populations. How prevalent is sexual coercion and acquaintance rape on college campuses?

It's very widespread on campuses. Marcia McCoy and I recently asked college men if they had ever been in any of three situations: First, have you ever wanted to have sexual intercourse and made a sexual advance to a woman, she said no, and you stopped your advances? Second, have you ever been in a situation where you made an advance, she said no, you continued making sexual advances, but for some reason sexual intercourse did not occur? And finally, have you ever been in a situation where you made sexual advances, the woman said no, and you engaged in sexual intercourse with her even though she never changed her mind? That third situation was our definition of rape.

A very large proportion, 16 percent, of the men said they had been in that rape situation—much larger than I had really anticipated. And there were even more men, 46 percent, who endorsed the second situation.

What motivated the men in those situations?

We asked them what was going through their minds at the time. The men who stopped making advances were more likely to endorse self-statements that indicated respect for the woman and the relationship: "I don't want to lose her friendship"; "I believe her when she says no." The group that continued, but didn't have sex, tended to endorse: "I want to have sex, but not bad enough to force her."

The men in the rape situations were more likely to endorse items that said: "I want sex so much I don't care what she wants," or "This is a challenge to see how far I can get."

What are some of the traditional, stereotypical attitudes held by the men who you found were inclined to engage in coercion?

We typically measure traditionality using the Attitudes Toward Women Scale. We found that traditional men regarded it as worse for a woman to be drunk than for a man to be drunk. They felt that telling dirty jokes should be the prerogative of men. They would disagree with statements that say that women and men should take equal leadership roles, or that job promotion should be solely related to ability.

In the literature we typically say "traditional men." I'm not sure exactly why we do that as opposed to saying "sexist men," because in both cases people are limiting what they find acceptable for women to do on the basis of sex.

In addition to having traditional gender-role attitudes, what traits distinguish men who perpetrate sexual coercion?

Other studies show that men who rape are more likely to believe rape myths. Rape myths include things such as: "If women dress in tight outfits, they're 'asking for rape,'" or "Any healthy woman could avoid being raped if she really wanted to, so a woman who was raped wasn't really trying to escape." There's also evidence that men who rape have engaged in sex earlier and have higher expectations about how much sex they should engage in and what they're entitled to.

643

Are there factors that predispose a woman to be a victim of sexual coercion?

That can be a very sensitive issue, because it can seem like blaming the victim even to pose that question. Pat Harney and I investigated factors that increase the likelihood of victimization, looking at cultural, situational, and personal factors. We concluded that all women are at risk, but there are some factors that can increase or decrease the level of risk.

One thing that puts women at risk is living in a rape-prone culture. Peggy Reeves-Sanday, an anthropologist, did a study looking at rape-free versus rape-prone cultures from 1750 B.C. to 1960. She found that the rape-prone cultures were more likely to have male dominance in terms of political power and stereotyped gender roles, and to accept violence, including interpersonal violence and war.

Other risk factors could include being on a date where the man initiated, paid, and drove, or being with a man who has very sexist attitudes. It could include alcohol intoxication—there is a lot of evidence that rape is more likely to occur when both the perpetrator and the victim are intoxicated. If a woman is involved with many different men, then the chances of running across a rapist are increased.

Age is another risk factor. Women are at greater risk in their teens and early twenties than they are later. Males in that age range are most likely to be perpetrators, and they tend to rape women who they know, which may be women their own age.

The risks seem to be similar for black and white women. Koss and Russell reported higher rates of victimization among Native American women and lower rates among Asian American women. But it's not clear whether that relates to actual risk factors or if that relates to reporting.

In terms of personality factors, such as traditionality, no clear trends have emerged. However, several studies, including one that Lisa Brenner and I did, found that women who have been sexually abused as children are more likely to be raped as adults. We're still unclear about causes for this link.

How common is it for men to be victims of sexual coercion?

If sexual coercion is defined broadly, then it is clearly a problem for men as well. A study that Stephen Cook and I did asked women and men whether they had engaged in sexual intercourse when they did not want to for any one of a variety of reasons. We found that more men than women reported having engaged in unwanted sexual intercourse—62 percent of the men, and 47 percent of the women. But when men engaged in sexual intercourse when they didn't want to, it was not always due to coercion by their sexual partners.

Some men reported engaging in unwanted sexual intercourse because when a woman makes a sexual advance, they feel they cannot say no, out of worry that she'll think there is something wrong with them. More men than women also said that they engaged in sexual intercourse when they didn't want to because they felt peer pressure, they needed to get more experience, they needed something to talk about, or because they didn't want to appear shy, afraid, homosexual, or impotent.

There were also certainly some reports of situations where their partner was coercive. That could include verbal coercion such as saying, "If you really loved me, you would do this," or "Everybody's doing it." There were also some reports of a partner who threatened self-harm.

How do the consequences of acquaintance rape and stranger rape differ for the person who is victimized?

The consequences of acquaintance rape are just as serious as the consequences of stranger rape. However, there are differences. Women who are raped by acquaintances are more likely to have difficulty with trust, because they were raped by someone they trusted. They are more likely to blame themselves, and also to have other people blame them. They're more likely to be affected by rape myths, such as, "You were just out on a date with him, and he didn't call you, so you're crying rape," or "You led him on." Acquaintance rape is also very much less likely to be reported than stranger rape.

Do you plan to use your research to educate people about acquaintance rape?

Yes. Jayme Jones-Coben and I have already done one study on how to change students' attitudes about rape. She wrote a lecture that tried to dispel rape myths and had it presented to introductory psychology students. We told them about the prevalence and consequences of rape, emphasizing that rape often occurs between acquaintances, and suggesting what men can do to help the situation, including listening to what women have to say and respecting women's "No."

Four weeks later, supposedly unrelated to this lecture, they received a questionnaire about attitudes relating to rape. We found that students who heard the lecture accepted rape less, accepted rape myths less, and had more empathy toward rape victims, whether they heard the lecture from a male or a female.

What signs can women look for to help them make judgments about whether they are getting involved with a man who could become sexually coercive in a dating situation?

There are no absolute guarantees. However, some things that I would worry about are a man who has sexist attitudes, who insists on making all of the decisions on a date, or who indicates any acceptance of violence. The first time he doesn't take no for an answer about anything, or indicates that they, as a couple, are going to do what he wants regardless of what she wants, I would be concerned.

To avoid being victims of sexual coercion, women should try to be as clear as they can in their own minds about what sexual activity they do or do not want to engage in. Then try to convey that to the other person. It can be difficult to know when to bring up the topic, but sometimes, realistically, we know that people in this culture interpret nonsexual behavior as indicative of sexual interest. For example, if I were with someone who said, "Do you want to go back to my place?" I think that at that time I might feel more comfortable if I were to clarify the situation. So I might say, "I just need to tell you that I would be happy to go talk, but I don't want to engage in sex."

Do you think that if a woman says no in a nonsexual context that a man is more likely to listen?

Yes. Sandy Andrews and I did a study where we videotaped a man and a woman supposedly out on a date, and at various points in the tape we incorporated a segment where the woman says, "I hope you don't misinterpret my going to your apartment on the first date, but seriously, I don't want to do anything more than kiss tonight." We found that when the woman told him this, the male college student viewers rated her as less likely to want any sexual behavior beyond kissing. They said that in that situation they would be less likely to attempt sexual behavior beyond kissing, and that they would feel less "led on." Over half the men said they would feel more positive toward a woman who took such an approach, and only 12 percent said they would feel more negative.

What should a woman do if she has taken proper precautions but suddenly finds herself in a situation where a man is forcing her physically?

If a man starts to make a verbal or mild physical advance that she doesn't want, I would suggest the first time she say, "No," pleasantly. But if he continues and doesn't respond to what she says, then I think it's important not to worry about making a scene, not to worry about hurting his feelings. I would recommend that she say, "No," really strongly—I mean yell, "No!"

Ginna Beal and I found that it was very effective for a woman to label the behavior as rape. If she said, "This is rape and I'm calling the cops," it was very effective in causing men, even men who had been coercive in the past, to say they would stop their advances. It's also effective for a woman to use physical force if she's in a situation where she can do that. But there are some situations where the man has a weapon or where she's just not in a position to use physical force.

Dealing with Rape

Although rape is a society-wide problem, it is the rape victim who experiences the direct, personal violation. The suggestions offered below may reduce a woman's chances of being raped. However, following these suggestions offers no guarantee of avoiding rape. Even a woman who leads an extremely cautious and restricted life may be raped. We first address strategies for preventing stranger rape, followed by recommendations relevant for acquaintance rape.

Reducing the Risk of Stranger Rape
Rape prevention consists primarily of making it as difficult as possible for a rapist to make you his victim. Many of the following suggestions are commonsense measures against other crimes as well as rape.

1. Do not advertise that you are a woman living alone. Use initials on your mailbox and in the phone book; even add a fictitious name.

2. Install and use secure locks on doors and windows, changing door locks after losing keys or moving into a new residence. A peephole in your front door can be particularly helpful.

3. Do not open your door to strangers. If a repairman or public official is at your door, ask him to identify himself and call his office to verify he is a reputable person on legitimate business.

4. When you are in situations where strangers may be encountered, demonstrate self-confidence through your body language and speech to communicate that you will not be intimidated. Research reveals that rapists often tend to select as victims women who exhibit passivity and submissiveness (Richards et al., 1991).

5. Lock your car when it is parked and drive with locked car doors.

6. Avoid dark and deserted areas and be aware of the surroundings where you are walking. This may help if you need an opportunity to escape. Should a driver ask for directions when you are a pedestrian, avoid approaching his car. Instead, call out your reply from a safe distance.

7. Have house or car keys in hand before coming to the door, and check the back seat before getting into your car.

8. Should your car break down, attach a white cloth to the antenna and lock yourself in. If someone other than a uniformed officer in an official car stops to offer help, ask this person to call the police or a garage but do not open your locked car door.

9. Wherever you go it can be very helpful to carry a device for making a loud noise, like a whistle, or even better, a small pint-sized compressed air horn available in many sporting goods and boat supply stores. Sound the noise alarm at the first sign of danger.

Many cities have crime-prevention bureaus that will provide further suggestions and home-safety inspections.

What to Do in Threatening Situations Involving Strangers
When a woman is approached by a man or men who may intend to rape her, she will have to decide what to do. *Each situation, assailant, and woman is unique: There are no absolute rules* (Fischhoff, 1992).

1. Run away if you can.

2. Resist if you cannot run. Make it difficult for the rapist. Many men, upon locating a potential victim, test her to see if she is easily intimidated. Resistance by the woman is responsible for many thwarted attempts (Bart & O'Brien, 1984; Cohen, 1984; Fischhoff, 1992; Furby & Fischhoff, 1992; Siegel et al., 1989). Active and vociferous resistance — shouting, being rude, causing a scene, running away, fighting back — may deter the attack.

3. Ordinary rules of behavior do not apply. Vomiting, screaming, or acting crazy — whatever you are willing to try — can be appropriate responses to an attempted rape.

4. Talking can be a way to stall and give you a chance to devise an escape plan or another strategy. It can be helpful to get the attacker to start talking ("What has happened to make you so angry?"), to express some empathy ("It is really discouraging to lose a job"), or to negotiate ("Let's take time to talk about this"). Even when talking does not prevent an assault, it may reduce the degree of violence (Prentky et al., 1986).

5. Self-defense classes are a resource for learning techniques of physical resistance that can injure the attacker(s) or distract them long enough for you to escape.

6. Remain alert for an opportunity to escape. In some situations it may be initially impossible to fight or elude an attacker. However, you may later have a chance to deter the attack and escape —for example, if the rapist becomes distracted or a passerby comes on the scene.

Reducing the Risk of Acquaintance Rape

1. When dating someone for the first time, seriously consider doing so in a group situation or meeting him at a public place. This will allow you to assess your date's behavior in a relatively safe environment.

2. Watch for inclinations that your date may be a controlling or dominating person who may try to control your behavior. A man who plans all activities and makes all decisions during a date may also be inclined to dominate in an intimate setting.

3. If the man drives and pays for all expenses, he may think he is justified in using force to see that he gets

Many women take self-defense training to protect themselves from assault.

"what he paid for." If you cover some of the expenses, he may be less inclined to use this rationale to justify acting in a sexually coercive manner (Muehlenhard, 1988; Muehlenhard & Schrag, 1991; Muehlenhard et al., 1991).

4. Avoid using alcohol or other drugs when you definitely do not wish to be sexually intimate with your date. Consumption of alcohol and/or other drugs, by both victim and perpetrator, is commonly associated with acquaintance rape (Boeringer et al., 1991; Koss et al., 1988; Muehlenhard & Schrag, 1991). Drug intoxication can both diminish your capacity to escape from an assault and reduce a perpetrator's reluctance to engage in assaultive behavior.

5. Avoid behavior that may be interpreted as "teasing." Clearly state to your date what you do and do not wish to do in regards to intimate contact. For example, you might say, "I hope you do not misinterpret my inviting you back to my apartment. I *definitely* do not want to do anything more than relax, listen to some

music, and talk." If you are interested in initiating an exploration of some kind of early intimate contact, you might say, "Tonight I would like to hold you and kiss, but I would not be comfortable with anything else at this point in our developing relationship." When men are recipients of such direct communication, their inclinations to force unwanted sexual activity or to feel "led on" are likely to be markedly reduced (Muehlenhard & Andrews, 1985; Muehlenhard et al., 1985).

6. If, despite direct communication about your intentions, your date behaves in a sexually coercive manner, you may "use a strategy of escalating forcefulness — direct refusal, vehement verbal refusal, and, if necessary, physical force" (Muehlenhard & Linton, 1987, p. 193). In one study the response rated by men as most likely to get men to stop unwanted advances was the woman vehemently saying, "This is rape, and I'm calling the cops" (Beal & Muehlenhard, 1987). If verbal protests are ineffective, reinforce your refusal with physical force

such as pushing, slapping, biting, kicking, or clawing your assailant. Men are more likely to perceive their actions as at least inappropriate, if not rape, when a woman protests not only verbally but also physically (Beal & Muehlenhard, 1987; Muehlenhard & Linton, 1987; Shotland & Goodstein, 1983).

What to Do If You Have Been Raped

If a woman has been raped, she will have to decide whether to report the attack to the police.

1. It is advisable to report a rape, even an unsuccessful rape attempt. The information a woman provides may prevent another woman from being raped.

2. When a woman reports a rape, any information she can remember about the attack will be helpful — the assaulter's physical characteristics, voice, clothes, car, even an unusual smell.

3. A woman who has been raped should call the police as soon as possible; she should not bathe or change her clothes. Semen, hair, and material under her fingernails or on her apparel all may be useful in identifying the man who raped her.

4. It may be very helpful to contact a rape crisis center, where qualified staff members may assist you in dealing with your trauma. Most large urban communities in the United States have such programs. If you are unable to make the contact yourself, have a friend, family member, or the police make the call.

5. Finally, it is important to remember that many women will mistakenly blame themselves for the rape. However, the victim has not committed a crime — the man who raped her has.

OUR SEXUALITY

Rape of Males

Health professionals who work with rape survivors know that men are raped. However, statistics on the frequency of rapes of males are extremely difficult to obtain. Men are probably less likely than women to report that they have been raped (Harney & Muehlenhard, 1990; Mezey & King, 1989).

Only rarely do men report being sexually coerced by women who employ threats of bodily harm, and this type of assault is undoubtedly a very uncommon phenomenon. However, in recent years such cases have been reported with increasing frequency (Smith et al., 1988). It is very difficult to assess just how rare this offense is because most men would probably be intensely embarrassed or humiliated to acknowledge that their presumed male prerogative to initiate and control sexual encounters had been usurped by one or more female assailants.

A large percentage of the rapes of males are perpetrated by heterosexual men, who often commit their crime with one or more cohorts. As in rape of women, violence and power is often associated with the sexual assault of men. The possibility of being raped is a very serious issue among male homosexuals because they are often the victims of such attacks.

Rape of inmates in penal institutions is a serious problem (Cotton & Groth, 1982; Lockwood, 1980). Men who do the raping typically consider themselves to be heterosexual. When released they usually resume sexual relations with women. The men who are raped often experience brutal gang assaults. Such a man may become the sexual partner of one particular dominant inmate for protection from others (Braen, 1980).

The idea that mature males can be raped by women has been largely rejected because it has been assumed that a man cannot function sexually in a state of extreme anxiety or terror. However, this common impression is not accurate, as illustrated in this account of what happened to a 27-year-old, 178-pound male truck driver:

One night he had been drinking and left a bar with a woman companion he had not known previously. They went to a motel where he was given another drink and shortly thereafter fell asleep. He awoke to find himself naked, tied hand and foot to a bedstead, gagged, and blindfolded. As he listened to voices in the room, it was evident that several women were present.

When the women realized that he was awake, he was told that he had to have sex with all of them. He thinks that during his period of captivity four different women used him sexually, some of them a number of times. Initially he was manipulated to erection and mounted. After a very brief period of coitus, he ejaculated. He was immediately restimulated to erection and the performance was repeated. Following the first two coital episodes, he did not ejaculate again until he was seen in therapy. After several more coital experiences, it became increasingly difficult for him to maintain an erection. When he couldn't function well, he was threatened with cas-

The Aftermath of Rape

The vast majority of rapes that occur outside prisons and jails are perpetrated by males upon female victims. However, as noted in the box "Rape of Males," the research and treatment community is becoming increasingly aware that nonimprisoned men also can be raped by either males or females. Because the majority of people who are raped are females, it follows that most of our knowledge about the short- and long-term effects of rape have been gleaned from studies of female survivors of rape.

Emotional Repercussions. Given the characteristics of rape — the physical violation and psychological trauma it inflicts and our societal attitudes about it — it is understandable that many rape survivors suffer long-lasting emotional effects. The emotional repercussions women experience following rape or attempted rape have been labeled *rape trauma syndrome* (Burgess & Holmstrom, 1974a, 1974b, & 1988).

tration and felt a knife held to his scrotum. He was terrified that he would be cut and did have some brief improvement in erective quality. (Sarrel & Masters, 1982, pp. 121–22)

Philip Sarrel and William Masters (1982) reported on 11 men who had been raped by women. None of the victims reported the assault, and none was able to talk about it until he became involved in therapy several years after the offense was committed. A common feeling among the male victims was that there was something drastically wrong with them because they had responded sexually in circumstances they thought would render any normal man incapable of erection. Labeling themselves as abnormal kindled sexual performance anxieties and feelings of inadequacy as men. All these victims suffered from a "postassault syndrome," characterized by impaired sexual functioning and emotional distress, which was comparable to the rape trauma syndrome previously described for women.

Researchers Gillian Mezey and Michael King (1989) of Great Britain recently reported the results of a survey of 22 men who had been sexually victimized by other men. All of these attacks occurred outside of prison in the general community. Eleven of the victims knew their assailants to be homosexual, three heterosexual, and three bisexual. In the remaining five cases, the sexual orientation of the assailant was not clear. The immediate and long-term responses of these male victims "were very similar to those described in female victims of rape" (p. 205). The majority of the attacked men (17) were victims of forced anal intercourse. Five were masturbated by their assailants, three of whom ejaculated. "These victims expressed profound disgust and confusion at responding in this way" (p. 206).

Alfred Kinsey and his associates were perhaps the earliest sex researchers to acknowledge the ability of the human male to function sexually in a variety of severe emotional states, when they noted that "the rec-

ord suggests that the physiologic mechanism of any emotional response (anger, fright, pain, etc.) may be the mechanism of sexual response" (Kinsey et al., 1948, p. 165). More recently, the eminent Scottish endocrinologist John Bancroft (1980) cited evidence from human and other animal research indicating that sexual responses can occur in situations that induce extreme anxiety. This finding that males may respond sexually in situations involving intense fear and degradation is paralleled by the observation that "most women lubricate and some women respond at orgasmic levels while they are being sexually molested" (Sarrel & Masters, 1982, p. 118). Sexual response during an assault, particularly if it is at an orgasmic level, may be a source of great confusion and anxiety to both female and male rape survivors. In some instances they may find their sexual response to be more upsetting than the physical trauma and social humiliation produced by the assault.

There are usually two phases of rape trauma. The first, known as the *acute phase,* begins immediately following the rape and may continue for hours, days, or often several weeks. During the first few hours after the attack, a woman will tend to react in either an expressive or controlled manner. In the expressive reaction, she will likely be crying and obviously upset. In the controlled reaction, a woman will appear subdued and matter-of-fact. She may, however, experience the expressive reaction at a later time. The feelings many victims report during the acute phase cover a wide range, often including shame, anger, fear, nervousness, guilt, self-blame, and a sense of powerlessness (Murnen et al., 1989; Ruch et al., 1991; Rynd, 1988). Physical symptoms, such as nausea, headaches, sleep disorders, and nightmares, are also commonly associated with the emotional trauma (Duddle, 1991; Rynd, 1988). Some physical symptoms may be due to the assault itself and not to the emotional trauma (Beebe, 1991; Slaughter & Brown, 1992). Injuries such as bruises, abrasions, and vaginal or rectal tears may take time to heal.

Fear and nervousness often continue during the second phase, called the *long-term reorganization phase,* which may last for several years (Sales et al., 1984). The woman may fear retaliation by the rapist, and she may change her place of residence frequently during this time. She may have fearful or negative feelings about sexual relations, particularly intercourse. One long-term study of rape survivors revealed that 40% refrained from sexual contact for six months to a year after the assault. Almost three out of four of these women reported that the frequency of their sexual activity remained below preassault levels for as long as four to six years after the attack. Their major sexual problems occurred in the area of sexual desire and arousal. Orgasmic difficulties, painful intercourse, and vaginismus were less common (Burgess & Holmstrom, 1979). Another study provided similar evidence. Out of a sample of 222 rape survivors, 60% reported one or more sexual problems that surfaced after the attack. The most common difficulties were fear of sex and lack of arousal and desire (88% reporting). Only 25% of the women in this sample indicated having orgasm problems (Becker et al., 1984). These findings suggest that a rape interferes less with the survivor's physiosexual response than with the psychological aspects of her sexual activity. Rape survivors may associate sexual touches or sex talk with the trauma of their assault. As a result these sexual stimuli may be more likely to induce anxiety than sexual desire or arousal in the postassault period.

Women often find that supportive counseling, either individually or in groups, can help ease the trauma caused by rape (Burgess & Holmstrom, 1988; Roth et al., 1988). It is very important "to begin counseling the victim as soon after the assault as possible to help repair emotional damage" (Burgess & Holmstrom, 1988, p. 43). Research has shown that women who receive help soon after an assault experience less severe emotional repercussions than women whose treatment is delayed (Duddle, 1991; Stewart et al., 1987). Most rape survivors find that they need to talk about their assault and the emotionally rending feelings that they experience in its aftermath. Often the process of reviewing the event allows them to gain control over their painful feelings and to begin the process of healing.

A Partner's Response to Rape.   The rape of his partner may be a difficult experience for a man. In a sense he also is victimized by the assault. He may feel a range of emotions including rage, disgust, and helplessness. He may be confused and unsure about how he should react to his lover's victimization. This lack of direction may prove costly, because his reactions can have a profound impact on both his lover's recovery and the future of their relationship. In the following paragraphs, we offer some suggestions for how a man may participate meaningfully in his partner's recovery. These recommendations are adapted from *Sexual Solutions* (1980), an excellent book by Michael Castleman. Although they are directed to the male partners of female victims, they are also applicable to people whose same-sex partners have been violated and to female partners of male assault victims.

Before reviewing the following suggestions, take some time to consider how you might respond to a partner who has been raped. What kinds of actions might be helpful? Harmful?

The last thing a rape survivor needs is to have her judgment questioned ("Why did you park on a dark side street?"). Equally counterproductive is the

Supportive counseling can help ease the trauma suffered by a rape victim.

response of the partner who gets sidetracked by focusing his attention on his own imagined shortcomings ("I should have been along to protect you"). The woman has just finished dealing with a violent man (or men), and being confronted with a similar emotional state in her partner (motivated by his desire for revenge against the assailant) is probably not in her best interests.

What she does need is to be listened to. A person comforting a rape survivor might understandably try to divert her attention from the terrible event. However, professionals who work with survivors of sexual assault have found that many of these people need to talk repeatedly about the assault to come to terms with it. A partner can help by encouraging his lover to discuss the rape in any way that she is able.

A rape survivor may recover more quickly when she is able to decide for herself how to deal with the assault. A man may be inclined to ease his partner's burden by taking charge and deciding what should be done in the aftermath of a rape. However, "she should make every decision in response to the assault. She was the person attacked. The important thing is for her to regain a sense of control over her life after being stripped of that control by her attacker(s)" (Castleman, 1980, p. 177). Her partner may suggest alternatives and act as a sounding board while she weighs her options. Nevertheless, the woman should ultimately make all the decisions, unless she is unable to do so.

In the days, weeks, and even months following the rape, a partner can continue to provide empathy, support, and reassurance to a rape victim. He can encourage her to resume a normal life and support her at those moments when she feels particularly vulnerable, fearful, or angry. He can be there to listen, even if it means hearing the same things over and over again. In the event that her assailant is prosecuted, she may be in particular need of support and understanding throughout the often arduous legal proceedings.

Rape victims may need more than their lovers or families can provide. Some may require short- or long-term therapy to help ease the trauma of rape and reconstruct their lives. Partners may recognize these needs and encourage their lovers to seek professional help. Similarly, partners of sexually assaulted women may also experience severe conflicts and deep feelings of rage and guilt that they need help coping with (Burgess & Holmstrom, 1988; Cohen, 1988). These men may find that a close friend, family member, or professional therapist will listen as they voice their pain and anger. "Men who take care of their own emotional needs tend to provide better support to their lovers" (Castleman, 1980, p. 181).

Resuming sexual activity after a rape may present problems for both the victim and her partner. Rape may precipitate sexual difficulties for the woman; she may not want to be sexually intimate for quite a while. However, some women may desire relations very soon after the attack, perhaps for assurance that their lovers still care for them and do not consider them "tainted." Some women may prefer not to have intercourse for a while but instead just want to be close and affectionate. Deciding when and how to engage in intimate sharing is best left up to the woman. Her partner's support in this matter is very important. Even when sexual intimacy resumes, it may be some time before she is able to relax and again respond the way she did before the attack. A patient, understanding, sensitive partner can help her reach the point where she is again able to experience satisfying sexual intimacy.

Reporting the Rape. A recent survey of several hundred rape victims revealed that individual characteristics of the rapists and the victims had no appreciable impact on the probability that a rape would be reported to the police. Rather, how a woman perceived the legal strength of her case appeared to exert the greatest influence on her decision whether to report the assault. Women in this sample were inclined to report the rape when one or more of the following conditions were met: when the rapist was a stranger, when he stole a significant amount of personal property, when there was serious injury, and when the woman was married (Lizotte, 1985). Another study found that rapes perpetrated by strangers in which the victim's home was broken into, a weapon employed, or significant personal injury incurred were much more likely to be reported than were rapes that occurred in a dating or social situation (Williams, 1984).

Women who report a rape to the police and prosecute the offender will be involved in legal proceedings that will include a recounting of the assault. In the past the judicial system has been insensitive and sometimes psychologically brutal to rape survivors. In recent years there has been considerable improvement as the police and court system have attempted to be more sensitive and supportive. Some cities have instituted *rape victim advocate programs.* These provide a counselor to work with the woman, beginning with the initial report and continuing throughout the prosecution process.

Women who choose not to report a rape to the police or to tell anyone else are likely to have the same traumatic psychological reactions to their experience as women who report rape. Furthermore, they may have even more problems coping because they do not have the opportunity to express and resolve their feelings. Sometimes the trauma of the rape surfaces later when a woman seeks help for a problem apparently unrelated to the attack.

In summary, rape is usually a very traumatic experience. The passage of time combined with support from others can help alleviate its effects, and counseling may also be helpful. We hope that the many women who are survivors of this crime will seek help in resolving a trauma that can interfere significantly with their lives.

Sexual Abuse of Children

Child sexual abuse is defined as an adult engaging in sexual contact of any kind with a child (inappropriate touching, oral–genital stimulation, coitus, etc.). Such interaction is considered coercive and illegal in that the child victim is not considered mature enough to provide informed consent to sexual involvement. *Informed consent* implies the possession of adequate intellectual and emotional maturity to understand fully both the meaning and possible consequences of a particular action. Certainly one of the most reprehensible aspects of child sexual abuse is that the adult perpetrator obtains his or her sexual gratification by exploiting the naiveté, immaturity, and trust of a child.

Most researchers distinguish between non-relative child sexual abuse, referred to as **pedophilia** or **child molestation,** and **incest,** which is sexual contact between two people who are related (one of whom is often a child). Both forms of child sexual abuse are illegal in every state. Incest includes sexual contact between siblings as well as sexual contact between children and their parents, grandparents, uncles, or aunts. Sexual contact between first cousins is a gray area; not all state legal codes contain laws against these unions. Although incest may occur between related adults, more commonly it involves a child victim and an adult relative (or older sibling) perpetrator. Although its definition may vary slightly from culture to culture, incest is one of the most widely prohibited sexual behaviors throughout the world.

There are some gray areas in the definition of child molestation. For instance, if a 21-year-old male has sexual intercourse with a 15-year-old female, is he guilty of pedophilia, statutory rape, or simply bad judgment? The issue is often further complicated when his partner willingly participates and may, in fact, have been the initiator. Each state has its own legal codes that specify at what age sexual interaction between an adult and a younger person is considered child molestation (usually if the younger person is under age 12); statutory rape (generally 12 to 16 or 17); and a consenting sexual act (the age of consent in the United States generally ranges from 16 to 18 but in some states is 21). The legal codes may appear ludicrous at times, particularly in cases involving teenage interactions where one partner is technically an adult and the other technically a minor, though only one or two years separate their ages. Incest is illegal regardless of the ages of the participants. However, an incestuous relationship between consenting adult relatives is considerably less likely to precipitate legal action than one involving an adult and a child.

Incest occurs at all socioeconomic levels. However, it appears to occur with greater frequency in families disrupted by a variety of problems including severe marital conflict, spouse abuse, alcoholism, unemployment, and emotional illness. It is commonly assumed that father–daughter incest is the most prevalent, but studies have shown that brother–sister and first-cousin contacts are more common (Canavan et al., 1992; Finkelhor, 1979; Hunt, 1974; Stark, 1984). However, father–daughter sexual abuse is far more likely to be reported to authorities, a fact that has no doubt led to the confusion over which type of incestuous pattern occurs most frequently.

Sexual relations between brothers and sisters are seldom discovered, and when they are, they do not typically elicit the extreme reactions that father–daughter sexual contacts often do. Furthermore, it is not uncommon for participating siblings to look favorably upon their shared experiences, particularly if no coercion was involved (Finkelhor, 1980; Justice & Justice, 1979; Story & Story, 1983). Sexual abuse by a parent, however, often has a devastating impact on the child victim.

The incestuous involvement of a father (or stepfather) and his daughter often begins before the female child understands its significance. Frequently it starts as a kind of playful activity involving wrestling, tickling, kissing, and touching. Over time the father may gradually include touching of the genitals and breasts, perhaps followed by oral or manual stimulation of the genitals and intercourse. In most cases the father does not need to use physical force but relies on his position of authority or the pair's emotional closeness to get what he wants. He may pressure his daughter into sexual activity by reassuring her that he is "teaching" her something important, by offering rewards, or by exploiting her need for love. Later, when she discovers that the behavior is not appropriate or finds her father's demands to be unpleasant and traumatizing, it may be difficult for her to escape from a well-established pattern of exploitive sexual activity. Occasionally, a daughter may value the relationship for the special recognition or privileges it brings her. The incestuous involvement may come to public attention when she gets angry with her father, often for nonsexual reasons, and "tells on him." Sometimes a mother may discover, much to her horror, what has been transpiring between her husband and daughter. However, just as often she may be aware of such behavior but allow it to continue for various reasons. These may include shame, fear of reprisals, concern about having her family disrupted if her husband is jailed, or the fact that the incestuous activity allows her to avoid her husband's sexual demands.

Once detected, a father who engages in sexual relations with his child may be prosecuted under state criminal codes. Sometimes an entire family may be disrupted, with the father imprisoned, the mother facing economic difficulties, and perhaps the victim and other siblings placed in foster homes. Separation or divorce may result. These potential consequences of revealing an incestuous relationship place tremendous pressures on the child. For these and other reasons, she may be extremely reluctant to tell anyone else in her family, let alone public authorities.

Prevalence of Child Sexual Abuse

It is difficult to make an accurate estimate of the incidence of either incest or pedophilia. For reasons previously mentioned, a child victim of incest frequently does not reveal what is occurring at the time — and may in fact not utter a word about it until she reaches adulthood, if then. Furthermore, concealment by families and powerful social taboos against such activity significantly reduce the chances that incestuous behavior will come to public attention. However, some studies on the problem of sexual abuse in the home have led researchers to conclude that incest occurs with a much higher frequency than previously imagined (Russell, 1984; Stark, 1984).

It is also difficult to make an accurate estimate of the frequency of pedophilia in American society. Acts of child molestation are unlikely to be reported at the time they occur for several reasons. First, a child may not recognize that what has transpired is improper behavior. Second, he or she may be unable to distinguish between expressions of affection and illicit sexual contact; the fact that the offender is often a friend may further confuse him or her. A third reason for low reporting stems from the fact that even when a child does inform his or her parents of improper sexual advances, the parents may not believe the child or may be reluctant to expose the child to the stress of legal proceedings. This reluctance to prosecute may be compounded when the offender is a friend or acquaintance of the family.

In your opinion, how common is sexual abuse of children in American society? Are the perpetrators of such abuse more commonly strangers or friends and relatives of the victims? And are the victims of such abuse more commonly females or males? Think about these questions for a couple of minutes before reading on.

When you read a statement like "One out of four American females is sexually abused during her youth," keep in mind that this estimate represents the combined statistics of sexual abuse by nonrelatives and relatives. A significant portion of the overall abuse rate consists of incestuous abuse by relatives. Because of the low reporting of child sexual abuse at the time that it occurs (for reasons previously outlined), researchers tend to rely more heavily on reports provided by adults regarding their childhood experiences with sexual abuse. To get a sense of the magnitude of child sexual abuse, consider the following statistics, obtained from three recent surveys of adult populations:

1. A 1985 report issued by the United States Department of Health and Human Services estimated that one in every four or five girls and one in every nine or ten boys is sexually abused before the age of 18. In over 90% of the cases of child sexual abuse uncovered by this investigation, the child was abused in the home by a close relative, family friend, or neighbor.

2. A telephone survey of almost 3000 adults, commissioned by the *Los Angeles Times* in July 1985, revealed that 22% of the respondents indicated having been sexually abused as children (27% of the women and 16% of the men). Almost 70% of the abuse was perpetrated by friends and relatives; 93% of the victims said that their abusers were men.

3. The results of the first survey of a nationally representative sample of adults questioned about childhood sexual abuse were published in 1990. In this study 2626 randomly selected American women and men, drawn from all 50 states, were interviewed over the telephone. The anonymity of all participants was assured by the use of random-digit dialing. Of the 1481 women who responded, 27% indicated having been sexually victimized as a child, while 16% of the 1145 men responded similarly. Approximately one in four of the females and one in seven of the males who reported sexual abuse indicated having been victimized by relatives (Finkelhor et al., 1990).

Although clinical literature has indicated that more girls than boys are victims of sexual abuse, recent research has suggested that the number of young boys who are sexually molested in the United States may be substantially higher than previously estimated (Bera et al., 1991; Watkins & Bentovim, 1992). Furthermore, awareness is increasing among mental health professionals that some children are being sexually abused by women (Elliott, 1992; Wolfers, 1992). The belief that women sometimes sexually victimize children has been slow to emerge, both because of the prevailing notion that child sexual abuse is a male activity and because "this subject is more of a taboo because female sexual abuse is more threatening — it undermines feelings about how women should relate to children" (Elliott, 1992, p. 12).

The Aftermath of Child Sexual Abuse

There is increasing evidence that child sexual abuse can be a severely traumatizing and emotionally damaging experience with long-term negative consequences for the victim (Beitchman et al., 1992; Boyer & Fine, 1992; Frazier & Cohen, 1992; Young, 1992). Clinical contact with adult survivors of child sexual abuse often reveals memories of a joyless youth filled with pain. Survivors speak of their loss of childhood innocence, the contamination and interruption of normal sexual development, and a profound sense of betrayal at the hands of a beloved family member or trusted friend.

A number of factors have been shown to influence the severity of a child victim's response to her or his abuse. "In general, the more intrusive the abuse, the more violent the assault, the longer the sexual molestation has occurred, and the closer the relationship of the perpetrator to the victim, the worse the prognosis and the greater the need for long-term treatment" (Krugman et al., 1991).

Many of the victims of child sexual abuse have difficulty forming intimate adult relationships, particularly with men (Felitti, 1991; Harter et al., 1988; Jackson et al., 1990; Janeway, 1981; Maltz & Holman, 1987). When relationships with men are established, they are frequently devoid of emotional and sexual fulfillment (Jackson et al., 1990; Meiselman, 1978). Sexual abuse is not uncommon in the histories of women who seek treatment for sexual difficulties (Maltz, 1988; McGuire & Wagner, 1978). Other difficulties commonly found in sexual abuse survivors include low self-esteem, guilt, shame, depression, a sense of alienation from others, a lack of trust in others, revulsion at being touched, drug and alcohol abuse, obesity, elevated suicide rates, and a predisposition to being repeatedly victimized in a variety of ways (Felitti, 1991; Gomes-Schwartz et al., 1985; Harter et al., 1988; Koss & Dinero, 1989; Massie & Johnson, 1989).

In recent years a variety of treatment programs have emerged to help survivors of child sexual abuse. These treatment strategies range from individual therapy to group and couples-oriented approaches. Such programs are designed to help individuals resolve issues regarding abuse experiences and their emotional aftermath (Cahill et al., 1991; Cornell & Olio, 1991; Maltz, 1988; Patten et al., 1989; Zimpfer, 1987). Most large metropolitan areas in the United States also have self-help support organizations for survivors of sexual abuse. (For those readers who wish more information about how to seek professional therapeutic assistance, we suggest reviewing the guidelines outlined in Chapter 17.)

The Offender

Who is the person who commits sexual offenses against children? What kind of personality traits and behavioral characteristics would you expect to find in a child sexual abuser? Think about this for a few moments before reading on.

A range of studies has revealed that the pedophile offender is most commonly a male, perhaps a teenager but often middle-aged or older, who is shy, lonely, conservative (particularly in the area of sexual attitudes), possesses limited sexual knowledge, and is often very moralistic or religious (Bauman et al., 1984). They are likely to have poor interpersonal and sexual relations with other adults, and they may feel socially inadequate and inferior (Alford et al., 1984; Bauman et al., 1984; Segal & Marshall, 1985). Their child victims are often family friends, neighbors, or acquaintances. Relating to these children sexually may represent a way of coping with powerful feelings of inadequacy that are likely to emerge in socio-sexual relationships with other adults. A child, as a nonadult, is less threatening. Thus, sexual behavior directed at a child may be an attempt to establish a relationship seemingly unavailable to him in the adult world.

Alcoholism, severe marital problems, sexual difficulties, and poor emotional adjustment are additional problems frequently experienced by people who molest children (Johnston, 1987; Kolodny et al., 1979; Levin & Strava, 1987). Also, these offenders have often been sexually victimized themselves during their own childhoods (Gaffney et al., 1984; Groth, 1979; Seghorn et al., 1987).

The man who engages in an incestuous relationship with his own child shares many of the characteristics of the pedophile or child molester. He is often economically disadvantaged, a heavy drinker, unemployed, devoutly religious, emotionally immature, and very conservative (Furniss, 1985; Meiselman, 1978; Rosenberg, 1988; Stark, 1984). His behavior may result from general tendencies toward pedophilia, severe feelings of inadequacy in adult sexual relations, or rejection by a hostile spouse; it may also be an accompaniment to alcoholism or other psychological disturbances (Rosenberg, 1988). Not uncommonly, the man who molests his own child comes from a family where patterns of incest were modeled for him by parents, siblings, or both (Delson & Clark, 1981). He also frequently has certain distorted ideas about adult – child sex — for example, that a child who does not resist desires the sexual contact, that adult – child sex is an effective way for children to learn about sex, that a father's relationship with his daughter is enhanced by having sexual contact with her, and that a child does not report contact because she enjoys it (Abel, 1984).

Prevention of Child Sexual Abuse

Specialists in the field of child sexual abuse are becoming increasingly focused on developing more effective strategies for preventing the sexual victimization of children. This is essential because the available evidence indicates that most children do not reveal that they have been victimized, and when they do, families are often reticent to seek outside help (Finkelhor, 1984a). The experiences of health professionals who work with victims suggest that many children could have avoided being victimized if they had been provided with some important messages such as their right to say no, the difference between "okay" and "not-okay" touches, and how to cope with an adult's attempt to coerce them into inappropriate intimate contact.

Perhaps the best prospects for reducing the high levels of child sexual abuse in our society lie in developing effective programs to be implemented in the early stages of a child's public education. As indicated in Chapter 13, American parents are very reticent to talk about sex with their children. Therefore, it is probably unrealistic to expect better parent–child communication to resolve the issue. Furthermore, parents are often the perpetrators of the sexual abuse of children. The following list of suggestions, drawn from the writings of a number of child abuse specialists, offers some suggestions for preventing child sexual abuse that may be helpful to parents, educators, and other adult caregivers of children:

1. It is important to present prevention-oriented material to children when they are still very young because as many as 25% of child sexual abuse victims are younger than age seven (Finkelhor, 1984a). Be sure to include boys because they too may be abused.

2. Educators and parents will be more effective if they avoid complicated discussions of ethics, social responsibility, and complex notions of appropriate sexual activity. A more realistic approach is to keep things simple and "to translate the notions of sexual abuse into concepts that make sense within the world of the child" (Finkelhor, 1984b, p. 3)

3. It is wise to avoid making a discussion of child sexual abuse unduly frightening. A child may develop so much fear that she or he will feel powerless and incapable of acting effectively in an abuse situation. It is important that children be sufficiently concerned that they will be on the lookout for potentially abusive adult behavior. However, we also want them to be confident in their ability to avoid such a situation should it occur.

4. Take time to carefully explain the differences between okay touches (pats, snuggles, and hugs) and not-okay touches that make a child feel uncomfortable or confused. Not-okay touches can be explained as touching under the panties or underpants or touching areas that bathing suits cover. In discussing touches that are not-okay, be sure to indicate that a child does not have to touch an adult in these same areas even if the adult says it is all right. It is also a good idea to talk about not-okay kisses (prolonged lip contact or tongue in mouth).

5. Encourage children to believe that they have rights — the right to control their bodies and the right to say no when they are being touched in a way that makes them uncomfortable.

6. Encourage children to tell someone right away if an adult has touched them in a way that is inappropriate or has made them do something about which they are uncomfortable. Emphasize that you will not be angry with them and that they will be okay when they tell, even if someone has told them that they will get in trouble. Stress that no matter what happened, it was not their fault, and they will not be blamed. Also, warn them that not all adults will believe

Specialists in the field of child sexual abuse sometimes use anatomically correct dolls to educate children about "okay touches." These dolls may also be used in discussions with very young victims to clarify the nature of the abuse that has occurred.

them. Tell them to keep telling people until they find someone like you who will believe them.

7. Discuss with children some of the strategies that adults may use to gain compliance with their deviant sexual demands. For example, tell them to trust their own feelings when they think something is wrong, even if an adult who is a friend or relative says that it is okay and that they are "teaching" them something about which they need to learn. Given that many adults use the "this is our secret" strategy, it can be particularly helpful to explain the difference between a secret (something they are never to tell — a bad idea) and a surprise (a good idea because it is something they tell later to make someone happy).

8. Discuss strategies for getting away from uncomfortable or dangerous situations. Let them know that it is okay to scream, yell, run away, or get assistance from a friend or trusted adult.

9. Encourage children to state clearly to the adult who touches them inappropriately that they will tell a particular responsible adult about what went on. Interviews with child sexual abuse offenders have revealed that many would be deterred in their abusive actions by a child saying that she or he would tell a specific adult about the assault (Budin & Johnson, 1989; Conte et al., 1989; Daro, 1991).

10. Perhaps one of the hardest things to incorporate in this prevention discussion, particularly for parents, is the message that private touching can be a very joyous and pleasurable experience, as they will discover when they grow older and meet someone they care for or love. Without some discussion of the pos-

itive aspects of sexuality, there is a risk that a child will develop a very negative view of any kind of sexual contact between people, regardless of the nature of their relationship.

What kinds of responses might be appropriate or helpful in the event you discovered that your child was involved in a sexual encounter with an adult? As you consider this question, think in terms of what might be most beneficial for the emotional health of your child.

The emotional trauma a child experiences as a result of a sexual encounter with an adult may be magnified by excessive parental reactions to revelations or discovery of such an activity. The child, when reporting to the parent, may merely be relaying a sense of discomfort over something he or she does not fully understand. When the parents understandably react with extreme agitation, the child is likely to respond with increased emotional negativity. He or she may now have a sense of being implicated in something terrible and may come to feel extremely guilty over having participated in such an event. Children may feel guilty about such experiences even without parental displays of distress because they sense the guilt of the person who molests them.

It is important that parents respond appropriately to instances of child abuse involving their children. Such acts should not be ignored! While parents can try to remain calm in the face of their child's revelation, they should take great precautions to see that the child is not alone with the offending party again. In many instances children are repeatedly molested by the same person, and they may come to feel a sense of obligation and guilt. It is essential to ensure that the child is protected from further experiences of this kind. In addition, it is essential to report the offender to the police to protect other children, because it is very likely that your child is not the offender's only victim.

Sexual Harassment

Sexual harassment, which may generally be defined as unwanted sexual advances from individuals in the workplace or an academic setting, is widespread within the fabric of U.S. society. In the following sections, we discuss relevant information about this form of sexual victimization as it occurs both on the job and in educational environments.

Sexual Harassment in the Workplace

Working Women United Institute, a New York – based research and resource center founded in 1975 to deal exclusively with sexual harassment on the job, offers a brief and succinct definition of this behavior: "Sexual harassment is any unwanted attention of a sexual nature from someone from the workplace that creates discomfort and/or interferes with the job" (Bartlett, 1982, p. 22).

Many working people are subjected to sexual harassment on the job. This form of sexual victimization, while perhaps not as extreme as sexual abuse of children or rape, is nevertheless a major concern that is receiving increasing attention.

Sexual harassment creates anxiety and tension in the workplace.

In spite of the recent unprecedented national media coverage of law professor Anita Hill's charge that she was sexually harassed by Supreme Court nominee Clarence Thomas, some people may still consider sexual harassment an unimportant or trivial issue. However, victims perceive this problem very differently, as the following account reveals:

> A woman in her late forties was hired as an executive secretary to the head of a small business in California. Her duties included a heavy correspondence load, keeping the social schedule of her boss and his wife, paying all his personal and household bills, and also arranging dates with, buying gifts for, and making motel reservations for the many young women whom he recruited for one-night stands. She was then summoned in the morning to hear about his sexual exploits, and to rehearse with him the details of an overnight business trip he had concocted as an excuse for his wife.
>
> When she objected to such nonbusiness duties, she was told that she was lucky, at her age, to hear about sex at all. When he began to accompany his morning rehearsals with pats on her buttocks and requests for blow jobs, she objected more strongly, but still she felt guilty about having gone along with his lies up to then. He told her she was a "dirty old woman," and she felt ashamed, as if she might somehow have invited his advances. After a number of incidents in which he unzipped his pants in front of her, she finally quit the job she badly needed. Though she had done the secretarial work with great efficiency (and he had hired two women to replace her), he gave her poor work references, and wouldn't support her claim for unemployment insurance. (Lindsey, 1977, p. 47)

How common are such experiences? A number of studies have shown that sexual harassment is extremely widespread. A survey of more than 17,000 federal employees found that 42% of the women and 15% of the men surveyed had been sexually harassed (U.S. Merit Systems Protection Board, 1981). A recent update of this national survey found that the incidence of harassment in 1988 was essentially the same as reported earlier (U.S. Merit Systems Protection Board, 1988). In 1976 *Redbook* magazine printed a questionnaire on sexual harassment that was returned by 9000 women. Approximately 88% of the respondents said that they had personally been subjected to sexual harassment at work (Safran, 1976). The *Redbook* respondents were certainly not a representative sample of the general population. However, the high incidence revealed by the survey suggested that sexual harassment is a very common problem for working women. Interviews with several hundred randomly selected Connecticut women revealed that 50% of the interviewees who had ever been employed had experienced sexual harassment in the workplace (Loy & Stewart, 1984). Over 50% of randomly selected Los Angeles women, interviewed by phone, stated that they had experienced job-related sexual harassment (Gutek, 1985). A survey of 496 Missouri nurses revealed that 82% had experienced sexual harassment on the job (Grieco, 1987). Indeed, the abundant evidence of large-scale sexual harassment in the workplace led one writer to suggest that "unwanted sexual attention may be the single most widespread occupational hazard in the workplace today" (Garvey, 1986, p. 75).

In the last few years, there have been a number of court decisions that have interpreted Title VII of the 1964 Civil Rights Act, which prohibits discrimination in employment on the basis of sex, as also prohibiting unwelcome sexual advances or requests for sexual favors. In 1980 the Equal Employment Opportunity Commission issued guidelines derived from the Civil Rights Act that impose liability on companies for sexual harassment by supervisors unless the company takes immediate and appropriate action. These guidelines, revised in 1986, emphasize that both verbal and physical harassment are illegal. Furthermore, they also provide legal recourse for other employees if a coworker uses sex to obtain job advancement. Thus, if employee A has sex with a boss and gets promoted, employee B, who is equally qualified for the higher-level position, may file suit against the employer for sexual discrimination.

There is evidence that employers are becoming increasingly sensitive to the issue of sexual harassment, perhaps motivated in part by a number of court decisions that have awarded large payments to victims. More and more large companies (including CBS, General Electric, General Motors, IBM, and General Telephone) are establishing programs for supervisors that clarify what harassment is and when a company can be liable for such invasive and offensive actions by its supervisors, coworkers, and even customers.

Varieties of Sexual Harassment on the Job. Sexual harassment on the job can appear in many forms. A common situation involves a boss or supervisor who requires sexual services from an employee as a condition for keeping a job or getting a promotion. This is a particularly insidious form of harassment because when an employee is fired for noncompliance, the supervisor may invent a reason for the termination that can be damaging to the victim's future employment prospects. Employees are well aware of this possibility and thus may feel great pressure to go along with their employers' demands. Even if the employee does not get fired, she (or he) may suffer other, less dramatic consequences that are nevertheless quite damaging. A person may be denied promotion, be demoted to a lesser job, receive a reduction in pay, have vacation requests denied, be assigned to less desirable work, and so forth. Sometimes job seekers find that sexual availability is a condition for being hired. A prospective employer may even require a "sample" before putting a new person on the payroll.

What if a worker is subjected to obscenities or made the constant target of sexual jokes? Is this sexual harassment? We certainly believe so, and apparently the courts share this view. In one case a woman engineer — whose coworkers made her job intolerable by such abusive behaviors as loudly speculating about whether she was a virgin and passing around an obscene cartoon about her — complained to her supervisor and was then promptly fired. After several years of trying to obtain legal redress, she was compensated on all counts. The coworkers were found guilty of sexual harassment, and each had to pay her $1500. The company was required to reinstate her in a higher position and pay all back wages.

Sometimes workers are coerced into providing sexual services to customers or clients of the firm for which they work. This is also clearly a form of sexual harassment for which a company can be liable.

A U.S. Federal District Court judge in Jacksonville, Florida, recently ruled that a display of pornographic pictures in a Jacksonville shipyard constituted sexual harassment. In this important decision, the court broadened the concept of workplace sexual harassment by maintaining that the offensive display of licentious photographs of women helped to promote the stereotype of women as sexual objects rather than competent workers.

Effects of On-the-Job Sexual Harassment on Victims. The financial ramifications of refusing to endure sexual harassment on the job may be devastating, especially for people in lower-level positions such as clerical and blue-collar workers. Many victims, particularly if they are supporting families, cannot afford to be unemployed. Many find it exceedingly difficult to look for other jobs while maintaining their present employment. If they are fired for refusing to be victimized, they may be unable to obtain unemployment compensation (unfortunately, harassment is sometimes seen as insufficient reason for quitting a job); and when they do obtain it, compensation will probably provide only half of their former income. Thus, a person who quits or is fired as a result of sexual harassment faces the prospect of severe financial difficulties.

The victim of sexual harassment may also suffer a variety of adverse emotional and physical effects (Hamilton et al., 1987). In two separate surveys of sexually harassed women, 75% and 78%, respectively, reported experiencing some negative effects including feeling angry, humiliated, ashamed, embarrassed, cheap, nervous, irritable, and unmotivated (Loy & Stewart, 1984; MacKinnon, 1979). Many of these women also felt guilty, as though they had done something to encourage the harassment; some felt that they alone had been singled out for such abuse, an often mistaken notion that can result in a sense of alienation from coworkers. The sense of degradation and helplessness reported by many victims of sexual harassment is similar to that experienced by many rape victims (Safran, 1976). These feelings of isolation, helplessness, and guilt, together with the very real threat of financial disaster, may cause a victim to acquiesce to the exploitive sexual demands encountered on the job. Very few comply because they feel "flattered" by the sexual attention they receive (MacKinnon, 1979; Safran, 1976).

Finally, many victims of sexual harassment report a variety of psychosomatic symptoms that stem directly from the pressures associated with their victimization. These include headaches, stomach ailments, back and neck pain, and a variety of other stress-related ailments.

How to Deal with Sexual Harassment in the Workplace. If you face sexual harassment at work, a number of options are available to you. The suggestions listed below, some of which are adapted from an excellent article by Karen Lindsey (1977), provide guidelines for dealing with this exploitive abuse:

1. If the harassment includes actual or attempted rape or assault, you can file criminal charges against the perpetrator.

2. If the harassment has stopped short of attempted rape or assault, you may wish to confront the person who is harassing you. State in clear terms that what he or she is doing is clearly sexual harassment, that you will not tolerate it, and that if it continues you will file charges through appropriate channels. You may prefer to document what has occurred and your response to it in a letter directed to the harasser (keep a copy). In such a letter, you should include specific details of previous incidents of harassment, your unequivocal rejection of such inappropriate overtures, and your intent to take more serious action if they do not stop immediately.

3. If the offender does not stop the harassment after direct confrontation, it may be helpful to discuss your situation with your supervisor and/or the supervisor of the offender.

4. If neither the harasser nor the supervisors respond appropriately to your concern, you may want to gather support from your coworkers (you may not be the only victim in your company). Discussing the offense with other sympathetic women and men in your workplace may produce sufficient pressure to terminate the harassment. Be sure of your facts, though, because such actions could result in a slander lawsuit.

5. Sometimes you can get results by using unorthodox tactics such as an anonymous posting of the offender's name or picture along with the message, "Warning: This person is a sexual harasser."

6. If your attempt to deal with this problem within your company does not work or if you are fired, demoted, or refused promotion because of your efforts to end harassment, you can file an official complaint with your city or state Human Rights Commission or Fair Employment Practices Agency (the names may vary locally). You can also ask that the local office of the federally funded Equal Employment Opportunity Commission investigate the situation.

7. Finally, you may wish to pursue legal action to resolve your problem with sexual harassment. Lawsuits can be filed in federal courts under the Civil Rights Act. They can also be filed under city or state laws prohibiting employment discrimination. One lawsuit can be filed in a number of jurisdictions. A person who has been a victim of such harassment is most likely to receive a favorable court judgment if she or he has first tried to resolve the problem within the company before taking the issue to court.

Students protest against sexual harassment on campus.

Sexual Harassment in Academic Settings

Sexual harassment also occurs in educational settings. Across the United States, students often find themselves in the unpleasant situation of experiencing unwanted sexual advances from their professors or supervisors. Both sexes are vulnerable to this form of harassment. However, most commonly the perpetrators are male professors or instructors who harass female students.

There are some differences between this type of harassment and that which occurs in the workplace. For one thing, a student who is faced with unwanted sexual advances often has the option of selecting a different instructor or advisor. In contrast, workers in an employment setting tend to have fewer alternatives for avoiding or escaping the harassment while still keeping their jobs. However, students may experience coercive compliance pressures associated with the need to obtain a good grade, a letter of recommendation, or a desirable work or research opportunity (Riger, 1991). Students also tend to be more naive than workers about the implications of becoming sexually involved with someone who is in a position to give or withhold aid that may be very important to their successful pursuit of a career. When one is young and easily impressed by people with prestige and/or power, there is a very real potential for inappropriate exploitation of this naiveté. Furthermore, recent evidence has suggested that sexual harassment in the classroom can negatively affect a student victim who "might wonder whether her academic success has been due to her ability or her professor's sexual interest in her" (Satterfield & Muehlenhard, 1990, p. 1).

Just how common is sexual harassment in academia? In two studies of undergraduate women, approximately one-third of the respondents reported having been the target of one or more incidents of sexual harassment (Benson & Thomson, 1982; Wilson & Kraus, 1981). More recently, a survey of several hundred college undergraduates revealed that 28% of the females and 12% of the males had experienced some form of sexually harassing behavior (Roscoe et al., 1987). Another survey of 215 undergraduates at a small university revealed that 29% of the females and 20% of the males had been the target of one or more incidents of sexual harassment perpetrated by professors (Mazer & Percival, 1989). Surveys of female graduate students have revealed that almost half have experienced sexual advances from their professors or supervisors (Glaser & Thorpe, 1986; Robinson & Reid, 1985).

What should you do if you are a victim of sexual harassment on campus? Think about this for a minute or two before reading on.

How to Deal with Sexual Harassment on Campus. Some students elect to avoid or escape the harassment by dropping a class, finding another faculty advisor, or even leaving school. However, we would advise someone who feels that she or he is being harassed to report it, if for no other reason than to curtail these inappropriate actions and reduce the likelihood that other students may be victimized by the same professor (it is common for people who harass students to have multiple targets). You may wish to speak to the chairperson or dean who supervises the offending individual. If you are not satisfied with that person's response, contact the campus officer or department that handles matters dealing with civil rights or affirmative action. You need not be concerned about grade discrimination or loss of position. Federal affirmative action guidelines prevent these forms of discrimination against people who, in good conscience, file legitimate claims of sexual harassment. Furthermore, a professor guilty of such action is not likely to continue to behave in an harassing or discriminatory fashion toward you because he or she will likely be closely monitored (repeat infractions may result in termination of employment).

Summary

Rape

The legal definition of rape varies from state to state, but most laws define rape as sexual intercourse that occurs under actual or threatened forcible compulsion that overcomes the earnest resistance of the victim.

Although evidence strongly suggests that rape is widespread, it is exceedingly difficult to obtain accurate statistics on the actual number of rapes and rape survivors in the United States.

Many contemporary attitudes and beliefs regarding rape stem from the historical low status of women.

Males in our society often acquire callous attitudes toward women that, when combined with a belief that "might makes right," provide a cultural foundation for rape and other acts of sexual coercion.

The many false beliefs about rape tend to hold the victim responsible for the crime and excuse the attacker.

Significant changes are occurring in rape laws regarding legal definitions and prosecution proceedings.

Rape is often a product of socialization processes that occur within certain rape-prone societies — societies that glorify masculine violence, teach boys to be aggressive, and demean the role of women in the economic and political aspects of life.

Extensive evidence suggests that exposure to sexually violent media may contribute to more accepting attitudes toward rape, decrease one's sensitivity to the tragedy of rape, and perhaps even increase men's inclinations to be sexually aggressive toward women.

Rapists frequently reveal extensive histories of sexual offenses, rape and violence fantasies, and being sexually abused in their childhoods. They also may exhibit displaced anger toward women and distorted perceptions of their rape behavior.

There is no singular pattern that characterizes the violent act of rape, and there is a wide range of individual differences among rapists. From the perspective of motivational intent, rapes can be categorized as anger rapes, power rapes, sadistic rapes, or sexual gratification rapes.

The majority of rapes are acquaintance rapes, where the perpetrator is known to the victim.

Sexual coercion in dating situations is quite prevalent. Both sexes experience sexual coercion, but women are more likely than men to be physically forced into unwanted sexual activity.

Rape survivors often suffer severe emotional difficulties that are manifested in the two phases of the rape trauma syndrome, the acute phase and the long-term reorganization phase.

Women often find that supportive counseling, either individually or in groups, can help ease the trauma caused by rape.

A rape survivor's recovery from her ordeal may be facilitated by a partner who listens and provides support and encouragement.

There are some rape-prevention tactics that may help reduce the chances of a woman being raped.

Women who choose not to report a rape to police or to tell anyone else may have more problems coping with their trauma than people who do tell others, because they do not have the opportunity to express and resolve their feelings.

Sexual Abuse of Children

Child sexual abuse refers to sexual contact between an adult and a child.

A distinction is generally made between non-relative child sexual abuse, called pedophilia or child molestation, and incest involving sexual contact between an adult and a child relative.

It is difficult to obtain accurate estimates of the frequency of incest and pedophilia in American society. Estimates of the number of girls sexually victimized range from 20% to 27%, whereas comparable estimates for boys range from 10% to 16%.

The majority of child sexual abusers are male relatives, friends, or neighbors of their victims.

Recent research suggests that the number of boys who are sexually molested in the United States may be substantially higher than has been reported.

Child sexual abuse can be a traumatic and emotionally damaging experience with long-term negative consequences for the child.

Survivors often experience a loss of childhood innocence, a disruption of their normal sexual development, and a profound sense of betrayal. Other damaging consequences include low self-esteem and difficulty establishing satisfying sexual and emotional relationships as adults.

There are a number of treatment programs for victims of child sexual abuse, ranging from individual therapy to group and couples-oriented approaches.

Most individuals who engage in pedophilia are middle-aged or older males who are shy, lonely, conservative, and often very moralistic or religious. They frequently have poor social and sexual relations with other adults and may feel inadequate and inferior.

Fathers who engage in incest with daughters are often economically disadvantaged, heavy drinkers, unemployed, religious, and very conservative.

Not uncommonly, pedophiles were sexually victimized themselves during their childhoods, while men who engage in incest often grew up in families where patterns of incest were modeled.

Prevention of Child Sexual Abuse

It is important to talk to children about protecting themselves from sexual abuse. Things children need to know include the difference between okay and not-okay touches, the fact that they have rights, that they can report abuse without fear of blame, and strategies for getting away from uncomfortable situations.

Sexual Harassment

Sexual harassment is any unwanted attention of a sexual nature from someone on the job that creates discomfort and/or interferes with the job.

Title VII of the 1964 Civil Rights Act prohibits sexual harassment in all its forms. A company can be liable for such coercive actions by its supervisors, coworkers, and customers.

Victims of sexual harassment may experience a variety of negative financial, emotional, and physical effects.

Sexual harassment also occurs in educational settings. Most commonly, perpetrators are male professors or instructors who harass female students.

◎ *Thought Provokers* ◎

1. How do false beliefs about rape perpetuate the belief that the victim is responsible, rather than the attacker? In your opinion, what effect does this belief have on the prosecution of rape? On its incidence? On the survivor?

2. Many people perceive a woman who wears "suggestive clothing" and is then raped as somehow responsible for her own rape. In contrast, a man who dons an expensive suit, carries lots of cash, and wears a Rolex watch is seldom, if ever, held responsible for being robbed on the street. What are your thoughts about this inconsistency in assigning the label "victim precipitation" to these two events? Is it ever appropriate to label a victim responsible for her or his own victimization?

3. If your child were a victim of sexual abuse, what would you do to reduce the potentially adverse effects of such an experience? What steps would you take to prevent the recurrent victimization of your child?

4. Do you believe that sexual harassment by professors is a significant problem on your campus? What experience, if any, have you or your friends had with this form of sexual victimization? How might a student effectively deal with instances of sexual harassment by a professor?

Suggested Readings

Bart, Pauline; and O'Brien, Patricia (1985). *Stopping Rape: Successful Survival Strategies.* New York: Pergamon Press. An excellent and very helpful overview of various strategies for reducing the risk of becoming a victim of sexual assault.

Bass, Ellen; and Davis, Laura (1988). *The Courage to Heal.* New York: Harper & Row. This powerful, moving book is aimed at assisting women survivors of child sexual abuse to recover from the emotional aftermath of being sexually victimized.

Beneke, Timothy (1982). *Men on Rape.* New York: St. Martin's Press. This provocative book deals with men's responsibility in stopping rape. Beneke provides numerous insights into what men think about women and rape.

Brady, Katherine (1979). *Father's Days.* New York: Dell. A courageous and powerful true story of a woman's sexual victimization by her father.

Brownmiller, Susan (1975). *Against Our Will: Men, Women, and Rape.* New York: Simon & Schuster. Offers a powerful, illuminating examination of rape from the feminist perspective that rape is an act of power and domination.

Colao, Flora; and Hosansky, Tamar (1983). *Your Children Should Know.* New York: Bobbs-Merrill. This very fine book, written in an engaging style, provides a wealth of information about preventing child sexual abuse and strategies for coping with such occurrences. Children, parents, educators, and health professionals all might profit from reading this excellent text.

Grauerholz, Elizabeth; and Koralewski, Mary (Eds.) (1990). *Sexual Coercion: A Sourcebook on Its Nature, Causes, and Prevention.* Lexington, Mass.: Lexington Books. This valuable collection of articles provides several illuminating perspectives on the nature of sexual coercion in its various forms, together with insights into how it may be prevented.

Groth, A. Nicholas (1979). *Men Who Rape.* New York: Plenum. Written by the director of a sex offender program in Connecticut, this book provides important insights into the character and motivation patterns of rapists.

MacKinnon, Catherine (1979). *Sexual Harassment of Working Women.* New Haven, Conn.: Yale University Press. This book offers an excellent, comprehensive discussion of the nature, extent, and impact of sexual harassment.

Maltz, Wendy; and Holman, Beverly (1987). *Incest and Sexuality: A Guide to Understanding and Healing.* Lexington, Mass.: Lexington. This excellent book helps sexual abuse survivors and their partners understand and recover from the effects of sexual abuse.

McGovern, Kevin (1985). *Alice Doesn't Baby-Sit Anymore.* Portland, Ore.: McGovern and Mulbacker Books. A children's storybook designed to teach children, parents, and educators how to avoid child sexual abuse. The author of this superb book is a clinical psychologist with extensive experience in the treatment of sex offenders and survivors of sexual victimization. Price: $8.95, which includes handling and shipping. Make checks payable to Alternatives to Sexual Abuse, P.O. Box 25537, Portland, OR 97225.

Parrot, Andrea; and Bechhofer, Laurie (Eds.) (1991). *Acquaintance Rape: The Hidden Crime.* New York: Wiley. This very fine up-to-date book provides in-depth analysis of the nature and extent of acquaintance rape together with excellent suggestions for its treatment and prevention.

Rush, Florence (1981). *The Best Kept Secret: Sexual Abuse of Children.* New York: Atlantic. A superb, painfully illuminating discussion of the sexual abuse of children. The author details the historical, political, social, and even religious factors that have sanctioned and perpetuated child–adult sex through the ages.

Russell, Diana (1982). *Rape in Marriage.* New York: Macmillan. This book summarizes the results of a comprehensive study of marriage rape. Russell provides an excellent analysis of the prevalence of wife rape, its connection to wife battery and alcoholism, and the underlying cultural attitudes that contribute to what she calls "the crime in the closet."

Resources

Rape crisis centers are listed in the white pages of the phone books of many cities.

CHAPTER 22
Sex for Sale

Pornography
Prostitution

*T*his chapter examines two broad areas of business in which money is exchanged for sexual stimulation, and explores the social and legal issues these activities raise.

Pornography

Pictorial and written representations of sexuality are not modern inventions. Cave drawings depicted sexual activity. Ancient Greek and Roman societies used sexual themes to decorate housewares and public architecture. The ancient Indian love manual *Kama Sutra,* dating from about A.D. 400, summarized philosophies of sexuality and spirituality in its description of specific sexual techniques. Graphic representations of coitus in Japanese *schunga* paintings and woodcuts from the 1600s and 1700s were regarded as art masterpieces.

A clear-cut contemporary definition of **pornography** is difficult to establish. The United States judicial system has not been able to establish a consistent definition, and individual opinions vary greatly on what is considered to be pornography. Generally speaking, pornography is written, visual, or spoken material, depicting or describing sexual conduct or genital exposure, that is arousing to the viewer. This definition is broad, however; within it the continuum could range from suggestive advertisements commonly seen on billboards and in magazines to explicit video portrayals of sexual interaction and sexually oriented violence, including torture and murder. The legal controversies surrounding pornography center on what is to be legally defined as "obscene," a term that implies a personal or societal judgment that something is offensive. In our discussion of relevant legal issues, pornography will be used as a collective term for visual and written materials sold for the purpose of sexual arousal. We will, however, further refine this definition in a later section on the effects of sexually explicit materials.

Sexual scenes on a Greek vase.

A Japanese *schunga* painting.

Four Legal Issues

The legal controversies relating to pornography have centered on four issues: the evaluation of what is obscene, regulations concerning the dissemination of sexually explicit materials, the constitutional right of free speech, and sexual discrimination ordinances.

Attempts at a Legal Definition. Pornography itself is not illegal, but materials considered to be obscene are. This leads us to the dilemma faced by the courts in determining what constitutes obscenity. Early U.S. courts considered material to be obscene if it depraved and corrupted the user. The courts then faced the problem of establishing that a person had been depraved by the materials. The first major challenge to this legal definition of obscenity occurred in the *Roth* v. *United States* case (354 U.S. 476), decided by the U.S. Supreme Court in 1957. This and subsequent decisions have established three criteria for evaluating obscenity. First, the dominant theme of the work as a whole must appeal to prurient interest in sex. Second, the work must be patently offensive to contemporary community standards. Third, it must be without serious literary, artistic, political, or scientific value (*Miller* v. *California*, 413 U.S. 15, 1973).

The subjectivity of these criteria is reflected in Supreme Court Justice Potter Stewart's comment that obscenity is difficult to define intelligently, "but I know it when I see it" (*Jacobelis* v. *Ohio*, 379 U.S. 197, 1965), as well as in local differences in interpretation. Community standards of obscenity can vary dramatically. In some areas, particularly in large cities, all manner of explicit sexual films are openly advertised and shown. In other areas, particularly in small communities, magazines such as *Playboy* have been banned. Some school boards have eliminated books they found objectionable from classrooms and libraries (see the box "Books Banned in Schools"). Courts, communities, and pornographic entrepreneurs still

OUR SEXUALITY

Books Banned in Schools

School boards and their appointed book-review committees can legally ban books from classroom use or the library, and have increased their book banning activities in recent years (Hochman, 1992). Many books have been banned from various schools. John Steinbeck's *Grapes of Wrath* was banned from classroom use in Kanawha, Iowa, because a parent complained that the work was "profane, vulgar, and obscene"; his book *Of Mice and Men* was removed from a high school library in Oil City, Pennsylvania, because it referred to prostitution and contained "vulgarity and profanity." A high school library in Milton, New Hampshire, removed Aleksandr Solzhenitsyn's work *One Day in the Life of Ivan Denisovich* because it contained "language you wouldn't allow to be used in the home." The school board of Issaquah, Washington, removed *The Catcher in the Rye*, by J. D. Salinger, from classroom use, claiming that it represented an "overall Communist plot" and contained numerous profanities. The Middleville, Michigan, school board banned the same book after several parents complained that it "violates the word of God." The school board of Miller, Missouri, banned Aldous Huxley's *Brave New World* because many parts of the book "make that kind of sex look like fun." The school board in a middle school in Eugene, Oregon pulled *The Clan of the Cave Bear* from the school library. Even the *American Heritage Dictionary* has been removed from a high school because, among other things, a "bed" was defined as a "place for lovemaking." The school board in Anchorage, Alaska, also removed this dictionary, because it contained too many "dirty words" (Doyle, 1982).

struggle with the legal definition of obscenity. The 1986 Attorney General's Commission on Pornography Report did not expand or clarify the legal definition of obscenity.

Regulating the Dissemination of Pornography. There have been several legal approaches to the regulation of obscene materials. In 1969 the U.S. Supreme Court ruled that private possession in the home was not a crime, nor was it subject to government regulation (*Stanley* v. *Georgia*, 394 U.S. 557). However, the dissemination of pornography is closely regulated. Federal laws prohibit broadcasting, mailing, importation, and interstate transport of obscene materials.

Most of these pornography dissemination statutes stem from the Comstock Act of 1873 (mentioned in Chapter 11), which made it a felony to deposit any materials of "indecent character" in the U.S. mail. During the first eight years of his involvement in the New York Society for the Suppression of Vice, self-appointed censor Anthony Comstock supervised the destruction of 27,584 pounds of books; the confiscation of 1,376,939 "obscene" songs, poems, pamphlets, and catalogs; and the recording of 976,125 names and addresses of people on mailing lists for pornography (Kilpatrick, 1960). Federal mailing laws have also been invoked in contemporary times in the prosecution of purveyors of obscene materials, and the 1986 Attorney General's Commission on Pornography recommended increasing funds for the enforcement of these laws.

There are other ways of regulating the dissemination of pornography. Many cities limit the areas where adult bookstores and movie houses can be located. Containment of bookstores and movie houses by zoning and land-use regulations attempts to protect nonusers of pornography from being visually assaulted by offensive material on the basis of the right to freedom from involuntary exposure

Due to zoning ordinances, high concentrations of pornographic shops and "adult" entertainments have arisen in some cities.

to pornography. Because of zoning ordinances, high concentrations of pornographic establishments have arisen in some cities. The "Combat Zone" in Boston and North Beach in San Francisco are examples of such areas.

Freedom of Speech. In a 1957 decision the Supreme Court declared that the U.S. Constitution's First Amendment guarantee of freedom of speech and of the press did not apply categorically to obscene materials. Vigorous arguments against this position have been presented by civil libertarians as well as by some of the justices of the Supreme Court. They maintain that any censorship is unconstitutional and therefore support the unrestricted availability of pornography to adults. The American Civil Liberties Union (ACLU) opposes many of the recommendations of the 1986 Attorney General's Commission on Pornography as "unconstitutional proposals which strike not only the First Amendment directly, but intrude upon civil liberties values like due process, privacy, and choice" (American Civil Liberties Union, 1986, p. 4).

Sexual Discrimination. A number of communities across the United States have considered laws establishing pornography as a form of sexual discrimination. These laws would be similar to those that allow people to file complaints against discrimination in employment: Individuals could press civil suits against the mak-

First Amendment rights regarding obscene materials have been tested in several recent cases. (a) A 1989 exhibit of Robert Maplethorpe's photographs was ordered closed by Cincinnati authorities because several of the photographs were considered pornographic under local obscenity laws. (b) The original image of four classical Greek statues on the cover of the Tin Machine album Tin Machine II was considered too obscene for release in the United States, so the group created a special U.S. version of the cover with the statues' genitalia removed.

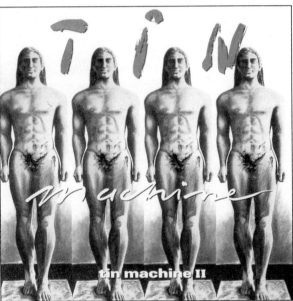

ers, distributors, or exhibitors of sexually explicit depictions of the subordination of women. Proponents of such laws and ordinances maintain that pornography harms a woman's opportunities for equal rights because it fosters exploitation and subordination based on sex.

Opponents of this type of legislation believe that such laws would infringe on freedom of personal choice by giving the courts power to interpret and rule on a wide variety of sexual images. They are also concerned about the antisexual bias in the proposed laws: Sexual explicitness is singled out as the target of these proposed laws and defined as degrading to women, rather than sexist images in general (Vance, 1985). They also maintain that eliminating pornography would not alleviate discrimination toward women. Historically, women have been oppressed when pornography was not a significant part of the culture. For example, pornography did not lead to the burning of witches in early American times (Duggan et al., 1985). One research study actually found that the political, economic, and legal status of women is higher in states with higher circulation rates of non-violent, soft-core pornography. The researchers maintained that their results indicated a political tolerance where gender equality and pornography flourish (Baron, 1990).

Effects of Sexually Explicit Materials

Questions about the effects of pornography have been debated extensively in recent years from different philosophical perspectives, and a considerable body of research is emerging. Some of the key questions being raised have to do with whether sexually explicit materials have significant effects on behavior, what those effects are, and what messages pornography may transmit about human relationships.

In the late 1960s, President Johnson appointed a Commission on Obscenity and Pornography to study the effects of sexually explicit materials. This commission studied events following the legalization of pornography in Denmark, analyzed findings of various self-report and survey research studies in the United States, and offered recommendations. The commission found that after pornography was legalized in Denmark in the late 1960s there was an initial increase in the number of Danish people who purchased pornographic materials. After a few years, however, sales to Danes decreased, and foreign tourists purchased most of the pornography. The commission noted that the legalization and increased availability of pornography did not result in an increase in reported sex offenses, although a cause-and-effect relationship in this regard is difficult to establish. (For example, there may have been increased tolerance and reduced prosecution of lesser offenses such as exhibitionism.) Also, the commission's analysis of current research found that imprisoned sex offenders had not had more exposure to pornography than had other prison inmates or nonprison populations. In its summary of research on the effects of sexually explicit materials, the commission concluded that no significant, long-lasting changes in behavior were evident in college-student volunteer research subjects after being exposed to pornography. On the basis of this information, the commission's 1970 report recommended repealing all laws prohibiting access to pornography for adults. However, the U.S. Senate and President Nixon rejected the commission's recommendations.

Controversy and concern about the effects of pornography have continued, and research in this area has expanded. (Research results are limited by several factors. Most subjects are undergraduate male college students rather than a sample of the general population. In addition, the experimental setting is artificial, and it is difficult to know how reported attitudes will affect actual behavior in daily life [Green, 1985].) As research has increased, the categorization of sexually explicit materials has become more distinct. Much of the current research separates sexually explicit materials into three groups: violent and aggressive pornography, degrading and dehumanizing pornography, and mutually consenting and pleasurable erotica. Central to both violent and degrading pornography is the depiction of an unequal balance of power for the purpose of sexual stimulation and entertainment. Violent pornography involves aggression or brutality; the violence takes the form of rape, beatings, dismemberment, and even murder. Degrading pornography objectifies and denigrates its subjects (Donnerstein et al., 1987). In contrast, "erotica can be defined as depictions of sexuality which display mutuality, respect, affection, and a balance of power" (Stock, 1985, p. 13). Erotica offers "a spontaneous sense of people who are there because they want to be, out of shared pleasure" (Steinem, 1980, p. 37).

Do you think sexually violent pornographic images have increased or decreased in the last 20–30 years? Arrive at your own conclusion before reading on.

Although an analysis of the last 30 years of *Playboy* magazine found that sexually violent depictions had decreased (Scott & Cuvelier, 1987), several other studies found that the prevalence of violence toward women in pornography and in mass-media depictions in magazines, record covers, films, and videos had increased significantly since the 1960s (Check, 1984; Malamuth & Spinner, 1980; Penrod & Linz, 1984). Another study found that one-third of the sex episodes in pornographic books involved some type of emotional or physical force and that the number of rape depictions doubled from 1968–1974 (Smith, 1976). The violent and degrading nature of these materials is likely a response to the marketplace. One study examined college men's reactions to pictures of women half nude and bound. Some of the women in the pictures were portrayed as being distressed and others as enjoying themselves. Almost 80% of the men in the study found pictures of distressed women more erotic than those of women portraying enjoyment (Heilbrun & Seif, 1988).

Research has indicated that exposure to violent pornography in young volunteer subjects may lead to increased tolerance for sexually coercive or aggressive behavior, to greater acceptance of the myth that women want to be raped, and to increased hostility toward a female accomplice in laboratory studies (Rosen & Beck, 1988). Exposure to violent pornography also reduces sensitivity to rape victims (Linz, 1989). In Chapter 21 we presented research indications that exposure to depictions of violent sex may, in some cases, encourage men to commit rape.

A newer focus of research has been to examine the effects of degrading pornography. Sexual depictions that degrade, debase, and dehumanize women are a common pornographic theme. Women are presented as sexual playthings, eager to accommodate every sexual urge of any man (Zillman & Bryant, 1982). This type of material may be most prevalent in mainstream X-rated videos. One study found that subjects who viewed pornography videos or films on their own initiative at least once a month were more accepting of rape myths, more accepting of violence against women, and more likely to report that they would rape women and force them to engage in unwanted sex acts (Check, 1985). What research has not determined is what is the cause here and what the effect.

Many of the studies examining the effects of nonviolent but degrading pornography show results similar to the effects of exposure to violent pornography. One study found that after about five hours of exposure to nonviolent stag films, subjects considered rape to be a lesser offense than prior to viewing the films.

Men's sexual callousness toward women also increased, as indicated by their increased support of such statements as "a woman doesn't mean no until she slaps you." In addition, subjects were less compassionate toward rape victims and less supportive of the women's movement after seeing the films (Zillman & Bryant, 1982). Another study demonstrated that increased acceptance of the myth that women want to be raped remained two months after the exposure to degrading pornography (Linz, 1985).

How do you think these laboratory studies translate into changes in behavior in daily life? Give this some thought before reading on.

An important question about changes in attitudes that occur in research experiments is whether these attitudes influence real-life behavior. A leading researcher has hypothesized:

> The data suggest that the type of media effects found in the research . . . may indirectly affect actual aggression against women. This may occur in two ways. First, it appears that in combination with other factors, attitudes that are relatively accepting of violence against women may contribute to the likelihood that a person will commit aggressive acts. Of course, media messages are only one of the many sources that can influence attitudes and in many cases changed attitudes will not necessarily alter behavior. A second way in which the media may indirectly affect behavior is by contributing to the social climate. For example, if a person's attitudes become more tolerant of violence against women this may not necessarily affect his own aggressive behavior but may influence how he reacts to a friend's boasting about sexual aggression, his reactions to a rape victim or even his vote as a member of a jury in a rape trial. Such responses may influence the aggressive behavior of others. Clearly, there is a need for additional research concerning these propositions. (Malamuth, 1985, p. 110)

One of the most important points in this research concerns reactions to violence. Most researchers in this area have found that the violent nature of material, whether it is sexual or not, is associated with aggressive tendencies in men (Scott & Schwalm, 1988). Leading researchers criticized the Meese Commission Report because it ignored the "inescapable conclusion that it is violence, whether or not accompanied by sex, that has the most damaging effect upon those who view it, hear it or read about it. . . . The most clear and present danger. . . is all violent material in our society, whether sexually explicit or not, that promotes violence against women" (Donnerstein & Linz, 1986, p. 59).

How do you think pornography affects intimate relationships between men and women? Develop your own ideas before reading further.

Besides the questions already raised about the effects of violent or degrading pornography are concerns about its impact on intimate relationships between women and men. One criticism of pornography is that it contributes to unrealistic expectations about sexuality. Pornography often stresses performance and conquest rather than pleasure. It perpetuates the myths that a real man is always ready for sex and that sex can be obtained without regard for the other person or the complex nature of the man himself (Zilbergeld, 1978). Exposure to pornography can increase acceptance of male dominance and female servitude (Zillman & Bryant, 1988a). In addition, women are often portrayed in pornography as intensely responsive to just about any stimulation from men. When women do not react in such a manner in real life, men may feel cheated, and both women and men may doubt their own perfectly normal sexuality. One research study of undergraduate students and the general population found that after repeated exposure to pornography, men and women became less satisfied with the physical appeal and sexual performance of their sexual partners (Zillman & Bryant, 1988b). Sexual expectations derived from pornography may also cause conflict in relationships. For example, 10% of a randomly selected group of women said that they had been upset by being asked to do something their male partners had seen or read in pornographic pictures, movies, or books (Russell, 1980).

How do the effects of exposure to erotica compare to the effects of exposure to violent and degrading pornography? Come to your own conclusions before reading further.

Equally important to the issues related to exposure to violence is that the studies of exposure to erotica have not shown significant adverse effects (Donnerstein et al., 1987). A partial solution to the potential problems with pornography would be for erotica to be as available as sexually violent and degrading materials (Check, 1984). Research has also suggested that education dispelling rape myths can change attitudes in a positive direction (Donnerstein et al., 1987). Educational programs that deal with the myths and stereotypes about women and rape may reduce the negative impact of violent and dehumanizing media images of sexuality (Linz et al., 1987).

In 1986 the U.S. Attorney General's Commission on Pornography addressed numerous issues, and in its report reached drastically different conclusions and made radically different recommendations than did the 1970 commission. The report concluded that violent pornography caused sexually aggressive behavior toward women and that degrading pornography fostered accepting attitudes toward rape and had some causal relationship to sexual violence. The commission members disagreed substantially about the effects of mutually consensual sexually explicit erotica; some viewed erotica as harmless and potentially beneficial, while others believed it to be destructive to the moral environment of society by promoting promiscuity and sex outside of marriage. Among the 92 recommendations in the report were many advocating more vigorous law enforcement and prosecution related to obscene materials. It recommended citizen activity to file complaints, to pressure the legal system, and to monitor and boycott newsstands, videocassette stores, and bookstores selling objectionable sexually explicit materials. Additional recommendations included prosecuting consensual sexual activity occurring in "adults-only" bookstores and prohibiting obscene cable television programming and "Dial-a-Porn" telephone services (phone numbers a person can call to hear sexual talk). The report placed special emphasis on child pornography and encouraged increased enforcement efforts of the criminal laws now in place related to the production, sale, and distribution of child pornography. In addition, contrary to earlier Supreme Court rulings that private possession of pornography in the home is not a crime, the report recommended that possession of child pornography become a felony (U.S. Attorney General's Commission on Pornography, 1986).

Many of the report's conclusions and recommendations have generated considerable dissent and disagreement. To begin with, the composition of the commission was biased; 6 of the 11 members had been involved in some type of opposition to sexually explicit materials prior to their appointments, and none of the members had a history of opposition to the restriction of sexually explicit materials (American Civil Liberties Union, 1986; Kurtz, 1985). In addition, many critics maintained that the commission's goal was to establish the dangers of sexually explicit materials and to justify greater government control rather than to engage in an objective, balanced inquiry (American Civil Liberties Union, 1986; Wooster, 1986).

Two commission members, behavioral scientist Judith Becker and journalist and editor Ellen Levine, wrote a dissenting opinion to the report in which they expressed concern that the materials presented in the hearings were not representative of materials available, and that testimony during the hearings did not accurately represent the positive and negative effects of sexually explicit materials. The ACLU's critique stated, "Materials which presented alternative viewpoints [or] reached conclusions not consistent with the presuppositions of the Commission . . . were suppressed or ignored" (1986, p. 1). Another researcher stated:

> Pornography is not contagious. . . . For example, the eleven members of the Meese Commission on Pornography (1986) exposed themselves to vast amounts of pornography, but . . . None has admitted to having been turned into a marauding and predatory paraphiliac practitioner of sexual violence, which, if the predictions of their report were correct, they should have been. (Money, 1988, pp. 167–68)

The ACLU was also concerned about the use of public tax money for the commission's study. "Every dollar spent on the legal 'fight' against pornography is a dollar taken from the struggle against murder, rape, robbery, extortion, and the corruption of public institutions. A decision to expend scarce enforcement resources on 'crimes' of consensual individual behavior in preference to other priorities ought to be rejected" (1986, p. 155).

The 1986 Attorney General's Commission on Pornography Report and its advocates and critics have intensified the issue of government regulation and enforcement of "morality." The social significance of the commission's report goes beyond its specific findings: the report is much more a documentation of attitudes toward sexual morality and the role of government that have gained acceptance during the Reagan era than of current scientific knowledge. A journalist explained, "The findings of presidential commissions are often a kind of mirror of the public sensibility of the time — one reason, perhaps, that the latest porn report is so different from the 1970 one" (Stengle, 1986, p. 17).

Definitions of and perspectives on pornography, as well as pornography itself, have changed with time. However, the issues involved, such as freedom of speech, the role of law, effects on human relationships, and considerations of personal and public morality, remain controversial.

Prostitution

Prostitution refers to the exchange of sexual services for money. In prostitution, sexual contact is treated as a commodity (de Zalduardo, 1991). Prostitution is typically thought of in terms of a woman selling sexual services to a man, although transactions between two males are also common. Payment for a man's services to a woman are less usual. Involvement of children in prostitution also occurs (see the box "Teenage Prostitution and Child Pornography"). Prostitution is generally characterized by sexual contacts with multiple partners, with whom the contract for the exchange of sexual services for money is explicit. Prostitution is illegal in every state of the United States except Nevada.

Prostitution has existed throughout history. However, the significance and meaning of prostitution have varied in different times and societies. In ancient Greece the practice was tolerated. During some periods of Greek history, certain types of prostitutes were valued for their intellectual, social, and sexual companionship. Prostitution was part of revered religious rituals in other ancient societies. Sexual relations between prostitutes and men often took place within temples and were seen as sacred acts; in some cultures the man in this transaction was considered to be a representative of the deity. In medieval Europe prostitution was tolerated, and the public baths provided opportunities for contacts between customers and prostitutes. In England during the Victorian era, prostitution was viewed as a scandalous but necessary sexual and social outlet for men: It was a lesser evil for a man to have sexual relations with a prostitute than with another man's wife or daughter (Taylor, 1970).

Who do you think is a prostitute's typical customer, or "John"? Develop your own ideas before reading further.

Prostitutes exist because there is a demand for their services (Cohen, 1980). Many customers regularly visit prostitutes; one study found that 93% of the men interviewed had contact once a month or more frequently (Freund et al., 1991). Customers of prostitutes are usually white, middle-aged, middle-class, and married (Adams, 1987); they patronize prostitutes for various reasons. Sex with a prostitute provides sexual contact or release without any expectation of intimacy or future commitment, offers an opportunity to engage in sexual techniques that a partner will not permit, and eliminates the risk of rejection.

No single theory can explain the motivation for being a prostitute. A combination of psychological, social, environmental, and economic factors is involved. Economic incentive is often the primary motivation for becoming a prostitute (Rio, 1991). Studies have also reported a high incidence of childhood sexual abuse in the history of female prostitutes; one researcher found that prostitutes have a 46–60% incidence of childhood sexual abuse, with physical force involved in nearly one-fourth of the cases (Bachmann et al., 1988).

Some prostitutes work on a part-time basis and otherwise pursue conventional school, work, or social lifestyles. Prostitutes may be delinquent school dropouts and runaways or well-educated adults. "Prostitutes have exceedingly diverse life histories, aspirations, and present life conditions" (de Zalduardo, 1991, p. 241). People who work as prostitutes on a temporary, part-time basis and have other occupational skills can more easily leave prostitution. Many of these men and women have not identified themselves as prostitutes, or "professionals" (Davis, 1978). The full-time prostitute, who is alienated from traditional values and has identified herself or himself as part of the subculture (being arrested facilitates this

ETHICAL/LEGAL ISSUES IN HUMAN SEXUALITY

Teenage Prostitution and Child Pornography

Experts estimate that there may be as many as 2.4 million teenage prostitutes in the United States (United States General Accounting Office, 1982). Teenagers often become prostitutes as a means of survival after they have run away from home. Other options for earning money are limited or nonexistent. As one prostitute has stated:

> There's no doors opened to us. . . . How are you going to be able to hold down a job if you have no high school diploma, if you're not able to take a shower every day, if you don't have clean clothes to wear to work? And let's say you came out here because of "certain circumstances" at home. You're scared out here. (Hersch, 1988, p. 35)

Most teenage prostitutes come from dysfunctional families: Approximately 95% have been victims of sexual abuse, and most have been abandoned by their families (Rios, 1991). Approximately 70% of runaways who come to emergency shelters have been sexually molested or severely physically abused (Hersch, 1988). Most teenage prostitutes did not perform well in school and have poor self-images. One study of adolescent male prostitutes found two dominant themes in their earlier lives: They were likely to have had an unstructured and unsupervised home life, and they also felt rejected by peers at school and had few friends (Price et al., 1984).

The children who become prostitutes are often seeking adult attention and affection, and they believe at first that prostitution is a life of glamour and adventure. However, in reality they must cope with the extreme dangers of street life, including serious risks of contracting the virus that causes AIDS, through either sexual contact or shared needles (many adolescent prostitutes are IV-drug abusers).

Pornographers are able to find children — usually between the ages of 8 and 16 — who will participate in making pornographic photographs, videotapes, or movies in exchange for friendship, interest, or money, or as a result of threats. One study found that many of the children were related by blood to the pornographers (Burgess et al., 1984). Some children, particularly the very young, may not know their photographs are used as pornography. Commercially pro-

duced child pornography has declined due to the Protection of Children Against Sexual Exploitation Act of 1977, stricter law enforcement, and media attention. Federal law bars the importing of child pornography from other countries; it is a felony to sell child pornography; and possessing child pornography is illegal in 13 states (Cohn, 1988). However, home-made, underground child pornography is still produced (Baker, 1980). The 1986 U.S. Attorney General's Commission on Pornography Report focused a great deal of attention on the prevention of and interventions against this problem. More aggressive law-enforcement strategies to find, prosecute, and penalize child pornographers are underway (Molotsky, 1988). Many of the consumers of child pornography also were sexually abused children (Cohn, 1988).

Children involved in prostitution and pornography often suffer emotional distress and have poor life adjustment. Many develop a concept of themselves as objects to be sold. They frequently have problems with employment because of the stigma of their past and their dissatisfaction with the lower pay of a regular job. They may have difficulty establishing meaningful relationships and are likely to become involved in crime. Many children who have been involved in pornography suffer from depression, anxiety, guilt, and self-destructive and antisocial behavior (Burgess et al., 1984).

identification), typically has little education and few marketable skills. These people usually find it very difficult to become successfully independent of prostitution. Legal problems, health hazards, and fear of personal injury are serious concerns of prostitutes. However, according to one study, 70% of the 46 street prostitutes interviewed reported enjoying intercourse with customers at least some of the time (Savitz & Rosen, 1988).

AIDS is also a concern with prostitution. In parts of Africa, sex with prostitutes is a primary mode of transmission of the HIV virus, which causes AIDS. One study found that 85% of 1000 prostitutes tested in Nairobi, Kenya, were infected with the HIV virus (Lambert, 1988). HIV-infection rates among prostitutes in the United States are in general much lower and vary greatly from one geographic area to another. HIV-infection rates among prostitutes in several U.S. studies averaged 12% and varied from 0% in brothels in Las Vegas to 57% in northern New Jersey (Lambert, 1988). Since March 1986 prostitutes in county-licensed brothels in Nevada are required to be tested monthly for HIV antibodies (Leads from the MMWR, 1987), and some brothel owners now require customers to use condoms to prevent HIV infection (Chaze et al., 1987). Prostitutes of low socioeconomic status are much more likely to be infected with HIV than are high-priced prostitutes (Lambert, 1988). The greatest risk factor for prostitutes for HIV infection is intravenous drug abuse or having sex partners who are IV-drug abusers. Women with unprotected vaginal exposures also appear to be at greater risk than those whose male partners always use condoms (Leads from the MMWR, 1987). Male prostitutes who service other men are at great risk of becoming infected and transmitting the virus that causes AIDS (Decker, 1987).

Female Prostitutes

There are various types of female prostitutes who service male customers. The variations relate to such characteristics as the public visibility of the woman, the amount of money she charges, and her social class. We look at a few different categories, defined roughly in terms of the method a woman uses to contact customers. These include *streetwalkers,* women who work in brothels or massage parlors, and *call girls.*

Streetwalkers can be seen on the streets of most large cities. They solicit customers on the street or in bars. They are often from lower socioeconomic backgrounds, charge less than do other types of prostitutes for their services, and must share a large portion of their earnings with their pimps (discussed later in this chapter). Streetwalkers are at the bottom of the hierarchy of prostitution (Diana, 1985). The prostitutes in this group are most likely to have histories of traumatic family backgrounds (Rio, 1991). Because of their visibility, streetwalkers are easily subject to arrest. Most streetwalkers repeat the cycle of arrest, short jail sentences, and release many times throughout their careers. Even in the few cities where laws inflict penalties on the customer as well as the prostitute, the male customers of streetwalkers and other prostitutes are rarely arrested.

A **brothel** is a house in which a group of prostitutes work. Brothels were common in earlier American history and remain so in some other countries. They

Streetwalkers can be seen on
the streets of most large cities.

are legal in some areas of Nevada today. Brothels range from expensive establishments to run-down, seedy places. They are usually managed by a "madam" who acts as the hostess and business manager of the house. Prostitutes who work in brothels in areas where prostitution is illegal are somewhat more protected from arrest than are streetwalkers because they are less visible to the police. Prostitutes are also less vulnerable to physical assault from their customers within the brothel setting.

Massage parlors are often seen as a modern "quick-service" version of brothels. Manual stimulation (a "local" or "hand finishing") or oral stimulation to orgasm is often arranged for a fee once the customer is in the massage room. The customer also can often dictate in what state of dress or undress he would like his masseuse to be. Intercourse may or may not occur as part of the "massage." Most of the massage parlor customers in one study were white-collar businessmen over the age of 35 (Velarde & Warlick, 1973). Zoning and business-license laws are sometimes used to attempt to control the location or existence of massage parlors.

Call girls generally earn more than other kinds of prostitutes. They often come from middle-class backgrounds. Call girls frequently offer social companionship as well as sexual services for their customers. Their customer contacts are usually made by personal referral, and they often have several regular customers. Their public visibility is minimal, and their risk of arrest is much less than that of the streetwalker. Call girls charge more for their services and provide themselves with attractive wardrobes and apartments—all part of their business expenses. They are also more likely than other types of prostitutes to be given goods such as

Call girls are the "elite" of female prostitutes and obtain their customers through escort services and personal referral rather than chance street encounters.

clothing or living accommodations by regular customers. A case study of call girls is described in Chapter 2, in the box "The Elegant Prostitute."

Male Prostitutes

Men who provide sexual services for women in exchange for money and gifts are called **gigolos.** The role of a gigolo is most similar to that of a call girl, because he usually acts as a social companion as well as a sexual partner. His customers are usually wealthy middle-aged women seeking the attentions of attractive young men. There is often a pretense on the gigolo's part of romantic interest in the woman. The exchange of money for services is less explicit than in most interactions between female prostitutes and male customers. It is unknown how common this type of male prostitution is, but it is probably far less common than female prostitution.

Male prostitutes who cater to homosexual men are probably as numerous as female prostitutes but have not been studied as extensively. Like female prostitutes, male prostitutes who cater to homosexual men can be classified into different groups. *Hustlers* make contact with customers on the streets, in gay bars or bath houses, or in public parks or toilets. Most hustlers come from chaotic family backgrounds and live in a social milieu of drug abuse and unstable personal relationships (Wilson, 1991). (The recent movie *My Own Private Idaho* provided a vivid

OTHER TIMES, OTHER PLACES

Prostitution in the American West in the Late 1800s

Prostitution permeated both the rural and the urban American West in the 1800s. Prostitutes gravitated toward mining towns, construction sites, military outposts, cattle terminals, supply stations, and larger urban centers of the frontier. They sold companionship and sex in dance halls and gambling joints, in brothels, in shacks and tents off the streets, or in traveling "cat wagons." Prostitutes

were among the poorest women on the frontier, and they usually remained destitute throughout their lives. They were often European immigrants or from ethnic groups such as Oriental, Mexican, or Native American.

Some black women became prostitutes after the close of the Civil War. Their previous experiences in American society had exposed them mostly

to unskilled or agricultural labors; most remained uneducated and untrained. Thrust into a society that did not want them, left with no means of support, some turned to prostitution in the West. The appearance of the black brothel represented an extension of the cultural interaction that generations of black women had been taught in slavery. Sexual availability without matrimonial protection permeated the experiences of female slaves. Long eliminated from the inner circles of profit, advancement, and status, black women did nonetheless understand the art of survival. For some the transformation from slave to prostitute arose from the debilitating social and economic effects of bondage (Butler, 1985).

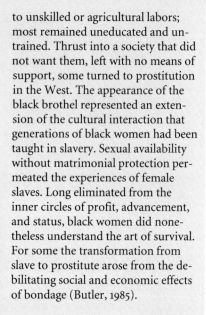

Prostitutes' "cribs" like these were common throughout the West in the 1890s. This photo was taken in the Yukon Territory.

fictional portrayal of the lives of a group of young hustlers.) *Call boys* work similarly to call girls. They have regular customers and are often social companions as well as sexual partners. Call boys find their customers through advertisements (often in gay newspapers) or through personal referrals. *Kept boys* are partially or fully supported by an older male. *Peer-delinquent prostitutes* often work in small groups and use homosexual prostitution as a vehicle for assault and robbery. Most peer-delinquent prostitutes are between 14 and 17 years old. Their usual modus operandi is for one or more of them to solicit a customer who is willing to pay to perform fellatio on them; they then rob and physically assault the customer. Peer-delinquent prostitutes often define their contacts with customers as a demonstration of their masculinity and heterosexuality to their peers. However, beneath this facade many have strong homosexual feelings (Allen, 1980).

Some male prostitutes consider themselves to be heterosexual. They have concurrent female sexual partners and usually return to a heterosexual lifestyle after a brief career in prostitution. Like peer-delinquent prostitutes, they often restrict their homosexual activities to those in which they assume the more masculine role; for example, allowing customers to perform fellatio on them but not reciprocating (Reiss, 1964).

ETHICAL/LEGAL ISSUES IN HUMAN SEXUALITY

Prostitution and the Law

The legal status of prostitution has been debated for some time in the United States. There are several arguments for maintaining its status as a criminal offense. One view is that if prostitution were not a punishable offense, many women would take it up and it would be more difficult to enforce any restrictions on prostitution activities. Another argument is that it is the responsibility of government to regulate public morals, and the absence of laws against prostitution signifies government tolerance of commercialized vice (United Nations Study on Traffic in Persons and Prostitution, 1959).

Arguments against the criminal status of prostitution center on the difficulty of effective prosecution. Prostitution flourishes despite criminal sanctions against it, as it has throughout history in most societies where it has been prohibited. Other arguments are concerned with the possible negative results of outlawing prostitution. For instance, its criminal status may encourage connections with organized crime and hamper the rehabilitation of prostitutes (who

may find it difficult to find other kinds of work once they have a criminal record). There are also arguments that center on discrimination in applying penalties. Customers and prostitutes are equally responsible in the vast majority of cases, but it is the prostitute, not the customer, who is arrested and prosecuted.

There are at least two alternatives to the criminal status of prostitution. One is its *legalization*; the other is *decriminalization*. If legalized, prostitution could be regulated, licensed, and taxed by the government. In some European cities, prostitutes are registered and required to follow certain procedures such as periodic STD checks to maintain their licenses. If prostitution were decriminalized, criminal penalties for engaging in prostitution would be removed; however, prostitutes would be neither licensed nor regulated. Laws concerning solicitation and laws against the involvement of minors would remain, even if prostitution were legalized or decriminalized.

The rationale for legalization or decriminalization is based on several

factors. Prostitution is usually considered a "victimless crime," an act that does not harm the people engaged in it. (However, prostitution may not be victimless in all senses because, as we have seen, the prostitute is often the victim of abuse from customers and pimps and of discriminatory laws and social stigmas.) Decriminalizing or legalizing prostitution would perhaps allow the criminal justice system to expend more efforts combating crimes that harm people or property (Morris, 1973). Also, if prostitution were legal, its association with organized crime might be weakened. And the victimization of prostitutes by pimps, customers, the judicial system, and others who profit at their expense would perhaps also be reduced.

Some prostitutes have organized for political change and mutual support. The prostitutes' union, COYOTE (Cast Out Your Old Tired Ethics), acts as a collective voice for the prostitutes' concerns; what ultimate impact this organization will have on U.S. laws pertaining to prostitution remains to be seen.

Economics and Profit from Prostitution

For many men and women who sell sexual services, prostitution is a way of earning a living; most view their work as an economic opportunity (Diana, 1985). Recognizing the connection between prostitution and economic disadvantage, the 1959 United Nations Commission study of prostitution concluded that creating other economic opportunities for women was important for its prevention.

Although women and men usually become prostitutes to earn money for themselves, the practice also profits many other parties. In fact, it may not be as lucrative for the prostitute as it is for the other people involved, either directly or indirectly. Pimps, the criminal justice system, referral agents, and hotel operators all benefit financially from prostitution (Diana, 1985). *Pimps* are men who "protect" prostitutes (usually streetwalkers) and live off their earnings. (Women are more likely than men to have pimps.) The illegality of prostitution contributes to the prostitutes' need for a pimp. Pimps bail the women in their "stables" out of jail when they are arrested. They may offer companionship, a place to live, clothing, food, and in some cases, drugs. They often assume a highly controlling, authoritarian, sometimes abusive relationship with their prostitutes while being supported by the women's earnings. Pimps may keep as much as 95% of the streetwalkers' earnings, which they often invest in ostentatious clothing and cars that represent the pimp's status and his prostitutes' earning power (Young, 1970).

Because prostitution is illegal, police officers, attorneys, judges, bail bondsmen, and jailers spend part of their work time attempting to control, litigate, or process prostitutes through the judicial bureaucracy. In this way prostitution provides some of the business for the criminal justice system. (Some people argue that the time and money spent in actions against prostitution impede the judicial system's effectiveness in working with more serious crimes.) Organized crime is also often involved in prostitution and profits from it (Sheehy, 1973).

Referral agents also make money from prostitution. Cabdrivers, hotel desk clerks, and bartenders get cash tips from customers as well as from prostitutes for helping establish the contact. Prostitutes who work out of their apartments may have to give doormen, hotel proprietors, and elevator operators an ongoing supply of tips, high rental fees, or sexual services (or any combination thereof) so that they will not report them to the authorities.

Summary

Pornography

A clear definition of pornography and obscenity has yet to be established by the judicial system. The criteria established by the Supreme Court in attempting to decide what is obscene are that the dominant theme of the work as a whole must appeal to prurient interest, be offensive to contemporary community standards, and be without serious literary, artistic, political, or scientific value.

Legal regulation of pornography occurs through mailing laws and zoning of pornography outlets. The U.S. Constitution's First Amendment guarantee of freedom of speech and of the press does not apply categorically to obscene materials. Some communities have considered laws establishing pornography as a form of sexual discrimination.

The increased availability and legalization of pornography in Denmark was not followed by an increase in reported sex offenses.

There are conflicting data on the effects of pornography. The 1970 Commission on Obscenity and Pornography reported that pornography did not have significant, long-lasting effects. However, more recent research has suggested that sexually violent and degrading materials could have a significant impact on attitudes toward women and could promote the myth that women want to be raped. The controversial 1986 Attorney General's Commission on Pornography Report maintained that sexually violent and degrading pornography caused sexual aggression toward women.

Research has found that nonsexual violence in media materials was associated with aggressive tendencies in men. However, the Meese Commission Report ignored research in this area.

Characteristics of erotica include mutual affection, respect, and pleasure. Unlike violent and degrading pornography, erotica has no known significant negative effects.

Prostitution

Prostitution refers to the exchange of sexual services for money. Many prostitutes have a childhood history of sexual abuse. Streetwalkers, women in brothels or massage parlors, and call girls are general categories of female prostitutes.

Male prostitutes who service women are called gigolos. Male prostitutes who service homosexual men may be categorized as hustlers, call boys, kept boys, or peer-delinquent prostitutes.

Prostitutes most at risk of contracting or transmitting HIV, the virus that causes AIDS, are IV-drug abusers, have sexual partners who are IV-drug abusers, or do not use condoms consistently during sexual encounters.

Women or men who turn to prostitution do so, in part, for economic opportunity. However, pimps, the criminal justice system, organized crime, referral agents, and hotel operators also profit from prostitution.

∽ *Thought Provokers* ∽

1. When did you first encounter pornographic material? How did it affect you?

2. What effects, if any, do you think violent and degrading pornography and erotica have on intimate relationships between men and women?

3. What kinds of laws about prostitution make sense to you? How do you justify your point of view?

Suggested Readings

American Civil Liberties Union (1986). *Polluting the Censorship Debate.* Washington, D.C.: American Civil Liberties Union. A summary and critique of the Final Report of the Attorney General's Commission on Pornography.

Butler, Anne (1985). *Daughters of Joy, Sisters of Mercy.* Urbana: University of Illinois Press. A detailed book about the lives and the socioeconomic impact of prostitutes in the American West in the late 1800s.

Delacoste, Frederique; and Alexander, Priscilla (1987). *Sex Work: Writings by Women in the Sex Industry.* Pittsburgh: Cleis Press. This edited book is written by women in the sex industry — prostitutes, nude dancers, porn movie actresses, and workers in massage parlors — who speak out about their work.

Donnerstein, Edward; Linz, Daniel; and Penrod, Steven (1987). *The Question of Pornography.* New York: Free Press. Offers a comprehensive summary of the scientific research on the effects of sexually explicit images and legal and regulatory issues.

Millett, Kate (1976). *The Prostitution Papers.* New York: Ballantine Books. A critical exploration into the social role of prostitutes in our society; presents an argument against legalization and for decriminalization.

Rio, Linda (1991). "Psychological and Sociological Research and the Decriminalization or Legalization of Prostitution." *Archives of Sexual Behavior* 20, 205–18.

U.S. Attorney General's Commission on Pornography (1986). *Final Report of the Attorney General's Commission on Pornography.* Washington, D.C.: U.S. Justice Department. A two-volume, 1960-page report of the testimony, analysis, and recommendations of the commission; includes dissenting opinions of commission members.

Glossary

Abortion The spontaneous or medically induced removal of the contents of the uterus during pregnancy.

Acquaintance rape Forced sexual assault by a friend, acquaintance, or date.

Acquired immunodeficiency syndrome (AIDS) A catastrophic illness in which a virus invades and destroys the ability of the immune system to fight disease. The AIDS virus appears to be passed primarily through sexual contact, needle sharing among intravenous drug abusers, or less commonly, through administration of contaminated blood products.

Adrenogenital syndrome (AGS) [ad-rē'-nō-JĔN-i-tal] A condition that results when a female fetus's adrenal glands malfunction and produce abnormally high amounts of androgen, inducing masculinization of the external genitals.

AGS *See* Andrenogenital syndrome.

Afterbirth The placenta and amniotic sac following their expulsion through the vagina after childbirth.

AIDS *See* Acquired immunodeficiency syndrome.

AIDS-related complex (ARC) A less-severe form of AIDS that manifests in people infected with the AIDS virus. A substantial number of cases of ARC eventually progress to AIDS.

AIS *See* Androgen insensitivity syndrome.

Amenorrhea [a-men'-o-RĒ-a] The absence of menstruation.

Amniocentesis [am'-nē-o-sen-TĒ-sis] A procedure in which amniotic fluid is removed from the uterus and tested to determine if certain fetal birth defects exist.

Amniotic fluid The fluid inside the amniotic sac surrounding the fetus during pregnancy.

Amniotic sac A sac of tissue inside the uterus that encloses the fetus and the amniotic fluid.

Ampulla [am-POOL-la] Upper portions of the vas deferens that undergo muscle contractions during the emission phase of ejaculation.

Anaphrodisiac [an-ah-frōh-DIZ-ē-ak] A substance that allegedly inhibits sexual desire and behavior.

Androgen insensitivity syndrome (AIS) A condition resulting from a genetic defect that causes chromosomally normal males to be insensitive to the action of testosterone and other androgens. These individuals develop female external genitals of normal appearance.

Androgens [AN-droh-jens] A class of hormones that promotes the development of male genitals and secondary sex characteristics and influences sexual motivation in both sexes. These hormones are produced by the adrenal glands in males and females and by the testes in males.

Androgyny [an-DRAW-jin-ē] A blending of typical male and female behaviors in one individual.

Anorgasmia [AN-or-GAZ-mē-uh] A sexual difficulty involving the absence of orgasm in women.

Antiandrogens A group of drugs that blocks the action of testicular and adrenal androgens.

Aphrodisiac [ah-frō-DIZ-ē-ak] A substance that allegedly arouses sexual desire and increases the capacity for sexual activity.

ARC *See* AIDS-related complex.

Areola [a-RĒ-ō-la] The darkened circular area surrounding the nipple of the breast.

Autosomes [AW-tuh-somes] The 22 pairs of human chromosomes that do not significantly influence sex differentiation.

Bacterial vaginosis A vaginal infection, usually caused by a bacterium called *Gardnerella vaginalis*, that may be the most common form of vaginitis among American women.

Bartholin's glands Two small glands slightly inside the vaginal opening that secrete a few drops of fluid during sexual arousal.

Basal body temperature A method of birth control based on temperature changes before and after ovulation.

Bisexual A person who feels sexual attraction to or has sexual contact with members of both sexes.

Blastocyst [BLAS-tō-sist] Multicellular descendant of the united sperm and ovum that implants on the wall of the uterus.

Brothel A house in which a group of prostitutes works.

Bulb The base of the penis.

Bulbourethral glands [bul'-bō-yoo-RĒ-thral] *See* Cowper's glands.

Calendar method A method of birth control based on abstinence from intercourse during calendar-estimated fertile days.

Candida albicans A yeastlike fungus ordinarily found in the vagina. When excessive amounts of it develop, a vaginal inflammation called candidiasis results.

Candidiasis [kan-de-DĪ-a-sis] An inflammatory infection of the vaginal tissues caused by the yeastlike fungus *Candida albicans*.

Case studies A method of research that involves in-depth study of one or more subjects who are examined individually.

Castration Surgical removal of the testes or ovaries.

Cavernous bodies The structures in the shaft of the penis and clitoris that engorge with blood during sexual arousal.

Celibacy [SEL-a-ba-sē] Historically defined as the state of being unmarried, currently defined as not engaging in sexual behavior.

Cerebral cortex The thin outer layer of the brain's cerebrum, or "gray matter," that is responsible for higher mental processes including perceiving, thinking, and remembering.

Cerebral hemispheres The two sides (left and right) of the cerebrum.

Cervical cap A plastic or rubber cover for the cervix that provides a contraceptive barrier to sperm.

Cervix [SER-viks] The small end of the uterus, located at the back of the vagina.

Cesarean delivery [sē-SĀR-ē-an] A childbirth procedure in which the infant is removed through an incision in the abdomen and uterus.

Chancre [SHAN-ker] A raised, red, painless sore that is symptomatic of the primary phase of syphilis.

Chancroid A bacterial sexually transmitted disease characterized by small bumps in the region of the genitals, perineum, or anus that eventually rupture and form painful ulcers with a foul discharge.

Child molestation Sexual contact between an adult and child, usually when the child is under the age of 12.

Child sexual abuse Sexual abuse involving contact between an adult and a child. A distinction is generally made between non-relative child sexual abuse (called pedophilia or child molestation) and incest involving sexual contact between a child and adult who are relatives.

Chlamydial infection [clah-MID-ē-al] Urogenital infection caused by the bacterium *Chlamydia trachomatis*. Chlamydial infections are the most prevalent and among the most damaging of all sexually transmitted diseases.

Chorionic villus sampling (CVS) [ko-rē-ON-ik VIL-us] A prenatal test that detects some birth defects.

Chromosomes [KRO-muh-somes] The structures in the nucleus of each cell that contain the genes that provide information for the transmission of inherited characteristics.

Cilia [SIL-ē-a] The hairlike filaments in the inside of the fallopian tubes that propel the egg along to the uterus.

Circumcision [ser'-kum-SIZH-un] Surgical removal of the foreskin of the penis.

Climacteric [kli-MAK-ter-ik] Physiological changes that occur during the transition period from fertility to infertility in both sexes.

Clitoral hood The skin that covers the clitoris.

Clitoris [KLI-to-ris] A highly sensitive structure of the female external genitals, the only purpose of which is sexual pleasure.

Cohabitation Living together and having a sexual relationship without being married.

Coitus A technical term for penile-vaginal intercourse.

Colostrum [ka-LOS-tram] A thin fluid secreted by the breasts during late pregnancy and the first few days following delivery.

Combination pills Contraceptive pills containing both estrogen and progestin.

Coming out The process of becoming aware of and disclosing one's homosexual identity.

Companionate love A type of love characterized by friendly affection and deep attachment based on extensive familarity with the loved one.

Complete celibacy Engaging neither in masturbation nor in interpersonal sexual contact.

Condom A latex or membrane sheath that fits over the penis and is used for protection against unwanted pregnancy and sexually transmitted diseases.

Conjunctivitis [kon-junk'-ti-vī-tis] Inflammation of the mucous membrane that lines the inner surface of the eyelid and the exposed surface of the eyeball.

Consensual adult statutes Laws that maintain that private, consensual sexual behavior between adults is not illegal.

Consensual extramarital relationship A sexual and/or emotional relationship that occurs outside the marriage bond with the consent of one's spouse.

Constant dose combination pill A type of birth control pill containing a constant daily dose of estrogen and progestin.

Contraception Techniques, drugs, or devices to prevent conception.

Coprophilia [cop-rō-FIL-ē-uh] A sexual paraphilia in which a person obtains sexual arousal from contact with feces.

Corona [ko-RŌ-na] The rim of the penile glans.

Corpora cavernosa *See* Cavernous bodies.

Corpus luteum A yellowish body that forms on the ovary at the site of the ruptured graafian follicle and secretes progesterone.

Corpus spongiosum *See* Spongy body.

Cowper's glands Two pea-sized glands located alongside the base of the urethra in the male that secrete an alkaline fluid during sexual arousal.

Cremasteric muscle A muscle located in the spermatic cord that elevates the testicles when voluntarily or involuntarily contracted.

Cremasteric reflex Involuntary contractions of the cremasteric muscle induced by stroking the inner thigh.

Crura [KROO-ra] The innermost tips of the cavernous bodies that connect to the pubic bones.

Cryptorchidism [krip-TOR-ki-dizm] A condition in which the testicles fail to descend from the abdominal cavity to the scrotal sac.

Cunnilingus [kun-i-LIN-gus] Oral stimulation of the vulva.

CVS *See* Chorionic villus sampling.

Cystitis An inflammation of the urethra or bladder, characterized by discomfort during urination.

Date rape Forced sexual assault by an acquaintance when on a date.

Decriminalization Removing criminal penalties for activities previously defined as criminal.

Demographic bias A kind of sampling bias in which certain segments of society (such as caucasian, middle-class, white-collar workers) are disproportionately represented in a study population.

Desire stage According to Helen Kaplan's model of sexual response, the first step in the sequence of human sexual response.

DHT-deficient male Chromosomally normal (XY) male who develops external genitalia resembling those of a female as a result of a genetic defect that prevents the prenatal conversion of testosterone into DHT.

Diaphragm A birth control device consisting of a latex dome on a flexible spring rim. The diaphragm is inserted into the vagina with contraceptive cream or jelly and covers the cervix.

Direct observation A method of research in which subjects are observed as they go about their activities.

Douching Rinsing out the vagina with plain water or a variety of solutions. It is usually unnecessary for hygiene, and too-frequent douching can result in vaginal irritation.

Ductus deferens *See* Vas deferens.

Dysmenorrhea [dis'-men-o-RĒ-a] Pain or discomfort before or during menstruation.

Dyspareunia [DIS-puh-ROO-nē-uh] Pain or discomfort during intercourse.

Ectopic pregnancy [ek-TOP-ik] Implantation of a fertilized ovum in a location other than the uterus, usually in the fallopian tubes.

Effacement Flattening and thinning of the cervix that occurs before and during childbirth.

Either/or question A question that allows statement of a preference.

Ejaculation The process whereby semen is expelled from the body through the penis.

Ejaculatory ducts [e-JAK-yoo-la-to'-rē] Two short ducts located within the prostate gland.

Ejaculatory inhibition A sexual difficulty whereby the male does not ejaculate inside the vagina.

Elective abortion Medical procedures performed to terminate pregnancy.

Emission phase The first stage of male orgasm, in which the seminal fluid is gathered in the urethral bulb.

Endocrine system [EN-dō-krin] A system of ductless glands that produces hormones and secretes them directly into the bloodstream.

Endometriosis [en'-dō-MĒ-trē-ō-sis] A condition in which uterine tissue grows on various parts of the abdominal cavity.

Endometrium [en'-dō-ME-trē-um] The tissue that lines the inside of the uterine walls.

Epididymis [ep'-i-DID-i-mus] The structure along the back of each testicle in which sperm maturation occurs.

Episiotomy [e-pis'-ē-OT-ō-mē] An incision in the perineum that is sometimes made during childbirth.

Erectile inhibition A sexual difficulty whereby a man's penis does not become erect in response to sexual stimulation.

Erection The process of the penis or clitoris engorging with blood and increasing in size.

Erogenous zones Areas of the body that are particularly responsive to sexual stimulation.

Estrogens [ES-troh-jens] A class of hormones that produces female secondary sex characteristics and affects the menstrual cycle. Also found in lesser amounts in males.

Ethnographers [eth-NOG-ra-fers] Anthropologists who specialize in studying the cultures of different societies.

Excitement phase William Masters and Virginia Johnson's term for the first phase of the sexual response cycle, in which engorgement of sexual organs and an increase in muscle tension, heart rate, and blood pressure occur.

Exhibitionism The act of exposing one's genitals to an unwilling observer.

Experimental research Research conducted in precisely controlled laboratory conditions so subjects' reactions can be reliably measured.

Expulsion phase The second stage of male orgasm, during which the semen is expelled from the penis by muscular contractions.

Extramarital relationship Sexual interaction by a married person with someone other than his or her spouse.

Faking orgasms A sexual difficulty whereby a person pretends to experience orgasm during sexual interaction.

Fallopian tubes [fa-LŌ-pē-an] Two tubes in which the egg and sperm travel, extending from the sides of the uterus.

Fellatio [fel-Ā-shē-ō] Oral stimulation of the penis.

Fetally androgenized female Chromosomally normal (XX) female who, as a result of excessive exposure to androgens during prenatal sex differentiation, develops external genitalia resembling those of a male.

Fetishism [FET-ish-iz-um] Obtaining sexual excitement primarily or exclusively from an inanimate object or a particular part of the body.

Fimbriae [FIM-brē-a] Fringelike ends of the fallopian tubes into which the released ovum enters.

First-stage labor The initial stage of childbirth in which regular contractions begin and the cervix dilates.

Follicle-stimulating hormone (FSH) A pituitary hormone. Secreted by a female during the secretory phase of the menstrual cycle, it stimulates the development of ovarian follicles. In males, it stimulates sperm production.

Foreplay Usually defined as the kissing, touching, or oral–genital contact preceding coitus.

Foreskin A covering of skin over the penile or clitoral glans.

Frenulum [FREN-yoo-lum] *See* Frenum.

Frenum A highly sensitive, thin fold of skin that connects the foreskin with the underside of the penile glans.

Frotteurism A fairly common paraphilia in which a person obtains sexual pleasure by pressing or rubbing against another in a crowded public place.

FSH *See* Follicle-stimulating hormone.

Fundus The upper, rounded portion of the uterus.

Gardnerella vaginalis A bacterium that causes bacterial vaginosis.

Gay A homosexual, particularly a homosexual man.

Gender The state of being masculine or feminine.

Gender assumption Assumptions about how people are likely to behave based on their maleness or femaleness.

Gender dysphoria [dis-FŌR-ē-a] *See* Transsexual.

Gender identity How one psychologically perceives oneself as either male or female.

Gender nonconformity A lack of conformity to stereotypic masculine and feminine behaviors.

Gender role A collection of attitudes and behaviors that are considered normal and appropriate in a specific culture for people of a particular sex.

Genes The basic units of heredity, carried on the chromosomes.

Genitals The sexual organs of males and females.

Genital tubercle The area on a fetus that develops into the male or female external genitals. It is undifferentiated prior to six weeks of fetal age.

Genital warts Viral warts that appear on the genitals. The warts are primarily sexually transmitted.

Gigolos Men who provide social companionship and sexual services to women for financial gain.

Giving permission Providing reassurance to one's partner that it is OK to talk about certain specific feelings or needs.

Glans The head of the penis or clitoris; richly endowed with nerve endings.

Gonadotropins Pituitary hormones that stimulate activity in the gonads (testes and ovaries).

Gonads The male and female sex glands — ovaries and testes.

Gonorrhea [gon-ō-RĒ-a] A sexually transmitted disease that initially causes inflammation of mucous membranes.

Graafian follicle [GRAF-ē-an FOL-i-kal] A small swelling on the ovary from which a mature ovum is discharged.

Grafenberg spot Glands and ducts located in the anterior wall of the vagina below the urethra. Some women may experience sexual pleasure, arousal, orgasm, and an ejaculation of fluids from stimulation of the Grafenberg spot.

Granuloma inguinale A very rare disease that may be spread either sexually or nonsexually. Initial symptoms are small, painless, pimple-like bumps on the genitals or thighs that eventually ulcerate and emit a sour odor. The disease may result in extensive tissue destruction and permanent scarring of the genitals.

Group marriage Several adults living together, each maintaining what are considered marital relationships with more than one other group member.

Gynecology [gi'-na-KOL-ō-jē] The medical practice specializing in women's health and in diseases of the female reproductive and sexual organs.

HCG *See* Human chorionic gonadotropin.

Hermaphrodites [her-MAF-roh-dites] People with ambiguous or contradictory sex characteristics.

Herpes A disease, characterized by blisters on the skin in the regions of the genitals or mouth, that is caused by a virus and is easily transmitted by sexual contact.

Heterosexual person A person whose primary social, emotional, and sexual orientation is toward members of the other sex.

Homophobia Irrational fears of homosexuality, the fear of the possibility of homosexuality in oneself, or self-loathing toward one's own homosexuality.

Homosexual person A person whose primary erotic, psychological, emotional, and social orientation is toward members of the same sex.

Hormone replacement therapy (HRT) The use of supplemental hormones during and after menopause.

Hormones Chemical substances produced by endocrine glands that affect the functioning of other organs.

HRT *See* Hormone replacement therapy.

Human chorionic gonadotropin (HCG) [kō-rē-ON-ik gon'-a-dō-TRŌ-pin] A hormone that is detectable in the urine of a pregnant woman about a month after conception.

H-Y antigen [AN-ti-jen] A substance present in males that triggers the transformation of the embryonic gonads into testes.

Hymen [HĪ-men] Tissue that partially covers the vaginal opening.

Hypogonadism Impaired hormone production in the testes that results in androgen deprivation.

Hypothalamus [hy-poh-THAL-ah-mus] A critical brain structure that plays a major role in controlling the production of sex hormones and the regulation of fertility and menstrual cycles through its interaction with the pituitary gland.

Hysterectomy [his′-te-REK-tō-mē] The surgical removal of the uterus.

Incest Sexual interaction between close relatives other than husband and wife.

Induced abortion Medically induced removal of the contents of the uterus during pregnancy.

Inguinal canal The canal through which the testes travel during fetal development from inside the abdomen to the scrotum.

Inhibited sexual desire (ISD) A sexual difficulty involving lack of interest in sexual fantasy and activity.

Interstitial cells [in′-ter-STISH-al] Cells located between the seminiferous tubules that are the major source of androgen in males.

Intrauterine device (IUD) A small, plastic device that is inserted into the uterus for contraception.

Introitus [in-TRŌ-i-tus] The opening to the vagina.

Intromission Insertion of the penis into the vagina.

ISD *See* Inhibited sexual desire.

IUD *See* Intrauterine device.

Kegel exercises A series of exercises that strengthen the muscles underlying the external female or male genitals.

Klinefelter's syndrome A rare condition characterized by the presence of two X chromosomes and one Y (XXY).

Klismaphilia [klis-ma-FIL-ē-uh] A very unusual variant in sexual expression in which an individual obtains sexual pleasure from receiving enemas.

Labia majora [LĀ-bē-a ma-JO-ra] The outer lips of the vulva.

Labia minora [LĀ-bē-a min-OR-a] The inner lips of the vulva, one on each side of the vaginal opening.

Legalization Making legal previously defined illegal activities and regulating, licensing, or taxing the activities.

Lesbianism Female homosexuality.

Lesbian A female homosexual.

Leukorrhea A general term applied to a variety of vaginal infections characterized by an excessive discharge.

Leydig's cells *See* Interstitial cells.

LH *See* Luteinizing hormone.

Libido A term commonly used to denote sexual motivation.

Limbic system A subcortical brain system composed of several interrelated structures that influences the sexual behavior of humans and other animals.

Lochia [LŌ-kē-a] A reddish, uterine discharge that occurs following childbirth.

Longitudinal study A research study that evaluates a group of subjects at several, intervening points to assess how certain behaviors may have changed.

Lubrication inhibition A sexual difficulty that involves a lack of lubrication during sexual interaction.

Luteinizing hormone (LH) [LOO-tē-n′-īz-ing] The hormone secreted by the pituitary gland that stimulates ovulation in the female. In males it is called interstitial cell hormone (ISCH) and stimulates production of androgens by the testes.

LVG *See* Lyphogranuloma venereum.

Lymphogranuloma venereum (LVG) A rare sexually transmitted disease that first appears as small painless papules on the genitals.

Mammary glands [MAM-ar-ē] Milk glands in the female breast.

Mammography [mam-OG-ra-fē] A highly sensitive X-ray test for the detection of breast cancer.

Mastectomy Surgical removal of the breast(s).

Masturbation Stimulation of one's own genitals to create sexual pleasure.

Menarche [me-NAR-kē] The initial onset of menstrual periods in a young woman.

Menopause Cessation of menstruation due to the aging process or surgical removal of the ovaries.

Menstrual phase The phase of the menstrual cycle when menstruation occurs.

Menstrual synchrony The development of congruent menstrual cycle timing that sometimes occurs among women who live in close proximity.

Menstruation [men′-stroo-Ā-shun] The sloughing off of the built-up uterine lining that takes place if conception has not occurred.

Midwife A woman who has had training as a birth attendant.

MIS *See* Müllerian-inhibiting substance.

Miscarriage The spontaneous expulsion of the fetus from the uterus early in pregnancy, before it can survive on its own.

Molluscum contagiosum A sexually transmitted disease, caused by a pox virus, that is characterized by small, painless lesions.

Mons veneris A triangular mound over the pubic bone above the vulva.

Mucosa [myoo-KŌ-sa] Collective term for the mucous membranes, moist tissue that lines certain body areas such as the penile urethra, vagina, and mouth.

Mucous method A birth control method based on determining the time of ovulation by means of the cyclical changes of the cervical mucus.

Müllerian ducts A pair of ducts in the embryo that develop into female reproductive organs.

Müllerian-inhibiting substance (MIS) A substance secreted by the fetal testes that causes the Müllerian ducts to shrink rather than develop into internal female structures.

Multiphasic pills Birth control pills that vary the dosages of estrogen and progestin during the cycle.

Multiple orgasms More than one orgasm experienced within a short time period.

Mutative relationship A kind of dynamic love relationship in which both partners and the relationship itself continually generate change.

Mutual empathy The underlying knowledge that each partner in a relationship cares for the other and knows that the care is reciprocated.

Myometrium [mi′-o-MĒ-trē-um] The smooth muscle layer of the uterine wall.

Myotonia [mi-o-TO-nē-a] Muscle tension.

Necrophilia [nek-rō-FIL-ē-uh] A rare sexual paraphilia in which a person obtains sexual gratification by viewing or having intercourse with a corpse.

Neisseria gonorrhoeae The name of the bacterium that causes a gonorrhea infection.

NGU *See* Nongonococcal urethritis.

Nipple The central pigmented area of the breast, which contains numerous nerve endings. In women, the nipple also contains the milk ducts.

Nocturnal emission Involuntary ejaculation during sleep, also known as a "wet dream."

Nocturnal orgasm Involuntary orgasm during sleep.

Nonconsensual extramarital sex Engaging in an outside sexual relationship without the consent (or presumably the knowledge) of one's spouse.

Nongonococcal urethritis (NGU) An inflammation of the male urethral tube caused by other than gonorrhea organisms.

Nonresponse The refusal to participate in a research study.

Oophorectomy [ō-of-ō-REK-tō-mē] Surgical removal of the ovaries.

Open marriage A marriage in which spouses, with each other's permission, have intimate relationships with other people as well as the marital partner.

Open-ended question A type of question that allows a respondent to share any feelings or information she or he thinks is relevant.

Oral–genital stimulation Mouth to genital contact to create sexual pleasure.

Orchidectomy The surgical procedure for removing the testes.

Orgasm A series of muscular contractions of the pelvic floor muscles occurring at the peak of sexual arousal.

Orgasm phase A term coined by Masters and Johnson to describe the third phase of the sexual response cycle in which rhythmic muscular contractions of the pelvic floor occur.

Os The opening in the cervix that leads to the interior of the uterus.

Outercourse Noncoital forms of sexual intimacy.

Ovary Female gonad that produces ova and sex hormones.

Ovulation [ō-vyoo-LĀ-shun] The release of a mature ovum from the graafian follicle of the ovary.

Ovum The female reproductive cell.

Pap smear A screening test for cervical cancer.

Paraphilia Term used to describe uncommon types of sexual expression.

Paraphrasing A listener summarizing the speaker's message in his or her own words.

Partial celibacy Not engaging in interpersonal sexual contact but continuing to engage in masturbation.

Passionate love State of extreme absorption in another person. Also known as romantic love.

Passing Appearing to be heterosexual and avoiding presenting oneself as homosexual.

Pedophilia Sexual contact between an adult and a child.

Pelvic inflammatory disease (PID) An infection in the uterus and pelvic cavity.

Penis A male sexual organ consisting of the internal root and external shaft and glans.

Perimetrium [per-i-MĒ-trē-um] The thin membrane covering the outside of the uterus.

Perineum [per'-a-NE-am] The area between the vagina and anus of the female and the scrotum and anus of the male.

Petting Physical contact including kissing, touching, and manual or oral genital stimulation but excluding coitus.

Peyronie's disease Abnormal fibrous tissue and calcium deposits in the penis.

Pheromones Certain odors produced by the body that relate to reproductive functions.

Phimosis A condition characterized by an extremely tight penile foreskin.

PID *See* Pelvic inflammatory disease.

Pituitary gland A gland located in the brain that secretes hormones that influence the activity of other endocrine glands.

Placenta A disc-shaped organ attached to the uterine wall and connected to the fetus by the umbilical cord. Nutrients, oxygen, and waste products pass between mother and fetus through its cell walls.

Placenta previa [pla-SEN-ta PRĒ-vē-ā] A birth complication in which the placenta is between the cervical opening and the infant.

Plateau phase Masters and Johnson's term for the second phase of the sexual response cycle, in which muscle tension, heart rate, blood pressure, and vasocongestion increase.

PMS *See* Premenstrual syndrome.

Population In research, all the subjects within a given group of people.

Pornography Visual and written materials of a sexual nature that are used for purposes of sexual arousal.

Postpartum period The first several weeks following childbirth.

Premarital sex A term commonly used to categorize coitus that occurs before marriage.

Premature ejaculation A sexual difficulty whereby a man ejaculates so rapidly as to impair his own or his partner's pleasure.

Premenstrual syndrome (PMS) Symptoms of physical discomfort and emotional irritability, also called premenstrual tension, that occur 2 to 12 days prior to menstruation.

Prepared childbirth Birth following an education process that can involve information, exercises, breathing, and working with a labor coach.

Prepuce [PRĒ-poos] The foreskin or fold of skin over the glans penis or clitoris.

Preputial glands Small lubricating glands located in the foreskin of the penis.

Priapism Prolonged and uncomfortable penile erection.

Primary erogenous zones Areas of the body that contain dense concentrations of nerve endings.

Prodromal symptoms Symptoms that give advance warning of an impending herpes eruption.

Progestational compounds A class of hormones, which includes progesterone, that are produced by the ovaries.

Progesterone The hormone produced by the corpus luteum of the ovary that causes the uterine lining to thicken.

Progestin-only pills Contraceptive pills that contain a small dose of progestin and no estrogen.

Proliferative phase The phase of the menstrual cycle in which the ovarian follicles mature.

Pronatalism Attitudes and policies that encourage parenthood for all couples.

Prophylactic *See* Condom.

Prostaglandins Hormones that are used to induce uterine contractions and fetal expulsion for second-trimester abortions.

Prostate gland [PROS-tāt] A gland located at the base of the bladder that produces about 30% of the seminal fluid released during ejaculation.

Prostatitis [pros-tuh-TY-tis] Inflammation of the prostate.

Prostitution The exchange of sexual services for money.

Pseudohermaphrodites Individuals whose gonads match their chromosomal sex, but whose internal and external reproductive anatomy has a mixture of male and female structures or structures that are incompletely male or female.

Psychosexual therapy Treatment designed to help clients gain awareness of their unconscious thoughts and feelings that contribute to their sexual problems.

Psychosocial Refers to a combination of psychological and social factors.

Puberty The stage of life between childhood and adulthood during which the reproductive organs mature.

Pubic lice Lice that primarily infest the pubic hair and are transmitted by sexual contact.

Pubococcygeal (PC) muscle A muscle surrounding the vaginal opening.

Random sample A randomly chosen subset of a population.

Rape Sexual intercourse that occurs without consent as a result of actual or threatened force.

Reciprocity The principle that when we are recipients of expressions of liking or loving, we tend to respond in kind.

Refractory period The period of time following orgasm in the male during which he cannot experience another orgasm.

Relationship contract A mutually agreed on set of rules, plans, and philosophies related to an interpersonal relationship.

Replicability A study's ability to be repeated with a different group of participants in order to determine whether the results of the research are reproducible.

Representative sample A type of limited research sample in which every individual in the total population about which one wishes to draw inferences has an equal chance (probability) of being included.

Resolution phase The fourth phase of the sexual response cycle as outlined by Masters and Johnson, in which the sexual systems return to their nonexcited state.

Retrograde ejaculation Process by which semen is expelled into the bladder instead of out of the penis.

Root The portion of the penis that extends internally into the pelvic cavity.

Rugae [ROO-jē] The folds of tissue in the vagina.

Sadomasochism (SM) [SĂ-dō-MAS-ō-KIZ-um] The act of obtaining sexual arousal through receiving (masochism) or giving (sadism) physical or psychological pain.

Scabies A highly contagious infestation by tiny, parasitic mites that may be transmitted by sexual contact.

Scrotum [SKRŌ-tum] The pouch of skin of the external male genitals that encloses the testicles.

Secondary erogenous zones Areas of the body that have become erotically sensitive through learning and experience.

Secondary sex characteristics The physical characteristics other than genitals that indicate sexual maturity, such as body hair, breasts, and deepened voice.

Second-stage labor The middle stage of labor, in which the infant descends through the vaginal canal.

Secretory phase The phase of the menstrual cycle in which the corpus luteum develops and secretes progesterone.

Self-selection The bias introduced into research study results due to participants' willingness to respond.

Semen A viscous fluid ejaculated through the penis that contains sperm and fluids from the prostate, seminal vesicles, and Cowper's glands.

Seminal fluid *See* Semen.

Seminal vesicles [SEM-i-nal VES-i-kuls] Small glands adjacent to the terminals of the vas deferens that secretes an alkaline fluid (conducive to sperm motility) that constitutes the greatest portion of the volume of seminal fluid released during ejaculation.

Seminiferous tubules [sem'-i-NI-fer-us] Thin, coiled structures in the testicles in which sperm are produced.

Sensate focus A process of touching and communication used to enhance sexual pleasure and to reduce performance pressure.

Sex Biological maleness and femaleness.

Sex chromosomes A single set of chromosomes that influences biological sex determination.

Sex flush A pink or red rash that appears on the chest or breasts during sexual arousal.

Sexual addiction The need to engage in excessive sexual activity to relieve feelings of depression, anxiety, loneliness, and worthlessness.

Sexual aversion Extreme and irrational fear of sexual activity.

Sexual differentiation The process whereby the individual develops physical characteristics distinct from those of the other sex.

Sexual harassment Unwanted attention of a sexual nature from someone at the workplace.

Sexually transmitted diseases (STDs) Diseases that are transmitted by sexual contact. Term includes, but is not limited to, diseases traditionally called venereal disease (VD).

Sexual orientation Sexual attraction to one's own sex (homosexual) or the other sex (heterosexual).

Shaft The length of the clitoris and penis between the glans and the body.

Shigellosis A sexually transmitted bacterial infection characterized by diarrhea, fever, and inflammation of the large intestine.

SM *See* Sadomasochism.

Smegma A cheesy substance of glandular secretions and skin cells that sometimes accumulates under the foreskin of the penis or hood of the clitoris.

Socialization The process whereby our society conveys behavioral expectations to the individual.

Sodomy An ill-defined legal category for noncoital genital contacts such as oral–genital and anal intercourse.

Speculum An instrument with two blades used to open the vaginal walls during a gynecological exam.

Sperm The male reproductive cell.

Spermatic cord [sper-MAT-ik] A cord attached to the testicle that contains the vas deferens, blood vessels, nerves, and cremasteric muscle fibers.

Spermatogenesis [sper'-ma-tō-JEN-e-sis] Sperm production.

Spermicides Chemical substances used in contraceptives that kill sperm.

Spongy body A chamber that forms a bulb at the base of the penis, extends up into the penile shaft, and forms the penile glans.

Spontaneous abortion *See* Miscarriage.

Statutory rape Intercourse with a person under the legal age of consent.

Stereotype A generalized notion of what a person is like that is based only on that person's sex, race, religion, ethnic background, or similar criterion.

STDs *See* Sexually transmitted diseases.

Stop–start technique A treatment technique for rapid ejaculation, consisting of stimulating the man's penis to the point of impending orgasm and then stopping until the preejaculatory sensations subside.

Stranger rape Rape of a person by an unknown assailant.

Survey A research method in which a sample of people are questioned about their behaviors and/or attitudes.

Swinging The exchange of marital partners for sexual interaction.

Syphilis A sexually transmitted disease caused by a spirochete called *Treponema pallidum.*

Systems therapy Treatment that focuses on interactions within a couple relationship and on the functions of the sexual problems in the relationship.

Taxonomic survey Surveys aimed at classifying people into behavioral categories for statistical comparisons.

Testicle *See* Testis.

Testis Male gonad inside the scrotum that produces sperm and sex hormones.

Testosterone A major male hormone produced by the testes.

Third-stage labor The last stage of childbirth, in which the placenta separates from the uterine wall and comes out of the vagina.

Toxemia [toks-Ē-mē-a] A dangerous condition during pregnancy in which high blood pressure occurs.

Toxic shock syndrome (TSS) A disease that may cause a person to go into shock, occurring most commonly in menstruating women.

Trachoma [tra-KŌ-ma] A chronic, contagious form of conjunctivitis caused by chlamydial infections.

Transsexual A person whose psychological gender identity is opposite to his or her biological sex.

Transvestism Deriving sexual arousal from wearing clothing of the other sex.

Trichomoniasis [trick-ō-mon-I-ah-sis] A form of vaginitis caused by a one-celled protozoan called *Trichomonas vaginalis*.

Trimesters Three-month segments dividing the nine months of pregnancy.

Trophoblast cells [TROF-ō-blast] Cells of the placenta that secrete human chorionic gonadotropin (HCG).

True hermaphrodites Exceedingly rare individuals who have both ovarian and testicular tissue in their bodies. Their external genitals are often a mixture of male and female structures.

TSS *See* Toxic shock syndrome.

Tubal sterilization Female sterilization accomplished by cutting the fallopian tubes.

Turner's syndrome A rare condition characterized by the presence of one unmatched X chromosome (XO). Turner's syndrome individuals have normal female external genitals, but their internal reproductive structures do not develop fully.

Tyson's glands Small glands under the corona of the penis on either side of the frenum.

Urethra [yoo-RĒ-thra] The tube through which urine passes from the bladder to outside the body.

Urethral bulb The portion of the urethra between the urethral sphincters in the male.

Urethral sphincters Two muscles, one located at the base of the bladder in both sexes and another located below the prostate in the male.

Urethritis An inflammation of the urethral tube.

Urology [yoo-ROL-ō-jē] The medical specialty dealing with reproductive health and genital diseases of the male and urinary tract diseases in both sexes.

Urophilia [yoo′-rō-FIL-ē-uh] A sexual paraphilia in which a person obtains sexual arousal from contact with urine.

Uterus A pear-shaped organ inside the female pelvis, within which the fetus develops.

Vagina A stretchable canal in the female that opens at the vulva and extends about four inches into the pelvis.

Vaginal spermicides *See* Spermicides.

Vaginismus [vaj-in-IZ-mus] A sexual difficulty in which a woman experiences involuntary spasmodic contractions of the muscles of the outer third of the vagina.

Vaginitis [vaj′-a-NĪ-tis] Inflammation of the vaginal walls caused by a variety of vaginal infections.

Validating The process of indicating that a partner's point of view is reasonable, given some assumptions that one may not share with one's partner.

Vas deferens [vas DEH-fur-renz] A sperm-carrying tube that begins at the testicle and ends at the urethra.

Vasectomy [va-SEK-tō-mē] Male sterilization procedure that involves removing a section from each vas deferens.

Vasocongestion The engorgement of blood vessels in particular body parts in response to sexual arousal.

Vasovasostomy Surgical reconstruction of the vas deferens after vasectomy.

Vernix caseosa [VER-niks kas′-EO-sa] A waxy, protective substance on the fetus's skin.

Vestibular bulbs [ves-TIB-yoo-lar] Two bulbs, one on each side of the vaginal opening, that engorge with blood during sexual arousal.

Vestibule [VES-ti-byool] The area of the vulva inside of the labia minora.

Viral hepatitis [hep-a-TĪ-tis] A disease in which liver function is impaired by a viral infection.

Virgin A person who has not experienced coitus.

Voyeurism [voi-YUR-iz-um] The act of obtaining sexual gratification by observing undressed or sexually interacting people without their consent.

Vulva The external genitals of the female, including the mons veneris, labia majora, labia minora, clitoris, and urinary and vaginal openings.

Wolffian ducts The internal duct system of the embryo that develops into male reproductive structures.

XYY males A chromosomal anomaly that results when a normal ovum is fertilized by an atypical sperm bearing two Y chromosomes. XYY males develop normal sex organs and characteristics of males and are masculine in appearance.

Yes or no question A question that asks for a one-word answer and thus provides little opportunity for discussing an issue.

Zoophilia [zōō-FIL-ē-uh] A paraphilia in which a person has sexual contact with animals.

Zygote [ZĪ-gōt] The single cell resulting from the union of sperm and egg cells.

Bibliography

Abel, E. (1980). Fetal alcohol syndrome. *Psychological Bulletin,* 87, 29–50.

———. (1984). Opiates and sex. *Journal of Psychoactive Druga,* 16, 205–216.

Abel, G. (1981). The evaluation and treatment of sexual offenders and their victims. Paper presented at St. Vincent Hospital and Medical Center, Portland, Ore., October 15.

———, Barlow, D., Blanchard, E., & Guild, D. (1977). The components of rapists' sexual arousal. *Archives of General Psychiatry,* 34, 895–903.

———, Becker, J., & Cunningham-Rather, J. (1984). Complications, consent, and cognitions in sex between children and adults. *International Journal of Law and Psychiatry,* 7, 89–103.

———, Becker, J., Mittleman, M., Cunningham-Rathner, J., Rouleau, J., & Murphy, W. (1987). Self-reported sex crimes of nonincarcerated paraphiliacs. *Journal of Interpersonal Violence,* 2, 3–25.

Abrahams, J. (1982). Azoospermia before puberty. *Medical Aspects of Human Sexuality,* 1, 13.

Abramowicz, M. (1987). Drugs that cause sexual dysfunction. *The Medical Letter,* 29, 65–70.

———. (Ed.) (1990). Drugs for HIV infection. *The Medical Letter on Drugs and Therapeutics,* 31, 11–13.

———. (Ed.) (1990). Treatment of sexually transmitted diseases. *The Medical Letter on Drugs and Therapeutics,* 32, 5–10.

Adams, F. (1987). The role of prostitution in AIDS and other STDs. *Medical Aspects of Human Sexuality,* 21, 27–33.

Adams, G., Adams-Taylor, S., & Pittman, K. (1989). Adolescent pregnancy and parenthood: A review of the problem, solutions, and resources. *Family Relations,* 38, 223–229.

Adams, J. (1973). *Understanding Adolescence.* Boston: Allyn and Bacon.

Adamson, G., & Gare, D. (1980). Home or hospital births? *Journal of the American Medical Association,* 243, 1732–1736.

Addiego, F., Belzer, E., Comolli, J., Moger, W., Perry, J., & Whipple, B. (1981). Female ejaculation: A case study. *Journal of Sex Research,* 17, 13–21.

Adducci, C., & Ross, L. (1991). Common urethral injuries in men. *Medical Aspects of Human Sexuality,* October, 32–44.

Adler, J., Duignan-Cabrera, A., & Gordon, J. (1991). Drums, sweat, and tears. *Newsweek,* June 24, 46–53.

———, McCormick, J., Bingham, C., King, P., & Annin, P. (1992). Abortion's long siege. *Newsweek,* April 27, 44–47.

Adler, N., Hendrick, S., & Hendrick, C. (1986). Male sexual preference and attitudes toward love and sexuality. *Journal of Sex Education and Therapy,* 12, 27–30.

Agnew, J. (1986). Hazards associated with anal erotic activity. *Archives of Sexual Behavior,* 15, 307–314.

Ainslie, J., & Feltey, K. (1991). Definitions and dynamics of motherhood and family in lesbian communities. *Marriage & Family Review,* 17, 63–85.

Akers, R. (1985). *Deviant Behavior: A Social Learning Approach,* 3rd ed. Belmont, Calif.: Wadsworth.

Alan Guttmacher Institute (1991). Abortion in the United States. *Facts in Brief.* New York, NY, Alan Guttmacher Institute.

Alder, C. (1985). An exploration of self-reported sexually aggressive behavior. *Crime and Delinquency,* 31, 306–331.

Alderman, P. (1988). The lurking sperm. *Journal of the American Medical Association,* 259, 3142–3176.

Alexander, N., & Anderson, D. (1987). Immunology of semen. *Fertility and Sterility,* 47, 192–205.

Alexander, S. (1984). Improving sex education programs for young adolescents: Parent's views. *Family Relations,* 33, 251–257.

Alford, J., Kasper, C., & Baumann, P. (1984). Diagnostic classification of child sexual offenders. *Corrective and Social Psychiatry,* 30, 40–46.

Algood, C., Newell, G., & Johnson, D. (1988). Viral etiology of testicular tumors. *Journal of Urology,* 139, 308–310.

Allen, D. (1980). Young male prostitutes: A psychosocial study. *Archives of Sexual Behavior,* 9, 399–426.

Allen, J., Philliber, S., & Hoggson, N. (1990). School-based prevention of teenage pregnancy and school dropout: Process evaluation of the national replication of Teen Outreach Program. *American Journal of Community Psychology,* 18, 505–524.

Allen, M., & Marte, C. (1992). HIV infection in women: Presentations and protocols. *Hospital Practice,* March 15, 155–162.

Allgeier, E. (1981). The influence of androgynous identification on heterosexual relations. *Sex Roles,* 7, 321–330.

Al-Nozha, M., Ramia, S., Al-Frayh, A., & Arif, M. (1990). Female to male: An inefficient mode of transmission of human immunodeficiency virus (HIV). *Journal of AIDS,* 3, 193–194.

Allon, N., & Fishel, D. (1979). Singles bars. In N. Allon (Ed.)., *Urban Life Styles.* Dubuque, Ia.: Brown.

Alper, J. (1991). Environmentalists: Ban the (population) bomb. *News & Comment,* May 31, 1247.

Alpern, D. (1986). A *Newsweek* poll: Sex laws. *Newsweek,* July 14, 38.

Althof, S., & Turner, L. (1992). Self-injection therapy and external vacuum devices in the treatment of erectile dysfunction: Methods and outcome. In R. Rosen & S. Leiblum (Eds.), *Erectile Disorders.* New York: Guilford Press.

Altman, L. (1983). Increase in testicular cancer prompts call for self-examination. *New York Times* News Service, May 3.

Alzate, H. (1985). Vaginal eroticism: A replication study. *Archives of Sexual Behavior, 14,* 529–537.

————, & Hoch, Z. (1986). The ``G spot'' and ``female ejaculation'': A current appraisal. *Journal of Sex and Marital Therapy, 12,* 211–220.

————, & Londono, M. (1984). Vaginal erotic sensitivity. *Journal of Sex and Marital Therapy, 10,* 49–56.

Ambrosio, A., & Sheehan, E. (1991). The just world belief and the AIDS epidemic. *Journal of Social Behavior and Personality, 6,* 163–170.

American Academy of Pediatrics and American College of Obstetricians and Gynecologists (1983). *Guidelines for Perinatal Care.* Evanston, Ill.

American Cancer Society (1991). Cancer Statistics, 1991. (Reprinted from *Ca-A Cancer Journal for Clinicians, 41,* 19–36.)

American Civil Liberties Union (1986). *Polluting the Censorship Debate.* Washington, D.C.: American Civil Liberties Union.

American College of Obstetricians and Gynecologists (1984). *Urinary Tract Infections.* Washington, D.C.: ACOG.

————. (1985). *Dysmenorrhea.* Washington, D.C.: ACOG.

————. (1991). Carcinoma of the breast (*ACOG Technical Bulletin No. 158*). Washington, D.C.: ACOG.

American Psychological Association (1975). Press release, January 24.

————. (1990). Ethical principles of psychologists. *American Psychologist, 45,* 390–395.

Ames, K. (1991). And donor makes three. *Newsweek,* September 30, 60–61.

Ames, T. (1991). Guidelines for providing sexuality-related services to severely and profoundly retarded individuals: The challenge for the nineteen-nineties. *Sexuality and Disability, 9*(2), 113–122.

Amick, A., & Calhoun, K. (1987). Resistance to sexual aggression: Personality, attitudinal, and situational factors. *Archives of Sexual Behavior, 16,* 153–163.

Anand, K., Phil, B. & Hickey, P. (1992). Halothane-morphine compared with high-dose sufentanil for anesthesia and postoperative analgesia in neonatal cardiac surgery. *The New England Journal of Medicine, 326,* 1–9.

Andersen, B., Anderson, B., & deProsse, C. (1989). Controlled prospective longitudinal study of women with cancer: I. Sexual functioning outcomes. *Journal of Consulting and Clinical Psychology, 57,* 683–691.

Andolsek, K. (1990). *Obstetric Care: Standards of Prenatal, Intrapartum, and Postpartum Management.* Philadelphia: Lea & Febiger.

Andre, T., & Bormann, L. (1991). Knowledge of acquired immune deficiency syndrome and sexual responsibility among high school students. *Youth and Society, 22,* 339–361.

Andrews, W. C., & Mishell, D., Jr. (1988). OC labeling changes: New perspectives on the pill. *Dialogues in Contraception, 2*(6), 5–8.

Annon, J. (1974). *The Behavioral Treatment of Sexual Problems,* Vol. I. Honolulu: Enabling Systems.

Ansell, J. (1991). The crooked penis: Causes and treatment. *Medical Aspects of Human Sexuality,* Setpember, 32–38.

Anthony, E., Green, R., & Kolodny, R. (1982). *Childhood Sexuality.* Boston: Little, Brown.

Apfelbaum, B. (1980). Why we should not accept sexual fantasies. In B. Apfelbaum (Ed.)., *Expanding the Boundaries of Sex Therapy.* Berkeley, Calif.: Berkeley Sex Therapy Group.

Apuzzio, J., & Hoegsberg, B. (1992). PID: Hard to find, essential to treat. *Patient Care,* March 30, 30–54.

————, & Leo, M. (1991). Herpes in the pregnant woman. *Medical Aspects of Human Sexuality,* June, 55–58.

Aradi, N. (1988). The partner's role in impotence. Paper presented at the American Association of Sex Educators, Counselors, and Therapists Twenty-First Annual Meeting, San Francisco, April 27–30.

Aral, S., & Holmes, K. (1991). Sexually transmitted diseases in the AIDS era. *Scientific American, 264,* 62–69.

————, Mosher, W., & Cates, W., Jr. (1992). Vaginal douching among women of reproductive age in the United States: 1988. *American Journal of Public Health, 82,* 210–214.

————, Vanderplate, C., & Magder, L. (1988). Recurrent genital herpes: What helps adjustment? *Sexually Transmitted Diseases, 15,* 164–166.

Arbesfeld, D., & Thomas, I. (1991). Cutaneous herpes simplex virus infections. *American Family Physician, 43,* 1655–1664.

Archer, J., & Lloyd, B. (1985). *Sex and Gender.* New York: Cambridge University Press.

Arentewicz, B., & Schmidt, G. (Eds.). (1983). *The Treatment of Sexual Disorders.* New York: Basic Books.

Armentrout, J., & Burger, G. (1972). Children's reports of parental child-rearing behavior at five grade levels. *Developmental Psychology, 7,* 44–48.

Asch, A., & Rousso, H. (1985). Therapists with disabilities: Theoretical and clinical issues. *Psychiatry, 48,* 1–12.

Athanasiou, R., Shaver, P., & Tavris, C. (1970). Sex. *Psychology Today,* July, 39–52.

Atkin, C. (1982). Changing male and female roles. In M. Schwarz (Ed.)., *TV and Teens: Experts Look at the Issues.* Reading, Mass.: Addison-Wesley.

Atwood, J. (1981). The role of masturbation in sociosexual development. Ph.D. dissertation, University of New York at Stony Brook.

————, and Gagnon, J. (1987). *Journal of Sex Education and Therapy, 13,* 35–41.

Austin, H., Louv, W., & Alexander, W. (1984). A case-control study of spermicides and gonorrhea. *Journal of the American Medical Association, 251,* 2822–2824.

Austrom, D., & Hanel, K. (1985). Psychological issues of single life in Canada: An exploratory study. *International Journal of Women's Studies, 8,* 12–23.

Bacchetti, M., & Moss, A. (1989). Incubation period of AIDS in San Francisco. *Nature, 338,* 251–253.

Bachman, G. (1992). Using androgens to increase libido. *Medical Aspects of Human Sexuality, 26,* 6.

Bachmann, G. (1991). Sexual dysfunction in the older woman. *Medical Aspects of Human Sexuality,* February, 42–45.

———, Moeller, T., & Benett, J. (1988). Childhood sexual abuse and the consequences in adult women. *Obstetrics and Gynecology, 71,* 631–642.

Bachrach, C. (1984). Contraceptive practice among American women, 1973–1982. *Family Planning Perspectives, 16,* 253–259.

Backerman, I. (1991). Premenstrual syndrome. Lecture presented at the Behavioral Medicine Lecture Series, Portland Adventist Medical Center, Portland, Ore., April 18.

Bailey, J. M., & Pillard, R. (1991). A genetic study of male sexual orientation. *Archives of General Psychiatry, 48,* 1089–1096.

———, Willerman, L., & Parks, C. (1991). A test of the maternal stress theory of human male homosexuality. *Archives of Sexual Behavior, 20,* 277–293.

Baird, P., Sadovnick, A., & Yee, I. (1991). Maternal age and birth defects: A population study. *Lancet, 337,* 527.

Baker, C. (1980). Preying on playgrounds. The sexploitation of children in pornography and prostitution. In L. Schultz (Ed.), *The Sexual Victimology of Youth.* Springfield, Ill.: Thomas.

Baker, D., Gonik, B., Milch, P., Berkowitz, A., Lipson, S., & Verma, U. (1989). Clinical evaluation of a new herpes simplex virus ELISA: A rapid diagnostic test for herpes simplex virus. *Obstetrics and Gynecology, 73,* 322–325.

Baker, J. (1990). Lesbians: Portrait of a community. *Newsweek,* March 12, 24.

Baker, L., & Nagata, F. (1978). A group approach to the treatment of heterosexual couples with sexual dissatisfactions. *Journal of Sex Education and Therapy, 4,* 15–18.

Baker, S., Thalberg, S., & Morrison, D. (1988). Parents' behavioral norms as predictors of adolescent sexual activity and contraceptive use. *Adolescence, 23,* 278–281.

Bancroft, J. (1980). Psychophysiology of sexual dysfunction. In M. Dekker (Ed.), *Handbook of Biological Psychiatry.* New York: Dekker.

———. (1992). Foreword. In R. Rosen & S. Leiblum (Eds.), *Erectile Disorders.* New York: Guilford Press.

———. Sanders, D., Davidson, D., & Warner, P. (1983). Mood, sexuality, hormones and the menstrual cycle: III. Sexuality and the role of androgens. *Psychosomatic Medicine, 45,* 509–516.

———. Sherwin, B., Alexander, G., Davidson, D., & Walker, A. (1991). Oral contraceptives, androgens, and the sexuality of young women: I. A comparison of sexual experience, sexual attitudes, and gender role in oral contraceptive users and nonusers. *Archives of Sexual Behavior, 20,* 105–120.

———. Sherwin, B., Alexander, G., Davidson, D., & Walker, A. (1991). Oral contraceptives, androgens, and the sexuality of young women: II. The role of androgens. *Archives of Sexual Behavior, 20,* 121–135.

Bangs, L. (1985). Aging and positive sexuality: A descriptive approach. Ph.D. dissertation, U.S. International University.

Banmen, J., & Vogel, N. (1985). The relationship between marital quality and interpersonal sexual communication. *Family Therapy, 12,* 45–58.

Barbach, L. (1976). *For Yourself: The Fulfillment of Female Sexuality.* Garden City, N.Y.: Doubleday.

Barbaree, H., Marshall, W., & Lanthier, R. (1979). Deviant sexual arousal in rapists. *Behavior Research and Therapy, 17,* 215–222.

Barbieri, R. (1988). New therapy for endometriosis. *New England Journal of Medicine, 318,* 512–514.

Barfield, R., Wilson, C., & Mcdonald, P. (1975). Sexual behavior: Extreme reduction of postejaculatory refractory period by midbrain lesions in male rats. *Science, 189,* 147–149.

Barlow, D., Mills, J., Agras, W., & Steinman, D. (1980). Comparison of sex-typed motor behavior in male-to-female transsexuals and women. *Archives of Sexual Behavior, 9,* 245–253.

———, Silverstein, C., & Bieber, I. (1980). New frontiers in human sexuality. *Contemporary Psychology, 25,* 355–359.

Baron, L. (1990). Pornography and gender equality: An empirical analysis. *The Journal of Sex Research, 27,* 363–380.

Baron, R. (1986). Self-presentation in job interviews: When there can be "too much of a good thing." *Journal of Applied Social Psychology, 16,* 16–28.

Barrett, C., Austin, H., Louv, W., Alexander, W., & Hadler, S. (1992). Risk factors for hepatitis B virus infection among women attending a clinic for sexually transmitted diseases. *Sexually Transmitted Diseases, 19,* 14–18.

Barrett-Connor, E., & Bush, T. L. (1991). Estrogen and coronary heart disease in women. *Journal of the American Medical Association, 265,* 1861.

Bart, P., & O'Brien, P. (1984). Stopping rape: Effective avoidance strategies. *Signs, 10,* 83–101.

———, & ———. (1985). *Stopping Rape: Successful Survival Strategies.* New York: Pergamon Press.

Bartell, G. (1970). Group sex among the mid-Americans. *Journal of Sex Research, 6,* 113–130.

Barth, R., Fetro, J., Leland, N., & Volkan, K. (1992). Preventing adolescent pregnancy with social and cognitive skills. *Journal of Adolescent Research, 7,* 208–232.

Bassett, L., & Butler, D. (1991). Mammography and early breast cancer detection. *American Family Physician, 43,* 547–557.

Batchelor, E. (Ed.) (1980). *Homosexuality and Ethics.* New York: Pilgrim Press.

Bauer, H., Greer, C., Chambers, J., Tashiro, C., Chimera, J., Reingold, A., & Manos, M. (1991). Genital human papillomavirus infection in female university students as determined by a PCR-based method. *Journal of the American Medical Association, 265,* 472–477.

Bauman, K. (1973). Volunteer bias in a study of sexual knowledge, attitudes, and behavior. *Journal of Marriage and the Family, 35,* 27–31.

Bauman, R., Kasper, C., & Alford, J. (1984). The child sex abusers. *Corrective and Social Psychiatry, 30,* 76–81.

Baumeister, R. (1988). Masochism as escape from self. *Journal of Sex Research, 25,* 28–59.

Baxter, D., Marshall, W., Barbaree, H., Davidson, P., & Malcolm, P. (1984). Deviant sexual behavior: Differentiating sex offenders by criminal and personal history, psychometric measures, and sexual response. *Criminal Justice and Behavior,* 11, 477–501.

Beach, F. (Ed.) (1978). *Human Sexuality in Four Perspectives.* Baltimore: Johns Hopkins University Press.

Beal, G., & Muehlenhard, C. (1987). Getting sexually aggressive men to stop their advances: Information for rape prevention programs. Paper presented at the Annual Meeting of the Association for Advancement of Behavior Therapy, Boston, November.

Beatty, W. (1979). Gonadal hormones and sex differences in nonreproductive behaviors in rodents: Organizational and activational influences. *Hormones and Behavior,* 12, 112–163.

Beck, J., & Davies, D. (1987). Teen contraception: A review of perspectives on compliance. *Archives of Sexual Behavior,* 16, 337–368.

Beck, J. G., Bozman, A., & Qualtrough, T. (1991). The experience of sexual desire: Psychological correlates in a college sample. *The Journal of Sex Research,* 28, 443–456.

Beck, M. (1989). Baby blues, the sequel. *Newsweek,* July 3, 62.

———. (1990). The politics of breast cancer. *Newsweek,* December 10, 62–65.

———. (1992). Menopause. *Newsweek,* May 25, 71–79.

———, Wickelgren, I., Quade, V., & Wingert, P. (1988). Miscarriages. *Newsweek,* August 15, 46–49.

Becker, E. (1978). *Female Sexuality Following Spinal Cord Injury.* Bloomington, Ill.: Accent Special Publications.

Becker, H., & Maraist, F. (1987). Immediate breast reconstruction after mastectomy using a permanent tissue expander. *Southern Medical Journal,* 80, 154–160.

Becker, J., & Kaplan, M. (1991). Rape victims: Issues, theories, and treatment. *Annual Review of Sex Research,* 2, 267–272.

Becker, J., Skinner, L., Abel, G., Axelrod, R., & Chicon, J. (1984). Sexual problems of sexual assault survivors. *Women and Health,* 9, 5–20.

———, ———, ———, & ———. (1986). Level of postassault sexual functioning in rape and incest victims. *Archives of Sexual Behavior,* 15, 37–49.

Beckman, A., Sherman, K., Myerson, D., Daling, J., McDougall, J., & Galloway, D. (1991). Comparative virologic studies of condylomata acuminata reveal a lack of dual infections with human papillomaviruses. *The Journal of Infectious Diseases,* 163, 393–396.

Beebe, D. (1991). Emergency management of the adult female rape victim. *American Family Physician,* 43, 2041–2046.

Beitchman, J., Zucker, K., Hood, J., DaCosta, G., Akman, D., & Cassavia, E. (1992). A review of the long-term effects of child sexual abuse. *Child Abuse and Neglect,* 16, 101–118.

Bell, A., & Weinberg, M. (1978). *Homosexualities: A Study of Diversity Among Men and Women.* New York: Simon & Schuster.

———, ———, & Hammersmith, S. (1981). *Sexual Preference: Its Development in Men and Women.* Bloomington: Indiana University Press.

Bell, R. (1971). The sexual exchange of marriage partners. *Sex Behavior,* 1, 70–79.

Belzer, E. (1981). Orgasmic expulsions of women: A review and heuristic inquiry. *Journal of Sex Research,* 17, 1–12.

———, Whipple, B., & Moger, W. (1984). On female ejaculation. *Journal of Sex Research,* 20, 403–406.

Bem, S. (1974). The measurement of psychological androgyny. *Journal of Consulting and Clinical Psychology,* 42, 155–162.

———. (1975). Sex role adaptability: One consequence of psychological androgyny. *Journal of Personality and Social Psychology,* 31, 634–643.

———. (1979). Theory and measurement of androgyny: A reply to the Pedhazer–Tetenbaum and Locksley–Colton critiques. *Journal of Personality and Social Psychology,* 37, 1047–1054.

———. (1980). Beyond androgyny: Some presumptuous prescriptions for a liberated sexual identity. In J. Sherman and F. Denmark (Eds.)., *The Future of Women: Issues in Psychology.* New York: Psychological Dimension.

———, & Lenney, E. (1976). Sex typing and the avoidance of cross-sex behavior. *Journal of Personality and Social Psychology,* 33, 48–54.

———, Martyna, W., & Watson, C. (1976). Sex-typing and androgyny: Further explorations of the expressive domain. *Journal of Personality and Social Psychology,* 34, 1016–1023.

Bennett, S. (1984). Family environment for sexual learning as a function of father's involvement in family work and discipline. *Adolescence,* 19, 609–627.

Benson, D., & Thomson, G. (1982). Sexual harassment on a university campus: The confluence of authority relations, sexual interest, and gender stratification. *Social Problems,* 29, 236–251.

Benson, R. (1985). Vacuum cleaner injury to penis: A common urologic problem? *Urology,* 25, 41–44.

Bera, W., Gonsiorek, J., & Letourneau, D. (1991). *Male Adolescent Sexual Abuse.* Newbury Park, Calif.: Sage.

Beral, V., Bull, D., Darby, S., Weller, I., Carne, C., Beecham, M., & Jaffe, H. (1992). Risk of Kaposi's sarcoma and sexual practices associated with foecal contact in homosexual or bisexual men with AIDS. *The Lancet,* 339, 632–635.

Berard, E. (1989). The sexuality of spinal cord injured women: Physiology and pathophysiology. *Paraplegia,* 27, 99–112.

Beretta, G., Chelo, E., & Zanollo, A. (1989). Reproductive aspects in spinal cord injured males. *Paraplegia,* 27, 113–118.

Berg, B., & Wilson, J. (1991). Psychological functioning across stages of treatment for infertility. *Journal of Behavioral Medicine,* 14(1), 11.

Berg, S., & Harrison, W. (1981). Spectinomycin as primary treatment of gonorrhea in areas of high prevalence of penicillinase-producing N. gonorrhoeae. *Sexually Transmitted Diseases,* 8, 38–39.

Berger, C., Gold, D., Andres, D., Gillett, P., & Kinch, R. (1984). Repeat abortion: Is it a problem? *Family Planning Perspectives,* 16, 70–75.

Berger, R. (1982). *Gay and Gray.* Urbana: University of Illinois Press.

———. (1990). Passing: Impact on the quality of same-sex couple relationships. *Social Work*, 35, 328–332.

Bergman, A., & Nalick, R. (1991). Genital human papillomavirus infection in men: Diagnosis and treatment with a laser 5-fluorouracil. *Journal of Reproductive Medicine*, 36, 363–366.

Bermant, G., & Davidson, J. (1974). *Biological Bases of Sexual Behavior*. New York: Harper & Row.

Berndt, R., & Berndt, C. (1951). *Sexual Behavior in Western Amhem Land*. New York: Viking Fund Publications in Anthropology.

Bernstein, L., Ross, R., & Henderson, B. (1992). Prospects for the primary prevention of breast cancer. *American Journal of Epidemiology*, 135, 142–152.

Berrill, K., & Kane, R. (1992). *Anti-Gay/Lesbian Violence, Victimization & Defamation in 1991*. Washington, D.C.: National Gay & Lesbian Task Force Policy Institute.

Bianchi, N. (1991). Sex determination in mammals: How many genes are involved? *Biology of Reproduction*, 44, 393–397.

Bidwell, R., & Deisher, R. (1991). Adolescent sexuality: Current issues. *Pediatric Annals*, 20, 293–302.

Bieber, I., Dain, H., Dince, P., Drellich, M., Grand, H., Gundlach, R., Kremer, M., Rifkin, A., Wilbur, C., & Bieber, T. (1962). *Homosexuality*. New York: Vintage Books.

Bierce, A. (1943). *The Devil's Dictionary*. New York: World.

Blair, C., & Lanyon, R. (1981). Exhibitionism: Etiology and treatment. *Psychological Bulletin*, 89, 439–463.

Blanchard, R., Clemmensen, L., & Steiner, B. (1987). Heterosexual and homosexual dysphoria. *Archives of Sexual Behavior*, 16, 139–152.

———, Legault, S., & Lindsay, W. (1987). Vaginoplasty outcome in male-to-female transsexuals. *Journal of Sex and Marital Therapy*, 13, 265–275.

———, Steiner, B., & Clemmensen, L. (1985). Gender dysphoria, gender reorientation, and the clinical management of transsexualism. *Journal of Consulting and Clinical Psychology*, 53, 295–304.

Bleibtreu-Ehrenberg, G. (1991). Pederasty among primitives: Institutionalized initiation and cultic prostitution. *Journal of Homosexuality*, 20, 13–31.

Blendon, R., Donelan, K., & Knox, R. (1992). Public opinion and AIDS: Lessons for the second decade. *Journal of the American Medical Association*, 267, 981–986.

Bloch, D. (1978). Sex education practices of mothers. *Journal of Sex Education and Therapy*, 4, 7–12.

Block, J. (1976). Issues, problems, and pitfalls in assessing sex differences. *Merrill-Palmer Quarterly*, 22, 283–308.

———. (1983). Differential premises arising from differential socialization of the sexes: Some conjectures. *Child Development*, 54, 1335–1354.

Bloom, F., Lazerson, A., & Hofstadter, L. (1985). *Brain, Mind, and Behavior*. New York: Freeman.

Blum, M. (1984). Vaginal candidiasis transmitted by noncoital sex. *British Journal of Sexual Medicine*, 11, 144.

Blumstein, P., & Schwartz, P. (1983). *American Couples*. New York: Morrow.

Bly, R. (1990). *Iron John*. New York: Addison-Wesley.

Boag, F., Houang, E., Westrom, R., McCormack, S., & Lawrence, A. (1991). Comparison of vaginal flora after treatment with clotrimazole 500 mg vaginal pessary or a fluconazole 150 mg capsule for vaginal candidiasis. *Genitourinary Medicine*, 67, 232–234.

Boeringer, S., Shehan, C., & Akers, R. (1991). Social contexts and social learning in sexual coercion and aggression: Assessing the contribution of fraternity membership. *Family Relations*, 40, 58–64.

Bogren, L. (1991). Changes in sexuality in women and men during pregnancy. *Archives of Sexual Behavior*, 20, 35–46.

Bohlen, J., Held, J., Sanderson, M., & Patterson, R. (1984). Heart rate, rate-pressure product, and oxygen uptake during four sexual activities. *Archives of Internal Medicine*, 144, 1745–1748.

Bolch, O., & Warren, J. (1973). In vitro effects of Emko on Neisseria gonorrhoeae and Trichomonas vaginalis. *American Journal of Obstetrics and Gynecology*, 115, 1145–1148.

Bollen, N., Tournaye, H., Camus, M., Devroey, P., Staessen, C., & Van Steirteghem, A. (1991). The incidence of multiple pregnancy after in vitro fertilization and embryo transfer, gamete, or zygote intrafallopian transfer. *Fertility and Sterility*, 55, 314–319.

Bolognesi, D. (1991). Paper presented at the Seventh Annual International Conference on AIDS, Florence, Italy, June.

Bolton, F., & MacEachron, A. (1988). Adolescent male sexuality: A developmental perspective. *Journal of Adolescent Research*, 3, 259–273.

Bond, S., & Mosher, D. (1986). Guided imagery of rape: Fantasy, reality, and the willing victim myth. *Journal of Sex Research*, 22, 162–183.

Bongaarts, J. (1982). Infertility after age 30: A false alarm. *Family Planning Perspectives*, 14, 75–78.

Booth, A., & Johnson, D. (1988). Premarital co[chhab[chi[chta[chtion and marital success. *Journal of Family Issues*, 9, 255–272.

Borgatta, L., Piening, S., & Cohen, W. (1989). Association of episiotomy and delivery position with deep perineal laceration during spontaneous delivery in nulliparous women. *American Journal of Obstetrics and Gynecology*, 160, 294–297.

Boswell, J. (1980). *Christianity, Social Tolerance, and Homosexuality*. Chicago and London: University of Chicago Press.

Boucher, C., O'Sullivan, E., Mulder, J., Ramautarsing, C., Kellam, P., Darby, G., Lange, J., Goudsmit, J., & Larder, B. (1992). Ordered appearance of zidovudine resistant mutations during treatment of 18 human immunodeficiency virus–positive subjects. *The Journal of Infectious Diseases*, 165, 105–110.

Boyer, D., & Fine, D. (1992). Sexual abuse as a factor in adolescent pregnancy and child maltreatment. *Family Planning Perspectives*, 24, 4–19.

Bradford, J., & Bourget, D. (1987). Sexually aggressive men. *Psychiatric Journal of the University of Ottawa*, 12, 169–175.

———, Boulet, J., & Pawlak, A. (1992). The paraphilias: A multiplicity of deviant behaviors. *Canadian Journal of Psychiatry*, 37, 104–107.

Braen, G. (1980). Examination of the accused: The heterosexual and homosexual rapist. In C. Warner (Ed.)., *Rape and Sexual Assault.* Germantown, Md.: Aspens Systems.

Brambati, B., Tului, L., Simoni, G., & Travi, M. (1991). Genetic diagnosis before the eighth gestational week. *Obstetrics & Gynecology,* 77, 318–323.

Brandt, A. (1985). *No Magic Bullet.* New York: Oxford University Press.

Brashear, D., & Munsick, R. (1991). Hymenal Dyspareunia. *Journal of Sex Education & Therapy,* 17, 27–31.

Brecher, E. (1971). *The Sex Researchers.* New York: New American Library.

———. (1984). *Love, Sex and Aging.* Boston: Little, Brown.

Bremer, J. (1959). *Asexualization.* New York: Macmillan.

Brenner, P. (1988). The menopausal syndrome. *Obstetrics and Gynecology,* 72, 6S–11S.

Bretl, D., & Cantor, J. (1988). The portrayal of men and women in U.S. television commercials: A recent content analysis and trends over 15 years. *Sex Roles,* 18, 595–610.

Bretschneider, J., & McCoy, N. (1988). Sexual interest and behavior in healthy 80-to-102-year-olds. *Archives of Sexual Behavior,* 17, 109.

Briddell, D., & Wilson, G. (1976). Effects of alcohol and expectancy set on male sexual arousal. *Journal of Abnormal Psychology,* 85, 225–234.

Bright, P. (1987). Adolescent pregnancy and loss. *Maternal-Child Nursing Journal,* 16, 1–12.

Brinton, L., Reeves, W., Brenes, M., Herrero, R., Gaitan, E., Tenoria, F., de Britton, R., Garcia, M., & Rawls, W. (1989). The male factor in the etiology of cervical cancer among sexually monogamous women. *International Journal of Cancer,* 44, 199–203.

Britton, G., & Lumpkin, M. (1984). Battle to imprint for the 21st century. *Reading Teacher,* 37, 724–733.

Britton, T. (1988). Personal communication.

Brody, E., Ottey, F., & Lagrandade, J. (1976). Early sex education in relation to later coital and reproductive behavior: Evidence from Jamaican women. *American Journal of Psychiatry,* 133, 969–972.

Broering, J., Moscicki, B., Millstein, S., Policar, M., & Irwin, C. (1989). Sexual practices among adolescents. Paper presented at the Annual Meeting of the Society for Adolescent Medicine, San Francisco, March.

Bromberg, W., & Coyle, E. (1974). Rape: A compulsion to destroy. *Medical Insight,* 22, 21–25.

Brookmeyer, R. (1991). Reconstruction and future trends of the AIDS epidemic in the United States. *Science,* 253, 37–42.

Brooks, A. (1985). Serial marriages keep divorce courts busy. *The Oregonian,* February 13, B1.

Brooks-Gunn, J., & Ruble, D. (1983). Dysmenorrhea in adolescence. In S. Golub (Ed.)., *Menarche.* Lexington, Mass.: Lexington Books.

Brown, E. (1988). Affairs: The hidden meanings have major impact on therapeutic approach. *Behavior Today,* October 24, 3–4.

Brown, J., & Hart, D. (1977). Correlates of females' sexual fantasies. *Perceptual and Motor Skills,* 45, 819–825.

Brown, M., & Zimmer, P. (1986). Personal and family impact of premenstrual symptoms. *Journal of Obstetrical, Gynecological and Neonatal Nursing,* 15, 31–38.

Brown, R., Cromer, B., & Fischer, R. (1992). Adolescent sexuality and issues in contraception. *Obstetrics and Gynecology Clinics of North America,* 19, 177–190.

Brown, W. (1987). Hormones and sexual aggression in the male: Commentary. *Integrative Psychiatry,* 5, 91–93.

Brownmiller, S. (1975). *Against Our Will: Men, Women, and Rape.* New York: Simon & Schuster.

Brubaker, R., & Wickersham, D. (1990). Encouraging the practice of testicular self-examination: A field application of the theory of reasoned action. *Health Psychology,* 9, 154–163.

Brunham, R. (1991). The concept of core and its relevance to the epidemiology and control of sexually transmitted diseases. *Sexually Transmitted Diseases,* 18, 67–68.

Bryner, C. (1989). Recurrent toxic shock syndrome. *American Family Physician,* 39, 157–164.

Budin, L., & Johnson, C. (1989). Sex abuse prevention programs: Offenders' attitudes about their efficacy. *Child Abuse and Neglect,* 13, 77–87.

Budoff, P. (1987). Cyclic estrogen–progesterone therapy. In M. Walsh (Ed.)., *The Psychology of Women.* New Haven, Conn.: Yale University Press.

Buffum, J. (1988). Substance abuse and high-risk sexual behavior: Drugs and sex—the dark side. *Journal of Psychoactive Drugs,* 20, 165–168.

Buhrich, N. (1976). A heterosexual transvestite club: Psychiatric aspects. *Australian and New Zealand Journal of Psychiatry,* 10, 331–335.

Bullard, D. (1988). The treatment of desire disorders in the medically ill and physically disabled. In S. Leiblum and R. Rosen (Eds.)., *Sexual Desire Disorders.* New York: Guilford Press.

Bullough, V., Bullough, B., & Smith, R. (1983). Comparative study of male transvestites, male to female transsexuals, and male homosexuals. *Journal of Sex Research,* 19, 238–257.

Bumpass, L., Martin, T., & Sweet, J. (1991). The impact of family background and early marital factors on marital disruption. *Journal of Family Issues,* 12, 22–42.

Bureau of the Census (1985). *U.S. Statistics at a Glance: Annual Summary of Demographic and Economic Indicators.* Washington, D.C.: Government Printing Office, June.

Burger, R., & Guthrie, T. (1974). Why circumcision? *Pediatrics,* 54, 362–364.

Burgess, A., Hartman, C., McCausland, M., & Powers, P. (1984). Response patterns in children and adolescents exploited through sex rings and pornography. *American Journal of Psychiatry,* 141, 656–662.

———, & Holmstrom, L. (1974a). Rape trauma syndrome. *American Journal of Psychiatry,* 131, 981–986.

———, & ———. (1974b). *Rape: Victims of Crisis.* Bowie, Md.: Robert J. Brady.

———, & ———. (1979). Rape: Sexual disruption and recovery. *American Journal of Orthopsychiatry,* 49, 648–657.

———, & ———. (1988). Treating the adult rape victim. *Medical Aspects of Human Sexuality,* January, 36–43.

Burkhart, B. (1983). Acquaintance rape statistics and prevention. Paper presented at the Acquaintance Rape and Rape Prevention on Campus Conference, Louisville, Ky., December.

Burstein, B., Bank, L., & Jarvik, L. (1980). Sex differences in cognitive functioning: Evidence, determinants, implications. *Human Development, 23,* 289–313.

Burt, M. (1980). Cultural myths and supports for rape. *Journal of Personality and Social Psychology, 38,* 217–230.

Bush, C., Bush, J., & Jennings, J. (1988). Effects of jealousy threats on relationship perceptions and emotions. *Journal of Social and Personal Relationships, 5,* 285–303.

Buss, D. (1989). Sex differences in human mate preferences: Evolutionary hypotheses tested in 37 cultures. *Behavioral and Brain Sciences, 12,* 1–49.

Butler, A. (1985). *Daughters of Joy, Sisters of Mercy.* Chicago and London: University of Chicago Press.

Butterworth, C., Jr., Hatch, K., Macaluso, M., Cole, P., Sauberlich, H., Soong, S., Borst, M., & Baker, V. (1992). Folate deficiency and cervical dysplasia. *Journal of the American Medical Association, 267,* 528–533.

Buunk, B., & Bringle, R. (1987). Jealousy in love relationships. In D. Perlman & S. Duck (Eds.)., *Intimate Relationships.* Newbury Park, Calif.: Sage.

Buvat, J., Buvat-Herbaut, M., Lemaire, A., Marcolin, G., & Quittelier, E. (1990). Recent developments in the clinical assessment and diagnosis of erectile dysfunction. *Annual Review of Sex Research, 1,* 265–308.

Byrne, D. A., Ervin, C., & Lamberth, J. (1970). Continuity between the experimental study of attraction and ``real life'' computer dating. *Journal of Personality and Social Psychology, 16,* 157–165.

Byrne, D., & Murnen, S. (1988). Maintaining loving relationships. In R. Sternberg & M. Barnes (Eds.), *The Psychology of Loving.* New Haven, Conn.: Yale University Press.

———, Clore, G., & Smeaton, G. (1986). The attraction hypothesis: Do similar attitudes affect anything? *Journal of Personality and Social Psychology, 51,* 1167–1170.

Cadman, D., Gafni, A., & McNamee, J. (1984). Newborn circumcision: An economic perspective. *Canadian Medical Association Journal, 131,* 1353–1355.

Cado, S., & Leitenberg, H. (1990). Guilt reactions to sexual fantasies during intercourse. *Archives of Sexual Behavior, 19,* 49–71.

Cadwallader, M. (1975). Marriage as a wretched institution. In Jack DeLora & Joann DeLora (Eds.)., *Intimate Lifestyles: Marriage and Its Alternatives.* Pacific Palisades, Calif.: Goodyear.

Caggiula, A. (1970). Analysis of the copulation-reward properties of posterior hypothalamic stimulation in male rats. *Journal of Comparative and Physiological Psychology, 70,* 399–412.

———, & Hoebel, B. (1966). Copulation-reward site in the posterior hypothalamus. *Science, 153,* 1284–1285.

Cahill, C., Llewelyn, S., & Pearson, C. (1991). Treatment of sexual abuse which occurred in childhood: A review. *British Journal of Clinical Psychology, 30,* 1–12.

Cain, R. (1991). Relational contexts and information management among gay men. *Families in Society,* June, 344–352.

Calderone, M. (1965). The sex information and education council of the U.S. *Journal of Marriage and Family, 27,* 533–534.

———. (1983). Fetal erection and its message to us. *SIECUS Report, 11,* 9–10.

Cale, A., Farouk, M., Prescott, R., & Wallace, I. (1990). Does vasectomy accelerate testicular tumour? Importance of testicular examinations before and after vasectomy. *British Medical Journal, 300,* 370–371.

Campbell, S. (1976). Double-blind psychometric studies on the effects of natural estrogens on post-menopausal women. In S. Campbell (Ed.)., *The Management of the Menopausal and Post-Menopausal Years.* Baltimore: University Park Press.

Campion, M. (1992). The adequate cervical smear: A modern dilemma. *Journal of Family Practice, 34,* 273–275.

Canavan, M., Meyer, W., & Higgs, D. (1992). The female experience of sibling incest. *Journal of Marital and Family Therapy, 18,* 129–142.

Capewell, A., McIntyre, M., & Elton, R. (1992). Postmenopausal atrophy in elderly women: Is a vaginal smear necessary for diagnosis? *Age and Aging, 21,* 117–120.

Caplan, B. (1975). In the foreword of Brodyaga, L., Gates, M., Singer, S., Tucker, M., and White, R. *Rape and Its Victims: A Report for Citizens, Health Facilities and Criminal Justice Agents.* Washington, D.C.: U.S. Department of Justice, November.

Carey, P., Howards, S., & Vance, M. (1988). Transdermal testosterone treatment of hypogonadal men. *Journal of Urology, 140,* 76–79.

Carnes, P. (1983). *Out of the Shadows: Understanding Sexual Addiction.* Minneapolis: Compcare Publication.

———. (1986). Progress in sexual addiction: An addictive perspective. *SIECUS Report,* July, 4–6.

———. (1991). *Don't Call It Love.* New York: Bantam Books.

Carrera, M. (1981). *Sex: The Facts, The Acts, and Your Feelings.* New York: Crown.

Carroll, J., Volk, K., & Hyde, J. (1985). Differences between males and females in motives for engaging in sexual intercourse. *Archives of Sexual Behavior, 14,* 131–139.

Carson, J., Russell, L., Taragin, M., Sonnenberg, F., Duff, A., & Bauer, S. (1992). The risks of blood transfusion: The relative influence of acquired immunodeficiency syndrome and non-A, non-B hepatitis. *The American Journal of Medicine, 92,* 45–52.

Carson, S. (1988). Sex selection: The ultimate in family planning. *Fertility and Sterility, 50,* 16–19.

Carswell, R. (1969). Historical analysis of religion and sex. *Journal of School Health, 39,* 673–683.

Carter, A., Cohen, E., & Shorr, E. (1947). The use of androgens in women. *Vitamins and Hormones, 5,* 317–391.

Cash, T., & Janda, L. (1984). The eye of the beholder. *Psychology Today,* December, 46–52.

Castleman, M. (1980). *Sexual Solutions.* New York: Simon & Schuster.

———. (1981). Men, lovemaking and cramps. *Medical Self-Care,* Spring, 21.

Catalano, P., Merritt, A., & Mead, P. (1991). Incidence of genital herpes simplex virus at the time of delivery in women with known risk factors. *American Journal of Obstetrics and Gynecology,* 164, 1303–1306.

Catalona, W., Smith, D., Ratliff, T., Dodds, K., Coplen, D., Yuan, J., Petros, J., & Andriole, G. (1991). Measurement of prostate-specific antigen in serum as a screening test for prostate cancer. *The New England Journal of Medicine,* 324, 1156–1161.

Cates, W. (1991). Teenagers and sexual risk taking: The best of times and the worst of times. *Journal of Adolescent Health,* 12, 84–94.

———, & Stone, K. (1992). Family planning, sexually transmitted diseases and contraceptive choice: A literature update: Part I. *Family Planning Perspectives,* 24, 75–84.

Centers for Disease Control (1984a). *Morbidity and Mortality Weekly Report,* 33, 43–44; 49.

———. (1984b). Fetal alcohol syndrome: Public awareness week. *Morbidity and Mortality Weekly Report,* 33, 1–2.

———. (1985a). 1985 STD treatment guidelines. *Morbidity and Mortality Weekly Report Supplement,* September.

———. (1985b). *Chlamydia trachomatis* infections. *Morbidity and Mortality Weekly Report Supplement,* August 23.

———. (1987). Self-reported changes in sexual behaviors among homosexual and bisexual men from the San Francisco City Clinic cohort. *Morbidity and Mortality Weekly Report,* 36, 187–189.

———. (1988a). Guidelines for the prevention and control of congenital syphilis. *Morbidity and Mortality Weekly Report,* 37 (Supplement S–1).

———. (1988b). Guidelines for effective school health education to prevent the spread of AIDS. *Morbidity and Mortality Weekly Report,* 37, 1–13.

———. (1989). Update: Acquired immunodeficiency syndrome—United States, 1981–1988. *Morbidity and Mortality Weekly Report,* 38, 229–236.

———. (1990). Hepatitis C rarely transmitted by sex. *CDC AIDS Weekly,* November 5, 11.

———. (1991a). Premarital sexual experience among adolescent women—United States, 1970–1988. *Morbidity and Mortality Weekly Report,* 39, 929–932.

———. (1991b). Pelvic inflammatory disease: Guidelines for prevention and management. *Morbidity and Mortality Weekly Report,* 40, 1–26.

———. (1991c). Primary and secondary syphilis—United States, 1981–1990. *Morbidity and Mortality Weekly Report,* 40, 314–316.

———. (1991d). The HIV/AIDS epidemic: the first 10 years. *Morbidity and Mortality Weekly Report,* 40, 357–358.

———. (1991e). Characteristics of, and HIV infection among, women served by publicly funded HIV counseling and testing services—United States, 1989–1990. *Morbidity and Mortality Weekly Report,* 40, 195–203.

———. (1992a). Sexual behavior among high school students. *Morbidity and Mortality Weekly Report,* 40, 885–888.

———. (1992b). The second 100,000 cases of acquired immunodeficiency syndrome—United States. *Morbidity & Mortality Weekly Report,* 41, 28–29.

———. (1992c). Hysterectomy prevalence and death rates for cervical cancer—United States, 1965–1988. *Morbidity and Mortality Weekly Report,* 41, 17–19.

Chapman, J. (1984). Sexual anhedonia: Disorders of sexual desire. *Journal of the American Osteopathic Association,* 82, 709–714.

Chapman, L. (1991). Expectant fathers' roles during labor and birth. *Journal of Obstetrics, Gynecology & Neonatal Nursing,* 21(2), 114–120.

Chasnoff, I., Griffith, D., Freier, C., & Murray, J. (1992). Cocaine/polydrug use in pregnancy: Two-year follow-up. *Pediatrics,* 89, 284–289.

Chaze, W., Hawkins, S., & Lord, M. (1987). Fear of AIDS chills sex industry. *U.S. News and World Report,* February 16, 25.

Check, J. (1984). Mass media sexual violence: Content analysis and counteractive measures. Paper presented at a meeting of the American Psychological Association, Toronto, August.

———. (1985). Psychoticism and habitual pornography consumption as mediators of the effects of exposure to violent and nonviolent pornography. Paper presented at the meeting of the International Society for the Study of Individual Differences, San Feliú de Guixols, Spain, June.

———, & Malamuth, N. (1983). Sex role stereotyping and reactions to depictions of stranger versus acquaintance rape. *Journal of Personality and Social Psychology,* 45, 344–356.

Cherfas, J. (1991). Sex and the single gene. *Science,* 252, 782.

Cherlin, A. (1981). *Marriage, Divorce, Remarriage.* Cambridge, Mass.: Harvard University Press.

Cherniak, D., & Feingold, A. (1973). *VD Handbook.* Montreal: Montreal Press.

Chessare, J. (1992). Circumcision: Is the risk of urinary tract infection really the pivotal issue? *Clinical Pediatrics,* February, 100–104.

Chez, R. (1991). Identifying maternal/fetal risks before pregnancy. *Medical Aspects of Human Sexuality,* April, 54–58.

Chiasson, M., Stoneburner, R., Lifson, A., Hildegrandt, D., Ewing, W., Schultz, S., & Jaffe, H. (1990). Risk factors for human immunodeficiency virus type 1 (HIV-1) infection in patients at a sexually transmitted disease clinic in New York City. *American Journal of Epidemiology,* 131, 208–220.

Chin, J., & Mann, J. (1990). HIV infections and AIDS in the 1990s. *Annual Review of Public Health,* 11, 127–142.

Chiriboga, D., & Thurnher, M. (1980). *Journal of Divorce,* 3, 379–390.

Chitwood, D., & Comerford, M. (1990). Drugs, sex, and AIDS risk. *American Behavioral Scientist,* 33, 465–477.

Christensen, A., Oei, P., & Callan, V. (1989). The relationship between premenstrual dysphoria and daily ratings dimensions. *Journal of Affective Disorders,* 16, 127–132.

Christmas, J. (1992). The risks of cocaine use in pregnancy. *Medical Aspects of Human Sexuality,* 26(2), 36–43.

Christopher, F. (1988). An initial investigation into a continuum of premarital sexual pressure. *Journal of Sex Research,* 25, 255–266.

————, & Cate, R. (1984). Factors involved in premarital decision making. *Journal of Sex Research*, 20, 363–376.

————, & ————. (1988). Premarital sexual involvement: A developmental investigation of relational correlates. *Adolescence*, 23, 793–803.

Chung, W., & Choi, H. (1990). Erotic erection versus nocturnal erection. *The Journal of Urology*, 143, 294–297.

Clanton, G. & Smith, L. (1977). *Jealousy*. Englewood Cliffs, N.J.: Prentice-Hall.

Clark, R., & Hatfield, E. (1989). Gender differences in receptivity to sexual offers. *Journal of Psychology and Human Differences*, 2, 39–55.

Clarke, E., Hatcher, J., McKeown-Eyssen, G., & Lickrish, G. (1985). Cervical dysplasia: Association with sexual behavior, smoking, and oral contraceptive use? *American Journal of Obstetrics and Gynecology*, 151, 612–616.

Clarke, G. (1985). In the middle of a war. *Time*, August 12, 46.

Clarke, J. (1978). The unmarried marrieds: The meaning of the relationship. In J. Eshleman and J. Clarke (Eds). *Intimacy, Commitment, and Marriage*. Boston: Allyn and Bacon.

Cleek, M., & Pearson, T. (1985). Perceived causes of divorce: An analysis of interrelationships. *Journal of Marriage and the Family*, 47, 179–183.

Clement, U., & Pfäfflin, F. (1980). Changes in personality scores among couples subsequent to sex therapy. *Archives of Sexual Behavior*, 9, 235–244.

Clements, M. (1992). Should abortion remain legal? *Parade*, May 17, 4–5.

Clerici, M., Berzofsky, J., Shearer, G., & Tacket, C. (1991). Exposure to human immunodeficiency virus type 1–specific T helper cell responses before detection of infection by polymerase chain reaction and serum antibodies. *The Journal of Infectious Diseases*, 164, 178–182.

Clifford, R. (1978). Development of masturbation in college women. *Archives of Sexual Behavior*, 7, 559–573.

Cochran, S. (1988). Paper presented at the Annual American Psychological Association Convention, Atlanta, August.

Cochran, W., Mostetler, F., & Tukey, J. (1954). *Statistical Problems of the Kinsey Report on Sexual Behavior in the Human Male*. Washington, D.C.: The American Statistical Association.

Cocores, J., & Gold, M. (1989). Substance abuse and sexual dysfunction. *Medical Aspects of Human Sexuality*. February, 22–31.

Coen, S. (1978). Sexual interviewing, evaluation, and therapy: Psychoanalytic emphasis on the use of sexual fantasy. *Archives of Sexual Behavior*, 7, 229–241.

Cogen, R., & Steinman, W. (1990). Sexual function and practice in elderly men of lower socioeconomic status. *Journal of Family Practice*, 32, 162–166.

Cohen, B. (1980). *Deviant Street Networks*. Lexington, Mass.: Lexington Books.

Cohen, D., & Rose, R. (1984). Male adolescent birth control behavior: The importance of developmental factors and sex differences. *Journal of Youth and Adolescence*, 13, 239–252.

Cohen, L. (1988). Providing treatment and support for partners of sexual-assault survivors. *Psychotherapy*, 25, 94–98.

Cohen, P. (1984). Resistance during sexual assaults: Avoiding rape and injury. *Victimology*, 9, 120–129.

Cohn, B. (1988). A fresh assault on an ugly crime. *Newsweek*, March 14, 64–65.

Coker, A., Hulka, B., McCann, M., & Walton, L. (1992). Barrier methods of contraception and cervical intraepithelial neoplasia. *Contraception*, 45, 1.

Cole, D. (1987). It might have been: Mourning the unborn. *Psychology Today*, July, 64–65.

Cole, S. (1991). Preface to the special issue on sexual exploitation of persons with disabilities. *Sexuality and Disability*, 9(3), 179–183.

Coleman, E., & Edwards, B. (1986). Sexual compulsion vs. sexual addiction: The debate continues. *SIECUS Report*, July, 7–10.

Colino, S. (1991). Sex and the expectant mother. *Parenting*, February, 111.

Coll, C., Hoffman, J., VanHouten, L., and Oh, W. (1987). The social context of teenage childbearing: Effects on the infant's care-giving environment. *Journal of Youth and Adolescence*, 16, 345–360.

Comfort, A. (1972). *The Joy of Sex*. New York: Crown.

Communicable Disease Summary (1985). AIDS update. Oregon Health Division, 34, 1–3.

Confino, E., Tur-Kaspa, I., DeCherney, A., Corfman, R., Coulam, C., Robinson, E., Haas, G., Katz, E., Vermesh, M., & Gleicher, N. (1990). Transcervical balloon tuboplasty. *Journal of the American Medical Association*, 264, 2079–2082.

Connell, E. (1991). Contraceptive options for the woman over 40. *Medical Aspects of Human Sexuality*, April, 20–24.

————, & Grimes, D. (1990). Contraceptive advances: Part II: IUDs and barrier methods. *The Female Patient*, 15, 14–28.

Connell, J. (1992). Seeking common ground. *Oregonian*, April 5, B1–B4.

Connor, J. (1980). The Pinks and the Blues. In *Nova*. Boston: WGBH Transcripts.

Conte, J., Wolf, S., & Smith, T. (1989). What sexual offenders tell us about prevention strategies. *Child Abuse and Neglect*, 13, 293–301.

Contraceptive Technology Update (1987). Candidates for IUD use must meet these carefully developed criteria. December, 151.

———— (1988a). Debate continues over OC use by women over age 40. September, 101–111.

———— (1988b). Limited human trials underway on SHUG reversible vasectomy device. June, 72–73.

———— (1988c). Female condom may soon appear on markets in U.S., Britain. September, 75.

Cooney, B. (1991). Letting go of guilt and fear: Dancing in a canyon. *Wingspan*, October/December, 7.

Coope, J. (1976). Double-blind cross-over study of estrogen replacement. In S. Campbell (Ed.)., *The Management of the Menopausal and Post-Menopausal Years*. Baltimore: University Park Press.

Cooper, A. (1986). Progestogens in the treatment of male sex offenders: A review. *Canadian Journal of Psychiatry*, 31, 73–79.

————, & Cernovovsky, Z. (1992). The effects of cyproterone acetate on sleeping and walking penile erections in pedophiles: Possible implications for treatment. *Canadian Journal of Psychiatry*, 37, 33–37.

Cora-Bramble, D., Bradshaw, M., & Sklarew, B. (1992). The sex education practicum: Medical students in the elementary school classroom. *Journal of School Health*, 62, 32–34.

Coreil, J., & Parcel, G. (1983). Sociocultural determinants of parental involvement in sex education. *Journal of Sex Education and Therapy*, 9, 22–25.

Cornelius, D., Chipouras, S., Makas, E., & Daniels, S. (1982). *Who Cares? A Handbook on Sex Education and Counseling Services for Disabled People.* Baltimore: University Park Press.

Cornell, W., & Olio, K. (1991). Integrating affect in treatment with adult survivors of physical and sexual abuse. *American Journal of Orthopsychiatry*, 61, 59–69.

Cos, L., Valvo, J., Davis, R., & Cockett, A. (1983). Vasovasostomy: Current state of the art. *Urology*, 22, 567–575.

Cotton, D., & Groth, A. (1982). Inmate rape: Prevention and intervention. *Journal of Prison and Jail Health*, 2, 45–57.

Coughlin, P. (1990). Premenstrual syndrome: How marital satisfaction and role choice affect symptom severity. *Social Work*, 35, 351–355.

Counts, R. (1992). Second and third divorces: The flood to come. *Journal of Divorce and Remarriage*, 17, 193–200.

Cowley, G., & Rosenberg, D. (1992). A needle instead of a knife. *Newsweek*, April 13, 62.

Cox, C. (1983). Second marriages: Better while they last. *Psychology Today*, February, 72.

Cox, D. (1988). Incidence and nature of male genital exposure behavior as reported by college women. *Journal of Sex Research*, 24, 227–234.

Crawford, E., Schutz, M., Clejan, S., Drago, J., Resnick, M., Chodak, G., Gomella, L., Austenfeld, M., Stone, N., Miles, B., & Thomson, R. (1992). The effect of digital rectal examination on prostate-specific antigen levels. *Journal of the American Medical Association*, 267, 2227–2228.

Crawford, S. (1988). Lesbian families: Psychosocial stress and the family-building process. In Boston Lesbian Psychologies Collective (Eds.)., *Lesbian Psychologies*. Urbana: University of Illinois Press.

Creasman, W. (1991). Estrogen replacement therapy: Is previously treated cancer a contraindication? *Obstetrics and Gynecology*, 77, 308–312.

Crocket, Takihara H., & Cosentino, M. (1984). The varicocele. *Fertility and Sterility*, 41, 5–11.

Cromer, B., McClean, C., & Heald, F. (1992). A critical review of comprehensive health screening in adolescents. *Journal of Adolescent Health*, 13, 15S–65S.

Crooks, R. (1991). Incidence of rape victimization among female college students enrolled in human sexuality courses. Unpublished research.

Csikszentmihalyi, M. (1980). Love and the dynamics of personal growth. In K. Pope (Ed.)., *On Love and Loving*. San Francisco: Jossey-Bass.

Cunningham, D., Fulgham, D., Rayl, D., Hansen, K., & Alexander, N. (1991). Antisperm antibodies to sperm surface antigens in women with genital tract infection. *American Journal of Obstetrics and Gynecology*, 164, 791–796.

Cunningham, G., Cordero, E., & Thornby, J. (1989). Testosterone replacement with transdermal therapeutic systems. *Journal of the American Medical Association*, 261, 2525–2531.

Curran, J. (1980). Economic consequences of pelvic inflammatory disease. *American Journal of Obstetrics and Gynecology*, 138, 848–851.

Curtis, R., & Miller, K. (1988). Believing another likes or dislikes you: Behavior making the beliefs come true. *Journal of Personality and Social Psychology*, 51, 284–290.

Cutler, W., Garcia, C., & McCoy. (1987). Perimenopausal sexuality. *Archives of Sexual Behavior*, 16, 225–234.

————, Preti, G., Krieger, A., Huggins, G., Garcia, C., & Lawley, H. (1986). Human axillary secretions influence women's menstrual cycles: The role of donor extract from men. *Hormones and Behavior*, 20, 463–473.

Cuzick, J., Terry, G., Ho, L., Hollingworth, T., & Anderson, M. (1992). Human papillomavirus type 16 DNA in cervical smears as predictor of high-grade cervical cancer. *The Lancet*, 339, 959–960.

Cvetkovich, G., Grote, B., Lieberman, J., & Miller, W. (1978). Sex role development and teenage fertility-related behavior. *Adolescence*, 13, 231–236.

Cwayna, K., Remafedi, G., & Treadway, L. (1991). Caring for gay and lesbian youth. *Medical Aspects of Human Sexuality*, July, 50–57.

Dagg, P. (1991). The psychological sequelae of therapeutic abortion–denied and completed. *American Journal of Psychiatry*, 148, 578–585.

Dahlheimer, D., & Feigal, J. (1991). Bridging the gap. *Networker*, January/February, 44–53.

Dailey, D. (1978). The pregnant male. *Journal of Sex Education and Therapy*, 4, 43–44.

Daling, J., Sherman, K., Hislop, T. G., Maden, C., Mandelson, M., Beckmann, A. M., & Weiss, N. (1992). Cigarette smoking and the risk of anogenital cancer. *American Journal of Epidemiology*, 135, 180–189.

Daniels, N. (1992). HIV-infected professionals, patient rights, and the 'switching dilemma.' *Journal of the American Medical Association*, 267, 1368–1371.

Daniels, S. (1981). Critical issues in sexuality and disability. In D. Bullard and S. Knight (Eds.), *Sexuality and Physical Disability: Personal Perspectives*. St. Louis, Mo.: Mosby.

Darling, C., & Davidson, J. (1986). Enhancing relationships: Understanding the feminine mystique of pretending orgasm. *Journal of Sex and Marital Therapy*, 12, 182–196.

————, ————, & Conway-Welch, C. (1990). Female ejaculation: Perceived origins, the Grafenberg spot/area, and sexual responsiveness. *Archives of Sexual Behavior*, 19, 29–47.

————, ————, & Passarello, L. (1992). The mystique of first intercourse among college youth: The role of partners, contraceptive practices, and psychological reactions. *Journal of Youth and Adolescence*, 21, 97–117.

————, & Hicks, M. (1982). Parental influence on adolescent sexuality: Implications for parents as educators. *Journal of Youth and Adolescence*, 11, 231–245.

Darling, C. A., Davidson, J. K., Sr., & Conway-Welch, C. (1990). Female ejaculation: Perceived origins, the Grafenberg spot/area, and sexual responsiveness. *Archives of Sexual Behavior*, 19, 29–47.

Daro, D., (1991). Child sexual abuse prevention: Separating fact from fiction. *Child Abuse and Neglect*, 15, 1–4.

DaVanzo, J., Parnell, A., & Foege, W. (1991). Health consequences of contraceptive use and reproductive patterns. *Journal of the American Medical Association*, 265, 2692–2696.

Davenport, W. (1965). Sexual patterns and their regulation in a society of the Southwest Pacific. In F. Beach (Ed.)., *Sex and Behavior*. New York: Wiley.

————. (1978). Sex in cross-cultural perspective. In F. Beach (Ed.)., *Human Sexuality in Four Perspectives*. Baltimore: Johns Hopkins University Press.

Davidson, J. (1984). Response to ``Hormones and human sexual behavior'' by John Bancroft, M.D. *Journal of Sex and Marital Therapy*, 10, 23–27.

Davidson, K., & Hoffman, L. (1986). Sexual fantasies and sexual satisfaction: An empirical analysis of erotic thought. *Journal of Sex Research*, 22, 184–205.

————, Darling, C., & Conway-Welch, C. (1989). The role of the grafenberg spot and female ejaculation in the female orgasmic response: An empirical analysis. *Journal of Sex and Marital Therapy*, 15, 102–119.

Davies, J. (1992). Female genital mutilation—a practice that should have vanished. *Midwives Chronicle & Nursing Notes*, February, 33.

Davis, B., & Noble, M. (1991). Putting an end to chronic testicular pain. *Medical Aspects of Human Sexuality*, April, 26–34.

Davis, G., Balart, L., Schiff, E., Lindsay, K., & Bodenheimer, H. (1989). Treatment of chronic hepatitis with recombinant interferon alpha. *The New England Journal of Medicine*, 321, 1501–1506.

Davis, N. (1978). Prostitution: Identity, career, and legal-economic enterprise. In J. Henslin and E. Sagarin (Eds.)., *Studies in the Sociology of Sex*. New York: Schocken Books.

Davison, G., & Neale, J. (1990). *Abnormal Psychology*, 5th ed. New York: Wiley.

Dawson, D. (1990). Trends in use of oral contraceptives: Data from the 1987 National Health Interview Survey. *Family Planning Perspectives*, 22(4), 169.

Dawson, K. (1982). Serving the older gay community. *SIECUS Report*, 11, 5–6.

Day, N., Robles, N., Richardson, G., Geva, D., Taylor, P., Scher, M., Stoffer, D., Cornelius, M., & Goldschmidt, L. (1991). The effects of prenatal alcohol use on the growth of children at three years of age. *Alcoholism: Clinical and Experimental Research*, 15, 67–71.

Day, R., & Hook, D. (1987). A short history of divorce: Jumping the broom—and back again. *Journal of Divorce*, 10, 57–73.

De Amicis, L., Goldberg, D., LoPiccolo, J., Friedman, J., & Davies, L. (1984). Three-year follow-up of couples evaluated for sexual dysfunction. *Journal of Sex and Marital Therapy*, 10, 215–228.

Dean, C. (1987). Psychiatric morbidity following mastectomy: Preoperative predictors and types of illness. *Journal of Psychosomatic Research*, 31, 385–392.

De Bruyn, M. (1992). Women and AIDS in developing countries. *Social Sciences and Medicine*, 34, 249–262.

Decker, J. (1987). Prostitution as a public health issue. In H. Dalton, S. Burris and the Yale AIDS Law Project (Eds.)., *Aids and the Law; A Guide for the Public*. New Haven, Conn.: Yale University Press.

Deckers, P., & Ricci, A., Jr. (1992). Pain and lumps in the female breast. *Hospital Practice*, February 28, 67–94.

Degler, C. (1980). *At Odds: Women and the Family in America from the Revolution to the Present*. Oxford: Oxford University Press.

Deitch, C. (1983). Ideology and opposition to abortion: Trends in public opinion, 1972–1980. *Alternative Lifestyles*, 6, 6–26.

DeLamater, J. (1983). An interpersonal and interactional model of contraceptive behavior. In D. Byrne and W. Fisher (Eds.)., *Adolescents, Sex and Contraception*. Hillsdale, N.J.: Erlbaum.

Delaney, J., Lupton, M., & Toth, E. (1976). *The Curse, A Cultural History of Menstruation*. New York: Dutton.

Delgado, J. (1969). *Physical Control of the Mind*. New York: Harper & Row.

Deln, Bart. (1978). *The Sex Offender*. Boston: Beacon Press.

Delson, N., & Clark, M. (1981). Group therapy with sexually molested children. *Child Welfare*, 50, 161–174.

Démare, D., Briere, J., & Lips, H. (1988). Violent pornography and self-reported likelihood of sexual aggression. *Journal of Research in Personality*, 22, 140–153.

DeMaris, A., & Leslie, G. (1984). Cohabitation with the future spouse: Its influence upon marital satisfaction and communication. *Journal of Marriage and the Family*, 46, 77–84.

————, & Rao, K. (1992). Premarital cohabitation and subsequent marital stability in the United States: A reassessment. *Journal of Marriage and the Family*, 54, 178–190.

DeMartino, M. (1970). How women want men to make love. *Sexology*, October, 4–7.

D'Emilio, J., & Freedman, E. (1988). *Intimate Matters*. New York: Harper & Row.

Demetriou, E., Sackett, R., Welch, D., & Kaplan, D. (1984). Evaluation of an enzyme immunoassay for detection of *Neisseria gonorrhoeae* in an adolescent population. *Journal of the American Medical Association*, 252, 247–250.

Demsky, L. (1984). The use of Depo-Provera in the treatment of sex offenders. *Journal of Legal Medicine*, 5, 295–322.

Dennerstein, L., Burrows, G., Wood, C., & Hyman, G. (1980). Hormones and sexuality: The effects of estrogen and progestogen. *Obstetrics and Gynecology,* 56, 316–322.

———, Wood, C., & Burrows, G. (1977). Sexual response following hysterectomy and oophorectomy. *Obstetrics and Gynecology,* 49, 92–96.

Denny, N., Field, J., & Quadagno, D. (1984). Sex differences in sexual needs and desires. *Archives of Sexual Behavior,* 13, 233–245.

Deno, D. (1982). Sex differences in cognition: A review and critique of the longitudinal evidence. *Adolescence,* 17, 779–788.

Derogatis, L., Meyer, J., & Gallant, B. (1977). Distinctions between male and female invested partners in sexual disorders. *American Journal of Psychiatry,* 134, 385–390.

DeVisto, P., Kaufman, A., Rosner, L., Jackson, R., Christy, J., Pearson, S., & Burgett, T. (1984). The prevalence of sexually stressful events among females in the general population. *Archives of Sexual Behavior,* 13, 59–67.

de Zalduondo, B. (1991). Prostitution viewed cross-culturally: Toward recontextualizing sex work in AIDS intervention research. *The Journal of Sex Research,* 28, 223–248.

Dew, M. (1985). The effect of attitudes on inferences of homosexuality and perceived physical attractiveness in women. *Sex Roles,* 12, 143–155.

Dhabuwala, C., Kumar, A., & Peirce, J. (1986). Myocardial infarction and its influence on male sexual function. *Archives of Sexual Behavior,* 15, 499–504.

———. (1977). Human sexual development: Biological foundations for social development. In F. Beach (Ed.), *Human Sexuality in Four Perspectives.* Baltimore: Johns Hopkins University Press.

Diamond, M. (1979). Sexual identity and sex roles. In V. Bullough (Ed.), *The Frontiers of Sex Research.* Buffalo, N.Y.: Prometheus Press.

———. (1982). Sexual identity, monozygotic twins reared in discordant sex roles and a BBC follow-up. *Archives of Sexual Behavior,* 11, 181–186.

———. (1991). Hormonal effects on the development of cerebral lateralization. *Psychoneuroendocrinology,* 16, 121–129.

———, Johnson, R., & Ehlert, J. (1979). Comparison of cortical thickness in male and female rats: Normal and gonadectomized young and adult. *Behavioral and Neural Biology,* 26, 485–491.

Diana, L. (1985). *The Prostitute and Her Clients: Your Pleasure Is Her Business.* Springfield, Ill.: Thomas.

Dickinson, R. (1949). *Atlas of Human Sex Anatomy.* Baltimore: Williams & Wilkins.

DiClemente, R., Durbin, M., Siegel, D., Krasnovsky, F., Lazarus, N., & Comacho, T. (1992). Determinants of condom use among junior high school students in a minority, inner-city school district. *Pediatrics,* 89, 197–202.

———, Ries, C., Stoller, E., Straits, C., Olivia, G., Haskin, J., & Rutherford, G. (1989). *The Journal of Sex Research,* 26, 188–198.

Diczfalusy, E. (1992). Contraceptive prevalence, reproductive health, and international morality. *American Journal of Obstetrics and Gynecology,* 166, 1037–1043.

Dion, K. L., & Dion, K. K. (1987). Belief in a just world and physical attractiveness stereotyping. *Journal of Personality and Social Psychology,* 52, 775–780.

Dixen, J. (1985). Bisexual panel presentation at the Society for the Scientific Study of Sex Western Regional Conference, Palm Springs, Calif., January 12.

Dodson, B. (1974). *Liberating Masturbation.* New York: Betty Dodson.

Dolin, R., Graham, B., & Greenberg, S. (1991). The safety and immunogenicity of a human immunodeficiency virus type 1 (HIV-1) recombinant gp160 candidate vaccine in humans. *Annals of Internal Medicine,* 114, 119–128.

Dombrowski, M., Wolfe, H., Welch, R., & Evans, M. (1991). Cocaine abuse is associated with abruptio placentae and decreased birth weight, but not shorter labor. *Obstetrics & Gynecology,* 77, 139–141.

Domingue, P., Dadhu, K., Costerton, J., Bartlett, K., & Chow, A. (1991). The human vagina: Normal flora considered as an in situ tissue-associated, adherent biofilm. *Genitourinary Medicine,* 67, 226–231.

Donnerstein, E., & Berkowitz, L. (1981). Victim reactions in aggressive erotic films as a factor in violence against women. *Journal of Personality and Social Psychology,* 41, 710–724.

———, & Linz, D. (1984). Sexual violence in the media: A warning. *Psychology Today,* January, 14–15.

———, & ———. (1986). The question of pornography. *Psychology Today.* December, 56–59.

———, ———, & Penrod, S. (1987). *The Question of Pornography.* New York: Free Press.

Dorfman, L., Derish, P., & Cohen, J. (1992). Hey girlfriend: An evaluation of AIDS prevention among women in the sex industry. *Health Education Quarterly,* 19, 25–40.

Dorfman, R., & Shipley, T. (1956). *Androgens: Biochemistry, Physiology and Clinical Significance.* New York: Wiley.

Dormont, P. (1989). Life events that predispose to erectile dysfunction. *Medical Aspects of Human Sexuality,* April, 17–19.

Dorner, G. (1988). Neuroendocrine response to estrogen and brain differentiation in heterosexuals, homosexuals, and transsexuals. *Archives of Sexual Behavior,* 17, 57–76.

Dörner, G. (1976). *Hormones and Brain Differentiation.* Amsterdam: Elsevier.

———. (1977). Sex-hormone-dependent brain differentiation and reproduction. In J. Money and H. Musaph (Eds.), *Handbook of Sexology.* New York: Elsevier/North-Holland Biomedical Press.

Doshi, M. (1987). Accuracy of consumer performed in-home tests for early pregnancy detection. *American Journal of Public Health,* 76, 512–514.

Doty, R., Ford, M., Preti, G., & Huggins, G. (1975). Changes in the intensity and pleasantness of human vaginal odors during the menstrual cycle. *Science,* 190, 1316–1318.

Downey, L. (1980). Intergenerational change in sex behavior. A belated look at Kinsey's males. *Archives of Sexual Behavior,* 9, 267–317.

Doyle, J. (1985). *Sex and Gender.* Dubuque, Ia.: Brown.

Doyle, R. (1982). American Library Association Office of Intellectual Freedom. Personal correspondence.

Dressel, P., & Avant, W. (1983). Range of alternatives. In R. Weg (Ed.)., *Sexuality in the Later Years: Roles and Behavior.* New York: Academic Press.

Drew, W., Blair, M., Minor, R., & Conant, M. (1990). Evaluation of the virus permeability of a new condom for women. *Sexually Transmitted Diseases,* 17, 110–112.

Droegemueller, W. (June 1984). Pelvic inflammatory disease: Changing management concepts. *Drug Therapy,* 131–147.

Dubovsky, S. (1991). When sexual dysfunction masks anxiety and depression. *Medical Aspects of Human Sexuality,* October, 22–30.

Dubow, E., & Luster, T. (1990). Adjustment of children born to teenage mothers: The contribution of risk and protective factors. *Journal of Marriage and the Family,* 52, 393–404.

Duchin, S., Ledger, W., Schulze, R., & Speroff, L. (1989). OCs: Risks, benefits, guidelines. *Patient Care,* March, 89–111.

Duckworth, J., & Levitt, E. (1985). Personality analysis of a swingers' club. *Lifestyles: A Journal of Changing Patterns,* 8, 35–45.

Duddle, M., (1991). Emotional sequelae of sexual assault. *Journal of the Royal Society of Medicine,* 84, 26–28.

Duggan, L., Hunter, N., & Vance, C. (1985). False promises: New antipornography legislation in the U.S. *SIECUS Report,* 13, 1–5.

DuRant, R., & Sanders, J. (1989). Sexual behavior and contraceptive risk taking among sexually active adolescent females. *Journal of Adolescent Health Care,* 10, 1–9.

Dweck, C. (1975). Sex differences in the meaning of negative evaluation in achievement situations: Determinants and consequences. Paper presented at a meeting of the Society for Research in Child Development, Denver, April.

Easmon, C., Hay, P., & Ison, C. (1992). Bacterial vaginosis: A diagnostic approach. *Genitourinary Medicine,* 68, 134–138.

Easterday, C., Grimes, D., & Riggs, J. (1983). Hysterectomy in the United States. *Obstetrics and Gynecology,* 62, 203–212.

Edeiken, S. (1987). Mammography and palpable cancer of the breast. *Cancer,* 61, 263–265.

Edell, D. (1989). Dr. Dean Edell's medical journal. *Medical Self Care,* January/February, 23–24.

Edgerton, M. (1984). The role of surgery in the treatment of transsexualism. *Annals of Plastic Surgery,* 13, 473–476.

Ehrhardt, A. (1977). Prenatal androgenization and human psychosexual behavior. In J. Money and H. Musaph (Eds.)., *Handbook of Sexology,* New York: Elsevier/North-Holland Biomedical Press.

———. (1985). The psychobiology of gender. In A. Rossi (Ed.)., *Gender and Life Course.* New York: Aldine.

———, Meyer-Bahlburg, H., Rosen, L., Feldman, J., Veridiano, N., Zimmerman, I., & McEwen, B. (1985). Sexual orientation after prenatal exposure to exogenous estrogen. *Archives of Sexual Behavior,* 14, 57–75.

Ehrlich, G. (1988). Sexual concerns of patients with arthritis. *Medical Aspects of Human Sexuality,* March, 104–107.

Eigner, E., Kabalin, J., & Kessler, R. (1991). Penile implants in the treatment of Peyronie's Disease. *Journal of Urology,* 145, 69–72.

Eisen, M., & Zellman, G. (1987). Changes in incidence of sexual intercourse of unmarried teenagers following a community-based sex education program. *The Journal of Sex Research,* 23, 527–544.

———, ———, & McAlister, A. (1985). A health belief model approach to adolescents' fertility control: Some pilot program findings. *Health Education Quarterly,* 12, 185–210.

Eisner, T., Conner, J., & Carrel, J. (1990). Systemic retention of ingested cantharidin by frogs. *Chemoecology,* 1, 57–62.

Ekstrand, M., & Coates, T. (1990). Maintenance of safer sexual behaviors and predictors of risky sex: The San Francisco Men's Health Study. *American Journal of Public Health,* 80, 973–977.

Elder, J. (1988). The undescended testis: Hormonal and surgical management. *Surgery Clinics of North America,* 68, 983–1005.

Elia, J. (1987). History, etymology, and fallacy: Attitudes toward male masturbation in the ancient Western world. *Journal of Homosexuality,* 14, 1–19.

Elias, S., & Simpson, J. L. (1991). Sampling the chorionic villi. *Contemporary OB/GYN, Technology,* 11–28.

Eliasson, R., & Lindholmer, C. (1976). Functions of male accessory genital organs. In E. Hafez (Ed.)., *Human Semen and Fertility Regulations in Men.* St. Louis, Mo.: Mosby.

Elkind, D. (1967). Egocentrism in adolescence. *Child Development,* 38, 1025–1034.

———. (1985). Egocentrism redux. *Developmental Review,* 5, 218–226.

Ellerbrock, T., Bush, T., Chamberland, M., & Oxtoby, M. (1991). Epidemiology of women with AIDS in the United States, 1981 through 1990. *Journal of the American Medical Association,* 265, 2971–2975.

Elliott, M. (1992). Tip of the iceberg? *Social Work Today,* March, 12–13.

Ellis, A. (1966). *Sex Without Guilt.* Secaucus, N.J.: Lyle Stuart.

Ellis, B., & Symons, D. (1990). Sex differences in sexual fantasy: An evolutionary psychological approach. *The Journal of Sex Research,* 27, 527–555.

Ellis, D., & Hewat, R. (1985). Mothers' postpartum perceptions of spousal relationships. *Journal of Obstetric, Gynecologic, and Neonatal Nursing,* 14, 140–146.

Ellis, L., & Ames, M. (1987). Neurohormonal functioning and sexual orientation: A theory of homosexuality-heterosexuality. *Psychological Bulletin,* 101, 233–258.

———, Burke, D., & Ames, M. (1987). Sexual orientation as a continuous variable: A comparison between the sexes. *Archives of Sexual Behavior,* 16, 523.

Ellison, C. (1980). A critique of the clitoral model of female sexuality. Paper presented to the American Psychological Association, Montreal, September 4.

Emmanuel, N., Lydiard, R., & Ballenger, J. (1991). Fluoxetine treatment of voyeurism. *American Journal of Psychiatry,* 148, 950.

Engelmann, U., Schramek, P., Tomamichel, G., Deindl, F., & Senge, T. (1990). Vasectomy reversal in central Europe: Results of a questionnaire of urologists in Austria, Germany and Switzerland. *Journal of Urology,* 143, 64–67.

Epstein, A. (1988). Decoy: One potential drug that would lure the AIDS virus to a false target. *Scientific American,* March, 32–34.

Erickson, W., Walbek, N., & Seely, R. (1988). Behavior patterns of child molesters. *Archives of Sexual Behavior, 17,* 77–86.

Erlichman, K. (1989). Lesbian mothers: Ethical issues in social work practice. *Women and Therapy, 8,* 207–224.

Essex, M. (1985). Paper presented at an international conference on AIDS, Atlanta, April.

Esterberg, K. (1990). From illness to action: Conceptions of homosexuality in The Ladder, 1956–1965. *The Journal of Sex Research, 27,* 65–80.

European Study Group. (1989). Risk factors for male to female transmission of HIV. *British Medical Journal, 298,* 411–415.

Everitt, B., & Bancroft, J. (1991). Of rats and men: The comparative approach to male sexuality. *Annual Review of Sex Research, 2,* 77–118.

Expert Committee on Pelvic Inflammatory Disease (1991). *Sexually Transmitted Diseases, 18,* 46–64.

Fagot, B. (1978). The influence of sex of child on parental reactions to toddler children. *Child Development, 49,* 459–465.

———, Leinbach, M., & O'Boyle, C. (1992). Gender labeling, gender stereotyping, and parenting behaviors. *Developmental Psychology, 28,* 225–230.

Fahrner, E. (1987). Sexual dysfunction in male alcohol addicts: Prevalence and treatment. *Archives of Sexual Behavior, 16,* 247–257.

Falk, G., & Falk, U. (1980). Sexuality and the aged. *Nursing Outlook, 28,* 51–55.

Fallon, B., Miller, R., & Gerber, W. (1981). Nonmicroscopic vasovasostomy. *Journal of Urology, 126,* 361.

Farber, N. (1992). Sexual standards and activity: Adolescents' perceptions. *Child and Adolescent Social Work, 9,* 53–76.

Farley, T., Rosenberg, M., Rowe, P., Chen, J., & Meirik, O. (1992). Intrauterine devices and pelvic inflammatory disease: An international perspective. *Lancet, 339,* 785–788.

Faundes, A., Cochon, L., Brache, V., Alvarez-Sanchez, F., & Tejada, A. S. (1991). Ovulatory dysfunction during continuous administration of low-dose levonorgestrel by sudermal implants. *Fertility and Sterility, 56,* 27–31.

Faux, M. (1984). *Childless by Choice.* New York: Anchor Press.

Faye, R., & Farber, M. (1989). The neuroendocrine regulation and dysfunctions of the menstrual cycle. *Medical Aspects of Human Sexuality,* April, 90–97.

Fedoroff, J. P. (1991). Interview techniques to assess sexual disorders. *Families in Society: The Journal of Contemporary Human Services,* March, 140–145.

Fein, G., Johnson, D., Kesson, N., Stork, L., & Wasserman, L. (1975). Sex stereotypes and preferences in the toy choices of 20-month-old boys and girls. *Developmental Psychology, 11,* 527–528.

Feinauer, L. (1988). Relationship of long term effects of childhood sexual abuse to identity of the offender: Family, friend, or stranger. *Women and Therapy, 7,* 89–107.

Feingold, A. (1988). Cognitive gender differences are disappearing. *American Psychologist, 43,* 95–103.

———. (1992). Good-looking people are not what we think. *Psychological Bulletin, 111,* 304–341.

Feldman-Summers, S., & Jones, G. (1984). Psychological impacts of sexual contact between therapists and other health care practitioners and their clients. *Journal of Consulting and Clinical Psychology, 52,* 1054–1061.

———, & Norris, J. (1984). Differences between rape victims who report and those who do not report to a public agency. *Journal of Applied Psychology, 14,* 562–573.

Felitti, V. (1991). Long-term medical consequences of incest, rape, and molestation. *Southern Medical Journal, 84,* 328–331.

Felsman, D., Brannigan, G., & Yellin, P. (1987). Control theory in dealing with adolescent sexuality and pregnancy. *Journal of Sex Education and Therapy, 13,* 15–16.

Fenster, L., Eskenazi, B., Windham, G., & Swan, S. (1992). Caffeine consumption during pregnancy and fetal growth. *Obstetrical and Gynecological Survey, 47,* 148–149.

Fergusson, D., Lawton, J., & Shannon, F. (1988). Neonatal circumcision and penile problems: An 8-year longitudinal study. *Pediatrics, 81,* 537–540.

Fielding, J. (1978). Adolescent pregnancy revisited. *New England Journal of Medicine, 299,* 893–896.

Filips, J. (1991). Norplant. *Oregonian,* January 20, L1, L4.

Findlay, J., Place, V., & Snyder, P. (1989). Treatment of primary hypogonadism in men by the transdermal administration of testosterone. *Journal of Clinical Endocrinology and Metabolism, 68,* 369–373.

Findlay, S. (1991). AIDS: The second decade. *U.S. News and World Report,* June 17, 20–22.

Finkelhor, D. (1979). *Sexually Victimized Children.* New York: Free Press.

———. (1980). Sex among siblings: A survey on prevalence, variety, and effects. *Archives of Sexual Behavior, 9,* 171–194.

———. (1984a). *Child Sexual Abuse: Theory and Research.* New York: Free Press.

———. (1984b). The prevention of child sexual abuse: An overview of needs and problems. *SIECUS Report, 13,* 1–5.

———, Hotaling, G., Lewis, I., & Smith, C. (1990). Sexual abuse in a national sample of adult men and women: Prevalence, characteristics, and risk factors. *Child Abuse and Neglect, 14,* 19–28.

Fischhoff, B. (1992). Giving advice: Decision theory perspectives on sexual assault. *American Psychologist, 47,* 577–588.

Fischl, M., Richman, D., & Hansen, N. (1990). The safety and efficacy of zidovudine (AZT) in the treatment of subjects with mildly symptomatic human immunodeficiency virus type 1 (HIV) infection. *Annals of Internal Medicine, 112,* 727–737.

Fish, L., Fish, R., & Sprenkle, D. (1984). Treating inhibited sexual desire: A marital therapy approach. *American Journal of Family Therapy, 12,* 3–12.

Fisher, B., Bauer, M., Margolese, R., Poisson, R., Pilch, Y., Redmond, C., Fisher, E., Wolmark, N., Deutsch, M., Montague, E., Saffer, E., Wickerham, L., Lerner, H., Glass, A., Shibata, H., Deckers, P., Ketcham, A., Oishi, R., & Russell, I. (1985). Five-year results of a randomized clinical trial comparing total mastectomy and segmental mastectomy with or without radiation in the treatment of breast cancer. *New England Journal of Medicine, 312,* 665–673.

Fisher, M. (1991). Parents' view of adolescent health issues. Paper presented at the 18th annual meeting of the Society for Adolescent Medicine, Denver, Colo., March 14.

Fisher, T. (1987). Family communication and the sexual behavior and attitudes of college students. *Journal of Youth and Adolescence,* 16, 481–495.

———. (1988). The relationship between parent–child communication about sexuality and college students' sexual behavior and attitudes as a function of parental proximity. *Journal of Sex Research,* 24, 305–311.

Fisher, W. (1983). Gender, gender role identification, and response to erotica. In E. Allgeier and N. McCormick (Eds.)., *Changing Boundaries: Gender Roles and Sexual Behavior.* Palo Alto, Calif.: Mayfield.

———, & Gray, J. (1988). Erotophobia–erotophilia and sexual behavior during pregnancy and postpartum. *Journal of Sex Research,* 25, 379–396.

Fitch, W., & Hodge, E. (1988). Management of penile fracture: Maintenance of erectile function. Paper presented at the Eighty-Second Annual Assembly of Urologists, New Orleans, November.

Flaherty, J., & Dusek, J. (1980). An investigation of the relationship between psychological androgyny and components of self-concept. *Journal of Personality and Social Psychology,* 38, 984–992.

Flattum-Riemers, J. (1991). Norplant: A new contraceptive. *American Family Physician,* 44, 103–109.

Fleming, M., Cohen, D., Salt, P., Jones, D., & Jenkins, S. (1981). A study of pre- and postsurgical transsexuals: MMPI characteristics. *Archives of Sexual Behavior,* 10, 161–170.

Fletcher, J. (1991). Perinatal transmission of human papillomavirus. *American Family Physician,* 43, 143–148.

Follingstad, D., & Kimbrell, D. (1986). Sex fantasies revisited: An expansion and further clarification of variables affecting sex fantasy production. *Archives of Sexual Behavior,* 15, 475–486.

Fonow, M., Richardson, L., & Wemmerus, V. (1992). Feminist rape education: Does it work? *Gender and Society,* 6, 108–121.

Fontaine, P., & Toffler, W. (1991). Dorsal penile nerve block for newborn circumcision. *American Family Physician,* 43, 1327–1333.

Forbes, G. (1992). Body size and composition of perimenarchal girls. *American Journal of Diseases in Children,* 146, 63–66.

Ford, C., & Beach, F. (1951). *Patterns of Sexual Behavior.* New York: Harper & Row.

Foreman, H., Stade, B., & Schlesselman, S. (1981). Intrauterine device usage and fetal loss. *Obstetrics and Gynecology,* 58, 669–677.

Forgac, G., Cassel, C., & Michaels, E. (1984). Chronocity of criminal behaviors and psychopathology in male exhibitionists. *Journal of Clinical Psychology,* 40, 827–832.

———, & Michaels, E. (1982). Personality characteristics of two types of male exhibitionists. *Journal of Abnormal Psychology,* 91, 287–293.

Forrest, B. (1991). Women, HIV, and mucosal immunity. *The Lancet,* 337, 835–837.

Forrest, J., & Henshaw, S. (1987). The harassment of U.S. abortion providers. *Family Planning Perspectives,* 19, 9–13.

———, Singh, S. (1990). The sexual and reproductive behavior of American women, 1982-1988. *Family Planning Perspectives,* 22, 206–214.

Forrest, L., & Gilbert, M. (1992). Infertility: An unanticipated and prolonged life crisis. *Journal of Mental Health Counseling,* 14, 42–58.

Foster, M. (1992). Aberrant puberty. *Obstetrics and Gynecology Clinics of North America,* 19, 59–70.

Fowers, B., & Olson, D. (1986). Predicting marital success with PREPARE: A predictive validity study. *Journal of Marital and Family Therapy,* 12, 403–413.

Fowler, F., Wennberg, J., Timothy, R., Barry, M., Mulley, A., & Hanley, D. (1988). Symptom status and quality of life following prostatectomy. *Journal of the American Medical Association,* 259, 3018–3022.

Fox, B., & Joyce, C. (1991). Americans compete for control over sex. *New Scientist,* January 12, 23.

Fox, R. (1990). Bisexuality and sexual orientation self-disclosure. Paper presented at The Society for the Scientific Study of Sex Annual Western Region Conference, San Diego, Calif., April 25.

Franceschi, S., Serraino, D., Vaccher, E., & Tirelli, U. (1989). Homosexual role separation and spread of AIDS. *Lancet,* January 7, 42.

Frank, D. (1991). Sexual counseling with a developmentally disabled couple: A case study. *Perspectives in Psychiatric Care,* 27, 30–34.

Frank, E., Anderson, C., & Rubinstein, D. (1978). Frequency of sexual dysfunction in ``normal'' couples. *New England Journal of Medicine,* 299, 111–115.

———, ———, & ———. (1979). Marital role strain and sexual satisfaction, *Journal of Consulting and Clinical Psychology,* 47, 1096–1103.

———, ———, ———, & Enos, S. (1983). The love life of the American wife. *Ladies Home Journal,* February, 71–73, 116–119.

Franz, W., & Reardon, D. (1992). Differential impact of abortion on adolescents and adults. *Adolescence,* 27, 161–172.

Frazer, J. (1987). The dilemma of the perimenopausal female: A sexual/physical health issue. *Holistic Nursing Practice,* 1, 67–75.

Frazier, P., & Cohen, B. (1992). Research on the sexual victimization of women. *The Counseling Psychologist,* 20, 141–158.

Freedman, E., & D'Emilio, J. (1990). Problems encountered in writing the history of sexuality: Sources, theory and interpretation. *The Journal of Sex Research,* 27, 481–495.

Freeman, E., Rickels, K., & Sondheimer, S. (1992). Course of premenstrual syndrome symptom severity after treatment. *American Journal of Psychiatry,* 149, 531–533.

———, ———, Huggins, G., Celso-Ramon, G., & Polin, G. (1980). Emotional distress patterns among women having first or repeat abortions. *Obstetrics and Gynecology,* 55, 630–636.

Freud, S. (1953). Three essays on the theory of sexuality. In *Standard Edition,* Vol. VII. London: Hogarth Press. Originally published in 1905.

Freund, K. (1990). Courtship disorder. In W. Marshall, D. Laws, & H. Barbaree (Eds.), *Handbook of Sexual Assault: Issues, Theories and Treatment of the Offender.* New York: Plenum.

———. (1992). Chlamydia disease in women. *Hospital Practice,* February 15, 175–186.

Freund, M., Lee, N., & Leonard, T. (1991). Sexual behavior of clients with street prostitutes in Camden, N.J. *The Journal of Sex Research,* 28, 579–591.

Friday, N. (1980). *Men in Love.* New York: Delacorte.

Friedland, G., Saltzman, B., Rogers, M., Kahl, P., Lesser, M., Mayers, M., & Klein, R. (1986). Lack of transmission of HTLV-III/LAV infection to household contacts of patients with AIDS or AIDS-related complex with oral candidiasis. *New England Journal of Medicine,* 344–349.

Friedman, R., Hurt, S., Arnoff, M., & Clarkin, J. (1980). Behavior and the menstrual cycle *Signs,* 5, 719–738.

Friedrich, E. (1985). Vaginitis. *American Journal of Obstetrics and Gynecology,* 152, 247–251.

———. (1987). Vulvar vestibulitis syndrome. *Journal of Reproductive Medicine,* 32, 110–115.

Frisch, R. (1988). Fatness and fertility. *Scientific American,* March, 88–95.

———, & McArthur, J. (1974). Menstrual cycles: Fatness as a determinant of minimum weight for height necessary for their maintenance or onset. *Science,* 185, 949–951.

———, Wyshak, G., & Vincent, L. (1980). Delayed menarche and amenorrhea in ballet dancers. *New England Journal of Medicine,* 303, 17–19.

Fromm, E. (1965). *The Ability to Love.* New York: Farrar, Straus & Giroux.

Furby, L., & Fischhoff, B. (in press). Rape self-defense strategies: A review of their effectiveness. *Victimology.*

Furniss, T. (1985). Conflict-avoiding and conflict-regulating patterns in incest and child sexual abuse. *Acta Paedopsychiatrica,* 50, 299–313.

Furstenberg, F. (1984). Family communication and teenagers' contraceptive use. *Family Planning Perspectives,* 16, 163–170.

———, Brooks-Gunn, J., & Morgan, S. (1987). *Adolescent Mothers in Later Life.* Cambridge, Mass.: Cambridge University Press.

———, Menchen, J., & Lincoln, R. (1981). *Teenage Sexuality, Pregnancy, and Childbearing.* Philadelphia: University of Pennsylvania Press.

Furuhjelm, M., Karlgren, E., & Carstrom, K. (1984). The effect of estrogen therapy on somatic and psychical symptoms in postmenopausal women. *Acta Obstetricia et Gynecologica Scandinavica,* 63, 655–661.

Gadpaille, W. (1975). *The Cycles of Sex.* New York: Scribner.

Gaffney, G., Luries, S., & Berlin, F. (1984). Is there familiar transmission of pedophilia? *Journal of Nervous and Mental Disease,* 172, 546–548.

Gagnon, J. (1977). *Human Sexualities.* Glenview, Ill.: Scott, Foresman.

———. (1985). Attitudes and responses of parents to preadolescent masturbation. *Archives of Sexual Behavior,* 14, 451–466.

———, & Simon, W. (1987). The sexual scripting of oral–genital contacts. *Archives of Sexual Behavior,* 16, 1–25.

Gallagher, W. (1988). Sex and hormones. *Atlantic Monthly,* March, 77–82.

Gambert, S. (1991). Screen now for prostate cancer. *Medical Aspects of Human Sexuality,* February, 21–24.

Ganong, L., & Coleman, M. (1989). Preparing for remarriage: Anticipating the issues, seeking solutions. *Family Relations,* 38, 28–33.

Garcia, L. (1982). Sex-role orientation and stereotypes about male–female sexuality. *Sex Roles,* 8, 863–876.

Gardner, J. (1992). Descriptive study of genital variation in healthy, nonabused premenarchal girls. *Journal Pediatrics,* 120, 251–257.

———, Schuman, K., Slattery, M., Sanborn, J., Abbott, T., & Overall, J., Jr. (1991). Is vaginal douching related to cervical carcinoma? *American Journal of Epidemiology,* 133, 368–375.

Garnets, L., Hancock, K., Cochran, S., Goodchilds, J., & Peplau, L. A. (1991). Issues in psychotherapy with lesbians and gay men. *American Psychologist,* 46, 964–972.

Garnett, T., & Studd, J. (1991). Hormone replacement therapy: Indications and contra-indications. *Maternal and Child Health,* September, 276–281.

Gartrell, N. (1987). The lesbian as ``single'' woman. In M. Walsh (Ed.)., *The Psychology of Women.* New Haven, Conn.: Yale University Press.

Garvey, M. (1986). The high cost of sexual harassment suits. *Labor Relations,* 65, 75–79.

Gavzer, B. (1987). Why more older women are marrying younger men. *Parade,* May 24, 12–13.

Gaylin, N. (1991). An intergenerational perspective of marriage: Love and trust in cultural context. *Marriage and Family Review,* 16, 143–159.

Geary, D. (1989). A model for representing gender differences in the pattern of cognitive abilities. *American Psychologist,* 44, 1155–1156.

Gebhard, P. (1965). Situational factors affecting human sexual behavior. In F. Beach (Ed.)., *Sex and Behavior.* New York: Wiley.

———. (1966). Factors in marital orgasm. *Journal of Social Issues,* 22, 88–95.

———. (1971). Human sexual behavior: A summary statement. In D. Marshall and R. Suggs (Eds.)., *Human Sexual Behavior: Variations in the Ethnographic Spectrum.* Englewood Cliffs, N.J.: Prentice-Hall.

———. (1977). The acquisition of basic sex information. *Journal of Sex Research,* 13, 148–169.

———, Gagnon, J., Pomeroy, W., & Christenson, C. (1965). *Sex Offenders: An Analysis of Types.* New York: Harper & Row.

Geer, J., & O'Donohue, W. (1984). Premature ejaculation: Investigation of factors in ejaculatory latency. *Journal of Abnormal Psychology,* 93, 242–245.

Gelbard, M. (1988). Dystropic penile calcification in Peyronie's disease. *Journal of Urology, 139,* 738–740.

Geller, A. (1991). Sexual problems of the recovering alcoholic. *Medical Aspects of Human Sexuality,* March, 56–59.

Gelman, D., Foote, D., Barrett, T., & Talbot, M. (1992). Born or bred? *Newsweek,* February 24, 46–53.

Gendel, E., & Bonner, E. (1988). Gender identity disorders and paraphilias. In H. Goldman (Ed.), *Review of General Psychiatry.* Norwalk, Conn.: Appleton & Lange.

Genevie, L., & Margolies, E. (1987). *The Motherhood Report: How Women Feel About Being Mothers.* New York: Macmillan.

Gerrard, M. (1987). Sex, sex guilt, and contraceptive use revisited: The 1980s. *Journal of Personality and Social Psychology, 52,* 975–980.

Gerstman, B. B., Piper, J., Tomita, D., Ferguson, W., Stadel, B., & Lundin, F. (1991). Oral contraceptive estrogen dose and the risk of deep venous thromboembolic disease. *American Journal of Epidemiology, 133,* 32–37.

Geschwind, N., & Behan, P. (1982). Left-handedness: Association with immune disease, migraine, and developmental learning disorder. *Proceedings of the National Academy of Science, USA, 79,* 5097–5100.

——, & ——. (1984). Laterality, hormones, and immunity. In N. Geschwind & A. Galaburda (Eds.), *Cerebral Dominance: The Biological Foundations.* Cambridge, Mass.: Harvard University Press.

Gibbs, E. (1988). Psychosocial development of children raised by lesbian mothers: A review of research. *Women and Therapy, 8,* 65–75.

Gibbs, R. (1991). Herpes simplex virus infections in pregnancy. *Contemporary OB/GYN,* May, 85–86.

——, & Mead, P. (1992). Preventing neonatal herpes–current strategies. *The New England Journal of Medicine, 326,* 946–947.

Giguere, J., Stablein, D., Spaulding, J., McLeod, D., Paulson, D., & Weiss, R. (1988). The clinical significance of unconventional orchidectomy approaches in testicular cancer: A report from the testicular cancer intergroup study. *Journal of Urology, 139,* 1225–1288.

Gilbert, B., Heesacker, M., & Gannon, L. (1991). Changing the sexual aggression-supportive attitudes of men: A psychoeducational intervention. *Journal of Counseling Psychology, 38,* 197–203.

Gilbert, D., Hagen, R., & D'Agostine, R. (1986). The effects of cigarette smoking on human sexual potency. *Addictive Behaviors, 11,* 431–434.

Gilbert, H. (1991). Bad blood. *Northwest Magazine,* February 17, 8–13.

Gillespie, L. (1984). The diaphragm: An accomplice in recurrent urinary tract infections. *Urology, 24,* 25–30.

Gilmartin, B. (1977). Swinging: Who gets involved and how? In R. Libby and R. Whitehurst (Eds.)., *Marriage and Alternatives: Exploring Intimate Relationships.* Glenview, Ill.: Scott, Foresman.

Gilson, R. (1992). Sexually transmitted hepatitis: A review. *Genitourinary Medicine, 68,* 123–129.

Gilstrap, L., & Wendel, G. (1992). Syphilis rise calls for accurate diagnosis. *Contemporary OB/GYN,* March, 56–60.

Given, F., Jr., & Jones, H., III (1992). Self-administered cervical cancer screening. *Clinical Obstetrics and Gynecology, 35,* 3–12.

Gjerdingen, D., & Froberg, D., (1991). The fourth stage of labor: The health of birth mothers and adoptive mothers at six-weeks postpartum. *Family Medicine, 23,* 29–35.

——, —— & Fontaine, P. (1991). The effects of social support on women's health during pregnancy, labor and delivery, and the postpartum period. *Family Medicine, 23,* 370–375.

Glasser, M., Dennis, J., Orthoefer, J., Carter, S., & Hollander, E. (1989). Characteristics of males at a public health department contraceptive service. *Journal of Adolescent Health Care, 10,* 115–118.

Glenn, N., & Weaver, C. (1988). The changing relationship of marital status to reported happiness. *Journal of Marriage and the Family, 50,* 317–324.

Glick, P., & Lin, S. (1986). Recent changes in divorce and remarriage. *Journal of Marriage and the Family, 48,* 737–748.

——, & Norton, A. (1979). *1979 Update: Marrying, Divorcing, and Living Together in the U.S. Today.* Washington, D.C.: Population Reference Bureau.

Gochros, H. (1978). Counseling gay husbands. *Journal of Sex Education and Therapy, 4,* 6–10.

——. (1992). The sexuality of gay men with HIV infection. *Social Work, 37,* 105–109.

Goedert, J., Biggar, R., Winn, D., Greene, M., Weiss S., Grossman, R., Strong, D., & Blattner, W. (1984). Determinants of retrovirus (HTLV-III). antibody and immunodeficiency conditions in homosexual men. *Lancet,* September 29, 711–715.

Goeman, J., & Piot, P. (1992). Interaction between HIV infection and other STDs. *IPPF Medical Bulletin, 26,* 1–2.

Goethals, G. (1980). Love, marriage, and mutual growth. In K. Pope (Ed.)., *On Love and Loving.* San Francisco: Jossey-Bass.

Goetsch, M. (1991). Personal communications.

Gold, D., Ashley, R., Solberg, G., Abbo, H., and Corey, L. (1988). Chronic-dose acyclovir to suppress frequently recurring genital herpes simplex virus infection: Effect on antibody response to herpes simplex virus type 2 proteins. *Journal of Infectious Diseases, 158,* 1227–1234.

Gold, S., & Chick, D. (1988). Sexual fantasy patterns as related to sexual attitude, experience, guilt and sex. *Journal of Sex Education and Therapy, 14,* 18–23.

——, Balzano, B., & Stamey, R. (1991). Two studies of females' sexual force fantasies. *Journal of Sex Education & Therapy, 17,* 15–26.

Goldberg, C. (1986). Controlled trial of ``intervir-A'' in herpes simplex virus infection. *Lancet, 1,* 703–706.

Goldberg, D., Whipple, B., Fishkin, R., Waxman, H., Fink, P., & Weisberg, M. (1983). The Grafenberg spot and female ejaculation: A review of initial hypotheses. *Journal of Sex and Marital Therapy, 9,* 27–37.

Goldberg, M., Edmonds, L., & Oakley, G. (1979). Reducing birth defect risk in advanced maternal age. *Journal of the American Medical Association, 242,* 2292–2294.

Goldberg, P. (1968). Are women prejudiced against women? *Transaction*, April, 28–30.

Goldberg, S. (1983). Parent–infant bonding: Another look. *Child Development*, 54, 1355–1382.

Golden, G. (1989). Parental attitudes to infant's sex play determine child's later attitudes to sex. *Medical Aspects of Human Sexuality*, May, 73–97.

Golden, J. (1988). A second look at a case of inhibited sexual desire. *Journal of Sex Research*, 25, 304–306.

Goldenring, J., & Purtell, E. (1984). Knowledge of testicular cancer risk and need for self-examination in college students: A call for equal time for men in teaching of early cancer detection techniques. *Pediatrics*, 1093–1096.

Goldfarb, J., Mumford, D., Schum, D., Smith, P., Flowers, C., & Schum, C. (1977). An attempt to detect ``pregnancy susceptibility'' in indigent adolescent girls. *Journal of Youth and Adolescence*, 6, 127–144.

Golding, J., Siegel, J., Sorenson, S., Burnan, M., & Stein, J. (1989). Social support sources following sexual assault. *Journal of Community Psychology*, 17, 92–107.

Goldman, R., & Goldman, J. (1982). *Children's Sexual Thinking: A Comparative Study of Children aged 5 to 15 Years in Australia, Britain, and Sweden*. London: Routhedge & Kegan Paul.

Goldsmith, M. (1991). AIDS vaccines inch closer to useful existence. *Journal of the American Medical Association*, 265, 1356–1357.

Golub, S. (1983). *Menarche*. Lexington, Mass.: Lexington Books.

Gomes-Schwartz, B., Horowitz, J., & Sauzier, M. (1985). Severity of emotional distress among sexually abused preschool, school-age, and adolescent children. *Hospital and Community Psychiatry*, 36, 503–508.

Goodchilds, J., & Zellman, G. (1984). Sexual signaling and sexual aggression in adolescent relationships. In N. Malamuth and E. Donnerstein (Eds.)., *Pornography and Sexual Aggression*. Orlando: Academic Press.

Goodpasture, H. (1991). Antiviral drug therapy. *American Family Physician*, 43, 197–204.

Gooren, L. (1988). Hypogonadotropic hypogonadal men respond less well to androgen substitution treatment than hypergonadotropic hypogonadal men. *Archives of Sexual Behavior*, 17, 265–270.

———, Fliers, E., & Courtney, K. (1990). Biological determinants of sexual orientation. *Annual Review of Sex Research*, 1, 175–196.

Gordon, J., & Gorski, R. (1979). Sexual differentiation of the brain—implications for neuroscience. In D. Schneider (Ed.)., *Reviews of Neuroscience*, Vol. 4. New York: Raven Press.

Gordon, S. (1973). *The Sexual Adolescent*. North Scit[chuate, Mass.: Duxbury Press.

Gottman, J. (1991). Predicting the longitudinal course of marriages. *Journal of Marital and Family Therapy*, 17, 3–7.

———, & Krokoff, L. (in press). The relationship between marital interaction and marital satisfaction: A longitudinal view. *Journal of Consulting and Clinical Psychology*.

———, & Levenson, R. (1986). Assessing the role of emotion in marriage. *Behavioral Assessment*, 8, 31–48.

———, & ———. (1988). The social psychophysiology of marriage. In P. Noller & M. Fitzpatrick (Eds.), *Perspectives on Marital Interaction*. Philadelphia: Multilingual Matters.

———, Notarius, C., Gonso, J., & Markman, H. (1976). *A Couple's Guide to Communication*. Champaign, Ill.: Research Press.

Gouchie, C., & Kimura, D. (1991). The relationship between testosterone levels and cognitive ability patterns. *Psychoneuroendocrinology*, 16, 323–334.

Gould, L. (1989). Impact of cardiovascular disease on male sexual function. *Medical Aspects of Human Sexuality*, April, 24–27.

Gove, W., & Shin, H. (1989). The psychological well-being of divorced and widowed men and women. *Journal of Family Issues*, 10, 122–144.

Goy, R. (1970). Experimental control of psychosexuality. *Philosophical Transactions of the Royal Society of London Biological*, 259, 149–162.

Grafenberg, E. (1950). The role of urethra in female orgasm. *International Journal of Sexology*, 3, 145–148.

Graham, C., & Sherwin, B. (1992). A prospective treatment study of premenstrual symptoms using a triphasic oral contraceptive. *Journal of Psychosomatic Research*, 36, 257–266.

Gram, I., Austin, H., & Stalsberg, H. (1992). Cigarette smoking and the incidence of cervical intraepithelial neoplasia, grade III, and the cancer of the cervix uteri. *American Journal of Epidemiology*, 135, 341–346.

Granberg, D., & Granberg, B. (1980). Abortion attitudes, 1965–1980: Trends and determinants. *Family Planning Perspectives*, 12, 250–261.

Grauerholz, E., & Koralewski, M. (Eds.) (1990). *Sexual Coercion: A Sourcebook on its Nature, Causes and Prevention*. Lexington, Mass.: Lexington Books.

Gray, C., Koopman, E., & Hunt, J. (1991). The emotional phases of marital separation: An empirical investigation. *American Journal of Orthopsychiatry*, 61, 138–143.

Gray, L., & Saracino, M. (1991). College students' attitudes, beliefs, and behavior about AIDS: Implications for family life educators. *Family Relations*, 40, 258–263.

Greeley, A., Michael, R., & Smith, T. (1989). A most monogamous people: Americans and their sexual partners. *GSS Topical Report*, No. 17. Chicago, Il: NORC.

Green, G., & Clunis, D. (1988). Married lesbians. *Women and Therapy*, 8, 41–49.

Green, R. (1974). *Sexual Identity Conflict in Children and Adults*. New York: Basic Books.

———. (1979). Adults who want to change sex; adolescents who cross-dress; and children called ``sissy'' and ``tomboy.'' In R. Green (Ed.)., *Human Sexuality: A Health Practitioner's Text*, 2nd ed. Baltimore: Williams & Wilkins.

———. (1985). Exposure to explicit sexual materials and sexual assault: A review of behavioral and social science research. Paper presented at a hearing of the Attorney General's Commission on Pornography, Houston, September 12.

———. (1987). *The ``Sissy Boy'' Syndrome and the Development of Homosexuality*. New Haven, Conn.: Yale University Press.

———, Mandel, J., Hotvedt, M., Gray, J., & Smith, L. (1986). Lesbian mothers and their children: A comparison with solo parent heterosexual mothers and their children. *Archives of Sexual Behavior,* 15, 167–184.

Green, S., & Sollie, D. (1989). Long-term effects of a church-based sex education program on adolescent communication. *Family Relations,* 38, 152–156.

Greenberg, M., Rutledge, L., Reid, R., Berman, N., Precop, S., & Elswick, R. (1991). A double-blind, randomized trial of 5% podofilox and placebo for the treatment of genital warts in women. *Obstetrics and Gynecology,* 77, 735–739.

Greenberg, P. (1992). Immunopathogenesis of HIV infection. *Hospital Practice,* February 15, 109–124.

Greenburg, D. (1986). *Dan Greenburg's Confessions of a Pregnant Father.* New York: Macmillan.

Greene, R., & Field, S. (1989). Social support coverage and the well-being of elderly widows and married women. *Journal of Family Issues,* 10, 33–51.

Greene, W. (1991). The molecular biology of human immunodeficiency virus type 1 infection. *The New England Journal of Medicine,* 324, 308–317.

Greenwald, H. (1958). *The Call Girl.* New York: Ballantine Books.

———. (1970). *The Elegant Prostitute: A Social and Psychoanalytic Study.* New York: Walken.

Greenwood, S. (1989). No more UTI misery. *Medical Self Care,* January/February, 18–64.

Gregoire, A. (1992). New treatments for erectile impotence. *British Journal of Psychiatry,* 160, 315–326.

Grieco, A. (1987). Scope and nature of sexual harassment in nursing. *Journal of Sex Research,* 23, 261–266.

Grimes, D. (1991). Contraception and STDs. *Dialogues in Contraception,* 3(4), 1–8.

———, Forrest, J., Kirkman, A., et al. (1991). An epidemic of antiabortion violence in the United States. *American Journal of Obstetrics and Gynecology,* 165, 1263.

———, Mischell, D., Shoupe, D., & Lacarra, M. (1988). Early abortion with a single dose of the antiprogestin RU-486. *American Journal of Obstetrics and Gynecology,* 158, 1308–1312.

Grohmann, S., & MacDonell, K. (1992). Predicting the course of HIV infection. *Medical Aspects of Human Sexuality,* 26, 22–29.

Groth, A. (1979). *Men Who Rape.* New York: Plenum Press.

Groth, N. (1979). Sexual trauma in the life histories of rapists and child molesters. *Victimology,* 4, 10–16.

———, & Hobson, W. (1983). The dynamics of sexual assault. In L. Schlesinger and E. Revitch (Eds.), *Sexual Dynamics of Anti-Social Behavior.* Springfield, Ill.: Thomas.

Gruber, E., & Chambers, C. (1987). Cognitive development and adolescent contraception: Integrating theory and practice. *Adolescence,* 22, 211–219.

Gruen, D. (1990). Postpartum depression: A debilitating yet often unassessed problem. *Health and Social Work,* 15, 261–269.

Grunfeld, L. (1989). Workup for male infertility. *Journal of Reproductive Medicine,* 43, 143–149.

Gurian, B. (1988). Loss of father's libido after childbirth. *Medical Aspects of Human Sexuality,* 22, 102–116.

Gutek, B. (1985). *Sex and the Workplace.* San Francisco: Jossey-Bass.

Gwinn, M., Pappaioanou, M., George, R., Hannon, W., Wasser, S., Redus, M., Hoff, R., Grady, G., Willoughby, A., Novello, A., Petersen, L., Dondero, T., & Curran, J. (1991). Prevalence of HIV infection in childbearing women in the United States. *Journal of the American Medical Association,* 265, 1704–1708.

Haage, D. (1991). "Homophobia?" *Journal of Social Behavior and Personality,* 6, 171–174.

Hackenbruck, P. (1987). Adolescent sexuality: Differential development. Paper presented at Sexual Identity Issues of Adolescence, National Association of Social Workers, Vancouver, Wash., March.

Hage, M., Helms, M., Hammond, W., & Hammond, C. (1988). Changing rates of cesarean delivery: The Duke experience, 1978–86. *Obstetrics and Gynecology,* 72, 99–101.

Hagen, R., & D'Agostino, J. (1982). Smoking may be hazard to male sexual response. *Brain-Mind Bulletin,* 7, 3.

Halikas, J., Weller, R., & Morse, C. (1982). Effects of regular marijuana use on sexual performance. *Journal of Psychoactive Drugs,* 14, 59–70.

Halman, L. J., Abbey, A., & Andrews, F. (1992). Attitudes about infertility interventions among fertile and infertile couples. *American Journal of Public Health,* 82, 191–194.

Halpern, D. (1989). The disappearance of cognitive gender differences: What you see depends on where you look. *American Psychologist,* 44, 1156–1158.

Hamilton, E. (1978). *Sex, with Love.* Boston: Beacon Press.

Hamilton, G. (1983). *The Religious Case for Abortion.* Asheville, N.C.: Madison and Polk.

Hamilton, J. (1943). Demonstrable ability of penile erection in castrate men with markedly low titers of urinary androgen. *Proceedings of the Society of Experimental Biology and Medicine,* 54, 309.

———, Alagna, S., King, L., & Lloyd, C. (1987). The emotional consequences of gender-based abuse in the workplace: New counseling programs for sex discrimination. *Women and Therapy,* 6, 155–182.

———, Hartigan, P., Simberkoff, M., Day, P., Diamond, G., Dickinson, G., Drusano, G., & Egorin, M. (1992). A controlled trial of early versus late treatment with zidovudine in symptomatic human immunodeficiency virus infection. *New England Journal of Medicine,* 326, 437–443.

Hammarback, S., Damber, J., & Backstrom, T. (1989). Relationship between symptom severity and hormone changes in women with premenstrual syndrome. *Journal of Clinical Endocrinology and Metabolism,* 68, 125–130.

Hammerschlag, M. (1989). Chlamydial infections. *Journal of Pediatrics,* 114, 727–734.

Hampson, J. L., & Hampson, J. G. (1961). The ontogenesis of sexual behavior in man. In W. Young (Ed.), *Sex and Internal Secretions.* Baltimore: Williams & Wilkins.

Hand, J. (1970). Surgery of the penis and urethra. In M. Campbell and J. Harrison (Eds.)., *Urology*, Vol. 3. Philadelphia: Saunders.

Handsfield, H. (1991). Recent developments in STDs: I. Bacterial diseases. *Hospital Practice,* July 15, 47–56.

———. (1992). Recent developments in STDs: II. Viral and other syndromes. *Hospital Practice,* January 15, 175–200.

———, & Hammerschlag, M. (1992). *Chlamydia:* The challenge is diagnosis. *Patient Care,* February 15, 69–84.

———, & Schwebke, J. (1991). *Sexually Transmitted Diseases Clinical Practice Guidelines.* Seattle: Seattle-King County Department of Public Health.

Handyside, A., Penketh, R., Winston, R., Pattinson, J., Delhanty, J., & Tuddenham, E. (1989). Biopsy of human preimplantation embryos and sexing by DNA amplification. *Lancet,* February 18, 347–349.

Hanna, G. (1988). Gender differences in mathematical achievement among eighth graders: Results from twenty countries. Paper presented at the annual meeting of the American Association for the Advancement of Science, Boston, February.

Harahap, M., & Siregar, A. (1988). Circumcision: A review and a new technique. *Journal of Dermatology and Surgical Oncology,* 14, 383–386.

Harden, B. (1985). Tradition stalls progress of Africa's women: Pregnancy, farm work fill their lives. *The Oregonian,* July 9, A2.

Harker, L., & Thorpe, K. (1992). "The last egg in the basket?" Elderly primiparity: A review of findings. *Birth,* 19, 23–30.

Harley, V., Jackson, D., Hextall, P., Hawkins, J., Berkovitz, G., Sockanathan, S., Lovell-Badge, R., & Goodfellow, P. (1992). DNA binding activity of recombinant SRY from normal males and XY females. *Science,* 255, 453–456.

Harlow, H., & Harlow, M. (1962). The effects of rearing conditions on behavior. *Bulletin of the Menninger Clinic,* 26, 13–24.

Harlow, S., & Matanoski, G. (1991). The association between weight, physical activity, and stress and variation in the length of the menstrual cycle. *American Journal of Epidemiology,* 133, 38–49.

Harney, P., & Muehlenhard, C. (1990). Rape. In E. Grauerholz & M. Korlewski (Eds.), *Sexual Coercion: A Sourcebook on Its Nature, Causes, and Prevention.* Lexington, Mass.: Lexington Books.

———, & ———. (1991). Factors that increase the likelihood of victimization. In A. Parrot & L. Bechhofer (Eds.), *Acquaintance Rape: The Hidden Crime.* New York: Wiley.

Harnish, S. (1988). Congenital absence of the vagina: Clinical issues. *Medical Aspects of Human Sexuality,* July, 54–60.

Harold, E., & Way, L. (1983). Oral–genital sexual behavior in a sample of university females. *Journal of Sex Research,* 19, 327–329.

Harris, L., & Associates (1987). *Attitudes About Television, Sex and Contraceptive Advertising.* New York: Planned Parenthood.

Harris, R. (1988a). AIDS meeting suggests research gaps. *Science News,* June 25, 405.

———. (1988b). Exercise and sex in the aging patient. *Medical Aspects of Human Sexuality,* January, 148–159.

Harrop-Griffiths, J., Katon, W., Walker, E., Holm, L., Russo, J., & Hickok, L. (1988). The association between chronic pelvic pain, psychiatric diagnoses, and childhood sexual abuse. *Obstetrics and Gynecology,* 71, 589–593.

Hart, J., Cohen, E., Gingold, A., & Homburg, R. (1991). Sexual behavior in pregnancy: A study of 219 women. *Journal of Sex Education & Therapy,* 17, 86–90.

Harter, S., Alexander, P., & Neimeyer, R. (1988). Long-term effects of incestuous child abuse in college women: Social adjustment, social cognition, and family characteristics. *Journal of Consulting and Clinical Psychology,* 56, 5–8.

Hartman, A. (1991). Toward a redefinition and contextualization of the abortion issue. *Social Work,* 36, 467–468.

Hartman, W., & Fithian, M. (1974). *Treatment of Sexual Dysfunction.* New York: Jason Aronson.

———, & ———. (1984). Any man can: Multiple orgasmic response in males. Paper presented at the Regional Conference of the American Association of Sex Educators, Counselors, and Therapists, Las Vegas, October.

Harvey, S. (1987). Female sexual behavior: Fluctuations during the menstrual cycle. *Journal of Psychosomatic Research,* 31, 101–110.

Hasselbring, B. (1990). Heavenly bodies. *Oregonian,* October 14, NW25.

Hasset, J. (1978). Sex and smell. *Psychology Today,* March, 40–45.

Hatcher, R. (1988). *Contraceptive Technology 1988–1989.* New York: Irvington.

———, Guest, F., Stewart, F., Stewart, G., Trussell, G., Trussell, J., & Frank, E. (1990). *Contraceptive Technology 1990–1991,* 15th rev. ed. New York: Irvington.

———, ———, ———, ———, Trussell, J., Cerel, S., & Cates, W. (1986). *Contraceptive Technology 1986–1987,* 13th rev. ed. New York: Irvington.

Hatfield, E., & Rapson, R. (1987). Passionate love/sexual desire: Can the same paradigm explain both? *Archives of Sexual Behavior,* 16, 259–278.

———, & Sprecher, S. (1986). *Mirror, Mirror . . . The Importance of Looks in Everyday Life.* Albany: State University of New York Press.

Hawton, K., Catalan, J., & Fagg, J. (1992). Sex therapy for erectile dysfunction: Characteristics of couples, treatment outcome, and prognostic factors. *Archives of Sexual Behavior,* 21. 161–175.

Hazes J., Dijkmans, B., Vandenbroucke, J., et al. (1990). Reduction of the risk of rheumatoid arthritis among women who take oral contraceptives. *Arthritis and Rheumatism,* 33(2), 173.

Hearst, N., & Hulley, S. (1988). Preventing the heterosexual spread of AIDS. *Journal of the American Medical Association,* 259, 2428–2432.

Heath, D. (1984). An investigation into the origins of a copious vaginal discharge during intercourse—"enough to wet the bed"—that "is not urine." *Journal of Sex Research,* 20, 194–215.

Heath, R. (1972). Pleasure and brain activity in man. *Journal of Nervous and Mental Disease,* 154, 3–18.

Heaton, J., & Varrin, S. (1991). The impact of alcohol ingestion on erections in rats as measured by a novel bio-assay. *The Journal of Urology,* 145, 192–194.

Heidrich, F., Berg, A., & Bergman, J. (1984). Clothing factors and vaginitis. *Journal of Family Practice,* 19, 491–494.

Heilbrun, A., & Seif, D. (1988). Erotic value of female distress in sexually explicit photographs. *The Journal of Sex Research,* 24, 47–57.

Heim, N. (1981). Sexual behavior of castrated sex offenders. *Archives of Sexual Behavior,* 10, 11–19.

Heiman, J., & LoPiccolo, J. (1988). *Becoming Orgasmic: A Sexual Growth Program for Women.* Englewood Cliffs, N.J.: Prentice-Hall.

Heimer, L., & Larsson, K. (1964). Drastic changes in the mating behavior of male rats following lesions in the junction of diencephalon and mesencephalon. *Experientia,* 20, 460–461.

Hein, K. (1989). Commentary on adolescent acquired immunodeficiency syndrome: The next wave of immunodeficiency virus epidemic? *Journal of Pediatrics,* 114, 144–149.

Hellberg, D., Valentin, J., & Nilsson, S. (1983). Smoking as a risk factor in cervical neoplasia. *Lancet,* December 24–31, 1947.

Hendrick, C., & Hendrick, S. (1986). A theory and method of love. *Journal of Personality and Social Psychology,* 50, 392–402.

———, & ———. (1989). Research of love: Does it measure up? *Journal of Personality and Social Psychology,* 56, 784–794.

———, ———, & Adler, N. (1988). Romantic relationships: Love, satisfaction, and staying together. *Journal of Personality and Social Psychology,* 54, 980–988.

Henshaw, S. (1986). Trends in abortion, 1982–1986. *Family Planning Perspectives,* 18, 34.

———, Binkin, N., Blaine, E., & Smith, J. (1985). A portrait of American women who obtain abortions. *Family Planning Perspectives,* 17, 90–96.

———, & Matire, G. (1982). Abortion and the public opinion polls: Morality and legality. *Family Planning Perspectives,* 14, 53–60.

———, & Silverman, J. (1988). The characteristics and prior contraceptive use of U.S. abortion patients. *Family Planning Perspectives,* 20, 158–168.

Herdt, G. (1992). "Coming out" as a rite of passage: A Chicago study. In G. Herdt (Ed.), *Gay Culture in America,* Boston: Beacon Press.

———, & Boxer, A. (1992). Introduction: Culture, history, and life course of gay men. In G. Herdt (Ed.), *Gay Culture in America.* Boston: Beacon Press.

———, & Davidson, J. (1988). The Sambia ``Turnim-man'': Sociocultural and clinical aspects of gender formation in male pseudohermaphrodites with 5-alpha-reductase deficiency in Papua, New Guinea. *Archives of Sexual Behavior,* 17, 33–56.

Herek, G. (1988). Heterosexuals' attitudes toward lesbians and gay men: Correlates and gender differences. *Journal of Sex Research,* 25, 451–477.

———, Kimmel, D., Amaro, H., & Melton, G. (1991). Avoiding heterosexist bias in psychological research. *American Psychologist,* 46, 957–963.

Hernandez-Aguado, I., Alvarez-Dardet, C., Gili, M., Perea, E., & Camacho, F. (1988). Oral sex as a risk factor for *Chlamydia*-negative *Ureaplasma*-negative nongonococcal urethritis. *Sexually Transmitted Diseases,* 15, 100–102.

Herrell, R. (1992). The symbolic strategies of Chicago's Gay and Lesbian Pride Day Parade. In G. Herdt (Ed.), *Gay Culture in America.* Boston: Beacon Press.

Herrera, A., & Macaraeg, A. (1984). Physicians' attitudes toward circumcision. *American Journal of Obstetrics and Gynecology,* 148, 825.

Hersch, P. (1988). Coming of age on city streets. *Psychology Today,* January, 28–37.

———. (1991). Secret lives. *Networker,* January/February, 37–43.

———. (1991). What is gay? What is straight? *Networker,* January/February, 37–43.

Herzog, L. (1989). Urinary tract infections and circumcision. *American Journal of Diseases of Children,* 143, 348–350.

Hessol, N., Lifson, A., O'Malley, P., Doll, L., Jaffe, H. & Rutherford, G. (1989). Prevalence, incidence and progression of human immunodeficiency virus infection in homosexual and bisexual men in hepatitis B vaccine trials, 1978–1988. *American Journal of Epidemiology,* 130, 1167–1175.

Hill, J., & Kassam, S. (1984). Sexual competence in multiple sclerosis, *Female Patient,* 9, 81–84.

Hingson, R., Alpert, J., Day, N., Dooling, E., Kayne, H., Morelock, S., Oppenheimer, E., & Zuckerman, B. (1982). Effects of maternal drinking and marijuana use on fetal growth and development. *Pediatrics,* 70, 539–546.

Hinman, F. (1991). Screening for prostatic carcinoma. *The Journal of Urology,* 145, 126–130.

Hira, S., Kamanga, J., Macuacua, R., Mwansa, N., Cruess, D., & Perine, P. (1990). Genital ulcers and male circumcision as risk factors for acquiring HIV-1 in Zambia. *The Journal of Infectious Diseases,* 161, 584–585.

Hite, S. (1976). *The Hite Report: A Nationwide Study of Female Sexuality.* New York: Dell Books.

———. (1981). *The Hite Report on Male Sexuality.* New York: Knopf.

Hitt, J., Hendericks, S., Ginsberg, S., & Lewis, J. (1970). Disruption of male but not female sexual behavior in rats by medial forebrain bundle lesions. *Journal of Comparative and Physiological Psychology,* 73, 377–384.

Hochman, A. (1992). Chained to ideals. *Oregonian,* May 17, L1–L7.

Hodgen, G. (1991). Paper presented at annual meeting of the American Association for the Advancement of Science, Washington, D.C., February.

Hodgkin, J. (1988). Everything you always wanted to know about sex. *Nature,* 331, 300–301.

Hoeffer, B. (1981). Children's acquisition of sex-role behavior in lesbian-mother families. *American Journal of Orthopsychiatry,* 51, 536–544.

Hofferth, S., Kahn, J., & Baldwin, W. (1987). Premarital sexual activity among U.S. teenage women over the past three decades. *Family Planning Perspectives,* 19, 46–54.

Hoffman, M. (Ed.) (1992). *The World Almanac and Book of Facts 1992.* New York: Pharos Books.

———, & Saltzstein, H. (1967). Parent discipline and the child's moral development. *Journal of Personality and Social Psychology,* 5, 45–57.

Holden, C. (1992). Twin study links genes to homosexuality. *Research News,* January, 33.

Hollender, M. (1970). Women's coital fantasies. *Medical Aspects of Human Sexuality,* 4, 63–70.

Hook, E., Cannon, R., Nahmias, A., Lee, F., Campbell, C., Glasser, D., & Quinn, T. (1992). Herpes simplex virus infection as a risk factor for human immunodeficiency virus infection in heterosexuals. *The Journal of Infectious Diseases,* 165, 251–255.

Hooker, E. (1957). The adjustment of the male overt homosexual. *Journal of Projective Techniques,* 21, 18–31.

Hoon, E., Hoon, P., Rand, K., Johnson, J., Hall, N., & Edwards, N. (1991). A psycho-behavioral model of genital herpes recurrence. *Journal of Psychosomatic Research,* 35, 25–36.

Hooton, T., Hillier, S., Johnson, C., Roberts, P., & Stamm, W. (1991). *Escherichia coli* bacteriuria and contraceptive method. *Journal of the American Medical Association,* 265, 64–69.

Horney, K. (1967). *Feminine Psychology.* New York: Norton.

Hosken, F. (1989). Female genital mutilation—strategies for eradication. *The Truth Seeker,* July/August, 22–30.

Hoult, T., Henze, L., & Hudson, J. (1978). *Courtship and Marriage in America.* Boston: Little, Brown.

Hrebinko, R., Bahnson, R., Schwentker, F., & O'Donnell, W. (1990). Early experience with the DuraPhase penile prosthesis. *Journal of Urology,* 143, 60–61.

Hudson, B., Pepperell, R., & Wood, C. (1987). The problem of infertility. In R. Pepperell, B. Hudson, and C. Wood (Eds.), *The Infertile Couple.* Edinburgh: Churchill Livingstone.

Hufnagel, V. (1988). Male and female sexual surgery: The conspiracy against the uterus. Paper presented at the Twenty-First Annual Meeting of the American Association of Sex Educators, Therapists and Counselors, San Francisco, April.

———, & Golant, S. (1988). Hysterectomies and later health. *The Oregonian,* September 6, A9.

Huggins, S. (1989). A comparative study of self-esteem of adolescent children of divorced lesbian mothers and divorced heterosexual mothers. In F. Bozett (Ed.), *Homosexuality and the Family.* Binghamton, N.Y.: Harrington Park Press.

Hughes, C., Jr., Wall, L. L., & Creasman, W. (1991). Reproductive hormone levels in gynecologic oncology patients undergoing surgical castration after spontaneous menopause. *Gynecologic Oncology,* 40, 42–45.

Humphreys, J., Henneberry, J., Rickard, R., & Beebe, J. (1992). Cost-benefit analysis of selective screening criitiera for *chlamydia trachomatis* infection in women attending Colorado family clinics. *Sexually Transmitted Diseases,* 10, 47–53.

Hunt, M. (1974). *Sexual Behavior in the 1970s.* Chicago: Playboy Press.

———, & Hunt, B. (1977). *The Divorce Experience.* New York: Signet.

Hunter, E. (1991). For want of a child. *Oregonian,* October 20, L1.

Hurd, W., Gauvin, J., Kelly, M., Smith, A., Ohl, D., & Cummins, C. (1992). The effect of cocaine on sperm motility characteristics and bovine cervical mucus penetration. *Fertility and Sterility,* 57, 178–182.

Hurlbert, D., & Whittaker, K. (1991). The role of masturbation in marital and sexual satisfaction: A comparative study of female masturbators and nonmasturbators. *Journal of Sex Education & Therapy,* 17, 272–282.

Hurt, S., Schnurr, P., Severino, S., Freeman, E., Gise, L., Rivera-Tovar, A., & Steege, J. (1992). Late luteal phase dysphoric disorder in 670 women evaluated for premenstrual complaints. *American Journal of Psychiatry,* 149, 525–530.

Huston, A. (1983). Sex typing. In E. Hetherington (Ed.), *Handbook of Child Psychology: Vol. 4, Socialization, Personality and Social Development.* New York: Wiley.

Huston, R., Martin, L., & Foulds, M. (1990). Effect of a program to facilitate parent-child communication about sex. *Clinical Pediatrics,* 29, 626–630.

Hutt, C. (1973). *Male and Female.* New York: Penguin Books.

Hyde, J. (1991). *Half the Human Experience: The Psychology of Women,* 4th ed. Lexington, Mass.: Heath.

———, Fenneman, E., & Lamon, S. (1990). Gender differences in mathematics performance: A meta-analysis. *Psychological Bulletin,* 107, 139–155.

———, Krajnik, M., & Skuldt-Niederberger, K. (1991). Androgyny across the life span: A replication and longitudinal follow-up. *Developmental Psychology,* 27, 516–519.

———, & Linn, M. (1988). Gender differences in verbal ability: A meta-analysis. *Psychological Bulletin,* 104, 53–69.

———, & ———. (Eds.) (1986). *The Psychology of Gender.* Baltimore: Johns Hopkins University Press.

Ickovics, J., & Rodin, J. (1992). Women and AIDS in the United States: Epidemiology, natural history, and mediating mechanisms. *Health Psychology,* 11, 1–16.

Imperato-McGinley, J., Peterson, R., Gautier, T., & Sturla, E. (1979). Androgens and the evolution of male-gender identity among male pseu[chdo[chher[chmaph[chro[chdites with 5-;ga-reductase deficiency. *New England Journal of Medicine,* 300, 1233–1237.

Inglis, J., Ruckman, M., Lawson, J., MacLean, A., & Monga, T. (1982). Sex differences in the cognitive effects of unilateral brain damage. *Cortex,* 18, 257–276.

Isay, R. (1989). *Being Homosexual: Gay Men and Their Development.* New York: Farrar, Straus, Giroux.

Jack, B., & Culpepper, L. (1991). Preconception care. *Journal of Family Practice,* 32, 306–315.

Jacklin, C., Dipietro, J., & Maccoby, E. (1984). Sex-typing behavior and sex-typing pressure in child–parent interaction. *Archives of Sexual Behavior,* 13, 413–425.

Jackson, J., Calhoun, K., Amick, A., Maddever, H., & Habif, V. (1990). Young adult women who report childhood intrafamilial sexual abuse: Subsequent adjustment. *Archives of Sexual Behavior,* 19, 211–221.

Jacques, J., & Chason, K. (1979). Cohabitation: Its impact on marital success. *Family Coordinator*, 28, 35–39.

Jaffe, H. (1987). Paper presented at the Third International Conference on AIDS, Washington, D.C., June.

Jamison, P., & Gebhard, P. (1988). Penis size increase between flaccid and erect states: An analysis of the Kinsey data. *Journal of Sex Research*, 24, 177–183.

Jancin, B. (1989). Prenatal gender selection appears to be gaining acceptance. *Obstetrical and Gynecological News*, 23, 30.

Janeway, J. (1981). Incest: A rational look at the oldest taboo, *Ms.*, November, 61 ff.

Janoff-Bulman, R., & Golden, D. (1984). Attributions and adjustment to abortion. Paper presented at a meeting of the American Psychological Association, Toronto, August 24.

Japenga, A. (1984). Pornography: Fuel for rapists? *The Oregonian*, January 31, C1.

Jarrett, L. (1984). Psychosocial and biological influences on menstruation: Synchrony, cycle length, and regularity. *Psychoneuroendocrinology*, 9, 21–28.

Jefferson, T., Glaros, A., Spevack, M., Boaz, T., & Murray, F. (1989). An evaluation of the Minnesota multiphasic personality inventory as a discriminator of primary organic and primary psychogenic importance in diabetic males. *Journal of the American Medical Association*, 18, 117–125.

Jencks, S. (1992). Prostate-specific antigen: Improving its ability to diagnose early prostate cancer. *Journal of the American Medical Association*, 267, 2236–2238.

Jenks, R. (1985). Swinging: A replication and test of a theory. *The Journal of Sex Research*, 21, 199–210.

Jensen, B., Hoff, G., & Weismann, K. (1988). A comparison of an enzyme immunoassay and cell culture for detection of *Chlamydia trachomatis* in genitourinary specimens. *Sexually Transmitted Diseases*, 15, 123–126.

Jensen, S. (1986). Sexual dysfunction and diabetes mellitus: A six-year follow-up study. *Archives of Sexual Behavior*, 15, 271–284.

Jeremy, J., & Mikhailidis, D. (1990). Prostaglandins and the penis: Possible role in the pathogenesis and treatment of impotence. *Sexual and Marital Therapy*, 5(2), 155–165.

Jessamine, P., Plummer, F., Ndinya, A., Wainberg, M., Wamola, I., D'Costa, L., Cameron, D., Simonsen, J., Plourde, P., & Ronald, A. (1990). Human immunodeficiency virus, genital ulcers and the male foreskin: Synergism in HIV-1 transmission. *Scandinavian Journal of Infectious Diseases Supplement*, 69, 181–186.

John, E., Savitz, D., & Sandler, D. (1991). Prenatal exposure to parents' smoking and childhood cancer. *American Journal of Epidemiology*, 133, 123–132.

Johnson, C. A. (1991). Making sense of dysfunctional uterine bleeding. *American Family Physician*, 44, 149–157.

Johnson, S. (1985). TSS—Don't overlook less obvious cases. *Contemporary Obstetrics/Gynecology*, 25, 131–138.

Johnston, S. (1987). The mind of the molester. *Psychology Today*, February, 60–63.

Jones, E., Forrest, J., Goldman, N., Henshaw, S., Lincoln, R., Rosoff, J., Westoff, C., & Wulf, D. (1985). Teenage pregnancy in developed countries: Determinants and policy implications. *Family Planning Perspectives*, 17, 53–63.

———, & Forrest, J. (1992). Contraceptive failure rates based on the 1988 NSFG. *Family Planning Perspectives*, 24, 12–19.

Jones, M. (1992). The management of the mildly abnormal smear. *Maternal and Child Health*, February, 52–56.

Jones, W., Chernovetz, M., & Hansson, R. (1978). The enigma of androgyny: Differential implications for males and females. *Journal of Consulting and Clinical Psychology*, 46, 298–313.

Joseph, R. (1991). A case analysis in human sexuality: Counseling to a man with severe cerebral palsy. *Sexuality and Disability*, 9(2), 149–159.

Jouriles, E., Bourg, W., & Farris, A. (1991). Marital adjustment and child conduct problems: A comparison of the correlation across subsamples. *Journal of Consulting and Clinical Psychology*, 59, 354–357.

Judd, C., Kenny, D., & Krosnick, J. (1983). Judging the positions of political candidates: Models of assimilation and contact. *Journal of Personality and Social Psychology*, 44, 952–963.

Justice, B., & Justice, R. (1979). *The Broken Taboo: Sex in the Family*. New York: Human Sciences Press.

Kalash, S., & Young, J. (1984). Fracture of the penis: Controversy of surgical versus conservative treatment. *Urology*, 24, 21–24.

Kalisch, P., & Kalisch, B. (1984). Sex-role stereotyping of nurses and physicians on prime-time television. *Sex roles*, 10, 533–554.

Kanin, E. (1967). Reference groups and sex conduct norms. *Sociological Quarterly*, 8, 495–504.

———. (1969). Selected aspects of male sex aggression. *Journal of Sex Research*, 5, 12–28.

———. (1985). Date rapists: Differential sexual socialization and relative deprivation. *Archives of Sexual Behavior*, 14, 219–231.

Kaplan, D. (1991). Abortion: Just say no advice. *Newsweek*, June 3, 18.

———. (1992). Is Roe good law? *Newsweek*, April 27, 49–51.

Kaplan, H. (1974). *The New Sex Therapy: Active Treatment of Sexual Dysfunction*. New York: Brunner/

———. (1977). Hypoactive sexual desire. *Journal of Sex and Marital Therapy*, 3, 3–9.

———. (1979). *Disorders of Sexual Desire*. New York: Brunner/Mazel.

———. (1987). *The Illustrated Manual of Sex Therapy*. New York: Brunner/Mazel.

Kaplowitz, L., Baker, D., Gelb, L., Blythe, J., Hale, R., Frost, P., Crumpacker, C., Rabinovich, S., Peacock, J., Herndon, J., & Davis, G. (1991). Prolonged continuous acyclovir treatment of normal adults with frequently recurring genital herpes simplex virus infection. *Journal of the American Medical Association*, 265, 747–751.

Karlen, A. (1988). *Threesomes: Studies in Sex, Power, and Intimacy*. New York: Beech Tree/Morrow.

Kasper, A. (1985). Health and public policy. *Women and Health*, 10, 109–127.

Kassel, V. (1983). Long-term care institutions. In R. Weg (Ed.)., *Sexuality in the Later Years: Roles and Behavior*. New York: Academic Press.

Katz, J. (1976). *Gay American History.* New York: Avon Books.

Kaufman, A., Divasto, P., Jackson, R., Voorhees, D., & Christy, J. (1980). Male rape victims: Noninstitutionalized assault. *American Journal of Psychiatry,* 137, 221–223.

Keen, J. (1991). Colleges `degrade' rape victims. *USA Today,* June 11, A1–A2.

Keen, S. (1991). *Fire in the Belly.* New York: Bantam Books.

Keet, I., van Lent, N., Sandfort, T., Coutinho, R., & van Griensven, G. (1992). Orogenital sex and the transmission of HIV among homosexual men. *AIDS,* 6, 223–226.

Kegel, A. (1952). Sexual function of the pubococcygeus muscle. *Western Journal of Surgery,* 60, 521–524.

Kelley, K. (1985). Sex, sex guilt, and authoritarianism: Differences in responses to explicit heterosexual and masturbatory slides. *Journal of Sex Research,* 21, 68–85.

Kelly, J. (1982). Divorce: The adult perspective. In B. Wolman and G. Stricker (Eds.)., *Handbook of Developmental Psychology.* Englewood Cliffs, N.J.: Prentice-Hall.

———, & Rice, S. (1986). The aged. In H. Gochros, J. Gochros, and J. Fisher (Eds.)., *Helping the Sexually Oppressed.* Englewood Cliffs, N.J.: Prentice-Hall.

Kelly, M., Strassberg, D., & Kircher, J. (1990). Attitudinal and experiential correlates of anorgasmia. *Archives of Sexual Behavior,* 19, 165–181.

Kennedy, K., & Visness, C. (1992). Contraceptive efficacy of lactational amenorrhoea. *Lancet,* 339, 227–230.

Kennedy, S., & Over, R. (1990). Psychophysiological assessment of male sexual arousal following spinal cord injury. *Archives of Sexual Behavior,* 19, 15–27.

Kennell, J., Klaus, M., McGrath, S., Robertson, S., & Hinkley, C. (1991). Continuous emotional support during labor in a U.S. hospital. *Journal of the American Medical Association,* 265, 2197–2201.

Kenney, A., Guardado, S., & Brown, L., (1989). Sex education and AIDS education in the schools: What states and large school districts are doing. *Family Planning Perspectives,* 21, 56–64.

Kent, C. (1992). Health care goes to school. *Medicine and Health Perspectives,* January 6, 3–6.

Kettl, P., Zarefoss, S., Jacoby, K., Garman, C., Hulse, C., Rowley, F., Corey, R., Sredy, M., Bixler, E., & Tyson, K. (1991). Female sexuality after spinal cord injury. *Sexuality and Disability,* 9(4), 287–295.

Kilkku, P. (1983). Supravaginal uterine amputation vs. hysterectomy: Effects on coital frequency and dyspareunia. *Acta Obstetricia et Gynecologica Scandinavica,* 62, 141–145.

———, Gronroos, M., Hirvonen, T., & Rauramo, L. (1983). Supravaginal uterine amputation vs. hysterectomy: Effects on libido and orgasm. *Acta Obstetricia et Gynecologica Scandinavica,* 62, 147–152.

Kilmann, P., Sabalis, R., Gearing, M., Bukstel, L., & Scovein, A. (1982). The treatment of sexual paraphilias: A review of the outcome research. *Journal of Sex Research,* 18, 193–252.

Kilpatrick, A. (1987). Childhood sexual experiences: Problems and issues in studying long-range effects. *Journal of Sex Research,* 23, 173–196.

Kilpatrick, J. (1960). *The Smut Peddlers.* Garden City, N.Y.: Doubleday.

Kimbrell, A. (1991). A time for men to pull together. *Utne Reader,* May/June, 66–74.

Kimmel, D. (1978). Adult development and aging: A gay perspective. *Journal of Social Issues,* 34, 113–130.

Kinard, E., and Reinherz, H. (1987). School aptitude and achievement in children of adolescent mothers. *Journal of Youth and Adolescence,* 16, 69–78.

King, F. (1976). Roll me over, lay me down. In D. Stillman and A. Beatts (Eds.)., *Titters.* New York: Collier Books.

King, L. (1988). Editorial comment in response to Wiswell et al., 1987. *Journal of Urology,* 139, 883.

Kinsey, A., Pomeroy, W., & Martin, C. (1948). *Sexual Behavior in the Human Male.* Philadelphia: Saunders.

———, ———, ———, & Gebhard, P. (1953). *Sexual Behavior in the Human Female.* Philadelphia: Saunders.

Kirby, D. (1984). *Sexuality Education: An Evaluation of Programs and their Effects.* Santa Cruz, Calif.: Network Publications.

———, Waszak, C., & Ziegler, J. (1991). Six school-based clinics: Their reproductive health services and impact on sexual behavior. *Family Planning Perspectives,* 23, 6–16.

Kirchner, J. (1991). Syphilis: An STD on the increase. *American Family Physician,* 44, 843–854.

Kirkpatrick, M. (1982). Lesbian mother families. *Psychiatric Annals,* 12, 842–845; 848.

———, Roy, R., & Smith, K. (1981). Lesbian mothers and their children: A comparative study. *American Journal of Orthopsychiatry,* 51, 545.

Kite, M., Deaux, K., & Miele, M. (1991). Stereotypes of young and old: Does age outweigh gender? *Psychology and Aging,* 6, 19–27.

Kitson, G., Babri, K., Roch, M., & Placidi, K. (1989). Adjustment to widowhood and divorce. *Journal of Family Issues,* 10, 5–32.

Klagsbrun, G. (1985). *Married People: Staying Together in the Age of Divorce.* New York: Bantam Books.

Klaich, D. (1974). *Woman Plus Woman: Attitudes Towards Lesbianism.* New York: Simon & Schuster.

Klaus, M., & Kennell, J. (1982). *Parent–Infant Bonding,* 2nd ed. St. Louis, Mo.: Mosby.

Klein, H., & Cordell, A. (1987). The adolescent as mother: Early risk identification. *Journal of Youth and Adolescence,* 16, 47–58.

Klein, R. (1991). Universal precautions for preventing occupational exposures to human immunodeficiency virus type 1. *The American Journal of Medicine,* 90, 141–149.

Klitsch, M. (1988a). FDA approval ends cervical cap's marathon. *Family Planning Perspectives,* 20, 137–138.

———. (1988b). The return of the IUD. *Family Planning Perspectives,* 20, 19–40.

Knafo, D., & Jaffe, Y. (1984). Sexual fantasizing in males and females. *Journal of Research in Personality,* 19, 451–462.

Knapp, J., & Whitehurst, R. (1977). Sexually open marriage and relationships: Issues and prospects. In R. Libby and R. Whitehurst (Eds.)., *Marriage and Alternatives: Exploring Intimate Relationships.* Glenview, Ill.: Scott, Foresman.

Knussmann, R., Christiansen, K., & Couwenbergs, C. (1986). Relations between sex hormone levels and sexual behavior in men. *Archives of Sexual Behavior,* 15, 429–445.

Koblinsky, S., & Palmeter, J. (1984). Sex-role orientation, mother's expression of affection toward spouse, and college women's attitudes toward sexual behaviors. *Journal of Sex Research,* 20, 32–43.

Kochanek, K. (1991). Induced terminations of pregnancy: Reporting states, 1988. *Centers for Disease Control Vital Statistics Report,* 39, 1–31.

Kockott, G., & Fahrner, E. (1987). Transsexuals who have not undergone surgery: A follow-up study. *Archives of Sexual Behavior,* 16, 511–522.

Koff, W., & Scaletscky, R. (1990). Malformations of the epididymis in undescended testis. *Journal of Urology,* 143, 340–343.

Kohlberg, L. (1966). A cognitive-developmental analysis of children's sex-role concepts and attitudes. In E. Maccoby (Ed.)., *The Development of Sex Differences.* Stanford, Calif.: Stanford University Press.

Kojima, H., Wang, S., Kuo, C., & Grayston, J. (1988). Local antibody in semen for rapid diagnosis of *Chlamydia trachomatis* epididymitis. *Journal of Urology,* 140, 528–531.

Kolata, G. (1986). Maleness pinpointed on Y-chromosome. *Science,* 234, 1076–1077.

Kolodny, R. (1980). Adolescent sexuality. Paper presented at the Michigan Personnel and Guidance Association Annual Convention, Detroit, November.

———, Masters, W., & Johnson, V. (1979). *Textbook of Sexual Medicine.* Boston: Little, Brown.

Kools, A. (1992). Hepatitis A, B, C, D, and E: Update on testing and treatment. *Postgraduate Medicine,* 91, 109–114.

Koopman, P., Gubbay, J., Vivian, N., Goodfellow, P., & Lovell-Badge, R. (1991). Male development of chromosomally female mice transgenic for SRY. *Nature,* 351, 117–121.

Koppelman, A. (1988). A feminist model of women's sexual health. Paper presented at the Association for Women in Psychology, Bethesda, Md.

Korenman, S., & Viosca, S. (1992). Use of a vacuum tumescence device in the management of impotence in men with a history of penile implant or severe pelvic disease. *Journal of the American Geriatric Society,* 40, 61–64.

Kosnik, A., Carroll, W., Cunningham, A., Modras, R., & Schulte, J. (1977). *Human Sexuality: New Directions in American Catholic Thought.* New York: Paulist Press.

Koss, L., & Dinero, T. (1989). Discriminant analysis of risk factors for sexual victimization among a national sample of college women. *Journal of Consulting and Clinical Psychology,* 57, 242–250.

———, Gidycz, C., & Wisniewski, N. (1987). The scope of rape: Incidence and prevalence of sexual aggression and victimization in a national sample of higher education students. *Journal of Consulting and Clinical Psychology,* 55, 162–170.

———, ———, & Seibel, C. (1988). Stranger and acquaintance rape. *Psychology of Women Quarterly,* 12, 1–24.

Koss, M. (1992). The underdetection of rape: Methodological choices influence incidence estimates. *Journal of Social Issues,* 48, 61–75.

Koss, M., Dinero, T., Seibel, C., & Cox, S. (1988). Stranger and acquaintance rape: Are there differences in the victim experience? *Psychology of Women Quarterly,* 12, 1–24.

Kost, K., Forrest, J. D., & Harlap, S. (1991). Comparing the health risks and benefits of contraceptive choices. *Family Planning Perspectives,* 23, 54–61.

Kotloff, K., Tacket, C., Clemens, J., Wasserman, S., Cowan, J., Bridwell, M., & Quinn, T. (1991). Assessment of the prevalence and risk factors for human immunodeficiency virus type 1 (HIV-1) infection among college students using three survey methods. *American Journal of Epidemiology,* 133, 2–8.

Koup, R., Merluzzi, V., Hargrave, K., Adams, J., Grozinger, K., Eckner, R., & Sullivan, J. (1991). Inhibition of human immunodeficiency virus type 1 (HIV-1) replication by the dipyridodiazepinone B1-RG-587. *The Journal of Infectious Diseases,* 163, 966–970.

Krantzler, M. (1975). *Creative Divorce.* New York: New American Library.

Krieger, J., Coombs, R., Collier, A., Ross, S., Chaloupka, K., Cummings, D., Murphy, V., & Corey, L. (1991). Recovery of human immunodeficiency virus type 1 from semen: Minimal impact of stage of infection and current antiviral chemotherapy. *The Journal of Infectious Diseases,* 163, 386–388.

Kronmal, R., Whitney, C., & Mumford, S. (1991). The intrauterine device and pelvic inflammatory disease: The women's health study reanalyzed. *Journal of Clinical Epidemiology,* 44(2), 109–122.

Kroon, S., Peterson, C., Anderson, L., Rasmussen, J., & Vestergaard, B. (1990). Long-term suppression of severe recurrent genital herpes simplex infections with oral acyclovir: A dose-titration study. *Genitourinary Medicine,* 66, 101–104.

Krugman, R., Bays, J., Chadwick, D., Levitt, C., McHugh, M., & Whitworth, J. (1991). Guidelines for the evaluation of sexual abuse of children. *Pediatrics,* 87, 254–260.

Kuhns, J., & Arakawa, F. (1987). Hymens in newborn female infants. *Pediatrics,* 80, 399.

Kujansuu, E., Kivinen, S., & Tuimala, R. (1981). Pregnancy and delivery at the age of forty and over. *International Journal of Gynecological Obstetrics,* 19, 341–345.

Kulhanjian, J., Soroush, V., Au, D., Bronzan, R., Yasukawa, L., Weylman, L., Arvin, A., & Prober, C. (1992). Identification of women at unsuspected risk of primary infection with herpes simplex virus type 2 during pregnancy. *The New England Journal of Medicine,* 326, 916–920.

Kulin, H., Frontera, M., Demers, L., Bartholomew, M., & Lloyd, T. (1989). The onset of sperm production in pubertal boys. *American Journal of Diseases of Children,* 143, 190–193.

Kupperman, H., & Studdiford, W. (1953). Endocrine therapy in gynecologic disorders. *Postgraduate Medicine,* 14, 410–425.

Kurth, R., Binninger, D., Ennen, J., Denner, J., Hartung, S., & Norley, S. (1991). The quest for an AIDS vaccine: The state of the art and current challenges. *AIDS Research and Human Retroviruses,* 7, 425–433.

Lacayo, R. (1992). No matter what happens to Roe v. Wade, the doctors who perform abortions and their patients face formidable obstacles. *Time,* May 4, 27–32.

Lader, L. (1991). *RU 486: The Pill That Could End the Abortion Wars and Why American Women Don't Have It.* Reading, Mass.: Addison-Wesley.

Ladouceur, P., & Temple, M. (1985). Substance use among rapists: A comparison with other serious felons. *Crime and Delinquency,* 31, 269–294.

Laflin, M. (1985). Assertiveness as a predictor of sexual satisfaction. Paper presented at the Twenty-Eighth Annual Meeting of the Society for the Scientific Study of Sex, San Diego, Calif., September 19–22.

Lamb, M. (1982). Early contact and maternal-infant bonding: One decade later. *Pediatrics,* 70, 763–768.

Lambert, B. (1988). AIDS among prostitutes not as prevalent as believed, studies show. *New York Times,* September 20, B1.

Lammer, E., Chen, D., Hoar, R., Agnish, N., Benke, P., Braun, J., Curry, C., Fernhoff, P., Grix, A., Lott, I., Richard, J., & Sun, S. (1985). Retinoic acid embryopathy. *New England Journal of Medicine,* 313, 837–841.

Landa, A. (1990). No accident: The voices of voluntarily childless women—an essay on the social construction of fertility choices. *Women & Therapy,* 10(1/2), 139–158.

Landis, S., Schoenbach, V., Weber, D., Mittal, M., Krishan, B., Lewis, K., & Koch, G. (1992). Results of a randomized trial of partner notification in cases of HIV infection in North Carolina. *New England Journal of Medicine,* 326, 101–106.

Landry, M., & Zibello, T. (1988). Ability of herpes simplex virus (HSV). types 1 and 2 to induce clinical disease and establish latency following previous genital infection with the heterologous HSV type. *Journal of Infectious Diseases,* 158, 1382–1385.

Langevin, R., Paitich, D., & Ramsay, G. (1979). Experimental studies of the etiology of genital exhibitionism. *Archives of Sexual Behavior,* 8, 307–331.

———, ———, & Russon, A. (1985). Voyeurism: Does it predict sexual aggression or violence in general? In R. Langevin (Ed.)., *Erotic Preference, Gender Identity, and Aggression in Men.* Hillsdale, N.J.: Erlbaum.

Langfeldt, T. (1981). Sexual development in children. In M. Cook and K. Howells (Eds.)., *Adult Sexual Interest in Children.* London: Academic Press.

Larsen, A., & Olson, D. (1989). Predicting marital satisfaction using PREPARE: A replication study. *Journal of Marital and Family Therapy,* 15, 311–322.

Larsen, G., & Williams, S. (1990). Postneonatal circumcision: Population profile. *Pediatrics,* 85, 808–812.

Larsen, K., & Long, E. (1988). Attitudes toward sex roles: Traditional or egalitarian? *Sex Roles,* 19, 1–12.

Lauer, J., & Lauer, R. (1985). Marriages made to last. *Psychology Today,* June, 22–26.

Lauersen, N., & Graves, Z. (1984). Pretended orgasm. *Medical Aspects of Human Sexuality,* 18, 74–81.

Laurent, S., Garrison, C., Thompson, S., Moore, E., & Addy, C. (1992). An epidemiologic study of smoking and primary infertility in women. *Fertility and Sterility,* 57, 565–572.

Laury, G. (1987). Sexuality of the dying patient. *Medical Aspects of Human Sexuality,* 21, 102–109.

———. (1992). When women sexually abuse male psychiatric patients under their care. *Journal of Sex Education & Therapy,* 18, 11–16.

Lawrence, J., Kelly, J., Hood, H., & Brasfield, T. (1989). Behavioral intervention to reduce AIDS risk activities. *Journal of Consulting and Clinical Psychology,* 57, 60–67.

Laws, J., & Schwartz, P. (1977). *Sexual Scripts: The Social Construction of Female Sexuality.* Hinsdale, Ill.: Dryden Press.

Leads from the MMWR. (1987). Antibody to human immunodeficiency virus in female prostitutes. *Journal of the American Medical Association,* 257, 2011–2013.

Lederer, W., & Jackson, D. (1977). False assumption 3: That love is necessary for a satisfactory marriage. In F. Morrison and V. Borosage (Eds.)., *Human Sexuality: Contemporary Perspectives,* 2nd rev. ed. Palo Alto, Calif.: Mayfield.

Lederman, S. (1992). Estimating infant mortality from human immunodeficiency virus and other causes in breast-feeding and bottle-feeding populations. *Pediatrics,* 89, 290–296.

Lee, A., & Scheurer, V. (1983). Psychological androgyny and aspects of self-image in women and men. *Sex Roles,* 9, 289–306.

Lee, J. (1974). The styles of loving. *Psychology Today,* 8, 43–51.

———. (1988). Love-styles. In R. Sternberg & M. Barnes (Eds.), *The Psychology of Love.* New Haven, Conn.: Yale University Press.

Lee, N., Rubin, G., & Borucki, R. (1988). The intrauterine device and pelvic inflammatory disease revisited: New results from the women's health study. *Obstetrics and Gynecology,* 72, 1–6.

Lefèvre, J., Averous, S., Bauriand, R., Blanc, C., Bertrand, M., & Lareng, B. (1988). Lower genital tract infections in women: Comparison of clinical and epidemiologic findings with microbiology. *Sexually Transmitted Diseases,* 15, 110–113.

Lehnhoff, N. (1990). The fetal shell game. *Oregonian,* October 21, NW 29.

Leiblum, S., & Rosen, R. (1992). Couples therapy for erectile disorders: Observations, obstacles, and outcomes. In R. Rosen & S. Leiblum (Eds.), *Erectile Disorders.* New York: Guilford Press.

———, & Segraves, R. T. (1989). Sex therapy with aging adults. In S. Leiblum & R. Rosen (Eds.), *Principles and Practice of Sex Therapy.* New York: Guilford Press.

Leigh, B. (1989). Reasons for having and avoiding sex: Gender, sexual orientation, and relationship to sexual behavior. *Journal of Sex Research,* 26, 199–208.

———. (1990). The relationship of substance use during sex to high-risk sexual behavior. *The Journal of Sex Research,* 27, 199–213.

Leiter, E. (1984). Urethritis: Clinical manifestations and interrelationship with intercourse and therapy. *Sexuality and Disability,* 6, 72–77.

Lepor, H. (1992). New drug treatments for benign prostatic hyperplasia. *Medical Aspects of Human Sexuality,* 26(1), 39–44.

Letich, L. (1991). Do you know who your friends are? *Utne Reader,* May/June, 85–87.

LeVay, S. (1991). A difference in hypothalamic structure between heterosexual and homosexual men. *Science,* 253, 1034–1037.

Levin, R., & Levin, A. (1975). Sexual pleasure: The surprising preferences of 100,000 women. *Redbook,* September, 38.

———, & ———. (1975). The *Redbook* report on premarital and extramarital sex. *Redbook,* October, 51.

Levin, S., & Stava, L. (1987). Personality characteristics of sex offenders. *Archives of Sexual Behavior,* 16, 57–79.

Levine, M., & Troiden, R. (1988). The myth of sexual compulsivity. *The Journal of Sex Research,* 25, 347–363.

Levine, S. (1992). Intrapsychic and interpersonal aspects of impotence: Psychogenic erectile dysfunction. In R. Rosen & S. Leiblum (Eds.), *Erectile Disorders.* New York: Guilford Press.

———, & Althof, S. (1991). The pathogenesis of psychogenic erectile dysfunction. *Journal of Sex Education & Therapy,* 4, 251–266.

Levinson, D. (1978). *The Seasons of a Man's Life.* New York: Knopf.

Lewes, K. (1988). *The Psychoanalytic Theory of Male Homosexuality.* New York: Simon & Schuster.

Lewin, E. (1981). Lesbianism and motherhood: Implications for child custody. *Human Organization,* 40, 6–14.

Lewin, T. (1991). 5-year contraceptive seems headed for wide use. *The New York Times,* November 29, 43

Lewis, R. (1973). Parents and peers: Socialization agents in the coital behavior of young adults. *Journal of Sex Research,* 9, 156–162.

Lieberman, A. (1987). *Giving Birth.* New York: St. Martin's Press.

Lieblum, S., & Bachmann, G. (1988). The sexuality of the climacteric woman. In B. Eskin (Ed.)., *The Menopause: Comprehensive Management.* New York: Yearbook Medical Publications.

———, & Rosen, R. (Eds.). (1988). *Sexual Desire Disorders.* New York: Guilford Press.

Liebowitz, M. (1983). *The Chemistry of Love.* Boston: Little, Brown.

Lief, H. (1989). Sexology. *Journal of the American Medical Association,* 261, 2888–2889.

Lifson, A., Buchbinder, S., Sheppard, H., Mawle, A., Wilber, J., Stanley, M., Hart, C., Hessol, N., & Holmberg, S. (1991). Long-term human immunodeficiency virus infection in asymptomatic homosexual and bisexual men with nor-mal CD4+ lymphocyte counts: Immunologic and virologic characteristics. *The Journal of Infectious Diseases,* 163, 959–965.

———, Rutherford, G., & Jaffe, H. (1988). The natural history of human immunodeficiency virus infection. *Journal of Infectious Diseases,* 158, 1360–1366.

Lightfoot-Klein, H., & Shaw, E. (1991). Special needs of ritually circumcised women patients. *Journal of Obstetrics, Gynecology and Neonatal Nursing,* 20, 102–107.

Lind, P. (1992). Congenital syphilis: Old disease, new resurgence. *Pediatric Health Care,* 6, 12–17.

Linde, R., Doelle, G., Alexander, N., Kirchner, F., Vale, W., Rivier, J., & Rabin, D. (1981). Reversible inhibition of testicular steroidogenesis and spermatogenesis by a potent gonadotropin-releasing hormone agonist in men. *New England Journal of Medicine,* 305, 663–667.

Lindsey, K. (1977). Sexual harassment on the job. *Ms.,* November, 47 ff.

Linke, V. (1986). AIDS in Africa. *Science,* 231, 203.

Linn, M., & Hyde, J. (1989). Paper presented at the annual meeting of the American Association for the Advancement of Science, Washington, D.C., April.

Linz, D. (1985). Sexual violence in the media: Effects on male viewers and implications for society. Doctoral thesis, University of Wisconsin, Madison, Department of Psychology.

———. (1989). Exposure to sexually explicit materials and attitudes toward rape: A comparison of study results. *Journal of Sex Research,* 26, 50–84.

———, Donnerstein, E., & Penrod, S. (1987). The findings and recommendations of the Attorney General's Commission on Pornography. *American Psychologist,* 42, 946–953.

———, Wilson, B., & Donnerstein, E. (1992). Sexual violence in the mass media: Legal solutions, warnings, and mitigation through education. *Journal of Social Issues,* 48, 145–171.

Lish, J., Ehrhardt, A., Meyer-Bahlburg, H., Rosen, L., Gruen, R., & Veridiano, N. (1991). Gender-related behavior in development in females exposed to diethylstilbestrol (DES) in utero: An attempted replication. *Journal of the American Academy of Child and Adolescent Psychiatry,* 30, 29–37.

Lisk, R. (1966). Increased sexual behavior in the male rat following lesions in the mammillary region. *Journal of Experimental Zoology,* 161, 129–136.

Liskin, L., Benoit, E., & Blackburn, R. (1992). Vasectomy: New opportunities. *Population Reports,* Series D, No. 5, March.

———, & Blackburn, R. (1987). Hormonal contraception: New long-acting methods. *Population Reports,* 15, K58–K87.

———, Rinehart, W., Blackburn, R., & Rutledge, A. (1985). Minilaparotomy and laparoscopy: Safe, effective, and widely used. *Population Reports,* 13, 2.

Little, B., & Snell, L. (1991). Brain growth among fetuses exposed to cocaine in utero: Asymmetrical growth retardation. *Obstetrics & Gynecology,* 77, 361–364.

Litwin, M., & Richie, J. (1989). Urology. *Journal of the American Medical Association,* 261, 2896–2897.

Livson, F. (1983). Gender identity: A life-span view of sex-role development. In R. Weg (Ed.)., *Sexuality in the Later Years: Roles and Behavior.* New York: Academic Press.

Lizotte, A. (1985). The uniqueness of rape: Reporting assaultive violence to the police. *Crime and Delinquency,* 31, 169–190.

Lloyd, C. (1968). The influence of hormones on human sexual behavior. In E. Astwood and C. Cassidy (Eds.)., *Clinical Endocrinology,* Vol. 2. New York: Grune & Stratton.

Lo, B., & Steinbrook, R. (1992). Health care workers infected with the human immunodeficiency virus. *Journal of the American Medical Association,* 267, 1100–1105.

Lobo, R., & Whitehead, M. (1989). Too much of a good thing? Use of progestogens in the menopause: An international consensus statement. *Fertility and Sterility,* 51, 229–231.

Lockwood, D. (1980). *Prison Sexual Violence.* New York: Elsevier.

Loffer, F. (1984). Hysteroscopic sterilization with the use of formed-in-place silicone plugs. *American Journal of Obstetrics and Gynecology,* 149, 261–269.

Lohr, J. (1989). The foreskin and urinary tract infections. *Journal of Pediatrics,* 114, 502–504.

London, R., Murphy, L., Kitlowski, K., & Reynolds, M. (1987). Efficacy of alpha-tocopherol in the treatment of the premenstrual syndrome. *Journal of Reproductive Medicine,* 32, 400–404.

LoPiccolo, J. (1980a). Low sexual desire. In S. Leiblum and L. Pervin (Eds.)., *Principles and Practice of Sex Therapy,* New York: Guilford Press.

———. (1980b). The human sexual dilemma: New clinical approaches and perspectives. Paper presented in seminar in Portland, Ore., October 22.

———. (1982). Personal communication, July.

———. (1985). Advances in diagnosis and treatment of sexual dysfunction. Paper presented at the Twenty-Eighth Annual Meeting of the Society for the Scientific Study of Sex, San Diego, Calif., September 19–22.

———. (1989). Sexual dysfunctions: Advances in diagnosis and treatment. Workshop for Oregon Division of The American Association for Marriage and Family Therapy, Portland, Ore., April.

———. (1991). Counseling and therapy for sexual problems in the elderly. *Clinics in Geriatric Medicine,* 7, 161–179.

———. (1992). Postmodern sex therapy for erectile failure. In R. Rosen & S. Leiblum (Eds.), *Erectile Disorders.* New York: Guilford Press.

———, & Friedman, J. (1988). Broad-spectrum treatment of low sexual desire: Integration of cognitive, behavioral, and systemic therapy. In S. Lieblum and R. Rosen (Eds.)., *Sexual Desire Disorders.* New York: Guilford Press.

———, & Heiman, J. (1978). The role of cultural values in the prevention and treatment of sexual problems. In C. Qualls, J. Wincze, & D. Barlow (Eds.)., *The Prevention of Sexual Disorders.* New York: Plenum.

LoPresto, C., Sherman, M., & Sherman, N. (1985). The effects of a masturbation seminar on high school males' attitudes, false beliefs, guilt, and behavior. *The Journal of Sex Research,* 21, 142–156.

Lorincz, A., Reid, R., Jenson, B., Greenburg, M., Lancaster, W., & Kurman, R. (1992). Human papillomavirus infection of the cervix: Relative risk associations of 15 common anogenital types. *Obstetrics and Gynecology,* 79, 328–337.

Lothstein, L. (1980). The postsurgical transsexual: Empirical and theoretical considerations. *Archives of Sexual Behavior,* 9, 547–563.

———. (1984). Psychological testing with transsexuals: A 30-year review. *Journal of Personality Assessment,* 48, 500–507.

Lott, B. (1987). *Women's Lives: Themes and Variations in Gender Learning.* Monterey, Calif.: Brooks/Cole.

Loulan, J. (1984). *Lesbian Sex.* San Francisco: Spinsters Ink.

Lourea, D., Rila, M., & Taylor, C. (1986). Sex in the age of AIDS. Paper presented at the Western Region Annual Conference of the Society for the Scientific Study of Sex, Scottsdale, Ariz., January.

Lown, J., & Dolan, E. (1988). Financial challenges in remarriage. *Lifestyles: Family and Economic Issues,* 9, 73–88.

———, McFadden, J., & Crossman, S. (1989). Family life education for remarriage focus on financial management. *Family Relations,* 38, 40–45.

Loy, P., & Stewart, L. (1984). The extent and effects of the sexual harassment of working women. *Sociological Focus,* 17, 31–43.

Luciano, A., Turksoy, R., Carleo, J., & Hensrix, J. (1988). Clinical and metabolic responses of menopausal women to sequential versus continuous estrogen and progestin replacement therapy. *Obstetrics and Gynecology,* 71, 39–43.

Luker, K. (1975). *Taking Chances: Abortion and the Decision Not to Contracept.* Berkeley: University of California Press.

Lukes, C., & Land, H. (1990). Biculturality and homosexuality. *Social Work,* 35, 155–161.

Lunde, D., & Hamburg, D. (1972). Techniques for assessing the effects of sex hormones on affect, arousal and aggression in humans. *Recent Progress in Hormone Research,* 28, 627–663.

Lundstrom, B., Pauly, I., & Walinder, J. (1984). Outcome of sex reassignment surgery. *Acta Psychiatrica Scandinavica,* 70, 289–294.

Lynch, C., Sinnott, J., IV, Holt, D., & Herold, A. (1991). Use of antibiotics during pregnancy. *American Family Physician,* 43, 1365–1368.

Lynch, F. (1992). Nonghetto gays: An ethnography of suburban homosexuals. In G. Herdt (Ed.), *Gay Culture in America.* Boston: Beacon Press.

Maccoby, E. (1985). Address presented at a Symposium on Issues in Contemporary Psychology, Reed College, Portland, Ore., May.

MacDonald, A., Jr. (1981). Bisexuality: Some comments on research and theory. *Journal of Homosexuality,* 6, 21–35.

MacDonald, J. (1971). *Rape: Offenders and Their Victims.* Springfield, Ill.: Thomas.

MacFarlane, A., & McPherson, A. (1992). Sex and teenagers. *Health Visitor,* 65, 18–19.

MacLean, P. (1965). New findings relevant to the evolution of psychosexual functions of the brain. In J. Money (Ed.)., *Sex Research: New Developments.* New York: Holt, Rinehart & Winston.

MacLusky, N., & Naftolin, F. (1981). Sexual differentiation of the central nervous system. *Science,* 211, 1294–1303.

MacMillan, W., Deutchman, M., Hartman, K., & Hahn, R. (1992). Obstetric ultrasound by family physicians. *Journal of Family Practice,* 34, 186–200.

MacNamara, D., & Sagarin, E. (1977). *Sex, Crime, and the Law.* New York: Free Press.

Madore, C., Hawes, W., Many, F., & Hexter, A. (1981). A study on the effects of induced abortion on subsequent pregnancy outcome. *American Journal of Obstetrics and Gynecology,* 139, 516–521.

Malamuth, N. (1981). Rape proclivity among males. *Journal of Social Issues*, 37, 138–157.

———. (1982). Aggression against women: Cultural and individual causes. In N. Malamuth and E. Donnerstein (Eds.)., *Pornography and Sexual Aggression*. New York: Academic Press.

———. (1985). The mass media as an indirect cause of sexual aggression. Paper presented at a hearing of the Attorney General's Commission on Pornography, Houston, September 12.

———. (1986). Predictors of naturalistic sexual aggression. *Journal of Personality and Social Psychology*, 50, 953–962.

———, & Check, J. (1981). The effects of mass media exposure on acceptance of violence against women: A field experiment. *Journal of Research in Personality*, 15, 436–446.

———, & Spinner, B. (1980). A longitudinal content analysis of sexual violence in the best-selling erotica magazines. *Journal of Sex Research*, 16, 226–237.

———, Haber, S., & Feshback, S. (1980). Testing hypotheses regarding rape: Exposure to sexual violence, sex differences, and the ``normality'' of rapists. *Journal of Research in Personality*, 14, 121–137.

Malatesta, V., Pollack, R., Crotty, T., & Peacock, L. (1982). Acute alcohol intoxication and female orgasmic response. *Journal of Sex Research*, 18, 1–17.

Maletzky, B. (1987). Data generated by an outpatient sexual abuse clinic. Paper presented at the annual conference of the Association for the Behavioral Treatment of Sexual Abusers, Newport, Ore., May.

———, & Price, R. (1984). Public masturbation in men: Precursor to exhibitionism? *Journal of Sex Education and Therapy*, 10, 31–36.

Mallon, R. (1984). Demonstration of vestigial prostatic tissue in the human female. Paper presented at the Annual Regional Conference of American Association of Sex Educators, Counselors, and Therapists, Las Vegas, October.

Malloy, G., Herold, E. (1988). Factors related to sexual counseling of physically disabled adults. *Journal of Sex Research*, 24, 220–227.

Malloy, T., & Wein, A. (1988). Erectile dysfunction: Effects of pharmacotherapy. *Medical Aspects of Human Sexuality*, June, 42–48.

Maltz, W. (1988). Identifying and treating the sexual repercussions of incest: A couples therapy approach. *Journal of Sex and Marital Therapy*, 14, 142–170.

———. (1991). *The Sexual Healing Journey*. New York: HarperCollins.

———, & Holman, B. (1987). *Incest and Sexuality: A Guide to Understanding and Healing*. Lexington, Mass.: Lexington Books.

Mann, J. (1992). AIDS: The second decade: A global perspective. *The Journal of Infectious Diseases*, 165, 245–250.

Mannion, K. (1981). Psychology and the lesbian: A critical view of the research. In S. Cox (Ed.)., *Female Psychology: The Emerging Self*, 2nd ed., New York: St. Martin's Press.

Mano, H., & Chermann, J. (1991). Fetal human immunodeficiency virus type 1 infection of different organs in the second trimester. *AIDS Research and Human Retroviruses*, 7, 83–88.

Mansfield, P., Theisen, S. C., & Boyer, B. (1992). Midlife women and menopause: A challenge for the mental health counselor. *Journal of Mental Health Counseling*, 14, 73–83.

Margolies, L., Becker, M., & Jackson-Brewer, K. (1988). Internalized homophobia: Identifying and treating the oppressor within. In The Boston Lesbian Psychologies Collective (Eds.)., *Lesbian Psychologies*. Urbana: University of Illinois Press.

Margolis, C., & Goodman, R. (1984). Psychological factors in women choosing radiation therapy for breast cancer. *Psychosomatics*, 25, 464–466; 469.

Margolis, D., McMillen, M., Hashmi, H., Wasson, D., & MacArthur, J. (1992). Aggressive axillary evaluation and adjuvant therapy for nonpalpable carcinoma of the breast. *Gynecology & Obstetrics*, 174, 109–114.

Markos, A., Wade, A., & Walzman, M. (1992). Oral sex and recurrent vulvo-vaginal candidiasis. *Genitourinary Medicine*, 68, 61–62.

Markowitz, L. (1991). Homosexuality: Are we still in the dark? *Networker*, January/February, 27–35.

Marks, E. (1981). Review of behavioral psychotherapy (II).: Sexual disorders. *American Journal of Psychiatry*, 138, 750–756.

Marks, G., Richardson, J., Ruiz, M., & Maldonado, N. (1992). HIV-infected men's practices in notifying past sexual partners of infection risk. *Public Health Reports*, 107, 100–109.

Marmor, J. (Ed.). (1980). *Homosexual Behavior*. New York: Basic Books.

———. (1989). Nonsurgical treatment of impotence. *Medical Aspects of Human Sexuality*, April, 44–47.

Marshall, D. (1971). Sexual behavior on Mangaia. In D. Marshall & R. Suggs (Eds.)., *Human Sexual Behavior: Variations in the Ethnographic Spectrum*. Englewood Cliffs, N.J.: Prentice-Hall.

Marshall, S. (1989). Evaluation and management of simple erectile dysfunction in office practice. *Medical Aspects of Human Sexuality*, April, 5–8.

Marshall, W. (1981). The evaluation of sexual aggressives. Paper presented at the Third Annual Conference on the Evaluation and Treatment of Sexual Aggressives, San Luis Obispo, Calif., May.

———. (1988). The use of sexually explicit stimuli by rapists, child molesters, and nonoffenders. *Journal of Sex Research*, 25, 267–288.

———. (1989). Intimacy, loneliness and sexual offenders. *Behaviour Research and Therapy*, 27, 491–503.

———, & Barbaree, H. (1984). A behavioral view of rape. *International Journal of Law and Psychiatry*. 7, 51–77.

———, Eccles, A., & Barbaree, H. (1991). The treatment of exhibitionists: A focus on sexual deviance versus cognitive and relationship features. *Behaviour Research and Therapy*, 29, 129–135.

———, Payne, K., Barbaree, H., & Eccles, A. (1991). Exhibitionists: Sexual preferences for exposing. *Behaviour Research and Therapy*, 29, 37–40.

Martin, D., & Lyon, P. (1972). *Lesbian-Woman*. New York: Bantam Books.

Martinson, F. (1980). Childhood sexuality. In B. Wolman & J. Money (Eds.)., *Handbook of Human Sexuality.* Englewood Cliffs, N.J.: Prentice-Hall.

Marx, J. (1989). Circumcision may protect against the AIDS virus. *Science,* 245, 470–471.

Marx, R., Aral, S., Rolfs, R., Sterk, C., & Kahn, J. (1991). Crack, sex, and STD. *Sexually Transmitted Diseases,* 18, 92–101.

Maslow, A., & Sakoda, J. (1952). Volunteer-error in the Kinsey study. *Journal of Abnormal and Social Psychology,* 47, 259–267.

Massie, M., & Johnson, S. (1989). The importance of recognizing a history of sexual abuse in female adolescents. *Journal of Adolescent Health Care,* 10, 184–191.

Masters, W. (1983). Half a century of unnecessary sexual myths. *Journal of the American Medical Association,* 250, 244.

———, & Johnson, V. (1961). Orgasm, anatomy of the female. In A. Ellis & A. Abarbonel (Eds.)., *Encyclopedia of Sexual Behavior,* Vol. 2. New York: Hawthorn Books.

———, & ———. (1966). *Human Sexual Response.* Boston: Little, Brown.

———, & ———. (1970). *Human Sexual Inadequacy.* Boston: Little, Brown.

———, & ———. (1976). *The Pleasure Bond.* New York: Bantam Books.

———, & ———. (1979). *Homosexuality in Perspective.* Boston: Little, Brown.

———, & ———. (1986). *Masters and Johnson on Sex and Human Loving.* Boston: Little, Brown.

Matteo, S., & Rissman, E. (1984). Increased sexual activity during the midcycle portion of the human menstrual cycle. *Hormones and Behavior,* 18, 249–255.

Matthews, K. (1992). Myths and realities of the menopause. *Psychosomatic Medicine,* 54, 1–9.

Maugh, T. (1981). Male ``pill'' blocks sperm enzyme. *Science,* 212, 314.

May, R. (1969). *Love and Will.* New York: Norton.

Mazer, D., & Percival, E. (1989). Students' experiences of sexual harassment at a small university. *Sex Roles,* 20, 1–22.

McAninch, J. (1989). Editorial comment on the report of the Task Force on Circumcision. *Pediatrics,* 84, 667.

McArthur, L., & Resko, B. (1975). The portrayal of men and women in American television commercials. *Journal of Social Psychology,* 97, 209–220.

McBride, G. (1991). New U.S. advisory board on ethics in reproduction. *British Medical Journal,* 302, 490.

———. (1992). U.S. Supreme Court will decide women's right to abortion. *British Medical Journal,* 304, 271–272.

McBride, W. (1991). Spontaneous abortion. *American Family Physician,* 43, 175–182.

McCabe, M. (1987). Desired and experienced levels of premarital affection and sexual intercourse during dating. *Journal of Sex Research,* 23, 23–33.

———, & Delaney, S. (1992). An evaluation of therapeutic programs for the treatment of secondary inorgasmia in women. *Archives of Sexual Behavior,* 21, 69–87.

McCaghy, C. (1971). Child molesting. *Sexual Behavior,* August, 16–24.

McCarthy, B. (1988). Premature ejaculation: New conceptualizations in understanding, treatment, and prevention. Paper presented at the Thirty-First Annual Meeting of the American Association of Sex Educators, Counselors, and Therapists, San Francisco.

———. (1992). Sexual trauma: The pendulum has swung too far. *Journal of Sex Education & Therapy,* 18, 1–10.

McCarthy, J., & McMillan, S. (1990). Patient/partner satisfaction with penile implant surgery. *Journal of Sex Education & Therapy,* 16, 25–37.

McCauley, C., & Swann, C. (1978). Male–female differences in sexual fantasy. *Journal of Research in Personality,* 12, 76–86.

McClintock, M. (1971). Menstrual synchrony and suppression. *Nature,* 229, 244–245.

McClure, D. (1988). Men with one testicle. *Medical Aspects of Human Sexuality,* May, 22–32.

McConnel, J. (1977). *Understanding Human Behavior.* New York: Holt, Rinehart & Winston.

McCormick, C., & Witelson, S. (1991). A cognitive profile of homosexual men compared to heterosexual men and women. *Psychoneuroendocrinology,* 16, 459–473.

———, ———, & Kingstone, E. (1990). Left-handedness in homosexual men and women: Neuroendocrine implications. *Psychoneuroendocrinology,* 15, 69–76.

McCoy, H., McKay, C., Hermanns, L., & Lai, S. (1990). Sexual behavior and risk of HIV infection. *American Behavioral Scientist,* 33, 432–450.

McCoy, N., Cutler, W., & Davidson, J. (1985). Relationships among sexual behavior, hot flashes, and hormone levels in perimenopausal women. *Archives of Sexual Behavior,* 14, 385–394.

McCulloch, D., Young, R., Prescott, R., Campbell, I., & Clarke, B. (1984). The natural history of impotence in diabetic men. *Diabetologia,* 26, 437–440.

McCutchan, J. (1990). Effects of HIV on sexual functioning. Paper presented at The Society for the Scientific Study of Sex Annual Western Region Conference, San Diego, Calif., April 25.

McDougall, J. (1986). *Theaters of the Mind: Illusion and Truth on the Psychoanalytic Stage.* New York: Basic Books.

McFarlane, J., Martin, C., & Williams, T. (1988). Mood fluctuations: Women versus men and menstrual versus other cycles. *Psychology of Women Quarterly,* 12, 201–224.

McGinnis, T. (1982). *More Than Just a Friend.* Englewood Cliffs, N.J.: Prentice-Hall.

McGlone, J. (1978). Sex differences in functional brain asymmetry. *Cortex,* 14, 122–128.

McGovern, K. (1982). Personal communication, June 28.

———, Kirkpatric, D., & LoPiccolo, J. (1976). A behavioral group treatment program for sexually dysfunctional couples. *Journal of Marriage and Family Counseling,* 2, 397–404.

McGrew, M., & Shore, W. (1991). The problem of teenage pregnancy. *The Journal of Family Practice,* 32, 17–25.

McGuire, L., & Wagner, N. (1978). Sexual dysfunction in women who were molested as children: One response pattern and suggestions for treatment. *Journal of Sex and Marital Therapy*, 4, 11–15.

McKenna, J., McMillan, A., & Blakely, A. (1991). Cold sores and safer sex. *Lancet*, 338, 632.

McKinlay, J., McKinlay, S., & Brambilla, D. (1987). The relative contributions of endocrine changes and social circumstances to depression in mid-aged women. *Journal of Health and Social Behavior*, 28, 345–363.

McKinnon, K. (1979). *The Sexual Harassment of Working Women*. New Haven, Conn.: Yale University Press.

McLaren, A. (1990). *A History of Contraception: From Antiquity to the Present Day*. Cambridge, MA. Basil Blackwell.

McLaren, N., & Neiburg, P. (1988). Fetal tobacco syndrome and other problems caused by smoking during pregnancy. *Medical Aspects of Human Sexuality*, August, 69–75.

McNaught, B. (1991). Personal communication.

McNeil, E., & Rubin, Z. (1977). *The Psychology of Being Human*. San Francisco: Canfield Press.

McNiven, P., Hodnett, E., & O'Brien-Pallas, L. (1992). Supporting women in labor: A work sampling study of the activities of labor and delivery nurses. *Birth*, 19, 3–8.

McWorter, W. (1977). Flashing and dashing: Notes and comments on the etiology of exhibitionism. In C. Bryant (Ed.)., *Sexual Deviancy in Social Context*. New York: New Viewpoints.

Mead, M. (1949). *Male and Female: A Study of Sexes in the Changing World*. New York: Morrow.

———. (1963). *Sex and Temperament in Three Primitive Societies*. New York: Morrow.

Medical Letter, The (1987). Drugs that cause sexual dysfunction. 29, 65–68.

Medical Research International (1991). In vitro fertilization-embryo transfer (IVF-ET) in the United States: 1989 results from the IVF-ET registry. *Fertility and Sterility*, 55, 14–23.

Meeropol, E. (1991). One of the gang: Development of adolescents with physical disabilities. *Journal of Pediatric Nursing*, 6, 243–249.

Meiselman, K. (1978). *Incest*. San Francisco, Jossey-Bass.

Melman, A. (1992). Neural and vascular control of erection. In R. Rosen & S. Leiblum (Eds.), *Erectile Disorders*. New York: Guilford Press.

———, & Tiefer, L. (1992). Surgery for erectile disorders: Operative procedures and psychological issues. In R. Rosen & S. Leiblum (Eds.), *Erectile Disorders*. New York: Guilford Press.

Mendelson, J. (1976). Marijuana and sex. *Medical Aspects of Human Sexuality*, 10, 23–24.

Mendham, C., & Rees, C. (1992). A positive change. *Nursing Times*, 88(12), 34–35.

Mengel, M., Berg, A., Weaver, C., Herman, D., Herman, S., Hughes, V., & Koepsell, T. (1989). The effectiveness of single-dose metronidazole therapy for patients and their partners with bacterial vaginosis. *The Journal of Family Practice*, 28, 163–171.

Merriam, A. (1971). Aspects of sexual behavior among the Bala. In D. Marshall & R. Suggs (Eds.)., *Human Sexual Behavior: Variations in the Ethnographic Spectrum*. Englewood Cliffs, N.J.: Prentice-Hall.

Mertz, G., Benedetti, J., Ashley, R., Selke, S., & Corey, L. (1992). Risk factors for the sexual transmission of genital herpes. *Annals of Internal Medicine*, 116, 197–202.

Messenger, J. (1971). Sex and repression in an Irish folk community. In D. Marshall & R. Suggs (Eds.)., *Human Sexual Behavior: Variations in the Ethnographic Spectrum*, Englewood Cliffs, N.J.: Prentice-Hall.

Metcalf, M., Braiden, V., & Livesey, J. (1992). Symptom cyclicity in women with the premenstrual syndrome: An 8-year follow-up study. *Journal of Psychosomatic Research*, 36, 237–241.

Metzler, C., Noell, J., & Biglan, A. (1992). The validation of a construct of high-risk sexual behavior in heterosexual adults. *Journal of Adolescence Research*, 7, 233–249.

Meuwissen, I., & Over, R. (1991). Multidimensionality of the content of female sexual fantasy. *Behavior Research and Therapy*, 29, 179–189.

Meyer, J., & Dupkin, C. (1985). Gender disturbance in children. *Bulletin of the Menninger Clinic*, 1985, 49, 236–269.

Meyer, V. (1991). A critique of adolescent pregnancy prevention research: The invisible white male. *Adolescence*, 26, 217–222.

Meyer, W., Webb, A., Stuart, C., Finkelstein, J., Lawrence, B., & Walker, P. (1986). Physical and hormonal evaluation of transsexual patients: A longitudinal study. *Archives of Sexual Behavior*, 15, 121–138.

Meyer-Bahlburg, H. (1977). Sex hormones and male homosexuality in comparative perspective. *Archives of Sexual Behavior*, 6, 297–325.

Meyering, R., & Epling–McWherter, E. (1986). Decision-making in extramarital relationships. *Lifestyles: A Journal of Changing Patterns*, 8, 115–129.

Mezey, G., & King, M. (1989). The effects of sexual assault on men: A survey of 22 victims. *Psychological Medicine*, 19, 205–209.

Michael, R., Bonsall, R., & Warner, P. (1974). Human vaginal secretions; volatile fatty acid content. *Science*, 186, 1217–1219.

———, Keverne, E., & Bonsall, R. (1971). Pheromones: Isolation of male sex attractants from a female primate. *Science*, 172, 964–966.

Milan, R., & Kilmann, P. (1987). Interpersonal factors in premarital conception. *Journal of Sex Research*, 23, 289–321.

Miller, K., Losh, D., & Folley, A. (1992). Evaluation and follow-up of abnormal Pap smears. *American Family Physician*, 45, 143–149.

Miller, L. (1989). Nonsurgical treatment of sexual dysfunction associated with penile curvature. *Medical Aspects of Human Sexuality*, April, 123–128.

Milow, V. (1983). Menstrual education: Past, present and future. In S. Golub (Ed.)., *Menarche*. Lexington, Mass.: Lexington Books.

Mims, F., & Chang, A. (1984). Unwanted sexual experiences of young women. *Psychosocial Nursing*, 22, 7–14.

Mindel, A., Tovey, S., Timmins, D., & Williams, P. (1989). Primary and secondary syphilis, 20 years' experience. *Genitourinary Medicine,* 65, 1–3.

Minkoff, H. (1988). Herpes virus infection during and after pregnancy. *Medical Aspects of Human Sexuality,* April, 98–108.

Minton, J., Foecking, D., Webster, D., & Matthews, R. (1979). Caffeine, cyclic nucleotides, and breast disease. *Surgery,* 86, 105–109.

Mitchell, J. (1992a). Childless by choice. *Oregonian,* January 26, L1–L5.

———. (1992b). Faith, hope and disparity. *Oregonian,* June 14, L1–L5.

Mitsuya, H., & Broder, S. (1988). Inhibition of infectivity and replication of HIV-2 and SIV in helper-T cells by 2',3'-dideoxynucleosides in vitro. *AIDS Research and Human Retroviruses,* 4, 107–113.

Mittwoch, U. (1973). *Genetics of Sex Differentiation.* New York: Academic Press.

———, & Burgess, A. (1991). How do you get sex? *Journal of Endocrinology,* 128, 329–331.

Mohr, D., & Beutler, L. (1990). Erectile dysfunction: A review of diagnostic and treatment procedures. *Clinical Psychology Review,* 10, 123–150.

Molotsky, I. (1988). Pornography measure passes. *New York Times,* September 29, A24.

Monaghan, J. (1992). Norplant insertion and removal. *Patient Care,* March 15, 231–237.

Monat, R. (1982). *Sexuality and the Mentally Retarded.* San Diego, Calif.: College-Hill Press.

Moncrieff, M., & Pearson, D. (1979). Comparison of MMPI profiles of assaultive and non-assaultive exhibitionists and voyeurs. *Corrective and Social Psychiatry and Journal of Behavior Technology,* 25, 91–93.

Money, J. (1961). Components of eroticism in man: The hormones in relation to sexual morphology and sexual desire. *Journal of Nervous and Mental Disease,* 132, 239–248.

———. (1965). Psychosexual differentiation. In J. Money (Ed.)., *Sex Research, New Developments.* New York: Holt, Rinehart, & Winston.

———. (1967). Cytogenetic and other aspects of transvestism and transsexualism. *Journal of Sex Research,* 3, 141–143.

———. (1968). *Sex Errors of the Body: Dilemmas, Education, Counseling.* Baltimore: Johns Hopkins University Press.

———. (1970). Clitoral size and erotic sensation. *Medical Aspects of Human Sexuality,* 4, 95.

———. (1972). *Man Woman/Boy Girl.* Baltimore: Johns Hopkins University Press.

———. (1975). Ablatio penis: Normal male infant sex-reassigned as a girl. *Archives of Sexual Behavior,* 4, 65–72.

———. (1981). Paraphilias: Phyletic origins of erotosexual dysfunction. *International Journal of Mental Health,* 10, 75–109.

———. (1983). Food, fitness, and vital fluids: Sexual pleasure from Graham Crackers to Kellogg's Cornflakes. Paper presented at the Sixth World Congress of Sexology, May 27.

———. (1984). Paraphilias: Phenomenology and classification. *American Journal of Psychotherapy,* 38, 164–179.

———. (1986). *Lovemaps: Clinical Concepts of Sexual/Erotic Health and Pathology, Paraphilias, and Gender Transposition in Childhood, Adolescence, and Maturity.* New York: Irvington.

———. (1988). *Gay, Straight, and In-Between: The Sexology of Erotic Orientation.* New York: Oxford University Press.

———, & Bennett, R. (1981). Postadolescent paraphilic sex offenders: Antiandrogenic and counseling therapy follow-up. *International Journal of Mental Health,* 10, 122–133.

———, & Ehrhardt, A. (1972). Prenatal hormonal exposure: Possible effects on behavior in man. In R. Michael (Ed.)., *Endocrinology and Human Behavior.* London: Oxford University Press.

———, Hampson, J., & Hampson, J. (1955). An examination of some basic sexual concepts: The evidence of human hermaphrodism. *Bulletin of Johns Hopkins Hospital,* 97, 301–319.

———, & Lamacz, M. (1990). *Vandalized Lovemaps.* Buffalo, N.Y.: Prometheus Press.

———, Lehne, G., & Pierre-Jerome, F. (1984). Micropenis: Adult follow-up and comparison of size against new norms. *Journal of Sex and Marital Therapy,* 10, 105–116.

———, & Masica, D. (1968). Fetal feminization by androgen insensitivity in the testicular feminizing syndrome: Effect on marriage and maternalism. *Johns Hopkins Medical Journal,* 123, 105–114.

———, Prakasam, K. S., & Joshi, V. N. (1991). Semen-conservation doctrine from ancient Ayurvedic to modern sexological theory. *American Journal of Psychotherapy,* 45, 9–13.

———, & Primrose, C. (1968). Sexual dimorphism and dissociation in the psychology of male transsexuals. *Journal of Nervous and Mental Disorders,* 147, 472–486.

———, & Walker, P. (1977). Counseling the transsexual. In J. Money & H. Musaph (Eds.)., *Handbook of Sexology.* Amsterdam: Elsevier/North-Holland Biomedical Press.

———, & Yankowitz, R. (1967). The sympathetic-inhibiting effects of the drug Ismelin on human male eroticism, with a note on Mellaril. *Journal of Sex Research,* 3, 69–82.

Monier, M., & Laird, M. (1989). Contraceptives: A look at the future. *American Journal of Nursing,* April, 496–499.

Montagu, A., & Matson, F. (1979). *The Human Connection.* New York: McGraw-Hill.

Montauk, S., & Clasen, M. (1989). Sex education in primary care: Infancy to puberty. *Medical Aspects of Human Sexuality,* January, 22–36.

Mooney, T., Cole, T., & Chilgren, R. (1975). *Sexual Options for Paraplegics and Quadraplegics.* Boston: Little, Brown.

Mooradian, A. D., & Greiff, V. (1990). Sexuality in older women. *Archives of Internal Medicine,* 150, 1033–1038.

Moore, D., Winfield, A., Segars, J., & Herbert, C., III (1991). Selective fallopian tube canalization. *American Family Physician,* 43, 889–893.

Moore, R., & Gillette, D. (1990). *King Warrior Magician Lover.* San Francisco: Harper & Row.

———, Hidalgo, J., Sugland, B., & Chaisson, R. (1991). Zidovudine and the natural history of the acquired immunodeficiency syndrome. *The New England Journal of Medicine,* 324, 1412–1416.

Moore, S., & Rosenthal, D. (1991). Adolescent invulnerability and perceptions of AIDS risk. *Journal of Adolescent Research,* 6, 164–180.

Morales, A., Condra, M., Owen, J., Surridge, D., Fenemore, J., & Harris, C. (1987). Is yohimbine effective in the treatment of organic impotence? Results of a controlled trial. *Journal of Urology,* 137, 1168–1172.

———, ———, & Reid, K. (1990). The role of nocturnal penile tumescence monitoring in the diagnosis of impotence: A review. *Journal of Urology,* 143, 141–145.

Moran, M. (1992). Effects of sexual orientation similarity and counselor experience level on gay men's and lesbians' perceptions of counselors. *Journal of Counseling Psychology,* 39, 247–251.

Moreland, R., & Zajonc, R. (1982). Exposure effects in person perception: Familiarity, similarity, and attraction. *Journal of Experimental Social Psychology,* 18, 395–415.

Morgan, E. (1978). The Puritans and sex. In M. Gordon (Ed.)., *The American Family in Social-Historical Perspective.* New York: St. Martin's Press.

Morgan, L. (1989). Economic well-being following marital termination. *Journal of Family Issues,* 10, 86–101.

Morgan, R. (1991). Clinical aspects of pelvic inflammatory disease. *American Family Physician,* 43, 1725–1732.

Morin, J. (1981). *Anal Pleasure and Health.* Burlingame, Calif.: Down There Press.

Morokoff, P. (1986). Volunteer bias in the psycho[chphysiological study of female sexuality. *Journal of Sex Research,* 22, 35–51.

Morrell, M., Dixen, J., Carter, C., & Davidson, J. (1984). The influence of age and cycling status on sexual arousability in women. *American Journal of Obstetrics and Gynecology,* 148, 66–71.

Morris, N. (1973). The law is a busybody. *New York Times Magazine,* April 18, 58–64.

———, & Udry, J. (1978). Pheromonal influences on human sexual behavior: An experiential search. *Journal of Biosocial Science,* 10, 147–159.

Morse, E., Simon, P., Osofsky, H., Balson, P., & Gaumer, R. (1991). *Social Science and Medicine,* 32, 535–539.

Moseley, D., Fellingstad, D., Harley, H., & Heckel, R. (1981). Psychological factors that predict reaction to abortion. *Journal of Clinical Psychology,* 37, 276–279.

Moser, C., & Levitt, E. (1987). An exploratory-descriptive study of a sadomasochistically oriented sample. *Journal of Sex Research,* 23, 322–337.

Moses, A., & Hawkins, R. (1985). Two-hour in-service training session on homophobia. In H. Hidalgo, T. Peterson, & N. Goodman (Eds.)., *Lesbian and Gay Issues.* Silver Spring, Md.: National Association of Social Workers.

Mosher, D., & Anderson, R. (1986). Macho personality, sexual aggression, and reactions to guided imagery of realistic rape. *Journal of Research in Personality,* 20, 77–94.

———, & Tomkins, S. (1988). Scripting the macho man: Hypermasculine socialization and enculturation. *Journal of Sex Research,* 25, 60–84.

Mott, F., & Haurin, R. (1988). Linkages between sexual activity and alcohol and drug use among American adolescents. *Family Planning Perspectives,* 20, 128–137.

Moul, J., & Belman, B. (1988). A review of surgical treatment of undescended testes with emphasis on anatomical position. *Journal of Urology,* 140, 125–128.

Muccigrosso, L. (1991). Sexual abuse prevention strategies and programs for persons with developmental disabilities. *Sexuality and Disability,* 9(3), 261–266.

Muehlenhard, C. (1988). Misinterpreting dating behaviors and the risk of date rape. *Journal of Social and Clinical Psychology,* 6, 20–37.

———. (1989). Young men pressured into having sex with women. *Medical Aspects of Human Sexuality,* April, 50–62.

———, & Andrews, S. (1985). Open communication about sex: Will it reduce risk factors related to rape? Paper presented at the Annual Meeting of the Association for Advancement of Behavior Therapy, Houston, November.

———, & Falcon, P. (1990). Men's heterosexual skill and attitudes toward woman as predictors of verbal sexual coercion and forceful rape. *Sex Roles,* 23, 241–259.

———, Felts, A., & Andrews, S. (1985). Men's attitudes toward the justifiability of date rape: Intervening variables and possible solutions. Paper presented at the Midcontinent Meeting of the Society for the Scientific Study of Sex, Chicago, June.

———, Goggins, M., Jones, J., & Satterfield, A. (1991). Sexual violence and coercion in close relationships. In K. McKinney & S. Sprecher (Eds.), *Sexuality in Close Relationships.* Hillsdale, N.J.: Lawrence Erlbaum.

———, & Hollabaugh, L. (1989). Do women sometimes say no when they mean yes? The prevalence and correlates of women's token resistance to sex. *Journal of Personality and Social Psychology,* 54, 872–879.

———, & Linton, M. (1987). Date rape and sexual aggression in dating situations: Incidence and risk factors. *Journal of Consulting Psychology,* 34, 186–196.

———, & Long, P. (1988). Men's versus women's reports of pressure to engage in unwanted sexual intercourse. Paper presented at the Western Region Meeting of the Society for the Scientific Study of Sex, Dallas, May.

———, & MacNaughton, J. (1988). Women's beliefs about women "who lead men on." *Journal of Social and Clinical Psychology,* 7, 65–79.

———, & Schrag, J. (1991). Nonviolent sexual coercion. In A. Parrot & L. Bechhofer (Eds.), *Acquaintance Rape: The Hidden Crime.* New York: Wiley.

Mulligan, T. (1989). Impotence in the older man. *Medical Aspects of Human Sexuality,* April, 32–36.

———, & Palguta, R., Jr. (1991). Sexual interest, activity, and satisfaction among male nursing home residents. *Archives of Sexual Behavior,* 20, 199–204.

Mulligan, T., Retchin, S. M., Chinchilli, V. M., & Bettinger, C. B. (1988). The role of aging and chronic disease in sexual dysfunction. *Journal of the American Geriatrics Society, 36,* 520–524.

Munroe, R. (1980). Male transvestism and the couvade: A psychocultural analysis. *Ethos,* 8, 49–59.

Murdock, G. (1949). *Social Structure.* New York: Macmillan.

Murnen, S., Perot, A., & Byrne, D. (1989). Coping with unwanted sexual activity: Normative responses, situational determinants, and individual differences. *Journal of Sex Research,* 26, 85–106.

Murphy, A., Durmusoglu, F., Schlaff, W., Damewood, M., Hassiakos, D., & Rock, J. (1991). Laparoscopic cautery in the treatment of endometriosis-related infertility. *Fertility and Sterility,* 55, 246–251.

Murphy, N., & Fain, T. (1978). Psychobiological factors in sex and gender identity. Paper presented to the AASECT Conference in Portland, Ore., October 19.

Murstein, B. (1978). Swinging or comarital sex. In B. Murstein (Ed.)., *Exploring Intimate Life Styles.* New York: Springer.

———, Case, D., & Gunn, S. (1985). Personality correlates of ex-swingers. *Lifestyles: A Journal of Changing Patterns,* 8, 21–34.

Musher, D. (1991). Syphilis, neurosyphilis, penicillin, and AIDS. *The Journal of Infectious Diseases,* 163, 1201–1206.

Myers, B. (1984). Mother–infant bonding: The status of this critical-period hypothesis. *Developmental Review,* 4, 240–274.

Myers, L., Dixen, J., Morrissette, D., Carmichael, M., & Davidson, J. (1990). Effects of estrogen, androgen, and progestin on sexual psychophysiology and behavior in postmenopausal women. *Journal of Clinical Endocrinology and Metabolism,* 70, 1124–1131.

Myron, A., & Maguire, D. (1991). Pain perception in the neonate: Implications for circumcision. *Journal of Professional Nursing,* 7, 188–193.

Nachtigall, L., & Heilman, J. (1987). *Estrogen: The Facts Can Change Your Life.* New York: Harper & Row.

Nachtigall, R. (1991). Assessing fecundity after age 40. *Contemporary OB/GYN,* March, 11–33.

———, Becker, G., & Wozny, M. (1992). The effects of gender-specific diagnosis on men's and women's response to infertility. *Fertility and Sterility,* 57, 113–121.

Nadelson, C., & Notman, M. (1985). Behavioral-psychological aspects of pregnancy and abortion. In Z. DeFries, C. Friedman, & R. Corn (Eds.)., *Sexuality, New Perspectives.* Westport, Conn.: Greenwood Press.

Nadler, R. (1968). Approach to psychodynamics of obscene telephone calls. *New York Journal of Medicine,* 68, 521–526.

Narod, S., de Sanjose, S., & Victora, C. (1991). Coffee during pregnancy: A reproductive hazard? *American Journal of Obstetrics and Gynecology,* 164, 1109.

Narum, G., & Rodolfa, E. (1984). Sex therapy for the spinal cord injured client: Suggestions for professionals. *Professional Psychology: Research and Practice,* 15, 775–784.

National Cancer Institute. (1986). *Breast Exams: What You Should Know.* National Institute of Health Publication No. 86–2000.

National Center for Health Statistics (1991). *Advance Report of Final Natality Statistics, 1989,* 40, No. 8.

———. (1991). Annual summary of births, marriages, divorces, and deaths: United States, 1990. *Monthy Vital Statistics Report,* 39, 1–7.

———. (1991). *Monthly Vital Statistics Report,* 39, 9.

———. (1992). *Monthly Vital Statistics Report,* 40, No. 12.

National Gay & Lesbian Task Force. (1987). *Anti-Gay Violence, Victimization and Defamation in 1987.* Washington, D.C.: National Gay and Lesbian Task Force.

Nelson, J. (1980). Gayness and homosexuality: Issues for the church. In E. Batchelor, Jr. (Ed.)., *Homosexuality and Ethics.* New York: Pilgrim Press.

———. (1985). Male sexuality and masculine spirituality. *SIECUS Report,* 13, 1–4.

Nelson, R. (1988). Nonoperative management of impotence. *Journal of Urology,* 139, 2–5.

Nevid, J. (1984). Sex differences in factors of romantic attraction. *Sex Roles,* 11, 401–411.

Newcomb, M., & Bentler, P. (1980). Assessment of personality and demographic aspects of cohabitation and marital success. *Journal of Personality Development,* 4, 11–24.

Newcomer, S., & Udry, J. (1985). Oral sex in an adolescent population. *Archives of Sexual Behavior,* 14, 41–46.

———, & ———. (1985). Parent–child communication and adolescent sexual behavior. *Family Planning Perspectives,* 17, 169–174.

———, & ———. (1988). Adolescents' honesty in a survey of sexual behavior. *Journal of Adolescent Research,* 3, 419–423.

Nieschlag, E., Wickings, E., & Breuer, H. (1981). Chemical methods for male fertility control. *Contraception,* 23, 1–10.

NIH Consensus Conference (1991). Treatment of early-stage breast cancer. *Journal of the American Medical Association,* 265, 391–395.

Norman, J., & Harris, M. (1981). *The Private Life of the American Teenager.* New York: Rawson Wade.

Notelovitz, M. (1990). Management of the changing vagina. *Clinical Practice in Sexuality,* Special Issue, 16–17.

Novas, J., Meyers, S., & Gleicher, N. (1989). Obstetric outcome of patients with more than one previous cesarean section. *American Journal of Obstetrics and Gynecology,* 160, 364–367.

Nutter, D., & Condron, M. (1983). Sexual fantasy and activity patterns of females with inhibited sexual desire versus normal controls. *Journal of Sex and Marital Therapy,* 9, 276–282.

O'Carroll, R. (1991). Sexual desire disorders: A review of controlled treatment studies. *The Journal of Sex Research,* 28, 607–624.

O'Driscoll, K., Foley, M., MacDonald, D., & Stronge, J. (1988). Cesarean section and perinatal outcome: Response from the House of Horne. *American Journal of Obstetrics and Gynecology,* 158, 449–52.

Oesterwitz, H., Bick, C., & Braun, E. (1984). Fracture of the penis: Report of 6 cases and review of the literature. *International Urology and Nephrology,* 16, 123–127.

Oettinger, K. (1979). *Not My Daughter.* Englewood Cliffs, N.J.: Prentice-Hall.

Office of Technological Assessment, U.S. Congress. (1988). *Infertility: Medical and Social Choices.* Washington, D.C.: Government Printing Office.

O'Hare, M., Schlechte, J., Lewis, D., & Wright, E. (1991). Prospective study of postpartum blues. *Archives of General Psychiatry,* 48, 801–806.

Olasov, B., & Jackson, J. (1987). Effects of expectancies on women's reports of moods during the menstrual cycle. *Psychosomatic Medicine,* 49, 65–78.

Olds, J. (1956). Pleasure centers in the brain. *Scientific American,* 193, 105–116.

Olson, D., Fournier, D., & Druckman, J. (1987). *Counselor's Manual for PREPARE/ENRICH* (revised edition). Minneapolis, Minn.: PREPARE/ENRICH.

O'Neill, N., & O'Neill, G. (1972). *Open Marriage.* New York: Evans.

O'Neill, P. (1988). Prenatal: Neglect poses future health costs for society. *The Oregonian,* December 4, A1.

Onlofsky, J. (1977). Sex-role orientation, identity formation, and self-esteem in college men and women. *Sex Roles,* 3, 561–576.

Onorato, I., McCray, E., & The Field Services Branch (1992). Prevalence of human immunodeficiency virus infection among patients attending tuberculosis clinics in the United States. *The Journal of Infectious Diseases,* 165, 87–92.

Orlando [pseud.] (1978). Bisexuality: A choice not an echo. *Ms.,* October, 60.

Orr, D., Beiter, M., & Ingersoll, G. (1991). Premature sexual activity as an indicator of psychosocial risk. *Pediatrics,* 87, 141–147.

———, Langefeld, C., Katz, B., Caine, V., Dias, P., Blythe, M., & Jones, R. (1992). Factors associated with condom use among sexually active female adolescents. *Journal of Pediatrics,* 120, 311–317.

Orr, M. (1982). Sex education and contraceptive education in U.S. public high schools. *Family Planning Perspectives,* 14, 304–313.

Ory, H., Rosenfield, A., & Landman, L. (1980). The pill at 20: An assessment. *Family Planning Perspectives,* 12, 278–283.

Ory, S. (1992). New options for diagnosis and treatment of ectopic pregnancy. *Journal of the American Medical Association,* 267, 534–537.

Ostrov, E., Offer, D., Howard, K., Kaufman, B., & Meyer, H. (1985). Adolescent sexual behavior. *Medical Aspects of Human Sexuality,* 19, 28–31; 34–36.

Padawer, J., Fagan, C., Janoff-Bulman, R., Strickland, B., & Chorowski, M., (1988). Women's psychological adjustment following emergency cesarean versus vaginal delivery. *Psychology of Women Quarterly,* 12, 25–34.

Padesky, C. (1989). Attaining and maintaining positive lesbian self-identity: A cognitive therapy approach. *Women and Therapy,* 8, 145–156.

Padian, N. (1990). Paper presented at the sixth Annual International Conference on AIDS, San Francisco, June.

———, Shiboski, S., & Jewell, N. (1991). Female-to-male transmission of human immunodeficiency virus. *Journal of the American Medical Association,* 266, 1664–1667.

Page, D., Mosher, R., Simpson, E., Fisher, E., Mardon, G., Pollack, J., McGillivray, B., Chapelle, A., & Brown, L. (1987). The sex-determining region of the human Y chromosome encodes a finger protein. *Cell,* 51, 1091–1104.

Page, H. (1989). Estimation of the prevalence and incidence of infertility in a population: A pilot study. *American Fertility Society,* 51, 571–577.

Paige, K. (1978). The ritual of circumcision. *Human Nature,* 1, 40–48.

Palca, J. (1991). The sobering geography of AIDS. *Science,* 252, 372–373.

Palken, M., Cobb, O., Simons, C., Warren, B., & Aldape, H. (1991). Prostate cancer: Comparison of digital rectal examination and transrectal ultrasound for screening. *The Journal of Urology,* 145, 86–92.

Palson, C., & Palson, R. (1972). Swinging in wedlock. *Society,* 9, 43–48.

Pansky, M., Golan, A., Bukovsky, I., & Caspi, E. (1991). Nonsurgical management of tubal pregnancy. *American Journal of Obstetrics and Gynecology,* 164, 888–895.

Papadopoulos, C. (1991). Sex and the cardiac patient. *Medical Aspects of Human Sexuality,* August, 18–21.

Papini, D., Farmer, F., Clark, S., & Snell, W. (1988). An evaluation of adolescent patterns of sexual self-disclosure to parents and friends. *Journal of Adolescent Research,* 3, 387–401.

Paplau, L. (1981). What homosexuals want in relationships. *Psychology Today,* March, 28–38.

Parrot, A., & Allen, S. (1984). Acquaintance rape: Seduction or crime? Paper presented at the Eastern Regional Annual Conference of the Society for the Scientific Study of Sex, April.

———, & Bechhofer, L. (Eds.) (1991). *Acquaintance Rape: The Hidden Crime.* New York: Wiley.

Parrott, T. (1989). Summary of annual meeting of the section on pediatric urology. *Pediatrics,* 83, 591–596.

Parsons, J. (1983). Sexual socialization and gender roles in childhood. In E. Allgeier & N. McCormick (Eds.)., *Changing Boundaries: Gender Roles and Sexual Behavior.* Palo Alto, Calif.: Mayfield.

Pasquale, S. (1984). Rationale for a triphasic oral contraceptive. *Journal of Reproductive Medicine,* 29, 560–567.

Paterson, P., & Petrucco, A. (1987). Tubal factors and infertility. In R. Pepperell, B. Hudson, & C. Wood (Eds.)., *The Infertile Couple.* Edinburgh: Churchill Livingstone.

Patten, S., Gatz, Y., Jones, B., & Thomas, D. (1989). Posttraumatic stress disorders and the treatment of sexual abuse. *Social Work,* 34, 197–203.

Paul, J. (1984). The bisexual identity: An idea without social recognition. *Journal of Homosexuality,* 9, 45–63.

Pauly, I. (1974). Female transsexualism: Part II. *Archives of Sexual Behavior,* 3, 509–526.

———. (1990). Gender identity disorders: Evaluation and treatment. *Journal of Sex Education and Therapy,* 16, 2–24.

Pearlman, S. (1988). The saga of continuing clash in lesbian community, or will an army of ex-lovers fail? In Boston Lesbian Psychologies Collective (Eds.)., *Lesbian Psychologies.* Urbana: University of Illinois Press.

Pearson, L. (1992). The stigma of infertility. *Nursing Times,* 88(1), 36–38.

Peckman, M. (1988). Testicular cancer. *Acta Oncologica,* 27, 439–453.

Pelletier, L., & Herold, E. (1988). The relationship of age, sex guilt, and sexual experience with female sexual fantasies. *Journal of Sex Research,* 24, 250–256.

Penrod, S., & Linz, D. (1984). Using psychological research on violent pornography to inform legal change. In N. Malamuth & E. Donnerstein (Eds.)., *Pornography and Sexual Aggression.* Orlando: Academic Press.

Pepe, M., & Byrne, T. J. (1991). Women's perceptions of immediate and long-term effects of failed infertility treatment on marital and sexual satisfaction. *Family Relations,* 40, 303–309.

Pepitone-Rockwell, F. (1980). Counseling women to be less vulnerable to rape. *Medical Aspects of Human Sexology,* January, 145–146.

Perez, A., Labbok, M., & Queenan, J. (1992). Clinical study of the lactational amenorrhoea method for family planning. *Lancet,* 339, 968–970.

Perlman, J., et al. (1991). Re: "Vasectomy and the risk of prostate cancer." *American Journal of Epidemiology,* 134, 107–109.

Perry, J., & Whipple, B. (1981). Pelvic muscle strength of female ejaculators: Evidence in support of a new theory of orgasm. *Journal of Sex Research,* 17, 22–39.

Persky, H., Dresibach, L., Miller, W., O'Brien, C., Khan, M., Lief, H., Charnery, N., & Strauss, D. (1982). The relation of plasma androgen levels to sexual behavior and attitudes of women. *Psychosomatic Medicine,* 44, 305–319.

———, Lief, H., Strauss, D., Miller, W., & O'Brien, C. (1978). Plasma testosterone level and sexual behavior of couples. *Archives of Sexual Behavior,* 7, 157–173.

Peterman, T., Cates, W., & Curran, J. (1988). The challenge of human immunodeficiency virus (HIV). and acquired immunodeficiency syndrome (AIDS). in women and children. *Fertility and Sterility,* 49, 571–581.

Peterson, J., Hartsock, N., & Lawson, G. (1984). Sexual dissatisfaction of female alcoholics. *Psychological Reports,* 55, 744–746.

———, Kretchmer, A., Nellis, B., Lever, J., & Hertz, R. (1983). The *Playboy* readers sex survey, Part 2. *Playboy,* March, 90–92; 178–184.

Peterson, R. (1986). *Urologic Pathology.* Philadelphia: Lippincott.

Petitti, D., & Reingold, A. (1988). Tampon characteristics and menstrual toxic shock syndrome. *Journal of the American Medical Association,* 259, 686–687.

Petrovich, M., & Templer, D. (1984). Heterosexual molestation of children who later become rapists. *Psychological Reports,* 54, 810.

Pfeiffer, E. (1975). Sex and aging. In L. Gross (Ed.)., *Sexual Issues in Marriage.* New York: Spectrum.

Pfenninger, J. (1992). Colposcopy in a family practice residency. *Journal of Family Practice,* 34, 67–72.

Pfuhl, E. (1978). The unwed father: A "non-deviant" rule breaker. *Sociological Quarterly,* 19, 113–128.

Phelan, J., Ahn, M., Diaz, F., Brar, H., & Rodriguez, H. (1989). Twice a cesarean, always a cesarean? *Obstetrics and Gynecology,* 73, 161.

Phillips, R., Tuomala, R., Feldblum, P., Schachter, J., Rosenberg, M., & Aronson, M. (1992). The effect of cigarette smoking, chlamydia trachomatis infection and vaginal douching on ectopic pregnancy. *Obstetrics & Gynecology,* 79, 85–90.

Phipps, W., Cramer, D., Schiff, I., Belisle, S., Stillman, R., Albrecht, B., Gibson, M., Berger, M., & Wilson, E. (1987). The association between smoking and female infertility as influenced by cause of the infertility. *Fertility and Sterility,* 48, 377–382.

Phoenix, C., Goy, R., Gerall, A., & Young, W. (1959). Organizing action of prenatally administered testosterone propionate on the tissues mediating mating behavior in the female guinea pig. *Endocrinology,* 1959, 65, 369–382.

Piazza, M., Chirianni, A., Picciotto, L., Guadagnino, V., Orlando, R., & Cataldo, P. (1989). Passionate kissing and microlesions of the oral mucosa: Possible role in AIDS transmission. *Journal of the American Medical Association,* 261, 244–245.

Pietropinto, A., & Simenauer, J. (1979). *Husbands and Wives.* New York: Times Books.

Pinhas, V. (1985). Personal communication, June.

———. (1989). Treatment of sexual problems in chemically dependent women. *The Female Patient.*

Platz-Christensen, J., Larsson, P., Sundstrom, E., & Bondeson, L. (1989). Detection of bacterial vaginosis in Paponicolaou smears. *American Journal of Obstetrics and Gynecology,* 160, 132–133.

Pleck, J., Sonenstein, F., & Swain, S. (1988). Adolescent males' sexual behavior and contraceptive use: Implications for male responsibility. *Journal of Adolescent Research,* 3, 275–284.

Plummer, F., Simonsen, J., Cameron, D., Ndinya-Achola, J., Kreiss, J., Gakinya, M., Waiyaki, P., Cheang, M., Piot, P., Ronald, A., & Ngugi, E. (1991). Cofactors in male–female sexual transmission of human immunodeficiency virus type 1. *The Journal of Infectious Diseases,* 163, 233–239.

Polit-O'Hara, D., & Kahn, J. (1985). Communication and adolescent contraceptive practices in adolescent couples. *Adolescence,* 20, 33–43.

Pollack, A. (1991a). Colposcopy: Indications and technique. *Medical Aspects of Human Sexuality,* September, 42–49.

———. (1991b). Norplant: What you should know about the new contraceptive. *Medical Aspects of Human Sexuality,* January, 38–42.

———, & Girvin, S. (1992). When should an IUD be removed and replaced? *Medical Aspects of Human Sexuality,* 26(2), 46–58.

Pollack, S. (1990). Lesbian parents: Claiming our visibility. *Women & Therapy,* 10(1/2), 181–194.

Pomeroy, S. (1975). *Goddesses, Whores, Wives, and Slaves: Women in Classical Antiquity.* New York: Schocken Books.

Pomeroy, W. (1965). Why we tolerate lesbians. *Sexology,* May, 652–654.

Potts, J. (1992). Chlamydial infection: Screening and management update, 1992. *Postgraduate Medicine,* 91, 120–126.

Potts, M. (1991). The challenge of the 1990s. *IPPF Medical Bulletin,* 25, 1–4.

Pratt, C., & Schmall, V. (1989). College students' attitudes toward elderly sexual behavior: Implications for family life education. *Family Relations,* 38, 137–141.

Pratto, F., Bargh, J. (1991). Sterotyping based on apparently individuating information: Trait and global components of sex stereotypes under attention overload. *Journal of Experimental and Social Psychology,* 27, 26–47.

Prentky, R., Burgess, A., & Carter, D. (1986). Victim responses by rapist type: An empirical and clinical analysis. *Journal of Interpersonal Violence,* 1, 73–98.

Prescott, J. (1986). The abortion of ``The Silent Scream.'' *The Humanist,* 46, 10–17.

———. (1989). Affectional bonding for the prevention of violent behaviors: Neurological, psychological and religious/spiritual determinants. In L. Hertzberg (Ed.), *Violent Behavior. Vol. 1: Assessment and Intervention.* New York: PMA Publishing.

Preston, B., Poiesz, B., & Loeb, L. (1988). Fidelity of HIV-1 reverse transcriptase. *Science,* 242, 1168–1171.

Preston, S. (1975). Estimating the proportion of American marriages that end in divorce. *Sociological Methods and Research,* 3, 435–460.

Price, V., Scanlon, B., & Janus, M-D. (1984). Social characteristics of adolescent male prostitution. *Victimology,* 9, 211–221.

Price, W., Dimarzio, L., & Gardner, P. (1986). Bio[chpsychosocial approach to premenstrual syndrome. *American Family Physician,* 33, 117–122.

Prince, V., & Bentler, P. (1972). Survey of 504 cases of transvestism. *Psychological Reports,* 31, 903–917.

Prior, J., & Vigna, Y. (1987). Conditioning exercise and premenstrual symptoms. *Journal of Reproductive Medicine,* 32, 423–428.

———, & ———. (1991). Ovulation disturbances and exercise training. *Clinical Obstetrics and Gynecology,* 34, 180–190.

Proctor, F., Wagner, N., & Butler, J. (1974). The differentiation of male and female orgasm: An experimental study. In N. Wagner (Ed.)., *Perspectives on Human Sexuality.* New York: Behavioral Publications.

Przbyla, D., & Byrne, D. (1984). The mediating role of cognitive processes in self-regulated sexual arousal. *Journal of Research in Personality,* 18, 54–63.

Pugeat, M., Lejeune, H., Dechaud, H., Emptoz-Bonneton, A., Fleury, M., Charrie, A., Tourniaire, J., & Forest, M. (1987). Effects of drug administration of gonadotropins, sex steroid hormones and binding proteins in humans. *Hormone Research,* 28, 261–273.

Purcell, S. (1985). Relation between religious orthodoxy and marital sexual functioning. Paper presented at a meeting of the American Psychological Association, Los Angeles, August 25.

Purifoy, F., Martin, C., & Tobin, J. (1983). Age-related variation in female sexual arousal. Paper presented at the Twenty-Sixth Annual Meeting of the Society for the Scientific Study of Sex, Chicago, November 18–20.

Puzo, M. (1969). *The Godfather.* Greenwich, Conn.: Fawcett Books.

Quadagno, D., & Sprague, J. (1991). Reasons for having sex. *Medical Aspects of Human Sexuality,* June, 52.

Quinsey, V., Chaplin, T., & Upfold, D. (1984). Sexual arousal to nonsexual violence and sadomasochistic themes among rapists and non–sex-offenders. *Journal of Consulting and Clinical Psychology,* 52, 4, 651–657.

———, & Upfold, D. (1985). Rape completion and victim injury as a function of female resistance strategy. *Canadian Journal of Behavior Science,* 17, 40–50.

Rabe, T., Thuro, H., Goebel, K., Borchardt, C., Grunwald, K., & Runnebaum, B. (1992). Lipid metabolism in Norplant-2 users: A two-year follow-up study. *Contraception,* 45, 21.

Rachman, S. (1966). Sexual fetishism: An experimental analogue. *Psychological Record,* 16, 293–296.

Rada, R. (1975). Alcoholism and forcible rape. *American Journal of Psychiatry,* 132, 444–446.

———. (1976). Alcoholism and the child molester. *Annals of the New York Academy of Sciences,* 273, 492–496.

Radar, C. (1977). MMPI profile types of exposers, rapists, and assaulters in a court service population. *Journal of Consulting and Clinical Psychology,* 45, 61–69.

Ragg, D. M., & Rowe, W. (1991). The effective use of group in sex education with people diagnosed as mildly developmentally disabled. *Sexuality and Disability,* 9(4), 337–352.

Rajfer, J., Aronson, W., Bush, P., Dorey, F., & Ignarro, L. (1992). Nitric oxide as a mediator of relaxation of the corpus cavernosum in response to nonadrenergic, noncholinergic neurotransmission. *The New England Journal of Medicine,* 326, 90–94.

Rao, M., Wilkinson, J., & Benton, D. (1991). Screening for undescended testes. *Archives of Disease in Children,* 66, 934–937.

Rapaport, R., & Burkhart, B. (1984). Personality and attitudinal characteristics of sexually coercive college males. *Journal of Abnormal Psychology,* 93, 216–221.

Raphael, S., & Robinson, M. (1980). *Alternative Lifestyles,* 3, 207–229.

Rapp, F. (1982). Structure and function of the virus: Latency of herpes simplex virus. Paper presented at the Herpes Symposium, Oregon Health Sciences University, Portland, April 2.

Reamy, K., & Reamy, E. (1991). The climacteric: Sexual myths and realities. *Medical Aspects of Human Sexuality,* September, 20–26.

Reamy, K. J. (1991). A management guide to postpartum problems. *Medical Aspects of Human Sexuality,* January, 20–24.

Rebeta-Burditt, J. (1978). *The Cracker Factory.* New York: Bantam Books.

Reid, K., Surridge, D., Morales, A., Condra, M., Harris, C., Owen, J., & Fenemore, J. (1987). Double-blind trial of yohimbine in treatment of psychogenic impotence. *Lancet,* 2, 421–423.

Reid, R. (1991). Premenstrual syndrome. *New England Journal of Medicine,* 324, 1208–1210.

Reilly, M., Lott, B., Caldwell, D., & Deluca, L. (1992). Tolerance for sexual harassment related to self-reported sexual victimization. *Gender and Society,* 6, 122–138.

Rein, M. (1985). Condoms and STDs: Do the former prevent transmission of the latter? *Medical Aspects of Human Sexuality,* 19, 113; 116–117.

Reinisch, J., Ziemba-Davis, M., & Sanders, S. (1991). Hormonal contributions to sexually dimorphic behavioral development in humans. *Psychoneuroendocrinology,* 16, 213–278.

Reiss, A. (1964). The social integration of queers and peers. In H. Becker (Ed.)., *The Other Side.* New York: Free Press.

Reiss, I. (1986). *Journey into Sexuality: An Exploratory Voyage.* Englewood Cliffs, N.J.: Prentice-Hall.

Remafedi, G. (1987a). Male homosexuality: The adolescents' perspective. *Pediatrics,* 79, 326–330.

———. (1987b). Adolescent homosexuality: Psychosocial and medical implications. *Pediatrics,* 79, 331–337.

Renshaw, D. (1987a). Management of impotence: Psychological considerations. *Clinical Therapy,* 9, 142.

———. (1987b). Painful intercourse associated with cerebral palsy. *Journal of the American Medical Association,* 257, 2086.

———. (1990). Short-term therapy for sexual dysfunction: Brief counseling to manage vaginismus. *Clinical Practice in Sexuality,* 6(5), 23–29.

———. (1991). Female "wet dreams." *Medical Aspects of Human Sexuality,* January, 63.

Research Forecasts, Inc. (1981). *The Tampax Report: A Summary of Survey Results on a Study of Attitudes Toward Menstruation.* New York: Tampax Incorporated.

Rice, S., & Kelly, J. (1987). Love and intimacy needs of the elderly: Some philosophical and intervention issues. *Journal of Social Work and Human Sexuality,* 5, 89–96.

Rich, A. (1976). *Of Woman Born.* New York: Norton.

Richards, L., Rollerson, B., Phillips, J. (1991). Perceptions of submissiveness: Implications for victimization. *The Journal of Psychology,* 125, 407–411.

Riche, M. (1988). Postmarital society. *American Demographics,* November 23–26, 60.

Rietmeijer, C., Krebs, J., Feorino, P., & Judson, F. (1988). Condoms as physical and chemical barriers against human immunodeficiency virus. *Journal of the American Medical Association,* 259, 1851–1853.

Riger, S. (1991). Gender dilemmas in sexual harassment policies and procedures. *American Psychologist,* 46, 497–505.

Riley, A. (1983). Androgens and female sexuality. *British Journal of Sexual Medicine,* 10, 5–6.

Rio, L. (1991). Psychological and sociological research and the decriminalization or legalization of prostitution. *Archives of Sexual Behavior,* 20, 205–217.

Ritz, S. (1981). How to deal with menstrual cramps. *Medical Self-Care,* Spring, 17–22.

Rivlin, M. (1992). Chlamydia in pregnancy: Who should be tested? *Medical Aspects of Human Sexuality,* 26, 27–31.

Robbins, M., & Jensen, G. (1978). Multiple orgasm in males. *Journal of Sex Research,* 14, 21–26.

Robbins, S., Templer, D., Brown, R., & Veaco, L. (1987). Parameters of sexual contact of boys with women. *Archives of Sexual Behavior,* 16, 379–384.

Roberto, L. (1983). Issues in diagnosis and treatment of transsexualism. *Archives of Sexual Behavior,* 12, 445–473.

Roberts, J. (1990). Is routine circumcision indicated in the newborn? An affirmative view. *The Journal of Family Practice,* 31, 185–196.

Robinson, G. (1989). Premenstrual syndrome: Current knowledge and management. *Canadian Medical Association Journal,* 140, 605–611.

———, Garner, C., Gare, D., & Crawford, B. (1987). Psychological adaptation to pregnancy in childless women more than 35 years of age. *American Journal of Obstetrics and Gynecology,* 156, 323–328.

Robinson, J. (1983). Cervical cancer: Occupational risks. *Lancet,* 2, 1496–1497.

Rodgers, C. (1987). Sex roles in education. In D. Hargraves & A. Colley (Eds.)., *The Psychology of Sex Roles.* New York: Hemisphere.

Rodman, H., Sarvis, G., & Bonar, J. (1987). *The Abortion Question.* New York: Columbia University Press.

Roel, J., & Gray, D. (1984). The crises of rape: A guide to counseling victims of rape. *Crises Intervention,* 13, 67–77.

Roeleveld, N., Vingerhoets, E., Zielhuis, G., & Gabreels, F. (1992). Mental retardation associated with parental smoking and alcohol consumption before, during and after pregnancy. *Preventive Medicine,* 21, 110–119.

Rogel, J. (1978). A critical evaluation of the possibility of higher primate reproductive and sexual pheromones. *Psychological Bulletin,* 85, 810–830.

Rogers, C. (1951). *Client-Centered Therapy: Its Current Practice, Implications, and Theory.* Boston: Houghton Mifflin.

Rohrbaugh, J. (1988). Choosing children: Psychological issues in lesbian parenting. *Women and Therapy,* 8, 51–64.

Roland, D., Greenleaf, W., Mas, M., Myers, L., & Davison, J. (1989). Penile and finger sensory thresholds in young, aging, and diabetic males. *Journal of the American Medical Association,* 18, 1–11.

Roman, L., Morris, M., Eifel, P., Burke, T., Gershenson, D., & Wharton, J. T. (1992). Reasons for inappropriate simple hysterectomy in the presence of invasive cancer of the cervix. *Obstetrics & Gynecology,* 79, 485–489.

Rooney, J., Felser, J., Ostrove, J., & Straus, S. (1986). Acquisition of genital herpes from an asymptomatic sexual partner. *New England Journal of Medicine,* 314, 1561–1564.

Rooth, F., & Marks, I. (1974). Persistent exhibitionism: Short-term response to aversion, self-regulation, and relaxation treatment. *Archives of Sexual Behavior,* 3, 227–248.

Roscoe, B., Goodwin, M., Repp. S., & Rose, M. (1987). Sexual harassment of university student and student–employees: Findings and implications. *College Student Journal,* 12, 254–273.

———, Kruger, T. (1990). AIDS: Late adolescents' knowledge and its influence on sexual behavior. *Adolescence,* 25, 39–48.

Rosen, M., Greenfield, A., Walker, T. G. (1991). Cigarette smoking: An independent risk factor for atherosclerosis in the hypogastric-cavernous arterial bed. *Urology,* 145, 759.

Rosen, R. (1991). Alcohol and drug effects on sexual response: Human experimental and clinical studies. *Annual Review of Sex Research,* 2, 119–179.

———, & Beck, J. (1988). *Patterns of Sexual Arousal*. New York: Guilford Press.

Rosenberg, M. (1988). Adult behaviors that reflect childhood incest. *Medical Aspects of Human Sexuality*, May, 114–124.

Rosenfeld, W., (1991). Sexually transmitted diseases in adolescents: Update 1991. *Pediatric Annals*, 20, 303–312.

Rosenkrantz, P., Vogel, S., Bee, H., Broverman, I., & Broverman, D. (1968). Sex-role stereotypes and self concepts in college students. *Journal of Consulting and Clinical Psychology*, 32, 287–295.

Rosenthal, E. (1991). New look at birth control choices. *The New York Times Health*, August 21, 5.

Rosenthal, S. (1987). *Sex over 40*. New York: St. Martin's Press.

Ross, M., & Arrindell, W. (1988). Perceived parental rearing patterns of homosexual and heterosexual men. *Journal of Sex Research*, 24, 275–281.

———, & Need, J. (1989). Effects of adequacy of gender reassignment surgery on psychological adjustment: A follow-up of fourteen male-to-female patients. *Archives of Sexual Behavior*, 18, 145–153.

Rossignol, A., & Bonnlander, H. (1991). Prevalence and severity of the premenstrual syndrome. Effects of foods and beverages that are sweet or high in sugar content. *Journal of Reproductive Medicine*, 36, 131–136.

Roth, S., Dye, E., & Lebowitz, L. (1988). Group therapy for sexual-assault victims. *Psychotherapy*, 25, 82–93.

Rothblum, E. (1989). Introduction: Lesbianism as a model of a positive lifestyle for women. *Women and Therapy*, 8, 1–12.

Rotheram, M., & Weiner, N. (1983). Androgyny, stress, and satisfaction. *Sex Roles*, 9, 151–158.

Rotolo, J., & Lynch, J. (1991). Penile cancer: Curable with early detection. *Hospital Practice*, June 15, 131–138.

Roumeliotou-Karayannis, A., Nestoridou, K., Mandalaki, T., Stefanou, T., & Papaevangelou, G. (1988). Heterosexual transmission of HIV in Greece. *AIDS Research and Human Retroviruses*, 4, 233–236.

Rousseau, L., Couture, M., Dupont, A., Labrie, F., & Couture, N. (1990). Effect of combined androgen blockade with LHRH agonist and flutamide in one severe case of male exhibitionism. *Canadian Journal of Psychiatry*, 35, 338–341.

———, Dupont, A., Labrie, F., & Couture, M. (1988). Sexuality changes in prostate cancer patients receiving antihormonal therapy combining the antiandrogen flutamide with medical (LHRH agonist). or surgical castration. *Archives of Sexual Behavior*, 17, 87–90.

Roy, R., & Roy, D. (1973). Is monogamy outdated? In E. Morrison & V. Borosage (Eds.)., *Human Sexuality: Contemporary Perspectives*. Palo Alto, Calif.: National Press Books.

Royston, J., Humphrey, S., Flynn, A., Marshall, J., & Zarzosa-Berez, A. (1984). An automatic electronic device (Rite Time). to detect the onset of the infertile period by basal body temperature measurements. *British Journal of Obstetrics and Gynaecology*, 91, 565–573.

Ruben, D. (1992). Saying no to nursing. *Parenting*, March, 21.

Rubenstein, C. (1983). The modern art of courtly love. *Psychology Today*, July, 39–49.

Rubin, J., Provenzano, F., & Luria, Z. (1974). The eye of the beholder: Parents' views on sex of newborns. *American Journal of Orthopsychiatry*, 44, 512–519.

Rubin, L. (1976). *Worlds of Pain: Life in the Working Class Family*. New York: Basic Books.

Rubin, R., Reinisch, J., & Haskett, R. (1981). Postnatal gonadal steroid effects on human behavior. *Science*, 1318–1324.

Rubin, Z. (1970). Measurement of romantic love. *Journal of Personality and Social Psychology*, 16, 265–273.

———. (1973). *Liking and Loving*. New York: Holt, Rinehart & Winston.

Rubinsky, H., Eckerman, D., Rubinsky, E., & Hoover, C. (1987). Early-phase physiological response patterns to psychosexual stimuli: Comparisons of male and female patterns. *Archives of Sexual Behavior*, 16, 45–55.

Ruch, L., Amedeo, S., Gartrell, J., & Coyne, B. (1991). The sexual assault symptom scale: Measuring self-reported sexual assault trauma in the emergency room. *Psychological Assessment: A Journal of Consulting and Clinical Psychology*, 3, 3–8.

Ruefli, T., Olivia, Y., & Barton, J. (1992). Sexual risk taking in smaller cities: The case of Buffalo, New York. *The Journal of Sex Research*, 29, 95–108.

Ruffin, M., & Van Noord, G. (1991). Improving the yield of endocervical elements in a pap smear with the use of the cytology brush. *Family Medicine*, 23, 365–369.

Rush, F. (1980). *The Best Kept Secret: Sexual Abuse of Children*. Englewood Cliffs, N.J.: Prentice-Hall.

Russell, D. (1980). Pornography and violence: What does the new research say? In L. Lederer (Ed.)., *Take Back the Night: Women on Pornography*. New York: Morrow.

———. (1984). *Sexual Exploitation: Rape, Child Sexual Abuse, and Workplace Harrassment*. Beverly Hills, Calif.: Sage.

———.1982). *Rape in Marriage*. Riverside, N.J.: Macmillan.

Ryan, K. (1992). Abortion or motherhood, suicide and madness. *American Journal of Obstetrics and Gynecology*, 166, 1029–1036.

Rynd, N. (1987). Incidence of psychosomatic symptoms in rape victims. *Journal of Sex Research*, 24, 155–161.

Saario, T., Jacklin, C., & Tittle, C. (1973). Sex role stereotyping in public schools. *Harvard Educational Review*, 43, 386–416.

Sabatelli, R., Meth, R., & Gavazzi, S. (1988). Factors mediating the adjustment to involuntary childlessness. *Family Relations*, 37, 388.

Sacco, W., Levine, B., Reed, D., & Thompson, K. (1991). Attitudes about condom use as an AIDS-relevant behavior: Their factor structure and relation to condom use. *Psychological Assessment: A Journal of Consulting and Clinical Psychology*, 3, 265–272.

Sacks, S., Fox, R., Levendusky, P., Stiver, G., Roland, S., Nusinoff-Lehrman, S., & Keeney, R. (1988). Chronic suppression for six months compared with intermittent lesional therapy of recurrent genital herpes using oral acyclovir: Effects on lesions and nonlesional prodromes. *Sexually Transmitted Diseases*, 15, 58–62.

Sadker, M., & Sadker, D. (1985). Sexism in the school room of the 80s. *Psychology Today*, 19, 54, 57.

Sadler, S. (1992). What it's really like to be pregnant. *Professional Care of Mother and Child,* February, 48.

Safran, C. (1976). What men do to women on the job: A shocking look at sexual harassment. *Redbook,* November, 148 ff.

————. (1981). Sexual harassment: The view from the top. *Redbook,* March, 47–51.

Safrin, S., Schachter, J., Dahrouge, D., & Sweet, R. (1992). Long-term sequelae of acute pelvic inflammatory disease. *American Journal of Obstetrics and Gynecology,* 166, 1300–1305.

Saghir, M., & Robins, E. (1973). *Male and Female Homosexuality: A Comprehensive Investigation.* Baltimore: Williams & Wilkins.

Salameh, W., McAdams, L., Bhasin, S., Peterson, M., Steiner, B., & Swerdloff, R. (1991). Marked suppression of gonadotropins and testosterone by an antagonist analog of gonadotropin-releasing hormone in men. *Fertility and Sterility,* 55, 156–164.

Sales, E., Baum, M., & Shore, B. (1984). Victim readjustment following assault. *Journal of Social Issues,* 40, 117–136.

Salholz, E. (1990a). The future of gay America. *Newsweek,* March 12, 20–25.

————. (1990b). Politics and the pill. *Newsweek,* February 26, 42.

Salisbury, N. (1991). Personal communication.

Salovey, P., & Rodin, J. (1985). The heart of jealousy. *Psychology Today,* September, 22–29.

Samet, J. (1991). Editorial commentary: New effects of active and passive smoking on reproduction? *American Journal of Epidemiology,* 133, 348–350.

Samuels, J., Vlaho, D., Anthony, J., & Chaisson, R. (1992). Measurement of HIV risk behaviors among intravenous drug users. *British Journal of Addiction,* 87, 417–428.

Sanday, P. (1981). The socio-cultural context of rape: A cross-cultural study. *Journal of Social Issues,* 37, 5–27.

Sanders, D., & Sambo, A. (1991). AIDS in Africa: The implications of economic recession and structural adjustment. *Health Policy and Planning,* 6, 157–165.

Sanders, G. (1982). Social comparison as a basis for evaluating others. *Journal of Research in Personality,* 16, 21–31.

————, & Cairns, K., & Mullis, R. (1988). Family influence on sexual attitudes and knowledge as reported by college students. Adolescence, 23, 837–846.

————, & Mullis, R. (1988). Family influences on sexual attitudes and knowledge as reported by college students. *Adolescence,* 23, 837–845.

Sarrell, P. (1980). Male rape. Paper presented at the Annual Meeting of the International Academy of Sex Research, Phoenix, Ariz., November.

————. (1988). Sex and menopause. Paper presented at the Twenty-First Annual Meeting of the American Association of Sex Educators, Counselors, and Therapists, San Francisco, April.

————. (1990). Genital blood flow and ovarian secretions. *Clinical Practice in Sexuality,* Special Issue, 14–15.

————, & Masters, W. (1982). Sexual molestation of men by women. *Archives of Sexual Behavior,* 11, 117–131.

Satterfield, A., & Muehlenhard, C. (1990). Flirtation in the classroom: Negative consequences on women's perceptions of their ability. Paper presented at the annual meeting of the Society for the Scientific Study of Sex, Minneapolis, Minn., November.

Saunders, D., Fisher, W., Hewitt, E., & Clayton, J. (1985). A method for empirically assessing volunteer selection effects: Recruitment procedures and responses to erotica. *Journal of Personality and Social Psychology,* 49, 1703–1712.

Saunders, J., & Edwards, J. (1984). Extramarital sexuality: A predictive model of permissive attitudes. *Journal of Marriage and the Family,* 46, 825–835.

Savitz, L., & Rosen, L. (1988). The sexuality of prostitutes: Sexual enjoyment reported by ``streetwalkers.'' *Journal of Sex Research,* 24, 200–208.

Saxer, J. (1989). *Chlamydia trachomatis* genital infections in a community-based family practice clinic. *Journal of Family Practice,* 28, 41–47.

Scanlon, J. (1974). Obstetric anesthesia as a neonatal risk factor in normal labor and delivery. *Clinics in Perinatology,* 1, 465–482.

Schachter, J. (1989). Why we need a program for the control of *Chlamydia trachomatis.* New England Journal of Medicine, 320, 802–804.

————, Moncada, J., Dawson, C., Sheppard, J., Courtright, P., Said, M., Zaki, S., Hafex, S., & Lorincz, A. (1988). Nonculture methods for diagnosing *Chlamydia* infection in patients with trachoma: A clue to the pathogenesis of the disease. *Journal of Infectious Diseases,* 158, 1347–1352.

Schaeffer, A. (1990). Editorial comment. *Journal of Urology,* 143, 226.

Schecter, M., Jeffries, E., Constance, P., Douglas, B., Fay, S., Maynard, M., Nitz, R., Willoughby, B., Boyko, W., & MacLeod, A. (1984). Changes in sexual behavior and fear of AIDS. *Lancet,* June 9, 1293.

Scheig, R. (1991). The hepatitis viruses: Who's at risk? *Medical Aspects of Human Sexuality,* March, 23–26.

Schiavi, R. (1990). Sexuality and aging in men. *Annual Review of Sex Research,* 1, 227–249.

————. (1992). Laboratory methods for evaluating erectile dysfunction. In R. Rosen & S. Leiblum (Eds.), *Erectile Disorders.* New York: Guilford Press.

Schifeling, D., & Hamblin, J. (1991). Early diagnosis of breast cancer. *Postgraduate Medicine,* 89(3), 55–61.

Schlegel, P. (1991). New treatment options for the infertile man. *Medical Aspects of Human Sexuality,* June, 22–31.

Schlesselman, J., Stadel, B., Murray, P., & Lai, S. (1988). Breast cancer in relation to early use of oral contraceptives. *Journal of the American Medical Association,* 259, 1828–1833.

Schmader, K., Studenski, S., & MacMillan, J. (1990). Are stressful life events risk factors for herpes zoster? *Journal of the American Geriatric Society,* 38, 1188–1194.

Schmidt, J. (1992). Localized prostate cancer: Prostatectomy versus interstitial implantation. *Journal of Surgical Oncology,* 49, 1–2

Schmidt, P., Nieman, L., Grover, G., Muller, K., Merriam, G., & Rubinow, D. (1991). Lack of effect of induced menses on symptoms in women with premenstrual syndrome. *New England Journal of Medicine,* 324, 1174–1179.

Schneebaum, T. (1975). Notes and observations on Mascho Amarataire and Huachipairi. In C. A. Tripp, *The Homosexual Matrix.* New York: McGraw-Hill.

Schneider, M., & Tremble, B.(1986). Gay or straight? Working with the confused adolescent. *Journal of Social Work and Human Sexuality,* 4, 71–82.

Schoen, E., & Fischell, A. (1991). Pain in neonatal circumcision. *Clinical Pediatrics,* 30, 429–432.

Schoen, E., Anderson, G., Bohon, C., Hinman, F., Poland, R., & Wakeman, E. (1989). Report of the Task Force on Circumcision. *Pediatrics,* 84, 388–391.

Schover, L. (1988). *Sexuality and Cancer.* New York: American Cancer Society.

———. (1989). Sexual problems in chronic illness. In S. Leiblum & R. Rosen (Eds.), *Principles and Practice of Sex Therapy.* New York: Guilford Press.

———, Friedman, J., Weiler, S., Heiman, J., & LoPiccolo, J. (1982). Multiaxial problem-oriented system for sexual dysfunctions. *Archives of General Psychiatry,* 39, 614–619.

———, & Jensell, S. (1988). *Sexuality and Chronic Illness.* New York: Guilford Press.

———, Thomas, A., Lakin, M., Montague, D., & Fischer, J. (1988). Orgasm phase dysfunction in multiple sclerosis. *Journal of Sex Research,* 25, 548–554.

Schreiner-Engle, P., & Schiavi, R. (1986). Lifetime psychopathology in individuals with low sexual desire. *Journal of Nervous and Mental Disease,* 174, 646–651.

———, ———, Veitorisz, D., and Smith, H. (1987). The differential impact of diabetes type on female sexuality. *Journal of Psychosomatic Research,* 31, 23–33.

Schrinsky, D. (1988). Personal communication, January.

Schultz, W., van de Wiel, H., Klatter, J., Sturm, B., & Nauta, J. (1989). Vaginal sensitivity to electric stimuli: Theoretical and practical implications. *Journal of the American Medical Association,* 18, 87–94.

Schuster, R. (1988). Sexuality as a continuum: The bisexual identity. In The Boston Lesbian Psychologies Collective (Eds.), *Lesbian Psychologies.* Urbana: University of Illinois Press.

Schwarcz, S., Bolan, G., Fullilove, M., McCright, J., Fullilove, R., Kohn, R., & Rolfs, R. (1992). Crack cocaine and the exchange of sex for money or drugs. *Sexually Transmitted Diseases,* 19, 7–13.

Schwartz, J., & Kaplan, D. (1992). They're only trying to help. *Newsweek,* January 27, 47.

Schwartz, L. (1989). Surrogate motherhood III: The end of a saga? *American Journal of Family Therapy,* 17, 67–73.

Schwartz, M., & Masters, W. (1988). Inhibited sexual desire: The Masters and Johnson Institute treatment model. In S. Lieblum and R. Rosen (Eds.)., *Sexual Desire Disorders.* New York: Guilford Press.

Schwartz, P. (1984). The changing nature of American relationships—heterosexual and homosexual. Paper presented at Regional Conference, American Association of Sex Educators, Counselors, and Therapists, Las Vegas, October.

———. (1990). The future is the past: Gay custody decisions. Paper presented at The Society for the Scientific Study of Sex Annual Western Region Conference, San Diego, Calif., April 25.

———, & Blumstein, P. (173). Bisexuality: Some sociological observations. Paper presented at the Chicago Conference on Bisexual Behavior, October 6.

Schwebke, J. (1991a). Gonorrhea in the '90s. *Medical Aspects of Human Sexuality,* March, 43–46.

———. (1991b). Syphilis in the '90s. *Medical Aspects of Human Sexuality,* April, 44–49.

Schweiger, U. (1991). Menstrual function and luteal-phase deficiency in relation to weight changes and dieting. *Clinical Obstetrics and Gynecology,* 34, 191–197.

Scott, J., & Cuvelier, S. (1987). Sexual violence in *Playboy* magazine: A longitudinal content analysis. *Journal of Sex Research,* 28, 534–539.

———, & Schwalm, L. (1988). Rape rates and the circulation rates of adult magazines. *Journal of Sex Research* 24, 241–250.

Scully, D., & Marolla, J. (1984). Convicted rapists' vocabulary of motives. Excuses and justifications. *Social Problems,* 31, 530–544.

Seagraves, K. (1989). Extramarital affairs. *Medical Aspects of Human Sexuality.* April, 99–105.

Seaman, B., & Seaman, G. (1978). *Women and the Crisis in Sex Hormones,* New York: Bantam Books.

Sedney, M. (1987). Development of androgyny: Parental influences.*Psychology of Women Quarterly,* 11, 311–326.

Segal, E. (1991). Social policy and intervention with chemically dependent women and their children. *Child and Adolescent Social Work,* 8, 285–290.

Segal, Z., & Marshall, W. (1985). Heterosexual social skills in a population of rapists and child molesters. *Journal of Consulting and Clinical Psychology,* 53, 55–63.

Seghorn, T., Prentky, R., & Boucher, R. (1987). Childhood sexual abuse in the lives of sexually aggressive offenders. *Journal of the American Academy of Child and Adolescent Psychiatry,* 26, 262–267.

Segraves, R. (1989). Effects of psychotropic drugs on human erection and ejaculation. *Archives of General Psychiatry,* 46, 275–284.

Segraves, R. T., & Segraves, K. (1992). Aging and drug effects on male sexuality. In R. Rosen & S. Leiblum (Eds.), *Erectile Disorders.* New York: Guilford Press.

Seibel, M. (1988). A new era in reproductive technology, *New England Journal of Medicine,* 318, 828–834.

Seibel, M. M., Freeman, M., & Graves, W. (1980). Carcinoma of the cervix and sexual function. *Obstetrics and Gynecology,* 55, 484–487.

Seligmann, J. (1984). The date who rapes. *Newsweek,* April 9, 91–92.

———. (1992). A condom for women moves one step closer to reality. *Newsweek,* February 10, 45.

———. (1992). Is my baby all right? *Newsweek,* June 22, 62–63.

———, & Church, V. (1992). A vote of no confidence. *Newsweek,* March 2, 75.

Semans, J. (1956). Premature ejaculation, a new approach. *Southern Medical Journal,* 49, 353–358.

Serbin, L. (1980). The Pinks and the Blues. In *Nova,* Boston: WGBH Transcripts.

Serdula, M., Williamson, D., Kendrick, J., Anda, R., & Byers, T. (1991). Trends in alcohol consumption by pregnant women. *Journal of the American Medical Association,* 265, 876–879.

Sevely, J., & Bennett, J. (1978). Concerning female ejaculation and the female prostate. *Journal of Sex Research,* 14, 1–20.

Shain, R., Miller, W., Holden, A., & Rosenthal, M. (1991). Impact of tubal sterilization and vasectomy on female marital sexuality: Results of a controlled longitudinal study. *American Journal of Obstetrics and Gynecology,* 164, 763–771.

Shainess, N., & Greenwald, H. (1971). Debate: Are fantasies during sexual relations a sign of difficulty? *Sexual Behavior,* 1, 38–54.

Shangold, M. (1980). Sports and menstrual function. *The Physician and Sports Medicine.* 8, 66–70.

———. (1985). Causes, evaluation, and management of athletic oligoamenorrhea. *Medical Clinics of North America,* 69, 83–95.

Shapiro, J. (1987). The expectant father. *Psychology Today,* January, 36–42.

Shaul, S., Bogle, J., Hale-Harbaugh, J., & Norman, A. (1978). *Toward Intimacy: Family Planning and Sexuality Concerns of Physically Disabled Women.* New York: Human Sciences Press.

Sheehan, K., Casper, R., & Yen, S. (1982). Luteal phase defects induced by an agonist of luteinizing hormone-releasing factor: A model for fertility control. *Science,* 215, 170–172.

Sheehy, G. (1973). *Hustling.* New York: Delacorte.

Sheeran, P. (1987). *Women, Society, the State and Abortion: A Structuralist Analysis.* New York: Praeger.

Sheinberg, M., & Penn, P. (1991). Gender dilemmas, gender questions, and the gender mantra. *Journal of Marital and Family Therapy,* 17, 33–44.

Sherfey, M. (1972). *The Nature and Evolution of Female Sexuality.* New York: Random House.

Sherwen, L. (1987). *Psychosocial Dimensions of the Pregnant Family.* New York: Springer.

Sherwin, B. (1988). A comparative analysis of the role of androgens in human male and female sexual behavior: Behavior specificity, critical thresholds and sensitivity. *Psychobiology,* 16, 416–425.

———. (1991). The psychoendocrinology of aging and female sexuality. *Annual Review of Sex Research,* 2, 181–186.

———, Gelfand, M., & Brender, W. (1985). Androgen enhances sexual motivation in females: A prospective crossover study of sex steroid administration in the surgical menopause. *Psychosomatic Medicine.* 47, 339–351.

Shoham, Z., Zosmer, A., & Insler, V. (1991). Early miscarriage and fetal malformations after induction of ovulation (by clomiphene citrate and/or human menotropins), in vitro fertilization, and gamete intrafallopian transfer. *Fertility and Sterility,* 55, 1–11.

Sholty, M., Ephross, P., Plaut, S., Fischman, S., Charnas, J., & Cody, C. (1984). Female orgasmic experience: A subjective study. *Archives of Sexual Behavior,* 13, 155–164.

Shostak, A. (1979). Abortion as fatherhood lost: Problems and reforms. *Family Coordinator,* 28, 569–574.

———, McLouth, G., & Seng, L. (1984). *Men and Abortions: Lessons, Losses and Love.* New York: Praeger.

Shoupe, D., Mishell, D., Jr., Bopp, B., & Fielding, M. (1991). The significance of bleeding patterns in Norplant implant users. *Obstetrics & Gynecology,* 77, 256–261.

Siegal, M. (1987). Are sons and daughters treated more differently by fathers than by mothers? *Developmental Review,* 7, 183-209.

Siegel, J., Sorenson, S., Golding, J., Burnam, M., & Stein, J. (1989). Resistance to sexual assault: Who resists and what happens? *American Journal of Public Health,* 79, 27–31.

Silber, S., & Cohen, R. (1984). Microsurgical reversal of tubal sterilization: Factors affecting pregnancy rate, with long-term follow-up. *Obstetrics and Gynecology,* 64, 679–682.

Siller, B., & Azziz, R. (1991). New ways of managing ectopic pregnancy. *Medical Aspects of Human Sexuality,* March, 30–39.

Silver, R., Straus, F., Vogelzang, N., Kellman, H., & Chodak, G. (1991). Response to orchidectomy following Zoladex therapy for metastatic prostate carcinoma. *Urology,* 37, 17–21.

Silverman, S. (1989). Scope, specifics of maternal drug use, effects on fetus are beginning to emerge from studies. *Journal of the American Medical Association,* 261, 1688–1689.

Simenauer, J., & Carroll, D. (1982). *Singles: The New Americans.* New York: Simon & Schuster.

Singer, J., & Singer, I. (1972). Types of female orgasms. *Journal of Sex Research,* 8, 255–267.

Singleton, C. (1987). Sex roles in cognition. In D. Hargraves & A. Colley (Eds.)., *The Psychology of Sex Roles.* New York: Hemisphere.

Sivin, I., Stern, J., Diaz, S., Pavez, M., Alvarez, F., Brache, V., Mishell, D., Jr., Lacarra, M., McCarthy, T., Holma, P., Darney, P., Klaisle, C., Olsson, S., & Odlind, V. (1992). Rates and outcomes of planned pregnancy after use of Norplant capsules, Norplant II rods, or levonorgestrel-releasing or copper TCu 380Ag intrauterine contraceptive devices. *American Journal of Obstetrics and Gynecology,* 166, 1208–1213.

Skene, A. (1980). Two important glands of the urethra. *American Journal of Obstetrics,* 265, 265–270.

Skolnick, A. (1992). Ultrasound may help detect breast implant leaks. *Journal of the American Medical Association,* 267, 786.

Slaughter, L., & Brown, C. (1992). Colposcopy to establish physical findings in rape victims. *American Journal of Obstetrics and Gynecology,* 166, 83–86.

Sloan, L., Gay, J., Snyder, S., & Bales, W. (1992). Substance abuse during pregnancy in a rural population. *Obstetrics & Gynecology,* 79, 245–248.

Sloane, E. (1985). *Biology of Women,* 2nd ed. New York: Wiley.

Smith, B., Cummings, M., Covino, J., Benes, S., Draft, K., & McCormack, W. (1991). Evaluation of ofloxacin in the treatment of uncomplicated gonorrhea. *Sexually Transmitted Diseases,* 18, 18–20.

Smith, D. (1976). The social content of pornography. *Journal of Communication,* Winter, 16–24.

Smith, J., & Smith, L. (1970). Co-marital sex and the sexual freedom movement. *Journal of Sex Research,* 6, 131–142.

———, & Midlarsky, E. (1985). Empirically derived conceptions of femaleness and maleness: A current view. *Sex Roles,* 12, 313–328.

Smith, P., Weinman, M., & Mumford, D. (1992). Knowledge, beliefs, and behavioral risk factors for human immunodeficiency virus infections in inner-city adolescent females. *Sexually Transmitted Diseases,* 19, 19–24.

Smith, R. (1985). Abortion, right and wrong. *Newsweek,* March 25, 16.

———, Pine, C., & Hawley, M. (1988). Social cognitions about adult male victims of female sexual assault. *Journal of Sex Research,* 24, 101–112.

Smith, T. (1990). Adult sexual behavior in 1989: Number of partners, frequency and risk. Paper presented at the annual meeting of the American Association for the Advancement of Science, New Orleans, La., February.

Smithyman, S. (1979). Characteristics of undetected rapists. In W. Parsonage (Ed.)., *Perspectives on Victimology,* Beverly Hills, Calif.: Sage.

Snellman, L., & Stang, H. (1992). Prospective evaluation of complications of local anesthesia for neonatal circumcision. *American Journal of Diseases of Children,* 146, 482.

Snyder, H. (1991). To circumcise or not. *Hospital Practice,* January 15, 201–207.

Sokolov, J., Harris, R., & Hecker, M. (1976). Isolation of substances from human vaginal secretions previously shown to be sex attractant pheromones in higher primates. *Archives of Sexual Behavior,* 5, 269–274.

Solimini, C. (1991). Cures for yeast infections. *New Woman,* May, 129.

Sollom, T. (1991). State legislation on reproductive health in 1990: What was proposed and enacted. *Family Planning Perspectives,* 23, 82–94.

Solomon, J. (1986). Does renal failure mean sexual failure? *RN,* 49, 41.

Soloway, M., Chodak, G., Vogelzang, N., Block, N., Schellhammer, P., Smith, J., Scott, M., Kennealey, G., & Gau, T. (1991). Zolodex versus orchidectomy in treatment of advanced prostate cancer: A randomized trial. *Urology,* 37, 46–51.

Sonda, L. P., Mazo, R., & Chancellor, M. (1990). The role of yohimbine for the treatment of erectile impotence. *Journal of Sex and Marital Therapy,* 16, 15–21.

Sonda, L., Mazo, R., & Chancellor, M. (1990). The role of yohimbine for the treatment of erectile impotence. *Journal of Sex and Marital Therapy,* 16, 15–22.

Sonenstein, F. (1986). Risking paternity: Sex and contraception among adolescent males. In A. Elster and M. Lamb (Eds.)., *Adolescent Fatherhood.* Hillsdale, N.J.: Erlbaum.

———, Pleck, J., & Ku, L. (1989). Sexual activity, condom use and AIDS awareness among adolescent males. *Family Planning Perspectives,* 21, 152–158.

———, ———, & ———. (1991). Levels of sexual activity among adolescent males in the United States. *Family Planning Perspectives,* 23, 162–167.

Sontag, S. (1972). The double standard of aging. *Saturday Review,* September 23, 29–38.

Soper, D. (1991). Disseminated gonococcal infection. *Contemporary Obstetrics and Gynecology,* February, 97–99.

———. (1992). The femal condom. *Medical Aspects of Human Sexuality,* 26(1), 14.

Sorenson, R. (1973). *Adolescent Sexuality in Contemporary America.* New York: World.

Soskolne, V., Aral, S., Magder, L., Reed, D., & Bowen, S. (1991). Condom use with regular and casual partners among women attending family planning clinics. *Family Planning Perspectives,* 23, 222–225.

Spanier, G. (1977). Sources of sex information and premarital sexual behavior. *Journal of Sex Research,* 13, 73–88.

———, & Furstenberg, F. (1982). Remarriage after divorce: A longitudinal analysis of well-being. *Journal of Marriage and the Family,* 44, 709–720.

Spector, I., & Carey, M. (1990). Incidence and prevalence of the sexual dysfunctions: A critical review of the empirical literature. *Archives of Sexual Behavior,* 19, 389–408.

Spence, J., & Helmreich, R. (1973). *Masculinity and Femininity: The Psychological Dimensions, Correlates, and Antecedents.* Austin: University of Texas Press.

———, ———, & Stapp, J. (1975). Ratings of self and peers on sex role attributes and their relation to self-esteem and conceptions of masculinity and femininity. *Journal of Personality and Social Psychology,* 32, 29–39.

Spencer, S., & Zeiss, A. (1987). Sex roles and sexual dysfunction in college students. *Journal of Sex Research,* 23, 338–347.

Spengler, A. (1977). Manifest sadomasochism of males: Results of an empirical study. *Archives of Sexual Behavior,* 6, 441–456.

Sperling, R., Friedman, F., Joyner, M., Brodman, M., & Dottino, P. (1991). Seroprevalence of human immunodeficiency virus in women admitted to the hospital with pelvic inflammatory disease. *The Journal of Reproductive Medicine,* 36, 122–124.

Speroff, L. (1991). A clinician's approach to therapy during a woman's transition years. *Contemporary OB/GYN,* August, 64–68.

———, Blas, R., & Kase, N. (1989). *Clinical Gynecologic Endocrinology and Infertility.* Baltimore: Williams & Wilkins.

Sprecher, S. (1989). Premarital sexual standards for different categories of individuals. *Journal of Sex Research,* 26, 232–248.

Spring-Mills, E., & Hafez, E. (1980). Male accessory sexual organs. In E. Hafez (Ed.)., *Human Reproduction.* New York: Harper & Row.

Stafford, R. (1991). The impact of nonclinical factors on repeat cesarean section. *Journal of the American Medical Association,* 265, 59–63.

Stampfer, M., Colditz, G., Willett, W., Manson, J., Rosner, B., Speizer, F., & Hennekens, C. (1991). Postmenopausal estrogen therapy and cardiovascular disease: Ten-year follow-up from the nurses' health study. *New England Journal of Medicine,* 325, 756.

Stanhope, R., & Brook, C. (1988). An evaluation of hormonal changes at puberty in man. *Journal of Endocrinology,* 116, 301–305.

Starcher, E., Kramer, M., Carlota-Orduna, B., & Lundberg, D. (1983). Establishing efficient interview periods for gonorrhea patients. *American Journal of Public Health,* 73, 1381; 1384.

Stark, E. (1984). The unspeakable family secret. *Psychology Today,* May, 42–46.

Starr, B., & Weiner, M. (1981). *The Starr–Weiner Report on Sex and Sexuality in the Mature Years.* New York: Stein & Day.

Steege, J., Stout, A., & Carson, C. (1986). Patient satisfaction in Scott and small-carrion penile implant recipients: A study of 52 patients. *Archives of Sexual Behavior,* 15, 393–399.

Stein, A. (1991). The chlamydia epidemic: Teenagers at risk. *Medical Aspects of Human Sexuality,* February, 26–33.

Steinberg, M., Juliano, M., & Wise, L. (1985). Psychological outcome of lumpectomy versus mastectomy in the treatment of breast cancer. *American Journal of Psychiatry,* 142, 34–39.

Steinem, G. (1980). Erotica and pornography: A clear and present difference. In L. Lederer (Ed.)., *Take Back the Night: Women on Pornography.* New York: Morrow.

Stenager, E., Stenager, E. N., Jensen, K., & Boldsen, J. (1990). Multiple sclerosis: Sexual dysfunctions. *Journal of Sex Education & Therapy,* 16, 262–269.

Stengel, R. (1986). Sex Busters. *Time,* July 21, 12–21.

Stern, E. (1987). Sex during pregnancy. *American Baby,* March, 71–79.

Sternberg, R. (1986). A triangular theory of love. *Psychological Review,* 93, 119–135.

———. (1988). Triangulating love. In R. Sternberg & M. Barnes (Eds.), *The Psychology of Love.* New Haven, Conn.: Yale University Press.

Steven-Simon, C., & White, M. (1991). Adolescent pregnancy. *Pediatric Annals,* 20, 322–331.

Stevenson, M. (1990). Tolerance for homosexuality and interest in sexuality education. *Journal of Sex Educaton & Therapy,* 16, 194–197.

———, & Stevenson, D. (1991). Beliefs about AIDS among entering college students. *Journal of Sex Education and Therapy,* 16, 201–204.

Stewart, A. (1987). Clinical and biochemical effects of nutritional supplementation on the premenstrual syndrome. *Journal of Reproductive Medicine,* 32, 435–441.

———, Stewart, M., & Tooley, S. (1992). Premenstrual syndrome: Is there a basis for a holistic approach. *Maternal and Child Health,* March, 86–88.

Stewart, B., Hughes, C., Frank, E., Anderson, B., Kendall, K., & West, D. (1987). The aftermath of rape. Profiles of immediate and delayed treatment seekers. *Journal of Nervous and Mental Disorders,* 175, 90–94.

Stiglitz, E. (1990). Caught between two worlds: The impact of a child on a lesbian couple's relationship. *Women & Therapy,* 10, 99–116.

Stimson, A., Wase, J., & Stimson, J. (1981). Sexuality and self-esteem among the aged. *Research in Aging,* 3, 228–239.

Stock, W. (1985). The effect of pornography on women. Paper presented at a hearing of the Attorney General's Commission on Pornography, Houston, September 11–12.

Stoller, R. *Sex & Gender.* (1968). New York: Science House.

———. (1971). The term ``transvestism.'' *Archives of General Psychiatry,* 24, 230–237.

———. (1972). Etiological factors in female transsexualism: A first approximation. *Archives of Sexual Behavior,* 2, 47–64.

———. (1977). Sexual deviations. In F. Beach (Ed.)., *Human Sexuality in Four Perspectives.* Baltimore: Johns Hopkins University Press.

———. (1982). Transvestism in women. Archives of Sexual Behavior, 11, 99–115.

———. (1985). *Observing the Erotic Imagination.* New Haven, Conn.: Yale University Press.

———, & Herdt, G. (1985). Theories of origins of male homosexuality. *Archives of General Psychiatry,* 42, 399–404.

Stone, M. (1976). *When God Was a Woman.* New York: Dial Press.

Stone, R., & Waszak, C. (1992). Adolescent knowledge and attitudes about abortion. *Family Planning Perspectives,* 24, 52–58.

Storms, M. (1980). Theories of sexual orientation. *Journal of Personality and Social Psychology,* 38, 783–792.

Strassberg, D., & Mahoney, J. (1988). Correlates of contraceptive behavior of adolescents/young adults. *Journal of Sex Research,* 25, 531–536.

———, ———, Schaugaard, M., & Hale, V. (1990). The role of anxiety in premature ejaculation: A psychophysiological model. *Archives of Sexual Behavior,* 19, 251–257.

Straus, M., & Baron, L. (1983). Sexual stratification, pornography, and rape in American states. Paper presented at the annual meeting, American Society of Criminology, Denver, Colo., November.

Straw, T. (1981). Visual impairment. In D. Bullard & S. Knight (Eds.), *Sexuality and Physical Disability.* St. Louis, Mo.: Mosby.

Strickler, J. (1992). The new reproductive technology: Problem or solution? *Sociology of Health & Illness,* 14, 111–132.

Strommen, E. (1989). "You're a What?": Family member reactions to the disclosure of homosexuality. In F. Bozett (Ed.), *Homosexuality and the Family.* Binghamton, N.Y.: Harrington Park Press.

Stuart, F., Hammond, C., & Pett, M. (1988). Inhibited sexual desire in women. *Archives of Sexual Behavior,* 16, 91–106.

Stubblefield, P., Fuller, A., & Foster, S. (1988). Ultrasound-guided intrauterine removal of intrauterine contraceptive devices in pregnancy. *Obstetrics and Gynecology,* 72, 961.

Stulberg, I., & Smith, M. (1988). Psychosocial impact of the AIDS epidemic on the lives of gay men. *Social Work,* 33, 277–281.

Sue, D. (1979). Erotic fantasies of college students during coitus. *The Journal of Sex Research,* 15, 299–305.

Sugarman, S., Hergenroeder, A., Chacko, M., & Parcel, G. (1991). Acquired immunodeficiency and adolescents. *American Journal of the Diseases of Children,* 145, 431–436.

Suggs, R. (1962). *The Hidden Worlds of Polynesia*. New York: Harcourt, Brace & World.

Suh, M., & Denworth, L. (1989). Operation rescue. *Ms.*, April, 92–94.

Sullivan, W. (1971). Boys and girls are now maturing earlier. *New York Times*, January 24.

Summit, R., & Kryso, J. (1978). Sexual abuse of children: A clinical spectrum. *American Journal of Orthopsychiatry*, 48, 237–251.

Susset, J., Tessier, C., Wincze, J., Bansal, S., & Malhotra, C. (1988). Effect of yohimbine HCL on erectile impotence—A double blind study. Paper presented at the Eighty-Second Annual Assembly of Urologists, New Orleans, La., November.

————, ————, ————, ————, ————, & Schwacha, M. (1989). Effects of yohimbine hydrochloride on erectile impotence: A double-blind study. *Journal of Urology*, 141, 1360–1363.

Swaab, D., & Fliers, E. (1985). A sexually dimorphic nucleus in the human brain. *Science*, 228, 1112–1115.

Sweeney, P., Onorato, I., Allen, D., Byers, R., & The Field Services Branch (1992). Sentinel surveillance of human immunodeficiency virus infection in women seeking reproductive health services in the United States, 1988–1989. *Obstetrics and Gynecology*, 79, 503–510.

Szoka, P., & Edgren, R. (1988). Drug interactions with oral contraceptives: Compilation and analysis of an adverse experience report database. *Fertility and Sterility*, 49, 31S–37S.

Taffel, S., Placek, P., & Kosary, C. (1992). U.S. cesarean section rates, 1990: An update. *Birth*, 19, 21–22.

Talamini, J. (1982). *Boys Will Be Girls: The Hidden World of the Heterosexual Male Transvestite*. Washington, D.C.: University Press of America.

Tannen, D. (1990). *You Just Don't Understand: Women and Men in Conversation*. New York: Ballantine Books (paperback edition, 1991).

Tanner, M., Pierce, B., & Hale, D. (1981). Toxic shock syndrome. *Western Journal of Medicine*, 134, 477–484.

Tanner, W., & Pollack, R. (1988). The effect of condom use and erotic instructions on attitudes toward condoms. *Journal of Sex Research*, 25, 527–541.

Tauber, M. (1979). Sex differences in parent–child interaction styles in a free-play session. *Child Development*, 50, 981–988.

Tavris, C. (1977). Masculinity. *Psychology Today*, January, 34.

————, & Sadd, S. (1977). *The Redbook Report on Female Sexuality*. New York: Delacorte.

Taylor, D. (1986). Development of perimenstrual symptom typologies. Paper presented at Western Society of Nursing Research, Portland, Ore.

Taylor, J. (1971). In R. Haber & C. Eden (Eds.)., *Holy Living*, rev. ed. New York: Adler.

Taylor, M., & Lockwood, W. (1981). Toxic-shock syndrome. *Journal of the Mississippi State Medical Association*, 22, 194–198.

Taylor, R. (1970). *Sex in History*. New York: Harper & Row.

Taylor-Robinson, D., & Thomas, B. (1991). Laboratory techniques for the diagnosis of chlamydial infections. *Genitourinary Medicine*, 67, 256–266.

Terpstra, D., & Baker, D. (1988). Outcomes of sexual harassment charges. *Academy of Management Journal*, 31, 185–194.

Terry, J. (1990). Lesbians under the medical gaze: Scientists search for remarkable differences. *The Journal of Sex Research*, 27, 317–339.

Tessler, A., & Krahn, H. (1966). Variocele and testicular temperature. *Fertility and Sterility*, 17, 201–203.

Teti, D., & Lamb, M. (1989). Socioeconomic and marital outcomes of adolescent marriage, adolescent childbirth, and their co-occurrence. *Journal of Marriage and the Family*, 51, 203–212.

Thomas, L. E. (1991). Correlates of sexual interest among elderly men. *Psychological Reports*, 68, 620–622.

Thompson, R. (1985). *The Brain*. New York: Freeman.

————. (1990). Is routine circumcision indicated in the newborn? An opposing view. *The Journal of Family Practice*, 31, 189–196.

Thoresen, J. (1984). Lesbians and gay men: Complements and contrasts. Paper presented at the Society for the Scientific Study of Sex Conference, Philadelphia, April 7.

Thornburg, H. (1981). Adolescent sources of information about sex. *Journal of School Health*, 51, 274–277.

————, & Aras, Z. (1986). Physical characteristics of developing adolescents. *Journal of Adolescent Research*, 1, 47–78.

Tiefer, L., Pederson, G., & Melman, A. (1988). Psychosocial follow-up of penile prosthesis implant patients and partners. *Journal of Sex and Marital Therapy*, 14, 184–201.

Tolstedt, B., & Stokes, J. (1983). Relation of verbal, affective, and physical intimacy to marital satisfaction. *Journal of Counseling Psychology*, 30, 573–580.

Toufexis, A. (1989). Too many mouths. *Newsweek*, January 2, 48–50.

Tourney, G. (1980). Hormones and homosexuality. In J. Marmor (Ed.)., *Homosexual Behavior*. New York: Basic Books.

Toussie-Weingarten, C., & Jacobwitz, J. (1987). Alternatives in childbearing: Choices and challenges. In L. Sherwen (Ed.)., *Psychosocial Dimensions of the Pregnant Family*. New York: Springer.

Trimble, J., Gay, H., & Docherty, J. (1986). Characterization of the tumor-associated 38-kd protein of herpes simplex virus Type II. *Journal of Reproductive Medicine*, 31 (supplement)., 399–409.

Tripp, C. (1975). *The Homosexual Matrix*. New York: McGraw-Hill.

Trussell, J. (1988). Teenage pregnancy in the United States. *Family Planning Perspectives*, 20, 262–273.

————, & Westoff, C. (1980). Contraceptive practice and trends in coital frequency. *Family Planning Perspectives*, 12, 246–249.

Trussell, J., Warner, D., & Hatcher, R. (1992). Condom slippage and breakage rates. *Family Planning Perspectives*, 24, 20–23.

Tucker, V., & Cho, C. (1991). AIDS and adolescents. *Postgraduate Medicine*, 89, 49–53.

Tullman, G., Gilner, F., Kolodny, R., Dornbush, R., & Tullman, G. (1981). The pre- and post-therapy measurement of communication skills of couples undergoing sex therapy at the Masters and Johnson Institute. *Archives of Sexual Behavior*, 10, 95–99.

Turner, L., Althof, S., Levine, S., Risin, C., Bodner, D., Kursh, E., & Resnick, M. (1989). Self-injection of papaverine and phentolamine in the treatment of psychogenic impotence. *Journal of Sex and Marital & Therapy*, 15(3), 163–176.

————, Froman, S., Althof, S., et al. (1990). Intracavernous injections in the management of diabetic impotence. *Journal of Sex Education & Therapy*, 16(2), 126.

Turque, B., Miller, M., King, P., & Duignan-Cabrera, A. (1991). The age of "outing." *Newsweek,* August 12, 22–23.

U.S. Attorney General's Commission on Pornography (1986). *Final Report of the Attorney General's Commission on Pornography.* Washington, D.C.: U.S. Justice Department.

U.S. Bureau of the Census (1978). *Statistical Abstract of the United States: 1978,* 99th ed. Washington, D.C.: U.S. Department of Commerce.

———. (1985). *Statistical Abstract of the United States: 1985,* 105th ed. Washington, D.C.: U.S. Department of Commerce.

———. (1988). *Statistical Abstract of the United States 1988.* Washington, D.C.: Government Printing Office.

———. (1990). Household and family characteristics: March 1990 and 1989. *Current Population Reports,* Series P–20, No. 447. Washington, D.C.: Government Printing Office.

———. (1991a). Marital status and living arrangements: March 1990. *Current Population Reports,* Series P–20, No. 450. Washington, D.C.: Government Printing Office.

———. (1991b). *Statistical Abstract of the United States 1991.* Washington, D.C.: Government Printing Office.

U.S. General Accounting Office (1982). *Sexual Exploitation of Children—A Problem of Unknown Magnitude.* Gaithersburg, Md. U.S. General Accounting Office.

U.S. Merit Systems Protection Board (1981). *Sexual Harassment in the Federal Workplace: Is It a Problem?* Washington, D.C.: U.S. Government Printing Office.

Ubell, E. (1984). Sex in America today. *Parade,* October 28, 11–13.

Udry, R., Billy, J., Morris, N., Groff, T., & Raj, M. (1985). Serum androgenic hormones motivate sexual behavior in adolescent boys. *Fertility and Sterility,* 43, 90–94.

United Nations Commission. (1959). Study on Traffic in Persons and Prostitution. ST/SOA/5D/8.

Upton, G. (1987). Contraception for the perimenopausal patient. *Obstetrics and Gynecology Clinics of North America,* 14, 207–227.

Utian, W. (1990). Current thoughts on postmenopausal hormone replacement therapy. *Clinical Practice in Sexuality,* Special Issue, 22–24.

Valdiserri, R., Arena, V., Proctor, D., & Bonati, F. (1989). The relationship between women's attitudes about condoms and their use: Implications for condom promotion programs. *American Journal of Public Health,* 79, 499–501.

Vance, C. (1985). Is it really a novel law? *Psychology Today,* April, 40.

Vanderbilt, H. (1992). Incest, a chilling report. *Lear's,* February, 49–77.

Vander Mey, B. (1988). The sexual victimization of male children: A review of previous research. *Child Abuse and Neglect,* 12, 61–72.

Van de Wiel, H., Jaspers, J., Weijmar-Schultz, W., & Gal, J. (1990). Treatment of vaginismus: a review of concepts and treatment modalities. *Journal of Psychosomatic Obstetrics & Gynecology,* 11, 1–18.

Van Dis, H., & Larsson, K. (1971). Induction of sexual arousal in the castrated male rat by intracranial stimulation. *Physiological Behavior,* 6, 85–86.

van Haastrecht, H., van den Hoek, J., & Coutinho, R. (1991). Evidence for a change in behavior among heterosexuals in Amsterdam under the influence of AIDS. *Genitourinary Medicine,* 67, 199–206.

Van Wyk, P. (1984). Psychosocial development of heterosexual, bisexual, and homosexual behavior. *Archives of Sexual Behavior,* 13, 505–544.

Vaughn, E., & Fisher, A. (1962). Male sexual behavior induced by intracranial electrical stimulation. *Science,* 137, 758–760.

Vazi, R., Best, D., Davis, S., & Kaiser, M. (1989). Evaluation of a testicular cancer curriculum for adolescents. *Journal of Pediatrics,* 114, 150–162.

Veith, J., Buck, M., Getzlaf, S., Van Dalfsen, P., & Slade, S. (1983). Exposure to men influences the occurrence of ovulation in women. Paper presented at the Ninety-First Convention of the American Psychological Association, Anaheim, Calif., August 27.

Velarde, A., & Warlick, M. (1973). Massage parlors: The sensuality business. *Society,* 11, 63–74.

Vella, S., Giuliano, M., Pezzotti, P., Agresti, M., Tomino, C., Floridia, M., Greco, D., & Zanussi, C. (1992). Survival of zidovudine-treated patients with AIDS compared with that of contemporary untreated patients. *Journal of the American Medical Association,* 267, 1232–1236.

Vellacott, I., & O'Brien, P. (1987). Effect of spironolactone on premenstrual syndrome symptoms. *Journal of Reproductive Medicine,* 32, 429–434.

Ventura, S. (1992). Advance report of new data from the 1989 birth certificate. *Centers for Disease Control Monthly Vital Statistics Report,* 40, 1–31.

Verp, M., Harrison, H., Ober, C., Oliveri, D., Amarose, A., Lindgren, V., & Talerman, A. (1992). Chimerism as the etiology of a 46,XX/46,XY fertile true hermaphrodite. *Fertility and Sterility,* 57, 346–349.

Verschoor, A., & Poortinga, J. (1988). Psychological differences between Dutch male and female transsexuals. *Archives of Sexual Behavior,* 17, 173–178.

Vikram, B., & Vikram, R. (1988). Prevention of impotence in patients with prostate cancer. *Medical Aspects of Human Sexuality,* March, 29–33.

Vincelette, J., Baril, J., & Allard, R. (1991). Predictors of chlamydial infection and gonorrhea among patients seen by private practitioners. *Canadian Medical Association Journal,* 144, 713–721.

Vinick, B. (1978). Remarriage in old age. *The Family Coordinator,* 27, 359–363.

Vinson, R., & Epperly, T. (1991). Counseling patients on proper use of condoms. *American Family Physician,* 43, 2081–2085.

Voeller, B. (1991). AIDS and heterosexual anal intercourse. *Archives of Sexual Behavior,* 20, 233–269.

Walbroehl, G. (1984). Sexuality during pregnancy. *American Family Physician,* 29, 273–275.

Walfish, S., & Myerson, M. (1980). Sex role identity and attitudes toward sexuality. *Archives of Sexual Behavior, 9,* 199–203.

Walker, E., Katon, W., Neraas, K., Jemelka, R., & Massoth, D. (1992). Dissociation in women with chronic pelvic pain. *American Journal of Psychiatry, 149,* 534–537.

Walker, L. (1979). *The Battered Woman.* New York: Harper & Row.

Wall, E., Sinclair, A., Nelson, J., & Toffler, W. (1989). The relationship between assessed obstetric risk and maternal–perinatal outcome. *Journal of Family Practice, 28,* 35–40.

Wallerstein, E. (1980). *Circumcision.* New York: Springer.

Walling, M., Andersen, B., & Johnson, S. (1990). Hormonal replacement therapy for postmenopausal women: A review of sexual outcomes and related gynecologic effects. *Archives of Sexual Behavior, 19,* 119–137.

Walnut Creek Contraceptive Drug Study (1981). A prospective study of the side effects of oral contraceptives. NIH Publication No. 81–564, 111, 9.

Walster, E., & Walster, G. (1978). *A New Look at Love.* Reading, Mass.: Addison-Wesley.

Walters, D. (1991). The gathering momentum against tobacco: Action by physicians is needed on all fronts. *Canadian Medical Association Journal, 144*(2), 135–136.

Wang, P., Cong, S., Dong, X., Chen, Z., & Ma, C. (1991). A genetic study of human interferon-induced repair of DNA damage in hepatitis B patients. *Mutation Research, 262,* 125–128.

Ward, S., Chapman, K., Cohn, E., White, S., & Williams, K. (1991). Acquaintance rape and the college social scene. *Family Relations, 40,* 65–71.

Warner, E., & Strashin, E. (1981). Benefits and risks of circumcision. *Canadian Medical Association Journal, 125,* 967–976, 992.

Warren, M. (1982). Onset of puberty later in athletic girls. *Medical Aspects of Human Sexuality, 4,* 77–78.

Watkins, B., & Bentovim, A. (1992). The sexual abuse of male children and adolescents: A review of current research. *Journal of Child Psychology and Psychiatry, 33,* 197–248.

Watson, R. (1985). Gardnerella vaginalis: Genitourinary pathogen in men. *Urology, 25,* 217–222.

———, & DeMeo, P. (1987). Premarital cohabitation vs. traditional courtship and subsequent marital adjustment: A replication and follow-up. *Family Relations, 36,* 193–197.

Weg, R. (1983). The physiological perspective. In R. Weg (Ed.)., *Sexuality in the Later Years: Roles and Behavior.* New York: Academic Press.

Weidiger, P. (1976). *Menstruation and Menopause.* New York: Knopf.

Weinberg, G. (1973). *Society and the Healthy Homosexual.* New York: Anchor.

Weinberg, M., Williams, C., & Moser, C. (1984). The social constituents of sadomasochism. *Social Problems, 31,* 379–389.

Weinberg, T. (1987). Sadomasochism in the United States: A review of recent sociological literature. *Journal of Sex Research, 23,* 50–69.

———, & Bullough, V. (1988). Alienation, self-image, and the importance of support groups for the wives of transvestites. *Journal of Sex Research, 24,* 262–268.

Weinrich, J. (1990). Does childhood gender nonconformity predict adult high-risk behavior? Paper presented at The Society for the Scientific Study of Sex Annual Western Region Conference. San Diego, Calif., April 25.

Weinstein, E., & Rosen, E. (1991). The development of adolescent sexual intimacy: Implications for counseling. *Adolescence, 26,* 331–339.

Weinstock, H., Bolan, G., Hohn, R., Balladares, C., Back, A., & Oliva, G. (1992). *Chlamydia trachomatis* infection in women: A need for universal screening in high prevalence populations? *American Journal of Epidemiology, 135,* 41–47.

Weis, D. (1983). Affective reactions of women to their initial experience of coitus. *Journal of Sex Research, 19,* 209–237.

———, Rabinowitz, B., & Ruckstuhl, M. (1992). Individual changes in sexual attitudes and behavior within college-level human sexuality courses. *The Journal of Sex Research, 29,* 43–59.

Weisman, C., Plichta, S., Nathanson, C., Ensminger, M., & Robinson, J. (1991). Consistency of condom use for disease prevention among adolescent users of oral contraceptives. *Family Planning Perspectives, 23,* 71–74.

Weiss, B., Bassford, T., & Davis, T. (1991). The cervical cap. *American Family Physician, 43,* 517–523.

Weiss, T., Meffin, E., Jones, R., & Jones, W. (1992). Trends in causes and treatment of infertility at Flinders Medical Centre, Adelaide, 1976–1989. *Medical Journal of Australia, 156,* _311.

Weizman, R., & Hart, J. (1987). Sexual behavior in healthy married elderly men. *Archives of Sexual Behavior, 16,* 39–44.

Wells, B. (1983). Nocturnal orgasms: Females' perceptions of a ``normal'' sexual experience. *Journal of Sex Education and Therapy, 9,* 32–38.

Wells, J. (1991). The effects of homophobia and sexism on heterosexual sexual relationships. *Journal of Sex Education & Therapy, 17,* 185–195.

———, & Kline, W. (1987). Self-disclosure of homosexual orientation. *Journal of Social Psychology, 127,* 191–197.

Wendell, D., Onorato, I., McCray, E., Allen, D., & Sweeney, P. (1992). Youth at risk: Sex, drugs, and human immunodeficiency virus. *American Journal of Diseases of Children, 146,* 76–81.

Wertheimer, M. (1991). Against minimalism in breast cancer follow-up. *Journal of the American Medical Association, 265,* 396–399.

West, C. (1992a). Management of uterine fibroids. *The Practitioner, 236,* 117–121.

West, R. (1992b). Vasectomy and testicular cancer. *British Medical Journal, 304,* 729.

Wetzel, C., & Insko, C. (1982). The similarity-attraction relationship: Is there an ideal one? *Journal of Experimental Social Psychology, 18,* 253–276.

Wharton, C., & Blackburn, R. (1988). Oral contraceptives. *Population Reports,* A(7).

Whatley, M. (1987). Biological determinism and gender issues in sexuality education. *Journal of Sex Education and Therapy, 13,* 26–29.

Wheeler, M. (1991). Physical changes of puberty. *Endocrinology and Metabolism Clinics of North America, 20,* 1–14.

Whipple, B., & Komisaruk, B. (1988). Analgesia produced in women by genital self-stimulation. *Journal of Sex Research, 24,* 130–140.

————, Ogden, G., & Komisaruk, B. (1992). Physiological correlates of imagery-induced orgasm in women. *Archives of Sexual Behavior, 21,* 121–133.

Whitam, F. (1980). The prehomosexual male child in three societies: The United States, Guatemala, Brazil. *Archives of Sexual Behavior, 9,* 87–99.

Whitam, F. (1990). Homosexual transsexuals in female roles in Japanese "Ludruk" drama. Paper presented at The Society for the Scientific Study of Sex Annual Western Region Conference, San Diego, Calif., April 25.

White, J. (1990). Legal medications, illegal drugs and sexual dysfunctions in men: A review of the literature. Paper presented at The Society for the Scientific Study of Sex Annual Western Region Conference, San Diego, Calif., April 25.

White, L., & Booth, A. (1986). Children and marital happiness. *Journal of Family Issues, 7,* 131–147.

————, & ————. (1991). Divorce over the life span. *Journal of Family Issues, 12,* 5–21.

White, S., & DeBlassie, R. (1992). Adolescent sexual behavior. *Adolescence, 27,* 183–191.

Whitley, B. (1987). The relationship of sex-role orientation to heterosexuals' attitudes toward homosexuals. *Sex Roles, 17,* 103–113.

Whitley, R., Arvin, A., Prober, C., Corey, L, & Burchett, S. (1991). Predictors of morbidity and mortality in neonates with herpes simplex virus infections. *The New England Journal of Medicine, 324,* 450–454.

Wiest, W. (1977). Semantic differential profiles of orgasm and other experiences among men and women. *Sex Roles, 3,* 399–403.

Wikstrom, A., Hedblad, M., Johansson, B., Kalantari, M., Syrjanen, S., Lindberg, M., & von Krogh, G. (1992). The acetic test in evaluation of subclinical genital papillomavirus infection: A comparative study on peroscopy, histopathology, virology and scanning electron microscopy findings. *Genitourinary Medicine, 68,* 90–99.

Wilcox, A. (1987). Urinary hCG among intrauterine device users: Detection with a highly specific and sensitive assay. *Fertility and Sterility, 2,* 527–531.

Williams, L. (1984). The classic rape: When do victims report. *Social Problems, 31,* 459–467.

Williams, P., & Smith, M. (1979). Interview in The First Question. London: British Broadcasting System Science and Features Department film.

Williamson, M. (1992). Sexual adjustment after hysterectomy. *Journal of Obstetrics, Gynecology & Neonatal Care, 21*(1), 42–47.

Willson, J., & Carrington, E. (1987). *Obstetrics and Gynecology,* 8th ed., St. Louis, Mo.: Mosby.

————, ————, & Ledger, W. (1983). *Obstetrics and Gynecology,* St. Louis: Mosby.

Wilson, C., Turner, C., & Keye, W., Jr. (1991). Firstborn adolescent daughters and mothers with and without premenstrual syndrome: A comparison. *Journal of Adolescent Health, 12,* 130–137.

Wilson, D. S. (1991). Male prostitution and social skill deficiencies: Individual pathology or street-learned interaction styles. Paper presented at The Society for the Scientific Study of Sex Annual Western Region Conference, Humphrey's Half Moon Inn, San Diego, Calif.

Wilson, G. (1984). Alcohol and sexual function. *British Journal of Sexual Medicine.* 11, 56–58.

————, & Lawson, D. (1976). Effects of alcohol on sexual arousal in women. *Journal of Abnormal Psychology, 85,* 489–497.

Wilson, K., & Kraus, L. (1981). Sexual harassment in the university. Paper presented at the Annual Meeting of the American Sociological Association, Toronto, June.

Wilson, M. (1984). Female homosexuals' need for dominance and endurance. *Psychological Reports, 55,* 79–82.

Winslow, R. (1991). Use of birth control pill surges in U.S. *The Wall Street Journal,* August 20.

Wise, T., & Meyer, J. (1980). Transvestism: Previous findings and new areas for inquiry. *Journal of Sex and Marital Therapy, 6,* 116–128.

Wiswell, R., Enzenauer, R., Holton, M., Cornish, J., & Hankins, C. (1987). Declining frequency of circumcision: Implications for changes in the absolute incidence and male to female sex ratio of urinary tract infections in early infancy. *Pediatrics, 79,* 338–342.

Witelson, S. (1988). Neuroanatomical sex differences: Of no consequence for cognition? *Behavioral and Brain Sciences, 11,* 215–217.

Witelson, S. (1991). Neural sexual mosaicism: Sexual differentiation of the human temporo-parietal region for functional asymmetry. *Psychoneuroendocrinology, 16,* 131–153.

Witherington, R. (1991). Mechanical devices for the treatment of erectile dysfunction. *American Family Physician, 43,* 1611–1620.

Wofsy, C. Hauer, L., & Michaelis, B., Cohen, J. Padian, N., Evans, L., Levy, J. (1986). Isolation of AIDS-associated retrovirus from genital secretions of women with antibodies to the virus. *Lancet,* March 8, 527–529.

Wolchik, S., Brauer, S., & Jensen, K. (1985). Volunteer bias in erotica research: Effects of intrusiveness of measure of sexual background. *Archives of Sexual Behavior, 14,* 93–107.

Wolfe, L. (1981). *The Cosmo Report.* New York: Arbor House.

Wolfers, O. (1992). Same abuse, different parent. *Social Work Today,* March, 13–15.

Women on Words & Images (1972). *Dick and Jane as Victims.* Princeton, N.J. Women on Words & Images.

————. (1975) *Channeling Children: Sex Stereotyping on Prime Time TV.* Princeton, N.J.

Woods, E. (1991). Contraceptive choices for adolescents. *Pediatric Annals, 20,* 313–321.

Woods, N. (1986). Socialization and social context: Influences on perimenstrual symptoms, disability, and menstrual attitudes. In V. Olesen and N. Woods (Eds.)., *Culture, Society, and Menstruation.* Washington D.C.: Hemisphere.

———, Lentz, M., Mitchell, E., Lee, K., Taylor, D., & Allen-Barash, N. (1987). Women's health: The menstrual cycle/pre-menstrual symptoms: Another look. *Public Health Reports*, 106–112.

Wooster, M. (1986). Reagan's smutstompers. *Reason*, April, 26–33.

World Health Organization Task Force on Methods for the Regulation of Male Fertility (1990). Contraceptive efficacy of testosterone-induced azoospermia in normal men. *Lancet, 2*, 955.

Wright, J., Bissonnette, F., Duchesne, C., Benoit, J., Sabourin, S., & Girard, Y. (1991). Psychosocial distress and infertility: Men and women respond differently. *Fertility and Sterility*, 55, 100–108.

Wright, M., & McCary, J. (1969). Positive effects of sex education on emotional patterns of behavior. *Journal of Sex Research*, 5, 162–169.

Wyatt, G. E. (1991). Child sexual abuse and its effects on sexual functioning. *Annual Review of Sex Research*, 2, 249–254.

Wyers, N. (1987). Homosexuality in the family: Lesbian and gay spouses. *Social Work*, 32, 143–148.

Yamada, D., Hattori, N., Kurimura, T., Kita, M., & Kishida, T. (1988). Inhibition of growth of HIV by human natural interferon in vitro. *AIDS Research and Human Retroviruses*, 4, 287–294.

Yates, A., & Wolman, W. (1991). Aphrodisiacs: Myth and reality. *Medical Aspects of Human Sexuality*, December, 58–64.

Yates, E., Barbaree, H., & Marshall, W. (1984). Anger and deviant sexual arousal. *Behavior Therapy*, 15, 3, 287–294.

Young, L. (1992). Sexual abuse and the problem of embodiment. *Child Abuse and Neglect*, 16, 89–100.

Young, W. (1970). Prostitution. In J. Douglas (Ed.), *Observations of Deviance*. New York: Random House.

Zabin, L., & Clark, S. (1981). Why they delay: A study of teenage family planning clinic patients. *Family Planning Perspectives*, 13, 205–217.

———, Hardy, J., Streett, R., & King, T. (1984b). A school-, hospital- and university-based adolescent pregnancy prevention program. *The Journal of Reproductive Medicine*, 29, 421–426.

———, Hirsch, M., Smith, E., & Hardy, J. (1984a). Adolescent sexual attitudes and behavior: Are they consistent? *Family Planning Perspectives*, 16, 181–185.

Zakin, D. (1984). Perforation of the bladder by the intrauterine device. *Obstetrical and Gynecological Survey*, 39, 59–66.

Zatuchni, G. (1984). *Current Problems in Obstetrics and Gynecology, Medical Aspects of Human Sexuality*, 4–37.

Zaviacic, M., Zaviacicova, A., Holoman, I., & Molcan, J. (1988a). Female urethral expulsions evoked by local digital stimulation of the G-spot: Differences in the response patterns. *Journal of Sex Research*, 24, 311–318.

———, ———, ———, ———, Dolezalova, S., Holoman, K., Zaviacicova, A., Mikulecky, M., & Bradil, V. (1988b). Concentrations of fructose in female ejaculate and urine: A comparative biochemical study. *Journal of Sex Research*, 24, 319–325.

Zazove, P., Caruthers, B., & Reed, B. (1991). Genital human papillomavirus infection. *American Family Physician*, 43, 1279–1291.

Zelnick, M., & Kantner, J. (1977). Sexual and contraceptive experiences of young unmarried women in the United States, 1976 and 1971. *Family Planning Perspectives*, 9, 55–71.

———, & ———. (1978). First pregnancies to women aged 15–19: 1976 and 1971. *Family Planning Perspectives*, 10, 11–20.

———, & ———. (1980). Sexual activity, contraceptive use, and pregnancy among metropolitan-area teenagers: 1971–1979. *Family Planning Perspectives*, 12, 230–237.

———, & Kim, Y. (1982). Sex education and its association with teenage sexual activity, pregnancy and contraceptive use. *Family Planning Perspectives*, 14, 117–126.

Zilbergeld, B. (1975). Group treatment of sexual dysfunction in men without partners. *Journal of Sex and Marital Therapy*, 1, 204–214.

———. (1978). *Male Sexuality: A Guide to Sexual Fulfillment*. Boston: Little, Brown.

———. (1992). *The New Male Sexuality*. New York: Bantam Books.

———, & Kilmann, P. (1984). The scope and effectiveness of sex therapy, *Psychotherapy*, 21, 319–326.

Zillmann, D., & Bryant, J. (1982). Pornography, sexual callousness, and the trivialization of rape. *Journal of Communication*, Autumn, 10–21.

———, & ———. (1988a). Effects of prolonged consumption of pornography on family values. *Journal of Family Issues*, 9, 518–544.

———, & ———. (1988b). Pornography's impact on sexual satisfaction. *Journal of Applied Social Psychology*, 18, 438–453.

Zimpfer, D. (1987). Group treatment for those involved with incest. *Journal for Specialists in Group Work*, 12, 166–177.

Zini, D., Carani, C., Baldini, A., Ghizzani, A., & Marrama, P. (1990). Sexual behavior of men with isolated hypogonadotropic hypogonadism or prepubertal anterior panhypopituitarism. *Hormones and Behavior*, 24, 174–185.

Zorgniotti, A. (1991). Update on pharmacologic erection. *Medical Aspects of Human Sexuality*, January, 28–30.

———, & Lizza, E. (1991). Physical examination of the patient with impotence. *Medical Aspects of Human Sexuality*, September, 54–59.

Zuger, B. (1989). Homosexuality in families of boys with early effeminate behavior: An epidemiological study. *Archives of Sexual Behavior*, 18, 155–165.

Zussman, L., Zussman, S., Sunley, R., & Bjornson, E. (1981). Sexual response after hysterectomy–oophorectomy: Recent studies and reconsideration of psychogenesis. *American Journal of Obstetrics and Gynecology*, 140, 725–729.

Credits

Photographs

Frontispiece part and chapter opener photographs by Robert Farber © 1992. Computer enhancement by Hal Rucker, Rucker/Higgans Design. **Page 4:** © Jean-Claude LeJeune/Stock Boston. **6:** The Bettmann Archive. **8:** Giraudon/Art Resource, New York. **9, left:** The Bettmann Archive. **9, right:** The Minneapolis Institute of Arts. **10–12:** The Bettmann Archive. **14: A Buddhist wedding:** © Katrina Thomas/Photo Researchers, Inc. **B Jewish wedding:** © David Wells/The Image Works. **C Hindu wedding:** © Bernard Pierre Wolff 1973/Photo Researchers, Inc. **D Christian wedding:** Courtesy of Robin Heyden. **22:** © Suzanne Arms Wimberley. **27:** Wallace Kirkland, Life Magazine. **31:** Art Phillips/Bettmann News Photos. **34:** Courtesy of Farrall Instruments, Inc. **40:** Courtesy of T.T. Puck, *The Mamalian Cell as Microorganism*, 1972, Holden Day, Inc., Oakland, CA. **49:** From *Man and Woman, Boy and Girl*, fig. 5.5 by J. Money and A. Erhardt © 1972 Baltimore: Johns Hopkins University Press. **64, left:** © Leonard Freed/Magnum Photos, Inc. **64, right:** Jerry Howard/Stock Boston. **65:** Suzanne Arms Wimberley/Jeroboam, Inc. **66, top left:** © Wayne Lottinville/New England Stock Photo. **66, top right:** © Kathleen L. Kliskey/New England Stock Photo. **66, bottom:** © Art Phaneuf 1991/New England Stock Photo. **67:** © Bernard Boudreau/Shooting Star. **72:** © Robert Azzi 1980/Woodfin Camp & Associates. **58:** Courtesy Dr. D. Laub, Palo Alto, CA. **73:** © Lorraine Rorke/The Image Works. **80:** © William Thompson. **81:** © T. Corinne. **82:** Judy Chicago, 1979. Photo by Mary McNally. **94:** SIU Biomedical Communications/Photo Researchers, Inc. **97:** Petit Format/Photo Researchers, Inc. **99:** © Baron Wolman. **101:** © Carl Miller. **102:** © Deni McIntyre/Photo Researchers, Inc. **122:** © Joel Gordon 1992.

124: © D.D. Kunkel, University of Washington. **127:** © John Walsh/Photo Researchers, Inc. **136:** SIPA Press/Art Resource, New York. **137:** © Justine Hill. **156:** © Charles Gatewood/The Image Works, Inc. **186:** Culver Pictures, Inc. **187:** © Joel Gordon 1991. **201:** © John Huet/Leo de Wys, Inc. **204:** © Sandra Weiner/The Image Works, Inc. **207:** © Mary Ellen Mark/Archive Pictures, Inc. **218:** Dan Chidester/The Image Works, Inc. **229:** © Harriet Gans/The Image Works, Inc. **234:** © Michael Siluk/The Image Works, Inc. **238:** © Joel Gordon 1981. **245:** © David Pratt 1991/Postive Images. **246:** Courtesy of the Trustees of the Britsh Museum. **259:** Natural Photography © Robert Vernon Wilson. **261:** Robert Foothorap/Jeroboam, Inc. **271:** © Alain McLaughlin 1992. **290, right:** © Alain McLaughlin/Imapct Visuals. **292:** © Mahoney/The Image Works, Inc. **293:** © Alain McLaughlin/Impact Visuals. **294, 295:** © Alain McLaughlin 1992. **298, left:** © Bettye Lane/Photo Researchers, Inc. **298, right:** © Joel Gordon 1991. **301:** © Joel Gordon 1981. **302:** © Joel Gordon 1985. **304:** © Dion Ogust/The Image Works, Inc. **310:** Sophia Smith Collection/Smith College. **316:** Courtesy of Ortho Pharmaceutical Corporation. **320, left:** © Joel Gordon 1991. **320, right** © Joel Gordon 1992. **322:** © William Thompson. **325, 326 left, top center:** © William Thompson. **326, bottom center:** © Gail Kefauver. **328:** © Alain McLaughlin/Impact Visuals. **329:** © William Thompson. **332, bottom** © William Thompson; IUD courtesy of Planned Parenthood Association, San Mateo County, CA. Wide World Photos. **350:** Federation of Feminist Women's Health Centers. **354:** courtesy of IVF Clinic, Stanford Medical Clinic. **361:** © David Scharf 1982/Peter Arnold, Inc. **362:** © Alain McLaughlin/Impact Visuals. **371:** © Lennart Nilsson, from *A Child is Born,* Dell Publishing. **375:** © Fotographia/Westlight. **366, top:** Bettmann Newsphotos. **366, bottom:** New York Daily News. **372, top, bottom right:** © Lennart Nilsson, from *A Child is Born,* Dell Publishing. **372, bottom left:** © Lennart Nilsson, from *Behold Man,* Little, Brown & Co. **373:** Petit Format/Science Source/Photo Researchers, Inc. **378:** © Howard Sochurek/The Stock Market. **383:** © John Brook. **387:** © Joseph Nettis/Stock Boston. **388:** © SIU/Photo Researchers, Inc. **389:** © Beth Elkin. **394:** © John Brook. **395:** Medala, Inc. **401:** © Alex Harris. **402:** © Phelps/Rapho. **403:** © Frederick Bodin/Stock Boston. **407:** © Kit Hedman/Jeroboam, Inc. **410:** © Barbara Rios/Photo Researchers, Inc. **416:** © Gale Zucker/Stock Boston. **425:** © Doug Nunuez/Picture Group. **427, right:** © Jean-Claude LeJeune/Stock Boston. **428:** © Comstock, Inc., New York. **435:** © Spencer Grant/Stock Boston. **438:** © Elizabeth Hamlin/Stock Boston. **441:** © Joel Gordon 1978. **453:** © Art Phaneuf/New England Stock Photo. **454:** © Charles Harbutt/Archive Pictures, Inc. **459:** © Erik Heinila/Shooting Star. **461, left:** © Joel Gordon 1988. **461, right:** © James Motlow/ Jeroboam, Inc. **471, left:** © MacDonald Photography/Unicorn Stock Photos. **471, right:** © Alain McLaughlin/Impact Visuals. **472:** © Joan Liftin/Actuality, Inc. **473:** © Jerry Howard/Positive Images. **481:** © Bachmann/Image Works, Inc. **493:** © Judy S. Gelles/Stock Boston. **519:** Courtesy of F.E. Young and Company. **541:** © Patricia Schwarz. **543:** © Spencer Grant/The Picture Cube. **545:** © Joel Gordon 1988. **547:** © Evan Johnston/Jeroboam, Inc. **562, 567, 569, 571, 578:** Centers for Disease Control, Atlanta, GA. **579:** Alon Reininger/Woodfin Camp & Associates. **581:** © Alain McLaughlin/Impact Visuals. **594:** © Bob Daemmrich/Stock Boston. **609:** © Jean C. Pigazzi/Archive Pictures. **618:** © Carl Miller. **633:** © Lionel Delevingne/Stock Boston. **647:** © Spencer Grant/Photo Researchers, Inc. **651:** © Joel Gordon 1992. **659:** Mary Ellen Mark Library. **661:** © Richard Tauber 1992. **665:** © Marilyn Humphries/Impact Visuals. **671:** Museum of Fine Arts, Boston. **682:** © David Woo/Stock Boston. **672:** SIPA Press/Art Resource. **686:** Amon Carter Museum, Forth Worth, TX. **674:** © Nita Winter. **675:** "Larry and Bobby Kissing" © 1979 The Estate of Robert Mapplethorpe. **Tin Machine cover art before and after:** Courtesy of Isolar, New York. **684:** © Kirk Condyles/Impact Visuals. **685:** © Sydney Freelance/Gamma Liaison Network.

Excerpts

165: From *Human Sexual Response* by William H. Masters and Virginia E. Johnson. Little, Brown and Company, 1966. **101:** Breast self-examination information from the American Cancer Society. **105:** Lines from "She Shall Be Called Woman" from *Collected Poems* (1930–1973) by May Sarton, reprinted by permission of W.W. Norton & Company, Inc. Copyright © 1974 by May

Index